Fundamentals of Law Office Management: Systems, Procedures, and Ethics

Second Edition

The West Legal Studies Series

Your options keep growing with West Legal Studies

Each year our list continues to offer you more options for every area of the law to meet your course or on-the-job reference requirements. We now have over 140 titles from which to choose in the following areas:

Administrative Law	Family Law
Alternative Dispute Resolution	Federal Taxation
Bankruptcy	Intellectual Property
Business Organizations/Corporations	Introduction to Law
Civil Litigation and Procedure	Introduction to Paralegalism
CLA Exam Preparation	Law Office Management
Client Accounting	Law Office Procedures
Computer in the Law Office	Legal Research, Writing, and Analysis
Constitutional Law	Legal Terminology
Contract Law	Paralegal Employment
Criminal Law and Procedure	Real Estate Law
Document Preparation	Reference Materials
Environmental Law	Torts and Personal Injury Law
Ethics	Will, Trusts, and Estate Administration

You will find unparalleled, practical support

Each book is augmented by instructor and student supplements to ensure the best learning experience possible. We also offer custom publishing and other benefits such as West's Student Achievement Award. In addition, our sales representatives are ready to provide you with dependable service.

We want to hear from you

Our best contributions for improving the quality of our books and instructional materials is feedback from the people who use them. If you have a question, concern, or observation about any of our materials, or you have a product proposal or manuscript, we want to hear from you. Please contact your local representative or write us at the following address:

West Legal Studies, 3 Columbia Circle, P.O. Box 15015, Albany, NY 12212-5015

For additional information point your browser at
www.westlegalstudies.com

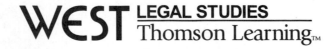

Fundamentals of
Law Office Management:
Systems, Procedures,
and Ethics

Second Edition

Pamela I. Everett
Saddleback College

Africa • Australia • Canada • Denmark • Japan • Mexico • New Zealand • Philippines
Puerto Rico • Singapore • Spain • United Kingdom • United States

NOTICE TO THE READER

Publisher does not warrant or guarantee any of the products described herein or perform any independent analysis in connection with any of the product information contained herein. Publisher does not assume, and expressly disclaims, any obligation to obtain and include information other than that provided to it by the manufacturer.

The reader is notified that this text is an educational tool, not a practice book. Since the law is in constant change, no rule or statement of law in this book should be relied upon for any service to any client. The reader should always refer to standard legal sources for the current rule or law. If legal advice or other expert assistance is required, the services of the appropriate professional should be sought. The Publisher makes no representation or warranties of any kind, including but not limited to, the warranties of fitness for particular purpose or merchantability, nor are any such representations implied with respect to the material set forth herein, and the publisher takes no responsibility with respect to such material. The publisher shall not be liable for any special, consequential, or exemplary damages resulting, in whole or part, from the readers' use of, or reliance upon, this material.

West Legal Studies Staff:
Business Unit Director: Susan Simpfenderfer
Executive Editor: Marlene McHugh Pratt
Acquisitions Editor: Joan Gill
Developmental Editor: Rhonda Dearborn
Editorial Assistant: Lisa Flatley
Executive Marketing Manager: Donna Lewis
Channel Manager: Nigar Hale
Executive Production Manager: Wendy Troeger
Production Editor: Laurie A. Boyce
Cover Design: Lauri Baram

Printed in the United States of America.
 2 3 4 5 6 7 8 9 10 XXX 05 04 03 02 01 00

For more information, contact Delmar, 3 Columbia Circle, PO Box 15015, Albany, NY 12212-0515; or find us on the World Wide Web at http://www.westlegalstudies.com

Library of Congress Cataloging-in-Publication Data

Everett, Pamela I.
    Fundamentals of law office management : systems, procedures and ethics / Pamela I.
  Everett.–2nd ed.
      p. cm.
  Includes bibliographical references and index.
  ISBN 0-7668-0881-5
  1. Law offices--United States. I. Title.

KF308 .E94 2000
340'.068–dc21   99-059723

Dedication

This text is dedicated to my mother, IRENE T. BUNNELL, whose love is an inspiration to me.

Preface

A law office is an exciting place to work. It provides employees with a stimulating environment that is rich with opportunities to learn and grow. It is a world that speaks its own language, has its own systems, and contains elements that are not found in other offices. Like other industries, law is a business - but it conducts its business differently from other industries. Without proper education in the business of law in general, students are not prepared for a career in law. Students must have knowledge of the business of law, know how a law office functions, and understand the legal world.

Learning law is a difficult task. There is much to learn to prepare a student for a successful legal career. In addition to substantive and technical courses, knowledge of the business of law is important to understand how the substantive material is delivered to a client. Nonsubstantive subjects, such cultural elements of an office, are important to learn so that one feels comfortable in a legal environment. These elements are just as important as the mechanics of doing the job.

Fundamentals of Law Office Management: Systems, Procedures and Ethics, Second Edition, is directed to students who choose a legal career, whether as a manager, paralegal, secretary or attorney. It will inform the student how a law office is managed rather than how to manage a law office. Therefore, students who have no management aspirations will find that this text contains vital information, as well as those who have management goals.

ORGANIZATIONS OF THE TEXT

Law Office Management: Systems, Procedures and Ethics Second Edition has three goals and is organized in three sections to accomplish those goals:

Section 1. *To provide knowledge of the industry.* The first five chapters of the text—The legal Marketplace, The Legal team, Personnel Relations, Client Relations, and Paralegal Ethics and Client Relations—provide an overview of the legal industry. These chapters explain the parameters and policies of the business of law, and provide a strong foundation upon which to build a legal career. The information contained in these chapters is essential to understand why law firms conduct business differently from other industries.

Section 2. *To provide knowledge of how a law office functions.* Chapters six through ten—Legal Fees, Timekeeping, Billing and Financial Management, Managing the Clients' funds Account, and Technology in the Law Office—introduce students to the functions and procedures common to a law office environment. Understanding how legal offices function will make students' transition into legal employment easier.

Section 3. *To provide essential skills.* The last four chapters—Law Office Systems, Docket Control Systems, Records and File Management, and Law Library Organization and Management—provides students with essential skills that will be utilized throughout their legal career.

The text is organized to accommodate a sixteen-week semester course, although it is also conducive to a shorter schedule. The chapters are placed so that they may be assigned in sequential order to give the student requisite information to go on with the subsequent chapters.

FEATURES

The text has many features to contribute to a student's learning experience, including:

◆ Chapter objectives are included at the beginning of each chapter. These objectives highlight the main concepts of the chapter and provide a preview of what is to come. They act as a checklist for the student to review after the chapter is read to make sure all of the concepts were learned.

◆ Key words are emphasized in four ways. First, new terms are highlighted in bold print within the chapter. Second, each new term is defined in the margin adjacent to the paragraph in which it is found. This helps students learn the definition at the time the material is read, and increases comprehension of the material. Third, a list of key terms is included at the end of each chapter. Fourth, a comprehensive glossary is found at the end of the text.

◆ Exhibits are used to illustrate concepts throughout the text. Photographs, charts, and diagrams provide visual reinforcement of the material. In addition, many chapters contain profiles of people in various types of legal positions that give a real live example of the concepts presented in the text.

◆ Ethics alerts appear throughout the text and call attention to important ethical information. An Ethics Alert symbol appears in the margin next to the coverage of an ethical principle. In addition, the pertinent material is italicized within the body of the chapter.

◆ A summary at the end of each chapter highlights and summarizes the main points in the chapter. The summary is not a substitute for reading the chapter, but helps students study for exams.

◆ Chapter Review questions are listed at the end of each chapter. These questions review the main points of the chapter and test the student's comprehension of the material. These questions can be assigned as homework or class discussion. Answers to these questions are found in the teacher's manual.

◆ Each chapter contains examples for discussion at the end. These examples stimulate class discussions and can also be used for group projects. These examples bring the chapter contents to life by illustrating how they are used in a law office. Suggested responses are found in the teacher's manual.

◆ Various types of assignments are included at the end of each chapter. Some are easily completed and others require more effort. Most are individual assignments, but can also be used for group assignments. Suggested answers are found in the teacher's manual.

◆ The Appendix contains material that will help students understand the text and complete homework assignments. They include practical information that will be helpful on the job, such as time management tips for paralegals, and an article describing marketing activities that can be performed by nonlawyer personnel. In addition, the appendix contains reference material that is useful during the course, as well as on the job, such as a list of associations for legal assistants and managers, the codes of ethics for the National Association of Legal Assistants, and the National Federation of Paralegal Associations.[i]

CHANGES IN THE SECOND EDITION

The Second Edition has been prepared to further the text's goals. Course material has been updated, outdated material deleted, and new exhibits, photos and illustrations have been added. Many new features make the text more user-friendly and makes the

[i]**NOTE:** The terms *paralegal* and *legal assistant* are used interchangeably throughout this text with no substantive difference between the two.

material fun to learn. It has been completely overhauled while keeping its original continuity and organization.

New Chapters

Three new chapters have been added:

Chapter 5—Legal Assistant Ethics and Client Relations: In the first edition, legal assistant ethics were combined with attorney ethics, as well as disbursed throughout the book. This vital topic required more coverage and emphasis, as many important topics were not adequately covered in the First Edition. Topics include the evolvement of paralegal ethics, paralegal ethics and client relations, and the unauthorized practice of law.

Chapter 9—Managing the Clients' Funds Account: This topic was originally included in the Financial Management chapter. Since many paralegals have responsibility for maintaining a clients' funds account without being responsible for the financial accounting for a law office, this important material was easily missed. To do the subject justice, the information needed to be expanded and the author felt that this subject was important enough to have its own chapter. This chapter will prepare a student to manage a firm's trust account. Topics covered in this chapter include types of funds held in the clients' funds account, maintaining the trust account, interest on the account and trust account abuses.

Chapter 10—Technology in the Law Office. Now that technology is an essential part of every law office, a new chapter on technology has been added. This new chapter will acquaint the student with the various applications used in a law office. While it does not go into detail how to use the software, it gives an overview of the different types of software essential to law offices. It gives the student a background in Internet technology and discusses how the Internet is used in the law office. Among the topics in this chapter are common law office software, the Internet, Intranets and Extranets, electronic mail and technology ethics.

Chapters Combined

It was suggested that some chapters be combined to make the material easier to comprehend. The Billing and Financial Management chapters were combined into a new Chapter 8. In addition, the Records Management and File Management chapters are combined into a new chapter 13. Most of the material that was originally in these chapters remain intact, although updated and reduced slightly.

NEW FEATURES

The Second Edition has a number of new and useful features:

◆ More professional profiles. I received many comments that the profiles of paralegals found in Chapter 1 of the First Edition were very popular and helpful to students. Therefore, this feature has been expanded to include more professional profiles throughout the book. This feature allows a student to see how the chapter material relates to individuals and communicates another's viewpoint about the topic.

◆ Technology Section. The various technology used in the every-day systems and procedures of a law office has been included in each applicable chapter, such as timekeeping, billing and docket control. While it is not the intent of the course to give specific instruction on software, the section illustrates how technology increases the efficiency of a particular process. It also illustrates how technology is incorporated into various law office systems.

◆ Tech Tips Sidebar. To enhance the material in the technology section, a tech tips sidebar is included in most chapters. It lists the different software available for a particular topic. Its purpose is not to be an exhaustive list, but to be an example only. Neither the author nor the publisher endorse or recommend the software listed in the sidebar.

◆ Cyber Sites Sidebar. The cyber sites sidebar lists web sites that pertain to the chapter material. This feature will be very useful to instructors as well as students. Students can gain additional information about the subject matter by researching the topic on the Internet. Instructors can assign Internet research assignments using this sidebar material. Since web sites change often, the author cannot guarantee the reliability of all web sites listed in this sidebar.

◆ Of Interest Sidebar. There are many "Of-Interest" sidebars that enhance the chapter material by giving illustrations or tips pertaining to the chapter material.

◆ Trends Sidebar. This sidebar discusses trends in the marketplace that pertain to the subject matter of the chapter. It replaces the future trends section in the First Edition.

◆ Chapter Illustration. This new section has been added to the end of each chapter to reinforce the chapter material in a "real world" context. The section follows one law firm, Brown, White & Greene, from its formation (chapter 1) through its growth. Students are introduced to the firm's employees, and follow them throughout the book as they apply the concepts in the chapter. The characters experience the every-day problems and successes that average law offices experience. Its story format will amuse the student, as well as reinforce the material in the chapter. The story approach to the material will give the student a different perspective of the material and will illustrate how an average small firm is managed. This section can also be used for class discussion.

◆ Self-Test. This feature, at the end of each chapter, makes purchasing a separate study guide unnecessary. The self-test is a list of questions about the chapter material. The student can test their comprehension of the material by answering the questions and comparing their answers with the correct answer found in Appendix A. The questions are comprehensive and cover all of the material in each chapter.

SUPPLEMENT PACKAGE AND ANCILLARY MATERIALS

The author and the publisher offer supplemental materials to make the delivery of the material easy and increase the comprehension of the material. The following materials are included with adoption of the text:

◆ Test bank on CD. This feature allows easy compilation of test questions for exams. Multiple choice, true/false, fill-in, matching and essay questions are included.

◆ Instructor's Manual. An instructor's manual is included that contains teaching tips, suggestions for class discussions, answers to Chapter Review and Discussion questions, and lecture outlines. The teacher's manual consists of the following:

  ◆ An outline of each chapter. This outline will assist the instructor in planning lecture material.

  ◆ A list of key words and their definitions. This list will aid the instructor in planning lecture material.

  ◆ The answers to the chapter review questions found at the end of each chapter.

  ◆ The answers to the discussion questions found at the end of each chapter, and provide the instructor with suggestions on where to direct the discussion questions.

- ◆ Answers to the assignments at the end of each chapter.
- ◆ Teaching pointers and suggestions and includes group assignments and activities.
- ◆ Transparency masters for each chapter. The transparencies are illustrations, conceptual outlines, graphs, and charts to aid in the delivery of the material. Also included is a chapter outline showing where each transparency is to be used in the lecture material. This outline will act as a guide to the instructor's use of the transparency masters.
- ◆ Test bank that consists of multiple choice, true/false and short answer questions. The instructor may use all, or some, of the questions as they see fit.
- ◆ Powerpoint presentation slides. Chapter highlights are provided in Powerpoint software to facilitate lecture delivery.
- ◆ Web Page. A web page is available that will post updates to the text material, allow for direct feedback, and give additional teaching and learning tips to the instructor and student. The web site will also contain links to various web sites that contain information applicable to the text material. The web page can be found at www.Westlegalstudies.com
- ◆ Videos. Free to qualified adopters
- ◆ "I Never Said I was a Lawyer" Paralegal Ethics Video. This tape is non-state specific and can be used in all paralegal programs.
- ◆ Court TV Videos. Available for a fee
  - ◆ New York v. Ferguson—Murder on the 5:33: The Trial of Colin Ferguson
  - ◆ Ohio v. Alfieri—Road Rage
  - ◆ Flynn v. Goldman Sachs—Fired on Wall Street: A Case of Sex Discrimination?
  - ◆ Dodd v. Dodd: Religion and Child Custody in Conflict
  - ◆ Fentress v. Eli Lilly & Co., et al.—Prozac on Trial

ACKNOWLEDGMENTS

The Second Edition of this text would not be possible without the help of many people. Special thanks to Rhonda Dearborn of West Legal Studies who worked tirelessly on this project. I am very grateful for her dedication and expertise. Thanks also to Joan Gill of Delmar and all of the "behind the scenes" people at Delmar who contributed to this text. A heartfelt "thank you" to Stacy Williams and Jennifer La Bounty, my assistants, who worked hard on many aspects of this project.

My appreciation is extended to the reviewers who reviewed the text and offered their suggestions and comments. The effort required for a book review is substantial and certainly appreciated. I seriously considered each and every comment and suggestion, and implemented most of them. The reviewers' contributions make this edition a great text—***thank you very much.***

Reviewers of the Second Edition:

Barry S. Grossman
Nebraska College of Business, NE

Stacey Hoffpauir
Remington College, LA

Maureen K. Kappler
Elgin Community College, IL

Gayle Mozee
Santa Clara University, CA

Edward O'Boyle
Gwinnett College of Business, GA

Christopher Sadler
Denver Paralegal Institute, CO

Ellis Schein
Pace Institute, PA

Leigh Anne Chavez
Albuquerque Technical
Vocational Institute

Donna Donathon
Marshall University

Marjorie Fishman
Athens Area Technical College

Anne Kastle
Edmonds Community College

Laurine R. Kreipe
formerly of Washburn
University of Topeka

Jennifer Labosky
Davidson County
Community College

Kathryn Myers
Saint Mary-of-the-Woods
College

H. Margaret Nickerson
William Woods College

Kathleen Mercer Reed
University of Toledo

Michele Rehwinkle
Tallahassee Community
College

Hon. Gene Schnelz
Madonna University

George D. Schrader
Auburn University
at Montgomery

Jane Lee Sutton
J. S. Reynolds Community
College

Last, but certainly not least, thanks to my family whose love, understanding and support of mom, grandma, daughter and sister makes life beautiful and hard work worth the effort.

To the Student

After teaching this class for twenty years, I've heard many comments and opinions from my students. They told me of their desires for this course and what material is useful for them. I appreciate all their comments, and sincerely hope to continue receiving them.

Many students have told me that the material in this text made their transition into their new legal career easier—and that is the goal of this text. If this text helps you understand the legal world better, then it has succeeded in reaching its goals. I'd like to hear from you. Let me know what you like, and didn't like, about this text. Just drop me an email from our web site.

You've made a wise decision to pursue a legal career. It will challenge and exhilarate you, as well as satisfy your personal and professional goals. Sincere best wishes in your studies and career development.

Pamela Everett

Contents

CHAPTER

4

The Attorney-Client Relationship   118

CHAPTER

5

Paralegal Ethics and Client Relations   166

CHAPTER

6

Legal Fees   198

CHAPTER

7

Timekeeping   242

CHAPTER

9

Managing the Client Funds Trust Account   309

CHAPTER

10

Technology in the Law Office 327

CHAPTER
11

Law Office Systems   370

The Legal Marketplace

OBJECTIVES

After completion of this chapter, a student should be able to do the following:

◆ Describe the structure and organization of small, medium, and large firms.

◆ Explain the autocratic, democratic, managing partner, committee, and combination management styles.

◆ Discuss the differences between a sole proprietorship, partnership, professional corporation, boutique firm, office-sharing association, and legal clinic.

◆ Discuss the differences between corporate legal departments, private companies, and government agencies.

◆ List the potential employment opportunities for legal assistants.

◆ Identify the changes that have affected the legal marketplace.

INTRODUCTION

Legal clinic: Low-cost firms with standard fees for standard services.

Boutique: A law firm that offers services in one area of law only.

Most employers of legal assistants are attorneys. Both legal assistants and attorneys are unique professionals whose talents and personalities are as diverse as their numbers. They work in many different types of law offices: small firms, large firms, corporate legal departments, **legal clinics,** government agencies, and **boutique,** or specialized, firms. All of these offices have similarities, yet they are different. Each law office has its own structure, organization, and combination of personalities.

The purpose of this chapter is to provide an overview of the different types of law office settings and discuss the various management styles. Comments from legal assistants working in the various types of law offices will give an idea of the diversity of law offices. This chapter will supply the foundation for a more in-depth discussion of elements that are common among all law offices and provide a familiarity with the diversity of the legal marketplace.

This chapter describes the structure and organization of law firms. Then, it examines the three categories of the marketplace in which attorneys practice law: private law firms, private industry, and government agencies. Finally, it discusses opportunities for legal assistants and the changing marketplace of law firms.

STRUCTURE AND ORGANIZATION

For a law office, *structure* refers to its many parts that are brought together to form a whole. *Organization* refers to the management of each part so that all parts function together as one unit. The structure and organization of a law office depend on the needs and desires of its attorneys, especially senior attorneys who own the firm. These components are not rigid but are subject to change. Variables such as the economy and the changing needs of society influence a law office's structure and organization. A legal assistant must be flexible to bend with organizational changes.

The structure and organization of a law office are determined by four characteristics: size, specialty, management style, and form.

Size

The size of a law office is measured by the number of attorneys employed by that office. The size differential varies according to the population of the geographic area of the office. For example, in large metropolitan areas, such as New York, Chicago, and Los Angeles, the average size of law firms is larger, so the size differential is larger. The size differential for a highly populated area is as follows:

Small office: 1 to 35 attorneys

Medium office: 36 to 100 attorneys

Large office: 101 or more attorneys

In areas of average to large populations, the size differential is somewhat smaller:

Small office: 1 to 25 attorneys

Medium office: 26 to 80 attorneys

Large office: 81 or more attorneys

In rural areas with smaller populations, the size differential is smaller yet:

Small office: 1 to 15 attorneys

Medium office: 16 to 60 attorneys

Large office: 60 or more attorneys

The number of branch offices a firm has also determines its size. For example, a large law firm with 200 attorneys may have those attorneys disbursed in several branch offices. A branch office may employ only three to four attorneys, thereby constituting a small office. However, the size of a law firm is calculated by the total number of attorneys employed by the firm, including the attorneys in all of its branch offices.

Small Firm   Small firms are the preferred setting for practicing law for most lawyers in the United States. The average size of a small firm is three to four attorneys. A small firm may be less formal and less structured. Most of a small firm's clientele are individuals.

Medium Firm   The size of a medium firm depends on the area of the United States in which it is located. Medium firms tend to attract entrepreneurial clients who are cost conscious (see Exhibit 1.1).

Merger: The union of two or more law firms to form one law firm.

Megafirm: A firm that employs more than 300 attorneys and has branch offices throughout the world.

Large Firm   Four traditional types of large law firms exist: local, regional, national, and international. A local firm is located in one geographic area with no branch offices, a regional firm has branch offices within a specific region, a national firm has branch offices within the United States, and an international firm has branch offices in other countries as well as in the United States.

The **merger** boom of the 1980s brought the creation of a new type of larger firm: the **megafirm.** Megafirms employ three hundred or more attorneys and have branch offices all over the world.

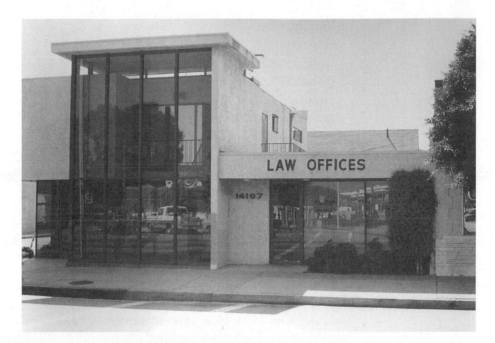

EXHIBIT 1.1 Medium Firms Tend to Attract Entrepreneurial Clients Who Are Cost Conscious

Large firms are formal and highly structured. They employ many types of support personnel and, for the most part, service large corporate clients. Most large firms have branch offices in major American cities to meet the needs of their corporate clients that conduct business in other areas of the country. Many large firms have offices in other countries.

Specialties

As society has become more complex, law has become more complex as well. Thousands of new laws are passed each year, and it has become increasingly difficult for attorneys to keep abreast of the many changes. This has forced attorneys to specialize in a particular area of law.

The transition to specialization in law is analogous to that in the medical profession. Before World War II, doctors and lawyers were "general family practitioners." They took care of all the legal and medical needs of a family from birth to death. Now, however, the complexities of law and medicine have made general practice unfeasible for the welfare of the client and the patient.

The areas of law in which a firm's attorneys specialize help determine the firm's clientele and its need for staff, equipment, and materials. For example, a criminal attorney does not need a plush office in which to greet clients since he will probably meet clients in jail. A business law specialist, who offers clients a wide range of services, will need a tax department, corporate department, litigation department, labor relations department, and contract department. The firm must have a large support staff and a sophisticated computer system. A professional office environment is necessary to greet business clients and conduct conferences.

In 1990, the American Bar Association (ABA) identified 278 attorney specialty areas, some of which are the following:

Administrative	Admiralty	Antitrust
Aviation	Bankruptcy	Business
Civil rights	Commercial	Communications
Consumer	Contract	Corporate
Construction	Criminal	Education

Employment	Energy	Entertainment
Environment	Family	Franchise
Government	Health	Immigration
Insurance	International	Labor
Landlord-tenant	Military	Natural resources
Mergers and acquisitions	Patent, copyright, and trademark	Transportation
Tribal	Trusts and estate planning	

Cybertort: Actions for damages resulting from libelous material posted on the Internet. Also included is posting material that is protected by copyright or trademarks, such as magazines and photos.

A new specialty that is gaining popularity is **cybertort,** or actions for tortuous activity arising from Internet postings.

A number of states have developed plans for the recognition of legal specialties. In some states, attorneys whose law practice consists of a particular area of law can designate themselves a specialist. In others, the state bar monitors a certified specialist program. An attorney must pass a specialty exam in addition to a bar exam in order to be a certified specialist.

According to a census conducted by the ABA Standing Committee on Specialization in late 1996, there are more than 21,000 specialists in the United States, a 17 percent increase from 1995. New specialty areas, such as elder law and health law increased tremendously. Most of the certified lawyers are certified by ten states, with the vast majority found in California, Florida, and Texas. There are over twenty-four specialty areas found in the various state-sponsored specialist programs. Attorney specialties fluctuate according to outside factors such as the economy, legal trends, and social concerns. For example, in the late 1980s, attorneys specializing in Employee Retirement programs were in the most demand. In the early 1990s, environmental attorneys were in the most demand. When the recession hit in the mid 1990s, bankruptcy specialists were in the highest demand. As the recession subsided, corporate and transactional specialties were prominent. At the millennium, technology skyrocketed which transferred the demand from corporate to intellectual property and patent specialists.

Legal assistants specialize in the same areas as attorneys. They may also be recognized as a specialist. Specialty exams are administered by the two national paralegal associations and are described in Chapter 2.

According to a survey conducted by Matthew Bender and *Lawyers Weekly* (March 1997), specialists earn more than general practitioners. They charge more for their services because they get more complex cases and are considered experts in the area. "Specializing makes life easier," says John Shea, a personal injury specialist in Richmond, Virginia. "You build up a body of knowledge so you can do things efficiently. It's very difficult, if not impossible, to do a lot of things well." Lawyers in small towns and rural areas find it very difficult to specialize because the community demands a variety of legal services. Other general practitioners also find this difficult because they prefer the diversity that general practice provides.

Management Styles

One very important aspect of the practice of law is not taught to attorneys in most law schools: managing their business. Consequently, many attorneys have suffered from poor office management, which has resulted in reduced profits, increased attorney discipline proceedings, and office disorganization. These problems are reflected in dissatisfied clients.

Since the early 1970s, attorneys have realized the importance of effective management. Before this, attorneys ran their business by "panic management," which, unfortunately, still exists today.

Culture: The working environment of a law firm, consisting of intangible elements such as the social environment, employee relationships, and attitudes.

A law office's environment is referred to as its **culture,** which includes such intangible elements as the sharing of work assignments, recognition, autonomy, responsibility, attitudes toward the community and family, and social atmosphere. A firm's management style is also part of its culture.

Two distinct managerial areas are addressed by any law firm: administrative (financial, office systems, and so forth) and governance (associates, client relations, personnel, marketing, and the like). The combination of approaches used in these two areas is the management style of the firm. Attorneys, growing tired of chaos, have developed five management styles that are used in most law firms in the United States: autocratic, democratic, managing partner, committee, and combination.

Autocratic: Relating to government by one person with unlimited power.

Autocratic In an **autocratic** form of management, one person makes all the decisions for the firm (see Exhibit 1.2). This style is most often found in small offices with one employing attorney. In small offices with more than one attorney, the autocrat is usually attorney who formed the law firm or controls the major clients of the firm. However, an autocrat is also found in larger offices.

An autocrat in a small office makes all the decisions for the firm, and a secretary, legal assistant, or both help implement the decisions. In a larger office, an autocrat makes all the decisions, and an office manager implements them. Small firms with strong leadership have prospered under this type of management. Successful autocrats gain the respect of their associates and usually ask for their input before making major decisions. Like any good leader, they can motivate their staff and associates and delegate responsibility well.

Some autocrats have poor management skills and do not request input from their staff when making decisions. They become tyrants who intimidate staff and clients. An autocratic management style combined with poor leadership skills causes low employee morale and reduces productivity.

Despite the authoritarian nature of this type of management, it is generally effective in getting things done. An autocrat is usually a "born boss" and gladly accepts management responsibility. Many attorneys would rather leave the management decisions to another so that they can devote their time to their clients. Strong leadership is an essential element of the success of prosperous law firms.

Democratic There are two types of the democratic form of governance: those in which all attorneys in the firm have a vote on management policy and those in which only owners of the law firm have a vote in management policy.

In small offices with fewer than fifteen attorneys, usually all attorneys participate in the firm's management. In larger offices, only owners participate in making management decisions.

Legal administrator: Experienced manager who is hired to manage a law firm. Has the authority of a managing partner.

Actual management duties are accomplished in a democratic management style: In a large firm, the decisions of the firm are delegated to a **legal administrator,** who accomplishes the task or delegates it to an appropriate person. The administrator is a full-time administrator whose only duty is to implement the decisions of the

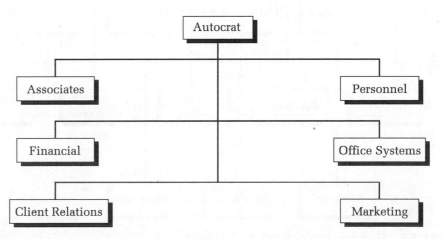

EXHIBIT 1.2 Autocratic Organizational Chart

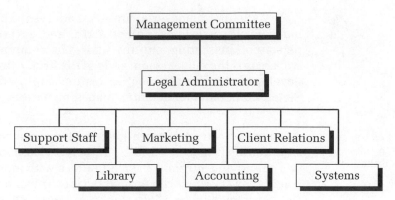

EXHIBIT 1.3 Democratic Organizational Chart for a Large Firm

attorneys. In a small firm, a part-time manager/legal assistant whose management duties are shared with paralegal duties implements the decisions (see Exhibit 1.3).

In a smaller firm, each attorney is assigned an area of management, such as equipment procurement, personnel relations, or billing. Each attorney then performs management duties with the assistance of a secretary, legal assistant, or both. This form of democratic management style is shown in Exhibit 1.4.

Since people hold many opinions as to how a firm should be managed, complete agreement on a topic is rare in this type of management style. Unless a senior partner or another leader takes control of this group, a consensus of opinion is difficult to reach. Consequently, action is delayed because decisions are delayed. In addition, some attorneys have neither the desire nor the skill to handle management functions. Some attorneys in this management style view their participation in management as a burden, taking time away from their cases and resulting in lower billing for a firm. Generally, this style of management is ineffective and expensive for a firm.

Managing Partner   In the managing partner style of management, one of the owners of a firm is designated the managing partner, who is responsible for managing the firm. In smaller firms, a managing partner manages a firm in addition to practicing

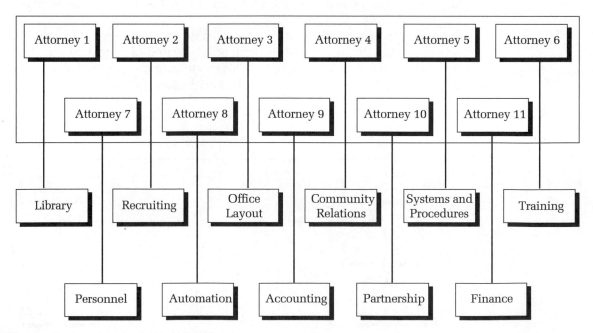

EXHIBIT 1.4 Democratic Organizational Chart

Office manager: A person hired to assist a managing partner or legal administrator with management functions of a firm.

law. This person delegates duties to a legal assistant, secretary, or office manager to carry out the decisions. The delegated person is a part-time office manager in addition to being responsible for other duties.

In medium firms, the managing partner spends more time on management duties but is encouraged to continue to practice law so as not to lose legal skills, therefore contributing to the firm's income. The average managing partner spends about 40 percent of the time practicing law. The managing partner often has an **office manager,** legal administrator, or both to assist in the firm's management responsibilities. The managing partner is the head of the firm and often is a senior attorney of the firm. An example of this type of structure is shown in Exhibit 1.5.

In large firms, a managing partner may devote all the time to management functions, and employs an administrator and perhaps many office managers to manage individual areas of a firm, as shown in Exhibit 1.6. These management professionals have no duties other than management functions.

The managing partner style of management is the style most commonly used in law offices in the 1990s. A managing partner with the necessary management and leadership skills is an effective manager. This person must be capable of delegating day-to-day decisions to others while maintaining control. This style of management is closely related to the autocratic style, especially in a small firm.

Committee Some firms rely on a committee structure for management. This management style is normally found in large firms. Committees form when the firm cannot agree on a leader or when no strong person emerges after the founder retires.

The terms of committee membership are generally limited, and members rotate from committee to committee to participate in the various areas of management. Management committees generally consist of five to seven members and may comprise senior partners only, a mixture of senior and junior partners, a mixture of partners and associates, or a mixture of partners, associate office managers, and legal assistants (see Exhibit 1.7).

A firm may have various committees, the most common of which are the following:

Associate personnel (including legal assistants)

Automation and technology

Client relations

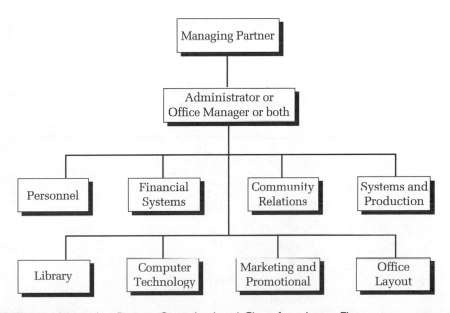

EXHIBIT 1.5 Managing Partner Organizational Chart for a Large Firm

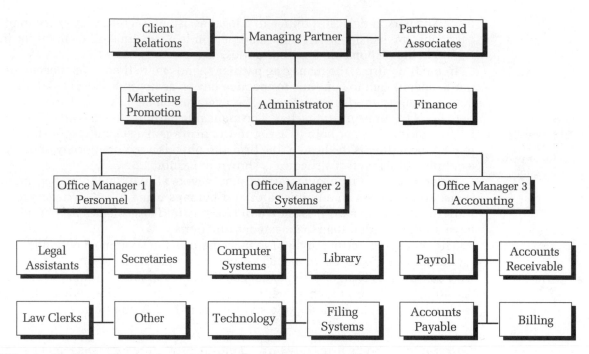

EXHIBIT 1.6 Managing Partner Organizational Chart for a Medium Firm

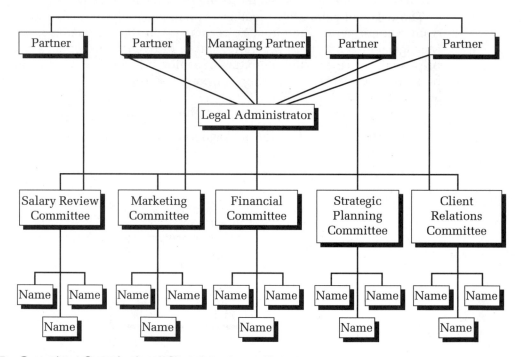

EXHIBIT 1.7 Committee Organizational Chart for a Large Firm

> Community relations
> Compensation
> Employee training
> Equipment and supplies
> Finance and accounting
> Marketing
> Office facilities and furnishings

Office space and layout
Partnership matters
Recruiting
Strategic planning
Support personnel
Systems and procedures

Executive committee: A committee comprising the heads of the various committees in a law firm.

An **executive committee** composed of heads of the various management committees coordinates the activities of the committees, as shown in Exhibit 1.8. In medium to large firms, a legal administrator helps coordinate the various committees and is responsible for implementing the decisions. In large offices, the administrator delegates responsibilities to an office manager or managers and sits on each committee.

Many problems may occur with this type of structure. It has been said that a committee is composed of the unwilling, picked from the unqualified, to do the unnecessary. Closely related committees may duplicate efforts. Attending committee meetings may be difficult for some attorneys, especially trial attorneys. Some committee members may be weaker because of no management training or knowledge of the subject area. An example would be when the committee members take time to educate themselves about computers. Adding this extra step causes delays to take place in the decision process. Additionally, committee work requires the use of the firm's greatest asset: the time of its attorneys. Committees are normally ineffective, especially in times of change.

Combination A combination management style is one that uses two or more management styles at the same time, such as managing partner and committee or democratic and committee (see Exhibit 1.9).

TRENDS ➤➤➤

Law Firm Names

Law firms are changing their names. Names that consist of the owner's last names separated by commas and an ampersand (&) are often very long and cumbersome. Firms are dropping the commas and ampersand from their names as well as a name or two. For example, Pierce, Atwood, Scribner, Allen, Smith & Lancaster is now Pierce Atwood. When Thompson & Mitchell merged with Coburn & Croft, the new name did not become Thompson, Mitchell, Coburn & Croft; it is Thompson Coburn. Receptionists are pleased with this new trend.

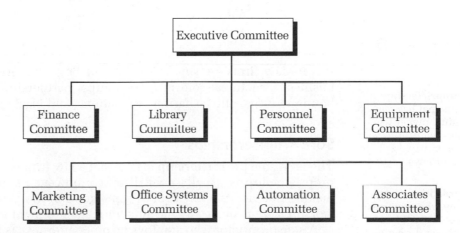

EXHIBIT 1.8 Executive Committee Organizational Chart

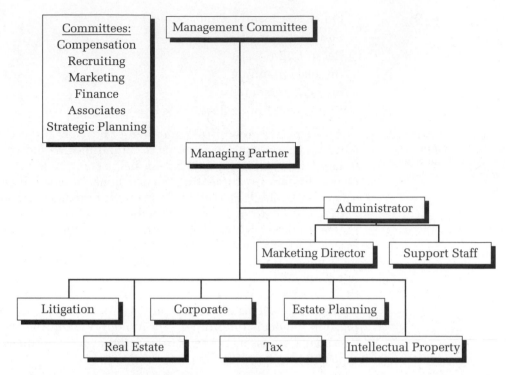

EXHIBIT 1.9 Combination Organizational Chart for a Large Firm

Forms of Management

Management takes two forms: centralized and decentralized. Having a centralized form of management means that an entire law firm is managed from one source, whether by autocratic, democratic, managing partner, or committee style of management. Having a decentralized form of management means that a law firm is managed in segments, or in many areas. For example, in a decentralized form of management, branch offices may have their own management structure and may not rely on a parent firm for management direction. Each branch may have a different management style, with one managed by committee and another managed by a managing partner.

In a large law firm, each department, identified by areas of law, may manage itself in an **autonomous,** or independent, manner. In this form of decentralized management, the managing partner of each department sits on an executive committee to make decisions involving the whole firm and is solely responsible for management decisions of the department.

Autonomous: Being self-governing, independent, and subject to its own methods of management.

PRIVATE LAW FIRMS

Private law firms are small, medium, or large and are organized into six different business structures: sole proprietorships, partnerships, professional corporations, boutique firms, office-sharing associations, and legal clinics.

Sole proprietorship: A business that has one individual owner who operates the firm. A sole proprietor may employ other attorneys.

Sole Proprietorships

The term **sole proprietorship** means that a law firm is owned by one attorney. A sole proprietorship is usually a small office; however, it may employ thirty attorneys, making it a medium law firm in some areas of the United States. Most sole proprietorships are managed by the autocratic management style.

A sole proprietor who employs no other attorneys is a **sole practitioner.** Sole practitioners who do not specialize in a particular area of law are **general practitioners.**

Sole practitioner: An attorney who practices law alone. A sole practitioner does not employ other attorneys.

General practitioner:
An attorney who does not specialize but accepts cases in all areas of law.

The American Bar Association estimated in 1999 that 46 percent of all attorneys in private practice are sole practitioners. A new attorney who has just graduated from law school is most likely to be a general practitioner. The cost of opening a law office is very high, and because of financial concerns, a new attorney will accept almost any type of case. A new lawyer is also developing a client base, so it is important to work for as many clients as possible. As a new attorney's client base, skill, and reputation increase, more opportunities for specialization present themselves. Attorneys who live in rural areas and small towns normally are general practitioners because the needs of the community require more general legal services. The five most common specialties for sole proprietors are family law, real estate, torts and personal injury, criminal defense, and probate and estate planning. In small towns, attorneys specialize in either family law or estate planning.

Sole practitioners constitute the largest category of lawyers in private practice. Before World War II, most attorneys in the United States were sole practitioners—approximately 60 percent. By the late 1950s, the percentage of sole practitioners had declined to 40 percent. In 1990, 19 percent of the entire lawyer population were sole practitioners.

Some sole practitioners work only for attorneys, not for clients. They are called **contract attorneys,** or temporary lawyers. They work for temporary agencies much in the same way as temporary support staff personnel. The temporary agency contracts them out to law firms and corporate legal departments to work on a project basis. The project may last a few days or many months. This form of sole practice is gaining popularity both with the lawyers and with the firms for which they work.

Contract attorney:
Attorneys who work for law firms on an assignment basis or as an independent contractor.

Most contract attorneys are recent bar admittees. However, experienced, reputable attorneys are choosing contract work over the more traditional employment for various reasons. Some lost their jobs to corporate downsizing, whereas others recently relocated to new areas, had babies, or decided that the partnership track was not for them. A large portion of contract attorneys, about 25 percent by some estimates, are sole practitioners who accept contract work to compensate for slow periods in their own business. According to the U.S. Bureau of Labor Statistics, there were 40,000 contract attorneys in the United States in 1995, up from 10,000 in 1992. By 2005, the number is expected to increase 56 percent.

Contract attorneys are subject to the same canons of ethics as their employing firms. Ethical issues faced by contract attorneys are addressed in ABA Formal Opinion 88-356, which defines a temporary lawyer as a lawyer engaged by a firm for a limited period time, either directly or through a lawyer placement agency. They are bound by the same rules of confidentiality and conflict of interest, disclosure, and fee-sharing rules, as described in Chapter 4.

Law firms are realizing that they can utilize the talent and skill of a contract attorney at a fraction of the cost of an employee and realize the following benefits from using contract attorneys:

◆ An opportunity to try out potential hires
◆ Less administrative work
◆ Ability for small firms to accept bigger cases without hiring additional personnel
◆ Staff attorneys relieved from mundane work
◆ Positions covered for attorneys who are out on sick leave or on vacation
◆ Reduced employee costs, such as benefits and employee related expenses

Contract attorneys realize the following benefits from accepting temporary assignments:

◆ Sole practitioners able to supplement their practice
◆ Affords a lawyer the time needed to find the right job or to pursue other endeavors, such as continuing education

◆ Flexible hours for lawyers who juggle work and family
◆ Work as little or as much as you would like
◆ Ease of relocation to a new area
◆ More control over work schedules

A sole proprietor may change the type of organization as time goes by. A sole proprietor may promote an associate to ownership status, thereby evolving the firm into a partnership. A sole proprietor may also incorporate a business and turn it into a professional corporation.

Advantages and Disadvantages to a Sole Practice

Advantages	Disadvantages
Receives all profits	Responsibility for all a firm's expenses
More freedom and independence	No assistance with caseload and court appearances from other attorneys
Opportunity to make all the decisions for a firm	Usually a lower income and no guaranteed paycheck
Familiarity with all facets of a firm's operation	Difficulty taking time off for vacations; long work hours
	Need to handle all areas of a business: managing, bringing in clients, preparing documents, and making court appearances
	Difficulty specializing at first
	Usually unable to afford the latest equipment and the newest technology
	Abandonment of clients if attorney should die or become incapacitated

A Typical Sole Practitioner The office of Eric Norby consists of one attorney, one secretary, and one legal assistant. The management style of the firm is autocratic, and the legal assistant, Cindy Upcraft, assists Eric in the management duties. In addition to her paralegal duties, Cindy is responsible for billing, accounts receivable, and accounts payable. She also does some light bookkeeping to prepare records for the accountant.

Eric does family law, estate planning, probate, criminal, and landlord-tenant work. Cindy handles the day-to-day maintenance of cases under Eric's supervision, except for probate cases, from an initial client interview to the close of a case. The firm utilizes the services of a freelance probate legal assistant to handle the probate cases. Since the office is small, the probate legal assistant works out of her home and bills the firm hourly for her time.

Cindy is busy with paralegal and management functions, so she relies heavily on the legal secretary, Carol Vinnecomb. Carol is very experienced in wills and family law matters and prepares the necessary paperwork under the direction of the legal assistant and the attorney. She is responsible for all clerical functions and is also responsible for receptionist duties and for greeting clients who come into the office.

Cindy and Carol each have a personal computer. Eric has not yet overcome his fear of computers, so he relies heavily on his staff for functions requiring their use.

Everyone in the office works very hard. Cindy works a lot of overtime and, on occasion, weekends. She is underpaid for her skills and knows she could make more money in a larger firm. However, she likes the family atmosphere of a small office and the close client contact.

Partnerships

A partnership is a law firm formed by two or more attorneys. Attorneys work cooperatively on cases that are taken in by the firm, and the partners share in the profits.

Linda J. Metcalf, legal assistant, works for Roger W. Moister, Jr., a sole proprietor in Atlanta, Georgia. The office specializes in bankruptcy, and Roger is also a bankruptcy trustee. The office also handles civil litigation matters. When asked about the structure of her office, Linda states:

"I am the office. I do everything here. I manage the office and am responsible for everything except for reconciling bank statements. In addition to my paralegal duties, which consist of completing all bankruptcy documents and monitoring the litigation cases in bankruptcy adversary proceedings, I have a lot of client contact.

"My job is always different. Each day brings a new challenge. There is never a dull moment. I worked for a large company for twenty years, and I like a small firm much better. I am appreciated here, and I learn more with a variety of work.

"There is a lot of pressure in a small office. We have many cases. My salary may be lower than [it would be in] other firms, but my bonuses are better. I do not get paid for overtime, but I receive compensatory time off. I like the small atmosphere and team concept of my job. I also like the control I have with my management responsibilities."

Jeanne M. O'Neill, a certified legal assistant **(CLA),** works for a sole proprietor, Jeffrey Mazor, in Florida. She supervises the legal assistants in her office and has other administrative functions. Her office has one major client, a very large bank in her area. The firm does a variety of work for the bank, including forfeiture and seizure, bankruptcy, and collections. She states:

"I am exposed to more variety of work when working for a small firm. I have more responsibility and work independently. I have more control over the cases. If I do a good job, my boss will reward me with a bonus. This would not happen in a large firm where bonuses are structured and approved by the governing body.

"I like the close family atmosphere. We don't have as many benefits and 'comforts' in a small firm, but we do have a very good, high-quality computer system. My attorney and the office are very organized. Anyone in the office can answer a client's question if the attorney is out—*as long as it does not require giving legal advice.* The structure of our office allows maximum productivity for the firm. Since we are very experienced legal assistants in our firm, the attorney just supervises our work. The advantages far outweigh the disadvantages."

CLA: Certified legal assistant. A certification that is granted after a legal assistant passes an exam given by the National Association of Legal Assistants.

Partnerships

A partnership is a law firm formed by two or more attorneys. Attorneys work cooperatively on cases that are taken in by the firm, and the partners share in the profits. Three classes of attorneys work in a partnership: partners, associates, and nontraditional, such as contract attorneys, as more specifically detailed in Chapter two.

Choosing a partner is an important decision. A potential partner must be dependable, reliable, and trustworthy. Each partner in a firm is liable for the decisions and conduct of other partners. If one partner obligates a firm, all partners are liable for the obligation. If one partner commits fraud or is unethical, the other partners are also liable. Some partnerships are finding relief from this personal liability for the acts of other partners by forming a **limited liability company.**

Limited liability company: A company formed to shield its owners and their assets from liability arising from the misconduct of other owners or employees.

Limited liability companies (LLCs) were created to shield partners and their assets from the liabilities of other partners' malpractice or other problems. Each state has different protections and different requirements, a situation that has created problems for regional and national firms. While LLCs have made many partners feel more secure in their partnership structure, this form of partnership has created other issues. For example, some clients do not like the fact that senior partners are no longer responsible for the unprofessional conduct of associates. Because of these and other problems, some partnerships and megapartnerships have chosen not to become an LLC.

Advantages and Disadvantages to a Partnership

Advantages	Disadvantages
Other lawyers can handle a case if an attorney becomes ill or goes on vacation	Need for discipline in work habits
More opportunity for specialization	Exposure to risk—liability of all attorneys in a partnership for the malpractice and obligations of a partner or associate
Assistance from other attorneys or networking with other attorneys in a firm	Inability to accept a case pro bono (for no fee) or for a reduced fee without partners' approval
Partners to share the expenses of a firm	Need to be able to compromise
More security	
Potentially higher income	
More opportunity for community involvement and marketing activities	

A Typical Partnership   The law firm of Goldes, Levin & Strong is composed of six full partners, three junior partners, ten associates, nineteen secretaries, thirteen legal assistants, seven law clerks, and one legal administrator. The firm also employs one receptionist, one full-time bookkeeper, one case manager, and five file clerks.

The business is run by a managing partner, Helane Strong. Helane is a senior partner because she was one of the founders of the firm. She was chosen to be the managing partner because of her management background before she became an attorney. Helane devotes 80 percent of her time to management duties; she spends the remaining 20 percent on tax work. The administrator is responsible for the day-to-day management of the firm and reports directly to Helane.

The firm specializes in business organizations and works for business clients. It has four departments: business litigation, tax, corporate, and contracts. Each department has at least one partner. Seven attorneys make up the business litigation department; three attorneys, including Helane, work in the tax department; five attorneys form the corporate department; and four attorneys are in the contracts department.

The firm employs one secretary for each attorney and one legal assistant for every two attorneys, except in the litigation department, which employs one legal assistant for each attorney. The law clerks are organized in a pool and work for all the attorneys as needed.

The firm is managed by a combination style: managing partner and management committee. It has one management committee composed of all six partners. The managing partner, Helane, is the chairman of the management committee. The committee meets once each month, at which time decisions are made. Helane carries out the decisions of the committee and delegates tasks to the administrator.

The administrator is directly responsible for all personnel, all systems, and the general functioning of the firm. He is also responsible for ensuring that all timekeeping records are turned in so that clients may be billed timely. If a personnel dispute occurs, the administrator attempts to resolve it. If it is a problem the administrator cannot resolve, he asks for Helane's assistance.

All the legal assistants in the firm specialize in one of four areas of law: business litigation, tax, corporate, and contracts. The secretaries also specialize. The firm has a sophisticated computer system. Each secretary, legal assistant, legal administrator, and attorney has a computer. The computers are linked by a network so that each person has access to all departments of the firm.

The employees are satisfied with their compensation, which is comparable to that provided by other firms in the area. Most of the legal assistants enjoy working as a specialist. Others, however, find the work too repetitive and would like more variety.

CYBERSITES
Law Firms on the Web

Need more information about law firms? Check out the following Web sites:

Large Firms

Pierce Atwood—www.pierceatwood.com. East coast law firm with 80+ attorneys. Has client relations and technology pages. Describes its nonlegal subsidiary, PA Strategies, a consulting division. Access to firm newsletter on-line.

Anderson Kill & Olick—www.andersonkill.com. Law firm of 150+ attorneys. Has newsletter page and description of branch offices. Contains an interesting page of information regarding vacated judgments.

Large International Firms

Arent Fox Kintner & Kahn, PLLC—www.arentfox.com. Voted best large-firm Web site by *Legalonline*. Firm has 100+ attorneys. Site contains firm brochure and many other features

Crowell & Moring LLP—www.crowellmoring.com. Firm has 240+ attorneys. Site contains pro bono area, newsletters, seminar announcements, and information regarding its nonlegal subsidiary, C&M International, Ltd.

Medium Firms

Schuyler, Roche & Zwirner, PC—www.srzlaw.com. Firm with 40+ attorneys. Site has client relations page, including their philosophy regarding communication with clients.

Venture Law Group—www.venlaw.com. Firm with 70+ lawyers. Specialists in representing deal-intensive technology companies and venture capital banking firms in Silicon Valley, California.

Moye Giles O'Keefe Vermeire & Garrell LLP—www.mgovg.com. Voted best medium-firm Web site by *Legalonline*. Contains interesting articles on legal ethics and has many other interesting pages.

Boutique Firms

Kapilan Meyers Rosen & Louik, PC—www.kmrlmedmal.com. Medical malpractice and personal injury law firm. Employs seven attorneys and two doctors. Newsletter on-line.

Birch, Steward, Kolasch & Birch, LLP—www.bskb.com. Law firm that specializes in intellectual property. They give seminars and have an on-line newsletter of patent and trademark issues.

The Tax Prophet—www.taxprophet.com. Voted the best small-firm Web site by *Legalonline*. Sole practitioner who specializes in tax matters.

Oppedahl & Larson—www.patents.com

Small Firms

Law Offices of Seth J. Arnowitz—www.ctattorney.com. Sole practitioner who specializes in real estate litigation.

Law Offices of Richard L. Armstrong—www.armstlaw@law-armstrong.com. Small firm that has interesting links to clients' Web sites. Does pro bono work for a women's center (pregnancy counseling).

Law Offices of J. B. Baugh—http//firms.findlaw.com/jbbough/about.com. Sole proprietor in northern Alabama specializing in civil litigation and mediation.

Sole practitioner web site—www.solaw.com.

Foreign Firms

Rotheras Solicitors—www.rotheras.demon.co.uk. Firm of 15+ attorneys in Nottingham, England. Has interesting lawyer joke page.

Chan Robles & Associates—www.chanrobles.com. International firm in the Philippines. Office is open twenty-four hours a day to accommodate international clients. Site contains links to many international legal databases and many links to various government agencies. Firm has many nonlegal subsidiaries, including a consulting company, a CPA firm, a collection firm, training services, and a publishing company.

Professional Corporations

A law firm or an individual lawyer who wishes to incorporate will form a professional corporation. A professional corporation is different from a general corporation in that all its shareholders must be of the same profession. Doctors own professional medical corporations, and lawyers own professional legal corporations. Attorneys purchase shares in a professional corporation as they would in a public corporation. The number of shares an attorney owns determines the attorney's ownership percentage in a corporation. In most states, only attorneys may own shares in a professional legal corporation.

Dividend: A payment according to the profitability of a firm and the number of shares of stock owned by an attorney.

All attorneys employed by a professional corporation, including the shareholders, are employees of the corporation and receive a salary for their work. In addition, the shareholders receive **dividends** according to the profitability of the corporation and the number of shares they own. A professional corporation may have one shareholder or many shareholders.

The organization of a professional corporation is like that of other, nonprofessional corporations (see Exhibit 1.10). The corporation is considered a separate entity unto itself. Therefore, shareholders are not generally personally responsible for the corporation's debts. The shareholders elect a board of directors by voting their shares. The board of directors is the policy-making body of the corporation, and it elects officers: president, vice-president, secretary, and treasurer. The officers are responsible for the day-to-day management of the corporation. A shareholder may be a director and an officer.

One-half of the existing law firms in 1985 were professional corporations. Attorneys incorporated because they received certain tax advantages, mainly pension benefits. However, the tax reform acts of 1984 and 1986 took away many of those advantages, and a professional corporation has become less attractive to attorneys. Even though the tax advantages have decreased, many attorneys still prefer to be incorporated because of the reduced liability they are offered as shareholders. For example, in a partnership, if partner Sam Smith purchased a $300,000 computer system for his partnership, each partner would be individually liable for the debt if the firm could not pay for the equipment. In a professional corporation, only the corporation would be responsible for the debt.

EXHIBIT 1.10 Professional Corporation Organizational Chart

Professional Profile

Sandra Allen is a litigation specialist with the medium-size firm of Ramey, Flock, Jeffers, Crawford, Harper & Collins, a defense firm in Tyler, Texas. Its clients are mainly insurance companies. Sandra's duties are focused on discovery matters, collections, and the evaluation of medical records. She also assists the attorneys in jury selection. Of her job, she states:

"I enjoy the structured environment of this firm. It is well managed by a professional legal administrator and has very clear written policies for the entire firm. The office manager acts as a liaison between the attorneys and support staff. It is a prestigious firm where everyone knows each other.

"Some senior attorneys in this firm have a difficult time delegating responsibility to a legal assistant. My duties are rather routine. I am not given as much responsibility as I would like. All and all, though, I like working here."

Christine Johansson is a litigation specialist with a medium-size firm in Santa Fe, New Mexico. She is working on two complex litigation cases, for which she is in charge of controlling the documents and witness files. She is putting the documents on a computerized system to track information about the case. She states:

"My work is very interesting. I love computers. My firm is not [so large that] you lose contact with people. I like the variety of personalities in a medium firm. There is still a family atmosphere here. I used to work for a small firm where I did everything. I like this better because I specialize and my duties are more focused in one area.

"There seems to be more pressure here than in the small firm I used to work [for]. This firm can afford better computer equipment and the latest technology. Small firms don't have the latest technology. There are more opportunities here."

P.C.: Professional corporation.

Some firms organized as professional corporations may themselves consist of professional corporations. For example, Anderson & Kopecki, Professional Corporation (**P.C.**), employs Randall Anderson, P.C., an individual who is a professional corporation, and Sharon Kopecki, P.C., another individual who is a professional corporation. The firm pays the individual professional corporations for the services of the attorneys. The attorneys are paid a salary from their own corporation.

A sole practitioner may be a professional corporation. The sole practitioner would be the only shareholder as well as a director and an officer. All sizes of firms may incorporate and become a professional corporation.

Advantages and Disadvantages to a Professional Corporation

Advantages	Disadvantages
Limited liability, with the corporation, not other attorneys within the firm, responsible for contracts and certain torts of employed attorneys	Need to comply with state corporate requirements
Some tax benefits	Increased employee taxes and insurance expenses
Flexibility	Need for a majority vote of directors to make major decisions
More employee benefits	Some increased taxes
	Possibly a problem with corporate status if a firm has multistate offices
	Increased recordkeeping

A Typical Professional Corporation Major, Pierce & Saunders is a large, international, megafirm professional corporation that employs 740 attorneys—446 of whom are individual professional corporations—in fourteen offices around the world. It has 287 shareholders. The shareholders elect ten members to serve on a board of directors. The board of directors elects four officers—president, vice-president, secretary, and treasurer—who are responsible for the management of the firm.

The corporation has a centralized form of management that is organized into five groups: administration, policy, financial, marketing, and operations. Each group comprises many committees. For example, the financial group encompasses a compensation committee and an investment committee. The members of the compensation committee determine compensation and benefits for employees as well as a bonus structure. The financial committee determines how to invest the firm's funds and monitor its retirement program.

The firm employs seven legal administrators, one of whom is the chief legal administrator. The chief legal administrator is like the corporate chief operating officer. This person serves on all committees and is responsible for implementing the committees' decisions. The corporation also employs twenty office managers who work under the direction of the legal administrators. Each branch office has an office manager, and the larger branches have a legal administrator. The administrator or office manager in each branch reports to corporate headquarters and must submit monthly reports and time records. Corporate headquarters handles all the billing for the branch offices.

In addition to hundreds of support staff, this firm employs other nonlawyer specialists: accountants, information systems specialists to manage the firm's computer system, librarians to manage the various libraries, communications specialists to manage the telephone systems, human resource managers to manage personnel, and marketing managers to handle marketing activities.

Corporate headquarters is the largest of the branches. All major decision makers for the firm are located here. The corporation has a very sophisticated mainframe computer system. Each branch office is linked to the mainframe so that the branch can have access to information contained at corporate headquarters.

The firm is highly departmentalized. Corporate headquarters has fifteen departments:

Tax	General litigation
Family law	Estate planning, trusts, and probate
Contracts	Real property
Bankruptcy	Corporate
Commercial litigation	Labor
Patents, trademarks, and copyrights	Tort
Environmental	International
Admiralty and maritime	

The branch offices do not have all of these departments. Each branch office has different departments and specialties according to the needs of the clients. For example, the Hong Kong office was formed primarily to help one of the firm's major corporate clients establish a manufacturing plant there. That branch office consists of a contracts department, a corporate department, and a labor department.

The legal assistants in this firm are highly specialized. Some of them like highly specialized work, and others do not. Some say the work is too repetitive. However, they are all among the highest-paid legal assistants in their area and have a lot of employee benefits, including retirement benefits after they have been with the firm for five years.

Some legal assistants thrive on the politics and bureaucracy of this large firm, and others do not. Some feel the red tape is burdensome. Some complain that the firm is too large for them to feel "connected," or part of a family.

Boutique Firms

The trend toward specialization brought a new type of law firm in the 1980s: the boutique firm. A boutique firm is a small firm in which attorneys specialize in only one or possibly two areas of law. These firms are replacing the small general practice that assisted the public in various areas of law and are normally found in highly populated areas. A boutique firm may be a sole proprietorship, partnership, or professional corporation.

Examples of the specialties of a boutique firm are government contracts, domestic law, taxes, intellectual property, labor law, workers' compensation, and so on.

Advantages and Disadvantages to a Boutique Firm

Advantages	Disadvantages
Ability to concentrate on one area of law and become expert in that area	Need to work with a specific type of client
Networking with other attorneys	Tendency to lose touch with other areas of law
Opportunity to work with a specific type of client	

A Typical Boutique Firm   The law firm of Ellingboe, Rialto, Loh & Young is a professional corporation that employs four attorneys. All four attorneys are shareholders of the corporation. The attorneys specialize in estate planning and probate: Nancy Ellingboe specializes in estate and gift tax, Ernest Rialto in trust administration, Pete Loh in wills, and Alexandria Young in probate. The firm employs four legal assistants, four secretaries, an office manager, and a receptionist. One secretary and one legal assistant are assigned to each attorney.

Ellingboe, Rialto has a committee style of management, with all four attorneys on the executive committee and each attorney responsible for one of four areas of management: financial, personnel, administrative systems, and community relations. The office manager carries out the decisions of the executive committee and works with all the attorneys for the general management of the firm.

The library in the firm is very small and consists of only the books needed for estate planning and probate. The firm has a state-of-the-art computer system with the latest applicable software, which enables the staff to prepare documents in a few minutes. The firm has streamlined its systems to increase the volume of work. It has a good reputation in the legal community. In addition to high salaries, the staff enjoys many benefits.

Office-Sharing Associations

Changes in the economy, law, technology, and the practice of law in general have made sole practice too expensive for most lawyers. Higher capital contributions are required for the office equipment, a library, furniture, and supplies required to start a business. In addition, the costs of office space and employee wages have skyrocketed. Attorneys are forced to devise alternative methods of practice to maximize their profit margin. Office-sharing associations, also called legal associations, are a popular alternative.

Two types of office-sharing arrangements are utilized: the suite concept and the firm concept.

Suite Concept   The suite concept developed in the 1970s. With this arrangement, one attorney, group of attorneys, or management company leases out an entire floor of an office building and builds individual offices in various sizes. The suite is decorated and equipped with a full law library, a conference room, a copier and fax equipment, a telephone system, a receptionist area, and other law office essentials. The individual offices are subleased—either furnished or unfurnished—to lawyers whose rent proportionately pays the costs of the operation and of the general upkeep of the suite. The attorneys pay each time they use the fax machine or the copier, and these costs are added to their monthly bill.

Deborah Ebert is a senior litigation legal assistant and paralegal administrator for the Newport Beach, California, branch office of Latham & Watkins, a large professional corporation of approximately 413 attorneys. The firm is managed by a committee style, and Deborah serves on a management committee. Her tenure on the committee is for two years. Each committee has a representative from each branch office, but not all have a legal assistant representative.

"I really enjoy my administrative functions," states Deborah. "However, my time spent on administrative functions is not calculated in my annual billing requirement of 1,600 hours. I must work extra hours to fulfill my billing requirements. It is all worth it at bonus time because those extra hours and management functions are calculated into my bonuses.

"I enjoy the team approach in this office. You have more support in a large firm than a smaller firm. There are always people available to help you if you should get in a bind. In this firm, we have legal assistant assistants to help us. I share a secretary with another legal assistant, and we have floater secretaries [secretaries not assigned to a permanent job] to fill in any gaps. All our secretaries are well trained.

"There are opportunities here that are not available in a smaller firm. We are trendsetters in our paralegal program, which provides a career ladder and advancement opportunities for our legal assistants. Another advantage of working for a large, prestigious firm is the respect and recognition one receives from all aspects of the legal community.

"When I worked in a smaller firm, I had more variety of duties. I used to calendar dates in the smaller firm, but I do not have to do that here. I also did more legal research in the smaller firm. Here, we have law clerks and associates who do most of the research. Also, there were more opportunities to assist the attorney at trial in a smaller firm."

Jean Evers works for the large firm of Poyner & Spruill in Raleigh, North Carolina. Poyner & Spruill is a regional firm of approximately 120 attorneys. The firm has many specialty areas. Jean specializes in environmental law.

"The best thing about working for a large firm is the ability to specialize," states Jean. "You can concentrate on a project more intensely. In a small firm, you bounce from project to project and work on a project in bits and pieces. Since environmental law is a fairly new area, I have been able to watch the law evolve in this area.

"Large firms have more support staff available. In the smaller firm, I did filing, copying, and clerical work. All those functions are done by other people here. There is higher technology here, which is a big help. I am paid more money and have better benefits, including retirement, which was not available in the small firm. I also feel that my status as a legal assistant is higher in a large firm."

A suite usually offers secretarial or paralegal services or both on an as-needed basis, thereby cutting employee costs. If an attorney employs a secretary and a legal assistant, additional space can be rented for them.

A suite is usually elegantly decorated and gives the impression of a large, prosperous firm. Management functions are the responsibility of a suite owner, with no input from the tenants. The attorneys have the benefits of a larger firm—networking and referrals from other lawyers—while maintaining the autonomy of a sole practice.

Firm Concept In the firm concept, an attorney rents an office that is vacant in an established firm. The renting attorney may arrange to do work for the law firm in lieu of paying rent. The renting attorney has the use of the firm's receptionist services and facilities. Arrangements are made for use of the firm's support staff services, or the attorney may rent additional space for a secretary and a legal assistant.

This type of arrangement allows a young lawyer to begin the practice of law without high start-up costs. It is also used as a "trial marriage" if a firm is considering hiring an attorney. The attorney and the firm can see whether they are compatible without making any commitments to each other.

The obvious disadvantage to this type of arrangement is that a renting attorney is subject to the needs of a law firm. If the firm grows and needs an extra office, the renting attorney must move. In addition, if the attorney is very busy, the attorney may find that doing the firm's work for payment of rent a burden.

Advantages and Disadvantages to an Office-Sharing Association

Advantages	Disadvantages
Lower overhead	Lack of personalized attention to clients through a community secretarial pool
Freedom and independence	
Networking with other attorneys	No say in the management decisions of an office
More opportunities to specialize, depending on the referrals of other attorneys in the suite	
Nice office environment	
No management headaches	
Access to a full library and facilities	

A Typical Office-Sharing Association

When Tony Florentine passed the bar exam, he desired to practice law as a sole practitioner and to specialize in family law. He had limited funds to start his practice, so he rented an office in a suite of twenty-two other sole practitioners. The owner of the suite is also a practicing attorney in the suite.

The suite is spacious, with a large, very plush reception area. It has a complete law library with all the books and periodicals Tony will need. It also has a secretarial service with computerized word processing equipment to service attorneys who have no staff. Tony utilizes the secretarial service, so he has no need for a full-time secretary.

Since he is a new attorney, he also works on other types of cases in addition to family law. He advises other attorneys in the suite of his desire to specialize and asks them to refer all the family law matters they do not want to him. In return, he will refer cases he does not want or is not qualified to handle to them.

Tony is happy with the arrangement, although he has had some difficulty with the secretarial service. He once needed some work done immediately to take to court for a hearing, but the secretarial service was too busy with other attorneys' work to drop everything for him. Consequently, he was not prepared for his court hearing. Since then, he has hired a part-time secretary who also does some paralegal work.

He also has a problem with Sally Whitefeather, one of the receptionists. She does not answer his calls promptly and hangs up on his clients. At times, he does not get important messages left by clients. Tony complained about this to the suite owner, who indicated he would remedy the situation. However, Sally has continued in her poor work habits, and Tony is upset because he can do nothing to remedy the situation.

Tony has practiced in the suite for two years, which has been enough time for his practice to grow considerably. He has become associated with two other sole practitioners who are leaving the suite to form a partnership. They have asked Tony to come with them and join their firm as a full partner. In this partnership, Tony will be able to practice family law exclusively, and he is glad to accept their offer.

Legal Clinics

Legal clinic: Low-cost firm with standard fees for standard services.

Legal clinics are lower-cost law firms with standard fees for standard services. They emphasize low overhead and high volume. They advertise heavily through the media and have convenient locations to serve clients. Legal clinics offer services at reduced rates because they do not spend money on expensive offices and employees are paid lower salaries. Legal assistants do most of the paperwork on a case, leaving an attorney free to make court appearances. Systems are streamlined and fully

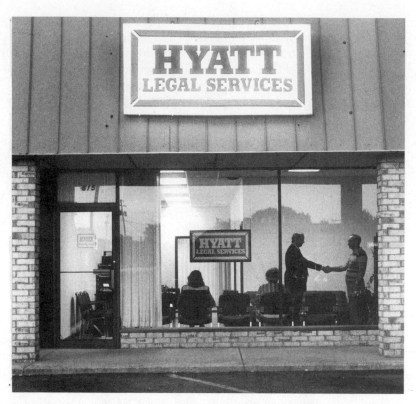

EXHIBIT 1.11   Legal Clinics Emphasize Low Overhead, High Volume, and Convenient Locations

computerized, allowing a clinic to do a high volume of work. Legal clinics are privately owned and are structured as partnerships or professional corporations. One such clinic is shown in Exhibit 1.11.

Clinics are located in malls, storefront offices, or heavily trafficked areas and offer clients evening and weekend appointments. A typical office has no frills and is not elegantly furnished.

Low- to middle-income people are typical clients of a legal clinic. Although some legal clinics may take litigation cases with complex issues, most of their cases are standard divorces, bankruptcies, probate matters, and wills. A legal clinic usually has neither the resources nor the time to take a complex litigation case. A survey administered by Kent State University indicated that the average client would not retain a legal clinic if the issues were complex or involved a criminal matter.

Legal clinics are small offices that belong to a larger firm. A managing attorney for each office hires support staff and makes policy for that office. Although each managing attorney must report to headquarters, each individual office has its own management style, usually autocratic, and is run independently of other offices.

The managing attorney is responsible for an office's profitability, and each office is monitored by headquarters. All income received by each office is sent to headquarters, which pays the expenses of the office. Each office must pay the main office a percentage of its income, usually 30 to 40 percent. After the main office deducts its percentage, it subtracts the smaller office's expenses, and the managing attorney receives the remainder of the income. Staff attorneys and support staff salaries are considered an expense of the office. The main office provides each smaller office with management and training support, accounting services, promotion, and advertising.

Attorneys who work for legal clinics are eligible for partnership as in other private law firms. However, various levels of partnerships exist in a legal clinic (see Exhibit 1.12). A managing attorney may be a low-level partner, entitled to a low percentage of the profits. For example, a managing attorney who is a partner may be

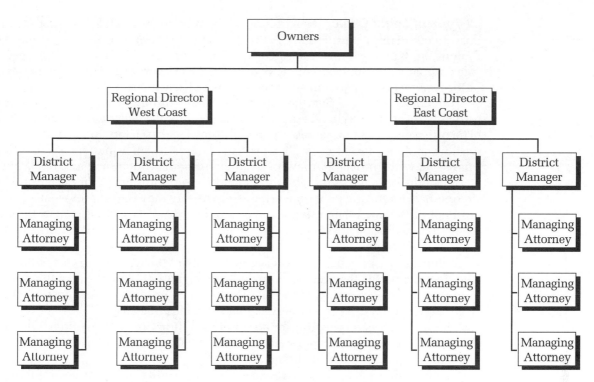

EXHIBIT 1.12 Legal Clinic Organizational Chart

entitled to a small percentage of the profits of a district or region rather than of the entire law firm.

Legal clinics emerged in the late 1970s and enjoyed great success for about fifteen years. Television advertisement and client convenience contributed to their success. Now, however, there are very few legal clinics. The concept, while appealing for many low- to middle-income clients, suffered from many problems that eventually caused their demise. They found that it was impossible to standardize fees for a large area because of the diversity of each region. Overhead increased to the point that clinics were forced to raise their rates. Technology streamlined case management, allowing private firms to reduce their prices to compete with legal clinics. It was not long before their rates were the same or, in some cases, higher than those charged by private law firms. Attorneys were paid a fraction of what their friends in private law firms were making, so they quit in droves, taking their clients with them. To further escalate the downslide, internal squabbles among clinic owners caused mismanagement and chaos.

Advantages and Disadvantages to a Legal Clinic

Advantages	Disadvantages
A headquarters to handle the promotion of a firm	Pressure from a main office to be profitable
Support in the areas of consultations, training, and management	Need to report to a main office
	Inability to take cases with complex issues
A main office to handle accounting and complaints	Usually a lower income
	Income that is dependent on clients paying promptly
A headquarters to handle most management functions	Work on evenings and weekends
	Inability to specialize
	Usually inability to afford the latest equipment and technology

A Typical Legal Clinic   Neighborhood Legal Services is a legal clinic based in Dallas, Texas. It is a partnership with two major partners, Judy Miller and Monica Valentino, who each own 35 percent of the company. The remaining 30 percent of the company is disbursed among regional directors and district managers. Managing attorneys receive a percentage of the profits of their district.

Neighborhood Legal Services has many offices throughout the United States. One office is located in Tyler, Texas, and consists of one managing attorney: Bill Lowe. The office employs one secretary, one full-time legal assistant, one part-time legal assistant, and one receptionist. It represents clients in such matters as dissolution of marriage, wills, probate, unlawful detainer, minor civil matters, and bankruptcy.

Since the office does a high volume of cases, appointments for clients are limited to one-half hour. Clients who work during the day may request an evening or weekend appointment. When clients come into the office, they are given an information sheet to complete. This sheet is then given to the legal assistant or attorney who will interview a client.

When a file is opened, the case is given to one of the legal assistants, who prepares the documents for the attorney's review and signature. Bill reviews the documents and makes changes or signs the documents. Since Bill is in court most of the time, a legal assistant handles the day-to-day maintenance of a case.

The secretary is responsible for all the clerical functions of the office. When he gets busy, he may ask the receptionist to help him. The secretary is also responsible for submitting all reports to the home office.

The full-time legal assistant has a lot of responsibility in this office. He is very busy and finds the constant ringing of the telephone a distraction. He works a lot of overtime and must work two Saturdays a month, like Bill and the other employees in the office. His salary is low, but he gets paid for overtime and likes the variety of work. He is the type of person who thrives on pressure and works very well in this type of environment.

PRIVATE INDUSTRY

Private industry includes companies formed for purposes other than providing legal services and consists of all sizes of businesses: small, medium, and large. A company often employs its own attorneys. A private industry legal department is located within the company that employs it. It is most often called an in-house legal department and has one client: the company.

Private industry uses two types of legal departments: corporate legal departments for very large corporations and legal departments for smaller private companies.

Corporate Legal Departments

Outside counsel: A private law firm retained to do legal work for a corporation.

Preventive law: Legal information designed to avoid legal problems before they occur.

In-house counsel: An attorney who is an employee of a corporation and works in the corporation's legal department.

The emergence of corporate legal departments for large corporations, such as the one shown in Exhibit 1.13, is relatively new. Some years ago, corporate legal departments consisted of an attorney and a secretary, who delegated a corporation's legal work to **outside counsel.** Outside counsel is a separate law firm responsible for all the legal work of a corporation.

Since the late 1970s, however, legal and business issues have become more complex, thereby increasing a corporation's legal demands considerably. Corporations hire their own attorneys to meet their legal needs and to practice **preventive law,** or law designed to avoid legal problems. With attorneys monitoring a project from its inception, the possibility of legal problems in the future is reduced. At the same time, corporations were under pressure to reduce costs. These issues forced corporations to handle more matters in-house and to monitor the activities of outside counsel closely. The use of the services of **in-house counsel** increased 300 percent from 1978 to 1993.

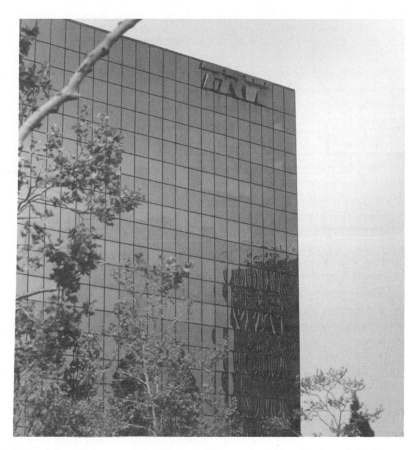

EXHIBIT 1.13 Legal Departments of Large Corporations Employ Legal Assistants, Many of Which are Corporate Specialists

A corporate legal department functions as a part of the whole corporation around the projects of the corporation. For example, an automobile manufacturing company introducing a new line of automobiles would require the contribution of each department of the company. Sales and marketing would work on the automobile's promotion, personnel would hire additional staff as necessary, engineering would be responsible for designing the automobile, manufacturing would be responsible for producing the automobile, legal would be responsible for contracts with dealers to sell the automobile and for any patent requirements, and the executive department would supervise all departments.

The type of business a corporation is in influences the legal needs of the corporation. A manufacturing corporation has a greater need for a large patent department than does a service corporation. A chemical corporation has a greater need for environmental attorneys than does a banking corporation.

The head attorney in a corporate legal department is called a **general counsel.** Frequently, the general counsel is also an officer of the corporation, usually a corporate secretary or vice president. A general counsel reports directly to the president of the corporation. Increasingly, a general counsel is responsible for the legal requirements of the corporation, such as minutes, stock transfers, and state filing requirements.

Corporate legal departments have both centralized and decentralized forms of organization. Most corporate legal departments are centralized. Centralized legal departments are located in corporate headquarters and provide legal services for all a company's departments and locations. All attorneys can be found in the legal department, under the authority of a general counsel. This form of organization is shown in Exhibit 1.14.

General counsel: An attorney in charge of a corporate legal department; often an officer of the corporation.

EXHIBIT 1.14 Corporate Legal Department Organizational Chart

In a decentralized form of organization, corporate headquarters consists of a general counsel and a few attorneys. Other attorneys are disbursed among the various departments of the corporation and function independently of the general counsel. For example, a labor attorney works in the personnel department, a patent attorney in manufacturing and engineering, and a collection attorney in sales.

The management style of a corporate legal department must conform to the management style of the whole corporation. Therefore, a legal department is not autonomous in its management decisions. For example, if it is necessary for a legal department to hire additional personnel, the decision must be approved by the personnel department in most corporations. The personnel department will then take over the hiring process and be responsible for finding qualified applicants.

The concerns of a corporate legal department are different from those of traditional law firms. For example, public relations and attracting clients are not concerns to a corporate attorney. Corporate legal departments must prepare and adhere to department budgets, which are subject to management approval outside a legal department.

Corporate legal departments are small, medium, or large. The size of a legal department depends on how much legal work is done in-house. A corporate legal department that handles a corporation's litigation will have a large litigation staff. Corporate legal departments that handle corporate secretary functions and patents only and send all other work to outside counsel will have a smaller staff.

According to a 1998 survey conducted by the American Corporate Counsel Association (ACCA), the size of corporate legal departments range in size from 1 to 617 attorneys. More than 20 percent of in-house counsel are their clients' sole attorney (21.5 percent). The majority of corporate attorneys (38.2 percent) work in legal departments of less than five attorneys. Twenty-five percent work in legal departments with six to twenty attorneys, and 15 percent of corporate attorneys work in legal departments of more than twenty-one attorneys. The survey reported one legal department with more than 600 attorneys. The survey also revealed the following about legal departments:

◆ They have become more diverse.
◆ Cost control is their most pressing issue.
◆ There is a significant increase in participation in pro bono services.
◆ Time management and keeping up with the flow of new information are challenges to them.

Advantages and Disadvantages to a Corporate Legal Department

Advantages	Disadvantages
Less pressure	No say in the management policy of a corporation
Fewer hours of work than required of private attorneys and legal assistants	Red tape
Good employee benefits	Need to report to other departments of a corporation
Security	Usually not as much compensation as received by private attorney
Opportunity to specialize	Need to interact with the other departments of a company, which often delays actions

A Typical Corporate Legal Department   ABC Corporation manufactures computer circuit boards used in the airline industry. The legal department at ABC is small, consisting of one general counsel, one office administrator, twelve attorneys, six legal assistants, ten secretaries, one file clerk, and one case manager.

The general counsel does not practice law; he interacts with other departments of the corporation and delegates assignments to the attorneys. Three attorneys are patent attorneys, three are corporate attorneys, one is a labor specialist, three are litigation attorneys, and two are contract attorneys. Two of the legal assistants are patent assistants, two are corporate assistants, and two handle warranty disputes for the corporation. Each attorney is assigned a secretary, except the patent attorneys, who share the services of one secretary.

The corporation has a contract with Major, Pierce & Saunders, a very large international law firm, to handle all its litigation. Major, Pierce employs attorneys who practice in all areas of law. It also has branch offices in many major cities in the United States, which is convenient for ABC.

ABC has a lot of litigation since its circuit boards are used in airplanes of all sizes all over the country. If injuries are sustained because an airplane malfunctioned in an area where the circuit board is located, ABC is sued. ABC's litigation attorneys monitor outside counsel's management of the litigation cases. They are apprised of each step in every case. The attorneys at Major, Pierce receive direction and authority from ABC's litigation attorneys.

Other areas of ABC's legal department also use the services of outside law firms. If the corporate or contract attorneys should get behind, they will ask for assistance from outside counsel.

The office manager is responsible for the general management of the department and reports to the general counsel. She spends 33 percent of her time on budgeting and accounting, 20 percent on personnel administration, 20 percent on practice support and office systems, 15 percent on information support systems, and 12 percent on other management functions.

The legal assistants enjoy their company benefits and are treated as professionals by other employees of the corporation. They seldom work overtime or weekends, and they have good salaries. People who used to work as legal assistants in the legal department have been promoted to management positions in other departments of the corporation.

Private Companies

Private industry includes smaller companies formed to provide nonlegal services or products to the public and services directly to law firms. The legal needs of these companies are more targeted than those of large corporations (see Exhibit 1.15). For example, a real estate company would employ its own real estate attorney and legal assistant

EXHIBIT 1.15 The Legal Needs of Private Industry Companies are More Targeted Than Those of Corporate Legal Departments

to handle real estate contracts and closings. A small company that specializes in franchise work would employ a legal staff to handle franchise contracts and transactions.

Private companies, although smaller than large corporations, have the same structure as a corporation. Management decisions are made not by the attorneys but by company management—unless an attorney is part of the management of a company. Unlike an attorney in a corporate legal department, one in a private company may not be an officer or a manager of the company.

Some private companies are also divided into departments. The departments are fewer and smaller than those in a large corporation. As in a large corporation, each department functions together around projects of the company.

Legal assistants have successfully utilized their paralegal training for careers in private companies and obtained the following positions:

Insurance underwriter	Corporate bond department manager
Law firm administrator	Employee benefits manager
Recruiting coordinator	Association manager
Law firm marketing specialist	Writer
Rehabilitation counselor	Teacher
Corporate personnel director	Career counselor
Consultant	Politician
Commercial arbitrator	Sales marketer
Sales representative	Negotiator
Legal software trainer	Convention marketer
Law librarian	Editor
Investigator	Environment specialist
Real estate broker	Stockbroker
Litigation consultant	Paralegal program director
Civil rights analyst	Computer-related positions

Freelance paralegal: Contracts his or her services out to law offices and works under the supervision of an attorney.

Self-Employed Paralegal Services Legal assistants are also forming their own private companies. They are independent contractors and are self-employed. There are two types of self-employed legal assistants: **freelance** (or contract) **paralegals** and

Professional Profile

Jennifer Sawyer, CLA, a trademark legal assistant at the corporate headquarters of Tupperware, International, in Miami, Florida, is experienced in real estate, litigation, and intellectual property, specializing in defense work. For Tupperware, she monitors trademarks, submits new trademarks for research, handles all trademark and copyright infringements, and monitors litigation. She states:

"Working for a corporate legal department is great because you only have one client. I have worked for many private law firms in general practice, and I like specialized work better than general practice. I also don't work much overtime, [as] I used to do in a private firm. The salary and benefits are better in a corporate legal department."

Marie Smith, CLA, is a corporate legal assistant for US West Communications in Salt Lake City, Utah. She is the custodian of records for her company and responds to subpoenas and telephone records requests. She is involved in a variety of legal work, including criminal investigations, workers' compensation, and labor disputes. She testifies as the custodian of records on behalf of her company and represents the company in employment hearings. She also reviews and tracks legislation for the company. Of her work, she states:

"My company is very supportive of continuing education. They will pay for courses and seminars and let us off to attend them. We also have the very latest in technology, which makes my job easier.

"We receive no overtime pay. Sometimes the bureaucracy of a large company can be a hassle. Once, I needed a particular form, and I had to order a form to order another form to get the form I needed. You learn to work within the constraints of the red tape, though."

independent paralegals. Freelance paralegal services offer their services to attorneys, and independent paralegals offer their services to the public.

Freelance Paralegal Services   Freelance paralegal services are offered to attorneys on a **contract basis.** A freelance legal assistant is not an employee of a firm but works for the firm on an independent contract basis. Attorneys have increased the use of freelance paralegal services since the early 1980s to control high employee costs.

Contract basis: Working as an independent contractor on a per case or assignment basis. The person is not an employee of the firm.

A variety of paralegal services are available in the United States. The organizations offering these services range from companies with one legal assistant to firms that have many legal assistants and employ attorneys. Most freelance legal assistants specialize in one area of law. The most common specialty areas are litigation, corporate, real estate, and probate. A freelance legal assistant may come to an attorney's office, work out of the home, or rent an office.

A specialty area that is popular for freelancers is a paralegal service that provides computerized litigation support. A law firm that does not have sophisticated computer capabilities or the staff to handle a complex litigation case may contract with a service to computerize the many documents, thereby saving thousands of dollars on new equipment and additional staff. The scope and sophistication of computer services offered by paralegal firms runs the gamut from coding data entry to building specialized databases and storing data on in-house mainframes.

CYBERSITES
Freelance Paralegals on the Web

I.P. Paralegal Services—www.ipparalegal.com
Paralegal Services—www.freeyellow.com/members/paralegal/index

California Association of Independent Paralegals—
    www.paralegals.org/members/region/CAIndependent

Freelance paralegal services are sole proprietorships, partnerships, and corporations. Most freelance paralegal services are sole proprietorships consisting of one legal assistant. If the paralegal service incorporates, it may not incorporate as a professional corporation but may incorporate as a general corporation or limited liability company.

Freelancing offers legal assistants versatility in scheduling work around family obligations.

Independent paralegal: A person who does law-related work for the general public without the supervision of an attorney.

Independent Paralegal Services **Independent paralegal** services offer their services directly to the public. Most have their own offices. While the legality of this form of paralegal service is controversial, the number of independent paralegal businesses is growing every day. It is important for legal assistant students to understand the difference between a freelance paralegal service and an independent paralegal service.

Many independent paralegals do business as legal typing or form preparation services that offer clerical help and forms on a variety of basic or routine cases, such as bankruptcy, uncontested divorces, and landlord tenant matters. Some independent paralegals work for nonprofit organizations, such as women's shelters. They charge less than attorneys. *Independent paralegals cannot give legal advice or represent clients in court,* but they can help people complete their own paperwork and represent themselves. Despite their limitations, independent paralegals are carving out a niche among consumers who want to handle their own legal problems or cannot afford the services of an attorney. A more in-depth discussion of this issue is found in Chapter 5.

ETHICS ALERT

CYBERSITES

Independent Paralegals on the Web

Alternative Legal Solutions—www.altlegal.com

Paralegal Plus—www.paralegal-plus.com

Find a Paralegal—http://legalalt.hypermart.net/finda.htm

Advantages and Disadvantages to Freelancing

Advantages	Disadvantages
Freedom and independence	Inability to see an entire case through to the end
Opportunity to work for many different attorneys	Income fluctuates
Opportunity to specialize	Need to pay for one's own taxes, insurance, and benefits
Ability to choose one's own work	No paid sick leave and holidays
	Many rush assignments

Before starting a career as a freelance legal assistant, one should have at least three to five years' experience in a law office setting; a diploma or certificate from a paralegal program alone is not sufficient. Most attorneys utilizing the services of freelance legal assistants are new sole practitioners. They are not experienced enough to supervise a new legal assistant adequately. Freelancing is not the place to receive on-the-job training. Freelancing also requires risk since there is no steady income and clients may be slow to pay for services. It is highly recommended that freelancing be given careful consideration and be entered into only when you are experienced and feel very comfortable with your skill level.

Professional Profile

Alice Penny is the owner of Paralegal Services of North Carolina, Raleigh, North Carolina. She employs six people: one office manager and five legal assistants. Her company does land title research; public document filing, search, and retrieval; real property foreclosure; estate administration; background investigations; and corporate work. Alice started her company in 1988 after more than thirty years' legal experience.

Alice began accepting outside work while still employed by a large firm in Raleigh. She moonlighted in order to test the market for freelance paralegals and to build a clientele before she quit her job. Of her company, she states:

"I started my own business to be my own boss. But then I found out that being one's own boss is a myth. I have many bosses. My clients are my bosses. I have found that the stress level is higher with your own business. I have to wear all of the hats: management, marketing, promotion, advertising, administrator, and do the paralegal work. I have all of the headaches of running a business. On the other hand, having your own business is exciting and rewarding, in spite of the hard work."

Attorney Service and Nonprofit Companies   Many companies offer services to legal offices. Companies that offer essential services include service of process, messenger, court filings, preparation of demonstrative evidence, corporate record checking and retrieval, courier services, and investigations. Law book and legal periodical companies need legal editors and knowledgeable salespeople. Companies that produce legal software use educated legal assistants to develop the software, sell the software, and train people how to use the software. Bonding companies are used by law firms in many different types of cases. A legal assistant familiar with the legal process can be very successful in an attorney service company.

Private companies vary in their organization and structure. Some are small companies, while others are large corporations. Most companies offer their employees opportunities for advancement and increases in salary.

Nonprofit, charitable organizations also employ attorneys and legal assistants. Organizations such as the American Association of Retired Persons (AARP) and religious organizations such as Catholic Charities offer legal services to members of their particular group. While nonprofit organizations cannot afford to pay top wages, many legal assistants have found the work challenging and rewarding.

Advantages and Disadvantages to a Private Company

Advantages	Disadvantages
Good benefits	No say in the management policy of a company
Fewer hours of work than in a private law firm	Red tape
Security	Need to report to other departments of a company
Opportunity to specialize	
Usually less stress	

A Typical Private Company   Sandy Varella just graduated from paralegal school. She is a single mother who has been employed by a computer company for many years and is used to a good salary. When she began looking for a job as a legal assistant, she was discouraged to discover that law firms would not pay her very much as a legal assistant trainee. It would be difficult for her to take a cut in pay to pursue her goal of being a legal assistant.

She was just about to give up her dream when she read an ad in the newspaper that read, "Paralegal position. Computer experience essential." She got the job and went to work for International Computer Manufacturing Company (ICM).

ICM manufactures computers and software for business and industry. It has five departments: retail, medical, legal, grocery, and education. Sandy works in the legal department, which consists of two computer marketing consultants, two computer programmers, two attorneys, and one legal assistant: Sandy.

The department develops software for law offices. It has software for computerized litigation support, timekeeping systems, spreadsheets, billing, and word processing. The attorneys develop the functions of the software. Sandy's job is to go into the offices of the company's customers and train the staff to use the software. She gives seminars on the various ways the software can be used in a legal office. Her computer background and paralegal education made her a perfect candidate for the job.

Sandy is thrilled with her new position. She is considered an expert in her field and enjoys meeting people. Her hours are flexible, so she can be home when her children get home from school. She did not have to take a cut in pay—she makes more money than she did before.

GOVERNMENT AGENCIES

Legal assistants work in four main areas of government offices:

◆ Chief government lawyers; for example, attorneys general, and corporation counsel
◆ General counsel of individual agencies
◆ Individual agencies; for example, enforcement departments, and civil rights divisions.
◆ Individual legislators, individual legislative committees, legislative counsel, or legislative drafting offices

Government agencies vary in their administration systems, as do private law firms. Some organizations are more complex than others, and agencies have diverse legal needs as well as organizational size, structure, power base, and so on. An agency's need for legal assistants varies with these elements.

Four types of government agencies employ legal assistants: federal, state, county, and city.

Federal Agencies

The federal government is the largest employer in the United States. At the time of this writing, Uncle Sam employed approximately three million workers and hires 300,000 new employees each year to replace retiring or terminating employees. The government classifies workers into groups that fall within an occupational struc-

Professional Profile

Debbie Dee, a legal assistant in Durham, North Carolina, works for Lawyers Title Insurance Corporation of North Carolina. She manages the office, responds to title problems, and performs underwriting functions. She hires and trains legal assistants who work for the company. Of her job, she states:

"Opportunities in the title insurance industry are challenging. I have a lot of autonomy. The company is reputable, and I work in a good atmosphere.

"The company is structured differently than a private law firm. Most law firms are run by attorneys like a small business. This company is managed like a large corporation, which gives legal assistants more room for advancement. I make good money and have very good benefits."

Alice Verstegan is a legal assistant investigator for the California State Bar, Los Angeles, in the attorney discipline division. When a client submits a complaint against an attorney, Alice investigates the matter and reports her findings to the trial section of the state bar. She was a freelance legal assistant before her position with the state bar. She states:

"I really love my job with the state bar. I have a lot of client contact and find the cases very interesting. I freelanced for many years before coming here. I still freelance a little in my spare time. I just received a promotion to senior investigator. It is my second promotion in one year. I like the upward mobility this position has to offer."

ture. There are twenty-two occupational groups that include 441 different occupations. They are classified under the General Schedule, GS-000 through GS 2100 (see Exhibit 1.16). Each group is further subdivided into subgroups that have their own numerical code.

The government's existing classification system includes an occupational structure which groups similar jobs together. The Wage Grade Trades and Labor Schedule offers an additional 36 occupational group (WG-2500 through WG-9000). GS-900, entitled the Legal and Kindred Group, is where paralegals are placed. There are fifteen grades within each group and ten steps within each grade as shown on Exhibit 1.17. Pay steps are earned on the basis of length of employment and the employee's work performance.

The federal government utilizes a two-tiered approach for legal assistants: legal clerk/technician and paralegal specialist. A legal clerk/technician position is a stepping-stone to a paralegal specialist position. It is mainly clerical but involves some basic paralegal duties. The salary level of a legal clerk starts at GS-4 and usually does not go beyond GS-9.

A paralegal specialist is classified under GS-950 within that series. A paralegal specialist can start as low as GS-5 and go as high as GS-15. According to the *Handbook of Occupational Groups and Series* published by the federal government, a paralegal specialist performs the following duties:

> The specialists analyze the legal impact of legislative developments and administrative and judicial decisions, opinions, determinations, and rulings on agency programs; conduct research for the preparation of legal opinions on matters of interest to the agency; perform substantive legal analysis of requests for information under the provisions of various acts; or other similar legal support functions which require discretion and independent judgment in the application of a specialized knowledge of laws, precedent decisions, regulations, agency policies and practices, and judicial or administrative proceedings.

SERIES	DESCRIPTION OF GROUP
GS-000	Miscellaneous
GS-100	Social science, psychology, and welfare
GS-200	Personnel management and industrial relations
GS-300	General administrative, clerical, and office services
GS-400	Biological science group
GS-500	Accounting and budget
GS-600	Medical, hospital, dental, and public health
GS-700	Veterinary medical science
GS-800	Engineering and architecture
GS-900*	Legal and kindred
GS-1000	Information and arts
GS-1100	Business and industry
GS-1200	Copyright, patent, and trademark
GS-1300	Physical science
GS-1400	Library and archives
GS-1500	Mathematics and statistics
GS-1600	Equipment, facilities, and services
GS-1700	Education
GS-1800	Investigation
GS-1900	Quality assurance, inspection, and grading
GS-2000	Supply group
GS-2100	Transportation

EXHIBIT 1.16   Federal Government General Schedule Occupational Structure

STEP	1	2	3	4	5	6	7	8	9	10
GS-1	13,662	14,118	14,572	15,024	15,481	15,748	16,195	16,647	16,666	17,093
GS-2	15,361	15,727	16,236	16,666	16,851	17,347	17,842	18,338	18,883	19,329
GS-3	16,761	17,319	17,878	18,437	18,996	19,554	20,113	20,672	21,231	21,789
GS-4	18,815	19,443	20,070	20,697	21,324	21,952	22,579	23,206	23,833	24,461
GS-5	21,051	21,753	22,456	23,158	23,860	24,562	25,264	25,966	26,668	27,370
GS-6	23,464	24,247	25,029	25,811	26,593	27,375	28,158	28,940	29,722	30,504
GS-7	26,075	26,943	27,812	28,681	29,549	30,418	31,287	32,155	33,024	33,893
GS-8	28,878	29,840	30,803	31,765	32,728	33,690	34,653	35,615	36,578	37,540
GS-9	31,897	32,961	34,024	35,088	36,152	37,215	38,279	39,343	40,406	41,470
GS-10	35,126	36,297	37,468	38,640	39,811	40,982	42,153	43,324	44,496	45,667
GS-11	38,593	39,879	41,165	42,452	13,378	45,024	16,310	47,596	48,882	50,168
GS-12	46,254	47,796	49,339	50,881	52,423	53,966	55,508	57,050	58,592	60,135
GS-13	55,004	56,837	58,670	60,504	62,337	64,170	66,003	67,837	69,670	71,503
GS-14	64,998	67,164	69,331	71,497	73,663	75,830	77,996	80,162	82,329	84,495
GS-15	76,456	79,005	81,554	84,103	86,652	89,201	91,750	94,299	96,848	99,397

EXHIBIT 1.17 General Schedule Salary Structure

*GS pay is adjusted geographically to account for higher costs of living (approximately 5.6 to 12 percent higher). Pay for positions outside the United States are 10 to 25 percent higher. (Note: The General Schedule is adjusted periodically. This schedule is current as of December 1998.)

According to William P. Statsky in *Essentials of Paralegalism,* the following federal agencies employ the largest number of paralegal specialists:

Department of Health and Human Services

Department of Justice

Court system

Department of Treasury

Department of Transportation

Department of the Army

Department of the Anterior

Equal Employment Opportunity Commission

General Services Administration

Department of Energy

Department of State

Department of Labor

The main selling points of federal employment are job security and benefits. Additionally, federal employment is generally not affected by fluctuations in the economy as are other areas of the legal marketplace. However, political changes can influence staffing levels. Each presidential administration may have different public policy priorities that result in greater levels of federal employment in some programs and declines in others. Layoffs have occurred but are generally uncommon. The federal government offers 140 law-related careers for the paralegal (*Paralegal Reporter,* National Federal of Paralegal Associations, 1998).

A paralegal specialist in the federal government usually specializes in one particular area of law. Often, a legal assistant in this position becomes as familiar with a particular area of law as the attorneys in the office, if not more so. As attorneys come and go in the government, a legal assistant becomes the ongoing foundation of many government law offices.

Since deficit reduction, lawyers are still employed, but some positions are being filled by legal assistants. For example, the Bureau of Prisons, an agency of the Department of Justice, has a program in which a legal assistant is placed in almost every federal prison in positions that were once filled by lawyers.

Legal assistants in government have more autonomy than legal assistants in private law firms. According to federal standards, a legal assistant may or may not be supervised by an attorney. Paralegal specialist is considered a professional position, guaranteeing career mobility and tenure. In addition, legal assistants employed by the federal government may represent their agency before federal administrative tribunals. One area of the federal government that employs legal assistants is the Legal Services Corporation, commonly known as Legal Aid.

Indigent: Poor or needy.

Legal Services Corporation The Legal Services Corporation of the federal government establishes legal service offices in communities to service **indigent,** or poor or needy, people of a community. Whereas indigent people accused of crimes have access to a public defender for free legal representation, indigent people involved in civil disputes may receive free legal service through legal aid offices. A legal aid office is structured very much like a private legal clinic except it is not privately owned. Legal aid offices use the services of legal assistants extensively. A legal assistant in these offices has a great amount of responsibility but is not highly paid because of the limited resources of the office.

State Agencies

State government agencies function like federal government agencies except they report to state government officials rather than federal government officials. The opportunities for employment in state government continue to increase. State attorney general offices employ many legal assistants.

County Agencies

County government provides many legal services for its constituents. Among the employment opportunities at the county level are positions in the offices of county counsel, who represent a county when the county is sued; district attorneys; public defenders; public administrators; and court clerks. The governing body of county governments is the county supervisors.

Most often, legal assistants employed by county governing offices are not assigned to a particular attorney but are organized in pools, working for many attorneys on an assignment basis. Most counties have structured review procedures and periodic pay raise schedules.

City Agencies

Legal offices in city government include a city attorney's office and other governing offices. A city attorney represents a city if the city is sued and handle other matters as well. Each city structures its city attorney office differently. For example, some city

A retired Army officer, Felix Hernandez embarked on a new career in the paralegal field. Of his work, he states:

"For 20 years, I was in the U.S. Army, retiring as a major in 1994. While still in the army, I was visiting with another officer about life after the military. My friend had just discovered the new, fast-growing paralegal profession. With an undergraduate degree in political science and a graduate degree in human resources, I liked what I heard. I enrolled in classes, and the rest is history.

"I am now employed as a victim advocate in the juvenile division of a district attorney's office. My main jobs are first to notify the victim when the alleged juvenile offender will be appearing in court. The victim is sometimes required to be present or given the option of being present, depending on the case. Second, I escort the victim to the juvenile hearings if he or she is required or wishes to be present. Finally, if the alleged criminal is found guilty, I follow up on the restitution to the victim. This involves monitoring the money to be repaid for compensation for the victim's property damages or medical bills.

"I love my job because of its variety. It is also gratifying being on the side of the 'good guys.' "

attorneys are appointed by a city counsel, and some are elected by the people. Some city attorneys handle criminal cases, and others handle only civil cases, leaving the criminal cases to a district attorney. Larger cities employ many attorneys, and others employ only one attorney to monitor the work of outside council, much like a corporate legal department. Smaller cities may not have a city attorney but engage the services of a private law firm to represent their interests.

Advantages and Disadvantages to a Government Agency

Advantages	Disadvantages
Benefits	Stringent hiring process
Job security	Bureaucracy
Job protection	No overtime pay, in most cases
Upward mobility	Strict standards of conduct
Availability of positions all over the world	Pay raises that are controlled by politicians
	Stress due to politics
	Work that can be routine

OPPORTUNITIES FOR LEGAL ASSISTANTS

When paralegal training programs were developed in the early 1970s, the law firm was the only legal assistant employer. This had changed dramatically by the early 1990s. Businesses of all types were requiring greater efficiency while fighting budget cuts. Government regulations were increasing, which increased the demand for personnel with legal training.

The opportunities for legal assistants in private industry are growing. A paralegal education offers myriad opportunities. A traditional law firm is not the only potential employer; many alternatives can be found in the legal marketplace.

THE CHANGING MARKETPLACE

Certain changes that have occurred since the early 1970s have had a dramatic effect on the practice of law in traditional law firms. The event that has influenced the traditional delivery of legal services the most is the landmark and legendary decision of *Bates v. State Bar of Arizona*, 433 U.S. 350 (1977). The decision in this case opened the advertising door for attorneys. Before this decision, attorneys were prohibited from advertising their services to the general public. With guidelines from state bar associations, attorneys have entered the advertising arena. This has forced attorneys into an area for which they were neither prepared nor equipped: marketing and promotion. Some attorneys have an aversion to marketing because they view it as degrading for the profession. Others have no time to devote to learning marketing techniques. Therefore, the law firms with good marketing skills and high advertising budgets have gained exposure in the marketplace, which has resulted in an increased clientele.

Four other changes are also responsible for altering traditional law firms:

1. An increasing emphasis on the management and profitability of a firm
2. A declining public perception of attorneys and the legal profession
3. An increasing number of attorneys in the United States
4. Technology

Technology

What does the future hold for the legal marketplace? One cannot predict, but one thing is certain: change. According to a recent survey conducted by Pitney Bowes management services, an office support outsourcing firm, 87 percent of the firms surveyed said that legal services will change more in the years to 2005 than it has in the past fifty years. Technology is the catalyst to those changes.

Technology will change the way in which paralegals perform research, file documents, and communicate with clients. The Internet will play an important role in the delivery of legal services. Paralegals will continue their education through on-line courses and distance education.

Law firms will become more global, and there will be an increase in international law firms. Law firms will create alliances with CPA firms and other businesses. Law firms will continue to develop nonlegal subsidiaries to better serve their clients.

Nonlegal Subsidiaries

The 1980s saw the emergence of **nonlegal subsidiaries.** Law firms and individual attorneys are opening nonlegal businesses that utilize their legal expertise, such as the following:

Management consulting	Publishing
Specialized newsletter publication	Professional association formation
Environment consulting	Public relations
Seminars	Government contracting
International trade consulting	Personnel relations

For example, a mid-Atlantic law firm found that it was doing a lot of research for human resource vice presidents, so it formed an association for human resource vice presidents. For a fee, it offers seminars, a newsletter, consultations, and special research services. This association is managed by nonlawyer personnel and has been lucrative for the firm (see Exhibit 1.18).

Legal Insurance Plans

Traditional law firms, especially smaller firms, are becoming more involved with prepaid group legal services. Almost all the states ethically permit lawyers to participate in a plan of this type.

A prepaid group legal plan operates just like a medical insurance plan. Large insurance companies already offer such plans to large employers, such as General Motors and Chrysler Motor Corporation. Each employee pays a monthly fee for legal insurance. When an employee needs a lawyer, the insurance company pays the legal fees.

EXHIBIT 1.18   Example of Legal Subsidiary
Reprinted with permission of Corporate Creations.

Two types of plans are available: an access plan and a comprehensive plan. When a person has an access plan, services include legal advice; the performance of simple, nonlitigation procedures, such as writing a will; and preventive legal procedures. An access plan typically costs an employee $9 to $25 a month.

A comprehensive plan includes all types of legal services, including litigation procedures. It is limited to certain types of cases but is designed to meet 90 percent of the legal needs of an average family. Comprehensive plans cost $40 to $150 a year.

Some large companies offer legal insurance to their employees and staff an office of attorneys to meet the needs of the employees. Other insurance companies contract with private attorneys to work for their insureds for a reduced hourly fee. In 1995, 18 million people were covered by some type of prepaid group legal plan. This trend is expected to increase.

SUMMARY

Most employers of legal assistants are attorneys. The structure and organization of a law office depends on the needs and desires of its attorneys, especially senior attorneys who own the firm.

The structure and organization of a law office are determined by four characteristics: size, specialty, management style, and form. The marketplace in which attorneys practice law is divided into three categories: private law firms, private industry, and government agencies.

The size of a law office is measured by the number of attorneys it employs. Small firms are still the pre-ferred way to practice law for most lawyers in the United States. Four types of large law firms exist: local, regional, national, and international. Large firms are formal and highly structured.

As society has become more complex, law has become more complex. This has forced attorneys to specialize in a particular area of law. The transition to specialization in law is analogous to specialization in the medical profession.

A firm's structure and the areas of law in which its attorneys specialize determine the firm's clientele and its need for staff, equipment, and materials. Numerous attorney specialties exist in the United States, and a number of states have developed plans for the recognition of legal specialties.

Two distinct managerial areas are addressed in any law firm: administrative (financial, office systems, and so on) and governance (associates, client relations, personnel, marketing, and so on). The combination of approaches used in these two areas is the management style of the firm.

Attorneys have developed five management styles that are used in most law firms in the United States: autocratic, democratic, managing partner, committee, and combination.

Two forms of management are defined: centralized and decentralized. In a centralized form of management, an entire law firm is managed from one source, whether by autocratic, democratic, managing partner, or committee style. In a decentralized form of management, an office is managed in segments, or in many areas.

Private law firms are organized into six different business structures: sole proprietorship, partnership, professional corporation, boutique firm, office-sharing association, and legal clinic.

Private industry consists of all types of businesses: small, medium, and large. Two types of legal departments are identified: corporate legal departments for very large corporations and legal departments for smaller, private companies.

Freelance paralegal services are offered to attorneys on a contract basis. A variety of freelance paralegal services are available in the United States. A new area of specialty that gained prominence in the 1980s is paralegal services that provide computerized litigation support. Numerous private companies also provide support services for attorneys.

Four types of government agencies employ legal assistants: federal, state, county, and city.

Certain changes that have occurred since the early 1970s have had a dramatic effect on the practice of law in traditional law firms. These changes have forced attorneys into an area for which they were neither prepared nor equipped: marketing and promotion. The needs of society and the individual client have changed since the days of the family lawyer.

CHAPTER ILLUSTRATION

Robert Black and Dennis White are new attorneys who were classmates in law school. Dennis wants to practice general litigation, family, and criminal law. Robert is interested in specializing in intellectual property. When they graduated from law school, Dennis wanted to start his own business but could not afford to purchase the necessary supplies and equipment to establish his own office, so he rented an office in an office-sharing facility.

This law suite is equipped with a law library, secretarial service, receptionist service, and fax and copying services. Dennis's rent gives him access to the suite amenities. There are about twenty lawyers in the suite who practice in various areas of law, mostly general practice. Each of the twenty lawyers in the suite is a sole practitioner. Some have their own secretaries, and others use the secretarial service. Dennis is pleased with the office-sharing arrangement.

Robert pounded the pavement for a job in intellectual property in corporate legal departments but was unsuccessful. He started doing some general practice work to help him get by. Dennis convinced him to establish his practice in the office suite. Dennis told him that an attorney in his suite was looking for a contract attorney who did intellectual property work and suggested that he may also get referrals

from other attorneys. Robert joined the office and works on intellectual property cases and general litigation cases.

After a couple of years, their clientele had increased so that both men were very busy attorneys. They found that their practices were too busy to rely on the secretarial service, so they hired a secretary, Tricia Bunnell, to work for both of them.

After a year, their businesses had outgrown the law suite. They were ready to establish their own practice and agreed to practice law together. Dennis found an office in a new professional building and rented it. They discussed the form of their business. They discussed the advantages and disadvantages of a partnership and corporation. They wanted neither the liability of a partnership nor the structure of a corporation. They agreed that a limited liability company (LLC) would be the right form of business for them.

Each agreed to contribute $25,000 to get the business started. Robert's friend, Grant Greene, a tax specialist who worked for the IRS, was looking for a new job and wanted to join in the business. However, Grant had no money to contribute to the start-up endeavor. Grant became a junior partner, owning 10 percent of the firm. When Grant could pay his contribution of $25,000, he would be promoted to full partner. Therefore, Robert owned 45 percent, Dennis

45 percent, and Grant 10 percent. Since Robert had management experience, the partners agreed that he would be the Managing Partner.

On the first day of May, their law firm opened. They celebrated as they hung out their shingle "Law Firm of Black, White & Greene, LLC."

CHAPTER REVIEW

1. What are the four things that determine the structure and organization of a law office?

2. What has forced attorneys to specialize?

3. What are the five management styles used in most law firms?

4. What is the difference between centralized and decentralized management?

5. What is the most common management style of a private law firm?

6. What are the three types of attorneys found in a partnership?

7. How does a legal clinic differ from a private law firm?

8. What is outside counsel?

9. What is the head attorney in a corporate legal department called?

10. What caused the demise of the legal clinic?

11. What are the two managerial areas found in a law firm?

12. What five changes since the early 1970s have influenced the practice of law?

13. What are the disadvantages to partnerships?

14. What is a nonlegal subsidiary?

15. What is an LLC?

EXAMPLES FOR DISCUSSION

1. The Books Are in the Safe

It all came apart in less than a year: a booming products liability boutique headed by an ex-partner from a big firm—the scion of one of Maryland's most prominent legal families, an author, and a lecturer—in partnership with two of his old buddies, one a law school classmate.

Attorney Edward S. Digges of Annapolis, Maryland, left Baltimore's Piper & Maybury in 1984 and set up his own firm with David A. Levin and James T. Wharton. David and James were busy lawyering. Edward was the managing partner, who took on all the onerous administrative tasks—billings, for example.

Then, in February 1989, client Dresser Industries sued the firm, charging that Edward had overbilled it by more than $2 million. His busy partners now found the time to demand to see the books, only to be told they were in the safe and not available. The next month, though, they saw the books and came to the conclusion that Edward had cheated them out of $1 million in compensation. They forced Edward out of the firm.

By September, Dresser won a motion for summary judgment, a determination of issues without a trial, against David and James for $3.1 million in damages for the overbillings, in part because expert witnesses testified that the two partners failed to come up with a mechanism that would have allowed them to oversee Edward's billings.

In January 1990, Edward pleaded guilty in federal court to fraud. He was sentenced to thirty months in prison, fined $30,000, and ordered to pay $1 million in restitution. (Reprinted with permission from *The National Law Journal,* Monday, April 23, 1990, p. 29.)

1. What went wrong with this partnership?
2. Why did David and James have to pay the client $3.1 million instead of Edward?
3. How could this situation have been avoided?
4. If you were involved in a partnership, what steps would you take so that this situation would not happen to you?

2. Consolidated Edison Company

Arthur Lonergan, Jr., director of administration, Law Department, Consolidated Edison Company in New York, states:

"As corporate and government agencies, we differ from private firms. They pay their lawyers more—substantially more—than we can afford to pay ours.

"So how do we keep our people? The work itself is interesting and diversified, and the hours and benefits are much better than in a private firm, so the quality of life for our attorneys is better. We are getting more into bonuses for lawyers and starting to compete with other law departments. You simply won't see corporations competing for salaries with large law firms. Recruiting candidates from top schools is difficult, but we are getting plenty of excellent attorneys from lateral moves and second-tier law schools.

"There is constant pressure to reduce the use of outside counsel. But it causes problems. As our workload increases, we need more staff, though there is often budget pressure to reduce staff. We are capable of doing the outside work, but we need people. When setting staffing levels at budget time, corporations and [government] agencies need to make exceptions based on increased workloads for law departments. Unfortunately, when we do expand, we hire lawyers but not corresponding support staff. So, for example, legal secretaries may support three or four lawyers in departments, versus a smaller ratio in big firms. Automation has been helpful to us in this strategy." (Reprinted with permission from *The National Law Journal* © 1991 New York Law Publishing Company.)

1. What are the differences between a corporate legal department and a private law firm?
2. What are the similarities?

3. What concerns does a corporate legal department have that a private law firm does not have?
4. What concerns does a private law firm have that a corporate legal department does not have?

3. Too Many Lawyers

The legal services industry grew 382 percent in the twelve-year period from 1977 to 1989. By comparison, the food and auto industries grew 91 percent and 40 percent, respectively. More than one million lawyers were licensed to practice law in 2000. In 1960, there was one lawyer for every 630 persons. In 1987, there was one lawyer for every 375 persons. In the year 2000, there was one lawyer for every 275 persons.

1. How will this growth affect the practice of law in general?
2. How will this growth influence the legal assistant profession?
3. How will this growth affect society in general?

ASSIGNMENTS

1. Interview two sole proprietors in your area. What are the differences between the two? Write a report comparing the following:
   a. Years of experience
   b. Income level
   c. Office structure
   d. Management style
   e. Type of clientele
   f. Number of hours worked each week
   g. Office setup and staff
2. Before you enrolled in this class, did you have an idea of your "ideal" place of employment? Do you know what your employment needs are? If not, take a minute to think about it. To determine your needs, consider the following:
   a. Do you need to be in a luxurious, prestigious environment?
   b. Do routine tasks bore you?
   c. Do you enjoy interacting with many people or do you work better alone?
   d. Would you be happy doing research in a law library all day?
   e. Do you enjoy working with high technology?
   f. Do people with serious problems upset you?
   g. Do you work well under pressure?
   h. Are you flexible?

   i. Are you an organized person?
   j. Would working more than 40 hours a week bother you?
   k. What are your talents?
   l. Do you desire to travel in your work?
   m. What are your strengths?
   n. What are your weaknesses?

Write your answers to the above questions on a piece of paper and put it in a safe place to review later. Be candid with yourself. In what type of environment do you need to work to reach your maximum potential? When you have completed your paralegal training, review this assignment and make any changes you feel appropriate. This list will help you in your job search.

3. Based on the information in this chapter, describe the law office that will satisfy your employment needs. Describe the "ideal" law office in which you would like to work. Describe your expectations. Keep the description of your ideal office in a safe place and review it after you have completed your paralegal training. When you start looking for a job, concentrate your efforts on offices that come close to your description.
4. Research the Web sites of the law firms listed on page 15. Pick one firm and answer the following questions:
   a. What are the specialties of the firm?

b. Does the Web site list the attorneys in the firm? If so, what are their qualifications?

c. Does the site have links to other Web sites? If so, which ones?

d. Does the Web site list the firm's philosophy or mission statement? If so, what is it?

e. Does the Web site offer reference material for legal research?

f. Does the firm offer a newsletter? If so, download and print it.

g. Does the firm have a nonlegal subsidiary? If so, name them.

h. What did you find especially interesting about the Web site?

5. Does your state formally recognize legal specialties? If so, which specialties? Research this area and report on the following:

a. What are the qualifications of an attorney to be a specialist?

b. What are the requirements for certification?

c. What are the areas of specialties?

d. What is the duration of certification?

6. Research the five management styles in terms of structure, organization, behavior techniques, and policies. Prepare a report of your findings and conclude with your opinion of the management style that is the most effective and ineffective.

7. Compare centralized and decentralized forms of management. In what cases would a decentralized form of management be effective? Ineffective? In what cases would a centralized form of management be effective? Ineffective?

8. Contact an insurance company that offers prepaid group insurance, and ask for a copy of a policy. Review the policy and write a report answering the following questions:

a. What are the services offered?

b. What are the requirements?

c. What are the costs?

d. How many people are enrolled in the plan?

9. Compare a corporate legal department with a traditional law firm. What are the differences? What are the similarities?

SELF-TEST

How well did you grasp the material in the chapter? Test yourself by answering the following questions and check your answers against the answers found in Appendix A.

1. What four things determine the structure and organization of a law office?
2. How is the size of a law office measured?
3. What factor determines the size differential of law offices?
4. In what size firm does the majority of lawyers prefer to practice?
5. What are the four types of large law firms?
6. How did "megafirms" come into existence?
7. What has forced attorneys to specialize?
8. How do specialty areas affect a law firm?
9. What is Cybertort?
10. What is a law office's culture?
11. What are the five management styles used in the majority of law firms today?
12. What is an autocratic form of governance?
13. What are the two types of democratic governance?
14. What is a Legal Administrator?
15. What is an office manager?
16. Why is the managing partner encouraged to practice law in addition to management duties?
17. What is an executive committee composed of?
18. What is combination management style?
19. What are the two forms of management?
20. What is a sole proprietor?
21. What is a general practitioner?
22. What are the five most common specialties for sole proprietors?
23. What are the advantages of sole practice?
24. What are the disadvantages of sole practice?
25. What is a contract attorney?
26. What are the three classes of attorneys that work in a partnership?
27. What constitutes a full partner?
28. What constitutes a junior partner?
29. What do the terms "nonequity" or "special" partner mean?
30. What is an LLC?
31. Who may own shares in a professional legal corporation?
32. What is the function of the board of directors of a professional corporation?
33. What is a boutique firm?
34. What are the two types of office-sharing arrangements?
35. What motivates an attorney to seek an office-sharing arrangement?
36. What is a legal clinic?

37. What are the two factors that have been responsible for a legal clinic's success?

38. What factors are responsible for a legal clinic's failure?

39. What type of cases do legal clinics take?

40. What is an "outside counsel"?

41. What is preventative law?

42. How does a corporate legal department function?

43. What is the head attorney in a corporate legal department called?

44. What form of organization does a corporate legal department have?

45. What is an in-house counsel?

46. What are some areas in private industry in which legal assistants have utilized their paralegal training?

47. What is a freelance paralegal service?

48. What is an independent paralegal?

49. Where do freelance paralegals work?

50. How many years of experience should a paralegal have before they freelance?

51. What four types of federal government agencies employ paralegals?

52. What federal agencies are the largest employers of paralegals?

53. What is the General Schedule?

54. What is a legal clerk?

55. What is the Legal Services Corporation?

56. What are some examples of legal assistant employment opportunities in county government?

57. Under what classification on the General Schedule of occupational classification do paralegals fall under?

58. What events have impacted the practice of law?

59. What is a nonlegal subsidiary?

60. Describe prepaid legal insurance plans.

KEY WORDS

Autocratic
Autonomous
Boutique
CLA
Contract attorney
Contract basis
Culture
Cybertort
Dividends
Equity partner
Executive committee
Freelance paralegal
General counsel
General practitioner
Independent paralegal
Indigent

In-house counsel
Legal administrator
Legal clinic
Limited liability company
Megafirm
Merger
Nonequity partner
Nonlegal subsidiary
Office manager
Outside counsel
P.C.
Preventative law
Sole practitioner
Sole proprietorship

CHAPTER

2

The Legal Team

OBJECTIVES

After completion of this chapter, a student should be able to do the following:

◆ Describe the titles, functions, and duties of each member of a legal team.

◆ Describe the functions and differences of the different categories of attorneys in a law firm.

◆ Describe the history, present position, and responsibilities of a law office administrator and a law office manager.

◆ Explain the difference between an office administrator and an office manager.

◆ Identify the various types of managers in a large firm.

◆ Describe tiered legal assistant programs.

◆ Explain how different law office staff contribute to a legal team.

◆ Describe the types of outside services and consultants contracted by a law office and how they contribute to the delivery of legal services.

◆ List the many employment opportunities for a person with a paralegal education.

INTRODUCTION

The purpose of this chapter is to introduce the various types of personnel that work in the legal marketplace and to briefly describe their job duties. It is important to understand how the legal team functions together and to illustrate how legal assistants interact with other staff. Although no two law offices are alike and employees' duties may vary, a general description of the duties of law office staff will be very helpful to a new legal assistant to understand fully each member's contribution to the legal team.

After a brief history of law office personnel, this chapter will discuss the various types of personnel in a law office and their responsibilities. Personnel will be dealt with according to size and type of firm. The various services law firms use will also be covered. After completing this chapter, you should understand the components of a dynamic legal team.

HISTORICAL PERSPECTIVE

In the 1940s and 1950s, legal personnel consisted of an attorney and a secretary. The management duties of a law firm were the responsibility of both and most often were not given high priority. In the 1960s, the American Bar Association (ABA) determined that attorneys' incomes were below those of other professionals. To discover the reason, the ABA conducted a survey that compared attorneys' businesses with those of other professionals and found that attorneys' lack of attention to law office management resulted in their decreased incomes. The survey also revealed that other professionals employed assistants and delegated routine work to their assistants. The ABA found that lawyers' incomes would increase if their efficiency increased. Therefore, the legal assistant and legal administrator professions were born.

The advent of the legal assistant and legal administrator roles changed the traditional law firm. By delegating routine tasks to legal assistants and management duties to legal administrators, lawyers could realize greater efficiency and increased incomes. But attorneys were slow to recognize the full benefits of these new positions.

A 1963 Prentice Hall survey of 311 Missouri attorneys revealed that 63 percent would not use the services of nonlawyer assistants. Of the 37 percent who would use those services, approximately 66 percent would hire nonlawyer assistants part time and saw them performing clerical functions.

It only took five years for part of this attitude to change. In surveys conducted in 1968, 60 percent of attorneys indicated they would hire nonlawyer assistants. However, the majority would hire them only for clerical functions. Many lawyers resisted delegating legal tasks to nonlawyers.

Despite the resistance of attorneys, the legal assistant profession flourished. In addition to economics and efficiency, four elements contributed to its growth:

◆ *Promotion by Bar Associations.* The ABA established the Special Committee on Lay Assistants for Lawyers in 1968. This committee encouraged employment of legal assistants. The ABA adopted a formal definition of a legal assistant and guidelines for using legal assistant services (see the "Legal Assistant" section later in this chapter). State bar association committees for law office economics extensively promoted the use of legal assistant services. Today, many state bar associations have legal assistant divisions or committees.

◆ *Growth of Paralegal Education.* Many paralegal educational programs emerged, training qualified legal assistants. These legal assistants demonstrated their skills and capabilities to attorneys while on the job.

◆ *Organization of Legal Assistants and Managers.* Legal assistants and law office managers organized nationally and locally. These organizations worked hard to educate attorneys on the benefits of employing nonlawyer assistants. (Appendix B lists national and state associations for legal assistants and related associations.)

◆ *Restructuring of Other Professions.* Other professions, such as the medical, dental, architectural, and teaching professions, realized the benefits of employing assistants and demonstrated these benefits by increased incomes and efficiency.

Today, legal assistants, legal administrators, and law office managers are recognized as essential members of a legal team.

Legal Team Members

A law firm's need for staff varies according to the size and specialty of the firm. For example, a general practitioner would need a staff with skills in various areas of law. A boutique firm would need a staff with skills in its specialty. A large law firm would need more management personnel than a small law firm.

A person with a paralegal education and experience has management opportunities in a law office. Many law firms promote their legal secretaries and legal assistants to management positions instead of hiring outside people. This trend is especially true of small and medium law offices. Legal assistants are enhancing their paralegal education with management courses, with the goal of managing a law office or becoming a paralegal manager.

Certain types of legal personnel can be found in each law office: attorney, legal administrator or office manager, legal assistant, law clerk, secretary, and receptionist. One person may fill more than one position. For example, the legal assistant may also be an office manager or law clerk, and a secretary may also be the receptionist.

Attorney

An attorney is the captain of a legal team. According to a 1990 survey of the National Association of Law Placement, 27,000 new lawyers enter the profession each year, and the number of attorneys in the United States reached one million in the year 2000. In 1990, 20 percent of the nation's attorneys were women. In 2000, 40 percent were women.

Rainmaker: An attorney responsible for client development for a firm.

The attorney is the captain of the legal team. Four categories of attorneys exist: rainmakers, owners, associates, and nontraditional. **Rainmakers** are known as such because they bring in the clients that provide the firm with work. Rainmakers are often very active in community organizations and bar associations. They are usually senior members of the firm. Some rainmakers serve on clients' boards of directors. Because of their outside civic activities, they may have a lower annual billable hour requirement than other attorneys in the firm—that is, the firm does not require them to bill as many hours to clients (see Chapter 7).

CYBERSITES

Locating an Attorney on the Web

American Bar Association—www.abanet.org

Martinedale Hubbel Corp.—www.martindale.com

West Legal Directory—www.wld.com

Yahoo Law Directories—www.yahoo.com/business_and_economy/company/law/directories

Owners, whether sole proprietors, partners, or shareholders, maintain client relations and train associates. They are responsible to the clients and supervise associates. Owners are more likely to be rainmakers than are other attorneys.

Equity partner: A partner who is entitled to a portion of the firm's profits and is responsible for a portion of the firm's losses.

Partners　Partners are not considered firm employees who are entitled to a salary. They are paid out of firm profits according to the percentage of the firm they own, as shown in Exhibit 2.1. In addition, partners contribute money to a partnership endeavor and pool their money to capitalize the business. The percentage of a firm that a partner owns depends on the category of the partner. Some law firms have multiple classes of partner, but most firms have two categories: full partner and junior partner (see Exhibit 2.1).

A full partner, also known as **equity partner,** has an equal voice in management policies and shares equally in the profits of the law firm. Within the class of full partner is the senior partner. A senior partner is usually a firm's founder, has more seniority than other partners, or controls the cases of the majority of clients.

Nonequity partner: A partner who is not entitled to a portion of the profits and is not responsible for a portion of the losses of a firm.

Junior partners are newly admitted to a partnership and generally have little input in the direction of the firm. In some firms, the term **nonequity partner,** or special partner, is used to indicate the noncapital position of a junior partner. They are entitled to a smaller portion of the profits. An attorney will remain a junior partner for a certain amount of time until promoted to full partnership.

One advantage of junior partnership status is that a junior partner is not required to contribute money into the partnership to equal the contribution ratio of the other full partners. The time spent as a junior partner gives an attorney an opportunity to save for a partnership contribution. As can be seen in Exhibit 2.2, the percentage of nonequity partners at large firms is increasing.

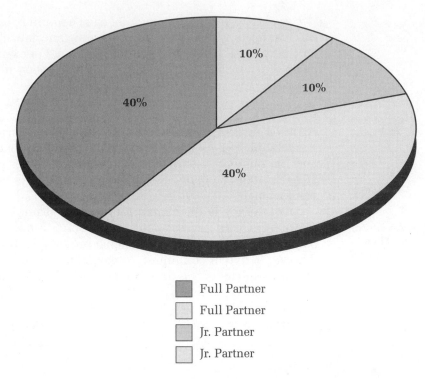

Full Partner
Full Partner
Jr. Partner
Jr. Partner

EXHIBIT 2.1 Firm Ownership by Partner Level

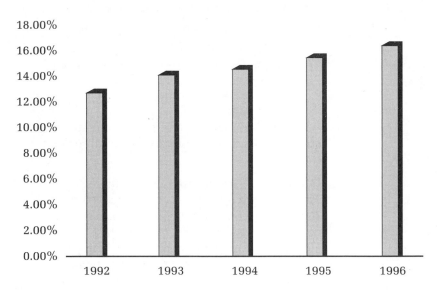

EXHIBIT 2.2 Percentage of Nonequity Partners at Large Firms
Reprinted with permission from the *National Law Journal.* Source: National Assn. For Law Placement, (1997).

Associates Associate attorneys are employees of a firm and are not entitled to a percentage of the firm's profits. They are paid a salary for their work. Associates do much of the work and often have a higher annual billable requirement than partners (see Chapter 7). Associates may be eligible for partnership in a firm when they have been employed by the firm for a certain length of time.

Before the 1940s, associates were employed for as long as twenty years before they were eligible for partnership. During the 1970s and 1980s, the average length of time an attorney had to be employed to reach the goal of partnership was five to seven years. Figures compiled by the National Association of Law Placement indicate that, during that period, the average length of time required before associates were considered for partnership status was 6.7 years in firms of twenty-five or more lawyers. However, since 1990, the length of time has increased, and some firms are reevaluating whether associates should be promoted at all.

Because of business constraints and competition in the marketplace, firms are promoting fewer associates to partnership status. They are finding that it is important to **leverage** an associate to the fullest extent possible. Leveraging is making a profit on the work of others. Studies have shown that the higher the ratio of associates to partner, the higher a partner's income. Therefore, it is not profitable for partners to promote associates in most cases.

A **leverage ratio** is a formula used to identify the number of leveraged income earners per partner. If a sole proprietor employs one associate, the ratio is 1:1. If a sole proprietor employs three associates, the ratio is 1:3. Legal assistants are also income producers for a law firm. Since they do not generate as high an income as an associate, their ratio is calculated at one-half of that of an associate, or .5. In other words, it takes two legal assistants to equal one associate in a leverage ratio. Therefore, if a sole practitioner employs two associates and two legal assistants, the ratio is 1:3. If a partnership of two attorneys employs five associates and two legal assistants, the ratio is 1:3, as shown here:

$$\frac{5 + (2 \times .5) = 6}{2 \text{ partners}} = \text{Ratio 1:3}$$

The leverage ratio varies according to firm size as shown in Exhibit 2.3.

Some firms have a limit on the number of associates they will promote to partner. A firm with seven or eight senior associates may promote only two or three to junior or full partner in order to maintain leverage. The remaining senior associates may become **permanent associates.** They receive a salary and fringe benefits but are not entitled to share

Leverage: The ability to make money from the work of others.

Leverage ratio: A formula used to identify the number of income-producing employees per owner.

Permanent associates: An employed attorney who is not eligible for a partnership in, or ownership of, a firm.

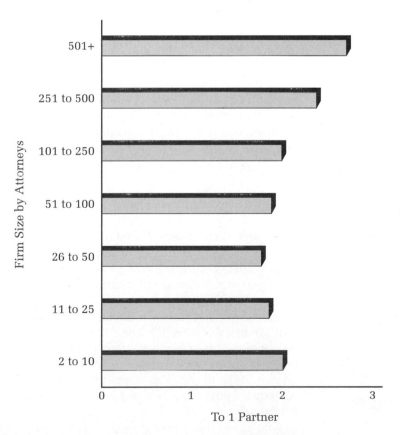

EXHIBIT 2.3 Relationship of Firm Size to Attorney-to-Partner Ratio

Reprinted with permission from the *National Law Journal.* Source: National Assn. For Law Placement (1994).

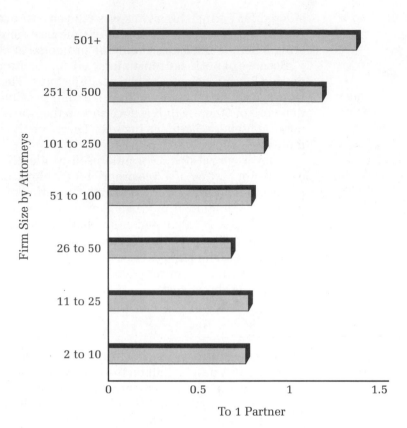

EXHIBIT 2.4   Relationship of Firm Size to Associate-to-Partner Ratio

Reprinted with permission from the *National Law Journal.* Source: National Assn. For Law Placement (1995).

in the firm's profits. The number of associates to partner, referred to as the associate-to-partner ratio, varies according to size of firm, as shown in Exhibit 2.4.

There are four classes of associates: senior associate, associate, junior associate, and nontraditional associates. Senior associates and associates supervise junior associates. Junior associates assist senior associates. A junior associate is usually a new attorney with little experience. Junior associates are analogous to an apprentice who must go through a period of training before they advance in the profession.

Nontraditional   In 1985, a large Cleveland partnership created a new position of **staff attorney** within its firm. A staff attorney is neither a partner nor an associate but is hired as a permanent employee with no possibility of advancement within a firm. Since then, firms have created forty-four separate classifications for firm lawyers that are neither partner nor associate. Among these classifications are counsel, staff attorney, special counsel, contract attorney, and advisory counsel (usually used for retired partners). The use of nontraditional attorneys is increasing as the potential for new partners is decreasing.

The term "of-counsel" refers to a semiretired former partner or an attorney who is affiliated with a firm on a part-time basis. An attorney who is well known may also be of-counsel to a law firm to help attract clients to the firm. In this capacity, the of-counsel attorney would be considered a rainmaker. An of-counsel attorney may be an employee of the firm or paid as a consultant only. Most of-counsel positions are not **equity** positions, which means that they are not entitled to a share of the firm's profits.

Law firms have established a variety of arrangements for their **of-counsel** positions. This has resulted in some confusion regarding the exact role of the of-counsel. The ABA, in its Model Code, defined an of-counsel as "A lawyer . . . [who] has a con-

Staff attorney: An employee of a law firm who has no advancement opportunities.

Equity: A right of ownership in a firm, entitling the holder to a portion of the profits.

Of-counsel: An attorney affiliated with a firm on a part-time basis.

tinuing relationship with the lawyer or law firm other than as a partner or associate." This definition allows for a variety of functions, and law firms apply the of-counsel designation for various reasons. The of-counsel position carries no clearly defined job description or duties.

OF INTEREST . . .

What do the letters after the attorney's name mean?

JD—Juris Doctor: Granted to a person on graduation of law school if the graduate has a bachelors degree

LLB—Bachelor of laws: Granted to a person on graduation of law school if the graduate does not have a bachelors degree

LLM—Master of laws: Granted to a person who has a JD and who successfully completes graduate course work in an area of law

Esq.—Esquire: Used for attorneys as a title of respect, such as "Honorable" is used for judges

---

Legal Administrator

MBA: Masters of business administration degree.

A legal administrator manages the business of a law firm. Some legal administrators have a law degree, but most have a masters of business administration (**MBA**) degree. A legal administrator's compensation is related to experience, size of firm, and geographic location.

Legal administrators have also been called office managers. However, the two are different. A legal administrator is responsible for making major business decisions for a firm. An office manager is under the direction of a legal administrator or a managing partner and does not have the authority of the administrator. Three major differences distinguish a legal administrator and an office manager:

◆ An administrator attends all partnership or committee meetings, although the administrator has no right to vote on issues.

◆ An administrator has the authority to hire and discharge staff personnel and administer salaries within approved guidelines.

◆ An administrator has the authority to make major purchases of furniture and equipment and to make financial decisions for a firm.

Before the legal administrator profession existed, secretaries acted as office managers and were asked to assume management functions under the direction of a managing attorney. In the late 1960s, the legal administrator profession emerged to assume management functions. Most office managers were promoted from legal secretary positions and had the status just above support staff but below associate. Most were hired to take over accounting and personnel functions and were regarded as administrative assistants to a managing partner.

Eventually, firms reviewed the amount of time managing partners devoted to management duties and determined that they would make more money if managing partners spent that time on billable matters. Management functions could be performed by an administrator at less cost to a firm. Therefore, the legal administrator position evolved to assume the duties of a managing partner, and some administrators are now partner-level employees, advising owners on key operational decisions.

Role of Administrator in a Large Firm   A legal administrator in a large firm is an experienced business executive, enjoying the same status and compensation as an attorney. A legal administrator may be referred to as chief operating officer or executive director. In most cases, however, an administrator is under the direction of a managing partner or executive committee.

Most senior legal administrators come from outside the legal profession. They have advanced degrees and years of senior-management-level experience. They are expert delegators and have strong leadership skills.

Role of Administrator in a Small Firm In a small firm, a legal administrator has the same responsibilities but on a smaller scale. Most often, the administrator's authority is not as great as in a large firm. This person may have other duties in addition to management responsibilities, such as paralegal or accounting work, and often has the title of office manager under the direction of the managing attorney. Owners of small firms are more autocratic and are possessive of the decision-making process.

While an administrator's areas of responsibility are similar in large and small firms, a small-firm administrator does not have the resources of a large-firm administrator. For example, while a large-firm administrator would have information specialists on staff, a small-firm one would have to be familiar with the available technology. In addition, small-firm administrators are responsible for training new personnel, whereas large-firm ones would delegate training to an employee or office manager.

TRENDS ▶▶▶

The Certified Legal Manager

The Association of Legal Administrators developed a voluntary certification program for managing partners, legal administrators, and office managers. The program requires the applicant to meet certain qualification requirements, pass an exam, and accumulate continuing education credits. The exam consists of four areas: financial management, human resources management, legal industry, and office management systems. Those who pass the exam receive the designation of certified legal manager (CLM).

The management areas for which an administrator has responsibility are divided into eight categories:

1. Financial management
   - Planning
   - Forecasting
   - Budgeting
   - Analysis
   - Billing and collections
   - Banking
   - Investments
   - Tax planning and reporting
   - Payroll and pension plans
2. Personnel management
   - Recruitment, selection, and placement
   - Orientation, training, and development
   - Performance evaluation
   - Salary and benefits
   - Discipline and termination
   - Workers' compensation
   - Organization analysis
   - Resource allocation

3. Systems management
   - ◆ Systems analysis
   - ◆ Operational audits
   - ◆ Procedures manual
   - ◆ Information services
   - ◆ Information storage and retrieval
   - ◆ Telecommunications
   - ◆ Litigation support
   - ◆ Legal practice systems
4. Facilities management
   - ◆ Lease negotiations
   - ◆ Space planning and design
   - ◆ Office renovation
   - ◆ Purchasing and inventory control
   - ◆ Reprographics
   - ◆ Reception
   - ◆ Mail and messenger services
5. General management
   - ◆ Policy making
   - ◆ Strategic planning
   - ◆ Business development
   - ◆ Risk management
   - ◆ Quality control
   - ◆ Organizational development
6. Practice management
   - ◆ Lawyer recruiting
   - ◆ Lawyer training and development
   - ◆ Legal assistant supervision
   - ◆ Work product quality control
   - ◆ Professional standards
   - ◆ Substantive practice systems
7. Marketing
   - ◆ Client profitability analysis
   - ◆ Business opportunities forecasting
   - ◆ Client development planning
   - ◆ Law firm visibility and image enhancement
   - ◆ Advertising
8. Leadership

Whether a legal administrator performs all these functions or delegates them to an office manager or managers depends on the size of the firm and the amount of authority given the legal administrator by the attorneys in the firm. The managing attorney or attorneys may not be willing to release some responsibilities to an administrator and may keep some for themselves. How an individual law firm accomplishes administrative tasks depends on the policies of the firm.

Law Office Manager

A law office manager works under the direction of a legal administrator or managing partner. In a small firm, an office manager performs all management functions. In a

EXHIBIT 2.5 Hierarchy of Managing Partner, Legal Administrator, and Office Managers

large firm, specialized office managers perform specific management functions under the supervision of a legal administrator, as shown in Exhibit 2.5. Each manager's duties vary according to the needs of the firm, as shown in Exhibit 2.6.

CPA: Certified public accountant.

Financial Manager A financial manager, usually a certified public accountant (**CPA**), is responsible for the various financial aspects of a firm. Duties consist of handling billing and collections, payroll, accounts payable, and investments.

Personnel Manager A personnel manager is responsible for managing the various aspects of a firm's human resources. This manager's duties include six tasks:

◆ Manage employee benefits
◆ Monitor vacation and sick leave
◆ Establish promotion and salary increase guidelines
◆ Hire and fire employees
◆ Interview prospective new employees
◆ Develop personnel policies and procedures

Administrative Manager An administrative manager is responsible for systems management. This person develops and maintains systems used in various areas of a firm. This manager's duties include five tasks:

◆ Manage file maintenance systems (see Chapter 12).
◆ Manage general office systems such as calendaring and tickler systems (see Chapter 10)
◆ Manage substantive systems (see Chapter 9)
◆ Write procedures for each system (see Chapter 9)
◆ Change systems as the need arises

Facilities Manager A facilities manager is responsible for managing the facilities of a firm, which include the office property, grounds, and structure. For employees to be productive, the office area must have enough space for all employees, be organized, and be structured in a manner that encourages productivity. The duties of a facilities manager include six tasks:

◆ Supervise parking conditions for employees and clients
◆ Plan the office area to accommodate current and future employees and maximize the use of space (includes assessing needs; deciding where to locate

the library, conference rooms, copy center, and receptionist; and ensuring accessibility to the various centers for the employees)
◆ Supervise security systems for the premises
◆ Supervise cleaning services for the premises
◆ Plan employee safety in case of a disaster
◆ Plan records preservation in case of a disaster

Marketing Manager A marketing manager is responsible for marketing and advertising. This is a new position in law firms and gained prominence in the late 1980s. Large firms employ a full-time marketing manager. Smaller firms hire marketing consultants. According to a survey conducted by Market Intelligence, a research firm, about one-third of all midsize and large firms have a full-time marketing manager on staff. Large firms are twice as likely as midsize firms to employ a marketing manager. The duties of a marketing manager include nine tasks:

◆ Prepare and analyze client surveys to determine firm strengths and weaknesses (see Chapter 4)
◆ Direct the firm in defining a target market
◆ Direct advertising activities

LEGAL ADMINISTRATOR

Legal Administrator wanted for growing law firm of 25 attorneys. Previous law firm management experience necessary. Bachelors degree in business required; MBA a plus. Must have excellent organizational, communication and training skills. Must be knowledgeable of computer systems and law firm accounting methods. Firm located in financial district. Excellent salary and benefits. Send resume and cover letter to Bunnell, Shuran and Kehl, P.O. Box 245, San Francisco, CA 94104.

MARKETING MANAGER

Large New York international law firm of Bristol, Snell, Procunier & Valentino has opening for marketing manager to coordinate the firm's public relations and client development program. Must have five years marketing experience and have strong writing and communication skills. Must be detail oriented to coordinate seminars, produce newsletter, and coordinate client surveys. Excellent salary, benefits, and working environment. Please send cover letter and resume to Legal Administrator, Bristol, Snell, Procunier & Valentino, 111 Eighth Avenue, New York, NY 10001.

OFFICE MANAGER

Office manager needed for corporate legal department of large, Fortune 500 company. The ideal candidate will have at least two years management experience in budget development, personnel management, and training. Must have a bachelors degree. Professional position that reports to general counsel. Must be a self-starter and computer literate. Send resume and cover letter to Dept. of Human Resources, ABC Corporation, 9000 Corporate Way, Chicago, IL.

MANAGEMENT

Seeking innovative manager to oversee general management of small law firm specializing in family law. Position requires experience with Novell LAN/WAN networks and PC applications, including Windows and WordPerfect. Must have knowledge of employment and labor laws and have previous management experience, preferably in a law firm. Send resume and salary history to 5507 Longview, Paradise, CA 95969.

EXHIBIT 2.6 Requirements for a Law Office Manager Vary Depending on the Firm's Needs

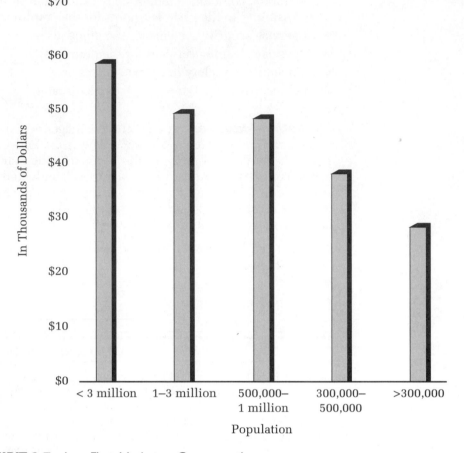

EXHIBIT 2.7 Law Firm Marketers Compensation

Reprinted with permission from the *National Law Journal.* Source: National Law Firm Marketing Assn. (1994).

◆ Direct promotional activities, such as client seminars and entertainment
◆ Prepare a firm newsletter and brochure (see Chapter 4)
◆ Direct public relations activities, such as press releases
◆ Monitor the public's perception of the firm
◆ Prepare marketing plan
◆ Monitor and update Web site and electronic advertising

As Exhibit 2.7 illustrates, law firm marketing specialists are highly compensated, as well as law firm managers as shown in Exhibit 2.8. For more information about law firm marketing, contact the National Law Firm Marketing Association (see Appendix B).

Legal Assistant Manager   A legal assistant manager, sometimes called a paralegal manager, is found in offices with many legal assistants and is generally a senior legal assistant with many years of experience. A legal assistant manager is responsible for supervising legal assistants and may also do paralegal work, shown as illustrated in Exhibit 2.9. Among the duties of a legal assistant manager are eleven tasks:

Liaison: A person responsible for communication between groups; a spokesperson.

◆ Direct the personnel matters of legal assistants and act as a **liaison** between legal assistants and firm management
◆ Supervise legal assistants
◆ Coordinate the paralegal workload and assign responsibilities
◆ Train legal assistants

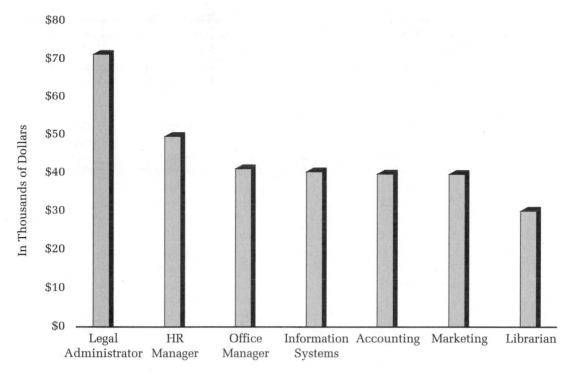

EXHIBIT 2.8 Median Compensation for Law Firm Managers

Reprinted with permission of the *National Law Journal.* Source: Altman Weil Penza's Survey of Law Firm Economics (1997).

◆ Verify that paralegal duties are performed in accordance with an attorney's instructions and act as a liaison between legal assistants and attorneys

◆ Evaluate legal assistants' performance (see Chapter 3)

◆ Oversee the firm's paralegal program

◆ Establish policies and guidelines relating to the effective utilization of legal assistant services

◆ Recruit, interview, and hire new legal assistants

◆ Conduct orientation and training sessions for new legal assistants

◆ Maintain personnel records for legal assistants

For more information about legal administrators and legal assistant managers, contact the Association for Legal Administrators, the Legal Assistant Management Association, and the National Association for Law Firm Marketing (see Appendix B).

Professional Profile	**Diane Mortenson,** owner of Direct Legal Management, is a marketing consultant for law firms. She started out in the legal field as a paralegal and worked as a paralegal for many years before obtaining her masters degree in management and pursuing a career in management. Of her responsibilities, Diane states:

"Marketing consultants are responsible for a number of areas. We set up and monitor seminars and workshops for clients and produce a firm newsletter. We establish and maintain databases and circulate client surveys. We also train and assist the attorneys in client development and help them with client relations, particularly in the area of client communication. One of our major duties is setting up a marketing plan to attract the firm's target market and develop marketing materials." She said that law firm marketing professionals are needed especially for large international law firms that establish a presence in another country. "A marketing professional who knows the needs and trends of a particular country is extremely valuable." She said that law firm marketing is not just for large firms. Smaller firms, especially boutiques, benefit greatly from the services of a law firm marketing specialist.

What does it take to be a good paralegal manager? There are a number of qualities absolutely essential for a good paralegal manager.

1. *The Ability to Work under Pressure.* Paralegal managers receive pressure from legal assistants as well as from attorneys. This is a position where the individual is literally caught in the middle and sits on a fence determining, on a case-by-case basis, which side of the fence to jump to.

2. *Analytical Skills.* The ability to gather facts from two disputing sides (usually an attorney and a paralegal) and to make sense from these facts is essential. It's helpful to have highly tuned mind reading skills as it seems no one actually communicates verbally—there is just an incredible amount of mind reading going on.

3. *Quality Writing and Speaking Skills.* In order to train legal assistants well, a paralegal manager must be able to communicate verbally as well as in writing.

4. *Practical/Common Sense.* A legal assistant manager must have the ability to take fiction and turn it into reality.

5. *Adaptable Personality.* A paralegal manager must take on multiple personalities in order to deal with the quiet, sensitive individual as well as the boisterous, high-strung individual.

6. *High Productivity.* A legal assistant manager is expected not only to take care of the hiring, firing, training, financial accounting, and space considerations but is frequently also expected to do some kind of legal work and to produce it in a very reliable fashion.

7. *Superior Organizational Skills.* The ability to keep training, hiring, and most important, vacation schedules in order!

8. A good legal assistant manager must also be *assertive* and *aggressive,* remembering there is a fine line between these two. One must tread this as if walking a tightrope.

9. *Patience.* Patience is a virtue that a legal assistant manager must have and instill in the legal assistants as well as the attorneys. In the legal profession, there is no room for impatience as everyone suffers.

10. *Attention to Detail.* The legal assistant manager must pay close attention to detail and catch *all* mistakes coming from *all* directions. It is like being a mother—you make everything work, and people just expect it.

11. *The Ability to Handle Three Things at Once.* I like to refer to this as "multipurpose programming," whereby multiple jobs can be done in one fell swoop.

12. A Sense of Humor. Last but not least, without a sense of humor, a legal assistant surely would not survive more than five minutes.

EXHIBIT 2.9   Profile of a Paralegal Manager

Reprinted with permission from *Legal Assistant Today.* Copyright 1998, James Publishing, Inc. For subscription information, call (800) 394-2626.

Legal Assistant

Definition   What is a legal assistant? What is the difference between a legal assistant and a paralegal? There is a difference of opinion as to the meanings of the two terms. In some areas of the country, a legal assistant is an entry-level paralegal or paralegal's assistant. Elsewhere, there is no difference. In other areas, the term "legal assistant" refers to the person whereas "paralegal" describes the legal assistant's work. For example, a legal assistant does paralegal work.

The ABA has set a definition of legal assistant as well as various legal assistant organizations as follows:

> "A legal assistant or paralegal is a person, qualified by education, training or work experience who is employed or retained by a lawyer, law office, corporation, governmental agency or other entity and who performs specifically delegated substantive legal work for which a lawyer is responsible." (1997)

As adopted by the National Federation of Paralegal Associations (NFPA) in 1987:

> "A paralegal/legal assistant is a person qualified through education, training or work experience to perform substantive legal work that requires knowledge of legal concepts and

is customarily, but not exclusively, performed by a lawyer. This person may be retained or employed by a lawyer, law office, governmental agency, or other entity or may be authorized by administrative, statutory or court authority to perform this work."

As adopted by the National Association of Legal Assistants (NALA) in 1995:

"Legal assistants, also known as paralegals, are a distinguishable group of persons who assist attorneys in the delivery of legal services. Through formal education, training and experience, legal assistants have knowledge and expertise regarding the legal system and substantive and procedural law which qualifies them to do work of a legal nature under the supervision of an attorney."

As adopted by the American Association for Paralegal Education (AAfPE) in 1998:

"Paralegals perform substantive and procedural legal work for others as authorized by law which work, in the absence of the paralegal, would be performed by an attorney. Paralegals have knowledge of the law gained through education and work experience which qualifies them to perform legal work. Paralegals adhere to recognized ethical standards and rules of professional responsibility."

These definitions are very broad, allowing attorneys, legal administrators, and paralegal managers to define a legal assistant's role in their particular law office. Since they delegate tasks to the legal assistants, they determine the legal assistant's level of responsibility.

Education　According to the 1997 Paralegal Compensation and Benefits Report created by the NFPA, the majority of its respondents (53 percent) have a bachelors degree, 7 percent have a masters degree, and 21 percent have an associate degree. According to a national survey conducted by *Legal Assistant Today* magazine in 1999, the higher the legal assistant's education, the higher their salaries, as shown in Exhibit 2.10.

In the early 1980s, the AAfPE (see Appendix B) was organized. This association has contributed much to the success of the paralegal profession. Educators and employers agree that a legal assistant's education is of utmost importance. The days when a legal assistant without a paralegal education or advanced degree receives on-the-job training are over. According to the 1998 salary survey conducted by *Legal Assistant Today* magazine, 67.5 percent of responding paralegals had a paralegal credential.

According to a resolution passed by the AAfPE, paralegals are qualified to do entry-level work with a college degree (associates or Bachelors degree) and a paralegal credential. The basis for the resolution are the following:

◆ Formal education is more learner-friendly than on-the-job training from busy attorneys.
◆ Those without an education will now find it more difficult to move forward as paralegals.
◆ More respect will be accorded to paralegals as a distinct profession, working with attorneys as part of the legal services delivery team. Paralegals will receive more respect and recognition.

% OF PARALEGAL	DEGREE	AVERAGE SALARY	% INCREASE FROM 1998
15	No degree	$35,019	−1.7
31.3	Associates	$33,762	−7.8
47.4	Bachelors	$35,586	+3.1
6.2	Masters	$36,714	+1

EXHIBIT 2.10　Paralegal Compensation by Education

Reprinted with permission from *Legal Assistant Today* magazine.

A legal assistant who meets certain qualifications can be certified through the NFPA by taking its PACE exam (established in 1996) or through NALA by taking its CLA exam (established in 1976). Both certifications are voluntary. According to the 1998 salary survey conducted by *Legal Assistant Today* magazine, 12 percent of the responding legal assistants were CLAs. Additionally, some states, such as California, offer voluntary state certification.

OF INTEREST . . .

Certification versus Noncertification

As of May 1998, there are 9,211 CLAs and 700 certified specialists in the United States. Not all paralegals agree that certification is essential for career growth. It is debatable among paralegals whether certification enhances a paralegal's employability and professional status. What paralegals are saying:

Pro Certification

"I think legal assistants should be certified—it looks better."

"The exam should be taken for no other reason than for yourself. Do I understand my profession? Am I on top of what is going on? Use it to sell yourself and your knowledge as a paralegal."

"Passing an exam is one way to tell the world that you know your stuff."

Con Certification

"I have been a paralegal for seventeen years. What will a certification exam do for me? All I know is that NALA or NFPA will make more money off me."

"The profession's love of rules and egotistic recognition is damaging to the future of many of its practitioners. Certification overkill!"

"Certified paralegals don't make more money than uncertified paralegals, so what's the point?"

Legal Assistant Today, *September 1998.*

Specialization Legal assistants specialize in the same areas as attorneys. Since a course in all the various specialties cannot be found in paralegal educational programs, legal assistants have learned their specialties on the job by working for a specialist. Others have taken a class in some of the more popular specialties. Today, legal assistants are realizing advantages to specializing in two and perhaps three areas to increase their marketability. Specialty exams are available from the NFPA and the NALA in some specialty areas. For example, as of this writing, the NALA offers specialty exams in bankruptcy, civil litigation, corporate/business law, intellectual property, estate planning and probate and real estate.

The specialty with the highest number of legal assistants is litigation. Litigation courses are taught in paralegal programs, and many other specialties involve the litigation process. Among the duties of a litigation legal assistant are the following fourteen tasks:

◆ Perform legal research and prepare research memoranda
◆ Conduct factual research and investigation
◆ Interview clients and witnesses
◆ Draft and prepare legal documents
◆ Analyze legal documents
◆ Perform records research
◆ Assist attorneys at depositions
◆ Prepare jury instructions and prepare deposition summaries

- Assist attorneys at hearings and trials
- Prepare trial exhibits and notebooks
- Prepare clients for depositions and trials
- Maintain and organize files
- Develop and maintain litigation support databases
- Coordinate demonstrative evidence for trial

Specialization can increase a paralegal's salary. According to a survey conducted by the NFPA in 1997, the smallest areas of specialization that have the largest salaries are trade regulation, telecommunications, and international law (more than $40,000). Paralegals practicing in family, public, and criminal law were paid the least (less than $27,000). The 1999 survey conducted by *Legal Assistant Today* magazine revealed different results. The highest paid specialties were intellectual property, corporate, and environmental law. In Silicon Valley, California, paralegals in corporate securities and patent law are commanding salaries in excess of $70,000. Pat Lyden, human resources director at Gray, Cary, Ware & Freidenrich in Palo Alto, said, "We've had to pay a premium to all those [paralegals] in patent and trademark positions just to make sure that we don't lose the good employees we already have."

The most popular specialties for paralegals are the following:

- Administrative law
- Admiralty law
- Bankruptcy law
- Corporate law
- Criminal law
- Elder law
- Employer benefits law
- Entertainment law
- Environmental law
- Family law
- Intellectual property law
- Labor law
- Litigation
- Native American law
- Personal injury law
- Probate and estate planning
- Public law
- Securities law
- Transactional law
- Workers' compensation law

Paralegal Responsibilities by Firm Structure   Legal assistants work in private law firms, corporate legal departments, private industry, and the government as shown in Exhibit 2.11. The "Utilization of Legal Assistants among Private Practitioners" survey, conducted in 1998 by the ABA Standing Committee on Legal Assistants, revealed that 99 percent of large firms employ paralegals and that only 34.8 percent of small firms (three or fewer attorneys) employ paralegals. The survey also revealed the following:

- Paralegals are used most extensively in business/corporate, probate/estate planning, and litigation practices.
- The most important skills desired in paralegals are organization, communication, and computer literacy.

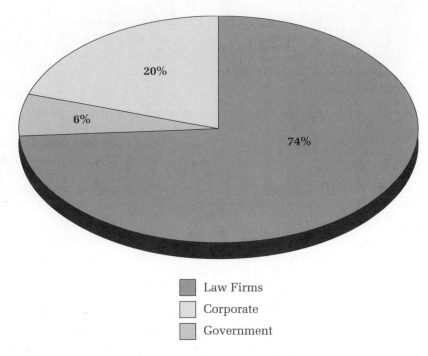

EXHIBIT 2.11　Where Do Paralegals Work?

Reprinted with permission from *Legal Assistant Today.* Copyright 1998, James Publishing, Inc. For subscription information, call (800) 394-2626.

◆ The least important skills are conducting legal research and preparing legal memos.

◆ Almost 66 percent of the respondents require their paralegals to have an associate or bachelors degree, while 25 percent require an ABA-approved education.

The average law office employs one paralegal for every six attorneys. There is no fixed goal with respect to the ratio of attorneys to paralegals. Some areas of law are paralegal intensive (litigation) and some are not (criminal).

A legal assistant in a small firm has different duties and responsibilities than a legal assistant in a large firm. In a small firm, the legal assistant may have duties in addition to paralegal work, such as office management and clerical work. This legal assistant may also work in a number of areas of law as demanded by the employer.

TRENDS ➤➤➤

Pro Bono Activities for Paralegals

Paralegals contribute to the community by volunteering their time and expertise in the following pro bono activities:

• Help an attorney work on a case for an indigent client

• Assist the local bar association's volunteer legal services program

• Assist the elderly in obtaining Social Security as authorized by law

• Represent children in court through a court-appointed special advocate as authorized by law

• Participate on paralegal advisory boards of a local college to ensure quality education

• Volunteer as a small-claims adviser for small-claims court

• Tutor a paralegal student

• Volunteer at local shelters

• Serve on the board of directors of local agencies, such as the YWCA of Hospice Homes

In a large firm, a legal assistant's duties are more narrow and structured. A large firm, having more resources than a small firm, allows a legal assistant to specialize and focus on a few duties and areas of expertise. Office managers handle the management, secretaries handle the clerical work, and file and calendar clerks handle filing and calendaring. In a small firm, the attorney supervises the legal assistant. In a large firm, the legal assistant may have many supervisors: the legal assistant manager, legal administrator, supervising attorney, and managing partner.

Available technology is different in small firms. According to a 1998 technology survey conducted by the ABA, 76.2 percent of paralegals at large firms (80 or more attorneys) have full access to the Internet, compared to only 18.6 percent in small firms (fewer than 20 attorneys). The survey also found that small firms have older technology than do large firms.

Another area of difference is upward mobility. In a small firm, legal assistants have fewer opportunities to advance than in larger organizations. Few small firms develop levels for their paralegal employees. Corporate legal departments offer their paralegals advancement opportunities inside and outside the legal department. Large firms create paralegal programs that have levels according to the legal assistant's education, experience, and seniority.

The late 1980s saw the beginning of tiered paralegal programs in law offices. A tiered paralegal program provides upward mobility for a legal assistant by establishing categories of paralegal positions. An inexperienced legal assistant would start at step (or level) 1 and move up the paralegal ladder to higher positions with greater responsibility and pay. For example, legal assistants in the legal department of 3M Company are placed on one of four levels; legal aid, legal assistant, advanced legal assistant, and senior legal assistant. Main Street Insurance Company has six steps, as shown in Exhibit 2.12. Promotions are based on demonstrated abilities.

Paralegals perform substantive and clerical tasks. The smaller the firm, the more likely the paralegal will do some clerical work. However, it is considered an inefficient use of a legal assistant's time to have them perform clerical tasks because clerical duties are normally considered firm overhead and not billed to the client. According to a survey conducted by *Legal Assistant Today* magazine in 1997, only 31 percent of responding paralegals had no clerical responsibilities. Twenty-five percent devoted one to five hours to clerical duties, and 43 percent devoted more than five hours to clerical duties.

Legal assistants reported that the following ten substantive tasks are most commonly performed:

◆ Draft legal documents
◆ Legal research

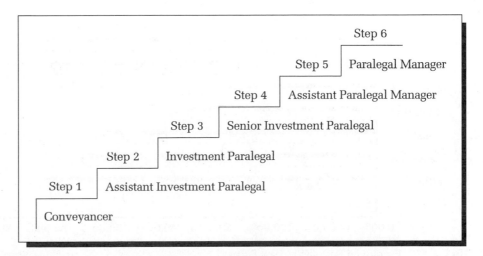

EXHIBIT 2.12 Main Street Insurance Company's Tiered Paralegal Program

◆ Client meetings and communication
◆ Trial preparation
◆ Investigation
◆ Drafting discovery
◆ Negotiations
◆ Record review and analysis
◆ Review medical records
◆ Project management

Salary and Benefits Salaries vary by geographic area. On a national scale, the average salary for 1999 was $35,115 (*Legal Assistant Today,* February, 1999). According to the 1999 *Legal Assistant Today* magazine salary survey, legal assistants in corporate legal departments were paid higher salaries than paralegals in private law firms or government positions. Additionally, as previously stated, specialists made more money than generalists, with intellectual property being the highest-paid specialty mentioned by the survey respondents. Sixty-one percent of the survey respondents received a bonus, the average of which was $1,475. Slightly more than 55 percent (55.8 percent) of the respondents felt that they were fairly paid.

Benefits vary greatly by employer. Generally, large firms and corporate legal departments offer their employees a better benefits package than do small firms or small private industry companies. Results of various surveys of the legal profession indicate that benefits are declining. As legal offices become more cost conscious, benefits are normally the first area in which to cut costs. The benefits reported in *Legal Assistant Today* magazine's 1998 salary survey are shown in Exhibit 2.13.

Future Growth In 1998, there were about 300,000 legal assistants in the United States, and the figure is projected to rise. According to recent figures released by the

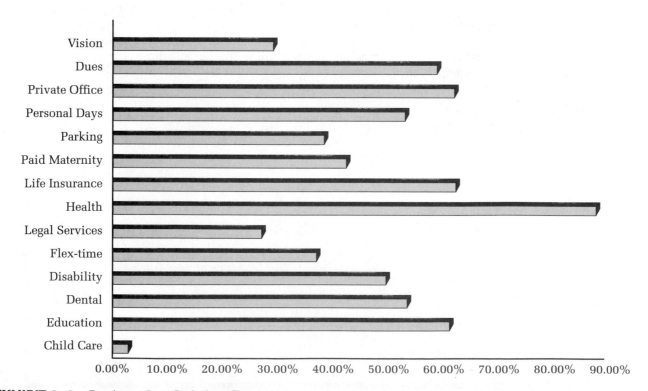

EXHIBIT 2.13 Employee Benefits in Law Firms

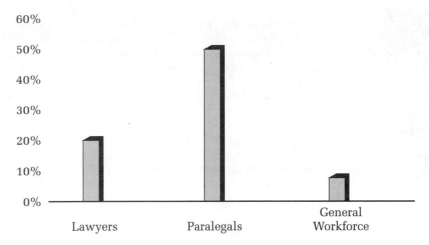

EXHIBIT 2.14 Projected Job Growth for the Paralegal Profession
Source: *National Law Journal,* February 17, 1997. Reprinted with permission.

Bureau of Labor Statistics, paralegal positions are expected to increase 58 percent between 1994 and 2005, more than four times the job rate for the general workforce. According to several surveys, areas demanding the most paralegals are employment, health care, and intellectual property law. Projected job growth in the paralegal profession is shown in Exhibit 2.14.

Altman & Weil, national legal consultants, predicts that corporate legal departments will hire more paralegals than law firms and will replace some attorney positions with paralegals. The Bureau of Labor Statistics indicated that private industry, consisting of insurance companies, banks, and title insurance companies, will also increase their paralegal staff.

CYBERSITES

Where to Find Information on the Paralegal Profession on The Web

NFPA—www.paralegals.org. The National Federation of Paralegal Association's home page is a paralegal's dream come true. It offers at least seventeen e-mail discussion groups. If you need an answer to a question about the paralegal profession, you will find it on the Internet.

Legal resources—www.paralegals.org/Legal Resources/home.html

Job listings—www.paralegals.org/Center/StateEmploy/home.html

California Association of Independent Paralegals—
www.paralegals.org/Members/RegionI/CAIndependent/caip.html

West Coast Association of Paralegals—www.paralegals.org/Members/RegionI/West
Coast/home.html

State and local paralegal associations—hg.org/assistants-assoc.html

Paralegal Education Program Directory—
www.paralegals.org/Members/Choice/school/state.html

Discussion groups—www.ljx.com/forumpages/paralegals.html

NALA—www.nala.org. Among other things, NALA offers an Internet campus where paralegals can learn new skills or brush up on current skills. In partnership with West Publishing Company, the campus was developed to educate paralegals and prepare paralegals for the NALA exam. A paralegal can earn continuing education credits on this site.

AAfPE—www.aafpe.org. This site provides information regarding educational programs.

While **Donna Barr** no longer calls herself a paralegal, she firmly states that without her paralegal background she could not perform in the position she now holds. Barr has been a real estate paralegal, office services supervisor, and paralegal manager for a major law firm. An attorney for whom Barr worked suggested to the Archdiocese that (1) hiring an in-house paralegal to manage its properties would be more cost-effective than its traditional policy of hiring outside counsel and that (2) he knew an excellent paralegal to be the first to hold the position.

That happened five years ago. Since then, Barr has used her knowledge of real estate law and the managerial skills she gained as a paralegal to manage the Archdiocese's properties and work with outside counsel. She continues to support the paralegal profession by teaching real estate law, introduction to the profession, and law office administration in the paralegal studies program at the Community College of Aurora.

A Typical Legal Assistant   According to NFPA's 1997 survey of 4,129 legal assistants in the United States, the typical legal assistant is characterized by the following:

◆ Is thirty-eight years old, white (91 percent), and female (92 percent)

◆ Has a bachelor's degree (53 percent)

◆ Makes $34,514 per year

◆ Works in a private law firm (71 percent)

◆ Has been employed as a paralegal for seven to ten years (85 percent)

◆ Received a bonus of $2,094 (64 percent received a bonus)

◆ Received the following benefits: vacation (90 percent), sick leave (78 percent), life insurance (68 percent), fully paid medical insurance (52 percent), and retirement plan (45 percent)

Responding paralegals reported that attorney contact and responsibility were their areas of greatest satisfaction. Among the areas of least satisfaction were bonus, salary, and secretarial support.

For more information regarding the legal assistant profession, contact a national or local paralegal association (see Appendix B).

Law Clerk

A law clerk is a law student, usually in the second or third year of law school, and typically works for a law firm on a part-time basis. Clerking supplements a law student's education.

Some firms have elaborate programs to attract the best law students from the best law schools. They want to establish a relationship with a student so that the student will consider being employed by that firm on graduation.

A law clerk's duties are performing legal research, writing memorandums of law, and preparing case briefs. Some third- or fourth-year law students may also draft legal documents. Legal assistants also do research, write memorandums, and draft legal documents. A law clerk is distinguished from a legal assistant by the following:

◆ Law clerks are normally temporary employees of a firm.

◆ Although law clerks are educated in the law, they receive very little practical procedural education. Although a law clerk may draft a motion, chances are the clerk does not know the format, requirements, and method for getting the document filed with a court.

◆ A law clerk has little practical knowledge of the forms required for an action.

◆ A clerk's time may or may not be billed to a client.

◆ Law clerks will usually not make a career out of clerking.

Legal Secretary

In the 1970s, the traditional legal secretary was responsible for all clerical tasks, some paralegal work, and some management duties. This "supersecretary" was an attorney's right arm. In the 1990s, a legal secretary was responsible for clerical tasks. Today, legal secretaries are technology specialists and are given more responsibility. The new millennium introduces a change in the secretary's job title from legal secretary to administrative assistant. Many of today's legal assistants started their legal careers in the role of legal secretary.

The typical duties of a legal secretary include fourteen tasks:

◆ Prepare legal documents and correspondence from dictation or instruction or both, organizing in order of priority and proofing as necessary
◆ Compose and prepare routine correspondence
◆ Record and prepare the minutes of meetings
◆ Prepare statements for services rendered
◆ Read and route incoming mail
◆ Locate the appropriate file and attach it to correspondence to be answered by an employer
◆ Sort, fold, insert, seal, address, and stamp outgoing mail
◆ Schedule appointments
◆ Screen calls and greet clients or visitors
◆ Place outgoing calls
◆ File correspondence and other documents
◆ Schedule appointments and court hearings and reconfirm them
◆ Respond to clients as directed
◆ Interact with clients, attorneys, and other personnel as directed
◆ Desktop publishing
◆ Develop spreadsheets
◆ Develop and manage databases
◆ Perform on-line research

E-mail: Electronic mail. A system that allows employees to communicate with one another on computer terminals.

Voice mail: An electronic recording device that delivers a message to the recipient of a call if that person is unable to answer the telephone.

The advent of legal assistants, legal administrators, and computers changed the role of a legal secretary. The days of one secretary for each attorney are over. Attorneys are drafting documents and correspondence on their own computer. They are also able to research a case directly from their computer terminal. With **e-mail** capabilities, attorneys and legal assistants can send memos to other members of a firm without secretarial assistance. **Voice mail** allows an attorney or a legal assistant to receive telephone calls without secretarial assistance.

As attorneys become computer literate, their need for secretarial assistance decreases. For example, one large firm hired fifty-three new attorneys in an eighteen-month period without hiring an additional secretary. It is not uncommon for a secretary to support three or four attorneys, legal assistants, or both. A firm strives for a ratio of one secretary for three attorneys. This places pressure on secretaries and lawyers to increase efficiency to reduce rush assignments.

The Bureau of Labor Statistics predicts that legal secretarial positions will increase by 24 percent during the period from 1994 and 2005. They also predict changes in the secretarial workforce in general. Secretaries' areas of responsibility are increasing along with their salaries. There is an increasing demand for legal secretaries on a temporary basis. According to a 1998 survey developed by The Affiliates, a temporary legal placement service, attorneys rated the value of legal secretaries working on a temporary basis. Half said "very valuable" and 39 percent said "somewhat valuable." Eighty-two percent of the law firms surveyed have temporary legal secretaries as a permanent part of their budgets.

Maureen Schell has been a legal secretary for fifteen years. She started by working as a secretary for Sears and was promoted to the legal department, where the lawyers specialized in labor and employment law. She found it very interesting. Her fifteen-year career took her to various departments, a very large international law firm, and now a medium firm in Los Angeles: Milbank, Tweed, Hadley & McCloy. She states that:

"When I went to a law firm, I was very surprised at the difference. There is a hierarchy in a law firm that was not found in the legal department. The first law firm I worked for was a very strict, traditional firm. I worked for two corporate attorneys. When I went to work for Milbank, I had to learn to do things differently. They have different policies here. They are not as strict as my other firm. I think it is because the attorneys are young and are bringing new ideas to the firm."

Maureen works for three attorneys in the real estate section of the firm. Two of her bosses are under the age of thirty-two and are computer literate. They produce their own correspondence and documents. Only the older attorneys dictate to their secretaries. She feels that it is because of her bosses' computer literacy that she is able to handle the work of three attorneys.

Maureen makes a very good salary. She has good benefits, including retirement. She receives a Christmas bonus plus an annual bonus based on the firm's profitability. She is evaluated once a year.

"I like my work. This is a good firm with good people. They have good management, and all the employees pull together as a team. My bosses trust me and have confidence in my abilities. I feel appreciated. The only thing I dislike about the job is that sometimes I have to work under pressure. I can handle pressure, but there are times when it becomes just too much when three attorneys need their work done immediately. Communication is the key to success in a busy law office."

The National Association of Legal Secretaries (NALS) offers two voluntary certifying exams for legal secretaries. The Accredited Legal Secretary (ALS) is an entry-level certification that requires a candidate to pass a one-day exam. The Professional Legal Secretary (PLS) is an advanced certification that requires a candidate to pass a two-day exam.

For more information about the legal secretarial profession, contact the National Association of Legal Secretaries (see Appendix B).

Receptionist

A receptionist is responsible for answering the telephone and greeting clients. This person is often a client's first contact with a law firm. The manner in which the client is greeted sets the stage for the attorney-client relationship. It is important that the client's first experience be a positive one.

A receptionist's duties vary according to the size and the structure of a firm. In a large firm, a receptionist may have no other duties than to answer the telephone. In a smaller firm, a receptionist may have additional duties, including the following:

◆ Greet clients
◆ Answer the telephone and take and deliver messages
◆ Receive, open, date, and sort mail and deliver it to a secretary
◆ Update and maintain a law library
◆ Collect, stamp, and post daily mail
◆ Perform errands as directed
◆ Open and close files
◆ Maintain attorney time records, a supply inventory, and a master schedule
◆ Order supplies and request service or repair when necessary
◆ Assist with office billings
◆ Perform clerical duties as directed
◆ Make photocopies as requested

The receptionist, being the first contact with a law firm, should be knowledgeable about such things as what seminars the firm is planning, how client disputes are solved, and who practices what kinds of law and for what clients. It is important for law firms to realize that 99 percent of their business starts with a telephone call to a receptionist.

As more telephone systems become automated, the need for a receptionist will decline. This position will be absorbed by technology. Although law firms will need a person to greet clients as they come into the office, an administrative assistant will soon fill this position.

Other Personnel

Other law office personnel are found in law offices according to size, specialty, and need. Large law firms need specialized personnel to handle specific areas. Small firms combine responsibilities and duties. The following sections describe the types of personnel who can be found in a law office setting.

Law Librarian A librarian manages the most valuable tool in a law office: information. Law librarians are also known as information resource managers or information systems directors. In addition to maintaining a library, they have a thorough knowledge of research manuals and legal databases. They also assist attorneys and legal assistants in their research projects. Some librarians have law degrees, but most have a masters degree in library science.

The role of a law librarian changed with the information explosion of the 1980s and 1990s. The trend in hiring law firm librarians has coincided with an increased use of **legal databases** and **nonlegal databases.** As information becomes more accessible, a manager is needed to handle it. Salaries for information systems directors have also increased.

Among the duties of a law librarian are ten tasks:

◆ Provide research services to attorneys and legal assistants. Most librarians are generalists and are familiar with most areas of law. However, librarians increasingly tend to specialize in a particular area of law.

◆ Acquire, retain, and preserve library materials. The American Library Association defines collection development as "the process of planning, building and maintaining a library's information resources in a cost-effective and user-relevant manner."

◆ Maintain a library. This includes filing supplements and pocket parts, shelving books, and organizing library materials (see Chapter 14).

◆ Develop and maintain a catalog and index of all library materials.

◆ Establish library policy. Establish loan policies and procedures and monitor a firm's library loan program.

◆ Manage and organize court form files and brief banks.

◆ Keep attorneys and legal assistants informed of library acquisitions and train a firm's employees on the use of a library.

◆ Manage the financial aspects of a library, such as accounts payable and budgets.

◆ Manage library staff such as assistant librarians.

◆ Plan for library growth.

Some librarians have additional duties outside a library, such as managing legal assistant or secretarial staff. Some librarians may also manage a firm's central filing area.

In small and medium firms, legal assistants and experienced legal secretaries act as librarians. Many legal assistants are finding the librarian profession an exciting and challenging adjunct to their paralegal education. Legal assistants are often excellent candidates for the position of librarian.

Legal database: An organized collection of statutes, case law, administrative rulings, and legal memorandums.

Nonlegal database: An organized collection of nonlegal information such as medical information, business statistics, and the like.

Calendar Clerk   A calendar clerk keeps track of all court hearings, depositions, and other important dates for a law firm. This clerk works closely with all staff and also keeps track of the statute of limitations on cases.

Proofreader   A proofreader reviews documents for typographical, grammatical, and syntactical errors. A proofreader also compares versions of contracts and highlights areas of change.

Legal Assistant Aid   An aid, clerk, or paralegal assistant helps a legal assistant with functions such as finding files and documents, photocopying, and performing general file maintenance. An aid may be an intern who is studying to be a legal assistant and works for a firm on a part-time basis. The type of experience gained in this position is very valuable for legal assistant students.

Information Systems Manager   An information systems manager is responsible for the computer system and technology of an office. Some large firms also employ a functional manager and technical specialists to meet their computer needs. A functional manager is in charge of a specific application area. Technical specialists are responsible for training and for the maintenance of various systems. Other terms for an information systems manager include database administrator, systems specialist, and information resource manager. Large firms employ information systems managers on a full-time basis. Other firms hire consultants for this function.

Legislative Analyst   A legislative analyst tracks legislation that affects clients. This person has access to legal databases that monitor all types of legislation: federal, state, and administrative hearings. This information helps attorneys keep abreast of the rapid changes in the law. In addition, an attorney may alert business clients of legislation that would affect their enterprise. Many legal assistants are finding a legislative analyst position a viable option for employment possibilities.

Investigator   An investigator examines cases and interviews witnesses. Many large firms and small boutiques that handle criminal matters employ their own investigator. Other firms use the services of outside investigator firms.

Messenger   A messenger, also called a courier or a runner, runs errands for a firm. Typical duties include delivering documents, filing documents with a court, and serving summonses. Most firms bill a client for the services of their messenger.

Service of process: The personal delivery of summonses, complaints, or other legal documents to a defendant or respondent.

Process Server   A process server is responsible for **service of process.** This person may work sporadic hours in order to "catch" an elusive defendant. Most firms bill a client for the services of a process server. A firm's investigator may also serve documents. Many firms contract with an outside firm for service of process.

Recruiter   A recruiter seeks out new attorneys and law clerks. Some very large firms employ full-time recruiters. Other firms use outside recruiter firms. Some firms give their administrator recruitment responsibilities.

Case Coordinator   A case coordinator has responsibility for the successful management of a case, usually a complex litigation case. This person will determine staffing needs; develop a strategy, timetables, and responsibilities; and supervise a project. A case coordinator will keep clients and attorneys apprised of progress. Legal assistants are often case coordinators.

Clerks   A clerk handles clerical or administrative assignments according to the needs of a supervisor. This person's responsibilities include numbering and indexing documents, creating file folders, and preparing bindings, trial exhibits, and trial notebooks. Clerks often work under the supervision of a legal assistant. A firm may bill a client for a clerk's time.

Accountant   Most large and many medium firms employ their own full-time accountant. Smaller firms use outside accountant services. The duties of a law firm accountant include handling accounts receivable, accounts payable, and collections; balancing a checkbook; and preparing financial statements.

Billing Clerk   A billing clerk assists an accountant or financial manager with a firm's billing. This person prepares the bills and monitors each client's ledger card or account summary. Large firms may employ many billing clerks. In smaller firms, an office manager or secretary performs this function.

File Clerk   A file clerk works in a firm's file room and is responsible for maintaining the firm's filing. This person opens and closes files and files documents. Large firms may employ many file clerks. In smaller firms, a secretary performs this function.

Photocopy Clerk   A photocopy clerk is responsible for photocopying a firm's documents. A full-time photocopy clerk is found only in large firms. In smaller firms, secretaries and legal assistants are responsible for their own photocopying needs.

Outsourcing

Outsourcing: A firm's use of outside services for support functions.

A firm's need for support staff is being replaced by **outsourcing,** which is the use of outside companies for support staff functions, such as copy center, facilities management, and mail room services. An outside service will install its own equipment and employees to manage, for example, a firm's photocopy and mail room centers. When a law firm has overflow work, an outside company uses its own off-site facilities to accommodate the overload. Outsourcing is spreading to other major areas of the firm, such as information management, records management, and even legal research and law libraries. The trend to outsource began with downsizing and cost-cutting policies. According to a recent survey, the respondents indicated that they received greater cost-efficiency with their outsourced functions. Larger firms report greater use of outsourcing services.

In addition to relying on outsourcing for support staff functions, law firms also utilize the services of a number of outside firms to meet other staffing needs.

Attorney Service   An attorney service picks up documents from a law firm and files them with a court for a monthly charge. This service also serves papers. In addition, some attorney services prepare subpoenas and notices. Most law firms use an attorney service instead of employing their own process servers.

Computerized Litigation Support Service   For firms with limited computer capabilities, a computerized litigation support service will organize and computerize documents in complex cases. Many of these services are owned and operated by experienced legal assistants. Small firms that do not have the resources to handle a complex litigation case find that they can accept such a case with the assistance of these services.

Paralegal Service   Firms use outside paralegal services for assistance with rush assignments or with overloads (see Exhibit 2.15). In addition, they use freelance legal

The Wave of the Future

PARALEGAL SERVICES

of NORTH CAROLINA,® INC. *is a firm of free-lance paralegals whose principals have over 50 years of combined experience in private law firms and with the judicial system. Being a nationwide public document search and retrieval company, we offer legal support to attorneys, corporations, financial institutions and document search and retrieval companies throughout North Carolina and across the United States.* PARALEGAL SERVICES *was founded upon confidentiality, accuracy and service. Our policy is to provide the best of those qualities to our clients.*

Over the years, PARALEGAL SERVICES *has earned and maintains a reputation for professionalism and excellence. That reputation has been built through a determined effort to provide our clients with the most prompt, accurate services available while maintaining a realistic fee schedule. We look forward to continuing this tradition through our service to you.*

ESTATE ADMINISTRATION

With more than 30 years of experience in probate settlement, our paralegals offer the complete marshalling of assets, preparation and filing of probate documents including but not limited to, the Federal and State death tax returns. Also on staff is a former Assistant Probate Clerk who is experienced in the private sector of estate administration as well. Our intent is to provide you with support in estate settlement and to be a liaison which will allow attorneys more time to practice law.

INCORPORATIONS

We offer complete incorporating services to the legal profession. Our firm can serve as your registered agent/office in North Carolina for a nominal fee. PARALEGAL SERVICES prepares all necessary documentation and confirms the date of filing by telephone. We take all necessary actions to expedite the filing which includes reserving your corporate name in advance to prevent having your filings rejected. We check desired names, confirm their availability, prepare the request and forward your name reservation certificate to you. PARALEGAL SERVICES acts as a "one stop shop" for these services nationwide.

DEPOSITION/TRIAL TRANSCRIPT SUMMARIES

Through our experienced staff, we provide summaries of those lengthy depositions and trial transcripts. All summarizations are prepared by professional paralegals who understand confidentiality as well as your needs for prompt service.

EXHIBIT 2.15 Brochure of a Freelance Paralegal Service

assistants to do deposition summaries and other paralegal duties on an ongoing basis. Attorneys also use specialized paralegal services, such as probate or bankruptcy, to expand their client base without expanding their facilities. Freelance paralegal services is a growing market for experienced legal assistants.

Employment Agency Most firms have an ongoing relationship with employment agencies for temporary staffing and employee recruitment. Temporary workers are paid by an employment agency instead of a law firm. In the past, employment agencies were called when an employee was sick or on vacation or for general backup work. With the trend to outsource clerical functions, temporary employees are working steady in law firms. Firms are utilizing temporary clerical workers, or temps, instead of employing their own clerical staff because doing so is more cost-effective.

Firms are also using the services of temporary employment agencies for attorneys (see nontraditional attorneys on page 50).

Using temporary services has several other advantages:

◆ Temps are available quickly.
◆ Temps provide additional help without adding employees.
◆ The services of temps can be billed to a client at a lower rate than that of an employed legal assistant.
◆ Temps are not entitled to firm benefits, and employee taxes are paid by an outside agency.

Using temporary services also has its disadvantages:

◆ Contracting with many different temps in the same capacity results in an incontinuity of work flow.
◆ Temps are likely to lack commitment to a firm's goals.
◆ A firm has little choice in selecting the temporary worker.
◆ Confidentiality or conflict-of-interest problems may arise.

Photocopy Service A photocopy service copies records in large photocopy projects. Often, a service accepts large photocopy projects from a firm. This service saves a firm money in purchasing additional photocopy equipment and hiring additional staff.

Bonding Company Bonding companies provide bonds for litigation cases, probate cases, notary needs, or other requirements. Most firms have an ongoing relationship with one or two bonding companies.

Records Search Company Record search companies search records in any secretary of state's office to give an attorney the information required. They also file documents and register companies in the various secretary of state offices. Some records search companies can search other records in the various states.

Expert witness: A person who testifies at trial on the basis of professional expertise.

Consultants Law firms utilize a myriad of consultants. Consultants assist law firms with management advice, intrafirm training, and **expert witness** testimony. The specialties of a law firm determine its need for specialized consultants. Consultants are also used to assist attorneys in evaluating cases. Donohue Rajkowski was the first law firm in the state of Minnesota to hire a full-time salaried consultant. The consultant works in the area of personal injury and health-related litigation and interprets medical information and claims.

Consultants may be employed by a firm or utilized by a firm on an "as-needed" basis. Most large and midsize firms use the services of some sort of consultant for marketing. Consultants are also used extensively as expert witnesses for trials.

The following is a sample list of consultants used by attorneys:

Accountants	Computer experts
Public relations experts	Environmental experts
Engineers	Actuaries
Financial planners	Legal search consultants
Nurses and doctors	Investment bankers
Accident reconstructionists	Scientists
Lobbyists	Psychologists
Metallurgical experts	Economists

Law firm employees and outside services function together like a team to give a client the best possible representation. An attorney cannot represent a client adequately without the expertise of the rest of the team. Most often, a client will see a receptionist, a secretary, and a legal assistant before seeing an attorney. A client's first impression of a firm starts with the support staff. The support staff is just as essential to good client relations as an attorney.

SUMMARY

In the 1940s and 1950s, legal personnel consisted of an attorney and a secretary. The advent of technology and the legal assistant and legal administrator roles changed the traditional law firm. As legal assistants and legal administrators gained prominence, they are now recognized as essential members of a legal team.

A law firm's need for staff varies according to its size and specialty. Certain types of legal personnel can be found in most law offices: attorneys, legal administrators or office managers, legal assistants, law clerks, secretaries, and receptionists. Other law office personnel are found in law offices according to size, specialty, and need. In addition to the services of their own personnel, law firms utilize the services of a number of outside firms and consultants.

CHAPTER ILLUSTRATION

When Black, White & Greene opened its doors, the secretary who worked for them in the office suite, Tricia Bunnell, went with them. She helped Robert Black, the managing partner, with management duties and soon found the workload to be too heavy. The firm hired a secretary to work for Dennis White. Audra Everett is an experienced secretary who worked for a very large firm in the area. She has extensive experience and a background in litigation and intellectual property, which is just what Dennis needed to help him with a large business litigation case he was working on. The case involved a business owned by the mayor of the city and received a lot of media coverage.

After the trial, Dennis received a very favorable outcome for his client. The firm received a lot of media attention that made the firm highly visible in the marketplace. Soon the telephone rang off the hook with new clients, and the three attorneys were having difficulty meeting the demand.

They contacted the local paralegal association and placed an ad for a legal assistant in the association's newsletter. Before long, they had many resumes from qualified legal assistants. They chose Milton Nollkamper, a paralegal with a bachelor's degree in business and an associate arts degree in paralegal studies from Saddleback College. Milton had litigation experience and also worked as a trademark and intellectual property paralegal for Nissan Motor Corporation. He was perfect for the job.

The firm's litigation practice continued to grow. Grant was able to save enough money to make a full financial contribution to the partnership and received the status of full partner. The firm wondered whether its existing staff could handle the workload. They decided to retain the services of a freelance paralegal service that specialized in litigation management and a contract attorney to assist in the litigation cases. The firm found it necessary to invest in new computer equipment and additional office space to accommodate the additional staff.

Soon the workload increased to the point that they needed an additional attorney. Patrizia Boen just graduated from law school after many years as a paralegal. She could step right into the litigation cases but needed support staff to help her. The firm could not justify hiring a secretary and a legal assistant, so it hired a legal assistant who also performed secretarial functions for Patrizia: Melvin Goldberg. He also worked for Grant. Tricia assisted Robert in his management duties and was promoted to office manager in addition to her secretarial duties. The firm now consisted of the following staff:

Robert Black,	managing partner
Dennis White,	senior partner
Grant Greene,	junior partner, now full partner
Patrizia Boen,	associate
Tricia Bunnell,	secretary/office manager
Audra Everett,	secretary
Milton Nollkamper,	legal assistant
Melvin Goldberg,	legal assistant/secretary

The firm outsourced the following services:

Litigation Services,	freelance paralegal service
George Templeton,	contract attorney

In addition, the firm used the services of Speedy Attorney Service and All in One Process Service. The firm also outsourced its large photocopy projects to Compex Corporation.

The partners are pleased with the growth of the firm and are working hard. Generally, their clients are satisfied with the firm's services.

CHAPTER REVIEW

1. What elements contributed to the use of the services of nonlawyer assistants?

2. What are the differences between an office manager and a legal administrator?

3. What is the difference between the responsibilities of an administrator in a large firm and those of an administrator in a small firm?

4. What two variables dictate the scope of an administrator's responsibilities?

5. What are a legal assistant manager's responsibilities?

6. In what type of legal office do most paralegals work?

7. What is a tiered paralegal program?

8. What are the differences between a law clerk and a legal assistant?

9. What is outsourcing?

10. What is a "nontraditional" attorney?

EXAMPLES FOR DISCUSSION

I Want Out

A New York attorney stated, "As I become more exposed to the adversarial system, the more I hate it. I work at a large, well-respected firm where no one engages in lowball [deceptive] tactics. Unfortunately, some opposing counsel do not operate as my firm does. I am beginning to reconsider whether I want to be a lawyer because of the unpleasant encounters with ruthless, dishonest, and manipulative attorneys who accuse me of 'bad faith' and 'delay tactics' when there is no foundation for such accusations. I am a relatively new attorney, and if this is what practicing law is all about, I want out. If it weren't for this unpleasant aspect of the profession, I would love being a lawyer."

1. Describe a scenario that might have caused these comments.
2. If you were the manager of this firm, how would you respond to this attorney's comments?
3. What advice would you give this attorney?
4. What are some possible solutions to this attorney's problem?

Definition

Four national organizations have defined a paralegal. The definitions are found on pages 58 and 59. Compare the definitions, note the similarities and differences, and answer the following questions:

1. What are the similarities?
2. What are the differences?

3. Are the differences significant? If so, how?
4. Do the differences affect the profession as a whole?

The New Legal Assistant

Brenda Starr, a legal secretary, had been employed by Ray Shuran, a sole practitioner, for many years. Starr was Shuran's right arm. She performed management duties, secretarial duties, and some paralegal duties. He was extremely busy, and she worked late and most weekends. Shuran was concerned that Starr had too much work to do, so he employed a part-time law clerk to do research. When the law clerk quit to pursue her own law practice, Shuran hired a legal assistant to do research and the paralegal work currently assumed by Starr.

When the new legal assistant came to work, Starr automatically resented his presence. She resented that the legal assistant was doing work that Starr used to do. She had a difficult time letting go of some of her responsibilities. When the legal assistant requested clerical services, Starr would reluctantly provide them only if Shuran's work was completed.

1. What is the reason for this conflict?
2. What could Shuran do to remedy the situation?
3. If you were the new legal assistant, how would you handle the problem?
4. If you were Callahan, how would you handle the problem?

ASSIGNMENTS

1. Most legal assistants have chosen paralegalism as their second career, and have had experience in another area of business or industry. Some legal assistants have experience as legal secretaries and others have no legal experience. Many legal assistants have been able to apply their past experience to their present position as a legal assistant. You have unique qualities to bring to the paralegal profession. You have skills and talents you have learned in your past experience, even if you have not had experience in the business or legal world. It is time for you to access your talents and abilities and apply them to your future goals. On a sheet of paper, write down talents, abilities and skills you have gained in the past. If you have no business experience, list the abilities and skills you have learned at home, church or community organization. You will need them to answer the next question.

2. Chapter 2 contains a description of the duties of the various types of legal personnel. It also contains options for your paralegal education. How many of your talents and abilities could apply to members of the legal team other than a legal assistant? Consider outside services and consultants. What other options are open for you?

3. List all members of the legal team of Black, White and Greene that is described in the Chapter Illustration section of Chapter 2. After you name each member, insert a description of their duties in the law firm.

4. Interview any one of the following persons. Ask the interviewee to describe his job and actual job duties. Report your findings to your class and compare them with those reported by other students. Do the functions and duties of the positions reported differ?
   a. Attorney
   b. Legal administrator
   c. Legal assistant
   d. Legal secretary
   e. Word processor
   f. Law clerk
   g. Receptionist
   h. File clerk
   i. Messenger
   j. Calendar clerk

5. Contact two or three offices in your area that have a tiered paralegal program and answer the following questions about each:
   a. How many steps does the program have?
   b. What is the title of each step?
   c. What are the qualifications for each step?
   d. How does one advance?
   e. What is the compensation for each step?

   Compare the programs. Which one do you think is the best? Why?

6. Look in the telephone book and list all the types of businesses under "Attorney Services." What different services are offered attorneys?

7. List all the job opportunities a legal assistant education offers. Consider outside attorney service companies, consultants, and law office personnel other than legal assistants. What areas interest you? What additional training or education would you need to pursue a career in these areas?

8. The law firm of Smith, Jones & Brown has three partners, six associates, and six legal assistants. Calculate the leverage ratio as illustrated on page 49.

9. Access the Internet sites found on page 65. Prepare a report about what each Internet site offers the paralegal student.

10. Access the Internet sites found on page 65. Find the area that discusses paralegal salaries and benefits. Compare your findings with the paralegal salaries and benefits discussed in this chapter. Have they increased? Decreased?

SELF-TEST

How well did you grasp the material in the chapter? Test yourself by answering the following questions and check your answers against the answers in Appendix A.

1. The advent of what two professions changed the traditional law firm?
2. For what reasons were the legal assistant and legal administrator professions developed?
3. How have legal assistants and legal administrators increased a lawyer's efficiency?
4. What factors have contributed to the growth of the legal assistant profession?
5. What determines a firm's need for personnel?
6. What are the five categories of attorneys?
7. What do "rainmakers" do?

8. What do associates do?
9. What is leveraging?
10. What is a leverage ratio?
11. What is a permanent associate?
12. What is a staff attorney?
13. What does the term "of-counsel" mean?
14. What do legal administrators do?
15. What is the significant difference between an office manager and an administrator?
16. What are the three major differences between an administrator and an office manager?
17. What is the status of a legal administrator in a large firm?
18. What are some other terms used for a legal administrator?
19. What is the difference between the responsibilities of an administrator in a large firm and an administrator in a small firm?
20. What are the seven main areas of an administrator's responsibilities?
21. What two factors dictate an administrator's responsibilities?
22. What other types of office managers are there?
23. What is a legal assistant manager's responsibilities?
24. What is a "tiered" paralegal program?
25. How does a legal assistant advance in a tiered paralegal program?
26. In what area do the majority of legal assistants specialize?
27. What did members of the Legal Assistant Management Association say should be the minimum educational requirement for legal assistants?
28. What is a law clerk?
29. Why do some firms have elaborate programs for their law clerks?
30. What do law clerks do?
31. What are the differences between a law clerk and legal assistant?
32. What do legal secretaries do?
33. What do receptionists do?
34. What do law librarians do?
35. What do investigators do?
36. What do messengers do?
37. What do recruiters do?
38. What do process servers do?
39. What do case coordinators do?
40. What is outsourcing?
41. What does an attorney service do?
42. What do paralegal services do?
43. What are the advantages of using a temporary employee?
44. What are the disadvantages of using a temporary employee?

KEY WORDS

CPA
E-mail
Equity
Equity partner
Expert witness
Legal database
Leverage

Leverage ratio
Liaison
MBA
Nonequity partner
Nonlegal database
Of-counsel

Outsourcing
Permanent associates
Rainmaker
Service of process
Staff attorney
Voice mail

Personnel Relations

OBJECTIVES

After completion of this chapter, a student should be able to do the following:

- ◆ Explain the objectives of law office management.
- ◆ Discuss employee motivation.
- ◆ Describe the management role.
- ◆ Identify the necessary skills and functions for effective management.
- ◆ List the various considerations in hiring the right employee.
- ◆ Identify appropriate interview questions.
- ◆ List the necessary ingredients of job satisfaction.
- ◆ Outline the evaluation process.
- ◆ Discuss legal assistant compensation and the laws affecting compensation.
- ◆ Explain the difference between an exempt employee and a nonexempt employee and how a legal assistant qualifies for exempt status.
- ◆ Discuss the elements of the team approach and working as a team to benefit a client.

INTRODUCTION

For a legal team to function at its peak, it must be managed effectively so that each team member contributes his maximum potential. Many elements contribute to effective personnel management.

A law firm's personnel are its most important resource—and the most expensive. Most people find either great satisfaction or dissatisfaction in their work. Finding the right place to work is essential to personal character building, self-esteem, and overall happiness in life. People spend one-third of their life at work, so it is important that they choose a positive working environment.

Whether an office is a pleasant or unpleasant place to work is the responsibility of both the employees and management. Management is responsible for developing an environment where employees can grow personally and professionally. Employees are responsible for contributing their skills and talents to the organization. Everyone involved with the firm, including clients, benefits when employees are happy with their work.

Management's personnel policies greatly affect a firm's environment. Employees' relationships to management also affect a firm's environment. How management and employees interact with each other influences a firm's environment. This chapter is devoted to describing the perspectives of both management and employees.

First, this chapter will look at employee relations from management's perspective. It will discuss the many duties and responsibilities a manager has in relation to personnel and various methods of ensuring positive personnel relations. Second, the chapter will look at employee relations from an employee's perspective. It will discuss what employees can expect from management and their responsibilities to an employer. Third, the chapter will combine both perspectives and discuss how management and employees work together as a team for the benefit of a firm, employees, and clients.

MANAGEMENT OBJECTIVES AND EMPLOYEE RELATIONS

Management is defined by Peter Drucker, a prominent management consultant, as "the method of using available resources to achieve desired goals" (*The Practice of Management,* published by Harper and Morners, 1954). Just as a conductor directs members of an orchestra to produce beautiful music, a manager directs employees to work in harmony together to achieve a firm's goals. If one member of an orchestra is playing an instrument incorrectly or is missing, the desired outcome is affected. In the same way, if one member of a legal team does not contribute to a firm, services to a client are affected.

Managers work with and through other people to achieve a firm's goals. A manager cannot perform all aspects of a business, just as an orchestra leader cannot play all the instruments in an orchestra. According to Drucker, a manager's performance can be measured by two characteristics: efficiency and effectiveness. *Efficiency* is doing things right, and *effectiveness* is doing the right thing. The most important characteristic is effectiveness, which includes choosing appropriate objectives and methods to reach those objectives. For a positive employment environment to exist, a manager must be effective. Good personnel relations are a test of effective management.

Each employee must have a clear understanding of his position on a legal team and of how his position relates to achieving the goals of a firm. Before this understanding can be attained, employees must clearly comprehend a firm's objectives.

Objectives are the purpose of a firm—the reasons for its existence. The goals and objectives of a firm are the reasons for management decisions and policies. Effective management guarantees success in achieving a firm's goals. Ineffective management guarantees failure in achieving a firm's goals.

Although law firms differ in structure and management style, most have basically the same three main objectives:

◆ Provide quality legal services to the client
◆ Provide growth and profit for the firm
◆ Provide growth and satisfaction for the employees

A government agency may have different objectives. Although some government agencies are required to produce enough income to make themselves profitable for the government, others operate within a budget set by the government as a service to the people. An example of a government agency's objectives is as follows:

◆ Provide quality legal services to the government or people
◆ Operate within the budget set by the government
◆ Provide growth and satisfaction for the employees

Since a corporate legal department has one client—the corporation—its goal is to keep legal expenses low and within a budget. An example of a corporate legal department's objectives is as follows:

◆ Provide quality legal services to the corporation.
◆ Keep outside legal costs low, and operate within the budget set by the corporation.
◆ Provide growth and satisfaction for the employees.

Growth and satisfaction for employees is an objective of each type of legal office. Since people are the most important resource of a firm, each person's productivity must be maximized. The methods used to maximize employee productivity have been set forth in management theories. Managers are responsible for implementing those theories. They are also responsible for carrying out five managerial functions.

The Manager's Role in Personnel Relations

A manager is responsible for all aspects of personnel relations. In large firms, a manager in charge of personnel may report to an administrator. In smaller firms, an administrator or manager is directly responsible for personnel relations. In firms with no administrator or manager, a managing attorney is responsible for personnel.

A manager's role is influenced by external and internal conditions. External conditions consist of economic conditions, government regulations, and laws. Internal conditions include the nature and structure of a firm, nature of the work, and nature of the employees.

External Conditions   Changes in our economy directly affect the personnel policies of any organization. The decisions to hire additional staff, lay off staff, or grant a bonus or raise are influenced by the economy. In addition, many government regulations and laws influence personnel relations. More laws are being passed each day in this area, and court decisions also establish laws with which employers must abide. A manager must be knowledgeable of all laws and keep abreast of court decisions relating to personnel issues. Since laws relating to personnel relations are changing each day, a manager and a firm must be flexible to change personnel policy if the law should mandate it.

Internal Conditions   Internal conditions include the nature of a firm, nature of the work, and nature of the firm's employees. Several elements make up the nature of a firm, such as objectives, strategies, structure, and size. A small boutique firm will have different personnel needs than a large megafirm. The specialty of a firm, or the nature of the work, influences management's staffing requirements. The nature of the employees includes whether employees work independently or in groups.

Functions of a Personnel Manager

A personnel manager, or a law office manager responsible for personnel relations, has five functions: planning, controlling, organizing, leading, and staffing.

Planning   Human resource planning covers all areas of the human resource field. Before managers can control, organize, lead, or staff, they must make plans that define the purpose and direction of a firm. This process is called **forecasting** and includes strategic planning and long-range planning for a firm. Forecasting involves anticipating a firm's future need for personnel and making plans accordingly.

Human resource planning is divided into four areas:

◆ Establishing human resource objectives
◆ Assessing current human resource conditions
◆ Designing and evaluating human resource activities
◆ Monitoring and evaluating the results of activities

Another aspect of planning is conducting a **human resource audit.** An audit assesses the strengths and weaknesses of current employees and helps a manager develop training plans.

Planning also includes deciding what needs to be done, when it needs to be done, how it needs to be done, and who will do it. Managers integrate human resources into

Forecasting: Planning for the future by anticipating future events.

Human resource audit: A determination of the strengths and weaknesses of current employees.

a firm's plans by developing a human resource plan that supports the firm's goals and objectives.

The goal of human resource planning is to develop personnel policies and programs that will achieve a firm's objectives. The ultimate objective of a human resource plan is to maximize a firm's effectiveness by maximizing employee effectiveness and productivity.

Controlling   Controlling is the process of ensuring that actions conform to plans. Since implementing plans requires action, controlling actions is the next managerial function. Controlling cannot take place unless a plan exists, and a plan has little chance of success unless activities are controlled and efforts are made to monitor its progress.

Control has three main elements:

◆ Establishing standards of performance.

◆ Measuring current performance and comparing it against established standards.

◆ Taking action to correct performance that does not meet established standards.

Controlling includes evaluating activities. For activities to be evaluated, standards must be set. If standards are set too high for employees to meet, employee frustration develops; if they are set too low, employees will not be challenged in their work. Standards must be realistic, attainable, and challenging.

Adherence to a budget is a common method of measurement. If a plan is proceeding within budgeted amounts, it is considered a good plan. If not, some changes need to be made to the plan or the budget. Other methods of measurement include employee evaluations and questionnaires.

The action taken to correct performance that does not meet established standards might include offering training programs for existing employees, firing an employee, or restructuring a work group.

Win-lose management:
A form of personnel control in which the policies of management are directed totally to profits and disregard employee needs.

When making personnel policies to control employees, managers must consider the needs of the employees. When management makes policies that disregard the personal needs of employees, it is **win-lose management.** Win-lose management has eight consequences:

◆ The atmosphere in an office becomes competitive and hostile.

◆ Time and energy are diverted from the main issues.

◆ Creativity, sensitivity, and empathy are eliminated from an office environment.

◆ Authority conflicts become more frequent and bitter.

◆ Important organizational decisions are increasingly made by an isolated, elitist group.

◆ New ideas are discouraged.

◆ Deadlocks are created, and decisions are delayed.

◆ Nonaggressive people are discouraged from participation.

Organizing   The organizing function requires a manager to coordinate the resources of a firm to maximize productivity and effectiveness. The more integrated the work of a law firm, the more effective the firm will be in delivering legal services to a client. The more organized the work, the more productive the firm. The more productive the firm, the more profitable the firm.

Different firms have different organizing objectives. For example, a large firm may be organized into several departments, with various subgroups working within each department, whereas a small firm may have only one or two specialties that require organization on a smaller scale. One firm may have one legal assistant for every four attorneys, whereas another firm may have one legal assistant for each attorney. Management's responsibility is to organize a firm in a manner that will be effective for the firm and will allow the firm to accomplish its goals.

INTERPERSONAL	INFORMATIONAL	DECISIONAL
Figurehead	Monitor	Entrepreneur
Leader	Disseminator	Conflict resolver
Liaison	Spokesperson	Negotiator
Motivator	Investigator	Resource allocator

EXHIBIT 3.1   Leadership Roles

Leading   A firm must have strong leadership if it is to maximize productivity and effectiveness. Employees look to firm management for direction.

Leading involves working directly with people. It includes determining what is to be accomplished and how to accomplish it. This requires a manager to assume three roles—interpersonal, informational, and decisional—as shown in Exhibit 3.1.

The title of manager does not give a person the essential skills to manage people. Results of an employee relations test indicated that many managers are not doing what many experts feel should be done to ensure good employee-employer relations:

◆ Almost 50 percent of the managers who took the test did not understand that people repeat behavior that is rewarded.

◆ Almost 70 percent did not believe that finding a mutually satisfactory solution to a problem is a way to handle a grievance.

◆ Almost 50 percent did not understand that improving quality will reduce operating costs.

Ideal managers recognize two things about their job. First, they realize that a business is not a democracy. Management is not elected by popular vote; it is placed in power by an arbitrary decision of a small group of people who are in positions of power. The people who appoint managers expect them to act like managers. Certain decisions are made by managers alone; managers cannot delegate those decisions, and they cannot abdicate their position of responsibility.

Second, ideal managers know that people need to grow, need to contribute, and need to assume power up to their level of ability. Effective managers have responsibility for decisions, but they pass on decisions that can be handled by capable people under them. They set high standards and command excellent and consistent performance. They also recognize their subordinates' right to question and share in decision making about things that affect them. They know they can get superior results from a person as long as that person has some say in how, where, and when an effort is applied.

Leadership includes the ability to motivate employees to reach their maximum potential. A law office that motivates employees gives employees an opportunity for growth by assigning tasks with adequate responsibility and direction.

Employees' contributions must be acknowledged to encourage them in their work. Kenneth H. Blanchard, in his book *One Minute Manager,* mentions the importance of praising employees for a job well done. A good manager takes advantage of every opportunity to acknowledge employees for doing a good job, meeting a deadline, or showing enthusiasm for a project.

Staffing   Staffing includes such duties as recruitment, screening, interviewing, testing, hiring, firing, job analysis, job description, and personnel record keeping. Successful staffing ensures that the right people are hired for the right jobs.

Staffing is the most important function of a manager. It is important for the success of the firm to employ the right employees. Employees impress clients; a client who is not satisfied with an employee can be dissatisfied with the entire firm. Good client relations require the involvement of all staff members. An employee with a poor attitude or other personal problems can negatively affect a firm's environment and damage the firm.

OF INTEREST . . .

Leadership Checklist

___ Am I sincerely interested in people? How do I show it?

___ Am I a good listener?

___ Do I look for opportunities to sincerely compliment others?

___ Is my speech free of sarcasm or prejudice?

___ Do I seek the opinions of others?

___ Do I enjoy giving credit to others?

___ Am I earnestly enthusiastic in my speech?

___ Am I trustworthy and confident?

___ Do I interrupt others when they are talking?

___ Do I tend to argue?

___ Do I give unsolicited advice?

___ Do I criticize others openly?

___ Do I attempt to look good by making others look bad?

___ Am I too positive?

___ Do I tend to exaggerate?

___ Does my voice sound threatening?

___ Do I attempt to impress others by using large and unusual words?

___ Do I use the pronoun "I" too much?

___ Do my stories tend to reflect too much credit on me?

___ Do I tend to brag about my achievements?

___ Do I enjoy proving others wrong?

Hiring employees is expensive. In addition, a firm with a high turnover rate is not operating at 100 percent efficiency. Studies have shown that an attorney with a new legal assistant is 20 percent less efficient. It takes at least three months for a new employee to be productive. During that training period, other employees are filling in or important tasks are not getting done. An example of the average cost of hiring a new legal assistant is shown in Exhibit 3.2.

FUNCTION	COST
Recruitment and interview—manager's time, 10 hours	$ 700
Follow-up interviews—attorney's time, 2 hours	$ 800
First-day initial orientation—manager's time, 4 hours	$ 280
First-day orientation—attorney's time, 2 hours	$ 800
Ineffective time—new legal assistant's time, the equivalent of two weeks' salary	$ 3,200
Reduction in efficiency—attorney's time, 2 weeks at 20% reduction	$ 6,400
Training—senior paralegal's time, 3 days	$ 1,680
Payroll taxes and benefits during ineffective time, 30%	$ 4,158
Total	**$18,018**

Manager's time calculated at $70 per hour.

Attorney's time calculated at $400 per hour.

Senior legal assistant's time calculated at $70 per hour.

New legal assistant's time calculated at $40 per hour.

EXHIBIT 3.2 Typical Cost of Hiring a New Legal Assistant—Per Employee

The Hiring Process

The hiring process consists of four steps: planning, recruitment, selection, and training.

Planning The first step in planning a position is to determine whether the position should be filled at all. At this time, the external and internal conditions of a firm are examined. If the economic environment is not stable, the position may be able to be restructured or eliminated. If it is a necessary position, management must decide whether to hire a new person or to promote from within the firm.

Promoting from within a firm offers many advantages, including the following:

◆ The selection cost of hiring a new employee is eliminated.
◆ The loss in productivity is reduced because the employee already knows the structure and procedures of the firm.
◆ Promotions encourage employee loyalty.
◆ A promoted employee receives recognition, which increases employee morale.

Promoting within a firm also has disadvantages. Among the most common is the difficulty of making a transition from one position to another. A legal secretary who is promoted to legal assistant after completing a paralegal education is often still viewed as a secretary by other employees. A legal assistant who is promoted to manager is often still viewed as a legal assistant and has difficulty assuming a position of authority.

If no viable candidates are available from within a firm, candidates are recruited from outside the firm. Before a manager is ready to recruit candidates, the position must be carefully detailed in a position description that includes a hiring specification of the ideal candidate. The **position description** contains the title, duties, and responsibilities for that position; an example is shown in Exhibit 3.3. The **hiring specifications** identify the education, experience, skills, and capabilities required.

Before a position description can be prepared, a law office manager must have a clear understanding of the position and the necessary qualifications of the prospective employee. The manager must know all aspects of the position, including the temperament and expectations of the supervising attorney. An exit interview with the outgoing employee is helpful to gain a clear understanding of a position. An interview with the supervising attorney is also important to understand the attorney's expectations.

Several questions need to be answered before a position description can be prepared:

◆ To what area of the law or specific tasks will this employee be assigned?
◆ Will this employee have contact with clients? If so, what are desirable qualities for positive client contact?
◆ What specific training should the employee possess?
◆ What specific experience should the employee possess?
◆ If a former employee is being replaced, what strengths and weaknesses of the former employee contributed to a marginal, adequate, or superior job performance?
◆ What necessary skills are required?
◆ What special requirements are required by the attorney for whom the employee will work?
◆ What are the minimum and maximum salaries paid for this position?
◆ What is the minimum educational requirement?

When preparing a position description, a manager must give careful thought to establishing requirements for the position. Requirements must be reasonable and must relate to the position. If a candidate is required to have seven years' computer experience, the manager must be able to show why three years' experience is not enough.

Position description: A document that describes the duties and responsibilities of a position.

Hiring specifications: The requirements for a position.

Law Offices of Black, White & Greene

Position Description
Litigation Legal Assistant

Department: Litigation   Supervising Attorney: Dennis White
Hours: 8:30 to 5:00   Level: Grade P-2—$24,000–$30,000 a year
Overtime Required: Some   Nonexempt position

Brief Position Summary: Assistant to litigation attorney specializing in business litigation. Heavy trial and discovery work.

Major Duties: Draft and answer discovery documents, including interrogatories, and produce documents. Prepare client for deposition, assist attorney in depositions, and summarize depositions. Perform legal research and prepare memorandums of law. Draft motions and other litigation documents. Prepare trial materials and trial notebooks. Organize documents and file. Document deadline control.

Recurring Duties: Interview witnesses and conduct investigations.

People Contact: Heavy—clients, opposing counsel, witnesses.

Work Group: Dennis White, Esq.; Grant Greene, Esq.; Audra Everett, secretary; Melvin Goldberg, secretary; and Milton Nollkamper, paralegal.

Skills: Good writing and communication skills. Good organization skills. Computer skills on IBM-compatible computers with knowledge of WordPerfect, WestLaw, timekeeping software, and database management.

Education: Bachelors degree and paralegal certificate. Bachelor's degree may be substituted for substantial experience.

Experience: Minimum of three years' recent litigation experience. At least one year's experience in complex litigation.

Other Requirements: Ability to speak Spanish a plus. Some clients and witnesses are Spanish-speaking people. Since Jennifer Jones is very precise, the ideal candidate must pay attention to details.

_____   _____

Tricia Bunnell, Manager   Approved: Robert Black, Esq.

EXHIBIT 3.3   Position Description

TECH TIPS
Human Relations Software

The following is a sample of human relations software:

People Manager—Contains employment information about each employee, such as marital status, dependents, citizenship verification, compliance with the Equal Employment Opportunity Commission, emergency contact, hire date, job history, pay rate, and supervisor. Also performs attendance tracing and review schedule.

HR Task Counselor—Tracks employee records, including training schedule, benefit administration, performance reviews, performance notices, and policy manual.

People Trak LT Applicant Tracking—Monitors applicant information to match positions and candidates. Matches skills and titles, salary requirements, drug testing, and information on Equal Employment Opportunity.

Software mentioned in this sidebar is for informational purposes only and is not for the purpose of endorsing products.

LAW	PROHIBITS	COVERS
Title VII of Civil Rights Act	Discrimination based on race, color, religion, sex, or national origin	Employers with fifteen or more employees, governments, unions, employment agencies
Equal Pay Act	Sex differences in pay for equal work	Private employers
Executive Orders 11246 and 11375	Discrimination based on race, color, religion, sex, or national origin (affirmative action)	Federal contractors and subcontractors
Age Discrimination in Employment Act	Age discrimination against those between the ages of forty and seventy	Employers with twenty or more employees, unions, employment agencies, training programs
Rehabilitation Act	Discrimination based on physical or mental handicap (affirmative action required)	Federal contractors, federal government
Veterans Readjustment Act	Discrimination against disabled veterans (affirmative action required)	Federal contractors, federal government
Civil Rights Act	Discrimination on the basis of sex, race, or religion. Discourages quotas and prohibits courts from requiring promotion of unqualified people	
Family Leave Act	Employees entitled a leave of twelve weeks per year for, (a) birth of a child, (b) adoption or foster care of a child, (c) care of seriously ill child or spouse, (d) illness	Employers of fifty or more employees
Americans with Disabilities Act	Discrimination based on physical disabilities	Private and government employers
Immigration Reform and Control Act of 1986 (IRCA)	Discrimination in hiring or termination on the basis of national origin or citizenship status; requires employers to verify eligibility of employees	
Employee Polygraph Protection Act of 1988	Requiring applicants or employees to submit to lie detector tests, except under limited circumstances	
Worker Adjustment and Retraining Notification Act (WARN)	Employers must provide sixty days notice and disclosure of plant closings or mass layoffs	Employers of 150 or more
Bankruptcy Code	Discrimination against an employee because she/he filed bankruptcy	

EXHIBIT 3.4 Federal Employment Laws

Recruitment   Many avenues of recruitment are open: employment agencies, newspaper advertising, legal assistant associations, and word of mouth. Whatever the route chosen, the recruitment process must meet employment guidelines set by federal and state governments.

The federal government has established staffing guidelines in various legislative acts, including the Fair Labor Standards Act of 1938, the National Labor Standards Act, and seven other acts that are discussed in Exhibit 3.4 (see also Appendix C).

In addition, individual states have their own employment and compensation laws. Unlike traditional conflict-of-laws problems in which federal laws supersede state laws, in matters concerning employment, the prevailing law is the law that sets the highest standard. Although a manager manger will probably not know all state and federal employment laws in detail, she must be familiar with employment guidelines imposed by those laws.

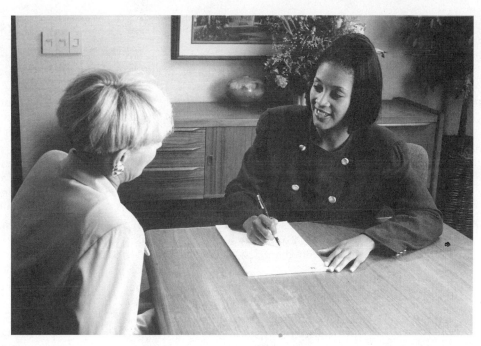

EXHIBIT 3.5   Law Firm Manager and Legal Assistant in an Employment Interview

A firm's employment application must comply with federal and state guidelines. Questions on the application that pertain to an applicant's age, sex, race, height, or weight violate federal regulations. Necessary information, such as date of birth, can be obtained after an applicant is formally hired.

Selection   A manager needs to understand that an applicant is probably nervous during an interview (see Exhibit 3.5). At the beginning of an interview, a manager should make every effort to calm an applicant. Casual conversation is one method to give an applicant an opportunity to relax.

The next step is for a manager to describe the position in detail. A profile of the supervising attorney and of those in the work group is also helpful. An applicant should also be informed of the requirements of the position.

The last part of an interview is for a manager to find out as much as possible about a job candidate. This involves asking questions.

The most important area in which to guard against federal law violations is interviewing. *To be sure not to discriminate in terms of race, color, religion, sex, or national origin, an interviewer must carefully structure interview questions to comply with the law.* This process can be difficult. To comply with federal guidelines, follow the recommendations given in Exhibit 3.6.

If all the dos and don'ts in Exhibit 3.6 seem rather complicated, a manager can apply the **ouch formula** to interview questions. *Ouch* is an acronym for proper interview questions. Questions must be objective, uniform and consistent and must have job relatedness.

An objective question solicits information that is verifiable or measurable. Examples of objective questions are the following:

◆ Do you have paralegal training?
◆ What is your educational background?
◆ Who was your previous employer?
◆ Who was your supervisor at your previous employer?
◆ Do you have experience in bankruptcy?

ETHICS ALERT

Ouch formula: An acronym for proper interview questions.

CATEGORY	IT IS LAWFUL TO:	IT IS UNLAWFUL TO:
Sex	restrict employment to one sex if it can be proven that the position requires an employee of a certain sex.	ask an applicant's sex. Physical labor does not justify excluding women.
Race or color	ask about distinguishing physical characteristics, such as scars.	ask an applicant's race, or skin, eye, or hair color, or ask height or weight questions if they are not relevant to the job.
Address	ask an applicant's address and how long the applicant has lived at current and previous addresses.	ask about foreign addresses that would indicate national origin; ask for the name or relationship of a person with whom an applicant resides; ask whether an applicant owns or rents a home.
Birthplace	request that an applicant produce a birth certificate or other proof of U.S. citizenship after employment.	ask for an applicant's birthplace or the birthplace of an applicant's spouse, parents, or other relatives; ask any questions that indicate religion or customs.
Military record	ask about education and experience in the service as they relate to the job.	ask type of discharge.
Photograph	ask for a photograph after hiring for identification purposes.	request a photograph before hiring, either on the application or after the interview. If desired, request that an applicant submit one at her option.
Citizenship	ask whether an applicant is a U.S. citizen and, if the applicant is hired, request that she or he submit proof.	ask in what country an applicant maintains citizenship; ask whether an applicant's parents or spouse is a U.S. citizen.
Ancestry or national origin	ask what language an applicant reads, speaks, or writes fluently.	ask questions pertaining to an applicant's lineage, ancestry, birthplace, or native language; ask about an applicant's parents' or spouse's national origin.
Car	ask whether an applicant would have any transportation problems if hired.	ask whether an applicant owns a car, unless the applicant must have a car to do the job.

EXHIBIT 3.6   The Dos and Don'ts of Interviewing

All questions must be uniform in application. In other words, they must apply to female as well as male applicants. They must apply to older as well as younger applicants and to minority as well as nonminority applicants. The questions must be asked of all applicants, regardless of sex, age, or background.

Questions must be consistent among applicants. If a manager asks one applicant one set of questions and another applicant another set of questions, the manager is not being consistent. Although each question does not have to be verbatim every time it is asked, its purpose for gaining information must be the same for all applicants.

Questions must be related to the position. If an employee does not need a car for the position—as one might if the position were messenger—all questions regarding vehicle ownership would be inappropriate. If a legal assistant will have secretarial assistance, some questions regarding secretarial skills may be inappropriate.

During the interview, a manager should look for certain characteristics. Although exceptions exist, a manager can spot "danger signals" that alert him or her to potential problems with an applicant. Asking an **open question** that requires a narrative answer is a good method to obtain information. A manager can learn a lot about an applicant by listening carefully. Some danger signs to look for are the following:

Open question: A question that requires a narrative answer and cannot be answered yes or no.

◆ *Job Hopping.* If an applicant's previous working experiences have been short, the applicant may be a job hopper. A manager can expect that the applicant will do the same with this position and not remain employed for more than a year.

CATEGORY	IT IS LAWFUL TO:	IT IS UNLAWFUL TO:
Education	ask about an applicant's academic or professional education; ask what school an applicant attended.	ask about a school's national, racial, or religious affiliation; ask how an applicant acquired a foreign language.
Experience	ask about an applicant's work experience and which countries the applicant has visited.	
Conviction and court records	ask about convictions that relate to an applicant's fitness to *perform* a particular job.	ask about arrests; ask about convictions that are not related to a job function and responsibilities.
Relatives	ask for the names of an applicant's relatives already employed by the firm; ask for the names and addresses of a minor's parents or guardian.	ask for the names or addresses of an adult applicant's relatives.
Emergency	ask for the names of *persons* to notify in case of an emergency.	ask for the names of *relatives* to notify in case of an emergency.
Organizations	ask about an applicant's membership in an organization if the organization's name or character does not reveal the applicant's race, religion, color, or ancestry.	ask an applicant to list all the organizations and lodges to which she or he belongs.
Credit rating		ask any questions about an applicant's credit rating, charge accounts, or other related information.
References	ask who referred an applicant to the firm; ask for the names of people willing to give professional or character references.	require an applicant to submit a religious reference.
Union	state the firm's philosophy on unionization.	ask questions about an applicant's feelings toward unions; ask about prior union activity or membership.
Miscellaneous	notify an applicant that any misstatement or omission of facts may be cause for dismissal.	

EXHIBIT 3.6 *Continued*

Having many employers in relatively short period of time may indicate that an applicant is dissatisfied easily.

◆ *Long Commute.* An applicant's address on an application form will indicate the applicant's area of residence. If it is far from the office, the applicant will spend a lot of time commuting. Although some people do not mind a long commute, others grow tired of it, especially in populated areas with congested traffic, and employees tend to seek employment closer to home after a while.

◆ *Poor Health.* Although a manager may not ask applicants whether they are healthy, a sharp eye can see whether an applicant is having health problems. It is important to hire a healthy person. Frequent absences due to health problems can be disruptive to a firm. In addition, employee absence is expensive for a law firm. A firm of 25 employees loses an average of $15,075 a year from absences and a firm with 105 employees loses over $60,000 per year due to absences.

◆ *Improper Termination Notice to Previous Employer.* If an applicant did not give proper notice to a former employer, this may be an indication that the applicant left abruptly, leaving the employer in a difficult position. The applicant might do the same in new employment. If an applicant is still employed, a desire to give proper notice is a good sign that the applicant accepts responsibility.

◆ *Questionable Reasons for Leaving Previous Employment.* Why did an applicant leave previous employment? If an applicant says she left because she was not

---

OF INTEREST . . .

The Most Commonly Asked Interview Questions

Why should we hire you rather than someone else?

Can you work under deadlines and pressure?

What kind of salary are you worth?

How long would it take you to make a contribution to our firm?

How long would you stay with our firm?

Why do you want to work for us?

Tell us about yourself.

What do you think of your last boss?

How would you describe your own personality?

What is your outstanding strength?

What is your greatest weakness?

Do you consider yourself dependable? Why?

What are your long- and short-term goals?

What is your opinion of the company for which you last worked?

Can you manage people?

What interests you the least about the available position?

What interests you the most about the available position?

Why did you leave your last job?

What did you like least about your last job?

What salary range are you looking for?

What are your three biggest accomplishments?

What would you do if. . . ?

In what type of position are you most interested?

What jobs have you had, how were they obtained, and why did you leave?

What do you know about our firm?

---

given responsibility and challenging work, this answer indicates that the applicant is a self-starter who desires to increase skills. A danger signal is if an applicant had personality conflicts with previous co-workers. This information alerts a manager that the applicant may have problems working with others. However, other problems, such as sexual harassment, may have caused the applicant to leave previous employment. Flexibility in judgment is required in this area.

◆ *Negative Relationship with Previous Employer.* Watch for indications of a negative relationship with a previous employer. If an applicant had a poor relationship with a previous employer, it could be an indication that the applicant resists direction or is upset easily.

After an interview, a manager will choose the most desirable candidates and call them back for additional interviews and interviews with the supervising attorney. Some firms administer tests to determine an applicant's knowledge, grammar skills, and computer skills.

Often, the selection process is difficult, especially when many desirable candidates apply for a position. Personality and how well a candidate "fits" with a firm are considered. An applicant's references and previous employers must be checked before the successful candidate is chosen. Often, management will use a rating sheet, such as the one shown in Exhibit 3.7, when making the final decision.

APPLICANT EVALUATION FORM

4 = Superior   3 = Qualified   2 = Marginal   1 = Unqualified

Applicants	TRAINING			SKILLS						PERSONAL			OTHER		TOTAL
	Bachelor's Degree	Paralegal Certificate	Experience	Computer Skills	WestLaw/Lexis	Writing	Management experience	Substantive area 1	Substantive area 2	Appearance	Demeanor	Communication	Organization skills	Follow Instructions	
1. Mary Edwards		3	3	3	1	3	1	4	1	3	2	2	3	2	31
2. Bob Fulton	4	3	1	2	1	2	2	2	1	3	3	2	2	3	31
3. Linda Wall	4	4	4	3	3	3	3	4	3	3	4	3	4	3	48
4. Marleen Granger		4	4	4	3	2	1	3	3	3	3	3	3	3	39
5.															
6.															
7.															
8.															

Date: 4-12-xx   Manager: Benita Fowler   Recommendation: Linda Wall

EXHIBIT 3.7   Applicant Rating Sheet

TECH TIPS
Human Relations Software

The following is a sample of related software:

SurveyWin—Assists the manager in creating employee surveys. Contains sample templates.

The Survey Genie—Develops surveys and formulates date. It comes in two versions: employee and customer survey.

Computer Training—Software that trains employees in a number of office software. Employees learn at their own pace. Includes skills assessment.

Trainlog—Tracks employee training. Also conducts hazard assessment with links to personal protective equipment requirements. Contains training certificate templates.

Software mentioned in this sidebar is for informational purposes only and is not for the purpose of endorsing products.

When a selection is made, all applicants are notified by letter and thanked for applying for the position. The finalists' applications are kept in case another opening occurs or the selected employee does not work out. Many firms put new employees on a sixty- or ninety-day probation period. This is a good policy to be sure that the right person was hired for the right job.

Orientation and Training   When a new employee is hired, the orientation period begins. It is management's responsibility to provide the necessary training program for a new employee. It takes time for a new employee to become familiar with firm employees, surroundings, systems, and policies. With adequate training, a new employee can function at 100 percent productivity in about three months.

EMPLOYEE OBJECTIVES AND MANAGEMENT RELATIONS

CEMEC principle: An acronym to describe employee expectations.

Good management-employee relations require a joint effort. Managers expect employees to do the job for which they were hired in an efficient and productive manner. Employee expectations can be best described in the **CEMEC principle.** CEMEC is an acronym that stands for communication, education, motivation, evaluation, and compensation.

Communication

Effective communication is an essential ingredient in the success of any endeavor—personal or business. Communication involves body language, tone of voice, listening, and speaking.

The first communication an employee has with a firm is usually the employment interview. During the interview, it is management's responsibility to communicate the position to an applicant. An applicant must have a firm understanding of the position so that she or he can accept or reject the position. Often management does not adequately communicate essential aspects of a position, such as attorney expectations, firm policy, and responsibilities. Time constraints often interfere with a manager's ability to describe adequately a position. It is common for a legal assistant to accept a position only to discover that the position is quite different from what she or he expected.

Communication between a legal assistant and a supervising attorney is crucial. It is the attorney's responsibility to communicate adequately an assignment. However, it is the legal assistant's responsibility to give the attorney feedback on the communication. For example, if an area of the communication is not clear to the legal assistant, the legal assistant must clarify the communication. If the legal assistant does not do this, the attorney will assume that the communication was clear and fully understood. The same principle applies to all members of the legal team.

Communicating with fellow employees is an essential part of every position within a law office. Every communication should be carefully phrased so that no one is offended or embarrassed by it. An improper remark, spoken in jest, could have damaging results for an employee and, indirectly, a firm.

Each member of a legal team must promote open communication by doing the following:

◆ Accepting responsibility for his ideas and feelings
◆ Being open to the ideas and feelings of others
◆ Experimenting with new ideas
◆ Helping others to be open with their ideas and feelings by exhibiting a nonjudgmental attitude

Openness, honesty, and integrity create an atmosphere for open communication. Fear is the inhibiting element of open communication: fear of rejection, fear of looking stupid, or fear of loss of respect by co-workers. Each team member's contribution is valuable, but only when it is shared with others.

OF INTEREST . . .

Nonverbal Communication

What is your body language communicating at a job interview?

Direct eye contact: Self-confident, assertive

Firm handshake: Friendly, sincere

Avoiding direct eye contact: Cold, evasive, indifferent, insecure

Shaking head: Disagreeing, shocked, disbelieving

Yawning: Bored

Patting on back: Encouraging, congratulatory, consoling

Scratching the head: Bewildered, disbelieving

Smiling: Contented, understanding, encouraging

Biting the lip: Nervous, fearful, anxious

Tapping feet: Nervous

Folding arms: Angry, disapproving, disagreeing

Raising eyebrows: Disbelieving, surprised

Narrowing eyes: Disagreeing, resentful, angry

Flaring nostrils: Angry, frustrated

Wringing hands: Nervous, anxious, fearful

Leaning forward: Attentive, interested

Slouching in seat: Bored, relaxed

Sitting on edge of seat: Anxious, nervous, apprehensive

Shifting in seat: Restless, bored, nervous, apprehensive

Hunching over: Insecure, passive

Erect posture: Self-confident, assertive

Education

When a legal assistant is hired by a law office, a period of training will ensue. It is unrealistic to expect a new employee—even an experienced legal assistant—to "hit the ground running" in a new position. It is up to a law firm to give employees a

Buddy system: A system of putting two employees together for training purposes.

certain level of competency by providing on-the-job training. Often, a new legal assistant will be trained by the person she is replacing. If this is not possible, a senior legal assistant or legal assistant manager will train the new employee. Sometimes, a firm will put a new employee with an experienced employee in the same capacity, who trains the new employee. This is called the **buddy system.**

The buddy system has many advantages. It brings employees together to promote friendships and gives a new employee someone at the firm with whom he is familiar. This facilitates the new employee's integration into the firm. It also trains the new employee from the perspective of a peer.

The buddy system also has disadvantages. Often, a veteran legal assistant who is training a new legal assistant falls behind on work and perceives training as an inconvenience. Or the veteran legal assistant may not have the same duties as the new legal assistant, thus making the training inadequate.

Mentoring is a successful method of legal assistant training. A mentor is an experienced legal assistant or attorney from whom a new legal assistant can learn. Mentoring is not a structured training program but occurs during the course of employment. All new legal assistants should have a mentor.

Motivation

Motivation is vital, yet it cannot be measured. Motivation can only be assumed to exist by observing performance and behavior. Abraham Maslow, a prominent management theorist, opined that one person cannot motivate another, that personal motivation must come from within an individual. Therefore, management cannot motivate an employee. However, management can provide employees with a working environment that is conducive to personal motivation. In the proper working environment, employees can be motivated to do their best. A positive working environment is one where employees are recognized for their achievements, have adequate responsibility, are creative, and have advancement opportunities.

Working Conditions Working conditions have a major effect on overall job satisfaction. Poor working conditions increase turnover and decrease efficiency. Good working conditions decrease turnover and increase efficiency.

Good working conditions include the following:

◆ *Policy*—Reasonable office policies fully set forth in an office manual, with grievance procedures and an appeal process established and explained
◆ *Health and Safety*—Good lighting and a clean, comfortable environment with regulated heating and air conditioning
◆ *Tools*—Updated tools and equipment, including technology

Poor working conditions include these:

◆ *Policy*—Strict and unreasonable office policies that are neither documented nor enforced, with no grievance procedures or appeal process established
◆ *Health and Safety*—Poor lighting and a dirty, messy environment with unreliable heating and air conditioning
◆ *Tools*—Outdated tools and equipment, including technology

Ergonomics: An area of science concerned with health issues in the workplace.

The emerging field of **ergonomics** is defining acceptable and unacceptable standards for employees' health and safety. Ergonomic concerns include office furniture, computers, and equipment that maximize employee health and safety. It is an employer's responsibility to provide ergonomically acceptable equipment—such as computer glare screens and keyboard stands—because the employer is responsible for an employee's health problems acquired at work. The U.S. Occupational Safety and Health Administration (OSHA) is considering setting standards that would require ergonomically correct conditions.

TRENDS ➤➤➤

Why Do Employees Leave?

The *Harvard Business Review* suggests the following are reasons people leave their jobs:

- Job content
- Inadequate level of responsibility
- Negative company culture
- Disputes with colleagues
- Inadequate salary
- No management effort to motivate them
- Lifestyle/work/family concerns
- No communication or input on issues
- Lack of resources or support
- Lack of recognition
- Do not identify with the organization
- No team commitment or involvement
- Work is not fun anymore
- Lack of equity
- Don't feel appreciated
- No pride in the work product
- No prospects for promotion or growth
- Incompetent management
- Poor working conditions
- Inadequate salary and benefits

Good working conditions also include an environment that is conducive to positive working relationships and free from personality conflicts and sexual harassment problems.

Sexual Harassment Every person has a right to pursue a career free from sexual harassment and suggestive remarks. According to the National Association for Female Executives, 77 percent of the women it surveyed felt that sexual harassment was a problem. Fifty-three percent had been sexually harassed or knew of someone who had been sexually harassed. Sixty-four percent of those sexually harassed did not report the incident. Of the 36 percent who reported the incident, 52 percent said it was not resolved to their satisfaction.

Government agencies have issued guidelines intended to interpret employment laws as they pertain to sexual harassment. Federal guidelines have established that sexual harassment is a violation of title VII of the Civil Rights Act. These guidelines hold that an employer is responsible for the actions of its employees and define sexual harassment as follows:

> Unwelcome sexual advances, requests for sexual favors, and other verbal or physical conduct of a sexual nature constitute sexual harassment when (1) submission to such conduct is made either explicitly or implicitly a term or condition of an individual's employment, (2) submission to or rejection of such conduct by an individual is used as the basis for employment decisions affecting such individual, or (3) such conduct has the purpose or effect of substantially interfering with an individual's work performance or creating an intimidating, hostile, or offensive working environment.

Sexual harassment can take many forms, can be either verbal or nonverbal, and is often difficult to recognize. It is highly subjective. What is offensive to one person may not be offensive to another. Any instances of sexual harassment, or suspected sexual harassment, must be immediately reported to management.

Most employers have established policies concerning sexual harassment and written policies that define sexual harassment. The written policies describe the type of conduct an employer considers unacceptable. Most policies are contained in an employee handbook.

Evaluation

Informal evaluation: A procedure by which an employee's work is evaluated verbally. It occurs in an informal manner.

Formal evaluation: A procedure by which an employee's work performance is evaluated and rated in writing. It occurs annually or biannually.

Two types of evaluation take place: informal and formal. **Informal evaluation** occurs daily when employees' mistakes are corrected or employees are told they did a good job on a project. **Formal evaluation** occurs once or twice a year. A formal evaluation is in writing, followed by a performance interview with the employee and evaluators.

The purpose of a formal performance interview is to do the following:

◆ Discuss openly and candidly how an employee's performance meets an employer's requirements
◆ Make suggestions on how to correct weaknesses
◆ Follow up after a time period to report on the progress being made, giving any additional suggestions that might help
◆ Discuss an employee's professional development
◆ Set goals for the following year
◆ Access an employee's professional goals
◆ Give an employee suggestions on how to enhance professional development

---

OF INTEREST . . .

Tips for the Formal Evaluation

1. Problems arise if a performance evaluation is not based upon common agreement on what primary duties will be rated and how they will be measured. The evaluation session will start with a lack of mutual agreement concerning the performance management process which will effect the evaluation's outcome.

2. Both the supervisor and employee must adequately prepare for the evaluation session. If the employee has kept good records of his/her accomplishments, the performance evaluation meeting will be easier. The supervisor prepares for the evaluation by gaining feedback from clients and co-workers about the employee's performance.

3. Don't allow the evaluation discussion to be one sided. If you believe the supervisor's comments to be unfair or wrong, be sure to bring them to his/her attention.

4. If there is a disagreement on an issue, a communication problem could arise if the supervisor tends to turn to power or avoidance modes rather than working with the employee to reach a mutual understanding about the issue.

5. End the meeting on a positive and amicable note.

6. At the end of the evaluation, make a record of the areas discussed, plans and commitments made and follow-up accordingly.

7. Evaluate how you handled the discussion. Could you have communicated your position better? If so, how?

Often, an employee's raise and bonus are based on the review process. Goals set at these sessions state what an employee would like to achieve in the next year. At the next annual performance interview, achievement of these goals is discussed.

Employers rate employees using a performance review sheet, such as the one shown in Exhibit 3.8. This sheet identifies several areas of performance that are important to the position and the firm. Each area is discussed, and an employee is asked

Law Offices of Black, White & Greene
Performance Evaluation

Name: Title:

Employee No.:   Date:

Rating Factors

5 = Outstanding: Gives exceptional performance; demonstrates rare ability
4 = Excellent: Gives high-quality performance; demonstrates above-standard ability
3 = Good: Consistently meets job requirements; gives excellent performance in some areas
2 = Satisfactory: Meets job requirements; requires supervision for some tasks
1 = Needs Improvement: Occasionally performs below standards; requires close supervision
0 = Unsatisfactory: Gives unacceptable performance; fails to meet minimum job requirements

Performance Objectives   **Achieved**   **Not Achieved**

Analysis of Performance against Objectives:

Performance Factors Analysis:

Description	Rating	Description	Rating
Quantity of work		Control	
Quality of work		Oral communication	
Problem analysis		Written communication	
Decision making		Staff development	
Planning and organization		Job knowledge	
Delegation		Collaboration and teamwork	
Innovation		Responsiveness to change	
Initiative		Persuasiveness	
Persistence		Leadership	
Ability to work with others		Professional presence	
Judgment		Job enthusiasm	

Overall Performance:

☐ Unsatisfactory   ☐ Needs Improvement   ☐ Satisfactory   ☐ Good   ☐ Excellent   ☐ Outstanding

---

Comments Explaining Overall Performance Rating:

Employee Comments: (Attach extra sheet if needed)

Goals for Next Year:
1.
2.
3.

All items recorded on this form have been discussed and are understood between us.

Employee Signature	*Title*	*Date*
Attorney Signature	*Title*	*Date*
Management Signature	*Title*	*Date*

EXHIBIT 3.8 Performance Evaluation Form

TECH TIPS
Performance Appraisals Software

The following is a sample of related software:

Employee Appraiser—Contains standard paralegals to help the manager write employee reviews. It contains Coaching Advisor, which offers suggestions of how to help employees improve their performance.

Performance Now—Writes employee reviews. Contains material in all major sections of an employee review.

Absentee Calendar Online—Tracks employee absences using a coding system and calendar format to help managers spot patterns of abuse. Tracks hours worked and timekeeping. Also records employee data, such as emergency contacts, information on Equal Employment Opportunity, review dates, and more.

Software mentioned in this sidebar is for informational purposes only and is not for the purpose of endorsing products.

to sign the performance review and is given a copy of the review. A copy of the review becomes a permanent part of the employee's personnel file.

Some of the areas considered in the performance evaluation are the following:

◆ Courtesy to clients
◆ Punctuality
◆ Dependability
◆ Communication skills
◆ Leadership capabilities
◆ Initiative
◆ Work habits
◆ Willing to work overtime
◆ Skills rating
◆ Job performance

Most firms go to great lengths to ensure that performance evaluations are objective. However, when a person evaluates the performance of another, a certain amount of subjective judgment is involved. What one supervising attorney considers superior may be only satisfactory to another. A performance interview is the setting to discuss any disagreements a legal assistant may have with an evaluation.

If a legal assistant is not satisfied with a performance evaluation after a thorough discussion with the evaluator or evaluators, she or he should immediately take steps to resolve the problem. Since performance evaluations are a permanent part of one's record, one should be assertive in resolving the problem. The legal assistant should contact the firm's administrator to determine what steps can be taken to remedy the situation. Firms often have an appeal process available to employees.

Compensation

For employees to be satisfied with their work, they must be compensated adequately. Although many experts in the field have said that money is not a motivator in employee productivity, money contributes to employees' overall satisfaction with their work. Employees cannot give their best effort to a firm when their morale is low because of personal financial problems.

Employees should be satisfied with their wages at the time employment is accepted. If an employee accepts a low salary, anticipating high raises and bonuses, the employee is doing her- or himself and the profession a disservice.

OF INTEREST . . .

Performance Evaluation Dos and Don'ts

Don't rely on attorneys to remember all the great things you did during the year. Prepare a one-page memo outlining your accomplishments and submit this to your supervisors before the review process begins.

Don't wait for the review to get feedback on your performance. Ask for input from the attorneys every time you complete a project and record their comments on a performance log.

Don't focus solely on your needs during the review. Ask about the needs of the firm. Consider your relationship with your employer as that of a partnership and make it clear to the reviewer that you understand such needs as cost-cutting, efficiency, and increased billable hours. Stay focused on why the firm is in business in the first place.

Don't be afraid to toot your own horn. Nobody knows what you have been doing better than you do. Be mentally prepared to discuss your accomplishments and the reasons that you deserve more responsibility. Keep a log of your accomplishments.

Don't assume that you know what is expected of you. Ask what the expectations are of each new assignment so that you can adjust your performance to meet explicit needs. Understand the expectations of the job.

Don't wait until the review to talk about a raise. Often, salary decisions have already been made at this point. Research what paralegals in your community are being paid and discuss this information with your supervisor before the review process begins. This kind of objective data is more convincing than an emotional appeal for more money.

Before a position is accepted, a legal assistant should contact a local paralegal association and ask for a salary survey. Most local paralegal associations have salary information for legal assistants according to education, experience, and specialty.

Generally, a new legal assistant should not accept anything less than the average salary in the appropriate category. If a legal assistant accepts a low salary, it will reflect itself on the next salary survey and bring the average down. This will affect all legal assistants in the area. Accepting a low basic salary will also influence a legal assistant's future earning power because raises, and sometimes bonuses, are based on that salary. A legal assistant's total compensation consists of salary, raises, bonuses, and benefits. A legal assistant's employment status also affects compensation.

Basic Salary Structure   A good compensation plan is a goal of a firm. To establish a basic compensation structure, firms consider the following:

◆ *Marketplace*—What other firms in the area pay their employees
◆ *Job Analysis*—Study of the activities, duties, and responsibilities of a job
◆ *Job Description*—Detailed description of a job and the skills required to perform it
◆ *Job Evaluation*—Determination that establishes the value of a job and puts a monetary value on the job

Often, a firm may assign points to each function and skill required for a job and then assign a monetary value to each point. In a position with a salary range—$24,000 to $32,000, for example—an employee with a low point value would be entitled to the lower salary, an employee with a high point value would be entitled to a higher salary, and an employee with an average point value would be entitled to a salary in the middle of the range. Exhibit 3.9 shows a sample form for assigning point values and salary equivalents.

Raises and Bonuses   Raises are based on the consumer price index and on merit, base salary, tenure, or incentive. Bonuses are based on merit, base salary, tenure, or incentive.

FUNCTIONS AND SKILLS	MAXIMUM POINTS	TOTAL POINTS
Education	10	
General experience	10	
Related experience	10	
Responsibility	10	
Supervisory responsibility	10	
Management responsibility	10	
Client contact	10	
Ability to travel	10	
Coordinating responsibility	10	
Training responsibility	10	
Total	100	

Note: 0–30 = Grade 1; 31–60 = Grade 2; 61–80 = Grade 3; 81–100 = Grade 4

EXHIBIT 3.9 Sample Point Values and Salary Structure

Consumer price index: An index that determines the annual increase in the cost of living.

Raises are usually given as a percentage of the base pay. When calculating raises, the **consumer price index** may be considered. If the consumer price index indicates that the cost of living rose 3 percent during the year, a raise will usually include a 3 percent cost-of-living increase in addition to a percentage increase based on merit, tenure, or incentive. According to a 1999 salary survey conducted by *Legal Assistant Today* magazine, the average raise for a legal assistant was $1,859. A raise is rarely over 15 percent of the base salary.

Merit raises and bonuses acknowledge above-average quality and quantity of work. Studies have shown that merit raises, properly given, will raise productivity 50 to 90 percent and efficiency 50 to 125 percent.

Some administrators feel that merit raises and bonuses weaken employee morale because some employees will receive a higher raise or bonus than others. To eliminate this problem, some firms give employees a bonus based on base salary. Each employee, regardless of merit, will receive the same bonus according to his classification of employment. For example, attorneys receive 8 percent of their base salary, legal assistants 5 percent of their base salary, and secretaries 3 percent of their base salary. Studies have shown that although this will eliminate employee dissension over bonuses, it does not encourage employees to work harder.

Raises and bonuses are based on tenure when an employee is rewarded for longevity with a firm. Incentive raises and bonuses are given when an employee reaches a goal set by a firm. According to the 1999 salary survey conducted by *Legal Assistant Today* magazine, 66 percent of responding legal assistants received a bonus, the average of which was $1,506.00. The highest bonus reported was $22,000. Private law firms paid the highest average bonus. A breakdown of average bonus by type of firm is as follows:

Corporate	$1,272
Government	$ 214
Law firm	$1,749
Other	$ 619

Not all law firms offer bonuses to their employees. Statistics have shown that employees in large firms receive fewer bonuses than those in small firms. Surveys also indicated that bonuses appear to be used primarily as rewards rather than to offset a low base salary.

Firms have various methods of determining raises and bonuses. Some use performance evaluations on which to base salary increases. A large firm may form a committee

TECH TIPS

The following is a sample of Human Resource Software:

People Works—A CD-ROM that contains the complete text of laws and regulations of OSHA, The Department of Labor, the Equal Employment Opportunity Commission, and state agencies. An updated version will be sent to subscribers each month. Includes compliance information and modules to help managers put situations into prospective.

Oshalog.200—Tracks injury and illness information to identify problems and trends. Helps the manager comply with OSHA's injury/illness log requirements. Creates safety plans.

Employee Manual Maker—Helps the manager develop, revise, and update the employee policies manual.

Policies Now—Assists management in developing company policies that comply with federal requirements. Contains policy revisions schedule. Automatically jumps to Internet sites with relevant legal information. Also contains human resource forms. Updated.

Software mentioned in this sidebar is for informational purposes only and is not for the purpose of endorsing products.

to evaluate salary increases and performance reviews and determine salary increases. In a small firm, a managing partner or senior partner may determine bonuses.

To ensure a satisfied and motivated staff, each decision affecting an employee's compensation must be made in a fair and objective manner. Firms go to great lengths to protect objectivity in their compensation standards.

Benefits

Studies have indicated that companies with good benefits enjoy a higher degree of employee loyalty. As medical expenses increase and the cost of medical insurance skyrockets, firms with good medical benefits are attracting solid employee relationships. Employees of firms with few or no benefits are leaving to join firms with benefits. Some benefits, such as retirement plans, are contingent on longevity with a firm and encourage employees to stay with the firm.

Firms' benefit plans vary with the size of a firm. Small firms and sole practitioner offices tend to offer fewer benefits for their employees. The cost of benefits is often too high for small firms to afford. Large firms and corporate legal departments usually have the better benefit packages that are more likely to include employee retirement and savings plans. Some large firms offer other benefits, such as health club memberships, company cars, and company charge accounts. In addition, most firms will pay for continuing education and membership dues in paralegal or other professional associations.

Some firms offer their employees some innovative benefits, such as job sharing and flex schedules, telecommuting, wellness programs, personal family counseling, tuition reimbursement, travel discounts, theater passes, store discounts, urgent family care, free legal services, and a massage on company time. The benefits reported in *Legal Assistant Today* magazine's 1998 salary survey are shown in Exhibit 2.13 in Chapter 2.

When calculating compensation, always include benefits in the total. Whereas one firm with few benefits may offer a higher salary, the total compensation may be greater with an office offering a lower salary and a good benefits package.

FLSA: Federal Labor Standards Act.

Exempt: A professional status that exempts an employee from overtime compensation.

Nonexempt: A nonprofessional status that requires payment of overtime.

Laws Affecting Compensation

The federal government has passed laws that establish minimum wage and overtime requirements, and prohibit wage discrimination. The Federal Labor Standards Act (**FLSA**) designates the parameters within which an employee may be designated exempt or nonexempt.

Exempt and Nonexempt Status

The terms **exempt** (professional) and **nonexempt** (nonprofessional) refer to minimum wage and overtime requirements.

Employees who are exempt are paid an annual or monthly salary and are not entitled to overtime compensation. Employees who are nonexempt are paid by the hour and are entitled to overtime compensation for all hours worked in excess of forty a week. Even though an employer may inform a nonexempt employee of his yearly "salary," that employee is actually paid by the hour. In return for X hours of work a year, the employer will pay the employee X dollars. If an employer docks the pay of a "salaried" employee who comes in late, leaves early, or must take time off for personal needs, the employee is not a salaried employee by the true sense of the word. A true salary is paid to exempt employees only.

The FLSA sets the standards of who may be exempt employees. Executives, professional employees, and administrative employees who satisfy specific requirements established by the Department of Labor are considered exempt employees. Whether an employee is exempt depends on the work. To be exempt, an employee must do work that is directly related to management objectives, goals, and policies.

Some legal assistants may qualify for exemption depending on their work responsibilities. According to case law, a legal assistant must exercise independent judgment with little or no supervision of an attorney in order to be exempt. It has been argued that most legal assistants exercise the skill, discretion, and individual judgment required to be considered exempt. If a legal assistant operates entirely under the supervision of an attorney, the legal assistant will be considered nonexempt. Legal secretaries, regardless of administrative assistant and office manager job titles, are considered nonexempt employees.

A survey conducted by the NFPA in 1997 indicated that 56 percent of responding legal assistants in its organization were considered exempt and 41 percent were considered nonexempt (3 percent no response). The exempt and nonexempt status of paralegals is an issue that has been long debated. As of this writing, a little more than half the paralegals in the United States have exempt status. The issue was brought before the Department of Labor for a determination. In April 1995, the Department of Labor ruled that a paralegal is a production worker and therefore does not qualify for exempt status. The same year, the Department of Labor sued the Dallas law firm of Page & Addison for classifying its paralegals exempt and refusing to pay overtime. The firm stated that the paralegals' work is substantive and therefore qualifies for exempt status. The jury agreed.

The controversy has caused law firms to think carefully about classifying their paralegals. Some firms are placing their junior paralegals in the nonexempt status and their senior paralegals in exempt status. The reasoning behind the difference is that the senior paralegal performs more management functions than a junior paralegal and the junior paralegal requires more supervision.

Some paralegals do not want to be exempt because they want to be compensated for overtime. They say that the higher wage paid to exempt paralegals is not high enough to compensate them for all the extra hours required. Others, even those who make more money with nonexempt status, prefer the prestige that exempt status brings them.

Do not let this controversy confuse you. Legal assistants are certainly professional. A legal assistant's level of professionalism has nothing to do with exempt or nonexempt classification. The work is challenging, and the rewards are great.

THE TEAM APPROACH

Team approach: A management theory in which management and employees work together for the benefit of an organization.

Many different concepts have been proposed for integrating management and employees for an effective organization. Many theories and approaches have been developed as well as techniques to maximize a firm's productivity. A popular approach applied in many law firms and private industry is the **team approach.**

The basic theory behind the team approach is that by aligning an organization's needs with the needs of its employees, the organization will benefit from the em-

TRENDS ➤➤➤

How Should You Submit Your Resume?

First of all, your resume and cover letter must be perfect. Once perfect, how should it be submitted to the prospective employer? Fax? E-mail? Snail mail? Hand delivered? A survey developed by Office Team revealed that the majority of top executives were neutral on the subject, but some (21 percent) indicated that they prefer to receive resumes the old-fashioned way—by snail mail. These executives indicated that they prefer the mailed version because of what it reveals about the candidate's professionalism: their choice of paper, quality of printing, and layout of the document. It indicates that the prospective employee has extended a greater effort to personalize the information.

Employment experts advise, however, that the ideal approach is to fax or e-mail the resume for expediency and indicate that a hard copy is in the mail. The survey's results indicated that employers like to receive resumes:

By mail	21%
By fax:	8%
By e-mail:	4%
Hand delivery:	1%
No preference:	66%

As technology is performing more functions for management, many candidates are including a scanable resume that is scanned into the company's computer system. Some companies may want two versions of your resume: one for management to read and one for the computer to read. Prepare your resume so it maximizes the computer's ability to "read" your resume by preparing it according to the following tips:

- Use white paper printed on one side only.
- Submit an original, not a photocopy. Laser printed is preferable.
- Do not fold or staple.
- Use standard fonts such as Times New Roman, Palatino, Arial, Helvetica in 10 to 14 points (12 is preferable—avoid Times 10 point).
- Don't condense spacing between letters.
- Use bold or all caps for section headings only.
- Avoid italics, underline, shadows.
- Avoid lines, graphics, and boxes.
- Do not use a two-column format.
- Place your name at the top on its own line.
- List the phone number on its own line.
- Do not center headings—put them flush left.
- Use key words that coincide with the position advertisements.

Tip: When faxing your resume, set the fax to "fine mode." The recipient will get a better quality copy.

ployees' personal motivation, energy, and drive as well as benefit employees by being a vehicle for achieving their personal goals.

Studies have shown that the team approach plays an important role in the personal satisfaction of employees, success of an enterprise, and good service to a client. To have a successful team, all members must function together. As on a good football team, individual contributions to a work team are dimmed when the contributions of other team members are considered. It is important that all team members feel that they belong to the team and are recognized for their contribution.

Legal Assistant Today magazine, in its search for the best law firm in 1997, asked its readers to nominate the best firm to work for and to indicate what made the firm so desirable. The legal assistants who responded to the survey were mainly from small firms. They responded that respect and a professional attitude were very important to them. One respondent said, "Paralegals [in this firm] are treated fairly, respectfully, and as professionals. We are recognized and utilized as valuable assets to the firm." Another wrote, "Each partner is concerned with the career development and potential of each legal assistant. They develop you as an individual and a team player and encourage our professional growth."

One method of the team approach consists of the five Cs: each member of the legal team must exhibit commitment, competency, constructive feedback, creativity, and cooperation.

Commitment

Building a strong team in a law office involves a commitment to the objectives of a firm. Each member of a football team knows the objective of the team and has the same goal: to win football games. Each team member makes an individual contribution to achieving the goal. Likewise, each member of a legal team should have the same objectives: (1) provide quality legal services to the client, (2) contribute to the profitability of the firm, and (3) derive personal satisfaction and growth from work.

A commitment to a firm is not made on one's first day of employment. Making this commitment requires trust in an organization and in its people. Once an individual can trust the motives of an organization—know that the organization will support him in achieving individual as well as company goals—a sense of loyalty develops. For this sense of loyalty to build, employees must know that they are an integral part of a team in control of their own destiny within an organization. Then, a sense of belonging to the organization exists, and a positive sense of self-esteem develops.

Competency

To be part of a dynamic team, each employee must be competent. Employees rely on one another. Since employees are responsible for different aspects of a project, it is important that team members have confidence in the contribution of other team members. If one member's contribution has to be redone or is substandard, it affects the entire project and the contribution of other team members. Incompetent employees will affect a firm's environment by creating dissent and inefficiency.

Graduating from paralegal school will not make a legal assistant competent—but it will give a legal assistant the tools to begin the journey to competency. Education, experience, on-the-job training, and continuing education are the keys to competency.

Experience   When legal assistants graduate from paralegal school, their legal education has just begun. Once paralegal skills are learned, legal assistants are constantly upgrading those skills by on-the-job experience. Studies have shown that it takes three years to learn a job completely. Does that mean that it will take three years to be competent? No. *Webster's New Collegiate Dictionary* defines competent as "having requisite or adequate ability or qualities." Each day a legal assistant works, something new is learned. Competency is always increasing.

On-the-Job Training   Training is closely related to other personnel activities. For example, planning identifies a firm's needs. These needs can be filled either by hiring new personnel or by increasing the skills of current employees through training. One purpose of a formal evaluation is to identify any problem areas. When a problem area is identified, it can be eliminated by proper training.

On-the-job training is effective because it concentrates on subject areas relevant to a job. Many paralegal programs offer an internship course that allows students to demonstrate their skills and receive exposure to the real legal world. A student observes an experienced legal assistant who has learned the tricks of the trade and therefore benefits directly. The experienced legal assistant is a role model for the student and can illustrate how a task relates to other tasks. In a classroom, it is difficult to get a real-life feel for the subject matter.

Many large firms conduct their own training programs. Firms that do not offer formal training programs encourage workers to attend seminars. Most firms will pay for, and give employees the requisite time off to attend, a seminar.

Continuing Legal Education The law is always changing and evolving. Law that is learned this year and next year will change and have to be relearned. Continuing legal education is essential to keep abreast of the changes in the law. A legal assistant must be flexible with the law and be willing to devote time to continuing legal education.

Most law firms and legal offices will pay for an employee's continuing education if it pertains to the job. Some firms have a policy of paying for all continuing education because they feel it will benefit the firm in the long run by increasing competency levels. Some firms and legal departments will even reimburse employees for expenses incurred to obtain an advanced degree or college education.

Constructive Feedback

Giving constructive feedback is closely related to communicating effectively and is essential for successful employer-employee relationships. A legal assistant who works hard on a project needs to know whether the work satisfies a supervising attorney. If areas did not meet the attorney's expectations, the legal assistant needs to know about them. If areas exceeded the attorney's expectations, the legal assistant needs to know about them. Constructive feedback motivates people to reach personal goals and improve their work. This allows each employee to grow in her or his chosen field. Unfortunately, constructive feedback is often overlooked in a busy law office and frequently must be requested.

Constructive criticism:
A negative performance evaluation that is given for the purpose of providing instruction and direction.

A legal assistant should be prepared for possible negative feedback, often called **constructive criticism.** Many people avoid giving negative feedback for fear that they will damage an employee's morale. Actually, usually so little positive feedback is given in a law office that negative feedback is perceived as a drastic event rather than as a challenge in a series of positive feedback events. Constructive criticism, although sometimes disturbing, is essential to improving job performance.

Employment evaluations and reviews are part of the feedback process. Evaluation is the process that appraises performance. It should occur often—preferably after a legal assistant completes a project. Being deprived of this feedback is losing an opportunity to learn and grow.

Constructive feedback also includes praise and recognition for a job well done. Employees who receive little recognition for their work begin to lose the motivation to work hard and do their best on a project.

Each member of a legal team must be kept apprised of the status of a case. Just as a football player must have knowledge of the plays of a game, employees must know what is going on before they feel like an integral part of a team. As captain of a team, an attorney is responsible for keeping staff apprised and giving adequate instructions in assigning work.

Creativity

For a person to grow, a job must give him an opportunity for creativity. Opportunities for creativity are great when company procedures are flexible, all team members interact as peers, and decision making involves all team players. A person who is given the responsibility to complete a project in a manner consistent with her competency level is given an opportunity to be creative.

Everyone has the ability to be creative. Research has proven that one need not have a high intelligence quotient (IQ) to be creative. Creativity is encouraged by increasing activities that exercise the following attributes:

◆ *Open Mind*—Willingness to change one's viewpoint and approaches and try new things and experiences.

◆ *Curiosity*—Spirit of inquiry; realization that one has much to learn; an enjoyment of learning

◆ *Ability to Concentrate*—Ability to delve below the surface of situations; willingness to apply energy and efforts to solve problems; enjoyment of working on complex problems; willingness to spend considerable time alone thinking

◆ *Persistence*—Willingness to keep working on a problem until a satisfactory solution is found; patience in working out solutions

◆ *Confidence*—Willingness to risk being ridiculed by others for unconventional ideas and approaches; optimism and enthusiasm about finding and implementing solutions to problems

◆ *Cooperation*—Ability to work productively with others to define problems, formulate solutions, and implement action plans; flexibility in adapting to the reality of situations

The essence of creativity is identifying a need and meeting it in an original and effective way. An element inherent in all legal cases is a problem or issue. A lawyer's job is to solve problems and resolve issues to the satisfaction of a client. A legal assistant's job is to help a lawyer find effective solutions. Examples of being creative in a legal case include applying the law in a unique manner, persuading a jury in an imaginative manner, and developing a system to make a law office run more smoothly.

A creative person is also a critical thinker. A critical thinker questions "facts" and will not be satisfied until all information is known. A critical thinker obtains a complete understanding of a situation and more easily produces a creative solution for a client.

Many legal assistants are afraid to assert their creativity for fear it will be rejected by others. A good place to start asserting creativity is to develop solutions to problems or develop a system to make a project easier. For example, Cheryl Miller is a legal assistant who spends a lot of time going through files to obtain information. She wanted an easier way to gather the information, so she developed a case flow cover sheet that listed all the documents in a file (see Chapter 12). She uses the cover sheet in all the files she reviews. When the office manager saw how efficient the system was, every legal assistant was required to complete a case flow cover sheet for their files. Cheryl's creativity ultimately saved the firm money.

Cooperation

Cooperation is essential for the success of a solid team. Interacting with other employees is essential in any job. Service to a client, being one of an employee's goals, requires flexibility in work habits. Occasionally, it is necessary to step outside the boundaries of a position to help a co-worker.

Cooperation is not always easy to attain. In a legal environment, it is easy to be abrupt to a co-worker. The nature of legal work is stressful, and stressful working conditions express themselves in personality conflicts. Stress reduction should be a goal of all team members.

Personality Conflicts   Like personal relationships, business relationships are subject to strain from time to time. On a whole, the business of law is more stressful than other industries because of constant deadlines and the immediate needs of clients. A legal team is under more pressure to perform quality work in less time as clients become more fee sensitive.

CYBERSITES
Job Search Web Sites

At the beginning of 1997, 1.2 million jobs were advertised on the Internet and 1 million resumes were circulating online according to the Electronic Recruiting Index published by the Internet Business Network. There are many benefits to recruiting online:

- The Internet is available 7 days a week, 24 hours a day.
- It's easy to use.
- Job postings reach a global marketplace including passive job seekers.
- Firms can target specific competencies.
- It costs less than newspaper advertisements.

There are numerous sites to help you with your job search. Some sites are free while others charge a fee to access resumes or post jobs.

Careers—www.careers.org. Contains links to hundreds of career-oriented sites.

Jobtrak—www.jobtrak.com. Database of job opportunities for students. In its "Search Tips" section, it provides information such as how to conduct an effective job search, networking, business protocol, letters, resumes, and personality tests.

Monster Board—www.monster.com. Contains job listings for U.S. and international jobs in all fields. In its career center, it offers information on resumes, relocation services, employer job postings, and seminar notices.

Career Path—www.careerpath.com Contains a database that can search job listings posted in all the major newspapers. Resume postings. This site was voted the number-one job site by Media Matrix.

NFPA—www.paralegals.org. In the career center, the NFPA posts job openings for paralegals in the United States. Offers information on salary, resume writing, opportunities, and career advancement.

Paralegal's Guide to U.S. government jobs—www.attorneyjob.com/paralegalcareers.html

American Lawyer—www.AmLawJOBS.com.

Espan—www.espan.com

The Job Market—www.thejobmarket.com

Online Career Center—www.occ.com

JobBank USA—www.jobbankusa.com

Career Mosaic—www.careermosaic.com

Job Web—www.jobweb.com

123 Jobs—www.123jobs.com

Job Search Tips—www.tcm.com/hr-careers/career/seekers.htm

Job Guide on the Internet—www.dbm.com

Each person has her or his own personality traits and style of handling stress. Good management understands the personalities of lawyers and support staff and must be careful to match the right support staff to the right lawyer. A mismatch can have disastrous effects on staff and on the productivity of a firm. For example, some secretaries and legal assistants can handle—and even thrive on—working for an aggressive and disagreeable lawyer, whereas others work well with a soft-spoken, pleasant attorney.

Stress affects every member of a team, from an attorney to a messenger. The ability to get along with people is a particular challenge in a law office environment. A harried employee may make a sharp comment to another employee—not because of a personality conflict but because of stress. The second employee, being sensitive, takes the comment personally, feeling that it was a direct attack. Consequently, the

The law firm's policy manual should contain a written statement prohibiting termination or other retribution for paralegals who blow the whistle on attorneys committing ethical violations or criminal acts. The firm's top management, including the paralegal manager, should communicate this policy on a regular basis to the paralegal staff.

The policy manual should also outline the following steps for paralegals who either spot such activity, or who are asked to commit acts which they consider unethical or illegal:

- Speak first to the attorney. Is the act really illegal, or are there mitigating circumstances of which you are not aware?
- If the attorney does not address these concerns adequately, report the problem to the paralegal manager, who should approach the firm's ethics committee or managing partner.
- If the firm does not take the action the issue requires, report the activity to the ethics committee of the state bar association.

EXHIBIT 3.10   What to Do about an Illegal Activity

Copyright 1993 by James Publishing, Inc. Reprinted with permission from *Legal Assistant Today.*

relationship of these two people begins to deteriorate, eventually affecting the entire working environment of the firm.

Conflicts are a source of personal and organizational malfunction. Most personality conflicts are a result of lack of communication. An effort should always be made to improve a conflicting situation before terminating employment. People citing a personality conflict as the reason for leaving prior employment are looked on with suspicion by potential employers. The key to success in dealing with personality conflicts is communicating and addressing issues directly to the offending person.

Constant Deadlines   One source of stress for legal assistants is meeting constant deadlines. Deadlines and time constraints are inherent in the practice of law. Legal assistants are often under pressure to complete a task before a deadline. Therefore, time management skills are essential for a legal assistant. Often, time management skills are acquired by experience. Many organizations provide time management seminars and help employees acquire necessary time management skills.

Unethical Behavior   Another source of conflict for a legal assistant is to observe unethical behavior. Whether the perpetrator is an attorney or a legal assistant, the circumstance puts a legal assistant in a compromising position. The unethical act must be corrected, and the legal assistant must exercise tact and good judgment in this situation. The legal assistant may bring the problem to the attention of the perpetrator and strongly suggest that the situation be corrected, or the legal assistant may bring the problem to management's attention and let management handle the problem. *Whichever option is chosen, the legal assistant must not allow any unethical behavior to pass unnoticed or unreported.* Exhibit 3.10 lists some suggestions for handling knowledge of an illegal activity.

ETHICS ALERT

There are many different methods of reducing stress. Experts in this area recommend stress reduction activities to sustain health. Exhibit 3.11 provides some suggestions for reducing stress.

1. *Relaxation.* Take ten minutes out of the day to sit quietly, take deep breaths, and relax all the muscles in your body.

2. *Release.* Release worries and concerns. Eighty percent of what we worry about never happens, 15 percent are beyond our control, and 5 percent are within our control.

3. *Recreation.* Take the time to have fun and to exercise.

4. *Refuse.* Practice ways of saying no to tasks that will overburden you. Avoid feeling overloaded with work and feeling guilty about saying no. Make realistic demands on yourself.

5. *Reorganize.* Get rid of unnecessary clutter and low-priority projects. List high-priority projects and complete them first.

6. *Reevaluate.* Reevaluate all your projects. Are they all as urgent as you think? Set new priorities and prepare project lists in order of priority.

7. *Refocus.* Refocus in a positive direction. Choose to see situations positively instead of negatively.

8. *Recuperate.* Get plenty of rest and take care of yourself.

9. *Reduce standards.* Often, we place high demands on ourselves. Must we always be right? Allow yourself some room to be wrong and forgive yourself for mistakes.

10. *Recognize.* Be aware of stress signals such as sore eyes, stiff neck, rapid heartbeat. Then retreat to a place where you can relax.

EXHIBIT 3.11   Ten Rs to Reduce Stress

CONCLUSION

Personnel relations can mean success or failure for a firm. The cost of replacing employees is very high. Employees of a small office may have more independence than employees of a large office, but small firms have reported problems usually not found in a large law office—for example, small legal clinics have more employment disputes than other firms.

Attrition: A reduction in workforce due to death, termination, retirement, or resignation.

A firm that loses a member of its team is disrupted until a replacement can be found. Firms with high **attrition** rates suffer from constant disorganization when an employee's position is vacant. Studies have shown that it takes an employee at least two or three months to become a productive member of a team. During the time of vacancy and training, someone's job is not getting done, and this affects the whole team. Chaos and confusion dominate the team, which is reflected in poor service to a client. Imagine a football team trying to play a game with half its fullbacks missing.

A firm's environment is never static; it is in constant transition. The dynamics of a firm's environment ebb and flow at the direction of the team members. Each person is responsible for her own contribution to a firm's environment. A positive firm environment consists of positive employees—those with the team spirit, a high degree of motivation, confidence, and the five Cs.

SUMMARY

Management is defined by Peter Drucker as "the method of using available resources to achieve desired goals." Managers work with and through other people to achieve a firm's goals. Good personnel relations are a test of effective management.

Although law firms differ in structure and management style, most firms have basically the same objectives. Many of a government agency's and corporate legal department's objectives may be different than a law firm's, but growth and satisfaction for employees is an objective of each type of legal office.

The manager is responsible for all aspects of personnel relations. The manager's role is influenced by external and internal conditions. External conditions include economic conditions, government regulations, and laws. Internal conditions include the nature and structure of a firm, the nature of the work, and the nature of the employees.

A personnel manager has five functions: planning, controlling, organizing, leading, and staffing. The goal of human resource planning is to develop personnel policies that will achieve a firm's objectives. Controlling is the process of ensuring that actions conform to plans. The organizing function requires a manager to coordinate the resources of a firm to maximize productivity and effectiveness. Leading involves determining what is to be accomplished and how to accomplish it. Staffing includes such duties as recruitment, screening, interviewing, testing, hiring, firing, job analysis, job description, and personnel record keeping.

The hiring process consists of four steps: planning, recruitment, selection, and training. The manager must complete a position description for the position which includes hiring specifications. Before a position description can be prepared, the manager must have a clear understanding of the position and the necessary qualifications of the prospective employee.

The government has established employment guidelines in various legislative acts. In addition, individual states have their employment laws and guidelines. The firm's employment application must comply with federal and state guidelines. The most important area to guard against federal law violations is the interviewing process. A manager may apply the ouch formula to interview questions to remain within interviewing requirements.

There are certain characteristics a manager should look for when interviewing a prospective employee. They are job hopping, long commute to work, poor health, improper termination notice to previous employer, reasons for leaving, and poor relationship with previous employer. Management often uses an applicant evaluation form when making a final decision.

Good management-employee relations require a joint effort. Employee expectations can be best described in the CEMEC principle, which consists of communication, education, motivation, evaluation, and compensation.

Working conditions have a major effect on motivation and overall job satisfaction. The emerging field of ergonomics is defining acceptable and unacceptable standards for employees' health and safety. Good working conditions also include an environment that is conducive to positive working relationships free from personality conflicts and sexual harassment problems.

Two types of evaluation take place: informal and formal. Informal evaluation occurs daily when employees' mistakes are corrected or they are told they did a good job on a project. Formal evaluation occurs once or twice a year in a performance review.

For employees to be satisfied with their work, they must be compensated adequately. A good compensation plan is a goal of a firm. Often, a firm may assign points to each function and skill required for a job and then assign a monetary value to each point. The federal government has passed laws that establish minimum wages and overtime requirements, and prohibit wage discrimination. The FLSA designates the parameters within which an employee may be designated exempt or nonexempt. The terms *exempt* (professional) and *nonexempt* (nonprofessional) refer to minimum wage and overtime requirements. Some legal assistants qualify for exemption, depending on their work responsibilities.

Many different concepts have been proposed for integrating management and employees for an effective organization. A popular approach applied in many law firms and private industry is the team approach. The basic theory behind the team approach is that by aligning an organization's needs with the needs of its employees, the organization will benefit from the employees' personal motivation, energy, and drive as well as benefit employees by being a vehicle for achieving their personal goals. Studies have shown that the team approach plays an important role in the personal satisfaction of employees, success of an enterprise, and good service to a client. One method of the team approach consists of the five Cs: each member of a legal team must exhibit commitment, competency, constructive feedback, creativity, and cooperation.

Personnel relations can mean the success or failure for a firm. A firm that loses a member of its team is disrupted until a replacement can be found. A firm's personnel relations affect its environment. For this reason, a firm's environment is never static; it is in constant transition.

CHAPTER ILLUSTRATION

Robert Black is the managing partner for Black, White & Greene. Tricia Bunnell is his assistant and has gained the title of office manager. Robert asked Tricia to develop human resource policies and procedures for the firm. In order to do this, she must conduct a human resource audit of the firm's existing staff to determine whether the staff should be re-structured to increase productivity and to plan for the future needs of the firm.

She began by asking each employee to list and describe each area of her or his job and to rate the frequency of each task. When she received the reports, she found the following:

- Some employees' tasks could be delegated to a subordinate employee.
- Some employees were not adequately trained to complete certain tasks.
- Some employees were overloaded with work, while others were underutilized.
- Secretaries were spending too much time filing and copying documents, causing them to fall behind on their secretarial work.

After discussing the findings with Robert, they developed the following plan:

- Hire a file clerk to handle the filing.
- Legal assistants were to delegate their clerical functions, such as file maintenance, to the secretaries.
- The complex litigation legal assistants were to receive training in handling complex litigation.
- The senior legal assistant was to delegate all deposition summaries to the junior legal assistant.
- Each employee would be evaluated once a year.

Goal 1

To accomplish goal 1, Tricia prepared a position description for the file clerk position. After a discussion with the secretaries who were currently performing the function, she determined the major duties and requirements for the position and included all the main areas in a position description, as shown in Exhibit 3.3. After Robert and the secretaries reviewed the position description, Tricia began the recruiting process by placing an ad in the classifieds section of the local newspaper. She also called the local college and submitted the position with the paralegal program director.

The first day, Tricia received about fifteen resumes, the second day twenty-five, and the third day thirteen. She then eliminated all resumes with typos or grammatical errors to arrive at twenty-five resumes worthy of consideration. Of those resumes, some applicants did not have the requisite backgrounds, some were overqualified, and others were underqualified. Two applicants appeared to be job hoppers. After eliminating those candidates, she arrived at ten qualified applicants for the position. She wrote each rejected applicant a letter, thanking them for their interest, and set appointments for the qualified applicants.

Before her first appointment arrived, Tricia developed her interview questions. She formulated them using the ouch formula and made sure that each question complied with the law. She also developed an applicant rating sheet like the one shown in Exhibit 3.6. She and Robert interviewed the applicants and compared their ratings. There were two applicants

who were tied for first place: Lori Smith and Kay Bowen. They were called back for a second interview. Kay Bowen received the most points after the second interview and was hired as the firm's file clerk.

On Kay's first day of work, Tricia conducted her orientation. She introduced her to all the members of the firm and described the firm's policies and procedures. For her training on filing procedures, Tricia used the buddy system and delegated the training to Audra, the most experienced secretary in the firm.

Goal 2

With Kay performing the filing for the firm, the secretaries were now ready to maintain the files and keep them current for the legal assistants. This task involved maintaining the status worksheets and categorizing documents. The secretaries required training on the correct method of the file maintenance. The most logical person to train the secretaries was the most experienced legal assistant, Milton, who developed a training program for the secretaries and delivered the training.

Goal 3

Specialized training was required to make sure the complex litigation legal assistants were knowledgeable about all areas of managing a complex litigation file. Since Milton was a member of the local paralegal association, he received information on all their educational programs. A workshop on complex litigation was being presented in three weeks, so the firm paid for him to participate. Tricia told him to watch for all workshops pertaining to complex litigation and encouraged him to attend them.

Goal 4

The junior legal assistant, Melvin, was given the responsibility to summarize depositions. To ensure that he had the proper training, he signed up for a refresher course in trial preparation at the local college. To assist Melvin, the firm also contracted the services of Depo Sum, a paralegal service that specialized in deposition summaries. Tricia spoke with the owner of Depo Sum, who agreed to come to the firm to supplement Melvin's training for deposition summaries.

Goal 5

Prior to the human resource audit, the firm had no policy for evaluating its employees. This was one area of concern for the employees who requested a formal evaluation process. After a discussion with Robert and the other attorneys of the firm, it was determined that the attorneys were the most qualified to evaluate their staff. However, most of the attorneys expressed concern about the process because they had little or no experience in the evaluation process. It was important that the attorneys receive training in this area before developing a formal plan.

The firm contacted a human resources consultant to educate the attorneys on the process. The consultant agreed to train the attorneys and the staff on the process. The consultant also developed an evaluation form for the firm like the one shown in Exhibit 3.8. While this was very expensive for the firm, the firm felt that it was extremely important that the evaluations be as objective as possible to maintain employee morale.

The evaluations were scheduled for the employment anniversary of each employee. When Melvin was evaluated, he was dissatisfied with his rating. He felt that he should have been given a higher rating. Audra was marked down on her evaluation because she had a tardiness problem. While her performance was excellent in many areas, her tardiness imposed undue hardship on other employees. She was admonished and encouraged to be punctual. Dennis White, her boss, gave her a formal warning about her tardiness. Audra agreed to be punctual and was convinced that her performance evaluation would improve after she resolved her punctuality problem. Milton's evaluation was so good that he now wants a raise.

Part of each employee's evaluation is to set goals for the year. Goals included improving on areas of performance and learning new skills. While some employees were dissatisfied with areas of the evaluation, for the most part they were very pleased with the process. With the exception of Melvin, the employees felt that the evaluations were fair.

With reference to compensation, the employees, except Milton, felt that they were fairly compensated. With the evaluations completed, the firm can now consider raises and bonuses for the employees.

The human resources audit took the firm one year to complete and implement. While it was being developed, the firm contracted with a temp agency for a temporary secretary to fill Tricia's position while she worked on the audit. Now that the audit is completed, Tricia can assume her secretarial duties. Robert has other plans, however. He decided to make Tricia a full-time office manager to handle the management of the law firm. She accepted. The temporary secretary, Pam Cody, was offered the position as a full-time employee, and she accepted. Tricia, too, was happy with her promotion.

The audit was a time-consuming and expensive program. However, the firm was rewarded for its hard work and commitment by creating a culture that is positive and cohesive. The employees work together as a team and are included in management's policy development.

CHAPTER REVIEW

1. Describe the internal and external conditions that affect a firm's management.

2. What are the five functions of a personnel manager? Which is the most important?

3. What are the four areas of human resource planning?

4. What are the three main elements of control?

5. What are the three roles of a leader?

6. What are the four steps of the hiring process?

7. What is the ouch formula?

8. What danger signals do managers look for in an interview?

9. What is the CEMEC principle?

10. What are the reasons for conducting a performance evaluation? What are some of the areas of performance considered?

11. What issues are considered when establishing a compensation plan?

12. What is the difference between an exempt employee and a nonexempt employee?

13. What is the team approach?

14. What are the five Cs of the team approach?

EXAMPLES FOR DISCUSSION

1. Iron Fist Management Style

The legal department of the Federal Contracts Agency is a government agency consisting of five attorneys, three legal assistants, and five secretaries. The office manager is known for managing the department with an iron fist. She is a retired accountant, committed to staying within the budget of the agency and earning recognition for reducing costs. She thinks that if very strict rules are implemented, productivity will increase and the department's reputation will increase.

When Sam Weeks was hired as a legal assistant for the department, the office manager gave him a three-page memo of rules. The memo stated:

Notice to Employees

1. Nothing will be placed on the top of the desk except essential working tools (no pictures, plants, etc.).
2. Desk drawers must be neat and tidy at all times and subject to unannounced inspections.
3. All tardiness (even five minutes) will be deducted from pay.
4. No personal telephone calls will be allowed except in extreme emergencies. Each employee's phone is equipped with a monitoring device that monitors all calls. Personal calls will be deducted from the paycheck for both time and charges.
5. Breaks are permitted only for attending to bathroom duties.
6. Absolutely no personal conversation with other employees will be permitted. All conversation must be work related.
7. Errors in work will not be permitted and will be monitored.
8. All supplies must be accounted for. When a pen runs out of ink, it may be turned in for a new pen. No pens will be issued unless accompanied by a used pen. This applies to scissors, staplers, hole-punchers, highlighters, etcetera.

1. What goal of the firm is the office manager overlooking?
2. What management theory is the office manager exhibiting?
3. What management theory is the office manager disregarding?
4. What management functions are missing with this office manager?
5. What leadership qualities are missing in this office manager?

2. Carolyn's Bad Day

Carolyn Albers, a real estate paralegal, knew the trial date of the Twin Lakes real estate case was quickly approaching. She also knew that she needed to complete a summary-of-events project before the trial. Since the case was complicated, she needed instruction from her boss, Michael Myogeto.

Michael is extremely busy. He is always in a meeting, in court, or with clients. Whenever Carolyn tried to talk to him, he was always too busy. Carolyn wrote him notes and slipped them under his door. They were never acknowledged.

After repeated attempts, Carolyn went by Michael's office and found him on the telephone. She went in his office to wait until he got off the phone. When he hung up, Carolyn requested instruction on the events summary for the Twin Lakes case.

"You mean you haven't started that yet?" said Michael.

"I've been waiting for your instructions," said Carolyn.

"Just do a summary of the events that occurred from the purchase of the property to foreclosure. You don't need to include Rick Everett's participation or Jennifer Hemstreet's participation. Be sure to include all activities of all the brokers and salespeople. Check the deposition for information," said Michael as he picked up his briefcase and left for court.

Carolyn returned to her office and sat down in her chair. She thought about what Michael had said: Do not include the activities of Rick Everett or Jennifer Hemstreet but include the activities of all salespeople and brokers. "But Rick Everett was a broker acting in the capacity of a salesman in one aspect of this case," thought Carolyn. "Is he confused? Am I confused? What do I do with Everett? Include him? I'll check the deposition. But . . . what deposition? There are seventeen depositions in this case! Which one did he mean? I guess I'd better review them all."

Carolyn, unsure of Michael's instructions and unable to meet with him again, reviewed all the depositions and could not find the answer to her question. She decided to be safe and include Rick Everett in the broker and salesperson categories. Time was running out. This extra work caused Carolyn to work late each night. The Friday before the trial, she was not finished with the summary, so she came into the office on Saturday and Sunday to complete it. She finally finished the project Sunday evening and put it on Michael's desk.

Carolyn arrived at the office early on Monday morning to make sure Michael was ready for trial. Michael was not there early but came in at his usual 9:30 A.M. When Carolyn asked him about the trial that morning, Michael said,

"I'm not going to trial on the Twin Lakes real estate case. We settled the case last Wednesday."

Carolyn was furious! This was not the first time this had happened. She immediately set an appointment with the administrator to request a change in supervising attorneys.

1. What were the consequences of Michael's lack of communication?
2. Take a guess at approximately how many hours Carolyn unnecessarily worked on the project. Carolyn's billable rate is $50 an hour. How much money did Michael's actions cost the firm?
3. Carolyn has requested a transfer, but no opening exists for her in any other area of the firm. Carolyn has threatened to quit the firm. If you were the administrator, what would you do to resolve the problem?

4. If you were Carolyn, what would you do?

5. What areas of the team concept are missing here?

3. The Big Bonus

A management policy of Noguchi & Black is that all employees keep all compensation matters confidential. No one knows how much another employee makes or the amount of his raise or bonus.

Noguchi & Black establishes bonuses based on merit. Each legal assistant is required to bill 1,500 hours a year for wages. If a legal assistant bills more than 1,500 hours a year, that legal assistant is rewarded with a bonus according to the number of excess hours billed.

Larry Esteban heard through the grapevine that Elizabeth Rinehart received a very large bonus because of the hundreds of hours of overtime she worked. Larry felt that was strange since it was common knowledge that Elizabeth refused to work overtime. She was never in the office on the weekends Larry was in. Elizabeth was always too busy to help another legal assistant. She appeared to be the last person that should be given a large bonus.

1. What could be the problem here?

2. What elements could have contributed to Elizabeth's bonus?

3. What are the consequences of this problem?

4. How could the problem be avoided?

5. If you were the administrator, what would you do to solve the problem?

4. Evaluation, Please!

Adam Knight is a litigation paralegal for the corporate legal department of Reysack Corporation. His boss, Mary Mlenek, asked him to do a research memorandum on a case involving contributory negligence. Adam was excited about the project because it was the first time he had researched this area of law and he was interested in the subject. He worked very hard on the project, reading all the cases he could find on it. He proudly turned in the project before the deadline.

A week went by without Mary mentioning the memorandum. Adam knew the trial was approaching and was anxious to find out whether the memorandum helped the client. He decided he would ask Mary about it when she got back from court in the afternoon. Before she returned, however, Adam noticed that Stuart Kline, the other litigation paralegal, was in the library doing research and had Adam's memorandum in front of him.

When Adam asked Stuart what he was doing, Stuart replied, "Oh . . . I'm doing research on contributory negligence for Mary."

"But I did that already," said Adam.

"Yes, but . . . Mary said that you completely missed the point and asked me to do it over."

Adam was shocked. He was embarrassed and humiliated in front of a co-worker and felt sure that Stuart thought he did inferior work.

1. What were the consequences of Mary's lack of constructive feedback?

2. What should Mary have done?

3. Imagine that you are Mary and have trouble giving constructive criticism. What do you say to Adam?

4. If you were the office manager, how would you resolve the situation?

5. What area or areas of the team concept are missing?

5. The Deposition Dilemma

Polly Ferraro is a legal assistant with the large firm of Major, Ingles & Hernandez. Her boss, Franklin Rush, informed her that his case was going to trial next Thursday and a few depositions had to be summarized before the trial. She said she would be happy to summarize them but was shocked to see a stack of ninety-five depositions brought into her office.

Perplexed and worried that she could not complete the assignment, Polly immediately started to summarize the depositions. While doing so, she overheard a conversation between Mike Gekeler and Marilyn Ling, two other legal assistants. Mike told Marilyn that he had completed his work and had nothing to do.

Polly hurried into Mike's office, where he was reading a magazine with his feet up on his very empty, very clean desk. She told him of the predicament she was in and asked him to help her with the depositions.

"Summarize depositions? No way! I hate to summarize depositions. I'm a corporate legal assistant, Polly, not a litigation legal assistant," stated Mike smugly. "I told myself I was through summarizing depositions, and I meant it. No, I won't help you with them."

1. What might be the consequences of Mike's lack of cooperation?

2. How might Mike's response ultimately affect the firm and the client?

3. If you were Polly, what would you do?

4. If you were the office manager, what would you do?

5. What area or areas of the team concept are missing?

6. The Demise of Shea & Gould

Shea & Gould, a prominent New York law firm of 230 attorneys, was formed in the early 1960s by William A. Shea, a prominent attorney. Shea Stadium was named after him for his efforts in forming the Mets baseball team. His firm enjoyed a prestigious clientele and was very prosperous.

Problems emerged at his firm in 1985 when he retired as managing partner and there was no one available with the leadership skills necessary to lead the firm. An executive committee was responsible for management decisions that were implemented by various managing partners who lacked the necessary skills to lead the firm. The business was decentralized and diversified.

Dissention among the partners grew, and the firm's structure was chaotic. Although the firm remained profitable, the partners and employees were dissatisfied with the firm's compensation program. Employees were leaving in droves. One partner was quoted as saying, "The firm has no economic problems, no serious debt. What it lacks is a social fabric, harmony as a unit."

A management consultant was retained to create a better compensation structure and a more structured firm government, but it was too late. The firm's intellectual property department defected to join another firm and took $20 million in business with them. Panic set in, and the firm could not recover. It finally dissolved and closed its doors forever. One partner summed it up this way: "A law firm has to exist for more reasons than just making money. Otherwise, you just keep selling out to the highest bidder."

1. What was missing from this firm's governance?
2. What should have been done to stop its demise?
3. What aspects of the CEMEC principle are missing here?
4. What aspects of leadership are missing here?

ASSIGNMENTS

1. For each of the following situations, taken from *Law Office Economics and Management Manual,* volume 1 (published by Clark, Boardman, Callaghan), answer the following questions:

   a. Which of the five Cs are present or lacking?

   b. What motivator is missing, or what demotivator is present?

   c. If you were manager of the firm, what would you do to solve the problem?

   d. With what management function is the problem associated?

   Situation 1: "Sometimes policies set by law firms can be infuriating! In our office, we have a policy of not replacing equipment until it is completely worn out. In my opinion (which is never asked for, incidentally) this is false economy. There are many breakdowns, especially in dictating equipment and computers—causing errors and lost time, costing far more than any money the policy might save. This doesn't count the frustration that comes from retyping copy that has been erased from the computer!"

   Situation 2: "At one time, I was asked to train an individual for a job equal to or better than mine. I did my very best, taking every opportunity to explain, illustrate, and guide him through all the details of his job. But he didn't listen to me. Then, that fateful day came when he really goofed! A procedure he should have followed was ignored. The error came to the attention of my boss. My boss came directly to me and criticized me for not training the new man properly. Can you imagine that? After all the years of faithful service I've given to the firm, my boss had to show me so little respect and confidence!"

   Situation 3: "I have been with our firm for many years. My boss has given me much responsibility, and I feel challenged by the work I have to do. However, my title is still secretary. Clients or other people coming into the office can't recognize me from any one else by my title. Even on the telephone, people refuse to talk to me as soon as they discover that I am a secretary. I am sure I could be of much more service to the firm if my title described what I do—office manager or administrative assistant or something like that. It would also give me a feeling that I am progressing within the firm and my profession."

   Situation 4: "In my work experience, I have been fortunate to have a boss believe that individuals can accept responsibility if it is given properly. She recognized that there are many things in the firm that I can do as well as or better than her or any of the lawyers. So she patiently taught me what to do—and as soon as she saw that I could do it on my own, the job became my responsibility, and I incorporated it into my routine. Because of this trust on her part, I feel greatly motivated and very loyal to her and to the firm."

Situation 5: "For the past eight years, I have worked for and with numerous lawyers and countless law students. I think the biggest dissatisfaction I experienced is the lack of organization on the part of these people. As a legal assistant, I could help organize the office in many ways and relieve the burden of a lawyer. But somehow, this responsibility is not shared. The lawyers feel that their training somehow includes office organization—but no one would ever notice it! They are overburdened with paperwork, visiting clients, and telephone calls. We could help them so much if they would only let us. One doesn't have to have a law degree to organize an office—or do much of the paperwork and telephoning that is necessary. They just have to show a little confidence in us. Instead, they blame us for errors that come from their poor management."

Situation 6: "I am quite certain that the most satisfying experience that I have had in the legal profession has not been working with other people but the extra responsibility given me on occasion. Occasionally, I am given the opportunity to sit down with a yellow pad and see what I can work out on this matter or that. Sometimes, my solutions are accepted with few changes. This makes me feel good— useful to the firm. Also, I am given opportunities to get away from the stale routine of work by traveling out of the city and the state for my firm, taking care of other company business."

Situation 7: "I am a former legal secretary. I enjoy being associated with a profession that helps people in desperate need. This aspect is satisfying and rewarding. But I have always wanted to be closer to the cases, to talk to the people involved, and to know more about the cases I was working on. Finally, the dull routine of typing, filing, and mailing got to me, so I went to paralegal school. After graduation, I expected more challenging assignments, but they never came. The lawyers in my firm still see me as a secretary—not a paralegal."

Situation 8: "Where can I go? I was hired as a legal assistant nine years ago, and I'm still doing much the same work as when I was hired. New legal assistants come into the firm and do much the same work I am doing—and for the same pay. I have no future but to summarize depositions for the rest of my working life. It is a pretty bleak outlook!"

Situation 9: "I began working in law offices over thirty years ago. I was really excited about my job and the people I worked for. It wasn't long until I discovered that there were many things in the office that were off limits to me. I was to do only as I was told and nothing more. There are many courses I could have taken at the university and special courses elsewhere to make myself more valuable to the firm. But the firm did not encourage continuing legal education and would not pay for any courses. Even though I wanted to better myself to benefit the firm, I knew it would be of no use."

2. Talk to two or three of your friends about the environment at their work. Are your friends motivated? If so, why? If not, why not?

3. On the evaluation form shown in Exhibit 3.8, evaluate your boss. If you are not working, evaluate a parent or spouse. Would you recommend this person for a raise?

4. Conduct a human resource audit at your place of employment or home. Are employees or family members 100 percent productive? If not, why not? Could some positions be eliminated or restructured to save money? If so, how? Write a report to your instructor detailing your recommendations for improvement.

5. Prepare a position description for your position at work. If you are not working, prepare a position description for your duties at home or in a club. Ask your supervisor, parent, or club leader as well as your co-workers what their concept of your position is. Do their understandings of your position correspond to yours? What are the differences, if any?

Source: Reprinted with permission from *Law Office Economics & Management Manual* Vol. 1, published by Clark Boardman Callaghan, 155 Pfingsten Road, Deerfield, IL. 60015.

SELF-TEST

How well did you grasp the material in the chapter? Test yourself by answering the following questions and check your answers against the answers found in Appendix A.

1. What is a law firm's most important resource?
2. Why is finding the right place to work important?
3. What two characteristics are a measure of effective management?
4. What are the three main objectives for a law firm?
5. What are the three objectives of a government office?
6. What are the three main objectives of a corporate legal department?
7. What are the external conditions that influence management?
8. What are the internal conditions that influence management?
9. What are the five functions of a personnel manager?
10. What is forecasting?
11. What are the four areas of human resource planning?
12. What is the goal of human resource planning?
13. What is the controlling process?
14. What are the three main elements of control?
15. What happens if management's standards are set too high?
16. What happens if management's standards are set too low?
17. What are the consequences of win-lose management?
18. What is the organization function?
19. What is the leadership function?
20. What is the staffing function?
21. What are the four steps in the hiring process?
22. What are four advantages of promoting from within the firm?
23. How are prospective employees recruited?
24. What questions on employment applications violate federal regulations?
25. What is the ouch formula?
26. What is one method to calm an applicant during an interview?
27. What are some danger signs a manager should look for when interviewing an applicant?
28. What is the CEMEC principle?
29. What is the inhibiting factor of open communication?
30. What is the buddy system?
31. What is a mentor?
32. What two things do poor working conditions produce?
33. What two things do good working conditions produce?
34. Working conditions consist of three things. What are they?
35. What are the two types of evaluation?
36. What is formal evaluation?
37. What is informal evaluation?
38. What are some of the areas considered in a formal performance evaluation?
39. What should a legal assistant do if she or he is unhappy with the formal performance evaluation?
40. What four things do firms consider when establishing a compensation structure?
41. What are raises based on?
42. What are bonuses based on?
43. What is often considered when calculating raises?
44. What do merit raises and bonuses acknowledge?
45. What is a raise or bonus based on tenure?
46. What type of firm usually offers fewer benefits?
47. What does FLSA stand for?
48. What does FLSA do?
49. What does "exempt" mean?
50. What does "nonexempt" mean?
51. What is the basic theory behind the team approach?
52. Studies have shown that the team approach plays an important role in what three things?
53. What are the five Cs of the team approach?
54. What are the three things to which each employee should be committed?
55. Making a commitment requires trust in two things. What are they?
56. What are the keys to competency?
57. Why is continuing legal education important?
58. What attributes increase creativity?
59. Why is the legal business more stressful than other businesses?
60. What is the basis of most personality conflicts?
61. If a legal assistant observes unethical behavior, how should the legal assistant handle the problem?

KEY WORDS

Attrition	FLSA	Nonexempt
Buddy system	Forecasting	Open question
CEMEC principle	Formal evaluation	Ouch formula
Constructive criticism	Hiring specification	Position description
Consumer price index	Human resource audit	Team approach
Ergonomics	Informal evaluation	Win-lose management
Exempt		

The Attorney-Client Relationship

OBJECTIVES

After completion of this chapter, a student should be able to do the following:
- ◆ Describe the variables affecting client relations.
- ◆ Explain a bar association's involvement in client relations.
- ◆ Discuss a lawyer's ethical responsibilities to a client.
- ◆ Explain what clients expect from their lawyers.
- ◆ Describe the various methods lawyers use to attract clients.
- ◆ Describe the difference between public relations and advertising.
- ◆ Identify when an attorney-client relationship begins and ends.
- ◆ Explain how a legal assistant participates in an attorney-client relationship.
- ◆ Define confidentiality, the attorney-client privilege, and the attorney work-product doctrine.
- ◆ Check for conflicts or potential conflicts.
- ◆ Identify the various types of discipline that may be imposed on lawyers.

INTRODUCTION

Law firms would not exist without clients, just as other businesses would not exist without customers. Since the legal business has become more competitive, attracting and retaining clients has become a major part of it—requiring the efforts of each member of a legal team.

Often, a client's first exposure to a law firm is through one of the firm's employees: receptionist, secretary, or legal assistant. A client's first impression of a firm—formed within the first three minutes—is often dependent on interaction with employees. An unfriendly receptionist greeting a potential client in an unprofessional manner influences whether the client will retain a firm. If clients do not retain a firm, the firm will cease to exist.

An attorney-client relationship is personal. Establishing rapport with a client so that the client will trust a firm is an essential element of this relationship. Although an attorney has the ultimate responsibility to maintain an attorney-client relationship, the attorney's employees play a major role in positive—or negative—attorney-client relationships. Actually, the relationship is between a client and a legal team. Legal assistants have a direct responsibility to participate in an attorney-client relationship.

Legal assistants are not ultimately responsible for an attorney-client relationship. However, for legal assistants to have a complete understanding of how a law office functions, they must understand this vital area of law office management. They must understand the boundaries within which a lawyer must function because a legal assistant must also function within those boundaries. For a legal assistant to spot potential ethics problems, she or he must have knowledge of the parameters of an attorney-client relationship.

As explained in Chapter 3, one goal of a law firm is to provide quality legal services to a client. Another goal is to ensure the firm's profitability. An attorney-client relationship is directly related to these goals. Positive attorney-client relationships are rewards for quality legal services. Satisfied clients pay their bills and recommend others to a firm, which ensures the firm's profitability.

The purpose of this chapter is to provide an overview of the unique relationship between a client and a legal team. First, this chapter will discuss the variables that affect an attorney-client relationship, including the roles of a bar association, an attorney, a legal assistant, and a client. Second, it will describe the various methods firms use to obtain clients. Third, it will examine the five major elements of an attorney-client relationship—the five Cs. Finally, the chapter will review attorney discipline—the consequences of not adhering to ethical guidelines concerning an attorney-client relationship. Throughout, the chapter will present ethical guidelines concerning an attorney-client relationship.

VARIABLES AFFECTING CLIENT RELATIONS

Before the 1970s, lawyers enjoyed fairly stable relationships with their clients. Most firms had an ongoing relationship with their clients that lasted for many years. This guaranteed a secure client base for a firm, and a client was guaranteed legal services from attorneys who understood the client's business and legal needs. During this time, the demand for lawyers exceeded the supply of lawyers. Because of this, law firms were managed to satisfy lawyers' needs.

Since the 1970s, however, certain variables have affected the traditional attorney-client relationship. Firms that previously rendered services to an ongoing and stable clientele have found that relationship threatened by economics, a demand for varied specialties, marketing, and business management changes. For law firms to succeed in the 1990s, they must be managed to satisfy clients' needs.

The economic flux of the United States has caused changes in the economics of the practice of law and business in general. Higher overhead and equipment costs have raised the price of legal services to the point that the average middle-class person cannot afford them. Large corporations, in an attempt to reduce their legal costs, have hired their own in-house attorneys, decreasing the demand for outside legal services. Law has become more complex, which has expanded the need for legal specialties. Increased government regulations have burdened businesses, which has caused them to turn to legal specialists for assistance.

To add to these pressures, the number of lawyers in the United States continues to increase. A client now has many choices of lawyers, and the supply of lawyers exceeds the demand. Young, more aggressive lawyers with impressive skills have caught the eye of many clients. This has caused traditional law firms to enter an area once forbidden for established, sophisticated firms: marketing and advertising.

Another change that occurred in the two decades leading up to the early 1990s is the development of laws that define, govern, and protect a client. An attorney is now bound by rules that have been established by legislatures and bar associations that set parameters and guidelines for an attorney-client relationship and provide for remedies if a client is damaged by an attorney.

Role of Bar Associations

Attorney-client relationships, as well as other areas of a lawyer's role in society, are governed by state bar associations. Every state bar association has adopted a code of professional responsibility by which every lawyer in that state must abide. This code

Joint venture: A grouping of two or more persons for a common goal.

governs an attorney's conduct in various areas, including an attorney-client relationship. The code of professional responsibility provides a **joint venture** approach to the attorney-client relationship and provides a model by which the responsibilities in any representation are allocated between the attorney and the client.

The American Bar Association (ABA) adopted rules of ethics known as the Model Code of Professional Responsibility (Model Code). Originally adopted in 1969, it was last amended in 1980. In 1983, this code was replaced by the Model Rules of Professional Conduct (Model Rules), amended in 1987 and 1989. A lawyer's professional responsibility to clients is described in the ABA's Model Rules as well as in statutory and case law. These rules act as a framework to guide an attorney in the role of lawyer.

The ABA is a voluntary national organization. Because a lawyer does not have to belong, the ABA has no authority to bind a lawyer to its rules. However, individual state bar associations have adopted the ABA's rules as their code of professional responsibility.

Some state bar associations have adopted the ABA's Model Rules entirely, with no changes. Other states have adopted those rules in part, making amendments as they see fit. Still other states have adopted the ABA's Model Code, in whole or in part, without replacing it with the new Model Rules. And other states have established their own ethical rules, using the ABA's rules as a guide. Always check an individual state's rules before relying on the ABA's.

Compulsory organization: An organization to which all persons of the same class must belong.

Many state bar associations are **compulsory organizations.** For these associations, every lawyer in the state must belong to the association and abide by its code of ethics.

Role of the Lawyer

Lawyers are clients' representatives, officers of the legal system, and public citizens having special responsibilities for the quality of justice. As a client's representative, a lawyer performs three functions—the three As: adviser, advocate, and agent.

Adviser　As an adviser to a client, a lawyer will do five things:

◆ Exercise independent judgment for the client
◆ Be candid no matter how unpleasant the advice may be
◆ Discourage illegal or fraudulent conduct
◆ Inform the client of adverse consequences
◆ Apprise the client of the proposed course of action

ETHICS ALERT

Model Rule 2.1 states:

In representing a client, a lawyer shall exercise independent professional judgment and render candid advice. In rendering advice, a lawyer may refer not only to law, but to other considerations such as moral, economic, social and political factors that may be relevant to the client's situation.

The client sets the objective of an attorney-client relationship and makes the ultimate decisions. For the client to do so intelligently, the lawyer must inform the client of the relevant facts and issues and advise the client of the law regarding those facts and issues. A lawyer may be disciplined if he is negligent in advising a client of all relevant issues of the case (see *Shear v. Hornsby & Whisenand,* 17 Fla. L. Weekly D1897 [3d Dist. Ct. App. opinion filed August 1992]).

Advocate　As a client's advocate, a lawyer will carry out three obligations:

◆ Represent the client before a court or tribunal
◆ Make reasonable efforts to expedite litigation consistent with the interest of the client
◆ Not bring a claim that has no basis in fact, to harass another

Rule 3.1 of the Model Rules states:

A lawyer shall not bring or defend a proceeding or assert or controvert an issue therein, unless there is a basis for so doing that is not frivolous, which includes a good faith argument for an extension, modification or reversal of existing law. A lawyer for the defendant in a criminal proceeding or the respondent in a proceeding that could result in incarceration, may nevertheless so defend the proceeding as to require that every element of the case be established.

An advocate has a duty to use legal procedure and substantive law to the fullest benefit of a client. However, an advocate also has a duty to society and the legal system. An attorney also must act in the best interests of society and uphold the integrity of the legal system.

An advocate has an obligation to reject frivolous cases that take up a court's time and resources. A case is considered frivolous if an action is taken primarily to harass a person or to injure another maliciously. An example of a malicious action commenced to harass or injure another is a domestic case in which a woman consistently drags her former husband into court every two or three months seeking an increase in child support, when a need for the increase cannot be supported by the facts.

A matter is also considered frivolous if a lawyer is unable to make a good-faith argument for a change in existing law. If a lawyer believes that a law or court ruling is wrong, the lawyer may challenge that law through the courts. If the challenge has no merit, the proceeding is considered frivolous.

OF INTEREST . . .

Case was Frivolous

A Pennsylvania man was fired by U.S. Steel in 1968. He felt the firing was unjustified and sued U.S. Steel for wrongful termination. He lost the case in 1971, but continued his feud with U.S. Steel for 28 years—until 1999. When he realized that his battle with U.S. Steel was futile, he blamed God for not bringing him justice in his dispute with U.S. Steel.

The complaint alleged "God was the sovereign ruler of the universe and took no corrective action against the leaders of U.S. Steel for their extremely serious wrong which ruined my life." It also complained that God failed to restore his youth and grant him the guitar-playing ability of famous guitarists. God also failed to resurrect his mother and pet pigeon. The plaintiff argued that if God failed to appear in court, he must lose by default.

In addition to God, the complaint listed other defendants including former presidents Ronald Reagan and George Bush, several television networks, all fifty states, every single American, the Federal Communications Commission, all federal judges and the 100th through 105th congresses. The plaintiff represented himself and appeared in pro per. U.S. District Judge Norman Mordue found the lawsuit frivolous.

Agent As a client's agent, a lawyer will perform four duties:

◆ Seek results advantageous to the client while being honest and fair with others.
◆ Be a spokesperson for the client.
◆ Negotiate on the client's behalf.
◆ Abide by the client's decisions after informing the client of the issues of the case and the ramifications of the client's decision.

Rule 1.2(a) of the Model Rules states:

A lawyer shall abide by a client's decision concerning the objective of representation . . . and shall consult with the client as to the means by which they are to be pursued. A lawyer shall abide by a client's decision whether to accept an offer of settlement of a matter. In a criminal case, the lawyer shall abide by the client's decision, after consultation with the lawyer as to a plea to be entered, whether to waive jury trial and whether the client will testify.

It is generally agreed that a lawyer has ultimate authority and responsibility to control the procedural elements and tactics of a client's case. However, when it comes to a settlement or binding a client to any provision of a contract, the client must consent. Lawyers have been disciplined for making decisions beyond their authority, against their client's wishes, and prejudicial to their client's interests. States differ on this subject. The extent of a lawyer's authority to bind a client is set forth in state statutes.

Role of the Legal Assistant

The attorney is ultimately responsible for an attorney-client relationship. The client may sue the attorney if a breach occurs in an attorney-client relationship. If a legal assistant participates in a breach of an attorney-client relationship or violates any ethical rule, the attorney will be disciplined since the attorney is responsible for the legal assistant's actions.

ETHICS ALERT

Legal assistants are not bound by the rules of professional conduct of state bar associations. They are, however, considered lawyers' agents. As such, *every legal assistant is ethically obligated to comply with the code of professional responsibility.* Therefore, legal assistants must be familiar with the ABA Model Rules as well as the code of professional responsibility of the state.

OF INTEREST . . .

Ten Tips for Working with Clients

1. Keep clients informed.
2. Forward all correspondence to the client.
3. Maintain a chronology and daily diary of events.
4. Prepare a list of client demands.
5. Complete inventories and financial information sheets.
6. Ask clients to assist with depositions and interrogatories.
7. Treat opposing counsel and party with courtesy.
8. Thoroughly explain all proceedings to the client.
9. Prepare client for depositions and court appearances.
10. Prepare the client for mediation and settlement conferences.

Role of the Client

Clients' perceptions of the quality of legal services they receive are based on several factors. At a conference of the American Marketing Association, three professors reported the results of their study into how business executives evaluate outside legal counsel. The 341 respondents were chief executive officers (CEOs) or general counsels of large corporations. This survey indicated that the following were important to these CEOs, listed in order of importance:

◆ Results obtained from a firm's work
◆ Counsel and advice
◆ Expertise in a specific area
◆ Personal interest taken in a client's legal matters
◆ Quality of a written product
◆ Keeping a client informed of a firm's progress

Of course, clients' opinions will vary by industry and individual. Another survey was taken of sixty-five CEOs of large Chicago companies. The following results were important to those CEOs, in order of importance:

◆ A compatible personality
◆ Proven experience in a particular issue
◆ Evidence of giving clients proper attention
◆ Accessibility
◆ Understanding a client's priorities

The four items clients generally want most from attorneys are commitment, integrity, commentary, and fairness in fees. Clients have listed commitment to their case as the most important element of an attorney-client relationship. Surveys have shown that clients are not as interested in results as they are in an attorney's zeal in representing them. Most important is that an attorney show an interest in a client's case and in the client as a person.

Surveys show that cost is not an important criteria when clients evaluate legal counsel. A busy Washington, D.C., lawyer, overwhelmed with work, decided to raise her fees so that she could take on less work without losing money. After she raised her fees, her workload did not decrease but continued to increase.

Clients want lawyers who will help them meet their business or personal goals. To do this, a lawyer must take a personal interest in a client and the client's business. Often, a busy lawyer with a heavy trial schedule does not have the time to take a personal interest in clients. Legal assistants can help lawyers by conveying to clients a message that a firm is interested in them.

Since the advent of the Total Quality Management (TQM) movement, law firms and businesses in general have focused on customer service and satisfaction as a major element of their company policy. Law firms have found that despite brilliant legal work done on the client's behalf, some clients were dissatisfied with the service because it lacked that "personal" touch. According to Milton W. Zwicker in his article "What Clients Really Want from Their Lawyers," clients want the following ten traits from their lawyers:

◆ Really listen to what the client has to say.
◆ Ask the client what the client thinks about the subject.
◆ Do not belittle or reject the client's concerns.
◆ Treat the client like a person, not a file.
◆ Speak to the client, not "at" the client.
◆ Tell the client how much the legal services will cost.
◆ Be available when the client needs the attorney.
◆ Do not brag about past successes; rather, show the client expertise.
◆ Keep the client informed.
◆ Let the client know that the legal team cares about the client's case.

CULTIVATING CLIENTS

Satisfied clients are the best source of new clients for a firm. In general, 50 percent of new clients come from the recommendations of existing and former clients, 30 percent come from the recommendations of people who are not clients but would be if the occasion should arise (friends, associates, relatives), and 20 percent come from marketing activities.

Marketing activities consist of client surveys, advertising, and other promotional activities.

Marketing Activities

A firm's marketing activities are stated in a marketing plan. This plan is an essential element of successful client cultivation. It analyzes several variables that affect a firm's practice, such as external and internal conditions. The beginning of the planning stage includes gathering information about a firm, a firm's clients, and a firm's employees. This requires asking who, what, when, where, and why questions. A client questionnaire is often sent to clients to determine their perception of a firm. Once all the necessary information is gathered, marketing strategies are developed and placed into the plan.

Marketing plans are time consuming and expensive, and, as of this writing, only 41 percent of the law firms that market their services have a marketing plan.

Client Surveys   As client satisfaction becomes increasingly important to law firms, they are conducting client surveys on a regular basis to assess client satisfaction and identify areas of future need. Client surveys are gaining popularity as an essential element of a marketing strategy for law firms. An example of a client survey appears in Exhibit 4.1. For an article on how to develop a client survey, see Appendix F.

A marketing manager analyzes the information from client surveys to determine a firm's strengths, weaknesses, opportunities, and roadblocks. This is called **positioning** a firm. A position statement includes a description of a firm's position in the legal community as it relates to competitive firms and resources.

A firm then establishes a **target market** for its strategic plan. A target market is a group the firm wants to attract as clients. After an analysis of a firm's position, a marketing plan directed to the target market is developed.

Positioning:
Determining a firm's strengths and weaknesses in relation to those of other firms in the community.

Target market: A group of people a firm wants as clients.

Marketing Strategies   Average attorneys have little or no education in marketing strategies and find themselves dealing in a foreign area when asked to prepare a marketing plan for a firm. Most attorneys do not want to be involved in marketing activities. Many attorneys have an aversion to marketing. Attorneys seem to object to the term *marketing* and use other terms, such as *business development* or *practice de-*

Client Questionnaire
Black, White & Greene LLP
1212 Main St.
Anytown, IL

Thank you very much for consulting our office regarding your legal problem. We appreciate your trust and confidence. We are interested in improving our legal services and would appreciate your assisting us by completing this questionnaire. Your response will be confidential. Please use the following measurements: 5 = extraordinary, 4 = excellent, 3 = good, 2 = fair, 1 = poor.

1. Did you feel our office personnel were friendly and treated you courteously?
2. Why did you select our office originally?
3. Did our office keep you adequately informed regarding your legal matter? If not, do you have any suggestions on how we might improve this area?
4. What was the nature of the legal work we did for you?
5. Did you feel the lawyer spent sufficient time with you on your legal matter?
6. Did you feel that sufficient attention and time were devoted to your legal matter?
7. Were your telephone inquiries answered to your satisfaction?
8. Were you satisfied with your dealings with the office staff?
9. Do you feel that our fee for services was reasonable for the work performed?
10. We would appreciate any comments that you might have that will help us improve our service to our clients. Please use the reverse side of this sheet if necessary.

THANK YOU very much for your time and courtesy in completing this questionnaire.

EXHIBIT 4.1   Sample Client Survey

velopment, said a marketing director at a midsize firm. Attorneys, feeling unfamiliar in this area, are hiring professional marketing people to handle marketing strategies for a firm (see Chapter 2). The emergence of this new professional for law firms has a promising future as attorney marketing becomes an integral part of law firm management. Law firm marketing directors have various titles, including director of client services, director of communications and business development, and economic development director.

TRENDS ▶▶▶

Attorney Brokers?

The importance of marketing for law firms is increasing. To remain competitive, law firms must increase their marketing budgets and put a greater emphasis on marketing activities. When ethical restraints against solicitation are relaxed, law firms will have their own sales force like other businesses. There will be an emergence of "for profit" referral services to help businesses find the right attorney. Companies already go through brokers and agents for insurance and real estate. What about an attorney broker?

Law firms use various methods to attract clients. Marketing personnel go to great lengths to position a law firm to a specific target market. Once a target market has been determined, a firm's efforts and money are directed toward attracting those clients to the firm. Methods for attracting clients to the firm include advertising in print, radio, television and the Internet; publishing law firm newsletters and brochures; sponsoring seminars; and providing leadership for community organizations.

Some firms involve employees, including legal assistants, in the marketing process. Once a plan has been developed, assignments are delegated to a firm's employees. Among the marketing tasks a legal assistant can perform are the following:

◆ Organize marketing activities, such as seminars and company brochures
◆ Measure marketing progress as results
◆ Question clients and former clients about their level of satisfaction with a firm
◆ Collect and maintain written materials about a firm and send them to clients
◆ Collect legislation and other information that affects a client and send it to the client
◆ Collect success stories about the firm and its attorneys and insert them into a company brochure
◆ Create and maintain a client relations database

Appendix D contains an article written by Jay Foonberg, Esq., titled "111 Ways a Nonlawyer Can Help a Firm in Marketing and Client Relations."

Advertising

"All business entrusted to us will be attended to with promptness and fidelity." The year was 1853, and this ad appeared in the *Iroquois Journal* as reported by *U.S. News and World Report* on December 24, 1984 (p. 10). It was placed by a young attorney, Abraham Lincoln, and his partner. In addition to newspaper advertising, Lincoln wrote letters soliciting business from the railroads, the wealthiest clients in Illinois in the 1800s. Such advertising was common at that time in the United States.

In 1908, the ABA adopted the first national standards for ethical conduct governing lawyers titled the Canons of Professional Ethics. These canons were patterned after the first code of ethics for lawyers, adopted by the Alabama Bar Association in 1887. Canon 27 banned lawyer advertising, including solicitation. The canons were adopted by individual states to control the conduct of lawyers and their marketing efforts. This was done to avoid "extravagant, artful, self-laudatory brashness" that could mislead laypersons and cause public distrust of the legal system. It was assumed that every lawyer had an established clientele that would spread the word of the lawyer's skill and abilities, thereby making advertising unnecessary. It was considered demeaning of the profession to advertise. It was also believed that advertisements had a negative effect on society. For example, the ABA felt that advertising divorce services might encourage the breakdown of the family unit.

In the 1970s, public interest groups and groups of lawyers began to question the validity of the advertising ban relative to the Sherman Antitrust Act and the free-speech guarantees of the First and Fourteenth Amendments to the U.S. Constitution.

"Do you need a lawyer? Legal services at very reasonable fees." The year was 1976, and this ad appeared in the *Arizona Republic.* It was placed by two young attorneys, Van O'Steen and John Bates, who opened a legal clinic in Phoenix. They were trying to attract the below-average to middle-income client in need of legal assistance.

The ad resulted in disciplinary action by the Arizona State Bar Association against the two Phoenix attorneys to suspend them from practicing law. The case, *Bates v. State Bar of Arizona,* 433 U.S. 350 (1977), was heard by the U.S. Supreme Court, which ruled that the ban on lawyer advertising was a violation of First Amendment guarantees of lawyers' right to advertise. The Court further found that the advertising restriction on lawyers was a restraint of trade. Justice Harry A. Blackmun wrote for the majority and declared that the First Amendment guaranteed lawyers the right to advertise. The primary dissenter was former Chief Justice Warren E. Burger, who was appalled at the prospect of his colleagues being involved in a price war. He insisted that "the public needs protection from the unscrupulous and incompetent practitioner anxious to prey on the uninformed." Justice Burger, until his retirement in 1986, continued to discourage lawyer advertising. In a speech made at a convention of the ABA in 1985, Justice Burger said, "My advice to the public is never, never, never, under any circumstances, engage the services of a lawyer who advertises." He went on to label advertising as pure shysterism and to say that he would dig ditches before advertising.

After the *Bates* decision, the ABA was faced with a dilemma. The *Bates* decision established a lawyer's right to advertise but did not address what type of advertising was appropriate. It quickly went to work to establish the ABA Task Force on Advertising (currently the ABA Commission on Lawyer Advertising), which conducted public hearings within six weeks of the *Bates* decision. It recommended two alternative amendments to the Model Code of Professional Responsibility to allow attorney advertising. Although it recognized that it could not prohibit attorney advertising, its goal was to impose strict regulations. The proposals adopted in February 1978 included a list of twenty-five types of information lawyers were permitted to communicate in an advertisement. Included in the list were provisions allowing the announcement of fields of practice, professional memberships, foreign-language ability, and six provisions governing fees. The list was preceded by a requirement that any such information be presented in a "dignified manner." The term *dignified manner* was further defined in later case law.

Lawyers' advertisements began to test the regulations. A California lawyer ran a score card of his murder trials and their dispositions in a newspaper. Another attorney, Ken Hur, ran a television ad in Madison, Wisconsin, which he played a convict whose final words from the electric chair were that he wished he would have called Hur's legal clinic. A Connecticut firm ran an ad of an actor taking a chain saw to furniture while a voice-over talked about better ways to divide community property. Each of these ads was subject to scrutiny by the state bars, which tried to ban them. In 1980, the U.S. Supreme Court heard the case of *Central Hudson Gas & Electric Corporation v. Public Service Commission of New York,* 447 U.S. 557 (1980). In that case, the Supreme Court developed a four-part test to determine whether a state's restriction of lawyer advertising was unconstitutional. It ruled that in order to enjoy First Amendment protection:

TECH TIPS
Marketing Software

Software has been developed that automates routine marketing-related tasks. They can track histories of contacts and generate follow-up lists and reminders to ensure that contacts are not lost. Firms can plan campaigns or visit contacts regularly. The following is a sample of related software.

Legal Ease—Cole Valley Software, Inc.
Interface—Interface Software, Inc.
Consumer Advice—www.myservice.com

Software mentioned in this sidebar is for informational purposes only and is not for the purpose of endorsing products.

◆ The advertisement must not concern unlawful activity or be misleading
◆ There must be a substantial state interest in the regulation
◆ The regulation must directly advance the asserted interest
◆ The court will ask whether the regulation is more extensive than necessary

ABA Model Rule 7.2 regulates lawyers' advertising activities by imposing the following guidelines:

ETHICS ALERT

(a) . . . [A] lawyer may advertise services through public media, such as a telephone directory, legal directory, newspaper or other periodical, outdoor advertising, radio or television, or through written or recorded communication.
(b) A copy or recording of an advertisement or communication shall be kept for two years after its last dissemination along with a record of when and where it was used.
(c) A lawyer shall not give anything of value to a person for recommending the lawyer's services except that a lawyer may:
    1. pay the reasonable costs of advertisements or communications permitted by this Rule;
    2. pay the usual charges of a not-for-profit lawyer referral service or legal service organization; and
    3. pay for a law practice in accordance with Rule 1.17.
(d) Any communication made pursuant to this rule shall include the name of at least one lawyer responsible for its content.

In addition to the ABA's Model Rules, states have devised their own rules concerning attorney advertisements. Every state now has incorporated advertising regulations in their ethics rules. In fact, in the fifteen-month period from April 1991 to June 1992, more advertising regulatory activity took place than in the fifteen years since the *Bates* decision. The Supreme Court's expansion of commercial free speech, coupled with aggressive regulatory efforts, ensures that the advertising debate will continue into the foreseeable future.

Have lawyers changed their mind about marketing through advertising? The 1989 Illinois Institute of Technology study "Attitudes and Opinions on Marketing Legal Services—Survey of Lawyers in Chicago" found the following:

◆ Lawyers feel anxious and apprehensive about marketing.
◆ Lawyers feel that advertising increases legal fees.
◆ Radio and television advertisements are liked the least.
◆ Community involvement and "getting around" are the preferred methods of marketing.

Attorneys have used the following advertising techniques: print media, radio, television, and the Internet.

Print Media Advertising in print media includes letterheads, newspapers, periodicals, and the Yellow Pages. In regulating print media advertisements, the ABA adopted Model Rule 7.1:

> A Lawyer shall not make a false or misleading communication about the lawyer or the lawyer's services. A communication is false or misleading if it:
> (a) contains a material misrepresentation of fact or law, or omits a fact necessary to make the statement considered as whole or materially misleading;
> (b) is likely to create an unjustified expectation about results the lawyer can achieve, or states or implies that the lawyer can achieve results by means that violate the Rules of Professional Conduct, or other law; or
> (c) compares the lawyer's services with other lawyers' services, unless the comparison can be factually substantiated.

Letterheads: Although not circulated among the public like other, more conventional print advertising, an attorney's letterhead has been determined to be an advertising medium and therefore is subject to Model Rule 7.1. The material placed on an attorney's letterhead may not be false or misleading.

Rules regarding specialty advertising vary by state. In those states that have certified specialist programs, only attorneys who have passed an exam in that area may advertise themselves as a certified specialist in that area of law (see Chapter 2). Some states, especially those with no specialist program, prohibit the use of the term *specialist* on letterheads and promotional material. ABA Model Rule 7.4 states in a pertinent part:

> A lawyer may communicate the fact that the lawyer does or does not practice in particular fields of law. A lawyer shall not state or imply that the lawyer has been recognized or certified as a specialist in a particular field of law except . . . (c)(1) if such certification is granted by the appropriate regulatory authority to grant such certification. . . .

Illinois attorney Gary E. Peel indicated on his letterhead that he was "certified as a civil trial specialist by the National Board of Trial Advocacy." The Illinois Attorney Registration and Disciplinary Commission accused Peel of violating its ethical rules pertaining to the specialist prohibition. The Illinois Supreme Court agreed and said that the title was misleading (*In re Peel*, 126 Ill. 2d 397 [1989]). The U.S. Supreme Court heard the case and disagreed with the Illinois ruling (*Peel v. Illinois*, 110 S.Ct. 2281 [1990]). The Court ruled that a state cannot completely ban statements that are not misleading, such as certification as a specialist by bona fide organizations such as the National Board of Trial Advocacy. Illinois and other states were forced to amend their rules to accommodate the U.S. Supreme Court's ruling.

TRENDS ▸▸▸

Attorneys' Letterheads Less Traditional

Traditionally, law firm letterheads had the same style: firm name centered at the top of the page in black with partners' and associates' names listed. In 1992, Baker & McKenzie became the first major firm to have its name in a brilliant red color across the top of the stationery. Now, law firms are having stationery printed in two colors and are creating firm logos and letterheads with a less traditional look. Partners' and associates' names are being left off the letterhead. Producing new letterheads every time there was a change in the firm proved to be too expensive. Another money-saving trend is to print the letterhead on laser printers at the same time a letter is printed. However, a survey conducted by Altman Weil Pensa titled "Comparative Study of Law Firm Identity Systems" indicated that such practices make a poor impression on clients.

SHELDON S. GOODMAN

ATTORNEY AT LAW

A PROFESSIONAL CORPORATION

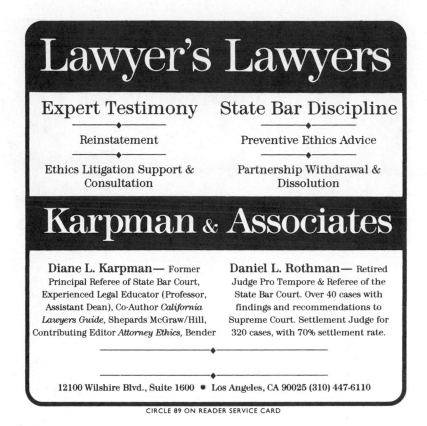

EXHIBIT 4.2 Ad from a Bar Association Periodical (*California Lawyer*)

Reprinted with permission of Karpman & Associates.

Newspapers: Advertising in the newspaper was the original method lawyers used to reach the public. The ads originally appeared in the classifieds section of a newspaper, but in the 1980s, lawyers have found that a much more lucrative location is the business page. Now, attorney ads are found in all areas of the newspaper.

Periodicals: Law firms also advertise in various periodicals, including magazines and newsletters. Once a firm's target market is identified, ads are placed in periodicals directed to that market. For example, an attorney specializing in defending attorneys in discipline proceedings would place an ad in bar association periodicals, such as the ad shown in Exhibit 4.2. A firm specializing in construction defect litigation would place an ad in a homeowners' association newsletter, such as the ad shown in Exhibit 4.3.

Yellow Pages: The most common method of attorney advertising is a listing in the Yellow Pages of the telephone book (see Exhibit 4.4). More lawyers advertise in the Yellow Pages than any other method by an overwhelming percentage. In some communities, more space in the Yellow Pages is dedicated to lawyer ads than to any other product or service. According to the ABA Commission on Lawyer Advertising, people find attorneys through the Yellow Pages more than any other method of selection, more so than bar-sponsored lawyer referral services, prepaid legal plans, and other forms of advertising. The Yellow Pages Publishers Association reported that consumers looked up attorneys about 350 million times, making it the eighth most frequently referenced classification in the Yellow Pages.

Most attorneys who advertise in the Yellow Pages feel that their money is well spent. Pennsylvania attorney Mark David Frankel reserved the entire back cover of two Yellow Page directories. He said, "Since we began using the back cover in April 1994, we've seen a 75 percent increase in clients. And they're the types of cases we want."

However, there are some disadvantages to Yellow Pages advertising. According to Los Angeles sole practitioner Susan Lavian, a full-page Yellow Pages ad is expensive. A full-page, black-and-yellow ad with a photo in the Los Angeles Yellow Pages costs about $6,000 a month. In addition, there are added overhead costs in hiring additional

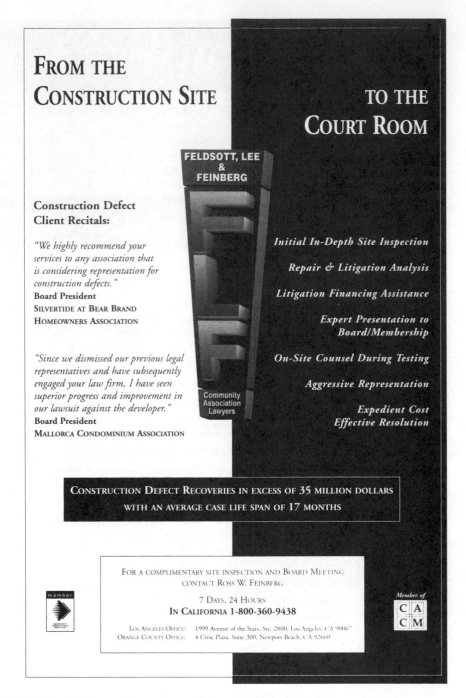

EXHIBIT 4.3 Ad from a Homeowners' Association Newsletter
Reprinted with permission of Feldsott, Lee & Feinberg.

staff to screen calls and follow up on the calls. Ms. Lavian indicated that out of every 100 calls, 25 percent are cases she would take, 10 percent bring in referral income, and the remainder are put on her mailing list.

Radio Advertising on the radio is becoming more common. Often, law firms will sponsor segments of a radio program, such as news or special announcements. Producing a radio talk show about the law, with an attorney moderator, is a popular method of exposing a firm to the public. The Los Angeles firm of Sheppard, Mullin, Richter & Hampton sponsors *The NewsHour with Jim Lehrer* for about $200,000 a year. The firm reported that the sponsorship has surpassed print advertising in terms of name recognition.

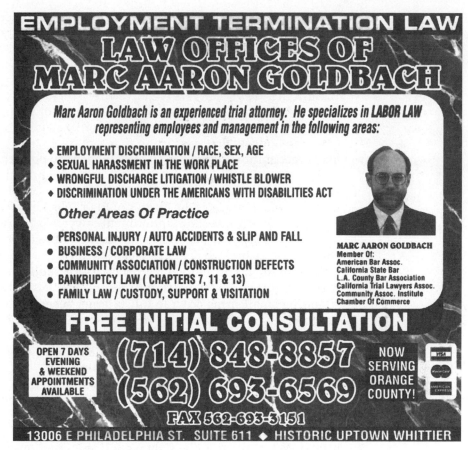

EXHIBIT 4.4 Ad from the Yellow Pages

Television Lawyers take advantage of the public exposure afforded them by television advertisement. Revenues for lawyer television advertising were $82 million in 1989 and exceeded $100 million in 1990. Attorneys who advertise on television have reported a return of $6 to $10 on every dollar spent on television advertising. One firm that advertises its personal injury services reported a 300 percent return on each dollar spent on television advertising.

This type of advertising has come under the scrutiny of state bar associations, and many attorneys have been disciplined for advertising messages that mislead the public. For example, an attorney advertised, "If you are injured in an automobile accident, or at work, call me. No fee until I win for you." The California State Bar found this advertising to be misleading because, even though the case was a **contingency** case, the client incurred fees for costs, such as filing fees, investigation fees, depositions, and so on. The attorney was required to stop this advertisement and develop a new one. The new advertisement said the same thing, except it had a disclaimer stating, "Does not include fees for costs."

Concerns about television advertising have prompted state legislation. The Iowa and New Jersey Supreme Courts require that television advertisements be "predominantly informational." The key consideration in evaluating the content of lawyer advertising is that it not be false, misleading, or deceptive. Many state bar associations have special task forces to regulate lawyers' television ads, and some have considered banning television ads, especially dramatic ones. The ABA Commission on Advertising presented awards to firms with the most dignified television ads. The Awards for Dignity in Lawyer Advertising was established in 1992 to illustrate what the commission feels is a dignified ad.

Television advertising was largely responsible for the legal clinic's success. Jacoby & Meyers Legal Clinic started advertising on television in the early 1970s and quickly expanded to 150 offices nationwide by 1977. It sparked their competitors to follow

Contingency: A case in which a lawyer receives a percentage of the recovery rather than a flat amount of money.

suit, resulting in many television ads in the 1980s. Since the 1980s, however, lawyer television ads have decreased substantially. Legal networks have emerged in reaction to the high costs of television advertising. Individual lawyers belong to such networks and contribute advertising dollars to the network, which then places the ad on television.

Currently, fewer lawyers are advertising on television because they find that it is not cost-effective. Since television ads hit a lot of people who do not purchase legal services, the high cost of television advertising is not a wise expenditure in an advertising budget. However, if the firm's purpose is to promote its image and create name recognition, television advertising is very powerful.

Another method of promoting a firm through television is to host a television show. Frederic G. Levin of Levin, Middlebrooks, Mabie, Thomas, Mayes & Mitchell in Pensacola, Florida, is the creator of Blab Television, which produces *Law Line.* On this show, Levin interviews prominent lawyers on various legal subjects of interest to the public. Levin indicates that in the approximately five years following the show's first airing, the firm's gross fees tripled.

The *Internet:* The Internet has become an essential tool for law firms. A 1998 ABA survey reported that 99 percent of responding large law firms and 80 percent of responding small firms provide full Internet access to their employees. Lawyers use the Internet to locate experts, research opinions, retrieve court rules and information, and obtain continuing education credits. Lawyers also use the internet to advertise their services and promote their firms (see Exhibit 4.5). This form of electronic advertising is called **netvertising.**

Netvertising:
Advertising products or services on the Internet.

In November 1994, five law firms had home pages on the Internet. Seven months later, that figure grew to 500. Lawyers' presence on the Internet has grown 341,000 percent. A 1997 ABA survey indicated that 61 percent of its respondents marketed services on the Internet, and that number increases each month. If a lawyer does not have a Web site, most likely they are listed in an on-line directory, such as Martindale Hubbell, which lists 900,000 attorneys on its Internet site (www.martindale-hubbell.com). According to a 1999 study conducted by Pitney Bowes Management

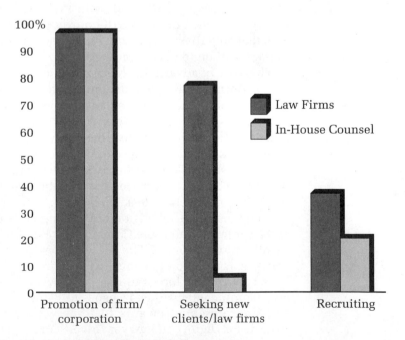

EXHIBIT 4.5 Why Law Offices Have Web Sites

Source: Pitney Bowes Management Services study on the use of technology in the legal profession; 200 lawyers at the nation's largest law firm and 100 in-house counsel at major corporations were surveyed.

Services, 95 percent of firms use their Web site to promote the firm, 75 percent use it for client development, and 32 percent use it to recruit new associates.

However, marketing over the Internet poses ethical problems. The ABA has not issued a specific rule for Internet advertising, but it applies Model Rule 7.1 to Web sites. About twenty states in early 1999 issued ethics opinions regarding the Internet. Most states have concluded that advertising on the Internet is acceptable if it complies with their other advertising guidelines.

Since the Internet has no state boundaries, it is difficult to determine which state rules apply. To determine which rules apply to a Web site, the following factors are considered:

◆ The state in which members of the firm are authorized to practice;

◆ The state in which the firm is seeking clients; and

◆ The state in which the firm practices; and

◆ The Web site's content.

If the Web site's content is for information purposes only (e.g., newsletters, articles, or public information), chances are that it would not fall under the jurisdiction of advertising rules. An example of a law firm Web site is shown in Exhibit 4.6. If the Web site's content is for the purpose of attracting clients (e.g., attorney biographies or areas of specialties), it would fall under the jurisdiction of the state's ethics rules.

Virtually every state has incorporated Rule 7.1 into its ethics rules prohibiting false and misleading information and lawyer comparisons in advertisements. As such, phrases used in Web sites such as "best lawyers," "highly qualified," and "expert" have been determined to violate Model Rule 7.1 since they serve to compare attorneys to other attorneys. As of this writing, only Texas and Florida have specific rules regarding Web site advertising. These rules require the Web page to be submitted to them for approval before they are posted.

Many lawyers view their Web sites as an electronic brochure. While some aspects of a Web site is analogous to print advertising, other elements are unique to cyberspace. In the very near future, the legal profession will promulgate rules specifically directed toward the use of the Internet to cultivate clients.

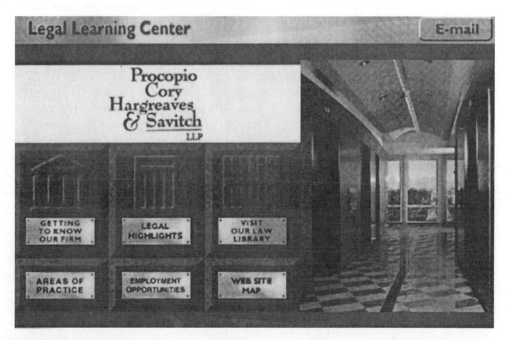

EXHIBIT 4.6 Example of Law Firm Web Site

Source: Reprinted with permission of Procopio Cory, Hargreaves, & Savitch, LLP and SiteLab International.

CYBERSITES

The Siskind Top Twenty Law Firm Web Sites

After reviewing over 400 law firm Web sites, the following are listed as the best twenty by Siskind. They are listed in alphabetical order:

Alexander, Rappazini & Graham—www.seamless.com

Arent Fox Kintner Plotkin & Kahn—www.arentfox.com

Bowie & Jensen—www.charm.net/~bowjen

Bricker & Eckler—http://benet-npl.bricker.com/welcome

Brobeck, Phleger & Harrison—www.broceck.com

Cushman, Darby & Cushman—www.cushman.com

Faegre & Benson—www.faegre.com

Frederikson & Byron—www.fredlaw.com

Gordon & Flickson, PC—www.ggtech.com

Joseph C. Grasmick, Esq.—www.grasmick.com

Hale & Dorr—www.haledorr.com

Kilcullen, Wilson & Kilcullen—www.attny.com

Jeffery Kuester—www.Kuesterlaw.com

Ralph Losey, Esq.—http://seamless.com/rcl/rcl

Moye, Giles, O'Keefe, Vermeire & Gorress—www.mgovg.com

Pepper & Corrazzini, LLP—www.commlaw.com

Robert L. Sommers, Esq.—www.taxprophet.com

Sharyn R. Sooho, Esq.—www.divorcenet.com

Venable, Naetjer, Howard & Civiletti, LLP—http://venable.com

Wasserman, Schneider & Babb—www.customs.com

Promotional Activities

Law firms have undertaken other activities to promote their business, including sponsoring seminars, joining community organizations, writing articles for trade publications, speaking at conferences or continuing education classes, and publishing brochures and newsletters.

Seminars   Some firms, especially large firms, sponsor and conduct seminars for their clients. A firm with a large corporate client may give an educational seminar to that client, free of charge, in areas that are of interest to that client. This helps keep the corporate client informed and creates a personal rapport with the client.

Statistics indicate that 89 percent of all large firms host client seminars. In smaller firms with twenty to fifty attorneys, 63 percent conduct at least one seminar a year. Firms may also cosponsor seminars with other organizations, such as banks, real estate companies, and accounting firms.

Community Organizations   A potential client base exists in various community organizations. Groups such as the Rotary Club, Lions Club, Elks Club, and Moose Lodge are known for networking opportunities for various professionals. Some community organizations allow only one representative from each profession.

Articles   Writing articles for legal or nonlegal publications gives an attorney and a firm exposure. In addition, writing on a particular area of law that other attorneys rely on gives an author a reputation of "expert" in the field. Often, the author is invited to speak publicly on the subject. Attorneys may also post the articles they write on a Web site.

Public Speaking Speaking at lawyers' conventions, continuing education courses, and organizational meetings give an attorney and a firm exposure. Although not directed at the public for cultivating clients, being known as an expert in a particular field gives a firm an opportunity for referrals from other attorneys. When an attorney refers a client to a firm, that client has the potential of referring other clients to the firm.

Brochures Most law firms have brochures, such as the one shown in Exhibit 4.7. Typically, a law firm brochure is eight to twenty pages in length, is professionally designed (83 percent), and includes inserts showing a firm's practice areas (70 percent) and lawyer biographies (60 percent). Midsize firms are more likely than large firms to include biographical information about their owner or owners. Fifty-seven percent of all brochures are illustrated with photos or drawings, and 38 percent include photos of a firm's lawyers.

Corporate general counsel receive five to ten law firm brochures each week. More often than not, these hit the wastebasket unread. Charles E. Rapport II, senior vice president and chief legal officer of the Bank of New York's thirty-five-lawyer legal department, states, "I have in front of me right now one of the finest glossies I've ever seen. I'm sure it cost more than our company's annual report, and I resent it. Legal fees are high enough that it annoys me to think that I'm paying for their advertising. I would much prefer to receive a typed firm resume than one of these twelve-page glossies with useless pictures." However, firm brochures are considered an effective marketing tool by most attorneys.

Newsletters Almost three-fourths of all large firms publish a newsletter. A newsletter can help a firm attain a variety of goals, including the following:

◆ Reminding clients of their obligation to file reports with government agencies
◆ Informing clients about new developments in the law
◆ Informing clients about services available from the firm

Jones, Day, Reavis & Pogue, a 900-lawyer firm with offices in more than a dozen cities, distributes *Bits and Bytes* from its information systems services group. The first issue of the newsletter came out in 1988. The quarterly newsletter describes programs that are available to lawyers and nonlawyers and gives information about the firm.

Some newsletters are more focused in one subject area. The law firm of Kilpatrick & Coty, a 150-lawyer firm based in Atlanta, publishes a bimonthly automation newsletter dealing with computer hardware and software issues.

A combination of four different trends has contributed to the success of the law firm newsletter:

◆ Desktop publishing and laser printers
◆ Increased usage of personal computers in law firms
◆ Awareness of increasing demands for technical support
◆ Spread of multiple offices that are connected to a computer network

Newsletters are used to get referrals, obtain clients, keep existing clients, and create visibility, as shown in Exhibit 4.8. Newsletters are also tied to promotional strategies. For example, articles published in newsletters can be sent to prospective *welcome to the*

B&B

LAW OFFICES of
Boyd & Boyd, P.C.

403 Masonic Street
Dyersburg, Tennessee 38024
901-285-8900

*we thank you
for choosing
our law firm*

* * * *

We appreciate your confidence in us. We will do all we can to earn your continued faith.

If you are a new client, you will benefit from knowing some things about your new law firm, and this booklet will help explain our office procedures so you can best follow the progress of your legal matter. If you are an "old" valued client, perhaps this will refresh your recollection. We will try to answer each of your questions as best we can. And we truly welcome your friendship and comments.

Why Choose a Firm of Lawyers?

In this age of specialization, we have divided our staff into various categories based on each lawyer's training, knowledge, and experience. By choosing our firm, you are getting more than one lawyer who will be interested in your case and who will use his or her knowledge in seeing that your case is properly handled.

How Will I Know Which Lawyer In the Firm Is Best for Me?

Choosing the lawyer on our staff who can best represent you will be carefully done so that you can take full advantage of our skills. Accordingly, it may not be possible, or even advantageous, to have one attorney handle all of your legal matters. However, our weekly staff meetings are designed to keep each of us informed of all developments. One lawyer will be responsible for the overall progress of your case, but from time to time another lawyer may perform certain duties within the case itself. Please do not be disturbed if your case is handled by a different attorney within our firm. "Your lawyer" will still be your lawyer. This is merely another sign to you that we are doing our best to handle your case as professionally as possible.

How Will I Be Kept Informed of My Case?

We intend to keep you informed whenever there is something important happening concerning your case. Therefore, we normally send you copies of all incoming and outgoing correspondence and other documents which relate to your case. These materials are stamped "For Your Information", and you should look them over carefully to see if any mistakes or misunderstandings have occurred or if we have missed any point which you think might be important.

In addition, you should receive a letter from us about every 60 days concerning the status of your case, if it takes several months to resolve.

Although we would like to talk to you every week, this is not very practical, so we ask you to call us only if you have important new information. If you change your address or job, or if there is a mistake or misunderstanding in any of the materials we have sent you. Much of this information can be given to the secretary or to the legal assistant without the necessity of talking to your lawyer, and your lawyer will then call you back if it is necessary to discuss the information with you.

What Do I Do When I Have a Question?

We are interested in your questions. We want you to ask them. Unfortunately, much of a lawyer's time and duties take him or her out of the office for trials and other work, even for days at a time. Also, like all professional people, we frequently have clients in our office, and cannot manage to answer all our calls. In that case, ask the secretary; you will be pleased at how informed and helpful she can be. If she cannot answer your question, she will get the answer for you, or arrange to have your legal assistant or attorney contact you. Oftentimes she will refer you to the legal assistant handling your case, who will be familiar with the details of your matter and will be in a position to discuss it with you. Above all, leave a message so we know your concern in advance. If you do that, we will always try to get an answer back to you even if your attorney is out of the office when you call.

Who is the Legal Assistant?

As an essential part of our team, our office employs Legal Assistants to handle various aspects of your matters. These are highly trained and very competent persons who have taken special college courses to be able to assist the lawyers in rendering legal services. If a legal assistant is assigned to your case, you will normally be introduced to that person during your initial visit to our office. If you have any questions about your case or matter or need to furnish additional information, call the legal assistant first. If the legal assistant feels that you need to talk to the lawyer handling the case, you will be put in touch with that lawyer as soon as possible.

EXHIBIT 4.7 Sample Law Firm Brochure

clients and distributed at trade conferences. Newsletters can also be posted on a firm's Web site. To save money, firms are posting their newsletters on their Web sites and sending postcards to clients announcing that the newsletter may be read on the Web site.

On the whole, newsletters are read and are useful. They generate goodwill and enhance client relations. General counsels state that they appreciate a little free legal advice and that a firm increases its recognition through newsletters. James T. Treadway, Jr., general counsel of New York's PaineWebber Group's fifty-five-lawyer in-house legal department and executive vice president of PaineWebber, says newsletters could be the best form of marketing. But he cautions that they must get to him quickly—within seventy-two hours of the latest legal development. "I want to see two or three one-line observations at the end as to what this development means and what issues are left unaddressed that we should be aware of," says Tread-

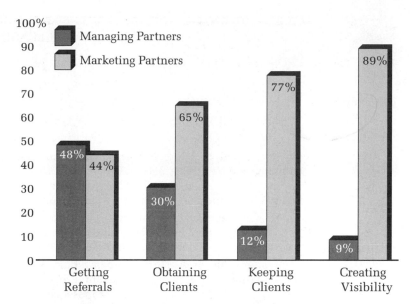

EXHIBIT 4.8 How Managing Partners and Marketing Directors Rate Newsletters
Source: National Law Firm Marketing Association survey on newsletters to clients.

way. "It shows me that the firm understands how it translates real-life issues to PaineWebber."

Public Relations

Most professionals do not know the difference between advertising and public relations. These are different methods of communicating a firm's services to the public. Advertising involves purchasing media space to promote a firm's practice and build a firm's image. Public relations is developing and maintaining a favorable public image between a law firm and a community. Advertising is purchased; public relations is not.

Public relations consists of participation in community and social activities as well as the publicity a firm receives on high-exposure cases. Once a firm gets its name in a newspaper, the chances of the paper repeating its name are very slim—unless the firm has another story that is newsworthy. A firm cannot dictate when the agencies of mass communication will run a story or where the story will be located in a newspaper. A journalist has complete control over a story and may leave out important information, such as the firm's location and phone number.

Law firms hire public relations firms to increase the firm's visibility and create a positive public image. The public relations firm teams up with the law firm in its marketing strategies to create press releases and advertisements for the firm, such as the one shown in Exhibit 4.9.

Advertising allows a firm to repeat publicity as often as it would like. Repetition is very important in building awareness of a firm and its specialties. Most important, a firm has total control over a message conveyed to the public and may include information it feels is important to attract new clients. In addition, an advertisement can be scheduled to appear at specific times when potential clients would most likely see it.

Public relations has more credibility than advertising since its source is presumably objective and nonbiased. Making reprints of public relations news stories and sending them to clients is a clever marketing tool.

NEWS RELEASE

FROM: Law offices of Black, White & Greene LLP

FOR IMMEDIATE RELEASE
<u>REAL ESTATE ATTORNEY AYERS CALLS ON LAWYERS TO
DEMONSTRATE RELIABILITY OF TIME-SHARE INDUSTRY</u>

LOS ANGELES, CA, June 6, 1993—"As an industry that has come into its own and has already passed the billion dollar mark, time-sharing doesn't need to prove its viability any longer. What it does need to prove is its *reliability.* And real estate attorneys must aid in that process, by ensuring that the time-share projects they structure or represent are well planned and honestly presented to the public."

That statement reflected the tone of remarks presented today by Robert Black, partner in charge of the Real Estate Department of the Law Offices of Black, White & Greene, to the Real Estate Section of the California State Bar Association.

A leader in the area of time-share law, Black explained the basic concept of real estate time-sharing and discussed existing and proposed state and federal regulations for the industry. "In addition to the many proposed state regulations, which are often needed to ensure consumer protection in this relatively new industry, I think we will see greater self-regulation by the industry. That will occur simply because reputable developers will insist on it to guarantee their credibility," he said.

"Image is the key today in time-share projects," Black added. "Not only must the projects we represent be structured honestly, employ ethical marketing techniques, and obtain sufficient capitalization, but they must also be seen to possess those attributes. And we must work with regulators, not against them, to see that the industry is established on a strong regulatory foundation."

A member of the National Timesharing Council of the American Land Development Association, Black serves on the NTC's State and Federal Regulations and Standards and Ethics Committee. He was co-chairman of the NTC—National Association of Real Estate Licensed Law Officials committee that drafted the model time-share law now being considered for state-by-state implementation.

As an attorney, Black has represented numerous developers of both domestic and foreign time-share projects over the past eight years. His articles on time-share law have appeared in such publications as *Real Estate Update, Resort Timesharing,* and the *National Law Journal.*

In addition to his law and real estate industry activities, Black is Chairman of the Board of Commissioners of the Los Angeles Housing Authority, a member of the California Real Estate Commission, and advisor to the American Resort Commission.

A graduate of the University of Southern California and UCLA School of Law, Black lives in Santa Monica, California.

EXHIBIT 4.9   Sample Press Release

Solicitation

ETHICS ALERT

Solicitation of clients is one of the most complicated—and ethically dangerous—areas in which attorneys and legal assistants work. The rules vary from jurisdiction to jurisdiction and include such areas as in-person contact, direct-mail solicitation, conduct of agents, and the Internet. However, the various rules do not define exactly what solicitation is, so it must be determined by case law that defines the term. One of the most difficult questions in lawyer solicitation involves multistate compliance with rules. *What is proper in one state may be improper in another.*

The ABA has strict rules prohibiting lawyers' direct solicitation of potential clients. Its Model Rule 7.3 has four parts dealing with solicitation as follows:

(a) A lawyer shall not by in-person or live telephone contact solicit professional employment from a prospective client with whom the lawyer has no family or prior professional relationship when a significant motive for the lawyer's doing so is the lawyer's pecuniary gain.

(b) A lawyer shall not solicit professional employment from a prospective client by written or recorded communication or by in-person or telephone contact even when not otherwise prohibited by paragraph (a) if:

    (1) the prospective client has made known to the lawyer a desire not to be solicited by the lawyer; or

    (2) The solicitation involves coercion, duress or harassment.

(c) Every written or recorded communication from a lawyer soliciting professional employment from a prospective client known to be in need of legal services in a particular matter, and with whom the lawyer has no family or prior professional relationship, shall include the words "Advertising Material" on the outside envelope and at the beginning and ending of any recorded communication.

(d) Notwithstanding the prohibitions in paragraph (a), a lawyer may participate with a prepaid or group legal service plan operated by an organization not owned or directed by the lawyer which uses in-person or telephone contact to solicit memberships or subscriptions for the plan from persons who are not known to need legal services in a particular matter covered by the plan.

Generally, a lawyer may not personally contact a person, unrelated or unassociated with the lawyer, and inform that person of the legal services the lawyer has to offer if the lawyer's objective is monetary gain. The justification for the prohibition is that lawyers are trained in the art of persuasion and that people in need of legal services may be emotionally vulnerable and subject to overreaching. The U.S. Supreme Court stated in *Ohralik v. Ohio State Bar Association,* 426 U.S. 447 (1978), "In-person solicitation is a practice rife with possibilities for overreaching, invasion of privacy, the exercise of undue influence fraud."

For example, if a lawyer is attending a cocktail party one evening and is speaking to an acquaintance who informs the lawyer that she is deeply in debt and is considering bankruptcy, the lawyer may not inform the acquaintance of his ability to represent her in the bankruptcy proceeding. However, if the acquaintance mentions her desire to file bankruptcy and requests the lawyers' services, the lawyer may accept the case without being accused of soliciting.

Direct Mail Through time, the ABA's rules have changed with case law rulings. For example, in 1988, Model Rule 7.3 prohibited direct-mail solicitation. The Supreme Court ruled in *Shapero v. Kentucky Bar Association,* 108 S.Ct. 64 (1988), that direct-mail solicitation was constitutionally protected free speech. The Court said that lawyers could send mail specifically to those known to be in need of services, such as accident victims, judgment debtors, and foreclosure defendants. In 1989, the ABA modified Rule 7.3 to comply with the court's ruling but added a provision that all such direct-mail advertisements be clearly labeled as such.

Direct-mail advertising has never been a popular form of advertising with bar associations. In 1989, Florida attorneys were mailing 700,000 direct-mail solicitations per year, 40 percent of which were aimed at accident victims or their survivors. The Florida Bar Association conducted a random sampling of recipients of the direct-mail campaign that revealed that 45 percent believed that the solicitation was designed to take advantage of gullible people, and 27 percent reported having a lower regard for the legal profession because of the mailings. The Florida Bar Association sought to ban direct-mail solicitation to accident victims and their families, and the lawyers challenged the ban.

The case of *Florida Bar v. Went For It, Inc.,* was heard by the Florida Supreme Court, which rejected the ban but imposed a thirty-day waiting period for direct-mail solicitation to accident and wrongful death victims and their families. The waiting period was challenged in federal court and the U.S. Court of Appeals for the Eleventh Circuit, which found the thirty-day waiting period unconstitutional and a violation of free speech. The U.S. Supreme Court heard the case (115 S.Ct. 897 [1995]) and overruled the federal courts' decisions. It ruled that the thirty-day waiting period was proper.

At the time the Supreme Court heard the case, twenty state bar associations and eight local bar associations joined in an **amicus curiae** brief, urging the court to implement the waiting period. The case has sparked state bar associations to consider restrictions on solicitation and television advertising. Maryland adopted a similar rule and extended the thirty-day ban to solicitation of criminal and traffic defendants. The U.S. Court of Appeals for the Fourth Circuit rejected the ban for criminal and traffic defendants (*Ficker v. Curran,* 96-2724), stating that criminal defendants are in immediate need of legal assistance and would not benefit from the thirty-day waiting period.

Wisconsin also considered implementing the thirty-day ban but, before doing so, conducted a survey of more than 500 accident victims to determine whether such restriction was necessary. The survey resulted in the findings shown in Exhibit 4.10. Wisconsin's State Bar President, David Saincheck, was quoted as saying, "It is pretty clear . . . that the public is nowhere near as negative about [direct mail] as attorneys might think."

An example of a direct-mail piece targeted to a specific audience (homeowners) is shown in Exhibit 4.11. An example of a direct-mail piece that violates the ABA Model Rules is shown in Exhibit 4.12.

E-mail Indiscriminate posting of e-mail messages to consumers promoting services or products is defined as **Spam.** In April 1993, Phoenix lawyer Lawrence Canter of the firm Canter & Siegal posted an advertisement for immigration services to thousands of Internet newsgroups without regard for the subject matter of the newsgroup. The firm received thousands of angry e-mails, including death threats. His endeavor resulted in hundreds of complaints that led to his suspension for one year for violating several ethics rules, including the following:

◆ Failure to label his e-mail as advertising material
◆ Failure to submit a copy of the e-mail to the state bar disciplinary authorities

Amicus curiae: Friend-of-the-court brief that states the position of the author relating to a case pending before the court.

Spam: To send unsolicited commercial e-mail messages to large numbers of persons on the Internet on an indiscriminate basis.

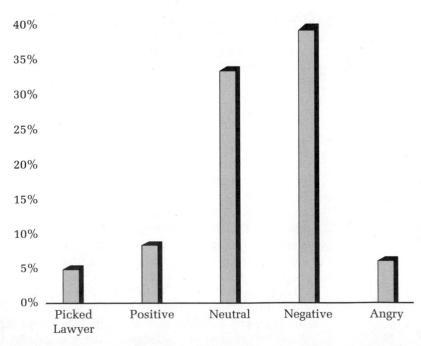

EXHIBIT 4.10 Results of the Wisconsin State Bar Association Survey of Direct-Mail Advertising

---

JAMES F. ROBERTS

IRVINE OFFICE	*Attorney at Law*	BREA OFFICE
18300 VON KARMAN	1-800-244-4882	770 S. BREA
SUITE 820		SUITE 207
IRVINE, CALIFORNIA 92715		BREA, CALIFORNIA 92621
FAX: (714) 863-9002		FAX: (714) 256-1070
TELEPHONE: (714) 863-1313		TELEPHONE: (714) 256-1065

October 27, 1992

Dear Homeowner:

This is not a summons to appear in court and I am not a bill collector. I help people avoid probate and I save them money; I am an estate planning attorney.

Doing nothing or doing the wrong things can actually cost you money. To prevent this from happening to you, I am inviting you to a FREE seminar meeting on family estate planning. We'll discuss living trusts, wills, health power, conservatorship, and a number of other topics of vital importance and . . . I'll answer your questions.

If all of your assets equal $60,000 or more, your estate will have to go through probate in California, and, if you own real property in other states you may have to hire an attorney and go through probate in those states as well.

If you're like me, you don't want any part of a process that takes 6% to 10% of everything you own, requires mounds of paperwork, and often takes two years or longer before the people you care about can claim their rightful inheritance.

There are many reasons why you don't want to go through probate. We'll be discussing those as well as discussing other important legal documents you should have to protect yourself now and in the future. I could not begin to cover these in a letter; that's why I'm inviting you and your family and friends to a FREE educational meeting.

I've been in business for over eleven years; I have set up more than 2,500 Living Trusts. The key is quality, customized legal documents that do a good job for you, follow your wishes, and keep you in control.

For your convenience, I'm presenting two seminars:

Tues., Nov. 10, 9:00 A.M.	Tues., Nov. 17, 7:30 P.M.
Velvet Turtle Restaurant	Holiday Inn (Off Harbor)
1450 N. Harbor, Fullerton	222 W. Houston, Fullerton
(Free Breakfast Meeting)	(Refreshments)

Seating is limited, so please call 1-800-244-4882 for reservations. Don't wait until it's too late to plan. You need this information to PROTECT yourself and your loved ones.

Sincerely,

James F. Roberts
Estate Planning Attorney

EXHIBIT 4.11   Sample of an Unsolicited Direct-Mail Advertisement

◆ Making reference to himself as an "immigration lawyer" in violation of a rule on government specialization
◆ Engaging in conduct prejudicial to the administration of justice

Another question regarding electronic advertising is whether a lawyer's participation in chat rooms and list servers constitutes solicitation. Some attorneys have admitted that their participation in such activities is solely for the purpose of generating business. If so, is that wrong? If it is, would every chat room session have to include a header with the phrase "Advertising Material?" Answers to these and other questions are currently being addressed by the ABA and individual states. In the next few years, new regulations of lawyers' solicitation activities over the Internet will be implemented.

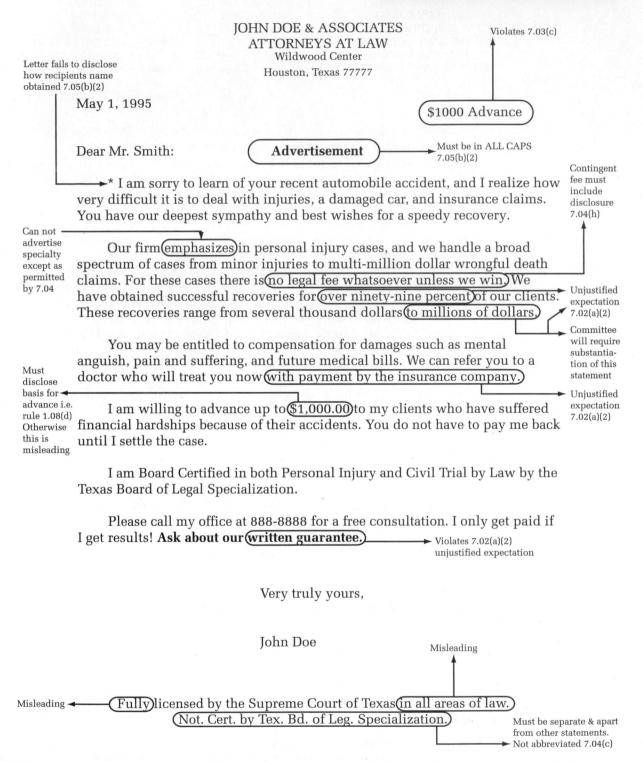

Not In Compliance

JOHN DOE & ASSOCIATES
ATTORNEYS AT LAW
Wildwood Center
Houston, Texas 77777

Violates 7.03(c)

Letter fails to disclose
how recipients name
obtained 7.05(b)(2)

May 1, 1995

$1000 Advance

Dear Mr. Smith: **Advertisement**

Must be in ALL CAPS
7.05(b)(2)

Contingent
fee must
include
disclosure
7.04(h)

* I am sorry to learn of your recent automobile accident, and I realize how very difficult it is to deal with injuries, a damaged car, and insurance claims. You have our deepest sympathy and best wishes for a speedy recovery.

Can not
advertise
specialty
except as
permitted
by 7.04

Our firm emphasizes in personal injury cases, and we handle a broad spectrum of cases from minor injuries to multi-million dollar wrongful death claims. For these cases there is no legal fee whatsoever unless we win. We have obtained successful recoveries for over ninety-nine percent of our clients. These recoveries range from several thousand dollars to millions of dollars.

Unjustified
expectation
7.02(a)(2)

Committee
will require
substantia-
tion of this
statement

You may be entitled to compensation for damages such as mental anguish, pain and suffering, and future medical bills. We can refer you to a doctor who will treat you now with payment by the insurance company.

Must
disclose
basis for
advance i.e.
rule 1.08(d)
Otherwise
this is
misleading

Unjustified
expectation
7.02(a)(2)

I am willing to advance up to $1,000.00 to my clients who have suffered financial hardships because of their accidents. You do not have to pay me back until I settle the case.

I am Board Certified in both Personal Injury and Civil Trial by Law by the Texas Board of Legal Specialization.

Please call my office at 888-8888 for a free consultation. I only get paid if I get results! **Ask about our written guarantee.**

Violates 7.02(a)(2)
unjustified expectation

Very truly yours,

John Doe

Misleading

Misleading ◄ Fully licensed by the Supreme Court of Texas in all areas of law. Not. Cert. by Tex. Bd. of Leg. Specialization.

Must be separate & apart
from other statements.
Not abbreviated 7.04(c)

EXHIBIT 4.12   Sample of a Direct-Mail Piece That Violates the ABA Model Rules
Reprinted with permission of The State Bar of Texas. *Texas State Bar Journal, 58*(7), p. 663. July, 1995.

Capper: A person who is paid to obtain cases for a lawyer.

ETHICS ALERT

Cappers   A **capper** is a person paid to get business for an attorney. Potential cappers include insurance adjusters, medical personnel, and police officers. An insurance adjuster or police officer investigating an accident is able to recommend an attorney to an accident victim. If the victim retains the lawyer, the capper is paid a fee. *This type of activity is highly illegal* and, unfortunately, occurs often.

Cappers are very creative in their solicitation efforts. They hang out in emergency room lobbies waiting for automobile accident victims. They come equipped with retainer agreements already completed so that all they have to do is fill in a victim's name and have the victim sign the agreement.

Exceptions to Solicitation Prohibitions   An attorney may inform a potential client of services if no financial benefits will be gained by doing so. For example, a lawyer employed by a public defender's office may inform a potential indigent client of his services without being accused of solicitation. A public defender and a district attorney are employed by a county or state and receive a salary from taxpayer dollars. Therefore, they will not increase their income by representing a client.

In addition, sponsored attorney referral services are exempt from capping allegations. These services charge a small fee to put an attorney on a list. When clients call a referral service for a recommendation, the service will give them an attorney's name and telephone number. The attorney agrees to charge the referred client a reduced fee for a consultation. After the consultation, the attorney sends the referral service a fee for the referral. An employee of an attorney referral service cannot be accused of soliciting for referring a client to an attorney, even though the attorney compensates the service.

Also exempt from solicitation allegations are attorneys employed by prepaid legal service plans. An attorney employed by an insurance plan may inform a member of the plan of the availability of legal services. Since the attorney is employed by the insurance company, the attorney's income will not increase by representing the member. The client will receive legal services at a reduced rate, and the fees will be paid by the insurance company.

There are other circumstances that are not considered overreaching and in which the prohibition against direct solicitation is not necessary. These circumstances are direct communications with a family member or current or former client, a person who requests the information, and a pro bono client. However, in some cases states have ruled that a pro bono client may be subject to the solicitation ban. Although the attorney may receive no monetary gain from representing the client, if the case is a high-profile case, the attorney would receive name recognition from media attention and would realize future profits.

Staff Referrals A firm's employees can refer their friends to the attorneys in their firm. *A problem occurs, however, if an employee is compensated for a referral.* Even a small gratuity or thank-you gift is considered payment for a referral in some states and is not allowed under ABA Model Rule 7.2(c). Therefore, if a legal assistant refers a friend to a firm, the legal assistant may not receive any compensation for the referral.

Departing Attorneys An attorney terminating employment with a firm may contact clients and inform them of the departure. However, case law rulings state that clients are a firm's property and not an individual attorney's property. It is considered improper for an attorney to try to persuade clients to leave a firm with the attorney. It is the client's decision to choose the attorney or the firm.

THE ATTORNEY-CLIENT RELATIONSHIP

An attorney-client relationship consists of many elements, including trust, loyalty, honesty, openness, and understanding. When any of these elements is missing from the relationship, the relationship suffers. When an attorney-client relationship suffers, it affects the entire firm.

When Does the Attorney-Client Relationship Begin?

Traditionally, determining when an attorney-client relationship began was based in contract law and principles of agency. Prior case law stated that the relationship began with the client request that the lawyer act on the client's behalf and the lawyer's agreement to represent the client. Some courts have ruled that no attorney-client relationship exists unless a written contract exists.

Recent case law indicates that determining when an attorney-client relationship begins is based on other factors that do not involve a written agreement. The Iowa Supreme Court used three conditions to test when an attorney-client relationship exists:

◆ The client sought legal advice
◆ The advice sought was within the areas of the lawyer's competence
◆ The lawyer gave, or agreed to give, the advice sought

Michigan ethics opinion states that an attorney-client relationship can begin from a brief, informal conversation in person or by telephone where legal advice was given although no fee was charged and no contract of employment was signed. If a lawyer gives gratuitous advice, he or she is held to the same standard of care as if formerly retained. Therefore, an attorney-client relationship may exist without a formal agreement and may be implied by a lawyer's conduct. If a lawyer's conduct would make a person believe that the lawyer is acting on the person's behalf, an attorney-client relationship is established. For example, in a Minnesota case, *Togstad v. Vesely, Otto, Miller, & Keefe,* 291 N.W. 2d 686 (1980), the court found that although the attorney did not agree to take the client's case, his action in telling the client that he did not think she had a case established a lawyer-client relationship. The client was awarded $650,000 because the lawyer did not warn her about a statute of limitations. However, the existence of an attorney-client relationship and the circumstances surrounding a case must be determined on a case-by-case basis.

Most frequently, an attorney-client relationship is created by an expressed agreement to represent a client. Paying a fee is only one element of the existence of a lawyer-client relationship. When a lawyer is consulted, is advised of facts, and agrees to take a case on the request of a client, a relationship is established.

The Five Cs of Client Relations

The attorney-client relationship consists of five major areas known as the five Cs of client relations: competence, commitment, communication, conflict of interest, and confidentiality.

The attorney is ultimately responsible for ensuring that the five Cs are performed. A lawyer's staff, especially legal assistants, must also be attentive to the five Cs.

Competence   The law has always recognized the importance of competent legal representation. However, the profession did not especially require lawyer competence until after 1970 when the ABA Model Code was amended to include lawyer competence.

Rule 1.1 of the Model Rules states:

ETHICS ALERT

> A lawyer shall provide competent representation to a client. Competent representation requires the legal knowledge, skill, thoroughness and preparation reasonably necessary for the representation.

A lawyer is expected to have knowledge of the principles of law applicable to the client's problem. In addition, a lawyer is expected to know procedural rules and rules for all the courts in which the lawyer practices. Legal assistants are helpful in this area. A new attorney is seldom knowledgeable about these rules and often relies on legal assistants for this information.

Legal skills include technical skills such as the ability to draft documents, review documents, conduct research, and perform administrative tasks, such as record keeping. Some important legal skills—such as analysis of **precedent,** evaluation of evidence, and legal drafting—are required in all legal problems. Perhaps the most basic legal skill is determining what kind of legal problems a situation may involve.

Precedent: A court decision on a question of law that gives authority or direction on how to decide a similar question of law in a later case with similar facts.

The standard of thoroughness required by the ABA Model Rules is the degree of thoroughness ordinarily employed by lawyers undertaking similar matters.

Adequate preparation requires necessary legal research and investigation of the facts of a case. Attorneys have been disciplined for neglect and inadequate preparation, specifically, for failure to ascertain basic statutory points of law readily ascertainable by any member of the bar. This rule does not, however, require that an attorney investigate remote theories of law or every fact of a case, unless the circumstances reasonably indicate the need for such investigation.

An attorney need not be experienced in an area of law before accepting a case. It is not possible for a lawyer to be an expert in all fields of law. If an attorney is inexperienced in an area of law before accepting a case in that area, the attorney must make an effort to become knowledgeable in that area without jeopardizing the client's case. For example, an attorney who has had no experience in probate may accept a probate case if, through diligent research and study, the attorney can become knowledgeable about probate without exposing the client's case to risk.

A lawyer who knows that he does not have the necessary skills to undertake a complex matter is bound by the Rules of Professional Responsibility of many states either to decline the case or to associate another attorney on the case who is competent in the subject matter. Lawyers have been suspended from the practice of law for failure to gain the necessary knowledge or to associate another lawyer on a complex case. If a lawyer chooses to associate another lawyer, that lawyer must have the client's consent. Furthermore, the fees charged the client cannot be increased because of the involvement of the additional lawyer.

Commitment   Commitment to a client's case forbids a lawyer to neglect the case. Prejudicial delay is clearly a violation of an attorney's commitment to a client. In addition, failure to act promptly may cause a client needless anxiety, worry, and frustration.

Rule 1.3 of the Model Rules states:

A lawyer shall act with reasonable diligence and promptness in representing a client.

This rule imposes a duty on a lawyer to be committed to a client's matter with reasonable speed and readiness. The case of *Mendicino v. Magagma,* 572 P. 2d 21, 23–24, states, "Lawyers . . . everywhere are, themselves, on public trial. . . . The procrastination of one of us results in the condescension of all and, in this context, we must stand responsible for each other as we discharge our obligation to our clients, the courts, and the public at large."

In addition to possibly damaging a client, a lawyer's procrastination and delay interfere with the administration of justice. Some examples of a lack of commitment to a client's case are the following:

◆ Failure to begin an action
◆ Failure to appear at hearing
◆ Failure to file pleadings
◆ Filing of carelessly drafted pleadings
◆ Failure to respond to interrogatories
◆ Failure to respond to correspondence from opposing counsel
◆ Failure to correct a known defect in a case
◆ Failure to notify clients of a lawyer's new office address or telephone number

Zeal: Enthusiastic and diligent devotion.

Commitment to a client's case also includes loyalty to the client. Under the ABA Model Code, this duty is expressed as zealousness. The term **zeal** first appeared in formal standards of conduct in ABA Canon of Professional Ethics 15, which states, in part, "[T]he lawyer owes entire devotion to the interest of the client, [and should] apply zeal in the maintenance and defense of his rights and the exertion of his utmost learning and ability, to the end that nothing be taken or withheld from him, [save] by the rules of law, legally applied." The term *zeal* suggests the frame of mind appropriate in advocacy but not appropriate in a lawyer's role as adviser. Although a lawyer must represent a client with zeal, the lawyer's zeal must always respect the decisions made by the client.

Communication   The obligation to communicate with a client has been recognized throughout the history of the legal system and the legal profession as one of a lawyer's primary duties. Breach of that duty is a very serious failure. However, attorneys' failure to communicate with clients is the most common complaint clients have about attorneys.

Rule 1.4 of the Model Rules states:

(a) A lawyer shall keep a client reasonably informed about the status of a matter and promptly comply with reasonable requests for information.
(b) A lawyer shall explain a matter to the extent reasonably necessary to permit the client to make informed decisions regarding the representation.

A lawyer can keep clients informed by doing the following:

◆ Advising them of the status of their affairs in a timely manner
◆ Responding to their requests for information
◆ Responding to clients' letters and telephone calls
◆ Notifying them of changes in the lawyer's address and telephone number
◆ Apprising them of any reason why the lawyer cannot provide them with diligent representation
◆ Advising them of the proper course of action and the risks involved and possible alternative action
◆ Informing them of their rights, especially in criminal cases

◆ Advising them on both the legal and the practical aspects of a matter
◆ Providing them with copies of all documents received or prepared in their case

The duty to communicate effectively is also necessary to maintain public confidence in the legal profession. Warren Burger states in *The Role of the Law School in Teaching Legal Ethics and Professional Responsibility*, "The findings of . . . polls . . . [suggest] that the public's perception of lawyers is that . . . lawyers do not care whether their clients fully understand what needs to be done and why."

Providing a client with information relates to two areas of the client's case: informing the client of the status of the case and advising the client of the law to allow the client to make informed decisions concerning the case. Therefore, a lawyer must communicate information sufficient to permit a client to appreciate the significance of a case.

Communication reassures a client that matters of importance are not being left unresolved, prevents prejudice to a client's rights, and preserves the trust and confidence that clients normally expect of their lawyers.

ETHICS ALERT

Conflict of Interest A lawyer may not represent one client whose interests are adverse to another client, even if the two representations are unrelated, unless the client consents and the lawyer believes the representation will not adversely affect a client. This rule has its roots in a lawyer's duty of loyalty to a client. It is generally agreed that a greater obligation is owed to a former client than to a potential client.

Rule 1.7 of the ABA Model Rules states:

(a) A lawyer shall not represent a client if the representation of that client will be directly adverse to another client, unless:
　(1) the lawyer reasonably believes the representation will not adversely affect the relationship with the other client; and
　(2) each client consents after consultation.
(b) A lawyer shall not represent a client if the representation of that client may be materially limited by the lawyer's responsibilities to another client, or to a third person, or by the lawyer's own interest unless:
　(1) The lawyer reasonably believes the representation will not be adversely affected; and
　(2) The client consents after consultation. When representation of multiple clients in a single matter is undertaken, the consultation shall include explanation of the implications of the common representation and the advantages and risks involved.

The first part of the rule states that a lawyer may not act as an advocate against a person whom the lawyer represents in another matter, even if it is totally unrelated. Doing so would cause the attorney's loyalty and commitment to the client to be compromised. The client is likely to doubt the loyalty of a lawyer who opposes him or her in an unrelated matter.

The second part of the rule refers to an attorney representing multiple clients in the same matter. For example, a husband and wife who seek a divorce and agree on the division of property may ask a lawyer to prepare the appropriate documents for the action. In some cases, this may limit the attorney in representing either the husband or the wife. If the division of the community property is unequal, the attorney would be limited in asserting the rights of the damaged party because the attorney represents both parties.

Representing both parties may subject an attorney to a malpractice claim. In *Ishmael v. Millington*, 241 Cal. 2d 520 (1966), the court upheld a judgment for malpractice when the attorney represented both sides in a dissolution of marriage. Courts have expressed concern that a lawyer's representation of one client may be diminished to avoid antagonizing a second client. However, according to ABA Model Rule 1.7, an attorney may represent both parties in a matter if the lawyer believes that the representation would not be limited.

Rule 1.9 of the ABA Model Rules states:

(a) A lawyer who has formerly represented a client in [a] matter shall not thereafter represent another person in the same or a substantially related matter in which that person's interests are materially adverse to the interests of the former client unless the former client consents after consultation.

(b) A lawyer shall not knowingly represent a person in the same or substantially related matter which a firm with which the lawyer formerly was associated had previously represented a client whose interests are materially adverse to that person and about whom the lawyer has acquired information protected by Rule 1.6 and 1.9(c) that is material to the matter; unless the former client consents after consultation.

(c) A lawyer who has formerly presented a client in a matter or whose present or former firm has formerly represented a client in a matter shall not thereafter

(1) use information relating to the representation to the disadvantage of the former client except as Rule 1.6 (confidentially) would permit or require with respect to a client or when the information has become generally known, or

(2) Reveal information relating to the representation except as Rule 1.6 or 3.3 would permit or require with respect to a client.

The reason for this rule is the potential for the violation of a lawyer's duty of loyalty to a former client as well as the risk that confidential information gained in a prior representation will be used to the disadvantage of the former client.

When a client retains an attorney in a law firm, the client retains every attorney in the firm. Therefore, *two attorneys in the same firm cannot represent two sides of a dispute because to do so would be a conflict of interest.* An attorney in an office-sharing arrangement may refer the opposing party to an attorney in the same suite if the two attorneys do not hold themselves out to be members of the same firm, the files are kept separate, and the clients' confidences are guarded.

There are three types of conflicts: direct conflict, potential conflict, and positional conflict. With a **direct conflict,** an attorney or firm has a direct relationship with, or financial interest in, an entity or person who is likely to be involved in the case. For example, one of the firm's attorneys may own stock in the opposing party or be related to the opposing party. With a **potential conflict,** a member of the firm may not be directly related to the opposing party but may have ties to the opposing party from a past or current relationship. For example, an attorney's daughter may be engaged to the opposing party's son. Another type of potential conflict is when a firm's employees have worked for the opposing party and may have knowledge of confidential information. This type of conflict must be determined on a case-by-case basis. A **positional conflict** arises when a firm agrees to represent a client's competitor. Clients, especially large corporate clients, are insisting that their attorneys demonstrate their loyalty by not representing their competition.

Most law firms today, especially large ones, build extensive databases to track their clients' and potential conflicts of interest. Some firms create their own conflict-checking software, but most firms use commercial software, such as the ones listed in the Tech Tips sidebar. Conflict-checking software traces companies' hierarchies, affiliates, and officers and displays relationships among adverse parties and identifies their opposing counsel. Conflicts can be easily spotted.

TECH TIPS
Conflict-Checking Software

The following are examples of software that check for potential conflicts of interest:

Conflict Search—Tremco Legal Solutions, Inc.

LegalKey—Legal Key Technologies, Inc.

LegalTRAX™ Open—Software iNTelligence, Inc.

Software mentioned in this sidebar is for informational purposes only and is not for the purpose of endorsing products.

ETHICS ALERT

Confidentiality One major characteristic that differentiates a law firm from business in other industries is the requirement that all matters within that office be kept confidential. *Information a legal team learns from or about a client during representation of that client is confidential.*

Rule 1.6 of the ABA Model Rules states:

(a) A lawyer shall not reveal information relating to representation of a client unless the client consents after a consultation, except for disclosures that are impliedly authorized in order to carry out the representation, and except as stated in (b).

(b) A lawyer may reveal such information to the extent the lawyer reasonably believes necessary:

(1) to prevent the client from committing a criminal act that the lawyer believes is likely to result in imminent death or subsequential bodily harm; or

(2) to establish a claim or defense on behalf of the lawyer in a controversy between the lawyer and the client, to establish a defense to a criminal charge or civil claim against the lawyer based upon conduct in which the client was involved, or to respond to allegations in any proceedings concerning the lawyer's representation of the client.

The primary justification for the strict rules on confidentiality is the desirability of complete candor between client and lawyer. Confidentiality not only facilitates the full development of facts essential to proper representation but also encourages people to seek legal assistance at an early stage.

Whenever attorneys get together, the primary topic of conversation are the cases they are working on. "I had a case where the plaintiff . . . " "While working on a bankruptcy case, I discovered that . . . " "I've been in trial all day on a drunk driving case where the defendant . . . " Are these attorneys breaking the confidentiality rule? The answer is, maybe. If the attorney reveals facts of the case that would reveal the client's identity, the confidentiality rule has been violated. Otherwise, the confidentiality rule has not been violated. If the statements were made to other attorneys within the same firm, the attorney may reveal the client's identity since the entire firm represents the client.

Technology is adding to the burden of keeping a client's case confidential. Lawyers and staff members who work on cases away from the office are taking advantage of remote access technology and can access the firm's computers from home, hotel rooms, and other remote areas. This remote access leaves the firm's computer vulnerable to others who are not authorized access to the information. For example, temporary help and contract attorneys who have no long-term commitment to the firm learn passwords and log-in codes to the firm's computer. On occasions, disgruntled employees and contract workers have gained access to a computer by remote access and done great harm to the firm's computer system. Every employee should guard computer information by performing backups regularly. Passwords should be changed often and laptops guarded against theft.

Exceptions to the Confidentiality Rule Exceptions to the confidentiality rule include the following:

◆ A client may consent to a lawyer's divulging confidential information, but only after full disclosure and consultation.

◆ A lawyer may reveal a client's intentions to commit a crime and the information necessary to prevent a crime.

◆ If a client commits perjury, an attorney has an obligation to reveal the perjury. Perjury is a fraud on the court, and the Model Rules require total candor with the court. The Model Rules further forbid lawyers to "knowingly use perjured testimony or false evidence" or to "knowingly make a false statement of law or fact." The lawyer is obligated to encourage the client to rectify the fraud and reveal the fraud to the court.

◆ If a law or a court order requires a lawyer to disclose otherwise confidential information, the lawyer may do so.

◆ A lawyer may reveal a client's confidences to collect fees and defend him- or herself against claims of criminal or unethical conduct arising out of her representation of the client.

◆ The ethical rule of confidentiality is distinguished from the attorney-client privilege rule. The scope of the attorney-client privilege is much more limited than the confidentiality rule.

The principle of confidentiality is based on two bodies of law: the rule of confidentiality established in professional ethics and the attorney-client privilege (which includes the work-product doctrine).

Attorney-Client Privilege The purpose of the attorney-client privilege is to encourage full and frank communication between attorneys and their clients and promote broader public interests in the observance of law and administration of justice. Attorney-client privilege permits a client to refuse to testify and to keep an attorney from testifying in a legal proceeding about communications made between the two in strict confidence. The privilege applies only to communications between lawyer and client and does not apply to information that the firm learns on its own during the representation.

In order for a communication between an attorney and client to be privileged, it must be made in confidence, must be made to obtain legal advice, and must be with an attorney. The client runs the risk of losing the privilege if third persons (i.e., other than the lawyer's agents and employees) are present during the consultation. However, the courts have ruled that, in some circumstances, a third party may be present during the consultation without voiding the attorney-client privilege. For example, a prisoner in conference with his or her attorney does not waive the attorney-client privilege by the presence of a guard.

A comparison of the attorney-client privilege and confidentiality follows:

◆ Attorney-client privilege protects only information covered by attorney-client communication. It does not protect the facts generating the confidences or the knowledge of the client.

◆ Information that is open to the public is not covered by the attorney-client privilege. However, the lawyer's obligation to keep information confidential includes information that is public.

◆ Attorney-client privilege includes information that the lawyer obtains from the client only. Confidentiality includes all information "relating to the representation of a client" regardless of its source.

◆ Attorney-client privilege prevents disclosure in the litigation process. Confidentiality prevents disclosure anywhere at any time, even after the death of the client.

Legal assistants often witness the development of attorney-client privilege. If a legal assistant attends a conference, such as the initial client interview, wherein the client reveals the facts of her case to the attorney and requests legal advice, the legal assistant has witnessed the development of attorney-client privilege. As an agent of the attorney, the legal assistant is protected and may be present without damaging the attorney-client privilege. However, if the client brings a friend to the meeting, the confidential nature of the communication that creates attorney-client privilege is breached. Legal assistants must be cautious to guard attorney-client communications and alert the attorney where a potential breach of attorney-client privilege is possible.

Other information the lawyer learns about the client that could hurt or embarrass a client is protected under confidentiality rules or the attorney work-product doctrine.

Attorney Work-Product Doctrine The attorney work-product doctrine requires that information an attorney learns in representation of a client be kept confidential and not be revealed to third parties. For information to be protected under this doctrine, it must be obtained by an attorney through the attorney's investigation and analysis of a case. Opposing counsel may not require disclosure of this information.

The cases of *Dabny v. Investment Corporation of America,* 82 F.R.D. 464 (1979), and *United States v. Cabra,* 622 F. 2d 182 (5th Cir. 1980), extend the work-product privilege to legal assistants. Legal assistants are most often the first members of a legal team to become aware of sensitive issues and confidential documents. Some examples of legal assistants' work products that are subject to the work-product doctrine include the following:

◆ Interoffice memorandums discussing case status or case strategy
◆ Telephone memos of conversations with clients, witnesses, and others related to the investigation
◆ Notes of meetings with clients
◆ Document-screening and site inspection notes
◆ Investigation memos and interview notes
◆ Document production notes
◆ Case memorandums and task assignment documents
◆ E-mails

When Does the Attorney-Client Relationship End?

When a client retains an attorney, he or she may end the relationship at any time without justifying the termination. When an attorney agrees to take a client's case, the commitment creates an obligation that the lawyer will continue the case until judgment, settlement, or resolution. If a lawyer wants to end a relationship with a client and the client will not release the lawyer from the obligation, in most cases the lawyer must have the court's permission. To get the court's permission, the lawyer must show that good cause exists for terminating the attorney-client relationship. Permission may be denied if withdrawal would adversely affect the opposing party or the client or interfere with the administration of justice, as would withdrawal on the eve of trial.

ETHICS ALERT

Model Rule 1.16, directed toward declining or terminating representation, states:

(a) Except as stated in paragraph (c), a lawyer shall not represent a client or, where representation has commenced, shall withdraw from representation of a client if:

1. The representation will result in violation of the rules of professional conduct or other law;

2. The lawyer's physical or mental condition materially impairs the lawyer's ability to represent the client; or

3. The lawyer is discharged.

(b) Except as stated in paragraph (c), a lawyer may withdraw from representing a client if withdrawal can be accomplished without material adverse effect on the interests of the client, or if:

1. The client persists in a course of action involving the lawyer's services that the lawyer reasonably believes is criminal or fraudulent;

2. The client has used the lawyer's services to perpetrate a crime or fraud;

3. A client insists upon pursuing an objective that the lawyer considers repugnant or imprudent;

4. The client fails substantially to fulfill an obligation to the lawyer regarding the lawyer's services and has been given reasonable warning that the lawyer will withdraw unless the obligation is fulfilled;

5. The representation will result in an unreasonable financial burden on the lawyer or has been rendered unreasonably difficult by the client; or

6. Other good cause for withdrawal exists.

(c) When ordered to do so by a tribunal, a lawyer shall continue representation notwithstanding good cause for terminating the representation.

(d) Upon termination of representation, a lawyer shall take steps to the extent reasonable practicable to protect a client's interests, such as giving reasonable notice to the client, allowing time for employment of other counsel, surrendering papers and property to which the client is entitled and refunding any advance payment of fee that has not been earned. The lawyer may retain papers relating to the client to the extent required by other law.

Under the ABA Model Rules, a lawyer may terminate an attorney-client relationship if any of ten conditions exist:

1. The client insists on a claim or defense that cannot be supported by a good-faith argument on existing law.
2. The client acts unlawfully or insists that the lawyer do so.
3. The client makes it unreasonably difficult for the lawyer to be effective.
4. Before the case goes to court, the client insists that the lawyer act contrary to the lawyer's judgment and advice.
5. The client deliberately disregards an agreement with the lawyer as to fees or expenses.
6. The lawyer's continued employment is likely to result in a violation of an ethics rule.
7. The lawyer is unable to work with cocounsel, to the detriment of the client's interest.
8. The lawyer has physical or mental problems that make it difficult to provide the client with an effective representation.
9. The client consents to the withdrawal.
10. Any other reason is found by the court to be good cause for withdrawal.

A lawyer must still protect a client's interest even after the lawyer has either withdrawn or been terminated from a case. If, for example, a lawyer is terminated or withdraws from employment four days before a court hearing and the client has not retained other counsel, the attorney must take all steps necessary to protect the client's rights, including appearing at the hearing and requesting a continuance for the client.

In some cases, the permission of the court is required before an attorney may withdraw from representation. Each state varies as to this requirement and the circumstances surrounding attorney withdrawal.

ATTORNEY DISCIPLINE

Attorneys who fail to abide by the ethical rules of their state are subject to discipline by their state bar association or other attorney disciplinary agency. Most state bar associations have rules governing discipline. In 1989, the ABA adopted the Model Rules for Lawyer Disciplinary Enforcement, which replaced earlier versions of the rules.

If a client complains to a state bar about an attorney, the state bar or other attorney disciplinary agency will investigate the matter, and a hearing will be held to determine whether the attorney has violated a rule. The attorney is entitled to be represented by an attorney. If the attorney is found guilty, the state bar or other agency may impose discipline on the lawyer in any one of five ways: admonition, reprimand, probation, suspension, or disbarment. Other forms of discipline may be used with these five in some circumstances.

Admonition

Admonition: A reprimand given to a lawyer.

Admonition, also known as a private reprimand or private reproval, is the least severe form of discipline. When it is imposed, a state bar or other attorney disciplinary agency declares an attorney's conduct improper but keeps the information private.

The charge, facts of the case, proceedings, and outcome go into the attorney's file, and no further action is taken on the matter. However, if the attorney faces similar charges in the future, the state bar or other attorney disciplinary agency will consider past offenses when imposing discipline.

For example, a client complained that his attorney consistently failed to return telephone calls. The attorney was contacted and asked why she had not communicated with the client. If the attorney's failure was by oversight or inadvertence, the attorney will be admonished to be more responsive to the client. The matter will be closed, and the attorney's file will be documented that the admonishment occurred.

Reprimand

Reprimand: A formal rebuke; to strongly criticize.

Reprimand, also known as public censure or public reproval, is a form of discipline that publicly declares an attorney's conduct improper. A state bar or other attorney disciplinary agency publishes the name of the attorney, facts surrounding the discipline, and the form of reprimand in newspapers, magazines, journals, and other publications.

An attorney who is reprimanded loses client confidence. The attorney's reputation and the firm's reputation suffer when a reprimand is published.

For example, an attorney was reprimanded for failing to maintain accurate records of his client funds trust account. The attorney was responsible for managing funds from the sale of client's business and received and deposited into the client trust account funds from the sale of the client's business. He wrote checks on behalf of the client resulting from the sale of the business. Two of the checks were returned for insufficient funds, and the attorney quickly deposited the requisite funds into the client funds account to satisfy the checks. On investigation by the disciplinary agency, it was found that the attorney had mismanaged his client funds account and was publicly reproved. In addition, the attorney had to complete four hours of training in client trust account management. The matter was published in a state bar association magazine.

Probation

Probation: A form of discipline that allows a person convicted of an offense to forgo more drastic punishment under supervised conditions.

When an attorney is on **probation,** a state bar or other disciplinary agency imposes certain conditions that must be met for the lawyer to continue to practice law. Probation may be ordered alone or with an admonition or reprimand. Probation also may be imposed as a condition on reinstatement of a suspended or disbarred attorney. The conditions of probation may include the following:

◆ Quarterly or semiannual reports on caseload status
◆ Supervision by a local disciplinary committee member
◆ Periodic audits of trust accounts
◆ Participation in local drug or alcohol abuse programs
◆ Passing of the Professional Responsibility section of the state bar exam
◆ Other limitations on the attorney's practice

For example, an attorney represented a client in a personal injury case. The attorney filed a complaint and shortly thereafter gave the case to another attorney without the client's knowledge and consent. Although she was the attorney of record, she failed to monitor the other attorney's work and failed to perform further work for the client. The court dismissed the complaint for failure to prosecute.

The client complained to the state bar, and, on investigation, the state bar found that the attorney had a prior record of discipline. The state bar ruled that the attorney was guilty of failure to competently perform legal services, improper withdrawal, and failure to return unearned fees. She was ordered to pay restitution to the client and was placed on three years' probation.

Suspension

Suspension: The temporary cessation of the right to practice law as punishment for wrongdoing.

A more severe form of discipline, **suspension** means that an attorney may not practice law for a specific period of time, usually from six months to three years. After the period of suspension has ended, the attorney may apply for **reinstatement,** or restoration of the right to practice law. The attorney must be able to prove **rehabilitation,** or restoration to a useful life, and may be put on probation as a condition of reinstatement.

Reinstatement: The restoration of a right that had ceased.

A suspended attorney must notify all clients, usually in writing, that he or she has been suspended. The attorney also must find clients another attorney if they so request. If the suspension jeopardizes a client's case, the suspended attorney must be diligent to minimize the client's inconvenience or damage caused by the suspension.

Rehabilitation: Restoration to a useful life through education and therapy.

A suspension is open to public scrutiny. The name of the attorney, facts of the case, and findings of the state bar or other attorney disciplinary agency are published in newspapers, magazines, or other periodicals. Suspension not only interrupts an attorney's career and ability to earn a living but is also damaging to the attorney's and the firm's reputation.

For example, an attorney worked for a distribution company owned by his father. The company contracted with a packing company that packed, stored, and sold the product. The attorney began to defraud the packing company by underpaying them and using false invoices. The case was litigated, and the jury found the attorney guilty of five counts of aiding and abetting mail fraud and conspiracy to commit mail fraud. The state bar investigated and found that the attorney's conduct involved multiple acts of wrongdoing based on his convictions. His license to practice law was suspended for three years.

Disbarment

Disbarment: The taking away of a lawyer's right to practice law.

Disbarment, the most drastic attorney discipline, terminates a lawyer's status as a lawyer and cancels the attorney's license to practice law. Disbarments are subject to public scrutiny. The name of the attorney, facts of the case, and findings of the state bar are published in newspapers, magazines, or other periodicals.

Some state bar associations do not have the ultimate authority to disbar an attorney. Since disbarment directly affects an attorney's ability to make a living, some states require that all disbarment proceedings be appealed or reviewed by the state's high court. The state court will review the allegations and the facts of the case and will either **confirm** (verify) or **overrule** (reject) the disbarment and order a suspension, reprimand, or other form of discipline.

Confirm: To corroborate or verify (ratify) the ruling of a lower court.

A disbarred attorney may not practice law in any other state. When an attorney applies for membership in a state bar of another state, the application asks whether the attorney is disbarred in another state. If a disbarred attorney lies on the application and the lie is discovered, the attorney will be immediately disbarred again and prosecuted for fraud.

Overrule: To reject or supersede an existing judicial opinion; to invalidate.

Disbarment is not always permanent. An attorney may apply for reinstatement after a sufficient amount of time has elapsed, usually about five years. The attorney must show proof of rehabilitation. Reinstatement may have conditions imposed, such as probation.

For example, an attorney was paid $20,000 to represent two clients in a civil case. She failed to perform the work, and the case was set for a hearing to determine whether the case should be dismissed. The attorney did not show up at the hearing, and the case was dismissed. The attorney failed to refund unearned fees to the client.

In a second matter, the same attorney represented a different client in a personal injury case. The client made numerous attempts to reach the attorney, but without success. Subsequently, the attorney settled the case without the client's knowledge or consent. She signed the client's name to the settlement draft and deposited the money into the client funds trust account. The attorney failed to notify the client that settlement funds were received and did not disburse the funds to the client. On investigation, the disciplinary agency found that the attorney had a prior record of similar acts of misconduct and that she had caused great harm to her clients. The attorney was disbarred for misappropriation of funds, failure to competently perform legal services, failure to refund unearned fees, failure to communicate, failure to notify clients of receipt of settlement funds, failure to disburse settlement funds, failure to maintain client funds in trust, and failure to cooperate in disciplinary proceedings.

Other Forms of Discipline

Other forms of discipline frequently imposed with the five standard forms of discipline include the following:

◆ Restitution, if a lawyer has stolen client's funds.

◆ Payment of costs.

◆ Limitation on practice.

◆ Requirement that a lawyer take the Professional Responsibility exam.

◆ Resignation. Occasionally an attorney will resign his or her license to practice law instead of going through disciplinary proceedings. If the grievance is serious enough to warrant disbarment, an attorney will resign to avoid publication of his or her conduct. When an attorney resigns, the resignation is published, but the actions of the attorney and the facts of the case are not published since resignation halts disciplinary and investigative proceedings.

Clients who have been damaged by the ethical violations of their attorneys may sue them for damages in addition to reporting them to disciplinary authorities.

Civil and Criminal Liability   To be licensed as an attorney, a person must be of high moral character. If an attorney is convicted of a crime or commits an illegal act, regardless of client involvement, a state bar association or other attorney disciplinary agency will consider the crime a moral offense and therefore subject the attorney to discipline. In addition, an attorney will be subject to any sentence or fines imposed by a judge in a criminal matter.

If an attorney's breach of an ethical rule involves fraud or any other civil offense, the client also may sue the attorney in civil court and may recover damages. If an attorney fails to act competently or represent a client diligently, the client may sue the attorney for malpractice.

Attorney Malpractice   A negligent attorney may be sued for malpractice. The case may be tried through the state court system or without court involvement through **arbitration.**

Arbitration: The resolution of a dispute without court involvement.

Most attorneys carry malpractice insurance to cover the costs of malpractice suits and arbitration. The price of this insurance has risen tremendously since the early 1970s because of the high cost of claims paid successful litigants. No matter how diligent a firm represents its clients, mistakes are made. In the practice of law, mistakes are costly not only for the firm but also for the client. Most legal malpractice claims have their origin in the breakdown of the attorney-client relationship. A client who has been treated professionally, courteously, and respectfully will rarely file a formal malpractice claim against an attorney. A disgruntled client, one who has been treated unprofessionally and without respect, is more likely to file a malpractice claim to make the attorney's life just as miserable.

In a conventional malpractice case, the plaintiff must prove the following four elements:

◆ The existence of an attorney-client relationship

◆ That the attorney's action (or inaction) was negligent

1. Failure to properly calendar a matter or event.

2. Failure to properly refuse engagement as an attorney or to disengage from previously accepted cases and clients.

3. A suit against a former client for unpaid legal fees. (Sued clients usually retaliate with legal malpractice claims.)

4. Inadequate knowledge of the law or failure to adequately investigate underlying facts.

5. Poor client relations.

6. Personal or financial involvement with clients.

7. Malicious prosecution and abuse of process claims by a former opponent.

8. Conflicts of interest.

9. Inadequate protection of client's interests (for example, failure to file or record security documents for a client's loan).

10. Lack of documentation (for example, failure to notify a client of a settlement offer).

EXHIBIT 4.13 The Ten Most Common Malpractice Claims, by Frequency
Reprinted with permission of *Legal Assistant Today* magazine. Copyright by James Publishing, Inc.

◆ That the attorney's action (or inaction) caused injury to the client
◆ The nature and amount of damages to the client

Stephen M. Blumberg and Willis S. Boughman researched legal malpractice claims and published their findings in their book *Preventing Legal Malpractice: California Case Studies.* They found the ten most common legal practice claims, which are shown in Exhibit 4.13. They also found that certain types of cases experienced more malpractice claims than others, as shown in Exhibit 4.14.

An attorney breaching a provision of the code of ethics damages his or her reputation and the reputation of the firm in addition to costing the firm high malpractice insurance rates. Therefore, the importance of good client relationships cannot be overemphasized.

CONCLUSION

Lawyers are paid for satisfying clients. Therefore, client satisfaction should be the basis for measuring law firm performance. Studies have shown that clients, in general, are not satisfied with how lawyers communicate with them or handle their legal matters. If all members of a legal team devoted their efforts to strengthening the attorney-client relationship, a firm would be rewarded by satisfied clients telling their friends about the firm. The future of every law firm rests on its ability to attract and hold satisfied clients. Lawyers do not build law firms—clients do.

By Percentages:
Plantiff personal injury practices see the highest number of legal malpractice suits.

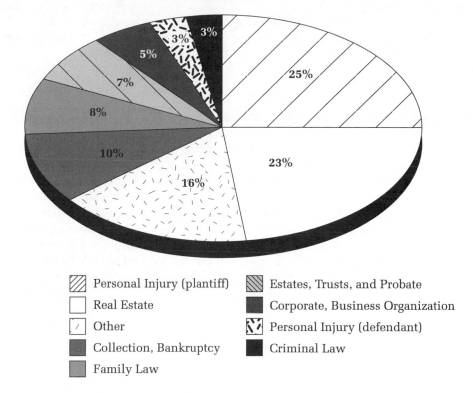

▨ Personal Injury (plantiff)	▨ Estates, Trusts, and Probate
☐ Real Estate	▩ Corporate, Business Organization
⟋ Other	⟦⟧ Personal Injury (defendant)
▨ Collection, Bankruptcy	⬛ Criminal Law
▨ Family Law	

EXHIBIT 4.14   Frequency of Malpractice Claims, by Type

Reprinted with permission of *Legal Assistant Today* magazine. Copyright by James Publishing, Inc.

SUMMARY

Before the 1970s, lawyers enjoyed fairly stable relationships with their clients. Since the 1970s, however, certain variables have affected the traditional attorney-client relationship. The economic flux of the United States and rules governing the attorney-client relationship have caused changes in the traditional relationship.

Lawyers are clients' representatives, officers of the legal system, and public citizens having special responsibility for the quality of justice. As a client's representative, a lawyer performs three functions: adviser, advocate, and agent.

A firm's marketing activities are set forth in a marketing plan. This plan is an essential element of successful client cultivation.

Law firms use various methods to attract clients, including advertisements, promotional activities, public relations, and solicitation. Each state has devised its own rules concerning attorney advertisements. Advertising in a newspaper was the original method lawyers used to reach the public. The most common method of advertising is listing in the Yellow Pages of a telephone book. Most recently, lawyers have taken advantage of the public exposure afforded them by Internet advertising, known as netvertising.

Some firms promote their business by sponsoring and conducting seminars for their clients. Writing articles for legal or nonlegal publications gives an attorney and a firm great exposure. Speaking at lawyers' conventions, continuing education courses, and organizational meetings also gives an attorney and a firm exposure.

The ABA Model Rules and the states' codes of professional responsibility have strict rules prohibiting lawyers' direct solicitation of potential clients. A lawyer may not approach a person and inform that person of the legal services he has to offer.

A capper is an agent of an attorney paid to obtain business for the attorney. Cappers have been known to be very creative in their solicitation efforts. Paying a capper for business is illegal.

The attorney-client relationship consists of five major areas known as the five Cs of client relations. They are competence, commitment, communication, conflict of interest, and confidentiality.

The law has always recognized the importance of competent legal representation. Four things are required to represent a client competently: legal knowledge, skill, thoroughness, and preparation. The legal skills required of a lawyer include technical skills such as the ability to draft documents, review documents, conduct research, and perform administrative tasks, such as record keeping.

Commitment to a client's case forbids a lawyer to neglect the case. ABA Model Rule 1.3 imposes a duty on a lawyer to be committed to a client's matter with reasonable promptness. Commitment to a client's case also includes loyalty to the client.

The obligation to communicate with a client has been recognized throughout the history of the legal system and profession as one of a lawyer's primary duties. Lack of communication is a client's biggest complaint against an attorney.

A lawyer may not represent one client whose interests are adverse to another client, even if the two representations are unrelated, unless each client consents and the lawyer believes he or she is able to represent the one client without adversely affecting the other. The reason for this rule is that without it, a lawyer's duty of loyalty to a former client may be violated, and confidential information gained in a prior representation may be used to the disadvantage of the former client.

One major characteristic that differentiates a law firm from businesses in other industries is the requirement that all matters within that office be kept confidential. Even though court actions are public record, a client's case cannot be discussed outside the office.

Attorneys who fail to abide by the ethical rules of their state are subject to discipline. Admonition is the least severe form of discipline. Reprimand is a form of discipline that publicly declares an attorney's conduct improper. When an attorney is on probation, a state bar or other attorney disciplinary agency imposes certain conditions that must be met for the lawyer to continue to practice law. A more severe form of discipline, suspension, means that an attorney may not practice law for a specific period. Disbarment, the most drastic attorney discipline, terminates a lawyer's status as a lawyer and cancels the attorney's license to practice law.

An attorney breaching a provision of the code of ethics damages one's reputation and the reputation of the firm in addition to costing the firm high malpractice insurance rates.

CHAPTER ILLUSTRATION

The law firm of Black, White & Greene continued to grow. Robert felt that it was time that the firm prepared a formal marketing plan to position the firm in the legal community. He and Tricia decided that the first step was to develop and circulate a client survey to determine the firm's strengths and weaknesses.

The survey was completed and distributed to current and past clients. Approximately 40 percent of the questionnaires were returned. The majority of the clients were satisfied with the service they received from the firm, and others gave the firm helpful suggestions on improving its service. Among the areas that needed improvement were keeping the client adequately informed and communicating with clients in a prompt manner. Some clients indicated that their telephone calls were not promptly returned. Tricia quickly prepared a new policy that allowed an attorney to delegate returning telephone calls to the paralegals. She circulated a memorandum that set forth the guidelines for the returned calls, including cautioning the paralegals against giving legal advice, accepting a case, and communicating legal fees to a client.

The next step was to identify the firm's target market. Because of Dennis White's successful outcome in a business litigation case that received favorable publicity, the firm was attracting small and medium business clients. Robert and Tricia agreed to target their marketing efforts at the business community, offering intellectual property and litigation services to them. The marketing plan was developed to reach the target market, and the firm committed $100,000 to the advertising budget.

Tricia and Robert determined that print advertising and direct mail were the best vehicles to market its services. They placed an ad in the business-to-business Yellow Pages. They also researched what magazines and periodicals were utilized by the local business community. They determined that the *County Business Journal* was the most popular periodical for businesses, so they placed a full-page ad in the *Journal.* Although expensive, they determined that the ad would receive the best exposure there.

Robert and Tricia also determined that the firm should join the local Chamber of Commerce, an organization of business owners in the community. The Chamber has breakfast meetings once a week and offers many benefits to its members. Robert joined and attends regularly. With his participation, the firm became known to many local businesses.

Robert and Tricia wanted to involve the entire firm in the firm's marketing plan. Robert expects the attorneys to participate in marketing activities with the assistance of the paralegals and secretaries. Dennis agreed to write an article on business litigation for the newspaper, and Grant agreed to participate in the next educational seminar being offered by the local bar association. Milton was assigned to watch the newspaper for announcements of new businesses in the county to mail them the firm's brochure. Audra volunteered to prepare a firm newsletter containing Dennis's articles and general information about the firm.

The marketing plan was completed and implemented. Although it took time, effort and money, the firm's marketing strategy was successful, and the firm received the exposure it desired. The firm's client list was getting longer.

One of the firm's new clients was Tinker Town Toy Company, a toy manufacturer. Tinker has a dispute with County Construction Company, which was contracted to build a new manufacturing facility for Tinker. According to Tinker, the facilities were built contrary to the contract and are totally inadequate. County refuses to remedy the situation and fix the problems. Tinker wants to sue. Grant accepted the case and filed a complaint on behalf of Tinker.

The case went into the discovery stage, and Grant scheduled the deposition of Henry Gonzales, County's president. At the deposition, Grant learned that County is a wholly owned subsidiary of Statewide Construction, Inc. Grant thought for a moment and immediately terminated the deposition. "What's going on?" County's attorney asked. "I'll talk to you later," said Grant.

Grant went into the file room and looked in the firm's closed files. There it was. *Statewide Construction, Inc. v. Carpenters Local 101.* The firm represented Statewide two years ago. Statewide Construction is the firm's client. Now the firm is suing a subsidiary of its client, a direct conflict of interest. "Oops," said Grant.

Grant went directly to Tricia and asked her about the firm's policy for checking conflicts. Tricia said, "I'm right now in the process of reviewing the various conflict software available to determine which one is best for the firm. But I haven't chosen one yet. As soon as I do, we'll have to go back into all the files since the beginning and input all the clients in the database. Then the database will be searched whenever a case is opened."

"That's great, but it won't help us now! I need to talk to Robert."

Grant conveyed to Robert his problem with the Tinker case. They knew they were in trouble. Grant immediately contacted Tinker and talked to the president about the problem. "The firm must immediately withdraw as your attorney," said Grant. Tinker's president was furious and said, "But then we'll have to start the case over with new attorneys. That will delay this problem even longer! We've already paid you thousands of dollars. Your negligence has hurt this case, and we are going to take this matter to the State Bar Disciplinary Committee!" He then hung up the phone.

Two weeks later, Grant received a telephone call from Alice Verstegan, investigator for the state bar. She informed him that the Tinker matter is under investigation. Grant cooperated with Alice during the investigation. In five months, the investigation was finished. Alice informed Grant that the state bar had made the following findings:

◆ The firm was negligent in not checking for conflicts when it accepted the case.

◆ The negligence delayed the client's case and resulted in financial damage to the client.

◆ The firm must reimburse Tinker the amount of its attorney's fees, or $34,500.

◆ The firm must implement a conflict-checking program immediately. A legal management consultant would visit the firm in thirty days to check on the program and will submit a report to the state bar reporting the status of the program.

◆ Since there were no prior discipline proceedings and the firm cooperated with the investigation, the state bar would give the firm an admonishment and put the firm on probation for two years. During the two-year period, the firm must submit quarterly reports informing the state bar of the firm's management policies and have no further client complaints.

Everyone in the firm felt the effects of the discipline. Robert and Tricia made sure that every employee received comprehensive ethics training. Now more than ever, the firm's relationship with its clients is the primary focus of the firm, and it has a state-of-the-art conflict-checking program.

CHAPTER REVIEW

1. What factors have affected the traditional attorney-client relationship?

2. What are the functions of a lawyer when representing a client (the three As)?

3. What four things do clients want from their attorneys? Which one do they consider the most important?

4. What types of marketing activities do firms employ?

5. What is the name of the case that permits lawyers to advertise?

6. What is the most common of attorney advertising?

7. What are the exceptions to "solicitation" allegations?

8. What are the five Cs of client relations?

9. What is attorney-client privilege?

10. What are the differences between confidentiality and attorney-client privilege?

11. How does the attorney work-product doctrine affect legal assistants?

12. What are the five types of attorney discipline?

EXAMPLES FOR DISCUSSION

1. New Client

Tim Hemstreet is a sole practitioner. He advises you, his legal assistant, that he is planning to visit a potential client in the hospital who, he read in the newspaper, had been involved in a serious accident. He plans to inform her of his services to retain her as a new client.

1. Is his conduct ethical?
2. Tim informs you that the potential client is his sister. Is his conduct ethical?
3. Tim informs you that he plans to offer his services to the potential client for free because she has six children under the age of seven years. Is his conduct ethical?
4. Tim informs you that he plans to offer his services to the potential client for free because the accident is suspected to be an attempted murder plot by her husband, the governor of the state. He expects the case to draw nationwide media attention that would give him fame and fortune. Is his conduct ethical?
5. Tim asks you to visit the potential client in the hospital to retain her as a client. He offered to give you a "substantial bonus" if you get a signed retainer agreement. Is his conduct ethical? Is your conduct ethical?
6. Which ABA Model Rule applies to this situation?

2. The Battles' Battle

Brenda Battle made an appointment with Gary Athman, a well-known divorce attorney. During the client interview, Brenda told Gary that she wanted a divorce and requested legal advice as to her rights. Gary informed her of her legal rights and counseled her on separate and community property. He also made recommendations on the steps she should take before beginning proceedings. Brenda did not retain Gary to handle her divorce proceedings but paid him for his time and his legal advice.

Two weeks later, Sam Battle, Brenda's estranged husband, made an appointment with Gary. He asked Gary to begin divorce proceedings against Brenda.

1. Should Gary represent Sam against Brenda? If so, why? If not, why not?
2. What ethical rule or rules apply to this case?

3. Where Is the Client?

Client Steven Bristol was scheduled to have his deposition taken regarding his lawsuit against the city. He had forgotten when the deposition was scheduled but was certain it was coming up soon. He contacted his lawyer to ask for the date of the deposition. The secretary told him the attorney was in court but took his name and number and said he would ask the attorney to return Steven's call. The attorney did not return Steven's call, so two days later, Steven phoned the attorney again.

Again, the attorney did not return Steven's call. Steven made two more attempts to contact the attorney for the deposition date and each time received the same reply from the secretary. Two weeks later, Steven was at work when he received a telephone call from his attorney's secretary:

"Mr. Bristol! Where are you? We are all here in the office ready to take your deposition! We're waiting for you. When will you be here?"

"What!" said Steven. "I had no idea my deposition was today. I've called you four times over the last two weeks to determine the date and could get no information at all! I have made no arrangements with my work to be gone this afternoon, and I have an important meeting to attend. What type of law firm do you run down there, anyway?! Tell the attorney that I want to speak to him immediately!"

Steven's deposition had to be canceled, the court reporter was sent home, and Steven's attorney and the city's attorney wasted an afternoon because of lack of communication.

1. What do you suppose Steven's response was when he received a bill for legal fees and court reporter costs for that afternoon?
2. How did this incident affect the attorney-client relationship?
3. How should the situation have been handled?
4. Which one of the five Cs of client relations does this situation illustrate?
5. What ethical obligation did the attorney violate?
6. How could a legal assistant have helped in this situation?

4. The Initial Client Interview

Norma Hunter, a legal assistant, works for the law firm of Everett & Mullins, a respected medium-size law firm. Her supervising attorney is Rick Everett, who specializes in criminal defense work. Norma assists Rick in the initial client interview by taking notes to be sure that they do not miss any facts. She often accompanies Rick to the jail to interview incarcerated clients. Rick was called to represent Charles Nix, a man accused of raping and murdering several women in the area. Rick and Norma went to the jail to interview Charles. The arraignment was scheduled for the next week.

As they entered the interview room, Charles was present, as was a guard who would not let Charles out of his sight. Halfway through the interview, Rick was called out of the room to answer a telephone call. While he was gone, Charles continued his story and asked Norma many questions that affected his rights. He also asked Norma for some legal advice concerning his case.

1. What should Norma's response be?
2. Does attorney-client privilege apply to this situation?
3. Does attorney-client privilege apply to the time Rick was out of the room?
4. If you were Norma, what would you do?
5. If you were Norma, how would you protect attorney-client privilege?

5. The Web Page

You are a legal assistant for sole practitioner, Irene Bunnell. Irene asked you to be in charge of developing a Web page for the firm. She gives you the following directions:

A. The title of the Web page is "The Best Lawyer in Town."
B. It must contain her biography.
C. It must contain the following phrase: "a specialist in family law, criminal law, and probate." (Your state has no recognized specialist program.)
D. It must include a list of her recent clients, including some comments they made about what great service they received from her.
E. It must include a list of articles she wrote for the local bar association and include links to the articles.
F. It must include her picture and a picture of her law office shingle.

1. What ABA Model Rule applies to Irene's Web page?
2. What elements are ethical?
3. What elements are unethical?

ASSIGNMENTS

1. For each situation, answer the questions given with the situation as well as the following questions:
   a. What is the attorney's ethical responsibility to the client?
   b. Under what section in the ABA's Model Code does the situation fall, if any?

   Situation 1: Attorney Pascal Chastain has received a notice of trial in the case of *Jensch v. Quenzer.* The trial will be held in ninety days. Numerous depositions have been taken in the case, but one more is necessary for the trial. It is the deposition of the eyewitness in the matter and is the most important deposition. The bill for the previous depositions exceeds $1,000 and has not been paid. Pascal's client originally agreed to pay the bill but now says he is unable to do so. In addition, the client has not paid his legal fees to Pascal's firm in three months and says he cannot do so. The court reporting service will not provide any more services to the firm until its bill is paid. All discovery must be completed thirty days before trial. What should Pascal do?

   Situation 2: John Korengold asks Rose Riley to represent him in an action against the county. After hearing John's story, making an independent investigation of the facts, and researching the applicable law, Rose concludes that present law does not support John's position but that an argument exists for a change in the law. Should Rose take the case?

   Situation 3: A disastrous airplane crash occurred at Los Angeles airport, and many people were killed. Lee Erickson specializes in airplane accident litigation and was interviewed on a local television show after the crash. During the interview, Lee remarked that the families of the victims should seek representation with attorneys experienced in air crash matters and that his firm is one of the few with such experience. If Lee's primary reason for granting the interview was to solicit clients, was the interview proper?

After the air crash, Lee placed an ad in the newspaper that gave the name, address, and telephone number of the firm and stated, "We specialize in air crash matters. No charge for initial consultation." Was the ad proper?

Lee paid a personal visit to each of the victims' families. After expressing condolences, he advised them of their rights against the airline and informed them that his firm would represent them against the airline. Was Lee's conduct proper?

Situation 4: Zoua Xiong represented Darla Schlattman and Janet Jeffrey by preparing a partnership agreement for their business venture. Darla and Janet revealed to Zoua certain confidential information about their personal financial situations. A year later, the partnership has broken up, and Darla has asked Zoua to represent her in litigation against Janet. Should Zoua accept the case?

Situation 5: Eric Anderson's firm is representing Ernest Walker in a wrongful death action resulting from an automobile accident. Eric has worked extensively on the case, which has received substantial publicity in the local news media, including allegations that Ernest was under the influence of drugs at the time of the accident. A friend asks Eric whether the news reports are true concerning the condition of his client. What should Eric say?

Situation 6: Angela Pavek is representing Paula Erdmann in a matter involving a claim by the Internal Revenue Service (IRS) for unpaid income taxes for the years 1985–88. Paula has informed Angela that before consulting Angela, she gave the IRS false financial statements for the years in question. What should Angela do?

Situation 7: Theresa Enrica is on an annual retainer for Bendix Corporation to handle all its litigation. Bendix consults Theresa on a complex workers' compensation matter. Theresa has had minimal training and no experience in such matters. Should she accept the case?

Situation 8: At the trial of a civil case, *McCauley v. Jeffers,* judgment was for client Molly McCauley, but she was not satisfied with the amount of damages awarded. She felt that she should have received more money. Client Molly demanded that her attorney, Patrizia Boen, appeal the matter on the basis of jury prejudice as evidenced by the small amount of the judgment. Ms. Boen polled the jury and does not believe that a good-faith argument can be made in support of Molly's position. She informed Molly that she did not believe that an appealable issue exists, but Molly insisted that the matter be appealed. What should Ms. Boen do?

Situation 9: Rochelle Betterly is a new legal assistant in a small law firm. She has a conversation with her attorney, at which time the attorney informs her that she will give Rochelle 10 percent of the fees on all legal cases Rochelle refers to the firm. What should Rochelle do?

Situation 10: Renee Farber has interviewed Brett Atkinson regarding a civil lawsuit for damages sustained by Brett as a result of a fight he was involved in at a downtown bar. Brett wants to sue a man for assault and battery. Renee reviews the documents and investigates the matter. She finds that Brett started the fight and that his opponent has filed many complaints against Brett for harassment. She also learns that Brett filed three previous lawsuits against this person for separate incidents of assault and battery. All three lawsuits were dropped when it was learned that Brett instigated each confrontation. Should Renee take the case?

2. Look in the telephone directory of your phone book, under "Attorneys." Do you see any "improper" ads? If so, why are they improper?

3. Interview friends who recently retained the services of a lawyer. Do they feel that the lawyer provided them with good legal services? Why or why not? What impressed your friends about the services? What upset your friends about the services? Where do their comments fall in the five Cs of client relations?

4. Obtain a copy of your state bar association's magazine, journal, or newsletter. Notice the section dealing with disciplined attorneys. What were the ethical violations that caused the attorneys' discipline? Report your findings to the class.

5. You are the office manager for a medium-size law firm in a large metropolitan area. Business is slow, and no new clients have retained your

firm in a long time. The owners of the law firm want to promote the firm and have put you in charge of developing a marketing plan to attract clients. Your target market is small and medium businesses since your firm specializes in real estate and business litigation. You have a budget of $100,000. Describe your plan in a written report. For each item, include a breakdown of cost and describe the members of the legal team who will be involved.

6. Obtain a copy of your state's code of professional responsibility. Compare it with the provisions of the ABA Model Code in the text. Do the two differ? If so, in what ways?

7. Create a client survey (see Appendix F for instructions).

8. For Black, White & Greene, write the client relations policies you would establish for the firm. Include the following:

A. Marketing strategies;
B. Assign marketing assignment to various personnel;
C. Firm policy regarding client referrals;
D. Confidentiality requirements;
E. Conflict of interest policy;
F. Client communications and legal advice;
G. Procedures for reporting unethical behavior;
H. Advertising guidelines and ethics;
I. Newsletter;
J. Seminars;
K. Press releases;
L. Community programs;
M. Client surveys.

SELF-TEST

How well did you grasp the material in the chapter? Test yourself by answering the following questions and check your answers against the answers found in Appendix A.

1. What are the four things that have affected the traditional attorney-client relationship?
2. What type of approach does a state bar's code of ethics provide?
3. What is the name of the rules of ethics adopted by the ABA?
4. As a client's representative, a lawyer performs what three functions (the three As)?
5. As an adviser, the lawyer performs what five functions?
6. As a client's advocate, what three functions will the lawyer perform?
7. As a client's agent, what four functions will the lawyer perform?
8. Who is ultimately responsible for the attorney-client relationship?
9. Who is responsible for a legal assistant's actions?
10. Are legal assistants bound by the Rules of Professional Responsibility of state bar associations?
11. Legal assistants are considered lawyers' _____ .
12. As lawyers' agents, legal assistants are obligated to comply with what?
13. What are the four factors clients want from their attorneys? Which is the most important?
14. What is the best source of new clients for a firm?
15. What percentage of new clients come from recommendations of former clients?

16. What percentage of new clients comes from marketing activities?
17. What kind of plan is a firm's marketing strategy stated in?
18. What is "positioning" a law firm?
19. What is a target market?
20. Why was attorney advertising banned by the ABA?
21. In the case of *Bates v. State Bar of Arizona,* what was the U.S. Supreme Court's ruling?
22. How was the term *dignified manner* defined?
23. What is the most common method of advertising?
24. What are the key considerations in evaluating the content of lawyer television advertising?
25. Why does the ABA promote the Dignity in Lawyer Advertising Award?
26. Why are fewer lawyers participating in television advertising?
27. What is Netvertising?
28. What Model Rule is applied to Internet advertising?
29. What are some of the problems associated with advertising on the Internet?
30. What information about a lawyer's services is prohibited in Internet advertising?
31. What type of firm is most likely to sponsor seminars for their clients?
32. Why do firms conduct seminars for clients?
33. What goals can a firm newsletter help a firm attain?
34. What four different trends participated in the demand for newsletters?
35. What is public relations?

36. What is the difference between public relations and advertising?

37. Why does public relations have more credibility than advertising?

38. What is the general rule against soliciting?

39. Why can lawyers not make the first contact with a potential client?

40. What was the U.S. Supreme Court's ruling in *Shapero v. Kentucky Bar Association?*

41. What is spam, and what happened to an attorney who spammed?

42. What is a capper?

43. Who is exempt from solicitation accusations?

44. What types of people are potential cappers?

45. When may an attorney inform a potential client of his or her legal services?

46. When does a problem occur if an employee refers a friend to an attorney?

47. If an attorney terminates his or her employment with the law firm, is the attorney entitled to take all of his or her clients with him or her? Why?

48. What are some of the elements of the attorney-client relationship?

49. What determines when the attorney-client relationship begins?

50. What were the three factors the Iowa Supreme Court used to test when an attorney-client relationship exists?

51. Is payment of a fee essential for an attorney-client relationship to exist?

52. What are the five Cs of the attorney-client relationship?

53. What four things are required to represent the client competently?

54. What are the legal skills required of a lawyer?

55. What is "thoroughness" as required by the ABA Model Rules?

56. What does adequate preparation consist of?

57. Must an attorney decline a case if he or she has no experience in the applicable area of law?

58. If the case is complex and the lawyer knows that he or she does not have the skill or experience to take the case, the attorney may do one of two things. What are they?

59. If the lawyer chooses to associate another lawyer on the case, what must the attorney obtain?

60. Can the attorney charge the client increased fees if he or she associates another lawyer on the case?

61. Who is responsible for the legal assistant's work?

62. What does commitment to a client's case forbid the lawyer to do?

63. What are some examples of a lack of commitment to a client's case?

64. What does "zeal" mean?

65. What is clients' most common complaint of their lawyers?

66. What are some of the things a lawyer can do to keep clients informed?

67. Providing the client with information relates to two areas of the client's case. What are they?

68. When may a lawyer represent a client whose interests are adverse to another client?

69. What client is owed a greater obligation by the lawyer? Former or potential?

70. When a client retains an attorney, what does the client retain?

71. Can two attorneys in the same firm represent two sides of a dispute? Why?

72. What is a direct conflict of interest?

73. What is a potential conflict of interest?

74. What is a positional conflict of interest?

75. What is one of the major factors that differentiates a law firm from other industries?

76. What are the reasons for confidentiality?

77. What are the exceptions to the confidentiality rule?

78. What is attorney-client privilege?

79. What three factors must be present for a communication between an attorney and client to be privileged?

80. What are the differences between confidentiality and attorney-client privilege?

81. What is the attorney work-product doctrine?

82. What are some examples of a legal assistant's work product that are subject to the work-product doctrine?

83. When may a client terminate the attorney-client relationship?

84. When must an attorney obtain the court's permission to withdraw from a case?

85. According to the ABA Model Rule 1.16, under what circumstances may an attorney terminate the attorney-client relationship?

86. If a lawyer has withdrawn or been terminated, what must the lawyer do?

87. What are the five ways an attorney can be disciplined by the state bar?

88. What is an admonition?

89. What is a reprimand?

90. What is probation?

91. What is suspension?

92. What is disbarment?

93. Who has the ultimate authority to disbar an attorney in most states?

94. Is disbarment permanent?

95. What are some other forms of discipline for an attorney?

96. If an attorney fails to act competently, what is the client's recourse?

97. If an attorney is negligent, what may the attorney be sued for?

98. What type of firm is sued for malpractice the most often?

99. What is the basis for measuring a law firm's performance?

KEY WORDS

Admonition
Amicus curiae
Arbitration
Capper
Compulsory organization
Confirm
Contingency
Direct conflict

Disbarment
Joint venture
Netvertising
Overrule
Positioning
Positional conflict
Potential conflict
Precedent

Probation
Rehabilitation
Reinstatement
Reprimand
Spam
Suspension
Target market
Zeal

Paralegal Ethics and Client Relations

OBJECTIVES

After completion of this chapter, a student should be able to do the following:

◆ Understand how paralegal ethics have evolved.

◆ Describe the disciplinary authority of paralegal associations.

◆ Develop their competency.

◆ Prepare a goodwill letter.

◆ Define legal advice and know what activities constitute legal advice.

◆ Guard against conflict-of-interest violations.

◆ Erect a Chinese wall around a person with a conflict of interest on a case.

◆ Understand the importance of keeping client's matters confidential.

◆ Identify the three main areas of the unauthorized practice of law.

◆ Identify an independent paralegal and discuss the issues surrounding them.

◆ Understand what activities constitute the unauthorized practice of law.

INTRODUCTION

A number of factors contribute to our ethical values: family, friends, religious up-bringing, education, environment, and past experiences. The *Living Webster Encyclopedic Dictionary* defines ethics as "the principles of morality, or the field of study of morals or right conduct." Morality and ethics are intangible. They cannot be defined as honest versus dishonest, right versus wrong, or good versus bad. There are many gray areas in between. Sometimes it is difficult to determine what is ethical because of the many gray areas involved in ethical issues.

Our personal characteristics influence the degree to which we can recognize ethical issues. People with good intentions sometimes violate ethical standards because they are unaware of ethical boundaries or do not give their actions serious thought. It is important to establish a foundation of ethical standards before you are faced with an issue. This foundation is established through education and knowledge of ethics and professional responsibility.

Many organizations—such as national and state bar associations; national, state, and local paralegal associations; and the courts—have developed ethical guidelines for paralegals to follow. Legal assistants are not lawyers and therefore are not bound by the attorney's state bar code of ethics by which attorneys must abide. However, legal assistants are lawyers' agents, and as such, they are morally bound to adhere to the lawyers' code of professional conduct and be familiar with the attorney's ethical responsibility to the client. A legal assistant cannot be **incarcerated** or prosecuted by a state bar or governing agency for unethical behavior. It is the client and the employing firm or attorney that suffer from a paralegal's unethical conduct.

Incarcerated:
Imprisoned; confinement to a jail or penitentiary.

166

Without a mechanism in place to enforce paralegal adherence to ethical codes, legal assistants comply with ethical codes to protect their employers from liability. Law firms expect a high standard of conduct from their employees. Therefore, legal assistants must adhere to strict ethical guidelines and be knowledgeable about what ethical behavior is expected from them.

EVOLVEMENT OF PARALEGAL ETHICS

Role of Bar Associations

The paralegal profession was born in the 1960s out of concern for the legal profession as it was structured. The rising cost of legal services was preventing low- and middle-income people from access to the legal system. This caused the organized bar and the lawyers themselves to examine their profession. A study conducted by the American Bar Association (ABA) in the early 1960s revealed that lawyers' businesses were not as profitable as other professionals, such as doctors, dentists, and architects. To discover the reason, the ABA took a hard look at the other professions. They found some distinct differences. Doctors and dentists were professionally managed and used assistants. The ABA considered the use of legal assistants and determined that it would (1) increase lawyers' efficiency, (2) decrease costs to the client, and (3) increase the attorney's profitability. Thus the paralegal profession was born.

In 1967, the ABA promoted the concept of legal assistants and established a committee on legal assistants in 1968. The committee, now called the ABA Standing Committee on Legal Assistants, promotes the paralegal concept and conducts surveys of attorneys regarding their utilization. Although attorneys were slow to accept legal assistants, today they are a common and essential member of the legal team.

The first formal paralegal educational programs were established in the early 1970s. In 1971, there were eleven paralegal programs in the entire country. In 1974, the ABA adopted guidelines for paralegal education and curriculum and began its approval process of paralegal programs in 1975. The ABA has attempted to further define the role of the legal assistant and to educate attorneys in the effective utilization of legal assistants by adopting the ABA Model Guidelines for Legal Assistant Services.

The ABA Model Guidelines contain ten guidelines, as follows:

Guideline 1: A lawyer is responsible for all of the professional actions of a legal assistant performing legal assistant services at the lawyer's direction and should take reasonable measures to ensure that the legal assistant's conduct is consistent with the ABA Model Rules of Professional Conduct.

Guideline 2: Provided the lawyer maintains responsibility for the work product, a lawyer may delegate to a legal assistant any task normally performed by the lawyer except those tasks proscribed to one not licensed as a lawyer by statute, court rule, administrative rule or regulation, controlling authority, the ABA Model Rules of Professional Conduct, or these Guidelines.

Guideline 3: A lawyer may not delegate to a legal assistant:

A. Responsibility for establishing an attorney-client relationship.

B. Responsibility for establishing the amount of a fee to be charged for a legal service.

C. Responsibility for a legal opinion rendered to a client.

Guideline 4: It is the lawyer's responsibility to take reasonable measures to ensure that clients, courts, and other lawyers are aware that a legal assistant, whose services are utilized by the lawyer in performing legal services, is not licensed to practice law.

Guideline 5: A lawyer may identify legal assistants by name and title on the lawyer's letterhead and on business cards identifying the lawyer's firm.

Guideline 6: It is the responsibility of a lawyer to take reasonable measures to ensure that all client confidences are preserved by a legal assistant.

Guideline 7: A lawyer should take reasonable measures to prevent conflicts of interest resulting from a legal assistant's other employment or interests insofar as such other employment or interests would present a conflict of interest if it were that of the lawyer.

Pro bono: Latin for "for the good"; used to describe work or services performed free of charge for indigent people.

Guideline 8: A lawyer may include a charge for the work performed by a legal assistant in setting a charge for legal services.

Guideline 9: A lawyer may not split fees with a legal assistant nor pay a legal assistant for the referral of legal business. A lawyer may compensate a legal assistant based on the quantity and quality of the legal assistant's work and the value of that work to a law practice, but the legal assistant's compensation may not be contingent, by advance agreement, upon the profitability of the lawyer's practice.

Guideline 10: A lawyer who employs a legal assistant should facilitate the legal assistant's participation in appropriate continuing education and **pro bono** public activities.

In addition to these ten guidelines, the ABA adopted Model Rule 5.3, which states the following:

With respect to a non-lawyer employed or retained by or associated with a lawyer:

a. A partner in a law firm shall make reasonable efforts to insure that the firm has in effect measures giving reasonable assurances that the person's conduct is compatible with the professional obligations of the lawyer;

b. A lawyer having direct supervisory authority over the non-lawyer shall make reasonable efforts to ensure that the person's conduct is compatible with the professional obligations of the lawyer; and

c. A lawyer shall be responsible for the conduct of such persons that would be a violation of the Rules Professional Conduct if engaged in by a lawyer if:

1. The lawyer orders or, with the knowledge of the specific conduct, ratifies the conduct involved; or

2. The lawyer is a partner in a law firm in which the person is employed, or has direct supervisory authority over the person, and knows of the conduct at a time when its consequences can be avoided or **mitigated** but fails to take responsible **remedial** action.

Mitigated: To make less severe; alleviation, reduction, abatement, or diminution of a penalty or punishment imposed by law.

Remedial: Affording a remedy; giving means of obtaining redress.

Further, ABA Ethical Consideration 3-6 states: "A lawyer often delegates tasks to clerks, secretaries and other lay persons. Such delegation is proper if the lawyer maintains a direct relationship with his client, supervises the delegated work, and has complete professional responsibility for the work product. This delegation enables a lawyer to render legal service more economically and efficiently."

In addition to the ABA, some local and state bar associations have also adopted guidelines for the use of legal assistants. Exhibit 5.1 lists some of the guidelines, by state. Limitations of delegable tasks differ widely. Some states prohibit legal assistants from attending real estate closings, while other states allow it. Some states prohibit legal assistants from supervising will executions, while other states allow it. Paralegals must be familiar with their state's ethical boundaries.

Role of Paralegal Associations

During the 1970s, two national paralegal associations were established: the National Federation of Paralegal Associations (NFPA) and the National Association of Legal Assistants (NALA). The NFPA is an association of local paralegal associations and individual members. The NALA is an association of individual members and has local paralegal groups affiliated with it. Numerous local and state paralegal associations were also established.

Each national association established a code of ethics for which their members are responsible. These codes are set forth in Appendix G. The NFPA has an enforcement committee that investigates an alleged violation. If the committee finds that misconduct occurred, it may impose any of the following sanctions:

◆ Letter of reprimand
◆ Counseling
◆ Attendance at an ethics course approved by committee
◆ Probation
◆ Suspension of authority to practice
◆ Revocation of authority to practice

STATE	RULES
Colorado	CBA Legal Assistant Committee Guidelines for the Utilization of Legal Assistants (1986)
Connecticut	Lawyers' Professional Responsibility Obligations concerning Paralegals (1985)
Florida	Florida Statute 57.104 (1980)
Georgia	Advisory Opinion 21 of the State Bar Disciplinary Board, State of Georgia
Idaho	Idaho State Bar Resolution 94-7 (1994)
Illinois	5 ILCS 70/1.35 (1996)
Iowa	Ethical Guidelines for Legal Assistants in Iowa (1988)
Kansas	Guidelines for the Utilization of Legal Assistants in Kansas (1988)
Kentucky	Supreme Court Rule 3.700, Provision Relating to Paralegals (1989)
Michigan	Guidelines for the Utilization of Legal Assistant Services (1993)
Missouri	Practicing with Paralegals—Answers to Frequently Asked Questions and the Missouri Bar Guidelines (1987)
New Hampshire	Supreme Court Rule 35 (1993)
New Mexico	SCRA 1986, Judicial Pamphlet 16 (1986)
New York	The Expanding Role of the Legal Assistant in New York
North Carolina	Guidelines for Use of Nonlawyers in Rendering Legal Services
North Dakota	Rules of Professional Conduct, Supreme Court Amendment (1996)
Rhode Island	Supreme Court Provisional Order No. 18—Guidelines for Use of Legal Assistants (1990)
South Carolina	Guidelines for the Utilization by Lawyers of the Services of Legal Assistants (1981)
South Dakota	Supreme Court Rule 92-5 (1992)
Texas	General Guidelines for the Utilization of the Services of Legal Assistants by Attorneys (1981)
Virginia	Education standards and Professional Responsibility Guidelines of Legal Assistants in the Commonwealth of Virginia (1994)

EXHIBIT 5.1 Paralegal Utilization Rules, by State

Source: *The Handbook on Paralegal Utilization.* Reprinted with permission of the California Alliance of Paralegal Associations.

◆ Imposition of a fine
◆ Assessment of costs
◆ Referral to the appropriate authority if criminal activity is found.

Some state and local paralegal associations have developed their own ethical code, while others have adopted the ethical codes of a national paralegal association. A few local paralegal associations have an ethical standards committee to impose discipline on their members who violate their codes. Discipline ranges from recommended counseling to cancellation of membership. As of this writing, only one paralegal's membership has been so canceled. Paralegal ethical standards committees have no authority to impose stricter discipline. It has been a problem to monitor adherence to the organization's ethics code. Unless the violation is reported to the association, the association is unaware of the violation.

PARALEGAL ETHICS AND CLIENT RELATIONS

We discussed the five Cs of client relations in Chapter 4 as they relate to the attorney. The same elements apply to legal assistants. The five Cs of client relations are competence, commitment, communication, conflict of interest, and confidentiality.

Competence

It is important to the effective representation of a client that all members of the legal team be competent. A legal assistant has an obligation to strive for increased competency. The four aspects of a lawyer's competency also apply to legal assistants: legal knowledge, skill, thoroughness, and preparation.

You acquire legal knowledge in school and continuing legal education. Applying that knowledge to clients' cases creates skill. Your knowledge and skill are continuously growing. You will increase your knowledge and skill by experience and continuing your legal education. The NALA expects its members to complete a certain number of continuing education units in order to maintain active status in their association.

Thoroughness is accomplished by adequate preparation. A law office relies heavily on its staff for various aspects of a case. A busy lawyer with little time to research a case relies on the legal assistant (or law clerk) for the research. If the research is not thorough, the lawyer has no way of knowing it unless he or she did the research him- or herself or was "surprised" at a court hearing.

Even minor errors can cause irreparable harm in a legal case. Typographical errors, wrong dates, wrong names, or a comma in the wrong place can have dire consequences to a client's case. Failing to prepare a document correctly or being sloppy in work habits affect thoroughness. It is vital to be meticulous about every detail in a task.

Surprisingly, technology has been responsible for a lack of thoroughness. A task can be accomplished faster, and it is easy to rely on technology to be thorough for us.

OF INTEREST . . .

Common Time Wasters

The following are things that waste time and affect the efficiency of paralegals:

Accepting too many jobs at one time

Attempting to blame people for mistakes

Changing priorities unnecessarily

Commuting

Daydreaming

Delayed decisions

Excessive clutter

Excessive neatness

Failure to delegate

Failure to let subordinates work on their own

Failure to set priorities

Failure to set standards

Fatigue

Inability to say no

Inadequate planning

Inadequate staffing

Incompetent staff

Interruptions

Lack of authority to carry out responsibilities

Lack of clear objectives

Lack of concentration

Lack of information

Lack of methods for handling recurring problems

> ## ▶ OF INTEREST . . .
>
> ### Paralegal's Sloppy Work Habits Cost Firm Half Million Dollars
>
> A complaint was delivered to a California firm when the responsible paralegal was away from her desk. The paralegal found the Complaint 38 days later, long after the twenty-day response period had expired. The court awarded the plaintiff a default judgment for $562,489.
>
> The firm attempted to reverse the judgment on the grounds that the Complaint got lost on the paralegal's desk, but the court refused to vacate the default judgment. On appeal, the appellate court refused to reverse the decision and the U.S. Supreme Court declined to hear the case.
>
> The firm investigated the incident and informed the court that an effective system is in place so that the incident does not happen again. The problem could have been avoided if the paralegal had neater work habits.

We tend to be lazy in the details. A legal assistant cannot afford to be lazy with details. Many legal malpractice lawsuits have their origin in minor, inadvertent errors that caused a client great harm. Thoroughness is one of the most important aspects of paralegal work.

Canon 9 of the NALA's Code of Ethics and Professional Responsibility provides the legal assistant with the following ethical guideline in this area:

> A legal assistant shall work continually to maintain integrity and a high degree of competency throughout the legal profession.

Section 1 of the NFPA Model Disciplinary Rules states:

> A paralegal shall achieve and maintain a high level of competence. A paralegal shall achieve competency through education, training and work experience. A paralegal shall participate in continuing education in order to keep informed of current legal, technical and general developments. A paralegal shall perform all assignments promptly and efficiently.

How do you know when you are competent? It is like being in love; you will know it when it happens. The more you perform certain tasks, the more competent you become. As you are exposed to various aspects of a task, you gain knowledge about that task. This exposure comes from experience. The more knowledgeable you become, the more skillful you are. The more skillful you are, the more thorough you are. The more thorough you are, the more competent you are.

For example, say that an attorney represents a client to incorporate the client's business. The paralegal is responsible for many of the tasks associated with forming a corporation. The attorney, with the assistance of the paralegal, prepared and filed the articles of incorporation. The client called the attorney to inquire about when the remainder of the corporate documents would be ready so that he could set and plan the first meeting of the board of directors of the corporation. The attorney asked the paralegal how long it would take to get the remainder of the documentation ready for the first meeting, and the paralegal said that they would be completed in ten days. The attorney told the client, and they set the first meeting of the board of directors for ten days hence.

Two days before the first meeting, the paralegal realized that she did not order the corporate seal, stock certificates, and other corporate supplies. She called the company that prepares the corporate supplies, and they informed her that the earliest the corporate materials could be ready was in five business days.

The paralegal told the attorney of the problem. The board of directors' meeting had to be postponed. The attorney was furious and knew that the client spent a lot of time setting the meeting date because it was difficult to get the entire board of directors together. Some board members lived in adjacent counties and had to rearrange their schedules to attend the meeting. The attorney called the client, saying that they had to postpone the meeting. The client was furious. The consequence of the paralegal's mistake are the following:

- ◆ The client and other board members were inconvenienced.
- ◆ The formation of the corporation was delayed.
- ◆ The attorney's trust in the paralegal suffered.
- ◆ The client's trust in the attorney suffered.
- ◆ The attorney-client relationship suffered.

Commitment

Legal assistants must be committed to the client's case. Since legal assistants are actively involved in cases, a legal assistant can easily identify potential problems and be assertive to bring potential problems to the attorney's attention. Legal assistants may then assist the attorney in preventing a problem before it interferes with the attorney-client relationship. Eight areas that indicate a lack of commitment and that will alert legal assistants to possible problem areas are the following:

- ◆ Failure to begin an action
- ◆ Failure to appear at hearing
- ◆ Failure to file pleadings
- ◆ Filing carelessly drafted pleadings
- ◆ Failure to respond to interrogatories
- ◆ Failure to respond to correspondence from opposing counsel
- ◆ Failure to correct a known defect in a case
- ◆ Failure to notify clients of a lawyer's new office address or telephone number

For example, an attorney represents a client in a case involving the client's apartment unit. The client's tenants are suing her for construction code violations. The client is very upset about the lawsuit and calls the attorney every day to learn of new developments. The attorney refers the calls to a paralegal. Every time the client calls, she complains about the lawsuit and the problems she has with her tenants. Each telephone call takes at least fifteen to twenty minutes of the paralegal's time. The case is moving slowly, and there are few if any new developments to report.

The client called to talk to the paralegal. When the paralegal heard that the call was from the client, he had no new information to give to her and did not take her call. The client called the next day and then the next. The paralegal, being busy with other projects, did not return her calls. The paralegal's lack of responsiveness to the client not only is unprofessional but also indicates a lack of commitment to the client's case.

Communication

Legal assistants can greatly assist an attorney in communicating with clients. Most often, when a client requests information about a case, a response from anyone in the firm will be sufficient. Legal assistants, being responsible for the day-to-day maintenance of a case, usually have information about the case readily available. In addition, a legal assistant is usually in the office. If a client gets into the habit of requesting information from a legal assistant, who is almost always available, it will relieve the attorney from returning numerous telephone calls after a day in court. Legal assistants are often the bridge between a distraught client and a busy attorney and contribute to easing the concerns of clients.

Responding to a client's correspondence or request for a status report consists of writing a letter to the client or telephoning the client with the information. Often, attorneys will not respond to a client's request because they have nothing new to tell

---

Black, White & Greene, LLP
Attorneys at Law
234 Main St.
Anytown, PA 00000
(999) 555-9876

Date

Clarence Client
345 Broadway St.
Anytown, Pa 00000

Dear Mr. Client:

This letter is written to inform you of the status of your case for the thirty-day period from January 1 through January 30.

There has been no activity on your case within this thirty-day period. However, we will keep you informed of future events as they occur.

If you should have any questions or comments, please do not hesitate to contact us at any time.

Sincerely,
Black, White & Greene

Milton Nollkamper, Legal Assistant to Dennis White

MN:pe

EXHIBIT 5.2   Sample Goodwill Letter, No Activity

Goodwill letter: Letter written to create rapport and good relations.

the client. If this is the case, a legal assistant can respond to the client's concerns, and this will enhance the attorney-client relationship. A legal assistant may draft a letter for the attorney's review without being specifically directed to do so. **Goodwill letters** are easily written, and if nothing has happened on the client's case in a month, a short letter to that effect should keep the client satisfied. The time it takes to write a simple letter comes back to the firm a hundredfold by way of satisfied clients. When the only correspondence a client receives from an attorney is a bill, the client begins to lose confidence in the attorney, and the attorney-client relationship suffers. Examples of goodwill letters are shown in Exhibits 5.2 and 5.3.

For example, a client called an attorney for updated information about his case. The attorney, being involved in trial, did not come into the office and did not return the client's call. The client called the next day. The paralegal received the attorney's phone messages and noticed that the client called again. The paralegal called the client and told him that the attorney was in trial and asked whether she could help him. The client wanted to know whether they had received a deposition transcript that was taken of the adverse party. The paralegal told the client that she would check and get back to him. The paralegal documented the file that the conversation took place and called the court reporter to find out the status of the deposition. She learned that the transcript would be ready in a week and called the client to inform him. In addition, she wrote the client a goodwill letter and repeated the information. The goodwill letter served two purposes: It gave client the requested information in writing so that the client's records are complete and served to document the file that the conversation took place.

Legal Advice   Paralegals and other nonattorney staff are constantly communicating with clients. Unlike other industries, the legal profession places strict boundaries on paralegal-client communication. The legal assistant must have a firm understanding

---

Black, White & Greene, LLP
Attorneys at Law
234 Main St.
Anytown, PA
555-9876

Date

Clarence Client
345 Broadway St.
Anytown, Pa

Dear Mr. Client:

This letter is written to inform you of the status of your case for the period January 1 through January 30.

The opposing attorney contacted us on January 15 and expressed a desire to take your deposition. However, no deposition date has been scheduled. We will inform you in the event your deposition is requested by the opposing attorney.

If you should have any questions or comments, please do not hesitate to contact us at any time.

Sincerely,
Black, White & Greene

Milton Nollkamper, Legal Assistant to Dennis White

MN:pe

EXHIBIT 5.3   Sample Goodwill Letter, Activity

ETHICS ALERT

of what is legal advice and what is not. *If the legal assistant suspects that the information the client seeks requires legal advice, the attorney must respond to the client.* Further, a client must be informed that the legal assistant is not an attorney and cannot give legal advice. But what is legal advice?

There is no definitive definition of legal advice. An article written by Barbara Rosen for *Legal Assistant Today* magazine in August 1995 describes the problem Susan Kaiser, policy vice president for the NFPA, had to determine the definition. She was helping the NFPA draft its ethical code and asked attorneys for the definition of legal advice. She was directed to the ABA for a definition. She said, "But when I asked the ABA myself, I was passed from department to department. I was finally told, 'We have no definition. Check the court cases in each state to see what they say.'"

ETHICS ALERT

Without researching each state's case laws concerning legal advice, a general guideline for legal advice is this: *If a legal assistant applies knowledge of the law to the facts of a case and renders an opinion, it is legal advice.* This would include the following activities:

◆ Recommending a course of conduct or action to a client
◆ Evaluating a case and predicting the possible outcome
◆ Evaluating a case and suggesting a course of action
◆ Explaining the client's rights or obligations to a client
◆ Independently interpreting statutes, decisions, or legal documents to a client

Court cases have ruled that legal advice requires knowledge that can be obtained only through a law school education and is therefore the exclusive domain of lawyers. This area is especially difficult for experienced paralegals who have worked in a specialized area of law for many years. They know the law and the answers to questions. Although a paralegal is very knowledgeable in her field, she cannot answer a client's questions if it requires applying the facts of the case to her knowledge. Sharon Cohron, chair of the NALA's Professional Development Committee, said, "You can't even shrug, shake your head, or make a facial expression to indicate your opinion." She warns paralegals to be careful of "hot" questions, such as "What are my options?," "How do you interpret this?," and "What does this mean?" (*Legal Assistant Today,* August 1995). Prefacing an opinion with "If I were you" or "If it were my problem, I would . . ." does not negate the legal advice. The impact on the client is the same as if the advice was not prefaced with a personal opinion.

If a paralegal is asked a question that requires legal advice, she or he must ask the attorney for the answer even though she or he may know the answer. She or he may then relay the information to the client. However, it must be the exact legal opinion of the attorney without any expansion or interpretation by the legal assistant. The legal assistant must add that it is not the paralegal's opinion since, as a legal assistant, she or he cannot give legal advice.

In addition to verbal legal advice, *a legal assistant must be careful not to sign a letter to a client containing legal advice.* A legal assistant may draft the letter for the attorney's approval and signature, but the legal assistant may not sign the letter.

There are a couple of exceptions to the prohibition of legal assistants giving legal advice. The case of *Johnson v. Avery,* 393 U.S. 484 (1969), lifting the legal advice prohibition from inmates to encourage them to help each other prepare **postconviction writs.** This case created the "jailhouse lawyer."

Another exception is that you may give legal advice to a client you are representing at an administrative hearing if the administrative agency allows nonattorney representation. Additionally, some states allow nonattorney legal advice in their pro bono program. As a rule of thumb: if you are not sure whether it is legal advice, it probably is. It is better to error on the side of caution and not give the advice.

Consider the following five examples.

1. Your friend has a dispute with his landlord. Under the terms of the lease, the landlord agreed to replace the roof of his house. The landlord did not replace the roof, and the roof leaked and damaged your friend's property. Your friend asks you for advice. You review the lease and tell your friend that the landlord

ETHICS ALERT

Postconviction writs: A written judicial order to perform a specified act or giving authority to have it done after a criminal conviction.

Black, White & Greene, LLP
555 Main St.
Anytown, State, 000000
(555) 321-1234

Clarence Client
234 Fourth St.
Anytown, State 000000

Re: Marriage of Client

Dear Mr. Client:

Enclosed is a copy of the documents that were filed with the court this date.

As you will note, the bank account with Gimme Money Bank has been listed as separate property. According to the information you provided us, the bank account was a gift from your deceased father so would be considered your separate property and not subject to division by the court.

The opposing party has scheduled your deposition for June 4 at 10:00 in our offices. I will contact you prior to that time to discuss your testimony.

Sincerely,

Milton Nollkamper, Legal Assistant

EXHIBIT 5.4 Sample Letter Containing Legal Advice

breached the lease by not replacing the roof and that he does not have to pay the rent. You are giving legal advice. You are applying your knowledge of landlord-tenant law to the facts of your friend's case and giving him an opinion.

2. At a party, a woman finds out that you are a paralegal. "I had an auto accident about a year ago," she groans. "My attorney still hasn't filed the complaint with the court. If he was your attorney, would you fire him?" You answer, "You bet I would." Your reply is legal advice. You are applying your knowledge of personal injury cases to the facts of the woman's case.

3. A patent attorney from the law firm across the hall does not know family law as well as you do. "My divorce client asked me what chance she has of getting custody of the children," he says. "What do you think I should tell her?" You say, "Tell her it's about 80/20 in her favor." Your response is not legal advice because the comment is made to an attorney. If you made the same comment to a nonattorney, it would be legal advice. Since the attorney is responsible for giving legal advice to clients, he is responsible for verifying the legal assistant's information before he relays it to his client.

4. You and your supervising attorney are interviewing a new client. The attorney had to leave the room. While the attorney was gone, you made the following comments to the client: "A plaintiff is a person who starts a lawsuit. A defendant is a person being sued. If the attorney decides to proceed with your case, you'd be the plaintiff. From what you've told us so far, it sounds like your complaint would be based on a claim of negligence and intentional infliction of emotional distress." The first two sentences would not be legal advice because you are not applying the facts of the client's case to the definitions. The next two sentences are legal advice.

5. A client called to speak to your supervising attorney, who was not available. The client asks you whether you think she could win her case. You say, "You have to remember that I am a legal assistant and cannot give you a legal opinion, but in my personal opinion, I think you have a very good case." The statement is inappropriate. Your personal opinion is based on your legal knowledge as it applies to the client's case and is therefore legal advice.

Identifying the Legal Assistant   When communicating with clients, legal assistants must always identify themselves as a legal assistant so that the client understands that the legal assistant is not an attorney. *All business cards and law firm stationery must clearly identify the paralegal's status.* If the legal assistant writes a letter to clients or others on law firm stationery, the term "legal assistant," "paralegal," or other appropriate title must follow the legal assistant's name. This will ensure that no one is confused as to the paralegal's status.

In an ethics opinion issued by the NFPA, it urged paralegals to always disclose their title and jurisdiction on all professional electronic communication to avoid any misunderstanding about their status. All e-mails, whether over the Internet or an **intranet,** should have the paralegal's title and jurisdiction. It should also include a disclaimer, such as "Nothing in this e-mail message should be construed as a legal opinion or legal advice."

Accepting a Case   Another area of a paralegal's communication with clients that is forbidden is accepting a case. *It is the attorney's responsibility to accept or reject a case.* Accepting a case creates the attorney-client relationship, for which the attorney is responsible. A comment that can be construed as accepting a case is forbidden to nonlawyers.

For example, a paralegal received a telephone call from a potential client who said, "I was involved in an automobile accident about ten months ago, and I want to sue.

ETHICS ALERT

Intranet: A private collection of information that is viewed by Internet Web browser software and is accessible only to authorized members of a private network; a private Internet site.

ETHICS ALERT

Statute of limitations:
The time period after an offense within which a lawsuit must be filed.

Does your firm handle such cases?" The paralegal replied, "Yes, we do. We'd have to get started on your case right away because the **statute of limitations** expires in two months. When was the exact date of the accident?" The potential client said, "June 23." "Okay," said the paralegal. "I'm going to send you a questionnaire for you to complete and return." "Okay," said the client.

The paralegal sent the potential client the questionnaire, but he did not return it. The paralegal did not hear from him until four months later. "How's my case going?" asked the potential client. The paralegal forgot about the previous call and searched the client list for the potential client but could not find him. "I think you have the wrong law firm," responded the paralegal. "No," said the potential client. "This is the right firm." Paralegal gave the call to Attorney. The next time the firm heard from the potential client, it was in the form of a legal malpractice suit for abandoning a client and missing the statute of limitations.

Even though the paralegal's comments did not intend to accept the case, the potential client perceived her comments as such. If he would have returned the questionnaire, the paralegal would have given it to an attorney and set an appointment for the potential client to consult with the attorney. However, that process was not made clear to the potential client. The paralegal's mistake was not following up on return of the questionnaire.

The following are the results of the paralegal's mistake:

◆ The statute of limitations expired that prevented the potential client from pursuing his case.
◆ The paralegal was admonished by the firm, resulting in damage to her reputation.
◆ The firm had to defend the lawsuit and ethics complaint, costing it money and damaging its reputation.

Conflict of Interest

Canon 8 of the NFPA's Model Code of Ethics and Professional Responsibility states:

> A paralegal shall avoid conflicts of interest and shall disclose any possible conflict to the employer or client, as well as to prospective employers or clients.

ETHICS ALERT

Although legal assistants do not represent clients, case law from 1985 to the present has opened a new area of concern for legal assistants: nonlawyer conflict of interest. Legal assistants have access to confidential information about a case. Furthermore, they are included in strategic planning meetings for a case and obtain knowledge about how a firm manages its cases. If the legal assistant terminates employment with one firm to become employed by another firm, she or he may work for a firm that represents the opposing party on a case she or he handled for the previous firm. *This presents a conflict of interest for the legal assistant.*

In the case of *Quinn v. Lum* (Haw. Ct. App.), attorney Richard Quinn filed suit against his former legal secretary, Rogerlene Lum, for accepting employment with Cronin, Fried, Sekiya & Kekina. Quinn's firm was known for specializing in representing doctors and hospitals in medical malpractice cases. The Cronin firm was known for representing plaintiffs in medical malpractice cases. Quinn held that Lum was exposed to confidential information in case review meetings about a case in which the Cronin firm represented the plaintiffs. He requested a **temporary restraining order** to stop Cronin's hiring of Lum.

Temporary restraining order: An emergency judicial remedy of brief duration that may issue only in exceptional circumstances and only until the trial court can hear arguments or evidence on the issue.

The court denied Quinn's temporary restraining order, but the Cronin firm agreed that Ms. Lum would not work on the case the firm had with Quinn.

In a California case, *In re Complex Asbestos Litigation,* an attorney who represented many plaintiffs in asbestos cases hired a legal assistant, Michael Vogel, who had previously worked for one of the defendant's attorneys. The defendant's attorney filed a motion to disqualify the plaintiffs' attorney on the basis of Mr. Vogel's conflict of interest.

The court granted the defendant's attorney's motion and disqualified the plaintiffs' attorney from representing plaintiffs in all the cases on which Vogel worked. In addition, the plaintiffs' attorney was fined $10,000 for failing to ensure confidentiality. The plaintiffs' attorney was also ordered to review all the files on which Mr. Vogel worked and to delete any information that Vogel contributed to the case. On appeal, the appellate court upheld the lower court's ruling and set forth two options for a firm hiring a legal assistant from opposing counsel's firm: The hiring firm must (1) obtain a written waiver from the former employer or (2) construct a **Chinese wall,** also known as a cone of silence or a screen, around the new legal assistant and prohibit the legal assistant from working on any case with the legal assistant's former employer. If the new firm does not do so, it is subject to disqualification and sanctions.

Chinese wall: Prohibits a person from working on or discussing a case if that person has a conflict of interest.

A Chinese wall imposes the following restrictions:

◆ The firm must educate all employees about the importance of the Chinese wall.

◆ The isolated person may not discuss the case with others or be near others who are working on the case. All firm employees must be aware of the wall that is constructed around the employee.

◆ The isolated person may not have access to files and documents of the case. The subject case files must be "flagged" in a manner that is identifiable from a distance and is obvious to all who see the file that it is subject to a Chinese wall.

◆ The client must be notified of the potential conflict and of the firm's efforts to isolate the person from those working on the case.

Freelance legal assistants, working for various firms on a per case basis, have a particular duty to guard against conflict of interest. If a freelance legal assistant worked on a case for one firm, she or he may not work on the same case for another firm. To do so would damage the assistant's credibility and reputation and expose the second firm to conflict-of-interest allegations. It is important that all freelance legal assistants keep a list of cases on which they have worked and a current client list.

For example, a freelance paralegal worked on a very large, complex litigation case for one of her clients. The project took many months of the paralegal's time. When she was finished, she received a call from a new law firm that was one of the defendants in the complex case she was working on for the previous law firm. They requested that the freelance paralegal work in the same complex case for them. The freelance paralegal must decline the assignment, as accepting it would be a conflict of interest.

Confidentiality

Legal assistants have a lot of direct client contact. A lawyer's duty to maintain clients' confidences extends to legal assistants. The lawyer has an ethical responsibility to ensure that all employees understand the obligation of confidentiality.

ETHICS ALERT

Although court actions are public record, a client's case cannot be discussed outside the office. In addition, caution should be taken when discussing a client's case while in the office. Never discuss a client's case near the waiting area where other client's may be sitting. Conferring about a case in an elevator is also dangerous. When discussing a case with a co-worker, a legal assistant must make sure that the surroundings are private.

ETHICS ALERT

Confidentiality also extends to the maintenance of client's files. To ensure confidentiality, some firms number files so that a client's name is not on the outside of a file folder. Also, locked filing cabinets protect a client's confidentiality. Client files must be out of the view of other clients or other people not affiliated with the law firm. Some pointers to remember when meeting with clients are shown in Exhibit 5.5.

Caution should be given when communicating with clients by e-mail. If you transmit confidential information to a client by e-mail, the client must receive the communication on a secure server. If the communication is sent to the client and oth-

OF INTEREST . . .

Conflict of Interest Situations

If a paralegal suspects that there may be a conflict of interest, the paralegal must bring the situation before the supervising attorney. It is the supervising attorney's responsibility to make the ultimate decision of whether there is, or is not, a conflict of interest. Conflict of interest situations include:

- Changing Jobs: If a paralegal works at a law firm that is handling a legal matter on behalf of a client and then goes to work for another law firm that is handling the same legal matter on behalf of the adversary, there is a conflict of interest.

- Family and Personal Relationships: If a paralegal is related to, or close friends with, a party in a matter, a client, or someone involved in the matter, there may be a conflict of interest.

- Other Interests Outside Employment: If the paralegal is involved in an organization or is affiliated with an organization that is a party to a matter, there may be a conflict of interest.

Tips and Suggestions:

- If you suspect that you may have a conflict of interest in a matter, bring it to the supervising attorney's attention immediately. Provide only the information necessary to determine whether there is a conflict of interest.

- When you start a new job, ask for a list of legal cases that your new employer is handling. Review the list for possible conflicts. Identify possible conflicts of interest and have a Chinese wall erected around those cases.

ers have access to the client's e-mail, attorney-client privilege may be lost. Before electronically communicating with a client, be sure to ascertain whether the client is the only person with access to the e-mail.

For example, a paralegal and a friend were having dinner in a restaurant and were discussing how easy it is to get a credit card. The paralegal told her friend that abusing credit cards has caused many people to file bankruptcy. She said, "We filed bankruptcy for a couple a month ago. She is a housekeeper, and he is a painter. There is no way they could qualify for a personal loan, but they received three credit cards in the mail. After a while, they had $75,000 in credit card debt that will be discharged in their bankruptcy." Her friend said, "You mean Jose and Ann Hernandez?" "Uhh-hhh . . . how did you know?" asked the paralegal. "Remember? She is my housekeeper, and I referred them to your firm. I didn't know they had to file bankruptcy.

Confidentiality Tips for Client Meetings

1. Do not have case files on your desk that may reveal the identity of another client.
2. Do not accept telephone calls from other clients while meeting with a client. This not only jeopardizes the confidentiality of a client's matter but also conveys a message to the client you are meeting with that his matter is not as important as the other client's matter.
3. Always close your door while meeting with a client.
4. Never mention that a certain client visited your office.
5. Do not have a document relating to a client's case on your computer while meeting with a client. Close the file or use a screen saver.
6. Do not discuss other cases in the office with a client. The client may assume that you also discuss his or her case with others.

EXHIBIT 5.5 Tips for Client Meetings

They told me they wanted a will. Did they really have $75,000 in credit card debt? Wow!"

Even though the paralegal did not mention any names, she did reveal information that identified the clients. Her mistake revealed confidential information about her friend's housekeeper.

THE UNAUTHORIZED PRACTICE OF LAW

Rule 5.5 of the ABA Model Rules states:

> A lawyer shall not: (a) practice law in a jurisdiction where doing so violates the regulation of the legal profession in that jurisdiction; or (b) assist a person who is not a member of the bar in the performance of activity that constitutes the unauthorized practice of law.

Before we can understand what activities constitute the unauthorized practice of law, we must first understand the activities that constitute the authorized practice of law. However, there is no precise definition of the practice of law. A few states have attempted to define the practice of law by case law, but no generally accepted definition exists. Concerning the practice of law, ABA Ethics Code 3-5 states:

> It is neither necessary nor desirable to attempt the formulation of a single, specific definition of what constitutes the practice of law. Functionally, the practice of law relates to the rendition of services for others that call for the professional judgment of a lawyer. The essence of the professional judgment of the lawyer is his ability to relate the general body and philosophy of law to a specific legal problem of a client; and thus, the public interest will be better served if only lawyers are permitted to act in matters involving professional judgment.

Since there is no generally accepted standard or definition of the authorized practice of law, there is no generally accepted definition of the unauthorized practice of law. The activities that constitute the unauthorized practice of law are subject to case law interpretation of each state. In many states, the unauthorized practice of law is a crime. To ensure competent representation, states issue a license to those it feels are competent to represent others. Since legal problems often involve complex issues, only those with an adequate legal education are authorized to resolve legal problems for others. Therefore, all states have statutes that limit the practice of law to licensed attorneys. The public is jeopardized if incompetent persons attempt to represent others.

Court decisions throughout the country have identified various elements of the practice of law. The unauthorized practice of law is performing any of those elements without authorization. The main elements are summarized by the following three tasks:

- ◆ Representing clients in court or government agency proceedings
- ◆ Preparing legal documents
- ◆ Giving legal advice

Representing Clients in Court or Government Agency Proceedings

Legal assistants may not represent a client in court. However, many states allow law students to represent clients in court under a lawyer's supervision in certain types of cases. The law student must meet certain qualifications and be registered with the court. In some states' lower courts, paralegals are allowed to make court appearances in certain uncontested matters if they meet certain qualifications. For the most part, however, paralegals may not appear in court on behalf of a client.

In the case of *People v. Alexander,* 53 Ill. App. 2d 299, 202 N.E. 2d 841 (1964), a law clerk appeared in court to advise the court that his employing attorney was involved in a trial and was unable to attend. The clerk informed the court that the case had not yet been settled. The clerk was prosecuted for the unauthorized practice of law even though he just relayed factual information to the court. At the clerk's trial, the court ruled that the clerk's appearance was an unauthorized practice of law, but the appellate court overruled the decision, stating, "[I]f apprising the court of an employer's engagement or inability to be present constitutes the making of a motion, we must hold that clerks may make such motions for continuances without being guilty of the unauthorized practice of law."

Paralegals may represent clients before many federal or state administrative agencies. The Administrative Procedure Act states, "A person compelled to appear in person before an agency or representative thereof is entitled to be accompanied, represented and advised by counsel or, if permitted by the agency, by other qualified representative." Some agencies have no requirement for the representation. Others have certain requirements that an individual must meet in order to represent a person. For example, immigration regulations provide that nonattorneys become certified representatives before the Board of Immigration Appeals.

Paralegals are also prohibited from representing a client at a deposition. While paralegals may attend depositions with their supervising attorney, they may not ask the **deponent** questions. In the California Municipal Court case of *People v. Miller,* a paralegal was prosecuted for the unauthorized practice of law for representing a client in a deposition because the employing attorney had a schedule conflict. Although the paralegal originally intended to simply accompany the deponent to the deposition, the opposing counsel badgered the deponent to tears. The paralegal tried to calm the client by asking her a couple yes-or-no questions to clarify some statements that could be misconstrued. The paralegal was prosecuted for the unauthorized practice of law. At the hearing, he was convicted of a misdemeanor and fined.

Deponent: A person whose deposition is taken.

Preparing Legal Documents

Preparing legal documents is a task that legal assistants perform often. A problem arises when legal documents are prepared *without the attorney's direct supervision.* Legal documents include preprinted legal forms. Some may argue that completing a form is not a complicated task, but courts have ruled that completing a court form for a client requires knowledge obtained by a law school education and constitutes giving legal advice. Paralegals may prepare the forms under the supervision of an attorney or for their own case if they represent themselves but may not complete forms for another person. Typing and legal secretarial services that choose a legal form for a customer or that tell the customer what information to put on the form have been found guilty of the unauthorized practice of law. There have been other court rulings that said that even informing a person what form to use constitutes the unauthorized practice of law. In addition, paralegals have been prosecuted for the unauthorized practice of law for completing legal forms for the general public.

There are exceptions to this rule. In the 1930s, state and local bar associations entered into a series of "turf agreements" with other professions, such as accountants, real estate agents, and bankers, that set forth what those professionals could and could not do in the legal area. Nonattorneys who are real estate salespersons often complete sales offer forms for their clients; such forms are binding legal documents. However, they are not prosecuted for the unauthorized practice of law pursuant to the turf agreements.

Experts disagree on where to draw the line in this area. Some states forbid their court clerks to tell a person who wants to process their own divorce what forms to use. Other states courts employ paralegals and other nonattorney staff solely for that purpose. They help **pro se** parties complete their paperwork consisting of legal forms for dissolutions of marriage, restraining orders, and small-claims cases. Without this assistance, wrong and incomplete forms are filed, causing delays in the court system. Helping pro se litigants complete their paperwork ensures that their rights are protected and their case is heard in a timely manner. These nonattorneys are giving legal advice as defined by case law in some jurisdictions, but they are contributing a

Pro se: For one's own behalf; appearing for oneself in court.

service to the public and the court system. No one is complaining about their potential unauthorized practice of law activities.

Some states are establishing laws and guidelines for nonattorneys to be able to complete forms for the public. Others are considering it. The Bankruptcy Code allows nonattorneys—bankruptcy petition preparers—to prepare bankruptcy forms for others under their guidelines. Exhibit 5.6 contains those guidelines. Some states, such as California, also allow nonattorneys to prepare forms in certain areas of law without prosecution for the unauthorized practice of law, if they register with each county in which they do business. You will see the law in this area change rapidly as states pass legislation to relax restrictions on the unauthorized practice of law.

A nonattorney who does not work under the supervision of an attorney and prepares bankruptcy petitions for a fee must conform to the following rules, or face fines of up to $500 for each offense:

Rule 1: A bankruptcy petition preparer must sign his/her name and print his/her name, address, and social security number on the petition.

Rule 2: A bankruptcy petition preparer must furnish a debtor with a copy of the document at the time the document is presented to a debtor for signature.

Rule 3: No bankruptcy petition preparer may sign a document on behalf of a debtor.

Rule 4: No bankruptcy petition preparer may use the word "legal" (or any similar term) in any advertisement or advertise under any category that includes the word "legal" in its name.

Rule 5: A bankruptcy petition preparer may not collect court or filing fees from a debtor.

Rule 6: Within 10 days after the date of filing, a bankruptcy petition preparer must file a declaration under penalty of perjury disclosing any fee received from a debtor for services rendered. The declaration must include any fees paid within 12 months immediately prior to filing and include any unpaid fees charged a debtor. If the fee exceeds a reasonable sum, the court may, upon motion of the debtor, trustee or creditor, order the excess fee to be turned over to the trustee and the debtor may exempt those recovered funds. A bankruptcy petition preparer has 30 days after service of an order in which to turn over any excess funds.

Rule 7: If a case or proceeding is dismissed because of the neglect or intentional disregard of a bankruptcy petition preparer, the bankruptcy court will inform the District Court. Upon motion of a debtor, creditor, trustee or U.S. Trustee, and after hearing, the District Court may order the bankruptcy petition preparer to pay the debtor the following:

1. Debtor's actual damages;
2. The greater of $2,000 or twice the amount paid to the bankruptcy petition preparer; and
3. Reasonable attorney's fees and costs.

If a trustee or creditor moves for damages, the bankruptcy petition preparer must pay the movant an additional $1,000, plus reasonable attorneys fees and costs. Additionally, a debtor, trustee, creditor, or U.S. Trustee may bring a civil action against a bankruptcy petition preparer. If the court finds that a bankruptcy petition preparer engaged in fraudulent conduct, the unauthorized practice of law, intentional neglect, or misrepresented his/her experience or education, the court may enjoin the bankruptcy petition preparer from such conduct. If the court finds that a bankruptcy petition preparer has continually engaged in improper conduct, or has not paid a penalty, the court may enjoin him/her from further work in the bankruptcy preparation business. Additionally, the bankruptcy petition preparer may be required to pay attorney's fees and costs of the action.

Any document filed for a debtor by a bankruptcy petition preparer must contain a certification disclosing the bankruptcy petition preparer's name, address, and social security number.

EXHIBIT 5.6   Rules for Bankruptcy Petition Preparers

ETHICS ALERT

Certificate of service: A document appended to the end of a legal document that contains the date and place of mailing.

Probate: A court procedure by which a will is proved to be valid or invalid; refers to the legal process wherein the estate of a decedent is administered.

Paralegals may draft and prepare pleadings, *but they may not sign the pleadings.* Every pleading or other document filed with the court (except **certificates of service**) must be signed by the attorney of record. The attorney's signature is verification that the attorney read and knows the contents of the document.

Giving Legal Advice

There have been many court rulings that have dealt with the area of legal advice and the unauthorized practice of law. In the 1970s, Dacey, a nonlawyer, wrote a book entitled *How to Avoid Probate.* The book provided forms and instructions on how to complete the forms for probating a decedent's estate through **probate.** He was prosecuted for giving legal advice and the unauthorized practice of law (*New York County Lawyer's Association v. Dacey,* 28 A.D. 2d 161, 283 N.Y.S. 2d 984). The court ruled that publication of forms and instructions on how to complete the forms did not constitute legal advice if the instructions were directed toward the public and not individual clients.

Since that time, many self-help legal books directed to the public have been published. Nolo Press, a legal book publisher in California, has a number of books written for this purpose. Nolo Press is not without its problems regarding the unauthorized practice of law. In 1998, the Texas Supreme Court informed Nolo Press that it was investigating it to determine whether its books and software constitute the unauthorized practice of law and whether Nolo books and software should be banned in Texas. Court's subcommittee on the unauthorized practice of law. The Texas Supreme Court dropped its investigation after a new law was passed exempting legal publishers from UPL allegations. Nolo's Web site contains details about the case (www.nolo.com).

Legal "kits" followed self-help books. Legal kits contain the requisite forms for a particular area, such as wills, trusts, and dissolutions of marriage, along with instructions on how to complete the forms. The publishers were prosecuted for the unauthorized practice of law. Consistent with the *Dacey* ruling, the courts ruled that the legal kits did not constitute the unauthorized practice of law because they are directed to the public rather than to an individual client. Today, legal kits for dissolution of marriage, bankruptcy, and will preparation are available in most stationery stores and are also available in software products.

There are a number of legal software products available by Nolo Press, Parsons Technology, Inc., and others. These products have been attacked for the unauthorized practice of law. In 1999, a Texas Federal Judge ruled that Parsons Technology, Inc.'s *Quicken Family Lawyer '99* software constituted the unauthorized practice of law and was therefore banned from the state of Texas. The software is an interactive legal software product that enables people to create their own legal documents such as wills and contracts. The court ruled that the software illegally functioned as a lawyer and placed the software in a new category—cyberlawyer. According to the Judge, the software went beyond providing instructions on how to fill out a legal document. Parsons' lawyers argued that the computer program did not constitute the unauthorized practice of law because there is no direct personal contact that creates an attorney-client relationship. Parsons' attorneys plan to appeal the ruling. The *Quicken Family Lawyer* software is the first self-help legal product to be banned anywhere in the United States since the *Dacey* case in 1967.

The majority of court rulings, however indicate that the kits and books themselves do not constitute legal advice as long as they are not sold in conjunction with personalized assistance in completing the process. A problem arises when you apply the information directly to a client's matter. For example, you can write a book about completing a petition for dissolution of marriage but cannot complete a petition for a client without the supervision of an attorney. You can direct a person to read a self-help legal book but cannot tell the person what the book says or, some experts would say, direct the person to a particular chapter or page.

Independent Paralegals

Independent paralegals provide legal services directly to the public in areas such as divorce, bankruptcy, immigration, and landlord-tenant matters at reduced rates. They direct their services to low- and moderate-income people who cannot afford an attorney. The cases are normally routine, uncomplicated cases with no complex issues. Independent paralegals are distinguished from freelance paralegals because they work directly for the public and do not work under an attorney's supervision. Freelance paralegals work for attorneys on an independent contractor basis under their direct supervision.

CYBERSITES

Freelance and Independent Paralegal Sites on the Web

Freelance

Corporate and Criminal Research Services, Inc.—www.criminalresearch.com

Ideal, Inc., Legal Support Index—www.i-deal.com

Paralegal Consultant Associates—www.paraconn.com

Advanced Business Solutions—www.advancedsol.com

JSB Legal Search and Paralegal Service (Alaska)—www.jsblegal.qpg.com

BWD Services—www.bwdlegal.com

Delaney & Associates Networking Services (California)—delaneyassoc.qpg.com

Independent

Divorce Services (Arizona)—www.paralegal-plus.com

Independent Paralegal Network—www.themisintl.com

Paralegal Services (California)—www.aparalegalservice.com

Sabina & Associates Paralegal Services (Canada)—www.sabinaparalegal.com

A Legal Alternative Paralegal Service (Arizona)—www.legalalternative.com

Association of Independent Paralegals (California)—
    www.paralegals.org/members/region1/CAIndependent

Independent paralegal services emerged in the early 1970s. In 1972, Ralph Warner, cofounder of Nolo Press and author of *The Independent Paralegal's Handbook: How to Provide Legal Services without Going to Jail,* helped launch the Wave Project, a chain of do-it-yourself divorce centers. Wave centers provided typing and information services to the public for $50 to $75.

Since the early 1970s, many independent paralegals have been prosecuted for the unauthorized practice of law. In a well-publicized case, *Florida Bar v. Furman,* 376 So. 2d 378 (1979), Rosemary Furman operated Northside Secretarial Service and helped customers prepare legal forms for their own cases. She was convicted of the unauthorized practice of law for giving them advice on the correct information to insert on the forms. The court prohibited her from helping customers complete the forms. She could prepare the forms, but only with information given by her customers. Furman protested that her customers did not know legal terminology or the correct form to use and that such a restriction would result in forms being completed incorrectly, and this would be a disservice to her clients. The court eventually imposed a jail sentence on her for failing to abide by its order. Her sentence was canceled in 1984 after she agreed to close her business.

In the late 1980s, the State Bar of California found that there was "an overwhelming unmet need" for better access to legal services for low- and moderate-income people. The bar created a commission to study whether independent paralegal services could meet this need. The committee, called the Public Protection Committee, held hearings of laypersons and members of the legal community and found that independent paralegals could help meet this need. The committee issued a report that recommended that the California Supreme Court adopt a rule authorizing independent paralegals to engage in the practice of law in bankruptcy, family law, and landlord-tenant law in uncomplicated, routine cases. The report caused an uproar in the state bar, and its president at the time vowed that it would "never see the light of day."

Scrivener: A clerk or scribe; a notary.

In late 1998, California enacted SB 1418, which allows paralegals to do "**scrivener-type**" services for the public if they register with the county and post a bond. They may help clients who are representing themselves by completing, filing, and serving legal documents. They may make legal information available to customers but may not offer legal advice. They are identified as "Legal Document Assistants." In 2003, the legislation expires and will be reconsidered at that time. Other states are enacting similar legislation or are considering similar legislation.

Contrarily, in 1999 the North Carolina Bar Association's Real Estate Section hired a consumer protection advocate to investigate independent and freelance paralegals who work in the real estate area without proper supervision by an attorney. The consumer protection advocate will submit complaints to the state bar association or attorney general's office for prosecution.

An organization with its roots in California, Help Abolish Legal Tyranny (HALT) estimates that as many as 128 million Americans—more than half the U.S. population—have no access to legal services. It also estimated that U.S. consumers could save 1.3 billion per year on matters such as divorces, wills, bankruptcy, and incorporations by using independent paralegals instead of lawyers. Today, many Wave centers are still operative. In their first twenty years of operation, Wave centers handled more than 50,000 divorces, saving consumers around $20 million in attorneys' fees.

Are independent paralegals fulfilling an unmet need for lower cost legal services? The question can be answered by the public's response to independent paralegals. The Central District of California is the largest bankruptcy court in the nation. More than 50 percent of its bankruptcy filings are prepared by independent paralegals called bankruptcy petition preparers. Some are qualified and some are not, causing havoc in the court system. To eliminate the havoc and control the situation, the Congress passed legislation to regulate bankruptcy petition preparers at 11 U.S.C. § 110, the full text of which is found in Exhibit I. The rules for bankruptcy petition preparers are found in Exhibit 5.6.

The battle against independent paralegal services continues today. It has created a need to separate independent paralegals from paralegals who work under the supervision of attorneys, called traditional paralegals. Traditional paralegals object to independent paralegals using the term *paralegal* or *legal assistant* in their title because they see the two as distinct professions. Attempts have been made to codify and define the term *paralegal* as one who works under the direct supervision of an attorney.

In California's SB 1418 mentioned previously, persons who provide independent paralegal services to the public are titled "legal document assistants." and "Unlawful Detainer Assistants." Traditional paralegals object to this term because it is too close to the title "legal assistant." In California, the opposition campaign was spearheaded by the California Alliance of Paralegal Associations (CAPA), which states that independent paralegal activities are scrivener-type work and CAPA sees the role of paralegals as much more substantive. Other terms for independent paralegals are "legal technician," "legal document assistant," "public paralegal," and "limited law advisers."

A landmark case further identifying the unauthorized practice of law in California is the case of *People v. Landlords Professional Services,* 215 Cal. App. 3d 1599; 264 Cal. Rptr. 548 (1989), which stated that the following actions, when clerical, do not constitute the unauthorized practice of law.

◆ Giving customers written instructions and legal information needed to handle their own cases, even detailed instructions containing specific advice

◆ Providing the appropriate court forms for the customer's use

> **TRENDS ➤➤➤**
>
> **The California Legal Document Assistant**
>
> In January, 1999, the California Legislature approved SB 1418 which created the Legal Document Assistant (LDA) and Unlawful Detainer Assistant (UDA). The bill allows independent paralegals to assist members of the general public with preparation of their legal documents if they register in each county in which they do business and post a $25,000 bond. To qualify as a LDA or UDA, one must have:
>
> 1. A high school diploma or general equivalency diploma and at least two years of law-related experience under the supervision of an attorney or at least two years experience providing self-help service; or
>
> 2. A baccalaureate degree in any field and either a minimum of one year law-related experience under the supervision of a licensed attorney, or a minimum of one year experience providing self-help service; or
>
> 3. A certificate of completion from a paralegal program that is institutionally accredited but not approved by the American Bar Association that requires successful completion of a minimum of 24 semester units, or the equivalent, in legal specialization courses; or
>
> 4. A certificate of completion from a paralegal program approved by the American Bar Association.
>
> The LDA and UDA receive a registration number and identification card that identifies the LDA. The card contains a picture of the LDA and contains the statement "This person is not a lawyer" in bold type. At the bottom of the card the statement "The county clerk has not evaluated this person's knowledge, experience or services" is printed in bold type. The registration number must be on all contracts, letterhead, business cards, and advertisements.
>
> If the County Clerk finds that an applicant does not meet the qualifications, or has been convicted of a felony or misdemeanor, or has had a civil judgment against them for fraud or misrepresentation, an applicant's registration may be denied. The denial may be appealed to the Director of the Department of Consumer Affairs.
>
> The law prohibits LDAs and UDAs from the following activities:
>
> 1. Make false or misleading statements to the consumer;
>
> 2. Guarantee or promise anything unless the LDA has a reasonable factual basis to make the guarantee or promise;
>
> 3. Make any statement that the LDA or UDA can or will obtain favors or has special influence with a court or agency;
>
> 4. Provide assistance or advice which is the unauthorized practice of law pursuant to California law;
>
> 5. Give legal advice, explanation, opinion, or recommendation about possible legal rights, remedies, defenses, options, selection of forms, or strategies. However, an LDA may give the customer written materials that explain procedures and list the forms needed.
>
> Registration is valid for two years, after which the registration may be renewed. The law expires January 1, 2003, at which time it will be reviewed and deleted or extended. For more information, contact the California Association of Independent Paralegal's Web site at www.caip.com.

◆ Typing the forms at the direction of the customer
◆ Filing the papers so that they will be accepted by the court
◆ Having the forms served as directed by the customer

Abuses

The lack of regulation of the paralegal profession, especially independent paralegal services, has created problems for the paralegal profession as a whole. Laypersons with little or no paralegal education or experience are starting independent paralegal services and processing legal cases for the public. The documents filed on their customers' behalf are often wrong or incomplete, causing great harm to the client and damage to the court system. Since there are few laws governing these services, damaged clients often have no recourse against the paralegal service. If a client was damaged by an attorney, they could sue the attorney for malpractice or complain to the state bar about the attorney's conduct.

Foreclosure: To shut out; a termination of all rights of the mortgagor in the property covered by the mortgage.

In 1998, a Florida man who ran an independent paralegal business was convicted of six counts of the unauthorized practice of law, a misdemeanor, and was sentenced to two years in jail. The defendant, Jesse Toca, had no paralegal education or experience but represented clients who were facing **foreclosure** by preparing motions and giving them legal advice. He ran a "pay for delay" scheme. A juror at his trial, Susan Finnerin said, "It was shocking how he was able to tie up the justice system repeatedly" (*Legal Assistant Today,* November 1998).

"Fly-by-night" independent paralegal programs are programs or independent paralegal services that are unqualified and that damage their customers and the paralegal profession, such as the one shown in the advertisement in Exhibit 5.7. The advertisement contains numerous inaccuracies and false statements and misleads the

---

Make Over $200,000 a Year Working at Home Part Time

"I work only two evenings a week. I only have a high school education, and it took only ten days (one Saturday a week for ten weeks) to learn how to be a Board Certified Independent Paralegal. I made $245,000 last year doing legal work in my spare time."

Two years ago, James Jones was a construction worker working for $12.50 an hour. Today, he is a wealthy entrepreneur with his own paralegal business.

Owns a Ranch in Flower Falls and a $750,000 home in Roland Heights

After attending our prestigious paralegal school, James now enjoys frequent vacations to Europe and has been around the world twice!

At our school, James learned how to help others with their divorces, bankruptcies, wills, name changes, incorporations, and landlord-tenant matters. At first he started out by charging his clients a nominal fee but then learned that the demand was so great he tripled his fees and reduced his hours.

Hottest Profession in the Country

The Department of Labor said that the paralegal profession was one of the hottest professions in the country. Start NOW to become part of the fastest-growing profession in the United States. In just ten tutorial visits, you can become a Board Certified Independent Paralegal, certified by the prestigious Professional Paralegal Bar Association of the United States of America, of which Jones is the president. For the low price of $1,200 per lesson, you can learn the secrets of successful independent paralegals. The fee includes software and manuals.

NO legal education required!

NO legal experience required!

We'll teach you all you need to know!

Cruises the Bahamas Six Months a Year in His Own Private Yacht

A FREE seminar is offered at the Holiday Inn, 346 Main St., Anytown, on Saturday, June 30, at 10 A.M. The seminar is sponsored by the prestigious Professional Paralegal Bar Association. At this seminar, you will find out how becoming an independent paralegal is the easiest and most lucrative home business in the country. CALL NOW (999) 555-5555 for your reservation in this seminar. The first ten calls will receive a FREE $50 manual entitled "How to Sue Any SOB for Millions without a Lawyer."

James Jones Is Booked to Make Over $400,000 Next Year

The time is NOW to get started. Riches await you. Because of the demand for this program, all the Monday and Wednesday evening tutorial classes are filled, and there is a waiting period of over ten months. There are still a few seats left in our Tuesday/Thursday evening tutorial sessions and two seats left for the Saturday session. HURRY! Call (999) 555-5555 for a schedule of classes at a location near you.

EXHIBIT 5.7 Sample Advertisement Promoting an Independent Paralegal Service public. With the limited knowledge that the public has about the paralegal profession, they are not aware of these inaccuracies. The program offered in the advertisement is actually a promotion for a paralegal school that teaches its students how to operate an independent paralegal service by purchasing its software and program at a very high price. No legal education or experience is required. Graduates of the program are calling themselves paralegals and doing legal work for the public. The public has no way of knowing whether the independent paralegal service is operated by knowledgeable, experienced paralegals or by one with no paralegal training.

Exhibits 5.8, 5.9 and 5.10 are examples of notices sent to people who were being evicted from their home or apartment. The independent paralegal service searches court records for new **unlawful detainer** actions and mails the notice to the evictees. One of the methods used by the independent paralegal service to delay a customer's eviction proceedings is filing bankruptcy for the customer. Unsophisticated people subject to eviction proceedings often are not aware of the ramifications of a bankruptcy proceeding and suffer its consequences for years in the future. To curb this illegal activity, the California legislature passed a law making access to unlawful detainer court records restricted to authorized personnel only. However, this type of activity still exists today. The passage of AB 1418 is expected to regulate those who provide unlawful detainer services to the public and eliminate this type of activity.

Without some type of regulation, these illegitimate programs and services will continue to proliferate. Regulating independent paralegals is currently being considered by many states and will be developed in the next decade. One thing is for sure: The debate over the unauthorized practice of law will continue into the twenty-first century.

> **Unlawful detainer:** A statutory procedure whereby a landlord can legally evict a tenant in default on the rent.

Brown Legal Offices
(555) 555-1000

YOUR ACTION IS REQUIRED

Dear Tenant:

Your landlord has filed an EVICTION LAWSUIT against you. This is the first step in an action to EVICT you from your residence.

Please take note. You have only five (5) CALENDAR DAYS to file a response in person with the court. If you do not answer within these five days, you could lose the case by default. A Marshal will post a "FIVE-DAY NOTICE TO VACATE" within a few days.

Our office can help you STOP THIS ACTION. By calling NOW, we can help you get the time required to find a new residence or even stay in the premises you now occupy. Don't be forced out of your home with only a few days to relocate. We will extend the time or prevent the action. Don't be misled by other companies claiming to get you more than two months or that others only give you the forms to complete.

WE COMPLETE ALL FORMS FOR YOU. YOU ONLY NEED TO SIGN THEM.

DO NOT DELAY - CALL NOW

YOUR QUICK ACTION IS A MUST. Call us today for an appointment. You will need to bring this letter and any other documents you have received.

EVENING/WEEKEND APPOINTMENTS ARE AVAILABLE
OUR COMPLETE FEE IS ONLY $50.00
WE FILE ALL COURT DOCUMENTS
WE CAN COME TO YOU

EXHIBIT 5.8 Sample Independent Paralegal Service Letter to a Tenant Facing Eviction #1

EXHIBIT 5.9 Sample Independent Paralegal Service Letter to a Tenant Facing Eviction #2

SPEEDY PARALEGAL SERVICES
(555) 555-2000

DEAR TENANT:

An EVICTION LAWSUIT has been filed against you by your landlord. The purpose of the lawsuit is to evict you from your premises. **REMEMBER This OFFICE IS HERE TO HELP YOU!!!!!**

If you have been served with a Court summons, you only have five (5) days "including weekends" in which to file a proper legal response. If you fail to answer within this time period, your landlord may win a JUDGMENT BY DEFAULT AND WILL THEN HAVE THE MARSHAL POST A "FIVE-DAY NOTICE TO VACATE" AND HAVE YOUR DOORS LOCKED AT YOUR RESIDENCE WITHIN A FEW DAYS.

If you have received your notice **CALL ME IMMEDIATELY!!!! "YOU MUST ACT IMMEDIATELY." TIME IS OF THE ESSENCE!!!!!!**

All County Paralegal Services will help you prepare your legal documents, including any legal defenses and follow-up consultation.

WE CAN HELP YOU TO REMAIN IN YOUR PREMISES FOR UP TO FOUR MONTHS. RESPONDING TO THIS LETTER WILL GET YOU ADDITIONAL TIME TO RESOLVE YOUR SITUATION.

Call our office as soon as you receive this letter and have a Counselor come out to your home with no trouble to you, or come in to one of our offices. Office hours are 8:00 A.M. to 8:00 P.M. seven days a week. **"REMEMBER YOU MUST ACT NOW"**

WE MAKE HOME CALLS
24-HOUR SERVICE
BANKRUPTCY CONSOLATION

EXHIBIT 5.10 Sample Independent Paralegal Service Letter to a Tenant Facing Eviction #3

OFFICIAL NOTICE

OUR RECORDS INDICATE THERE IS A NOTICE OF TRIAL/HEARING

TO ALL PARTIES:

PLEASE TAKE NOTICE that your Answer–Unlawful Detainer case has been set for COURT TRIAL on _____ at _____ [time] _____ in Division _____ of the _____ [name of court and address]_____ .

RESPONDING TO THIS NOTICE WILL GIVE YOU ADDITIONAL TIME TO RESOLVE YOUR SITUATION.

REMAIN IN YOUR PREMISES UP TO SIX (6) MONTHS

CALL TODAY FOR MORE INFORMATION

International Paralegal Services
Bankruptcy * Eviction Defense
24-Hour Service

CONCLUSION

According to Therese Cannon in her book *Ethics and Professional Responsibility for Legal Assistants,* legal assistants can advance professionalism through commitment to the following eight areas:

1. Public service
2. Education
3. High standards of ethical conduct
4. Excellence
5. Strong work ethic
6. Integrity and honor
7. Development of the whole person
8. Exercising good judgment, common sense, and communication skills

It is important that all paralegals exhibit the professionalism that comes from a commitment to these elements to ensure that the paralegal profession will be strong and continue to grow in future decades.

SUMMARY

Many organizations—such as national and state bar associations; national, state, and local paralegal associations; and the courts have developed ethical guidelines for paralegals to follow. Legal assistants are not bound by the attorney's state bar code of ethics but comply with them to protect their employers from liability.

In 1967, the ABA promoted the concept of legal assistants and developed guidelines for lawyers' use of them. In addition to the ABA's guidelines, some local and state bar associations have adopted guidelines for the use of legal assistants as well as the two national paralegal associations: NFPA and NALA. Some state and local paralegal associations developed their own ethical code or adopted the ethical code of a national paralegal association.

The same elements of the five Cs of client relations discussed in Chapter 4 apply to legal assistants. They are competence, commitment, communication, conflict of interest, and confidentiality.

The four aspects of a lawyer's competency apply to legal assistants: legal knowledge, skill, thoroughness, and preparation. You acquire legal knowledge in school and continuing legal education, and applying that knowledge to clients' cases creates skill. Thoroughness is accomplished by adequate preparation. The more knowledgeable you become, the more skillful you are. The more skillful you are, the more thorough you are. The more thorough you are, the more competent you are.

Knowledge of the eight areas that indicate a lack of commitment will alert legal assistants to possible commitment problem areas.

Legal assistants can greatly assist an attorney in communicating with clients. Responding to a client's correspondence or request for a status report consists of writing a letter to the client or telephoning the client with the information. A legal assistant may draft a letter for the attorney's review without being specifically directed to do so. When communicating with clients, a legal assistant must have a firm understanding of what is legal advice and what is not. If a legal assistant applies knowledge of the law to the facts of a case and renders an opinion, it is legal advice. If a paralegal is asked a question that requires legal advice, she or he must ask the attorney for the answer even though she or he may know the answer. A legal assistant must also be careful not to sign a letter to a client containing legal advice and must always identify her- or himself as a legal assistant so that the client understands that the legal assistant is not an attorney. Another area of a paralegal's communication with clients that is forbidden is accepting a case. It is the attorney's responsibility to accept or reject a case.

A lawyer's duty to maintain clients' confidences extends to legal assistants. Confidentiality also extends to the maintenance of client's files. Be careful when communicating with clients by e-mail. Transmitting information to an unsecured e-mail address may interfere with attorney-client privilege.

The activities that constitute the unauthorized practice of law are subject to case law interpretation of each state. Court decisions throughout the country have identified various elements of the practice of law. Legal assistants may not represent a client in court. However, paralegals may represent clients before many federal or state administrative agencies. Paralegals are also prohibited from representing a client at a deposition.

When legal assistants prepare legal documents, a problem arises when the documents are prepared without the attorney's direct supervision. Experts disagree on where to draw the line in this area. Some states forbid their court clerks to tell a person who wants to process his or her own divorce what form to use. Other states courts employ paralegals and other nonattorney staff solely for that purpose. Some states are establishing laws and guidelines for nonattorneys to be able to complete forms for the public. Paralegals may draft and prepare pleadings, but they may not sign the pleadings.

There have been many court rulings that have dealt with the area of legal advice and the unauthorized practice of law. The majority of court rulings indicate that legal "kits" and books themselves do not constitute legal advice as long as they are not sold in conjunction with personalized assistance in completing the process.

Independent paralegals provide legal services directly to the public in areas such as divorce, bankruptcy, immigration, and landlord-tenant matters. They direct their services to low- and moderate-income people who cannot afford an attorney. When independent paralegal services emerged in the 1970s, their owners were prosecuted for the unauthorized practice of law.

In the late 1980s, the State Bar of California found that there was "an overwhelming unmet need" for better access to legal services for low- and moderate-income people and that independent paralegals can help meet that need. Contrarily, the North Carolina Bar Association's Real Estate Section hired a consumer protection advocate to investigate independent and freelance paralegals who work in the real estate area without proper supervision of an attorney. The battle against independent paralegal services continues today.

The lack of regulation of the paralegal profession, especially independent paralegal services, has created problems for the paralegal profession as a whole. "Fly-by-night" independent paralegal programs are unqualified and damaging to their customers and the paralegal profession.

It is important that all paralegals exhibit the professionalism that comes from a commitment to ethical behavior to ensure that the paralegal profession will be strong and continue to grow in future decades.

CHAPTER ILLUSTRATION

The law firm of Black, White & Greene was still reeling from the Tinker Town Toy conflict of interest problem that plagued them in Chapter 4. Tricia worked hard to get their conflict-checking system up and running. They hired outside data processing people to go through every case the firm has handled and input all parties and other pertinent information into the system. Now, before the firm accepts a case, they will check their conflicts system to determine whether the firm has a potential or direct conflict of interest.

Tricia arranged for all the employees to be trained on the system, including each attorney. As Milton was being trained, he noticed that he may have a conflict of interest in a case the firm was handling against MidTown Manufacturing Company. He noticed that MidTown was represented by the law firm for which he used to work. He remembered working on the case, but he could not remember much about it. He thought that he had better bring it to Robert's and Tricia's attention.

He consulted with Robert and Tricia about the potential conflict problem. The case is Patrizia Boen's case, so Milton has not worked on it. Melvin, Patrizia's paralegal, has worked on it. However, to avoid any more conflict-of-interest problems, Robert and Tricia decided to erect a Chinese wall around Milton as it pertained to the MidTown Manufacturing case.

Tricia immediately prepared a memorandum to all employees explaining that Milton must be isolated from the MidTown Manufacturing case. All employees were forbidden to discuss the case around Milton, and he could not be near anyone when they were working on the case. They gathered the files containing the MidTown case and transferred it to bright-red folders. The folders had large letters on the front: "SUBJECT TO CHINESE WALL ERECTED AROUND PARALEGAL MILTON NOLLKAMPER." Patrizia Boen, the responsible attorney, was instructed to keep the file in her office in a locked filing cabinet. The file was not to be filed in the general filing area with the other clients' files, where Milton could see it. She was to work on the case in her office with the door closed. Melvin was also instructed to work on the case in his office with the door closed. In addition, Patrizia was instructed to inform her client, JB Asphalt Service, of the potential conflict and the efforts of the firm to isolate Milton from the case. Patrizia was also directed to obtain a release from JB indicating that they are aware of the potential conflict of interest and that they have been informed about the efforts of the firm to isolate the employee with the conflict.

With the Chinese wall firmly erected around Milton, the firm was comfortable with their efforts to eliminate the MidTown conflict. But a conflict of interest was not the only problem they would have with the MidTown case.

Melvin was working on JB Asphalt's response to MidTown's request for the production of documents.

Patrizia wrote Melvin a memo with instructions on how to prepare the response. The memo told him to object to requested documents 10 through 15 as being protected under attorney-client privilege and documents 18 through 21 as subject to the attorney work-product doctrine. He was instructed to submit the other requested documents. Melvin was instructed to obtain all the requested documents from the client. The response was due in thirty days. Melvin obtained all the documents from JB and started to draft the response. He got sick with the flu and did not come to work for a week. Patrizia was getting ready to go on vacation to Europe and was starting to panic because her work was not getting done because Melvin was out sick. The other paralegal, Milton, was isolated from the MidTown case, so he could not step in to help Melvin with the response. Melvin returned to work the day Patrizia was leaving for Europe.

The MidTown response was not the only deadline that faced Melvin when he returned. His desk was piled high with files that needed to be processed before Patrizia left for Europe. He was overwhelmed. Patrizia instructed him, "We have to get the complaints done on the two eminent domain cases today. They have to be filed tomorrow. Call MidTown's attorney and get a continuance on the responses until I return." "OK," said Melvin. Melvin called MidTown's attorney, who was not available. His secretary told him that he would return his call. He worked on the two eminent domain complaints and completed them. Patrizia reviewed them, signed them, and left for Europe.

The next day, MidTown's attorney returned Melvin's call. Melvin informed him that Ms. Boen was out of town and would return in two weeks. He requested a continuance on the responses until after she returned. MidTown's attorney blew up. "What! You want a continuance? This case is set to go to trial in two months! No, you may not have a continuance. Get that response to me today!" Melvin tried to explain the situation. He told him that he was ill for a week, putting the project behind schedule. "I don't want to hear your excuses," said MidTown's attorney. "I'd better have that response today, or I'll ask the court for sanctions against you!"

Melvin went right to work on the response. He was under pressure to get them done before 4 P.M., the time when the messenger was coming to pick it up to deliver it to MidTown's attorney. He quickly prepared it, included all the documents, signed Patrizia's name to it, and sent it off with the messenger.

At 7 P.M. that evening, as Melvin relaxed in front of the television set, he remembered Patrizia's memo about the response. "Ohhhh shi——!" Melvin jumped into his car and went directly to the office. He found the memo in the file. "Object to requested documents 10 through 15 as being protected under attorney-client privilege and documents 18 through 21 as subject to the attorney work-product doctrine." Melvin's response did not object to anything. He included those protected documents. He knew he was in trouble. The documents he attached that were subject to privilege are very important. They show their client in a negative light, and if the opposition sees them, they may lose the case. He had to get the response back.

Melvin called MidTown's attorney the first thing in the morning. "I have to have the response back," Melvin said. "It is incorrect." "What do you mean it's incorrect?" asked MidTown's attorney. "It contains all the documents I requested, and it is signed by Ms. Boen." "But," said Melvin, "she did not sign it. I was in a hurry to get it to you, and I signed it." "I don't believe you," MidTown's attorney responded. "You know that a paralegal can't sign pleadings. No, I won't return it to you. Have Ms. Boen call me as soon as she returns."

When Patrizia returned, Melvin told her what happened. She turned pale. She consulted with Robert and Tricia about the problem. They all agreed that Melvin should be fired, and he was.

The attorneys in the firm expect that their staff know the ethics involved in legal practice, but this problem alerted them to the possibility that their employees' ethics training needed improvement. Tricia consulted with an attorney who specialized in ethics and hired him to develop and conduct ethics workshops for the firm. The workshops were conducted every Wednesday evening for two months, and attendance was mandatory for all employees, including the attorneys.

CHAPTER REVIEW

1. Who conceived of the concept of legal assistants, and why was the profession created?

2. How is a legal assistant's competence increased?

3. What are the eight things that indicate a lack of commitment to a client's case?

4. What is legal advice?

5. What five activities constitute giving legal advice?

6. What are the exceptions to legal assistants giving legal advice?

7. A legal assistant may not accept a case. Why?

8. When does a legal assistant have a conflict of interest?

9. What are some things a legal assistant can do to keep a client's matter confidential?

10. What three activities are the main elements of practicing law?

11. What is the unauthorized practice of law?

12. What determines the unauthorized practice of law for each state?

13. What is an independent paralegal?

14. According to *People v. Landlords Professional Services,* what clerical activities are not the unauthorized practice of law.

15. What are some abuses of the lack of regulation of the paralegal profession?

EXAMPLES FOR DISCUSSION

1. Adapted from Louisiana State Bar Association v. Edwins, *540 So. 2d 294 La. (1989)*

Stacy Williams is a freelance paralegal doing business in New York City under the name Prompt Paralegal Service. She employs her daughter as a secretary. Stacy works mainly for attorneys who need extra help in the area of litigation support.

One afternoon, Stacy was contacted by Tim Hemstreet, an attorney with an office in Washington, D.C. He asked Stacy for some help on a case he had in New York. He asked Stacy to serve a defendant and prepare some interrogatories for him. He was impressed with Stacy's abilities and soon gave her more work. One morning, Hemstreet telephoned Stacy with a proposal. Tim wanted to develop a New York clientele and needed a branch office. He proposed to use Stacy's office as a New York branch office. He would list Stacy's office address as a branch office and would split office expenses with her. Stacy could still be a freelance paralegal, but Tim wants her to make his cases her first priority. Stacy agreed. The first thing Stacy did was take down the sign in front of her office that read "Prompt Paralegal Service" and exchanged it for a sign that said "Law Offices." If someone should walk in looking for an attorney, the secretary would direct the client to Stacy, who would interview the client, prepare a fee agreement, and get the case started.

Tim was busy with his Washington, D.C., cases and was never in the New York office. Stacy handled all his New York cases. She prepared complaints, answers, motions, and discovery. She faxed drafts of the documents she prepared to Tim for his approval and review. Tim would okay the documents and instructed Stacy to sign the pleadings for him. When Stacy complained about signing his name, he sent her a signature stamp of his signature so that all she had to do was stamp the document with the signature stamp. Soon, he became so confident in Stacy's abilities that he told her not to bother faxing the documents to him for his review. He was too busy to look them over. He told her to just sign the pleadings and file them with the court. Tim made all the court appearances, but Stacy did all the rest of the work for his New York clients.

1. Did Stacy violate any ethical guidelines? If so, what are they?

2. Did Tim violate any ethical guidelines? If so, what are they?

3. If you were Stacy, how would you handle the situation?

4. If you were Tim, what would you do differently?

5. If the State Bar of New York learned of Stacy's and Tim's arrangement, what would they do to Stacy? To Tim?

2. Adapted from In re Anderson, *79 B.R. 482; Bankr. S.D. Cal. (1987)*

Janis is a factory worker employed by a paper manufacturing company. She is having financial difficulties and wanted to know more about bankruptcy. She noticed an ad in the newspaper placed by J. R. Elms & Associates, a local independent paralegal service that advertised that they specialized in bankruptcy. Janis called for more information, and Joe Elms came to her house for an interview.

Joe told Janis that J. R. Elms was a legal typing service. He explained that he was not an attorney and could not give her legal advice. He gave her a questionnaire to complete that lists her assets and liabilities and creditors' names and addresses. Janis had only a few creditors. She owed her home mortgage and a couple of credit card companies. Her credit card debt totaled $2,500. Janis asked Joe a number of questions pertaining to the consequences of bankruptcy. He said, "Bankruptcy no longer has a stigma attached to it. Everyone is filing bankruptcy now." She asked him what the difference was between a Chapter 7 bankruptcy and a Chapter 13 bankruptcy. Joe told her that she was ineligible to file a Chapter 13 bankruptcy (although she was) and that a Chapter 13 would cost her more money. She asked Joe whether she would lose her house if she filed for Chapter 7. He said yes. She also asked him whether she would be able to keep her income tax refund that she expected to get. He said yes. She told Joe that she was expecting to receive some money from her grandmother as an inheritance and asked whether she would have to report it. Joe responded, "No, don't worry about it. I'll handle everything for you." She paid Joe the total fee for the bankruptcy. He assured her that he would handle everything and asked her to sign an agreement and guarantee that read:

> I, the undersigned, hereby authorize J. R. Elms & Associates, a legal scrivener service, to transcribe the information submitted herewith, in order for them to complete the proper legal forms for me to file bankruptcy. I consider myself competent to represent myself in court and do not expect J. R. Elms & Associates to give me any legal advice or present me in court or in any manner whatsoever.

1. Did Joe engage in the unauthorized practice of law? How?
2. Did Joe give Janis legal advice? When?
3. How would Joe's activities not be construed as unauthorized practice of law?

3. Do Independent Paralegals Contribute a Service or Break the Law?

There is a controversy surrounding independent paralegal services and the unauthorized practice of law. Proponents of independent paralegals doing work directly for the public list the following in support of their position:

◆ Low-income people cannot afford the services of a licensed attorney and have no background or training to process legal cases for themselves. Without low-cost assistance, they would have no access to the legal system.

◆ Independent paralegals contribute a service to the community by making the legal system more accessible to people.

◆ Independent paralegals contribute a service to the legal system by helping pro se parties process cases for themselves correctly.

◆ The cases processed by independent paralegals are normally routine and uncomplicated and do not involve complex issues. They are the types of cases that attorneys normally delegate to paralegals under their supervision.

Opponents to independent paralegals list the following in support of their position.

◆ There is no adequate regulation of independent paralegals. Therefore, unqualified persons can become independent paralegals, and this does great harm to the reputations of qualified paralegals and harm to the customers they serve.

◆ Completing forms and documents for others has been determined in jurisdictions as giving legal advice, an activity forbidden to paralegals.

◆ Independent paralegals have no law school education, so are unable to spot complicated issues that require more sophisticated legal services, to the detriment of their customers.

◆ Paralegals should abide by the law and not step outside the boundaries of the law.

1. Should independent paralegals be allowed to prepare documents for the public without an attorney's supervision?
2. When should independent paralegals be authorized to do work for the public?
3. When should independent paralegals not be authorized to do work for the public?
4. Should independent paralegals be licensed?
5. If independent paralegals should be licensed, should traditional paralegals be licensed also?
6. If independent paralegals should be licensed, who should the licensing agency be?
7. What qualifications should an independent paralegal have?

4. Conflicts of Interest

As seen in this chapter, a firm can be disqualified from a case if its legal assistant worked on the case when employed by the opposing law firm. Do you think that legal assistants should be subject to the same rules on conflicts of interest as those governing lawyers? Do you think that different conflict rules should be applied to government lawyers and paralegals? Why or why not?

5. Adapted from De Vaux v. American Home Assurance Co., 387 Mass. 814, 444 N.E. 2d 355 (1983)

A client called an attorney's office seeking legal advice for injuries she received in a fall in a department store. The secretary told the client to write a letter to the store informing them of her fall and injuries and arranged for the client to receive a medical examination with the store's doctor. She also told the client to write a letter to the attorney requesting legal assistance. The client wrote the letters and personally delivered the attorney's letter to the attorney's office, but it was misfiled and not seen by the attorney.

The client called the attorney a number of times, but the attorney did not return her calls. After three years, the statute of limitations expired, and the client sued the attorney for malpractice. In his answer, the attorney stated that he was never retained to represent the client and that no attorney-client relationship was established. The client stated that the secretary was the attorney's agent and therefore had *apparent authority* to establish the attorney-client relationship and that the client reasonably relied on the attorney's secretary. Her reliance established the attorney-client relationship. *Apparent authority* was defined as "authority that results from conduct by the principal which causes a third person reasonably to believe that a particular person has authority to enter into negotiations or make representations as his agent." The attorney asserted that the secretary had no authority to establish the attorney-client relationship. Where there is no attorney-client relationship, there can be no breach of duty and therefore no liability. The client claimed that the attorney placed the secretary in a position in which prospective clients might reasonably believe that she had the authority to establish the attorney-client relationship.

1. How do you think the court ruled in this case?
2. Did the secretary create the appearance of having the authority to establish the attorney-client relationship?
3. What aspects of the five Cs of client relations apply to this case?
4. What were the secretary's ethical violations, if any?
5. What were the attorney's ethical violations, if any?

6. If you were the secretary, what would you have done?
7. If you were the attorney, what would you have done?
8. What ABA ethical rule(s) was violated?

6. Are the Restrictions on the Unauthorized Practice of Law Too Stringent?

Do you think some activities that currently constitute the unauthorized practice of law should be allowed? If so, what activities? When should the activity be allowed? When should they not be allowed? How would relaxing the restrictions on the unauthorized practice of law affect the legal profession? The paralegal profession? The public? The court system?

7. Clerical versus Substantive Legal Work

The case of *People v. Landlords Professional Services* found on pages 185 and 186 lists the clerical activities that do not constitute the unauthorized practice of law. When would those activities be considered the unauthorized practice of law? What is the difference between clerical and substantive activities? What activities would not be considered clerical? Discuss.

ASSIGNMENTS

1. Look in the telephone book for ads from independent paralegals. Clip them out and insert each one on a separate sheet of paper. Also, find ads for freelance paralegal services. What are the differences in the ads? Do you see any ads that violate rule 4 of Exhibit 5.6 prohibiting the word *legal* in the company's name or advertisements?
2. Describe what a legal assistant must do when changing employment to avoid potential conflicts of interest.
3. Describe some things a legal assistant can do to increase competence. What are some things a legal assistant can do if her or his workload is too heavy to ensure thoroughness?
4. Refer to Exhibit 5.1 and find your state. Obtain a copy of the state's regulation concerning legal assistants. If your state is not listed, contact your state or local paralegal association and ob-

tain a copy of its code of ethics. Prepare an outline of a legal assistant's ethical responsibilities in your jurisdiction.
5. Role play the situations described in the examples to legal advice found on pages 175 and 176. What would be the correct response in each situation?
6. Review the advertisement in Exhibit 5.7 and list all its inaccuracies and false or misleading statements made. If you cannot prove that some statements are false, how can you assume that some statements are false?
7. Research the Web sites listed on page 184. What are the differences between the services offered by freelance legal assistants and independent legal assistants? What are the rates for independent paralegal services? What type of activities do they advertise?

SELF-TEST

How well did you grasp the material in the chapter? Test yourself by answering the following questions and check your answers against the answers found in Appendix A.

1. What factors contribute to our ethical values?
2. How does the *Living Webster Encyclopedia Dictionary* define ethics?

3. Ethics cannot be defined as honest versus dishonest, right versus wrong, or good versus bad. Why?

4. What factors contribute to how we can recognize ethical issues?

5. Why do people with good intentions sometimes violate ethical standards?

6. How is the foundation of ethical standards established?

7. What organizations have developed ethical guidelines for paralegals to follow?

8. Are legal assistants bound to an attorney's state bar code of ethics? Why?

9. Legal assistants are lawyers' _____ .

10. Can a legal assistant be prosecuted by a state bar or governing agency for unethical behavior?

11. Who suffers from a paralegal's unethical conduct?

12. Why must legal assistants abide by ethical codes?

13. Why was the paralegal profession established?

14. What did the ABA study conducted in the early 1960s reveal?

15. What differences did the ABA find between the legal profession and other professions?

16. The ABA determined that legal assistants could enhance the legal profession by what three things?

17. What is the ABA's legal assistant committee called?

18. When were the first formal paralegal education programs established?

19. When did the ABA begin its approval process of paralegal programs?

20. What is the name of the two national paralegal associations?

21. What are the sanctions that NPFA's Ethical Enforcement Committee can impose on legal assistants who violate its code of ethics?

22. Why has it been a problem to monitor adherence to an organization's ethical code?

23. What are the five Cs of client relations for legal assistants?

24. What are the four aspects of a lawyer's competency that apply to legal assistants?

25. How do you acquire legal knowledge?

26. How do you create skill?

27. How do you increase your knowledge and skill?

28. How do you develop thoroughness?

29. What factors affect thoroughness?

30. Why has technology been responsible for a lack of thoroughness?

31. What are the eight areas that indicate a lack of commitment to a client's case?

32. How can legal assistants assist an attorney in communicating with clients?

33. What is a goodwill letter?

34. Who may give legal advice to a client?

35. What is a general guideline for legal advice?

36. What five activities constitute legal advice?

37. Why is the prohibition against giving legal advice difficult for experienced paralegals?

38. If a legal assistant is asked a question that requires legal advice, what must she or he do?

39. May a legal assistant sign a letter that contains legal advice?

40. What are the exceptions to the prohibition of legal assistants giving legal advice?

41. What is the name of the case that created the "jailhouse lawyer"?

42. Why must legal assistants always identify themselves as a legal assistant?

43. Why is a legal assistant prohibited from accepting a case?

44. What is nonlawyer conflict of interest?

45. What is a Chinese wall?

46. What restrictions does a Chinese wall impose?

47. Why must freelance paralegals keep a list of cases on which they have worked?

48. How can a legal assistant ensure that a client's matter is kept confidential?

49. Why must an e-mail sent to a client be sent on a secure server?

50. What are the exceptions to the confidentiality rule?

51. How are the activities that constitute the unauthorized practice of law determined?

52. What three activities are determined to be the unauthorized practice of law?

53. When may paralegals represent clients?

54. May a paralegal ask a client questions at a deposition?

55. When does a paralegal's preparation of documents constitute the unauthorized practice of law?

56. Legal documents includes preprinted legal _____ .

57. How have courts ruled concerning completion of a legal form?

58. Many courts employ nonattorneys to assist people with what function?

59. Why do courts employ nonattorneys to assist people in pro se cases?

60. May a legal assistant sign a pleading?

61. Why must an attorney sign a pleading?

62. How did the court rule on the *Dacey* case?

63. Why did the Texas Supreme Court investigate Nolo Press?

64. What is a legal "kit"?

65. How did the courts rule concerning legal "kits"?

66. Where can you find a legal "kit"?

67. When does a problem arise in relation to a legal "kit"?

68. What is an independent paralegal?

69. What is a freelance paralegal?

70. What is the difference between an independent paralegal and a freelance paralegal?

71. What is the Wave Project?

72. What did Wave centers do?
73. What was the court's ruling in the *Florida Bar v. Furman?*
74. Why was Furman's jail sentence commuted?
75. What was the name of the committee formed by the State Bar of California in the late 1980s?
76. What did the committee do?
77. What was the committee's finding?
78. What did the committee's report recommend?
79. What kind of reaction did the committee's report receive from the State Bar of California?
80. What type of services will California's SB 1418 allow?
81. According to California's SB 1418, what may independent paralegals not do?
82. What are independent paralegals called pursuant to SB 1418?
83. When does SB 1418 expire?
84. Why did the North Carolina Bar Association hire a consumer protection advocate?
85. What does HALT stand for?
86. What does HALT promote?
87. What is a traditional paralegal?
88. Why do traditional paralegals and CAPA object to the title "legal document assistants"?
89. What are some other terms for independent paralegals?
90. What is the name of the case that lists the clerical activities that are not considered to constitute the unauthorized practice of law?
91. What has created problems for the paralegal profession and independent paralegals?
92. What are "fly-by-night" paralegal programs?
93. Why are "fly-by-night" paralegal programs dangerous?
94. How are unqualified paralegals allowed to proliferate?
95. What are the eight things to which a paralegal must be committed to ensure professionalism?

KEY WORDS

Certificate of service
Chinese wall
Deponent
Foreclosure
Goodwill letter
Incarcerated
Intranet
Mitigated
Postconviction writs
Probate
Pro bono
Pro se
Remedial
Scrivener
Statute of limitations
Temporary restraining order
Unlawful detainer

Legal Fees

OBJECTIVES

After completion of this chapter, a student should be able to do the following:

◆ Describe the various types of fees charged in a law office.

◆ Discuss the advantages and disadvantages of each type of fee.

◆ Explain the rules and ethics that apply to lawyers and legal assistants regarding fees.

◆ Describe other methods of producing profits besides fees.

◆ Explain the factors considered when determining a reasonable fee.

◆ Explain liens for fees.

◆ Describe a legal assistant's ethical responsibility concerning fees.

◆ Identify requirements for fee agreements.

INTRODUCTION

Mark up: To add a percentage on the cost of an item for profit.

The manner in which law firms charge for their services makes the practice of law different from other businesses. A retail store prices its product according to the product's cost; a merchant **marks up** the product to ensure a profit. Law firms use different methods to price their product: They charge for lawyers' and legal assistants' services. A thorough knowledge of legal fees will prepare a legal assistant student to participate in firm profitability and management.

One of the goals of a law firm is to make a profit, and legal fees are a major part of law firm profitability. Other goals—to provide quality legal services at reasonable prices and to ensure employee growth—cannot be compromised to achieve profitability. Keeping a law firm profitable while satisfying clients is a constant challenge for legal management.

A law firm goes to great lengths to establish a fee structure that is reasonable and maximizes profitability. In the competitive legal marketplace, it is a challenging task to keep fees affordable for a client and profitable for a firm. To do this, firms use various types of fees and charge different fees for different services. Developing a fee structure is not an arbitrary process; many issues are considered before a fee structure is established.

ETHICS ALERT

This chapter will discuss the history of legal fees, the various types of fees, the ethics involved in getting paid for legal services, the issues involved in setting fees, and fee agreements. Even though legal assistants may not set fees, knowledge of the methods used to do so will give them an understanding of law firm management. The chapter will explain when the different fees are used and the advantages and disadvantages of a particular fee from the client's and management's perspectives. It also will discuss the division of fees and other forms of law firm income.

Bar associations are actively involved in setting guidelines concerning legal fees. This chapter will review bar association guidelines and examples of fee agreements. Since legal assistants often draft fee agreements, these examples will enable legal assistant students to become familiar with fee agreement provisions. Last, the chapter will review legal assistants' ethical responsibilities concerning legal fees.

HISTORICAL PERSPECTIVE

Throughout history, lawyers' fees have been the subject of debate and controversy. At the time of the Roman republic, legal services were free of charge—rendered for the honor and personal satisfaction the advocate received by providing them. As Roman law became more complex, providing legal services became more complicated, and the advocates requested money or some other form of compensation for doing so. This practice was highly scandalous, and a law was passed prohibiting advocates from charging for their services.

With the fall of the republic, lawyers again sought monetary compensation for their services. Emperor Augustus decreed this practice unlawful and assessed lawyers who charged for their services a fine of four times the amount charged. However, this decree did not eliminate lawyers' attempts to charge for their services.

After hearing arguments on the advantages and disadvantages of lawyers' fees, Emperor Claudius passed a law permitting lawyers to accept a fee as long as the fee did not exceed a certain amount. Under this law, however, a client was under no legal obligation to pay a lawyer a fee.

The ancient practice of providing gratuitous legal services certainly has not prevailed into modern times, but accountability for a fee has remained. Society's reluctance to pay lawyers has created the requirement that a lawyer's fee be reasonable and proper. To ensure that a lawyer's fee is reasonable and proper, bar associations have established rules and guidelines that govern legal fees. Various types of fees have evolved to ensure client satisfaction, reasonableness, and profit for a firm.

TYPES OF FEES

To gain a complete understanding of the rate factor, one must have an understanding of the types of fees charged to clients. The different types of fees are retainer, hourly, flat (or fixed), task based, contingency, statutory, referral, premium, and combination.

Retainer Fees

A considerable amount of confusion arises over the meaning of the term *retainer*. The legal profession has used the term for decades—but with different meanings. It is common to hear the statement "The client has retained the firm." This means that the client has secured the services of the law firm. It also may mean that the client has paid the firm a retainer fee. But what type of retainer fee? Four types of retainer fees are used: true, nonrefundable chargeable, nonrefundable nonchargeable, and refundable chargeable. To avoid commingling client's and attorney's funds, some states require that all retainers received as advance payment of fees be deposited in an attorney's **client funds account,** which is an account that is established exclusively for clients' funds and cannot be used for any other purpose. When a fee is earned, the attorney may withdraw those funds and deposit them into the firm's operating account.

Client funds account: A bank account established exclusively for clients' funds; an attorney may not use this account for any other purpose; also called a client trust account.

True Retainer A true retainer fee is paid to a law firm to ensure the firm's availability to a client. No services are provided in return for the fee. This type of fee was prevalent before the 1960s, when few law firms existed. A client paid a true retainer fee to secure a firm's loyalty and availability to the client and to ensure that the firm would not accept a case against the client.

No standard amount was used for a true retainer fee; the fee was agreed on between the client and the firm. The payment schedule was also subject to agreement: The fee could be paid annually, biannually, quarterly, or monthly.

Since the 1960s, it is rare for a law firm to receive a true retainer fee. Increased competition in the legal arena and the advent of ethical rules that mandate a lawyer's loyalty to clients and former clients have made a true retainer fee unnecessary.

Nonrefundable Chargeable Retainer A nonrefundable chargeable retainer fee is paid in advance of representation, is not refundable to a client in most circumstances, and is applied toward the total fee. If a client's case should end before the retainer fee is used or if the client should discharge the firm, the remaining retainer fee is not returned to the client. For example, if the fee for a divorce is $2,000 and a lawyer requires a $1,000 nonrefundable chargeable retainer, the $1,000 is applied as advance payment for the $2,000 fee but is not returned to the client if the client has second thoughts about filing for divorce or terminates the attorney-client relationship.

Nonrefundable chargeable retainers are also used to make an attorney available to a client. For example, when a client needs to have access to an attorney by telephone, the client will pay a firm a nonrefundable chargeable retainer for anticipated services for the coming month. Any time spent by the attorney is deducted from the retainer. The remaining retainer at the end of the month is not returned to the client. If the client should not use the attorney's services during the month, the client is not entitled to reimbursement of the fee. This type of fee encourages a lawyer's availability and gives the client a priority on the lawyer's time.

Nonrefundable Nonchargeable Retainer A nonrefundable nonchargeable retainer is paid to a firm at the beginning of a case and is not applied to a client's bill. It is not returned to a client should the client decide not to retain the firm or elect to discharge the firm for any reason. This type of retainer is often called a sign-up bonus.

Lawyer hopping: Going from lawyer to lawyer for advice and representation.

Many firms use nonrefundable nonchargeable retainers to ensure client loyalty to a firm. It also discourages a client from **lawyer hopping,** or seeking advice and representation from a series of lawyers, which is very time consuming for lawyers. This type of retainer also tests a client's commitment to a case. Some clients are willing to pay this type of fee for the services of a prominent lawyer.

Each state has its own rules governing nonrefundable retainer fees. In some states, conditions are imposed on nonrefundable retainers, and in others nonrefundable retainers are not allowed. A New York lawyer charged his criminal client a nonrefundable fee of $15,000, and a fee agreement was signed indicating the nonrefundable nature of the fee. A month later, the client discharged the attorney and demanded a refund of the fee. The request was denied, and the client filed a grievance against the lawyer. At the grievance hearing, the court found that the nonrefundable nature of the fee was attorney misconduct, and the attorney was suspended from practicing law for two years. On appeal, the New York Court of Appeals upheld the two-year suspension and stated that the nonrefundable fee agreement interfered with the client's right to discharge the lawyer and was a form of economic coercion against that right (*In the Matter of Cooperman,* March 17, 1994, New York Court of Appeals).

Refundable Chargeable Retainer A refundable chargeable retainer fee is applied to a total fee and is returned if a client terminates an attorney-client relationship. This type of retainer is used in cases in which a client will likely not pay the bill.

For example, Melissa Edwards secured the services of Consuelo Lagos to defend her in a lawsuit filed by her landlord. Consuelo told Melissa that the firm would charge $200 an hour for each hour spent on the case and requested a $2,000 refundable retainer fee that would be applied toward her bill. In essence, the retainer fee was prepayment for ten hours of Consuelo's time. The $2,000 was collected from Melissa and deposited in the firm's client funds account, and Consuelo would withdraw the money as the fee was earned.

Consuelo answered the complaint and began negotiations with the landlord's attorney. After about five hours' work, they reached a settlement, and the landlord dismissed his case against Melissa. Consuelo withdrew $1,000 from the funds account as payment of the fee and returned the remaining $1,000 to Melissa. Had the $2,000 retainer fee been nonrefundable and chargeable, the services fee would have been deducted from it, but Melissa would have received no money back. If the $2,000 had been a nonrefundable nonchargeable retainer fee, Melissa would have received no money back and also been sent a bill for $1,000 for Consuelo's time.

Advantages and Disadvantages of Retainer Fees

Advantages	Disadvantages
Client commits to a case and a firm.	Monitoring system is required.
Firm has certainty of income.	Some clients may resist retainer fees.
Retainers from corporate clients have marketing value.	Clients may lack clarity on how a retainer is applied.
Firm's risk of nonpayment is limited.	

Hourly Fees

Hourly fees are the most common fees charged. In some areas, they are the only acceptable method of charging clients. With hourly fees, a client is charged by the hour for each hour or portion of an hour spent on a case.

Clients are billed according to the hourly rate of a person working on a case. Different hourly rates are set for partners, associates, legal assistants, and law clerks. In addition, different hourly rates are established within those categories to compensate a person for education, experience, specialty, and seniority.

Hourly rates vary according to specialty, geographic area, and years of experience. An experienced antitrust attorney may charge $300 an hour in the Midwest and as much as $450 an hour in major metropolitan areas, such as New York. Some firms vary their hourly rates according to the type of client served; they charge higher hourly rates for corporate clients and lower hourly rates for individual clients. The reasoning is that corporate clients have more complex issues than individual clients.

A typical case will involve a senior attorney, a junior attorney, and a paralegal. A senior attorney may bill $250 an hour, a junior attorney $200 an hour, and a paralegal $100 an hour. It is not uncommon to have five or six different people working on a case, each with a different hourly rate.

Exhibits 6.1 and 6.2 show paralegal billing rates by region and years of experience as reported by the 1997 National Federation of Paralegal Associations (NFPA) Paralegal Compensation and Benefits Report.

Blended Hourly Rates   Instead of charging a client different hourly rates for different employees working on a case, a firm may offer the client a blended hourly rate, which is an average hourly rate of the people working on the case. For example, the average of a senior attorney billing at $250 an hour, a junior attorney at $200 an hour, and a paralegal at $100 an hour is $183 per hour. A client is billed $183 an hour for the time spent by each timekeeper. This eliminates complicated billing statements setting forth the billing rates of each person.

	$20–$30	$31–$40	$41–$50	$51–$60	$61–$70	$71–$80	$81–$90	$91–$110	$111–$130	$131–$150	≥$151
Region 1	4.5	1.8	6.7	9.9	10.8	17.5	19.7	17.0	8.1	2.7	1.4
Region 2	2.5	5.3	10.9	13.1	17.3	20.1	15.8	12.3	2.5	0.0	0.4
Region 3	1.1	2.1	9.0	11.7	13.8	22.3	17.6	17.6	3.2	1.1	0.5
Region 4	2.3	6.9	15.2	19.4	17.1	20.3	8.8	8.8	0.5	0.9	0.0
Region 5	0.0	10.3	33.3	14.1	20.5	17.9	1.3	1.3	0.0	1.3	0.0
Region 6	4.1	5.6	13.5	20.6	18.8	17.6	12.6	5.9	0.3	0.3	0.6
Region 7	3.7	3.7	13.9	13.0	18.5	25.3	13.9	6.8	0.9	0.3	0.0
Region 8	2.9	4.3	19.6	17.9	18.2	13.2	10.4	10.7	2.1	0.7	0.0
Region 9	3.8	6.7	17.6	17.1	20.5	17.1	6.2	7.6	3.3	0.0	0.0
Region 10	4.7	5.3	14.0	18.0	21.3	22.7	8.0	5.3	0.7	0.0	0.0
Region 11	1.6	3.8	13.0	17.9	16.8	28.3	13.6	3.8	0.6	0.0	0.5
Region 12	2.4	3.8	9.9	6.1	14.6	20.3	11.8	21.7	6.6	2.8	0.0

PERCENT OF RESPONDENTS BY REGIONS

1. New England	8%	Connecticut, Massachusetts, Maine, New Hampshire, Rhode Island, Vermont
2. Middle Atlantic North	10%	New Jersey, New York, Pennsylvania
3. Middle Atlantic South	7%	Delaware, Maryland, Virginia, District of Columbia, West Virginia
4. South East	9%	Florida, Georgia, North Carolina, South Carolina
5. East South Central	3%	Alabama, Kentucky, Tennessee
6. West South Central	12%	Arkansas, Louisiana, Mississippi, Oklahoma, Texas
7. East North Central	12%	Indiana, Michigan, Ohio
8. Upper Midwest	11%	Iowa, Minnesota, North Dakota, South Dakota, Wisconsin
9. Midwest Central	8%	Illinois, Kansas, Missouri, Nebraska
10. Pacific Northwest	5%	Alaska, Idaho, Montana, Oregon, Washington
11. Mountain	7%	Arizona, Colorado, New Mexico, Nevada, Utah, Wyoming
12. California/Hawaii	7%	California, Hawaii

EXHIBIT 6.1 Paralegal Billing Rates by Region
Source: 1997 NFPA Salary and Benefits Report.

	$20–$30	$31–$40	$41–$50	$51–$60	$61–$70	$71–$80	$81–$90	$91–$110	$111–$130	$131–$150	≥$151 or more
>1 year	13.0	8.0	22.0	13.0	16.0	18.0	5.0	3.0	1.0	0.0	1.0
1–3 years	5.0	9.7	21.4	19.8	17.0	15.0	7.5	2.5	1.7	0.3	0.0
3–5 years	2.4	3.9	19.9	12.1	21.8	19.9	10.2	7.1	1.6	1.1	0.0
5–7 years	1.9	5.1	18.0	19.0	21.5	16.8	9.2	6.0	2.2	0.3	0.0
7–10 years	3.1	4.2	12.5	15.0	18.8	22.1	12.1	9.6	1.7	0.6	0.2
10–12 years	1.9	4.1	8.2	14.8	17.0	22.1	15.8	12.3	2.8	0.3	0.6
12–15 years	1.3	2.4	9.1	15.8	13.5	25.3	14.5	14.8	2.7	0.7	0.0
15–20 years	1.4	2.1	7.4	11.3	11.3	20.5	18.0	20.8	4.9	1.4	0.7
<20 years	3.2	3.2	3.9	9.4	12.6	19.7	19.7	18.9	3.9	3.9	1.6

EXHIBIT 6.2 Billing Rates by Years of Experience
Source: 1997 NFPA Salary and Benefits Report.

For example, Ut Dong is the owner of a real estate development firm. Ut had an hourly fee agreement with Black, White & Greene. Ut consulted Grant Greene on a case for which he wished to retain Black, White & Greene. They had agreed on the usual fee agreement of $250 an hour for senior partners, $200 an hour for junior partners, $175 an hour for associates, $150 an hour for junior associates, and $100 an hour for paralegals.

Ut had a two-hour conference with Grant, explaining the case to him. Since the case was sizable, Grant included a senior and a junior partner in the conference. A week later, the junior partner spent two hours going over the case with an associate. The next day, the associate had a two-hour conference with a junior associate and two legal assistants to inform them about the case.

To apprise the law firm of the case and before any work was done, Ut received a bill, as shown in Exhibit 6.3, that sets forth the various hourly rates for each timekeeper. Exhibit 6.4 is an example of a bill for the same services using blended hourly rates.

Note that the bill for the blended hourly rate is less than the one for the straight hourly rate. This is because more time was spent by senior attorneys than by legal assistants. If legal assistants spent most of the time on the case, the blended rate would result in higher fees than the straight hourly rate.

Black, White & Greene, LLP

For services rendered for conference regarding real estate case:

SERVICES	HOURS	AMOUNT
Senior partner Grant Greene	2.0	$ 500
Senior partner Dennis White	2.0	500
Junior partner Patrizia Boen	4.0	800
Associate George Templeton	4.0	700
Junior associate Fran Smith	2.0	300
Paralegal Milton Nollkamper	2.0	200
Paralegal Julie Hemstreet	2.0	200
Total	18.0	$3,200

Hourly rates:

Senior partner Grant Greene	$250
Senior partner Dennis White	$250
Junior partner Patrizia Boen	$200
Associate George Templeton	$175
Junior associate Fran Smith	$150
Paralegal Milton Nollkamper	$100
Paralegal Julie Hemstreet	$100

EXHIBIT 6.3 Invoice for Straight Hourly Rate

Black, White & Greene LLP

For services rendered for conference regarding real estate case:

Personnel	18.0 hrs @ $175	$3,150

EXHIBIT 6.4 Invoice for Blended Hourly Rate

A straight hourly rate bill accurately reflects what actually happened, and a blended hourly rate does not. Clients differ in their preferences. Some may appreciate a detailed statement, whereas others prefer an abbreviated style.

Advantages and Disadvantages of Blended Hourly Rates

Advantages	Disadvantages
Schedules are less complicated than standard hourly rate schedules. Fees are easy to set, negotiate, and administer.	Senior attorney involvement that is assumed may not occur.
Clients are able to establish a legal budget when the number of hours is estimated.	Delegation to lowest hourly person is encouraged and may result in lower-quality service and higher costs to a client.
	Different levels of expertise and specialization are not recognized.
	Some clients may resist this type of fee.

Method for Determining Hourly Rates   Putting a monetary value on legal services requires a great deal of skill, knowledge, and management expertise. Too often, hourly rates are determined by what the market will bear or what the competition is charging rather than on sound management principles. To determine what rates need to be charged in order to obtain a desired level of income and profit for a firm, a number of variables must be considered. Among them are the following:

◆ Planned or budgeted expenses, excluding partner or shareholder compensation and benefits
◆ Anticipated billable time by partner, associate, or legal assistant
◆ Desired profit percentage
◆ Reasonable allocation of expenses by partner, associate, and legal assistant
◆ Firm collection rate—billings divided by cash receipts
◆ Billing rate—work-in-progress billable time versus past billed hours

Other variables are also considered:

◆ Local living standards
◆ Experience of attorney
◆ Attorney's seniority
◆ Client's ability to pay
◆ Rates of competitors
◆ Attorney's specialty
◆ Attorney's ability
◆ Rule of three for legal assistants
◆ Firm's prestige

The more experienced and reputable an attorney, the higher the hourly rate. A new associate attorney will have a lower hourly rate than an experienced senior partner. The reasoning is that an experienced attorney can produce work faster and with greater efficiency than an inexperienced attorney. Therefore, a higher rate is warranted for a more experienced legal professional.

To calculate an hourly rate, one must consider overhead, profit, salary, and billable hours. For example, a junior attorney right out of law school desires a salary of $60,000 per year. He is expected to bill 1,500 hours a year (6.25 hours a day) for the salary. Overhead is 50 percent of his salary, and profit for the firm is 25 percent of overhead plus salary. How much money per hour must the junior attorney charge?

$$\$60,000 + \$30,000 \text{ overhead} + \$22,500 \text{ profit} = \$112,500 \text{ total receipts}$$
$$\$112,500 \div 1500 = \$75.00 \text{ per hour}$$

Advantages and Disadvantages of Hourly Fees

Advantages	Disadvantages
Clients are familiar with the concept.	Clients may resist fee increases.
Rate schedules can be adjusted to recognize varying levels of experience, skill, and expertise.	Firm is not rewarded for high-risk cases.
Hours and rates are easily monitored by clients.	Variables such as a quick turnaround or significant results are not accounted for.
Lawyers are paid the same regardless of outcome.	Value is generally not recognized.
Rates are used to evaluate performance.	Efficiency may be penalized and inefficiency rewarded.

Flat Fees

Flat fee: One fee that is charged for an entire case; also known as a fixed fee.

A **flat fee,** or fixed fee, is a set fee for a service rendered. For example, a simple will, uncontested dissolution proceedings, or drunk driving defense are usually charged one fee for the entire case.

Per diem: Latin term meaning "by the day."

Per Diem Flat Fees   A **per diem** flat fee is a fee charged by an attorney for a day's work. It is based on an attorney's hourly rate for eight hours of the attorney's time. For example, if an attorney charges $150 an hour, the per diem charge would be $1,200 a day. Attorneys charge per diem fees when they are in trial and cannot anticipate the length of the trial.

Minimum and Maximum Flat Fees   In some cases, a firm may quote a client two flat fees: a minimum and a maximum. These types of flat fees are based on the outcome of a matter. If the outcome is extremely satisfying for the client, the maximum fee is charged. If the outcome is not as the client had hoped, the minimum fee is charged.

Method for Establishing Flat Fees   A law firm knows by experience approximately how long it takes to complete a certain type of case. If time records have been routinely kept, it is not difficult to compute an average of the time it takes to complete a case that falls in a particular category. An attorney's and legal assistant's times are estimated, and a flat fee is established based on their hourly rates for completion of the case. For example, for a simple will, a flat fee might be determined as follows:

Attorney	1 hour at $200 an hour =	$200
Legal assistant	1 hour at $100 an hour =	100
	Total cost	$300

Advantages and Disadvantages of Flat Fees

Advantages	Disadvantages
Clients favor flat fees because legal fees are fixed and they can budget accordingly.	Those setting the fees are unable to anticipate unforeseen events in a case.
Billing process is simplified.	The cost and time involved in a case may be underestimated.
Efficiency and expeditious handling of cases are encouraged.	Activities of the opposing party cannot be controlled and could produce more work than anticipated.
Fees are easy to set and can be adjusted.	
Use of technology and the services of legal assistants are encouraged.	Fees must be monitored closely to determine profitability.

Task-Based Fees

The trend toward task-based billing was created in the late 1990s by corporate legal departments who wanted to manage their legal costs more effectively and economically. It was developed as an alternative to hourly fees. For decades, various entities, especially corporate legal departments, have objected to hourly fees. They felt that charging by the hour encourages inefficiency and overstaffing projects. They also felt that hourly rates discourage delegating a task downward to a qualified member of the legal team with a lower hourly rate. Certain legal organizations, especially the American Corporate Counsel Association, would like to abolish the hourly fee.

To eliminate some of these problems, representatives from the Litigation Section of the American Bar Association (ABA), the American Corporate Counsel Association, and corporate legal departments coordinated by Price Waterhouse L.L.P. developed a task-based management system, which is shown in Exhibit 6.5. In a task-based system, legal work is categorized by phase. Each phase contains a list of tasks, and each task contains activities. Each task is given a specific fee or hourly rate that is appropriate to the level of complexity of the task. For example, in the pretrial pleadings and motions phase, there are six tasks: pleadings, preliminary injunctions, court-mandated conferences, dispositive motions, other written motions, and class-action

---

L100—Case assessment, development, and administration
      L110—Fact investigation/development
      L120—Analysis/strategy
      L130—Experts/consultants
      L140—Document/file management
      L150—Budgeting
      L160—Settlement/nonbinding ADR
      L190—Other case assessment, development, and administration

L200—Pretrial pleadings and motions
      L210—Pleadings
      L220—Preliminary injunctions/provisional remedies
      L230—Court-mandated conferences
      L240—Dispositive motions
      L250—Other written motions/submissions
      L260—Class-action certification and notice

L300—Discovery
      L310—Written discovery
      L320—Document production
      L330—Depositions
      L340—Expert discovery
      L350—Discovery motions
      L390—Other discovery

L400—Trial preparation and trial
      L410—Fact witnesses
      L420—Expert witnesses
      L430—Written motions/submissions
      L440—Other pretrial preparation and support
      L450—Trial and hearing attendance
      L460—Posttrial motions and submissions
      L470—Enforcement

L500—Appeal
      L510—Appellate motions and submissions
      L520—Appellate Briefs
      L530—Oral argument

EXHIBIT 6.5 Uniform Task-Based Management System—Litigation Code Set certification and notice. The pleadings task includes activities such as researching, drafting, editing, filing and reviewing complaints, answers, and cross-complaints. For the pleadings task, the firm charges X dollars or X dollars per hour. For the preliminary injunctions task, the firm charges X dollars or X dollars per hour.

Categorizing legal services by task offers corporate clients many advantages over hourly billing. They can budget for legal costs and can estimate how much a case should cost. Additionally, if all the corporation's outside counsel use the same codes, such as the uniform coding system shown in Exhibit 6.5, corporations can compare their attorney's invoices and see which firm's services are the most reasonable.

Most firms find task-based timekeeping difficult to implement. Timekeepers must consult a long and detailed code list every time they make an entry on their timesheets. This process has been estimated at 5 to 10 percent of the total time devoted to the case. As a solution to this problem, firms find it necessary to acquire software that will calculate the fees and track the profitability of each phase or task. According to a survey of 210 firms conducted by Altman Weil Pensa in 1995, 20 percent responded that they do not have sufficient systems in place to offer task-based accounting. Another 48 percent responded that their systems need improvement, and 19 percent indicated that their accounting system is sufficient. As more software is developed, more firms will be able to offer their clients this type of fee. Software will allow a firm to use the ABA-approved system (Exhibit 6.5) or develop individualized systems for each corporate client.

Paralegals who work for firms that charge task-based fees must be conscious of the budget and be careful not to exceed preset fee guidelines. For example, if a firm has projected that it would take twenty-five hours to summarize eight depositions, it has calculated its fee on the basis of that time prediction. If the paralegal should exceed the twenty-five hours, the firm's profit margin is affected. This kind of fee structure calls for strict discipline in work habits.

Law firms that want to work for insurance companies and Fortune 500 corporate legal departments are being forced to consider task-based billing seriously. In 1999, the Los Angeles law firm of O'Melveny & Myers reported that 22 percent of the firm's total billings are task based, and that number is expected to increase in the new millennium. However, task-based fees are not expected to replace the standard hourly rate fees schedule for most law firms.

TRENDS ➤➤➤

Alternative Fees

As clients become dissatisfied with current billing techniques, creative fee structures will be developed to satisfy the demand. Legal fee structures are predicted to change more in the first ten years of the new millennium than they have in the previous fifty years.

Advantages and Disadvantages of Task-Based Fees

Advantages	Disadvantages
Bills can be more detailed.	A sophisticated accounting system to track profitability is required.
Management reports can be more detailed.	
Clients can prepare a litigation budget.	Bills are more detailed.
Delegation is encouraged.	Specific coding system must be adhered to.
Efficiency is encouraged.	Requires monitoring by management.
Corporate clients prefer this type of fee.	

TECH TIPS

Task-Based Billing Software

The following is a sample of related software:

InstaTrack: Team Work Software, Inc.—73501.526@Compuserve.com
CLS/Summit: Computer Law Systems, Inc.—www.clswin.com
ADC's Perfect Practice: ADC Legal Systems, Inc.—www.adclegal.com
JavelanX: Barrister Information Systems Corp.—www.barrister.com
CompuTrac Law Firm Management System for Windows—CompuTrac.www.cTinc.com

Software mentioned in this sidebar is for informational purposes only and is not for the purpose of endorsing products.

Contingency Fees

Contingency fee: A fee consisting of a percentage of the possible recovery from a lawsuit.

A **contingency fee** is a fee based on a percentage of a client's recovery in a case. The average rate charged is thirty-three and one-third to 40 percent of the recovery. For example, if a client is awarded a judgment for $15,000, a lawyer might receive one-third of the recovery, or $5,000, for the fee, and the plaintiff would receive the remaining $10,000.

A typical contingency fee arrangement is as follows:

◆ 25 percent of sums recovered by way of settlement prior to filing a lawsuit

◆ Thirty-three and one-third percent of sums recovered after filing a lawsuit but before trial

◆ 40 percent of sums recovered within thirty days of commencing trial or after trial

◆ 45 percent of sums recovered if any judgment is appealed or if garnishment or any proceeding after judgment has to be brought to collect the judgment or any portion thereof

◆ 50 percent of sums recovered if a matter is subject to retrial as ordered by a trial or appellate court

Costs: Expenses of one side of a lawsuit that a judge orders the other side to reimburse; includes filing fees, service fees, and recording fees.

In addition to a contingency fee, a client must pay all **costs** of a litigation that may be advanced by a law firm. In complex litigation cases, costs can be substantial. The manner in which costs are deducted from the total amount of a judgment determines the amount of a client's recovery and an attorney's fee.

Two methods are used to calculate a contingency fee: the gross fee method and the net fee method. Exhibits 6.6 and 6.7 show these methods for a case in which a client was awarded a judgment for $15,000, had a costs bill of $1,000, and had a one-third contingency fee agreement with an attorney.

Some states require that attorneys use the net fee method. Contingency cases are mainly plaintiff matters, but defense cases also may be taken on contingency. A contingency fee for a defense contingency case is called a modified contingency fee.

Judgment	$15,000
Attorney's fee (one-third)	−5,000
Subtotal	10,000
Costs	−1,000
Total to client	$ 9,000

EXHIBIT 6.6 Gross Fee Method

Judgment	$15,000.00
Costs	−1,000.00
Subtotal	14,000.00
Attorney's fee (one-third)	−4,666.67
Total to Client	$ 9,333.33

EXHIBIT 6.7 Net Fee Method

Modified Contingency Fee In a modified contingency fee case, a lawyer's percentage is not based on the amount of the recovery; rather, the lawyer is paid a percentage of the difference between the amount at issue and the amount of the final judgment. For example, a lawyer represents an insurance company in a case with a potential liability of $1,000,000. The lawyer's fee is based on the difference between $1,000,000, which is the client's exposure, and the actual judgment. Therefore, if the judgment is for $250,000, the lawyer's fee is a percentage of $750,000, which is the difference between the amount of exposure ($1,000,000) and the total judgment ($250,000). This fee arrangement encourages the lawyer to obtain the best possible judgment for the insurance company. If the judgment is for $1,000,000, the lawyer essentially loses the case and gets a reduced hourly rate or a retainer fee as compensation.

Contingency Fee Considerations Four considerations are involved in taking a case on a contingency basis. They can be described by the acronym RISC: risk, inflation, significant expense, and cash flow.

Risk. An element of risk is involved in taking a case on a contingency. If a client should lose the case, the attorney is entitled to no fee; one-third of zero is still zero. In addition, the case may not adequately compensate the attorney for the amount of time expended on it. On the other hand, in large cases a firm may make more than it would if it charged a client by the hour. Another risk is that a judgment debtor will be unable to pay a judgment, which would render the judgment uncollectible.

Inflation. In large areas, courts are extremely crowded, and it is not uncommon to wait as long as five years for a trial date. A firm will work on a case for the entire five-year period until trial. In the event of appeal, the case may be active for a longer period. Furthermore, the losing party does not necessarily put a check in the mail the day of the judgment. The firm may have to collect the judgment, which takes more time and effort.

If it takes a firm five or more years to complete a case, the value of the dollar will most likely decrease during that period. In addition, the firm's expenses and the attorney's hourly rate will increase. Therefore, the dollars received at the end of the case are worth less than the dollars that could have been earned at the beginning of the case.

Significant Expense. Some cases require expert witnesses, investigation, and other expenses. Most often, the client cannot afford the services of an expert witness, so a firm will **advance,** or loan, these costs to the client, to be reimbursed at the end of the trial. In complex cases, the services of expert witnesses can cost tens of thousands of dollars. In short, litigating cases is very expensive and requires a large amount of cash resources.

Cash Flow. If a firm works on a case for five years on a contingency basis, it is expending time that is not paid by the client when the service is rendered. Had the attorney or legal assistant spent time on a case that billed the client by the hour, the firm would have received compensation for that time fairly soon after the client was billed. In a contingency case, the firm may wait as long as five or more years to be paid for its efforts. In the meantime, employees must be paid, overhead expenses must be paid, and the attorney must receive a salary. Spending a lot of time on contingency cases affects a firm's cash flow.

The ABA has restricted the types of cases that can be taken on a contingency. Cases that are taken on contingency include personal injury, medical malpractice, wrongful death, and other **tort** cases, or cases involving a legal wrong done to a person or a civil wrong that is not based on a contract.

ABA Model Rule 1.5(c) and (d) expressly prohibits contingency fee agreements in domestic relations cases. A lawyer cannot agree to represent a family law client for a

Advance: To pay money before it is due; to loan money.

Tort: A legal wrong done to a person; a civil wrong that is not based on a contract.

TECH TIPS

Software Manages Contingency Fees

Contingency Fee Management 4.0 by CPS, Inc., in Birmingham, Alabama, manages contingency fee cases by processing settlement checks, manages client's trust accounts, provides financial history of contingency cases, and is customizable to client's specifications. It tracks time spent on the matter and calculates the profitability of the case.

Software mentioned in this sidebar is for informational purposes only and is not for the purpose of endorsing products.

percentage of the client's property settlement. Contingency fees are also prohibited in criminal and other types of cases that vary by state:

(c) A fee may be contingent on the outcome of the matter for which the service is rendered, except in a matter in which a contingent fee is prohibited by paragraph (d) or other law. A contingent fee agreement shall be in writing and shall state the method by which the fee is to be determined, including the percentage or percentages that shall accrue to the lawyer in the event of settlement, trial or appeal, litigation and other expenses to be deducted from the recovery, and whether such expenses are to be deducted before or after the contingent fee is calculated. Upon conclusion of a contingent fee matter, the lawyer shall provide the client with a written statement stating the outcome of the matter and, if there is a recovery, showing the remittance to the client and the method of its determination.

    (d) A lawyer shall not enter into an arrangement for, charge, or collect:
1. Any fee in a domestic relations matter, the payment or amount of which is contingent upon the securing of a divorce or upon the amount of alimony or support, or property settlement in lieu thereof; or
2. A contingent fee for representing a defendant in a criminal case.

Contingency Fee Limits   Several states have put limits on contingency fees. It was felt that doing so would discourage lawsuits. High plaintiff's recoveries in personal injury and medical malpractice cases have affected automobile and medical malpractice insurance rates. It has been argued that a ceiling on contingency fees would reduce awards and judgments and therefore keep insurance rates down.

In California, for example, medical malpractice insurance premiums increased to the point that doctors were having difficulty paying them. They lobbied for a ceiling on contingency fees, which resulted in legislation adopting a sliding scale limitation on the amount of contingency fees that could be recovered in medical malpractice cases. Attorneys' contingency fees are structured in California medical malpractice cases as follows:

◆ 40 percent of the first $50,000 of recovery

◆ 33.33 percent of the next $50,000 of recovery

◆ 25 percent of the next $100,000 of recovery

◆ 10 percent of any amount of recovery over $200,000

Recovery means the net sum after costs are deducted.

Advantages and Disadvantages of Contingency Fees

Advantages	Disadvantages
Opportunity exists for large fees in large cases.	Risk is involved.
	Cash flow is affected.
Client faces no immediate payment of legal fees.	Inflation affects the value of the money.

Fees are easy to set.

Some clients have no other way to access the legal system.

Lawyer is encouraged to be efficient and aggressive.

Since attorneys advance costs that can be substantial, frivolous cases are discouraged.

Firm's money and resources must be invested.

Costs advanced can be substantial.

Client may resist if an award is lower than the client expected.

Some states are limiting contingent fees.

Statutory Fees

Statutory fees are set by statute and vary with each state. These fees are usually a structured percentage of a case. For example, attorneys may be paid statutory fees in probate or workers' compensation matters, in which case the amount of a fee is based on the value of an entire estate and may be calculated as follows:

◆ 7 percent of an estate up to $200,000
◆ 5 percent of the next $500,000
◆ 3 percent of the next $1,000,000
◆ 2 percent of funds in excess of $1,000,000

According to this schedule, an attorney representing an estate worth $1,000,000 would receive the following fee:

7 percent of $200,000	$14,000
5 percent of $500,000	25,000
3 percent of $300,000	9,000
Total fee	$48,000

If an attorney spends more time than usual, or a case is more complex than the average case, the attorney may request that a court grant **extraordinary fees,** which are added to the statutory fees.

Extraordinary fee: A fee that is awarded in addition to statutory fees and that compensates an attorney for extra work required by the circumstances of a case.

Advantages and Disadvantages of Statutory Fees

Advantages

Amount of the fee can be determined at the beginning of a case.

Amount is confirmed by a court, which reduces fee disputes.

Disadvantages

Unforeseen circumstances are not accounted for in the fee.

Extraordinary fees are subject to hearing and approval by a court.

Fees are paid at the end of a case.

Expenditure of time and resources is required.

Fees must be approved by a court.

OF INTEREST . . .

The Largest Attorneys Fee Ever!

The $206 billion settlement of state lawsuits against the tobacco industry generated the largest attorneys' fees award in history—$10 billion—and some experts predict that legal fees could be even higher. The attorneys' fees provision is a small part of a complex settlement agreement with the tobacco industry and represents about 5 percent of the total settlement package. Some lawyers involved in the case had contingency fee agreements from 20 to 40 percent of the recovery and are expected to enforce their fee agreements through litigation or arbitration. The outcome of the arbitration and litigation could increase the total attorneys' fees award substantially. A legal expert hired by the state of Texas to fight the litigation brought about by its attorneys to enforce the contingency fee agreements calculated that the Texas lawyers were asking for fees that amounted to $92,000 an hour.

Referral Fees

A referral fee is a payment for referring a client to a firm. Courts and bar associations have discouraged gratuitous referral fees, or fees for which no other service is rendered, and most states prohibit them. Model Rule 7.2(c) states:

> A lawyer shall not give anything of value to a person for recommending the lawyer's services except that a lawyer may:
> (1) pay the reasonable costs of advertisements or communications permitted by this Rule (advertising);
> (2) pay the usual charges of a not-for-profit lawyer referral service or legal service organization; and
> (3) pay for a law practice in accordance with Rule 1.17.

Those against referral fees feel that such a fee may unfairly increase a client's bill. They feel that referral fees damage the image of lawyers who receive payment for doing little or no work and that most clients are offended by referral fees. They also feel that referral fees are beneath the dignity of the legal profession.

Those in favor of referral fees feel that clients, being unfamiliar with lawyers' reputations, benefit by being referred to the most competent attorney who will give them excellent legal services. They feel that a client is protected against increased fees by other rules of professional conduct.

Rules against referral fees are difficult to enforce. Often, a client is not aware that a referral fee is paid. A few states allow referral fees if a client consents and the fee is reasonable.

Advantages and Disadvantages of Referral Fees

Advantages	Disadvantages
Money is received for little or no work expended.	Attorneys may be encouraged to refer cases to firms that pay the highest referral fee rather than to firms with the highest expertise in the area of law.
Reciprocation with other law firms is encouraged.	In states where referral fees are prohibited, attorneys may be subject to discipline.
Clients are referred to attorneys who can obtain the best results for them.	Fees to a client may be increased.
	Some clients resist referral fees.
	Referral fees may damage the image of lawyers in general.

Premiums

Premiums can be best described as tips. In some situations, if an attorney obtains an especially favorable result for a client, the client will give a firm a premium fee in addition to the usual attorney's fee, whether it is a contingency fee, flat fee, or hourly rate. Some firms negotiate a premium at the beginning of a case. If, for example, a client requires a case to be handled immediately, an attorney and staff are required to put aside other cases. The firm will be entitled to a higher fee. However, until it is known that the case was handled in such a manner, the client does not want to commit to paying the higher fee. To encourage the firm to handle the case in an expeditious manner, a client will offer the firm a premium fee if the outcome is satisfactory to the client. A premium fee may be payment of an increased hourly rate, a flat fee, or a contingency fee.

A premium gives a law firm an incentive to obtain the best possible result for a client. For example, a bank gives a law firm a case to collect $50 million in loans from a real estate developer. The bank agreed to an hourly rate of $X. However, if the firm can collect 80 percent of the loans within a certain amount of time, it would be entitled to a premium. If collecting the money took longer or resulted in a lesser amount, a premium would not be due.

A well-known example of a premium fee is when New York's Cravath, Swaine & Moore told the Federal Deposit Insurance Corporation (FDIC) that it would bill it

$300 per hour. If, however, it could recover more than $22 million from Michael Milliken, a junk bond trader, the firm was entitled to a premium that brought its hourly rate up to $600 an hour.

Advantages and Disadvantages of Premiums

Advantages	Disadvantages
Premiums are profitable for a firm.	Clear criteria are difficult to establish.
Efficiency is encouraged.	Clients may resist premiums.

Combination Fees

Combination fees are a combination of retainer, hourly, flat, contingency, statutory, referral, and premium fees. Possible combinations are the following:

◆ Nonrefundable nonchargeable retainer and hourly fee (no portion of the retainer is returned to a client or applied to the hourly fee)

◆ Nonrefundable nonchargeable retainer and flat fee (no portion of the retainer is returned to a client or applied to the flat fee)

◆ Nonrefundable nonchargeable retainer and contingency fee (no portion of the retainer is returned to a client or applied to the contingency fee; if the retainer is substantial, a lower contingency fee—20 to 25 percent—may be charged)

◆ Nonrefundable nonchargeable retainer and statutory fee (no portion of the retainer is returned to a client or applied to the statutory fee)

◆ Refundable chargeable retainer and hourly fee (the retainer is applied to prepay the hourly fee)

◆ Refundable chargeable retainer and flat fee (the retainer is applied to prepay a portion of the flat fee)

◆ Refundable chargeable retainer and contingency fee (the retainer is deducted from the contingency fee at the conclusion of a matter)

◆ Refundable chargeable retainer and statutory fee (the retainer is deducted from the statutory fee at the conclusion of a matter)

◆ Hourly fee and flat fee (the flat fee is charged up to a certain point in the case, and then the firm begins charging by the hour)

◆ Hourly fee and contingency fee (a reduced hourly rate and a reduced contingency rate are charged)

◆ Flat fee and contingency fee (the flat fee may apply to anticipated costs or be considered a nonrefundable retainer and will be deducted from the contingency fee)

◆ Hourly rate and premium (the hourly rate increases, depending on the outcome)

◆ Flat fee and premium (the flat fee increases, depending on outcome)

◆ Contingency fee and premium (either the contingency fee percentage is increased or an additional flat fee is charged, depending on the outcome)

OF INTEREST . . .

The O. J. Simpson Defense

Experts estimated that O. J. Simpson's legal costs exceeded $5 million for his trial. The estimate was made assuming seven lawyers charging $51,000 a day, a forensics expert for $5,000 a day, four DNA experts at $6,000 a day, and other additional investigation expenses. One eighteen-hour workday for seven lawyers charging between $400 and $650 an hour is at least $51,000 a day. Simpson's lead attorney, Robert Shapiro, charged Simpson $650 an hour. If he billed him eighteen hours a day, seven days a week, his bill would be $350,000 a month.

Source: USA Today, *August 5, 1994.*

Division of Fees

Bar associations have set guidelines for the division of fees among lawyers and with nonlawyers.

Division of Fees Among Lawyers

Most states prohibit attorneys' dividing, or splitting, fees with other attorneys who are not a member of their firm unless the division is in proportion to services rendered or the client consents. This would prohibit attorneys' sharing fees with other attorneys in an office-sharing arrangement in which the attorneys are not associated with one another.

Model Rule 1.5(e) states:

> A division of fee between lawyers who are not in the same firm may be made only if:
>
> (1) the division is in proportion to the services performed by each lawyer or, by written agreement with the client, each lawyer assumes joint responsibility for the representation;
>
> (2) the client is advised of and does not object to the participation of all the lawyers involved; and
>
> (3) the total fee is reasonable.

According to this rule, a lawyer must perform some work or share responsibility for a case in order to deserve a fee from another lawyer, unless the client consents to the contrary.

Fee splitting among lawyers is appropriate when an attorney is discharged in a contingency case. A new attorney will make arrangements with a former attorney to pay the former attorney a percentage of the fee based on the amount of his services rendered on the case. The extent of a fee division, responsibility, and services rendered varies from case to case and is subject to agreement between the attorneys. Although Model Rule 1.5(e) does not state that the amount of the fee must be disclosed to a client, various states have rules requiring such disclosure.

ETHICS ALERT

Division of Fees with Nonlawyers

A lawyer is prohibited from sharing fees with a nonlawyer except in certain circumstances. Those circumstances are found in Model Rule 5.4(a), which states:

> (a) A lawyer or law firm shall not share legal fees with a non-lawyer, except that:
>
> (1) an agreement by a lawyer with the lawyer's firm, partner, or associate may provide for the payment of money, over a reasonable period of time after the lawyer's death, to the lawyer's estate or to one or more specific persons;
>
> (2) a lawyer who purchases the practice of a deceased, disabled, or disappeared lawyer may, pursuant to the provisions of Rule 1.17, pay to the estate or other representative of that lawyer the agreed-upon purchase price; and
>
> (3) a lawyer or law firm may include non-lawyer employees in a compensation or retirement plan, even though the plan is based in whole or in part on a profit-sharing arrangement.

A lawyer may be in violation of this rule if the lawyer does any of the following:

◆ Provides services in association with a member of another profession, such as a tax consultant, real estate developer, or financial analyst

◆ Works as a salaried employee of a nonlawyer who charges clients more for legal services than the attorney's salary costs the employer

◆ Owns an interest in a corporation in which nonlawyers provide services traditionally provided by lawyers

◆ Pays nonlawyer personnel according to a percentage of the fees earned by a firm

◆ Pays nonlawyer consultants a percentage of the proceeds of contingent fee litigation

Most states have adopted this prohibition of dividing fees with nonlawyers. However, in 1990, the District of Columbia stunned the legal community by adopting a rule that nonlawyers may own a portion of a law firm and receive a portion of the law firm's profits in certain circumstances.

An argument supporting the prohibition of fee splitting with a nonlawyer is that a fee division may allow a lawyer's independent judgment to be controlled by a nonlawyer who is interested in his or her own profit rather than the legal needs of a client. *Prohibiting fee splitting also discourages nonlawyers from engaging in the unauthorized practice of law and referring clients to a lawyer for a percentage of a fee, known as capping.*

ETHICS ALERT

An argument against this prohibition is that it prevents the development of "full-service" law firms, in which members of different professions work together to meet the needs of clients, such as tax counseling and financial planning.

Law firms may, however, offer their employees compensation through a profit-sharing plan if the compensation relates to the net profits of the firm and not to fees received in a particular case. Law firms may also give a small percentage of a fee received to a nonprofit attorney referral service. Some states, however, have ruled that a referral service may charge only flat fees and may not charge a fee based on a percentage of the fee received from a client referred by the service.

OTHER FEES AND CHARGES

Traditionally, a lawyer's hourly rate was intended to pay the attorney's salary and overhead expenses (salaries of support staff, rent, taxes, supplies, equipment, and related expenses) and to provide profit for a firm. However, law firm expenses, overhead, and staff compensation have increased 2 to 4 percent more than revenues each year since 1979. Lawyers have not been able to raise their hourly rates fast enough to accommodate the increased expenses. This has resulted in a "profit crunch," which requires law firm management to devise ways to recoup overhead and expenses to retain profit earnings for a firm.

Emerging since the early 1980s are law firms charging clients additional fees. To reduce overhead, these firms are charging clients for services that were traditionally considered overhead and included in a lawyer's fee. In addition to professional and paraprofessional fees, law firms are charging for the services of other law firm personnel, hard costs, and soft costs.

Other Law Firm Personnel

Some law firms bill clients for the time of secretaries, proofreaders, litigation support personnel, messengers, and temporary personnel.

Secretaries The traditional role of secretary is eroding with advances in technology. The functions and responsibilities of secretaries are changing into an administrative position. With computers sitting on most attorneys' desks, attorneys are performing some of their own clerical functions. E-mail capabilities are changing a secretary's phone responsibilities. Firms are faxing rather than mailing documents. Secretaries are given more responsibility.

With the changes in a secretary's function comes the necessity that secretaries be trained in new technology. Since new technology and computer capabilities are being introduced often, secretarial training costs for computer programs have also increased. In addition, since legal secretaries are scarce, they are demanding higher salaries than ever before. Therefore, firms have a substantial investment in their secretarial staff.

For some firms, secretaries are moving out of the overhead category into the income producer category as the firms bill a client for a secretary's time.

Proofreaders Only large firms and some medium firms employ proofreaders. Most proofreading is done by secretaries in small and medium firms. Proofreaders are becoming obsolete because computers proofread documents and **redline** changes in documents. Firms that employ proofreaders often charge clients for their time.

Redline: To mark a document to indicate changes made by other parties.

Litigation Support Only firms that handle a lot of complex litigation hire litigation support personnel. Some use outside litigation support services for this function. In either case, firms pass this cost on to a client. If a firm utilizes the services of its own personnel, it will charge a client more than the **actual cost,** or true cost, of the service. If a firm uses an outside litigation support service, the firm may or may not charge more than the actual cost.

Actual cost: The true cost without consideration of a markup for profit.

Messengers Special messenger services have traditionally been billed to a client but were not considered a profit center for a firm. In the past, a firm would bill a client the actual cost of messenger services or include the services in the overhead of the firm. Now, however, whether an outside messenger service or in-house messenger is used, most firms charge a client more than the actual cost to increase a firm's profit. In large cities, firms that have their own messengers have a flat charge to each client for each delivery, plus out-of-pocket expenses. Some messengers charge for their time and have a flat rate for each run for each client to cover the costs of transportation.

Temporary Employees If additional staff is required because of an absent employee or an abundance of work, the expense of hiring them is passed on to the client. Temporary employees can be an attorney or a file clerk.

In the past, the services of law firm personnel were incorporated into an attorney's fee. It has been argued that this was unfair to clients who did not use those services. One client may require heavy secretarial time, and another may require none. Therefore, separate charges for these services were justified out of fairness to a client. However, if these services are taken out of the overhead of a firm and are no longer included in an attorney's hourly rate, the attorney's hourly rate should have been reduced.

Hard Costs

Hard costs, also called direct costs, are directly attributable to a client's case—such as filing fees, service fees, deposition expenses, on-line legal research, and so on.

Hard cost: A cost incurred for filing fees, service fees, deposition expenses, and so on.

The term *costs of litigation* should not be confused with the term *expenses of litigation.* Although the terms are almost synonymous, they have different legal definitions. Costs are recoverable by the prevailing party in some cases, and expenses are not recoverable. Costs are defined in state statutes and include filing fees, service fees, recording fees, and other fees as provided by statute. Expenses of litigation include investigator's fees, deposition fees, expert witness fees, and expenses of obtaining and presenting evidence.

A client usually must pay for all the costs and expenses of a case. Model Rule 1.8(e) states:

> A lawyer shall not provide financial assistance to a client in connection with pending or contemplated litigation, except that:
> (1) a lawyer may advance court costs and expenses of litigation, the repayment of which may be contingent on the outcome of the matter; and
> (2) a lawyer representing an indigent client may pay court costs and expenses of litigation on behalf of a client.

If a lawyer loses a contingency case and the client cannot afford to pay the costs and expenses, a court may not require the client to pay the costs and expenses. However, some states require a client to reimburse a lawyer for all expenses of litigation regardless of financial status or outcome of the case.

If a client is severely injured and cannot work, some states allow a firm to pay a client a reasonable sum for the client's living expenses when involved in lengthy litigation. The client must sign a promissory note to repay the firm out of the proceeds of the judgment. Some states do not allow lawyers to do this. In 1979, an Arizona lawyer was suspended for advancing an unemployed client $215 for living expenses, pending the outcome of his case.

The prohibition against payment of costs and expenses originates from an early common law that prohibited an attorney from financing litigation for a portion of a recovery. Modern-day reasoning for not allowing attorneys to pay for the expenses of litigation is to discourage lawyers from putting their own recovery before that of a client and therefore creating a conflict of interest.

Soft Costs

Soft cost: A cost incurred for photocopying, long-distance telephone calls, faxes, and so on.

Soft costs, also known as indirect costs, cannot be directly attributable to a client's case until applied to the client's case. These costs include overhead expenses for items such as the following:

Photocopies

Attorney's time in preparing forms or other multiple-use documents

Use of conference rooms

Housekeeping services for meetings and depositions

Use of substantive systems (substantive systems developed by law firm personnel to increase efficiency and decrease the amount of time spent on a project)

Local and long-distance telephone charges

Transportation and meals on occasions of overtime

Telex and fax communications

Supplies

Storage of documents

Destruction of documents

Use of computer and computer database

Interest on accounts receivable

Outside services (refer to Chapter 2)

Document production

Postage

Photocopies   Photocopies were the first and the most frequent soft cost charged. Firms charge for photocopies on a per copy basis, and their charges vary. When considering the cost of the equipment, paper, supplies, and maintenance contracts, the actual cost of each copy may be about 6¢. However, when you add the time and expense of an employee's time to make the copy, the actual cost increases. Firms have made their photocopy service a profit center, with some firms charging as much as 30¢ to 50¢ to $1 a copy. A firm rarely charges clients the actual cost for photocopies.

In high-volume litigation cases, some firms reduce charges after a set number of pages. Costs for outside duplication work are passed on, usually without a surcharge. Firms with their own binding equipment often charge for each item bound to cover the cost of supplies and machinery.

Attorney's Time in Preparing Forms or Multiple-Use Documents   With the advent of computers, standard documents such as complaints take very little time to complete. An attorney's time consists of changing a standard document to insert information particular to a client's case. This may take as little as five minutes of an attorney's time. If an attorney billed a client by the hour for preparation of a complaint that took five minutes, the firm would not be compensated for the value of the product to the client. Therefore, the attorney imposes an extra charge for multiple-use documents.

If a complex document is used in another case, can the attorney charge a new client for the actual time spent altering the document for the new client or the original time spent creating the document? This is a difficult question since the expense of the new document is negligible compared to what a client paid for the original document. Experts differ in this area. Opponents say that the original client should not pay to benefit another client. Proponents say that the value of the document to the new client is the same as the original client and that they should pay the same amount. In 1993, the ABA addressed this question in its Formal Opinion 93-379, which states that lawyers who charge a previous client by the hour cannot charge the new client the same amount for recycled work product. Some state bar associations have adopted the same prohibition.

Use of Conference Rooms   Some firms charge an hourly rate or flat fee for the use of conference rooms for meetings or depositions.

Housekeeping Services   In addition to charging for the use of conference rooms, firms will charge for housekeeping services to come in and clean a conference room after its use. This charge also might be assessed if a meal is served at an office. However, most firms bill a client for food costs without passing on housekeeping service costs.

Use of Substantive Systems   When a firm develops systems that streamline services rendered to a client being charged by the hour, the law firm is being penalized for its efficiency. Therefore, clients that benefit from the systems pay for the systems and are billed an extra charge similar to the multiple-use document charge. For example, a firm with a custom database system for discovery documents will save a client money organizing discovery documents. The cost of the database's development is paid for by the clients who use it.

Local and Long-Distance Telephone Charges   In addition to the time a lawyer spends on a telephone call, a client is billed for telephone charges. Some firms assess

---

TRENDS ➤➤➤

Technology Creating Soft Cost Dilemma

Technology is reducing overhead costs for law firms, including soft costs that are billed to the client. Many law firms bill clients for faxing documents, as much as $1.00 to $2.00 per page to cover telephone costs associated with the fax. Now that documents can be faxed directly from a computer workstation, questions of whether and how to charge for those faxes arise. There are also expenses associated with scanning a document into a computer to be faxed that cause concerns. The ABA issued an opinion regarding soft costs that lawyers should charge "no more than the direct cost associated with the service plus a reasonable charge for the overhead associated with the expense." Calculating the direct cost and overhead allocation creates problems for many firms. Some firms disagree with the ABA's opinion and charge "whatever the client is willing to pay" for soft costs. However, clients are becoming increasingly intolerant of soft costs which is causing some law firms to eliminate charging for them.

actual charges; others add a substantial percentage for profit and to cover the cost of equipment and line charges. Most firms charge clients for long-distance calls, and some charge clients message units for local calls. Expenses for the attorney's cell phone are also charged.

Transportation and Meals   Travel is the expense most often billed by attorneys. Some firms add on a percentage of the cost to cover a travel-accident insurance policy in force at a firm. Some attorneys charge a client for the amount of time spent traveling. **Portal-to-portal** charges mean that an attorney's clock starts to run when he gets into his car to travel to the courthouse for a hearing and does not stop until he gets out of his car at the office after the hearing. In addition, when traveling by air, attorneys often bill clients for the time spent on the airplane. Some attorneys double-bill by working on another client's case while traveling on behalf of a client who is being charged for that time. *This practice has ethical implications. Double-billing is considered unethical in most states.*

Travel time may be charged at an attorney's regular hourly rate or at a reduced rate. The argument in support of charging for travel time is that it is time taken away from other billable work. In addition to travel time, a client is charged for other travel expenses, such as hotels and meals.

If a firm is required to work overtime on a case, the firm will charge a client for meals for the staff as well as additional overtime charges.

Telex and Fax Communications   Many firms have a flat rate for most faxes, with an additional charge for phone-line charges. Firms that use telexes through their word processing units assess an operator and connect charge.

Most firms charge for sending faxes. These charges are usually in two parts: an amount associated with the telephone charge and a charge for each page. The amount for each page may decrease with the volume of a particular transmittal. Some firms also charge for incoming faxes—either a flat fee for each document or a fee for each page. Some firms charge as much as $1.75 per page for faxes.

Supplies   The costs of supplies are often billed to clients in complex litigation cases when a large quantity of supplies is used.

Storage of Documents   In cases that have a large volume of documents, storing the documents becomes a problem. Firms must increase their office space to provide for storage space, which costs a firm additional money for rent. Therefore, a firm will charge a client a storage fee if a case generates many documents. Firms that put documents on microfilm also will charge a client for this service as well as for storing the microfilm.

Destruction of Documents   If a client does not want documents returned at the end of a case, a firm will charge the client to destroy those documents, including the time for an employee to shred the documents.

Use of Computer and Computer Database   In a complex litigation case for which documents or other information is input into a firm's computer **database,** a client is charged for use of the database as well as for the space used on the firm's hard drive. The more computer space a client uses, the higher the charge is. The charge continues while the information is retained in the firm's computer.

Most firms also charge a client for use of legal research databases in addition to the time spent by the person doing the research. Since a firm is charged for each minute

Portal-to-portal: Of or relating to the time spent traveling from one place to another.

ETHICS ALERT

Database: A collection of information for computer retrieval.

of use, it recovers this cost by billing a client. The amount charged to a client can be the actual amount, a fixed rate for each minute on-line, or a "type-of-job" charge. Legal databases include WESTLAW and LEXIS.

Interest on Accounts Receivable Charging interest on a client's past-due account was previously taboo for the legal profession. However, with the increasingly high costs of overhead and interest rates, attorneys have followed other professionals in doing so. Some state bar associations have rules that state that an attorney must inform a client in writing of interest charges. A few states require a client's consent to charge interest on an account.

Document Production Firms may charge for work produced either by individual secretaries or in a word processing department. Some firms charge by the hour. Other firms charge by the page—usually for the final number of pages despite numerous revisions, although some firms charge each time a page is handled.

Postage Many firms charge a client for regular postage as well as overnight mail and private document delivery and space. No uniformity exists in recovering costs. A firm may impose all, some, or no soft charges. Soft costs charged to clients vary by area of the United States. In the Midwest, firms are less likely to charge clients soft charges. Some firms just add on 5 to 10 percent of the bill as a general overhead charge instead of listing every category separately. Photocopies, postage, and telephone charges are most likely included in this general overhead charge, but other costs, such as messenger and computer charges, are listed separately.

Soft costs represent about 30 percent of a typical legal bill. As technology continues to introduce new automation, we will see new soft costs emerge. If the market will bear such charges, attorneys will continue to assess them until clients scream. Soft costs that clients most often resent are photocopies over $1 per page, fax charges, and postage. A large corporate client that receives a bill from its attorneys for thousands of dollars resents being charged the postage used to send them the bill. They also object to high fax charges that are imposed at the law firm's discretion when many faxes are not absolutely necessary. In 1993, the U.S. Department of Energy paid one firm $175,000 for photocopies and $49,000 for faxes in one case.

In December 1993, the ABA addressed soft costs in its Formal Opinion 93-379, which states:

> A lawyer may not charge a client for overhead expenses generally associated with properly maintaining, staffing and equipping an office; however, the lawyer may recoup expenses reasonably incurred in connection with the client's matter for services performed in-house, such as photocopying, long distance telephone calls, computer research, special deliveries, secretarial overtime and similar services, so long as the charge reasonably reflects the lawyer's actual cost for the services rendered.

The ABA continued to state that it is improper for the lawyer to impose a surcharge on disbursements over and above the actual cost, unless the client agrees in advance to the amount of soft costs charged. When no specific cost is agreed on, the ABA stated that the lawyer is obligated to charge the client no more than the direct cost associated with the service (i.e., the actual cost of making a photocopy) plus a reasonable allocation of overhead expenses directly associated with the service (i.e., the cost of the photocopy machine operator's time to make the copy).

In 1998, the Law Firm Services Association surveyed 127 small firms about their policies regarding soft costs, the results of which are shown in Exhibit 6.8.

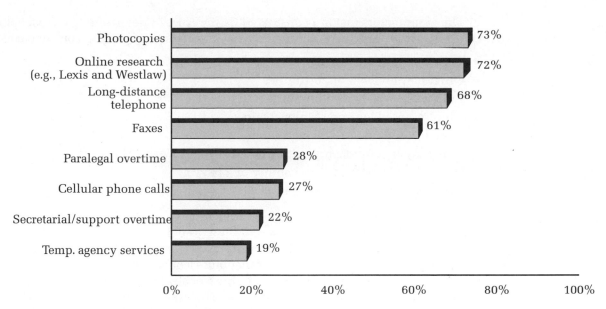

EXHIBIT 6.8 Percentage of Firms That Charge Soft Costs
Source: Law Firm Services Association's survey of 127 firms having mostly between one and forty attorneys.

STATUTORY AND JUDICIAL GUIDELINES

The ABA established rules and guidelines concerning legal fees for two reasons: (1) to preserve the effectiveness, integrity, and independence of the profession and (2) to give society reasonable access to the legal system. The two reasons seem to contradict each other. The first requires that lawyers be adequately compensated for their services, and the second requires that a compensation be reasonable for a client.

The ABA has set forth guidelines to help lawyers keep their fees reasonable. Eight factors are considered when calculating a reasonable fee.

Calculation of a Reasonable Fee

To set standards that will satisfy reasonableness without compromising a lawyer's compensation, the ABA set forth the ingredients of a reasonable fee in Model Rule 1.5(a), which states:

A lawyer's fee shall be reasonable. The factors to be considered in determining the reasonableness of a fee include the following:

1. The time and labor required, the novelty and difficulty of the questions involved, and the skill requisite to perform the legal service properly;
2. The likelihood, if apparent to the client, that the acceptance of the particular employment will preclude other employment by the lawyer;
3. The fee customarily charged in the locality for similar legal services;
4. The amount involved and the results obtained;
5. The time limitations imposed by the client or by the circumstances;
6. The nature and length of the professional relationship with the client;
7. The experience, reputation and ability of the lawyer or lawyers performing the services;
8. Whether the fee is fixed or contingent.

The eight factors that are considered by the ABA in determining a reasonable fee can be remembered by the acronym TOCATPET (think of petting your two cats):

- Time and labor required
- Other employment opportunities
- Customary fees in a community
- Amount involved and results obtained
- Time limitations
- Professional relationship with a client
- Experience, reputation, and ability of a lawyer
- Type of fee (fixed or contingent)

What constitutes a reasonable fee varies from case to case. Furthermore, federal and state laws, as well as case law, continue to define the elements that constitute reasonableness. ABA Informal Opinion 84-1509 ruled that Model Rule 1.5(a) applies to only unreasonably high fees rather than unreasonably low fees. On the basis of the rule, if a client sued an attorney for an unreasonable fee, a judge or arbitrator would consider the eight factors listed in the rule to determine whether the lawyer's fee was reasonable. One case may have one or two of the eight factors present, and another case may have more factors present. No standard weights are assigned to any factor, and no one factor is given more importance than another factor.

Most state bars' codes of professional responsibility list the factors that constitute reasonableness in their states. Some guidelines include more than the eight factors identified by the ABA.

Time and Labor Required　　The amount of time and labor required on a case is the basis of fee determinations. Each member of the legal team must keep an accurate accounting of the time spent on a matter, even though the case may be a contingency fee case or fixed fee case. This accounting need not be extremely detailed but must give some idea of the legal service performed during the time period. It also should reflect which lawyer or legal assistant performed the work. If the client should contest the fee, the firm can show the accounting of time expended on the matter. A judge will rule on the reasonableness of the amount of time spent and may adjust the time to eliminate excessive or unproductive time.

In addition to the time and labor required on a case, the novelty and difficulty of the questions involved and the skill necessary to represent a client are considered. A case with many complex issues not only requires more time but also calls on the skill and the experience of a lawyer to manage the issues effectively.

For example, a client retained a lawyer in a case involving a patent infringement of the client's computer software. The case was very complicated. Since the case involved a new area of law, few other cases involved the client's issue; this made research difficult. The case required the skill of a senior attorney because it was too complex for an inexperienced associate to handle. It also required more time than usual to be spent on research and discovery. The lawyer was entitled to a higher fee than usual because of these issues.

Other Employment Opportunities　　On occasion, the magnitude of a case will not allow a firm to accept other cases without significantly increasing its workforce and overhead. One case can consume the time of a law firm staff, which will not allow a firm to accept other cases. This severely affects the financial base for a firm.

Other employment opportunities also may be affected when a firm represents a party in a highly publicized, highly controversial case. If, for example, a firm represents a criminal defendant who has been accused of heinous crimes against people, defending that person is not going to win the firm any popularity contests.

To illustrate, suppose the owners of ABC Nursery School were accused of abusing the children in their care. The case received extensive media attention and included the longest criminal trial in decades. The proceedings lasted almost five years. The attorney who defended the owners could accept no other employment during the proceedings because the *ABC* case consumed all her time. Luckily, the lawyer had the support of her partners, who agreed to the representation and even agreed to contribute some of the firm's resources to the case. The lawyer commented that if the trial had lasted much longer, her firm would not have been able to continue and would have had to dissolve. In addition, because of the negative impression the case had on the public, the attorney's firm suffered a loss of other clients. The firm was entitled to larger fees for the effect the case had on it.

Customary Fees in a Community

The amount charged by other law firms in a community for a similar service is a consideration in calculating a reasonable fee. If a fee charged to a client is not wholly disproportionate to the fees charged by other firms in the area, it may be considered a reasonable fee.

Amount Involved and Results Obtained

A lawyer's fee must be reasonably comparable to the results a client obtains. A bill of $200 an hour for four hours spent negotiating a contract that saves a client $1,000,000 is disproportionate to the results of an attorney's efforts. On the other hand, a charge of $20,000 for litigating a case worth $15,000 is also disproportionate to the results obtained for a client.

In certain circumstances, a lawyer's fee may be more than the amount a client recovers in a case. A case that has a high value because it establishes precedent is an example of this type of circumstance. A case that challenges existing law requires more time and effort from an attorney. In some cases, however, the low value of a case will not justify the attorney's spending the extra amount of time or effort it takes to appeal the case. Few clients can finance an attorney to take a case to the U.S. Supreme Court.

In the 1950s, when civil rights laws were being litigated, attorneys found that they were not compensated for establishing precedent in this area. To remedy this problem, the legislature passed the Civil Rights Attorneys' Fees Act. This act stated that a successful plaintiff in a civil rights lawsuit would be awarded reasonable attorneys' fees, recognizing the low amounts of awards in comparison with the high cost of bringing an action. Other types of litigation award the cost of reasonable attorneys' fees to successful litigants.

Time Limitations

When the circumstances of a case are such that unreasonable time demands are imposed on a firm, the firm should be paid for this effort. Time limitations may require that a legal team suspend its work on other clients' cases to attend to the needs of one case. They also may require that attorneys, legal assistants, and other office staff work overtime to ensure the timeliness of a case. Therefore, a firm incurs additional expenses that should be paid by the client.

For example, a client who retains an attorney a week before the statute of limitations expires, the time period within which a lawsuit must be filed, is putting time constraints on the attorney, the legal assistant, the secretary, and other law firm personnel. The legal team must attend to this new client's case immediately, causing them to stop working on other clients' matters. The firm should be compensated for the inconvenience.

Professional Relationship with a Client

When a client provides a firm with many cases during a year, that client may be entitled to fee consideration from the firm. The concept of volume discounts is appropriate for law firms.

Experience, Reputation, and Ability of a Lawyer   The more experienced and reputable an attorney, the more that attorney should be compensated. The more experienced an attorney, the higher the attorney's hourly rate. The rationale for this is that an experienced lawyer will take less time to complete a project than an inexperienced lawyer.

Attorneys with a high profile who have received publicity for their performance in high-visibility cases will demand a higher fee for their work. An attorney's reputation affects a case. For example, a product liability attorney who has earned very high judgments for clients and has received publicity for this influences the manner in which an opposing party will litigate a case. If an attorney has a reputation for winning cases, an opposing defendant or insurance company will likely settle a case rather than go to trial.

Type of Fee   A contingency fee contains elements of risk for a law firm, and the firm should be compensated for all elements involved in taking a contingency case (RISC). Courts have generally awarded a higher fee for RISC factors in a contingency fee case. However, some courts have ruled that RISC factors are contained in an attorney's hourly rate. Some courts have felt that to increase a fee to include the RISC factors would encourage frivolous lawsuits.

Average cases involving a higher-than-average contingency fee have been held to be unreasonable. For example, in a personal injury case of average complexity and average recovery, a contingency fee of 50 percent has been determined to be unreasonable (*In re Kennedy,* 472 A. 2d 1317 [1984]). Such a standard has received various interpretations by different courts. If a client agreed to pay an attorney 50 percent of a recovery, some courts are reluctant to interfere with a valid fee contract between the client and the attorney. Other courts feel an obligation to supervise fee agreements. However, in general, contingency fees providing for an exorbitant percentage of a recovery have been held to be unreasonable (see *United States v. 115.128 Acres of Land,* 101 F. Supp. 796 D. N. J. [1951]).

Contingency fees can be set aside by a court and an hourly rate applied to a case. Events occurring after a fee agreement is signed may affect the reasonableness of a fee. For example, an attorney represented a client in a personal injury case for a one-third contingency fee. Doctors who treated the client filed liens, or charges, on the outcome of the suit for payment of medical services rendered the client, and an insurance company put a lien against the net recovery for the amount of past benefits paid the client. At the end of the case, after the attorney, doctors, and insurance company were paid, the client received nothing. The attorney's time records indicated that if billed by the hour, the attorney would have received about 10 percent of the contingency fee. Considering the events, the contingency fee was unreasonable, and the attorney's fee was reduced to reflect hourly compensation (see *MacKenzie Construction v. Maynard,* 758 F. 2d 97).

Lodestar and Multipliers

Lodestar: A method of calculating an attorney's fee using the attorney's hourly rate multiplied by the number of hours worked on a case.

A number of federal circuit courts adopted a two-step approach to calculating reasonable attorneys' fees: lodestar and multipliers. The term **lodestar** originated in the U.S. Court of Appeals for the Third Circuit in the case *Lindy Bros. Builders v. American Radiator & Standard Sanitary Corp.,* 487 F. 2d 161, and has been the basis of most fee awards in the court system since 1973. Calculation of a lodestar figure is accomplished by determining the number of hours reasonably spent in a case and applying the attorney's hourly rate thereto to arrive at a reasonable fee. A court will limit lodestar hours to hours reasonably expended and may discount hours spent unproductively. In addition a court may rule that an attorney's hourly rate is not reasonable, and make adjustments. In most cases, however, an attorney's established hourly rate is presumed to be reasonable.

Multiplier: An amount that is added to an attorney's lodestar fee to compensate for time limitations and risks.

Courts have determined that the factors listed in ABA Model Rule 1.5(a) (TOCAT-PET) are inherent in the lodestar calculation. For example, the complexity and difficulty of a case would reflect themselves in the number of hours expended. The experience, reputation, and skill level of an attorney would reflect themselves in the hourly rate.

Some courts have ruled that factors such as time limitations and contingency fees are not considered in lodestar calculations. If a court determines that lodestar does not adequately compensate for all factors of a case, the court may apply a **multiplier** to the lodestar figure, thereby increasing the fee. A court may award an additional flat fee or percentage to a lodestar figure to compensate an attorney for time limitations imposed by a client. As an example, if an attorney's lodestar is calculated to be $200 an hour and the attorney's time records indicate that he spent 100 hours on a case, a judge will calculate the lodestar fee at $20,000. To compensate the attorney for the RISC factors of a contingency case, the judge may increase the figure by 20 percent, or $4,000, for a total fee award of $24,000. Lodestar multipliers occur only in rare circumstances.

OF INTEREST . . .

Unreasonable Multiplier?

The law firm of Kaplan, Miller & Ciresi L.L.P. represented the state of Minnesota in its lawsuit against the tobacco industry. The tobacco industry agreed to pay the firm $444 million for attorneys' fees, but the manner in which that fee was calculated is in controversy. The fee agreement covering the firm's work for the state is explicit, with a complex formula detailing how the firm and tobacco industry agreed on $444 million. The agreement calls for $27.5 million, covering the firm's billable fees, to be multiplied by a lodestar multiplier of 14 for a total of $385 million. This sum was added to a "contingency component" of $58.8 million for a total of $444 million.

A multiplier is normally applied so that a fee fairly represents the risk a firm took in the case. No one disputes that the firm's risk was high when it began work on a contingency fee basis. More than 100 firm employees worked on the case, most of which were lawyers. They participated in document discovery, 300 depositions, 190 motions, 18 appeals, and a 74-day trial.

Professor Brickman, Professor of Teshinva University's Benjamin N. Cardozo School of Law and critic of large fees who has testified before Congress on the matter, has never heard of a multiplier anywhere near 14.

"Two or three is normal, and five is quite high," said Brickman. "This multiplier is not from this planet—it's hocus pocus." A lawsuit was filed to block payment of the fee.

Reprinted with permission of the National Law Journal, *September 14, 1998.*

Liens

Courts have ruled that payment of expenses of litigation without reimbursement creates a proprietary interest in a case. ABA Model Rule 1.8(j) prohibits a lawyer from acquiring an ownership or proprietary interest in a client's case, except under two conditions. The rule states:

> A lawyer shall not acquire a proprietary interest in the cause of action or subject matter of litigation the lawyer is conducting for a client, except that the lawyer may:
> (1) acquire a lien granted by law to secure the lawyer's fee or expenses; and
> (2) contract with a client for a reasonable contingent fee in a civil case.

Examples of an attorney acquiring a proprietary interest in a case include giving a client advice on various courses of action if the attorney stands to profit by one of the courses of action (allowing the outcome of a case to affect an asset of the attorney) and obtaining literary rights to a book about the case.

A lawyer may place two types of liens on a case: a charging lien and a retaining lien.

Charging Lien

Charging lien: A lien placed on a client's proceeds or judgment for payment of an attorney's fees.

ETHICS ALERT

A **charging lien** is placed on a judgment that a lawyer obtained for a client. The lien may be created by a specific contract or by a provision in a retainer agreement. When the client is paid the judgment, the lawyer is paid from the proceeds of the judgment. A charging lien will have priority over other liens, except tax liens. *In many states, a lawyer cannot place a charging lien on the judgment of an unrelated case or on alimony or child support.* Most states allow charging liens.

Retaining Lien

Retaining lien: A lien placed on property that belongs to a client and is in an attorney's possession.

ETHICS ALERT

A **retaining lien** allows a lawyer to retain papers, money, or other property received from a client until the lawyer is paid a fee. If the lawyer relinquishes the property on which the lien is placed, the lawyer may lose the lien. *In many states, a lawyer cannot place a lien on any property received for a specific purpose or on property received in an unrelated case.*

Controversy has arisen regarding retaining liens. Courts have questioned a lawyer's right to retain property that was entrusted to the lawyer for safekeeping. It is a lawyer's ethical responsibility to take reasonable steps to avoid prejudice to a client, and retention of a client's property may prejudice the client. Some states have ethical rules prohibiting a retaining lien, but several states allow retaining liens.

Other Liens

An attorney may secure payment of fees by having a client sign a promissory note secured by a deed on the client's property. Lawyers also may hold the pink slip to a client's car to secure payment of fees.

Legal Assistant Guidelines

A lawyer has full responsibility for a client's fee. However, legal assistants are agents of an attorney and are responsible for complying with guidelines concerning fees. Legal assistants must be careful in two areas of legal fees: quoting and setting.

Quoting Fees

ETHICS ALERT

Bate-and-switch: A tactic used in advertising to attract customers to a sale item and switch that item with one that is not on sale.

There has been much debate over whether legal assistants should quote fees to a client. Legal assistants will often be asked how much a firm charges for its services. In cases that have a flat fee established—such as for simple wills, uncontested divorces, bankruptcies, and some criminal cases—legal assistants are often permitted to quote fees to a client.

Legal assistants should be cautioned against quoting fees regardless of an attorney's authorization to do so. Cases have ruled that it takes the independent judgment of a person with a law school education to quote fees. Clients frequently do not know the law in their case and cannot determine their legal needs. A client who contacts an office for a simple will may in fact require complex estate planning to protect an estate. Only an attorney can identify potential issues in a case and anticipate potential problems that affect the fee. Since an attorney is ultimately responsible to a client for fees, the attorney should quote all fees.

An attorney is ultimately responsible for the acts of a legal assistant. A legal assistant who quotes a standard fee to a client may damage a potential attorney-client relationship if the client needs more than standard services. Firms have been accused of **bait-and-switch** tactics by clients who were quoted low fees and required more complex work. A legal assistant is not to blame in this circumstance. However, to avoid potential problems, legal assistants should not quote fees.

OF INTEREST . . .

Nine Ways Paralegals Can Help Reduce Legal Fees

1. *Promote Partnering:* Share responsibility for legal work with the client. In-house legal staff can perform some of the tasks performed by outside counsel.
2. *Scrutinize Discovery Procedures:* Establish clear procedures that streamline the discovery process.
3. *Act as Liaison:* Outline needs requirements of a case to avoid costly and unnecessary delays.
4. *Draft Detailed Retention Letters:* A retention letter summarizes the terms of the representation and prevents misunderstandings at the case's conclusion. The letter sets for the limits of the representations and helps staff keep within those limits during the course of the representation.
5. *Use Task-Based Billing:* Task-based billing sets limits on each task and helps paralegals stay within those limits.
6. *Employ Information Technology:* Use technology whenever possible to save time and reduce costs.
7. *Consolidate Vendor Contracts:* If the firm does a lot of business with an outside vendor, volume discounts can be negotiated and passed on to the client.
8. *Preapprove Disbursements:* Obtain approval from the client before incurring costs for such expenses as temporary staff and on-line legal research.
9. *Control Case Staffing:* Some firms overstaff a case, resulting in duplication of effort and wasted time bringing additional personnel up to speed. Set the staffing needs at the beginning of the case to avoid these costs.

Reprinted with permission of Legal Assistant Today *magazine, September 1997.*

ETHICS ALERT

Reasonable attorneys' fees: The amount of attorneys' fees determined by a governing entity to be reasonable.

Setting Fees   *A legal assistant may not set a fee.* A legal assistant does not have the requisite training to anticipate the facts and issues of a case and is not qualified to set a fee. This is an attorney's responsibility. Legal assistants who manage a law firm may be involved in fee setting from a management perspective, but all standard fees set by management must be reviewed and accepted by the attorneys in authority.

Recoverability of Legal Assistant Fees   In certain types of cases, the prevailing party in a lawsuit may be awarded attorneys' fees. This means that the losing party must pay the prevailing party's **reasonable attorneys' fees.** In the past, legal assistants' fees were not recoverable by a prevailing party. However, the U.S. Supreme Court considered this issue in the case of *Missouri v. Jenkins,* 109 S. Ct. 2463 (1989), and ruled that legal assistants' fees are recoverable. The Supreme Court stated, "By encouraging the use of lower cost legal assistants rather than attorneys wherever possible, permitting market rate billing of paralegal hours encourages cost-effective delivery of legal services."

However, what constitutes paraprofessional duties is an issue. A U.S. bankruptcy judge denied claims for legal assistants' fees when the duties were considered clerical in nature, such as photocopying, preparing envelopes, and mailing pleadings and orders. The judge stated that the costs for clerical duties are covered in professional hourly rates. The case was appealed.

Courts have ruled that the following criteria apply when an attorney's fee award may include expenses for paralegals:

◆ The service performed must be legal in nature.

◆ The performance of services must be supervised by an attorney.

◆ The qualifications of the person performing the services must be specified in the request to determine such qualifications.

◆ The nature of the service must be specified to allow the court to determine whether the service is legal or clerical.

OF INTEREST . . .

Recovery of Paralegal Fees—Cases

American Petroleum Institute v. United States, 52 F. 3d 1113 (Fed. Cir. 31996)

Beach Colony II v. California Coastal Com. (1985) 166 Cal. App. 3d 106

Brandt v. Schal Associates, Inc., 960 F. 2d 640 (7th Cir. 1992)

Buchanan v. U.S., 755 F. Supp. 319 (D. Or. 1990), aff'd 765 F. Supp. 642

Chambless v. Masters, Mates & Pilots Pension Plan, 885 F. 2d 1053 (2d Cir. 1989), cert. 496 U.S. 905

Citizens Against Rent Control v. City of Berkeley (1986) 181 Cal. App. 3d 213

Computer Statistics, Inc. v. Blair, 418 F. Supp. 1339 (S.D. Tex. 1976)

Connolly v. National School Bus Service, 1998 U.S. Dist. Lexis 1795 (1996) (N. Dist. Ill., Eastern Div.)

Consolo v. George, 58 F. 3d 791 (1st Cir. 1995)

County of San Luis Obispo v. Abalone Alliance (1986) 178 Cal. App. 3d 848

Guinn v. Dotson (1994) 23 Cal. App. 4th 262

Gullet v. Stanley Structures, 722 P. 2d 619, 222 Mont. 365 (1986)

Harman v. Lyphomed, Inc., 787 F. Supp. 772 (N.D. Ill. 1992)

Harris v. Railroad Retirement Board, 948 F. 2d 123 (2d Cir. 1991)

Hearn v. GE, 1996 U.S. Dist. Lexis 21897 (Mid. Dist. Alabama, So. Div.)

In re Continental Illinois Securities Litigation, 985 F. 2d 867 (7th Cir. 1993)

In re Grenoble Apartments, II, 145 Bankr. 43 (Bankr. D.S.D. 1992), vacated and remanded 152 B.R. 608 (D.S.D. 1993)

In re Sounds Distributing Corporation, 122 Bankr. 952 (W.D. PA 1991)

LA Shawn A. v. Barry, 1998 U.S. Dist. Lexis 2137, District of Columbia

Little Rock School District et al. v. Pulaski County Special School District #1, 959 F. 2d 71 (8th Cir. 1992)

Maltzer v. Provident Life & Accident Ins. Co., 843 F. Supp. 692 (M.D. Fla. 1993)

Margolin v. Regional Planning Corp. (1982) 134 Cal. App. 3d 999

Metro Data Systems, Inc. v. Durango Systems, Inc., 597 F. Supp. 244 (D. Ariz. 1984)

Miller v. Alamo, 983 F. 2d 856 (8th Cir. 1993)

Missouri v. Jenkins, 491 U.S. 274, 109 S. Ct. 2463, 105 L. Ed. 2d 229 (1989)

New Mexico Citizens for Clean Air v. Espanola Mer., 72 F. 3d 830 (10th Cir. 1996)

Niehus v. Liberio, 973 F. 2d 526 (7th Cir. 1992)

Occidental Chemical Corporation v. The Power Authority of the State of New York, 786 F. Supp. 316 (W.D. N.Y. 1992), aff'd at 990 F. 2d 726 (2d Cir. 1993)

Price v. Cole, 574 N.E. 2d 403 (Mass. App. Ct. 1991)

River Valley Preservation Project v. Metropolitan Transit Development Bd. (1995) 37 Cal. App. 4th 154

Ross v. Buckeye Cellulose Corp., 764 F. Supp. 1543 (M.D. Ga. 1991)

Salton Bay Marina, Inc. v. Imperial Irrigation Dist. (1985) 172 Cal. App. 3d 914

Stewart v. Sullivan, 810 F. Supp. 1102 (D. Hawaii 1993)

Sundance v. Municipal Court (1987) 192 Cal. App. 3d 268

U.S. Football League v. National Football League, 887 F. 2d 408 (2nd Cir. 1–9:39)

Wasson v. Secretary of Secretary of Department of Health and Human Services, 24 Cl. Ct. 482 (1991)

Court Denial Of Paralegal Fee Recovery

Edgewater Townhouse Homeowner's Association v. Holtzman, 845 P. 2d 122–L, 256 Mont. 182 (Montana 1993)

In re Speeds Billiards & Games, Inc. Debtor, 149 Bankr. 434 (E.D. Tex. 1993)

McCullough v. City of Oakland (1996) 46 Cal. App. 4th 1

Adapted from Handbook on Paralegal Utilization *by the California Alliance of Paralegal Associations.*

◆ The amount of time must be reasonable.

◆ The amount charged must reflect reasonable community standards.

Fees awarded to paralegals vary from $25 an hour (*Mason v. Oklahoma Turnpike Authority* 1997, W.L. 311880, U.S.C.A., 10th Cir. Okla. [1997]) to $250 an hour for a class-action suit (*Berchin v. General Dynamics Corp.* W.L. 465752, S.D.N.Y. [1996]). The recent case of *Spegon v. The Catholic Bishop of Chicago,* 989 F. Supp. 984 (1998), ruled that $90 an hour was an appropriate award for paralegal services.

FEE AGREEMENTS

A misunderstanding about fees is frequently a source of disputes between a client and a lawyer and erodes an attorney-client relationship. Studies have indicated that lawyers are reluctant to discuss fees with clients at the outset of a case. Fee agreements that result in disputes are informal, oral agreements that are often miscommunicated.

Model Rule 1.5(b) and (c) states:

(b) When the lawyer has not regularly represented the client, the basis or rate of the fee shall be communicated to the client, preferably in writing, before or within a reasonable time after commencing the representation.

(c) A fee may be contingent on the outcome of the matter for which the service is rendered, except in a matter in which a contingent fee is prohibited by law or by these rules. A contingent fee agreement shall be in writing and shall state the method by which the fee is to be determined, including the percentage or percentages that shall accrue to the lawyer in the event of settlement, trial or appeal, litigation and other expenses to be deducted from the recovery, and whether such expenses are to be deducted before or after the contingent fee is calculated. Upon conclusion of a contingent fee matter, the lawyer shall provide the client with a written statement stating the outcome of the matter and, if there is a recovery, showing the remittance to the client and the method of its determination.

The requirement that fee agreements be in writing is to prevent misunderstandings, enhance an attorney-client relationship, and provide protection for a lawyer in case of a fee dispute. Any ambiguity in a fee agreement is determined against the lawyer.

Some states require that all fee agreements be in writing. California, for example, requires a written fee agreement when fees in a case are expected to exceed $1,000. The agreement must contain an explanation of the fee, the nature of the services to be provided to the client, the responsibility of the lawyer, and the responsibility of the client.

Retainer Fee Agreements

Many states require that nonrefundable retainers, if allowed, be clearly explained to clients. A fee agreement must clearly state that the entire retainer will be nonrefundable on discharge and the circumstances surrounding the retainer (chargeable or nonchargeable). Exhibit 6.9 is an example of an agreement with a nonrefundable chargeable retainer clause.

Hourly Fee Agreements

Hourly agreements must set forth a schedule with the hourly rate of each employee clearly stated. All hard and soft costs must be indicated to avoid disputes about the entire fee. Exhibit 6.10 is an example of an hourly fee agreement.

Flat Fee Agreements (Fixed Fee)

Some states require that flat fees be in writing. If any additional charges are assessed, those charges must be clearly stated. Exhibit 6.11 is an example of a flat fee agreement.

Attorney-Client Fee Contract

This document (the "agreement") is the written fee contract that the law requires lawyers to have with their clients. We will provide legal services to you on the terms set forth below.

1. SCOPE OF SERVICES. You are hiring us as your attorneys, to represent you in the matter described on the attached Rate Schedule. We will provide those legal services reasonably required to represent you. We will take reasonable steps to keep you informed of progress and to respond to your inquiries. Unless you and we make a different agreement in writing, this Agreement will govern all future services we may perform for you.

2. MINIMUM FEE/DEPOSIT. You agree to pay us an initial deposit of $_____ by _____. Of the initial deposit, $_____ will be our minimum fee, paid in exchange for our agreement to represent you. The minimum fee is nonrefundable, but our hourly charges will be credited against it. The remainder of the initial deposit, as well as any future deposit, will be held in a trust account. You authorize us to use that fund to pay the fees and other charges you incur. Whenever your deposit is exhausted, we reserve the right to demand further deposits, each up to a maximum of $_____. You agree to pay all further deposits within _____ days of our demand. Except for the minimum fee, any unused deposit at the conclusion of our services will be refunded.

3. LEGAL FEES AND BILLING PRACTICES. You agree to pay by the hour at our prevailing rates for time spent on your matter by our legal personnel. Our current hourly rates for legal personnel (and other billing rates) are set forth on the attached Rate Schedule. The Rate Schedule also provides for periodic increases.

4. COSTS AND OTHER CHARGES.

(a) In General—We will incur various costs and expenses in performing legal services under this agreement. You agree to pay for those costs and expenses in addition to the hourly fees. The costs and expenses commonly include long-distance telephone calls, messenger and other delivery fees, postage, parking and other local travel expenses, photocopying and other reproduction costs, clerical staff overtime, word processing charges, charges for computer time, and other similar items. Except for the items listed on the Rate Schedule, all costs and expenses will be charged at our cost.

(b) Out-of-Town Travel—You agree to pay transportation, meals, lodging, and all other costs of any necessary out-of-town travel by our personnel. You will also be charged the hourly rates for the time legal personnel spend traveling.

5. BILLING STATEMENTS. We will send you periodic statements for fees and costs incurred. Each statement will be due within _____ days of its date. You may request a statement at intervals of no less than 30 days. If you do, we will provide one within 10 days.

6. DISCHARGE AND WITHDRAWAL. You may discharge us at any time. If you should discharge us, the minimum fee will not be returned to you. When our services conclude, all unpaid charges will immediately become due and payable.

7. DISCLAIMER OF GUARANTEE. Nothing in this agreement and nothing in our statements to you will be construed as a promise or guarantee about the outcome of your matter.

CLIENT   ATTORNEY

By _____   By: _____

Figure # _____

EXHIBIT 6.9   Sample Nonrefundable Chargeable Fee Agreement

Contingency Fee Agreements

According to Model Rule 1.5(c), a contingency fee agreement is the only type of fee arrangement that must be in writing. This section requires that a contingency fee agreement state whether the fee is calculated by a gross fee or by a net fee method. At the conclusion of a case, a client must receive a full accounting of the fee, including an itemization of the costs. Exhibit 6.12 is an example of a contingency fee agreement.

Attorney-Client Hourly Fee Contract

This ATTORNEY-CLIENT FEE CONTRACT ("Contract") is entered into by and between _____ ("Client") and _____ ("Attorney").

1. SCOPE AND DUTIES. Client hires Attorney to provide legal services in connection with _____. Attorney shall provide those legal services reasonably required to represent Client, and shall take reasonable steps to keep Client informed of progress and to respond to Client's inquiries.

2. DEPOSIT. Client shall deposit $_____ by _____. The sum will be deposited in a trust account, to be used to pay costs, expenses and legal fees. Client hereby authorizes Attorney to withdraw sums from the trust account to pay the costs and/or fees Client incurs. Any unused deposit at the conclusion of Attorney's services will be refunded.

3. LEGAL FEES. Client agrees to pay for legal services at the following rates: partners, $250 per hour; associates, $200 per hour; paralegals, $100 per hour; law clerks, $75 per hour. Attorneys and paralegals charge in minimum units of .2 hours.

4. COSTS AND EXPENSES. In addition to paying legal fees, Client shall reimburse Attorney for all costs and expenses incurred by Attorney, including, but not limited to, process servers' fees, fees fixed by law or assessed by courts or other agencies, court reporters' fees, long-distance telephone calls, messenger and other delivery fees, postage, in-office photocopying at $.30 per page, parking, mileage at $3.00 per mile, investigation expenses, consultants' fees, expert witness fees, and other similar items. Client authorizes Attorney to incur all reasonable costs and to hire any investigators, consultants, or expert witnesses reasonably necessary in Attorney's judgment.

5. STATEMENTS. Client shall pay Attorney's statements within 30 days after each statement's date. Client may request a statement at intervals of no less than 30 days.

6. LIEN. Client hereby grants Attorney a lien on any and all claims or causes of action that are the subject of Attorney's representation under this Contract. Attorneys lien will be for any sums due and owing to Attorney at the conclusion of Attorney's services. The lien will attach to any recovery Client may obtain, whether by arbitration award, judgment, settlement, or otherwise.

7. DISCHARGE AND WITHDRAWAL. Client may discharge Attorney at any time.

8. CONCLUSION OF SERVICES. When Attorney's services conclude, all unpaid charges shall become immediately due and payable. After Attorney's services conclude, Attorney will, upon client's request, deliver Client's file to Client, along with any Client funds or property in Attorney's possession.

9. DISCLAIMER OF GUARANTEE. Nothing in this Contract and nothing in Attorney's statements to Client will be construed as a promise or guarantee about the outcome of Client's matter.

Client   Attorney

By _____   By: _____

Figure # _____

EXHIBIT 6.10 Sample Hourly Fee Agreement

CONCLUSION

A Halifax lawyer, Peter Green, in a speech to the Nova Scotia Education Society, said, "The lawyer's fee is one of the least understood aspects of the practice of law, both within the profession and by the general public." The high cost of attorneys is the subject of many conversations. Attorneys' fees are expensive—so expensive that many people cannot afford them. In 1990, a well-known attorney stated that he could not afford his own fees.

When considering fees, one must consider the value of the service one receives. A lawyer's work involves people's lives, and the outcome of a case can dramatically affect the quality of a person's life. Consumers pay for a product for its value; they place a high value on an attorney's service to society.

Attorney-Client Fixed Fee Contract

This ATTORNEY-CLIENT FEE CONTRACT ("Contract") is entered into by and between _____ ("Client") and _____ ("Attorney").

1. SCOPE AND DUTIES. Client hires Attorney to provide legal services in connection with her dissolution of marriage. Attorney shall provide all services to bring the matter to conclusion, including filing all papers, appearing in court, and preparing a marital settlement agreement.

2. FIXED FEE. Client agrees to pay a fixed fee of $1,500 for Attorney's services under this Contract. The fixed fee is due by June 1. Attorneys shall have no obligation whatsoever to provide services to Client until the fixed fee is paid in full.

3. COSTS AND EXPENSES. In addition to the fixed fee, Client shall reimburse Attorney for all costs and expenses incurred by Attorney, including, but not limited to, long-distance telephone calls, messenger and other delivery fees, postage, in-office photocopying at $.50 per page, parking, mileage at $2.50 per mile, investigation expenses, consultants' fees, and other similar items. Client authorizes Attorney to incur all reasonable costs and to hire any investigators or consultants reasonably necessary in Attorney's judgment.

4. DEPOSIT. In addition to the fixed fee Client shall deposit $500.00 by June 1. The sum will be deposited in a trust account, to be used to pay for costs and expenses. Client hereby authorizes Attorney to withdraw sums from the trust account to pay the costs Client incurs. Any unused deposit at the conclusion of Attorney's services will be refunded.

5. STATEMENTS. Client shall pay Attorney's statements within 10 days after each statement's date.

6. DISCHARGE AND WITHDRAWAL. Client may discharge Attorney at any time. If Attorney withdraws before completing Attorney's duties under this Contract, Client may be entitled to a refund of some or all of the fixed fee, depending on the facts and circumstances.

7. DISCLAIMER OF GUARANTEE. Nothing in this Contract and nothing in Attorney's statements to Client will be construed as a promise or guarantee about the outcome of Client's matter.

Client   Attorney

By _____   By: _____

Figure # _____

EXHIBIT 6.11 Sample Flat Fee Agreement

SUMMARY

The various types of fees are retainer, hourly, flat, task based, contingency, statutory, referral, premium, and combination. A true retainer fee is paid to a law firm to ensure the firm's availability to a client. Hourly fees are the most common type of legal fees and in some jurisdictions the only acceptable method of charging clients. A flat fee is a set fee for a service rendered. A task-based fee is a flat rate for specific tasks in a matter. A contingency fee is a fee based on a percentage of a client's recovery in a case. A statutory fee is set by statute and varies with the state. A referral fee is a fee for referring a client to a firm. Premium fees can be best described as tips. Combination fees are a combination of any other types of fees.

Changes are occurring in the traditional delivery of legal services. Emerging since the early 1980s are law firms charging clients additional fees. Some law firms are now billing clients for the time of staff members and for costs, such as hard and soft costs.

The ABA established rules and guidelines concerning legal fees for two reasons: (1) to preserve the effectiveness, integrity, and independence of the profession and (2) to give society reasonable access to the legal system. To set standards that will satisfy reasonableness without compromising a lawyer's compensation, the ABA set forth the ingredients of a reasonable fee in Model Rule 1.5(a).

What constitutes a reasonable fee varies from case to case. The eight factors that are considered in de-

---

Attorney-Client Contingency Fee Contract

We will provide legal services to you on the terms set forth below.

Client hereby retains attorney to represent client in the matter of _____ for the purpose of recovering all compensation, benefits, and civil damages lawfully due client based on any contractual, governmental or tort liability arising out of the described occurrence. Attorney will provide all reasonably necessary legal services to obtain such compensation for client.

Attorney will advance all necessary and reasonable costs for preparing and presenting any claim or litigation covered by this agreement. Costs advanced will be reimbursed to attorney out of the gross recovery on behalf of client. The balance remaining will constitute the "net recovery," and attorneys' fees will be deducted from that amount.

Attorneys' fees will be set according to the following contingent fee schedule:

Claim	25% of net recovery	Litigation	30% of net recovery
Trial	40% of net recovery	Appeal	50% of net recovery

There will be a lien for reimbursement of costs advanced and payment of attorneys' fees on any recovery made for client. If there is no recovery, there will be no fee for legal services under this agreement.

Client understands that any recovery is contingent on establishing legal liability or contractual responsibility and that, furthermore, the collectability of any award or judgment is contingent on the existence of insurance or of funds and assets which can be levied upon. Client further understands that no particular result or amount of compensation can be guaranteed or promised by attorney.

Provisions respecting withdrawal or discharge of attorney: Attorney has the right to withdraw from the representation upon giving client reasonable notice to secure other counsel. Client has the right to discharge for any reason upon giving attorney reasonable notice. Attorney's compensation on discharge will be determined according to the services rendered up to the discharge date.

Attorney is authorized to associate other counsel on client's behalf any time attorney deems it necessary or desirable. Attorney will give client notice of any association and agrees that client's legal fees will not be increased by virtue of an association. Allocation of legal fees with associate counsel will be made according to the Rules of Professional Conduct of the State Bar of this State.

Client   "Attorney"

_____   _____

EXHIBIT 6.12   Sample Contingency Fee Agreement

---

termining a reasonable fee can be remembered by the acronym TOCATPET.

A number of federal circuit courts adopted a two-step approach to calculating reasonable attorneys' fees: lodestar and multipliers. Courts have determined that the factors listed in ABA Model Rule 1.5 (TOCATPET) are inherent in the lodestar calculation.

A lawyer may place two types of liens on a case: a charging lien and a retaining lien. A charging lien is placed on a client's judgment. A retaining lien allows a lawyer to retain papers, money, or other property received from a client until the lawyer is paid a fee. An attorney may also secure payment of fees by having a client sign a promissory note secured by a deed on the client's property.

A lawyer has full responsibility for a client's fee. Much debate has taken place over whether legal assistants should quote fees to a client. Legal assistants should be cautioned against quoting fees regardless of an attorney's authorization to do so. In addition, a legal assistant may not set a fee.

Many states require that nonrefundable retainers be clearly explained to clients. Hourly agreements must set forth a schedule with the hourly rate of each employee clearly stated. Some states require that flat fees be in writing. According to Model Rule 1.5(c), a contingency fee agreement is the only type of fee arrangement that must be in writing.

The law firm of Black, White, & Greene charges its clients four types of fees: hourly, fixed, statutory, and contingency. Certain criminal cases that Dennis White handles, such as drunk driving defenses, are charged a fixed fee. The firm averaged the amount of time Dennis and his paralegal, Milton, spends on drunk driving cases and applied their hourly rates to the total number of hours to arrive at a fixed fee of $1,500 for each representation. Robert and Tricia monitor the cases closely to determine whether the fixed fee is providing the firm with a profit. They found that some cases warranted additional time that was not originally anticipated but that others required less time than originally anticipated. Therefore, it averages out, and they are satisfied with the charge. If the firm's expenses increase, they will adjust the fee accordingly.

Associate Patrizia Boen handles personal injury cases for the firm and charges those clients a contingency fee. She charges 33⅓ percent of the recovery before trial, 40 percent thirty days before trial and trial, and 50 percent if the case is appealed. Her clients are required to deposit $500 in the firm's clients trust account for costs such as filing fees, service fees, and depositions. If the case exceeds those costs, the client must reimburse the firm out of the proceeds of the case. The firm uses the net fee method to calculate the contingency fee. Ms. Boen also handles the firm's workers' compensation cases. The fee for these cases is a 10 percent contingency fee and is set by statute.

Tricia and Robert monitor the contingency cases closely. The firm's computer keeps track of the employees' time spent on contingency matters. When discussing settlement, Patrizia can ask for a management report of the time spent on the case to determine the case's settlement value. She can also determine whether the case was profitable by looking at time reports. The firm has a policy that no more than 50 percent of Patrizia's caseload can be contingency cases because of the amount of time it takes to get paid on the case. It affects the firm's cash flow to have too many contingency cases.

George Templeton, the firm's contract attorney, handles probate and estate planning for the firm. The fee for probate cases is set by statute and is a percentage of the total amount of the estate. Most of the time, the probate cases involve issues that are not anticipated at the beginning of the case. To be compensated for these problems, George requests extraordinary fees from the probate court, which is always granted.

However, most of the firm's clients are charged an hourly rate for legal services. To establish their hourly rates, Tricia researched what the standard hourly rates were in the community. She calculated the rate after applying the firm's overhead expenses and profit margin to the rate schedule to arrive at the final schedule of hourly fees. She considered that a certain percentage of accounts receivable would not be collected and increased the rates accordingly. She came up with the following rate schedule:

Robert Black, senior attorney:	$300/hour
Dennis White, senior attorney:	$300/hour
Grant Greene, partner:	$275/hour
Patrizia Boen, associate:	$250/hour
George Templeton, contract:	$225/hour
Milton Nollkamper, paralegal:	$ 90/hour

In addition to direct costs, the firm also charges its clients for indirect, or soft, costs. It developed the following soft cost schedule:

Photocopies:	30¢/page
Faxes:	75¢/page
Long-distance telephone calls:	Actual cost plus 10 percent
Postage:	Actual cost
Employee overtime:	Time-and-a-half of hourly rate
Messenger service:	Actual cost plus 20 percent

A potential new client, Technology Enterprises, Inc., called and made an appointment with Robert to discuss the possibility of the firm handling all its business litigation. Technology Enterprises is a very large corporation with a corporate legal department of twenty-four attorneys. The company's general counsel met with Robert and told him that they are dissatisfied with their current attorneys and wanted to replace them with a new firm. He said that they were interviewing three firms in the area and would choose one to handle all their litigation. Since Black, White & Greene had such a good reputation in the business community, he requested that they submit a proposal describing their fees for litigation work. Robert was very excited about the possibility of working for this new client because they could provide the firm with a lot of work.

Robert went right to work on the proposal. He asked for the assistance of Tricia and of Audra, who was the desktop publishing expert in the firm. Robert wanted the proposal to stand out among their competition, so the firm hired a temporary secretary to fill in for Audra as she worked on this proposal.

The proposal included a complete history of the firm, a biography of its attorneys, and a list of major clients the firm represented. It included a history of the firm's successful cases. It also included a schedule of the firm's hourly rates and a list of costs billed to the client. The firm hired a professional photographer to take pictures of the firm and employees to put in the proposal.

Audra worked hard on the proposal, which, when she finished it, was beautiful. She had it professionally bound with a beautiful cover. It was quite impressive. Robert had the proposal personally delivered to Technology and was confident that they would get the account.

A week passed, and Robert heard nothing from Technology. He called the general counsel, who told him that they were reviewing all the proposals and had not made a decision yet. He commented on Robert's proposal as one of the most beautiful he had ever seen. Robert was sure that they would get the account and started thinking about hiring additional employees to handle all the work they would get.

A week later, Technology's general counsel called Robert, but Robert was not in. Robert returned the call the next day, but the general counsel was not in. Robert was very anxious and told Tricia to cancel all his appointments for the next two days so that he would be available when Technology called. They called the next day.

"Hello, Robert," said Greg Meyers, the general counsel of Technology Enterprises. "Hello, Greg," said Robert, "it's good to hear from you. Have you made your decision yet?"

"Yes we have, and I'm sorry to tell you that your firm was not chosen," said Greg. "We chose the Smith & Jones firm."

Robert was stunned. He was sure he did not hear him correctly. "What?" asked Robert.

Greg continued, "We chose the Smith & Jones law firm. It was a tough decision. Your proposal was by far the nicest, but the Smith firm charges its corporate clients task-based fees. We prefer task-based fees because it is easier to monitor cases and track our litigation expenses. We are moving away from hourly fees. Another problem with your proposal was the soft costs you charge. We have a problem paying for postage, faxes, and telephone charges. The Smith firm just adds a low monthly administrative fee to cover those things. I want to thank you for submitting your proposal and wish you much success."

Robert thanked him and hung up the phone. He was shocked and very disappointed. "Task-based fees?" he thought. "I've heard of them but don't quite understand how it works." He called Tricia into his office and told her the bad news. He instructed her to research task-based billing and to do whatever was required to implement it into the firm's fee structure. The next time a large client requests a proposal, they will be prepared.

CHAPTER REVIEW

1. Describe the four types of retainer fees. How is each used?

2. Explain the difference between straight hourly rates and blended hourly rates.

3. What variables are considered when determining a lawyer's hourly rate?

4. What variables are considered when determining a set fee?

5. What is task-based billing?

6. What is the difference between a contingency fee and a modified contingency fee?

7. What is the difference between the gross fee and net fee methods for calculating a contingency fee?

8. What four considerations are involved in taking a case on a contingency?

9. What are premium fees?

10. What are hard costs?

11. What are soft costs?

12. What eight factors are considered when determining a reasonable fee?

13. What is the lodestar approach to calculating a reasonable fee?

14. What is the difference between a charging lien and a retaining lien? In what circumstance is each used?

15. Why should legal assistants not quote fees?

EXAMPLES FOR DISCUSSION

1. The Fee Feud

Research Data, a large corporation, retained Attorney Cecilia Patino to represent it in a breach-of-contract action. Research Data agreed to pay Cecilia a one-third contingency fee. After filing suit and initiating discovery, Cecilia found the case to be more complex than she had originally anticipated, so she associated Melvin Hislop, a successful civil fraud specialist who agreed to handle the litigation. The attorneys agreed to share equally in the work and the fee. Research Data signed a new contingency agreement, incorporating Melvin into the agreement.

Research Data received a favorable outcome and paid the attorneys the contingency fee. When it came to splitting the fee, however, a dispute arose between the attorneys. Melvin alleged that Cecilia was not entitled to one-half fee because she did not do one-half the work on the case.

1. If you were the judge in this matter, how would you resolve the conflict?
2. Should Cecilia be given consideration because it was her case to begin with? If so, how much? If not, why not?
3. What Model Rule applies to this case?

2. High-Overhead Solution

Reingold & Feinstein found that its overhead and expenses were too high. It decided to hire an experienced law firm administrator to keep costs down and bring the profits of the firm up. As compensation, the firm offered the administrator a salary and a percentage of the profits. If the administrator did a good job, the percentage of the profits could be as much as one-fourth to one-third the administrator's total compensation. It was believed that such compensation would be an incentive for the administrator to produce greater efficiency and productivity, which would increase profits for the firm.

1. Was the administrator's compensation proper?
2. What area of the United States would condone such a financial arrangement?
3. What Model Rule applies to this case?
4. What are some possible repercussions of this arrangement?
5. Do any advantages accompany this arrangement? If so, what are they?

3. The Fee Is Mine!

Rachel Appledorn is a bankruptcy lawyer who represented Phyllis Swiftarrow in a bankruptcy case. During the bankruptcy, Phyllis was injured on the job and asked Rachel whether she would handle her new workers' compensation and personal injury case. Since Rachel is a bankruptcy lawyer, she referred the case to Ming Liao, a workers' compensation specialist. Ming, specializing in only workers' compensation cases, would not take the personal injury part of the case.

Rachel told Phyllis that she would continue to look for a personal injury lawyer and called many of her colleagues asking them whether they were interested in the case. Because the case involved complex issues for little recovery, the lawyers declined it. The statute of limitations had almost expired, so Rachel prepared and filed a complaint for Phyllis, listing Phyllis as in propria persona, or representing herself. Rachel continued to search for a personal injury attorney for Phyllis and mentioned to Ming that she was unable to find one. Ming recommended that Rachel call Albert Franzmeir, who agreed to take the case.

Phyllis indicated that she would agree to a referral fee for finding Albert. Rachel feels that she is entitled to the fee, but Ming insists that he is entitled to it. Albert says he does not want the case if it will involve a referral fee war between Rachel and Ming.

1. How would you resolve this problem?
2. In your opinion, who is entitled to the referral fee? Why?
3. What Model Rule applies in this case?
4. What are the advantages of paying a referral fee in this case?
5. What are the disadvantages of paying a referral fee in this case?

4. Attorney Referral Fees

Discuss attorney referral fees. Do you think they are proper? If so, why? If not, why not? Do you think there is a problem monitoring referral fees? How could they be monitored?

5. Creative Fee Structuring

Shannon Freer contacted Joel Olson to represent her in her personal injury case. She asked Joel to take the case on a contingency since most firms take personal injury cases on a contingency basis and she had no funds for a lawyer. Joel is a new sole practitioner, right out of law school, and is struggling to meet the overhead expenses of the office. He told Shannon that he could not afford to take the case on a contingency fee basis. Shannon was very impressed with Joel, however, and asked him to reconsider his decision.

1. What are some possible fee structures that could meet both Joel's and Shannon's needs?

6. Drill and Fill Dental Services

You go to the dentist twice a year to get your teeth cleaned. You heard that your dentist had devised a new method of charging for the service, but you were surprised to receive the following bill:

DRILL AND FILL DENTAL SERVICES

For dental services rendered on July 10:

Call for appointment

Receptionist time	0.2 hour	$ 7.00
Long-distance charges		2.00

Appointment Setup

Secretarial services	0.3 hour	12.00
One page in appointment book		0.25
Computer charges		10.00
Reminder card		5.00
Postage for reminder card		0.35
Copy of reminder card for file		0.50

Appointment

Receptionist services	0.2 hour	7.00
Use of reception area	0.8 hour	20.00
Magazine rental		5.00
Professional services		50.00
One set rubber gloves		10.00
Dental floss		0.05
Dental tools rental		10.00
Dental equipment rental		45.00
Free toothbrush		3.00

Billing

Bill preparation, secretarial services	0.3 hour	12.00
Dentist review	0.2 hour	25.00
Three photocopies		1.50
Postage		0.35
Total		$226.00

All accounts will be charged 18% annual interest if not paid within 15 days of date of invoice.

1. How do you react to the bill?
2. Are the charges proper?
3. Why do doctors and dentists not bill their patients as shown in the example?
4. Why do attorneys charge for soft costs?
5. Why are attorneys' charges and soft costs tolerated?

7. Who Pays to Educate the Lawyer?

Adam Hunt retained the services of Anne Sheridan in his case involving a title dispute on his property. Anne charged Adam $150 an hour for each hour she spent on the case. At the conclusion of the case, Anne gave Adam a bill as follows:

Client interview	1.0 hour	$150
Research	3.0 hours	450
Document preparation	1.0 hour	150
Conversation with title officer	0.5 hour	75
Total		$825

Adam paid the bill, thanked Anne, and left.

A week later, Mark Edwards retained the services of Anne with the same title problem on his property. He asked Anne how much the service would cost.

Since knowledge of the transaction was fresh in Anne's mind from Adam's case, Anne would not have to do research on the case. In addition, the necessary documents were in Anne's computer, so she would not need a full hour to prepare them. Altogether, it would only take Anne about two hours to handle Mark's case.

1. If Anne charged Mark $150 an hour based on her actual time, would it be fair that Adam paid for Anne's education to benefit Mark?
2. Could Anne qualify herself as an expert in this area to justify charging Mark a higher hourly rate than she charged Adam?
3. If Anne charged Mark an $825 flat fee, would this be fair to Mark?
4. If Anne charged Mark a lower flat fee, would this be fair to Adam?
5. What Model Rule applies to this case?

8. Bond or Bust

Brenda Camp gave Attorney Doug Lillehei $100,000 to pay for a bond in a foreclosure proceeding on her casino. When Brenda later failed to pay Doug's fees,

Doug argued that the $100,000 was given as partial payment of those fees and that he had advanced the remainder of the money for posting the bond. When the money from the bond was released, Doug indicated that he had a right to retain it because he had placed a retaining lien on it for attorneys' fees owed.

1. Who is entitled to the bond money?
2. What Model Rule applies to this case?
3. Was a retaining lien proper in this case?
4. If you were Doug, what would you have done in this case?

9. The Old Bait-and-Switch Tactic

Gail Dahl contacted Lawyer Susan Crowe to file bankruptcy. When Gail called the office, she talked with Jan Odegard, the legal assistant, and inquired how much a Chapter 7 bankruptcy would cost. Jan told her the fee was $650 and mailed her a questionnaire to complete for her appointment, which was set for a week later. The procedure for the firm is to have the legal assistant interview a client and then refer the client to a lawyer.

When Gail came in for her appointment, Jan interviewed her and told her again that the fee for the bankruptcy would be $650, payable in advance. Gail paid the fee to Jan. Gail was then interviewed by Susan. During the course of the interview, Susan discovered that Gail was the owner of a small business that was also heavily in debt. Further questioning revealed that Gail's business debts consisted of more than $350,000, with over 150 creditors. Since the business was a sole proprietorship, it would have to be included in the Chapter 7 bankruptcy.

Susan told Gail that because of the magnitude of the bankruptcy, the case would cost $1,500. Gail protested vehemently, stating that Jan told her it would cost $650 and she refused to pay more. Gail accused Susan of bait-and-switch tactics and threatened to file a complaint with the state bar.

1. What did this incident do to the reputation of Susan?
2. How did this incident affect the reputation of lawyers in general?
3. What did Jan do wrong?
4. What did Susan do wrong?
5. What did Gail do wrong?
6. How could this type of incident be avoided?

ASSIGNMENTS

1. You are a judge for fee disputes for lawyers and clients. To determine whether a fee is reasonable, consider the concepts discussed in this chapter, including the eight factors (TOCAT-PET) that contribute to the reasonableness of a fee. For each situation, list the issues involved and the factors that apply and make your ruling.

Situation 1: Anthony Vegas retained Howard O'Brien to represent him in his divorce proceedings. Anthony executed a fee agreement that provided for a nonrefundable retainer of $2,500. The agreement stated:

A client will pay a lawyer a nonrefundable retainer of $2,500, which is not to be affected by any possible reconciliation between the client and a spouse. Said retainer is to be credited against charges of $100 an hour.

After Howard had spent ten hours on Anthony's case, Anthony discharged Howard and gave no reason for doing so. Howard refused to refund the remainder of the retainer fee to Anthony. Anthony contested. Is Anthony entitled to a refund of the retainer?

Situation 2: A court determined a lodestar fee for a contingency case and doubled that fee to account for a "risk premium." The court determined that since the client's chance of success was 50 percent, a doubling of the lodestar was necessary to account for the lawyer's risk in taking the case. The client appealed the ruling to an appellate court, stating that the multiplier was excessive. Was it?

Situation 3: Paula O'Connor agreed to defend Glen Hageman in a criminal proceeding. Paula prepared a fee agreement calling for a flat fee of $15,000 to cover all services, including the trial. The fee was payable up front. Glen signed the agreement but paid no money. Three months later, after Paula had worked on the case, she refused to represent Glen further until she received the retainer. Glen had no money, so Paula demanded a $25,000 note secured by a second mortgage on Glen's vacation home. When Glen did not pay the fee, Paula started foreclosure proceedings on the home. Glen objected. May Paula foreclose on Glen's vacation home?

Situation 4: Ray Addington, a businessman, employed Ellen Henley regarding a contract action. Ellen stated that her hourly rate would be $200. When Ray indicated he had no money to pay on an hourly basis, Ellen presented a one-third contingency fee agreement, which Ray signed. Ellen participated in settlement negotiations for a year and obtained a settlement figure of $195,000 for her client. Under the contingency fee agreement, the lawyer's fee was $65,000. When payments were made to the lawyer, creditors, and subcontractors out of the settlement proceeds, nothing was left for Ray. Time sheets indicated that if Ellen had charged $200 an hour, her services would have been worth $20,000. Is a contingency fee appropriate in this case?

Situation 5: Donna DeMaster, owner of a piece of property worth $70,000, hired Bill Schuster to represent her in a quiet title lawsuit brought by Donna's brother. The case never went to trial but was settled because of the efforts of the parties' mother. No novel or difficult legal questions were involved, and the pleadings filed in the matter were not complicated. Bill charged Donna $23,000 for the representation. He kept no time records since he had the case on a one-third contingency basis. Is the fee excessive?

Situation 6: Al Houser paid Walter Krogen $45,000 to represent him in a felony case. Al pleaded guilty, did not go to trial, and was sentenced to one year in prison. He felt that the fee was excessive. Al's codefendant, who went to trial, paid his attorney $12,000. However, Walter stated that he spent more than 800 hours representing Al on the case. Was the fee appropriate?

Situation 7: Laura Albertson retained Leslie Olson regarding the final distribution of property from her divorce. A detailed retainer agreement set forth a minimum number of hours required for the representation and specified Leslie's hourly rate under two alternative time schedules. It also provided for the payment of additional attorneys' fees of a percentage of the net property distribution obtained for Laura. Was the fee agreement proper?

Situation 8: Meghan Schuh represented Joshua Anderson in a product liability case that was taken on a contingency and that included an appeal. The trial court ruled against Joshua, and Meghan sought an appeal of the ruling. However, Meghan had no experience with appellate work, so she hired an experienced appellate attorney to prepare the appeal and argue the case before the appellate court. In return for the appellate attorney's services, Meghan agreed to pay him 25 percent of the total fee. Meghan did not inform Joshua of her association of the appellate attorney. Did Meghan act properly?

Situation 9: Erin Brown's fee agreement with Nathan Moe entitled her to one-third of a gross recovery received by compromise or settlement prior to filing an insurance suit and 40 percent thereafter. The fee agreement also gave Erin a charging lien on any recovery. Erin opened the file, collected certain information, and notified the insurance carrier of the case. The carrier declined Nathan's claim. Suit was filed in the hope of receiving a favorable disposition from the insurance company, but no offer was forthcoming. Erin wrote Nathan a letter that stated that no further work would be done on the case and advised Nathan that he could seek other counsel, pursue the case himself, or have the matter dismissed. Nathan retained another law firm to represent his interests. When the second firm received his file from Erin, it was accompanied by a statement of Erin's charging lien on the proceeds of the case. Was Erin entitled to collect on the charging lien?

Situation 10: Sonia Feldbrugge represented Erica Lukk in a criminal case. During the course of representation, Erica was injured in an automobile accident and requested that Sonia represent her in the personal injury case. Sonia agreed to represent Erica for a one-third contingency fee. Erica's criminal matter ended, but she did not pay Sonia for that case. Erica owed Sonia $5,000 for the criminal case. Therefore, Sonia put a charging lien on the proceeds of the personal injury case for the $5,000 fee not paid in the criminal case. Was the lien proper?

2. Draft a contingency fee agreement for a one-third fee before trial, 40 percent if the case goes to trial, and 45 percent if an appeal is made. Use the examples in this chapter as a guide.

3. Draft a fee agreement that includes a nonrefundable nonchargeable retainer and hourly rates for the following:

Senior attorney at $200 an hour
Associate attorney at $150 an hour
Legal assistants at $75 an hour

4. Draft a fee agreement that includes a $5,000 refundable chargeable retainer and a flat fee of $10,000, using the examples in this chapter as a guide.

5. In your ficticious law firm, the owner's hourly rate is $225 an hour, senior attorneys $200 an hour, junior attorneys $175 an hour, legal assistants $125 an hour, and law clerks $100 an hour. Assuming that the owner and one senior attorney, one junior attorney, one legal assistant, and one law clerk work on a case, what would be the blended hourly rate?

6. For Black, White & Greene, write about their fee structure. For this exercise, it is OK to set fees. Include:

a. Hourly rates for all attorneys, legal assistants and law clerks;

b. Describe what types of cases are flat fee cases and the amount of each;

c. Describe what types of cases are contingency cases and the percentage factors;

d. Describe whether the firm calculates its fees by the gross fee or net fee method;

e. Describe the firm's policy of retainer fees and describe the type of retainer fee charged;

f. Describe the firm's policy concerning referral fees;

f. Describe the firm's policy on premium fees and combination fees;

g. Describe the firm's policy concerning hard costs;

h. Describe the firm's policy concerning soft costs and list all soft costs and the charges;

i. Describe the firm's policy concerning liens;

j. Describe the firm's policy regarding legal assistants quoting fees and describe what a legal assistant should do if a client asks the legal assistant for fee information.

SELF-TEST

How well did you grasp the material in the chapter? Test yourself by answering the following questions and check your answers against the answers found in Appendix A.

1. At the time of the Roman republic, how much did legal services cost?
2. Name the nine different types of fees.
3. Name the four types of retainer fees.
4. What is a true retainer fee?
5. Why is a true retainer fee used?
6. What is a nonrefundable chargeable retainer fee?
7. What is a nonrefundable nonchargeable retainer fee?
8. Why do many firms use nonrefundable retainers?
9. What is a refundable retainer?
10. What are hourly fees?
11. Hourly rates vary according to what three things?
12. What is a blended hourly rate?
13. What are the six factors used to determine hourly rates?
14. What is the most common fee found in law offices?
15. What is a flat (fixed) fee?
16. What is a per diem flat fee?
17. What are minimum/maximum flat fees?
18. How are flat fees established?
19. What is task-based billing?
20. What is a contingency fee?

21. What are the two methods of calculating the attorney's contingency fee?
22. What is the difference between the gross fee method and the net fee method of calculation?
23. What type of fee calculation gives the client the most money?
24. What is a modified contingency fee?
25. What are the four considerations in taking a case on a contingency fee basis?
26. Why have a number of states put limits on contingency fee?
27. What are statutory fees?
28. According to Model Rule 1.5(e), what are the three occasions when an attorney may divide a fee with another attorney?
29. According to Model Rule 5.4, what are the three occasions when a lawyer may share legal fees with a nonlawyer?
30. Why are lawyers prohibited from fee splitting with nonlawyers?
31. According to Model Rule 7.2(c), what are the three occasions when an attorney may pay a referral fee?
32. What are the four arguments against referral fees?
33. What are the two arguments for referral fees?
34. What are premium payments?
35. What are combination fees?
36. What are hard costs?

37. What is the difference between costs of litigation and expenses of litigation?

38. Why are attorneys not allowed to pay for the expenses of litigation?

39. What are soft costs?

40. What are some examples of soft costs?

41. What are the two reasons that the ABA established rules and guidelines concerning legal fees?

42. What are the eight considerations in determining a reasonable fee (TOCATPET)?

43. What is the lodestar calculation?

44. What are multipliers?

45. What are the two types of liens that an attorney may place to secure payment of fees?

46. What is a charging lien?

47. What is a retaining lien?

48. In addition to a charging lien and a retaining lien, what else may a lawyer do to secure payment of fees?

49. Who has full responsibility for a client's fee?

50. Why must legal assistants comply with attorney guidelines concerning fees?

51. What has case law ruled that a person must have to quote fees?

52. Whose responsibility is it to set fees?

53. What is the name of the case that ruled that legal assistant fees are recoverable?

54. What is most often the source of dispute between a client and a lawyer?

55. What is the essential ingredient for any fee agreement?

56. What type of fee must be in writing according to Model Rule 1.5(c)?

57. Why are written fee agreements desirable?

KEY WORDS

Actual cost
Advance
Bait-and-switch
Charging lien
Client funds account
Contingency fee
Costs
Database

Extraordinary fee
Flat fee
Hard cost
Lawyer hopping
Lodestar
Mark up
Multiplier

Per diem
Portal-to-portal
Reasonable attorneys' fees
Redline
Retaining lien
Soft cost
Tort

CHAPTER

Timekeeping

OBJECTIVES

After completion of this chapter, a student should be able to do the following:
◆ Define annual billable hours requirements.
◆ Explain what constitutes nonbillable time.
◆ Explain the difference between creditable and noncreditable nonbillable time.
◆ Calculate a billing in tenths of an hour.
◆ Complete a time sheet for billable and nonbillable time.
◆ Prepare management reports based on timekeeping records.
◆ Describe work on time sheets.
◆ Explain how coding is used on time sheets.
◆ Describe the various methods of timekeeping.
◆ Discuss timekeeping ethics.
◆ Describe the various features of timekeeping software.

INTRODUCTION

The knowledge and expertise of lawyers and legal assistants are the products law firms sell to their clients. Time is the vehicle by which they deliver their products. Compare a manufacturing firm and a law firm. A manufacturing firm has a product: a widget. Salespeople sell widgets to customers. Sales produce orders for widgets. Orders result in accounts receivable, and accounts receivable result in money. A law firm's products are knowledge and expertise of their lawyers and legal assistants. Marketing activities result in clients. Clients order the time and expertise of the legal team, which results in work in progress. Work in progress results in accounts receivable, and accounts receivable result in money.

Unlike widgets in a manufacturing firm that can be counted in inventory, knowledge and expertise are not tangible products. As a result, lawyers and legal assistants frequently have their own personal methods of recording their time. A firm that has minimal or no timekeeping policies gives lawyers and legal assistants an enormous amount of personal discretion about what to bill a client, what not to bill a client, how to describe time, and how much time to record on a particular project. Without proper training in timekeeping, timekeepers produce inaccurate time records that result in inaccurate client billing and management reports. Inaccurate billing causes law firms to lose clients and client goodwill. Inaccurate management records cause management to make decisions on the basis of incorrect information. Therefore, comprehensive guidelines and timekeeping policies are essential for the success of a law firm.

Managing time is a skill that requires effort. Since time is the vehicle by which a law firm delivers its product, it must be documented before its value can be realized. If it is not documented, its value is lost, and a firm loses its product. Unlike a manufacturing firm that may produce more widgets, a law firm may never recover lost time.

Lawyers and legal assistants are the primary timekeepers in a law office. A firm bills a client for their time, thereby obtaining its income. Other personnel, such as law clerks and secretaries, may also bill clients for their time, requiring them to keep time records. However, the main income producers for a firm are lawyers and legal assistants.

Timekeeping is an essential element of a legal assistant's job. Law firm management uses information derived from time records to bill clients, establish budgets, and prepare management reports. This chapter will prepare a student to develop timekeeping skills. The first section will introduce the timekeeping requirements of most law firms and will give an overview of a firm's expectations. The second section will explain how law firm management uses time records, and the third section will discuss the elements of timekeeping and describe how to keep time records. The fourth section will review various timekeeping methods. The fifth section will discuss timekeeping ethics, and the last section will give pointers on accurate timekeeping.

TIMEKEEPING REQUIREMENTS

Annual billable hours requirement: The number of hours a timekeeper is required to bill in a year.

Most law firms establish a minimum number of billable hours that must be produced by each timekeeper in a year. This is called an **annual billable hours requirement.** Since a firm bases its budget and financial forecasting on projected income produced by its timekeepers, it is very important that each timekeeper meet the annual requirement. In addition, a timekeeper's bonus, raise, or both may be based on whether an annual requirement is met. If it is exceeded, the timekeeper may expect a raise or bonus. If it is not, the timekeeper may not get a raise or bonus.

The number of annual billable hours required of a legal assistant varies with each firm. The chart in Exhibit 7.1 indicates the number of hours one must bill a day to meet the indicated annual billable hours requirement, assuming a 236-day work year.

Studies indicate that legal assistants are not required to bill as many hours as attorneys. According to a 1997 nationwide survey conducted by *Legal Assistant Today* magazine, 59 percent of legal assistants had an annual billable hour requirement. The average number of billable hours required ranged from 1,500 to 1,650 per year. The National Association of Legal Assistants (NALA) and the National Federation of Paralegal Associations (NFPA) surveyed their members in 1997 and arrived at their annual billable hours requirement, the results of which are shown in Exhibit 7.2.

HOURS A YEAR	HOURS A DAY
1,200	5
1,300	5.5
1,400	6
1,500	6.5
1,600	7
1,700	7.2
1,800	7.6
1,900	8
2,000	8.5

EXHIBIT 7.1 Annual Billable Hours a Day

NUMBER OF HOURS	NALA	NFPA	AVERAGE SALARY (NFPA)
Less than 250	1%	—	—
251–500	3%	—	—
501–750	1%	2.7%	$27,352
751–1,000	4%	3.9%	$24,268
1,001–1,250	8%	6.5%	$30,511
1,251–1,500	31%	18.6%	$33,255
1,501–1,750	30%	17%	$36,452
1,751–2,000	19%	8.9%	$37,483
More than 2,001	4%	4%	$38,321

EXHIBIT 7.2 Legal Assistant Annual Billable Hours Requirement
Source: 1997 NFPA Salary and Benefits Report.

Billable and Nonbillable Hours

The hours of a workday are placed in two categories: billable and nonbillable. Billable hours are directly applied to client's matters, while nonbillable hours are not applied to clients' matters. The average legal assistant spends 75 to 85 percent of a day on billable projects. Two types of nonbillable hours exist: creditable and noncreditable, as shown in Exhibit 7.3.

Creditable nonbillable hours are credited toward an annual billable hours requirement and include time spent in five types of activities:

Creditable nonbillable hours: The time that is applied to an annual billable hours requirement.

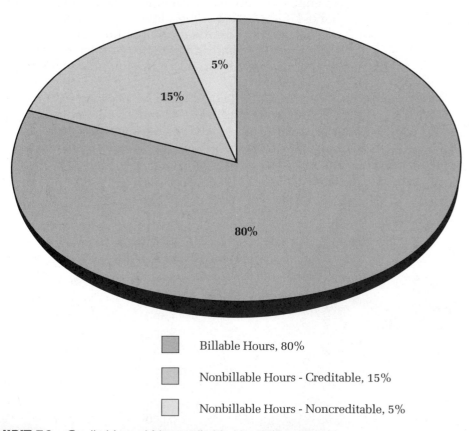

5%

15%

80%

▢ Billable Hours, 80%

▢ Nonbillable Hours - Creditable, 15%

▢ Nonbillable Hours - Noncreditable, 5%

EXHIBIT 7.3 Creditable and Noncreditable Nonbillable Hours

◆ Duties in serving on law firm committees
◆ Pro bono work, or work provided at no cost to a client
◆ Participation in management functions (e.g., completion of reports and attendance at law firm meetings)
◆ Administrative functions
◆ Training

Noncreditable nonbillable hours: The time that is not applied to an annual billable hours requirement.

Noncreditable nonbillable hours are not credited toward an annual billable hours requirement and include time spent in three types of activities:

◆ Educational activities, consisting of attendance at seminars, attendance at paralegal association conferences, and reading of trade journals
◆ Personal matters
◆ Paralegal association work

Firms differ in their application of creditable and noncreditable time. Many firms do not consider nonbillable time as a firm expense, but it is. If a firm with ten attorneys and three legal assistants had a one-hour staff meeting each week, the annual cost to the firm is as follows:

$$10 \text{ attorneys @ } \$200/\text{hr.} = \$2,000$$
$$3 \text{ legal assistants @ } \$100/\text{hr.} = \underline{\$\ \ \ 300}$$
$$\$2,300 \text{ per week} \times 50 \text{ weeks} = \textbf{\$115,000}$$

Ceiling: The maximum number of hours that may be spent on nonbillable projects.

Some firms put a **ceiling,** or maximum limit, on the number of creditable nonbillable hours to increase a timekeeper's billable hours. Others do not put a ceiling on creditable nonbillable hours if the time is spent on law firm business.

Some firms credit a legal assistant's educational activities, and some do not. If the state bar requires continuing education hours for lawyers, most firms will credit a lawyer's educational activities to the annual billable hours requirement. A firm and ultimately a client indirectly benefit from hours spent in educational activities. Increasing the expertise of a timekeeper ultimately results in increased efficiency and services for a client. Crediting time spent in educational activities and paying for those activities are ways a firm encourages continuing education for its timekeepers.

Some firms may also credit hours spent by a legal assistant on paralegal association work. If a legal assistant holds an office in a paralegal association, some firms believe that it results in advertising for the firm. Firms that support networking of employees may encourage their employees to become involved in association work by crediting hours spent on association business.

Most firms give attorneys a higher allowance for creditable nonbillable hours than they do legal assistants because attorneys are expected to participate in more marketing activities for a firm. For example, a lawyer would be given credit for activities such as working on pro bono cases, speaking at seminars, cultivating clients, and participating in community organizations.

Pad: To expand in a fraudulent manner.

Recording nonbillable time has traditionally been neglected or not required at all. Firms felt that the information was unimportant because it was not used for billing purposes. They also felt that requiring information on nonbillable time offered opportunities for a timekeeper to **pad,** or fraudulently add time to, time sheets to make up for unproductive time. Since law firms have become more competitive, however, marketing and planning a law firm's resources have become crucial. These activities require management of nonbillable time.

The information that emerges from the nonbillable categories of a time sheet will tell law firm management a lot about the efforts being expended by a timekeeper on the firm's behalf. These records are considered when an employee is evaluated and considered for a raise or bonus. Exhibit 7.4 shows the amount of billable and nonbillable hours of partners in 1997.

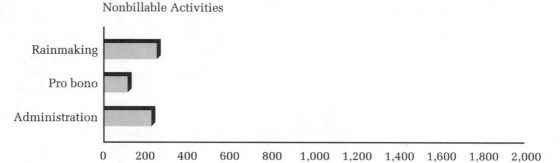

EXHIBIT 7.4 Billable and Nonbillable Hours of Partners—1997

Reprinted with permission of the *National Law Journal.* Source: National Assn. For Law Placement (1998).

Calculation of a Billable Hour

Each firm differs on the method used to calculate billable hours. Some firms require time calculated in hours, quarters of an hour, or tenths of an hour. Other firms require time to be documented in minutes. The most common method used is tenths of an hour. Decimal time entries are easily input into a computer. A billable hour is divided into ten 6-minute increments, as shown in Exhibit 7.5.

Since it is difficult to work on a project in 6-minute intervals, accurate timekeeping is difficult with this method. A legal assistant must become accustomed to watching the clock when a project begins and ends and also when the work is interrupted by a telephone call or co-worker.

Minimum Charges

Most law firms have a minimum-charge policy, which is the minimum amount of time they will charge on any project or aspect of a project. The most commonly used minimum charge is 0.2 hour, or 12 minutes. However, some firms' minimum charge may be as much as 0.5 hour, or 30 minutes. For example, a legal assistant makes a telephone call to opposing counsel. Opposing counsel is not available. The secretary takes the legal assistant's telephone number and tells the legal assistant that the attorney will return the call. The amount of time spent is approximately 1 to 2 minutes. The legal assistant charges the client 0.2 hour, or 12 minutes, for that activity according to the minimum-charge policy.

An argument opposing this practice is that clients are being overcharged. An argument in favor of this policy is that it takes the timekeeper time to make the transition from working on one file to working on another. When the legal assistant hangs up the telephone, she must document the time spent making the call and document the file for which the call was made. The legal assistant must retrieve the file of the next matter she will be working on and prepare her thoughts for the next matter. This

TIME INCREMENT	DECIMAL ENTRY
1–6 minutes	0.1 hour
7–12 minutes	0.2 hour
13–18 minutes	0.3 hour
19–24 minutes	0.4 hour
25–30 minutes	0.5 hour
31–36 minutes	0.6 hour
37–42 minutes	0.7 hour
43–48 minutes	0.8 hour
49–54 minutes	0.9 hour
55–60 minutes	1.0 hour
61–66 minutes	1.1 hours
67–72 minutes	1.2 hours
73–78 minutes	1.3 hours
79–84 minutes	1.4 hours
85–90 minutes	1.5 hours
91–96 minutes	1.6 hours
97–102 minutes	1.7 hours
103–108 minutes	1.8 hours
109–114 minutes	1.9 hours
115–120 minutes	2.0 hours

EXHIBIT 7.5   Time Increments in Tenths of an Hour

time is covered by minimum charges, and a law firm does not lose money when time-keepers make the transition from one file to another.

Billable Hour versus Actual Hour

Billable hour: Sixty minutes of time that are billed to a client.

A billable hour is different from an actual hour. An actual hour contains 60 minutes. A **billable hour** may contain as little as 5 minutes or as much as 8 hours. For example, a legal assistant must make five telephone calls to five different clients to inform them of hearing dates. Each telephone call takes a little over 1 minute, but each client is billed for 12 minutes—the 0.2-hour minimum charge. Therefore, the legal assistant has 1 billable hour for 5 minutes' actual time spent, as shown in Exhibit 7.6.

A billable hour may also be as much as eight actual hours because of nonbillable creditable or noncreditable time. For example, a legal assistant spent her day as shown in Exhibit 7.7.

An example of a legal assistant's time sheet that includes billable, creditable nonbillable, and noncreditable nonbillable time is given in Exhibit 7.8.

CLIENT	BILLABLE TIME	ACTUAL TIME
A	0.2 hour	1 minute
B	0.2 hour	1 minute
C	0.2 hour	1 minute
D	0.2 hour	1 minute
E	0.2 hour	1 minute
Total	1.0 hour	5 minutes

EXHIBIT 7.6   Billable Hours versus Actual Hours for Five Phone Calls

TIME	DESCRIPTION	BILLABLE HOURS	ACTUAL HOURS
9:00 A.M.–9:30 A.M.	Search for Jones file		0.50
9:30 A.M.–10:00 A.M.	Research for Jones file	0.5	0.50
10:00 A.M.–12:00 P.M.	Equipment committee meeting		2.00
12:00 P.M.–1:00 P.M.	Lunch		1.00
1:00 P.M.–1:15 P.M.	Conference with Jones re file	0.3	0.25
1:15 P.M.–2:00 P.M.	Conference with new copier vendors		0.75
2:00 P.M.–2:10 P.M.	Conference with attorney re Jones file	0.2	0.20
2:10 P.M.–3:10 P.M.	Review of time sheets for billing		1.00
3:10 P.M.–4:00 P.M.	Legal assistant staff meeting		0.80
4:00 P.M.–4:30 P.M.	Computer malfunction (tried to fix)		0.50
4:30 P.M.–5:00 P.M.	Interview with prospective secretary		0.50
Total hours		1.00	8.00

EXHIBIT 7.7 Billable Hours versus Actual Hours for a Legal Assistant's Day

Law Offices of Black, White, & Greene

Name: Peggy McIntire   Date: March 25, 2004

TIME	DESCRIPTION	CREDITABLE BILLABLE HOURS	CREDITABLE NONBILLABLE HOURS	NONCREDITABLE NONBILLABLE HOURS	TOTAL HOURS
8:30–9:00	Administration—read office memos and correspondence		0.5		
9:00–10:00	Smith v. Jones—office conference w/client	1.0			
10:00–10:15	Education—read paralegal association news			0.3	
10:15–10:30	Smith v. Jones—draft memo to file re meeting	0.3			
10:30–11:00	Shady Oak Corp. v. Industrial Metals—review complaint	0.5			
11:00–12:00	Administration—staff meeting		1.0		
12:00–1:00	Lunch			1.0	
1:00–1:30	Phone call from daughter			0.5	
1:30–3:15	Shady Oak Corp. v. Industrial Metals—draft answer to complaint	1.8			
3:15–3:20	Black v. Perry—take call from client	0.2			
3:20–3:30	Black v. Perry—prepare memo to attorney re telephone call	0.2			
3:30–3:45	Doss v. Frieholz—review produced documents	0.3			
3:45–3:50	Doss v. Frieholz—make telephone call to client	0.2			
3:50–4:00	Call to Linda re paralegal meeting			0.2	
4:00–4:30	Grey v. Rose—look for file		0.5		
4:30–4:40	Telephone call from husband			0.2	
4:40–5:00	Shady Oak Corp. v. Industrial Metals—prepare continuance motion	0.4			
Total Hours		4.9	2.0	2.2	8.5

EXHIBIT 7.8 Time Sheet with Billable and Nonbillable Hours

TIMEKEEPING RECORDS AND REPORTS

Management utilizes time records for seven purposes:

- ◆ Billing clients
- ◆ Compensating hourly employees
- ◆ Calculating employee productivity
- ◆ Planning
- ◆ Monitoring work in progress
- ◆ Projecting profitability
- ◆ Forecasting income

Billing Clients

Clients are billed according to the number of hours expended by a firm's timekeepers, unless they have a different fee arrangement, such as a flat fee or contingency fee. For cases that are billed hourly, computers generate bills on the basis of time records. Also, outside billing companies will prepare bills on the basis of time records.

Compensating Hourly Employees

Instead of having employees punch a time clock, law firms use time sheets to calculate an hourly employee's salary. A firm may also pay its nonemployees, such as freelance legal assistants, according to the time sheets they turn in.

Calculating Employee Productivity

Quota: An assigned goal.

Since law firms establish annual billable hours requirements, keeping track of the billable hours of each employee determines whether an employee will meet the **quota** set by a firm. By these records, management can determine whether an employee is productive.

In some firms, management will keep each timekeeper apprised of her or his creditable billable hours and give each timekeeper a report of billable hours monthly, quarterly, or biannually. These reports will allow a timekeeper to monitor accumulated billable hours to determine where she or he is in relation to her or his goal. For example, a legal assistant with an annual billable hours requirement of 1,800 hours must bill as shown in Exhibit 7.9 to be on schedule.

Planning

Time records provide information regarding the activity of a firm by type of case. Firms that provide services in various areas of the law will be able to calculate how much business they are doing in each area. In large and medium firms with departments established according to specialty, management can determine the activity of each department, as shown in the report in Exhibit 7.10. If management finds that a firm's bankruptcy department has increased its activity substantially, management may consider hiring another attorney and legal assistant or distribute the increasing workload accordingly. If a firm's tax department has decreased its activity substantially, the firm may decide to transfer employees into another department. Therefore, a firm manages its resources to accommodate the needs of clients. By comparing current figures with past years' figures, a firm can see its direction by the types of cases it is attracting. This type of information helps management direct the marketing efforts of a firm.

Exhibit 7.11 is an example of a management report by type of case. Type-of-case reports provide management with information on the time it takes to complete a certain type of case. This helps management establish fees for flat fee cases. For example, if a firm has records for the time spent on criminal cases for drunk driving defenses, it will

GOAL

1800 Hours

December 31 - 1800 Hours

September 30 - 1350 Hours

June 30 - 900 Hours

March 31 - 450 Hours

EXHIBIT 7.9   Legal Assistant's Billable Hours Goal

Law Offices of Black, White, & Greene
Quarterly Summary of Billable Hours by Department

Department	1st Qtr. Actual	1st Qtr. Proj.	2d Qtr. Actual	2d Qtr. Proj.	3d Qtr. Actual	3d Qtr. Proj.	4th Qtr. Actual	4th Qtr. Proj.
Antitrust	124.5	120.0	122.5	120.0	118.0	120.0	127.5	120.0
Litigation	860.0	950.0	875.0	950.0	980.0	950.0	989.0	950.0
Real estate	320.0	300.0	313.5	300.0	290.0	300.0	304.0	300.0
Bankruptcy	560.0	400.0	523.0	400.0	497.5	400.0	560.0	400.0
Tax	125.0	350.0	164.0	350.0	112.0	350.0	243.5	350.0
Total	1,989.5	2,120.0	1,998.0	2,120.0	1,997.5	2,120.0	2,224.0	2,120.0

SUMMARY

Quarter	Actual	Goal	Variance
1	1,989.5	2,120.0	(130.5)
2	1,998.0	2,120.0	(122.0)
3	1,997.5	2,120.0	(122.5)
4	2,224.0	2,120.0	(104.0)

EXHIBIT 7.10   Departmental Management Report

MANAGEMENT REPORT OF DRUNK DRIVING CASES	
CLIENT	TIME SPENT
A	10.3 hrs.
B	11.8 hrs.
C	16.2 hrs.
D	14.7 hrs.
E	13.5 hrs.
Total	66.5 hrs.

66.5 hr. ÷ 5 cases = 13.3 hr. for each case;

13.3 hr. × $175 an hr. = $ 2,327.50 set fee for each case

EXHIBIT 7.11 Type-of-Case Report

average the time and apply the attorney's and legal assistant's hourly rate to the average, thereby establishing a fixed fee. Time reports also monitor time spent on flat fee cases to determine whether the fee is too low or too high so that an adjustment can be made if necessary.

Monitoring Work in Progress

Monitoring the time spent on each case will inform management where a firm's resources are and are not being spent. For example, if no activity has occurred on a file during a sixty- or ninety-day period, a report of the amount of time spent on each case will alert management to potential neglect of that case. The responsible attorney will be informed and the file reviewed. If a large amount of time is being spent on one case, management will consider obtaining additional staff for the case.

Time records also allow management to monitor the workload of attorneys and legal assistants. These management reports give attorneys and legal assistants a realistic idea of their caseload and allow management to allocate work accordingly.

Projecting Profitability

Time records allow management to project the productivity of its timekeepers. For example, if a legal assistant is required to bill 1,500 hours a year, time sheets will reveal how close or how far the legal assistant is from meeting the goal. If a firm allows a legal assistant 20 percent of a day for nonbillable time creditable and noncreditable, the time sheets will also reveal whether the legal assistant spends too much time on nonbillable projects.

Forecasting Income

The number of billable hours projected for each timekeeper will determine the projected annual income of a law firm. A law firm budget is prepared from these projections. If the timekeepers meet their quotas and all fees are collected, a firm will receive its projected income. Exhibit 7.12 is an example of a firm's income projections.

Once a budget is prepared on the basis of anticipated income and expenses, management may plan for a firm's financial future. This planning includes retirement benefits, law firm investments, and long-term financial goals.

If a timekeeper fails to meet the quota or exceeds the nonbillable time allowance, the firm's income will decrease, and the firm must plan accordingly. The firm may cut expenses, reduce the owners' profit, eliminate an employee benefit, or lay off employees. A timekeeper's mismanagement of time affects the firm's cash flow, therefore

TIMEKEEPER	ANNUAL HOURS	HOURLY RATE	PROJECTED INCOME
Partner LuAnn Ephart	1,600	$200	$ 320,000
Partner Alex Webber	1,600	225	360,000
Associate Trevor Clarke	1,800	175	315,000
Associate Ina Davis	2,000	150	300,000
Legal assistant Blake Rowan	1,800	100	180,000
Legal assistant Wanda Lubovich	1,800	75	135,000
Total			$1,610,000

EXHIBIT 7.12   Income Projections

Amount of fees received			$12,000
Attorney's time	23 hrs. at $175	$4,025	
Legal assistant's time	59 hrs. at $75	4,425	
Total			$ 8,450
Unexpected profit			$ 3,550

EXHIBIT 7.13   Contingency Fee Case Report

affecting the entire firm. Managing time is an important skill for legal assistants. For time management pointers, see Appendix E.

A law firm also calculates the profitability of contingency cases by time records. When a contingency case has ended and a firm collects its fee, it calculates the profitability of the case by multiplying the amount of time spent on it by the attorney's and legal assistant's hourly rates. If the fee is higher than the figure calculated, the case was profitable. If it is lower, the case was not profitable. Exhibit 7.13 is an example of a report on a contingency fee case.

ELEMENTS OF TIMEKEEPING

Time sheets require eight pieces of information:

◆ Name of timekeeper
◆ Date
◆ File name
◆ Client number
◆ File number
◆ Amount of time expended, in tenths of an hour
◆ Description of work performed
◆ Name or initials of responsible attorney

Firms may require three additional pieces of information:

◆ Department code
◆ Task-based code numbers, if applicable
◆ Type-of-case code number

These entries will ensure that the appropriate client is billed for the time spent on the file and that management is supplied with appropriate information for its reports. An example of a time sheet is shown in Exhibit 7.14.

Law Offices of Black, White, & Greene
Time Record

Name: Peggy McIntire

Date: March 25, 2004

Client No.	File Name	Type	File No.	Description	Time
1001	*Dobmeyer v. Ferry*	102	1001-765	C/W Atty. Pflaum—R1–D1 answers to interrogs. T/C client re ans. to interrogs	2.3
3014	*Shady Oak Corp. v. Industrial Metals*	104	3014-223	R2 from oppos. counsel—D3 memo to file	0.6
2332	*In re Wilcox*	121	2332-405	P file for CH—summarize DP	1.5
5667	*People v. Anderson*	133	5667-101	T/C client re CT	0.2
3211	*Doss v. Frieholz*	105	3221-322	R negligent entrustment issue—D3 re research	2.4
Firm	Paralegal committee	151		Paralegal committee meeting	1.0
				Total	8.0

EXHIBIT 7.14   Time Sheet

The date on a time sheet is used to inform a client of the date a service was rendered and also to inform management of the timekeeper's performance for that day. The client's number, file name, and file number are essential so that the correct client and case are billed, especially if a client has multiple cases with an office. Firms also require legal assistants to insert the name or initials of their supervising attorney. This information is used in the event a discrepancy occurs as to the legal assistant's assignment for a client. The description area is used to inform a client and management of the work performed. The amount of time spent on a matter is documented in the time area in tenths of an hour.

It is important to be as clear as possible when describing work, even if it takes more time. This information is entered on a client's bill so that the client will know what work was done and the cost of that work. Billing disputes are as likely to be caused by a client's irritation at the way time is described as by the amount of time spent. For example, a client may resist paying $250 for a legal assistant's time spent "in conference with attorney" but would probably not resist paying for "planning trial strategy." Exhibit 7.15 gives examples of ineffective and effective descriptions.

Coding

To expedite the timekeeping process, law firms have developed codes for each function. A computer is programmed to pick up these codes and transform them into their proper meaning. Each firm develops its own coding system. An example of the types of codes used is shown in Exhibit 7.16.

Notice the column marked "Type" on the time sheet in Exhibit 7.14. This column is used for the type of case. Each type of case is given a specific number, and a computer is programmed to convert the numbers into the specific type of case. Exhibit 7.17 is an example of this type of coding.

INEFFECTIVE	EFFECTIVE
Work on case	Draft answers to third set of interrogatories
Review of file	Review first and second set of answers to interrogatories for inconsistencies
Conference with attorney	Conference with attorney re client's deposition
Telephone call to counsel	Telephone call to counsel re setting deposition date

EXHIBIT 7.15   Descriptive Entries are Important

C/W	Conference with
CT	Court trial
CH	Court hearing
D1	Draft of pleadings
D2	Draft of correspondence
D3	Draft of memorandum
D4	Draft of other
DP	Deposition
N/C	Nonchargeable
P	Preparation of
R	Research of
R1	Review of pleadings
R2	Review of correspondence
R3	Review of memorandum
R4	Review of other
RV	Revision of
TC	Telephone conversation with

EXHIBIT 7.16   Work Description Codes

Contingency Fee Law Firms

Time records are also important for law offices that do not bill clients by the hour. A firm working on personal injury cases on a contingency fee basis receives a percentage of the settlement at the end of a case. It needs time records to monitor the profitability of a case and monitor work in progress.

In addition, contingency attorneys are occasionally called on to produce time records. For example, if an attorney is terminated by a client, the attorney wants to get paid for work done to termination. If the case is a contingency case, the attorney is not paid until it is completed. The attorney may file a lien against the case, and to prepare the lien accurately, time records are essential. In court cases in which a former attorney has sued to recover a portion of a contingency fee, judges have requested time records to rule on the amount of the fee. Without these records, judges have difficulty evaluating the value of a former attorney's services to a client.

Time records are also valuable in fee disputes and other client complaints. They document an attorney's work on a case to disprove allegations of client abandonment or improper representation.

Another benefit of time records in contingency cases is in determining a case's settlement value. By keeping time records, attorneys are aware of the value of the time spent on a case. By comparing the time value multiplied by the timekeeper's hourly rates against settlement offers, an attorney can determine whether a settlement should be pursued. Exhibit 7.13 shows how profitability on a contingency case is calculated. It makes little economic sense to spend more time on a matter than the matter is worth. Through time records, contingency cases can be monitored to keep track of their value.

Litigation	
General	100
Real estate	101
Tort	102
Business	103
Corporate	104
Fraud	105
Domestic	
General	120
Uncontested	121
Contested	122
Custody	123
Adoption	124
Prenuptial	125
Name change	126
Criminal	
General	130
Misdemeanor	131
Felony	132
Driving while intoxicated (DWI)	133
Estate Planning	
General	140
Will	141
Trust	142
Probate	143
Litigation	144
Administration	
General	150
Attendance at meetings	151
Review of law firm correspondence	152
Continuing education	153
Law firm organization	154
Interviewing	155
Client development	156

EXHIBIT 7.17 Type-of-Case Codes

Corporate Legal Departments

Some corporate legal departments do not require time records from their attorneys and legal assistants because the departments do not prepare billing statements. However, these legal departments are finding that their management reports are not as comprehensive as those from legal departments that require time records from their employees. Therefore, many corporate legal departments require their attorneys and legal assistants to keep time records.

A corporate legal department services many departments of a corporation: finance, marketing, and sales. In addition, it may service subsidiaries of the corporation. These departments and subsidiaries are considered the legal department's clients.

Some corporate law departments bill each "client" for services rendered and are paid from that "client's" operating budget. Furthermore, documenting the time spent for each department or subsidiary gives management valuable information. When a legal department prepares its budget, time records are a valuable tool to justify additional staff or funding.

Corporate legal departments may be entitled to court-awarded legal fees if they prevail in litigation in addition to their outside counsel. A Delaware district court awarded Scott Paper Company in-house corporate counsel fees in a patent infringement case against Moore Business Forms (594 F. Supp. 1051 [D.Del 1984]). Scott's time records were evaluated when determining the fee award. Therefore, time records are essential to justify court-awarded legal fees.

Government Legal Offices

Timekeeping activities in government legal offices are becoming more common. In 1975, the California legislature mandated that the Attorney General begin billing legal services by individual case or project, therefore requiring a sophisticated timekeeping system.

Time records for government agencies are valuable tools when preparing budget proposals and management records. Management reports for a government office are usually very detailed to provide the government with statistics. In addition, lawyers employed by the U.S. government use timekeeping records for performance appraisals.

TIMEKEEPING SYSTEMS

Timekeepers have various methods of keeping track of time. Some track their time manually, and some use a computer or other devices. Manual time records are ultimately entered into a computer for billing and management reports. Each firm must examine the alternatives and select the appropriate system for its needs.

Manual Systems

Although manual systems may be obsolete, familiarity with them provides a general understanding of the essential elements of timekeeping. Additionally, many timekeepers keep their time records manually and then input them into the computer at the end of the day. This procedure may seem like preparing time sheets twice, but it ensures that the information put into the firm's computer system is accurate and complete. Furthermore, if a computer is not available because of a power failure or other reason, the timekeeper can keep time sheets up-to-date so that valuable time is not lost.

A time sheet is a permanent fixture of a timekeeper's desk. A time sheet can take the form of the one shown in Exhibit 7.14, or it may be like the diary shown in Exhibit 7.18. Entries are inserted on the time sheet daily or as a project is finished. In no case should a timekeeper delay completing the time sheet, as delay causes information to be lost, resulting in lost revenue for the firm. If a legal assistant who bills time at $75 an hour missed just one minimum-charge telephone call a day, the firm would lose $3,540 a year. Time sheets should be completed daily and, preferably, many times during the day. Timekeepers should never leave the office for the day without completing their time sheets. Legal consultants indicate that firms that require their timekeepers to keep an accurate accounting of their time make 15 to 30 percent more than those who do not.

It is recommended that timekeepers keep two types of time sheets: one for creditable projects and another for noncreditable projects. Legal assistants who keep track of noncreditable time are better able to manage time because they can see where their time is going. This allows the timekeeper to see whether she or he is spending more than 5 percent of the day on noncreditable activities.

When completing time sheets, include billable and nonbillable creditable activities. Management needs this information to prepare management reports. Additionally, the firm will have a permanent record of the time you spend on behalf of the firm, whether that time is for training an employee, looking for a file, or attending firm meetings. This information will be important when it comes time for a raise or bonus.

It is also beneficial to keep a separate time sheet documenting nonbillable noncreditable time. A written record of this time will help you develop your time management skills and monitor unproductive time. Five percent of your day (20 minutes

EXHIBIT 7.18 Example of Diary System

in an eight-hour day) is allotted for nonbillable noncreditable time. Keeping track of it will alert you if you are exceeding this guideline.

There are two methods of manual timekeeping systems: the long method and the short method.

With the long method, you document each activity as you start and stop it. For example, you start the day working on the ABC case. Before you begin, you write the entry on your time sheet. You note the time you begin and describe your activity. After 30 minutes, you are interrupted by a telephone call from your client in the Smith v Jones case. You note the time and complete your entry for the ABC case by inserting .5, indicating that you worked on the case for 30 minutes before the interruption. You then start a new entry for the Smith v Jones case and insert the telephone call from your client. You speak to the client for 10 minutes. When you are finished, you document your time sheet for .2 hr. and describe the telephone call. As you return to the ABC case, you make a new entry on your time sheet for the ABC case and describe your work again. You note the time and begin the clock running on the ABC assignment. Each time you stop working on a case, for whatever reason, you end your time sheet entry.

With the short method, you do not make a new entry each time you are interrupted. For example, you begin working on the ABC case and prepare your time sheet accordingly. After working on the case for 30 minutes, you are interrupted by a telephone call from your client in the Smith v Jones case. You note the time and make an entry on your time sheet for the telephone call: Smith v Jones case. You do not close out the first entry of the ABC case. The telephone call lasted 10 minutes and you document your time sheet with the telephone call and note the time so you may start the clock running on the ABC case. You finish working on the ABC case an hour later. You have a total of 1.5 hours on the ABC case and document your time sheet entry for the ABC case with 1.5 hours. This method will give you one entry per case per day on your time sheet. When using the short method, be sure to describe all of your activities performed for that client. The short method is more concise and makes inputting the information into the computer easier.

Firms differ on their requirements for submitting time sheets. Some require that they be submitted daily, some weekly, and some monthly. Be sure to make copies of your time sheets before you submit them.

A paralegal is working on the time sheet throughout the day. When it gets busy and there is a lot of activity, it is easy to overlook this very important task. Always have your time sheet handy. If you cannot complete an entry, at least write in the name of the case on which you worked and the time you started the activity. This entry will stimulate your memory of what transpired when you can complete your time sheet. You should never wait longer than the end of the day to complete your time sheet. It is the first task you do at the beginning of the day and the last task at the end of the day. Always end the day with a complete time sheet.

TRENDS ▶▶▶

Are Bonuses Connected to Billable Hours?

A prominent New York law firm, LeBoeuf, Lamb, Greene & MacRae, reported that it gives its attorneys two types of bonuses: nondiscretionary and discretionary. A nondiscretionary bonus is based on a percentage of the attorneys' base salary and is awarded if the attorneys met their annual billable hours requirement. The discretionary bonus is awarded to attorneys who have made exceptional contributions to the firm. Attorneys are eligible for the discretionary bonus if they billed 2,200 creditable hours, including up to 200 hrs of pro bono work. Among the attorneys who received the highest discretionary bonus were corporate and litigation associates who logged nearly 2,700 hours in one year. The amount of the discretionary bonus varied, but some associates earned as much as 25 percent of their base salaries.

Automated Systems

Manual timekeeping systems are becoming obsolete as firms take advantage of timekeeping software products. In a survey of law firms that was conducted by the American Bar Association (ABA) and Chicago-Kent College of Law in 1992, 86 percent of lawyers had a computer on or near their desks. In 1986, only 7 percent of surveyed lawyers used computers.

As lawyers become more comfortable with computers, more timekeepers will use them for timekeeping. Entering time information directly into a computer eliminates the need for data entry and saves a firm money. Management can produce daily reports more quickly than if data entry were required.

A timekeeper will enter the essential information directly into a computer or submit completed time sheets to a data entry clerk who will code and enter the information. A computer can be programmed to accommodate a firm's coding system regarding type of case, type of work performed, and timekeeper. For management to receive the many different management reports, all necessary information must be inserted into a computer.

More than 100 time and billing software packages existed in 1999. A listing of the most popular programs are listed in the Tech Tips sidebar on page 260. Most products have the following features:

◆ Record time, expense, and payment entries
◆ Produce client billing statements
◆ Age and track accounts receivable
◆ Produce management and productivity reports

Additionally, many programs will check for conflicts of interest and will accommodate task-based pricing of services.

Most of the products are marketed to small and medium law firms, although many of them will accommodate a large firm if additional software is purchased. For example, Timeslips Deluxe is designed strictly for time and billing but has additional software, Timeslips Deluxe Accounting Link, that will provide a general ledger and accounting link into thirty general ledger or accounting software programs. It also has other **add-on** features, such as a spellcheck and a remote timekeeper program.

Add-on: A software application that can be purchased to enhance the features of another software application; also called a plug-in.

EXHIBIT 7.19 Example of Navigator Screen in Timekeeping Software

Reprinted with permission of Sage U.S., Inc.

Icon: A picture that symbolizes a software application or function of an application.

Drop-down list: A list of activities that are listed in an area of the screen that is visible if the list is chosen.

Application: Software that has a specific function, such as word processing, spreadsheet, or database.

The basic screens of Timeslips Deluxe are listed as **icons** at the top of the screen and include time and expense, transactions, client, timekeeper, activity, file maintenance, and settings, as shown in Exhibit 7.19. Options are available by a **drop-down list** within each screen. The program can be customized to meet the needs of individual users.

Like most other programs, Timeslips includes an on-screen timer that captures time as events occur. This feature can be accessed from any other **application** and allows manual time entry and timing by way of a clock that measures time. This clock can be turned off and on. It is possible to enter projected time to be spent on a matter into the clock so the actual time can be compared to the projected time. This feature is useful for task-based billing projects.

The billing rates for each individual timekeeper is programmed into the system along with the firm's coding system. The program will permit the firm to apply a markup or markdown of a particular slip. The computer automatically translates the codes into descriptive details of the services rendered, and client bills are automatically generated. The system will track the time of each timekeeper and automatically apply each timekeeper's hourly rate to the charges. Software also tracks the productivity of fixed fee and contingency matters. Exhibit 7.20 is an example of a time entry screen and calendar of billed time.

Timeslips (as well as other programs) is capable of fifty different management reports in seven categories: slip analysis, bills and worksheets, client reports, client work in progress, user reports, activity reports, and system reports. An automated system saves a firm management time and provides management reports faster.

TIMEKEEPING ETHICS

The ethical implications of accurate timekeeping cannot be overemphasized. When tracking time, be aware of the following ethical guidelines:

◆ *Do not bill clients for work not performed.* Billing clients for work not performed is stealing. When working on a client's file, be sure to note the exact time when

EXHIBIT 7.20 Example of Time Entry and Tracking Screen in Timekeeping Software
Reprinted with permission of Versys Corporation.

TECH TIPS
Timekeeping and Billing Software

The following is a sample of related software:

Timeslips Deluxe: Timeslips Corporation—www.timeslips.com
Advanced/Network Billing: Compulaw—www.compulaw.com
*DDI*Law:* DDI, Inc.—(847) 647-2222
Distributed Time Entry 5.0: Advanced Productivity Software—
   www.advancedproductivity. com
PC Law Jr.: Alumni Software—www.pclaw.com
ProLaw: Impact Software Productions, Inc.—www.prolaw.com
TABS III, Jr.: Software Technologies, Inc.—www.softwaretech.com
Time & Profit: BytePro—www.bytepro.com
The Tussman Program: Tussman Programs, Inc.—(800) 228-6589
Amicus Attorney: Gavel & Gown Software—www.amicusattorney.com
Time Matters: Data.Txt Corporation—www.timematters.com
Carpe Diem: Prosoft Corporation—
StatusPro: CSS, Inc.—www.csspro.com
AboutTime: Versys Corporation—www.versys.com

For Large Firms

Javelan Practice Management System: Barrister Information Systems—
   www.barrister.com
CMS Open: CMS/Data Corporation—www.cmsdata.com
Elite: Elite Information Systems—www.elite.com

*Software mentioned in this sidebar is for informational purposes only and is not
for the purpose of endorsing products.*

ETHICS ALERT

you start and stop the work. If you should be interrupted by a telephone call from another client, note the time and stop the clock before you take the call. When you have finished the call and resume the previous client's project, note the time again. This will allow you to insert accurate time entries on your time sheet for both projects. Deduct the amount of time you spent on the telephone call from the time spent on the client's file.

◆ *Do not pad time sheets.* Be sure to insert accurate time entries for each client's case. Timekeepers with a heavy annual billable hours requirement may be tempted to include extra time on their time sheets, but should not give in to this temptation. If you completed a project in less time than anticipated, insert the correct time on your time sheet and bring it to the attorney's attention. If you think you spent more time than anticipated on a project, insert the correct time and bring it to the attorney's attention. It is the attorney's responsibility to adjust the time entry if necessary. Padding time sheets is more prevalent than one would expect. In a 1995 survey of corporate counsel, more than 80 percent estimated that at least 5 percent of all billings were padded, while more than 25 percent believed that billings were padded by 25 percent.

ETHICS ALERT

◆ *Do not bill a client for time spent on personal matters.* If you are working on a client's file while you receive a personal telephone call, note the time and deduct that time from the client's matter.

ETHICS ALERT

◆ *Do not double-bill.* If a legal assistant works on two matters at once, the time must be split between the two matters. For example, a legal assistant is traveling by air to another city to assist in a trial. The firm bills the client for travel time. While on the airplane, the legal assistant works on a file for another client and bills both clients for the time spent on the airplane. Legal assistants should work on the case for which she or he is being paid to travel.

ETHICS ALERT

◆ *Do not bill multiple clients for one activity.* If a legal assistant is preparing interrogatories that will be used in two cases, you cannot bill both clients for the same time spent on the project. For example, spending three hours on an activity that benefits two clients does not equal six hours of billable time. The time should be split between both clients to total the actual time spent on the activity. The ABA ruled in its Formal Opinion 93-379 that attorneys who bill by the hour cannot double-bill for recycled work product. Other state bars have similar opinions.

ETHICS ALERT

◆ *Do not apply an attorney's hourly rate to the services of a paralegal.* Firms that bill an attorney's rate for paralegal time are committing fraud. Webster Hubbell, President Clinton's friend and right-hand man in the Justice Department, pled guilty to charging clients for work that was completed by associates. He spent eighteen months in prison. If you discover that your firm is guilty of this practice, it should be brought to management's attention immediately.

ETHICS ALERT

OF INTEREST . . .

Burning the Midnight Oil

A partner in a respected Chicago law firm charged clients for 6,022 hours of work in 1993. This amounts to 16.5 billable hours a day, seven days a week, every week of the year. A review of his past billing record indicates that he billed about 5,000 hours a year for the previous three years at a billable rate of $350 an hour. Annual billings of 3,000 hours are extremely rare, and 5,000 hours of billing is virtually impossible.

An internal memorandum of this lawyer's firm specified that firm management, departmental, client relations, and general office matters are not billable. His colleagues described this lawyer as a tenacious litigator who regularly works long days and weekends, but they could not explain how he spent all the time that he was awake on billable matters.

Source: Wall Street Journal, *May 1994.*

Common Problems

Each timekeeper will experience at least one of the following situations. These common problems should be discussed with the firm's management or supervising attorney for guidance on a firm's policies.

◆ *The vanishing file:* Finding files is an ongoing challenge for most law firms. Files have been found in the attorney's office, desk, briefcase, and car trunk—anywhere but the file room. *Question:* How does a legal assistant document time spent looking for files? Should this time be creditable or noncreditable nonbillable hours? *Answer:* The time should not be billed to the client. A legal assistant's annual billable hours requirement should not be penalized because of a firm's mismanagement of files. Therefore, the time should be credited to the timekeeper's annual billable hours requirement as administrative time. If it is not creditable, the timekeeper would have to work extra hours to make up the time spent looking for files. It is an interesting exercise to keep track of time spent looking for files. Management would be surprised how much money file mismanagement costs a firm in unproductive time.

◆ *The chatty co-worker:* Every office has one. This employee tells co-workers her or his life story—twice—before starting work in the morning. Being polite to this co-worker is important to develop a positive firm culture, but it is also important to get work done. *Question:* How does a legal assistant handle this situation? *Answer:* A legal assistant can be both polite and assertive in this situation by commenting, for example, "Gee, I would love to hear all about this, but I must prepare this document by noon. Can we talk at lunch?" Also, subtle tactics, such as closing the office door, discourages a chatty co-worker.

◆ *Time constraints:* Clients are becoming more cost conscious, and many are requiring that a firm adhere to a budget for a case. Task-based billing projects require timekeepers to be especially aware of the amount of time spent on a matter. *Question:* If a legal assistant exceeds the allotted time for a project, what should she or he do with the extra time? *Answer:* The exact time spent on the matter should be included on the time sheet regardless of time restrictions. A note referencing the excessive time will alert management to the problem. Management or the attorney will catch the time and adjust the client's bill accordingly. Management monitors the time that each activity takes and uses this information to predict future charges. If in doubt, the timekeeper should consult management or the supervising attorney for guidance.

◆ *The waiting game:* The legal assistant has scheduled a meeting with the supervising attorney regarding a client's case. During the meeting, the supervising attorney takes telephone calls from other clients. The legal assistant must wait for the attorney to finish before resuming the meeting. *Question:* How should this time be documented? *Answer:* The time the legal assistant waits for the attorney to resume the meeting should not be charged to the client unless the timekeeper works on the case while waiting. The legal assistant should consult management or the supervising attorney in this situation or leave the meeting until the attorney finishes the call.

◆ *Travel time:* Is travel time billable or nonbillable? The firm may bill some clients for travel time and not others. Others bill clients a reduced rate for travel time. *Question:* If the firm bills a client for travel time, may the timekeeper work on another client's case while traveling? *Answer:* No. If the timekeeper did so, she or he would be guilty of double-billing.

◆ *Short telephone calls:* A legal assistant receives a series of short telephone calls on one case throughout the day. *Question:* Are the calls billed at a minimum charge separately, or are they aggregated? *Answer:* The legal assistant must use her or his own judgment in this situation. The general rule is that if the calls occur while the legal assistant is working on the case, the calls should be aggregated and included in the total time spent on the case. If the calls occur while the legal assistant is working on another case, the calls should be billed at the minimum charge. The answer depends on the firm's policy, the type of client, and the circumstances involved.

◆ *Minimum charges:* Most firms have a minimum charge, usually 12 minutes, or 0.2 hour. On occasion, a legal assistant may work on a matter for only 2 or 3 minutes. For example, a client calls and requests a copy of a document. The time it takes for the legal assistant to take the call and retrieve the document to give it to the secretary for copying is three minutes. *Question:* Should the legal assistant bill the client for the minimum charge, or not document the charge? *Answer:* Document the call. One solution is to document the charge as a minimum charge and attach a note to the supervising attorney that the matter took about three minutes. It is the supervising attorney's or management's responsibility to make the ultimate decision to charge or not charge the client.

TIMEKEEPING TIPS

Keep the Time Sheet Handy

Preparing a time sheet is the first thing a legal assistant does in the morning. Completing a time sheet is the last thing a legal assistant does in the evening. Since a legal assistant works with time sheets constantly (whether a manual or an electronic time sheet), a time sheet must be accessible at all times. As a project is begun, the file name, client name and number, and description of the work are documented on the time sheet. The time is noted. When the project is finished, the time is noted. The time can then be calculated in tenths of an hour and entered on the time sheet. It is helpful to finish a project once it is started. However, if a legal assistant is interrupted or must stop for another reason, the time is noted. The time the project is resumed is also noted. The interval time is deducted from the total amount of time for the project.

Record the Largest Amount of Time

When recording time in tenths of an hour, it is difficult to end a task on the exact 6-minute increment. If a legal assistant worked on a project for 40 minutes, does she bill the client 0.6 hour (36 minutes) or 0.7 hour (42 minutes)? It is generally accepted to put down the largest amount of time.

Document the Time as a Project Is Finished

Timekeepers who wait until the end of a week to complete time sheets are costing their firms a lot of money. It is very easy to forget about many short telephone calls. Missing just one a day will add up to thousands of dollars by the end of a year. With a billing rate of $75 an hour, not documenting one minimum-charge telephone call a day will total $3,540 by the end of a year:

$$0.2 \text{ hour a day} \times \$75 = \$15 \text{ a day}$$
$$\$15 \times 236 \text{ days a year} = \$3,540 \text{ a year}$$

Do Not Estimate Time

Timekeepers who wait until the end of a day to document time sheets usually estimate their time spent on a project. A timekeeper who thinks that she or he can accurately estimate time is fooling her- or himself and the firm. An experiment conducted by Altman, Weil & Pensa asked a number of attorneys to pick several files and estimate their time spent on each case. In every case, the attorney was either 50 percent too high or 40 percent too low. Other studies have consistently shown that time-keepers who estimate their time underestimate their time.

Be Accurate

If a legal assistant feels that it took too much time to complete a project, she or he may be tempted to reduce the recorded amount of time spent on the project. This is a disservice to the legal assistant. All time spent on a project must be recorded regardless of its billable nature. If a supervising attorney feels that the time spent on a project is not billable or is too high, it is the attorney's responsibility to reduce the cost to the client when the attorney reviews the bills.

If a legal assistant feels that she or he completed a project too quickly and should have devoted more time to it, she or he may be tempted to add to the amount of time. A legal assistant should not give in to this temptation. Each legal assistant works at her or his own pace. What is speedy to one legal assistant is average to another.

Be Descriptive and Concise

When describing time, a timekeeper should avoid using overly broad phrases such as "review of file" or "conference with lawyer." Descriptions should clearly identify the work performed, such as the reason a file was reviewed or the issues discussed at a conference. When describing telephone calls, include the name of the other party and the topic of conversation. Descriptions must be clear, brief, and concise.

Record All Nonbillable Time

If a firm does not require nonbillable time to be documented on time sheets, a legal assistant should develop a "nonbillable time" time sheet and record all nonbillable activities on it. This will come in handy at evaluation time.

Develop To-Do Lists

Putting projects on a to-do list will help a legal assistant give priority to projects and structure a day. Projects are placed in three categories: A, B, and C. A projects are urgent, B projects must be completed within a week, and C projects may be completed within a month. The list should be revised each week.

CONCLUSION

Timekeeping is a very important skill for all legal assistants. Accurate timekeeping is especially important in view of the current economic conditions—in which clients are pressured to keep legal fees down and law firms are pressured to maximize revenue.

SUMMARY

The knowledge and expertise of lawyers and legal assistants are the products law firms sell to their clients. Time is the vehicle by which lawyers deliver their products. Managing time is a skill that requires effort. Since time is a law firm's product, it must be documented before its value can be realized. If it is not documented, its value is lost, and a firm loses its product.

Lawyers and legal assistants are the primary timekeepers in a law office. Most law firms establish a minimum number of billable hours that must be produced by each timekeeper in a year. The number of annual billable hours required of a legal assistant varies with each firm.

The hours of a workday are placed in two categories: billable and nonbillable. Billable hours are directly applied to clients' matters; nonbillable hours are not applied to clients' matters. Creditable nonbillable hours are credited toward an annual billable hours requirement, and noncreditable nonbillable hours are not credited toward an annual billable hours requirement.

Each firm differs on the method used to calculate billable hours. The most common method used is tenths of an hour, in which a billable hour is divided into ten 6-minute increments. Most law firms have a policy of charging a minimum of 0.2 hour, or 12 minutes, on any project or aspect of a project.

Law offices that do not bill clients by the hour need time records to monitor the profitability of a case and monitor work in progress. When the time comes for a government office or corporate legal department to prepare its budget, time records become a valuable tool to justify additional staff or funding.

The ethical implications of accurate timekeeping cannot be overemphasized. Timekeepers should not bill clients for work not performed or time spent on personal matters, pad time sheets, double-bill, or apply an attorney's hourly rate to a paralegal's services.

Preparing a time sheet is the first thing a legal assistant does in the morning and the last thing a legal assistant does in the evening. Time should be documented as a project is finished. Timekeepers who wait until the end of a day to document time sheets usually estimate their time spent on a project. A person who thinks she or he can accurately estimate time is fooling himself and the firm.

CHAPTER ILLUSTRATION

Each attorney and paralegal at Black, White, & Greene, L.L.P., have an annual billable hours requirement. Their annual requirements are as follows:

Robert Black	1,200 (the remainder of the time is spent managing the firm)
Dennis White	1,750
Grant Greene	1,750
Patrizia Boen	2,000
George Templeton	2,000
Milton Nollkamper	1,500

The firm bills clients and prepares management reports on the basis of time sheet information. Each timekeeper prepares time sheets manually and gives them to the secretaries each Monday so that they can input the information into the computer system. They are comfortable with the system, and there are very few billing issues to resolve—except for Dennis.

Dennis has a problem getting used to documenting his time. He is disorganized by nature and forgets to write down important details about his work. He loses his time sheets, does not turn them in to Audra on time, and forgets to write down his work. There are many times that the firm had to delay billing because Dennis's time sheets were not turned in on time. Audra, Dennis's secretary, is very frustrated with this problem.

The firm tried different techniques to help Dennis with his timekeeping. One method that seemed to work was the diary method. Dennis kept a large appointment book on his desk and was instructed to write down his work in the book. It would be easier for him to lose a time sheet than a large book. Audra would then transfer the entries onto a time sheet and enter the information into the computer. However, Audra noticed that essential work was not being doc-

umented. She had to remind Dennis that the work was done and ask him to estimate the time spent on the work. Dennis would estimate the time but could not ensure the accuracy of his time sheet. Robert and Tricia were concerned that the firm was not being compensated for some of Dennis's work. Dennis's quota was not being met, but he was working hard. It was a constant struggle that was affecting the firm's profitability.

As we saw in Chapter 6, the firm lost a client because it did not have the ability to offer task-based billing to its clients. Robert instructed Tricia to research timekeeping software that would enable the firm to apply a fixed fee to each activity in a case. Tricia did so, and the firm installed the software on its computer system. The new timekeeping system had to be developed, and each employee had to be trained on its use. The new system requires each timekeeper to be more detailed in her or his description of work. They had to implement a more complex coding system that would require more effort from the firm's timekeepers.

The attorneys and paralegal grumbled a bit, but Dennis had a fit. "I don't like to keep track of time anyway. This system is even worse than the old system! I don't have time to put down every little detail. And look at these codes. There's hundreds of codes to remember! It's just too much," he complained.

"Dennis," said Robert. "Last month we lost Technology Enterprises as a new client because we could not offer task-based billing to them. That client could have brought hundreds of thousands of dollars to the firm. You're one-third owner of this firm. How much money do you think you would have received if we would have landed that client?"

"Hmm," said Dennis. "I didn't think of that. Hundreds of thousands of dollars?"

"Yes," said Robert. "Smith & Jones got Technology because they were able to offer them task-based billing. There is a trend of the major corporations to require task-based billing from their outside counsel. I want us to be in a position to be competitive with other firms for their business. Implementing this timekeeping system is the first step. We must do it. Otherwise, we won't be able to compete for the big clients."

"Okay," said Dennis. "I'll learn the system. Audra will have to help me. But if we can get a big corporate client with this system, it'll be worth the effort."

CHAPTER REVIEW

1. What is the annual billable hours requirement?

2. What activities are included in creditable nonbillable hours?

3. What is the difference between nonbillable creditable hours and nonbillable noncreditable hours?

4. Other than for billing clients, why does management use time records?

5. How does law firm management use time records to establish flat fees?

6. How does law firm management use time records to determine an employee's productivity?

7. Why do firms keep time records on contingency cases?

8. Why do corporate legal departments keep time records?

9. Why do government offices keep time records?

10. What six timekeeping activities are unethical?

EXAMPLES FOR DISCUSSION

1. The Lost File

Margaret Cleary is a legal assistant who works for a law firm that requires her to bill clients seven hours a day. One of Margaret's assignments was to prepare interrogatories on a real estate case. She entered the client's number, file name, file number, and date on her time sheet and went to the file room to retrieve the file. The file was not there. She spent 1.5 hours looking for the file, which was in the lawyer's briefcase. If Margaret does not bill for that time, those 1.5 hours are lost time and she must stay an extra 1.5 hours to make them up.

1. How should Margaret bill this time?

2. If you were Margaret and the supervising attorney told you to bill the client for the time, what would you do?

3. If you were the law firm administrator, how would you remedy this situation?

2. Overproductive Co-Worker

Bill Seewich and John Carruthers work closely on a large litigation case. They come in at the same time and leave together in the evening. They eat lunch together and seldom work weekends. Bill had occasion to review the firm's billing summary for the month and noticed that John reported working at least two to three hours a day more than Bill. Bill suspects that John is padding his time sheet.

1. What should Bill do?

2. What should the law firm administrator do?

3. The Opinion Letter

Gay Keel is a real estate legal assistant to Don Gonzales, the managing partner of a large law firm. Don told Gay to research a complex issue for Food Center Shopping Centers. Gay spent 5 hours researching the issue and gave Don a memo describing her findings. Don prepared an opinion letter for the client that was based on Gay's research. A week later, Gay discovered that Don had billed the client his hourly rate for the time Gay spent on the research.

1. If you were Gay, what would you do?

2. Suppose you informed Don of this problem and he did not resolve the problem, what would you do?

3. If you were the administrator for the firm, how would you handle the problem?

ASSIGNMENTS

1. Analyze Exhibit 7.8 and answer the following questions:
   a. Does a discrepancy exist between actual time spent and the total of billable time, creditable nonbillable time, and noncreditable nonbillable time? If so, why? Of how much?
   b. If this legal assistant must have 1,500 billable creditable hours a year, has she met her quota for the day?
   c. Has this legal assistant exceeded the average of spending 20 percent of her time on nonbillable items? If so, in what area?

2. You are the manager of a medium-size law firm. The managing partner has asked for a report on the state of the departments in the firm. You run the departmental management report shown in Exhibit 7.10. After analyzing this report, answer the following questions:
   a. What is the financial condition of each department?
   b. Which departments are profitable? Which are not?
   c. What are the net results for each department?
   d. What are your recommendations for improving the firm's financial picture?

3. On blank time sheets, keep a record of your time for one week. Use tenths of an hour for each function and develop codes that apply to your situation. At the end of the week, answer these questions:
   a. How much of your time did you spend productively?
   b. How much of your time did you spend nonproductively?
   c. How much time did you spend studying for class?
   d. How much time did you lose?

4. Contact the software companies listed in the Tech Tips sidebar on page 260. Review the features of each product and write a report about the products. List the features and make a recommendation of the product that you feel is the best value.

5. Interview legal assistants in your area who are required to keep time sheets. What are some common problems they encounter? What are their complaints about the timekeeping system in their firm? What do they enjoy about timekeeping? How long did it take them to learn timekeeping methods?

6. For your law firm, describe the timekeeping procedures. If you do not work in a law firm, describe the timekeeping system used in Black, White & Greene found on page 265. Assume that the firm uses a manual timekeeping system. Develop timekeeping policies and procedures. Develop a coding system and illustrate the system into your description. You may use the codes described in the text or develop your own. Describe what percentage of a timekeeper's time are billable and nonbillable time. Develop firm policies concerning nonbillable creditable and noncreditable time. Develop firm ethical considerations regarding timekeeping. Describe your firm's policy concerning time spent looking for a file, traveling from one place to another, and minimum charges.

SELF-TEST

How well did you grasp the material in the chapter? Test yourself by answering the following questions and check your answers against the answers found in Appendix A.

1. What is a law firm's product, and how is it produced?
2. What do inaccurate time records produce?
3. Why must a timekeeper's time be documented?
4. Who are the primary timekeepers in a law office?
5. What is an annual billable hour requirement?
6. What are billable hours?
7. What are nonbillable hours?
8. What are the two types of nonbillable hours?
9. What are creditable nonbillable hours?
10. What are noncreditable nonbillable hours?
11. What are some ways a firm encourages continuing education?
12. Why do most firms give attorneys a higher creditable nonbillable hours allowance?
13. What are some activities that would be included in an attorney's creditable nonbillable hour allowance?

14. What information will management obtain from nonbillable hours?

15. What is the most common method of calculating time?

16. What is the most common minimum charge?

17. How is the billable hour different from an actual hour?

18. Name the seven most common management reports derived from time records.

19. How do time records assist management in its marketing efforts?

20. How do time records assist management in setting flat fees?

21. How do time records assist management in monitoring work in progress?

22. How do time records allow management to monitor the profitability of a timekeeper?

23. How do time records allow management to calculate the profitability of contingency cases?

24. How do time records assist management in making financial forecasts?

25. What are the seven elements contained in all time sheets?

26. What additional information may time sheets contain?

27. Why do firms use codes for each function?

28. Why do contingency law firms keep time records?

29. Why do corporate legal departments require time records?

30. Why do government legal offices use time records?

31. What are the four basic features of most timekeeping software?

32. What are the six things a timekeeper may not do?

33. What is double-billing?

34. What is padding time sheets?

35. How should a legal assistant document personal telephone calls?

36. What is the first thing a legal assistant does in the morning?

37. What is the last thing a legal assistant does in the evening?

38. Why should you not wait until the end of the day to complete your time sheets?

39. Why should timekeepers not estimate their time?

40. Whose responsibility is it to reduce the cost of a project?

41. Why should a timekeeper record all nonbillable time?

42. Why should legal assistants maintain to-do lists?

43. When should a time sheet be completed?

KEY WORDS

Add-on	Billable hour	Icon
Application	Ceiling	Noncreditable nonbillable hours
Annual billable hours requirement	Creditable nonbillable hours	Pad
	Drop-down list	Quota

CHAPTER

8

Billing and Financial Management

OBJECTIVES

After completion of this chapter, a student should be able to do the following:

◆ Explain the importance of good communication with a client.
◆ Describe the importance of documenting all client communication.
◆ Draft an engagement letter.
◆ Explain the importance of billing frequently.
◆ Understand the difference between descriptive and brief bills.
◆ Prepare a descriptive bill.
◆ List the steps involved in collection procedures.
◆ Prepare collection letters.
◆ Describe a firm's ethical responsibility concerning billing.
◆ Discuss some problems of the billing process.
◆ Describe the factors that affect a firm's profitability.
◆ Calculate an employee's realization rate.
◆ Explain how firms structure their finance function.
◆ Explain the finance function differences between small, medium, and large firms and corporate legal departments.
◆ Identify the types of income and expenses in a law firm.
◆ Identify the various types of management reports and the purpose for each.
◆ Estimate projected law firm income and expenses.
◆ Calculate a firm's expense percentage and discuss the various ways it is used.

INTRODUCTION

Before the 1960s, lawyers had a reputation for casual billing practices. They billed their clients sporadically, some waiting as long as a year to bill for work done. Lawyers had few or no billing policies, and their incomes reflected this lack of policy.

Since the introduction of general business practices to law firms to encourage them to be more profitable, lawyers have realized the importance of appropriate and regular billing practices. As the practice of law becomes more competitive and expensive, firms can no longer afford to work for a client without receiving payment for their services on a regular basis.

Proper billing techniques result in bills being paid quickly, and improper billing techniques result in billing disputes that drain a firm's time and resources. Prompt payment of a firm's bills is important to the financial stability of the firm.

An administrator or manager is responsible for setting billing policies and preparing timely bills. A legal assistant's role in the billing process varies. A legal assistant in a small firm may be directly responsible for calculating and preparing bills. A legal assistant in a large firm may not be directly involved in the billing process. In every firm, however, a legal assistant participates in the billing process by submitting time records.

This chapter will discuss the elements involved in effective billing techniques. It will also explain the billing process and billing reports and give examples of various styles of bills. It will describe procedures for collecting overdue bills as well as how a firm handles fee disputes. Finally, it will discuss ethical billing practices and some problems firms encounter with their billing procedures.

THE ART OF BILLING

The goal of a good billing practice is to get a firm's bills paid as promptly as possible. To do this, a firm must make a client aware of the value received for each dollar spent. The more valuable a client perceives a service, the more quickly the client will pay a bill.

The manner in which bills are prepared contributes to the speed of payment. A client who cannot understand the charges or who is unaware of the work performed will not promptly pay a bill.

The billing process has four essential elements: communication, documentation, regular and frequent billing, and descriptive bills.

Communication

The most important aspect of the billing process is communication. Communication begins at an initial client interview and continues throughout an attorney-client relationship until the relationship is terminated. The client should have a clear understanding of the fees involved at the beginning of the case.

ETHICS ALERT

Initial Client Interview   A firm's fee structure is explained to a client at an initial client interview (see Exhibit 8.1). *A legal assistant may not explain a fee agreement to a client.* It is the lawyer's responsibility to communicate a fee agreement to a client.

A lawyer should also communicate expected hard and soft costs. Most clients do not realize that a flat fee does not include costs such as filing fees, photocopies, or other charges. A client's obligation for fees and costs should be clearly communicated and stated in a written fee agreement.

Although many attorneys discuss fees with clients, most do not inquire about a client's ability to pay. An attorney may discover that a prospective client mistakenly thinks that the opposing party will pay the fees or that the fees are payable out of the recovery. Knowledge of a client's ability to pay for legal services will enable an attorney to make an informed decision regarding acceptance of a matter. This can be a delicate area, and the manner in which it is handled affects an attorney-client relationship. If a case is a contingency or flat fee case, the client's ability to pay is less critical.

Ongoing Communication   A firm's communication responsibility does not end with the initial client interview. Communicating the cost of legal services to a client continues throughout an attorney-client relationship. An attorney is obligated to discuss steps of a client's case with the client. If a legal team informs a client of each aspect of a case, the client will not be surprised to see charges for those aspects on a bill. Many clients complain when they do not hear from their attorney for months and then receive a large bill. A client is surprised that a "simple matter" suddenly became complex. The client then blames the lawyer for making a simple matter complex to increase fees. Clients distrust their attorneys, causing an attorney-client relationship to deteriorate. This can be avoided by proper communication.

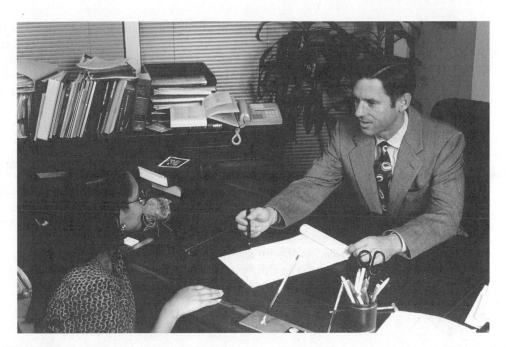

EXHIBIT 8.1 Explaining a Firm's Fee Structure and Billing Policies is an Essential Element of the Initial Client Interview

One way to keep clients informed is to send a client copies of all documents prepared or received on the client's behalf. An attorney often overlooks this function and relies on his staff to handle it. A legal assistant can take the initiative and send a client copies of all documentation. A transmittal letter stating that the documents are for the client's information will go a long way in strengthening the attorney-client relationship. The attorney, as well as the client, will appreciate the extra time it takes to do this.

ETHICS ALERT

Legal Assistant Communication At times, a client may contact a legal assistant with questions about a bill. These occasions give a legal assistant the opportunity to participate in client relations by showing a client compassion and understanding of the client's concerns. A legal assistant may discuss a situation with a client in an empathic manner *but may not give advice or suggest a solution to a problem.*

To help a client resolve a billing problem, all such calls should be directed to the attorney, a manager, or an administrator. If a client feels that charges are too high, only the responsible attorney or administrator has the authority to adjust the bill. If a client needs clarification on a bill, a legal assistant may answer the client's questions if the legal assistant knows the answers and the answers are within accepted parameters.

ETHICS ALERT

When communicating with clients, legal assistants must be aware of the parameters within which they can work. *A legal assistant may not discuss the duration of a case.* In other words, if a client asks a legal assistant how long a case will take, the legal assistant may not give an estimated amount of time. It is an attorney's responsibility to give the client this information. *A legal assistant may not estimate the cost of a matter.* All fee quotes are an attorney's responsibility. In addition, *a legal assistant may not give an opinion as to the possible outcome of a matter.* All client communication should be polite, compassionate, and professional. Every client should be treated as if he or she were a firm's only client.

ETHICS ALERT

Attorneys and legal assistants have a good concept of the legal process, but most clients do not. Often, a client has no idea of the steps necessary for a successful resolution to a problem. The client should clearly understand the intricacies of a case and a lawyer's strategy for the case. The client must also understand the process of the case to have a good concept of what the fee is purchasing. The lawyer should describe all strategy and give the client a range of hours and discuss what could shorten or lengthen the amount of time. This will increase the client's understanding of the matter. However, it is important to remember that *a legal assistant may not discuss strategy with a client.* A client's complete understanding of the fee structure will result in prompt payment of a firm's invoices.

Documentation

Engagement letter: A letter summarizing the scope of representation and the fee agreement between a lawyer and a client.

Engagement Letter

It is a good practice to send a new client an **engagement letter,** like the one shown in Exhibit 8.2, along with a copy of the fee agreement soon after the initial client interview. Often, during an initial interview, a client is upset or anxious about a case. Many clients sign fee agreements without taking the time to read or fully understand them. An engagement letter restates the terms of a representation as discussed in the interview. The client should sign a copy of the engagement letter and return it to the firm. American Bar Association (ABA) Model Rule 1.5(b) states:

> When the lawyer has not regularly represented the client, the basis or rate of the fee shall be communicated to the client, preferably in writing, before or within a reasonable time after commencing the representation.

Documenting Communication

All client communications should be documented. If a client discusses a bill with a member of the legal team, the conversation must be documented by a memo to the file as soon as possible after the conversation takes place.

Regular and Frequent Billing

Billing should be regular and frequent. Traditionally, lawyers have withheld billing until a substantial amount of time was spent on a case. With many law firms advancing costs, delaying the billing process was a very expensive practice. Lawyers were, in essence, lending interest-free money to their clients to finance a case. The cost of operating capital has forced lawyers to bill clients more frequently.

Monthly billing is the most common method of billing. Clients prefer to receive smaller monthly bills rather than larger infrequent bills. However, small firms and sole proprietors have difficulty meeting a monthly billing schedule, especially if a legal team is working hard to meet approaching deadlines. A sole proprietor preparing for trial is not thinking of billing. Nevertheless, small firms can least afford casual billing policies. A legal assistant is in a good position to urge that billing be done timely. A legal assistant may suggest hiring temporary help in times of crisis so that billing can be prepared on time.

Billing a client as soon as possible after a matter is completed is a crucial element of a good billing policy. It is a good practice to send a bill with the final documents. A delay in billing will lower a client's perception of the value of services rendered, as shown in the chart in Exhibit 8.3.

Descriptive Bills

Firms disagree on how descriptive bills should be prepared. Some feel that extremely descriptive bills are confusing to clients, and others feel that they are essential. Bills in flat fee cases need not be as descriptive as those in hourly cases. Bills should describe the service in a brief and concise manner. Studies have shown that individual clients want descriptive bills and that corporate that clients do not want very long itemized bills.

BLACK, WHITE, & GREENE
Attorneys at Law
2121 Broadway
Palo Alto, CA 90000

Date: June 1, 2004

Lila Peterson
234 56th St.
Palo Alto, CA 90000

Re: *Peterson v. Johnson*

Dear Ms. Peterson:

We are very pleased you have retained us in connection with the matter of *Peterson v. Johnson.* The purpose of this letter is to confirm the terms by which this office will represent you.

The scope of our representation will include negotiating settlement of the dispute with Rita Johnson. If the dispute cannot be negotiated to your satisfaction, we will commence to file suit in the Superior Court and proceed to take the case to trial.

You have agreed to pay us $275 an hour for Dennis White's time and $225 an hour for Grant Greene's time. You have agreed to pay us $100 an hour for legal assistant time and $75 an hour for law clerk time. You have also agreed to pay all costs incurred, which consist of filing fees if the suit is commenced ($120), service fees (approximately $50), and office costs. Office costs are $0.50 a copy for photocopies, the actual cost of long-distance telephone calls, and messenger costs, if needed. If the lawsuit proceeds to trial, there may be additional costs for discovery, such as motion fees, witness fees, and deposition costs. We will consult with you before incurring any discovery costs.

Ms. Peterson, it is very difficult to anticipate the total cost in a case such as yours. We expect, however, negotiation would take no more than ten hours. Litigating this matter will be quite costly, possibly requiring as much as one hundred hours to trial. We can give you the approximate cost of a trial as we approach the trial date.

You will be billed on the first of every month, for fees and costs incurred. You have agreed to pay our invoice within fifteen days of receipt. If the invoice is not paid within thirty days, you have agreed to pay the firm 15 percent per annum interest on all past-due amounts.

Be assured we will do our best to serve you effectively. We cannot guarantee the success of your venture, but we will represent your interests professionally and efficiently. If at any time you should have any questions or concerns, please contact me.

If you disagree with the above, please contact me as soon as possible. Thank you for retaining our firm. I am sure you will be pleased with our service. We look forward to serving you.

Sincerely,

Black, White & Greene

Dennis White, Attorney

Agreed and accepted this _____ day of _____, 2004.

_____

Lila Peterson

EXHIBIT 8.2   Engagement Letter

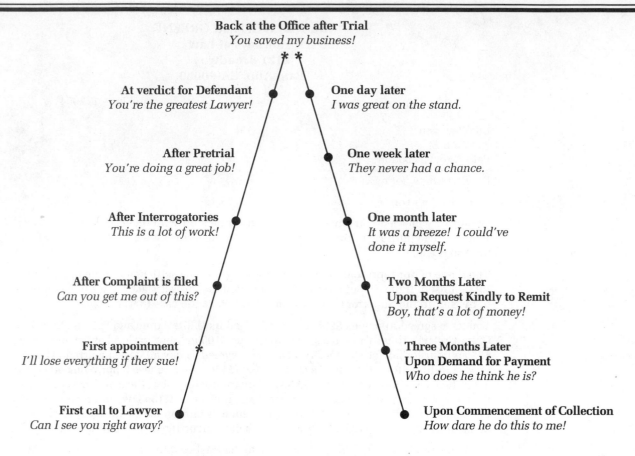

Back at the Office after Trial
You saved my business!
✻ ✻

At verdict for Defendant
You're the greatest Lawyer!

One day later
I was great on the stand.

After Pretrial
You're doing a great job!

One week later
They never had a chance.

After Interrogatories
This is a lot of work!

One month later
It was a breeze! I could've done it myself.

After Complaint is filed
Can you get me out of this?

Two Months Later
Upon Request Kindly to Remit
Boy, that's a lot of money!

First appointment
I'll lose everything if they sue!
✻

Three Months Later
Upon Demand for Payment
Who does he think he is?

First call to Lawyer
Can I see you right away?

Upon Commencement of Collection
How dare he do this to me!

✻ Proper Time to Discuss Fee Agreement

✻ ✻ Proper Time to Submit Final Bill

EXHIBIT 8.3 Client's Line of Gratitude

An average bill has twelve basic elements:

1. Name of the case
2. Billing period
3. Date of the work
4. Description of the work performed
5. Time increment of the work
6. Name of the person who performed the work
7. Hourly rate of the person performing the work
8. Cost of the work
9. Itemization of costs
10. Total costs
11. Total of fees and costs
12. Payment terms

THE BILLING PROCESS

Preliminary bill: A bill prepared for an attorney's review and consideration for adjustment.

Entries from time sheets are input into a computer for billing purposes. After the information is input, a **preliminary bill** is prepared. A lawyer reviews the preliminary bill and may add or subtract charges to it. Often, legal assistants are asked to assist an attorney in the review process.

BLACK, WHITE & GREENE
Attorneys at Law

FEE ADJUSTMENT MEMORANDUM

Date: _____   Responsible Lawyer: Robert Black

Client: ABC Corp. v. Huntington Driving Range

File No: 45-456   Matter: Litigation

Final Bill _____ Interim Bill _____ Date from _____ to _____

Atty. Initials	Hours × Rate	= Time-Dollar Value
RB	15 × $275	$4,125
Total time-dollar value:		$4,125

Adjustments		Add	Deduct
a.	Novelty or skill	_____	_____
b.	Amount involved	_____	_____
c.	Loss of other employment	_____	_____
d.	Ability to pay	_____	_____
e.	Statutory limit	_____	_____
f.	Internal fee schedule of firm	_____	_____
g.	_____	_____	_____
	TOTALS	_____	_____
Final fee		$_____	

EXHIBIT 8.4   Fee Adjustment Memorandum

The eight factors considered to determine the reasonableness of a fee are represented by the acronym TOCATPET (see page 222). A firm may be entitled to an increased fee if a case so warrants. If so, it is an attorney's responsibility to add these factors into the bill at the time of billing. In some cases, a decreased fee is appropriate. If the recovery for a client does not justify a large fee, an attorney may reduce it. An attorney may also reduce charges if he or she feels that they are too high.

To make adjustments to bills, many firms use a **fee adjustment memorandum.** The appropriate adjustments are made on the memorandum, and the memorandum is given to an administrator or billing manager, who will make the adjustments accordingly. An example of a fee adjustment memorandum is shown in Exhibit 8.4.

Fee adjustment memorandum: A form used by an attorney to increase or decrease a client's bill as appropriate.

Interest Charges

Charging interest on past-due accounts is generally accepted. However, some states require a client's consent to charge interest, and some states require that the agreement be in writing. Other states require notice to a client with an opportunity to pay without interest. Interest is generally discussed in an initial client interview and documented in an engagement letter.

As a rule, interest is rarely collected. It has been only slightly successful in encouraging clients to pay bills. Firms have also found compliance with state and federal regulations burdensome and not worth the effort.

Credit and Credit Cards

Lawyers often extend credit to their clients. Credit has traditionally been extended to people on the basis of their ability to pay. Banks go through sophisticated procedures to determine whether a person has the ability to pay for credit. Very few lawyers, however, determine their clients' ability to pay their bill before they extend credit. This has caused law firms to have severe collection problems.

To ease the financial burden on firms, lawyers have offered clients two credit alternatives: loans and the use of credit cards. A firm will enter into an agreement with a local bank or lending institution. On approval of credit, the lending institution will buy a client's contract from an attorney at a 5 to 10 percent discount. The client then becomes obligated to the lending institution instead of the firm for the attorney's services.

In 1974, the ABA sanctioned lawyers' use of credit cards as payment for legal fees. The ABA issued the following guidelines concerning the use of credit cards:

ETHICS ALERT

(2) No directory of any kind shall be printed or published with the names of individual attorney members who subscribe to the credit card plan.

(3) No promotional materials of any kind will be supplied by the credit card company to a participating attorney except possibly a small insignia to be tactfully displayed in the attorney's office indicating his participation in the use of the credit card.

(4) A lawyer shall not encourage participation in the plan, but his position must be that he accepts the plan as a convenience for clients who desire it, and the lawyer may not because of his participation increase his fee for legal services rendered to the client.

(5) Charges made by lawyers to clients pursuant to a credit card plan shall be only for services actually rendered or cash actually paid on behalf of a client.

(6) In participating in a credit card program the attorney shall scrupulously observe his obligation to preserve the confidences and secrets of his client.

BILLING SYSTEMS

Law firms have computerized billing systems. There are hundreds of billing software packages available to law firms today, most of which are combined with their time-keeping systems. Some software is appropriate for the small firm, while others are developed for the large firm. Some large firms have developed their own billing software.

When a final billing is ready to prepare for mailing, the computer automatically prepares the bills and includes the date of the service, a description of the service, the initials of the timekeeper, the amount of time expended, and the costs. The bill is detailed and also includes payments received on the account.

TECH TIPS
Time and Billing Software

The following is a sample of related software:

CLS/Summit: Computer Law Systems—www.clswin.com
Perfect Practice: ADC Legal Systems—www.adclegal.com
PCLAW: Alumni Computer Group, Inc.—www.pclaw.com
Attorney Tom: Total Office Management, Inc.—www.tominc.com
Legal Insight: Versys Corporation—www.versys.com
WinVantage Legal System: Advantage Computer Systems Corporation—www.advantage.com
ASA Legal Systems: ASA Legal Systems—www.asaint.com
Javelan®: Barrister Information Systems Corporation—www.barrister.com
CMS OPEN™: CMS/Data—www.cmsopen.com
CompuTrac: CompuTrac, Inc.—www.computrac.com
Juris: Juris, Inc.—www.juris.com
Orion: Orion Law Management Systems—www.orionlaw.com
ProLaw: ProLaw Software—www.prolaw.com
RTG Bills: RTG Data Systems—www.rtgsoftware.com
Timeslips Deluxe: Sage U.S., Inc.—www.timeslips.com

Software mentioned in this sidebar is for informational purposes only and is not for the purpose of endorsing products.

Fee allocation: When a percentage of the bill is given to the originating or supervising attorney as compensation.

Cost recovery system: A utility program that allows data to be transferred to a billing program by copier or telephone systems.

Most software packages will bill for other forms of legal fees in addition to hourly fees. These include contingency, flat fee, retainer, **fee allocation,** and split fee billing. Some software will accommodate task-based billing, while others will not. Some software products allow a **cost recovery system** to be integrated with the firm's copier and telephone system. By programming the copier before copies are made, copy charges are automatically picked up by the billing system and inserted on the bill. Telephone charges are billed in the same manner.

In addition to billing clients, the software will also track accounts payable and clients' trust account balances. Some programs will also do conflict checking and keep track of important due dates and appointments.

BILLING STYLES

Various billing styles are used by law firms. The style of a bill depends on the type of client, type of case, and policy of a firm. Some firms find long, detailed bills time-consuming and unnecessary. Other firms' clients demand detailed bills. Whenever a client questions a bill and contacts a firm for clarification, it delays payment of the bill. The rule of thumb is to be as descriptive as necessary to get a bill paid.

Billing an Hourly Fee Case

Two styles of hourly bills are used: detailed, shown in Exhibit 8.5, and brief, shown in Exhibit 8.6.

Billing a Flat Fee Case

If a firm represents a client on a flat fee basis, a detail of services performed is not necessary. However, some firms prefer to include a summary of services rendered to inform a client of the work done on a case. If the fee is paid before any work is done on the case, a bill is unnecessary, except for hard costs incurred. Normally, a flat fee includes all soft costs incurred. An example of a descriptive flat fee bill is shown in Exhibit 8.7; an example of a brief flat fee bill is shown in Exhibit 8.8.

Billing a Contingency Fee Case

If a firm represents a client in a complex contingency case with high costs, the firm may periodically bill the client for costs or require the client to deposit money in an attorney's client funds account for payment of costs. It is preferable, however, to bill a client periodically for costs to keep a cost bill reasonable. If a client has prepaid costs, a statement should indicate the amount left in a client funds account after the costs are deducted. Some firms indicate the amount of time spent on a contingency case even though a client is not billed for the time. This time entry is made so that a client will know that a firm is working on a case. An example of a bill for costs in a contingency case is shown in Exhibit 8.9.

Most often, however, a firm will wait until the end of a contingency matter to give a client an accounting of fees and costs. The money from a judgment or settlement is deposited into an attorney's client funds account, also known as the trust account, and the funds disbursed therefrom. Exhibit 8.10 is an example of a gross contingency fee accounting, and Exhibit 8.11 is an example of a net contingency fee accounting.

COLLECTION

Most lawyers find collecting bills the most distasteful part of their job. However, collection activities are a necessary part of the overall operation of a firm. Once time has been expended for a client, it cannot be repossessed and reused to benefit another

BLACK, WHITE & GREENE
Attorneys at Law

Date

Valued Client
234 56th St.
Anytown, CA 90000

Re: Client v. Johnson, et al.

For legal services rendered from January 1, 20XX, through January 31, 20XX

Date	Initials	Description	Time	Cost
1/5/xx	RJB	Conference with opposing atty re discovery	.3	$ 45.00
1/6/xx	RJB	Draft and review interrogatories	1.5	225.00
1/6/xx	MN	Draft interrogatories	2.0	150.00
1/6/xx	MN	Conference with client re interrogatories	.3	22.50
1/15/xx	MN	Review request for production of docs	.4	30.00
1/16/xx	RJB	Review request for production	.3	45.00
1/18/xx	PB	Prepare for deposition	2.0	250.00
1/24/xx	PB	Attend deposition	4.0	500.00
1/25/xx	PB	Conference w/DAC re deposition	.5	62.50
1/25/xx	MN	Conference w/JKL re deposition	.5	37.50

Total Fees $1,367.50

Costs

Photocopies, 68 × .25	$17.00
Depositions	345.00
Word processing, 9 pgs × 2.00	18.00
Long-distance telephone	6.50

Total costs $386.50

Total <u>**$1,754.00**</u>

Billing code:

RJB	Robert J. Black, senior partner	$150.00 hr.
MN	Milton Nollkamper, legal assistant	75.00 hr.
PB	Patrizia Boen, associate attorney	125.00 hr.

Payment due within 15 days of receipt.

EXHIBIT 8.5 Example of Detailed Hourly Statement

client. The collection process usually begins with sending reminder letters and may advance through renegotiating a contract or withdrawing to filing a lawsuit against a client or turning a matter over to a collection agency.

Sending Reminder Letters

Each firm has its own collection policy. Generally, accounts receivable are reviewed monthly, and collection activities begin when more than thirty days have passed since the last billing. At this time, a firm sends a client a mild reminder letter, such as the one shown in Exhibit 8.12.

If an account is sixty days past due, a more aggressive letter, such as the one shown in Exhibit 8.13, is sent, followed by a telephone call.

BLACK, WHITE & GREENE
Attorneys at Law

Date

Valued Client
234 56th St.
Anytown, CA 90000

Re: Client v. Johnson, et al.

For legal services rendered from January 1, 20xx, through January 31, 20xx

Professional services	$1,367.50
Costs	386.50
Total Due	**$1,754.00**

Payment due within 15 days of receipt.

EXHIBIT 8.6   Example of Brief Hourly Statement

BLACK, WHITE & GREENE
Attorneys at Law

Date

Valued Client
234 56th St.
Anytown, CA 9000

Re: Marriage of client

Initial client interview; conference with opposing attorney; prepare petition, summons and order to show cause papers; prepare marital settlement agreement, negotiation with opposing attorney, court hearings

Professional services		$3,000.00
Amount paid		1,000.00
Balance		**$2,000.00**
Costs		
Photocopies	$4.50	
Long-distance telephone	7.85	
Filing fee	120.00	
Total Costs		132.35
Total due		**$2,132.35**

$1,000 and costs due within 15 days.
Balance due at the time of trial.

EXHIBIT 8.7   Example of Descriptive Flat Fee Statement

BLACK, WHITE & GREENE
Attorneys at Law

Date

Valued Client
234 56th St.
Anytown, CA 90000
Re: Marriage of client

Professional services		$3,000.00
Amount paid		1,000.00
Balance		**$2,000.00**

Costs

Photocopies	$4.50	
Long-distance telephone	7.85	
Filing fee	120.00	
Total costs		132.35
Total due		**$2,132.35**

$1,000 and costs due within 15 days.
Balance due at the time of trial.

EXHIBIT 8.8   Example of Brief Flat Fee Statement

BLACK, WHITE & GREENE
Attorneys at Law

Date

Valued Client
234 56th St.
Anytown, CA 90000

Re: Client v. General Motors

For costs incurred

Photocopies	$4.50	
Long-distance telephone	7.85	
Filing fee	120.00	
Total costs		132.35
Amount in client funds account		**$500.00**
Total due		**$132.35**
Balance of client funds account		**$367.65**

EXHIBIT 8.9   Contingency Statement for Costs

BLACK, WHITE, & GREENE
Attorneys at Law

Valued Client
234 56th St.
Anytown, CA 90000

Date: _____

Re: Client v. State Farm Insurance Co.

Gross recovery:		$15,000.00	
Less 33⅓% attorney's fee		5,000.00	
Balance			$10,000.00
Less Costs			
1/4/xx	Filing fee	$120.00	
1/15/xx	Greg's Attorney Service, service fees	75.00	
1/26/xx	Mileage for interviewing witness	32.60	
2/5/xx	Private Eye Investigations	235.00	
2/8/xx	Wrecker Garage, storage of auto	532.00	
2/15/xx	The Photo Shop, photos	64.50	
3/15/xx	H.E. Sawitall, witness fees	22.50	
4/23/xx	Depo Service, depositions	321.00	
5/18/xx	Dr. Goode, medical report	175.00	
6/2/xx	Dr. Wright, medical report	125.00	
7/23/xx	Dr. Goode, medical lien	350.00	
9/15/xx	Speedy Messenger Service	45.00	
9/20/xx	Various long-distance telephone	27.50	
9/20/xx	Photocopies	68.30	
Total costs and disbursements			$2,193.40
TOTAL RECOVERY TO CLIENT			**$7,806.60**

EXHIBIT 8.10 Contingency Fee Accounting by Gross Fee Method

If payment is not received within two weeks of a sixty-day letter, a firm's collection department will telephone the client. If the client is unable to pay the entire bill, the firm will make payment arrangements at this time. It is important that a firm's collection staff be aware of state and federal laws concerning proper telephone collection procedures, especially the federal Fair Debt Collection Practices Act. Some states have enacted laws that prohibit frequent or harassing telephone calls. An attorney may be disciplined and fined for inappropriate collection techniques of staff members.

Renegotiating and Withdrawing

If a client still does not pay and an account is ninety days or more past due, a firm must decide on the correct collection procedure. At this point, the responsible lawyer becomes involved in the collection process. The lawyer will contact the client and discuss payment of the bill with the client. If a problem exists with the bill, the lawyer will try to work out the charges.

Each account is considered separately. If a client has been a very good client who has fallen on hard times, a firm may decide to give him or her more time, discount a bill, or even write it off completely. If a client has a case that is pending with the firm that is close to completion, the firm may decide to wait until the end of the case. In some cases, a firm will stop work for a client until a bill is paid or withdraw from a case completely.

BLACK, WHITE, & GREENE
Attorneys at Law

Date

Valued Client
234 56th St.
Anytown, CA 90000

Re: Client v. State Farm Insurance Co.

Gross recovery:			$15,000.00
Less costs			
1/4/xx	Filing fee	$120.00	
1/15/xx	Greg's Attorney Service, service fees	75.00	
1/26/xx	Mileage for interviewing witness	32.60	
2/5/xx	Private Eye Investigations	235.00	
2/8/xx	Wrecker Garage, storage of auto	532.00	
2/15/xx	The Photo Shop, photos	64.50	
3/15/xx	H.E. Sawitall, witness fees	22.50	
4/23/xx	Depo Service, depositions	321.00	
5/18/xx	Dr. Goode, medical report	175.00	
6/2/xx	Dr. Wright, medical report	125.00	
7/23/xx	Dr. Goode, medical lien	350.00	
9/15/xx	Speedy Messenger Service	45.00	
9/20/xx	Various long-distance telephone	27.50	
9/20/xx	Photocopies	68.30	
Total costs and disbursements			$ 2,193.40
Balance			12,806.60
Less 33⅓% attorney's fee			4,268.87
Total recovery to client			**$8,537.73**

EXHIBIT 8.11   Contingency Fee Accounting by Net Fee Method

BLACK, WHITE, & GREENE
Attorneys at Law

Date

Valued Client
1234 56th St.
Anytown, CA 90000

Re: Client v. Johnson

Dear Mr. Client:

Our records indicate that the attached invoice remains unpaid. If your payment has been mailed, please disregard this letter.

If you should have a problem with any aspect of the enclosed invoice, please contact me so we may discuss it. Otherwise, I look forward to receiving your check for $3,187.00 by return mail.

Thank you for your prompt attention to this matter.

Sincerely,

Tricia Bunnell
Administrator

EXHIBIT 8.12   Example of Thirty-Day Reminder Letter

BLACK, WHITE, & GREENE
Attorneys at Law

Date

Valued Client
1234 56th St.
Anytown, CA 90000

Re: Client v. Johnson

Dear Mr. Client:

Your account with our firm is seriously past due.

Please remit $3,187.00 by return mail, or we will be forced to take further action on this account.

Your immediate attention to this matter is imperative.

Sincerely,

Tricia Bunnell
Administrator

EXHIBIT 8.13   Example of Sixty-Day Collection Letter

ETHICS ALERT

Before a firm stops work or withdraws from a case, it must give careful consideration to an attorney's ethical responsibilities to a client. A lawyer may do nothing that would jeopardize a client's case. *If stopping all work on a case would jeopardize the case, a lawyer may not do so even though he or she may not be paid for her work.* The Michigan Supreme Court stated:

> Once a lawyer accepts a retainer to represent a client, he is obliged to exert his best efforts wholeheartedly to advance the client's legitimate interests with fidelity and diligence until he is relieved of that obligation either by his client or the court. The failure of the client to pay for his services does not relieve a lawyer of his duty to perform them completely and on time, save only when relieved as above.

If a client fails to pay a fee, a lawyer may withdraw from a case if the withdrawal will not prejudice the client. Some states require a court's permission to withdraw from a case for nonpayment of fees. Even with a court's permission, an attorney must take steps to protect a client's interest. An attorney must give a client reasonable notice and time to employ a new attorney.

In some states, withdrawal is not justified if a client is unable to pay a fee, as long as the lawyer is able to continue. The ABA permits a lawyer to withdraw from a case in six circumstances, one of which is nonpayment of fees. ABA Model Rule 1.16(b) states those six circumstances as follows:

> . . . [A] lawyer may withdraw from representing a client if withdrawal can be accomplished without material adverse effect on the interests of the client, or if:
> 1. the client persists in a course of action involving the lawyer's services that the lawyer reasonably believes is criminal or fraudulent;
> 2. the client has used the lawyer's services to perpetrate a crime or fraud.
> 3. the client insists upon pursing an objective that the lawyer considers repugnant or imprudent;
> 4. the client fails substantially to fulfill an obligation to the lawyer regarding the lawyer's services and has been given reasonable warning that the lawyer will withdraw unless the obligation is fulfilled.
> 5. the representation will result in an unreasonable financial burden on the lawyer or has been rendered unreasonably difficult by the client; or
> 6. other good cause for withdrawal exists.

Many states have passed ethical guidelines that prohibit a lawyer from withholding a client's property pending payment of fees. In addition, some states require attorneys to complete a case, even if fees have not been paid. For example, a lawyer may not wait until his or her fees are paid to file a final judgment in a divorce action. As discussed in Chapter 6, a lawyer may be entitled to a retaining lien on a final judgment but may not refuse to file the judgment.

Nine issues should be considered before withdrawing from a case:

1. A client's financial condition at the beginning of the representation and whether the lawyer had knowledge of the client's ability to pay
2. A client's sophistication as a consumer of legal services
3. Whether the fees and expenses were explained fully to the client
4. Whether the lawyer offered several different fee arrangements and the client selected a payment option with knowledge of the consequences of the selection
5. Whether the client has received periodic notice about costs as they were incurred and whether the actual charges remained in the range predicted
6. How long the fee has been outstanding
7. Efforts the client has made to submit partial payment
8. Efforts of the lawyer to negotiate a more lenient fee payment schedule
9. Whether there is a dispute about the fee

Suing

ETHICS ALERT

If an account is past ninety days, a firm may decide to sue a client. If a firm sues a client, the firm has the burden of proving the extent of the services rendered and the reasonableness of the fee. If an attorney has no time records, he or she will have a difficult time proving the validity of a bill. *Furthermore, if a judge finds a suit to recover fees unjustified, a lawyer may be subject to disciplinary action.* Lawsuits against clients are disfavored by the courts. Model Code EC 2-23 states that a lawyer should avoid suing clients:

> A lawyer should be zealous in his efforts to avoid controversy over fees with clients and should attempt to resolve amicably any differences on the subject. He should not sue a client for a fee unless necessary to prevent fraud or gross imposition by the client.

Suing a client should be the last resort. A high percentage of lawsuits for fees result in cross-claims for attorney malpractice. Some legal malpractice insurance companies prohibit their insureds from suing clients in court and demand that fee disputes be resolved in arbitration through a local or state bar association. An attorney will lose not only the goodwill of a client but also that of the client's friends and business associates.

Using a Collection Agency

The older an account, the more difficult it is to collect. A firm may decide to turn an account over to a collection agency. Most collection agencies operate on a contingency basis and are paid 50 percent or more of the amounts collected.

Most states allow lawyers to turn accounts over to a collection agency if all efforts by an attorney to collect a fee have failed. Other states prohibit the use of collection agencies because of their effect on an attorney-client relationship and on the profession's dignity.

Some states require an attorney to give notice to a client before turning an account over to a collection agency. It is standard practice for a firm to give a client at least two weeks' notice of collection agency involvement. This will give a client a chance to pay a bill before damaging the client's credit rating.

BILLING ETHICS

Lawyers are obligated under the code of professional responsibility of their states to deal honestly and fairly with clients. This admonition carries over to billing policies. Billing methods and disputes have contributed to the public's negative perception of lawyers. If clients cannot trust their lawyers to bill fairly and as agreed, they will not trust their lawyers' legal advice.

Four areas of unethical billing practices are the most common:

ETHICS ALERT

- ◆ *Applying a client's funds to a disputed fee.* An attorney may not apply funds held in a client funds account to a disputed fee.
- ◆ *Charging more than a client agreed to pay.* It is unethical to charge a client more than the client agreed to pay.
- ◆ *Charging for services not rendered to a client.* It is unethical to charge a client for services not rendered to the client.
- ◆ *Increasing a flat fee.* A firm that charges a flat fee at the outset cannot increase the fee if complications should arise, unless this possibility was discussed with the client and put into a fee agreement.

Fiduciary: Of, relating to, or involving great confidence and trust; a person who transacts business for another person, necessitating great confidence and trust by the second party and a high degree of good faith by the first.

Legal fee agreements are held to a higher standard than other contracts because of the **fiduciary** relationship between an attorney and a client. This relationship exists whenever a person transacts business for another person and requires a great deal of confidence and trust from the second party and a high degree of good faith from the first. In a fee dispute, any ambiguity in a fee agreement will be construed against a lawyer. A lawyer who deviates from reasonable and acceptable billing practices is running the risk of disciplinary action.

Legal Auditors

The lack of ethical billing practices has resulted in a new type of service that began in the late 1980s: that of a legal auditor. Large corporations have hired independent auditing firms to review their outside law firm bills to find overbilling. Areas of concern include billing for more lawyers than are necessary for a project, vague service descriptions, billing a lawyer's time for work a paralegal could have performed, and unreasonable office expenses, or soft costs. The sad truth is that auditors often find enough overbilling to return a profit to their clients after their fee is paid. Some legal auditors charge a percentage of the overbilling they find. According to a survey of the 1,000 largest corporations published in *Corporate Counselor,* auditing legal bills was the third most popular method of controlling legal costs. If overbilling was not prevalent, legal auditors would be unnecessary.

Clients of legal auditors, usually large corporations and insurance companies, indicate that it is the law firm's billing practices that irritate them most. Clients who pay $300 an hour for the lawyer's time are insulted to see charges for postage, faxes, and photocopies on their bill. In most cases, soft costs make up less than 10 percent of a legal bill but get more than half the client's attention and complaints.

CYBERSITES

Finding Legal Auditors on the Web

Examen—www.examen.com

Jurist Doctor—www.juristdoctor.com

Lex Tech—www.lextechonline.com

Power Legal Financial Management—www.dhdial.com

Sterling Third Party Administrator—www.sterlingtpa.com

Accountability Services—www.legalbills.com

Becerra (international)—www.becerra-es.com

Professional Profile	**Examen Legal Cost Management Service,** located in Sacramento, California, provides its clients with bill review services. Most of its clients are large corporate legal departments and insurance companies that submit their invoices from outside counsel for review.

When the invoices are received, Examen categorizes the entries by task. The categorization is similar to the Uniform Task Code and task-based billing (see Chapter 6). Examen then applies the client's billing policies and guidelines to the information and looks for compliance with them. The information is reviewed by an invoice analyst who notes any noncompliance with the client's billing policies. The information is also reviewed by a senior analyst and then by the company's quality control department, which makes sure that all the data are correct. A report is then sent to the client. A copy of the report may also be sent to the law firm at the client's request. If an entry is not in compliance with the company's guidelines, Examen may recommend that the entry not be paid or request follow-up information, depending on the client's billing guidelines.

For example, if a client's guidelines request that only one attorney attend a deposition without prior consultation, the invoice cannot contain an entry for two attorneys to attend the same deposition. If it does, the item is flagged and brought to the client's attention. If authorization was provided, the client will forward the authorization to Examen, who will note that on its report.

The company's primary function is to review law firm invoices for compliance with client guidelines and to provide its clients with a management report of legal services so that it can monitor their legal costs.

Examen employs attorneys, paralegals, and others. Paralegals are employed as invoice analysts.

Common Billing Problems

Two of the major problems clients complain about are ambiguous bills and high legal costs. Sally King, manager of legal administration for General Electric Company, lists ten problems as major contributors to ambiguous bills her company receives from law firms (reprinted with permission from the *National Law Journal*):

◆ *Vague service descriptions.* A description of the service performed must contain enough detail to allow the client to understand what was accomplished. Describing a service in a brief and concise manner can be difficult. A description that is too long and wordy can be ambiguous, and a description that is too short can be vague. An entry that describes a telephone conversation as "telephone conference with Attorney Smith" is inadequate. The entry should be "telephone conference with Attorney Smith re deposition."

◆ *Surprise total.* Sometimes, a client is expecting an invoice for $10,000 and a $50,000 invoice arrives instead. Law firms should try to anticipate expectations and keep clients informed to avoid unpleasant surprises.

◆ *Perceived poor work.* Some in-house lawyers are forced to spend a considerable amount of time rewriting and improving a brief written by outside counsel, only to receive a bill for the full amount of time spent by counsel on an inadequate work product.

Team churning: Making frequent changes in the legal team.

◆ *Team churning.* In some firms, especially large ones, a legal team is constantly changing. This is called **team churning.** This means that additional time must be spent scaling the learning curve at the client's expense. The client is paying for the same service two or three times. It destroys any efficiency associated with the effects of experience.

◆ *Interoffice conferences.* Clients frown on interoffice conferences between members of the legal team because they perceive the charge as paying for the legal team to chitchat. Law firms need to look closely at the proportion of conference time to the time spent on other activities as reflected in a bill.

◆ *Nickel-and-dime billing.* Some firms include line-item charges for postage, fax, and so on, amounting to less than $10 in a bill for tens of thousands of dollars. A variation on this theme may be a bill for $50,000, which is readily acceptable—followed a few days later with a "supplemental invoice" for a minimal amount.

◆ *Errors in arithmetic.* Such errors reveal that no real billing review has been performed.

◆ *Other glaring errors.* Some bills indicate time billed to the wrong client or matter. Others may show that an attorney has worked twenty-six hours in one day. As in the previous point, mistakes such as these raise questions about an entire bill.

◆ *Bill received months after work is completed.* When a bill is not timely, everyone who ever worked on, or was involved in, the matter has forgotten the complexity of the issues as well as the results obtained.

◆ *Bill directed to wrong person.* The in-house lawyer who works on a matter may not be responsible for getting bills paid. A bill should go to the person charged with this responsibility. That person, often the administrator, will obtain all appropriate reviews and approvals.

◆ *Padding.* Charging a client for services not performed is fraudulent and illegal. It is important to be precise in entering the amount of time spent on a matter. If a new member of the legal team works on a matter, a task may take longer than if an experienced member did the work. Clients are increasingly intolerant of inexperience and less willing to pay for a person's training. The time of an inexperienced person should be billed at a lower rate.

◆ *Clerical work.* Clients object to paying a paralegal for clerical work. Tasks such as typing, filing, photocopying, and indexing are generally considered clerical and part of the firm's overhead. From a management standpoint, a paralegal should not be performing clerical tasks because it is not a good use of the paralegal's time and training.

◆ *Review and revision.* These terms are vague and ambiguous unless they are used with a more descriptive entry informing the client what was reviewed and why.

◆ *Block billing.* **Block billing** is listing tasks in a one block summary to avoid listing all the work done. An example of block billing would be an entry for seven hours for "preparing for trial." Each activity of the trial preparation should be listed and the appropriate amount of time applied to each, as shown in Exhibit 8.14. Many courts do not permit block billing because it hinders them from applying lodestar to the task. A bankruptcy court completely disallowed blocked entries to determine lodestar in the case of *In re The Leonard Jed Company*, 103 B.R. 706 (Bankr. D. Md [1989]).

Block billing: Charging a client for services rendered in one large block of time rather than itemizing the tasks performed in that period of time.

Block Billing—Improper

| 1/05/xx | Prepare summary judgment motion | 7.5 hrs. |

Proper

DATE	DESCRIPTION	TIME
1/05/xx	Review correspondence, discovery, pleadings, and evidence re summary judgment motion	2.0
1/05/xx	Legal research re liability issue	1.0
1/05/xx	Draft summary judgment motion and supporting brief re liability of independent contractors	2.5
1/05/xx	Telephone conference with attorney Smith re extension of time to file summary judgment motion	.2
1/05/xx	Telephone conference with Judge Jones re extension of time to file summary judgment motion	.2
1/05/xx	Complete summary judgment motion and supporting brief and memoranda	1.6

EXHIBIT 8.14 Example of Block Billing

OF INTEREST . . .

Twelve Red Flags in Legal Bill Review

Task descriptions. Are the task descriptions detailed and informative? Every task description should identify the activity with sufficient detail to assess its necessity and relevance to the project.

Inadequate time entries. Itemized time entries are preferable to clock entries or no time entry at all. Itemized time entries enables the review to better ascertain the appropriateness of the time spent in relation to the significance and complexity of the task. All entries should include the date the work was performed.

Correspondent charge. Although most invoices will contain a total sum of the amount owed, there should be a charge after each particular task. This allows the firm to determine whether an overtime rate or inflated price was billed and to certify that the billing rates charged are those established at the inception of the case.

Timekeeper's identity. Identification of timekeepers should not be limited to three-letter initials unless they are identified elsewhere in the invoice. The entire name of the individual and title should appear on the bill along with the billing rate.

Appropriately staffed. Are there any unauthorized individuals billing time to the file? Are there too many professionals involved in the project? Overstaffing often lends to inefficiency and higher costs because of duplication of effort and time educating others.

Too much time? The time spent on an activity should be commensurate with the complexity and significance of the task.

Appropriate skill level. Are overqualified professionals performing tasks below their skill levels at standard billing rates? Examples include an associate charging for file organization or a senior partner billing for basic research.

Task justified? Excessive "file review" or other perfunctory phrases without stated reason should be further investigated to determine the purpose and necessity of task.

Interoffice conferences. Interoffice conferences are disliked by clients and should not be inserted on a bill.

Duplication of effort. Did two partners participate in a hearing when only one was needed? Did the paralegal attend all depositions unnecessarily? Did four associates contribute to one brief? Although such items may raise a red flag, at times they are justified. Be sure to communicate these events to the client.

Clerical charges. Charges for clerical tasks should not be on a bill.

Office expenses. Are office expenses authorized and appropriate? Be sure that office expenses are scrutinized and deleted when inappropriate.

*Reprinted with permission of **Legal Assistant Today** magazine.*

Client-Directed Billing Policies

Many large corporate legal departments, and insurance companies have developed their own billing policies for their outside law firms to follow. These policies direct the law firms how to prepare their bills and inform them of unacceptable billing entries. Their policies indicate what soft costs are reimbursable. They also indicate the procedures to be followed before incurring hard costs and the parameters of acceptable charges.

Some law firms object to client-directed billing policies. They say that the policies illegally restrict their practice of law and are therefore contrary to the code of professional responsibility because they create a conflict of interest between the independence of outside counsel and their clients. Some Montana defense attorneys refused to abide by their clients' billing rules because of a potential conflict of interest and fear of malpractice suits from dissatisfied clients, most of which were insurance companies. Some have been fired because of their refusal to adhere to their clients' billing policies.

These Montana attorneys filed suit in the Montana Supreme Court requesting it to rule on the legality of client-directed billing policies. Twelve national insurance companies were named in the suit. It is the first lawsuit to be brought to rule on the legality of client-directed billing. As of this writing, the case has not been heard. Proponents of the lawsuit point out that several state bar associations, including those of Tennessee and Kentucky, ruled that client-directed billing policies violate ethical codes. However, the majority of state bar associations see no ethical violations.

FEE DISPUTES AND ARBITRATION

Most of the complaints received by bar associations are complaints of legal fees. The Michigan Attorney Grievance Commission estimates that 80 percent of complaints filed are fee disputes.

According to the Fair Credit Billing Act, once a firm has been advised of a dispute regarding a bill, the firm may not take steps to collect the amount. The firm may, however, send periodic statements informing the client of the amount of the bill. The firm may not send collection letters, telephone the client, or sue the client until the dispute has been resolved.

To keep fee disputes out of the court system, most state bar associations have developed arbitration programs to resolve them. In many states, state and local bar associations offer an arbitration service to resolve attorney-client disputes.

Arbitration: The resolution of a dispute without court involvement.

Most state **arbitration** programs are voluntary; in some states, however, arbitration is mandatory. Arbitration procedures must be exhausted before a court action is filed. All arbitration programs allow clients to begin an action, and some allow attorneys to begin an action. An arbitrator or arbitration panel hears a dispute and makes a ruling. In some states, the arbitration panel comprises lawyers, and in other states, the panel consists of nonlawyers. Although clients have been reluctant to arbitrate fee disputes before a panel of lawyers, statistics have shown that many clients receive favorable results.

The ABA encourages lawyers to take advantage of bar-sponsored arbitration programs. The comment to Model Rule 1.5 states:

> If a procedure has been established for resolution of fee disputes, such as an arbitration or mediation procedure established by the bar, the lawyer should conscientiously consider submitting to it.

Each state differs in its arbitration procedures, although all arbitration procedures are similar. New Jersey's process starts with a client filing a request form with the secretary of the bar association's fee arbitration committee. The client must consent to be bound by the arbitration. To be sure the client understands the finality of the decision, the bar provides the client with an information booklet.

When a complaint is filed, the bar sends a questionnaire to the attorney, whose participation is mandatory. Besides asking the attorney to respond to the client's allegations, the bar asks for copies of the disputed bill as well as the fee agreement and time records.

Cases involving fees of $3,000 or more are heard by a panel with three members, usually two lawyers and one nonlawyer, who volunteer their time to the process. Smaller disputes are heard by a single arbitrator. Hearings are scheduled with at least ten days' written notice. There is no **discovery,** or acquisition of new information about acts or facts. All parties have the power of subpoena. No transcript of the proceeding is maintained because appeals are not allowed.

Discovery: The acquisition of notice or knowledge of given acts or facts; that which was previously unknown.

All proceedings are conducted in private. Rules of evidence are not observed. The burden of proof is on the attorney to show that the bill is reasonable. The eight factors determining the reasonableness of a fee (TOCATPET) are considered. A determination is mailed within thirty days.

The disciplinary board of the bar hears enforcement motions. If it finds that an attorney refused to comply with an arbitrator's ruling, it may ask the supreme court to suspend the attorney. Three such suspensions have occurred in New Jersey.

FINANCIAL MANAGEMENT

The goal of every law firm is to be profitable. Whether a firm is profitable depends on management's methods of managing firm resources. Accounting systems play an important role in managing the firm to maximize profitability.

Every law firm employee contributes to law firm accounting functions. Timekeeping duties, keeping track of costs, and doing a probate accounting are examples of accounting functions. A general knowledge of law firm accounting is essential to a well-rounded knowledge of law firms in general.

Law Firm Profitability and Realization

To be profitable, law firm management must consider certain factors that contribute to profitability. These factors are called profitability factors. Law firm profits are the result of two types of profitability factors: direct and indirect.

Direct profitability factors: Factors that affects a firm's profitability in a short period of time, usually one year.

Direct Profitability Factors   **Direct profitability factors** directly affect a firm's profitability in a short period, usually one year. Direct profitability factors consist of five elements: rates, utilization, leverage, expenses, and speed, the acronym for which is RULES.

Rates. Rates include the effective rates that are ultimately billed and collected, such as hourly fees and other types of fees. They are adjusted periodically to accommodate changes in the marketplace and increase profitability, and they allow the firm to remain competitive.

A firm must give careful consideration when setting hourly rates. If the rate is too high, the firm may lose potential clients. If it is too low, the firm will lose income. Hourly rates should be competitive with the firm's geographic area but high enough for the firm to make a profit.

Firms often do not charge enough for a legal assistant's time, especially senior legal assistants. Surveys indicate that clients are willing to pay for the expertise of an experienced legal assistant and would rather pay for the services of an experienced legal assistant than those of an inexperienced attorney. Legal assistants' hourly rates should reflect their expertise.

Utilization. Utilization includes the use of the chargeable hours of a firm's timekeepers and the ability to delegate responsibility to the lowest timekeeper. Law firms set the number of annual billable hours required of each timekeeper per year. It is important that each timekeeper meet the annual requirement because a firm estimates its income on annual billable hours expected from each timekeeper. If every timekeeper in a large firm produced two hours a week below the annual requirement, the firm would lose more than a million dollars of potential income.

Timekeepers in some firms also include law clerks, secretaries, and clerical staff. To be profitable, a task should be delegated to the least expensive employee capable of performing the task. A timekeeper's services are being effectively utilized if each is given adequate responsibility and challenge.

Leverage. Leverage is the number of profit contributors (associates and paralegals) for each owner. The more associates and paralegals for each owner, the higher the owner's income.

The leverage ratio of the number of profit contributors to owner differs in each firm. Some firms may have a one-to-four ratio (one profit contributor per four attorneys) or a four-to-one ratio (four profit contributors per attorney).

Expenses. Expenses directly affect a firm's profitability. To be profitable, management must control law firm expenses. Expenses eat up profits and can rapidly increase if management does not monitor them closely.

Expenses include staff salaries and benefits, supplies, and other costs of doing business. Expenses are the most flexible of the profitability factors. If expenses are too high, they are reduced. If expected income is not received, expenses are cut.

Compensation expenses: Employee expenses, including wages and benefits.

Operating expenses: Expenses other than compensation expenses that include occupancy costs, office operating costs, costs of professional activities, and general business expenses.

There are two types of expenses: compensation expenses and operating expenses. **Compensation expenses** include employees' compensation and are categorized into three categories: associates' and legal assistants' compensation; administrative staff salaries; and employee benefits. **Operating expenses** include all other expenses.

There are four categories of operating expenses: occupancy costs, office operating costs, costs of professional activities, and general business expenses. Occupancy costs include office rental, storage facilities, and utilities. Office operating costs include the day-to-day expenses involved in running the office, such as office equipment, computers, janitorial services, stationery, copying costs, and miscellaneous supplies. Professional activity costs include professional dues, continuing education, and client entertainment. General business expenses include telephone costs, library costs, insurance, taxes, and interest expenses.

The cost of doing business continues to increase. Expenses increase faster than attorneys can increase their fees. To maintain profitability, management is continually seeking ways to manage expenses.

Speed. The time it takes to perform a task, bill for the service and collect from the client contributes to a firm's profitability. If a bill is unpaid for 90 to 120 days, a firm's profitability for that project decreases. The sooner a bill is collected, the higher the firm's profitability.

Indirect profitability factors: Factors that indirectly affect a firm's profitability over a longer period, more than one year.

Indirect Profitability Factors

Indirect profitability factors indirectly affect a firm's profitability over a longer period, more than one year. Indirect profitability factors consist of five elements: strategy, culture, organization, reward systems, and environment, the acronym for which is SCORE.

Strategy. Strategy includes the firm's plans for reaching its profitability goals. It also includes the type of clients the firm serves, the geographical area(s) in which the firm practices, and the areas of specialties of the firm. Management is constantly studying these factors and making changes as warranted. For example, if statistics indicate that more clients require legal services in the area of intellectual property, the firm will add that area of law to its specialties.

Culture. A firm's culture is the firm's environment, including intangible factors such as employee behavior patterns, social policies, and employees' values. It also includes how employees interact and dress and the way clients are treated. A positive culture creates a positive working environment that results in fewer position vacancies and satisfied employees who maximize their contributions to a firm. A firm with a positive culture is more profitable than one with a negative culture.

Organization. Organization refers to a firm's organizational structure for managing its law practice as well as its business affairs. This includes the hierarchy of firm management and the structure of each department within the firm. A well-organized office is more profitable than a poorly organized office. The management structure, as discussed in Chapter 1, affects a firm's culture. An effective management structure increases a firm's profitability. An ineffective management structure is devastating to law firm profitability.

Reward systems. Reward systems include compensation plans, bonus plans, and other professional and personal reward systems for motivating people to contribute to the firm's profitability. These reward systems include benefits, retirement programs, savings programs, and profit-sharing plans. Reward systems are carefully planned into the firm's financial forecast. A firm with a low profit margin cannot afford the luxury of generous reward systems for its employees.

Environment. Environment includes the office area, support staff, and technology that a firm provides its employees for enhancing their productivity and effectiveness. This is closely related to culture because it affects culture. The environment affects profitability because it affects a firm's employees. Employees must have a thriving environment within which to contribute their best effort. Without such an environment, employees are not productive, therefore affecting a firm's profitability.

Both direct and indirect profitability factors are responsible for a firm's profitability. If one factor is dysfunctional, a firm suffers economically. If a circumstance occurs that immediately affects the firm, such as a large client leaving the firm, direct factors are adjusted. For example, expenses are decreased, leverage is increased, and utilization is maximized. If a circumstance occurs that affects long-term goals, such as rapid growth, indirect factors are adjusted. For example, the firm moves to a bigger building or creates an additional department.

Organization of the Financial Management Function

Prior to the 1960s, lawyers did not give much attention to the financial management of their firms. Since that time, lawyers have realized that the practice of law is a business in addition to a service and have implemented sophisticated business principles. Just as in other types of businesses, the success of a law firm depends on the financial decisions of the firm's management.

The finance function, or managing the firm's income and expenses, directly affects the success of the firm. This function consists of many areas, such as collection techniques, managing income and expenses, tax planning, and investment strategies. Each of these functions may be distributed among several financial specialists employed or retained by a firm.

The organization of a firm's finance function depends on the size of the firm. The larger the firm, the more complex its financial activities. As financial activities become more complex, more staff are required to monitor them.

Small Firms   In a small firm with a low volume of activity, the finance function is often performed by an attorney or office manager with the assistance of an outside bookkeeper or certified public accountant (CPA). Often, the office manager is a legal assistant who also performs paralegal duties. The office manager or attorney prepares the records for the accountant, who prepares the firm's financial reports and tax returns.

Some small firms use outside services for many financial management functions. They hire outside accountants who update the firm's accounting records once a month and may also have a payroll service. A payroll service will calculate the amount of payroll checks, prepare the checks and necessary tax forms, and deposit taxes with a bank. In addition to an accountant and outside payroll service, there are also outside billing services that will prepare bills and billing reports for the firm. Most small firms, however, use accounting software to manage their finances.

Controller: Also called a comptroller, an employee charged with certain duties relating to the financial affairs of the business.

General ledger: An accounting term used to describe the book that summarizes a business's financial accounts. Contains a separate account for every asset, liability, and expense.

Accounts payable: Accounts that a business owes for goods or services rendered.

Medium Firms   In medium law firms, financial activities are more complex. A **controller** or office administrator manages the finance function. The controller may perform the finance function or manage employees who do so. In some medium firms, the finance function is divided into two groups who report to the controller: a general ledger group and a billing and collections group, Exhibit 8.15. The general ledger group consists of a **general ledger** accountant, payroll clerk, cashier, and **accounts payable** clerk. The billing and collections group consists of billing clerk, timekeeping clerk, and collection clerk. Medium firms also use outside services as needed.

Large Firms   A large firm has sophisticated systems and a large staff of accountants to manage the firm's finances. The finance department is managed by the controller or office administrator. Some large firms have a financial administrator whose sole responsibility is to manage the financial affairs of the firm.

A large firm has many supervisors under the financial administrator or controller. Supervisors manage several clerks who perform accounting-related tasks. The supervisors found in a large firm are shown in Exhibit 8.16.

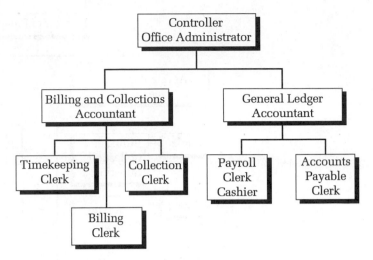

EXHIBIT 8.15   Financial Function—Medium Firm

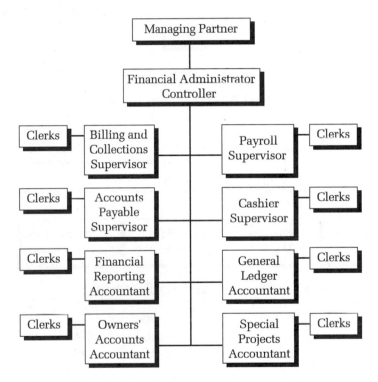

EXHIBIT 8.16   Financial Function—Large Firm

Megafirms   In a megafirm with many branch offices, a director of finance or chief financial officer is in charge of the financial aspects of the firm. The chief financial officer manages a staff of professional accountants. A megafirm has the same financial divisions as a large firm but because of the volume may divide them into two groups, with a manager managing each group, as shown in Exhibit 8.17.

Corporate Legal Departments   A corporate legal department's financial functions are handled by the corporation's finance department. The finance department is not a part of the legal department. The chief financial officer of the corporation is responsible for the finances of all departments within the corporation. The legal department submits a budget to the finance department, and the legal department is

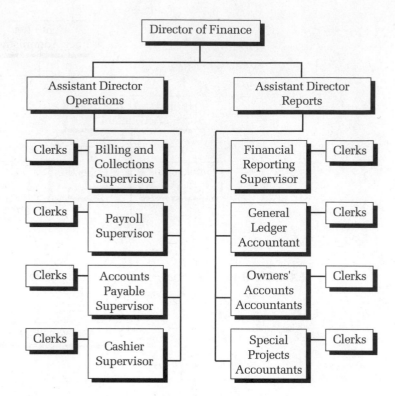

EXHIBIT 8.17 Example of Finance Function for Megafirm

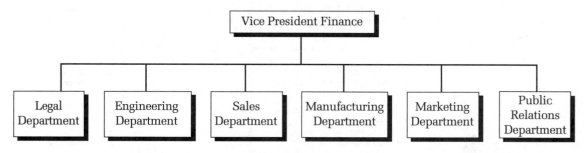

EXHIBIT 8.18 Financial Function—Corporate Legal Department

expected to adhere to the budget. All income and expenses are handled by the finance department, as shown in Exhibit 8.18.

The Realization Process

Realization: The process of turning time into cash.

For a law firm to be successful, it must have strong **realization** policies. Realization is the process of turning time into cash. This begins when a firm accepts a client and consists of five steps: getting, doing, recording, billing, and collecting for the work, as shown in Exhibit 8.19.

The realization process is turning time into cash. When a new client retains the firm, the firm spends time on the client's matter. The firm bills for the work done, and the client pays for the service. The firm uses part of the money to obtain new clients, and the process repeats itself. There may be a difference between the amount billed and the amount collected. This difference is reflected in a percentage of the amount collected, known as a realization rate.

Realization rate: The hourly rate of a timekeeper that the firm actually realizes when all accounts have been collected compared to the total amount billed.

Realization Rate A **realization rate** is the rate that the firm actually receives for work done. This rate may be different from the timekeeper's hourly rate. For exam-

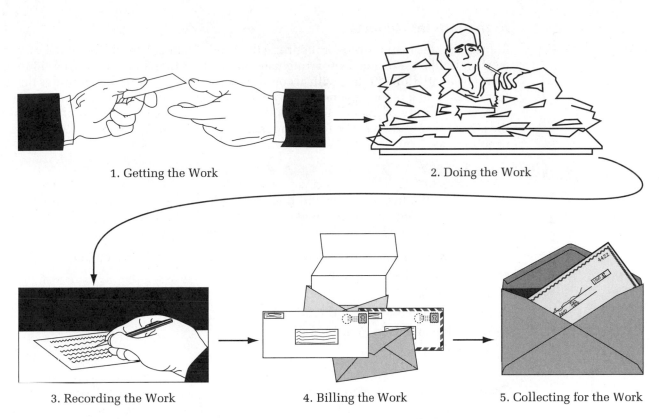

1. Getting the Work

2. Doing the Work

3. Recording the Work

4. Billing the Work

5. Collecting for the Work

EXHIBIT 8.19 The Realization Process is the Process of Turning Time into Cash.

ple, if a timekeeper's hourly rate is $100 an hour but the firm is unable to collect 10 percent of the timekeeper's bills, the realization rate is 90 percent of the hourly rate, or $90 an hour ($100 − $10 = $90). Management uses the realization rate to prepare the firm's budget. Anticipation of uncorrectable debts is an important function of the budgeting process.

A number of factors affect the realization rate: nonbillable time, **write-ups, write-downs,** and **write-offs.**

As we saw earlier in the chapter, a preliminary bill is prepared and given to the attorney for adjustment. A fee adjustment memorandum is prepared for some bills that need adjustment. A firm will write up a client's bill when the client receives a substantial benefit from the firm's work on the case and agrees to give the firm a premium. The timekeepers' realization rate is increased by the premium. A write-down is when some of the timekeeper's time is not billed to a client or is discounted. The timekeeper's realization rate is reduced. If a client's bill is uncorrectable, or written off, the timekeeper's realization rate is further reduced.

Management calculates a ratio of write-ups, write-downs, and write-offs from the fee adjustment memorandum. It strives for a 90 to 95 percent realization rate for each timekeeper, but an 80 percent realization rate is more common. To arrive at a timekeeper's realization rate, multiply the number of annual billable hours by the hourly rate and take 80 percent of that figure. A timekeeper with an annual billable hour requirement of 1,800 hours at $100 an hour would calculate the realization rate as follows:

$$\$100 \times 80\% \$ = \$80 \text{ an hour}$$
$$1{,}800 \times \$80 = \$144{,}000$$

The firm estimates its income from that timekeeper at $144,000. If that income is not realized, the firm's profitability is decreased. If the income is exceeded, the firm's profitability is increased, and the legal assistant may be entitled to a merit bonus.

Write-up: An increase in the amount owed because of a premium.

Write-down: A decrease in the amount owed because of a discount.

Write-off: A credit for the total amount owed.

Management Reports

Management is responsible for reporting the firm's financial condition to the owners or shareholders. Financial reporting used to be an arduous task requiring hours of manual calculations. Today, with accounting software, the computer compiles the information, and a report is generated by a few keystrokes on the computer.

A wide variety of financial reports are used, each conveying different aspects of the accounting function. The following sections discuss the types of financial reports used in a law firm.

Client Report   A client report can be cumulative or individual. A cumulative report lists all the firm's clients and their billing histories. An individual report lists one client's billing history. A client report may also be prepared for each attorney indicating the attorney's client base. The client reports describe six items:

◆ Attorney and legal assistant hourly rates and number of hours charged
◆ Amounts paid and unpaid
◆ Unbilled time
◆ Costs advanced, billed and unbilled
◆ Any adjustments in monthly billing
◆ Dates of service

Transaction Activity Report   A transaction activity report gives daily transaction entries per timekeeper. The information is derived from each timekeeper's daily time sheets. The report lists time spent, disbursements, and costs. The report monitors the amount of billable time spent per day per timekeeper. This report will alert management if a timekeeper is not producing the minimum amount required. It also monitors the activities of each timekeeper.

File Maintenance Report   A file maintenance report describes client file information and makes changes to file information, including client address and the names of the responsible attorney and legal assistant.

Work-in-Progress Report   A work-in-progress report describes details of unbilled hours and costs per timekeeper, including client totals. This report may also be aged. Aged reports of unbilled time are valuable information for attorneys working on contingency matters. The older the matter, the more costly it is for the firm.

Billing Report   A billing report consists of five items:

◆ Unbilled time and disbursements per client or case
◆ Draft bills
◆ Summary of bills with client totals and timekeeper totals
◆ Summary of client billing history, including amounts billed, amounts collected, and amounts uncollected
◆ Total amount of bills generated per month compared to budgeted amounts indicating variances.

Aging: Calculating the number of days an account has been unpaid.

Accounts Receivable Report   An accounts receivable report describes the amount of clients' outstanding bills and includes an **aging** report. This report alerts management to begin collection activities if a bill has been outstanding for a specific period of time. Aging puts accounts in four categories according to the age of that account as shown in Exhibit 8.20:

CLIENT	TOTAL	1–30 DAYS	31–60 DAYS	61–90 DAYS	OVER 90 DAYS
ABC Corp.	$ 26,786	$18,786	$ 6,000	$ 2,000	
U.R. Best, Inc.	$ 1,543	$ 1,543			
Flaky Jake	$ 9,765				$ 9,765
XYZ Corp.	$ 76,987	$25,765	$10,983	$20,811	$18,428
Ruth Addington	$ 7,543			$ 7,543	
Bob BigBoy	$ 10,456	$ 1,543	$ 5,321	$ 1,586	$ 2,000
Allgood Products	$ 1,245	$ 1,245			
Totals	**$134,325**	**$48,882**	**$22,304**	**$31,940**	**$30,193**
Percentages	**100%**	**36.5%**	**17%**	**24%**	**22.5%**

EXHIBIT 8.20 Aging Report

◆ 1 to 30 days
◆ 31 to 60 days
◆ 61 to 90 days
◆ Over 90 days

Cash Receipts Report   A cash receipts report describes income received per day, per week, per month, per quarter, or per year. Cash receipts are compared to the amount of projected income for a specific time period. This report allows management to make financial decisions concerning income and expenditures for the firm.

Practice Management Report   A practice management report varies according to the needs of the firm. In general, it includes five items:

◆ *Client investment summary.* A summary for each client of total amount billed and total unbilled with a calculation of the actual costs of providing the service.
◆ *Billing realization report.* A summary of each timekeeper's billings for the current month compared to the previous year showing year-to-date totals. This report describes amounts billed, amounts received, variance, and realization percentages per timekeeper. It is from this report that a timekeeper's realization rate is calculated.
◆ *Staff utilization report.* A summary of the billable hours and nonbillable hours for each timekeeper for the current month with year-to-date totals. This report informs the timekeeper of expected billable and nonbillable hours.
◆ *Fee analysis report.* A summary of fees generated by client, by area of law, by branch office, and responsible attorney. This report helps management in making marketing decisions and expansion plans. This report shows a firm's management what areas, or branch offices, are profitable and those that are not.
◆ *Type-of-case summary.* A summary of the average amount of time spent on a case per area of law. This report assists management in setting flat fees for a service. It also assists management in determining the profitability of a certain matter.

Compensation Report   A payroll report gives a summary of the firm's payroll, employee benefits, and tax liability.

Accounts Payable Report   An accounts payable report is a summary of all accounts payable, including year-to-date balances and aging reports. A record of all transactions with each vendor is compiled. As an invoice is received and paid, the computer updates each vendor's account so that a running total is kept for each vendor.

Budget Performance Report A budget performance report is a comparison of the firm's actual income and expenditures compared with budgeted income and expenditures.

Cash Flow Projection Report A cash flow projection report is used to anticipate monthly cash availability and to plan periodic partner distributions and law firm investments.

Cumulative: Increasing by successive addition; running total of each month's services and costs.

Cumulative Report A cumulative report provides a summary of services and costs. This report informs management of whether the firm's projected income expectations are being met and aids in financial planning for the firm.

Total Hours Report A total hours report provides management with a total number of hours billed to date and per hour average. This report informs management of whether the firm's projected billable hour expectations are being met. If not, management will require additional hours from the timekeepers.

Year-to-Date Report A year-to-date report provides totals for each client. This report assists management in its client relations program. It will alert management if a client is decreasing its activity with the firm. If so, the firm will increase its client relations with that client.

Adjustments Report An adjustments report provides management with the total amount of adjustments made in the bills as reflected on the fee adjustment memorandum. If the percentage of adjustments is too high, management will investigate the reason and resolve any problems that may exist.

Timekeeper Summary Report A timekeeper summary report is a summary of billable hours for each timekeeper that includes monthly charges and year-to-date totals. This report informs management if each timekeeper is producing the required billable hours. If not, management will alert the timekeeper to increase billable hours.

Work Log Summary Report A work log summary report is done by a timekeeper. This report informs management of each timekeeper's workload. If management believes that a timekeeper is spending too much time on a certain case or in a certain area, management will recommend changes.

Work Category Summary Report A work category summary report is done by a timekeeper. This report shows the charges and income by type of case. This report informs management of the volume of cases in a certain category. By averaging the time records of each case in a certain area, management can determine a standard flat fee for that type of case.

THE BUDGETING PROCESS

The budget is the key to law firm profitability. It contains guidelines that direct a firm's management in its financial decisions. It identifies how much money is needed to meet expenses. If an expense is underestimated, it will have an impact on the profitability of the firm. Studies have shown that firms that adhere to a budget are more profitable than those who do not.

A budget is prepared at the start of each year. Management uses one of two methods to prepare the budget: It may base its projections on the firm's activities of the previous year, or it may solicit input from the firm's employees. When developing a budget, a firm's management projects income, projects personnel costs, and projects operating expenses.

Income Projection

Gross income: Income received before payment of expenses.

In order to project the **gross income,** or income received before expenses are paid, for the year, management must estimate the amount of work required for existing clients and anticipate work from new clients. Variables in determining income from new clients include the economic environment, the firm's marketing activities and strategic planning, past experience in producing new clients, and competitive pressures.

Income generated from each timekeeper is considered when projecting a firm's income. Factors considered are annual billable hours, hourly rate, and realization rate for each timekeeper, as follows:

Billable hours × Hourly rate × Realization rate = Gross income

Exhibit 8.21 shows an example of income projections.

Personnel Costs Projection

Downsize: To reduce staff and expenses because of reduced income.

Budgeting for personnel costs requires management to anticipate personnel needs for the year. If management anticipates that fewer employees will be needed, the firm will **downsize,** and employees will be laid off. If additional personnel are anticipated, the cost thereof will be put into the budget. Budgeting for personnel costs requires management to anticipate associates' compensation, administrative staff salaries, employee benefit costs, and employee taxes.

If the firm is a sole proprietorship or partnership, the owners' salaries are not anticipated in personnel costs because they are paid out of the profits of the firm. If the firm is a professional corporation, the owners are employees of the corporation, and their salaries are included in personnel costs.

Operating Expense Projection

Four categories are estimated when projecting operating expenses: occupancy costs, office operating expenses, professional activity costs, and general business expenses.

Law Firm of Black, White & Greene
Projected Income for 2006

TIMEKEEPER	BILLABLE HOURS	HOURLY RATE	REALIZATION	TOTAL
R. Black, Esq.	1,600	$250.00	90%	$360,000.00
D. White, Esq.	1,600	250.00	90%	360,000.00
G. Greene, Esq.	1,800	200.00	85%	306,000.00
P. Boen, Esq.	1,900	175.00	80%	266,000.00
G. Templeton, Esq.	1,900	175.00	80%	266,000.00
M. Nollkamper, L.A.	1,800	100.00	85%	153,000.00
J. Hemstreet, L.A.	1,800	75.00	80%	108,000.00
M. Goldberg, L.A.	1,800	50.00	75%	67,500.00
Total projected gross income				**$1,886,500.00**

EXHIBIT 8.21 Example Income Projections

These costs can be estimated from the previous year's expenses. Management will increase each category as needed. If a firm expects a 15 percent increase in new client work, it will increase the expenses accordingly. If it expects a 15 percent decrease in new client work, it will decrease the expenses accordingly. Exhibit 8.22 shows a sample budget.

Calculating an Expense Percentage

When the budget is prepared, management can calculate an expense percentage by dividing expenses by income as follows:

$$\text{Expenses} \div \text{Income} = \text{Expense percentage}$$
$$\$1,048,575 \div 1,886,500 = 56\%$$

Per unit cost: The amount of money it costs to produce a product or provide a service.

Knowing the expense percentage will allow a firm to calculate the expenses it allocates to each timekeeper. This calculation is known as **per unit cost** and is used by businesses to determine how much it costs to produce a product or provide a service. For example, it costs the firm in Exhibit 8.23 $209,000 for timekeeper A to produce $380,000 in revenue and $37,125 for timekeeper H to produce $67,500 in revenue. Knowing the per unit cost of a timekeeper is helpful to calculate actual potential profits of each timekeeper. Actual profit expected is calculated by deducting the expense percentage of each timekeeper's gross fees, as shown in Exhibit 8.23.

Knowing the expense percentage of the firm has other uses. It is helpful when comparing the profitability of the firm with that of other firms. Management can also estimate partners' income without recalculating the expenses, as shown in Exhibit 8.24.

The lower the expense percentage, the more profitable the firm. A typical expense percentage is between 40 and 70 percent, with an average of 60 percent. If the expense percentage is over 70 percent, management must take measures to either increase income or decrease expenses.

Law Firm of Black, White & Greene
2006 Budget

Income		$1,886,500.00

(Derived from projected income)

Expenses

Compensation expense

Timekeeper compensation	$450,000.00	
Administrative	128,000.00	
Benefits	90,000.00	
Taxes	102,000.00	
Total Compensation Expense		$770,000.00

Occupancy expense

Rent	$24,000.00	
Utilities	12,500.00	
Storage	4,300.00	
Other _____		
Total Occupancy Expense		$40,800.00

Office operating costs

Stationery	$ 1,980.00	
Messenger	940.00	
Postage	1,575.00	
Supplies	1,890.00	
Miscellaneous	500.00	
Computers	19,485.00	
Software	1,460.00	
Printers	2,345.00	
Photocopier	5,678.00	
Furniture	2,864.00	
Filing cabinet(s)	3,500.00	
Calculators	750.00	
Janitorial	3,850.00	
Dictation	1,550.00	
Total office operating costs		$48,367.00

Professional Activities

Association dues	$ 950.00	
Other dues	200.00	
Seminars	3,000.00	
Continuing education	5,000.00	
Miscellaneous	500.00	
Other	300.00	
Total professional activities		$9,950.00

General Business Expenses

Advertising	$ 5,000.00	
Agency fees	2,340.00	
Legal periodicals	675.00	
Books	12,890.00	
Updates	21,000.00	
Subscriptions	1,850.00	
Miscellaneous	650.00	
Other	500.00	
Telephone	20,500.00	
Liability Insurance	40,053.00	
Office contents	3,000.00	
Workers' compensation	14,000.00	
Miscellaneous	500.00	
Business license	500.00	
Income taxes	50,000.00	
Business tax	5,000.00	
Miscellaneous	1,000.00	
Total business expenses		$179,458.00
Total projected expenses		**$1,048,575.00**
Total projected net income		**$ 837,925.00**

EXHIBIT 8.22 Example Budget

	BILLABLE HOURS	HOURLY RATE	REALIZATION RATE	TOTAL	EXPENSE (%)	TOTAL EXPENSE	NET PROFIT
A	1,600	$250	95%	$ 380,000	55%	$ 209,000	$171,000
B	1,600	250	90%	360,000	55%	198,000	162,000
C	1,800	200	85%	306,000	55%	168,300	137,700
D	1,900	175	80%	266,000	55%	146,300	119,700
E	1,900	175	80%	266,000	55%	146,300	119,700
F	1,800	100	85%	153,000	55%	84,150	68,850
	1,800	75	80%	108,000	55%	59,400	48,600
G	1,800	50	75%	67,500	55%	37,125	30,375
	TOTAL			**1,906,500**		**1,048,575**	**857,925**

EXHIBIT 8.23 Net Profit Per Timekeeper

Law Firm of Black, White & Greene

Projected Partners' Income
2006

Estimated Income	$1,906,500.00
Less expenses 55%	1,048,575.00
Net distributable income	857,925.00
Distributable income per partner (3)	$ 285,975.00

EXHIBIT 8.24 Projected Partner Income

SUMMARY

For a law firm to be successful, it must have strong billing policies that quickly turn time into cash. Realization is the process of turning time into cash and has five steps: getting, doing, recording, billing, and collecting for work. The realization rate is the hourly rate actually received for work done.

The goal of a good billing practice is to get a firm's bills paid as promptly as possible. The most important aspect of the billing process is communication. Communicating the cost of legal services to a client continues throughout an attorney-client relationship.

Legal assistants are often asked to answer a client's questions regarding a bill. A legal assistant should direct all inquiries to an office manager. A legal assistant may not negotiate a fee agreement. A legal assistant also may not inform a client of the possible duration or outcome of a matter. A legal assistant should document all client communication.

Billing should be regular and frequent. Monthly billing is the most common method of billing. Billing a client as soon as possible after a matter is completed is a crucial element of a good billing policy.

In recent years, clients have demanded descriptive bills, and the trend is to be as descriptive as possible.

The billing process begins when entries from a time sheet are input into a computer and a preliminary bill is prepared. Charging interest on past-due accounts is generally accepted, and lawyers often extend credit to their clients. To ease the financial burden on firms, lawyers have offered clients two credit alternatives: loans and the use of credit cards. In 1974, the ABA sanctioned lawyers' use of credit cards as payment for legal fees.

Firms use off-the-shelf time and billing software to prepare clients bills. Various styles of bills are used by law firms. The style of a bill depends on the type of client, the type of case, and the policy of a firm.

Each firm has its own policy for collecting accounts. Each account is considered separately. A lawyer may withdraw from a case if a client fails to pay a fee, if the withdrawal will not prejudice the client. Before a firm stops work or withdraws from a case, it must give careful consideration to an attorney's ethical responsibilities to a client. Suing a client should be the last resort.

To keep fee disputes out of the court system, most state bar associations have developed arbitration programs to resolve them. The ABA encourages lawyers to take advantage of bar-sponsored arbitration programs.

The success of a law firm depends on the financial decisions of the firm's management. The finance function directly affects the success of the firm. The organization of a firm's finance function depends on the size of the firm. Time is the product that law firms sell to clients. Two profitability factors are considered: direct profitability factors, consisting of rates, utilization, leverage, expenses, and speed, and indirect profitability factors, consisting of strategy, culture, organization, reward systems, and environment. A law firm's hourly rate for each timekeeper is an element of profitability. A timekeeper's realization rate is the amount the firm actually realizes from the timekeeper.

The budget is the key to law firm profitability. A budget is prepared at the start of each year. In order to project the gross income for the year, management must estimate the amount of work required for existing clients and anticipate work from new clients. Income generated from each timekeeper is considered when projecting a firm's income.

Management derives various reports from its accounting functions that help the firm plan its resources.

Four categories of operating expenses are estimated when projecting operating expenses: occupancy costs, office operating expenses, professional activities, and general business expenses. Knowing the expense percentage of the firm will allow the firm to calculate the amount of expenses it allocates to each timekeeper. The lower the expense percentage, the more profitable the firm.

CHAPTER ILLUSTRATION

The budgeting process for Black, White & Greene begins in November of each year. In November, Tricia reviews various management reports to anticipate the firm's needs for the next year. Each attorney is involved in the process and is asked to project any major expenses. For example, the firm did not replace Melvin when he was fired, so the firm expects to hire a new legal assistant in the coming year. Tricia increased the personnel cost projection accordingly. Dennis White was retained for a large contingency case and anticipates high litigation costs. Tricia increased the operating expenses projection accordingly.

The previous year, the firm's expense percentage was 55 percent of income, and its realization rate was 90 percent of total billings. This year, however, Patrizia Boen's realization rate is lower than last year, so Tricia expects a lower overall realization rate for the coming year. She calculated the realization rate for the firm at 85 percent for the new year. She made the adjustment in the income projection. She must also adjust the expenses for the firm to the lower income projection, so she reduced the expense projection 5 percent to maintain profitability. Tricia completed the new year's budget in December, and it was approved by Robert in January. The attorneys are expected to adhere to the budget and to report any extraordinary expenses so that they can be put into the budget.

Tricia handles the firm's finance function. The firm uses a popular time and billing software program that prepares descriptive, itemized bills for the clients. The software also includes an accounting function that tracks all the firm's accounts payable and accounts receivable. Tricia enters accounts payable information into the computer when she pays her bills.

Each timekeeper enters their time directly into the computer. The computer prepares hourly bills, flat fee bills, and contingency statements. Tricia recently upgraded the program to include task-based accounting functions. The computer is programmed to produce descriptive bills so that each client is aware of each service performed on his or her behalf.

The third week of the month, Tricia prepares preliminary bills on the basis of the timekeeping information input by the timekeepers. The preliminary bills are given to the responsible attorney for review. At times, mistakes are made that must be corrected. Additionally, there are times when the attorney will increase or reduce a charge if he or she feels that the adjustment is warranted. The responsible attorney makes these corrections on a fee adjustment memorandum and submits it to Tricia, who makes the needed adjustments. The final bills are then prepared so that they can be mailed on the first of each month.

Tricia is never late with the billing. She knows that the sooner clients receive their bills, the sooner the firm will be paid. Prompt and regular billing is important for the firm to meet its commitments. If an account goes unpaid for sixty days, the computer is programmed to charge the client interest at a reasonable interest rate. Tricia prints out an aging report to determine the collection letters needed.

Black, White & Greene has a standard policy of explaining its charges to the client in the initial client interview. A fee agreement is prepared and executed for every case. An engagement letter is sent immediately after the initial client interview that summarizes the fee agreement. The client is expected to sign the engagement letter and return it to Tricia. On a few occasions, fee disputes have arisen, in which case, the firm requires that the dispute be arbitrated by a fee arbitration panel of the local bar association.

George Templeton, the contract attorney for the firm, represented Janine Jamison in her divorce case. He charged her a flat fee of $2,000 for the representation. She paid $1,000 at the beginning of the case, the remainder of which was due before the hearing. One week before the hearing, George called her to discuss the case and to request payment. She told George that she would give him a check the day before the hearing, but she did not. George considered continuing the hearing, but the opposing party, Janine's estranged husband, would not grant a continuance because he was anxious to remarry. George had no alternative but to appear at the hearing.

After the hearing, George asked Janine for payment. She told him that she was fired from her job and had no money. George completed her divorce and sent her collection letters to collect the fee. When Janine received the third collection letter, she called George and told him that she did not feel she should pay the remainder of the fee because she did not get the amount of child support she expected.

She also accused George of conspiring against her with her ex-husband. George tried to explain to her that he did not conspire against her, but to no avail. Janine still refused to pay the remainder of the fee. George immediately submitted the dispute to the fee arbitration panel of his local bar association.

The bar association's fee dispute panel sent Janine a questionnaire to complete and asked her to describe her dispute. They also sent a questionnaire to George to complete and submit to them along with George's time records on the case. George asked Tricia for a client time report on the case. He sent the report with the questionnaire to the bar association, which set the matter for a hearing.

Both Janine and George appeared at the hearing and gave the panel their side of the story. Afterward, the panel ruled that George did not conspire against his client and that his representation of Janine was proper. They found, however, that he spent eight hours on the case. Applying his hourly rate of $200 to the amount of time records (lodestar) totaled $1,600, so they deducted $400 off the remaining balance owed. Janine was ordered to pay $600 instead of $1,000. She sent a check the next week.

CHAPTER REVIEW

1. What is the main goal of a firm's billing policy?

2. What are the five steps of the realization process?

3. What is the most important aspect of the billing process?

4. What is an engagement letter?

5. When communicating with clients, what are the things a nonlawyer should not do?

6. Why is regular and frequent billing important?

7. What is a preliminary bill?

8. Describe the two methods lawyers use to extend credit to their clients.

9. What elements are contained in a descriptive hourly bill that are not contained in a brief hourly bill?

10. What is the difference between an hourly bill and a flat fee bill?

11. What are the four most common unethical billing practices?

12. What is a legal auditor?

13. What are direct profitability factors?

14. What are indirect profitability factors?

15. What is a realization rate, and how is it calculated?

16. What are the three projections that management makes when preparing a budget?

17. What are the four types of operating expenses in a law firm?

18. What is an expense percentage, and how is it calculated?

EXAMPLES FOR DISCUSSION

1. United States v. DeLorean

In the 1984 white-collar criminal case of *United States v. DeLorean*, Howard L. Wietzman defended John DeLorean on charges of conspiring to possess and distribute cocaine. DeLorean was also prosecuted on fraud and racketeering charges. No fee agreement was made, and Wietzman kept no time records. He never quoted DeLorean a particular fee and waited one year to send DeLorean his first bill. He was known to "ballpark," or estimate, his fees. DeLorean paid Wietzman a total of $3.5 million.

At the time of DeLorean's acquittal, he was quoted as saying, "Without Mr. Weitzman, I would probably put my head in the oven." Later, however, a controversy arose over Wietzman's fee. Wietzman claims that DeLorean owes him an additional $683,392. DeLorean claims that Wietzman owes him a refund. When asked how he figured the additional fee that was due, Wietzman said, "How much would you pay to stay out of jail, pal? I owe him nothing. He owes me his life." The trial court will decide the outcome of the matter.

1. If you were the judge, how would you rule?
2. What are the issues in this case?
3. Are Wietzman's actions ethical?
4. What factors of reasonableness (TOCATPET) apply in this case?

2. The Sixfold Bill

Geraldo Hernandez, a real estate developer, was sued by six separate parties in six cases resulting from a dispute about the same development project. Geraldo thought it would be advisable to have all six cases handled by Robert Valentino. The fee agreement between Geraldo and Robert stated that Robert would charge an hourly rate of $250.

Robert filed six answers that were essentially identical to one another. A few weeks later, Geraldo received a bill showing the same amount of time, and applying the same hourly rate, for the preparation of each answer. The amount of time shown on the bill suggested to Geraldo that he was being charged six times the actual number of hours worked.

When Geraldo called Robert about the bill, Robert stated that since one answer took one-half hour to prepare, the other answers have the same value.

1. If you were Geraldo, what would you do?
2. When discussing fees, what should Robert have done? What should Geraldo have done?

3. Was Robert's answer justified?
4. Were Robert's billing policies ethical?

3. The Modified Agreement

Pete Moss retained Emily McGregor to negotiate a lease with Pete's landlord. Pete agreed to pay Emily $200 an hour. Emily sent Pete an engagement letter like the one shown on page 273.

As time elapsed, the negotiations with Pete's landlord became more complex. Because of the complexity, Emily felt that an increase in her hourly rate was warranted. She sent Pete a notice of fee increase that stated that her hourly fee was increased to $250 an hour because of the complexity of the issues. Pete refused to pay the increased fee, and Emily sued him for the difference.

1. If you were the judge, how would you rule?
2. What is the basis of your ruling?
3. If you were the manager of Emily's firm, what would you do to prevent this situation from happening again?

4. Hourly or Flat Fee?

You are the manager of a medium-size law firm. The managing partner is concerned about the profitability of the domestic relations department consisting of three attorneys and one legal assistant. The managing partner has asked you to prepare a report of the profitability of the department. He has also asked you to give him a report of the average cost and the average fee of each domestic relations case. He has also asked you to establish a flat fee for certain domestic cases and to recommend which cases should be on a flat fee basis.

1. What reports would you generate for the managing partner?
2. Where does the information for each report come from?
3. How reliable is the information in the report?

ASSIGNMENTS

1. From the records you kept for assignment 3 in Chapter 7, prepare a detailed hourly bill for your instructor for this class. If you have spent any money for the class, such as for supplies or books, include them in the bill as costs. Follow the format on page 278 for a detailed hourly bill.
2. You are an administrator for a small firm of two attorneys. Use the aging report on page 297 to complete the following tasks:
   a. Prepare a collection program for the accounts stated. Write reminder letters, using those in this chapter as a guide. For

accounts over ninety days past due, make a recommendation for the appropriate collection procedure. Use the following profiles to develop the appropriate collection program:

ABC Corporation—new client. The firm has wanted ABC as a client for a long time. ABC has given the firm a couple of cases to determine whether it will give the firm more cases.
T. R. Best—bankruptcy client.
Jake Wagner—criminal client. Jake was arrested on drug-dealing charges and acquitted.

XYZ Corporation—firm's largest client. The firm handles many cases for XYZ.

Addington—dissolution-of-marriage client. Ruth is a mother of four young children who is trying to find her husband, who abandoned the family. She works as a waitress and goes to night school, taking paralegal courses.

Bob Bradford Tires—tire manufacturer. The firm is defending the client in a product liability case.

Allgood Products—health food chain. The firm is providing corporate services. Allgood has a potential of becoming a large client.

   b. On the basis of the aging report, write a report to your instructor about the financial condition of the firm.

   c. The hourly rates of both attorneys in your firm are $250. Assuming that the figures in the over-ninety-days category in the aging report are uncollectible, what is your firm's realization rate? What is the realization rate for each attorney? Assume that each attorney has an equal amount of uncollectible income.

3. You are an administrator for a large law firm. The managing partner wants to start charging interest on all past-due accounts. He has asked you to research the applicable laws in your state concerning charging and collecting interest. He has asked you also to research the ethics opinions of the state bar concerning interest charges. Prepare a report of your findings that describes your firm's obligations and requirements concerning interest.

4. You are a dissatisfied client who disputes the fee charged by your lawyer. You want to arbitrate the dispute. Research the applicable arbitration programs in your area and prepare a step-by-step procedural guide for arbitrating fee disputes in your state.

5. You are an administrator for a large corporate legal department. You suspect that outside counsel is overbilling, and the general counsel wants to hire a legal auditor to review the firm's bills for the last six months. He asked you to help him choose a legal auditing company. Research the Internet sites of legal auditors listed in the Cybersites sidebar on page 285 and prepare a report listing the following for each company:

   a. Services

   b. Rates

   c. Company profile including length of time in business

   d. Recommendation

6. The law firm of Smith & Jones is a partnership owned by Steve Smith and Jerry Jones. In addition to the partners, the firm employs three associate attorneys and three legal assistants. The partners are required to bill 1,800 hours at $250 an hour. They have a 90 percent realization rate. The associates are required to bill 2,000 hours at $200 an hour. They have an 85 percent realization rate. The legal assistants are required to bill 1,800 hours. One legal assistant's hourly rate is $85 an hour, and she has an 85 percent realization rate. The other two legal assistants' hourly rate is $70 an hour. Legal assistant number 2 has a realization rate of 80 percent, and legal assistant number 3 has a realization rate of 75 percent. Calculate the firm's projected gross income for the year.

7. Smith & Jones has an expense percentage of 62 percent. On the basis of the projected income in question 1, calculate the firm's projected net income for the year.

8. On the basis of the income calculated in questions 6 and 7, calculate each partner's projected income for the year.

SELF-TEST

How well did you grasp the material in the chapter? Test yourself by answering the following questions and check your answers against the answers found in Appendix A.

1. What are the four essential elements of the billing process?

2. What is the most important aspect of the billing process?

3. Who has the responsibility to communicate the fee agreement to the client?

4. When discussing bills with clients, what may legal assistants *not* do?

5. Who has the authority to adjust a client's bill?

6. When communicating with clients, what may legal assistants *not* do?

7. When a legal assistant has a communication with a client, what must she or he do?

8. How will a firm be rewarded for a client's complete understanding of the case?

9. What is an engagement letter?

10. Why should billing be regular and frequent?
11. What type of law firm has difficulty meeting a monthly billing schedule?
12. When should a client be billed?
13. What happens to a client's perception of legal services as time goes by?
14. What is the most common method of billing?
15. What type of bills do individual clients prefer?
16. What are the twelve elements of an average bill?
17. What is a preliminary bill?
18. What is a fee adjustment memorandum?
19. What has caused law firms to experience collection problems?
20. What two methods do firms use to offer credit to clients?
21. What are the guidelines the ABA issued regarding the use of credit cards?
22. What is fee allocation?
23. What is a cost recovery system?
24. What determines the style of a bill?
25. What is the rule of thumb of billing styles?
26. What are the two styles of hourly bills?
27. What is a gross contingency fee accounting?
28. What is a net contingency fee accounting?
29. When do collection activities begin?
30. When does the lawyer become involved in collection activities?
31. If a lawyer withdraws from a case because of nonpayment of fees, what must the lawyer do?
32. What are the nine things to consider before withdrawing from the case?
33. If a firm sues a client, what must the firm prove?
34. When should a firm sue a client?
35. It is a standard practice to give a client at least _____ notice of collection agency involvement.
36. What has contributed to society's negative perception of lawyers?
37. What are the four most common unethical billing practices?
38. Why are legal fee agreements held to a higher standard than other contracts?
39. What is a fiduciary?
40. If a fee agreement is ambiguous, how is it determined?
41. What is a legal auditor?
42. What do legal auditors do?
43. What are the two major problems clients complain about?
44. What are the ten problems that are major contributors to ambiguous bills?
45. What are the majority of complaints received by bar associations?
46. What is team churning?
47. What is padding?

48. What is block billing?
49. What are client-directed billing policies?
50. Why do some attorneys object to client-directed billing policies?
51. If a fee is disputed, what must a firm do?
52. What have state bar associations done to keep disputes out of the court system?
53. What is arbitration?
54. What is discovery?
55. What determines the organization of a firm's finance function?
56. What are direct profitability factors?
57. When should a task be delegated downward?
58. What is leveraging?
59. What is a leverage ratio, and how is it calculated?
60. What are the two types of expenses?
61. What are the three categories of compensation expenses?
62. What are the four categories of operating expenses?
63. What do occupancy costs include?
64. What do office operating costs include?
65. What do professional activity costs include?
66. What do general business expenses include?
67. What are indirect profitability factors?
68. Of what elements does a law firm's culture consist?
69. What do reward systems consist of?
70. How does the environment affect a firm's profitability?
71. How is the finance function accomplished in a small firm?
72. Why do small firms use outside services for their finance function?
73. What is a CPA?
74. How is the finance function accomplished in a medium firm?
75. In some medium firms, the finance function is divided into what two groups?
76. What functions make up the general ledger group?
77. What are the functions of the billing and collections group?
78. Who manages the finance function in a large firm?
79. What finance supervisors are found in a large firm?
80. Who manages the finance function in a megafirm?
81. Who manages the finance function in a corporate legal department?
82. What is realization?
83. What are the five steps of the realization process?
84. What is a realization rate?
85. When is a realization rate used?
86. What factors affect a realization rate?
87. What is a write-up?
88. What is a write-down?
89. What is a write-off?

90. What is the most common realization rate?
91. How is a realization rate calculated?
92. What type of firm averages the highest ratio of legal assistants to attorney?
93. What type of firm averages the lowest ratio of legal assistants to attorney?
94. What is a client report?
95. What is a transaction activity report?
96. What is a file maintenance report?
97. What is a work-in-progress report?
98. What is a billing report?
99. What is aging?
100. What is an accounts receivable report?
101. What is a cash receipts report?
102. What is a practice management report?
103. What is a compensation report?
104. What is an accounts payable report?
105. What is a budget performance report?
106. What is a cash flow projection report?
107. What is a cumulative summary report?
108. What is a total hours report?
109. What is a year-to-date report?
110. What is an adjustments report?
111. What is a timekeeper summary report?
112. What is a work log summary report?
113. What is a work category summary report?
114. What is the key to a law firm's profitability?
115. When developing a law firm's budget, what does management do?
116. How does management project gross income?
117. What are the factors used to determine income from new clients?
118. What factors are considered when projecting a firm's income?
119. How does a firm budget for personnel?
120. How is an expense percentage calculated?
121. How is a firm's anticipated profit calculated?
122. What is the average expense percentage for law firms?

KEY WORDS

Accounts payable	Discovery	Operating expenses
Aging	Downsize	Per unit cost
Arbitration	Engagement letter	Preliminary bill
Block billing	Fee adjustment memorandum	Realization
Compensation expenses	Fee allocation	Realization rate
Controller	Fiduciary	Team churning
Cost recovery system	General ledger	Write-down
Cumulative	Gross income	Write-off
Direct profitability factors	Indirect profitability factors	Write-up

CHAPTER

9

Managing the Client Funds Trust Account

OBJECTIVES

After completion of this chapter, the student should be able to do the following:

◆ Know the type of funds to be deposited in a trust account.

◆ Prepare a client ledger sheet.

◆ Document financial transactions in the cash receipts and cash payments journals.

◆ Document trust account transactions correctly.

◆ Disburse funds from the trust account.

◆ Prepare monthly trust account statements.

◆ Close a client's trust account.

◆ Guard against trust account abuse.

INTRODUCTION

The client funds trust account is a bank account established exclusively for clients' funds. It is separate from a firm's general or operating account. Almost every firm is called on to handle money for its clients, sometimes in large amounts. For example, a firm may handle a personal injury claim for a client. When the case is over, medical bills, costs, and other expenses are paid out of the proceeds of the case. Money derived from the proceeds of the case is deposited in, and disbursed from, the clients' funds trust account. The attorney holds the funds "in trust" for clients and acts as a fiduciary by maintaining control of the funds.

Each state's bar association has rules governing the client funds trust account. *The attorney and law firm are bound by state professional responsibility codes to keep client funds completely separate from office and personal bank accounts.* This principle is known as **segregation of cash.**

A firm usually has one account for the funds of all its clients. Opening a separate account for each client is cumbersome and discouraged by the American Bar Association (ABA). However, if a firm anticipates that a case will have many large transactions, the firm may open a separate trust account for that case only. Large probate cases commonly have their own trust account.

Examples of the type of funds held in the trust account are funds for costs and expenses, estate proceeds, escrow funds, settlements, judgment payments, and fee advances.

ETHICS ALERT

Segregation of cash:
Keeping clients' funds separate from law firm funds.

TYPES OF FUNDS HELD IN THE TRUST ACCOUNT

Costs and Expenses

When a client retains a firm, a firm normally requests a deposit of money for payment of costs of the case. Since the exact amount of the costs is unknown at the commencement of a case, a lump sum is requested and is deposited in the trust account. As the costs are incurred, they are paid directly from the trust account. For example, a client pays the firm a lump sum of $500 for payment of costs, and that sum is deposited in the trust account. A complaint is prepared and needs to be filed with the court. A check for the filing fee is drawn on the client's trust account and sent to the court with the complaint. The amount of the check is deducted from the $500 deposit.

Estate Proceeds

There are numerous financial transactions in a probate case. Expenses owed by the decedent before death must be paid, some of which must be paid immediately to preserve the assets of the estate. The heirs may deposit some money for payment of the expenses, or existing cash from the decedent's bank account may be used. If the decedent has income due at the time of death, the income is deposited in the estate trust account. Additionally, the estate may receive periodic income from the sale of its assets that is used for the expenses of the estate. These transactions are managed from the estate's trust account.

Since there are many transactions in a probate case, it is more convenient for bookkeeping purposes to open a separate trust account for large estates. Meticulous records must be kept of each transaction. When the estate is closed and the assets are disbursed to the heirs, cash assets are disbursed from the trust account so that the firm has a permanent record of the disbursements. When all expenses have been paid, the law firm may pay itself from the cash in the trust account and return the remainder to the heirs. When all transactions are completed, the estate trust account is closed.

Escrow Funds

There are various reasons a firm will receive funds in escrow on behalf of a client. Law firms that handle real estate transactions will accept a down payment for the property and keep those funds in the trust account pending transfer of the property. Also, if the firm represents a client who is sued and owes payments to a creditor, the client deposits the money for the payment in the firm's trust account. The payments are paid from the law firm's trust account so that there is a record that the payments were made.

Another example of escrow funds is when a dispute arises regarding a debt. In this case, payments are made to the firm's trust account pending resolution of the dispute. For example, a client is a tenant of an apartment building and has a dispute with the landlord regarding the habitability of the apartment. The client refuses to pay the rent until the problems are fixed, but her obligation for the rent continues. The client pays the rent to the law firm's trust account instead of to the landlord. The attorney will transfer the rent when the repairs have been made. This procedure shows the tenant's good faith and ensures that the rent money will be available when repairs are made.

Settlements

When a case is settled, the trust account is used to accept the funds of settlement or judgment. Often, insurance companies make a check payable to the client and the lawyer. The client endorses the check, and the lawyer places the funds in the trust account. From these funds, costs and expenses are paid, as are the attorney's fees owed on the case. Other expenses, such as medical liens, are also paid directly from these funds. The client receives the balance after expenses are paid. Disbursing funds from the trust account creates a record that the payments were made.

Judgments

Judgments are normally paid to and from the attorneys' trust accounts. When a firm represents a judgment creditor, the firm receives the proceeds of the judgment from either the judgment debtor's attorney's trust account or directly from the judgment debtor. The payments are paid to the judgment creditor and the attorney so that the funds can be deposited into the judgment creditor's attorney's trust account. The funds are disbursed after deducting costs, expenses, and attorneys' fees. All payments are monitored by the attorneys so that if a dispute should arise, there are accurate records of each payment. Additionally, most people prefer adversarial financial transactions to be completed with the assistance of an intermediary to eliminate misappropriation allegations. Attorneys' trust accounts are used for this purpose.

Fee Advances

ETHICS ALERT

ETHICS ALERT

There is a disagreement among bar associations regarding whether fee advances are to be deposited in the trust account or are the attorney's property. The majority of bar associations have taken the position that they are the property of the client and should be deposited in the trust account. *The attorney may not withdraw the funds until the fees are earned and a monthly accounting is sent to the client.* For example, a client pays an attorney an advanced fee of $2,000, which is prepayment for ten hours of the attorney's time. The first month, the attorney spent four hours on the case. The attorney may withdraw $800 from the trust account after sending an invoice to the client indicating that the withdrawal was made and the services provided for the payment. *If the attorney withdraws the money before the usual billing period, the attorney may be violating the code of professional responsibility.*

Nonrefundable nonchargeable, or true retainer, fees that secure an attorney's availability may be deposited directly into the attorney's operating account. These funds are considered "earned on receipt" and are not considered prepayment for the attorney's services. Therefore, it is not necessary to deposit them in the trust account.

MAINTAINING THE TRUST ACCOUNT

Each law firm employee has the obligation to make sure that the client funds account is accurate and in compliance with the Code of Professional Responsibility. Legal assistants are often given the responsibility of maintaining a trust account, especially in small firms.

Rules for maintaining a trust account vary from state to state. Some states have specific record-keeping requirements for the trust account and require lawyers to annually verify their compliance with the states' requirements. Legal malpractice insurance companies also have specific rules governing how trust accounts are maintained. Most billing and accounting software packages monitor trust accounts along with the firm's other accounting functions. Each software package has its own methods and features. However, it is important to check the applicable rules governing trust accounts before relying solely on the computer for trust account accounting functions. Some legal malpractice insurance companies require that manual records of the trust account be kept in addition to electronic records in case of computer failure, energy shortages, and other disasters.

The following sections outline the procedures to maintain the clients' funds trust account. It is impossible to give precise instructions on the use of automated accounting programs because of the vast differences among software programs. It is recommended that manual procedures be followed in addition to computer records so that valuable information is not lost. The nine steps outlined in the following sections are essential elements of proper trust fund accounting.

Preparing the Client Ledger Sheet

As soon as a client retains a firm, a client ledger sheet is prepared, such as the one shown in Exhibit 9.1. The client ledger sheet documents the amount of fees and costs billed, amount paid, and trust account funds received and disbursed. When the client is billed or pays the firm money, the transaction is documented on the client ledger card. If the client gives the firm money to deposit in the trust account, that transaction is also indicated on the client ledger card. *It is important that money deposited in the trust account be listed separately on the client ledger sheet* (see Exhibit 9.1).

Automated software programs automatically prepare a client ledger sheet after the client's information is input. These ledger sheets may also be maintained by hand, or a printout of each ledger sheet may be made each time a change is made. If a ledger sheet is printed after a change is made, the firm will always have a **hard copy** of current trust account information, which is important to maintain the integrity of the system.

Hard copy: A copy of computer records on a sheet of paper.

Maintaining Journals

Cash receipts journal: Record of all deposits and cash received.

A **cash receipts journal** and a **cash payments journal** are maintained for the trust account, examples of which are shown in Exhibit 9.2. All money received for the trust account is entered in the cash receipts journal, and all checks written from the trust account are entered in the cash payments journal.

When manually entering information into the journals, the following information should be included:

Cash payments journal: Record of all checks written or cash disbursed.

- ◆ Date of transaction
- ◆ Name of payer
- ◆ Name of client
- ◆ Name of case
- ◆ Amount of transaction
- ◆ Check number
- ◆ Purpose and description of transaction (e.g., deposition of Harry Snow)

The cash receipts journal and cash payments journal are automatically generated by accounting software packages. The features of each package vary. Trust account software needs to be able to apply debits and credits to an individual client. Some packages have this capability, while others do not. Some need special setup procedures to accommodate the details necessary for trust account transactions.

The person responsible for the trust account must be very careful to enter all the information about the transaction into the system so that the computer can categorize the transactions correctly. When a check is written or a deposit made, the computer will require that a specific account be entered so that the entry will be posted to the correct account. The manner in which these entries are made is crucial. If they are not done correctly, the information will not be posted against the appropriate client's account. *This problem will cause the attorney to be subject to trust account abuse allegations.*

For example, client A deposited $500 in the trust account. The firm was filing a complaint on behalf of client A and required a filing fee from the trust account. When the check was written, the computer asked for an account to apply the transaction against. If the transaction is applied to a "filing fees" account, it will not be debited against client A's funds unless the computer is specifically set up for this type of information. It would be very difficult to reconcile the trust account, especially when the trust account contains the funds of many clients.

Name Lila Peterson
Address 234 56th St., Palo Alto, CA 90000
Matter: *Peterson v. Johnson*

File No. 94-126R
Phone 555-1234

Date	Description	Chk. No.	FEES			COSTS			TRUST FUNDS		
			Charged	Rec'd.	Balance	Adv.	Rec'd.	Balance	Rec'd.	Paid	Balance
1/7/95	Rec'd. from client	739							$1,500.00		$1,500.00
2/1/95	Feb. billing		$465.00		$450.00	$ 56.92		$ 56.92			
2/1/95	Payment of fees	840		$465.00	-0-		$ 56.92	-0-		$521.92	$ 978.08
3/1/95	Mar. billing		$650.00		$650.00	$145.23		$145.23			
3/1/95	Payment of fees	851		$650.00	-0-		$145.23	-0-		$795.23	$ 182.85
4/1/95	Apr. billing		$295.00		$295.00	$ 31.90		$ 31.90			
4/1/95	Payment of fees	863		$182.85	$112.15					$182.85	-0-

EXHIBIT 9.1 Client Ledger Sheet

Trust Account Receipts Journal

Month of _____ 20 _____

Date	Source	Person or Entity With Interest in Funds	Case or File No.	Amount	Total Daily Deposit

Trust Account Payments Journal

Month of _____ 20 _____

Date	Check No.	Payee	Purpose	Person or Entity With Interest in Funds	Case or File No.	Amount

EXHIBIT 9.2 Transactions must be documented in the Trust Account Receipts Journal and the Trust Account Payments Journal.

The client ledger sheets, cash receipts journal, and cash payments journal must balance with the client funds account. When trust account bank statements are received each month, the statement must be reconciled immediately.

ETHICS ALERT

Communicating with Clients

Immediately on receipt of the funds, the client must be notified that the funds were received. Most codes of professional responsibility do not state a specific time period within which the client must be notified, indicating only that it be immediately or as soon as possible after receipt. Lawyers have been disciplined for their delay in notifying clients of receipt of funds. The time period that constitutes a delay is determined on a case-by-case basis.

Documenting Transactions

Often, checks for settlement of a case are made payable to both the client and the lawyer. If this is the case, the client must endorse the check before it can be deposited into the trust account for disbursement. If the client cannot come into the office to endorse the check, it should be sent to the client by certified mail and mailed back to the lawyer by certified mail. The lawyer then endorses the check and deposits the check into the trust account. If the lawyer endorses the check first and then mails the check to the client for endorsement, the check may be lost in the mail or subject to theft.

Before the check is deposited, copies of the deposit slip and the front and back of the check are made. A copy is filed in the client's file and a copy is filed in a trust account receipts file. A trust account receipts file is necessary in case of an account dispute and will come in handy when the account is reconciled. The deposit is then entered in the system on the client ledger sheet and journals. When entering the deposit, be sure to include the payer, check number, and exact date of deposit.

TECH TIPS

Clients Funds Account Software

Many accounting software products have a trust account module built into them. A few products are created specifically for the trust account.

Trust Accounting System by Software Technology, Inc., www.stilegal.com
Brief Accounting by Brief, www.briefaccounting.com
Trust Account Platinum by golden Omega Software, www.goldenomega.com

Disbursing Funds

A check must clear the bank before any funds are disbursed. Normally, the funds will clear the bank in ten business days, but this time period varies with each bank. Some banks will make the funds immediately available pending clearance if prior arrangements are made.

ETHICS ALERT

When the check clears the bank, the funds may be disbursed. *The funds must be disbursed promptly after receipt to avoid allegations of commingling.* The exact meaning of "promptly" is determined on a case-by-case basis. All funds must be disbursed by check so that the firm will have a record that the check was negotiated. The responsible attorney or office manager signs each check.

All disbursements should have some written documentation describing what the payment is for. Payments for medical liens or other expenses should be accompanied by an invoice or a written statement. Disbursements for payment of attorney's fees and costs may be made after a statement is prepared for the client. If the disbursements are for settlement of a contingency case, the firm will prepare a contingency case accounting, which was illustrated in Chapter 8. The trust account check for fees and costs must be immediately prepared and deposited into the firm's general operating account. *Funds for payment of attorney's fees and costs must not be commingled with client funds.* Removing these funds as soon after billing as possible after an accounting will avoid allegations of commingling.

ETHICS ALERT

Reconciling the Account

Each month, the bank sends the firm a statement of transactions of the account. The trust account must be reconciled to the bank statement immediately. The account must balance to the penny. If the account does not balance, it is important to determine the

---

BLACK, WHITE & GREENE
Attorneys at Law

February 1, 200x

Valued Client
234 56th St.
Anytown, CA 90000

Re: Client v. Johnson, et al.

Statement of Trust Accounts

January 1, 200x to January 31, 200x

Date	Description	Rec'd	Disbursed	Balance
1/2/199x	Received from client	$1,500.00		$1,500.00
1/15/199x	Filing fee, Sup. Court		$ 120.00	1,380.00
1/23/199x	Service of John Doe		34.00	1,346.00
1/30/199x	Legal fees for month of January		1,000.00	346.00
Balance as of January 31, 200x				$346.00

EXHIBIT 9.3 Statement of Trust Account

cause immediately. As stated previously, state bar associations may randomly audit trust accounts, and some may do so without notice. Keeping the trust account reconciled will ensure accurate record keeping of the account.

Preparing Monthly Statements

Each month, a statement must be sent to each client informing him or her of the status of their trust account. If the client is billed monthly, this statement can be included on his or her monthly bill. An example of a monthly statement of trust account status is shown in Exhibit 9.3.

Closing an Account

When a case has ended, whether by settlement or judgment, the client's trust account is ready to be closed. All the funds in the account must be disbursed before closing, and each transaction must be documented on the client ledger sheet. If there are any funds remaining in the account, they must be returned to the client. Most firms wait until all checks have cleared the bank before closing.

Closing an account does not mean that the client funds account is closed, just that client's portion of the account. When an account is closed, the client ledger sheet must reflect a zero balance in the trust account section, as shown in Exhibit 9.4. A final accounting is prepared for the client and inserted into the client's file.

Keeping Records

Records of a trust account must be kept for auditing purposes or in the event of a malpractice claim. Individual state bar associations have their own trust account record retention schedules. Normally, trust account records should be kept for at least five years after the account is closed.

Name: Lila Peterson

Address: 100 Park St., Palo Alto, CA 90000

Matter: *Peterson v. Johnson*

File No. 94-126R

Phone: 555-1234

Date	Description	Chk. No.	FEES			COSTS			TRUST FUNDS		
			Charged	Rec'd	Balance	Adv.	Rec'd.	Balance	Rec'd.	Paid	Balance
1/7/95	Rec'd from client	300							$ 1,500.00		$ 1,500.00
2/1/95	Feb. billing		$465.00		$450.00	$ 56.92		$ 56.92			
2/1/95	Payment of fees	840		$465.00	-0-		$ 56.92	-0-		$ 521.92	$ 978.08
3/1/95	Mar. Billing		$650.00		$650.00	$145.23		$145.23			
3/1/95	Payment of fees	851		$650.00	-0-		$145.23	-0-		$ 795.23	$ 182.85
4/1/95	Apr. billing		$295.00		$295.00	$ 31.90		$ 31.90			
4/1/95	Payment of fees	863		$182.85	$112.15					$ 182.85	-0-
5/1/95	May billing		$540.00		$652.15	$ 86.50		$118.40			
6/1/95	ABC Ins. Co.	2031							$15,000.00		$15,000.00
6/15/95	Attorney's fees	901		$652.15	-0-		$118.40	-0-		$ 770.55	14,229.45
6/15/95	XYZ depositions	902								$ 245.00	13,975.45
6/15/95	Dr. Baker, M.D.	903								$ 675.00	13,330.45
6/15/95	Client	904								13,300.45	-0-

EXHIBIT 9.4 Client Ledger Sheet 2

INTEREST ON LAWYERS' CLIENT FUNDS ACCOUNT

Lawyers establish their trust accounts in an interest-bearing account. However, the firm does not receive interest on clients' funds. This interest is sent to state bar associations to fund legal programs for the indigent. The funds generating interest, when considered as an individual client's money, would not generate much interest if held in separate client accounts either because the amounts are too small or because the money is held for too short a time. However, the aggregate of all client funds held in a trust account can generate a substantial amount of interest.

The IOLTA (Interest on Lawyers' Trust Accounts) program was begun in England, Canada, and Australia in the 1960s. In the United States, it was introduced in Florida and now exists in most states. States have been developing IOLTA programs since 1981, when Congress changed the banking laws to allow some checking accounts to bear interest. All states in the United States have an IOLTA program.

As of June 1998, IOLTA programs have funded legal services for about 1.7 million poor people through its funding of legal aid programs, about $150 million per year. In 1998, it was estimated that $1 billion in interest has gone to legal services organizations in its seventeen-year history. Without IOLTA funds, these programs would not exist.

There are three types of IOLTA participation:

◆ Mandatory: All lawyers in the state must participate in IOLTA.

◆ Voluntary: All lawyers may choose whether to participate in IOLTA.

◆ Opt-out: All lawyers must participate unless they affirmatively choose not to participate.

Client security fund: A fund established to reimburse clients who have been damaged because of their attorney's fraudulent abuse of the trust account.

The money received for interest is transferred to the state bar or state bar foundation to fund law-related public interest programs for the indigent, elderly, or disabled, including legal aid, victim assistance programs, and **client security funds.** A client security fund allows clients who have been damaged by an attorney's illegal use of trust account funds to be reimbursed for their loss. A client security fund was recommended by the ABA in 1959. Since that time, the majority of states have established a client security fund.

Many attorneys were not supportive of the IOLTA program because of the additional administrative tasks the program requires. However, banks in many states voluntarily transfer the funds to the appropriate state bar agency, therefore taking the management burden off the law firms.

Opponents of IOLTA programs feel that interest on client funds should be paid to the client. They contend that technology exists today that easily calculates each client's share of the earned interest. Consequently, the legality of IOLTA programs was challenged in 1998 in the case of *Phillips v. Washington Legal Foundation* (96-1578), which was heard by the U.S. Supreme Court. The Court ruled that interest earned on client funds held in IOLTA accounts is the private property of the client. In the ruling, Chief Justice William H. Rehnquist said, "While the interest income at issue here may have no economically realizable value to its owner, possession, control and disposition are nonetheless valuable rights that inhere in the property."

This ruling caused a panic for IOLTA programs in the United States. IOLTA proponents feel that the ruling was logical but impractical. Since many people have small amounts in the trust account, the effort involved in providing the clients with a few pennies of interest and in eliminating IOLTA programs does not make sense. The National Association of IOLTA Programs (NAIP) secured the services of a law firm to address issues concerning the ruling. The Conference of State Supreme Court Chief Justices issued a unanimous resolution urging "continued operation of IOLTA programs in every jurisdiction." As of this writing, cases are pending that will clarify the ruling. In the meantime, IOLTA programs continue to function as usual and are confident that the constitutionality of its programs will be upheld.

Information about your state's IOLTA program can be found on the Web sites of various state bar associations. The Cybersites sidebar lists some sites that have IOLTA information.

CYBERSITES

Finding IOLTA Information on the Web

Kentucky Bar Association—www.kybar.org

Maryland Legal Services Corporation—www.mlsc.org

Center for Civic Values—www.civicvalues.org

National Legal Aid and Defender Association—www.nlada.org

Minnesota Bar Association—www2.mnbar.org/iolta

West Virginia Bar Association—www.wvbar.org.

Arizona Bar Association—www.azbar.org

TRUST ACCOUNT ABUSES

ETHICS ALERT

The clients' trust account has been abused by lawyers who have used client funds without authorization. *Misuse of the client funds trust account is grounds for discipline.*

It is because of past abuses that state bars closely monitor client trust accounts. Lawyers' trust accounts are under the jurisdiction of each state bar association that has authority to audit trust accounts. Each state bar association has its own procedures and requirements for auditing lawyers' trust accounts. In some states, the state bar may audit a firm's trust account at any time without provocation or reason, and other states audit only those accounts whose abuse is suspected. The law firm must open its client funds account to the state bar on request. If the account is not found in proper order, the attorney or firm is subject to disciplinary proceedings. Some state bar associations require banks to automatically notify it of any trust account overdrafts or bounced checks, whether they were honored or not. An overdraft is an indication of mishandling a trust account.

Common trust account abuses include the following:

Misappropriation: Using funds in the trust account for personal purposes.

◆ *Misappropriation.* **Misappropriation** includes writing personal checks from a trust account. If an attorney writes a personal check from the trust account, the attorney is essentially stealing clients' money. For example, an attorney represented a client in litigation against a school district. The attorney failed to file a complaint within the statutory time period. She was afraid of a legal malpractice lawsuit, so she did not inform the client of the missed deadline. Instead, she told the client that she settled the case for $10,000 and would send the client a check for $6,000 after deducting $4,000 for her attorney's fees. She sent the client a check from her trust account, thereby paying the client with other clients' funds. The attorney was disbarred for misappropriation of funds (*In re Barbara Baron Gonzales* [1997]).

◆ *Paying office expenses with client funds.* Using funds from the trust account to cover business expenses, debts, or overhead.

◆ *Withdrawing funds from the trust account of one client to meet another client's trust account obligations.* For example, a client retains a lawyer to represent her in a lawsuit against her employer. She agreed to deposit $500 into the trust account for costs, but she could not pay the money for a month. Her complaint had to be filed immediately, so the lawyer wrote a check from the trust account to pay the filing fee, therefore using other clients' funds for payment of her expenses. The funds were reimbursed when the client made her payment. This activity is a violation of trust account rules.

Check kiting: Using other clients' funds until a check clears the bank.

◆ *Check kiting.* **Check kiting** is when money is withdrawn from a recently deposited check before the check has cleared the bank, thereby using other clients' funds to cover the check. For example, a client retains a lawyer to represent her in a lawsuit that her neighbor filed against her. She paid $200 into the trust account for costs. However, her answer to the complaint had to be filed

Commingle: Mixing one person's funds with another person's funds.

before her check cleared the bank. The lawyer wrote a check from the trust account to pay the filing fee for the answer, therefore using other clients' funds.

◆ *Commingling.* **Commingling** includes mixing law firm funds with client funds. The attorney may not commingle client funds with law firm funds or personal funds. The only time an attorney may deposit firm funds into the clients' trust account is to cover monthly bank charges, such as service charges and check charges. If these expenses are incurred, the firm must deposit just enough money to cover those charges each month. If more money than is needed is deposited, the firm is commingling its funds with client funds. Many banks will waive the monthly charge for a clients' trust account.

◆ *Failure to promptly notify clients of receipt of funds.* Clients must be notified as soon as funds are received on the client's behalf. Although the exact time period is not specifically indicated in rules of professional conduct, an average allowable time period is within thirty days.

◆ *Failure to promptly disburse funds.* All expenses that are due to be paid from a trust account must be paid promptly. Failure to do so will subject the attorney to disciplinary proceedings. For example, a lawyer represents a client in her lawsuit against the city. The case settled for $30,000, and the lawyer deposited the funds in the trust account. The lawyer was obligated to pay medical liens from the proceeds. The lawyer deducted the liens and his attorney's fee and mailed the client a check for the balance. The lawyer deposited his attorney's fee in the firm's operating account. However, the lawyer did not pay the medical liens for nineteen months. During that time, his trust account balance was under the total of the liens, indicating mishandling of client funds. The lawyer was disciplined (*Blair v. State Bar,* 47 Cal. 3d 448 [1988]).

◆ *Failure to provide clients with an accounting of trust account funds.* Attorneys are obligated to provide periodic accountings of a client trust fund account. If there is activity on the account, an accounting should be sent monthly. If there is no activity on the account, an accounting may be sent quarterly, depending on the circumstances.

ETHICS ALERT

Although the attorney is ultimately responsible for the condition of the trust account, balancing the account is often delegated to a secretary or legal assistant. *A legal assistant not familiar with trust funds accounting principles may be exposing the firm to serious liability if allowed to maintain the firm's client funds account.*

ETHICS ALERT

If the client terminates the attorney-client relationship, all funds in the client funds account that have not been earned must be immediately returned to the client. In most states, a lawyer must have a client's permission to apply funds in the trust account to an outstanding legal bill. If the bill is disputed, most states require that the attorney return the client's funds and take other action to collect the unpaid fee.

Conclusion

As this chapter illustrates, the proper management of the client funds account is extremely important. Attorneys who have abused their clients' trust funds have been severely disciplined by state bars. If an attorney who works for a law firm that is a partnership abuses the trust account, each partner may also be subject to disciplinary proceedings. Managing the client funds account accurately has many benefits, including reduced legal malpractice insurance costs, reduced ethics problems, reduced client complaints, and reduced stress and anxiety.

TRENDS ➤➤➤

How Paralegals Help Attorneys Manage the Trust Account

Paralegals help attorneys manage the clients funds account by:

- Keeping the file organized to track expenses and receipts

- Maintaining a good file review system so each file is reviewed at least once a month.

- Inform the attorney when a settlement check, or other money that is to be deposited into the trust account, is received.

- When settlement checks come in, make sure they are deposited into the clients funds account immediately.

- Make sure all medical and other lienholders are paid from the proceeds of the case. Do not wait until directed to pay the liens.

- If there is a dispute as to the amount of a lien, all undisputed amounts must be paid. As soon as the dispute is resolved, the appropriate accounting functions are performed.

- Make sure the attorney's fee is deducted from the proceeds when funds are disbursed.

- Prepare an accounting for the client describing the transactions in the trust account.

- Make sure all client ledgers are accurate and up-to-date.

- Balance the trust account as soon as the bank statement is received.

SUMMARY

The client trust fund is a bank account established exclusively for client funds. The attorney and law firm are bound by professional codes of state bar associations to keep client funds completely separate from the office and personal bank accounts. A firm usually has one account for the funds of all its clients, except for large cases that require their own account. Examples of the type of funds held in the trust account are funds for costs and expenses, estate proceeds, escrow funds, settlements, judgment payments, and fee advances.

Rules for maintaining a trust account vary from state to state. Nine steps are essential elements of proper trust fund accounting: preparing a client ledger sheet, maintaining journals, communicating with clients, documenting transactions, disbursing funds, reconciling the account, preparing monthly statements, closing the account, and keeping accurate records.

The IOLTA program has been in effect for many years. Each state bar association determines its participation in IOLTA. The money received for interest is transferred to the state bar or state bar foundation to fund law-related public interest programs such as legal aid, victim assistance programs, and client security funds.

The legality of IOLTA programs was challenged in 1998 in the case of *Phillips v. Washington Legal Foundation,* which was heard by the U.S. Supreme Court. The Court ruled that interest earned on client funds held in IOLTA accounts is the private property of the client. Cases are pending that will clarify the ruling. In the meantime, IOLTA programs continue to function as usual and are confident that the constitutionality of its programs will be upheld.

Attorneys' trust accounts have been abused, so state bar associations closely monitor them. The attorney may not misappropriate, pay office expenses or other clients' expenses with client funds, participate in check kiting, or commingle client funds with law firm funds. Furthermore, attorneys must promptly notify clients of receipt of funds and promptly disburse funds. They must also provide clients with an accounting of trust funds. If a client terminates an attorney-client relationship, all funds in the client funds account that have not been earned must be immediately returned to the client.

CHAPTER ILLUSTRATION

Tricia, the office manager for Black, White & Greene, is responsible for the financial management for the firm. She delegates the firm's banking functions to the secretary, Pam Cody. Pam makes sure that all deposits are documented and that the bank accounts are reconciled.

Patrizia Boen, the attorney responsible for the firm's personal injury cases, settled a case for client

Sheldon Goodman. She negotiated the settlement with Fred Hull, a claims adjuster for Good Hands Insurance Company. Before accepting the settlement offer, she discussed it with Sheldon, who agreed to the settlement figure. Fred told Patrizia that the settlement check would be mailed that day in the names of the client and the firm. Patrizia told her secretary, Pam Cody, to telephone the client to have him come into the office in one week to endorse the settlement check. She was sure that the check would be there in a couple of days and would surely be there in one week.

Before Sheldon's appointment, Patrizia asked Pam whether the check had arrived. Pam replied that she had seen it but did not know where it was. She looked all over for it but could not find it. It was not on her desk, on Patrizia's desk, or in the file. Patrizia called Fred and asked him whether the check had been mailed. Fred told her that it was mailed to the firm one week ago and verified that the check was mailed to the correct address. The check was somewhere in the office, and Patrizia told Pam to find it.

Pam was searching for the check when Sheldon arrived to endorse it. "Have you found that check yet?" asked Patrizia.

"No," said Pam. "I've asked everybody. Kay [the file clerk] said she thought she saw a check come in when she was opening the mail, but she can't remember what case it was on. I'm having her go back through the daily logs for the week to find it."

"Okay. Sheldon is waiting in my office to sign the check. I'll have to tell him we are looking for it. This is very embarrassing. How can we lose a check for $45,000?"

Patrizia went back to her office to tell Sheldon the news. "The check has been misplaced. We are in the process of tracking it down. Normally, we are very organized and have systems in place to avoid this problem. I don't know what happened here. It may have been lost in the mail. I'll call you when we have the check. I'm sorry you made a trip down here for nothing."

"What! Can't find a check for $45,000? I took the morning off work to come here and missed an important meeting! Okay, I'll come back when you have the check."

Embarrassed, Patrizia apologized again and went into the file room, where Kay was searching the firm's daily mail logs. "Have you found that check?" asked Patrizia.

"I see here on the daily mail log that a check from Good Hands Insurance Company came in last Thursday. I've searched the file room, and it's not here. I'm sure I put it on your desk with the rest of the mail," said Kay.

"I've searched my office and Pam's desk. It's nowhere to be found. Okay, let's go back over everything we did last Thursday and find that check!"

Pam, Patrizia, and Kay spent hours tracing their activities on Thursday. They searched all files and finally found the check. It was in another file that Patrizia was working on that day. The check was picked up with other papers and put in the wrong file. Pam called Sheldon back to come in and endorse the check. He was not happy about leaving work early to do so.

Sheldon endorsed the check. "When will I get my money?" asked Sheldon.

Patrizia answered, "We have to wait ten business days for the check to clear before we disburse the funds."

"Ten business days? Boy, that's a long time. Why? Good Hands has millions. I'm sure the check is good. I need my money now!" said Sheldon.

"I know you're anxious for the money, Sheldon, but there's nothing I can do about it. The state bar has specific rules that require us to clear the check before disbursing funds from the trust account."

"Alright, I'll be in two weeks from today to pick up my check," said Sheldon.

Before Pam left for the day, she prepared the check for deposit. She copied the front and back and entered the amount on the client ledger sheet and journals. She prepared the deposit slip and put the check in the mail pick-up area to go out in the morning mail.

Two weeks later, Sheldon arrived on time for his appointment to disburse the funds. Patrizia did an accounting of the disbursements and had the checks ready when Sheldon arrived. The accounting showed the amount of settlement, payment for Sheldon's medical expenses, payment for costs and expenses, and her attorney's fees. Sheldon was happy to get the check to put a down payment on a new house he was purchasing.

Pam mailed the checks for the medical liens and deposited the attorney's fees into the firm's general operating account. One week later, Patrizia received a call from Sheldon. He was very upset.

"What kind of law firm are you running over there anyway?" exclaimed Sheldon. "My check bounced! What the———is going on?"

"Bounced? Are you sure? That can't be. Good Hands has plenty of money. I'll look into it and call you back," said Patrizia.

In a panic, Patrizia called Pam into her office. "Sheldon's trust account check bounced. Find out what's going on," Patrizia said.

Pam called the bank and inquired about the trust account balance. She discovered that it was overdrawn.

"Are you sure you deposited the check?" Patrizia asked Pam.

"Yes," responded Pam. "I remember specifically depositing the check. I made copies and documented the ledger. I specifically remember because I had to stay late so it would be ready for the morning mail. It must have been lost in the mail," said Pam.

"Mail rarely gets lost anymore," said Patrizia. "I'll check with Fred."

Patrizia called Fred and told him the problem. He asked Fred to cancel the check and issue another one. Fred checked his records and informed Patrizia that the check had already been cashed.

Patrizia was surprised. "Send me a copy of the front and back of the check. Something's very wrong here."

"Okay," said Fred. "But it'll take a couple of weeks to get a copy from the accounting department."

"I can't wait two weeks!" said Patrizia angrily. "I have checks bouncing out of the trust account. I have an angry client who is ready to complain to the state bar. On top of that, I start a big trial on Friday. Get me that check now!"

"Okay. I'll see what I can do," said Fred.

That afternoon, Pam received numerous telephone calls and complaints from Sheldon's doctors complaining that their checks bounced. The whole firm was in an uproar.

The next day, Fred faxed a copy of the check to Patrizia. "Oh no," said Patrizia as she went to Tricia's office. She showed Tricia the check. "Here's the problem. The check was deposited into the firm's operating account. Pam used the wrong deposit slip. We need to get those funds out of there immediately! Write a check from the operating account for $45,000 and get it into the trust account right away."

Tricia wrote the check and took it to the bank personally. Patrizia called Sheldon and told him what happened. She apologized and told him that she would prepare new checks. She had Pam call all the medical lienholders to apologize and tell them that they would receive new checks.

Patrizia issued new checks and had them ready when Sheldon came in. When Sheldon arrived, Pa-

trizia handed him the check. "Thanks," said Sheldon. "Oh, by the way, I received this lien from my doctor yesterday. It took him three months to send it to me. I forgot to tell you about it. We need to send him a check also."

Patrizia looked at the lien and sighed. "Well, okay, we'll pay it, but we'll have to cancel all of these checks and recalculate the disbursement. We use the net fee accounting method, which means that my fee and your share is deducted after liens and costs. My fee has now changed, and your share is different now, too. Can you wait while I recalculate this and prepare a new statement?"

Patrizia prepared a new statement and new checks and gave Sheldon the check. "Are you sure this one won't bounce?" asked Sheldon. "I can't tell you the problems I've had with this. My house fell out of escrow, and I'm in a real mess. I think you should pay for all the extra expenses I've incurred because of this problem."

"I'm sure we can work something out," said Patrizia.

Patrizia was relieved that the settlement was completed. She instructed Pam to close the trust account for Sheldon as soon as all the checks cleared the bank.

Three weeks later, Pam received the bank statement for the trust account and was reconciling the account. She noticed that a check for a medical lien from one of Sheldon's doctors was not cashed, so she called to inquire about it. She learned that they did not receive the check. "It must have been lost in the mail," Pam thought.

She went into Patrizia's office to tell her the news. She knew that Patrizia would not want to hear about this problem. As she walked in her office, Patrizia received a telephone call on her speaker phone. "Hello, Ms. Boen?"

"Yes," said Patrizia.

"This is Alice Verstegan from the state bar. We were informed by your bank that you had an overdraft in your trust account . . ."

CHAPTER REVIEW

1. What is segregation of cash?

2. What types of funds are deposited in a client funds account?

3. Why would a client have a separate, individual trust account?

4. When a firm is paid an advanced fee, when is it paid?

5. What are the nine steps of maintaining a trust account?

6. Why must trust account records be kept after it is closed?

7. What is IOLTA?

8. What are the three types of IOLTA participation?

9. For what are IOLTA funds used?

10. What are the eight ways a clients funds account is abused?

EXAMPLES FOR DISCUSSION

1. The Money Is in the Trust Account

Ellen is the legal assistant and office manager for Stephen Bristol, a sole proprietor. She was preparing a motion for client Fisher that must be filed with the court that afternoon. A $25 filing fee must accompany the motion. She prepared a check for the filing fee out of the office operating account and presented it to Mr. Bristol for signature. Mr. Bristol refused to sign the check, stating that payroll was due on Friday and that he was concerned there would not be enough money in the account to cover employee taxes. He instructed Ellen to take the money out of the trust account.

Ellen had checked the ledger card for client Fisher and informed Mr. Bristol that there was only $17 in Ms. Fisher's account. Mr. Bristol told Ellen that there was plenty of money in that account from other clients. He told Ellen to bill Ms. Fisher for the additional $8 and they could replace the money when she paid it.

1. Are Mr. Bristol's instructions ethical?
2. What should Ellen do?
3. What are some alternatives to the problem?

2. Those Pesky Little Details

Stephen Bristol, attorney for client Jane DeUlloa, settled her personal injury case for $45,000. The settlement check was made payable to Jane and Stephen. Stephen instructed Ellen, his legal assistant, to contact Jane so that she could come into the office to sign the check. When she did, Jane told Ellen that she was on her way to the airport for a three-week vacation to Europe and could not come into the office to endorse the check. Stephen was anxious to negotiate the check so that his attorney's fees could be paid as soon as possible. He needed the money to pay his state bar dues that were due next week. The check had to be deposited as soon as possible so that it would clear the bank in enough time to meet the deadline. He told Ellen to sign Jane's name to the back of the check and to deposit it. "Jane won't mind," he said. "She's as anxious as I am to obtain the funds."

1. Are Mr. Bristol's instructions ethical?
2. What should Ellen do?
3. What are some alternatives to the problem?

3. Does Interest Belong to the Client?

In light of the U.S. Supreme Court's ruling regarding IOLTA funds, discuss the following.

1. Do you think clients should be paid interest on funds in an attorney's trust account? If so, why? If not, why not?
2. If interest is the client's property, what will happen to legal aid programs for the poor?
3. If IOLTA funds are not available to fund legal aid programs, what are some alternatives?

ASSIGNMENTS

1. Make a client ledger sheet like the one shown in Exhibit 9.4 Document the following transactions on the client ledger sheet:
   a. 2/25/xx—Client retained firm and deposited $2,500 into the client funds account for advanced fees and costs.
   b. 3/1/xx—Billed client for $475 fees, which was paid out of the trust account.
   c. 3/10/xx—Filed complaint; filing fee $120 paid from trust account.
   d. 4/1/xx—Billed client for $860 in fees and $145 in costs; paid out of trust account.
   e. 5/1/xx—Billed client for $525 in fees and $27.80 in costs; paid out of trust account.
   f. 5/15/xx—Paid Fast Fingers Deposition Service $345 for deposition costs; paid out of trust account.
   g. 6/1/9x—Billed client for $395 fees and $15.20 costs; paid out of trust account.

   What is the balance of fees owed? Costs owed? Trust account? Prepare a statement of account like the one shown in Exhibit 9.3.

2. Contact your state bar association and obtain a copy of its rules and requirements for trust accounts. Prepare a memorandum to your instructor about the rules and recommend trust account maintenance procedures accordingly.

3. Information about disciplined attorneys is often published in state bar association periodicals. Obtain your state bar's magazine or periodical and review the section on disciplined attorneys. Note the cases in which attorneys are disciplined for trust account abuses. Prepare a report for the class on the attorneys' abuses and the discipline imposed.

SELF-TEST

How well did you grasp the material in the chapter? Test yourself by answering the following questions and check your answers against the answers found in Appendix A.

1. For what purpose is a client funds trust account established?
2. What is a fiduciary?
3. Who makes the rules concerning a client funds trust account?
4. What is segregation of cash?
5. How many trust accounts do firms have for their clients?
6. When is an individual trust account established for just one client?
7. What is probate?
8. What types of funds are held in a trust account?
9. Why are escrow funds held in a trust account?
10. Why are expenses of a case paid from the trust account?
11. Why do people prefer that adversarial financial transactions be handled through a trust account?
12. When may an attorney withdraw advance fee funds from the trust account?
13. What type of fees do not require to be deposited in the trust account?
14. Why are true retainer fees not required to be deposited in the trust account?
15. Who is often given the responsibility of maintaining a trust account?
16. What entity may require that manual trust account records be maintained?
17. Why keep manual records of a trust account?
18. What are the nine steps of proper trust fund accounting?
19. What is a client ledger sheet?
20. How are trust fund monies indicated on the client ledger sheet?
21. What is a hard copy?
22. What is a cash receipts journal?
23. What is a cash payments journal?
24. What seven items must be entered into the journals?
25. With what must the client ledger sheet and journals be balanced?
26. When should a trust account be reconciled?
27. When must a client be notified of the receipt of funds?
28. If a check is made payable to the client and lawyer, who must endorse the check first? Why?
29. If the check is mailed to the client for endorsement, how should the check be mailed?
30. Before a check is deposited into the trust account, what must be done?

31. Where are copies of the check filed?
32. What is a trust account receipts file?
33. What information about a deposit is inserted on the client ledger sheet?
34. What must happen before a check may be written against a deposit?
35. When must funds be disbursed?
36. Who signs a trust account check?
37. What must each disbursement have?
38. When should payment for attorneys' fees be deposited in the firm's operating account?
39. When is a trust account reconciled with a bank statement?
40. How is accurate record keeping of the trust account ensured?
41. When should a firm send a trust account statement to a client?
42. When is a trust account closed?
43. What do most firms do before closing a trust account?
44. When a client's account is closed, how is it reflected on the client ledger sheet?
45. Why are trust account records kept?
46. For how long should trust account records be kept?
47. Who receives interest derived from trust accounts?
48. For what is interest used?
49. What does IOLTA stand for?
50. In what countries did IOLTA have its origin?
51. What state was the first state in the United States to have an IOLTA program?
52. What are the three types of IOLTA participation?
53. Who receives interest derived from attorneys' trust accounts?
54. What types of programs do IOLTA funds sponsor?
55. What is a client security fund?
56. Why were many attorneys not supportive of the IOLTA program?
57. What is the name of the case that challenged the legality of IOLTA programs?
58. What was the Supreme Court's ruling?
59. What did the Conference of State Supreme Court Chief Justices say?
60. What has happened to IOLTA programs since the Supreme Court's ruling?
61. What happens to an attorney who abuses the trust account?
62. Who audits attorneys' trust accounts?
63. When are trust accounts audited?
64. Some state bar associations require that banks notify them of what event?
65. An overdraft in a trust account is an indication of what?

66. What are the common abuses of the client funds account?

67. What is misappropriation?

68. If an attorney writes a personal check from the trust account, what is he or she doing?

69. What office expense may be paid from the trust account?

70. What is check kiting?

71. What is commingling?

72. When may an attorney deposit a firm's funds into the trust account?

73. Who is ultimately responsible for the trust account?

74. Why must a legal assistant be familiar with trust account accounting principles?

75. If a client terminates the attorney-client relationship, what must be done with the funds in the trust account?

76. May an attorney apply funds in the trust account to an outstanding legal fee?

77. If an attorney in a partnership abuses the trust account, who may be subject to discipline?

78. What are the benefits of managing a trust account accurately and effectively?

KEY WORDS

Cash payments journal
Cash receipts journal
Check kiting

Client security fund
Commingle
Hard copy

Misappropriation
Segregation of cash

CHAPTER

10

Technology in the Law Office

OBJECTIVES

After completion of this chapter, a student should be able to do the following:

◆ Define the types of software most commonly used in a law office.

◆ Describe the origin of the Internet.

◆ Understand the essential elements of access to the Internet and the factors that contributed to its growth.

◆ Describe a Web site and its elements.

◆ Locate information on the Web.

◆ Search for information on the Web.

◆ Bookmark a Web site.

◆ Determine whether information on the Web is reliable.

◆ Know the features and benefits of an intranet and an extranet.

◆ Protect the confidentiality of information transmitted via the Internet.

◆ Subscribe to a listserv or newsgroup.

◆ Exhibit good netiquette.

◆ Write an appropriate e-mail message.

◆ Manage e-mail messages.

◆ Identify a potential ethical problem of a Web site.

INTRODUCTION

Technology is a tool that is used by legal professionals to deliver its product to a client. Effectively using this tool affects the quality of those services. It is necessary for lawyers and support staff to learn the tools and to learn them well. It is essential that all members of the legal team become proficient users of technology.

The technological advances made in the 1990s have transformed the average law office. The Internet and its technology have revolutionized the way law is practiced today. Before Internet technology, we were limited in our use of technology. Now, a wide variety of new technological opportunities are available to us. The first decade of the new millennium promises to excite us with even more technological advances.

The introduction of new technologies and rapid changes in existing technologies have been both a blessing and a curse. Upgrading existing technology and implementing new technology requires a tremendous capital investment as well as trained computer specialists to manage a firm's technology. While streamlining many tasks and automating routine functions, technology has placed new challenges on the legal team.

The primary challenge is keeping current with the latest technology. It is difficult for law firms, and for business in general, to keep up with the rapid changes in technology. New technologies are being developed faster than we can learn about them, and products become obsolete within months of their debut. As soon as one becomes proficient with a software product, it is upgraded to include new features that must be learned. This requires an investment of an employee's time and a firm's resources to train employees. To be trained adequately, employees must be trained often.

Another challenge is managing information. The legal team now has access to the information superhighway: the Internet. The Internet is exploding with information to enhance the practice of law. While access to this information enhances the delivery of legal services to a client, it has resulted in "information overload." The information must be managed properly in order for members of the legal team to be able to locate it. This has introduced new methods of information management of which all members of the legal team must be knowledgeable. Many legal professionals have difficulty with implementing new methods of information management.

Internet technologies have also increased the speed with which we receive and process information. Information is transmitted in seconds rather than days, and this increases the pressures on the legal team. These pressures require increased competence of law firm employees. Clients are increasingly intolerant of delays and mistakes.

Paralegals must be familiar with the common software used in legal offices and are expected to be able to operate the firm's computer system. The 1998 Technology Survey conducted by the National Federation of Paralegal Associations (NFPA) revealed that 55 percent of responding paralegals make software purchase decisions and that 42 percent of responding paralegals make hardware buying decisions for their firms. The 1999 Technology Survey conducted by *Legal Assistant Today* magazine revealed that 99.82 percent of paralegals use computers on a daily basis, with 46.4 percent classifying their computer skills as above average. It also revealed that technologically above-average paralegals earned an average of $3,197 a year more than technologically below-average paralegals.

This chapter will focus on the aspects of technology most frequently found in law offices. Since we are in the twenty-first century, it is assumed that the average person is knowledgeable about the basics of twentieth-century technology, such as computer hardware, software, and fax machines. First, this chapter will discuss the software most commonly found in law offices today and then the Internet and its impact on the legal profession. Next,this chapter will review intranets and extranets and how they are used in the law office. Finally, this chapter will discuss how emerging technologies have affected ethical rules and guidelines.

COMMON LAW OFFICE SOFTWARE

There are various types of software and thousands of software applications available in the legal marketplace to accommodate almost every aspect of a law office's functions, from specific practice areas to management tasks. Software applications can do almost anything, from assembling documents to helping a lawyer develop a trial strategy. As you are reading this, new software applications are being developed to further streamline legal tasks.

Software applications are developed specifically for the operating system used by the firm's computers. There are currently three major operating systems: Windows, Macintosh, and Unix.

Microsoft's Windows operating system is the most popular and widely used operating system used in law offices today. It has its origin in an operating system that was used in the 1970s and 1980s called MS-DOS (Microsoft Disk Operating System). Since Windows is based on the MS-DOS operating system, MS-DOS can be accessed from the Windows operating system. Most software in use today is designed for the Windows operating system.

Macintosh operating system is used exclusively on Macintosh computers manufactured by Apple Computer. It was the first operating system to use a graphical user interface and "point and click" technology. For many years, it was the most user-friendly operating system available. The Windows operating system is very similar to the Macintosh operating system.

The Unix operating system was created for computer programmers developing software. It is not as easy to use as Windows and is generally used by very large computers and servers. Unix is not used in most law offices.

A new operating system, Linux, emerged in late 1990s and is gaining prominence in the world of operating systems. Linux, distributed by Red Hat Software, was developed between 1991 and 1994 by Linus Torvalds, a student at the University of Helsinki. It is a variant of the Unix operating system and is used by some businesses as an alternative to the Windows operating system. The operating system is expected to grow at the rate of 25 percent by 2003.

Software applications are either custom or off-the-shelf. A custom software application is created exclusively for a law firm. It is created by computer programmers according to the parameters set by the firm's management. Employees using custom software are trained on its use by the software programmers. Off-the-shelf applications are created by software companies who market and distribute the software to the public. Training manuals are included with the software.

Some software manufacturers have developed **integrated software** applications. Integrated software combines many software applications into one program. An advantage of an integrated system is that the commands in the software are uniform, making the program easy to use. A disadvantage to integrated systems is that the individual features are generally less powerful than an individual application.

Manufacturers also "bundle" software together in one package, called office suites. Office suites combine several separate software applications, such as word processing, spreadsheet, database, and presentation programs, into one package. The applications have similar interfaces that interact with one another, making them easily integrated. This reduces training time and makes the various features of the software easier to use. It is also less expensive than purchasing each application individually. A popular office suite manufactured by Microsoft, known as Office 2000, consists of Microsoft Word (word processing), Excel (spreadsheet), Access (database) PowerPoint (presentation), and Outlook (personal information manager). Office suites can also be purchased with just two or three of the applications rather than all the ones listed here.

Most law firms use off-the-shelf computer applications and office suites. There are standard software applications used in a law office. The most common applications are word processing, spreadsheet, database, time and billing, case management (docket control), litigation support, substantive systems, court form generators, and browser.

Integrated software: A program that combines many different software applications into one program to make it easier to use.

Word Processing

Word processing software has been a standard application used in law firms since the 1960s. In the 1960s and 1970s, law firms had separate word processing departments that prepared only long, complicated documents, such as contracts and leases. In the 1980s, word processing programs became easier, eliminating the need for a separate department. Word processing tasks were given to clerical staff, mainly to secretaries. In the 1990s, all legal support staff were responsible for some word processing, and in the new millennium, everyone in the firm now uses word processing in one way or another.

The two most popular word processing systems used in law offices today are Corel's WordPerfect and Microsoft's MS Word. Until the late 1990s, WordPerfect was the standard word processor for law firms, with 97 percent of small firms and 84 percent of large firms using it. Word was the standard for corporate legal departments and other businesses. Since that time, however, many law firms have switched to Word not because it is a better product but because of the following:

◆ Firms use the Windows operating system, and because Microsoft makes both products, they feel that Word integrates better with Windows.

◆ Most clients use Word, and the firm can easily exchange documents with clients via disk or e-mail.

◆ Third-party software for WordPerfect, such as document management programs, are not as abundant as those for Word.

Both Word and WordPerfect contain a number of features that are used to create appealing documents. They both make preparing legal documents, such as pleadings, easy. In addition to producing the written word, one can also insert documents prepared in other applications, such as a spreadsheet, into the document. One can also insert multimedia into the document, such as video clips and sound. Features previously found in desktop publishing software are now found in the common word processor, making it an extremely functional software program.

Add-ons (plug-ins): A software application that can be purchased to enhance the features of another software application.

Software has been developed that adds features to the word processing program. These are called **add-on** (or **plug-in**) software. An example of a popular add-on is Hot-Docs by Capsoft Development Corporation. Hot Docs software consists of legal documents that are already prepared. The program uses the word processor's merge capabilities to create templates with customized prompt screens. This add-on allows routine documents to be produced by the word processor quickly and easily.

Spreadsheets

A spreadsheet application, such as Microsoft Excel, is used to crunch numbers. It is used in cases in which long, complicated accountings are prepared, such as a probate case. A typical spreadsheet application also prepares charts, graphs, and reports on the basis of the data. A spreadsheet program has numerous other uses.

Database

A database application, such as Microsoft Access, is a powerful application used by law firms and other businesses to manage information. Law firms use a database for its client list, to log marketing efforts, and to manage its brief bank. Once the information is input into a database, it can be managed in a number of ways. A firm can search a client database to check for conflicts, search a brief bank to find a document, and sort the information into various groups. There are a number of other uses for a database.

Time and Billing

Time and billing software is used by all the timekeepers in a firm. It prepares timekeeping reports and numerous other management reports. The timekeeping system is connected to the firm's billing system so that client invoices can be automatically generated. It is a very powerful program and is essential to every law office. More specific aspects of the software are discussed in Chapters 7 and 8.

Case Management and Docket Control

Case management software, also known as docket control software, is used to control calendars, monitor deadlines, and track essential law firm tasks. There are many case management software packages, each with different features. Abacus, the most popular docket control software in 1999, controls deadlines and calendars events critical to the effective management of a case. Deadlines found in court rules and civil procedure laws are programmed into the software and are automatically applied to a client's case. For example, thirty days after a complaint is served, an answer is due. The program automatically calculates the due date and enters it into the program. The program will warn the legal team of the approaching deadline so that the answer can be prepared before the due date.

This automatic calendaring feature has many benefits. It guards against missed deadlines, reduces employee time to enter due dates, and is updatable if the rules are changed. The program prints various types of case management reports. It allows users to program dates that are far in the future, such as statutes of limitations. If an event is scheduled that conflicts with an earlier entry, the program will alert the user of a conflict. It also has other features, such as document assembly and conflicts-of-interest checking. Case management software is more specifically described in Chapter 12.

Litigation Support

Litigation support applications, such as Summation Blaze, manage a complex litigation case. It keeps all necessary documents and information accessible for review, summarization, and organization, allowing the legal team to maintain control of various aspects of the case. It also allows information to be retrieved in many different ways that aids the lawyer in trial preparation and presentation. Litigation support systems follow an attorney into the courtroom where he or she can access all the information needed in seconds.

Complex litigation cases often involve thousands and sometimes millions of documents. These documents must be reviewed and organized in a manner that allows the legal team fast access to them. By inputting each document into a litigation support database, the information can be screened, sorted, and located quickly.

Scanned: Entering text or graphics into a computer by electronically changing the characters into a computer-readable format.

There are four types of litigation support software: abstract, full-text retrieval, document imaging, and a combination thereof. A document abstract system prepares an abstract, or summary, of a document's contents. A full-text retrieval contains the entire document instead of a summary. Document imaging allows documents to be electronically **scanned** into the computer. A combination has two and perhaps all three features.

Substantive Software Applications

Substantive law software, also known as legal specific software, is developed for use in a specific area of law. There are hundreds of software applications that aid a legal team in the practice of various areas of law. There is software that prepares a person's will or trust, prepares bankruptcy documents, manages collection cases, prepares family law documents, and prepares compliance forms.

For example, a bankruptcy software package directs the user in inserting all applicable information and will prepare the bankruptcy petition, schedules, and other required documents from the data. The forms are printed on a laser printer. The software keeps all information about a case in one place. Commerce Clearing House Incorporated (CCH) developed a software package, Section 16 Compliance Assistant, that helps a firm's clients comply with Security Exchange Commission (SEC) regulations. It helps the user prepare the forms and electronically files the forms directly with the SEC. Examples of the various types of substantive software available are shown in the Tech Tips sidebar.

Court Forms Generating

All the various courts require attorneys to use specific forms. These forms are mandated by a state agency responsible for designing the forms. In the early 1990s, law firms had to order these forms and keep a supply of all forms on hand. If the form was changed, a new supply had to be obtained. Managing court forms for the various courts was a headache for firm managers. Now, court forms are prepared by specific software packages, such as Proforma. The forms software is stored on the firm's server and are accessible by each workstation. The software program guides the user in preparing the forms, and they are printed on the firm's laser printer. Whenever there is a change in a form, the software is updated to accommodate the change. Forms-generating software not only made preparing the forms easier but made storage and management of the forms unnecessary as well.

TECH TIPS
Substantive Law Software

The following is a sample of related software:

Bankruptcy
> *Best Case Bankruptcy:* Best Case Solutions, Inc.
> *Bankrupted:* Blumberg Excelsior—www.blumberg.com
> *EZ Filing:* Zimmerman & Mohr, L.L.C.—www.ezfiling.com
> *Bankruptcy Plus:* Cornerstone Computer Group, Inc—www.cornerstone.com

Business Analysis
> *Business Insight 5.0:* Business Resource Software, Inc.

Collection
> *Easy Soft:* Easy Soft, Inc.—www.easysoft-usa.com
> *Abacus Totality:* Abacus Data Systems, Inc.—www.abacuslaw.com

Compliance
> *Lexpedite:* Lexis Document Services—www.netlds.com
> *ProFormWare:* ProformWare, Inc.—www.proformware.com
> *Section 16 Compliance Assistant:* CCH Incorporated

Corporate Law
> *Corporate Focus:* Two-Step Software, Inc.—www.twostep.com

Estate Planning
> *Estate Plan Plus:* ProBATE Software Publishing Co., Inc.—www.probate-software.com

Immigration
> *ImmForms Plus:* West Group—www.westgroup.com

Intellectual Property
> *WorldMark:* IPN, Ltd.
> *MicroPatent:* MicroPatent—www.micropat.com

Litigation
> *21st Century Lawyer:* Computerized Litigation Control Systems, Inc.

Personal Injury
> *Attorney's Medical Advantage:* West Group—www.westgroup.com

Probate and Fiduciary
> *Probate Plus:* ProBATE Software Publishing Co., Inc.—www.probate-software.com

Real Estate
> *Easy Soft:* Easy Soft, Inc.—www.easysoft-usa.com

Securities
> *Liveedgar:* Global Securities Information, Inc.
> *SECNOW:* West Group—www.westgroup.com

Tax
> *706 Plus—709 Plus:* ProBATE Software Publishing—www.probate-software.com

Software mentioned in this sidebar is for informational purposes only and is not for the purpose of endorsing products.

Browser

Browser: A software program that allows viewing and interaction with various kinds of resources available on the Internet.

Browsers are software programs that allow viewing and interaction with various kinds of resources available on the Internet. A browser is essential software for law firms. As of this writing, there are two major browsers: Netscape's Netscape Navigator and Microsoft's Internet Explorer. We will discuss browsers in more detail in the section on the Internet.

TECH TIPS

Most Popular Law Office Software Applications

According to the *Legal Assistant Today* Technology Survey conducted in 1999, the following products were the most prominently used software applications in a law office:

Word processors: WordPerfect by Corel (50.8%) and MS Word by Microsoft (46.4%)

Office suites: Corel Office 7 (www.corel.com) and Microsoft Office 97 Professional (www.microsoft.com/office)

Document generation: Hot Docs (www.capsoft.com)

Litigation support: Summation (47.4%) (www.summation.com)

Time and billing: Timeslips (48.6%) (www.timeslips.com)

Case management: Abacus Law (38.5%) (www.abacuslaw.com)

Operating system: Windows 95/98 (67.3%) (www.microsoft.com)

THE INTERNET

The Internet is a tremendous tool for individuals and organizations. Through the Internet, we have access to vast amounts of information at any time of the day or night through our computers. The Internet has been responsible for the development of new technologies that have revolutionized the way we do business.

Internet access is an essential tool for law firms, but as of 1999, not all firms offered their employees Internet access. A survey conducted by the Technology Resource Center of the American Bar Association (ABA) in 1998 found that Internet access is found mainly in large law firms. It also found that some firms, mainly small firms, restrict Internet use to certain employees. The ABA survey reported that 76.2 percent of paralegals at large firms have full access to the Internet, compared to only 18.6 percent of paralegals in smaller firms (twenty or fewer attorneys). The survey also showed that the most popular use of the Internet by law firms was for legal research, followed by client and colleague communication and access to court records.

History of the Internet

Network: Two or more computers connected to each other so they can share resources.

The Internet is a worldwide cooperative **network** of networks. It was designed by the RAND Corporation for the U.S. Department of Defense in the 1960s as a means of communication that would withstand nuclear war or other disaster. RAND developed it as a decentralized network so that it would function if one of its major components were destroyed or rendered inoperable. They called it ARPANET, named after the Advanced Research Projects Agency of the Department of Defense that funded it. It linked the scientific and research communities with U.S. defense contractors. The network could accommodate many different types of computers, and it grew quickly.

In 1983, ARPANET split into two networks: ARPANET and MILNET. The Department of Defense turned ARPANET over to the National Science Foundation's Office of Advanced Scientific Computing. In 1985, the network became NSFNET, which was a "backbone" to which other networks were connected. Access to NSFNET was provided free to any U.S. research and educational institution for noncommercial purposes. It was used primarily by scientists, academics, and nonprofit organizations. At this time, regional networks were created to bring electronic traffic from individual institutions to the NSF backbone service. As the net grew, new software applications were created to make access easier. This was the beginning of the Internet.

The National Science Foundation (NSF) prohibited commercial use of NSFNET but lifted the restriction in 1991. Also in 1991, the National Research and Education Network (NREN) was approved by Congress. The NREN was a $2 billion project to upgrade the NSFNET backbone. It promised to increase the speed of data transfer on the Internet so that the entire *Encyclopaedia Britannica* could be transmitted electronically in one second.

OF INTEREST . . .

Internet Facts

- The number of hosts to the Internet reached the one million mark in 1992.
- The phrase "surfing the Internet" was coined by Jean Armour Polly in 1992.
- NSFNET discontinued its function as the backbone of the Internet in 1995. It is now used solely for scientific research. The U.S. backbone now consists of interconnected network providers.
- China requires Internet users to register with police.
- Germany restricts some newsgroups carried through CompuServe.
- Saudi Arabia confines Internet access to universities and hospitals.
- Singapore requires political and religious content providers to register with the state.
- Internet publications in New Zealand can be censored and seized.
- In 1997, the Chinese government arrested Lin Hai for inciting to overthrow state power because she provided a U.S. Internet magazine with 30,000 e-mail addresses.
- In 1997, domain names reached two million.
- The first international connection to ARPANET was the University College of London and Royal Radar Establishment (Norway) in 1973.
- The first commercial presence on the Internet was The World (world.std.com) in 1991.
- The White House came on-line in 1993 (www.whitehouse.gov).
- The domain name "business.com" sold for $150,000.
- France sponsors an annual festival in recognition of the Internet: La Fete de l'Internet.

Internet Service Provider (ISP): A private company that provides access to the Internet for a fee.

Modem: A device that allows remote computers to transmit and receive data using telephone lines; short for modulator/demodulator.

Server: A large computer that contains a large amount of information and directs customers' inquiries to the Internet.

Protocol: The set of rules that two computers use to communicate with each other.

No one "owns" the Internet. The networks that use the Internet are owned and maintained by their owners, and some are publicly traded companies, such as America Online.

To access the Internet, one must have browser software and an **Internet Service Provider (ISP).** America Online and Earthlink are examples of an ISP. ISPs that are accessed by **modems** are often called dial-up services. ISPs maintain large computers known as **servers.** The ISP's server is connected either to larger regional networks or directly to the backbone sites that direct traffic on the Internet. An ISP is essentially a retailer of access to high-speed telephone lines. They get their access from telephone companies and charge a fee for their service.

Protocols

A **protocol** is a set of rules that ensures that different network software products can work together. Protocols dictate how the various systems on the Internet operate. The very existence of the Internet depends on people voluntarily agreeing to configure their software to the protocol standard. It is the language computers use to communicate with each other.

Protocol standards are set by the Internet Engineering Task Force (IETF), a large international community of network designers, operators, vendors, and researchers concerned with the smooth operation of the Internet. Some Internet protocols include **File Transfer Protocol (FTP)**, which allows entire files to be transferred between computers; **Telnet**, a protocol that allows a computer to connect with a remote computer as if it were local; and **Gopher**, which organizes Internet information into an index that can be searched and retrieved. Gopher was developed by two University of Minnesota students who named it after the school's mascot.

Today, there are tens of thousands of networks from around the world connected to the Internet. America Online was among the first commercial networks. The Internet's growth is phenomenal. In 1998, the Internet grew at a staggering rate of 20 percent a month.

Five factors are attributed to the Internet's sudden growth and prominence:

◆ Widespread use of personal computers and graphical user interfaces, such as the Windows operating system
◆ Elimination of commercial use prohibitions
◆ The creation of software applications specifically for use on the Internet
◆ The existence of a large body of electronically stored data
◆ Technological advances in computer hardware, such as modems and monitors

Domain Names

A **domain name** is a unique name that identifies an organization on the Internet. Domain names were created in 1986 by the NSF, AT&T, and Network Solutions, Inc. (NSI), through the InterNIC project. In 1993, the NSF turned over the registration and management of domain names to Network Solutions, Inc. In 1995, Network Solutions was acquired by the Science Applications International Corporation (SAIC), the largest employee-owned research and engineering company in the United States.

There have been many concerns over issuance of domain names. Among these are the following:

◆ A rise in conflicts between trademark owners and domain name registrants
◆ An increase in the commercial value of domain names requiring a more formal management system
◆ Internationalization of the Internet
◆ Too much U.S. government involvement in Internet activities

These concerns prompted the Clinton administration to issue its policy regarding domain name registration, known as the White Paper (www.ntia.doc.gov/ntia-home/domainname/). The government proposes to turn the domain name system over to a private U.S. corporation, the Internet Corporation for Assigned Names and Numbers (ICANN), which is comprised of an international group of Internet users. The new corporation is scheduled to be operational by September 30, 2000. This new corporation will devise a new registering system and be responsible for domain name disputes. It will also issue new type identifiers. The proposed new type identifiers are .nom for individuals, .info for information services, .shop for businesses offering goods to purchase, .firm for firms, .web for activities relating to the web, .arts for cultural activities, and .rec for recreational activities. As of this writing, it has not been determined what identifiers will be approved.

Domain names consist of the organization's name (or specific designation) and a suffix that describes the type of organization, known as a **type identifier.** The type identifier places organizations on the Internet into six categories, as shown in Exhibit 10.1. Type identifiers are used only for U.S. organizations. Organizations outside the United States have a country code to identify the country in which the organization is located. In 1999, there were 240 country codes, examples of which are shown in Exhibit 10.1.

File Transfer Protocol (FTP): A protocol that allows files to be transferred between computers.

Telnet: A protocol that allows a computer to connect with a remote computer.

Gopher: A protocol that organizes Internet information for search and retrieval.

Domain name: A unique name that identifies an Internet site.

Type identifier: A suffix attached to a domain name that identifies the type of organization.

A suffix at the end of a domain name identifies the type of organization:

.com—commercial
.edu—educational institution
.org—nonprofit organizations
.mil—military organization
.net—network provider
.gov—government institution

An additional extension identifies the country where the domain is located:

.au—Australia
.dk—Denmark
.ge—Germany
.uk—United Kingdom

EXHIBIT 10.1 Example of Domain Suffix and Country Codes

OF INTEREST . . .

Firm's Web Site Plays Major League Baseball

As baseball season opened, some Web-savvy fans looking for game schedules or live audio went to what seemed like the logical Web address for Major League Baseball: www.mlb.com. But enter that address into your browser, and you get the Web site of Morgan Lewis & Backius L.L.P. The firm's site is often mistaken for that of Major League Baseball at www.major-leaguebaseball.com, so much so that in March 1998, the firm got permission to add a link to the baseball site.

Now, apparently even people who know that www.mlb.com will not take them directly to the baseball site find it easier to enter the shorter address, scroll down, and then click on the Major League Baseball logo. "A lot of people go to our site and use it as a link," said Jennifer Schlagle, marketing and communications coordinator for Morgan Lewis's Philadelphia office.

The Morgan Lewis site went up in early 1996, about a year before the appearance of the Major League Baseball site. Jim Austin, a former publications manager at Morgan Lewis, was quoted in a September 1998 article in New York's weekly *Village Voice* as saying that the Morgan Lewis site initially received a lot of e-mail, some full of obscenities, from baseball fans complaining about the confusion between sites. He also said the firm set up the link to appease the fans.

Reprinted with permission of the **National Law Journal.**

To obtain a domain name, one must register with NSI or another registration service and pay the required fee. Information released in 1999 by NSI estimated that it had over four million registered domain names, less than 3 percent of its capacity. It also estimated that Internet users numbered 70 million in 1999 and was expected to be 477 million by 2002, an increase of almost 700 percent in three years.

The World Wide Web

The World Wide Web (WWW, or Web) is not the Internet. It is only one of the protocols that operate via the Internet. It was developed by Tim Berners-Lee in 1990 at the European Laboratory for Particle Physics (CERN) in Switzerland. It is managed by the World Wide Web Consortium (W3C), also known as the World Wide Web Initiative (www.w3c.org). The W3C is run by the Massachusetts Institute of Technology (MIT) and the French National Institute for Research in Computer Science (INRIA). It is funded by a number of large corporate members, including AT&T; Adobe Systems, Inc.; Microsoft Corporation and Sun Microsystems, Inc. The consortium's purpose is

Hypertext Transfer Protocol (HTTP): The protocol used by the World Wide Web.

Hypertext Markup Language (HTML): A software language used by documents posted on the World Wide Web.

Download: The method by which users access and retrieve a document, software, or other files from a central computer to their computers.

Shareware: Software that is distributed without initial cost. If the user likes the software, a nominal payment is expected.

Freeware: Free software.

Hyperlinks: A connection to another page or site that allows a person to navigate the Web.

Web site: A collection of linked pages grouped in a certain order.

Home page: The starting point of a Web presentation that contains a table of contents for the information that is available at the Web site, offering direct links to the different parts of the site.

to promote the Web by developing specification and reference software that will be freely available to everyone.

The protocol used by the Web is called **Hypertext Transfer Protocol (HTTP).** The Web is actually the name given to all documents written in a specific software language known as **Hypertext Markup Language (HTML).** It allows documents to be **downloaded** via HTTP. In order for a computer to read the HTML language, it needs browser software.

Plug-in software adds features to a browser and allows a person to view documents, hear sound, and view video images on the Web. Plug-in software is often **shareware** or **freeware,** or software that is free to the user. In 1999, the most popular plug-in software was Adobe Acrobat Viewer and Real Player for sound and video.

The Web delivers its information by **hyperlinks** to other pages or other areas on the Web. These hyperlinks enable readers to navigate through the Web. A collection of the linked pages, grouped together in an orderly manner, becomes a **Web site.**

Most Web sites contain levels. The number of levels of a Web site vary. Some contain as few as two levels, and some contain many levels. The levels are accessed through the first page of a Web site, known as the **home page.**

The Web has changed the way we do business and has enhanced our personal lives. We can do practically anything on the Web. We can bank, shop, gamble, play games, obtain a loan, participate in an auction, and some of you may be taking this class via the Web. It offers numerous benefits to us, and new uses for the Web are being created.

The legal profession uses the Web to publicize cases and manage the media in high-profile cases. For example, in the Unabomber case (*U.S. v. Theodore Kacyzynski,* CR.S-96-259 GEB), the court clerk was inundated with requests for information by the media. He developed a section of the court's Web page that was devoted entirely to that case where he published dockets, pretrial depositions, trial transcripts, and evidence. The media consulted the Web page instead of the clerk, making the clerk's life a lot easier. In the Oklahoma City bombing trial (*U.S. v. Timothy McVeigh*), a Web site was developed (www.okcitytrial.com) that published official transcripts of the trial. And last but certainly not least, the Kenneth Starr report of accusations against President Clinton was posted on the Web for the entire world to read, as were audiotapes of telephone conversations between Monica Lewinsky and Linda Tripp.

TRENDS ▶▶▶

Trends in Technology

The future promises some exciting technological innovations to intrigue us.

- The web will be personalized and be able to anticipate our interests. Web sites will be aware of their visitors and be able to customize the information it provides to suit the interests of individual visitors.

- Robotics technology is advancing. Soon robots will be available to homes to help with everyday tasks—like vacuuming and taking out the trash.

- Computers are needed everywhere. Instead of carrying a computer, we'll be able to wear one. The first device may be a device you wear like a hat.

- Voice activation will become common and handy to use in a car to help navigate from one place to another.

- Our appliances will be connected to a central home computer network that can be remotely controlled by our cell phones. We'll be able to turn on the oven from the office and water the lawn from the telephone while on vacation.

Locating Information on the Web

Before information on a Web site can be accessed, it must first be located. The Web contains millions of Web sites with hundreds of millions of pages of information. Finding the exact site can be tricky.

There are three basic ways to locate specific information on the Web: **Uniform Resource Locator** (URL), keyword search, and topical index.

Uniform Resource Locator (URL): An address of a Web site that directs a person to the information.

Uniform Resource Locator Each Web site is given an address known as a **Uniform Resource Locator (URL).** A typical URL has four main elements:

◆ Protocol

◆ Address of server where the data are located

◆ Domain name

◆ Type identifier

A URL for the Web displays each element of the address as follows: http:// (protocol) www(server) .domainname.(domain name) .com(type identifier) (e.g., http:// www.domainname.com)

To find the U.S. House of Representatives, you must first know its URL address. Many URLs can be found in periodicals and advertising materials. URL addresses are designed so that one can logically figure them out. The URL for the U.S. House of Representatives is http://www.house.gov. The "http" is the protocol, the "www" means World Wide Web, "house" is the domain name, and "gov." means that it is a government site (see Exhibit 10.1).

Almost all companies and corporations have Web sites ending with ".com," meaning that it is a commercial site. Most companies have secured a domain name that matches or closely resembles their name. To find a commercial Web site, enter its domain name after the protocol and then "www," as follows: http://www.microsoft.com. Your school can be located on the Web in the same manner, only ending with ".edu" (e.g., http://www.yourschool.edu). To locate a Web site outside the United States, substitute the type identifier with the country code, as follows: http://www.louvre.fr. With these basics, it is not difficult to locate most of the major Web sites.

Most Web sites consist of many sections, or pages, and it is possible to go directly to the page that contains the information desired. Each page has its own URL indicating the name of the directory in which the document is stored. This is known as the **pathname.** Subsequent pages in a URL are separated by a forward slash, as follows: Protocol://server.domainname/pathname/name of document (e.g., http://www. microsoft.com/products/msword).

Pathname: The URL address showing the path of where a certain document may be found on a Web site.

Certain rules apply to all URLs. There are no spaces in a URL. Each word of a domain name is run together (except some words in a domain name may be connected by a dash). A forward slash (/) is always used instead of backward slash (\). Domain names are not capitalized but are entered in all lowercase letters.

Keyword Search Each browser has a search feature that allows a keyword search. Enter the keyword of the desired site or information, and the browser will retrieve the Web sites that contain information about the words inserted. At times, there may be thousands of Web sites that contain the keywords, and it may take some time to review all of them before you find the one you want. For example, you want information about the U.S. House of Representatives. In the keyword search area of the browser, you enter "House of Representatives." The browser will retrieve all Web sites that contain the words "House" and "Representatives," including state houses of representatives. You will find the U.S. House of Representatives after reviewing the choices available. Clicking on the appropriate site will take you there.

Boolean search: A method of defining search criteria.

Proximity searching, or **Boolean search,** creates sets of words so that a search engine can narrow the search. It gives a search engine parameters within which to conduct the search, narrowing the outcome of a search. Boolean searches are constructed

OF INTEREST . . .

Why Is It Called "Boolean?"

George Boole (1815–1864) was an English mathematician who studied theories of logic. His theories of mathematical set creation formed the basis of modern computerized text searching.

using the words "and," "or," and "not" with your keywords. Connectors are also used, such as "w/5" to indicate "within five words" or "adj15" to indicate that the search words must be adjacent within fifteen words. An example of this concept is shown in Exhibit 10.2.

Search engine: An independent company that has indexed Internet sites and categorized them so that they can be found easily.

Topical Index Various Internet indexing companies exist that have categorized Internet sites into groupings of related fields, such as government, law, judiciary, and so on. There are many indexing companies, which are also known as **search engines,** some of which are listed in Exhibit 10.3. For example, to find the U.S. House of Representatives, go to the search engine's Web address (http://www.yahoo.com) and choose the category of the desired information (Government). You will come to a list

Searching for the URL of the House of Representatives in a search engine will return thousands of possible URLs because it will return all the sites that contain the word "house" and all the sites that contain the word "representative," as follows:

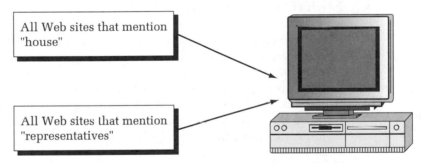

All Web sites that mention "house"

All Web sites that mention "representatives"

By inserting the word AND between House and Representatives, it instructs the computer to locate only those sites that contain both words, as follows:

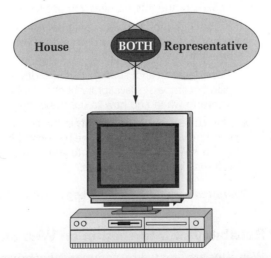

House   BOTH   Representative

EXHIBIT 10.2   Example of Boolean Search

All in One Search Page—http://www.albany.net
AltaVista—http://www.altavista.com
Clearinghouse for Internet Resource Guides—http://www.clearinghouse.net/search
Deja News—http://www.dejanews.com
Excite—http://www.excite.com
HotBot—http://www.hotbot.com
Infoseek—http://www.infoseek.com
Internet Public Library Web Searching—http://www.ipl.org.
Jump City—http://www.jumpcity.com
Liszt—http://www.liszt.com
Lycos—http://www.lycos.com
Magellan—http://www.mckinley.com
SavvySearch—http://savvy.cs.colostate.edu:2000
Search.Com—http://www.search.com
Trade Wave Galaxy Directory Services—http://galaxy.einet.net/www
Ultraseek—http://www.ultra.infoseek.com
U.S. Business Advisor—http://www.business.gov.
WebCrawler—http://www.webcrawler.com
World Wide Web Worm—http://www.cs.colorado.edu/www
Yahoo—http://www.yahoo.com

EXHIBIT 10.3 Example List of Search Engines

of government topics. Choose Law. You will see another, narrower list of choices. Choose Federal, which will bring up another list of choices, of which House of Representatives is one, as shown in Exhibit 10.4.

Web sites can be marked by a browser. This activity is known as **bookmarking.** When you bookmark a site, the URL is inserted in the Bookmarks section of the browser. To return to the Web site, access the list of bookmarked sites and choose the desired site. The browser will take you directly to the site.

Bookmarking: A part of browser software that marks a Web site so that its URL is accessible without searching for it.

TECH TIPS
Surfology 101

- Bookmark the Internet sites you use frequently and update your bookmark list regularly.

- Become comfortable with using Boolean search techniques for doing on-line research. It may take a little time and practice, but you will conduct more efficient searches, saving time for you and the client.

- Develop a research strategy that includes all the means available to you. A good research plan encompasses law library books, CD-ROMs, Westlaw and Lexis, and the Internet. Knowing when and how to use these resources effectively is a great time-saver.

- Stay current on developments in the field of electronic research, both factual and substantive. This is easily done by subscribing to listservs and newsgroups, some of which deliver e-mail updates to you. You should also read the computer and technology columns in legal publications.

Reprinted with permission of Legal Assistant Today *magazine © James Publishing Co.*

Reliability of Information on Web Sites

Web sites are created by commercial companies, organizations, associations, universities, the government, and individuals. You can find anything you want on the Web, but not all information is reliable. Verifying the accuracy of data on the Web is a

EXHIBIT 10.4   Example of Search Engine Search for the House of Representatives

problem. Commercial Web sites of reputable companies warrant their accuracy, as do those created by law librarians and archivists, but not all entities offer such warranties.

Anyone can post information on the Web regardless of age, background, and mental health. Almost all the Web sites created by the government and its agencies are reliable. Law school and university Web sites are also generally reliable. Some Web sites, especially those containing information about single subjects, are created by individuals

EXHIBIT 10.4 *Continued*

who may lack the knowledge and background necessary to rely on their information. Additionally, they may lack the resources necessary to update and maintain the Web site adequately, and so the information may be wrong, incomplete, or outdated.

There are certain things to look for to investigate the legitimacy of a Web site:

◆ Check to see whether the author of the Web site is identified.

◆ Determine the purpose of the Web site. Is it for the reader's benefit or the author's benefit?

◆ Do not judge a Web site by its home page. Home pages can be professional looking but may promote quack remedies or illegal activities.

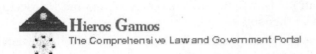

Friday, October 15, 1999

◄ Home | ALL OF HIEROS GAMOS | ⬍ |

Legal Associations - by name, address, telephone, fax and contact

I. **International** - World Jurist/IBA/UIA

II. **Special Associations** - Associations enhancing professionalism and service to clients.

    A. **Attorneys**

    B. **Legal Assistants & Paralegals**

    C. **Librarians**

    C. **Marketing & Administration**

    D. **Other**

III.   **Associations of Law Firms** - Alliances, Affiliations, Firm Associations

IV.   **Corporate Counsel**

V.   **Foundations/Institutes/Education Centers**

Other Sources

Information on Legal Associations

    Directory of Law Firm Associations, Alliances and Affiliations - Lex Mundi reprinted in Martindale Hubbell Volumes 1 and 2 - International
    Encyclopedia of Associations 1996 - Gale
    Articles on the Legal Profession accessible by the Internet

Internet Links

    Yahoo Index of Legal Organizations   **AustLII Legal Links - International Organisations**

    Georgetown University Legal Explorer   **Universita'di Bologna Research Guide International**
    International Law - Associations   **Organizations**

EXHIBIT 10.5   Example of Law Related Web Site

◆ Look for the date of the last update. If one is not available, the site may be outdated.

◆ Look at the site's links. If some have disappeared, it is a clue that the site is outdated.

CYBERSITES
Finding Review Guides on the Web

Argus Clearinghouse—http://www.clearinghouse.net/chhome

Mining Company—http://miningco.com

Readers Digest LookSmart—http://www.looksmart.com

Other Resources
Evaluating Internet information—http://www.medlib.med.utah.edu/navigator/discovery/eval

Evaluating quality on the Internet—http://www.tiac.net/users/hope/findqual

Thinking critically about Web resources—
    http://www.stemnet.nf.ca/Curriculum/Validate/validate

◆ Verify the information elsewhere. Some experts recommend verifying information by two other sources.

◆ Consult Web site review guides, some of which are listed in the Cybersites sidebar.

Law-Related Web Sites

The federal government is the largest contributor of material on the Web. Many of the law-related Web sites were developed by the government, law schools, law libraries, bar associations, and other legal organizations. Federal law materials, such as the U.S. Code, Code of Federal Regulations, Federal Court decisions, and hundreds of government agency regulations, can be found on the Web. The federal government operates the Government Information Locator Services (GILS) to help find precise information from the vast number of materials on the Web.

Because of the way the Web is constructed, Web sites are accessible from other Web sites by links. Almost all the leading law-related search engines contain links to court decisions, federal materials, state law resources, law reviews, and more, as shown in Exhibit 10.5. A listing of law-related search engines is shown in the Cybersites sidebar.

CYBERSITES

Finding Law-Related Search Engines on the Web

Federal Court Locator—http://www.law.vill.edu

Federal Judicial Center, Court Links—http://www.fjc.gov/govlinks.html

FedWorld Information Network—http://www.fedworld.gov

FindLaw—http://findlaw.com

Government Information Locator Service—http://info.er.usgs.gov/gils/index.html

Hieros Gamos—http://www.hg.org

Internet Sleuth Legal and Government Information—http://www.isleuth.com

JuriSearch—http://www.unilegal.com

LawCrawler—www.lawcrawler.com

LawGuru—http://www.lawguru.com/search

LawRunner—www.lawrunner.com

Meta-Index for U.S. Legal Research—http://gsulaw.gsu.edu/metaindex

Searching the Internet—http://lawlib.slu.edu/misc/direct.htm

Thomas—http://thomas.loc.gov

INTRANETS AND EXTRANETS

Web-based technology: Internet-like software applications.

Internet technology has been the foundation of new systems and software products, among them intranet and extranet programs. This technology, known as **web-based technology,** uses the www protocol, which is easy to use and understand. Law firms have taken advantage of this technology to create intranets and extranets.

Intranets

Intranet: A private collection of information that is viewed by Internet web browser software and is accessible only to authorized members of a private network; a private Internet site.

An **intranet** is a law firm's internal information distribution system that is based on Web technology. It differs from the Web because it is private and is accessible only by designated individuals, normally firm employees. It provides employees of a firm with the ability to access a variety of resources through one source.

Each person's computer is connected to the firm's server that stores the information. In order to accommodate the various types of information stored on an intranet, an intranet search engine is used. An intranet also uses specialized software, known as **groupware,** or software created specifically for use by groups. An index page di-

Groupware: Software created for and used by an intranet or extranet.

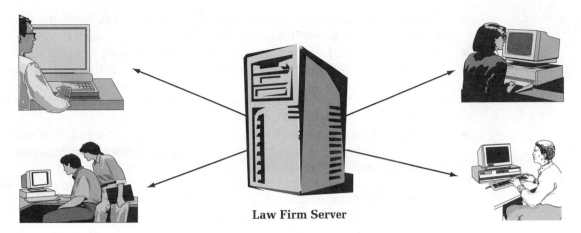

Law Firm Server

EXHIBIT 10.6   Example of Law Firm Intranet

rects the user to the information desired. The information is accessible from each person's individual workstation, as shown in Exhibit 10.6. Employees use their Internet browser software to access the information. The user just clicks on the desired subject matter. All the information is in one place, is easy to find, and can be searched easily.

Intranets are fairly new to law firms. As of 1998, only 20 to 30 percent of law firms had an intranet, and only 50 percent of corporate legal departments had one. However, as law firms realize the benefits of intranets, their numbers are expected to increase dramatically.

Intranets are custom made and designed according to a firm's specifications by professional intranet designers or in-house computer specialists. They generally have four or five levels that branch out from the top down:

Level 1:   The home page

Level 2:   Firm departments

Level 3:   Links within a department

Level 4:   Documents or databases to retrieve information

Level 5:   Forms, documents, or pages that contain the desired material.

Examples of the types of uses for an intranet are as follows:

◆ *Law firm calendar.* Law firm employees have their calendars posted to the intranet so that they are accessible to the entire firm. This facilitates scheduling events and locating an employee. Case management software is accessed from this area.

◆ *Continuing legal education.* Notices of upcoming educational seminars and workshops are posted or distributed to specific practice groups. Law firm

TECH TIPS

Intranet Groupware

Groupware that produces or creates features for an intranet are available. Among these are the following:

West Intranet Toolkit—Contains CiteLink™, which finds legal citation and creates hyperlinks to the full text of documents on Westlaw via the Internet. You can run a Westlaw check from the Start menu and add bookmarks to law-related Web sites.

Verity—An Intranet search engine.

Dow Jones Interactive Intranet Publishing Toolkit—Web subscription service about intranets.

Lotus Notes 5—Software that organizes an intranet or extranet.

Groupwise 5.5—Software that organizes an intranet or extranet.

On-line: Connected to the Internet or the World Wide Web.

employees can also access legal courses that are offered through the Internet and take the course **on-line** at their convenience.

◆ *Client information.* Law firm records pertaining to clients can be accessed, including client lists, matter lists, contact information, billing information, outstanding invoices, and the status of the client's case. This information is essential for conflict-of-interest checks and also displays client information immediately without searching through files and records.

◆ *Training.* Keeping employees informed about new features to a firm's software is a constant challenge for a law firm's management. Software manuals are accessed through an intranet, as is additional training on firm-specific systems. An employee can learn and be trained directly from the intranet according to the employee's schedule and is available immediately as the need should arise.

◆ *Discussion groups.* The firm can create discussion groups for the entire firm, firm management, individual practice areas, or case-specific groups. This feature reduces in-person meetings and keeps all interested persons abreast of the status of a case or changes in specific practice areas.

◆ *Internal directory.* A directory of all firm employees is accessed from the intranet, including telephone, address, home phone, cell phone, and department. An employee can be located quickly if needed.

Brief bank: A collection of documents that are used as a template to prepare new documents.

Template: A form document used as a guide to prepare new documents.

◆ *Brief bank.* A **brief bank** consists of form documents, such as letters, agreements, pleadings, and other documents that are used frequently. It also consists of legal research memoranda and briefs. These documents are used as a **template** to prepare new documents. Documents are prepared quickly without having to prepare them from scratch, saving the firm time and the client money.

◆ *Library resources.* Research materials are accessed from the intranet, including WestLaw and Lexis. Other research resources, such as legal research search engines or law-related Web sites, are also accessed from this location.

◆ *Management and firm policies.* Management memoranda are distributed through the intranet informing employees of new policies, firm announcements, employee benefits, and other firm news. The firm's employee manual is also posted. Vacation planning forms or other management forms are readily available when needed and can be downloaded and printed from the intranet. If the firm is recruiting new employees, a prospective employee can download an employment application from the firm's Web site and submit it via e-mail.

◆ *Practice area information and forms.* Whenever there is a change in the law, the employees in the applicable practice area can be immediately informed. If there is a change in a judicial form, the form is posted so that it is immediately available to anyone needing the form. This ensures that the firm has updated information at all times.

◆ *Time and billing.* A user's timesheets are completed through the intranet and submitted to management from the intranet. Preliminary bills are also reviewed from the responsible attorney's workstation. The firm's time and billing software is accessed in this area.

◆ *Access to courts.* Courts that accept electronic filing are accessed through the intranet. Documents are filed electronically through an individual workstation. Updated court information, such as calendars, dockets, and rules, are just a click away.

◆ *Marketing.* The intranet contains all the firm's marketing brochures and mailings, press releases, and advertisements. These materials can be incorporated into word processing documents.

Intranets require constant maintenance and updating. A firm's investment to produce, install, and maintain an intranet will come back to the firm quickly after implementation. A study conducted in 1998 by International Data Corporation of Framingham, Massachusetts, concluded that a firm will realize a return of 1,000 percent on its investment in an intranet.

Law firms, especially large firms, realize a number of benefits to distributing information electronically via an Intranet. An intranet enhances efficiency, maximizes the use of a firm's resources, reduces a firm's overhead, and increases employee productivity and satisfaction. Other benefits of an intranet are the following:

◆ An intranet centralizes operations from one source so that information can be found quickly and easily. This centralization prevents duplication of efforts, making a firm more efficient and profitable. More than one person can work on a project simultaneously, allowing for fast and efficient revisions.

◆ Information is distributed electronically, reducing the use of paper. Reducing paper saves the firm money for supplies, filing, and storage, including equipment and the extra space needed to produce and store the paper.

◆ Intranets allow a firm's work product to be reused easily, reducing duplication of efforts. This maximizes the firm's resources, increasing profits and employee productivity.

CYBERSITES

Finding Intranet Resources on the Web

Intranet Journal: http://www.brill.com/intranet—Offers links to intranet-related resources on the Internet, including a discussion forum.

Intranet Design Magazine: http://www.innergy.com/index—Articles and links to intranet information.

Intranet Exchange: http://innergy.com/ix/index—Discussion forum offered by the publishers of *Intranet Design* magazine.

Intranet Resource Center: http://www.clo.com/WebMaster/wm_irc—Offers links to information and resources regarding the design and implementation of an intranet.

Intranet Professional: http://mcq.com/IP/master.asp—Newsletter that contains articles regarding intranets, maintained by Howard McQueen.

TrialNet: http://www.trialnet.com—A company that develops intranets.

Extranets

Extranet: A Web-based interface to a private network; used to communicate directly with clients.

An **extranet** is a Web-based interface to a private network. It is a separate area of an intranet that is intended for private use of its members and selected outside entities. Larger than an intranet, extranets operate on the same Web-based platform.

An extranet is a private network that is accessible by a number of organizations, including selected firm employees, clients, outside counsel, and others who work together. An extranet offers the same benefits as an intranet: efficiency, improved quality of work, and enhancement of communication among people working together. An extranet also offers features such as access to calendars, scheduling, collaborative document drafting and editing, and distribution of messages to specific groups.

The difference between an intranet and an extranet is that an extranet is directed to different people and has different uses. Among the uses are direct client access and multijurisdictional litigation management.

Direct Client Access A law firm creates an extranet connection to its clients, especially large, corporate clients. Some firms may have more than one extranet, connecting multiple clients together. This connection is a separate system developed exclusively for the client and the client's cases. A firm provides the client with information regarding the client's cases to which the client has constant access. The client can also view its financial account with the firm as well as other information as needed. A firm can transmit documents, edit documents simultaneously,

Firm Server

EXHIBIT 10.7 Example of Firm-Centered Extranet

communicate via e-mail, and directly collaborate on a case. This type of extranet is known as a firm-centered extranet and is shown in Exhibit 10.7.

Clients also provide law firms with an extranet. Large corporations that use many law firms to handle their legal work provide their many outside counsels with an extranet to facilitate communication. This is especially helpful when preparing a case and handling the corporation's legal affairs. Responding to discovery requests often requires answers to technical questions that only the client can provide. Before extranets, the firm would request the information from the client, who would search through the records, prepare the information, and send it back to the firm. This was done several times for several cases. Sometimes the responses were complete, and at other times they were not, resulting in delay. Providing this information on an extranet allows many different firms immediate access to the information from their individual computers. This saves both the client and the firm time and money. An example of this type of extranet is shown in Exhibit 10.8.

Another advantage of an extranet is communicating with clients from another part of the world. Trying to communicate through time zones is difficult and causes delays. For example, with an extranet, a Japanese client has immediate access to the information provided it by its New York law firm and communicates with the firm regardless of the time of day or night. Extranets also reduce travel costs to attend strategy meetings with clients in another state or country.

EXHIBIT 10.8 Example of Client-Centered Extranet

Multijurisdictional Litigation It is not uncommon for forty or more law firms to join together on large class-action cases. A law firm involved in complex, multi-jurisdictional litigation uses an extranet to communicate with other counsel in the litigation. Attorneys share information through the extranet, such as witness lists, discovery, legal research, and so on. Sharing this information ensures that all parties have current and complete information and reduces duplication of effort. Each counsel involved with an extranet has access to pertinent information of the others, allowing the case to be prepared more completely and efficiently and in less time.

Attorney Charles Renfrew, partner at Leboef, Lamb, Greene & MacRae, said, "At times outside counsel find themselves reinventing the wheel—doing research that others have done for the client or work that the firm itself had done—but no one is easily able to locate the work, so it is easier to start from scratch than look through the files [to find it]" *National Law Journal,* "Clients Force Technology on Firms to Trim Costs," April 14, 1997.

Since extranets are new, not all firms have one. For these firms, extranets can be developed by using an outside extranet vendor, called extranet brokers. A broker provides a network server through which interested parties can connect. A number of firms can manage a complex case without the expense of implementing their own extranet. This type of extranet is known as a brokered extranet and is shown in Exhibit 10.9.

Extranet Security Since extranets contain sensitive, confidential information, they must be secure so that unauthorized individuals cannot access the information. Additionally, since extranets are connected to a firm's intranet, the private part of the firm's intranet must be protected. There are two types of security risks with an extranet: restricting access so that unauthorized persons do not have access to the system and protecting information in transit to and from other members in the extranet.

Restricting Access to Unauthorized Persons. There are several access control methods used to secure access to an extranet. A **firewall** is an electronic barrier

Firewall: A protective electronic barrier constructed around a network so that unauthorized persons cannot get through.

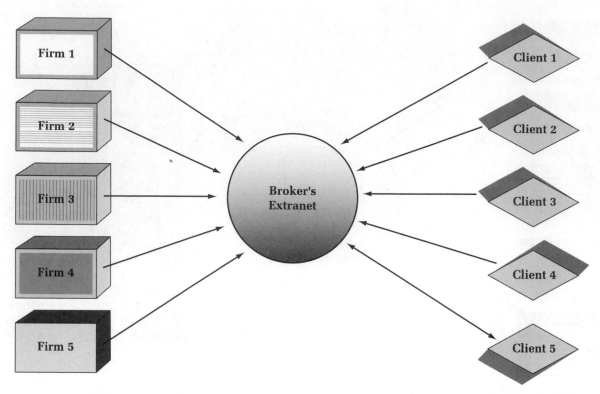

EXHIBIT 10.9 Example of Brokered Extranet

erected around the firm's network that will not allow an unauthorized person to get through to protected areas. It serves as a buffer between a firm's internal network and a number of external networks, including the Internet.

Perhaps the easiest security method to implement is to place the extranet in an undisclosed address on the Web. A private Web site can be hidden from search engines and its address provided only to those persons entitled to it. The address can be changed periodically so that unauthorized persons cannot find the site. The new address is given only to those entitled to it.

The most common security method is to require each user to use a special ID and password to gain entry to the extranet. A second-level password is required on some sites for additional protection. A second-level password can be changed or rotated according to a prearranged schedule. A company called SecurID has taken the ID/password security one step further. It issues a special card, similar to an ATM card, that displays a six-digit number. An ID, password, and card are required to access a system protected with SecurID.

Digital ID: A personal ID number that is encrypted and can be read only by the extranet.

The most recent security measure is a **digital ID.** A digital ID is a personal identification number or word issued to an individual or organization by an independent certifying authority. A digital ID solves the problem of losing a password or having a password stolen. A digital signature tells the recipient of the message or document that the person sending it is the correct person. It will also verify that the message or document sent has not been altered.

Users with digital IDs can obtain certificates from an outside vendor, Verisign, which will certify that the user is who he or she purports to be. To obtain a certificate, the user must provide personal identification that is validated by a credit bureau. Verisign is not the only vendor that issues certificates after verifying identity. Law firms may issue their own certificates to authorized persons. To issue identification certificates, a firm needs a certificate server, which is available from Microsoft, Netscape, Xcert, Entrust, and GTE.

It is important that the third-party vendor issuing certificates be reliable. As such, the regulation of digital signatures has been proposed. The Information Security Committee of the Science and Technology Section of the ABA published digital signature guidelines in 1997. Some states have also enacted some form of legislation pertaining to the use of digital signatures, some of which used the ABA guidelines as a model.

Protecting Information in Transit from One Computer to Another. Electronic transmissions sent through telephone lines are accessible to others. It is possible for others to tap into a transmission. Many law firms and corporate legal departments have a policy not to transmit confidential information through an extranet. According to the 1999 ABA Technology Survey, 50 percent of corporate legal departments, 60 percent of large firms, and 75 percent of small firms will not transmit confidential information over an extranet. For those firms that use extranets to transmit confidential information, each transmission must be secured to protect its confidentiality.

There are methods to ensure the privacy of electronic transmissions. Netscape, one of the most popular browsers, offers a Secure Sockets Layer (SSL), which is a protocol used to verify a server's identity to a client and a client's identity to a server. It also scrambles data in transit so that if it is penetrated, it cannot be read. Another product used for security is Secure HTTP (SHTTP), proposed by CommercNet. It is a protocol that is used with the HTTP protocol and is more extensive than SSL.

Cryptography: The method of scrambling information so that it is unreadable except by the person who holds the key to unscramble the information.

These security protocols use **cryptography** technology to **encrypt** and **decrypt** data. Cryptography is the process of securing private information that is passed through public networks by mathematically scrambling (encrypting) it in a way that makes it unreadable to anyone except the person holding the mathematical key that can unscramble (decrypt) it. Cryptography is not new technology; it was developed by the government many years ago as a method of keeping espionage activities secret. There are two types of cryptography that are in use today: same key and public key.

Encrypt: A way of coding the information so that if it is intercepted by a third party, it cannot be read.

With same-key cryptography, a message is encrypted and decrypted using the same key, which is passed along from one party to another. A more secure method is public-key cryptography, which uses a pair of different keys (one public, one private). A message encrypted with one key can be decrypted only with the other key and vice versa.

Decrypt: A way of decoding information so that it may be read.

Members of an extranet own a unique pair of keys. The public key is widely distributed among the extranet network and is used for encoding messages. The private key is held by one member of the network and is used to decrypt the incoming message, making it safe from interception. Controlling access to the encryption keys is important and requires close monitoring.

Other security methods are being developed every day. A New York company, Finger/Matrix, offers Check/One, which is a single finger scanner that limits access to the computer's data to individuals whose fingerprints identify them. Another security system scans an individual's retinas before granting them access to the system.

ELECTRONIC MAIL

Electronic mail (e-mail): An electronic message sent from one person to another through their computers.

Electronic mail (e-mail), is an electronic message system that allows communication from one person to another through their computers. It is one of the most commonly used features of technology used in law firms. In addition to receiving messages, a person can receive attachments to a message, such as documents, files, graphics, and computer programs. People can communicate with other people from around the world at any time of the day or night in seconds through e-mail.

Snail mail: The process of sending mail through the U.S. Postal Service.

In the early days of the Internet, almost 70 percent of the use of NSFNET was for personal messages, or e-mail. Today, many people prefer e-mail to **snail mail** because of its speed. In 1998, the Affiliates conducted a survey of 200 attorneys who worked for large law firms. The results of the survey found that 33 percent of the

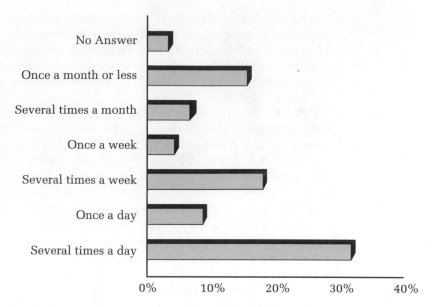

EXHIBIT 10.10   How Often Do Attorneys Communicate with Clients via E-Mail?

lawyers communicated with clients several times a day through e-mail, as shown in Exhibit 10.10.

E-mail passes to its destination through servers. To receive e-mail, one must have access to a server. An ISP provides each customer with an e-mail address that allows the customer to use the ISP's server. Like snail mail, each e-mail must contain an address so that the server will know where to deliver the e-mail. Each individual has his or her own e-mail address.

E-Mail Addresses

E-mail addresses normally have three main parts: username, domain name, and type identifier.

The username is the name of the person to whom the e-mail is sent. The same principles discussed in the World Wide Web section of this chapter apply to e-mail addresses. An e-mail address contains no spaces. Therefore, a username is not the persons' actual name consisting of a first name and a surname. A username contains no spaces and no uppercase letters. A username consists of a number of variations of the person's name, as follows: surname only (smith), or first initial and surname (jsmith), or first name and surname (johnsmith), or first name and surname separated by an underscore or hyphen (john_smith). A person's username may also be a nickname (cuddles). However, nicknames are rarely used in an office environment.

The second part of the e-mail address is the domain name. The domain name is the name of the organization that contains the server that transmits the e-mail. The username and domain name are separated by the axon symbol (@), which symbolizes the word "at." For private e-mail accounts, the domain name is the name of the ISP (e.g., jsmith@aol.com). For work-related e-mail accounts, the domain name is the name of the company (e.g., jsmith@microsoft.com).

The third part of the e-mail is the type identifier. It is separated by a dot or period (.) and is generally considered part of the domain name (e.g., .com).

E-mail addresses are always in lowercase letters. However, e-mail addresses are not **case sensitive.** This means that you can send an e-mail to Jsmith@Microsoft.com, JSMITH@MICROSOFT.COM, or Jsmith@MICROSOFT.com, and it will be delivered to the correct destination: jsmith@microsoft.com. However, some Internet addresses are case sensitive, and URLs are partially case sensitive. Therefore, it is good prac-

Case sensitive:
Requiring that all letters be in a specific case. If a letter is the wrong case, the information cannot be read.

tice to get used to entering all addresses in the correct case. E-mail addresses, as well as Web addresses, should be in all lowercase letters.

As of this writing, there is no comprehensive directory of e-mail or Internet addresses. However, there are several resources that are used to locate a person, some of which are listed in the Cybersites sidebar. If you cannot find a person in a directory, it is not difficult to figure out a person's e-mail address if you know the domain name of his or her place of work. Assume that his or her username is the first initial and surname.

E-mail addresses and Web addresses are different. For example, if you wanted to locate the White House on the Web, you would locate it through its URL: http://www.whitehouse.gov. If you wanted to send the president an e-mail message, you would do so by the president's e-mail address: president@whitehouse.gov.

CYBERSITES

Finding E-Mail Directories on the Web

555-1212.com—http://www.555-1212.com

Altavista—http://www.altavista.digital.com

AnyWho—http://www.anywho.com

Bigfoot—http://www.bigfoot.com

Find mE-mail—http://www.findmemail.com

Four11—http://www.four11.com

InfoSpace—http://www.infospace.com

Lookup—http://www.lookup.com

MESA—http://mesa.rrzn.uni-hannover.de/

Phonebooke—http://www.phonebooke.com

Switchboard—http://www.switchboard.com

Yahoo People Search—http://www.yahoo.com/search/people

Listservs and Discussion Groups

Listserv: A group of people who exchange information about a particular topic on the Internet.

There are thousands of groups and organizations that have their own discussion groups on the Internet. These groups exchange information and communicate with one another via e-mail. There are two types of discussion groups: newsgroups and mailing lists, which are also known as **listservs.** Newsgroups are public discussions on topics of general interest in which anyone with newsreader software can participate. A listserv contains a mailing list of e-mail addresses of people interested in the same subject. A member sends a message to a common e-mail address, and it is then distributed to everyone on the list. When someone replies to the message, the reply goes to everyone on the list. One need not participate in the discussion to be a member of a listserv. One may just read the material being posted without responding. This activity (or lack thereof) is called **lurking.**

Lurking: Not responding to messages posted on a listserv.

Listservs are either public or private and consist of two types: announcement type and discussion type. With an announcement-type list, you receive messages but cannot respond to the message. With a discussion-type list, every member can participate in the discussion. In addition, listservs are either moderated or unmoderated. In a moderated list, all messages are sent to a list moderator, who reviews them and makes a determination of whether it is appropriate to be distributed to the group. In an unmoderated list, each message is automatically sent to the group regardless of content.

There are thousands of law-related listservs, including many listservs for paralegals. The NFPA's Web site has links to paralegal listservs (http://paralegals.org) as well as the Washburn Legal Assistant's Society (listserv @lawlib.wuacc.edu/paralegal1). If you want to find a listserv on a specific topic and do not have a Web address, you can search the Law Lists Web site. Law Lists is compiled by Lynette Louis Jacques at the University of Chicago and is a database of listservs relating to the legal field (http://www.lib.uchicago.edu/cgibin.law-lists).

All you need to be a member of a listserv is an e-mail address and a subscription. Each group has specific directions on how to subscribe as well as how to cancel the subscription. On many Web sites, applicable listservs are listed from which subscription instructions and rules can be accessed.

To be good cybercitizens, it is suggested that each listserv participant become familiar with e-mail etiquette, known as Netiquette.

CYBERSITES

Finding Law-Related Listservs on the Web

Net-Lawyers—Discussion of study, practice, and marketing through the Internet. Topics include Web design, marketing, and legal Web sites and services. To subscribe: listserv@austin.onu.edu. To post: net-lawyers@peach.ease.lsoft.com.

Network2D-L—Focus on the latest legal technology. Topics include best legal word processor, scanner software, browsers, and voice dictation software. To subscribe: listserv@austin.onu.edu. To post: network2d-1@peach.ease.lsoft.com.

Bluesky—Focus on securities practice, students, and professors interested in blue sky law. Topics include contracts and preemption law, Proposition 211, Section 18, blue sky memoranda, and assets under management issues. To subscribe: listserv@law.umab.edu. To post: bluesky@law.umab.edu.

ABA-Tax—Focus on tax law and tax issues. Topics include repeal of the federal estate tax, debt versus equity issues, nonconvertible debt instruments, and federal insurance code. To subscribe: listserver@abanet.org. To post: aba-tax@abanet.org.

NFPA—Focus on issues relating to paralegal practice. Site has a number of listservs that discuss paralegal practice in general and by practice area. To subscribe: www.paralegals.org/Networks.

Netiquette

Netiquette: An informal code of conduct that governs e-mail communication.

Netiquette is a form of on-line etiquette. It is an informal code of conduct that governs the acceptable way for users to interact with one another through e-mail. The guidelines were informally developed by many different people on the Internet. There is no one authority or governing agency that makes and enforces the rules. The rules are enforced by the people using them. A disregard of the rules is considered rude and improper.

Some people receive hundreds of e-mails a day. Adhering to netiquette guidelines will make the process of managing e-mails easier for everyone. The following are rules to follow when communicating by e-mail:

◆ *Do not assume that your e-mail is private.* Do not send an e-mail that contains material that you would not want everyone at work to see. The firm's system administrator has access to e-mails to maintain the system, and e-mails are easily forwarded to others.

◆ *Never give your user ID or password to another person.* Another person can wreak havoc with your e-mail account. Since your e-mails can be viewed by the system administrator, all e-mails containing your user ID and password are presumed to be written by you.

◆ *Keep messages short and to the point.* Most busy people resent long e-mails that contain information not relevant to the subject matter.

◆ *Edit quotations.* Quotations should be edited to include only the relevant material to keep messages short.

◆ *Limit each message to one subject.* An e-mail should be limited to one subject, and that subject should be clearly indicated in the subject section of the e-mail.

◆ *Include your signature at the bottom of the e-mail.* A signature footer should include your name, position, affiliation, and e-mail address. It should not exceed four lines. A telephone number can be included.

◆ *Do not use words in all uppercase.* Words in all uppercase are considered shouting. If you want to capitalize a word to emphasize it, do so sparingly.

◆ *Use asterisks (*) to emphasize a point.* Some web browsers cannot bold a word, so words and phrases are emphasized by *asterisks around them.*

◆ *Use underscores before and after a title.* Some Web browsers cannot italicize words and phrases. To put a word or phrase in italics, such as the title of a book, use the underscore symbol before and after the title of a book: _Fundamentals of Law Office Management_.

◆ *Never send chain letters.* Chain letters clutter the system.

◆ *Spell out dates.* Because of the international nature of the Internet, understanding dates can be confusing. Do not list dates by the numbers (12/21/YY). Always spell out the month to avoid confusion: Dec 24, 2005, or 24 Dec 05.

◆ *Be careful what you say about others.* E-mails are easily forwarded, and a derogatory remark may come back to haunt you. An angry or a derogatory e-mail is known as a **flame**. Responding angrily to a flame will result in a flame war which is unpleasant for everyone.

◆ *Do not forward personal mail.* It is considered extremely rude to forward a personal e-mail to members of a listserv without the original author's permission.

◆ *Be careful with humor.* Without verbal communication and body language that can detect your intent, e-mails can be misinterpreted. Use **emoticons** to express your feelings. Commonly used emoticons are shown in Exhibit 10.11. Jokes may not be appreciated by co-workers and should not be distributed through an office's e-mail system. In 1998, two employees sued New York's Morgan Stanley for $30 million because of an offensive joke that was distributed by e-mail throughout the company. Employees have sued their employers for a hostile work environment because of offensive e-mails intended as jokes (*Daniels v. WorldCom,* WI. 91261 [N.D. Texas 1998] and *Schwenn v. Anheuser-Busch, Inc.,* WI. 166845 [N.D. Now York 1998]).

◆ *Use acronyms.* Acronyms shorten messages and should be used whenever possible. Make sure, however, that the recipient will understand the acronyms. Commonly used acronyms are shown in Exhibit 10.12.

◆ *Know your firm's e-mail policy.* In-house e-mail (e-mail sent to persons within the firm) are subject to a firm's e-mail policy. In-house e-mail should be regarded as memoranda used for office business. Personal e-mails should be kept to a minimum. There have been many controversies about personal e-mails sent at

Flame: An angry or a derogatory e-mail message.

Emoticons: Symbols used to express feelings in written e-mail communication.

:-) Happy	:-(Sad	:-o Surprised
:-I Indifferent	:-e Disappointed	:-< Mad
;-) Winking	:-& Tongue-tied	:-# Lips are sealed
:-I I Really angry	:-@ Screaming	:- Lips are sealed
:-D Laughing	:-(o) Yelling	:-] Grinning
8-) Wide-eyed	:-I Apathetic	:-] Smirk
:-[Sad sarcasm	;-(Feel like crying	:'-(Crying
%-) Happy but confused	:-* Kiss	:-\ Undecided
8-o Shocked	:-/ Skeptical	:-> Sarcastic smile
;^) Smirking smile	X-(Brain dead	>:-) Devilish
O:-) Angelic	:-P Sticking tongue out	

EXHIBIT 10.11   Emoticons

<BRB> Be right back	<BTW> By the way
<CUL> See you later	<F2F> Face to face
<FWIW> For what it's worth	<FYA> For your amusement
<FYI> For your information	<GMTA> Great minds think alike
<HHOK> Ha ha only kidding	<IMHO> In my humble opinion
<IOW> In other words	<LOL> Laughing out loud
<OIC> Oh, I see	<ROTFL> Rolling on the floor laughing
<SO> Significant other	<TIA> Thanks in advance
<TNX> Thanks	<WB> Welcome back
<WRT> With respect to	<WTG> Way to go
<BFN> Bye for now	<G> Grin
<HTH> Hope this helps	<IJWTK> I just want to know
	<OTOH> On the other hand

EXHIBIT 10.12 Common E-mail Acronyms

the office being the private property of the employee. Since e-mails at work are created on company time using company equipment, employers feel that e-mails are no different than letters and memos on company letterhead. Employees claim a right to privacy. Courts have agreed with the employer and have ruled that an e-mail sent at work, regardless of its nature, is the property of the employer.

◆ *Clearly identify yourself.* When communicating with clients or others regarding a case, it is important that each e-mail clearly states your status and that you are not an attorney. All e-mails should also state your full name, title, firm name, and return address.

◆ *Check e-mail daily.* Important information comes through e-mail that requires an immediate response. Additionally, e-mails can pile up, making review and response a time-consuming activity.

◆ *Request a return receipt.* Most e-mail software has the capability to request a receipt verifying when the message was viewed by the recipient. This can be important information, especially when notifying a party of important dates or events in a litigation or case. Return receipts for case information should be used as a matter of policy and the receipts retained.

◆ *Do not promote or advertise a product or service to a listserv.* Sending e-mails that contain promotional material or advertisements to a group, such as a listserv, is known as **spamming** and is unlawful. There are federal and state laws that prohibit using a computer to send unsolicited advertisements. A person who sends illegal junk e-mails may be fined $500 per e-mail sent.

◆ *Do not unsubscribe to the entire listserv.*

◆ *Use punctuation sparingly.* Be careful with punctuation. Many periods can separate thoughts (. . . . .), but the use of many exclamation marks looks like anger (!!!!!). Many question marks also signify strong emotion (??????????).

Spamming (spam): To send unsolicited commercial e-mail messages to large numbers of people on the Internet on an indiscriminate basis.

Managing E-Mail

Managing e-mail is a time-consuming process, especially if one participates in a number of listservs. E-mails should be considered documents, such as memoranda or letters. E-mails are no longer a casual mode of communication. It is an essential element of a law firm's communication system. Preserving the integrity of the system is important for all employees of a firm. Some people receive hundreds of e-mails a day. Netiquette helps, but many people have difficulty managing their e-mails.

An e-mail that requires a reply should be responded to immediately on receipt. E-mails that are unimportant and require no response should be deleted immediately.

OF INTEREST . . .

What Is "Spam"

The term "spam" refers to promotional material sent by e-mail to thousands, perhaps millions of people over the Internet. The term is not taken from a lunch meat product. It comes from a *Monty Python's Flying Circus* skit titled "The King of Spam" by S. Garfunkel. One of the most famous examples of spamming occurred in 1994 when an immigration lawyer advertised his services to members of about 5,000 listservs without regard for the subject of the listserv. He received over 30,000 replies, mostly flames that caused his ISP's server to crash. The ISP revoked his access rights, and he received a one-year suspension from the Arizona Supreme Court.

Examples of spam are the following:

- Unsolicited commercial messages
- Messages from individuals where the sender has not participated in the topical discussions of the list and the message is a commercial advertisement
- Messages that do not offer direct content to the topic being discussed
- Messages that have nothing in common with the topic of the list
- Messages like any of the above that are cross-posted to multiple mailing lists

OF INTEREST . . .

What Does the > Symbol Mean in E-Mails?

The > symbol is commonly seen in e-mails. It is called an annotate feature, and it is offered by individual software packages. Some software annotates a message automatically, and others have it as an option. When a user replys to an e-mail, the original message is repeated and enclosed in the > symbol. This allows the person responding to the message to view it while responding. A number of > symbols displays the number of times the message has been answered. For example, a message with >>> before it means that the message has been answered three times. When replying to a long message, delete the parts of the original message that are not applicable to the response.

Old e-mails should be deleted from the system periodically. However, not all e-mails should be deleted, and discretion should be used to identify which e-mails should be retained and which should be deleted.

Some e-mails that contain important information should not be deleted but should be stored permanently on the firm's server or printed and put in the file. Software exists that will automatically manage e-mails, known as **e-mail filters.** An e-mail filter is software that automatically manages e-mail. The software will automatically discard e-mails that contain profanity or sexually explicit material. It is also used to keep confidential e-mails confidential by not allowing them to be disseminated over a network. The software can be programmed to filter e-mails from a certain person who sends e-mails for harassment or flaming purposes. It also can be programmed to automatically delete old e-mails. E-mails are placed in three categories: the first category is permanently stored and not deleted, the second category is automatically deleted monthly, and the last category is automatically deleted weekly. Using an automatic system is convenient if e-mails are categorized correctly.

Keeping E-Mail Confidential

E-mail sent to clients that contain legal advice must be kept confidential to protect attorney-client privilege. An e-mail that is sent to a client is subject to interception by others over the Internet. Additionally, if the e-mail is sent to the client's work, others, such as the employer, may have access to the client's e-mail, waiving attorney-client privilege. If they are not secured, attorney-client privilege may be lost.

E-mail filters: Software that manages e-mail and that can be programmed to delete e-mails that contain profanity or offensive material.

In April 1999, the ABA Standing Committee on Ethics and Professional Responsibility issued its formal opinion 1999-01 addressing the confidentiality problem with e-mail. The opinion stated that a lawyer may transmit information to a client via e-mail without violating the Model Rules of Professional Conduct. It further stated that e-mail affords a reasonable expectation of privacy without the necessity of encryption.

National and state bar associations are developing rules and guidelines pertaining to e-mail. Some states have considered the confidentiality problem and have created a varying degree of rules that pertain to e-mail. Some states, including Iowa, require clients to acknowledge that they understand the confidentiality risks associated with e-mails. Other states, including Vermont and Illinois, have ruled that there is a reasonable expectation of privacy with e-mail.

Courts have considered whether the use of e-mail waives attorney-client privilege. Under most court decisions, if a lawyer takes reasonable precautions to protect confidentiality, attorney-client privilege will not be damaged even if eavesdropping occurs. Many people believe that encryption is the only method that ensures an e-mail communication to be secure. In addition, an e-mail from a lawyer to a client should contain the following warning:

> This message is intended for the use of the individual or entity to whom or which it is addressed and may contain information that is privileged, confidential, and exempt from disclosure under applicable law. If the reader of this message is not the intended recipient or the agent responsible for delivering the message to the intended recipient, you are hereby notified that any dissemination, distribution, or copying of this communication is strictly prohibited. If you have received this transmission in error, please notify us immediately.

TECH TIPS

Popular E-Mail Software and Resources

The following is a sample of related software:

SecurPC: RSA Data Security—cryptography software

For Your Eyes Only: Symantec—cryptography software

Secure Messenger E-Mail: Deming Internet Security—cryptography software

Pretty Good Privacy: PGPMail—cryptography software

Eudora Pro: Qualcomm—e-mail manager

Netscape Mail: Netscape—e-mail manager

Versign: Versign Corporation—third-party vendor that issues certificates for digital IDs and private keys for encryption software

MS Internet Mail—e-mail software program Microsoft

Pegasus Mail—e-mail software program Claris

At Guard: Real Network—e-mail software that includes firewalls

Software mentioned in this sidebar is for informational purposes only and is not for the purpose of endorsing products.

TECHNOLOGY ETHICS

The prominence of the Internet has created new ethical considerations that have caused existing ethical rules and guidelines to be reexamined. The three-year period of 1995 through 1998 saw the Internet emerge in nearly every major law firm in the United States. The speed with which the Internet has become an integral part of law offices has caused an immediate demand for ethical rules specifically directed to cyberspace, especially in the area of client development.

As we learned in Chapter 4, both national and state bar associations have rules pertaining to client development. We learned about the ABA's Model Rules concerning client development through advertising in Chapter 4. When the ABA's rules were developed in 1983, the Internet was not used for lawyer advertising or client development. Even though the rules have been amended since 1983, none of the changes have specifically addressed advertising issues in cyberspace. In the absence of specific cyberspace rules, the ABA applies its current rules to cyberspace, causing conflicts about defining what activity constitutes compliance and what activity does not, resulting in more questions than answers.

Some states have issued rules that specifically address the ethics of new technologies, and others are in the process of developing them. All state bar associations that have considered the subject of lawyer's advertising on the Web have concluded that advertising legal services on the Web is an ethical activity as long as the lawyers comply with other advertising rules.

Advertising

Are Web sites considered advertising? Most states say yes as more law firms promote themselves via the Web. A 1997 survey conducted by the ABA reported that 61 percent of respondents used the Web to market its services through a Web site. If an attorney from state A advertises over the Web in a manner that violates state B's advertising rules, can state B prosecute the offender? Since state B cannot impose its rules on a lawyer who practices in another state, how does the presence of a Web site in state B affect the rules? State B could complain to state A's bar association, which could investigate the lawyers' advertising practices, but state A could impose discipline only if the advertising violates its rules, not state B's rules.

The ABA and state bar associations apply their existing rules to the Web. As was discussed in Chapter 4, the ABA applies its Model Rule 7.1 to Web sites, which states the following prohibitions of advertising material in general:

◆ It cannot contain a misrepresentation.
◆ It cannot contain an omission of fact necessary making a statement misleading.
◆ It cannot create an unjustified expectation about the results the lawyer can achieve.
◆ It cannot compare the lawyer's services with those of other lawyers.

These rules are generally accepted restrictions on a law firm's advertisements, including its Web site. What is uncertain, however, is how the rule is applied to links contained on a firm's Web site. For example, phrases such as "expert," "best lawyers in town," and so on are deemed to be a comparison with other lawyer's services and are therefore prohibited. Suppose a client writes a newspaper or magazine article that discusses a firm's expertise and labels its lawyers "great lawyers." Would a link to the article on a firm's Web site be an ethical violation? If a Web site links to a nonlegal Web site for which a nonlawyer is responsible, must that person adhere to the advertising guidelines? Can a firm use links without being held responsible for the content of those links?

Another uncertain aspect of Web page advertising is its use of multimedia, such as video and sound. As we learned in Chapter 4, the ABA and state bar associations have strict rules regarding media advertisements on radio and television. Would Web sites that have multimedia features fall under the current media advertising restrictions?

Another question of Web advertising is whether it constitutes solicitation. As we learned in Chapter 4, solicitation of clients is an area forbidden to lawyers. Many legal Web sites tell their visitors about the firm and areas of practice. Some offer to send a visitor more information about the firm. Is the Web site guilty of soliciting?

The construction of a Web site may violate ethical rules. Professional Web page designers encourage the use of pictures on a Web site to make it appealing, and most legal Web sites contain pictures. However, some pictures may be misleading. For example, a

Web site that has a picture of a lawyer in a courtroom may be misleading if the lawyer lacks trial experience.

Domain Names

A firm's domain name is subject to ethical rules. Most firms choose a domain name that is similar to, or an acronym of, the firm name. Others, however, choose a domain name that communicates its expertise, such as "quickdivorce.com," "drunkdriving.com," and so on. Since most individuals search for a subject through a search engine by keywords, such as "divorce," "bankruptcy," and "drunk driving," firms with these domain names are easily located through a search engine. If the domain name is used as a locator only, is it proper and subject to ethics rules? Does the domain name "best-lawyers.com" constitute a comparison and therefore violate Model Rule 7.1?

E-Mail

ETHICS ALERT

E-mail presents an ethical problem not covered by current ethical rules. The ethical prohibition against client solicitation has been applied to e-mail. Many lawyers subscribe to listservs, some of which do so to promote their law practice. If a member of a listserv asks a lawyer a legal question and the lawyer responds, is it solicitation? *Lawyers have been accused of solicitation for listserv activities.*

Some firms' e-mails contain disclaimers to avoid solicitation allegations. An example of a disclaimer is as follows:

> Participation in a discussion of ideas and issues of common interest with respect to the various subjects covered on this listserv should not be construed as creating an attorney-client relationship between attorney and the participants. Nothing in this e-mail should be construed as legal advice or legal opinion. Participation in the discussions is not confidential or privileged, and any material submitted or comments made shall not be deemed to be confidential or privileged.

In 1988, the U.S. Supreme Court held that lawyers could send direct-mail advertisements to those persons known to be in need of legal services (discussed in Chapter 4). Some argue that e-mail falls under direct-mail guidelines. Others argue that e-mails are direct communication, not written communication, and are therefore subject to solicitation accusations. Some court rulings have stated that participation on a listserv constitutes solicitation. Others have ruled that it is not solicitation but, rather, a response to a potential client's request for information. Spamming is a clear violation of ethical rules, but there is no agreement as to what other e-mail activities are ethical violations.

CYBERSITES

Finding Ethics Sites on the Web

The American Legal Ethics Library—www.law.cornell.edu/ethics

Law Journal Extra, Professional Responsibility—
     www.ljextra.com/practice/professionalresponsibility/index

Legal Ethics—www.legalethics.com

Texas Center for Legal Ethics and Professionalism—www.txethics.org

ABA Center for Professional Responsibility—www.abanet.org/cpr/home

National Association of Bar Counsel—www.nobc.org

State Legal Advertising Restrictions—www.wld.com/direct/restrict

ABA/BNA Lawyers' Manual on Professional Conduct—
     www.bna.com/prodhome/bus/MOPC

Legal Ethical Opinions Database—www.mwbb.com/leo/leo

NetEthics—www.computerbar.org/netethic/netnav

Retention of Advertising Materials

Source codes: The coding used by HTML to program a Web site's material.

Most states require that advertising materials be retained for a certain period. The ABA suggests that a copy be retained for two years. It is uncertain how this rule applies to Web sites and what material must be retained. Must a copy of the Web site's **source codes** (HTML programming) be retained, or should a printed copy of the site itself be retained? Must hard copies of all the links on a Web site be retained? If so, this requirement puts a tremendous burden on law firms to monitor all links and note the numerous changes in the links. Some Web sites and/or its links change weekly. Retaining current copies for a certain time period would be extremely time consuming.

Multistate Compliance

The most difficult problem with cyberspace client development is how to apply ethical rules to marketing legal services to clients of other states. The Internet has no geographical boundaries; it is global. Lawyers doing business on the Internet have a worldwide client base. Complying with the various ethical rules of each state is a difficult task. Many questions arise from the multijurisdictional broadcast of a Web site:

◆ Is advising a client from another state deemed practicing law in that state? If so, must a lawyer be licensed in that state?

◆ Are lawyers subject to the ethical rules of other states in which they solicit business even though they practice in another state?

◆ Are lawyers subject to the ethical rules of states in which the Web site appears but in which they do not solicit clients?

◆ Must a firm maintain an office in those states in which they solicit clients?

◆ Is the appearance of a Web site in those states in which a lawyer does not solicit clients a misleading advertisement?

◆ Is soliciting clients from a state in which a lawyer is not licensed the unauthorized practice of law?

Unauthorized Practice of Law

The Web has many opportunities for the unauthorized practice of law. Lawyers must be licensed to practice law in their state. Giving legal advice is practicing law. Giving legal advice to a person in another state could be unauthorized in some cases.

Nonlawyers are portraying themselves as lawyers and giving bogus legal advice over the Internet. The unauthorized practice of law is defined as a crime in most states, and its definitions and elements are set forth in the statutes of the state. It is very difficult to prosecute these people because most states require that a defendant in a matter related to the unauthorized practice of law be physically present in the state while engaged in the unauthorized activity. If the act did not occur in the state, the state would have no jurisdiction over the perpetrator. California has closed this gap in jurisdiction by holding that one engages in the unauthorized practice of law if there is significant contact with California. In this case, the defendant's physical appearance may not be required to prosecute for the crime.

As of this writing, some states have started the process of supplementing their ethical rules to include technology guidelines. As we enter the first decade of the new millennium, we will see many new laws concerning Internet technology, among them ethics rules developed by national and state bar associations.

CONCLUSION

Technology has affected every aspect of our lives: the government, the manufacture and delivery of products, the economy, our households, transportation, communication systems, and business. We can now communicate with computers as we do with one another—through speech. It will not be long before computers will develop the capability to process information and to use logic to make decisions for us. Technology is a two-edge sword. While offering us numerous benefits, it also creates some challenges. As new technology is mastered, there will be others to give us new opportunities and new challenges.

SUMMARY

Technology is a tool that is used by legal professionals to deliver their products to clients. The technological advances made in the 1990s have transformed the average law office. The introduction of new technologies and rapid changes in existing technologies have been both a blessing and a curse. The primary challenge is keeping current with the latest technology. Another challenge is managing information. Paralegals must be familiar with technology and the common software used in law offices.

There are various types of software and thousands of software applications available in the legal marketplace to accommodate almost every aspect of a law office's functions, from specific practice areas to management tasks. Software applications are developed specifically for the operating system used by the firm's computers. There are currently three major operating systems: Windows, Macintosh, Unix, and Linux. Microsoft's Windows operating system is the most popular and widely used operating system used in law offices today.

Software applications are either custom or off-the-shelf. Some software manufacturers have developed integrated software applications. Manufacturers also bundle software together in one package, called office suites. Most law firms use off-the-shelf computer applications and office suites. The most common law office software applications are word processing, spreadsheet, database, time and billing, case management (docket control), litigation support, substantive systems, court form generators, and browser. Add-on, or plug-in, software has been developed that adds features to software programs.

The Internet is a tremendous tool for individuals and organizations and is an essential tool for law firms. The Internet is a worldwide cooperative network of networks. No one owns the Internet. The networks that use the Internet are owned and maintained by their owners, and some are publicly traded companies. Today, there are tens of thousands of networks from around the world connected to the Internet.

To access the Internet, one must have browser software and an Internet Service Provider (ISP). A protocol is a set of rules that ensures that different network software products can work together. Protocol standards are set by the Internet Engineering Task Force

(IETF), a large international community of network designers, operators, vendors, and researchers concerned with the smooth operation of the Internet.

A domain name is needed to be located on the Internet. It is a unique name that identifies an organization on the Internet. Domain names consist of the organization's name (or specific designation) and a suffix that describes the type of organization, known as a type identifier.

The World Wide Web (WWW, or Web) is not the Internet. It is only one of the protocols that operate via the Internet. The protocol used by the Web is called Hypertext Transfer Protocol (HTTP). The Web is actually the name given to all documents written in a specific software language, known as Hypertext Markup Language (HTML). The Web delivers its information by hyperlinks to other pages or other areas on the Web. The organization of these links constitutes a Web site. Most Web sites contain levels. The levels are accessed through the first page of a Web site, known as the home page. The Web offers us numerous benefits.

Before information on a Web site can be accessed, it must be located. There are three basic ways to locate specific information on the Internet: Uniform Resource Locator (URL), keyword search, and topical index. Almost all companies and corporations have Web sites ending with ".com," meaning that it is a commercial site. Most Web sites consist of many sections, or pages, and it is possible to go directly to the page that contains the information desired by its URL. Certain rules apply to all URLs.

Keyword searching, or Boolean search, gives a search engine parameters within which to conduct the search, thus narrowing the outcome of a search.

Various Internet indexing companies exist that have categorized Internet sites into groupings of related fields, such as government, law, judiciary, and so on. Web sites can be marked by a browser. This activity is known as bookmarking.

You can find anything you want on the Web, but not all information is reliable. Anyone can post information on the Web regardless of age, background, and mental health. The federal government is the largest contributor of material on the Web. Web sites are accessible from other Web sites by links.

Internet technology has been the foundation of new systems and software products, among them intranet and extranet programs. An intranet is a law firm's internal information distribution system that is based on Web technology. Each person's computer is connected to the firm's server that stores the information. An intranet also uses specialized software, known as groupware, or software created specifically for use by groups. Intranets are custom made and designed according to a firm's specifications by professional intranet designers or in-house computer specialists. It has many uses but requires constant maintenance and updating. Law firms, especially large firms, realize a number of benefits to distributing information electronically via an intranet.

An extranet is a Web-based interface to a private network, which is a network accessible by a number of organizations, including selected firm employees, clients, outside counsel, and others who work together. The difference between an intranet and an extranet is that an extranet is directed to different people and has different uses. Among the uses are direct client access and multijurisdictional litigation management. Since extranets contain sensitive, confidential information, they must be secure so that unauthorized individuals cannot access the information. There are two types of security risks with an extranet: restricting access so that unauthorized persons cannot access the system and protecting information in transit to and from other members in the extranet.

Electronic mail, known as e-mail, is an electronic message system that allows communication from one person to another through their computers. E-mail passes to its destination through servers. E-mail addresses normally have three main parts: username, domain name, and type identifier. E-mail addresses and Web addresses are different.

There are thousands of groups and organizations that have their own discussion groups on the Internet. There are two types of discussion groups: newsgroups and mailing lists, which are also known as listservs. Newsgroups are public discussions on topics of general interest in which anyone with newsreader software can participate. A listserv contains a mailing list of e-mail addresses of people interested in the same subject. Listservs are either public or private and consist of two types: announcement type and discussion type. There are thousands of law-related listservs, including many listservs for paralegals.

To be good cybercitizens, it is suggested that each listserv participant become familiar with e-mail etiquette, known as netiquette. Netiquette is a form of on-line etiquette. It is an informal code of conduct that governs the acceptable way for users to interact with one another through e-mail.

Managing e-mail is a time-consuming process, especially if one participates in a number of listservs. An e-mail that requires a reply should be responded to immediately on receipt. Some e-mails that contain important information should not be deleted but should be stored permanently on the firm's server or printed and put in the file. E-mail sent to clients that contain legal advice must be kept confidential to protect attorney-client privilege. National and state bar associations are developing rules and guidelines pertaining to e-mail. Under most court decisions, if a lawyer takes reasonable precautions to protect confidentiality, attorney-client privilege will not be damaged even if eavesdropping occurs.

The prominence of the Internet has created new ethical considerations that have caused existing ethical rules and guidelines to be reexamined. The speed with which the Internet has become an integral part of law offices has caused an immediate demand for ethical rules specifically directed to cyberspace, especially in the area of client development. In the absence of specific cyberspace rules, the ABA applies its current rules to cyberspace, causing conflicts about defining what activity constitutes compliance and what activity does not, resulting in more questions than answers. Some states have issued rules that specifically address the ethics of new technologies, and others are in the process of developing them.

Are Web sites considered advertising? Most states say yes as more law firms promote themselves via the Web. What is uncertain, however, is how the rules are applied to links contained on a firm's Web site. Another uncertain aspect of Web page advertising is its use of multimedia, such as video and sound. Another question of Web advertising is whether it constitutes solicitation. The construction of a Web site may also violate ethical rules. A firm's domain name is subject to ethical rules. E-mail presents an ethical problem not covered by current ethical rules. Spamming is a clear violation of ethical rules, but there is no agreement as to what other e-mail activities are ethical violations.

Most states require that advertising materials be retained for a certain period. The ABA suggests that a copy be retained for two years. It is uncertain how this rule applies to Web sites and what material must be retained. The most difficult problem with cyberspace client development is how to apply ethical rules to marketing legal services to clients of other states. The Web has many opportunities for the unauthorized practice of law. While offering us numerous benefits, technology also creates some challenges.

CHAPTER ILLUSTRATION

Part of Black, White & Greene's marketing budget for the year was dedicated to developing a Web site for the firm. Robert directed Tricia to begin the process. Tricia called a number of Web site design firms and obtained estimates. She chose Web Page Design, Inc., to design and create the firm's Web site. The firm's consultant, Jim Parks, owner of Web Page Design, Inc., determined that the first step was to obtain a domain name for the firm. He told Tricia that the domain name "blackwhitegreene.com" was available, so he registered it. When he received confirmation of the registration, he proceeded to the next step: establishing the contents of the Web page.

After consultation with Tricia and the attorneys in the firm, it was decided that the Web page would contain the following information:

◆ The firm's brochure
◆ A biography of the attorneys, including their pictures
◆ The firm's newsletter
◆ An e-mail link
◆ Links to other law-related sites

Jim worked with Audra to post the firm's newsletter and obtained all the information needed for the site. In a month, the Web page was completed, and it looked great. It contained a picture of the outside of the firm's building and a map showing directions to get to the firm. The firm brochure described the history of the firm and listed the attorneys in the firm, including George Templeton, the contract attorney. The name of each attorney linked to the attorney's biographical information, which showed a current picture of him or her, the date he or she graduated from law school, and each attorney's area of expertise. Each page of biographical information contained a link to the attorney's e-mail address so that the attorney could be contacted directly.

The site also contained links to the state bar association, the findlaw search engine, and a Web site for legal ethics. Since Grant's expertise was tax, the site also contained a link to a Web site that discussed recent changes in tax law.

Robert, the managing partner, was concerned about the ethical implications of the Web site. He was concerned about potential problems with communications being unsecured and potential solicitation accusations. After researching the state's ethical rules concerning Web sites, he decided that the site should contain a disclaimer. He called Jim and had the following disclaimer put on the site:

This Web site is intended to supply general information to the public. It is not intended to be advertising, solicitation, or legal advice. The legal information provided at this site is general and not specific. The reader should not assume that the legal information at this site applies to his or her specific situation without consulting competent counsel in his or her state. We cannot guarantee the accuracy of information contained on Web sites to which this site is linked. We do not intend the links on this Web site to be referrals or endorsements of any kind. This Web site is not an invitation for an attorney-client relationship. We do not wish to represent anyone from another state unless the party has a valid claim in this state. We do not guarantee that the e-mail to the firm will be secure. Do not send confidential or sensitive information over this e-mail system.

The Web page was posted to the Web. Tricia directed that the firm's Web site address, www.blackwhitegreene.com, be inserted on the firm's stationery and business cards. Tricia could now concentrate on the next technology upgrade for the firm: an intranet.

Tricia called TrialNet, a company that installs intranets for law firms, and hired them to install an intranet for the firm. TrialNet obtained intranet groupware that linked everyone's computer with the firm's server. When it was completed, the firm's employees had direct access to the firm's server. The intranet contained the firm's client list, calendar, brief bank, law library resources, Internet, policy manual, time and billing program, newsletter and marketing materials, and management forms, such as check requests, new client matter sheets, and personal leave requests. Each practice area had its own area for access to information and materials that pertain only to that specific practice area.

Everyone at the firm was extremely pleased with the intranet. They commented that it saved them a lot of time. Everything they needed was at their fingertips, and the intranet was easy to use. When all employees learned to use the intranet effectively, Tricia noticed that the firm's billing increased. Tricia credited the increase in profitability to the intranet because it increased employees' productivity.

It was a policy of the firm that employees check their e-mail daily. One day, Patrizia noticed that she received three e-mails from the same person—someone called sexymale@aol.com. She read the first e-mail message. It said that he was surfing the Internet and saw her picture on the firm's Web site. He told her that he thought she was beautiful and wanted to meet her. The other two e-mails relayed the same message. Patrizia was amused but did not respond.

Each day that Patrizia checked her e-mail, there was at least three e-mails from sexymale. Each day, the e-mails from sexymale became more intense. Sexymale professed his undying love and affection for Patrizia and was very anxious to meet her. He pleaded with her to meet him and respond to his e-mail.

Patrizia decided to respond to let him know that she was not interested in meeting him and had no intention of continuing a communication with him. Her response was nice but straightforward.

Sexymale would not accept Patrizia's rejection. He threatened to come to the office to meet her regardless of her disinterest. His e-mails became more frequent and threatening. Patrizia became concerned. "Who is this nut?" she thought to herself.

Sexymale's e-mails began to flood Patrizia's e-mail box with sexually graphic material. Some e-mails contained pornographic material. Since the firm's Web site contained a map, sexy-male could easily find his way to the office. Patrizia was frightened. She called the police and alerted the firm of the problem.

The police came out to the firm and took a police report. Patrizia told police detective Ryan, "I am frightened that this person may be stalking me. What can you do to protect me?"

"Do you have reason to believe that he is stalking you?" asked detective Ryan.

"No, but he knows where I work. He even has a map to the office from our Web site," said Patrizia.

Detective Ryan responded, "We can't do much without more evidence of actual stalking. We don't know who this guy is or where he lives. He may live in Timbuktu for all we know. If he is from another state, the matter is out of our jurisdiction. We will assign an investigator to the problem and do what we can to get him to stop. The investigator assigned to these types of cases gets hundreds of e-mail-related complaints a week. We just don't have the resources to thoroughly investigate them all."

When detective Ryan left, Patrizia submitted a complaint to America Online, sexymale's ISP. America Online said that it would investigate the matter but that the only thing it can do is give the perpetrator's identity to the police and cancel the person's account.

Tricia quickly installed an e-mail filter that blocked all Patrizia's e-mails from sexymale@aol.com. The e-mail filter program automatically sends a responding e-mail to sexymale that Patrizia does not accept e-mail from his address and to immediately cease sending further e-mails to her. The firm also installed a security system at the receptionist's desk that will alert police of an unauthorized visitor. The door between the reception area and the rest of the offices was kept locked and opened only to those authorized to get through.

Tricia called Jim Parks at Web Page Design and instructed him to take the attorneys' pictures off of the Web site immediately. She also told him to remove the map. Patrizia also took security precautions. She made sure that she was escorted out of the office by one of the other attorneys each evening and that her husband drove her to work each day. The atmosphere in the firm was tense.

Two weeks later, Patrizia received a telephone call from the police investigator assigned to her case. He told her that sexymale was a fifteen-year-old boy who lived in California with no criminal record. He said that he posed no threat to her or the firm. The investigator referred the case to juvenile authorities in California for further action. Patrizia was relieved. She e-mailed everyone in the firm about the update. Everyone in the firm was glad that the crisis was over and that the firm could get back to normal.

CHAPTER REVIEW

1. What is the difference between custom computer applications and off-the-shelf computer applications?

2. What are add-on software applications, and what do they do?

3. What is a substantive software application?

4. What is a protocol, and for what is it used?

5. Who manages the Web, and what is its purpose?

6. What are the four main elements of a URL?

7. What is a Boolean search, and what is its purpose?

8. What is an intranet, and for what is it used?

9. What is an extranet, and for what is it used?

10. What is a firewall, and what is its purpose?

11. What is cryptography, and what is its purpose?

12. What are the three main parts of an e-mail address?

13. What is a listserv, and how does it differ from a newsgroup?

14. What is netiquette, and who enforces it?

15. Why must e-mail to clients be kept confidential?

EXAMPLES FOR DISCUSSION

1. Does the domain name never-lose-a-case.com violate ABA Model Rule 7.1? If so, why? If not, why not?

2. Do you have experience with any of the most common software applications used in a law office? If so, which one(s)? Discuss your experiences with the features of each. What do you like and dislike about them?

3. Does your place of employment have an intranet or an extranet? If so, how is it used? What features does it contain? Has it improved your productivity? If so, how?

ASSIGNMENTS

1. The law firm of Black, White & Greene is replacing its computer applications because its current software is outdated. Your group has been given the responsibility of researching software applications for the firm. You are to research the software applications for word processing, spreadsheets, database, time and billing, case management (docket control), litigation support, substantive systems, court form generators, and browser. One group member is assigned to one type of application (word processing). Research the features, requirements, functionality, and cost of each product. Write a report to the managing partner, Robert Black, about each program researched, do a cost comparison, and make your recommendations. Your report should include the reason(s) you chose the product for the firm.

2. Conduct a search of lawyers' Web sites. Search by legal practice area. Note the domain names. Are any improper?

3. What are the cyberspace ethical guidelines for your state? Consult the Legal Ethics Web site (www.legalethics.com). Research the following areas for your state:

   a. Solicitation through Web pages and listservs
   b. Requirements for e-mail confidentiality
   c. Advertising guidelines for Web sites
   d. Activities that constitute UPL in cyberspace

4. Go to the Web site for the NFPA at www.paralegals.org and do the following:

   a. Choose What's New and click on the Surveys link. Choose NFPA's Technology Survey and read it. What software is used by the responding paralegals at their work?
   b. Return to the NFPA's home page. Choose "Getting Started." In the Helpful Articles section, you will see a list of articles relating to getting started in the paralegal field. Choose one and prepare a report for the class.
   c. Return to the home page and choose Networking. Chose Listservs. You will see a list of listservs in specific legal subject areas and a field where you can subscribe to the listserv. At the bottom of the page, there are instructions on how to subscribe to a student's listserv. Send an e-mail to students-request@paralegals.org and subscribe to the student's listserv.

5. Examine a software program or demo disk of a program that automates a law office administrative or practice area (e.g., case management, time and billing, litigation support, and substantive applications). Describe the functions the programs intend to automate and evaluate the effectiveness of the program.

6. Interview an information manager at a large law firm in your area. Prepare a report that describes his or her duties and responsibilities.

SELF-TEST

How well did you grasp the material in the chapter? Test yourself by answering the following questions and check your answers against the answers found in Appendix A.

1. What is the primary challenge of new technology?
2. What does adequate training entail?
3. How has access to the Internet created a challenge for the legal team?

4. For what are software applications specifically developed?
5. What are the three major operating systems?
6. What operating system is most commonly found in law offices?
7. In what operating system does the Windows operating system have its origin?

8. For what operating system is most software designed?

9. Which operating system was the first to use a graphical user interface?

10. For what is the Unix operating system used?

11. What is a custom software application?

12. What is an off-the-shelf computer application?

13. Who creates custom computer applications?

14. Who creates off-the-shelf computer applications?

15. What is an integrated software application?

16. What is an advantage to an integrated software application?

17. What is a disadvantage to an integrated software application?

18. What are office suites?

19. What are some advantages to an office suite?

20. What type of computer applications do most law offices use?

21. What software application has been used in law offices since the 1960s?

22. What are the two most popular word processing applications?

23. What word processing software was used by the majority of law offices in the early 1990s?

24. Why are law firms changing word processing applications?

25. What are add-on (or plug-in) software applications?

26. What does add-on software do?

27. For what is a spreadsheet application used?

28. For what is a database used?

29. For what type of tasks do law firms use a database?

30. What is time and billing software?

31. Who uses time and billing software?

32. What does a time and billing application do?

33. For what is case management software used?

34. What are the benefits of a case management application?

35. What are some other features of a case management application?

36. For what is litigation support software used?

37. How are documents in a litigation case managed by litigation support software?

38. What are the four types of litigation support software?

39. What is a document abstract system?

40. What is a full-text retrieval system?

41. What is a scanning?

42. What is substantive software applications?

43. What is court-forms-generating software?

44. What is a browser?

45. For what is a browser used?

46. What are the two major browser software programs?

47. What type of firm is more likely to restrict Internet use to certain employees?

48. What is the Internet?

49. Who designed the Internet?

50. For what government agency was the Internet designed?

51. For what purpose was the Internet designed?

52. What was the name of the first Internet?

53. For what does the name of the first Internet stand?

54. In 1983, the first Internet split into what two networks?

55. What government agencies controlled the two networks?

56. What was the name of the second Internet?

57. Who had access to NSFNET?

58. Who used NSFNET?

59. When was commercial use of the Internet allowed?

60. What does NREN stand for?

61. What is NREN?

62. Who owns the Internet?

63. To access the Internet, one must have what two things?

64. What is an ISP?

65. What is a modem?

66. What are an ISP's computers called?

67. To what is an ISP connected?

68. From what does an ISP get its access?

69. What is a protocol?

70. What does a protocol do?

71. Who establishes protocol standards?

72. What is IETF?

73. What is an FTP protocol?

74. What is a Telnet protocol?

75. What is a gopher protocol?

76. How did the gopher protocol get its name?

77. What five factors are responsible for the Internet's sudden growth?

78. What is a domain name?

79. Who created domain names?

80. What was the name of the domain name project?

81. What are some of the concerns over domain name registration?

82. What is the name of the government's policy toward domain name registration?

83. What is the government's proposed solution to some of the domain name concerns?

84. What is a type identifier?

85. What are the six categories of type identifiers?

86. How are countries outside the United States identified on the Internet?

87. How does one register a domain name?

88. What is the World Wide Web?

89. Who developed the Web?

90. Who manages the Web?

91. Who runs the W3C?

92. Who funds the W3C?
93. What is the W3C's purpose?
94. What is the protocol used by the Web?
95. What is the software language used by all documents on the Web?
96. What does a computer need to read the HTML language?
97. What is shareware?
98. What is the difference between shareware and freeware?
99. What is a hyperlink?
100. For what is hyperlinks used?
101. What is a collection of hyperlinks called?
102. What is the first page of a Web site called?
103. How does the legal profession use the Web to publicize and manage the media in high-profile cases?
104. What are the three basic ways to locate information on the Internet?
105. What is a Uniform Resource Locator?
106. What are the four main elements of a URL?
107. What type identifier do most companies use?
108. What does ".com" mean?
109. How do you locate a Web site that is outside the United States?
110. What is a pathname?
111. How are pages in a URL separated?
112. What are the rules that apply to URLs?
113. What is a keyword search?
114. What is a Boolean search?
115. What does a Boolean search do?
116. What is a search engine?
117. What does a search engine do?
118. What is bookmarking?
119. Who warrants the accuracy of their Web sites?
120. What seven things can you do to verify the accuracy of information on a Web site?
121. Who is the largest contributor of material on the Web?
122. Who is responsible for developing law-related Web sites?
123. What government service can be used to locate information on the Web?
124. What is an intranet?
125. What is Web-based technology?
126. How does an intranet differ from the Web?
127. What is groupware?
128. How is an intranet designed?
129. For what is an intranet used?
130. What does "on-line" mean?
131. What is a brief bank?
132. What is a template?
133. What type of firm realizes the most benefits from an intranet?

134. What are the benefits of an intranet?
135. What is an extranet?
136. What are the benefits of an extranet?
137. What is the difference between an intranet and an extranet?
138. What is a firm-centered extranet?
139. What is a client-centered extranet?
140. What is the difference between a firm-centered extranet and a client-centered extranet?
141. What is a brokered extranet?
142. What are the two types of security risks with an extranet?
143. What is a firewall?
144. What is the easiest security method to implement for an extranet?
145. What is the most common security method for an extranet?
146. What is a digital ID?
147. What is a digital ID certificate?
148. What is a Secure Sockets Layer?
149. What is Secure HTTP?
150. What is cryptography?
151. What does cryptography do?
152. What are the two types of cryptography?
153. What is same-key cryptography?
154. What is public key cryptography?
155. What is e-mail?
156. What is snail mail?
157. How does e-mail reach its destination?
158. Who provides a person with an e-mail address?
159. What are the three main parts of an e-mail address?
160. An e-mail user name contains no ____ and no _____.
161. What word does the axon symbol mean?
162. In what case are e-mail addresses?
163. What does "case sensitive" mean?
164. How are e-mail addresses and Web addresses different?
165. What is a listserv?
166. What is the difference between a listserv and a newsgroup?
167. What is lurking?
168. What are the two types of listservs?
169. What is an announcement-type listserv?
170. What is a discussion-type listserv?
171. What is a moderated listserv?
172. What is an unmoderated listserv?
173. What is netiquette?
174. Who enforces netiquette rules?
175. Why should you not assume that your e-mail is private?
176. Why should you not give your ID or password to another person?

177. Why should you keep e-mail messages short?
178. Why should you edit quotations?
179. Why should e-mail messages contain only one subject?
180. What information should be contained in your e-mail signature?
181. Why should you not use all caps in e-mail messages?
182. Why should you use asterisks to emphasize a point in an e-mail message?
183. Why should you use underscores to signify a book title?
184. Why should you never send chain letters via e-mail?
185. Why should you spell out dates in an e-mail message?
186. What is a flame?
187. Why should you not forward personal e-mail messages?
188. What is an emoticon and how is it used?
189. Why should you be careful with sending jokes via e-mail?

190. Why use acronyms in an e-mail message?
191. Why is it important to know your firm's e-mail policy?
192. Why should you clearly identify yourself when sending an e-mail to a client?
193. Why should you check your e-mail daily?
194. What is spam?
195. Why should you use punctuation sparingly?
196. When should an e-mail be permanently stored?
197. What is an e-mail filter?
198. Why should e-mail messages to clients be secured?
199. What is one method that ensures confidential e-mail messages?
200. Are Web sites considered advertising?
201. What four advertising prohibitions apply to Web sites?
202. Why have lawyers been accused of solicitation for web activities?
203. What are source codes?

KEY WORDS

Add-ons (plug-ins)
Bookmarking
Boolean search
Brief bank
Browser
Case sensitive
Cryptography
Decrypt
Digital ID
Domain name
Download
Electronic mail (e-mail)
E-mail filters
Emoticons
Encrypt
Extranet
File Transfer Protocol (FTP)
Firewall

Flame
Freeware
Gopher
Groupware
Home page
Hyperlinks
Hypertext Markup Language (HTML)
Hypertext Transfer Protocol (HTTP)
Integrated software
Internet Service Provider (ISP)
Intranet
Listserv
Lurking
Modem
Netiquette

Network
On-line
Pathname
Protocol
Scanned
Search engine
Server
Shareware
Snail mail
Source codes
Spam (spamming)
Telnet
Template
Type identifier
Uniform Resource Locator (URL)
Web site
Web-based technology

CHAPTER

11

Law Office Systems

OBJECTIVES

After completion of this chapter, a student should be able to do the following:

◆ Define the goals and purpose of systems in a law office.
◆ Describe the four types of systems and how they function.
◆ Identify the components of the four stages of systems development.
◆ Explain the difference between administrative and substantive microsystems.
◆ Develop a system, including forms, checklists, and written instructions.
◆ Discuss common problems with systems development.
◆ Explain how systems evolve.
◆ Describe third-party systems.

INTRODUCTION

Law offices, or any business for that matter, must have systems in order to function in an organized manner. A law office is a collection of systems working together to achieve its goals. Systems contribute to the orderly performance of legal work. Without them, confusion and chaos would occur. Legal assistants not only participate in a law office's systems but are involved with systems development and implementation as well.

This chapter will discuss the general concept of systems for an overall understanding of systems. It will then describe different types of systems, illustrate how systems are developed, explain systems evolvement, and examine third-party systems. A legal assistant will often use the skill of developing and implementing a system and will find this skill useful in any type of law firm.

WHAT IS A SYSTEM?

The *Oxford English Dictionary* defines a system as a "set or assemblage of things connected, or interdependent, so as to form a complex unity; a whole composed of parts in orderly arrangement according to some scheme or plan." Roberta Ramo, author of *How to Create System for the Law Office,* defines a law office system as "a documented logical method or way of handling transactions, procedures, or work flow in a law office so as to minimize waste, conserve professional time, and optimize productivity."

The purpose of a system is to streamline a task so that members of a legal team do not do unnecessary work, waste law firm resources, or make a mistake. As a result of a good system, a legal team will become more efficient, reduce costs to a client, reduce costs to a firm, increase client satisfaction, and increase profits for a firm.

The goals of a system are to maximize productivity, minimize waste, conserve resources, reduce errors, and produce high-quality work. Systems play a vital role in increasing employee efficiency. If there were no systems, there would be no organization of efforts, and chaos would result.

Systems are tools used to do the following:

◆ *Guarantee that a firm's products maintain their excellence.* Missed deadlines are common malpractice claims against lawyers, and it is embarrassing to inform a client that a court would not accept a document because it was incorrect. These errors are costly to a client and a firm. Systems reduce the possibility of error in deadlines and documents.

◆ *Guarantee that a firm's commodity—time—is used to its maximum potential.* A disorganized office wastes employees' time, and wasted time costs a firm money. Systems save time and increase the efficiency of their users. This results in increased profits for a firm.

◆ *Give each member of a legal team the benefit of the experience of another.* Each person involved in a system contributes his or her knowledge, experience, and know-how. Less experienced team members learn from the contributions of others. This increases the expertise of each team member.

◆ *Substitute for recollection.* Undocumented systems are stored in the heads or memories of their users. This does not benefit a firm or other team members. Memory is known to fail, especially when pressing matters occupy its space. A system will relieve the necessity of storing many facts in a person's memory, thereby reducing the amount of stress on the individual.

◆ *Improve language and legal skills.* Preparing standard documents enhances a user's language skills. Using a systematic approach to projects increases legal skills.

◆ *Promote delegation.* A system encourages delegation of tasks. A systems review highlights areas to be delegated downward. Without a system, delegation could be overlooked.

◆ *Preserve methods.* A system is documentation of a procedure that was successful in the past. As legal assistants gain experience in an area of law, they learn the right way to do a task and the wrong way to do a task. Documenting the right way preserves this experience for other legal assistants.

◆ *Systems save time and resources.* Using a system saves the firm's employees' time, making them more efficient. Increased efficiency results in increased profits for the firm. In addition, systems decrease the potential for a legal malpractice claim, saving the firm money.

TYPES OF SYSTEMS

Four types of systems exist: macrosystems, microsystems, minisystems, and subsystems (see Exhibit 11.1). A macrosystem is a large system within which microsystems are contained. A microsystem functions within a macrosystem and contains minisystems. A minisystem functions within a microsystem and contains subsystems. A subsystem is a small system that functions within a minisystem. All are interrelated and depend on one another. Each part relies on the other parts to accomplish its goals. A macrosystem cannot be successful without good microsystems, and microsystems cannot be successful without good minisystems.

A law firm comprises one macrosystem, two types of microsystems (substantive and administrative), many minisystems, and many subsystems.

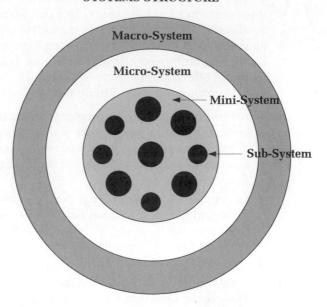

SYSTEMS STRUCTURE

Macro-System

Micro-System

Mini-System

Sub-System

EXHIBIT 11.1   Systems Structure

Macrosystems

The definition of the Greek word *macro* is "large." Therefore, we may define the term *macrosystem* as "large system." A firm's macrosystem consists of affiliated industries within which the firm must operate. An example of a part of a law firm's macrosystem is the U.S. court system.

Many elements affect a firm's macrosystem: technology, economy (U.S. and local), and government laws and regulations. When a change occurs in one of those elements, the firm's macrosystem feels its repercussions. These elements change often, and a firm must change with them.

Technology   Technology has changed the way in which we conduct business. E-mail, unheard of in the early 1980s, is a major source of communication in law firms today, and many firms are connecting their e-mail systems to those of their clients. This benefits the communication process and eliminates frustrating **telephone tag,** which occurs when someone calls a person who is unavailable and leaves a message and then is unavailable when the person returns the call. With the use of computers, law firms can deliver legal services in a more expeditious manner. As computer technology continues to streamline many legal tasks, systems must change to take advantage of this resource.

Telephone tag: A situation in which someone calls a person who is unavailable and leaves a message and then is unavailable when the person returns the call.

Economy   Eventually, the economy affects everyone—from a large corporation to a day laborer. In a recession, budgets are cut. Businesses cut budgets by reducing the amount of work given to their lawyers. People who cannot afford legal services find alternatives to their legal problems or go without legal representation. This eventually affects law firms, which must also cut their budgets. People are laid off because of lack of work—and the cycle continues.

When the economy changes, firms must also change to remain competitive. In a recession, firms may restructure their leadership and management policies to maintain their profitability. In addition, a firm may merge with another firm, therefore changing its entire macrosystem and its microsystems.

Government Laws and Regulations A firm whose clients are among highly regulated industries, such as public utilities, will have a different macrosystem than a firm whose clients are part of an unregulated industry. For example, some states impose state inheritance taxes on their citizens. These states establish inheritance tax agencies to collect the taxes, and law firms must interact with these agencies in probate cases. These agencies are part of a firm's macrosystem. If a state abolishes an inheritance tax or changes its laws and regulations, this affects a firm's system of completing probate cases and therefore affects its macrosystem and substantive microsystem.

Microsystems

A law firm has three goals: to provide quality legal services to clients, to attain growth and profit for the firm, and to provide growth and satisfaction for employees. A microsystem is a firm's methodology for reaching its goals.

A law office has two types of microsystems: administrative and substantive. These microsystems function together. A **substantive microsystem** supports goal 1, to provide quality legal services to clients. An **administrative microsystem** supports goals 2 and 3, to attain growth and profit for a firm and to attain growth and satisfaction for employees.

Substantive microsystem: A system of providing legal services to a client.

Administrative microsystem: A system relating to the management of a firm.

Administrative Microsystems Management develops and implements an administrative microsystem. The administrative microsystem consists of the firm's goals and objectives, resources, culture, and management style. Each of these microsystems contains minisystems, and the minisystems may contain subsystems.

There are many administrative minisystems. These minisystems include a firm's management policies and methods of implementing them. For example, a minisystem may be a firm's policy regarding employee vacations. A subsystem of that minisystem is the procedure for requesting a vacation, including preparing the required forms. Management's receipt of the form starts the second step in the minisystem: securing a replacement for the vacationing employee.

Many administrative minisystems are automated, such as conflict-of-interest checking, time sheet preparation, and others. For firms with an intranet (discussed in Chapter 10), the administrative minisystems are located on the firm's server and accessed from the employee's computer. Instructions for the minisystems can also be found on a firm's intranet.

Substantive Microsystems A firm's substantive microsystem is responsible for delivering legal services to a client. This system relates solely to the practice of law. It is specifically designed to contribute to greater efficiency in providing legal services. Lawyers and legal assistants who use substantive systems increase their productivity significantly.

The number of substantive microsystems in a firm varies according to the areas of law in which the firm practices. A small boutique firm specializing in one area of law will have one substantive microsystem and several minisystems. A large firm with many specialties and departments will have many substantive microsystems and minisystems, as shown in Exhibit 11.2.

Many substantive microsystems consist of software products specifically designed for a particular area of law. There are hundreds of such software packages on the market today. These products were discussed in Chapter 10, and a sample listing of substantive software is found on page 332.

Three methods are used to acquire a substantive microsystem: developing, evolving, and buying. Each of these methods is discussed later in this chapter.

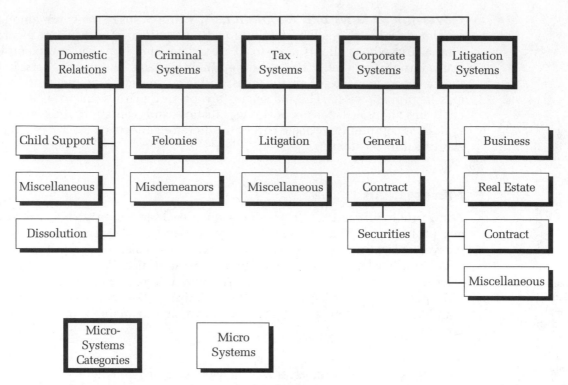

EXHIBIT 11.2 Substantive Microsystem and Minisystems for a Large Firm

Minisystems and Subsystems

A minisystem is a system within a microsystem. It is an intregal part of a microsystem. The type and number of minisystems depend on individual system users and the efforts of a firm to develop systems. Some minisystems die early, and others survive for as long as a firm exists.

Minisystems are constantly changing. Parts of a minisystem are improved, expanded, or changed as the law changes and as its users become more experienced. If a system is developed to the complete satisfaction of its users, changes may occur to a firm's macrosystem, such as changes in the law, that will affect the system. Therefore, minisystems are never fixed and permanent.

A minisystem must operate within substantive and administrative microsystems. For example, the ratios of legal assistants to attorneys and secretaries to an attorney—legal assistant team are considered an administrative minisystem. A substantive minisystem must function within this administrative minisystem. An administrative minisystem affects a substantive minisystem's development and the delegation of tasks within the substantive system.

Minisystems make the way a firm manages cases consistent. Each minisystem contains steps to complete a case. Each step is considered a subsystem. The number of subsystems in a minisystem depends on the procedural aspects of a case.

For example, an average civil litigation case is a microsystem that consists of ten activities, or minisystems, as shown in Exhibit 11.3.

1. Initial client contact
2. Conflict of interest check
3. Conduct initial client interview and complete questionnaire
4. Prepare summons and complaint
5. File complaint and issue summons
6. Serve summons and complaint
7. Commence discovery proceedings

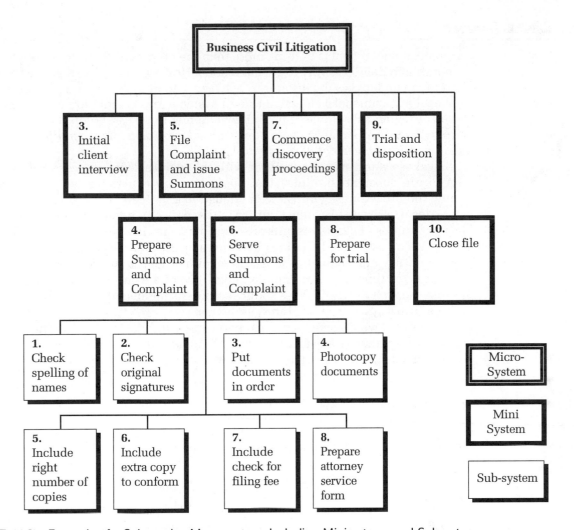

EXHIBIT 11.3 Example of a Substantive Macrosystem, Including Minisystems and Subsystems

8. Prepare for trial
9. Handle trial and disposition
10. Close file

Each minisystem can be broken down into tasks, or subsystems. For example, in the fifth minisystem (file complaint and issue summons), it is the secretary's responsibility to prepare the documents for court filing. Eight tasks are involved in this minisystem:

◆ Check spelling of all names
◆ Check to see whether the original is signed
◆ Put documents in correct order
◆ Photocopy documents
◆ Include appropriate number of copies for court
◆ Include additional copy to conform
◆ Include check for filing fee
◆ Prepare attorney service instruction form

Once all eight tasks, or subsystems, are completed, the minisystem (file complaint and issue summon) is completed, and the documents are ready to file with the court. If one of the tasks is overlooked, the documents will be filed incorrectly and rejected by a court clerk. This will result in delay and inefficiency. Each step of a subsystem is important to the success of a minisystem.

SYSTEMS DEVELOPMENT

ETHICS ALERT

Systems development is nothing more than the process of thinking through and documenting in detail the way to get a job done. How logically the steps are thought out and organized makes the difference between a good system and a poor system.

Legal assistants take an active role in systems implementation and development. They are often asked to assume the development process. *A lawyer must, however, supervise the work of a legal assistant and take ultimate responsibility for the supervision and management of a system.*

Legal assistants must be familiar with the requirements of a case before they can develop a substantive minisystem. Only through experience will legal assistants know the procedures of a case well enough to anticipate the next step. With experience, legal assistants become familiar with a case's standard documents and delegation of duties. Legal assistants also become familiar with the best methods to complete a task. They must also be familiar with a firm's administrative microsystem, and they must structure substantive minisystems to work within that microsystem. It takes time to gain complete knowledge of a firm's administrative micro-and minisystems. It normally takes about six months for an employee to become familiar with a firm's systems, procedures, and style.

Systems development involves choosing candidates, completing four stages (analysis, synthesis, organization, and finalization), and storing the system. It requires special skills and poses unique problems.

Candidate Selection

Certain areas of law are especially appropriate for systems development because they involve a series of routine tasks that are similar in each case. Those areas include the following:

Litigation	Dissolution of marriage
Adoption	Name change
Probate	Estate planning
Workers' compensation	Subrogation
Collection	Real estate
Corporate	Bankruptcy

Once a type of case is chosen, three questions must be answered:

1. Can this project be simplified?
2. Can this project be streamlined?
3. Can this project be improved to better serve the client?

If the answer to any of these three questions is yes, the project is a good candidate for a system. However, systems take time and effort to develop, and the effort should not be expended unless a system will be used. A hastily developed system will be more a hindrance than a help. A legal assistant must choose system candidates carefully. If a legal assistant occasionally works on probate cases, perhaps one or two a year, it would not be an effective use of the legal assistant's time to develop a comprehensive probate system. On the other hand, if a legal assistant works on probate cases 50 percent of the time, a firm would benefit from a probate system.

To develop the first system, a legal assistant should choose something that is easy and familiar, such as a routine project. If an office has established systems, a legal assistant may use them as a guide.

System development consists of four stages:

1. Analyze
2. Synthesize

3. Organize
4. Finalize

Stage 1: Analysis

Analyzing a system has four steps: review, separate, evaluate, and communicate.

Review The project chosen for systems development must be reviewed to determine whether it warrants the time and expense of systems development. If an existing system is being revised, it must be determined whether the system can be improved considerably. If revision would result in a slight improvement, a complete system revision should not be done; only necessary changes within the existing system should be made. Once the decision to develop a system has been made, all components must be reviewed to be sure all the necessary elements are available for analysis.

Separate For a system to be analyzed adequately, each step must be separated from the others. All the major activities are listed and broken down into smaller tasks and then steps. Writing down each step in a system gives a legal assistant the opportunity to see it. Seeing each step gives the legal assistant insight into ways to make the system better. Steps taken for granted are seen in the context of the entire system and therefore are understood better.

The first major activity in a substantive project is an initial client interview. This activity can be broken down into smaller increments, or tasks, and each task can be broken into smaller increments, or steps. After the steps have been broken into their smallest increments, the responsible team member for each task is listed. Exhibit 11.4 shows an organization chart that documents this breakdown.

TASK	STEP	WHO
1. Make appointment	Check attorney's calendar and enter appointment	Secretary
	Check paralegal's calendar and enter appointment	Secretary
	Send confirming letter	Secretary
	Give copies of letter to legal assistant	Secretary
	Give copies of letter to attorney	Secretary
2. Conduct initial consultation with legal assistant	Give introduction	Legal assistant
	Complete questionnaire	Legal assistant
	Give overview of case	Legal assistant
	Introduce attorney	Legal assistant
3. Conduct initial consultation with attorney	Review questionnaire	Attorney
	Give overview of case	Attorney
	Discuss strategy	Attorney
	Discuss fees	Attorney
	Check conflicts	Legal assistant
4. Sign retainer agreement	Prepare agreement	Legal assistant
	Review agreement	Attorney
	Sign agreement	Attorney
5. Set up file	Give questionnaire to secretary	Legal assistant
	Input client data	Secretary
	Set up client ledger	Secretary
	Incorporate file into filing system	Secretary

EXHIBIT 11.4 Initial Organization Chart

Evaluate Each step is now ready to be evaluated. For each step, the following questions are asked:

◆ Is it necessary?
◆ Could the step be delegated downward?
◆ Could this step be done easier?
◆ Could this step be done in less time? If so, how?
◆ Have problems occurred with this step in the past?
◆ Could the forms be made simpler?
◆ Could this step be combined with another?

Answers to these questions are written on an evaluation sheet in a comments section after each step, as shown in Exhibit 11.5.

Coding each step will allow a legal assistant to identify the status of each step quickly. Each step is coded by number or color. If coding is by number, each step is assigned a number according to importance, as follows:

1 = very important
2 = important
3 = somewhat important
4 = not important

If coding is by color, each step is highlighted with a different color highlighter, as follows:

Yellow = very important
Green = important
Pink = somewhat important
Orange = not important

Initial Client Interview

STEP	WHO	COMMENTS
Check attorney's calendar and enter appointment	Secretary	*OK*
Check paralegal's calendar and enter appointment	Secretary	*OK*
Send confirming letter	Secretary	*OK*
Give copies of letter to legal assistant	Secretary	*Could be eliminated*
Give copies of letter to attorney	Secretary	*Could be eliminated*
Give introduction	Legal assistant	*OK*
Complete questionnaire	Legal assistant	*OK*
Give overview of case	Legal assistant	*Could be eliminated*
Introduce attorney	Legal assistant	*OK*
Review questionnaire	Attorney	*OK*
Give overview of case	Attorney	*OK*
Discuss strategy	Attorney	*OK*
Discuss fees	Attorney	*OK*
Check conflicts	Legal assistant	*Could be done by secretary*
Prepare agreement	Legal assistant	*Could be done by secretary*
Review agreement	Attorney	*OK*
Sign agreement	Attorney	*OK*
Give questionnaire to secretary	Legal assistant	*OK*
Input client data	Secretary	*OK*
Set up client ledger	Secretary	*OK*
Incorporate file into filing system	Secretary	*OK*

EXHIBIT 11.5 Evaluation Sheet

Coding each step will save time when communicating the steps of a system to other team members and will give a legal assistant an overall view of how many steps in the system need change.

Communicate   After each step has been evaluated, it is time to identify other members of the team who will participate in the system. Each step should be discussed with them. It is best to call a meeting, as shown in Exhibit 11.6 than to discuss the system with them when they are in the middle of other projects. It is important to get their opinions of each step of the system that they will be expected to perform. Each team member should evaluate each step in order of importance. A legal assistant will then have their perception of each step in writing, which will be valuable information in the next step of systems development. Each team member should be asked the following questions:

◆ How would you rate each step in order of importance?
◆ Have you encountered problems with any of the steps? If so, what are they?
◆ What are your suggestions to correct the problems?
◆ Can any of the steps be delegated downward?
◆ Can any steps be eliminated?
◆ Must new steps be added?
◆ What can we do to make the system better?

Stage 2: Synthesis

Synthesize means "to make up by combining parts or elements." The synthesis stage has three steps: eliminate, delegate, and consolidate.

Eliminate   The first step in the synthesis stage is to eliminate all steps determined to be unnecessary. The effect of eliminating a step on the entire system is considered, and if it is minimal, the step should be eliminated.

EXHIBIT 11.6   Legal Team in Conference
Each step of the system should be discussed with team members who will use the system. It is also preferable to call a meeting for this purpose.

Delegate   When all unnecessary steps have been eliminated, the remaining steps are reviewed to determine which ones can be delegated downward. For example, in Exhibits 11.4 and 11.5, the legal assistant prepares a retainer agreement for the attorney's review. This is a necessary step in the initial interview process. Can this function be delegated to the secretary? If so, the appropriate changes for each function should be made.

ETHICS ALERT

When delegating functions, it is important to understand the limits within which support staff can operate. A systems developer must have a clear understanding of what a legal assistant can and cannot do. For example, it is recommended that legal assistants not quote fees. Case law has determined that quoting fees to a client requires an attorney's judgment and analysis of the issues. Therefore, a systems developer cannot delegate this function to anyone other than an attorney.

Delegating tasks is a skill. Delegating too much results in frustration and work overload, and delegating too little results in a lack of motivation. Effective delegation develops employees and allows them to grow personally. Successful delegators know that an employee needs increased responsibilities to grow personally. They also know that mistakes are common in the learning process and understand that the manner in which these mistakes are handled affect the growth process.

In order to delegate successfully, the delegator must have a clear understanding of the delegatee's abilities and trust the delegatee to perform at an acceptable level. A poor performer will receive fewer opportunities for increased responsibilities. To delegate over the person's abilities will have disastrous effects. The delegatee will become frustrated and lose confidence in her or his abilities. Delegating under a person's abilities sends a message of a lack of confidence in one's abilities, resulting in a lack of motivation.

Communication is the key to effective delegation. The duties and responsibilities must be clearly communicated, preferably in writing so there is no misunderstanding. After the task is communicated, the communication door must be left open for direction on each step of the process. When the task is finished, it is the delegator's responsibility to give feedback, whether it be constructive criticism, suggestions for improvement, or praise for a job well done.

Another, often overlooked aspect of delegation is authority and accountability. Many times, responsibility is delegated, but the authority necessary to adequately perform the task is withheld, resulting in failure. The person accepting the responsibility must also be held accountable for its success or failure. The responsible employee can then delight in an accomplishment or learn from mistakes made.

Consolidate   Consolidation is combining the new elements. A new organization chart that incorporates the changes is prepared, as shown in Exhibit 11.7.

Notice that some steps were eliminated, new steps were incorporated, and some steps were delegated downward. The material is now ready to be organized.

Stage 3: Organization

The two steps of the organization stage are establishing a chronological sequence and developing a master task list.

Establish a Chronological Sequence   After each step of a task has been consolidated, the steps are organized in chronological order. The following questions must be asked after this is done:

◆ Does the task flow?
◆ Does the sequence make sense?
◆ Should one step be completed before another?
◆ If the steps were reorganized, would it expedite the process?

Then, necessary changes are made in the organization of the steps.

Initial Client Interview

TASK	STEP	WHO
1. Make appointment	Check attorney's calendar and enter appointment	Secretary
	Check paralegal's calendar and enter appointment	Secretary
	Send confirming letter	Secretary
2. Conduct initial consultation with legal assistant	Give introduction	Legal assistant
	Complete questionnaire	Legal assistant
	Introduce attorney	Legal assistant
3. Conduct initial consultation with attorney	Review questionnaire	Attorney
	Give overview of case	Attorney
	Discuss strategy	Attorney
	Discuss fees	Attorney
	Check conflicts	Secretary
4. Sign retainer agreement	Prepare agreement	Secretary
	Review agreement	Attorney
	Sign agreement	Attorney
5. Set up file	Give questionnaire to secretary	Legal assistant
	Input client data	Secretary
	Set up client ledger	Secretary
	Incorporate file into filing system	Secretary

EXHIBIT 11.7 Organization Chart after Consolidation

Develop a Master Task List When each step has been put in its proper order, it is inserted on a master task list. This list is the skeleton from which a system will be developed. Each step is listed in chronological order. A master task list will do the following:

◆ Give a description of each task
◆ Describe specifically when each task is due
◆ Indicate the documents required to complete each task
◆ List the person responsible for completing each task and preparing the documents
◆ Give the order in which each task is to be completed
◆ List all actions to be taken (e.g., telephone client)
◆ Include telephone calls or court appearances
◆ Direct each team member to the appropriate checklist

A master task list should be self-explanatory, inclusive, and descriptive. It is reviewed with other members of a legal team for their opinions and suggestions. If other team members do not accept the organization of a project, it may be necessary to reorganize the project or make other changes.

Exhibit 11.8 is an example of a master task list for civil litigation.

When the final reorganization has been approved, a project is ready to go on to the final stage of systems development: finalization.

Stage 4: Finalization

The finalization stage is the most time-consuming aspect of systems development. This stage has four steps:

1. Preparing forms and checklists
2. Writing instructions

Civil Litigation

TASK	WHO	WHEN/HOW	√
1. Make appointment	Secretary	When client calls	A
A. Check calendars	Secretary	Before client hangs up	A
B. Send confirming letter	Secretary	Same day appointment is made	A
C. Send questionnaire—D1	Secretary	Enclose with letter—L-1	A
2. Conduct initial interview with legal assistant			
A. Review and complete questionnaire	Legal assistant	During interview	A
B. Introduce attorney	Legal assistant	After legal assistant interview	A
3. Conduct initial interview with attorney			
A. Review questionnaire	Attorney	During interview	A
B. Discuss strategy	Attorney	During interview	A
C. Discuss fees	Attorney	During interview	A
4. Sign retainer agreement			
A. Prepare agreement A-1	Secretary	When instructed by attorney	A
B. Review agreement	Attorney	When completed, during interview	A
C. Sign agreement	Attorney	At end of interview	A
5. Set up file			
A. Give questionnaire to secretary	Legal assistant	After reviewed	A
B. Input client data	Secretary	After receipt of questionnaire	A
C. Set up client ledger	Secretary	After data input	A
D. Open file	Secretary	After ledger setup	A
6. Prepare documents			
A. Draft summons and complaint P-1	Legal assistant	As soon after interview as possible	B
B. Give to attorney for review	Legal assistant	When draft is completed	B
C. Approve draft complaint	Attorney	As soon as possible	B
D. Prepare final summons and complaint	Legal assistant	As soon as possible	B
E. Give to attorney for review	Legal assistant	When final is completed	B
F. Approve final summons and complaint	Attorney	As soon as possible	B
G. Give to client for approval	Legal assistant	After attorney approval	B
H. Send cover letter	Secretary	After client approval—form L-1	B
I. Sign complaint	Attorney	Upon approval	B
7. File complaint			
A. Check spelling of names	Secretary	When complaint is received	C
B. Make six copies of summons and complaint	Secretary	After complaint is checked	C
C. Obtain check for filing fee	Secretary	After complaint is photocopied/use check request form M-45	C
D. Send original and four copies to court	Secretary	When check is received/use L-2	C
E. Insert one copy in file	Secretary	During process	C
F. Send copy to client with cover letter	Secretary	During process/use form L-3	C

(Note: √ column directs the reader to the appropriate checklist: A, B, or C.)

EXHIBIT 11.8 Master Task List

   3. Checking the system and following up
   4. Revising the system

     Prepare Forms and Checklists Forms consist of form letters, court documents, agreements and other documents. Documents of prior cases are reviewed to determine whether variations of the same document exist. If a document can be standardized, a form is developed, with information pertinent to each case left blank, such as client name and date. If special paragraphs should be inserted in certain circumstances, this is indicated by an **if clause:** "If corporation, insert paragraph A. If individual, insert paragraph B." The paragraphs are stored in a computer and are easily inserted in a document.

If a court document requires standard language, a form can be developed to insert information pertinent to each case. Each form can be used in every case of its type. By having these forms on a computer, it is a simple matter to insert a case caption and other pertinent information. A document is then ready for an attorney's signature. Exhibits 11.9 and 11.10 show a sample form pleading and a sample form letter, respectively.

The documents are reviewed and analyzed considering applicable laws and regulations. Whenever possible, terms such as *plaintiff, defendant,* or *debtor* should be used when developing forms. This will avoid the "he or she" differences and streamline the form. Lines or a specific "insert here" code are inserted to alert a user to enter the appropriate information in a form document. These codes can be **blind inserts,** which are entries that are seen on a computer screen but not printed and are available in most word processing software packages. *It is a lawyer's responsibility to proof and check all documents.* Approval of all form documents must be obtained before implementation.

Checklists are vital to the success of a system and are simple to create. Each step of a system is listed and includes the responsible team member. Places for the completion date and the team member's initials are also included. The responsible team member dates and initials the checklist as each task is completed. By doing this, each member of the team will be able to monitor each aspect of the project by looking at

If clause: A clause inserted in a form document alerting the preparer to insert the appropriate paragraph.

Blind insert: An entry in a form document alerting the preparer to insert material; seen on the computer screen but not printed.

ETHICS ALERT

Insert caption

Complaint for Personal Injuries

1. Plaintiff is a citizen of the State of Florida (or corporation with its principal place of business in the State of Florida) and Defendant is a citizen of the State of ***Insert state*** (or corporation organized under the laws of the State of ***Insert state*** having its principal place of business in ***Insert state***). The matter in controversy exceeds, exclusive of interest and costs, the sum of $50,000.00.

2. On or about ***Insert date*** on a public highway called ***Insert name of street*** in the city of ***Insert city and state***, Defendant drove his/her motor vehicle in such a negligent manner so as to strike Plaintiff as he/she was crossing said street.

3. As a result of the negligence of Defendant, Plaintiff was injured. Plaintiff has been prevented from transacting his/her business, suffered great pain of body and mind, and incurred expenses for medical attention at ***Insert name of hospital*** in a sum in excess of $50,000.

WHEREFORE, Plaintiff requests judgment against Defendant as follows:

1. For special damages in a sum in excess of $50,000;

2. For general damages in a sum in excess of $500,000;

3. For such other and further relief as the court may deem just and proper.

Dated: ***Insert date***

Law Offices of Black, White, & Greene

_____

Robert L. Black, Esq.

Doc.P-45 Rev.9/04

EXHIBIT 11.9   Form Pleading

Note: The document number, Doc. P-45 Rev.9/94, identifies the form and the date it was developed or revised.

BLACK, WHITE, & GREENE
2121 Broadway
Palo Alto, CA 90000
(555)123-4567

Insert date

Insert client name and address

Re: ***Insert case name***

Dear ***Insert client name***

Enclosed is the completed Complaint in the above matter.

Please review it carefully. If the Complaint requires correction, please contact Ms. Bunnell, Mr. Black's legal assistant, and inform her of the changes. If the Complaint meets with your approval, please sign in the appropriate place and return it to this office in the enclosed envelope. We will proceed to file it as soon as possible after receipt.

If you should have any questions or comments, please contact Ms. Bunnell or Mr. Black. Thank you for your prompt attention to this matter.

Sincerely,

Black, White, & Greene

Audra Everett, Secretary

sb

Encls.:

Doc.L-3, Rev.9/04

EXHIBIT 11.10 Form Letter

the checklist. If a question arises, the checklist will show the date a step was completed and the person who completed the step. Example checklists appear in Exhibits 11.11 and 11.12.

Checklists should contain a descriptive notation of when a step must be completed. If a document must be filed within ten days, is it ten days from the date of mailing? Date of receipt? Date of hearing? Is it ten calendar days? Ten business days? It is important to be specific.

Checklists are maintained in a computer so that they may be changed easily. Some firms have found that keeping master checklists in a computer reduces storage problems. When a checklist is needed, a hard copy is printed. The hard copy is usually kept in a client's file and is readily accessible to anyone working on the file.

Cross-index: To mark a document so that it can be easily found in a system.

When form and checklist documents are completed, they must be incorporated into a firm's computer system. Each one must be **cross-indexed** on the computer and identified to the system. To be easily located in a computer system, each form or checklist document must have an identifying number in the footer, usually in the order it will be used. Each document may be lettered and numbered to indicate the type of document and the use sequence, as follows:

L-1	First letter
P-1	First pleading
C-1	First checklist
A-1	First agreement

The document coding system must be developed so that the system may be expanded. For example, if all letters were coded 1 through 10, all pleadings 11 through 20, and all checklists 21 through 30, there would be room for only ten documents in each section. Adding an eleventh document would require completely renumbering the documents, changing the master task list, and rewriting the instructions. The letter-

Initial Client Interview

STEP	WHO	DATE COMPLETED	INITIALS
Check attorney's calendar and enter appointment	Secretary	_____	_____
Check paralegal's calendar and enter appointment	Secretary	_____	_____
Send confirming letter	Secretary	_____	_____
Give introduction	Legal assistant	_____	_____
Complete questionnaire	Legal assistant	_____	_____
Give overview of case	Legal assistant	_____	_____
Introduce attorney	Legal assistant	_____	_____
Review questionnaire	Attorney	_____	_____
Give overview of case	Attorney	_____	_____
Discuss strategy	Attorney	_____	_____
Discuss fees	Attorney	_____	_____
Prepare agreement	Secretary	_____	_____
Review agreement	Attorney	_____	_____
Sign agreement	Attorney	_____	_____
Give questionnaire to secretary	Legal assistant	_____	_____
Input client data	Secretary	_____	_____
Set up client ledger	Secretary	_____	_____
Incorporate file into filing system	Secretary	_____	_____

Doc.C-1, Rev.9/04

EXHIBIT 11.11 Checklist

Prepare Documents

STEP	WHO	DATE COMPLETED	INITIALS
Prepare documents			
A. Draft summons and complaint	Legal assistant	_____	_____
B. To attorney for review	Legal assistant	_____	_____
C. Approve draft complaint	Attorney	_____	_____
D. Prepare final complaint	Legal assistant	_____	_____
E. To attorney for review	Legal assistant	_____	_____
F. Approve final complaint	Attorney	_____	_____
G. To client for approval	Legal assistant	_____	_____
H. Send cover letter	Secretary	_____	_____
I. Sign complaint	Attorney	_____	_____
File summons and complaint			
A. Check spelling of names	Secretary	_____	_____
B. Make 6 copies of documents	Secretary	_____	_____
C. Obtain check for filing fee	Secretary	_____	_____
D. Send original plus 4 to court	Secretary	_____	_____
E. Insert one copy in file	Secretary	_____	_____
F. Send a copy to client with cover letter	Secretary	_____	_____

Doc.C-2, Rev.9/04

EXHIBIT 11.12 Checklist

and-number coding illustrated here will allow unlimited expansion of each section.

The master task list can be finalized at this point (see Exhibit 11.8).

Write Instructions Each system must have written instructions that explain how to use the system. Instructions are absolutely necessary and are often neglected. Many people will not take the time to prepare instructions when developing a system; this is a disservice to the system. As new people come into the firm and use the system, they must read the instructions to understand the system. A lack of written instructions will cause frustration and a lack of enthusiasm about the system.

Information for instructions is derived from the final master task list. This list is used as a guide. The first draft of the written instructions is prepared on the computer so that it may be revised easily. The written instructions are divided into four sections: information, requirements, instructions, and examples of forms and checklists.

The information section contains information about the goal and purpose of the system and the specific area of law for which the system was developed. If the system has limits, the reader is informed of them in this section. It is a good idea to refer the reader to additional sources of information.

All a system's requirements are listed in the requirements section. These include the following:

◆ Computer hardware
◆ Software, including version
◆ Titles of team members using the system
◆ Outside services, such as attorney service or courier
◆ Other supplies and requirements

The instruction section is the largest section. Written instructions are the basis of a system's evaluation. Without them, it would be difficult to determine whether a system was successful. They are also vital to a firm's training program.

The master task list is the beginning of the instructions section. The instructions should inform the reader when to use the system, how to use the system, and what each step of the system is. They should be as specific as possible. If there is a doubt about whether to include some information, it should be included; it is better to over-explain a step than to underexplain a step. Each form and checklist should be referenced, with instructions on how to complete it.

Instructions should include a section for special circumstances. No system can anticipate every situation that will arise in a case. The circumstances that a system will not accommodate should be indicated and the reader told what to do in those circumstances.

The forms and checklists section should include a hard copy, or printed copy, of every form and checklist. Each document should be presented in the order in which it is used. Each document must include the document number and a detailed description of where it can be found in the computer system. It should also contain the date it was developed or revised (see Exhibit 11.9). Whenever a form is revised, this information must be updated.

When a first draft of the instructions' four sections is completed, it is given to other team members for their review and approval. Some firms may require that management review and approve all systems. Documents and instructions may be finalized when final approval is received.

Check the System and Follow Up As a system is tested, necessary changes are noted. Any changes in the law that will affect the system must be incorporated by the attorney. Other team members are involved in this process. Problems or missed steps are noted. Depending on the area of law of the system, it is a good idea to complete one case using the new system before making a final determination of the success of the system. After the problems have been evaluated, the system is revised to eliminate those problems.

Revise the System   The revision step consists of the entire systems development process but on a smaller scale. Only one or two areas may need revision. Once the revised material has been analyzed, synthesized, and organized, the system is finalized by preparing a final draft of the forms, checklists, and written instructions. The system may now be implemented.

When a system is implemented, it will grow and evolve over time. As more people use the system, suggestions will be made to improve the system. The system must be flexible in order to be effective. The four stages of system development are shown in Exhibit 11.13.

Systems Storage

Systems are normally stored on the computer for easy access and revision. The system will be backed up in the firm's regular backup process. However, it is recommended that a hard copy of the system instructions and documents be kept in case of computer failure. A system in a hard-copy format can be reviewed easily.

The best method of storing a hard copy of the system is in a three-ring binder, in which individual documents and sections of the system can be easily updated and changed by page. If a system requires more than one binder, the same size and color of binder should be used for each section of the system. A one-and-a-half-inch binder usually works well. A smaller binder may cramp the documents, and a larger binder would be too heavy to handle if placed on a high shelf.

The binder should have a label holder on its spine to mark its contents. Putting a label on the spine with transparent tape is not a good way to mark the binder.

Tabbed dividers should be used in the binder to separate sections of the system. The dividers should be made of sturdy, heavy stock. Each tabbed divider should be

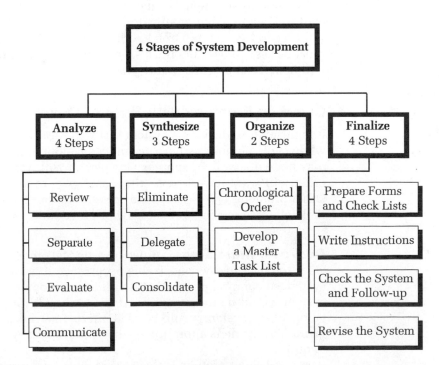

EXHIBIT 11.13   Four Stages of System Development

marked with the section of the system to which it relates: information, requirements, written instructions, forms, and checklists.

The front of the binder should contain a table of contents with corresponding page numbers. This will direct a user to the desired information with little effort.

The binder will contain copies of all documents and checklists. The checklists for each case are stored in the client's file and are completed as a task is completed. As a legal assistant proceeds to the next stage of a case, the appropriate checklist for that stage is copied from the system.

In a manual system, copies of checklists and forms are stored, and only one master original is kept. In a computerized system, original documents need not be copied; a form or checklist can be printed when needed.

Backup: Substitute; in computer systems, a copy of a system on a different disk.

An extra copy of a system is made and stored in the library. It is not necessary that each member of a team have a copy of the system as long as they know where the master original is located and it is accessible to them at all times. In many firms, storage is a problem and space is a premium. One master copy plus a **backup** copy are all that is needed and will make a system easier to update. In addition, since people are becoming conscious of our natural resources, unnecessary copies of documents are discouraged. For computerized systems, a backup of the entire system must be made and stored in a safe place.

Essential Skills for Systems Development

Sharp analytical skills are essential to produce a good system. But no matter how well a system is developed, it is only as good as its users. If users will not properly use a system, the system is wasted. One member of a team not participating in a system can cause the system to bog down and grind to a stop.

No matter how much time and expertise have been programmed into a system, the person using the system must have knowledge in the area of law and good work habits in order to use it properly. A good system will not compensate for poor work habits. A checklist can prompt a user when a document is due, but it cannot produce the document on time. Good planning and scheduling are required. Each member of a legal team must be a good time manager.

Developing a system is time consuming: The average systems development project takes about three months to complete. However, if planned and analyzed carefully, a good system is a tremendous asset to a firm. The system must be manageable, must be easy to use, and must save users' time. If all the steps are followed, a system will benefit its users for many years.

Common Problems with Systems Development

It is difficult to develop a system that will satisfy each member of a team, especially when each member participates in its development. What works well for one person may not work well for another. One person will want more steps in a system, and another will want fewer steps. It is a challenge to accommodate each person's needs. Other problems arise as a system ages and updates are not performed and when users look to a system as a source of law or procedure.

Desire for More Steps A person who feels that more steps should be added may want to cover every conceivable occurrence in a case. It is impossible to develop a system so comprehensive that it will accommodate every contingency of a case; the system would be too complicated to use. In addition, the time it would take to develop such a system would be prohibitive. Lawyers are good at playing the "what-if" game. This game is appropriate when developing systems, but one must know when to quit.

A good rule to follow is the 90 percent rule: If a situation can be expected to happen 90 percent of the time, it should be included; if a situation is expected to happen infrequently, it should be excluded. For example, suppose an attorney wants additional steps in a Chapter 11 bankruptcy system to include cases that involve individuals with an annual income of $750,000 or more. Chances are there will be few such cases. Therefore, it would not be practical to include such steps in the system. A good system is a simple system.

Desire for Fewer Steps

When functions in a system are divided among team members—secretary, legal assistant, and attorney—it is easy for a team member to underestimate the importance of another's tasks. Because he does not fully understand the importance of a function outside his own domain, he may eliminate a function as unnecessary. For this reason, it is vital to receive feedback from each member of a legal team working with a system. If the responsible team member considers a function important, it should not be eliminated. To do so would decrease the system's effectiveness and the team member's morale.

If a team member suggests eliminating a step, the step should be carefully evaluated before it is deleted. If it is found to be "somewhat important," it should be eliminated during the trial period of the system. If a problem occurs, the step can be reinstated. The system will be more successful if it is streamlined.

Need for Updates

Once a system has been operating successfully for some time, changes may occur that affect the system. The firm may change its software, which will affect the system. Or the law may change, requiring changes in the forms or procedures. The system should be reviewed periodically and updated accordingly.

A major problem with a system's success is that written instructions may not be updated to reflect changes in the system. The system's users are familiar with the system, so they may make periodic changes without referring to written material, therefore, the written material is not updated and becomes outdated. If a new person uses the system, the written instructions are incorrect, so the system is of no use to them. A system's written instructions must be updated with all revisions.

Use as an Information Source

A system should never be used as a source of law or procedure. It may be tempting for a legal assistant to consult a system for the answer to a procedural question instead of doing research in the library. Since a system was not developed to cover every contingency in a case, it is a poor source of information on a question concerning that area of law. Systems are not alternatives to learning but can help a user learn.

SYSTEMS EVOLVEMENT

Not all systems are developed from scratch; some systems evolve. As legal assistants work in an area of law, they become familiar with procedures in that area. They gain experience in the essential elements required. Most legal assistants keep an extra copy of each document they prepare to use as a form to prepare future documents.

Form files: A collection of copies of form documents and frequently used documents; these documents act as a guide when developing similar documents.

Most legal assistants keep these sample documents in **form files,** also known as brief banks (discussed in Chapter 10). As they collect these documents, they have the beginning of a system. During the course of a case, legal assistants develop their own personal checklists or have a checklist in their mind of projects to do. Eventually, legal assistants have the documents portion of a system developed on an "as-you-go" basis.

Putting together a formal system from existing documents, checklists, and methods that evolve over time involves the same four areas of systems development: analysis, synthesis, organization, and finalization. However, a systems developer will save a considerable amount of time in document preparation. Since all sample documents are prepared, all that is needed is to standardize them.

THIRD-PARTY SYSTEMS

Substantive minisystems can be purchased from several companies. These commercial systems are developed to accommodate many specialized areas of law. (See list in Chapter 10 on page 332). The first commercial systems on the market consisted of form letters, checklists, and written instructions. Now, commercial systems consist of computerized documents, written instructions, and some electronically filed documents.

When purchasing a commercial system, it is important to realize that the system was developed by someone's analysis of the necessary components of the system. This other person's logic composed the sequence of events and essential parts of the system. The method of analysis the author used should be reviewed to determine whether the system's divisions and subdivisions are adequate for the firm. Sample letters and documents should also be reviewed to determine whether they fit the firm's style.

Management needs to look for a couple of specific things when purchasing a system. First, is the system current? Outdated law or forms make a system obsolete. Second, can the system be changed or expanded? This is especially important as the law changes. Some companies offer updates to a system to accommodate these changes. Sometimes, the purchase price of a system is a small portion of its total cost; updates could make the system cost prohibitive. Third, can the system be expanded to include firm-specific documents and information? If a system cannot be expanded, it will soon become obsolete.

It is important that the forms in a system comply with a court's requirements. Each jurisdiction has different requirements for documents. For example, some federal district courts will not accept a form printed on a dot matrix printer, and some will not accept computer-generated forms.

Commercial substantive legal systems that are computerized can save a lot of time and be a valuable asset to a firm. These systems are programmed so that information entered on a master information sheet or initial client interview sheet is automatically inserted in the correct place on a form. This is done automatically by a computer rather than a lawyer or legal assistant. Commercial management systems offer the same feature. Information entered from a new-client form is automatically inserted on a client's ledger, a responsible attorney client list, and other management documents. Therefore, a secretary enters the information into the computer once rather than several times. The money a firm saves in terms of employee time greatly justifies the cost of the system.

CONCLUSION

Whatever the method used to obtain a system, legal assistants will be asked to participate in law firm systems. If a legal assistant spots an area in a system that can be improved, she or he should be assertive and bring it to the management's attention. The use of systems streamlines the practice of law and is essential for an organized, efficient law firm.

SUMMARY

Systems are tools used to streamline a task so that a legal team does not do unnecessary work, waste law firm resources, or make a mistake.

Four types of systems are used: macrosystems, microsystems, minisystems, and subsystems. A law firm comprises one macrosystem, two types of microsystems (substantive and administrative), minisystems, and subsystems.

Systems development is nothing more than the process of thinking through and documenting in detail the way to get a job done. It consists of four stages: analysis, synthesis, organization, and finalization.

Analyzing a current or new system has four steps: review, separate, evaluate, and communicate. The synthesis stage has three steps: eliminate, delegate, and consolidate. Organizing has two steps: establishing a chronological sequence and developing a master task list. Four steps constitute the finalization stage: preparing forms and checklists, writing instructions, checking the system and following up, and revising the system.

Each system must have written instructions that explain how to use the system. Information for written instructions is derived from a final master task list. Written instructions are divided into four sections: information, requirements, instructions, and examples of forms and checklists.

It is difficult to develop a system that will satisfy each member of a team, especially when each member participates in its development. It is impossible to develop a system so comprehensive that it will accommodate every contingency of a case. A good rule to follow is the 90 percent rule.

Once a system has been operating successfully for some time, changes may occur that affect the system. A major problem with a system's success is that written instructions may not be updated to reflect changes in the system. A system should never be used as a source of law or procedure.

Not all systems are developed from scratch; some systems evolve. Developing a formal system from existing documents, checklists, and methods that evolve over time involves the same four areas of systems development: analysis, synthesis, organization, and finalization.

Sharp analytical skills of a system's developer are essential to produce a good system. No matter how much time and expertise have been programmed into a system, the person using the system must have knowledge in the area of law and good work habits in order to use it properly. If all the steps of development are followed, a system will benefit its users for many years.

CHAPTER ILLUSTRATION

Dennis White—Black, White & Greene's litigation attorney—represents Secluded Homes Corporation in a very large business litigation case. The company is a large real estate developer in the area. It is being sued by the Washington County Home Owners' Association for construction defects found in their homes. The homes in the Washington County development are having problems with water and sewer drainage, and some homes' foundations are cracking. The case is expected to involve many parties and will generate thousands of documents to manage.

Since the case is expected to be so large, Dennis needs to hire a freelance paralegal to work exclusively on the case. The firm called the local paralegal association, and Dennis had many referrals, one of whom he hired. Julie Hemstreet is an experienced litigation paralegal with five years of experience. She has experience with large litigation cases and accepted the position. She would work exclusively on the case and would end her association with the firm when the case is finished.

Dennis called a meeting with Julie and Audra, his secretary, to discuss the case. The client was just served with a complaint that they must file an answer to in thirty days. He wants to file a cross-complaint against forty-five subcontractors. Dennis's case strategy needs a system that will organize the case from the beginning so that the team can manage it. He asked Audra and Julie to develop a system for the case.

The first step in the process is to research the marketplace for software that will accommodate the case. Audra and Julie received literature on ten case management software packages, each with similar features. Julie mentioned that she had experience working with the ComLit software package and that it was a good program. She felt that it would be perfect for the case. Tricia ordered the software, which they received ten days later.

Julie then went to work to develop the system. The first step was to make a list of tasks that needed to be done for the case. She consulted with Dennis and Audra and came up with an overview of the major tasks of the litigation. She incorporated the major tasks into the software and asked Audra to prepare the software for the case. The parties had to be entered, as did the dates on which the complaints and cross-complaints were filed. Audra did the necessary formatting, and Julie went to work dividing each task into segments. She developed a master task list of the essential elements of the case.

Julie reviewed the master task list with Dennis and Audra for their input. Dennis noted that some of the tasks that Julie was to be responsible for could be delegated to Audra. Audra also suggested some revisions to the list. After revision, the master task list was approved.

The next step of the development process was developing forms and checklists. This was a time-consuming process for Julie, but the case management software helped her because it contained sample forms that she could revise for use. She knew that some forms, such as form letters, would have to be changed as the need arose, and she made provision for it.

The largest area of the system was the discovery process, as they expected thousands of documents to be produced in the case. Julie developed a system that would organize the documents, gather essential information from them, and monitor them. The case management software is a full-text retrieval system that allows for all the information in the documents to be input into the computer. The documents can then be searched for their content and the information separated into categories. All information pertaining to one subject matter could then be found together. The system will allow the information to be organized in other ways, such as chronologically or by party.

When the discovery phase began and they received discovery documents, Julie gave each document an identifying number. The number was put on each document in a bar code that also contained other information, such as producing party, date of input and other information. The document was then scanned into the case management system. Audra was responsible for storing the hard copy of each document. She organized each document chronologically by its identifying number and stored them in a fireproof filing cabinet that was kept locked.

Julie prepared written instructions for each phase of the system. She asked Audra for help in preparing the instructions. Audra wrote down each step of the system for which she was responsible and inserted how she accomplished each step. Julie did the same and then integrated the instructions into one document.

When the system was completed, Julie printed out the instructions and cross-referenced the instructions with the applicable form and checklist. She inserted clear instructions on each form and checklist

on how they should be completed. All members of the team reviewed the system and were very pleased with it. The system was finished, just in time for all its aspects to be tested. While there were a couple of things that needed revision, most of the system worked very well.

The firm had the entire case organized. When Dennis took depositions of opposing parties, he took the system with him on his laptop computer. He had all the information about the case with him so that he could pinpoint his questions. When his client was deposed, Dennis was able to quickly counter tough questions with copies of the exact document that substantiated his point. Opposing attorneys on the case were very impressed with the system. Some felt intimidated by how organized and efficient Dennis was, considering the complexity of the case.

The system made preparing for trial very easy for Dennis. While opposing attorneys on the case struggled with managing the complex issues and thousands of documents, Dennis and Julie prepared the case quickly and easily.

Two weeks before trial, the parties attended a settlement conference. Dennis was ready. He could tell that the other attorneys did not want to try the case because of the magnitude of it. He also knew that he had the upper hand because he had such good control over the issues and evidence. He started settlement negotiations, and eventually the case was settled. The client was very pleased with the outcome of the matter. Dennis was also pleased. He knew that the system helped him greatly with the case.

Because the case settled, Julie was ending her contract with the firm. Dennis saw Julie as an integral part of his team and wanted her to stay with the firm to work on some other projects with him. He offered her a position as a full-time legal assistant to him, and Julie accepted. The system Julie developed was used as the system for other large litigation cases the firm handled.

CHAPTER REVIEW

1. What are the five basic goals of a system?

2. What are the four types of systems, and how do they function together?

3. What types of systems are found in a law firm?

4. What are the four stages of systems development?

5. Describe the four steps of stage 1, analysis.

6. Describe the three steps of stage 2, synthesis.

7. Describe the two steps of stage 3, organization.

8. Describe the four steps of stage 4, finalization.

9. What skills must a legal assistant have to develop a system?

10. How do systems evolve?

11. What should management consider when purchasing a third-party system?

EXAMPLES FOR DISCUSSION

1. What Happened?

Most people have encountered a service or business that seems totally disorganized. Disorganization usually means the lack of an effective system. Discuss with class members your experience with a business or service that did not function well and the possible reasons for the malfunction. Could a system have improved the service? What elements of systems planning were missing? What needed to be done to improve the system?

2. The Wrong Form

Brad Longstreet, a legal assistant at the firm of Henderson & Ruohniemi, created a system for dissolutions of marriage. It was a good system with written system requirements, instructions, and forms and checklists. Brad became ill and was replaced with a temporary legal assistant, Brenda Engstrom. Brenda followed the system and completed the documents for a simple dissolution and filed the documents with the court. When Brad returned, he discovered that the court had rejected the documents because one document was prepared on an outdated form. Brad was aware of the change in the form and tried to determine how Brenda could have filed the wrong form.

1. What step in the systems process was overlooked?
2. What must Brad do to keep the problem from happening again?
3. Should another step be added to Brad's system? If so, what step?

ASSIGNMENTS

1. Analyze your place of employment, home, or organization and answer these questions:
   a. What does the macrosystem consist of?
   b. How many microsystems are there?
   c. How many minisystems can you identify?
2. Prepare a checklist for a task you do often at work or home.
3. Prepare a form of a document you use often at work or school.
4. Choose an established system at your place of employment, home, or organization and answer the following questions:
   a. What are the problems of the system?
   b. How do these problems affect your work? The work of others? The final work product? The environment?
   c. What are your suggestions to improve the system?
5. Prepare a master task list of the system you have chosen and do the following:
   a. Analyze its components. What could you do to make the system better? What resources would you need? How would you delegate the tasks?

   b. Incorporate your changes and revisions in a new master task list. Is the system better?
   c. Present your final master task list to your employer, your family, or the head of your organization and report any comments to the class.
6. Prepare written instructions for the system you chose in assignment 4.
7. Research substantive system software programs. Compare the features of three programs and answer the following questions:
   a. What are the differences?
   b. What are the similarities?
   c. What tasks are automated?
8. For the law firm of Black, White & Green, describe:
   a. The macrosystem
   b. Minisystems
   c. Administrative minisystems including number of attorneys, legal assistants, and secretaries per attorney.
   d. Substantive minisystems
   e. Procedures to keep systems updated

SELF-TEST

How well did you grasp the material in the chapter? Test yourself by answering the following questions and check your answers against the answers found in Appendix A.

1. What is the purpose of a system?
2. What are a system's goals?
3. What seven things are systems used for?
4. What are the four types of systems?
5. What is a macrosystem?
6. What types of systems are found in law firms?
7. What does a law firm's macrosystem consist of?
8. What are the three main elements that affect a firm's macrosystem?
9. How many microsystems does a law firm have?
10. What are the two microsystems in a law firm?
11. What does a law firm's administrative microsystem consist of?
12. What is the purpose of a firm's substantive microsystem?
13. What determines the number of substantive microsystems in a law firm?
14. What are the three methods of acquiring substantive microsystems?
15. What is a minisystem?
16. What determines the type and number of substantive minisystems in a law firm?
17. Why are a firm's minisystems constantly changing?
18. What is a subsystem?
19. What determines the number of subsystems in a minisystem?
20. What is systems development?
21. Who has ultimate responsibility for the management and supervision of a system?
22. What are the four stages of systems development?
23. What are the four steps of systems analysis?
24. What are the advantages of coding each step?
25. Why is it important to discuss each step of the system with co-workers?
26. What are the three steps of the synthesis process?
27. What is important to remember when delegating functions?
28. How does a systems developer consolidate?
29. What are the two steps of the organization process?
30. What is the master task list?
31. What is the purpose of a master task list?
32. What are the four steps of the finalization process?
33. What is a form letter?
34. What is a blind insert?
35. What is a checklist?
36. Why are checklists maintained in a computer?
37. Why are form documents numbered?
38. Why are written instructions important for a system?
39. Where is information for written instructions obtained?
40. What are the four sections to the system's written instructions?
41. What does the information section of written instructions contain?
42. What does the requirements section of written instructions contain?
43. What is the purpose of the instructions section?
44. What is the beginning of the instructions section?
45. What is the basis of system evaluation?
46. What does the forms and checklist section of the written instructions contain?
47. How does one follow up on a system once it has been developed?
48. How is a system revised?
49. What is the best method to store a system?
50. How is a system divided into sections?
51. How many copies of the system should there be?
52. What are the essential skills one must have for systems development?
53. What are the four common problems of systems development?
54. How do systems evolve?
55. What is a commercial substantive minisystem?
56. What does a person look for when purchasing a system?

KEY WORDS

Administrative microsystem
Backup
Blind insert

Cross-index
Form files
If clause

Substantive microsystem
Telephone tag

CHAPTER

12

Docket Control Systems

OBJECTIVES

After completion of this chapter, a student should be able to do the following:

◆ List the elements of a docket control system.

◆ Explain what information is placed on a master calendar.

◆ Describe primary and secondary information.

◆ Explain how to maintain a tickler system.

◆ Explain how to tickle various types of due dates.

◆ Explain how to tickle statutes of limitations.

◆ Explain how to manage reminder dates.

◆ Describe the difference between a static and an automated computerized docket system.

◆ Explain the major features of automated docket control software.

◆ Set up a manual tickler system.

◆ Discuss the various forms and reports used in docket control systems.

◆ Describe file review.

INTRODUCTION

Scheduling a law firm's obligations is a great challenge for law firms, government agencies, and corporate legal departments. There are many deadlines in a law office, and a firm must have a scheduling system that controls those deadlines, allocates work so that projects are completed on time, and ensures that nothing is overlooked. An overlooked deadline can result in a legal malpractice suit, disciplinary proceedings, damage to a firm's reputation, or all of these.

Docket: An abstract or brief entry or the book or record containing such entries.

To meet this challenge, every firm relies on a **docket** control system. A docket control system is perhaps the most important system in a law office. The system is so important that professional liability insurance companies require applicants to describe their docket control systems on application forms in order to obtain legal malpractice insurance. According to recent statistics, 50 percent of all legal malpractice claims are a result of a missed court date or a critical deadline. A firm with no docket control system will not qualify for professional liability insurance.

Each member of a legal team takes an active role in a firm's docket control system and works with it every day. Secretaries and legal assistants in small firms may have total responsibility for the docket system. In larger firms, maintaining a firm's docket is the responsibility of docket coordinators or docket clerks. Since a legal assistant is responsible for the day-to-day maintenance of a case, the skill of controlling deadlines is essential. Every legal assistant and legal secretary must have knowledge of docket control systems.

This chapter will detail the essential elements of a docket control system and thoroughly explain and illustrate each element. It will examine calendaring systems, tickler systems, and file review systems. After reading this chapter, a student should be familiar enough with docket control systems to develop the skill of maintaining a firm's docket and be familiar with the features of docket control software.

ELEMENTS OF A DOCKET CONTROL SYSTEM

A good docket control system contains trial dates, court and hearing dates, deposition dates, meeting dates, filing deadlines, reminder dates, follow-up dates, appointments, and reminder dates.

A good, reliable system will perform 6 functions:

1. Meet time requirements
2. Expedite the completion of tasks
3. Promote good client relations
4. Ensure that professional liability insurance requirements are satisfied
5. Reduce stress
6. Avoid financial loss by reducing malpractice claims

The characteristics of a good system are as follows:

◆ Provides immediate and automatic calendaring
◆ Provides a double-check of entries
◆ Allows sufficient lead time in advance for completion of tasks
◆ Provides for follow-up to ensure actual performance of work
◆ Is easily maintained and operated

The type and sophistication of a docket control system varies according to the size of a firm, the type of firm, and the specialty of a firm. A firm's docket control system consists of a calendaring system, tickler system, and file review system.

CALENDARING SYSTEMS

A firm's calendar is a key component of the smooth operation of a law office. It is imperative that all members of the legal team manage their calendars correctly. There are two types of calendars: master and personal. Calendars come in two forms: computerized and manual. Calendaring skills are among the most important skills a legal assistant will learn. Mastery of calendaring skills is important to a legal assistant's success.

Master calendar:
Calendar that contains hearing and deposition dates for each attorney in the firm.

Two calendars are used in most law offices: **master calendar** and **personal calendar.** The calendars are categorized by the type of information inserted in the calendar.

Master Calendar

Personal calendar: An individual's calendar that contains the same information as a master calendar but also includes appointment dates, follow-up, deadlines, and personal information.

Firms vary by which information is inserted on a **master calendar.** However, all master calendars contain trial dates, hearing dates, and deposition dates for each attorney in a firm. The purpose of a master calendar is to locate an attorney and schedule future events.

A master calendar varies in size and format. Most firms have a computerized calendar program that provides a master calendar. A printout of the master calendar is distributed regularly to each member of a law firm. Large firms normally distribute a master calendar daily. A small firm that has few changes in the master calendar distributes it less often, normally weekly. Firms with an intranet do not distribute hard copies of the master calendar. These employees have immediate access to the most recent changes to the master calendar on their desktops. As a staff member makes changes or enters new information into the master calendar, it is immediately updated and accessible to all other firm employees.

Essential information on a master calendar includes the following:

♦ *Attorney.* First initial and last name of the attorney, or initials of the attorney.

♦ *Type of matter (trial, hearing, deposition).* If a trial or hearing is expected to last many days, a line or other designation is drawn through those days. If it is a motion, the type of motion is indicated. Abbreviations are appropriate to use.

♦ *Date and time.* If an event consists of several days, those days are included on the master calendar.

♦ *Name of case.* The case name is inserted on the master calendar. A client's surname is always indicated as the first name of a case, for example, *Client v. Name of Defendant* if the client is a plaintiff or *Client adv. Name of Plaintiff* if the client is a defendant.

♦ *Location.* If the matter is a trial or hearing, the court and the courtroom are indicated. If it is a deposition, the address of where it will be held is indicated.

Exhibit 12.1 is an example of a master calendar.

Personal Calendar

ETHICS ALERT

Statute of limitations:
The time period after
an offense within
which a lawsuit
must be filed.

Each member of the legal team has a **personal calendar.** A personal calendar contains two types of information: primary and secondary.

Primary information includes all the information inserted on the master calendar (court hearings, trials, and depositions). These dates are included in a personal calendar as well as the master calendar to ensure that the information is not missed. It is also necessary that the information be in front of the attorney and legal assistant at all times for scheduling purposes.

Primary information also includes the **statute of limitations** for each case for which the legal team is responsible. Statutes of limitations are entered in the personal calendar in red or in bold. *It is very important that statutes of limitations are not missed.* If a statute of limitation is missed, the client is barred from filing the action. The attorney becomes liable to the client for damages that may result in a legal malpractice lawsuit, disciplinary proceedings, or both. As an extra precaution, statutes of limitations are also entered in a tickler system (discussed later in this chapter).

Secondary information includes the following:

♦ Dates and times of appointments with clients
♦ Dates and times of conferences
♦ Other dates, such as bar association luncheons or continuing education obligations
♦ Personal reminders, such as birthdays and vacations dates

Some people combine primary and secondary information into one personal calendar. Others have a separate calendar for secondary information. Most personal calendars are computerized and are part of a firm's docket control software program, as shown in Exhibit 12.2. However, manual calendars, or calendars that are maintained by hand, are an essential element of a firm's calendaring policy in the event of computer malfunction.

A legal assistant's personal calendar is a duplicate of the attorney's personal calendar. If a legal assistant reports to more than one attorney, the legal assistant's personal calendar will contain information for each of those attorneys. These duplicate calendars are used to schedule events for the attorney. For this reason, it is important

Master Calendar				
MONDAY	**TUESDAY**	**WEDNESDAY**	**THURSDAY**	**FRIDAY**
1 JFH—9:00 Trial, Black v. Claridge, Sup. Ct. D-56 - - - - - ERN—9:00 Trial—Gardner v. Larson, Cir. Ct D-87 * * * *	2 * * * * * * * * * * * *	3 * * * * * * * * * *} BSD—9:00 Hrg. Motion to compel, Sand v. Waters, Sup. Ct. D12	4 WAC—10:00 Dep., Jacks v. Yawl, here REN—2:00 Dep., Tru v. Falz, here	5 PDF 9:00 Motion to quash, Pert v. Yerl, Cir. Ct., D-5
	PDF—10:00 Dep., Brown v. Redd, 346 Capitol St. LA, #787			
8	9 LCN—9:00 Disso Marriage of Yale, Sup. Ct. D-33	10 xxxxxxxxxxxxxxxxxxxxxxxxxxx BSD—10:00 Dep., Young v. Osterholm 1600 Main St., LA	11 xxxxxxxxxxxxxxxxxxx} NAD—1:00 Hrg. ++++ Luther v. Ti, Tax Ct., Rm. 9	12 +++++++++++++++++
15 +++++++++++++} 2:00 REN Dep., Tooly v. Hale, here ^^^^^^^^^	16 ^^^^^^^^^^^^^^^^^^^	17 _ _ _ _ _ _ _] ^^^^^^^^^^^^^^^^^^^^^^^^	18 ^^^^^^^^^^^^^^^^^}	19
22 HOLIDAY	23	24	25	26

EXHIBIT 12.1 Sample Master Calendar

to update personal calendars daily. A personal calendar may also contain a tickler system, as discussed later in this chapter.

Manual Calendaring Systems

Most professional liability insurance companies recommend that each attorney maintain a manual calendar in addition to a computerized calendar as a backup in the event the computerized system is not available. This backup system will ensure that valuable information is not lost. It is also a method of double-checking entries.

A manual calendar consisting of primary and secondary information may be a large appointment book, small appointment book, desk calendar, or an electronic calendar device. It may also be a hard copy of the information stored in the computer. Some attorneys use all three: an electronic calendar to transport to court, a large calendar for the person in charge of scheduling; and a desk calendar for the attorney's office. Legal assistants often use desk calendars for their schedules and have a separate calendar that is a duplicate of the attorney's calendar book.

Changing days
Move ahead or back
one day by clicking the
right (ahead) or left
(back) arrow.

Schedule conflicts
Shown in red.

Event Duration
Blocked out time is
shown in color.

Entering events
Double-click the
desired time. The New
Event dialog appears
(see page 10.)

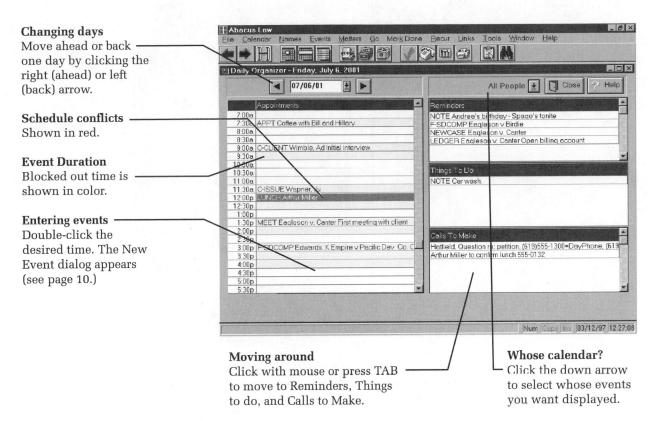

Moving around
Click with mouse or press TAB
to move to Reminders, Things
to do, and Calls to Make.

Whose calendar?
Click the down arrow
to select whose events
you want displayed.

EXHIBIT 12.2   Sample Personal Calendar
Reprinted with permission of Abacus Data Systems, Inc.

An electronic calendar, known as a personal desk assistant (PDA), such as the one shown in Exhibit 12.3, is compact and portable. It can connect to a computer so that information can be exchanged electronically without having to manually input new information. It contains many features that are convenient for attorneys, as shown in the Tech Tips sidebar.

Maintaining manual calendars requires good coordination. A legal secretary is usually given the responsibility of keeping the calendars current. However, each legal assistant must control her or his own calendars regardless of who is responsible for inputting the information.

Calendaring Procedures

Events are calendared as soon as possible after they are discovered. Waiting too long could have disastrous consequences. Documents from opposing parties that require a response or other action are entered into the docket system as they are received in the mail. Each document is stamped or initialed (or both) indicating that the event was docketed, and then the document is delivered to the appropriate attorney or legal assistant. The absence of the initials or stamp of a docket clerk on any document containing a hearing or deposition date indicates that the date was not docketed. In many firms, the pertinent file is pulled, the document put on top of the file, and the file delivered to the appropriate attorney so that the document can be reviewed with the file.

Events that require an action that are generated within the firm must also be calendared as soon as possible after they are discovered. The person responsible for maintaining the calendar enters the event into the system and also inserts the information on the attorney's and legal assistant's manual calendar.

Regular meetings, at least once or twice a week, should be set with the attorney, legal assistant, and legal secretary. Calendar meetings are often short, informal meetings.

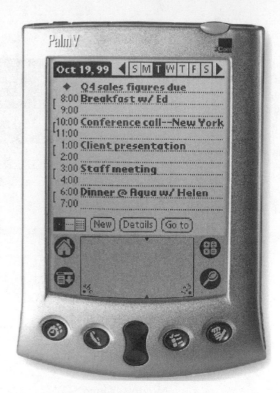

EXHIBIT 12.3 Example of a Personal Desk Assistant

Reprinted at permission of Palm Computing. 3com and the 3com logo are registered trademarks. Palm V and the Palm V logo are trademarks of Palm Computing, Inc., a 3com corporation or its subsidiary.

TECH TIPS

Handheld Personal Desk Assistant

There are many personal desk assistants (PDAs) on the market, each with different features and capabilities. A PDA contains a calendar, address book, to-do list, memo pad, e-mail retrieval, fax-sending capabilities, database, word processor, spreadsheet, and calculator. Products can be researched at CNET Computers at www.cnet.com. A description of a PDA is as follows:

Dimensions	3.3 × 4.9 × .8 inches
Weight (with battery)	.4 pounds
ROM memory	8 MB
RAM memory	8 MB
Screen size	3.9 inches
Resolution	240 × 320
Touch screen	Yes
Backlit display	Yes
Serial ports	Yes
Built-in speaker	Yes
Built-in microphone	Yes
Audio jacks	Yes
Modem	Yes
Handwriting recognition	Yes
Input method	Pen
Operating system	Windows 95/NT
Battery type	AAA
Adapter	Yes

If a secretary or legal assistant is responsible for the calendars of more than one attorney, calendar meetings should be held more often than for those who work for just one attorney. Calendars should be updated daily and the updated information shared with other members of the legal team. This will ensure that everyone has updated calendars.

OF INTEREST . . .

$750,000 a Day

A calendaring error can be very expensive. The Los Angeles firm of Latham & Watkins, learned the importance of accurate calendaring the hard way.

First Los Angeles Bank filed a legal malpractice suit in L.A. Superior Court that named Latham and Watkins. The bank complains that when the firm was defending it against an irate bank patron, Latham's miscalculation caused the firm to miss a deadline by one day, which resulted in a $750,000 liability, including interest against its client, First Bank. The underlying case concerns a customer, Patricia Teitel, who sued the bank for dishonoring her outstanding checks when her boss accused her of forgery.

A jury awarded Ms. Teitel $509,000 against the bank, $500,000 of which was punitive damages. The bank's efforts to get the amount reduced or win a new trial got mixed results during two trips to the California Second District Court of Appeal. The bank says it had a chance to win until its attorney gave the court the wrong date to issue an order, so the initial award became final.

Placing Events on a Calendar

Docket coordinator: A person in charge of a firm's docketing process.

Many medium and large firms have a docketing department that handles their docket. A **docket coordinator** is in charge of the docketing process. A legal secretary or legal assistant instructs the docket coordinator to insert an event on the docket by completing a docket request sheet, such as the one shown in Exhibit 12.4. Everyone in a firm should be familiar with a docket request sheet and should know how to use it. A docket request sheet contains the following information:

◆ Name or initials of the person requesting the docket entry
◆ Responsible attorney
◆ Name of case and file number, if applicable
◆ Type of matter (e.g., trial or deposition)
◆ Date and time
◆ Place (if court, indicate courtroom)
◆ Reminder dates
◆ Date the event was docketed
◆ Signature or initials of docket clerk indicating completion

---

Black, White & Greene

Docket Request Sheet

Requesting party _____ Responsible atty/LA _____

Case name _____ File no. _____

Event _____

Date _____ Time _____

Place _____

Reminder _____ Urging _____ Warning _____ Alert _____

Docketed on _____ [*date*] _____ By _____ [*name or initials*]

EXHIBIT 12.4 Sample Docket Request Sheet

Many different docket request sheets are used. These sheets are either purchased from a legal supply company or developed by the firm and printed on multipart, multicolored paper. Each docket request sheet should have an original and three copies, with each page a different color (e.g., white, blue, pink, and yellow). As a secretary or legal assistant completes the top white sheet, three copies of the information are automatically made. The requesting party keeps the bottom pink sheet as a record that the request was made. The remaining original and two copies are transferred to the docket coordinator. A docket clerk enters the information and signs and dates the docket sheet. The docket coordinator keeps the yellow sheet and returns the white original and blue copy to the requesting party, indicating that the docket entry was made. The secretary or legal assistant keeps the white original as a record that the event was docketed and as a reminder to enter the information into the manual calendars. The blue copy is given to the attorney so that he or she can enter the information into a manual calendar. This docketing process is shown in Exhibit 12.5.

If a firm has an intranet, a separate docketing department is not necessary. As soon as information is entered into the calendar, it is instantly distributed to all employees through the intranet. However, if manual calendars are kept, it is the secretary's responsibility to ensure that the information is inserted in the manual calendars.

In a small office, docketing is handled by a secretary or legal assistant, and the procedures are less formal. A secretary or legal assistant enters the docketing information directly into the firm's computer. A docket request sheet is used to inform other members of the legal team that an event was docketed so that they can insert the in-

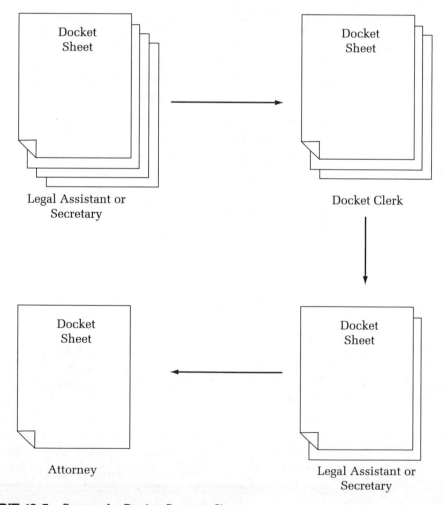

EXHIBIT 12.5   Route of a Docket Request Sheet

formation into their calendars. A docket request sheet consisting of an original and two copies is usually sufficient: The original is a record that the matter was docketed, one copy is given to the legal assistant to enter the information into a personal calendar, and the other copy is given to the attorney to enter the information into a personal calendar.

Calendaring Ethics

Members of a legal team consult their calendars many times throughout the day. Their calendars should always be handy so that they can be reviewed and revised easily. The calendars are usually kept on each person's desk. *It is important to keep all calendars, whether they are computerized or manual, out of the view of clients.* If there is a possibility that a client will visit your office, remove your calendars from view. Calendars contain names of other clients. To ensure the confidentiality of clients' cases, always keep calendars private.

TICKLER SYSTEMS

A tickler system, also known as a come-up system, is a method of controlling deadlines. It is used as a reminder and follow-up system. Documents must be filed with the court on time, and the filing of some documents triggers the clock to run on other deadlines. Every law firm has a system to control these deadlines. If no reminder system were implemented, a legal team would be in a constant state of panic.

For example, Jane Gavin was notified that her client, Flo Nygun, was served with a summons and complaint on June 1. Flo had thirty days in which to answer the complaint, which was due on July 1. Flo notified Jane of the service on June 3, which means that the complaint had to be answered within twenty-seven days. Jane entered July 1 into her calendar as the due date for the answer, without any additional reminders. On July 1, Jane informed her legal assistant, Jack Schrantz, to stop what he was doing and immediately draft an answer to Flo's complaint, which was due that day. Jack, already working on a rush project for Jane, had to drop what he was doing and draft the answer. The secretary had to stop in the middle of a very important project to prepare the answer. After a number of revisions had been made, a special courier was called to rush the answer to the courthouse. Jane's lack of planning and failure to implement reminder dates put undue pressure on her, the legal assistant, the secretary, and the courier. A tickler system uses reminder dates and specific tickler procedures to eliminate this pressure.

Tickler Procedures

A tickler system can be a separate system or integrated into a calendaring system. Most systems are integrated because it is preferable for scheduling purposes to have all information in one place: a calendar. Each member of the team can see the entire day's activities at a glance and plan accordingly. However, a busy litigation attorney with a heavy trial calendar may not have enough room on his or her personal calendar to insert tickler dates. A separate tickler or to-do list would be more appropriate. Each office has its own methods.

For example, in a manual system that combines the calendar and tickler systems, a legal assistant enters the daily schedule on the left side of her personal calendar as follows:

8:30	Meeting with Dave re calendar review
12:00	Paralegal association meeting, Jack's Restaurant
2:00	Conference with client Sanders re interrogatories
3:30	Deposition of N. Nelson re Davis v. Nelson, here

On the right side of her personal calendar, the legal assistant enters tickler dates:

Warning: Smith v. Johnson interrogs due 5/27*

Reminder: Galt v. Lowe Response to motion to compel due 6/3*

Due date: Answer of P. Lang due today, Anderson v. Lang

Due date: Answer to interrogatories due from Reed, Reed v. Jackson.

(Note: The asterisk [*] indicates documents to be prepared by the firm. Entries with no asterisk concern documents due from opposing parties.)

Exhibit 12.6 is an example of a desk calendar, with the daily schedule on one side and tickler information on the other.

Determining Due Dates

Before one can enter reminder dates, one must first determine the due date. Three dates are considered when determining due dates:

Trigger date: The date of an event that starts the clock running on a deadline.

Proof of service by mail: A document that informs the recipient of the date the attached document was mailed.

◆ **Trigger date.** The trigger date begins the clock running on an event. It is the date a document was served or delivered or the date it was mailed as indicated on a **proof of service by mail** form. In the previous example, the trigger date is the date that Flo Nygun was served with a summons and complaint: June 1. It started the thirty-day countdown to the deadline for the answer.

◆ *Due date.* The due date is the day a document is due, which is also known as the drop-dead date. If a due date falls on a holiday or weekend day, the due date is the next business day. In the previous example, the due date for Flo's answer was July 1, thirty days after she was served with the summons and complaint. If July 1 is a Saturday, the due date is the next business day: July 3.

◆ *Mail date.* The mail date is the date a document must be mailed to reach its destination by the due date. The exact number of days that should be set aside for mailing is determined by statute. For state court cases, the state statute is applied. For federal court cases, the federal statute is applied. Be sure to check the statute to determine the time period that should be set aside for the mail date. The federal statute requires that three days be set aside for mailing. In the

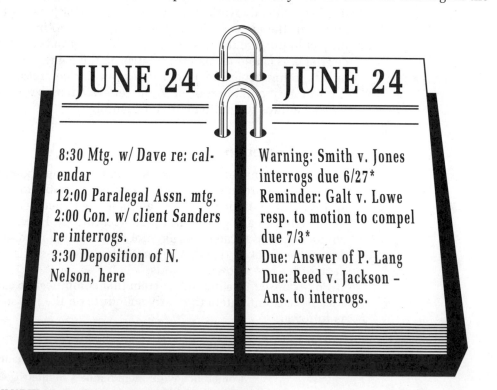

EXHIBIT 12.6 Sample Manual Desk Calendar

previous example, assume that Flo Nygun's case is a federal case and that Jane Gavin will mail the answer to the court. To reach the court on the due date, Flo's answer must be mailed three days before the due date: June 28 (July 1 is counted as the third day).

When counting days to determine the due date of a document, the first day is excluded and the last day is included. In other words, the trigger date is not counted. The first day after the trigger date, including holidays and weekend days, is the first day counted, and the due date is the last day counted. If the due date falls on a holiday or weekend day, the due date is the next business day.

ETHICS ALERT

In most jurisdictions, weekend days and holidays are counted except when a due date is less than eight days of the trigger date, at which time holidays and weekends are not counted. *Some states have different requirements; check local rules.* Extra time must be allowed for mailing.

For example, a firm received a cross-complaint that required an answer from a client in thirty days. The proof of service by mail indicated that the document was mailed on November 15. Calculate the due date as follows: You did not receive the cross-complaint on November 15 because of the days required for mailing. Federal law allows you to add three days to November 15 for mailing (November 18). November 18 is the date you received the cross-complaint and is not included in the count. Count thirty days, with day 1 starting on November 19. December 18 is the thirtieth day and is therefore the due date. If you are going to mail the answer to the court, subtract three days to allow for mail time to arrive at the mail date: December 15. To be timely, the answer to the cross-complaint must be completed and mailed on December 15.

ETHICS ALERT

A simpler method of counting days is to eliminate the two sets of three days for mailing because, in essence, they cancel each other out. Instead of adding three mailing days to the date of mailing as shown on the proof of service form, count thirty days from the date the document was mailed as shown on the proof of service form. You will arrive at the same due date that you would by adding and subtracting the mailing time ($30 + 3 - 3 = 30$). Mailing dates are important when determining due dates and are an essential element of calculating due dates. *Be sure to check your state's rule regarding the number of days allowed for mailing.*

Determining Reminder Dates For documents to be completed on time, reminder dates must be integrated into a docket system to remind an attorney and a legal assistant that action is required on a file. In addition, reminder dates must be integrated in the system to alert the legal team when a statute of limitations is due to expire, when documents are due from an opposing party, and when other important events are scheduled to take place.

Normally, there are four reminder dates:

1. *Reminder date.* A reminder date is the first of a series of reminders that a deadline is approaching. It is the least urgent of the reminders.
2. *Urging date.* An urging date is the second in a series of reminders that a deadline is approaching. It signifies that a deadline is getting very close and urges the legal team to take action on a matter.
3. *Warning date.* A warning date is the third and last reminder that a deadline is approaching. It is a warning that action must be taken or else a deadline may be missed. It signifies that no further reminders will be given before the due date.
4. *Alert date.* An alert date is an optional reminder date that is used when three reminders are not enough for a project to be completed.

The time intervals between these dates depend on the type of deadline imposed, the type of project, and where holidays and weekends fall on a calendar. The exact time intervals between reminder dates vary from a day to a year in some cases. State and federal statutes determine the time periods within which an event must happen, and reminder dates must work within these time frames. Establishing reminder date guidelines is subject to the discretion of firm management.

Appendix H provides a cheat sheet to help you calculate due dates and reminder dates.

Entering Reminder Dates   Placing reminder dates in the correct time intervals requires knowledge of the requirements of each type of project. Lengthy projects require four and sometimes more reminder dates, and short-term projects require one or two reminders. For most projects, three reminders are sufficient. Anticipating the need for reminders is essential so that the correct number of reminders will be inserted into the system. The more experience you gain with various calendaring projects, the better you can anticipate a project's tickler needs.

Reminder dates are used to manage projects. They keep a legal team on schedule by alerting them to the next step in a project. Placing reminder dates at the appropriate interval gives a legal team the necessary time to complete a project. For example, each reminder date signifies completion of a part of a project:

◆ Reminder date—ten days before due date: do research and review information to prepare document

◆ Urging date—seven days before due date: prepare draft document

◆ Warning date—three days before due date: finalize document

◆ Due date—file document

There are no specific rules that govern reminder date intervals. These time intervals are general guidelines and are very flexible. Some firms may set the reminder date for fifteen days before the due date instead of ten. Time intervals between reminder dates must be adjustable to accommodate holidays, weekend days, and other events. Although it is a simple matter to count back three or four days from a due date, attention must be given to holidays and weekends. A reminder date cannot be a weekend or holiday date. A docket clerk or secretary must know on what dates holidays and weekends fall so that reminder dates are not entered on those dates. If a matter is inadvertently calendared for a holiday or weekend date, it is likely to be overlooked.

For example, suppose that the tenth day before a due date is a Sunday. A reminder date cannot be entered there. Therefore, it would have to be entered on the next business day, Monday, which is the ninth day before the due date, or it could be entered on the Friday before, which is the twelfth day before the due date. This adjustment would require that all reminder dates be adjusted accordingly:

◆ Reminder date—ninth day before due date

◆ Urging date—sixth day before due date

◆ Warning date—two or three days before due date

Most computer tickler systems will let a docket clerk or secretary see what dates are holidays or weekends and will alert the docket clerk if an entry is inserted on a weekend date. Some software programs will automatically reject an entry on a holiday or weekend. Law firm holidays, retreats, or other events for which an office will be closed can be programmed into the computer so that no entries are made on those dates. Another example of tickling reminder dates around weekends and holidays is found in Exhibit 12.7.

Statutes of limitations. Monitoring statutes of limitations is extremely important. As noted previously, if a statute of limitations is missed, a client is prohibited from proceeding. Statute of limitations dates are entered into the calendar as well as the tickler system. Statutes of limitations are set by state and federal law. There are different statutes of limitations for different types of actions, and they vary by state. For example, a breach of written contract may have a four-year statute of limitations and a personal injury action a one-year statute of limitations. *Before calendaring reminder dates for a statute of limitations, always check the statute to determine the exact time period.*

ETHICS ALERT

Suppose a document is due thirty days from November 26, on December 26, which is a Sunday as shown on the following calendar. The due date will be December 27, and the answer will be calendared as follows:

December						
Sun	**Mon**	**Tues**	**Wed**	**Thur**	**Fri**	**Sat**
			1	2	3	4
5	6	7	8	9	10	11
12	13	14	15	16	17	18
19	20	21	22	23	24	25
26	27	28	29	30	31	

1. December 15 — Reminder date — do reseach and compile information to prepare answer.
2. December 20 — Urging date — draft answer — December 18 and 19 would be inappropriate urging dates because they are weekend dates.
3. December 23 — Warning date — finalize answer. Since three days before the due date is Christmas Eve, chances are the office will close early. Therefore, Christmas Eve would be an inappropriate warning date.
4. December 27 — Due date — file answer.

EXHIBIT 12.7 Sample Tickler System for Thirty-Day Deadline

For a one-year statute of limitation, four dates are entered:

1. Reminder date—120 days before due date
2. Urging date—60 days before due date
3. Warning date—30 days before due date
4. Due date—5 days before actual due date (just to be sure the statute is not missed; if a document is mailed, the due date is the mail date)

For a four-year statute of limitations, five dates are entered:

1. Reminder date—1 year before due date
2. Alert date—120 days before due date
3. Urging date—60 days before due date
4. Warning date—30 days before due date
5. Due date—5 days before actual due date (just to be sure the statute is not missed; if a document is mailed, the due date is the mail date)

Litigation and Case Documents. Litigation cases have many deadlines, the majority of which are thirty days. Normally, a standard thirty-day deadline has three reminder dates:

◆ Reminder date—ten days before the due date
◆ Urging date—seven days before the due date
◆ Warning date—three days before the due date

If a document will be mailed, the reminder dates for a thirty-day deadline are as follows:

◆ Reminder date—ten days before the mail date
◆ Urging date—seven days before the mail date

◆ Warning date—three days before the mail date
◆ Mail date—three days before due date (in federal cases, but subject to state statute)
◆ Due date—actual due date

In the previous example, Jane should have tickled the due date and entered three reminder dates:

◆ June 21—reminder date: get information together to prepare answer
◆ June 24—urging date: draft answer
◆ June 28—warning date: finalize answer
◆ July 1—due date: last day to file answer

If Jane were going to mail the answer to the court, she would have tickled the mail date and entered three reminder dates:

◆ June 18—reminder date: get information together to prepare answer
◆ June 22—urging date: draft answer
◆ June 25—warning date: finalize answer
◆ June 28—mail date: mail answer to the court
◆ July 1—due date: court receives answer

For a document that must be filed within fifteen days, such as a response to a motion, two reminders are sufficient. For example, a response that has a due date of June 23 needs two reminders:

◆ June 16—reminder date, seven days before due date: draft response
◆ June 20—warning date, three days before due date: finalize response
◆ June 23—due date: file response

Reminder dates of opposing parties. A document that is due from an opposing party must be documented to alert an attorney of a possible **default,** or failure to respond. When entering the due dates of opposing parties, it is not necessary to have numerous reminders; one entry is sufficient. A method should be devised to differentiate between due dates of clients and due dates of opposing parties. Various methods are used to differentiate between the two. If a computerized system is used, clients' information can be entered in italics, bold, or color. If a manual system is used, the information may be entered in red for a client and black for an opposing party, or an asterisk (*) may be inserted by information concerning a client or a "C" for a client and an "O" for an opposing party. Whatever method is chosen, it is important to be consistent.

Other reminder dates. Legal assistants and attorneys use a tickler system to remind them of several important dates and events. If a legal assistant requests that a client send documents, the legal assistant must have a reminder system to follow up. The circumstances of each event will dictate the dates of the reminders. If a legal assistant mails court documents to a client for approval or signature, enough time must be allowed for mailing and for the review of the documents. This will require additional tickler dates. In the previous example, if Jane sent the answer to Flo for her approval and signature, the tickler dates for the answer would be as follows:

◆ June 15—reminder date: get information together for answer
◆ June 20—urging date: draft answer
◆ June 21—alert date: complete answer
◆ June 22—mail date: send answer to client for approval and signature
◆ June 27—alert date: receive answer from client
◆ June 28—warning date: finalize answer
◆ July 1—due date: file answer

Default: Failure to respond within the required time.

If a document mailed to a client does not require filing with a court or is not subject to other deadlines, an entry must be made in a legal assistant's tickler system if the document is expected back. If an entry is not made, the event may be overlooked. The timing of the entry is subject to the legal assistant's judgment but should give the client enough time to review the document and return it to the legal assistant. If a client is a corporation and a document must be approved by corporate officers, the legal assistant must allow the client more time. An example of tickler entries for return of documents that were mailed on June 4 is as follows:

◆ June 14—reminder date: interrogatories back from client Jeffries?
◆ June 21—warning date: interrogatories back from client Jeffries? (mailed 6/4)

When the entry comes up on the legal assistant's tickler system on June 14, if the documents were received, the legal assistant eliminates the June 21 entry from the tickler system. If the documents were not received, the reminder date tag tells the legal assistant that a warning date will follow. The legal assistant then decides whether follow-up should be immediate or whether it can wait until the warning date. When the warning date comes up on June 21, the legal assistant contacts the client by mail, e-mail, or telephone and inquires about the status of the documents. If a letter is sent, a reply must also be tickled for about a week in the future. If a deadline is put in the letter, the legal assistant must insert that date into the tickler system and follow up as necessary.

Another area of use for the tickler system is to track verbal and office commitments. If a client, opposing counsel, or other person agrees to provide a legal assistant with information on a certain date, an entry is made to a tickler system to remind the legal assistant that the information is coming. If a legal assistant is scheduled to give a report at a law firm meeting, an entry is made in the legal assistant's tickler system to allow the legal assistant enough time to prepare the report.

Tickler systems are also used to complete work of an absent attorney or legal assistant. If an attorney is unexpectedly ill and must be out of the office for a period of time, the tickler system is consulted by other attorneys in the office who will temporarily take over the absent attorney's workload. This ensures that no project or deadline is overlooked in the attorney's absence.

Tickler systems schedule tasks to distribute work without undue stress and pressure on a legal team. Allowing sufficient time to complete a project also eliminates frustration caused by the absence of employees who are essential to the completion of the project or other unforeseen circumstances.

Basic Rule of Tickler Systems

The basic rule of a tickler system is that no item is removed from the system until it is completed. The system will keep a matter active until completed. Each morning, a secretary or other member of the legal team retrieves the tickler information and gives the attorney and legal assistant the information. Some secretaries will retrieve the appropriate file to correspond with the tickler entries and give it to the attorney or legal assistant. *An attorney or legal assistant should never be verbally reminded of tickler information.* If the information is verbally communicated, chances are that the information will get lost in a myriad of other matters on the minds of the attorney and legal assistant. It is important that an attorney and a legal assistant have written notification of reminder date information. Tickler reports are usually put on the attorney's or legal assistant's desk so that they are reminded whenever they look at it.

ETHICS ALERT

Docketing due dates and reminder dates correctly is only half the battle; getting the job done is the other half. The best docketing system in the world will not put the words down on paper. It is essential that each member of the legal team understands the importance of docketing procedures. Docket meetings with the attorney, legal assistant, and secretary should be priority meetings held at least once a week and preferably more often. Detailed to-do lists should be kept current and reviewed.

> **OF INTEREST . . .**
>
> **Docket Control Checklist**
>
> ☒ Double-check all entries.
> ☒ Reminders should have enough lead time to allow a task to be completed.
> ☒ Have regular calendar meetings.
> ☒ Train all employees how to use the system effectively.
> ☒ Always insert follow-up dates.
> ☒ Screen incoming mail for calendaring needs.
> ☒ Have procedures for handling deadlines in case of absence.
> ☒ Do not procrastinate.
> ☒ Do not leave projects to be completed on the due date.
> ☒ Always check statutes and rules.
> ☒ Do not assume anything.

COMPUTERIZED AND MANUAL DOCKETING SYSTEMS

There are two types of calendaring and docketing systems: computerized and manual. Of the computerized systems, there are two types: static calendar programs and automated docketing programs. Computerized docketing programs are found in most law firms today. Manual systems still exist in some areas, but they are being replaced by computerized systems.

Computerized Docket Control Programs

Computerized docket control software programs combine calendar and tickler systems into one system. In other words, the calendar contains both calendar and tickler information. Most law firms use docket control software to manage their calendars. There are hundreds of docket control software packages available for the legal marketplace. Some packages are directed to large firms, and others are more conducive to small firms.

Static calendar programs: A calendar program that requires entries to be made manually.

Static Calendar Programs A **static calendar program** allows the user to enter dates into the program, and the event will be noted on a specific date of the calendar. Both primary and secondary information are entered along with tickler dates. Static systems are sometimes associated with word processing programs, and calendar reports are printed in a word processing program, as shown in Exhibit 12.8. All dates, including tickler dates, are inserted manually. These programs are also known as PIMs (personal information managers). Most static systems are not specifically designed for a law office.

Static calendar programs are very similar to manual, hand-written systems. The only difference is that a computer is used to generate the information rather than a desk calendar or appointment book. Therefore, they are prone to error. For example, when a software program permits operators to enter case names, they may inadvertently schedule events for a single case under numerous different case names. Data entered for a case named American International Parts Corp. might have events scheduled for it under American International Parts, American Parts Corp., AIP Corp., or American International. When a report is generated for it, only information entered for American International Parts Corp. or American Parts Corp. will be generated, resulting in essential information entered under the other names being excluded and therefore missed.

Since tickler dates are calculated manually, it is possible for an entry to be scheduled for a holiday or weekend, resulting in lost information. Further consistency

Black, White & Greene

For week of May 1, 20xx, to May 5, 20xx

DATE	ATTY/LA	TYPE	CASE	TASK
5/1/xx	White	Reminder	Hopewell v. Miller	Answer of Jenkins
5/1/xx	Greene	Due date	ABC Corp.	Notice of annual mtg.
5/1/xx	Greene	Reminder	XYZ Corp.	File articles of incorp.
5/1/xx	Boen	Reminder	Goldberg Agmt.	Agmt. rec'd from client
5/1/xx	White	Due date	Reed v. Taylor	Req. for prod. of doc.*
5/1/xx	Boen	Due date	Keel v. Davis	Resp. to interogs. (Keel)*
5/2/xx	White	Reminder	DEF Corp.	Prep. contract
5/2/xx	White	Warning	Baxter v. Hemstreet	Trial brief*
5/2/xx	White	Urging	Hedfer v. Marine Co.	Answer of Dell*
5/2/xx	Boen	Warning	Tazmanian v. Yuan	Ans. to Yuan interogs.*
5/2/xx	Greene	Warning	Travel Time v. AA	Judgment expires 5/10
5/3/xx	Black	Due date	Estate of Pride	Final accounting*
5/3/xx	White	Due date	Beil Ins. Co.	File tax return
5/3/xx	Black	Reminder	Est. of Harold	File petition
5/4/xx	White	Urging	Hopewell v. Miller	Answer of Jenkins
5/4/xx	Boen	Warning	Noel v. Granger	Verification from Noel?
5/4/xx	Boen	Reminder	Allway v. Wier	Req. for prod. of docs.*
5/4/xx	Greene	Urging	XYZ Corp.	File articles of incorp.
5/4/xx	White	Due date	Sand v. See	Res. motion to compel*
5/4/xx	Black	Urging	Est. of Capp	Letters testamentary*
5/5/xx	White	Urging	DEF Corp.	Prep. contract
5/5/xx	White	Due date	Baxter v. Hemstreet	Trial brief

EXHIBIT 12.8 Sample Static Calendar System Tickler Report

problems arise when more than one person manages the calendar program. Static calendar systems are found in small firms and are not recommended for medium or large firms, especially those with heavy trial schedules. An example of a static calendar is shown in Exhibit 12.9.

Automated Docketing Programs Automated docketing programs are designed specifically for law firms. Two areas of automated docketing software set them apart from static calendaring programs: They prevent users from entering data incorrectly, and they apply preprogrammed court rules to schedule events. Such programs automatically calculate and schedule important dates, including tickler dates, and inserts them on a calendar. These programs are very powerful and provide the most

TECH TIPS

Static Calendar Programs

The following is a sample of related software:

Organizer: Lotus—www.lotus.com

Microsoft Outlook: Microsoft—www.microsoft.com

Calendar Creator: Broderbund—www.broderbund.com

Software mentioned in this sidebar is for informational purposes only and is not for the purpose of endorsing products.

Daily Calendar/To Do   Untitled

Wednesday, September 12, 2001

August 2001	September 2001	October 2001

🕐 **Calendar**

Time	Description
8 00	
15	
30	
45	
9 00	Hearing: People vs. Jones, Superior Court, Dept. 4
15	
30	
45	
10 00	
15	
30	
45	
11 00	
15	
30	
45	
12 PM	Lunch w/Fred – Fancy chicken Restaurant
15	
30	
45	
1 00	
15	
30	
45	
2 00	
15	
30	
45	
3 00	William Rogers – Appt. re will
15	
30	
45	
4 00	Staff Meeting
15	
30	
45	
5 00	
15	
30	
45	
6 00	
15	
30	
45	

☑ **To Do**

S	P	Category Description
F	1	DUE DATE: Gray vs. Addington – Statute of Limitations expires TODAY
F	2	WARNING: Jenkins vs. Brown – File complaint by 9/15
F	3	REMINDER: Neal vs. Armstrong – Start research for opposing to the motion to dismiss
F	3	Jones, adv. Smith – Client Jones to return information re Interrogatories

S=Status P=Priority

4/24/99 at 3:44 PM   Page 1

EXHIBIT 12.9   Sample Static Calendar System

accurate calculation of dates, warn users of approaching deadlines, and provide the best protection against missed deadlines.

Legal malpractice insurance companies are so impressed with automated docketing programs that some require their insureds to use one. Additionally, some insurance companies offer their insureds a discount on their premiums of up to 10 percent if they implement an automated docketing program. Insurance companies, such as Virginia Surety Insurance Corporation, will not insure a law firm that does not have this type of software in place.

Some consider automated docketing programs an essential tool for all law firms. Scheduling deadlines can be a complicated, time-consuming task. Law firms must adhere to many statutes regarding deadline rules. There are deadline rules for federal courts, federal appellate courts, the U.S. Supreme Court, state trial courts, state appellate courts, state supreme courts, and specialty-specific rules (e.g., bankruptcy rules, local rules of state courts, and local rules of federal courts). It is a monumental task to know all these rules to determine due dates correctly. Automated docketing programs contain databases that are preprogrammed with docketing rules so that the correct rule and its time frame are automatically applied to a client's matter. Calculating a due date in a manual system can take thirty minutes or more, but an automated program calculates it in seconds.

Some software programs have a conflict-checking feature that allows a user to check for a possible conflicts of interest, as shown in Exhibit 12.10. Additionally, some programs are tied to the firm's time and billing system so that all the clients' matters are centralized.

A number of different scheduling reports are automatically generated. Case management reports are included with some docket programs. A report that is handy for a firm's management to guard against files being overlooked is a malpractice alert report. This report lists all cases that have no activity scheduled for them. A firm's management can easily spot files that may be neglected or lost in the system. This report prevents cases from "slipping through the cracks" of a firm's filing system.

Experts agree that an automated docketing program should contain some key features to make it an effective program, including the following:

◆ *Preprogrammed court rules.* The program should apply preprogrammed court rules to a scheduling event. Court rules can be manually entered into the system or purchased from a legal vendor. It is important that the court rules be specific to the firm's jurisdiction and include all the courts in which the attorneys practice. It is important that the rules be current and that an update service is available to keep them so. Some rules, such as those of administrative agencies, may not available for purchase, so the system must be able to allow the user to program it with additional rules. This custom rule programming feature will allow other rules, such as firm-specific ones, to be programmed into it. For example, when a deposition is set, it triggers certain events, such as preparing a notice, serving the notice, scheduling a court reporter, reserving a conference room, and preparing for the deposition. Although some of these tasks are not contained in a statute or court rule, they can be programmed into the system to be implemented as needed. A legal assistant is reminded of each step of the process. An example of this feature is shown in Exhibit 12.11.

◆ *Automatic date scheduling.* This feature allows a user to enter a key event date, such as a trigger date, and the due date and reminder dates are automatically calculated and scheduled. The system automatically applies applicable court rules to the due dates and will not schedule a reminder on a holiday or weekend day. This process, if done manually, can be very complex. For example, when a case is set for trial, entering the trial date can trigger as many as fifty deadlines, such as discovery cutoff, witness lists, jury fees, settlement conferences, and so on. The system must be able to handle a complex scheduling process that considers the many variables involved.

◆ *Automatic reminders.* The program automatically generates reminders that an event is approaching. It automatically enters a reminder date, urging date,

To start:

1. Select *Tools/Conflicts of Interest* from the Menu Bar. The following window appears.

Names to check
Type in a name. Conflict Checking can be set to find references to specified names in your databases–even if the references are buried in a small note somewhere.

List of names
You can enter up to 200 names to check at once.

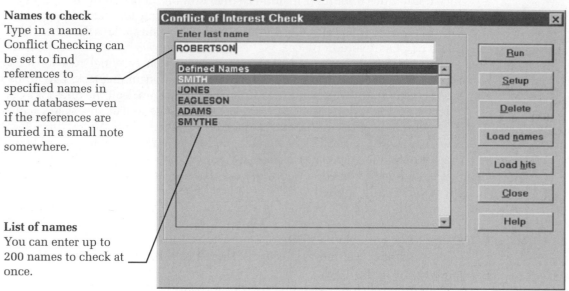

2. Enter the following last names and press ENTER after each name: SMITH, SMYTHE, JONES, EAGLE.

3. Click *Run.* A Hit List similar to the following appears.

The hits
Double-click on any hit to see the full details in context.

The misses
Highlight the names that are not a conflict and click **Delete.**

Sounds similar
You can setup conflicts checking to find similar sounding names.

The proof
Keep a printout to prove a conflict check was done.

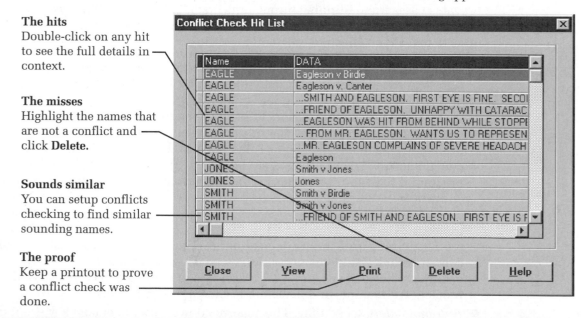

EXHIBIT 12.10 Example of Software That Checks for Conflicts of Interest
Reprinted with permission of Abacus Data Systems, Inc.

Data validation: A feature in automated docket control software that will not allow an incorrect entry.

warning date, and alert date. This feature must be flexible so that intervals between reminder dates can be adjusted according to the needs of the firm. An example of this feature is shown in Exhibit 12.12.

◆ *Data validation.* The program will automatically validate client matters so that an incorrect entry cannot be made. This **data validation** feature prevents the possibility

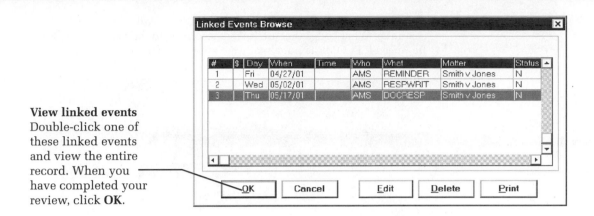

View linked events
Double-click one of these linked events and view the entire record. When you have completed your review, click **OK**.

Creating or Modifying a Rule

Select *File/Setup/Rules* and the Rules List appears. To modify an existing rule, you would highlight the rule and click Edit. For this example, we'll add a new rule called FILECOMP. Whenever you file a complaint, you must serve it.

This will be a short example with only one event after the filing of the complaint and serving it. When we're done, whenever you calendar an event with a What code of FILECOMP, the rule will automatically kick in and ask if you want to calendar the other event(s), which in this case is SERVCOMP.

Add a Rule
Click **Add**, a notice appears, click **OK**, and the Add Rule dialog appears as shown.

Rule Name
Enter FILECOMP for this example and click **OK**.

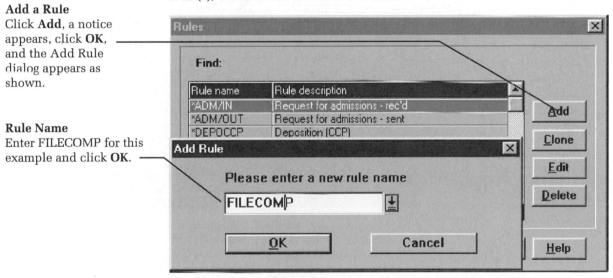

1. Click **Add** on the Rules list window. An information window appears that tells you the name of the rule will automatically be added to the What codes list. Click **OK** and the Add Rule window appears.

EXHIBIT 12.11   Example of Software That Preprograms Court Rules in a Docket Program
Reprinted with permission of Abacus Data Systems, Inc.

that two schedules are prepared for one client. For example, if a user attempted to enter information for American International Parts Corp. by inserting the name of the client as American Parts, the system would not accept the information and would direct the user to the correct name: American International Parts Corp. This feature will not tolerate errors in data entry and protects the integrity of the system.

2. Type FILECOMP in the Add Rule window. Every rule is simply a series of What codes that are linked according to the rule. Because FILECOMP is not already set up as a What code, a New What Code window appears.

Add the What codes
Every step in a rule must have a valid What code for the event. You can add it on-the-fly!

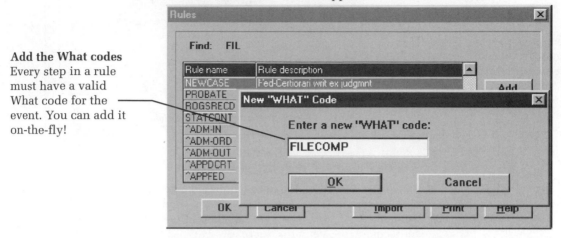

3. The Rule event editing window appears. In *What* enter SERVCOMP, in *Interval* enter 60, and in *Relative to event* enter 0.

What's next
Enter the What code for the next event in the rule.

Interval
Enter the days to be added (minus for subtracted) in calculating the date of this event.

Relative to event
The first event in a rule is always relative to event #0, the trigger event.

4. Our rule has one event, SERVCOMP, that will be automatically calendared 60 days after FILECOMP. Whenever you calendar an event with FILECOMP in the What field, *ABACUS LAW* will ask you if you want to add the other events from the Rule.

EXHIBIT 12.11 *(continued)*

◆ *Holiday scheduling.* Most docketing software programs come preprogrammed with a few of the most observed national holidays, such as Thanksgiving and Christmas. To be effective, this feature must be flexible to allow the user to insert other holidays that may be jurisdiction specific. For example, some courts close to observe Martin Luther King Jr.'s birthday, and others do not. Additionally, the system must be able to recognize other days a firm may be closed, such as days for a firm's retreats, the founding partner's birthday, or other non-workdays. Programming the software with these holidays ensures that reminder dates will not be inserted on those days.

First reminder
In the first Reminder field enter 1 to create a reminder on the day before.

Second reminder
In the second Reminder field enter negative seven (-7) to create a reminder to follow up a week later.

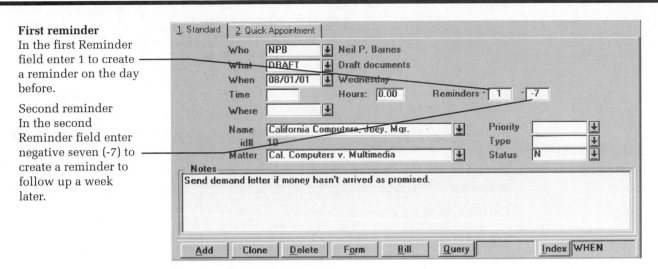

2. In Who enter NPB, in What enter DRAFT, then enter:
   - a 1 in the first Reminder field (to create a reminder for the day before)
   - a -7 (negative 7) in the second Reminder field (to create a reminder to follow up a week later

3. Click *Save* and select *Links/Events* from the Menu Bar. The following window appears.

View linked events
See the reminders in the Linked Events Browse window!

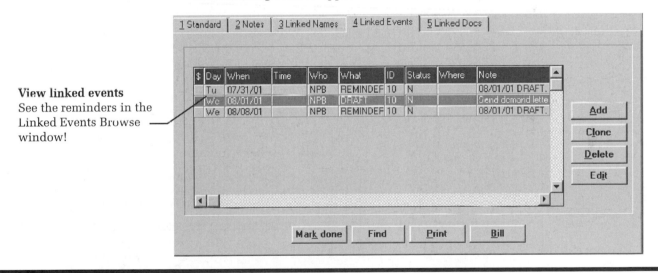

EXHIBIT 12.12   Example of Software That Automatically Generates Reminder Dates
Reprinted with permission of Abacus Data Systems, Inc.

Retroactive event recalculation: A feature in automated docketed software programs that automatically recalculates dates in the event of a change in a corresponding date.

◆ *Retroactive event recalculation.* **Retroactive event recalculation** allows entries to be recalculated if a rule changes. For example, if a court changes a rule that goes into effect on June 1, the program automatically recalculates entries made pursuant to the old rule and updates them to the new rule. This feature is also used if a trigger date changes or a matter is continued. It will automatically recalculate all dates attached to that event and adjust them to the new information.

◆ *Group scheduling.* The program provides for group scheduling, which is used by medium and large firms. For example, if a legal team consisting of three attorneys and two legal assistants are working on a specific case, the system provides all members of a legal team with scheduling information regarding that

BLACK, WHITE & GREENE
Tickler List
Hopewell v. Miller

For week of May 1, 20xx, to May 5, 20xx

DATE	ATTY/LA	TYPE	CASE	TASK
5/1/xx	White	Reminder	Hopewell v. Miller	Answer of Miller
5/4/xx	White	Urging	Hopewell v. Miller	Answer of Miller
5/4/xx	White	Due date	Rec'd docs from Miller?	

EXHIBIT 12.13 Sample Scheduling Report by Case

BLACK, WHITE & GREENE
Tickler List for Attny White and Legal Assistant Hemstreet

For week of May 1, 20xx, to May 5, 20xx

DATE	ATTY/LA	TYPE	CASE	TASK
5/1/xx	White	Reminder	Hopewell v. Miller	Answer of Jenkins
5/1/xx	Hemstreet	Reminder	Goldberg Agmt.	Agmt rec'd from client
5/1/xx	Hemstreet	Due date	Keel v. Davis	Resp. to interogs. (Keel)*
5/2/xx	Hemstreet	Warning	Baxter v. Hemstreet	Trial brief*
5/2/xx	White	Urging	Hedfer v. Marine Co.	Answer of Dell*
5/2/xx	Hemstreet	Warning	Tazmanian v. Yuan	Ans. to Yuan interogs.*
5/4/xx	White	Urging	Hopewell v. Miller	Answer of Jenkins
5/4/xx	Hemstreet	Warning	Noel v. Granger	Verification from Noel?
5/4/xx	Hemstreet	Reminder	Allway v. Wier	Req. for prod. of docs.*
5/4/xx	White	Due date	Sand v. See	Res. motion to compel*
5/5/xx	White	Due date	Baxter v. Hemstreet	Trial brief
5/5/xx	White	Warning	Hedfer v. Marine	Answer of Dell*
5/5/xx	Hemstreet	Due date	Tazmanian v. Yuan	Yuan's ans. to interogs.*
5/5/xx	Hemstreet	Reminder	Quick print v. Elkins	File stipulation*

EXHIBIT 12.14 Sample Scheduling Report by Legal Team

case. Whenever an event is scheduled for the case, each member of the team receives the information in his or her calendars.

◆ *Scheduling reports.* The program provides a number of scheduling reports. Examples of scheduling reports are those categorized by timekeeper by case, as shown in Exhibit 12.13, or by day, event, or team, as shown in Exhibit 12.14, or other desired topic. If this feature is not available, a hard copy of a large firm's calendar may be as large as fifty or more pages, making review cumbersome and wasting resources.

The information in an automated system is displayed in a calendar that resembles a personal calendar. It can be displayed in a number of different calendar formats: daily, weekly, or monthly, as shown in Exhibit 12.15. Court hearings and appointments are separated from reminder entries, with hearings and appointments on the left and tickler entries on the right, as in manual or static calendar systems.

There are many advantages to an automated docketing program. It increases accuracy, increasing productivity and therefore a firm's profits increase. An automated

TECH TIPS

Docket and Calendar Control Software

The following is a sample of related software:

Abacus Law: Abacus Data Systems, Inc.—www.abacuslaw.com

LawQuest: Bridgeway Software—www.bridge-way.com

CLS/SUMMIT: Computer Law Systems, Inc.—www.clswin.com

CaseMaster: Software Technology, Inc.—www.stilegal.com

Vision Docket: Compulaw—www.compulaw.com

DOCket: K&D Associates—www.docket.org

Legalex™: Alex Systems, Inc.—www.legalex.com

Software mentioned in this sidebar is for informational purposes only and is not for the purpose of endorsing products.

docket control program will pay for itself by way of reduced malpractice premiums and claims. It also contributes to positive client relations by increasing the efficiency of each member of the legal team. An example of some docketing software products are listed in the Tech Tips sidebar.

Manual Tickler Systems

A manual tickler system can still be found in some law offices today. Some use it as their primary system, and others use it in addition to a computerized system as a backup in the event the computer system should be unavailable for some reason and as an extra precaution against missed deadlines. Some legal malpractice insurance companies require a backup tickler system as a protection against missed deadlines. Compared to an automated system, manual tickler systems are less reliable, more time consuming, and are error prone.

The manual system that has been used by law offices since 1915 is the Basic System. It has been so successful that no changes have been made to it since that time. To set up a basic tickler system, the following materials are needed:

◆ A tin or wood box, 3½ inches deep
◆ One set of monthly divider cards, 3 × 5 inches
◆ Three sets of daily reminder cards, numbered 1 through 31
◆ Yearly divider cards, 3 × 5 inches, for three years
◆ Docket request sheets, plain 3 × 5 cards or paper in four different colors

All materials are readily obtainable at any stationery store and are inexpensive.

The monthly index cards are placed in the box in sequence. The three sets of daily reminder cards are placed behind the current month's divider, the next month's divider, and the next month's divider. The yearly cards are placed behind the monthly cards. Exhibit 12.16 shows an example of a basic manual tickler system.

A docket request sheet, such as the one shown in Exhibit 12.4, is used with this system. A docket request sheet can be developed on 3-by-5-inch cards or slips of paper of different colors. They also may be purchased from a legal supply store. They come in multipart sets with each page a different color. If docket request sheets are purchased from a legal supply store, they must have at least four pages in different colors. The original white page is for the due date, the pink slip for the warning date, the blue slip for the urging date, and the yellow slip for the reminder date (or other color coding scheme as the firm may choose). When a docket request sheet is completed, each page is inserted behind its corresponding date. Each morning, the tickler slips are pulled, and the appropriate action is taken.

Your Weekly Calendar

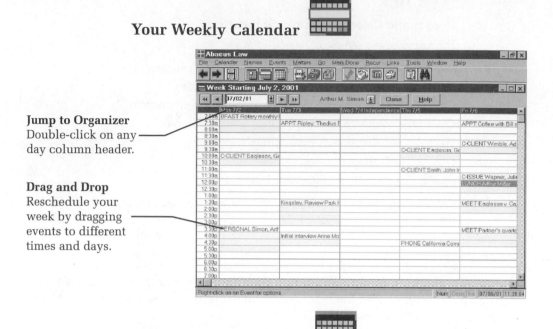

Jump to Organizer
Double-click on any day column header.

Drag and Drop
Reschedule your week by dragging events to different times and days.

Your Monthly Calendar

Jump to Organizer
Double-click on any day to see your Daily Organizer.

Highlights/Counters
Set up counters and highlights for priority events from *File/Setup/Calendar/Queries*.

Change Months/Years
Use the double arrows to change years, the single arrows to change months.

Tip: You can jump to another date by typing D and entering the date.

EXHIBIT 12.15 Example of Automated Docket System Calendars
Reprinted with permission of Abacus Data Systems, Inc.

When the current month ends, there should be no tickler sheets left behind a daily divider in that month. The daily divider cards in the current month are then transferred to the first month without daily divider cards. Tickler slips behind that month are then put behind the appropriate daily divider. Yearly index cards are used for long-range dates for events such as judgment renewal dates, stockholder meetings, tax return dates, statute of limitations, and review dates for wills and contracts.

To be effective, a manual system must be maintained. Nothing should be overlooked. A method should be devised to identify weekend and holiday dates so that

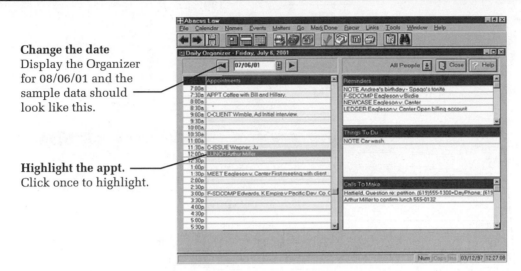

Change the date
Display the Organizer for 08/06/01 and the sample data should look like this.

Highlight the appt.
Click once to highlight.

2. Highlight the 1:00 p.m. appointment with George Eagleson and click the Rolodex on the Tool Bar. Your contacts list appears with George Eagleson's name highlighted. Click OK to display George's name record.

EXHIBIT 12.15 *(continued)*

no reminder sheets will be inserted behind that date. Red sticker dots can be put on those cards that represent weekend and holidays. When the daily cards are moved to the back of the system, the red dots are removed and inserted on the holiday and weekend dates of the current month.

FILE REVIEW SYSTEM

File review is another aspect of docket control systems. It is easy for an attorney who is responsible for many files to inadvertently ignore a file. A system must be devised in which a file cannot be ignored. Professional liability insurance companies require that a file review system be implemented.

Every file should be reviewed monthly. A busy attorney with many files often finds file review a burdensome but necessary task. It may be tempting for an attorney to postpone file review until a more convenient time (which never comes), but efforts should be made not to do so. Postponing file review defeats its purpose and results in loose habits. File review procedures should be strictly enforced.

Often, an attorney will delegate file review to an experienced legal assistant. Files that require no activity are calendared for the next month's review. This will ensure that no file will be overlooked or lost in the system. It is also a method of double-checking when documents are due.

When a file is reviewed, it must be documented as such. This is done by inserting the review date on a file review sheet, which is inserted in the file or taped to the cover of the file folder. When the file is reviewed, the review date is crossed out and a new date inserted, about thirty days from the current review date, as shown in Exhibit 12.17.

The docketing coordinator or secretary will insert the name of the file and the name of the attorney and/or legal assistant scheduled to review that file into the firm's docketing computer system. The computer inserts the date for file review on the attorney's or legal assistant's calendar, along with any pertinent notes for the next file review. Each morning, the docket coordinator or secretary pulls the files listed on

EXHIBIT 12.16 Sample Manual Tickler System

People v. Jackson, M.

FILE REVIEW

Date	By
~~5/16/~~	~~MHL~~
~~6/15/~~	~~MHL~~
~~7/12/~~	~~MHL~~
8/13/	MHL

*Strikethrough indicates file
was reviewed.

EXHIBIT 12.17 Sample File Review

the file review section of the calendar for that day and gives them to the attorney or legal assistant for review. When the file has been reviewed, a new review date is put into the system, usually for thirty days in the future, and the cycle continues.

Client Relations

Reviewing clients' files creates a good opportunity to promote positive client relations. One major complaint that clients have about their attorneys is that attorneys do not inform them of the status of their cases. Months go by without any communication from an attorney. An attorney or legal assistant may review the file each month, but unless the client knows this, the client is unaware of the efforts made on his or her behalf. Statistics have shown that clients who are regularly kept apprised of the status of their cases are satisfied clients. Statistics have also shown that regular contact with clients reduces the number of client telephone calls to an attorney or a legal assistant.

A short information letter should be sent to a client each time a file is reviewed to report the status of a case. If no activity has occurred on the file in the past thirty days, the client should be told this. If activity has occurred within the last thirty days, the client should be informed what the activity was and the status of the event.

Client relations is an area in which legal assistants can become valuable to a firm by taking the responsibility to prepare short information letters for either the attorney's or the legal assistant's signature. Attorneys can easily delegate this task to a legal assistant. If an attorney does not delegate this task, a legal assistant can take the initiative and prepare a letter without being formally told to do so, *as long as the attorney reviews the letter before it is mailed.* Goodwill letters, such as those found in Chapter 5 on pages 173 and 174, can be put in the computer system and quickly prepared. A firm will reap great rewards in good client relations from this small effort.

Being efficient in docket control systems and procedures requires time and experience. The time that a legal assistant or other legal support staff devote to learning effective docketing skills will reward them with an essential, marketable skill.

ETHICS ALERT

SUMMARY

There are many deadlines in a law office, and a firm must have a scheduling system that controls deadlines, allocates work so that projects are completed on time, and ensures that nothing is overlooked. A docket control system is perhaps the most important system in a law office. Each member of a legal team takes an active role in a firm's docket control system and works with it every day.

A good docket control system contains all trial dates, court and hearing dates, deposition dates, meeting dates, filing deadlines, reminder dates, follow-up dates, appointments, and personal and professional reminders. The type and sophistication of a docket control system varies according to the size of the firm, the type of firm, and the specialty of the firm.

A firm's calendar is a key component of the smooth operation of a law office. Two calendars are used in most law offices: master calendar and personal calendar. Each member of the legal team has a personal calendar. A legal assistant's personal calendar is a duplicate of the attorney's personal calendar.

Events are docketed as soon as possible after they occur. Regular meetings, at least once or twice a week, should be set with the attorney, legal assistant, and legal secretary to review calendars.

A tickler system, also known as a come-up system, is a method of controlling deadlines. Every law firm has a system to control deadlines called a tickler system, which consists of due dates and reminder dates. Three dates are considered when determining due dates: the trigger date, the mail date, and the due date. When counting days to determine the due date of a document, the first day is excluded and the last day is included. In most jurisdictions, weekend days and holidays are counted, except when a due date is eight days or less of the trigger date, at which time holidays and weekends are not counted. One must consider the time necessary to mail a document to determine a mail date.

For documents to be completed on time, reminder dates must be integrated into a docket system to remind an attorney and a legal assistant that action is required on the file. The time intervals between these dates depend on the type of deadline imposed, the type of project, and where holidays and weekends fall on a calendar. Placing reminder dates in the correct time intervals requires knowledge of the requirements of each type of project. There are no specific rules that govern reminder date intervals.

Legal assistants and attorneys use a tickler system to remind them of several important dates and events. Monitoring statutes of limitations is extremely important. Litigation cases have many deadlines that must be monitored. A document that is due from an opposing party must be documented to alert an attorney of a possible default, or failure to respond.

Other uses for a tickler system are to track verbal and office commitments, to complete the work of an absent attorney or legal assistant, and to schedule tasks to distribute work. The basic rule of a tickler system is that no item is removed from the system until it is completed. Docketing due dates and reminder dates correctly is only half the battle; getting the job done is the other half.

There are two types of calendar software used by law firms: static calendar programs and automated docketing programs. A static calendar program allows the user to enter dates into the program, and the event will be noted on a specific date of the calendar. Static calendar programs are very similar to manual, handwritten systems. Tickler dates are calculated manually, and it is possible for an entry to be scheduled for a holiday or weekend, resulting in lost information.

Automated docketing programs are designed specifically for law firms. Experts agree that an automated docketing program should contain key features that make it an effective program. The information in an automated system is displayed in a calendar that resembles a personal calendar. There are many advantages to an automated docketing program.

A manual tickler system can still be found in some law offices today. The manual system that has been used by law offices since 1915 is the Basic System. A docket request sheet is used with this system. When the current month ends, there should be no tickler sheets left behind a daily divider in that month.

File review is another aspect of a docket control system. Every file should be reviewed monthly. Often, an attorney will delegate file review to an experienced legal assistant. Reviewing clients' files creates a good opportunity to promote positive client relations. A short information letter should be sent to a client each time a file is reviewed to report the status of a case.

Client relations is an area in which legal assistants can become valuable to a firm by taking the responsibility to prepare short information letters. Being efficient in docket control systems and procedures requires time and experience.

CHAPTER ILLUSTRATION

Before Black, White & Greene installed their intranet, they used a static calendar system. The system consisted of a calendar program that displayed the calendar information in a number of formats: by day, by week, and by month. It also generated a to-do list that was posted to a specific date. Reminder information was put in the to-do list, and the date was entered so that the information would be displayed on the appropriate date. The program automatically blocked out the duration of a matter. For example, if an attorney was scheduled to attend a hearing for three hours, that information was inserted into the entry, and nothing could be inserted for that time period without a warning coming up on the screen.

Each secretary was responsible for her attorney's calendar. Audra was responsible for Dennis and George's calendar, Pam was responsible for Patrizia and Grant's calendar, and Tricia was responsible for Robert's calendar. Kay Bowen, the file clerk, was responsible for the master calendar and duplicating tickler information.

When the mail was delivered, the mail would be routed to the secretary for the attorney to whom the mail was directed. If a pleading or other document that required calendaring came in, these procedures would be followed:

◆ The secretary calculates the due date and tickler dates.

◆ The secretary inserts the due date and tickler dates into the calendar system.

◆ The secretary completes a docket request sheet and inserts her initials; attorney's initials; name of the case; description of the event; date, time, and place of the event; and reminder dates, if applicable.

◆ The secretary keeps the bottom yellow copy and puts it in a docket-pending file. The original and remaining three copies are given to Kay for her to put into the master calendar and duplicate tickler system. She then initials the document, which indicates that she inserted the information into the calendar and prepared a docket request sheet.

◆ When Kay receives a docket request sheet, she puts all primary information on the firm's master calendar. She puts secondary information, such as the reminder dates, on a separate firm follow-up calendar. Kay does not insert all secondary information into the follow-up calendar, such as appointments with clients, professional meetings, or personal information. The secretaries monitor that information and do not give them to her. Kay initials the docket request sheet, inserts the date the information was docketed, and retains the bottom blue copy as a record that the event was docketed. She returns the remaining original and two copies to the secretary.

◆ When the secretary receives the completed docket request sheet from Kay, she removes the slip from the docket-pending file. She gives the green copy to the attorney so that the attorney can insert the information into his or her calendar and gives the pink copy to the legal assistant to insert the information into his or her calendar. The original docket slip is inserted into the client's file.

Each Monday morning, Kay prints and distributes the master calendar to everyone in the firm. She also prepares a follow-up report of the reminder dates scheduled for each legal team and distributes it to the team's secretary. The secretary compares Kay's master calendar and follow-up report with hers to make sure that all reminder dates are inserted. When the reports are received, the secretary schedules a calendar meeting with the attorney and legal assistant. Each team schedules its own meeting around the attorney's availability and court schedule. At the calendar meetings, all three calendars are compared so that each team member has all the necessary information.

The firm also requires its attorneys to review each file monthly so that a file is not neglected. Each morning, the secretary retrieves all the files that need to be reviewed that day and puts them on the attorney's desk. When a file is reviewed, the date and the attorney's initials are put on the outside of the file folder. A new file review date for the next month is inserted. The attorney then gives the file to the secretary, who inserts the file review date into the calendar and returns the file to the file room.

Audra has difficulty setting calendar meetings with Dennis. He either has a court hearing or is too busy to meet with her and Julie, the legal assistant. When she sets a calendar meeting, Dennis often cancels it because of a rush project. Dennis often schedules appointments with clients or continues a hearing without informing her of the changes, making their calendar meetings critical. She has asked him to send her a quick calendar note when he does this, but to no avail. She has tried scheduling luncheon calendar meetings or meetings after work. Sometimes her efforts are successful, and sometimes they are not. There are times when two or three weeks may go by without a calendar meeting.

There have been many times that she schedules a meeting with a client or potential client at times that conflict with an appointment Dennis made. One time, the client showed up for an appointment, only to find that Dennis had a court hearing of which he did not inform Audra. This instance was embarrassing to her. This problem really frustrates Audra and Julie because they are unable to rely on the calendar to schedule appointments, motions, and depositions.

The calendar problem is not the only problem that frustrates Audra. Dennis has a problem performing his file review duties. He says that he is too busy to review the files and that he will do it on the weekend. He has good intentions to do it, and he works most Saturdays. However, other priorities interfere with file review, and it does not get done. Files are piled up in his office for review. He has an area in his office for these files: against the wall in piles four feet high. Many times, he has three- or four-piles of files to review. Whenever Audra cannot find a file, she knows exactly where to look—in Dennis' office against the wall.

One Monday morning, Audra tried to schedule a calendar meeting with Dennis. "Can we meet for twenty minutes around 10:00 this morning for calendar review?" asked Audra.

"No," replied Dennis. "I have that settlement conference on the Acme Products case this afternoon at 1:00. We have to put the finishing touches on the settlement brief. How is it coming?"

"I don't know," replied Audra. "I'll check with Julie."

Audra checked the calendar and saw that the settlement conference was not on the schedule for that day. It was scheduled for Wednesday of next week. She wondered whether she had made a mistake in the calendar and checked with Julie.

"I have the Acme Products settlement conference scheduled for next Wednesday also," said Julie. "I have research on the brief scheduled for tomorrow. Dennis's calendar must be wrong. Let's find out."

They went into Dennis's office and asked about the conference. "We have the Acme settlement conference scheduled for next Wednesday. I haven't started on it yet," said Julie.

Dennis replied, "It was scheduled for next Wednesday, but we had to move it up a week. It is this afternoon at 1:00. You haven't started on it yet? We have to get the brief done by noon today!"

"What?" exclaimed Julie. "You didn't tell us it was moved up a week. There is no way we can get it done in three hours!"

"We have to. Here's the file. Use the Backus Car Agency case's settlement brief as a guide and plug in the figures in the file."

"But . . . ," stammered Julie.

"No buts. Get started," said Dennis.

Both Audra and Julie went to work on the brief right away. The phone was ringing off the hook. Both Dennis and Julie instructed Audra that they could not accept telephone calls, so Audra took messages for them. She finally asked Pam to cover the phones for her until they got the settlement brief done, and Pam complied. It was 12:30. They were not finished. Dennis had to leave for court.

"How long until it's done?" asked Dennis.

"I need to put in information regarding the fraud allegation," said Julie. "To do it right, I need a few hours of research. The other parts of the brief can be done in an hour. What should I do?"

"Forget the fraud allegation," said Dennis. "I have to leave now to be there on time. As soon as you're finished, bring it to court. I'll be in Department 17."

"Okay," said Julie.

Julie completed the brief at 1:30 and rushed it to the courthouse. The freeway was jammed. It took her an hour to reach the courthouse, only to find the parking lot full. She had to park on a side street, blocks from the courthouse. She ran to the courthouse and got to the courtroom at 3:00. When Dennis saw her, he breathed a sigh of relief.

"The freeway was jammed, and I couldn't find a parking place," said Julie breathlessly.

"Thank God you made it," said Dennis as he took the brief. "I'll see you back at the office."

Audra and Julie were at their wits' end. Audra scheduled a meeting with Tricia and Robert to discuss the calendar problems. She was hoping that Tricia and Robert could give her a suggestion to fix the problems. At the meeting, Tricia and Robert told her that they were aware of the file review problem but did not know there were calendaring problems.

"What can I do?" asked Audra.

Tricia said, "We are currently installing an intranet that will centralize all our systems. One of the systems that will be centralized is the calendar system. We are purchasing an automated docketing program that will automatically do the calendaring for us. Everyone's calendar will be on the system and will be integrated with one another. A current master calendar and tickler system will be always available on everyone's computer. When you calendar something, it will automatically show up on Dennis's and

Julie's calendar. Whenever Dennis calendars something, it will automatically be put on your and Julie's calendars, so you won't have to worry about him not telling you about changes anymore. And the system will automatically recalculate reminder dates if a date changes. This new system should solve this calendar problem."

"Wow, great!" said Audra. "When will we get the system?"

"We've ordered it," said Robert. "It should be installed in about two weeks. But it will need to be set up, and we will need to input all our case data into it. This should take at least a month. We've made arrangements with Data Specialists to come in and set up the system at night and on weekends so they won't interfere with regular business. Then, everyone will need to be trained on the system."

"I think we should have the system up and running in a couple of months. Just hang in there until then."

"Okay," said Audra. "Now about file review."

CHAPTER REVIEW

1. What are the five characteristics of a good docket control system?

2. What are the three main areas of a docket control system?

3. What information is considered primary information?

4. What information is considered secondary information?

5. How are events placed on a calendar in a large firm? In a small firm?

6. Why would a firm maintain a manual calendar?

7. What three dates are considered when determining due dates?

8. What are the five reminder dates used in a tickler system?

9. How are the time intervals between reminder dates determined?

10. What is the basic rule of a tickler system?

11. What is a static computerized calendar system?

12. What is an automated docket control program, and what features are considered important for this system?

13. Why is a file review system important for good client relations?

EXAMPLES FOR DISCUSSION

1. Reluctant File Review

Richard Everett is a busy trial attorney specializing in personal injury cases. The medium firm for which he works has a monthly review for all files and sends a monthly status letter to clients. Richard's files do not get reviewed, however, and they pile up in his office, the walls of which are lined with piles of files. Whenever a file is missing from the file room, the firm's employees know where to find it: in Richard's office. Richard says that he does not have time to review all the files, with his heavy trial schedule, and files are becoming neglected.

1. You are the law firm's manager. What would you do to remedy the problem?

2. If Richard's files were given to a legal assistant to review, is it fair to the other attorneys who review their own files? Why or why not?

3. Should a legal assistant or other person selected to review the files have any special training or qualifications? If so, what?

2. Weekend and Holiday Projects

Sandy Esmay is the manager of a small firm. She hired a new secretary who is responsible for maintaining a computerized and manual tickler system for the firm. The secretary was instructed in the proper method of maintaining the tickler system. After six weeks had passed, an attorney approached Sandy in a panic and reported that he had missed a very important deadline. He accused the new secretary of not putting the information in the tickler system. Sandy insists that she inserted the information.

1. What could have happened here?

2. Where could Sandy go to determine whether she did insert the information?

3. You are the manager of the law firm. What procedures would you put in place so that the situation would not happen again?

3. Automated Systems

Do any students in the class have experience with a docket control system? If so, what type of system? What are the advantages and disadvantages of the system? Would any of the features of an automated docket control system described on page 411 improve the system? Discuss how a law firm could benefit from an automated docket control system.

4. Calendar Meetings and File Review Problem

Calendar meetings are an important aspect of docket control. As we saw in the Chapter Illustration, Audra had problems scheduling calendar meetings with Dennis. There were also problems with Dennis performing his file review duties. If you were Audra, how would you handle the problem? Do you think that Audra was right in discussing the problems with Robert and Tricia? What are some possible solutions to the file review problem? Do you think that Dennis will be upset with Audra for discussing the problems with Robert and Tricia? Why or why not?

ASSIGNMENTS

1. Robert Black, the managing partner, has assigned you to recommend an automated docket control software program for Black, White & Greene. Research the available programs and write a report about your findings. Compare features, capabilities, requirements, and price. Choose the product that you would recommend and state the reasons that you chose that product.

2. Make up a manual tickler system as described on page 419. Enter your class assignments into the system, scheduling your time to complete the assignments on time. Include reminder dates and follow-up dates. Also include any personal or professional obligations into the system.

3. Use the following calendars to determine the due dates and mail dates for the following scenarios (Note: Holidays are November 23 and 24 and December 25):

   a. Your client, Leona Ledford, was personally served with a summons and complaint on October 23 in the case of *Masters v. Ledford.* Her answer is due in thirty days.

   b. In the case of *Brozowski v. Thrifty Drugs,* your client, Rose Brozowski, was served with a cross-complaint by mail. The proof of service by mail form indicated that it was mailed on October 25. Her answer is due in thirty days. The case is a federal case that allows three days for mailing. You will mail the answer to the court.

   c. In the case of *Masters v. Ledford,* your client, Leona Ledford, was served with interrogatories by mail. The proof of service by mail form indicates that it was mailed on November 21. Her response is due in thirty days. The case is a state court case that allows five days for mailing. You will mail the response to the opposing party.

   d. The trial of *Stacy v. Pinkerton* is scheduled for December 18. A trial brief must be filed no later than ten days before trial. The brief contains many complex issues. It will be mailed to the court and the opposing counsel.

October						
Sun	Mon	Tues	Wed	Thur	Fri	Sat
1	2	3	4	5	6	7
8	9	10	11	12	13	14
15	16	17	18	19	20	21
22	23	24	25	26	27	28
29	30	31				

November						
Sun	Mon	Tues	Wed	Thur	Fri	Sat
			1	2	3	4
5	6	7	8	9	10	11
12	13	14	15	16	17	18
19	20	21	22	23	24	25
26	27	28	29	30		

December						
Sun	Mon	Tues	Wed	Thur	Fri	Sat
					1	2
3	4	5	6	7	8	9
10	11	12	13	14	15	16
17	18	19	20	21	22	23
24	25	26	27	28	29	30
31						

e. In the case of *Fullbright v. Kanner,* you received a motion to compel further answers to interrogatories of your client, Ron Kanner. The proof of service by mail indicates that the motion was mailed on November 13, and a response is due in fifteen days. The case is a federal case that allows three days for mailing. You will personally deliver the response to the court and the opposing party.

f. In the case of *People v. Gates,* your client wants to file an appeal. The verdict was rendered on October 3, and a notice of appeal was filed on October 17. Your appellate brief is due thirty days after the notice of appeal is filed, and the reply brief of the opposing party is due thirty days after the date your brief is due. You will mail your brief to the court. The court allows three days for mailing. What is the due date? What is the mail date? When is the reply brief of the opposing party due?

g. In the case of *Fullbright v. Kanner,* you mailed the opposing party a request for production of documents on November 3. A response is due in thirty days.

h. The trial of *Stacy v. Pinkerton* is scheduled for December 18. Subpoenas must be prepared and personally served on eight witnesses at least ten days before the trial. What is the last day the subpoenas may be served?

4. Calculate and enter reminder dates for scenarios a, b, d, e, and f.

5. Calculate and enter reminder dates for scenario c. You will mail the interrogatories to the client for review and signature before mailing them to the opposing party.

6. Your firm prepared a will for Robert Valentino, an elderly gentleman. On November 15, you mailed a copy of the will to him for his approval and comments before he comes into the office to sign the original will before witnesses. The appointment for the execution of the will has not yet been set. How would you enter this into a tickler system?

7. It is the morning of November 20. Your boss asks you to research and prepare a memorandum of law on an issue of comparative negligence as soon as possible. He asks you to get started right away. The memorandum is due on November 29, and he will provide you with additional information on November 24. How would you tickle this?

8. Your firm represents ABC Company in the case of *ABC Company v. XYZ Company.* The attorneys for XYZ Company filed a motion for summary judgment with a hearing date of December 8. Your opposition to the motion must be filed with the court no later than fourteen days of the date of the hearing. When is the due date of the response? It is a federal court case that allows three days for mailing. You will mail the response to the court. On what date must it be mailed to reach the court by the due date?

9. Your firm represents Ms. Grace in a slip-and-fall matter against Lucky Market. Her accident occurred on December 23 of last year. The statute of limitations is one year. How would you tickle the statute of limitations for her case?

10. In the case of *Johnson v. Mandle,* your client's brief in opposition to a motion is due within seven days of receipt of the motion. The proof of service by mail form indicates that the motion was mailed on October 26. It is a federal case that allows three days for mailing. Federal law also states that for deadlines of less than eight days, weekend and holiday dates are *not* counted. What is the due date? What is the mail date? How many reminders would you enter for the response?

SELF-TEST

How well did you grasp the material in the chapter? Test yourself by answering the following questions and check your answers against the answers found in Appendix A.

1. According to recent statistics, what percentage of malpractice claims are a result of a missed deadline?

2. Who has responsibility for a docket system in a small firm?

3. Who has responsibility for a docket system in a large firm?

4. Why must a legal assistant have knowledge of docketing procedures?

5. What types of information are contained in a docket control system?

6. How can a missed deadline have disastrous consequences for a firm?

7. What are the six functions of a good docket control system?

8. What are the characteristics of a good docket control system?

9. What are the two types of calendars used in a law office?

10. What information is contained on a master calendar?

11. What is the purpose of a master calendar?

12. How often do large firms distribute master calendars to employees?

13. How often do small firms distribute master calendars to employees?

14. How do firms with an intranet distribute their master calendars?

15. What essential information does a master calendar contain?

16. What two types of information does a personal calendar contain?

17. What does primary information include?

18. What is a statute of limitations?

19. What does secondary information include?

20. Why are manual calendars an essential element of a firm's calendaring policy?

21. Describe the various types of manual calendars.

22. Who is responsible to keep calendars current?

23. When should personal calendars be updated?

24. When are events docketed?

25. When are documents from opposing parties docketed?

26. What does a stamp or an initial on a document mean?

27. What does the absence of a stamp or an initial on a document mean?

28. Describe a calendar meeting.

29. What is a docket coordinator?

30. What is a docket request sheet, and for what purpose is it used?

31. What information is contained on a docket request sheet?

32. How many pages does a docket request sheet contain?

33. How are the copies of the docket request sheet used?

34. What is used to inform other members of the legal team that an event was docketed?

35. Why is it important to keep all calendars out of the view of clients?

36. What is a tickler system?

37. What would happen if a firm had no tickler system?

38. What is an integrated tickler system?

39. What type of information is inserted on the left side of a personal calendar?

40. What type of information is inserted on the right side of a personal calendar?

41. What three dates are considered when determining due dates?

42. What is a trigger date?

43. What is a due date?

44. If a due date falls on a holiday or weekend day, when is the due date?

45. What is a mail date?

46. How does one determine the number of days that should be set aside for mailing?

47. When counting days to determine a document's due date, what is excluded?

48. When counting days to determine a document's due date, what is included?

49. What day is counted as the first day when determining due dates?

50. Are weekend days and holidays counted when determining due dates?

51. When are weekends and holidays excluded from the day count?

52. Where would you find out a state's requirements for including weekends and holidays in a due-date calculation?

53. How do you compensate for mail time when determining due dates?

54. How is a legal team reminded that a deadline is approaching?

55. What are the four reminder dates?

56. How are the time intervals between reminder dates determined?

57. What governs the time intervals between reminder dates?

58. Why must time intervals between reminder dates be adjustable and flexible?

59. Why is it important to monitor statutes of limitations?

60. How many reminder dates does a one-year statute of limitations require?

61. How many reminder dates does a four-year statute of limitations require?

62. How many reminder dates does a thirty-day deadline require?

63. How many reminder dates does a fifteen-day deadline require?

64. What is a default?

65. How many reminder dates does a document that is due from opposing parties have?

66. What methods are used to differentiate between tickler entries for a firm's documents and those of opposing parties?

67. If a letter is sent that requires a reply, how is it tickled?

68. How is a tickler system used to track verbal and office commitments?

69. How is a tickler system used to complete the work of an absent attorney or legal assistant?

70. What is the basic rule of a tickler system?

71. Why should an attorney or a legal assistant never be verbally reminded of tickler information?

72. Docketing due dates and reminders is half the battle. What is the other half?

73. What are the two types of computerized docket systems?

74. What is a static calendar program?

75. What types of information are put into a static calendar program?

76. How are dates inserted into a static calendar system?

77. Static calendar programs are similar to what type of system?

78. How accurate are static calendar programs?

79. In what size of firm are static calendar programs found?

80. What are the two areas that set automated docketing software programs apart from static calendar programs?

81. Automated docketing programs contain databases that contain what information?

82. What does a malpractice alert report contain?

83. What are the key features of an automated docketing program?

84. What is automatic date scheduling?

85. What is data validation?

86. Why must the holiday scheduling feature be flexible?

87. What is retroactive event recalculation?

88. Why is the group scheduling feature important?

89. How is information in an automated docketing system displayed?

90. What are the advantages to an automated docketing program?

91. How do some firms use a manual tickler system?

92. What is the manual tickler system that has been used by law firms since 1915?

93. How is a manual tickler system used?

94. What type of method can be implemented into a manual tickler system that will identify weekend or holiday dates?

95. What is a file review system?

96. How often should each file be reviewed?

97. Why should an attorney not postpone file review?

98. How are files documented for file review?

99. How does file review promote good client relations?

KEY WORDS

Data validation
Default
Docket
Docket coordinator

Master calendar
Personal calendar
Proof of service by mail

Retroactive event recalculation
Static calendar programs
Trigger date

CHAPTER

13

File and Records Management

OBJECTIVES

After completion of this chapter, a student should be able to do the following:

◆ Organize a legal file.

◆ Maintain a legal file.

◆ Open a legal file.

◆ Perform a conflict-of-interest check.

◆ Discuss file organization procedures.

◆ Prepare a file for closing and retention.

◆ Discuss file retrieval procedures.

◆ Prune a file for closing and schedule it for destruction.

◆ Describe the essential considerations of records management.

◆ Discuss essential documents in a law firm.

◆ Explain when to keep or discard a document.

◆ Explain how filing systems are categorized.

◆ Categorize subjects.

◆ Discuss the various types of coding systems for files.

INTRODUCTION

A firm's file and records system is the nerve center of a law office. It is an active and vital part of the firm and must be properly managed and maintained. Every legal assistant will interact with a law firm's file and records system regardless of employer. An overview of a firm's file and records system will prepare legal staff members for employment in the legal marketplace by giving them an understanding of the rules and requirements necessary to maintain a system and to keep it running smoothly.

This chapter will instruct the legal assistant student of proper file management procedures to create professional, well-managed files. File maintenance concepts will be discussed, as will file retention and file destruction procedures. It will also discuss each element of a records management system and will give a student knowledge of the various filing systems used in today's law office. This knowledge will prepare a student to participate in a firm's file and records management system. A legal assistant student will be able to take this knowledge into any law firm and display excellent organizational skills.

CONSIDERATIONS OF RECORDS MANAGEMENT

A well-organized records management system provides benefits to law firms and their employees. For the law firm, the benefits are the following:

◆ Increased access to information
◆ Easier identification and processing of documents that require special handling
◆ Increased organization of an office as a result of established procedures in document retention
◆ Reduced costs for clerical, photocopy, filing equipment, and storage expenses

Employees enjoy four benefits:

◆ *Improved work product.* Necessary files and documentation are easily obtained to support each person's work.
◆ *Improved organization.* Unnecessary material is eliminated.
◆ *Increased productivity.* A legal assistant is allowed to spend time on billable projects rather than on trying to find files, documents, and pertinent information.
◆ *Improved use of office space.* A better arrangement of necessary equipment and space produces a comfortable working environment.

A records management system has eight general considerations:

ETHICS ALERT

◆ *Ability to find what you want when you want it.* The most common waste of time is searching for a document or file that is not accessible. Searching for misplaced records and files costs firms thousands of dollars per year in unproductive employee time. *A legal assistant with an annual billable hours requirement cannot bill a client for time spent searching for a file.* If a firm spent a fraction of the money it loses in unproductive employee time on a well-organized records management system, it would save thousands of dollars a year and increase employee productivity. Searching for a file or document in a disorganized office is frustrating and reduces employee morale. Disorganization ranks high on the list of causes of employee dissatisfaction.
◆ *Employee time involved in operating the system.* Employee time spent operating a records management system constitutes 80 percent of the cost of most systems. If the system is so complicated that it takes many people to keep it functioning or too much employee time to maintain it, it is not cost-effective and therefore is a poor system. Also considered is the training time that it takes for a new employee to learn a system. While an employee is learning a system, documents may be misfiled or not filed at all. The possibility of losing records because of misfiling is greater in a complicated system because employees consider misfiling easier than trying to figure out the system. Being too complicated disrupts the integrity of a system.
◆ *The amount and cost of floor space required for the system.* Office space is a very expensive commodity. Storing records is also very expensive. As a firm grows, its need for document storage grows. A firm will soon discover that it has outgrown an office because of increased storage needs. An office environment becomes cramped, and a move is inevitable and expensive.
◆ *Capital investment of durable equipment.* Filing cabinets and a storage system will ordinarily constitute 10 percent of the entire cost of a filing system. Many different types of storage equipment are available in various ranges of cost. Filing equipment must last a long time and be expandable.
◆ *Cost of supplies to maintain a system.* Supplies for maintaining a records management system constitute another 10 percent of its total cost. Supplies include file folders, file labels, fasteners, forms, and other miscellaneous items.

If a specialized file folder is required for a system, this will be more expensive and may not be readily available if it must be specially ordered. Unavailability of supplies can cause a backlog in a system.

◆ *Appearance of files and equipment.* The appearance of storage equipment is important to the working environment of a firm. A messy, unattractive filing area creates the impression of disorganization. A messy, disorganized file will not impress a client or a judge.

ETHICS ALERT

◆ *Confidentiality of files. A client's file may not be stored in an area where confidential information can be viewed by others.* A filing system must be secure and not accessible to other clients or nonemployees.

◆ *Safety of files.* A firm's records must be protected from theft, fire, and natural elements.

FILING SYSTEMS

The management and organization of a firm's filing system are essential to the smooth operation of a law firm. Each firm uses a different filing system, usually customized to the needs of the office. For a system to be effective, it must consist of a logical division of categories of records, and it must use a logical, efficient coding method.

The beginning of the computer revolution promised a "paperless" office. However, this has not evolved. The computer has generated more paper. Firms are running longer, more detailed reports, and computers allow for multiple revisions of documents. All this paper must be stored in a well-organized filing system.

Elements of a Filing System

The eight elements of an effective filing system are the following:

1. Retrievability
2. Functionality
3. Suitability
4. Flexibility
5. Consistency
6. Economy
7. Disposability
8. Security

Retrievability   A law firm's records must be accessible quickly. For a file to be retrieved quickly, it must be filed in an organized, logical manner. The categories of files must be logically divided and have little or no redundancy. Careful planning of categories will reduce the amount of time it takes to find a file.

Functionality   A law firm's records are considered by function (e.g., clients' files, the firm's business files, personnel files, and other files). When each function has been identified, categories are developed within each function. It would not be logical to file a firm's business records with its clients' files.

Suitability   Since the users of a system are document creators, a system must be suitable to them. A system must be easily understood by all employees and must follow an organization that each employee can comprehend. The more complex a system, the less suitable it is for employees; it is important that a system be simple.

Flexibility   No law firm is static; therefore, a filing system must be flexible to accommodate changes. In large offices, active files increase more than 25 percent a year, doubling in size every four years. As a firm grows, a filing system must grow with it. A system must have the flexibility to change without needing to be overhauled.

Consistency   To avoid confusion and chaos, a system must be consistent in its structure. Consistency develops familiarity among its users. When an employee becomes familiar with one part of a system, the other parts will be easy to understand. Consistency of structure reduces the level of uncertainty when looking for a record.

Economy   Economy of a filing system includes use of time and space. A filing system must not require a great deal of time to maintain. It must also be maintained in the least amount of space.

Disposability   A system must provide for timely disposition of records. If records are inactive or no longer viable, they are destroyed. Retention of inactive records that need not be retained uses valuable space and increases the time it takes to use and maintain a system.

ETHICS ALERT

Security   A filing system must consider confidentiality and damage. *Clients' records are confidential, and a system must ensure that confidentiality.* Additionally, clients' records must be protected from the elements, such as fire, water, and other natural elements.

Types of Filing Systems

There are three types of filing systems: centralized, decentralized, and automated.

Centralized   A centralized filing system has all the files located in one area and is normally managed by a file coordinator or clerk. A large firm and many medium-size firms have a centralized system. The files are stored in a centralized area and are maintained and controlled by one or more individuals, known as file clerks or file coordinators. In a centralized system, there is **controlled access,** which means that no one can remove a file without notifying the file clerk. When a file is needed, it is checked out of the file area and returned by the end of the day.

Controlled access: The access and retrieval of a firm's files are controlled by a specific system.

Decentralized   A decentralized system has files located in various areas, usually near the responsible attorney's office. Generally, a small firm will have a decentralized system. The files are stored in or near the responsible attorney's work area, and each attorney is responsible for maintaining his or her own files.

There are few totally centralized filing systems. Most lawyers like to keep their most active files in their work areas for easy retrieval as they are needed rather than returning them to a central file area at the end of the day. If this is the case, a system must be in place that documents the location of each file. This is known as **central file control** and is implemented for both centralized and decentralized systems.

Central file control: A system that documents the location of each file.

Automated Records Management   Firms are moving toward a paperless office by use of automated records management software programs. An automated records management program classifies files and folders in the same way a manual system does. Records management software tracks a file from its opening through its destruction. It assigns closed-file numbers and a file location in the inactive storage area. It has the capability of running numerous file reports.

Imaging: The process of scanning a paper document into a computer system.

An automated filing system consists of three parts: document entry, scanning, and retrieval. Each document in a file is scanned into a computer, referred to as **imaging.** The filing system software saves it in the appropriate file. Document retrieval software is used to retrieve a file or document by searching a database. A number of criteria can be used to search the database. The system will display the files that match the criteria and will display the documents in the file. A user can review, print, or fax documents directly from the system.

Filing System Classification

Classification: The process of separating items into categories.

A filing system, whether centralized, decentralized, or automated, consists of a logical division of categories of records. Dividing records into categories is known as **classification.** A good classification system increases accessibility and reduces complexity. The categories chosen will depend on a firm's size and specialties. A boutique law office specializing in one area of law would have fewer categories than a large firm practicing in many areas of law.

Records are divided into categories that have a logical connection to one another. There are four major categories for most law firm files: function, subject, topic, and subtopic. First their function is identified, then they can be categorized further by subject, topic, and subtopic. Knowing a record's function is essential before it can be located.

Function Categories   The first step in categorizing documents is to identify their functions. After their functions are identified, records are divided into subjects, and the subjects are further divided into topics:

    Clients' files (function)
        Criminal cases (subject)
            Burglary (topic)
    Personnel records (function)
        Performance evaluations (subject)
            Performance appraisals, June 2003 (topic)

Subject Categories   Functions are divided into subjects:

    I. Clients (function)
        A. Individual clients (subject)
        B. Business clients (subject)
    II. Area of law (function)
        A. Probate (subject)
        B. Real estate (subject)
        C. Corporate (subject)

Topic Categories   Subjects are further divided into topics:

    I. Clients (function)
        A. Individual clients (subject)
            1. Adams, Alice (topic)
            2. Benson, Bernadette (topic)
            3. Springer, David (topic)
        B. Business clients (subject)
            1. Quick Sell Real Estate (topic)
            2. Zono's Restaurant (topic)
            3. Velco Tire Company (topic)
    II. Area of law
        A. Probate
            1. Conservatorships
            2. Estate planning
            3. Guardianships

B. Real estate
 1. Litigation
 2. Title matters
 3. Leases
C. Corporate
 1. Agreements
 2. Minutes and meetings
 3. Labor relations

Subtopic Categories   Topics may be further divided into subtopics:

I. Clients (function)
 A. Individual clients (subject)
  1. Adams, Alice (topic)
   a. In re Marriage of Adams (subtopic)
   b. Bankruptcy of Alice Adams (subtopic)
   c. Star Financial Services v. Adams (subtopic)
  2. Benson, Bernadette (topic)
   a. Estate of Benson (subtopic)
   b. Name change of Benson (subtopic)
  3. Springer, David
   a. People v. Springer
   b. Marriage of Springer
   c. Springer v. Fedco
 B. Business clients
  1. Quick Sell Real Estate
   a. Copy Right v. Quick Sell
   b. Quick Sell v. Jackson
   c. Pride Shopping Center Lease
  2. Zono's Restaurant
   a. Jones v. Zono's
   b. Zono's v. Chunky Chickens
   c. Purchase of Busy Boy Burgers
  3. Velco Tire Company
   a. Madison v. Velco
   b. Jeffries v. Velco
   c. Velco v. Haniball
II. Area of Law
 A. Probate
  1. Conservatorships
   a. Conservatorship of Carey Carlson
   b. Conservatorship of Patricia Bolder
   c. Conservatorship of Frederick Kirch
  2. Estate planning
   a. Will of Carter Maxwell
   b. Will of Ester Lopez
   c. Trust of Zane Trent
  3. Guardianships
   a. Guardianship of Johnny Milestone
   b. Guardianship of Karen Fields
   c. Guardianship of Mary Walpert
 B. Real estate
  1. Litigation
   a. Manley v. Tripp
   b. Finley Development v. XYZ Architects
   c. Fischer v. Treadly
  2. Title matters
   a. Property of Gaines
   b. Property of Tyler
   c. Property of Gaston

3. Leases
   a. Goldenwest Cleaners
   b. Saleon Drugs
   c. Simeon Glass Company
C. Corporate
   1. Agreements
      a. Simpson and Quail Agreement
      b. Vision Lighting and Glass Components
      c. Harold Bookstore and Crown Books
   2. Minutes and meetings
      a. Vision Electronics Corporation
      b. Vision Lighting and Design
      c. Component Solutions
   3. Labor relations
      a. Velco Tire Company
      b. Vision Electronics Corporation
      c. Velco Tire Company

Coding Systems

A coding system is a method used to store files in a specified sequence. The sequence must be logical, follow a set of rules, and be simple to use. There are three methods of coding files: alphabetic, numeric, and alphanumeric.

Alphabetical Coding Systems   An alphabetical coding system, also known as a direct coding system, is the most common coding system used by small firms. A number of consultants feel that an alphabetical coding system is outdated, but small firms continue to use it because it is the easiest coding system to establish and maintain. In this system, a law firm's business records are arranged in alphabetical order by function, such as accounts receivable, accounts payable, and personnel. Client files are arranged in alphabetical order according to a client's surname, as shown in Exhibit 13.1.

Each file title or name is comprised of units, and each word is considered a unit. When filing, unit 1 is considered before unit 2, and unit 2 is considered before unit 3.

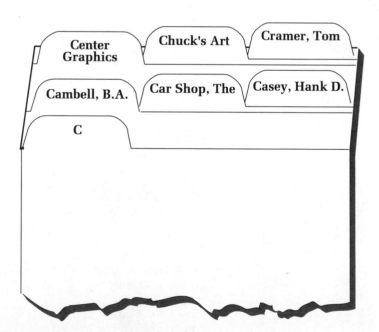

EXHIBIT 13.1   Alphabetical Client Files

Unit 1	Unit 2	Unit 3
Brown	John	T.
Great	Lakes	Realty

Although an alphabetical coding system seems easy, problems occur when employees have not been instructed in its rules. For the system to run smoothly, users must strictly adhere to the following alphabetical coding rules.

Rule 1. Always use the surname of an individual client as the first unit, as follows:

Unit 1	Unit 2	Unit 3
Brown,	John	T.

If the client is a business, the first name of the business is the first unit, as follows:

Unit 1	Unit 2	Unit 3	Unit 4	Unit 5
John	T.	Brown	Tire	Company

John T. Brown's file is filed under "B," and John T. Brown Tire Company is filed under "J."

Rule 2. File nothing before something. For example, Jane Roberts is filed before Jane Robertson, as follows:

Roberts, Jane A.

Robertson, Jane M.

Rule 3. Consider each unit when filing documents. If a firm has two clients named Jane Roberts, the third unit—middle name or initials—is considered:

Roberts, Jane

Roberts, Jane A.

Roberts, Jane E.

Roberts, Jane Michelle

Units include prepositions, conjunctions, and articles. Note that when the word *the* is used to begin a title, it is always the last unit:

Unit 1	Unit 2	Unit 3	Unit 4
Children's	Shop,	The	
A	Formidable	Feast	Restaurant

A Formidable Feast Restaurant is filed under "A," and The Children's Shop is filed under "C."

Rule 4. Ignore all punctuation and symbols when alphabetizing, and drop punctuation to determine a unit:

	Unit 1	Unit 2	Unit 3
A-1 Business Service	A1	Business	Service
A.A.A. Glass Co.	AAA	Glass	Co.
B&B Barbecue Equipment	BB	Barbecue	Equipment

Rule 5. Arabic and roman numerals are filed sequentially before alphabetic letters. Arabic numerals precede roman numerals. They are filed according to their number rather than the word that spells the number. For example, the first unit for The 21 Club is 21 instead of twenty-one:

Unit 1	Unit 2	Unit 3
21	Club	The
42nd	Street	Restaurant
IV	Brigade	The

Rule 6. Radio and television station call letters are identified as one unit, as follows:

Unit 1	Unit 2
KNBC	Television
WGN	Radio

Rule 7. File a record under its most commonly used name or title and cross-reference it under other names that might be used:

File Under	Cross-Reference Under
ATT	American Telegraph and Telephone
IRS	Internal Revenue Service

Rule 8. Always file under the client's name, regardless of his or her status in a case. If the client is the sole plaintiff, his or her name would always be first in the case. For example, in *Jones v. White,* if your firm represents the plaintiff, the case will be filed under J for Jones:

Jones, Stanley T. v. White, Mary L.

If your firm represents the defendant, list your client first and insert "adv." (adverse) instead of "v." (versus) to indicate that the client is the defendant:

White, Mary L. adv. Jones, Stanley T.

In this case, *Jones v. White* is filed under the client's surname: "W" for White.

In lawsuits with many plaintiffs and defendants, only the names of the first plaintiff and first defendant are used as the **primary case name,** which is the name used to identify a case. All parties are not included in the primary case name because the name would be too long. If a client's name is not in the primary case name, the primary case name is included on the client's file label, as follows:

Primary case name: The name used to identify a case, consisting of the first-named plaintiff and the first-named defendant.

Snow, Harry M. (Jones, Stanley T. v. White, Mary L.)

A cross-reference is required to refer the user to Harry Snow when a document is received concerning the *Jones v. White* case. If no index is available, a person searching for the *Jones v. White* case would be unable to find it because it is filed under the client's name: Snow, Harry M.

In an insurance defense firm or a corporate legal department with only one client, the client's name is not indicated on the label, as that name is the same for each file. Only the other party's name is indicated on the file label in such a case.

OF INTEREST . . .

Alphabetical Filing Tip

If an alphabetical entry is difficult, check the alphabetical sequence in a telephone book. For example, if you are not sure whether AAA Service is filed before AA Manufacturing, the telephone book will usually have the correct sequence. A telephone book is a good reference guide for alphabetical filing rules.

A firm may also have clients' files arranged alphabetically by subject, as shown in Exhibit 13.2. Subjects for clients' files are by area of law or responsible attorney. This method is more difficult than straight alphabetical coding because a user must know the subject before a file is accessible. A case may involve multiple areas of law, or a user may know that a client has a case with the firm but cannot remember the subject matter of the case. Firms that code files by subject must cross-index the case in an alphabetical listing by a client's name to locate the files.

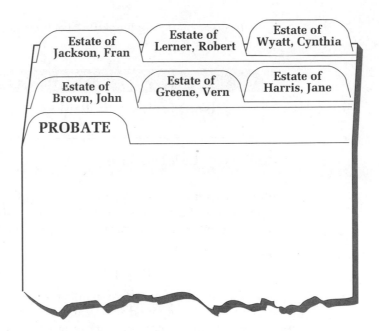

EXHIBIT 13.2   Clients' Files by Subject

Numeric Coding Systems

Files coded with numeric coding are arranged in numeric order according to a particular numbering pattern. Various numbering patterns are used, with management determining the one for a particular system. Management determines the order and progression in which the numbers or parts of numbers will be read.

Six different types of numeric systems are used: straight, coded, calendar, standard, account, and combination.

Straight Numbering   Straight numbering is consecutive numbering: 1, 2, 3, 4. A firm assigns a file number to each new matter as a file is opened. This is the least complicated numeric numbering system. By this numbering system, a firm keeps track of the number of cases it represents from the beginning of its operation. Numbering normally begins at 100.

In this type of system, a client with many cases will have files scattered throughout a filing system. A user must rely on an alphabetical index to find the proper file.

Coded Numbering   Coded numbering combines numbers with letters of the alphabet. Letters preceding the file number are used to further categorize files. The letters may be a responsible attorney's initials or the initials of a branch office or type of case. The file numbers are assigned sequentially:

AS123	Al Simpson's case, case no. 123
LA567	Los Angeles branch, case no. 567
LIT865	Litigation case, case no. 865

Coded numbering allows all of one attorney's files to be filed together or allows files to be filed by type of case or the cases of a branch office to be filed together. Color coding file labels is used to further categorize files. Exhibit 13.3 shows an example of coded numbering with color coding.

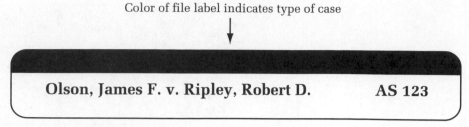

Color of file label indicates type of case

Olson, James F. v. Ripley, Robert D.   AS 123

EXHIBIT 13.3 Coded Numbering

Calendar Numbering Calendar numbering inserts the month and year a file was opened as part of the file number. After the calendar code, the case file is numbered sequentially. For example, case no. 0103341 would read as follows:

01	03	341
Year	Month (March)	File number

Calendar numbering will keep all files opened in one year together. It tells a firm how many files are opened in a year and in a month. This information is important for long-range planning and marketing projects. In addition, the file number tells a user the age of a case and that a case may be a candidate for closing.

Standard Numbering Standard numbering separates categories of numbers by a space, comma, period, or dash. Any number of considerations can be given the number. With a standard numbering system, a user gains information just by reading the file number.

Some firms further categorize case documents by separating documents by their type. These subfiles are known as volumes. A volume may have its own categorization and number. For example, a litigation case may have its own classification system as follows:

Folder 1	Volume .1	Correspondence
Folder 2	Volume .2	Pleadings and court documents
Folder 3	Volume .3	Medical records
Folder 4	Volume .4	Discovery
Folder 5	Volume .5	Legal research
Folder 6	Volume .6	Miscellaneous notes and reports

Each section may have up to ten volumes in each section. If a second correspondence volume is opened, that file would be volume .11. The third discovery volume would be volume .42.

For example, the file number 4/23-321.2 tells the user the responsible attorney, type of case, file number, and volume:

4	23	321	.2
Attorney's number	Type of case	File number	Volume number

When documents are logically categorized and consistent, all members of a legal team will know that volume 5 contains legal research and that volume 3 contains medical records. This system expedites retrieval of a document by directing a user to the subject matter of the document requested. For example, if a legal assistant needed to retrieve a medical report for the *Olson v. Ripley* case, he would retrieve file number 4/23-321.3.

Account Numbering Account numbering gives each client a permanent number, and all subsequent cases are filed with that account number. Each case is given a se-

Color of file label indicates court or other designation

01	07	4	23	.321	/3
Year	Month	Attorney	Type of case	File no.	Volume No.

EXHIBIT 13.4 Combination Coding

quential number after the account number, normally starting with 100. Client number 862's fourth case would be numbered 862-104. This type of coding system is used by firms that represent clients with a number of cases, such as collection cases for a large department store.

Combination Numbering It is not necessary to adhere to one style of numeric coding; many firms combine the coding styles. A calendar numbering system may be combined with a standard numbering system, as shown in Exhibit 13.4. The file number 0107-4/23.321.3 is interpreted as follows:

01	07	4	23	.321	.3
Year	Month	Attorney	Type of case	File number	Volume number

A coded numbering system may be combined with an account numbering system as follows:

LA	862	123
Attorney or branch office	Client number	File number

In addition, a firm may combine standard, calendar, and account numbering systems: The number 0107-4-23.867/341.3 is interpreted as follows:

01	07	4	23	.867	341	.3
Year	Month	Attorney	Type of case	Client	File number	Volume number

Alphanumeric Coding

An alphanumeric coding system is a numeric system that codes files alphabetically. A number is assigned to each letter of the alphabet, and each file is given a number that corresponds to the surname of a client. Files are then filed in alphabetical and numeric order:

A = 1	I = 9	Q = 17	Y = 25
B = 2	J = 10	R = 18	Z = 26
C = 3	K = 11	S = 19	
D = 4	L = 12	T = 20	
E = 5	M = 13	U = 21	
F = 6	N = 14	V = 22	
G = 7	O = 15	W = 23	
H = 8	P = 16	X = 24	

The first four or five letters of a client's surname are assigned a number according to their numeric value:

Abrams, E	A-B-R-A-M	1-2-18-1-13
Ackerman, D	A-C-K-E-R	1-3-11-5-18
Adams, N	A-D-A-M-S	1-4-1-13-19
Aggate, P	A-G-G-A-T	1-7-7-1-20
Ahart, Y	A-H-A-R-T	1-8-1-18-20

The cases are filed in numeric order but retain their alphabetical value. Therefore, when a new file is opened, it is given a number that pertains to its alphabetical value. For example, when Renee Aggerty's case is opened, her file would be given the number 1-7-7-5-18 (A = 1, G = 7, G = 7, E = 5, T = 18). The file would be filed between Aggate and Ahart according to its numeric value as follows:

Abrams, E	1-2-18-1-13
Ackerman, D	1-3-11-5-18
Adams, N	1-4-1-13-19
Aggate, P	1-7-7-1-20
Aggerty, R	**1-7-7-5-18**
Ahart, Y	1-8-1-18-20

Note that the file is in both numeric and alphabetical order.

Studies have shown that an alphanumeric coding system can increase retrieval and filing speed up to six times. Misfilings are also reduced. Another advantage is that a cross-index is in alphabetical and numeric order.

OF INTEREST . . .

Seven Causes of Misfiles

One of the things paperwork consultant Robert A. Shiff discovered while surveying hundreds of office employees is that we spend 20 to 30 percent of our time just looking for information.

Management engineers have put a dollar value on that lost time. Their estimates of the cost of a single misfile range from $61 to $73. Check your file drawers for these seven common causes of lost information:

1. Guide headings are too complex. Keep them simple. You don't have time to stop and decipher their meanings.

2. Headings aren't legible. Never handwrite your labels—especially in pencil, which will fade over time. Instead, type all file labels clearly, capitalizing only the first letter of each word. All caps are hard to read.

3. Files have too many or too few guides. Use no fewer than five and no more than 15 guides per drawer.

4. File drawers are overcrowded. Leave 3 to 4 inches of extra space per drawer. It can be frustrating and time-consuming to have to force files in and out—not to mention the paper cuts!

5. File folders are overstuffed. Make sure papers don't ride up, covering the guide.

6. Cross-references aren't used enough. Use a standard cross-reference form on colored stock showing the subject of the document, the date, and where it's located in the files.

7. Papers aren't indexed correctly. Before filing anything, write the correct file heading in the upper right-hand corner of each document, or underline it in colored pencil if it appears in the text.

Source: From 9 to 5. *The Dartnell Corporation. Reprinted with permission.*

Cross-Index

A cross index is a cross-reference of clients' files. All numeric coding systems must have an alphabetical cross index of clients with corresponding file numbers. In a firm with many cases, it is impossible to remember the file number of each case. Therefore, the name of the case and client must be cross-indexed alphabetically to locate a file.

All files and subfiles must be included on the index. Whenever a new subfile is opened, it is given a number and included on a cross-index. For example, a case has a combination numbering system, and a subfile is opened for each aspect of a litigation, as shown on page 442. All medical records are given the volume number of .3. As a file expands, new volumes are opened. The second medical records file is volume .31, and the third medical records file is .32. These new volumes must be inserted on a cross-index as they are opened, or no one will know they exist.

A **numeric index** must also be maintained. This index will inform the person assigning file numbers of the next number in sequence to be assigned. As a number is assigned to a file, the file name is inserted on the index. This index ensures that no two files will have the same file number.

Numeric index: An index in numeric order that lists files and the date opened. The purpose is to inform the file clerk of the next number in sequence when opening files.

Color Coding

Color coding is a common method of categorizing files. The use of color can categorize files according to a number of designations. Examples include type of case, type of document, responsible attorney, branch office, area of law, and year a file was opened. A user can quickly see the correct file by looking at the color of the file label or folder.

One problem with an alphabetical filing system is that retrieval time is increased if a client has many files. A user will have to go through each file before a specific file is found. This problem is solved with the use of colored file folders, colored file labels, colored stickers, or colored numbers.

A color is assigned to a particular area of law and may be a colored label or file folder as follows:

Litigation: Red

Probate: Black

Corporate: Blue

Real estate: Brown

Tax: Orange

Domestic: White

Criminal: Purple

Agency: Green

If a legal assistant was looking for John Brown's criminal case, she would look for a file with purple coding. If she were looking for John Brown's marriage dissolution file, she would look for a file with white coding.

In an office with more than one or two attorneys, color may be used to differentiate one attorney's files from another's as follows:

Morland Fischer's cases: Red

Loretta Ferro's cases: Blue

James Duncan's cases: Green

Michelle Gordon's cases: Yellow

A colored dot or sticker may also be added to the label to add additional information as follows:

Superior court case: Red dot

Municipal court case: Green dot

Federal court case: Yellow dot

EXHIBIT 13.5   Example of Colored Number Labels
Reprinted with permission of Smead Manufacturing Company.

Companies offer color alphabetic and numeric labels. The numbers or letters are inserted on the edge or top of a file folder so that they can be easily seen. When numbers are given a color, misfilings are easily spotted because a file with the contrasting color "pops out" from the rest of the files, as shown in Exhibit 13.5.

Some records managers maintain that color coding increases speed and accuracy in filing. Others claim that color coding is a waste of money and creates visual confusion. The answer is determined by the management of a firm. Each member of a legal team must know the meaning of each color before a system is effective. If too many colors are used, the system is too complicated.

Color may be applied to any system and may be used for paper or computer records. The many purposes that color has to offer a records management system is limited only by management's creativity and imagination.

File Retrieval

About 900 million documents are created each day in the United States. According to statistics, about 3 percent (or 2,700,000) are misfiled. If finding each misfiled document cost $100 (a conservative estimate), the cost associated with misfiling documents and files is astronomical. A file retrieval system must allow for easy access to files. It must also reduce the possibility of lost or misplaced documents and files. Procedures must be developed to facilitate file retrieval, and these procedures must be followed by each member of a legal team. Noncompliance with retrieval procedures results in lost files.

Firms employ file personnel who are responsible for maintaining a retrieval system. In small firms, a secretary or legal assistant may be responsible for file system maintenance in addition to other duties. In large firms, file clerks or file coordinators are employed whose sole responsibility is to maintain the system. An efficient system has a central person who is responsible for maintaining a system's procedures.

Requests for files from a centralized system are initiated by a requisition form similar to the one shown in Exhibit 13.6. The requisition form is completed and transferred to a file clerk, who retrieves and delivers the file. A written request has one important advantage over an oral request: It provides a record the request was made. A requisition form is also used to monitor a file's location.

File name _____ File no. _____

Requestor _____ Dept. _____

Date of request _____ Date required _____

Date file to be returned _____

Date file delivered _____

Follow-up dates _____

EXHIBIT 13.6 Sample File Requisition Form

A file must be accessible before it is retrieved. If management has established an understandable and precise coding system for a file, the file should be readily accessible. However, files may be in a location other than a file room for various reasons, including the following:

◆ An attorney is reviewing it.

◆ A legal assistant is working on it.

◆ A secretary is working on it.

◆ A law clerk has it in the library doing research.

◆ It is in the copy center having documents copied.

When a file is removed from the file area, its location must be traceable and monitored. Without a tracking system, time is wasted by searching an entire office for a file. A system used by firms for many years is an "out card" system, which is similar to the out card system used in law libraries. Bar code technology is also used to manage and retrieve files.

Out Card System   An out card is the size of a file folder, made of heavy vinyl, and has lines on the front on which to put names and dates, as shown in Exhibit 13.7. When a file is removed from the filing area, the responsible party inserts his or her name or initials and date on the out card, which is then placed in the location of the removed file. The person requesting the file knows the location of the file by looking at the last name on the out card.

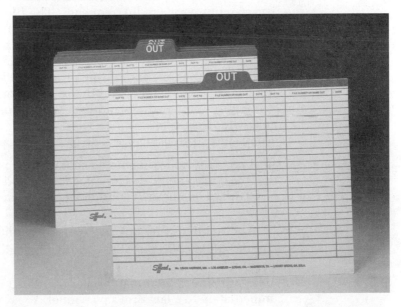

EXHIBIT 13.7   Example of Out Card System

Reprinted with permission of Smead Manufacturing Company.

Advantages to the out card system include the following:

◆ It shows that the file is being used and has not been misplaced.

◆ It enables a user to know the location of files at all times.

◆ It acts as a marker to indicate the proper place for a file.

This sounds like a simple and effective system. However, problems occur when employees do not put their names on the out card or do not use an out card. Many firms have problems getting staff to adhere to this simple procedure, so efforts are made to simplify the system further. Out cards are made to accommodate business cards of the firm's employees or requisition slips: Instead of writing his or her name, all the person has to do is insert a business card or requisition slip into the slot in the out card.

Out folders are also used. These are the same as out cards, except they will allow documents to be inserted in them. This is convenient for a file clerk who is waiting for a file to be returned to file documents. A clerk can file documents into the out folder until the absent file is returned.

Automatic data collection: The data entry method used in bar code technology.

Symbologies: Language used in bar code technology.

Bar Coding Bar codes are a fast, easy, and accurate data entry method used in a process known as **automatic data collection.** It appeared in the food industry in the early 1970s and has evolved into an effective and popular tool used in most businesses today. A number of bar code standards have been developed and refined over the years into accepted languages called **symbologies.** Bar codes are used as we check out of the grocery store or have a package delivered.

Bar coding technology is used by universities and libraries to manage circulation of books and journals. It is also used by businesses to manage inventory. Courts use bar code technology in their records management systems. Law offices have discovered that bar coding is excellent for managing records.

A bar coding system automates records management. Documents, files, books, and furniture may be bar coded. Firms using bar codes have reported that the system provides firms with more efficient document handling, an automated rather than manual master index, a more accurate index of files stored off-site, and decreased retrieval time.

A bar code is put on a label that is attached to a file, as shown in Exhibits 13.8 and 13.9. Whenever a file is removed from a central filing area, its bar code label is scanned by a portable data entry terminal that communicates its information back to the firm's computer via radio frequency. The file's new location is inserted into the computer, and the file database is automatically updated. As a file moves around the office, its location can be determined by using a portable bar code scanner. An office is easily inventoried using this system. A bar code is also read by other computerized programs, such as a time and billing program. When a timekeeper begins work on a file, the bar code is scanned, and the information is automatically entered into the timekeeping system. Medium and large firms especially benefit from using bar code technology for their files.

The six benefits to using bar code technology are the following:

1. *Accuracy.* Bar codes are more accurate than manual data entry. Studies show that the entry and read error rates for bar code technology is about one error in one million characters versus one error for every 300 characters in manual key entry.

2. *Ease of use.* Bar codes are easy to use and understand.

3. *Uniform data collection.* Bar code symbologies are universally understood and accepted.

4. *Timely feedback.* Information that is entered into a system is available immediately to a law firm's personnel.

EXHIBIT 13.8 Bar Coded Files

EXHIBIT 13.9 Example of Bar Coding Equipment
Reprinted with permission of Datamax®.

5. *Improved productivity.* Bar codes automate tasks, enabling a law firm's personnel to devote their time to other projects.

6. *Increased profitability.* Using bar code technology increases the efficiency of a firm's filing system. This results in increased employee efficiency, resulting in increased profitability.

Law office filing systems are as varied as the examples in this section. Whatever system is used, it is important to learn the system quickly and satisfactorily. One member of a legal team not adhering to the rules of a system can cause documents or files to be lost. Lost documents and files mean lost information and potential liability for a firm.

┌───┐
│ **OF INTEREST . . .**   │
│   │
│ **Tracing Lost Files**   │
│   │
│ In 1987, Todd Brockman, a student at the University of   │
│ Southern California, was doing an internship at Sun   │
│ Microsystems. An attorney in the office kept losing his   │
│ files. Brockman attached bar codes to the attorney's   │
│ files and developed a device that consisted of a bar   │
│ code generator and portable bar code scanner. Whenever   │
│ the attorney lost a file, he simply walked through the   │
│ office waving the magic scanner. When it beeped, he   │
│ found the missing file. Brockman programmed the device   │
│ so that it would display where the file was supposed to   │
│ be, even down to the exact filing cabinet. The device,   │
│ now called The Tracker, is sold by Todd's new technology │
│ company, CCG. It can also be used to find other lost   │
│ items, such as keys and office supplies.   │
└───┘

FILE OPENING

File opening consists of two steps: preclient files and file opening.

Preclient Files

Preclient: A person who consults an attorney but does not formally retain the services of the attorney.

Not all potential clients retain a firm. Some interview many attorneys before choosing a lawyer, and some just need some quick legal advice. These matters are known as **preclient** matters.

A firm keeps information about each person who consults with an attorney. If a lawyer or legal assistant takes notes during an initial interview, the notes are inserted into a **preclient file.** If a potential client returns to retain the firm, the notes are retrieved from the preclient file, and a client file is opened. A client file is not opened unless a client formally retains a firm. Normally, preclient files are coded alphabetically and kept at least one year. However, each law firm has its own retention period and coding method for preclient files.

Preclient file: A file containing notes of interview or consultation to be retrieved if the client retains the firm.

ETHICS ALERT

As we learned in Chapter 4, an attorney-client relationship is formed whenever an attorney gives a person legal advice. Even though a client does not formerly retain a firm, *if a person consults a lawyer about a matter, that person would be considered a client in many states.* As such, a preclient must be entered into a firm's conflict-checking system and the system checked before an appointment with a potential client. If there is a conflict of interest with a preclient, an attorney may not consult with the person.

File Opening Procedures

New case memorandum: A form used to provide information about a case so that a file may be opened.

A client file is opened immediately after a client retains a firm. A **new case memorandum** form, similar to the one shown in Exhibit 13.10, is completed by an attorney or legal assistant and given to a secretary or file clerk. The secretary or file clerk opens a file from the information on the new case memorandum form.

When a clerk or secretary receives a new case memorandum, the first step is to do a conflict check. Once a client has been cleared for conflicts, a client file is ready to be opened.

ETHICS ALERT

Conflict Check Each new client must be checked for a possible conflict of interest. *If a firm represented an adverse party at any time in the past or has another conflict, as described in Chapter 4, the firm has a conflict of interest in representing the new client.* A firm must reject a new client unless the conflicting client consents to the representation, although states vary on this requirement

ETHICS ALERT

A database is maintained with clients' names and the names of all parties to a matter in which the firm was involved. The database must be searched before a file is opened. *If a new client has a dispute with a previous client, the firm has a conflict in representing that client* (see Chapter 4). If a new client was an opposing party in a

Date _____ Responsible attorney _____

CLIENT INFORMATION

Name _____ New ☐   Old ☐

Address _____

City, State, Zip _____

Phone: Home _____ Work _____

Place of employment _____

Address _____

Department _____ Position _____

CASE INFORMATION

Matter name _____

Type of matter _____

Other party name _____

Address _____

Phone _____

Statute of limitations _____

FEE AND BILLING INFORMATION

Deposit received $ _____ _____ for Retainer ☐   Costs ☐   Fee ☐

Fee to be billed   ☐ Hourly   ☐ Contingency _____% Fixed fee of $_____

Payable _____

INSTRUCTIONS

_____

_____

Conflict check made by _____ on _____

File opened _____ File no. _____ By _____

EXHIBIT 13.10   New Case Memorandum Form

case and the new matter does not involve the firm's client, a firm must have written permission from the client in the previous matter to represent the new client in the new matter, although this requirement also varies by state. Careful attention must be given to this most important aspect of opening a file. Firms have been disciplined for conflict-of-interest violations.

A conflict check is the most important aspect of file opening procedures but is not limited to file opening. Each time a party makes an appearance in a case, a firm's client database must be checked to determine the new party's relationship to the firm, if any.

Most firms require some type of written record that a conflict check was made. As you can see in Exhibit 13.10, there is an area on the new case memorandum that must be completed when a conflict search is completed. *If the person conducting the conflict search suspects that there may be a problem with the representation, the attorney or manager must be notified immediately.*

Client File Opening   If a firm has no conflict of interest in representing a client, a client file may be opened. Each firm has different requirements for opening files. If a firm uses a numeric system, a clerk must consult a **file number index** to determine the next number for the file. The file number is inserted on the new case memorandum

TECH TIPS
Conflict Check Software

ConflictSearch software by Tremco Legal Solutions is designed specifically to conduct conflict searches. Originally developed as part of a time and billing software package, it now is a stand-alone product. To perform a search, a user just enters the information into a data screen, and the software automatically searches it and does a cross-reference check against all the information in the database.

Software mentioned in this sidebar is for informational purposes only and is not for the purpose of endorsing products.

form, and the file labels are prepared. If a firm uses a color coding system, a clerk prepares the file accordingly.

It is difficult to anticipate the size of a case when opening a file. Some firms open one main file and expand to additional files as the case develops. Other firms prepare one file folder for each area of the case, such as a folder for correspondence, a folder for pleadings, a folder for discovery, and so on. Each category may be given a different color folder or label to quickly identify it. Files with multiple folders are stored in an expandable accordion file with the file numbers inserted on the outside of the file, as shown in Exhibit 13.11.

A file clerk or secretary uses a new case memorandum as a checklist to complete file opening procedures. Many firms use an automated system that will guide a clerk to enter specific information into a firm's computer. Most automated systems are connected to other programs, such as a timekeeping, billing, and docket programs, and will automatically insert the required information into them when the information from a new client is input. This integration saves a clerk time because the information is entered into the system only once. Many automated software packages create file folder labels, print request slips, and prepare filing opening reports.

Common entries of both automated and manual systems include the following:

◆ *Conflict status.* The results of the conflict check are inserted on the new case memorandum. If a direct or potential conflict exists, the attorney or manager must be informed immediately. File opening procedures cease until the conflict has been cleared. If no conflict exists, file opening procedures may resume. The person performing the conflict search inserts his or her initials on the new case memorandum form as verification that the search was made.

ETHICS ALERT

◆ *Statute of limitations.* Some firms put the statute of limitations date on the outside of the folder in bold, red ink. *The date the statute of limitations expires must be put in the firm's tickler system to monitor it.* This information is integrated into a docket system.

◆ *Client information.* The client's name, address, telephone and fax numbers, and e-mail address are needed.

◆ *Subject matter.* The subject matter of the case is inserted.

◆ *Opposing parties.* The name, address, and telephone numbers of opposing parties are inserted. This information is important for future conflict searches and is put into the conflict database.

◆ *Responsible attorney.* The responsible attorney is inserted into the system. This ties the case to the responsible attorney for time and billing purposes. If a team is assigned, the names of all team members are inserted.

◆ *Date.* The date a file is opened is inserted. Some automated systems automatically put a file on the firm's case review schedule.

◆ *Billing information.* The type of fee charged, the amount, and billing instructions are inserted. The billing cycle is also inserted, such as monthly,

EXHIBIT 13.11   Client File That Contains
Multiple Folders
Reprinted with permission of Smead Manufacturing
Company.

quarterly, or contingency. This information is automatically integrated with the
billing program in an automated system.

◆ *Name of referring party.* The name of the person who referred the client to the
firm is inserted. This prompts the firm to send an acknowledgment or thank you
to the referring party. Preparing and sending this acknowledgment is part of the
file opening procedures.

◆ *Type of case.* The type of case is inserted. This information is used by a law
firm's management for statistics and marketing information. It also allows the
computer to track time spent on various types of cases.

The original new case memorandum is inserted into the client's file. Some firms
keep a copy of it in a separate binder in alphabetical order according to the client's
name. This binder is used as a cross-reference for numeric cases in the event that the
computer is not available. A new case report is circulated among the attorneys to inform them of the new client and the parties involved. This acts as a double check
against direct or potential conflicts of interest.

A firm's management may have other file opening requirements, such as inserting the client's name, address, and telephone number on the attorney's and legal assistant's client list or telephone directory. It is important that file opening procedures and information be accurate. Since the information is used in timekeeping, billing, and docketing programs, any errors at the file opening stage will affect other programs. Incorrect preliminary information results in incorrect reports, records, and other essential documents.

FILE MAINTENANCE

A legal assistant is responsible for maintaining clients' files in good order. The legal assistant may not be responsible for doing the actual clerical work involved, but the legal assistant most often directs the clerical work to be done accurately.

The manner in which files are maintained is changing with new technological advances. Before computers, a document was a sheet of paper. Now, documents consist of electronic documents, e-mails, photographs, video clips, digital images, diskettes, and CD-ROMs. Document management is moving toward image-based documents, called **rich media.** The Web is responsible for this transition because it is visual. As a result, there has been a shift from text-based to image-based media that is one of the biggest changes facing records management today. These innovations will continue to change the way that files and documents are managed into the first decade of the twenty-first century.

Rich media: Image-based technology that is visual rather than text oriented.

Document Categories

The first step in file maintenance is categorizing its documents. Documents are inserted into a file by category. For example, all correspondence is filed together in chronological order with the most recent on top, all notes are filed together in chronological order with the most recent on top, and so on. Filing correspondence, notes, pleadings, and court documents together results in messy, disorganized files.

Correspondence, pleadings, notes, and all other documents are filed in chronological order unless the case is large. In a small case, correspondence is inserted on the left side of the folder, and pleadings and other documents are inserted on the right side in chronological order with the most recent on top. A number of file folder products are available to help organize files. File partitions may be purchased as well as folders that have sections built into them, as shown in Exhibit 13.12. With a partitioned folder, categorizing documents is easier.

EXHIBIT 13.12 Partitioned File Folder
Reprinted with permission of Smead Manufacturing Company.

In a large or complex case, correspondence documents are further categorized by type, that is, by year or subject matter. They are filed chronologically within each group. Pleadings and discovery documents may be categorized by type as follows:

File 1: Pleadings

    Section I: Complaints

    Section II: Cross-complaints

    Section III: Answers

File 2: Discovery

    Section I: Interrogatories

    Section II: Requests for admissions

    Section III: Requests for production of documents

    Section IV: Deposition summaries

Case Cover Sheets

Case cover sheets are used to monitor the status of a case. They provide a synopsis of the events of a case. By looking at a case cover sheet, the attorney or legal assistant can see the current status of a case. A case cover sheet, such as the one shown in Exhibit 13.13, has been credited for saving valuable time searching the file for information.

Many docket control software programs automatically generate a case cover sheet that indicates due dates, tickler dates, and the date a task was completed. A case cover sheet may be put on top of a folder or in a file so that it can be viewed immediately on opening the file. Some firms keep case cover sheets or copies of them in a binder or on a computer so the status of each case can be updated and available without pulling the file from the file room. If a legal assistant needs to know when an answer to a complaint is due, she or he looks on the cover sheet instead of going through a file to find a certificate of service of the complaint. It takes a little time to maintain a case cover sheet, but the time it will save in searching files for information will be worth it.

Indexes

As a case grows and documents are categorized, indexes, such as the one shown in Exhibit 13.14, are used to direct a person to a document's exact location in a file. For example, as pleadings and court documents are received, they are filed chronologically in a small case. Each document is given a number that is put on a tab so that it can be found quickly. The tab is then inserted on a divider sheet and protrudes so that it can be seen easily. It is important not to put a tab on the actual document; tabs must be put on a separate divider sheet. Tabs may be purchased alone, or divider sheets may be purchased with tabbed numbers on them. Many indexing products are available.

A document is inserted behind its divider so that it can be located by lifting up the tabbed divider. As a new document is received, it is put on top of the previous document's divider sheet and given the next number in sequence.

The number, title of document, date, and party are inserted on an index sheet, which is placed on top of the applicable section. A specific document can be located quickly and easily. The use of cover sheets and indexes will keep files organized and decrease the time it takes to retrieve a document.

Tabs and indexes can be modified further to accommodate categorization of documents. For example, a file may be separated by section as follows:

Section I: Pleadings (complaints, cross-complaints, and answers)

Section II: Discovery documents

Case _____ No. _____

Attorney _____ S/L _____ Type of case _____

PLEADINGS

Complaint: Filed _____ Served _____ Ans. due _____ Ans. rec'd. _____

X Complaint: Served _____ Ans. due _____ Ans. filed _____

DISCOVERY

Int./RA propounded by _____ to _____

Served _____ Ans. due _____ Ans. rec'd. _____

Int./RA propounded by _____ to _____

Served _____ Ans. due _____ Ans. rec'd. _____

Int./RA propounded by _____ to _____

Served _____ Ans. due _____ Ans. rec'd. _____

Deposition of _____ Set for _____

by _____ Reporter _____ Depo. rec'd. _____

Deposition of _____ Set for _____

by _____ Reporter _____ Depo. rec'd. _____

Deposition of _____ Set for _____

by _____ Reporter _____ Depo. rec'd. _____

Prod. of docs. by _____ to _____

Served _____ Ans. due _____ Ans. rec'd. _____

Prod. of docs. by _____ to _____

Served _____ Ans. due _____ Ans. rec'd. _____

Prod. of docs. by _____ to _____

Served _____ Ans. due _____ Ans. rec'd. _____

Prod. of docs. by _____ to _____

Served _____ Ans. due _____ Ans. rec'd. _____

TRIAL

Trial date _____ Jury requested by _____ Fees posted _____

Settlement conference dates _____ _____ _____

Continuances _____ Requested by _____ to _____

EXHIBIT 13.13 Example of a Case Cover Sheet

Case: Smith, John J. v. Brown, Janis L. File no. 2003-596

No.	Description of Document	Date	Party
1	Summons and complaint for personal injuries	3/4/xx	Plaintiff
2	Proof of service of complaint	3/10/xx	Plaintiff
3	Answer to complaint	4/9/xx	Defendant
4	Cross-complaint	4/9/xx	Defendant
5	Answer to cross-complaint	5/7/xx	Plaintiff

EXHIBIT 13.14 Example Pleadings Index

Section III: Medical reports

Section IV: Other documents

Each document is numbered sequentially within each section as follows:

Document I-1: Plaintiff's complaint

Document II-1: Interrogatories

Document III-1: Medical report of Dr. Gunn, date June 10, 2001

Indexes should be developed for every category of file, except correspondence and miscellaneous notes. Exhibits 13.15 and 13.16 show examples of medical expenses and research indexes, respectively.

No loose papers should be in a file. Every document, regardless of size, must be secured by file fasteners. Systems can be developed to accommodate any type of document. For small pieces of paper, such as telephone messages, an envelope can be inserted in a file. Photographs should be put on a piece of paper or put in an envelope that is attached to the file with fasteners.

Document Management

Documents are generated in a law office in one of two ways: They are developed or received. A legal assistant will encounter many different types of documents and must make decisions regarding each document. Choosing which document to retain or discard requires judgment that is developed with time and experience.

Life Cycle of a Document   Every document has a life cycle and lives only as long as it serves its purpose. Since each document has a different purpose, each document

Case: Smith, John J. v. Brown, Janis L.		File no. 200203-596	
No.	**Description of Document**	**Date**	**Amount**
1	St. Jude Hospital	2/4/xx	$16,785.30
2	Dr. Frederick's, orthopedic surgeon	1/10/xx	4,521.70
3	Dr. Maynard, anesthesiologist	1/10/xx	987.00
4	Dr. Bunnell, physical therapist	1/19/xx	2,117.50

EXHIBIT 13.15   Example Medical Expenses Index

Case: Smith, John J. v. Brown, Janis L.		File no. 200303-596	
No.	**Case Name**	**Date**	**Subject**
1	Grand Trucking v. Henry, Gloria	2/4/82	Liability
2	Sanchez v. Bell Laboratories	11/15/72	Liability
3	ABC, Inc. v. VBF Corp.	6/8/86	Liability

EXHIBIT 13.16   Example Research Index

Document Creation

Document's Purpose

Yes RETAIN ? No

Active Files Destroy

Yes RETAIN ? No

Inactive Files Destroy

RETAIN ? No

Destroy

Permanent Storage

EXHIBIT 13.17 Life Cycle of a Document

has a different life cycle. Pleadings live as long as a litigation case, and correspondence may have a shorter life. Determining the life cycle of a document is vital to effective records and file management. Exhibit 13.17 shows a document's life cycle.

To determine the life cycle of a document, one must first identify a document's value. Three value determinations are used:

◆ *Operational value.* This refers to whether a document or information is needed on a day-to-day basis. A document that is referred to at least once a month has high operational value, while a document that is referred to less than once a month has low operational value. An example of a document with high operational value is an index of a firm's clients or cases.

◆ *Technical value.* This refers to whether a document or information has technical or procedural importance. An example of a document with technical value is instructions on how to operate a system or a change in court procedure.

◆ *Legal value.* This refers to whether a document or information is covered by statute or regulation. An example of a document with legal value is a pleading or corporate minutes.

For example, a notice of shareholders meeting has no operational value after the meeting is held. However, the document has legal value because it shows that the meeting was held and that the legal requirement of notice was accomplished. A letter confirming an extension of time to answer interrogatories has no operational value after the deadline has past, but it has legal value because it shows that the extension was given and may be evidence in a hearing on a motion to compel answers. A document describing a change in procedural rules of filing petitions for probate has technical and operational value until the procedure is learned.

To determine the value of a document, the following questions should be asked:

◆ Why would anyone refer to this document again?

◆ To what degree is this document needed for day-to-day business?

◆ When will the information in this document lose its validity? Two weeks? One month?

◆ Will this document be referred to often?

◆ Will this document be helpful information in the type of law in which I am working?

◆ Is this document covered by a statute or regulation?

◆ Has the statute of limitations expired on this document?

There are certain points in the life cycle of a document when a decision regarding its future must be made. These periods vary according to the type of document considered. The ultimate decision should be made by the responsible attorney.

Methods for Discarding Unnecessary Documents

Methods for Discarding Unnecessary Documents   The decision to dispose of a document is a difficult one for most people. However, keeping unnecessary documents is a waste of space and therefore costly for a firm. It also clutters files and makes files less manageable.

When making a decision to either keep or dispose of a document, the following questions should be asked:

◆ Is the document available elsewhere? Is it in the computer or on a disk where it is readily available?

◆ Is the material strictly for informational purposes? If the purpose of a document is to inform the recipient of information, once the recipient is informed, the document can be discarded.

◆ When would this information be needed? If there is no immediate answer and there is no legal reason to keep it, it is probably not worth saving.

◆ Is the information current? Often, files contain outdated information. If material is not part of a client's file, it may be discarded. It is a good idea to periodically review files to **purge,** or clear, them of outdated information.

Purge: To clear or discard.

Time management experts advise that document management decisions should be made as soon as a document is received. A document should be handled only once to efficiently manage time. However, if you cannot decide what to do with a document after asking yourself the previous questions, put the document in a "decision file" and review the document in one week. The office manager or supervising attorney can also give you guidance in this area.

Among the documents found in a typical law office are the following:

◆ Correspondence (client correspondence, law firm business correspondence, promotional mail and advertisements, and miscellaneous correspondence)
◆ Clients' case documents, such as pleadings
◆ Interoffice memos and reports
◆ Photocopies
◆ Meeting notes (notes from client conferences, law firm business meetings, and miscellaneous meetings, such as educational seminars)
◆ Rough drafts
◆ Articles and newspaper clippings

Correspondence. Filing experts have estimated that correspondence constitutes most of the documents received. However, not all correspondence is vital. All correspondence pertaining to a client's case must be filed in the client's file. If a document was faxed, the fax cover sheet must also be saved to show the date and origin of the fax. All incoming correspondence is **date stamped,** or marked with the date it was received, even fax cover sheets. Date-stamping correspondence when it arrives makes it easier to respond to a document in a timely manner and will eliminate paper glut. Envelopes need not be saved unless the correspondence was mailed certified or special delivery or unless the postmark or return address is important to a client's case. Some law firms have a policy to save all envelopes.

Promotional documents are a form of correspondence. If promotional material concerns a product or service that interests the recipient or someone else in the office, it should be saved or passed to an interested person. If the material is of no interest to anyone in the firm, it may be discarded.

The person to whom correspondence is sent is responsible for deciding whether to keep the material. If a decision is made to keep the material, it is filed in the appropriate file.

Clients' case documents. No document pertaining to a client's case may be discarded. Each document must be appropriately filed. If a document's importance or validity to a case is unclear, the responsible attorney should be consulted.

Interoffice memos and reports. Interoffice memos are important communication vehicles between a firm and its employees. A memo announcing an event or activity may be discarded after the event or activity has occurred. Memos regarding firm policies or systems are kept for future reference. All documents pertaining to employment reviews or benefits are retained. Memos regarding a client's case are filed in the client's file.

Photocopies. Excess photocopies cause files to bulge. If an original document is in a file, additional copies are unnecessary and should not be made. If a photocopy contains notes or highlighting that makes it different from the original, it should be retained. If a copy of a document is used often, as with a form, a photocopy should be made as it is needed. The original document should be marked to alert employees to make a copy of it instead of using the original. Placing the original in a sheet protector will discourage employees from using it rather than a copy.

A **courtesy copy** is a copy of a document sent to a person as a courtesy, or for informational purposes only. The recipient is considered a **secondary recipient,** and the person to whom the memo is sent is considered the **primary recipient.** A secondary recipient has no responsibility to retain the document but does have the responsibility of deciding what to do with the information. If the author of the document was within the organization, an official original will be filed in the appropriate file, so filing the courtesy copy is not necessary in most instances.

Meeting notes. Notes taken in a meeting with a client or on a client's behalf are always retained. If there is a misunderstanding of a meeting's discussions, the notes will be valuable documentation of the meeting's substance. For a law firm's meetings, pages of notes are often generated that are never referred to again. The decision to keep or

Date stamp: To stamp a document with the date it was received.

Courtesy copy: A document that is sent to a person for informational purposes only.

Secondary recipient: A person to whom a document is sent for informational purposes only.

Primary recipient: A person to whom a document is directed or addressed.

discard the notes of a law firm's meeting depends on the note taker's level of involvement in the meeting. If the note taker was in charge of the meeting, was required to report on the meeting, or do something as a result of the meeting, the notes are retained.

Rough drafts. Rough drafts of documents pose difficulties in deciding whether to retain them. As the terms of a contract are negotiated, many drafts are generated. As provisions are negotiated, they are modified. Rough drafts of agreements are important documents when negotiating a contract. A draft is written by one party to the contract and given to the other party for approval. Changes that are made are highlighted and marked to indicate the party who made them. Rough drafts are numbered as to the author of the changes, such as Party No. 1's Draft No. 1, Party No. 2's Draft No. 2, and so on. No rough draft of a contract is destroyed until the agreement has been fully negotiated and signed. Some law firms have a policy to retain all rough drafts of contracts in the event of future litigation. If the importance of the draft is unclear, the responsible attorney should be consulted.

Rough drafts of correspondence or pleadings are destroyed when the final document is completed. However, some firms may have a policy to determine the destruction of roughs drafts on a case-by-case basis. Be sure to have a solid understanding of your firm's policy before discarding rough drafts.

Articles and newspaper clippings. Various types of articles and newspaper clippings are of interest to a law office. A high-profile case will receive publicity, and a firm should keep all articles pertaining to a client's case.

Case law and changes in statutory law are often publicized when they occur. An article in a legal publication may be directly related to a client's case. An attorney or legal assistant may choose to keep the article for future reference as an aid in legal research.

When magazine and newspaper articles are kept, they should be clipped rather than retaining the entire magazine or newspaper. The name, volume number, and date of an article's source must be indicated on the article. The rest of the magazine or newspaper may be discarded or filed.

If it is beneficial to retain each issue of a particular magazine; firms file these in magazine files that require little space and help keep an office uncluttered. Some firms put periodicals on microfilm. However, before magazines are saved, a firm's librarian should be consulted to make sure that duplicate issues are not retained.

Managing Electronic Records

When is a message considered a record? The U.S. National Archives and Records Administration (NARA) defines a message as a record if it is "made or received in connection with the transaction of the organization's business, or it is preserved by the organization, or is appropriate for preservation." Managing electronic documents is similar to managing paper documents, with the exception that they require less space to store. After you have read a document, you make a decision to do one or more of the following: copy it, file it, write comments on it, forward it to someone in the firm, or dispose of it. These same actions are taken with an electronic document.

The files and subfiles into which electronic documents are stored must be similar in structure to the filing system for paper documents. Electronic documents are classified in the same manner as shown on page 436. The first step is to determine function categories. Then subject, topic, and subtopic categories can be identified. This hierarchy of folders is duplicated on the computer for electronic documents. For example, an e-mail regarding firm business, such as health benefits, should be filed in an electronic file as follows:

Firm policy (function)

Benefits (subject)

Health (topic)

Corres 2003 (type and year of document)

TRENDS ➤➤➤

Managing E-Mails

When is a message a record? Every organization has a different interpretation. The U.S. National Archives and Records Administration defines a message as a record if it is made or received by the company in connection with the transaction of the organization's business, or it is preserved by the origination or it is appropriate for preservation.

An informal study conducted in 1997 within a large government organization looked at the e-mail activity of a typical user. 149 e-mail messages sent to a typical user revealed:

- 16 career opportunities
- 25 promotional or advertising e-mails
- 7 miscellaneous
- 33 message received confirmation
- 68 valid work-related messages

The user was asked to identify the messages appropriate for filing. The user filed 35 messages. After filing, a records manager evaluated them and determined that only 10 of them were worthy of preserving. You need to decide which e-mail messages are worthy of retaining. Some unofficial guidelines to help you decide are as follows:

- Was the message developed in preparing reports, papers, or documents?
- Does the message reflect official actions taken?
- Does the message convey information on programs, policies, or decisions?
- Does the message convey statements of official policy or rationale for official decisions?
- Does the message document oral exchanges where official decisions were discussed?

In other words, retain the e-mail if it:

- Contains a decision or discussion of a decision
- Calls for a reply or action
- Concerns official business about a case
- Involves a significant member of your firm or your client

It is important to protect your electronic documents. After finalizing documents, you can move them to a similar directory structure in another part of the network where the directory is marked for "read only" access. This allows documents to be accessible to others in the firm but protects them from alteration. Electronic documents should be backed up each day to preserve them. Most firms have backup systems in place.

Just as with paper documents, automated documents must be managed according to a well-planned system. Some people may file an electronic document that was prepared for a client in the client's electronic file. Others may file it in an electronic folder by type of document. Others may have no destination for the electronic document and save it anywhere in the system the document may end up. A lack of planning causes confusion in the system.

A law office must have naming and saving rules for its electronic documents. Filing systems for electronic documents are similar to paper documents, with more complex cases requiring more classification of documents and more folders than smaller cases. Everyone in a firm should adhere to the rules; otherwise, a system will fail. A good system is easy to use, easy to remember, and is universally accepted by all employees.

A good document naming system makes it easy for a person to determine the document's contents by its name. A popular electronic filing system that is used in some law firms is to give each client an electronic file on the firm's computer system. As a document is prepared for a client, it is saved with a name that contains three components: the first four or five letters of the client's name or surname, the date of the document, and a code that indicates the type of document (e.g., CMP = complaint, ANS = answer, INT = interrogatories, LTR = letter). For example, a letter written for client Smith on June 14, 2002, would be named SMITH.020614.LTR. A complaint for client Johnson prepared the same day would be named JOHNS.020614.CMP. The document is saved in the applicable client's file, which lists all the documents in the folder in chronological order. One can look at the name of the document and get an idea of the document's contents.

Just as paper documents are stored on-site until they are no longer needed for current business, electronic documents remain on the network's hard drive until they are no longer needed, they can be disposed of, or the need to recoup hard drive space occurs. Electronic documents can be transferred to diskettes, CD-ROM, or tape for continued retention. A list of documents on disks can be created showing the locations of the documents on diskette or other media. Document management software makes this process easy.

Document Retrieval

Documents should never be removed from a file. When documents are removed from files, they are likely to get lost. If a specific document is needed from a file, the entire file should be requested. If a legal assistant needs a copy of a document, the document should be copied and immediately returned to its correct location in the file.

Automated Document Management

A recent survey reported that for 90 percent of the paper documents found in a law firm's files, one could find an electronic copy on the firm's computer system. Electronic documents have many advantages: They are stored in less space, are accessible at your fingertips, and are easily edited. There are also disadvantages: They are difficult to manage, are easily lost without a good filing system in place, and are difficult to search and review without opening the file. Many firms, especially medium and large ones, found help managing their electronic documents from document management software programs.

Automated document management software applications are multiuser, shared workgroup products that hook into the open and save commands of word processing or other application software. It allows a user to complete a profile of a document and to store the document on the firm's network or intranet. The software stores the profile information in a central database where it controls user access. The document's profile is updated automatically every time it is retrieved, edited, printed, archived, or deleted. It keeps track of clients, cases, authors, keywords, and other relevant information. A user can search the database for a document.

An automated document management system has other functions, including the following:

◆ Locates any document
◆ Calculates how much time attorneys, legal assistants, and secretaries spend editing documents and automatically enters that information into the billing system
◆ Moves seldom-used documents to remote storage
◆ Provides extra copies of documents in case the system fails
◆ Archives documents after a prearranged retention period is determined
◆ Keeps track of versions of documents

◆ Calculates the number of keystrokes typed and the number of pages printed for each document and automatically transfers the information to a time and billing system

◆ Makes a backup copy of the document

A document management software system tracks and manages every legal document created in a law office. Such a system is beneficial to firms because it helps employees locate information, ultimately saving a firm money.

Automated document management software is not used for a firm's records management functions. However, automated document management software will soon integrate records management features such as a file plan, classification tools, records retention processing and tracking file folders, boxes or electronic storage media.

Various software packages exist that help prepare legal documents. These software programs consist of a database of standard clauses that are used in standard contracts, leases, letters, memos, and other legal documents. They assist the document preparer by allowing a choice as to which clauses should be inserted into a document and then prompts the preparer for variable information, such as the party's name, address, and other fill-in-the-blank information. The software automatically assembles the document and opens it directly into the firm's word processing program.

Once prepared, the document is saved on the firm's network or intranet. The software can track multiple versions of a document, perform document comparisons, and save the document's criteria. The software contains a library of legal documents that can be accessed by all a firm's personnel. The library can be searched by a variety of search methods: full text, Boolean, and proximity.

There are other uses for this software. If an attorney wants to check on your productivity for a day, he searches for the documents that you prepared on a particular day and will get a list of all those documents. If a client calls and wants an immediate update, the system will search for all documents prepared for that client and list all the documents in the case. Because of this search capability, no document can be lost in the system.

Document management software can be purchased that contains documents directed to specific legal practice areas. Most packages are integrated with a firm's word processing system and can be integrated with other software applications, such as docketing and calendar programs, e-mail, and spreadsheet programs. Documents from the library may be "checked out" for use outside the network or intranet.

TECH TIPS

Automated Document Generation Software

DOCS Open: PC DOCS—www.pcdocs.com
GroupWise 5: Novell—www.novell.com
IManage Legal Office: TechLaw, Inc.—www.imanage.com
NovaDocs: Novation Corporation—www.novasoft.com
DocWise: Scan-Optics Inc.—www.scanoptics.com
Legal Counsel for DominoDoc: Global Compliance L.L.C.—www.lotus.com
LaserFiche Suite: Laserfiche—www.Laserfiche.com
Vista Plus: Quest Software, Inc.—www.quests.com
CanOpener: Abbot Systems—www.abbotsys.com
Worldox: World Software—www.worldox.com
DL Document Assembly: Blumberg Excelsior—www.blumberg.com
Perfect Law: Executive Data Systems, Inc.—-www.perfectlaw.com.

Software mentioned in this sidebar is for informational purposes only and is not for the purpose of endorsing products.

FILE CLOSING, RETENTION, AND DESTRUCTION

File Closing Procedures

When a case is completed, certain procedures must be followed before a file is a candidate for closing:

◆ A file must be reviewed to make sure that all final documents have been completed.
◆ The final bill must be paid.
◆ A disengagement letter must be sent to the client.
◆ Unnecessary documents must be discarded from the file, a procedure known as **pruning** a file.
◆ The status of a file must be changed from active to inactive.
◆ Original documents must be returned to the client.
◆ Any electronic records of the case must be deleted from a firm's computer system.

Pruning: To discard unnecessary documents from a file.

Final Documentation   When a case has been completed, a file must be double-checked to ensure that all documents have been completed and filed. If they have not, a file must remain active. Just because there has been no activity on a case for some time does not mean that it is completed. A case may have not been entered in the file review system, or a final document may have not been calendared. The final documentation, such as a final judgment or dismissal, may have been overlooked. It is important to carefully review a file before a file is a candidate for closing. This is often an attorney's responsibility but may be delegated to an experienced, senior paralegal.

If the appeal period has not expired, a case may not be closed. It is often a legal assistant's responsibility to calculate the appeal period or to know the status of a judgment. For example, if a judgment has not been completely satisfied, the file may not be closed until it is. If a judgment has been satisfied, final documentation must be filed with the court, indicating that the case is closed and that the judgment has been satisfied. If payments on a judgment have taken a long time, final documentation may have been overlooked.

Final Billing   A client's final bill must be paid before a case is closed. Legal assistants should double-check with management to ensure that the final bill has been paid before proceeding with file closing procedures. If the bill has been recently paid, final closing procedures should be delayed to allow a client's check to clear.

Disengagement Letter   Some firms send a disengagement letter with a final bill, while others wait until the bill has been paid. A disengagement letter promotes client relations and also substantiates that the client's perception of the status of the case is the same as the attorney's. It is often a legal assistant's responsibility to draft a disengagement letter for an attorney's signature. It is advisable to wait a couple of weeks after the letter is sent before closing a file. An example disengagement letter is shown in Chapter 4.

Pruning   Pruning a file eliminates unnecessary documents and compacts a file for storage. There are four considerations of pruning a file for closure. First, if the document is vital to the client, such as an original will or a deed, it must be returned to the client. Second, if a document pertains to an attorney's fiduciary duties to the client, it must be retained. Third, information that the firm needs to check for future conflicts of interest must remain in the file. Fourth, if the firm suspects that there may be a problem with the representation, such as legal malpractice or state bar action, all documents should be retained as evidence of the representation.

It is often a legal assistant's or secretary's responsibility to prune files. The person responsible for pruning files should be familiar with the case so that important documents are not discarded. Some experts recommend that the person pruning the file do so with the responsible attorney so that nothing is overlooked. Other experts say that an attorney reviewing files for closing is a waste of the attorney's time and therefore too costly for a firm.

All documents that are not essential to a case are either returned to the client or destroyed. However, some firms will not allow anything in a file to be discarded. In most cases, cover letters, extra copies (unless a copy is altered in some way), phone messages, drafts, and miscellaneous notes can be eliminated. All original documents, such as wills and deeds, are returned to the client by certified mail, return receipt requested. Each firm has specific pruning policies for its closed files.

ETHICS ALERT

Master client list: A list of active clients; does not include closed files.

Closed file list: A list of closed files by name, number, and closed file number.

Status Change Changing the status of a case from active to inactive involves changing the **master client list** and inserting the case on a **closed file list.** *The conflicts of interest database should be double-checked to determine whether all parties are in it.* The file is given a closed file number, and its retention period is determined (see "Records Retention" later in this chapter). Each firm has its own procedures for changing the status of a file. Legal assistants are often responsible for determining the retention period, but other file closing tasks are usually delegated to a secretary.

Documents Returned to the Client Original documents that are vital to a client, such as a will or deed, should be returned to the client. Some firms keep original wills for their clients. Normally, they are stored in a safe deposit box or other secure area. If a firm retains original wills, they should be removed from the file and stored in the will storage area. As noted previously, other records are a client's property and are returned to the client. An inventory of the items returned should be filed in the file. Some firms require that a copy be made of all important items that are sent to a client and the copies inserted in the closed file.

Case law and state bar opinions have ruled that materials in a client's file belong to the client. These materials include correspondence, pleadings, deposition transcripts, exhibits, experts' reports, and physical evidence. Opinions differ on whether a firm must give a client its work product, such as research memoranda, opinion letters, and notes. The case of *Sage Realty Corp. v. Mendelson,* 97 N.Y. Int. 0208 (1997), ruled that an entire file, including the attorney's work product, belongs to a client except for certain internal law firm memoranda. However, in some states, an attorney's work product need not be returned to the client. Be sure to check your state's rules and regulations before returning or destroying any documents.

Delete Electronic Records Electronic documents that are stored in a client's file on the firm's computer system are deleted from the system. Before doing so, they should be reviewed to determine whether they should be put into a firm's form files and knowledge bank (see Chapter 14). The electronic documents may be put on a diskette and the diskette inserted in the closed file, or a firm may have other filing procedures for diskettes of client documents.

File Closing Memorandum A file closing memorandum, such as the one shown in Exhibit 13.18, is prepared and acts as a checklist for file closing procedures. File closing memoranda are inserted into the closed file when the procedures are completed. A copy of it is stored in a closed file binder for future reference.

Inactive Records Storage

Inactive records are records that are seldom needed for the business of an office. They include office records that may be needed only once or twice a year and closed

Black, White & Greene, L.L.P.

FILE CLOSING MEMORANDUM

Open file no. *98-03-2043*	Closed file no. *C2004.326.05*
File name: *Jackson v. Holiday Inn*	Responsible attorney: *Robert Black*
Client: *Sarah Jackson*	Date file opened: *03/09/98*
Type of matter: *Personal injury*	Date file closed: *07/19/04*
Locator code: *Box 704-16 Offsite*	Destruction date: *07/19/14*

FUNCTION	INITIAL	DATE
Approval to close by responsible attorney	*RLB*	*7/10/04*
File purged	*TB & RLB*	*7/10/04*
Authorization that account balance is paid	*TB*	*7/08/04*
Client documents returned	*ALE*	*7/21/04*
All parties entered in conflict-of-interest database	*ALE*	*7/19/04*
Electronic documents deleted from computer system	*ALE*	*7/26/04*

EXHIBIT 13.18   Example File Closing Memorandum

clients' files. Inactive records should not be stored in the main filing area because they waste valuable floor and filing space. A law firm's management provides a less costly storage area for these records. Whatever storage method is used, a firm must employ an indexing system to locate and retrieve inactive files and records.

Inactive records are usually stored in filing cabinets or storage boxes outside the main storage area. Storage equipment and facilities must allow for the safety of the files so that they are not damaged by fire, water, or other natural elements. Each container, whether a cabinet or box, must be properly marked and labeled. Storage areas include a basement, back storage room, or off-site storage facility. Inactive files are also stored by micrographics and imaging technology.

Micrographics   An alternative method for storing inactive files is to microfilm them. Microfilm has been used in firms for many years and is especially useful for firms that store a large amount of records.

Medium and large firms may microfilm their inactive records, but sole proprietors and small firms with smaller storage needs often cannot justify the expense. When justifying the expense of micrographics, management considers space savings, durability, safety, and speed of reference.

Imaging   An imaging system is also used by large firms to store its closed files. This system consists of a control unit with a monitor, scanner and printer, CD-ROM storage unit, and software. The documents are scanned into the system, and an image of the document is saved on CD-ROMs, which will hold 250,000 documents on one disk. The disks are stored in a **jukebox,** which is a device that can hold many CD-ROMs. The imaging software will generate an index of all documents and identify the CD-ROM on which a document is found. In the event a document must be retrieved, it can be easily found and printed.

Best Evidence Rule   The **best evidence rule,** which requires a court to admit the best evidence that is available to a party under the existing situation, directly applies to micrographics and imaged records. Congress has expanded the basic concepts of this rule by the enactment of two statutes that pertain to these records: the Uniform Photographic Copies of Business and Public Records as Evidence Act of 1949 (UPA)

Jukebox: A device that contains many CD-ROMs and allows retrieval of a document on request.

Best evidence rule: The requirement that courts must admit the best evidence that is available to a party and procurable under the existing situation.

and the Uniform Rules of Evidence Act of 1974. These statutes permit the introduction of a microfilmed or imaged duplicate as evidence if the original document has been lost or destroyed, if certain conditions are met. However, other regulations have mandated the retention of certain original documents, such as contracts. If a question exists concerning the admissibility of an imaged or microfilmed document, statutes and state regulations should be consulted.

Inactive Storage Indexing Systems When inactive records are stored, they still must be accessible for retrieval. Therefore, all stored records are numbered and their storage media labeled. The closed file number and location are inserted on a closed file index for retrieval purposes. Firms use various systems to locate an inactive file.

Closed file coding. Most firms have a separate coding system for closed files. Firms that use an alphabetical coding system find that storing closed files alphabetically requires frequent reorganization. For example, a firm's closed files A–C are filed in one box or file drawer. As additional A–C files are closed, the box or drawer becomes too small, so the files must be moved to the next box or drawer. Putting C files in the D–F box will make that box or drawer too small, so each box or drawer must be reorganized.

To eliminate box and file drawer shuffling, closed files are arranged numerically. Calendar numbering is the preferred method for coding closed files. The calendar numeric code refers to the date a case is closed or the date a file is scheduled for destruction. With calendar coding, a file's age is quickly recognized.

Some firms that use numeric coding for active files change the file number when the file is closed. Others just insert a "C" before the number to indicate that the file is closed. Whatever coding method is used, it is imperative to keep an index of all closed files.

Closed file index. A closed file index is kept on the computer, and a hard copy is maintained as a backup in case of computer failure. The information should be in alphabetical order according to the client's surname and should include the location of all files.

The following information should be inserted on a closed file index:

◆ File name
◆ Active file number, if a numeric coding system
◆ Closed file number
◆ Date file was opened
◆ Date file was closed
◆ Location of file in storage (box or cabinet number or, if in microfilm or electronic format, the information pertaining to the location of the file)
◆ Short description of the disposition of the matter
◆ Date the file may be destroyed

Information for a closed file index is obtained from a closed file index form, such as the one shown in Exhibit 13.19. This form is completed by the person responsible for closing files. The form is inserted in the file or taped to the front of the file folder. A copy of the form can be used as a closed file index log.

Records Retention

ETHICS ALERT

Records retention is the time period during which records must be maintained by an organization because they may be needed for legal, operational, historical, or other purposes. These time periods are established by state and federal law. There are thousands of laws that pertain to records retention. *It is necessary that an organization develop a retention schedule that complies with the law.*

A retention schedule is a list of retention periods categorized according to type of document or case, as shown in Exhibit 13.20. Every firm should have an updated retention schedule and procedures for the retention of records. Many things must be

Name _____

Active file no. _____ Closed file no. _____

Date opened _____ Date closed _____

Location _____

Description _____

_____

_____

File destruction date _____

_____

EXHIBIT 13.19 Sample of Closed File Index Form

TYPE	PERIOD	COMMENCING FROM
Contract action	4 years	End of contract
Dissolution	5 years	Entry of final judgment or date when marital settlement agreement is no longer effective
Dissolution, child	5 years	Date children reach age of majority
Bankruptcy	5 years	Discharge
Probate	10 years	Final judgment
Estate planning	Permanent	
Tort claims	5 years	Collection of final judgment or dismissal
Tort, minor	5 years	Date child reaches age of majority
Real estate	5 years	Completion of transaction
Real estate contract	Permanent	
Leases	5 years	Termination of lease
Product liability	5 years	Judgment
Tax	10 years	Completion

Note: This schedule is for example only; each state has different guidelines.

EXHIBIT 13.20 Example of Retention Schedule

considered when determining the retention period for documents. Research has shown that 95 percent of all references to closed files occur within the first two years of closing. The responsibility for setting a retention period rests with management after researching legal requirements. Considerations vary, depending on whether a document is a business record or a client record.

When a file is closed, its retention period is indicated on the folder and inserted into a closed file index. This will help a file clerk determine the destruction date for the file. Records may be destroyed after the retention period expires. However, some records and files should be permanently retained. Courts and government agencies have imposed heavy fines for the inappropriate destruction of records.

A retention schedule integrated into a firm's computer system will automatically calculate a file's retention period. The computer will keep track of each file's location and the date each file is scheduled to be destroyed. However, no firm should rely on an automated retention schedule. Legal assistants must review a file before establishing a file's retention period. For example, a dissolution of marriage may have a retention period of five years after the dissolution is final. However, tax records must be retained for ten years. If the dissolution contained tax issues, it must be retained for ten, instead of five, years. A computerized system may not pick up all aspects of a case. Human interaction is essential before a file is scheduled for destruction. If a legal assistant is uncertain of a retention period, management or the responsible attorney should be consulted.

Business Records   For business records, management must consider statutes and regulations, any future need for the records and the statute of limitations.

Statutes and regulations. The law sets retention periods for business records as follows:

◆ The Internal Revenue Service may audit a tax return for three years after the return is filed. Therefore, it is prudent to keep income and expense records substantiating a tax return for at least three years.

◆ Personnel records are subject to many federal statutes. Various aspects of an employment relationship are the subject of different regulations. For example, payroll records should be kept for four years to meet the requirements of the Federal Insurance and Contributions Act (FICA) and the Federal Unemployment Tax Act (FUTA). Records of an employee's injury on the job should be kept for five years after the date of termination. An employee's medical records should be retained for thirty years after termination.

◆ Corporate records are permanent records and should not be destroyed.

Future need for records. The future need for business records is determined by a firm's management.

Statute of limitations. The statutes of limitations for lawsuits are set by each state. For example, in California, a breach-of-contract action must be brought within four years of the breach. Therefore, contracts should be retained for four years after the term of the contract expires.

Client Records

Considerations for the retention period for clients' records are statutes and regulations, any future need for records, statute of limitations, applicable age of majority if minors are involved, appeal period, and malpractice concerns.

Statutes and regulations. Very few legal requirements affect the retention of client records unless the records are kept in a **custodial** or fiduciary capacity.

Custodial: Relating to a person who has custody of another person or thing and is expected to act in its best interests.

Future need for records. The future need for records can be anticipated by the responsible attorney. Legal assistants should always consult with the responsible attorney regarding the future need for client records.

Statute of limitations. Records should be kept for as long as a statute is running. For example, if a judgment was obtained but was uncollectible, the judgment is good for ten years in some states and may then be renewed for another ten-year period. The file should not be destroyed until the judgment has been collected or the statute has expired.

Applicable age of majority. The statute of limitations on a minor's action begins to run when the child has reached the age of majority. If an action involves a four-year-old child, the child will reach age eighteen in fourteen years. If the statute of limitations is four years, the file should be retained for another four years. The total retention period is eighteen years after the case is closed.

Appeal period. A file should not be closed until the time period for an appeal has expired.

Malpractice concerns. The statute of limitations for professional liability varies by state. It ranges from six months to ten years after the firm's last contact with a client. A file should be retained for the appropriate time period pertaining to professional responsibility.

Records Destruction

When a file's retention period has expired, the file and its contents are destroyed by following established procedures. *To ensure confidentiality, records should never be disposed of in the trash can.* They must be destroyed.

In the past, businesses destroyed records by burning them. Today, however, environmental concerns discourage burning. Today documents are shredded in a shredder machine. Shredders are cost-effective, environmentally safe, and meet most business needs.

Before records can be shredded, they must be properly prepared. All clamps, paper clips, staples, and plastic covers must be removed. For very large amounts of shredding, a commercial disposal company provides "witnessed" destruction. The disposal company will haul the records off-site and destroy them in the presence of a supervisor. A supervisor will certify that the confidentiality of the records was preserved during destruction. This certification becomes a permanent record of the destruction process.

For smaller shredding projects, a firm shreds the documents. It is important that the shredding process be supervised. It is inappropriate to leave a shredder unattended because the confidentiality of the documents will not be protected.

Some firms make it a practice to recycle as much of their disposable records as possible. Preparing records for recycling requires extra effort. Only white paper is recyclable. Glossy paper and colored paper cannot be mixed with white paper. Some dealers will not take cardboard. All documents must be sorted, and staples, clips, and covers must be removed before the shredding process. After the white paper is shredded, it is taken to a recycling center.

Some state bar associations require that attorneys notify their clients by letter before destroying their files. A notification letter contains the following information:

◆ The date the file is scheduled for destruction
◆ The client's right to obtain or inspect the file
◆ Notice to the client that if he or she chooses to preserve the file, he or she is responsible for the cost thereof

Some firms insert their file closing and destruction policies in their retainer agreements. If a firm informs a client of its file destruction policy in its retainer agreement, it does not have to notify the client before destroying the file.

FILE AND RECORDS MANAGEMENT ETHICS

Law firm personnel must be aware of five ethical considerations when managing files and records: preserve a client's property, diligently perform conflict-of-interest checks, promptly return a client's property, retain records according to government regulations, and preserve a client's confidentiality.

Preserve Client's Property

An attorney is a client's agent and acts in a fiduciary capacity. *As such, the attorney must preserve a client's property and records in a safe environment and guard them against theft and damage.* Many firms require that clients' files be maintained in locked filing cabinets.

American Bar Association (ABA) Model Rule 1.15(a) states:

(a) A lawyer shall hold property of clients or third persons that is in a lawyer's possession in connection with a representation separate from the lawyer's own property. . . . [P]roperty shall be identified as such as appropriately safeguarded.

A law firm's personnel should be cautioned not to remove a file from the office. Some attorneys and legal assistants want to take files home to work on them in the evening, but they should be discouraged from doing so. There have been many files lost or damaged while in transit from the office to home. Some firms require that a file be copied and that only copies of necessary documents may be removed from the office.

Perform Conflict-of-Interest Checks

ETHICS ALERT

It is imperative that conflict checks be performed often. It is not just a file opening procedure. Each time a new party makes an appearance, the new party must be entered into the conflicts database. *Each time a potential client makes an appointment with an attorney, the database must be checked for conflicts.* The attorney must be informed of a potential conflict immediately.

Promptly Return File to the Client

ETHICS ALERT

If a client should terminate the attorney-client relationship, the file must be returned to the client promptly so that the client can continue legal representation elsewhere. Some firms hold the file pending payment of an invoice. Most state bar associations prohibit this activity and require attorneys to return the file regardless of the status of the client's account.

ETHICS ALERT

When a matter has been completed, the client is entitled to the original documents in his or her file. *Case law has ruled that all materials in the file, with the exception of certain internal memoranda, belong to the client.* Many firms duplicate the necessary documents and return the originals to the client. The duplicates are stored in inactive file storage, on microfilm, or on CD-ROMs to comply with a firm's retention schedule.

Retain Records

ETHICS ALERT

A firm must comply with records retention regulations set by state and federal governments. There are thousands of records retention laws and regulations, some of which conflict with one another. Once a schedule is established, it must be reviewed and approved by an attorney and be strictly adhered to. *A file must not be destroyed until its retention period has expired.* To do so would expose the firm to sanctions and/or fines.

The last sentence of ABA Model Rule 1.15 states:

> Complete record of such account funds and other property shall be kept by the lawyer and shall be preserved for a period of [five years] after termination of the representation.

The five-year period covers most legal malpractice statutes of limitations. However, some government regulations may require a longer period of retention. Whenever a rule conflicts, the record should be retained for the longer period.

Preserve Confidentiality

ETHICS ALERT

All clients' records and documents must be kept confidential. This was discussed in detail in Chapters 4 and 5, but the concept cannot be overemphasized. When closing and destroying clients' files, be sure to take steps to ensure their confidentiality.

CONCLUSION

File and records management procedures are important to the smooth operation of a law office. Understanding and complying with these procedures takes effort, but the effort will contribute to a legal assistant's success.

SUMMARY

A firm's files and records system is the nerve center of a law office. The management and organization of a firm's filing system are essential to the smooth operation of a law firm. A well-organized records management system provides benefits to law firms and their employees.

Law firm records are considered by function, including clients' files, a law firm's business files, personnel files, and other files. Since the users of a system are document creators, the system must be suitable to them. To avoid confusion, a system must be consistent in its structure.

There are three types of filing systems: centralized, decentralized, and automated. A centralized filing system has all the files located in one area and is normally managed by a file coordinator or clerk. A decentralized system has files located in various areas, usually near the responsible attorney's office. An automated filing system electronically stores files and records.

A filing system, whether centralized, decentralized, or automated, consists of a logical division of categories of records. Records are divided into categories that have a logical connection to one another. A coding system is a method used to store files in a specified sequence.

An alphabetical coding system is the most common coding system used by small firms. In this system, a law firm's records are arranged in alphabetical order according to a client's surname. Although this coding system seems easy, problems occur when employees have not been instructed in its rules.

Files may also be coded with numeric coding according to a particular numbering pattern. Six different types of numeric systems are used: straight, coded, calendar, standard, account, and combination. An alphanumeric system is also used, which is a combination of an alphabetical and numeric system.

A cross-index is a cross-reference of records. All files and subfiles must be included on a cross-index. A numeric index must also be maintained.

Color coding is a common method of categorizing files. Some records managers maintain that color coding increases speed and accuracy in filing. Color may be applied to any system and may be used for paper or computer records.

A file retrieval system must allow for easy access to files. Firms employ file personnel who are responsible for maintaining a retrieval system. File requests are initiated by a requisition form.

A file must be accessible before it is retrieved. When a file is removed from a filing system, its location must be traceable and monitored. One method used to trace files is an "out card." An out card is the size of a file folder, made of heavy vinyl, and has lines on the front on which to put names and dates.

Whenever someone removes a file, an out card is inserted in its place. Out folders are also used.

Bar codes are used to monitor files. Bar codes are a fast, easy, and accurate data entry method used in the process known as automatic data collection. Bar coding technology is used by universities and libraries to manage the circulation of books and journals. A bar coding system automates records management. A bar code is put on a label that is attached to a file. Medium and large firms especially benefit from using bar code technology for their files.

Not all potential clients retain a firm: Some interview many attorneys before choosing a lawyer, and some just need some quick legal advice. A firm keeps information about each person who consults with an attorney. As we learned in Chapter 4, an attorney-client relationship is formed whenever an attorney gives a person legal advice. A client file is opened immediately after a client retains a firm.

When a clerk or secretary opens a file, she or he must do a conflict check for a possible conflict of interest. A database is maintained with the names of clients and all parties to a proceeding in which a firm was involved. A conflict check is the most important aspect of file opening procedures but is not limited to file opening. A conflict check must be performed as each new party enters a case. Most firms require some type of written record that a conflict check was made. If a firm has no conflict of interest in representing a client, a client file may be opened.

A legal assistant is responsible for maintaining clients' files in good order. The first step in file maintenance is categorizing the documents. Correspondence, pleadings, notes, and all other documents are filed in chronological order unless the case is large. In a large case, documents are further categorized by type. Case cover sheets are used to monitor the status of a case.

Indexes are used to direct a person to a document's exact location in a file. Each document is given a number that is put on a tab so that it can be found quickly. A document is inserted behind its divider so that it can be located by lifting up the tabbed divider. The number, title of document, date, and party are inserted on an index sheet that is placed on top of the divider sheets. Indexes should be developed for every category of a case, except correspondence and miscellaneous notes.

Every document has a life cycle and lives only as long as it serves its purpose. To determine the life cycle of a document, one must first identify the document's value. After its value has been determined, a decision regarding its future must be made. Time management experts advise that document management decisions be made as soon as a document is received.

Filing experts have estimated that correspondence constitutes most of the documents received. Promotional documents are a form of correspondence. The person to whom correspondence is sent is responsible for deciding whether to keep the material. No document pertaining to a client's case may be discarded. Notes taken in a meeting with a client or on a client's behalf are always retained.

Complex agreements require many drafts that should be retained until the final agreement is signed. Some firms have a policy to keep all rough drafts of agreements. Rough drafts of correspondence or pleadings are destroyed when the final document is completed.

When magazine and newspaper articles are kept, they should be clipped rather than retaining the entire magazine or newspaper. If it is beneficial to retain each issue of a particular magazine; firms then file these in magazine files.

Today, documents do not consist only of paper. There are many types of documents: e-mail, word processing, spreadsheets, graphics, video clips, voice mail, and document images. After you have read an electronic document such as e-mail, you make a decision to do one or more of the following: copy it, file it, write comments on it, forward it to someone in the firm, or dispose of it. The files and subfiles into which electronic documents are stored must be similar in structure to the filing system for paper documents. Electronic documents remain on the network's hard drive until they are no longer needed, can be disposed of, or the need to recoup hard drive space occurs.

An automated document management system is an electronic filing system containing a database of documents that is updated automatically every time a document is created, retrieved, edited, printed, archived, or deleted. A document management system tracks and manages every legal document created in a law office. Once prepared, a document is saved on the firm's network or intranet.

When a case is completed, certain procedures must be followed before a file is a candidate for closing. When a case has been completed, a file must be double-checked to ensure that all documents have been completed and filed. If the appeal period has not expired, a case may not be closed. The final bill must be paid before a case is closed. Some firms send a disengagement letter with the final bill, and others wait until the bill has been paid. Pruning a file prepares a file for closing by eliminating unnecessary documents. Each firm has specific pruning policies for closed files.

Changing the status of a case from active to inactive involves changing a master client list and inserting the file on a closed file list. Original documents that are vital to a client, such as a will or deed, should be returned to the client. Electronic documents that are stored in a client's file on the firm's computer system are deleted from the system. A file closing memorandum is prepared and acts as a checklist for file closing procedures.

Inactive records are records that are seldom needed for the business of an office. Inactive records are usually stored in filing cabinets or storage boxes outside the main storage area.

An alternative method for storing inactive files is to microfilm or image them. Medium and large firms may image or microfilm their inactive records, but sole proprietors and small firms with smaller storage needs often cannot justify the expense. The best evidence rule, which requires a court to admit the best evidence that is available to a party under the existing situation, directly applies to imaged and microfilmed records.

When inactive records are stored, they still must be accessible for retrieval. Most firms have a separate coding system for closed files. Some firms that use numeric coding for active files change the file number when the file is closed. A closed file index is kept on the computer, and a hard copy closed file index log is maintained as a backup in case of computer failure. Information for the closed file index is obtained from a closed file index form.

Records retention is the time period during which records must be maintained by an organization because they may be needed for legal, operational, historical, or other purposes. A retention schedule is a list of retention periods categorized according to type of document or case. A retention schedule integrated into a firm's computer system will automatically calculate a file's retention period. However, human involvement is necessary to establish a file's retention period.

For business records, management must consider statutes and regulations, any future need for the records, and the statute of limitations. Considerations for the retention period for clients' records are statutes and regulations, any future need for records, statute of limitations if minors are involved, applicable age of majority, appeal period, and malpractice and business concerns.

When a file's retention period has expired, the file and its contents are destroyed by following established procedures. Today, documents are shredded in a shredder machine. Before records can be shredded, they must be properly prepared. Some state bar associations require that attorneys notify their clients by letter before destroying their files. Some firms insert its file closing and destruction policy into their retainer agreement.

A law firm's personnel must be aware of five ethical considerations when managing files and records: preserve a client's property, diligently perform conflict-of-interest checks, promptly return a client's property, retain records according to government regulations, and preserve a client's confidentiality.

CHAPTER ILLUSTRATION

When Black, White & Greene started their law firm, they had a decentralized filing system. Each attorney's files were stored in a filing cabinet in his or her secretary's area close to his or her office. Each secretary was responsible for opening files, and each legal assistant was responsible for maintaining the files. The secretaries were responsible for filing documents and keeping the files organized and indexed. Each attorney had his or her own file preferences: Robert and Dennis used partitioned folders, Grant used regular folders, and George wanted a folder for each type of document in a case. The firm used an alphabetical coding system for all files. Just one attorney, Patrizia, used color-coded labels to identify the file by type of case.

As the firm grew and the support staff grew busier, the secretaries had a problem keeping up with their filing duties. They did not like to file, so they would leave the filing until they completed their other, more pressing work. Consequently, the filing did not get done, and each secretary had a large pile of filing to do.

The secretaries handled this filing problem in different ways. Audra would come in on Saturdays to get caught up on her filing. Pam just threw the documents in the file without putting them in the proper order or placing them on an index sheet. Tricia collected the documents in a pile on her desk and watched the pile grow higher each day.

This filing backlog caused problems for the firm. When an attorney needed a document, it was not in the file. It was in the filing pile, and the legal assistant or secretary would have to search the piles of filing to find it. Robert and Grant, Pam's attorneys, always had messy files. They spent a lot of time going through loose documents to find the information they needed. They would give the messy files to Milton to organize and put the documents on index sheets. Milton resented this and felt that it was Pam's responsibility to keep the files in order.

When Tricia did her human resource audit (discussed in Chapter 3), Tricia found that filing interfered with the secretaries' productivity. She also found that the current filing system was fragmented and disorganized. It had no uniformity, which was important for the firm. She decided to overhaul the system to a centralized system, and she hired Kay Bowen as the firm's file clerk.

All the files were moved to a central area, and the secretaries were relieved from their filing responsibilities. Kay was responsible for filing documents. Tricia changed the coding for clients' files from alphabetical coding to a standard numeric system. This coding system will allow for file volumes, which would satisfy George's preference for separate folders for each type of document. The system would also accommodate files that had no volumes. Each attorney was given a number that was the first number in the code as follows:

2	45	321	.1
Attorney	Type of case	File number	Volume number

With this coding system, each attorney's files were filed together. Within each attorney's files, all cases of the same type were filed together. In addition, Tricia developed a color code that identified the year in which each case was opened. All files opened in 2000, for example, had the same color label. The age of the case was easily identified by looking at the file label.

Secretaries were responsible for opening a file. The attorney or legal assistant completes a new case memorandum and gives it to the secretary. Each secretary checks the conflicts database for a conflict of interest and, if there are no conflicts, opens the file. To determine the file number, the secretary consults the new file index, which gives the next number in sequence for each attorney. She enters the file number on the new case memorandum and makes a copy of it. The original memorandum is filed in the client's file, and the copy is filed in an alphabetical binder, which is used as a backup to the cross-index of clients' files. Once all file opening procedures are completed, the secretary prepares a new client memorandum and distributes it among the staff. The file is then given to Kay, who files it in the file room.

Kay is responsible for filing all documents and tracking the location of each file. If a file is needed, a file requisition slip is completed and given to Kay, who retrieves the file and inserts the person's name on an out folder. She then puts the out folder in the file's position in the file drawer. She signs and dates the file requisition form as evidence that the request was completed. The file requisition slip is stored in a "files out" file. As a file is returned, the requisition slip is removed from the files out file and inserted in a binder for future reference. If a file is not returned in a day or two, Kay knows where to find it.

When a file is ready to be closed, the attorney reviews it to make sure that all documentation has been completed. A file closing memorandum is signed by the responsible attorney, who transfers the file to Tricia, the office manager. Tricia checks to see whether the final bill has been paid: if it has been paid, she initials the file closing memorandum and transfers it and the file to the legal assistant. Legal assistants are responsible for file closing procedures.

When Julie receives the file, she first checks the conflicts database to verify that all parties are listed. Then the file is reviewed for any original documents that are to be returned to the client. After she makes a copy, she returns the original documents to the client with a disengagement letter that contains a notice informing the client that he or she is entitled to documents from the file. She gives the client thirty days to respond to the notice. If she does not hear from the client, she proceeds with file closing procedures.

She begins pruning the file and discarding all unnecessary documents. Then she changes the status of the case from active to inactive. She removes the case from the active files list and inserts it on the closed file list. She gives it a closed file number, which is a combination of calendar and straight coding systems. The first part of the number is the date the file is closed, and the second part of the number is the length of time the file must be retained according to the firm's retention schedule: 0203.10, which means that the file was closed in March 2002 and must be retained for ten years. She calendars the file for destruction for March 2012 and inserts the file into a numbered container. She inserts the number of the container, its location, and all other information on file closing memorandum and in the computer system. She then deletes the electronic file from the computer system. The closed file container is then transferred to storage, where the firm's inactive files are stored.

The new system was a definite improvement over the old system, but it was not without its problems. Some attorneys, especially Dennis, did not return files to the file room. He liked the convenience of having his files where he could get to them quickly. When Kay would come into his office looking for the files, he told her that he was not through with them. Files were piled up in his office. Robert and Tricia talked to Dennis about the importance of all employees following the rules of a filing system, but to no avail.

When the firm got an intranet (discussed in Chapter 10), Robert and Tricia realized that many aspects of the filing process could be automated. They researched records management programs and decided that they were not ready to transfer all their paper documents to electronic documents. However, they liked some of the features offered, such as automated file tracking, integrated conflict database, and file closing indexing and processing. They found a software package with these features. They purchased it and began the implementation process.

The first thing that had to be done was to put all their existing cases in the system. When a file was input, the system prepared a bar code label for the file, that transferred the information to the firm's time and billing system and automatically assigned a file number. The system was programmed with the firm's file coding system and automatically prepared a cross-index, list of cases, conflicts database, and file label. When a file was needed, the requester would e-mail the file requisition slip to Kay, who would scan the bar code, and the new location of the file would automatically be put into the database. Each member of the firm could access the database from the firm's intranet.

It took a long time to completely implement the automated system. An outside temporary service was called in to help Kay input all the files. After the files were in the system, each person had to be trained on the system. The secretaries, paralegals, and some of the attorneys loved the system. The other attorneys had difficulty adjusting to the "high tech" nature of the system. However, as they grew accustomed to it, they found the system very convenient and easy to use.

The firm could now boast of its state-of-the-art filing system. Now, if Dennis would just return all those bar coded files in his office, in his car, and in his home!

CHAPTER REVIEW

1. Describe the three types of filing systems.

2. Describe the classification of documents.

3. Describe the six types of numeric coding systems.

4. What is alphanumeric coding?

5. How are bar codes used in filing systems?

6. What is a preclient file?

7. Why is it important to do a conflict check for new clients?

8. When organizing a small file, how is correspondence filed?

9. What is the function of a case cover sheet?

10. What are the three value determinations for a document?

11. When may a document pertaining to a client's case be discarded?

12. What functions must be completed before a file is closed?

13. What is file pruning?

14. What is a closed file index?

15. What is a records retention schedule, and how is it developed?

16. What are the five ethical considerations of file and records management?

EXAMPLES FOR DISCUSSION

1. Alphabetical Client Files by Subject

The law firm of Smith & Jones utilizes a subject alphabetical system and separates client files by area of law: bankruptcy, criminal, domestic, litigation, probate, and real estate. Litigation was commenced on real property in Thomas Nelson's case. Sharon, the legal assistant, was given an assignment on the case and must retrieve the file. She knows that Thomas Nelson is deceased, and a case was opened.

1. If you were Sharon, in which category would you look for the file?
2. Do you see any problems with this coding system? What are they?
3. What are your suggestions for improving the system?

2. Missing Files

Julie is a legal assistant for a medium-size firm. She is having problems finding files in the office. The files are never in the central filing area, and out cards are not inserted where the missing files should be filed. After hours of searching, one attorney, the managing partner, is always responsible for removing the files without placing out cards in their places. The files are buried in his office, in the trunk of his car, or at his home.

1. What are the problems with the system?
2. What could be done about this problem?
3. What would you do about this problem?

3. Too Many Files

Darrel is a legal assistant for a small boutique firm specializing in personal injury cases. The firm has a policy to prepare five file folders per case as follows:

◆ Correspondence
◆ Pleadings
◆ Discovery
◆ Medical records
◆ Research

At the beginning of a case, there are few or no documents in many of the files. When Darrel must retrieve the file, he must retrieve all five files. Some employees retrieve only the file folder they need at the moment, causing the file to be fragmented and disbursed all over the law firm. The system is fine for large cases, but most of the cases are small. Darrel is very frustrated with the system and has been asked to develop new file maintenance procedures.

1. How should Darrel change file opening procedures?
2. What new file maintenance procedures should he recommend?
3. What file retrieval procedures should he recommend?

4. An Embarrassing Moment

Patrice Boen, associate of Black, White & Greene, was in trial on a complicated real estate litigation matter. She was in the process of cross-examination when the opposing party gave a different answer than he stated in his interrogatories. Ms. Boen, in an attempt to impeach his testimony, indicated that his interrogatory answers were contrary to his current testimony. She grabbed the file to find the interrogatories. The file was neither indexed nor organized, and Ms. Boen could not find the interrogatories. Five minutes passed as Ms. Boen thumbed through the file. The judge and jury watched her in silence. She stated that the interrogatories must be in another file and picked up another file to search for the interrogatories. As she did, twenty to thirty small phone message slips fell out of the file and scattered all over the courtroom floor. The judge and jury watched as she picked them up off the floor and then continued to search the file for the interrogatories. Needless to say, the judge, jury, and her client were not impressed.

1. If you were the judge, what would your impression of Ms. Boen be?
2. If you were on the jury, what would your impression of Ms. Boen be?
3. If you were Ms. Boen's client, how would you feel?
4. Do you think this disorganized file reflected on Ms. Boen's capability? How?
5. What needs to be done to improve the situation?

5. What About the Closed Files?

Smith & Jones law firm merged with Black & White law firm to form a new firm: Smith, Jones, Black & White. Before the merger, two attorneys from Smith & Jones, Bob Jackson and Sharon Fields, left the firm to form their own firm. The firm of Smith, Jones, Black & White have all of Smith & Jones' closed files, including the files of Bob and Sharon, who left the firm prior to the merger.

1. What is Smith, Jones, Black & White's obligation with regard to the closed files of Bob Jackson and Sharon Fields?
2. May they destroy the files? If not, why not? If they may, how?
3. If you were the managing partner of Smith, Jones, Black & White, what would you do with them?

ASSIGNMENTS

1. You are a probate legal assistant for a large firm. Three of the attorneys in the probate and estate planning department want to quit the firm and start their own boutique firm specializing in probate and estate planning. They want you to go with them and be the office manager for the new firm. You must set up the new firm's filing system. They have asked for a report that includes a descriptive report of the filing system. In your report:

   a. Describe the type of filing system you would choose and explain your choice.

   b. Describe the type of coding system you would choose and explain your choice.

   c. Include a list of materials needed to implement the system.

   d. Describe file opening procedures.

   e. Describe file maintenance procedures.

   f. Describe file closing procedures.

   g. Describe the storage and destruction of closed files.

2. Review the records management system at your place of employment. Write a report about the system and describe the following:

   a. What type of system is it?

   b. Do the system's users think the system is adequate? Inadequate? Why?

   c. How could the system be improved?

3. Set up files for all your school assignments. You may use regular file folders, partitioned file folders, or three-ring binders. Classify the assignments by function, subject, topic, and subtopic by establishing categories of documents, such as notes, quizzes, exams, and homework. Prepare an index sheet and tabbed dividers for each category. Choose a coding system for your files and use color where you feel appropriate.

4. Create a class cover sheet similar to the case cover sheet in Exhibit 13.13. Insert data from your course syllabus and include your grades received on each assignment, quiz, and exam. Insert it in front of your class file mentioned in assignment 3.

5. Your boss has asked you to research automated records management software. Choose three automated records management software products and write a report comparing the software (see page 464):

   a. List the common features of the software.

   b. Identify the hardware requirements of the software

   c. Explain how the firm can benefit from the software.

   d. Analyze the cost factor of the software.

   e. List any problems of the software.

   f. Make your recommendation for the firm to purchase one product.

6. File management is one of a legal assistant's main responsibilities and an area in which legal assistants and legal secretaries can demonstrate excellent organizational skills. A file is a package that contains a firm's product. The condition of the package communicates to the world a firm's perception of its product. The image files communicate to the world can be one of excellence and professionalism, or one of sloppiness and neglect. Good file management skills will help create a reputation of excellence for a firm. After completing this chapter, you will increase your organizational skills so you can accept the responsibility of file management with confidence. This very important skill will make you a valuable asset to any law office.

   Have you ever worked in an office with messy, disorganized files? If so:

   a. What was your perception of the organization?

   b. How much time was wasted finding the information you needed?

   c. What did the organization communicate by its files?

   d. What could have been done to eliminate the problem?

7. Create file and records management procedures for Black, White & Greene. Include:

   a. Procedures to retrieve a file

   b. Preclient files

   c. File opening procedures

   d. File organization

   e. File closing procedures

   f. File storage

   g. File storage procedures

   h. File destruction

   i. Alphabetical or numerical filing system

   j. How documents are filed in each client's file

SELF-TEST

How well did you grasp the material in the chapter? Test yourself by answering the following questions and check your answers against the answers found in Appendix A.

1. What are the four benefits a law firm realizes from a well-organized records management system?

2. What are the four benefits a law firm's employees realize from a well-organized record management system?

3. What are the eight considerations of a records management system?

4. Can a legal assistant bill a client for time spent searching for a file?

5. What is a cause of employee dissatisfaction?

6. What is responsible for 80 percent of the cost of most records management systems?

7. What two aspects constitute a poor records management system?

8. Why is the possibility of misfiling greater in a complicated filing system?

9. What is responsible for 10 percent of the cost of a filing system?

10. What else constitutes 10 percent of the cost of a filing system?

11. How may a specialized file folder for a system cause a backlog in the system?

12. A filing system must preserve the _____ of clients' files.

13. From what must a firm's files be protected?

14. What are the eight elements of an effective filing system?

15. When the function of a file is identified, what can then be developed?

16. Why is it important to keep a filing system simple?

17. How much does a large firm's active files increase in a year?

18. What must a filing system be to avoid confusion?

19. What does the economy of a filing system include?

20. When are records eliminated from an active system?

21. Why are inactive records not retained?

22. What are the three types of filing systems?

23. What is a centralized filing system?

24. Who manages a centralized filing system?

25. What type of firm uses a centralized filing system?

26. What is controlled access?

27. What is a decentralized filing system?

28. Who manages a decentralized filing system?

29. What type of firm uses a decentralized filing system?

30. What is an automated filing system?

31. What are the three parts of an automated filing system?

32. What is imaging?

33. What can a user do with an automated filing system?

34. What is classification?

35. What does a good classification system do?

36. What are the four major categories for most law firm files?

37. Before a document can be located, what must first be known?

38. After the function of a record is identified, what is it divided into?

39. After the subject is identified, what is it divided into?

40. What is a subtopic?

41. What is a coding system?

42. What are three coding methods?

43. What is the most common coding method used by small firms?

44. What coding system is the easiest to establish and maintain?

45. When a client's records are arranged in alphabetical order, what name is used?

46. What is the first unit of an individual client's file called?

47. What is the first unit of a business client's file name called?

48. File _____ before _____ .

49. The word "the" is always considered as the _____ unit.

50. When alphabetizing records, what do you do with all punctuation and symbols?

51. Where are arabic and roman numerals filed in an alphabetical system?

52. The call letters of a television station are considered _____ unit(s).

53. What is cross-referencing?

54. If the client is the sole plaintiff in a case, his name would be the _____ name in a case name.

55. If the client is the defendant, his name would be the _____ name in the case name.

56. What does "adversus" ("adv.") mean?

57. What is a primary case name?

58. In a corporate legal department or other firm with just one client, when is the client's name mentioned in the case name?

59. Why is subject alphabetical coding more difficult than straight alphabetical coding?

60. What must be used if a firm codes files by subject?

61. What are the six types of numeric coding systems?
62. What is straight numbering?
63. What numeric coding system is the least complicated?
64. Straight numbering normally begins at what number?
65. What is coded numbering?
66. How are files with a coded numbering system filed?
67. What is calendar numbering?
68. How are files with a calendar numbering system filed?
69. The file number in a calendar numbering system gives the user what information?
70. What is standard numbering?
71. What type of information does a standard numbering system convey?
72. What is a volume?
73. What is account numbering?
74. How are files with an account numbering system filed?
75. How are numbering systems combined?
76. What is alphanumeric coding?
77. How are files in an alphanumeric coding system filed?
78. What are the advantages to an alphanumeric coding system?
79. What is a cross-index, and how is it used?
80. What is a numeric index, and how is it used?
81. For what is color coding used?
82. What types of information can color coding convey?
83. For what purpose is a colored dot or sticker used?
84. How are misfilings reduced by giving file numbers a color?
85. According to statistics, what percentage of documents are misfiled?
86. What does noncompliance with retrieval procedures result in?
87. In a small firm, who is responsible for file system maintenance?
88. In a large firm, who is responsible for file system maintenance?
89. What does an efficient system have?
90. How is a file requested from a centralized filing system?
91. What advantage does a written request for a file have over an oral request?
92. For what reasons would a file not be available in a file room?
93. What is an out card system, and how is it used?
94. What are the advantages to an out card system?
95. When do problems occur with an out card system?
96. What is an out folder, and how is it used?
97. What is bar coding, and how is it used?
98. What is automatic data collection?

99. What are symbologies?
100. What are the advantages to bar coding?
101. How is bar code information communicated back to a firm's computer?
102. What is used to determine a file's location?
103. What type of firm benefits from using bar code technology?
104. What are the six benefits of using bar code technology?
105. What is a preclient?
106. When is a client's file formally opened?
107. What is a conflict check, and why is it necessary?
108. What information does a conflict check database contain?
109. What is the most important aspect of file opening procedures?
110. In addition to file opening, when must a conflict check be performed?
111. If there is a potential conflict of interest, what must be done?
112. What is a file number index, and for what is it used?
113. What is used as a checklist to complete file opening procedures?
114. When opening a file, what is done with the statute of limitations?
115. When opening a file, where does a clerk obtain billing information?
116. How is referral information used in file opening procedures?
117. How is type-of-case information used by a law firm's management?
118. What acts as a double-check against direct or potential conflicts of interest?
119. Why is it important that information generated when opening a file be accurate?
120. Who is responsible for maintaining clients' files in good order?
121. What are now considered documents?
122. What is rich media?
123. What is one of the biggest changes facing records management today?
124. What is the first step in file maintenance?
125. How is correspondence filed?
126. How are notes and pleadings filed in a small case?
127. Where is correspondence inserted in the folder in a small case?
128. Where are pleadings inserted in the folder in a small case?
129. How are documents categorized in a large case?
130. What is a case cover sheet, and how is it used?
131. Where is a case cover sheet located in a file?
132. Why do some firms keep an extra copy of a case cover sheet in a separate binder?
133. What is an index, and for what is it used?

134. How are indexing tabs used?

135. Where is a document inserted in an indexed system?

136. What information is inserted on an index sheet?

137. What categories of documents do not require an index?

138. How are photographs inserted into a file?

139. What are the two ways documents are generated in a law office?

140. What must be determined to identify a document's life cycle?

141. What are a document's three value determinations?

142. What is operational value?

143. What is considered high operational value?

144. What is technical value?

145. What is legal value?

146. How does one determine the value of a document?

147. Why should unnecessary documents not be kept?

148. What does it mean to purge a file?

149. When do time management experts advise that document decisions be made?

150. What types of documents are found in a typical law office?

151. Most of the documents received are what type of document?

152. What should be done with a fax cover sheet?

153. What is date stamping?

154. Why are documents date stamped?

155. When should envelopes be retained?

156. Who is responsible for deciding whether to keep or discard a document?

157. What document pertaining to a client's case may be discarded?

158. Who should be consulted if a document's importance is unclear?

159. What type of interoffice memo is always retained?

160. When should a photocopy of an original document be retained?

161. What is a courtesy copy of a document?

162. What is a secondary recipient?

163. What is a primary recipient?

164. What type of recipient has no responsibility to retain a document?

165. When are notes of a meeting with a client discarded?

166. When must a note taker in a law firm meeting retain notes of the meeting?

167. When is a rough draft of an agreement discarded?

168. When are rough drafts of correspondence and pleadings discarded?

169. What information is inserted on a magazine or newspaper article?

170. The files and subfiles into which electronic documents are stored must have what structure?

171. What is "read only" access?

172. Why are documents not removed from a file?

173. What are the advantages of electronic documents?

174. What are the disadvantages of electronic documents?

175. What are the functions of an automated document management system?

176. Most automated document management programs are integrated into what systems?

177. Where is an electronic document prepared for a client filed?

178. What type of rules must a firm have for electronic documents?

179. How will a filing system for electronic documents fail?

180. What are the characteristics of a good system?

181. A popular system that is used for saving electronic documents contains what three components?

182. Using the three components in answer 181 gives an electronic filing system what advantage?

183. What procedures must be followed before a file can be closed?

184. What is a disengagement letter?

185. What is pruning a file?

186. What is a file closing memorandum?

187. To determine whether a file is a candidate for closing, the file must be reviewed for what purpose?

188. What must be paid before a file is closed?

189. Who is responsible for drafting a disengagement letter?

190. Who has the responsibility for pruning files?

191. Why should an attorney review a file for closing?

192. Why do some experts recommend that an attorney not review files for closing?

193. When a file is closed, it changes its status from what to what?

194. Why should a conflict-of-interest database be checked when a file is closed?

195. What must be determined when a file is closed?

196. Who is usually responsible for file closing procedures?

197. If a firm retains a client's original will, where is it stored?

198. What happens to a client's electronic documents when a file is closed?

199. Why should inactive records not be stored in the active filing area?

200. What is used to locate and retrieve inactive files and records?

201. Where are inactive records stored?

202. What must be done to each inactive records container?

203. Storage areas include what three things?

204. What is micrographics?

205. What type of firm benefits from using micrographics to store records?
206. Why do smaller firms not use micrographics to store their inactive files?
207. What is imaging?
208. What items does an image system include?
209. How many documents will a CD-ROM hold?
210. What is a jukebox?
211. How is an imaged document located?
212. What is the best evidence rule?
213. What is the name of the two statutes that pertain to imaged records?
214. A closed file's number is listed on what?
215. Why do closed files with an alphabetical coding system create storage problems?
216. What is the preferred coding method for closed files?
217. What is a closed file index?
218. In what order should information be inserted on a closed file index?
219. What information should a closed file index contain?
220. Where is the information for a closed file index obtained?
221. Who completes the closed file index form?
222. What is done with a completed closed file index form?
223. What is records retention?
224. How are records retention time periods established?
225. For what purposes may an organization need inactive records?
226. When may records be destroyed?
227. When do 95 percent of all references to closed files occur?
228. Who is responsible for setting a retention period?
229. What is a retention schedule?
230. Why should a legal assistant not rely on an automated retention schedule?
231. When determining the retention period for business records, what three things are considered?
232. Who determines the future need for business records?
233. What are the six considerations for retaining client records?
234. Who determines the future need for client records?
235. When does the statute of limitations begin on a minor's action?
236. Why should records be shredded instead of disposing of them in the trash can?
237. What must be done to prepare records for shredding?
238. What is witnessed records destruction?
239. How are small shredding projects performed?
240. Why must a shredding project be supervised and not left unattended?
241. What type of paper is recyclable?
242. Who requires that an attorney notify the client before a file is destroyed?
243. What information does a notification letter regarding file destruction contain?
244. Some firms are notifying clients of their file destruction policy in what document?
245. Why should files not be removed from the office?
246. When should conflict-of-interest checks be performed?
247. If a client terminates the attorney-client relationship, when should a file be returned to a client?
248. Who must approve a records retention schedule?
249. Why must a file not be destroyed until the expiration of the retention period?
250. Why is knowledge of file and records management procedures important?

KEY WORDS

Automatic data collection	Date stamp	Preclient file
Best evidence rule	File number index	Primary case name
Central file control	Imaging	Primary recipient
Classification	Jukebox	Pruning
Closed file list	Master client list	Purge
Controlled access	New case memorandum	Rich media
Courtesy copy	Numeric index	Secondary recipient
Custodial	Preclient	Symbologies

Law Library Organization and Management

OBJECTIVES

After completion of this chapter, a student should be able to do the following:

◆ Describe the nature of law.

◆ Explain how laws are classified.

◆ Discuss the various types of law libraries.

◆ Discuss library organization.

◆ Describe the importance of updating.

◆ Discuss library technology.

◆ Identify the function of each book in the library.

◆ Explain how knowledge banks and form files are used.

◆ Find legal research sites on the Internet.

◆ Cite a case found on the Internet.

◆ Describe the duties of a law librarian.

◆ Update a law library.

INTRODUCTION

The law library has served as a symbol of the practice of law for centuries. Libraries are used as the background for a law firm's photographs and are displayed in the background of television commercials as attorneys advertise their services. Library shelves neatly lined with impressive, leather-bound law books greet clients as they enter a law firm, communicating a message of an attorney's expertise and knowledge of the law.

Two types of knowledge exist: knowledge we have about a subject and knowledge of where to find information about a subject. A law library is where attorneys and legal assistants obtain knowledge. Every law library is different. Each encompasses a world of knowledge that forms our society and documents the evolution of the United States. It is a place of excitement and frustration. It is a place where a legal assistant views a part of other people's lives. It is a place of continuing education. It is a legal professional's most important tool.

Millions of laws are in effect today. The United States is governed by the U.S. Constitution, the highest law in the land. Each state has a state constitution, the highest law in that state. Federal laws are enacted by Congress. Each federal agency, such as the Federal Drug Administration (FDA) and the Federal Aviation Administration (FAA), has laws that govern it. Each state has its own laws and laws that govern state agencies. In addition, each county and city has laws and ordinances that govern it.

Each individual in the country is bound by the U.S. Constitution, state constitution, federal law, federal agency law, state law, state agency law, county ordinances, and city ordinances. At this moment, the federal and state legislatures are busy enacting more laws. Organizing laws in an orderly manner so that each law is easily found is a huge undertaking.

Entering a large law library that contains thousands of books can be intimidating, to say the least. A legal assistant must be comfortable in a library setting because success as a legal assistant depends on it. Acquiring knowledge of libraries is the first step in understanding a law library. The second step is gaining knowledge of the contents of a law library. A legal assistant need not read every book in a library but should understand the function of each book.

The purpose of this chapter is to familiarize a prospective legal assistant with library management. Being familiar with this important tool is the beginning of using it effectively. The first section of the chapter will review the nature and classes of law. The second section will discuss law libraries and their maintenance. The third section will discuss law library technology. Finally, the chapter will discuss law librarians and their role in law library management.

THE NATURE OF LAW

Law has been defined as follows: "Law consists of enforceable rules governing the relationships between individuals and their relationships to society." Professor Holland, in *Elements of Jurisprudence,* defines law as "a general rule of external human action enforced by a sovereign political authority." Our legal system is based on a combination of civil law and common law.

Civil law is derived from Roman law and is based on a series of written laws. In advanced countries, laws were written as early as 2100 B.C. Cases were decided by applying written law to them. There are two main sources of written law: constitutions and statutes.

Stare decisis: The legal principle that a court will follow the decision of another court in a similar case.

Common law, also known as case law, evolved in England, where there were no written laws. During the reign of Edward I (1272–1307), some people, perhaps student lawyers, attended trials and reported what was said. Their accounts were later compiled into a series called the Yearbooks. Courts would consult the Yearbooks when making a ruling, establishing the doctrine of **stare decisis,** or standing by decisions. Cases were adjudicated by stare decisis, or following precedent, that is, following previous court decisions.

Codify: To arrange laws by subject.

The U.S. legal system utilizes both written law and case law with the exception of a few states. Most laws of the United States originated from English common law and were **codified,** or arranged, into written laws. In addition to establishing case law, U.S. courts interpret the statutes, and that interpretation sets a precedent.

Law Classification

One of the most important aspects of legal editorial work is classifying the law. The classification process entails placing law into categories. It is very similar to the classification process we learned in Chapter 13 when we classified documents so that they could be located quickly. Classification of the law was introduced in England in 1490. A man named Statham produced a subject-key index to all the cases in the Yearbooks, titled *Abridgment of the Yearbooks.* This was the first legal index published.

Today, we place laws into categories, and this helps us find them quickly. Laws are categorized according to function. When the function of a law is identified, it is categorized by subject. When the subject is identified, it is further categorized by topic and then subtopic, as we learned in Chapter 13. For example, statutes are classified by function: civil and criminal.

Civil statutes (function)

    Bankruptcy (subject)

        Chapter 7 (topic)

            Stockbroker liquidation (subtopic)

Criminal statutes (function)

    Felony (subject)

        Murder (topic)

            First degree (subtopic)

There are four million case laws, and 45,000 to 50,000 court decisions are made each year. If these decisions were not classified, it would be extremely difficult, if not impossible, to find a case. To eliminate this problem, case law is classified according to its subject matter. For example, a case dealing with probate is classified under the title "probate." A case regarding corporations is classified under the title "corporations." Understanding this classification process is important to understanding the law library.

There are four functions of law: type of action (civil or criminal), individuals involved (public or private), nature of the law (substantive or procedural), and source of the law (constitutions, statutes, and cases). This breakdown is shown in Exhibit 14.1.

Type of Legal Action   Two types of legal actions are filed: civil and criminal. In a criminal action, the government, state or federal, is the plaintiff in the action. The

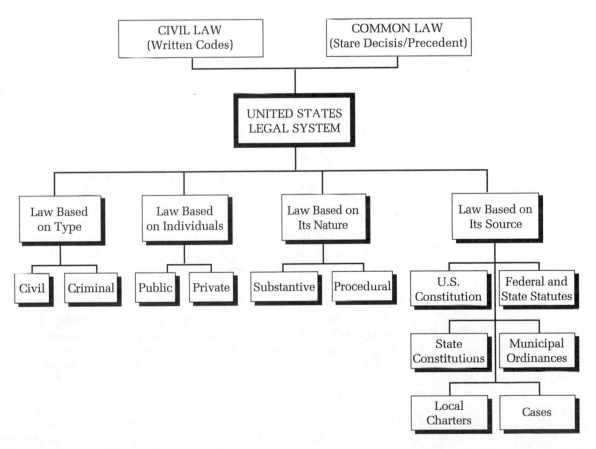

EXHIBIT 14.1   The Four Functions of Law

Source: Copyright 1987 by West Publishing Co. All rights reserved. Reprinted with permission from the National Association of Legal Secretaries [International], *The Career Legal Secretary,* rev. ed.

victim of a crime does not prosecute a criminal; crimes are considered an injury to society, so they are prosecuted by the government. A civil action is brought by one party against another party. Two types of remedies are available in a civil case: monetary relief and equitable relief. **Monetary relief** is compensation that consists of money that is paid to a party for an injury. **Equitable relief** is compensation other than money that is given to a party for an injury, such as the return of a person's property that was wrongfully taken.

Monetary relief:
Compensation by
money for an injury.

Equitable relief:
Compensation other
than money for an
injury.

Individuals Involved   Two types of laws apply to individuals: public laws and private laws. Public laws apply to everyone. Private laws apply only to individuals who fall under the jurisdiction of a law by circumstance. For example, property tax laws apply only to home owners.

Nature of the Law   A law can be either substantive or procedural in nature. **Substantive laws** are laws that govern society. They create, define, and regulate rights. If a substantive law is broken, the injured party is entitled to **damages,** or compensation for the injuries. How does one go about recovering damages? This question is answered in **procedural law,** which sets forth methods to enforce a person's rights and tells a person how to obtain relief.

Substantive law: A law
that creates, defines, or
regulates rights.

Damages:
Compensation for a
wrong or an injury.

Procedural law: A law
that defines procedures
of a lawsuit.

Source of the Law   A law is categorized by its source. Constitutional law encompasses the U.S. Constitution and the constitution of each state. Federal statutory law encompasses laws passed by the U.S. Congress. State statutory law encompasses laws passed by the state legislatures and local governments. Case law encompasses court decisions resulting from legal controversies.

CLASSES AND AUTHORITY OF LAW

There are three classes of law: primary authority, secondary authority, and search tools.

Primary Authority

Primary authority consists of laws made by the three branches of government: executive, legislative, and judicial. These are laws enacted by federal and state legislatures and administrative agencies. Primary authority is given the most weight and consideration in a case. Some disputes arise concerning the meaning or intent of a statute or both. The judicial branch of the government, the courts, interpret the statutes and apply them to the facts of a dispute. A court's ruling results in case law, which is also primary authority. In the U.S. legal system, a court's opinion constitutes a precedent to be followed in subsequent similar cases.

A legislature also enacts procedural law, which consist of laws governing the legal procedure used to redress wrong or injury. The judicial branch creates laws governing the rules and procedures of the court system. In addition, each court creates rules, called **local rules,** to be followed in that court only. These procedural laws and court rules are also primary authority. Therefore, primary authority consists of constitutions, statutes, judicial opinions, court rules, and administrative regulations and decisions.

Local rules: Rules
created by an individual
court that applies in
that court only.

Statutes   The most commonly used statutes are organized according to subject matter. The U.S. Code is categorized into fifty titles, each title being a separate topic. Each title is divided into sections.

Large libraries contain federal statutes, state statutes for their particular state, and the statutes of other states. Small libraries contain state statutes for their particular state and may or may not contain federal statutes.

Annotated: Referring to a publication that contains a law and other pertinent information about the law.

Unannotated: Referring to a publication that contains the text of a law only.

Pocket part: An addition to a book that updates its contents.

Reporter: A published volume of court decisions.

Series: A set of reporters in numeric order.

Slip opinion: A printed copy of a judicial opinion that is distributed soon after the decision is rendered.

Advance sheet: A softcover book of decisions that is circulated soon after a decision is rendered.

Full text: Consisting of a verbatim text that allows every word in a document to be retrieved by a researcher.

Statutes may be either **annotated** or **unannotated.** Annotated statutes contain historical information concerning amendments and additions to a statute, citations to judicial opinions interpreting a statute, and references to secondary sources that are relevant to a statute. Unannotated statutes contain a statute, delete repealed statutes, and insert all amendments and additions to a statute.

In a library, annotated statutes are placed where they are most accessible. Statutes that apply to a firm's jurisdiction are given priority over other state statutes. In large firms, more than one set of state statutes may be provided to accommodate a firm's employees. Placing statutes on a high shelf is not a good idea. Unannotated statutes are often placed in an attorney's or a legal assistant's office so that they are accessible whenever needed.

As new laws are passed, it is essential to have immediate access to them. Legal publishing companies provide an update service called Advance Legislative Service. New laws are published in **pocket parts,** which are additions that are inserted into a pocket inside the back cover of the applicable volume. A pocket part uses the same numbering system as the bound volume. It brings a law current to the beginning of the year. Every five or six years, a new edition of the U.S. Code is published with supplements being incorporated into the new volumes.

Pocket parts must be inserted into the back of the applicable volumes as soon as they are received. They should not be allowed to accumulate because employees will not have the most recent law at their disposal.

Judicial Opinions   Books called **reporters** contain the text of judicial opinions as they are made. Federal reporters report federal judicial opinions, and state reporters report state judicial opinions.

Thousands of volumes of reporters are published, and the volumes of each reporter are numbered consecutively. Since a reporter has hundreds of volumes, it may have more than one **series,** or set. When the volumes reach a high number, a publisher will name a new series and begin numbering its volumes from 1. For example, California Reports has four series: California Reports, 1950–1934; California Reports, 2nd series, 1934–1969; California Reports, 3rd series, 1969–1991; and California Reports, 4th series, 1991–.

Reporters contain hundreds of volumes and occupy a lot of shelf space in a library. They are placed in numeric order according to series, starting with the first series. Some libraries, especially small libraries, do not contain a first series because it is outdated and a library's space is limited. Other libraries may have a first series on microfilm or CD-ROM.

When an opinion is first printed, it is known as a **slip opinion.** Most law libraries do not receive slip opinions as they are made unless they are specifically requested. About four weeks after a slip opinion is printed, it is published in an **advance sheet,** which is a pamphlet that contains the **full text** of opinions released in the same time period. Advance sheets are sent to law libraries weekly and are placed at the end of a reporter set. After a period of time, the cases reported in the advance sheets are accumulated and bound together in a new volume. Once a new volume is received, the advance sheets may be discarded and the new volume placed at the end of the set. The case citations do not change.

Court Rules   Every law library contains court rules, which were first developed by the Judiciary Act of 1789, passed at the first session of Congress. They are court procedures that must be followed in cases before that court. They relate to such matters as filing papers, pretrial procedures, pretrial requirements, filing fees, and so on.

Court rules have three purposes:

1. To aid the court in expediting the business that comes before it
2. To establish uniform procedure for the conduct of a court's business
3. To provide parties to a lawsuit with procedural information and instructions on bringing the matter before a court.

In addition to court rules governing federal and state courts, each federal and state court creates local rules. Local rules may be different from court rules of general application.

The U.S. Supreme Court has rule-making authority over other federal courts. It has created rules for use in the federal district courts. In addition to these rules, individual lower federal courts have created rules that govern an individual court only. Every law library must have court rules for each court in which an attorney practices.

Court rules are placed in a library where they can be retrieved quickly. Large firms may have more than one copy of court rules to accommodate many employees.

Court rules are updated by a publisher or the particular court. Most often, they are contained in a three-ring binder to facilitate updating. When the updates are received, they must be quickly inserted into a volume.

Administrative Regulations and Decisions   Administrative law governs the powers and procedures of administrative agencies. Administrative agencies are established by Congress and are government entities, other than a court or legislative body, that affect the rights of people through their rules and decisions. Agencies make rules, adjudicate issues, provide licenses, distribute money, investigate matters, prosecute violators, mediate disputes, and exercise whatever other powers a legislature mandates. Agency regulations look very much like statutes.

There is no reporter of agency decisions, such as the West Reporter System for Federal Courts. Some agencies publish their own opinions. A few private publishers publish administrative and judicial opinions on particular subjects, such as the *United States Patents Quarterly*.

Many state administrative agencies exist. State agency administrative regulations and decisions are published chronologically, although some states codify their regulations. Some state administrative rulings are privately published in looseleaf reports or by services. State administrative agency rulings are not as uniformly published as federal administrative rulings.

Only large libraries contain administrative rulings. Since these rulings are very specialized, they should be accessible by the attorneys and legal assistants who utilize them. Administrative rulings are updated like reporters. In other words, many agencies provide a subscription service for their rulings.

Secondary Authority

Secondary authority is anything other than primary authority that aids a court in reaching a decision. At some point, primary source material reached such voluminous proportions that it was necessary to provide aids in identifying and explaining the law; secondary authority was developed for this purpose. Secondary authority is used to persuade. It is not considered in lieu of primary authority but is used in addition to primary authority.

Secondary authority includes commentary material written by legal scholars or experts in a particular field. It encompasses treatises, periodicals, dictionaries, and encyclopedias.

Treatises are legal commentaries on various subjects of law. Their purpose is to simplify and explain the law. Treatises can be either federal or state in nature.

Periodicals are booklets concerning articles about the law. The articles describe and analyze the law and, in some cases, make recommendations for changes in the law. To provide access to all the articles published in a legal periodical, indexes are published. The most established index service is the *Index to Legal Periodicals*, which dates back to 1908.

Every law library has a legal dictionary, and large libraries may contain more than one. Dictionaries do not restate the law or act as sources of the law. They are reference tools. However, if the meaning of a word is in dispute, the definition in a legal dictionary is quoted and is considered secondary authority.

Encyclopedias are volumes that contain statements on principles of law and are organized alphabetically by subject matter. They are categorized into broad topics that are subdivided into narrower topics and act as an index and guide to the law. Some states have encyclopedias devoted to their own laws.

Large libraries contain many volumes of secondary authority. Small libraries contain legal dictionaries and some periodicals but have very few treatises and encyclopedias. Volumes of secondary authority are placed according to their numeric order. Dictionaries are usually placed in a central area of a library.

As the law changes, editors will write some annotations to commentaries of treatises that supersede older annotations. Many treatises are updated by pocket parts, **restatements** are rewritten, and the new material is contained in an updated series. Other treatises are updated as the law changes.

The *Current Law Index* is published monthly. Most indexes are published quarterly and are accumulated to provide a new volume each year. Encyclopedia volumes have pocket parts and replacement volumes issued periodically. Legal dictionaries are not updated, but it is a good practice to replace them with a new volume every seven to ten years. Secondary authority is shown in Exhibit 14.2.

Search Tools and Form Books

Search tools help a researcher find primary authority. Form books help an attorney and legal assistant draft legal documents and assist in the procedures of a case. Search tools and form books are never cited as a source of law; they are tools only. Most libraries contain both.

Search tools consists of digests and citators. **Digests** are commonly-used search tools that list case citations that pertain to a particular subject or statute. The main body of a digest is arranged by topic like an encyclopedia. Each topic is divided into sub-topics. An example of a digest is shown in Exhibit 14.3.

A **citator** is a valuable addition to a law library. Citators give a researcher the current status of a law. Statutes are often **repealed,** or revoked, and case law is often **overruled.** It is important to know the status of a law before quoting it. A citator will inform a researcher whether a case was **affirmed** (confirmed), overruled, or mentioned in another case. A citator also provides a list of references to sources that were cited in a case. Each statute and case must be checked in a citator.

One main function of attorneys and legal assistants is drafting legal documents. Many types of legal documents are used: pleadings, contracts, wills, trusts, and deeds, to name a few. Form books contain samples of documents that attorneys have used successfully in the past. The forms are not comprehensive enough to be used in all situations, but they act as a guide. They are valuable tools for preparing documents. A variety of form books are available for each state.

Restatement: A series of volumes authored by legal scholars that describe the law, its changes, and future direction of the law.

Digest: A collection embodying the chief matter of numerous books, articles, court decisions, and so on, usually arranged alphabetically.

Citator: A set of books that provide the judicial history and interpretation of reported decisions.

Repeal: To abrogate or annul an existing law by the enactment of a statute that declares the former law revoked.

Overrule: To reject or supersede an existing judicial opinion; to invalidate.

Affirm: To confirm an existing judicial opinion.

EXHIBIT 14.2 Sample Secondary Authority
Source: West Publishing Co.

EXHIBIT 14.3 Sample Digest
Source: West Publishing Co.

LAW LIBRARY ORGANIZATION AND PROCEDURES

Every law office, corporate legal department, and government agency has a library or access to a law library. Some libraries consist of very few books, and others contain thousands of books. Most libraries contain electronic resources. The manner in which these resources are managed determines a library's organization.

Maintaining a library is extremely important. Every legal assistant should understand how a library is maintained. A comprehension of law library maintenance requires knowledge of its technology and systems. While no two law libraries are alike, they all have common elements.

Library Size

Law libraries are described according to size. A library's size depends on the size, specialties, and resources of a firm. A sole practitioner or a small firm in general practice may need a large library but may not be able to afford it. A small boutique firm with one specialty would not need a large library and would find a very small library sufficient.

Skeletal library: A small library containing only essential material.

Small libraries that contain only the books essential for the lawyers' needs are called **skeletal libraries.** These consist of state statutes, case reporters for a specific jurisdiction in which the lawyers practice, form books, and a legal dictionary. A skeletal library may also contain a treatise in a particular area of law. If more in-depth research is necessary, a researcher must go to a nearby county library or law school library or use an on-line legal database on the Internet. Some libraries give the public access to the entire library and others only to certain sections of the library. Some law schools forbid public access, and others charge for library use.

Complete library: A library containing a comprehensive collection of material.

Libraries that contain a comprehensive collection of the laws of the country are called **complete libraries.** These are very rare because of their cost. Complete law libraries are found in large law schools, some large agencies, courthouses, and major city libraries. A complete law library has over 300,000 hardcover volumes, microform, CD-ROMs, and access to legal and nonlegal databases. The largest complete law library in the United States is the Library of Congress in Washington, D.C., with more than two million volumes. Harvard Law School Library contains over 1,500,000 volumes. Large law libraries, such as the one shown in Exhibit 14.4, are found in large law firms, law schools, courthouses, and administrative agencies. An average large

EXHIBIT 14.4 A Large Law Library

library contains about 50,000 volumes, microform, CD-ROMs, and access to legal and nonlegal databases.

Types of Library Organization

Three types of library organization are used: centralized, decentralized, and satellite.

Centralized Organization A centralized library is found in one location that has been set aside by a firm. All library materials are found in one location. A centralized library provides a work area for those using the library, usually one seat for every five attorneys. A small firm with a centralized library may combine the library with the conference room. This combination creates problems by making the library inaccessible when a conference is being held. A large firm that occupies several floors of a building may designate one full floor as the library, depending on the size of the library. Most large firms have a centralized library.

Library cooperative: A group organized to pool library resources for the benefit of the group.

Sole practitioners and small firms that cannot afford large libraries often pool their resources and form a **library cooperative.** These firms are located in the same building or close to each other. A portion of a floor is dedicated to a centralized library for the participating lawyers. Each lawyer pays his or her proportionate share of the cost of the library. This arrangement works well for sole practitioners.

Decentralized Organization A decentralized library is distributed throughout a firm. The books are placed on bookshelves lining the office walls in the same location as the attorneys using them. For example, books used by a tax attorney are placed near the tax attorney's offices. Corporate law books are placed near the corporate attorney's offices. There is no library work area in a decentralized library. Attorneys and legal assistants use the books in their individual offices. Sole practitioners and small firms may have decentralized libraries.

Scattering a library throughout an office has three advantages:

1. The books are close to the attorneys and the legal assistants using them.
2. The books are decorative and give the office a nice appearance.
3. The books act as a noise buffer to keep an office quieter. For example, lining the walls of a copy room with books reduces noise from the copy machine.

The disadvantages of a decentralized library are that books are not readily accessible when needed, they are often misplaced, and they are kept in offices and not returned to the shelf.

Satellite Organization Satellite libraries are found in large firms with a large centralized library. A large firm that occupies several floors of a building locates a library in the brightest location, usually on the top floor. The attorneys and legal assistants must use the elevator and walk a distance to reach the library. Going back and forth to the library many times a day may be inconvenient. Some firms will remove specialty books from a central library and put a satellite library close to the employees using these books.

Tax and labor libraries are the most common satellite libraries. Satellite libraries are convenient for attorneys and legal assistants using the books but are difficult to maintain and control. In addition, other employees of a firm do not have convenient access to the books in a satellite library.

ETHICS ALERT

Library Maintenance

A law library must be maintained so that it is always current. The status of the law is of utmost importance to judges, lawyers, and clients. *The outcome of a client's case may depend on thorough legal research.* A California attorney was sued by a client for not adequately researching the issues of a case. In that case, the court awarded the client $100,000 (*Smith v. Lewis,* 13 Cal. 3d 349 [1975]). In another California case, an attorney was sanctioned for incorrectly citing a case. Because the law is changing and new cases are being decided daily, updated research may mean the difference between winning and losing a case.

Update service: A service that keeps books current.

Legal publishers provide an **update service** with their products. As new laws are made and enacted, they are automatically sent to subscribers. Supplemental material should be inserted into the proper books as soon as possible so that the attorneys and legal assistants have current law at their disposal. *The outcome of a client's case may depend on the timelines of this function.*

ETHICS ALERT

Law books must be updated constantly. In small and medium firms that do not employ a full-time librarian, it is often a legal assistant's duty to maintain a library. Library update services are also available. These are private companies that employ legal assistants or other personnel to go into legal offices and update their libraries for a fee.

Firms have a substantial investment in their library. The cost of maintaining a law library is very high. It is also expensive to keep the books and electronic resources current. Ninety percent of a law library's budget is spent to update law resources. The increased availability of information, such as legal and nonlegal databases and CD-ROMs, results in increased costs. Law firms are constantly challenged to maintain an adequate library and to keep costs down.

Library Checkout Systems

All libraries, whether centralized, decentralized, or satellite, must have a system that will locate every book in them. The system must reduce the possibility of lost or misplaced books. Books often leave the library for use in individual offices, are taken home, or are taken to court. It is easy for a book to be lost or misplaced. A misplaced book results in areas of the law not being accessible when needed. Legal assistants spend many frustrating hours looking for lost books.

A library checkout system consists of procedures to locate library materials. These procedures must be followed by each member of a legal team. Noncompliance with retrieval procedures results in lost library materials. A system is effective only if all employees participate in it.

The three most common systems used in law firm libraries are the out card, the bar code, and the library card system.

Out Card   A library out-card system is used like an out card system for files described in Chapter 13. An out card system is inexpensive and easy to set up and maintain. However, problems arise when employees do not take the time to write their names on the card or the cards fall off the shelf out of place. Library out cards also tend to cause a library to look messy.

Bar Code   Some firms have bar codes placed on their books, and the system is used like the one described in Chapter 13 for bar coded files. Bar coding makes it easy to check out books, maintains an accurate location of all books at all times, and is easy to operate. However, problems arise if the computer is down or the equipment is inoperable.

Library Card   A popular checkout system for library books is the library card system. Each book has a library card placed in a pocket on the inside cover of the book. A library card contains the book's name, author, and other pertinent information about the book. As the book leaves the library, the library card is placed into a card box or card holder behind the person's name taking the book. When the book is re-

TECH TIPS
Library Management Software

The following is a sample of related software:

> *Interliant:* Interliant—www.interliant.com (software for intranets and extranets)
> *TLC Total Library Computerization:* On Point, Inc.—www.onpointinc.com (for smaller libraries)
> *SydneyPLUS:* SydneyPLUS-ILS—www.ils.ca (software for special libraries)

Software mentioned in this sidebar is for informational purposes only and is not for the purpose of endorsing products.

turned, the person replaces the card in the book. This system is fast and easy for law firm employees and requires little effort to maintain. However, cards may be misplaced or lost, and books may be replaced without their cards being inserted.

LAW LIBRARY TECHNOLOGY

Technology has had a great affect on the traditional law library. Law libraries are no longer book depositories; they are now considered information management and transfer centers. Just as technology promised a paperless office, it now promises a bookless library. Some experts predict that an electronic library will be here soon. Others say that an electronic library is somewhere in the distant future. Technology has become a vital part of the law library but will not replace books until sometime in the future.

People, including attorneys, love books. Humans have been trained to absorb information from print media, and that is not likely to change soon. Recent sales figures from Amazon.com attest to this fact. However, law libraries are getting smaller because they are implementing technology by combining it with law books. Fewer books and more technology are being purchased.

Five types of technology are used in law libraries:

◆ On-line legal and nonlegal databases
◆ Microform
◆ CD-ROM
◆ E-mail and telefacsimile (fax) transmission
◆ The Internet

On-Line Legal and Nonlegal Databases

On-line legal and nonlegal databases are the most common type of technology found in law offices today. An on-line legal database is a database of laws compiled by a publisher who charges customers to use it. Legal research conducted with an on-line legal database is called **computer-assisted legal research** (CALR). Full-text copies of statutes, court opinions, regulations, agency rulings, and other material are available. They are accessed by a telephone line in the same manner used to make a telephone call. A **modem** is used to connect the telephone with the database. When a case or statute is found and a user desires a hard copy of a document, the database materials are downloaded from the central computer to the user's computer over telephone lines. The central computer and the user's personal computer "talk" to each other when sending and receiving information.

The two primary CALR systems are Westlaw, from IT Thompson's West Group, and Lexis, from Reed Elsevier, both of which provide access to full-text legal documents through a computer. Other on-line legal databases provide an **abstract system,** which does not provide the full text of a decision but instead provides an abstract, or summary, of a law.

Computer-assisted legal research: Legal research on a legal database accessed by computer.

Modem: A device that allows remote computers to transmit and receive data using telephone lines; short for modulator/demodulator.

Abstract system: A collection of abstracted, or summarized, documents.

Information may be quickly retrieved with a legal database. Learning to use CALR takes practice, training, and patience. One must know how to search a database and how to use the proprietary software necessary to access a database. One must learn how to conduct a search and how to narrow a search for faster results. Many law firms use CALR with book research for more comprehensive research projects.

Nonlegal databases operate the same as legal databases but contain nonlegal information. Many law firms subscribe to nonlegal databases and find them useful in cases that are technical in nature or that require specific information. For example, if a case involves the construction of a complex electrical plant, a lawyer may need the answer to a technical engineering question, or, in a personal injury or medical malpractice case, a lawyer may need a definition of a certain type of injury or medical treatment. Among the nonlegal databases used by law firms are Dun & Bradstreet's credit ratings, Standard & Poor's company profiles, and databases that provide economic statistics and stock market data.

Legal and nonlegal databases may also be accessed from the Internet. Westlaw is found at www.westlaw.com and Lexis Xchange at www.lexis-nexis.com. To access a database from the Internet, one needs an account and a password and must pay the requisite fees. Accessing a database from the Internet requires no specialized software (except a browser) and can be accessed from an individual computer. It is convenient for traveling attorneys and legal assistants.

Microform

Microform is the process of storing information photographically in reduced form. It involves printing miniature images of documents on film or paper and consists of microfilm and microfiche. Microfilm is 35-millimeter film that stores a large number of pages that run continuously in sequence and that need no alteration. Microfiche is a sheet of microfilm that comes in the form of a card that is used to store a small number of pages. One 100-foot roll of microfilm contains five large books. Six microfiche cards are needed to photograph one book. The new generation of microfiche, called ultrafiche, will hold more data than microfiche.

Microfilm is the most popular method of microform in law libraries. Volumes of books can be put on microfilm and stored in a small desk drawer. After documents have been photographed, the film is inserted into a reader/printer that enlarges the document on a screen for viewing. Each microform image can be converted into a hard copy if desired.

Microform is not new technology. Miniaturization of documents on paper has been used since the 1830s. Banks have been photographing records, mostly canceled checks, for storage purposes since 1930. Libraries began to use microform in the 1950s. The use of microform expanded into the legal profession in the 1960s and has been a popular method of storing records and documents. Law libraries are adding more microform than hard copy volumes to their libraries because microform is less expensive to purchase, store, and catalog.

Microform is especially useful for preserving volumes of out-of-print law books. Many books printed after 1850 were printed with acidic paper, and the pages are now crumbling into dust on library shelves. Since these books cannot be replaced, they are being put on microfilm. Microfilm will last about 200 years, so long-term preservation of the material is ensured.

CD-ROM

CD-ROM: Compact disk read-only memory. A computer disk that stores a large amount of data.

Megabyte: A computer term used to measure data: one megabyte contains about one million characters.

CD-ROM (compact disk read-only memory) disks can be found in our homes and offices and contain software, text, music, or movies. In a law library, a single 4.25-inch disc, 1/32 of an inch thick, stores about 300,000 manuscript pages, or 250 large law books. It is the equivalent of 1,500 conventional diskettes, or 600 **megabytes** (about 600 million characters) of data. CD-ROMs are found in most law libraries. A library can expand without the necessity of acquiring more library space and be accessible to traveling lawyers away from the office. Books that are not frequently used can be replaced by CD-ROM, freeing valuable library shelf space.

Legal publishers make material found in law books available on CD-ROM and sell the disks to their customers. CD-ROMs are available for every area of law, both federal and state. An example of a legal CD-ROM is West's *Federal Taxation Library,* which contains statutes, legal history, regulations, judicial decisions, administrative materials, and a digest of judicial decisions and administrative materials pertaining to federal taxation.

CD-ROM drive: A device that is connected to a computer and reads CD-ROM disks.

A **CD-ROM drive,** found on most individual computers today, is needed to access the material, which is displayed on a computer screen. CD-ROMs allow faster and more precise access to the information. A researcher can search the contents of a disk (250 law books) faster than through an on-line database. If a firm has a network or intranet, a CD-ROM drive is not necessary for each computer. Users can access the information from their computers through the network or the intranet. Firms use CD-ROM jukeboxes (Chapter 13) to make many disks available to users through a network or an intranet. A jukebox is a CD-ROM storage device that can hold as few as six and as many as 500 disks. With all of a firm's library material contained in a jukebox, lost or misplaced materials are a thing of the past.

With CD-ROMs, a large law firm with a centralized library can make portions of its library available to other areas of the firm, making access to the library more convenient. However, unless a firm has many CD-ROMs of the same title, only one person at a time has access to the information in 250 books rather than 250 people using 250 books.

One problem with CD-ROMs is that their data are often not current. As laws change, a disk must be updated by its publisher. Since laws change daily, providing current material has been a challenge for legal CD-ROM publishers. Because of the time and processes needed to produce and ship them, they are out of date when they are received. It is difficult to tell how current the material is on a CD-ROM or what changes have been made from a previous edition. Additionally, CD-ROMs contain only recent statutes. If a legal assistant needed to know what the law was twenty years ago, the information would not be available on CD-ROM.

User interface: The method of operation developed by a legal publisher for its CD-ROM products.

Law firms have been reluctant to replace law books with CD-ROMs and have had problems with CD-ROM technology. Each legal publisher's CD-ROMs operate differently because of their unique **user interface,** or screen methods of operation. They also use different search protocols, and this has caused training difficulties. With multiple CD-ROMs from different vendors, a user's ability to effectively use the products is reduced. Some CD-ROMs are not easily installed on networks and are not compatible with basic word processing programs.

It was forecast that CD-ROM technology would someday replace microform, but law firms have been reluctant to do so. The lifetime of a CD-ROM is currently ten to thirty years—not long enough to replace microform's longevity. Many people see CD-ROM technology as transitional until information contained on them is moved to the Internet. It has been predicted that CD-ROMs will become obsolete in the near future.

E-Mail and Telefacsimile (Fax) Transmission

Telefacsimile: A system of transmitting documents over telephone wires.

E-mail and **telefacsimile** (fax) machines send documents from one location to another electronically over telephone lines. E-mail and fax machines are standard equipment in law firms and large law libraries and bar association libraries. They give attorneys and legal assistants immediate access to materials not otherwise readily available to them.

As law firm libraries are stepping into their role of information centers, they must have access to a variety of information that may be needed by researchers. Bar association libraries that provide library services to their members deliver materials by e-mail or fax. Previously, legal assistants and other law firm personnel had to go to a library to copy materials. As cities become more congested, the time it takes to travel from one end of a city to another is a cost factor in obtaining the material. In addition, a library was inaccessible to firms a long distance away. E-mail and fax machines have solved these problems and have increased the accessibility of information.

Large firms with large libraries often lend materials to other firms and provide library materials to their branch offices. With the use of a fax machine, a book or document is sent over the telephone wires and need not leave the library, eliminating the need to monitor a book's or document's location. The fax machine has reduced the number of lost materials considerably.

The Internet

The Internet is the information superhighway that is absorbing other legal media types, such as print, CD-ROM, and on-line database services. Access to the information superhighway has put small firms on a par with large law firms that have large libraries and therefore offer more resources to a client. According to the 1999 Technology Survey conducted by the National Federation of Paralegal Associations (NFPA), more than 75 percent of the respondents conduct legal and factual research on the Internet.

Access to federal and state statutes and court decisions is available on the Internet for free. Access to this information is partially due to the assertive position of government agencies in placing their information on the Internet and to entrepreneurs who seek to bring viewers to their legal Web sites. These legal Web sites put the Internet in a position to be a serious research tool.

However, as of this writing, the Internet is not a better research tool than other, conventional types of technology used in law libraries. A great deal of information that lawyers and librarians need is not available from the Internet, such as secondary authority material. It is estimated that less than 20 percent of information is committed to the Internet, with the remainder found in books and on CD-ROM. Additionally, the credibility of the source of the information is uncertain, and the current nature of the material is questionable. Web sites that require a fee, such as Westlaw and Lexis Xchange, have an advantage because their publishers guarantee the reliability of the information.

Another problem with conducting legal research on the Web is its poor classification system, which makes law difficult to locate. The question is not whether the information is available on the Internet but how to find it. According to a recent Gartner Group study, a typical computer user spends up to 50 percent of their time searching for the information they need. The results from queries on a search engine are often so vast that it takes longer to do research on the Internet. For example, if a person searched for law regarding stockbroker bankruptcies, he may get hundreds of results that would have to be reviewed before the desired information is found.

The Internet is an important medium of gathering and disseminating information in new and powerful ways. The first decade of the new millennium will see a refinement of legal material available on the Internet, which will provide numerous benefits to law firm personnel.

Electronic Citation

The emergence of electronic legal research has created the need for new methods of citing the material. Traditional legal cites refer to the volume and page number of a law book, but if a case was not found in a law book, how is it cited?

The *Harvard Blue Book: A Uniform System of Citation* is used as a guide to legal citation. With reference to citing electronic documents, it states in rule 10.8.1(a):

> When a case is unreported and available on a widely used electronic database, then it may be cited to that database. Provide the case name, docket number, database identifier, court name, and full date of the most recent major disposition of the case. The data-

CYBERSITES

Finding Legal Research Sites on the Web

Findlaw—www.findlaw.com
The Legal List—www.lcp.com/The-Legal-List

Court Rules

www.llrx.com

General Regulations

www.access.gpo.gov

Federal Court Locator

www.law.vill.edu/Fed-Ct

Tech Legislation

www.lechlawjournal.com

Search Engines

www.fastsearch.com
www.lawcrawler.com
www.dejanews.com
www.dogpile.com

Legal Ethics

www.abanet.org
www.legalethics.com

Attorney Finders

www.martindale.com

Expert Witnesses

www.expertwitness.com

State Law

www.law.house.gov
www.prairienet.org/~scruffy

base identifier must contain enough information to enable a reader to identify the database and enable a reader to identify the database and find the case. If the database has identifying codes or numbers that uniquely identify the case (as do Lexis-Nexis and Westlaw after 1986), these must be given. Screen or page numbers, if assigned, should be preceded by an asterisk. . . . Cases that have not been assigned unique database identifiers should provide all relevant information.

The American Association of Law Libraries (AALL) recognized the need for a new citation format for electronic materials and recommended that a legal cite include the case name, year of the decision, specific court, a consecutively assigned case number, and paragraph number for the exact location of the quote. The case number is a consecutive number that refers to the number of decisions in a year. For example, the following case was the 235th decision in 1996:

Smith v. Jones	1996	6th Cir.	235	15
Case name	Year	Court	Number	Paragraph

In 1996, the ABA adopted the AALL's recommendation but suggested that the traditional site be included as follows:

Smith v. Jones	1996	6th Cir.	235	15	22 F. 3d 955
Case name	Year	Court	Number	Paragraph	Traditional cite

Many other groups have made recommendations for citing electronic documents, including the American Psychological Association and the Modern Language Association of America (MLA). While each group has slightly different recommendations, all seem to emphasize this basic format: name of author, title of document in quotes, version, date of document or last revision, protocol and address, and access path or directories. The MLA recommends that a Web site be cited as follows: For a professional site, name of page, host of page, date of last revision of site (if known), and URL (see Chapter 10) as follows:

Portuguese Language Page. U of Chicago. 1 May 1997. http://humanities.uchicago.edu/romance/port

The *Brief Guide to Citing Government Publications,* by the Government Publications Department, recommends the following citation format:

Name of law, code designation, date of law, URL, last revision date

For the Federal Register:

"Protection of Historic Properties." 59 Federal Register (3 Oct. 1994). ONLINE. Available: telnet://swais.access.gpo.gov . [26 Feb. 1996].

For the Congressional Record:

Ford, Rep. [TN]. "Tribute to Rhodes College Mock Trial Team." Congressional Record ONLINE 25 May 1995. GPO Access. Available: http://bubba.ucc.okstate.edu/wais/GPOAccess . [3 March 1996].

For Congressional bills: U.S. House. 104th Congress, 1st Session. H.R. 1950, Newborns' and Mothers' Health Protection Act of 1995. ONLINE. GPO Access. Available: http://www.lib.ncsu.edu/stacks/gpo/ <104th Congress>. [8 June 1995].

For GAO reports:

U.S. General Accounting Office. U.S. Vietnam Relations: Issues and Implications. ONLINE. GPO Access. 1995. Available: http://bubba.ucc.okstate.edu/wais/GPOAccess GAO "Blue Book" Reports. [30 Dec. 1995].

For statutes:

U.S. Code: Abandoned Shipwrecks (1995). Title 43 U.S. Code, Ch. 39 ONLINE. GPO Access. Available: telnet://swais.access.gpo.gov [1 Feb. 1996].

CO Rev Stat § 1-40-107 (1996 through 2nd Reg Sess, 60th Gen Ass)

For microform:

American Statistics Index (ASI*):* U.S. Department of Health and Human Services. 1992 AFDC Recipient Characteristics Study. Washington: The Department, 1994. (1994 ASI microfiche 4584-7).

Statistical Reference Index (*SRI*): Delaware. Department of Labor. Snapshot Delaware 93. Newark: Delaware Department of Labor, 1994. (1994 SRI Microfiche S1405-4).

As of 1999, no universally accepted citation system for electronic documents exists. The trend is for states to adopt the recommendations of the American Bar Association (ABA). In 1999, seventeen states had adopted, or shown an interest in adopting, the ABA's recommendation. Courts and legislatures are looking at the subject. It will be interesting to watch the evolution of this important area. The web sites listed in the following sidebar list sites will help you monitor this issue.

COURT FORMS, FORM FILES, AND KNOWLEDGE BANKS

Court form, form files, and knowledge banks are found in law libraries. Each employee in a law office must have access to court forms and knowledge banks. Court

CYBERSITES

Finding Electronic Citation Rules on the Web

VersusLaw—www.versuslaw.com

PaLAWnet—www.palawnet.com

Court of Appeals for the Fifth Circuit—http://courtstuff.com/5th/index.html

AALL Task Force on Citation Formats—www.aallnet.org/committee/citation/task_force.html

ABA Special Committee on Citation Issues—www.abanet.org/ftp/pub/citation/home.html

Harvard Blue Book, the Electronic Bluebook—http://members.aol.com/EBlueBook

MLA Handbook for Writers—www.mla.org/main_stl-nf.htm#sources

Basic Legal Citation, by Peter Martin—www2.law.corbell.edu/cgi-bin/foliocgi.exe/citation

Documenting Electronic Sources on the Internet, by Andrew Harback—http://falcom.eku.edu/honors/beyond-mla

How Technology Is Changing Citation, by Gene Tyburski—www.cirtualchase.com/LegalResearcher/Citation.htm

Citation of Legal and Non-Legal Electronic Database Information, by Elliot Person—www.michbar.org/publications/citation.htm

Electronic Citation Guide for Legal Materials, by Ruth Bohill—http://law.anu.edu.au/nglrw/lr3.htm

Guide to the Bluebook, by Jim Olmsted—www.law.uregon.edu/~olmsted/CITE%20FORM%20FAQS.html

Brief Guide to Citing Government Publications—www.lib.memphis.edu/gpo/citeweb.htm

forms are forms that are used in specific courts. Knowledge banks, also known as brief banks, are copies of work previously completed that may be used again or used as a guide to complete new projects.

Court Forms

Every law office must have an adequate supply of court forms, which are form documents used in a specific court. Each federal and state court has specific forms used by that particular court. Federal court forms and state court forms are available. Some court forms are used throughout all state courts, and others are used in a specific court only. Law offices use hundreds of court forms.

Court forms must be located quickly. All forms relating to a specific court must be clearly identifiable. In addition, court forms change often. Therefore, a library has a system to keep all forms current and up-to-date.

There are three methods of storing court forms: manually, on masters that are photocopied, and computer programs.

Court forms that are stored manually are filed in filing cabinets. These forms are rarely filed alphabetically by title. A legal assistant looking for wage garnishment forms would have a difficult time locating them in that type of an alphabetical system; for example, an affidavit for writ of garnishment would be found at the beginning of the alphabet and a writ of garnishment would be found at the end of the alphabet. A legal assistant would have to look through hundreds of forms to find the correct ones and would need to know the exact name of all the necessary forms to find them. If all wage garnishment forms were found in one place, it would save a legal assistant's time.

Court forms are normally organized alphabetically by subject matter. All forms relating to a particular subject will then be found in one place. Some firms store court forms by a numeric filing system. Each form is given a number, and each number gives a user information regarding a form, including subject and applicable court. File folders and labels may be color coded in a numeric system to further identify a form.

Photocopier-created forms are stored in three-ring binders to save space. The binders are indexed and divided into subjects. Only one copy of each form, the master form, is inserted into a binder. That form is photocopied when it is needed. Everyone using the form must understand the importance of returning the original form to the binder after photocopying. It is frustrating not have access to the correct form.

Problems with storage and access to court forms are solved with computer-generated forms. There are software programs that provide court forms and assist a user in completing them. They are printed after completion. Computer-generated forms are convenient and save space. All software containing court forms must be updatable to accommodate frequent changes in the forms. If an outdated form is used, a court may reject the document. Before using computer-generated forms, check with the court to determine its policy. Some courts require that a form be a specific color and will not allow printed forms unless they are produced on the correct color of paper. Additionally, some courts will not accept court forms printed on a dot-matrix printer.

Some courts undertake responsibility for distributing new court forms. Most courts, however, do not want to be burdened with this responsibility and so delegate it to a printing company, court form software company, or court forms service. The legal industry supports many court form service companies that will print and distribute forms to their subscribers. They will automatically send new and updated forms when these forms become effective. Automated court forms software is updated by the publisher.

Form Files

Forms other than court forms are used by a law office. These forms include deeds, corporate forms, and forms required by government agencies. These forms may be integrated into a firm's court form filing system or have their own filing system by subject.

Knowledge Banks

The knowledge of employees is a firm's most valuable asset. Managing this knowledge to its maximum potential is a challenge. One method used is a knowledge bank, which consists of samples of research and documents prepared by a firm and used in the same manner as form books. If used effectively, a knowledge bank will provide a firm with many benefits.

A knowledge bank contains briefs, research memoranda, opinion letters, pleadings, discovery requests, contracts, leases, and articles that may be useful in a future case. Eighty percent of work done in most law firms is not new. The work of attorneys and legal assistants is often similar to a previous case. If a firm can realize increased efficiencies on 80 percent of its work, it will increase productivity, resulting in increased profits. Keeping copies of briefs and research memorandums regarding an issue or subject saves employees' time in researching that issue again should a similar case arise. A knowledge bank helps ensure effective utilization of a firm's investment in its research and benefits clients by helping to provide better-quality, more efficient legal services at the lowest possible rates. Firms that keep copies of their work product in knowledge banks are generally more efficient than firms that do not.

When legal assistants and attorneys prepare a complex document or do comprehensive research on a subject, a copy of the document or research is deposited in the firm's knowledge bank. Some firms require their employees to look for law in a knowledge bank before doing research on a topic.

Before a knowledge bank is useful, its contents must be accessible. A work product retrieval system is used to retrieve its information. There are two types of work product retrieval systems: manual and automated.

A manual system is used by small firms. With a manual system, documents in a knowledge bank are filed alphabetically by subject to allow searchers to locate a document, such as a court form, quickly. However, many firms use a numeric coding system for their knowledge banks. A comprehensive index is required to locate the appropriate document. The index is prepared alphabetically by subject matter and contains the law or rule to which the document applies. If there is more than one subject matter, the document is cross-referenced to other topics. When a document is inserted into a knowledge bank, it is incorporated into the system by a research index memorandum form, such as the one shown in Exhibit 14.5.

A manual knowledge bank may also be kept in three-ring binders, with one binder containing documents for one subject. The subject is labeled on the outside of the binder, and the binders are organized in alphabetical order, or a legal assistant may organize a bank according to type of document, such as complaints, answers, interrogatories, and so on. Each binder is indexed like files, as shown in Chapter 13. Tabbed dividers are used with a document behind it to facilitate locating the appropriate document. An index, such as the one shown in Exhibit 14.6, is placed at the beginning of the form file so that its contents can be viewed easily. Each document in the bank should be given a reference number when it is indexed, and the index should contain a short summary of each document's contents. The number and manner of coding the materials vary.

Automated work product retrieval systems are used by medium and large firms that have large knowledge banks. A large knowledge bank must be automated to manage the high number of documents in it. Many document management software products are used for knowledge banks and were discussed in Chapter 13.

Research Index Memorandum

Name of case: _____

Type of document: _____

Author: _____

Year prepared: _____

Topic(s): _____

_____

Statutes and rules involved: _____

_____

Summary of material: _____

_____

_____

Index number: _____

Location: _____

EXHIBIT 14.5 Sample Research Index Memorandum Form

Complaint Knowledge Bank

TAB NO.	DESCRIPTION
1.	Complaint for personal injuries (auto accident)
2.	Complaint for personal injuries (slip and fall)
3.	Complaint for personal injuries (assault)
4.	Complaint for personal injuries (negligence)
5.	Complaint for medical malpractice
6.	Complaint for breach of contract
7.	Complaint for fraud
8.	
9.	
10.	

EXHIBIT 14.6 Sample Index Sheet for a Knowledge Bank

There are four types of automated work product retrieval systems: full text, index, abstracts, and a combination of these. A full-text system provides word-by-word search capabilities that will review the entire text of document to find the desired subject. An index system searches for documents by fields that are customized by a firm. An abstract system searches an abstract, or summary, of a document.

An automated system allows a user to search a knowledge bank database according to a number of parameters, including author, date, client, type, and subject. If a legal assistant is looking for a document that an attorney drafted for a particular client but cannot recall the date and name of the document, a search would list every document created by that attorney for that client. If a legal assistant knows that research was conducted on a particular subject but cannot remember who conducted it or the date, a search would list all documents prepared on a particular subject.

An automated system on a firm's network or intranet makes a knowledge bank available from each person's computer terminal. Attorneys and legal assistants locate a document on a computer and either view or print it without leaving their desk. Without a network, a knowledge bank is found on a dedicated computer in the library. Many librarians periodically circulate a list of the contents of a knowledge bank to inform attorneys and legal assistants of changes and additions to the bank.

ETHICS ALERT

Documents in knowledge banks become obsolete with changes in the law. Pruning a knowledge bank is an important but often overlooked task. When a change is made in the law or in the procedure of a case, obsolete documents must be removed from the system and replaced with a current document. The index must also be updated when a knowledge bank is pruned. *An attorney relying on outdated law or a legal assistant drafting an incorrect document has grave consequences for a firm and a client.* A document's date should be inserted on the document before inserting it into the knowledge bank. If a change occurs, the outdated nature of the document can be determined quickly and the document replaced with a current one.

ETHICS ALERT

Many legal assistants create and maintain their own knowledge banks. A personal knowledge bank is very helpful and saves a legal assistant time. Some legal assistants prepare a personal knowledge bank as samples of their work to show prospective employers and to take with them if they should leave a firm. Before so doing, however, a legal assistant should have explicit permission from the employer, preferably in writing. *Work that was created while employed belongs to the employer.* To keep a personal knowledge bank useful, a legal assistant must be diligent about pruning the bank and discarding obsolete documents to keep it updated.

CYBERSITES

Finding Sites of Interest to a Law Librarian on the Web

American Association of Law Libraries—www.aallnet.org
Integrated Library System Reports—www.ilsr.com
The Virtual Law Library—www.law.indiana.edu
Law Library Resource Exchange—www.llrx.com

Law Library Links

www.kieslerberman.com
www.law.vill.edu

THE LAW LIBRARIAN

The role of a law librarian is changing with the information explosion. The trend in hiring law firm librarians has coincided with the increased use of technology. As information becomes more accessible, a manager is needed to handle it. A librarian is this manager.

With the advent of technology, a librarian's role is changing into that of an information manager. As such, a librarian must be familiar with a firm's network and software programs. As more firms market their services on the Internet through a Web site, many librarians are considered a firm's Web master, who is responsible for designing, updating, and monitoring a firm's Web site. As the role of the librarian changes with technological changes, some have changed their title from librarian to information managers.

As libraries become smaller with the use of electronic resources, attorneys who are not familiar with electronic research resources depend on a librarian for their electronic research needs. Librarians that do research projects for a firm charge a client for their time. A librarian's billing rate is lower than an attorney's but higher than a paralegal's. An assistant librarian also bills a client for research. An assistant librarian's billing rate is usually the same as that of a junior paralegal.

Among the duties of a law librarian are the following:

◆ *Research.* Provide research services to attorneys and legal assistants. Most librarians are generalists and are familiar with most areas of law. However, librarians increasingly tend to specialize in a particular area of law.

◆ *Collection development.* Acquire, retain, and preserve library materials. The American Library Association defines collection development as "the process of planning, building and maintaining a library's information resources in a cost-effective and user-relevant manner."

◆ *Library maintenance.* File supplements and pocket parts, shelve books, and organize library materials, including CD-ROMs. Library maintenance is a daily function of a law librarian.

◆ *Indexing.* Develop and maintain a catalog and index of all library materials.

◆ *Establish library policy.* Establish loan policies and procedures and monitor a firm's library loan program.

◆ *Organization.* Manage and organize the court form files and knowledge bank.

◆ *Training.* Train the firm's employees on the use of a library and the firm's computer programs to keep attorneys and legal assistants informed of library acquisitions.

◆ *Management.* Manage the financial aspects of a library, such as accounts payable and budgets.

◆ *Personnel management.* Manage library staff, such as assistant librarians.

◆ *Planning.* Plan for library growth.

◆ *Web maintenance.* Manage the firm's Web site and keep it updated.

In addition, some librarians have duties outside the library, such as managing legal assistant or secretarial staff. Some librarians may also manage a central filing area.

A law librarian devotes full time to a firm's library and is found in large firms with large libraries. Most librarians in large firms have a master of library science degree, and some have a law degree. In small and medium firms, legal assistants and experienced legal secretaries act as librarians. Many legal assistants are finding the librarian profession an exciting and challenging adjunct to their legal assistant education. Legal assistants are excellent candidates for the position of librarian, as discussed in the Professional Profile.

CONCLUSION

The first decade of the twenty-first century offers exciting innovations to existing law library resources available through technology. We will also see changes to the manner in which we utilize the library. These changes will require us to develop new research and organizational skills to manage the information.

Professional Profile

Melonia Nixon had no particular interest in libraries and was somewhat disappointed in her first job. After earning her legal assistant certificate from Davidson County Community College, she was hired as a librarian and part-time receptionist at Womble, Carlyle, Sandridge & Rise in Winston-Salem, North Carolina.

"In those early days, there weren't many law firms in North Carolina that used legal assistants," she says. "Womble Carlyle needed a librarian. I'd had a legal bibliography course in my legal assistant program, and I'd written a manual on library procedures for it. Plus, I could do research, and they liked that."

The library at Wobble Carlyle was relatively well organized when Nixon took over. She did the updating and filed all the library material in addition to taking over for the receptionist during lunch and breaks. But Nixon soon was faced with managing a library for a firm that was experiencing phenomenal growth. Within two years, she was working in the library full time.

The firm's size increased from about thirty lawyers in one office to over 140 attorneys with offices in Winston-Salem, Raleigh, and Charlotte. Nixon manages the library operations for all three offices.

Nixon now has two full-time and two part-time assistants on her staff in the Winston-Salem office who file looseleaf services, handle photocopying requests, and shelve. Library assistants manage the libraries in each of the branch offices under Nixon's direction.

Nixon handles all the administrative work of the 15,000-volume main library and the two branch office libraries. She helps attorneys with research, including computer-assisted research. Lately, she has concentrated her efforts on automating the library and research operations. "Systems that worked for a small- and medium-size firm don't work for us now that we are so large," says Nixon. "Automation is a necessity.

"I've attended computer training courses to learn how to build databases and general reports to make managing the library more efficient and effective," she says. "I want to use the new technology to the fullest to continue building the library into an information resource for the attorneys and other employees."

Over the years, Nixon has learned a lot from other librarians by attending the American Association of Law Libraries (AALL) conventions and meetings of the Southeastern Chapter of AALL. "My job is not the same as it was ten years ago," she says. "The best advice I can give to others who manage law libraries is to plan for growth and change."

"I never thought I'd be in this career," she says, "but now I wouldn't trade what I do for anything."

Adapted by permission of James Publishing Company and Legal Assistant Today *magazine, September/October 1988.*

SUMMARY

The law library has served as a symbol of the practice of law for centuries as a symbol of an attorney's knowledge. Two types of knowledge exist: knowledge we have about a subject and knowledge of where to find information about a subject. A law library is where attorneys and legal assistants obtain knowledge.

Millions of laws are in effect today. Organizing laws in an orderly manner so that each law is easily found is a huge undertaking. Library management is a function of law office management.

The U.S. legal system consists of two types of law: written law and common law. Civil law is derived from Roman law and is based on a series of written laws. There are two main sources of written law: constitutions and statutes. Common law, also known as case law, evolved in England, where there were no written laws. The U.S. legal system utilizes both written law and case law, with the exception of a few states.

One of the most important aspects of legal editorial work is classifying the law, which is placing laws into categories. This helps us find laws quickly. If decisions were not classified, it would be extremely difficult, if not impossible, to find a case.

There are four areas of law: type of action, laws that applies to individuals, nature of law, and source of law. Two types of legal actions are filed: civil and criminal. Two types of laws apply to individuals: public laws and private laws. A law can be either substantive or procedural in nature, and a law is categorized by its source.

There are three classes of law: primary authority, secondary authority, and search tools. Primary authority consists of laws made by the three branches of government: executive, legislative, and judicial. A legislature also enacts procedural law, which consist of laws governing the legal procedure used to redress wrong or injury. Primary authority consists of constitutions, statutes, judicial opinions, court rules, and administrative regulations and decisions.

The most commonly used statutes are organized according to subject matter. Statutes may be either annotated or unannotated. In a library, annotated statutes are placed where they are most accessible.

As new laws are passed, it is essential to have immediate access to them. Pocket parts must be inserted into the back of the applicable volumes as soon as they are received to keep laws updated.

Books called reporters contain the text of judicial opinions as they are made. Thousands of volumes of reporters are published, and the volumes of each reporter are numbered consecutively. When an opinion is first printed, it is known as a slip opinion. Reporters contain hundreds of volumes and occupy a lot of shelf space in a library.

Every law library contains court rules. In addition to court rules governing federal and state courts, each federal and state court creates local rules. Court rules are placed in the library, where they can be accessible quickly. Court rules are updated by a publisher or the particular court.

Administrative law governs the powers and procedures of administrative agencies. There is no reporter of agency decisions, such as the West Reporter System for Federal Courts. State agency administrative regulations and decisions are published chronologically, although some states codify their regulations. Only large libraries will contain administrative rulings.

Secondary authority is anything other than primary authority that aids a court in reaching a decision. Secondary authority includes commentary material written by legal scholars or experts in a particular field. Treatises are legal commentaries on various subjects of law. Periodicals are booklets concerning articles about the law. Every law library has a legal dictionary, and large libraries may contain more than one. Encyclopedias are volumes that contain statements on principles of law and are organized alphabetically by subject matter. Large libraries contain many volumes of secondary authority. As the law changes, editors will write some annotations to commentaries of treatises that supersede older annotations.

Search books help a researcher find a primary authority. Search tools consists of digests and citators. A citator is a valuable addition to a law library.

Every law office, corporate legal department, and government agency has a library or access to a law library. Law libraries are described according to size. Small libraries that contain only the books essential for the lawyers' needs are called skeletal libraries. Libraries that contain a comprehensive collection of the laws are called complete libraries.

Three types of library organization are used: centralized, decentralized, and satellite. A centralized library is found in one location that has been set aside by a firm. A decentralized library is distributed throughout a firm. Satellite libraries are found in large firms with a large centralized library. Tax and labor libraries are the most common satellite libraries.

All libraries, whether centralized, decentralized, or satellite, must have a system that will locate every book in them. A library checkout system consists of procedures to locate library materials. The three most common checkout systems used in law firm libraries are the out card, bar code, and library card systems. A library out card system is used like an out card system for files described in Chapter 13. Some firms have bar codes placed on their books, and the system is used like the one described in Chapter 13 for bar coded files. A popular checkout system for library books is the library card system.

Technology has had a great affect on the traditional law library. Five types of technology are used in law libraries. On-line legal and nonlegal databases are the most common type of technology found in law offices today. Information may be quickly retrieved through a legal database. Nonlegal databases operate the same as legal databases but contain nonlegal information. Legal and nonlegal databases may also be accessed from the Internet.

Microform is the process of storing information photographically in reduced form. Microfilm is the most popular method of microform in law libraries. Microform is especially useful for preserving volumes of out-of-print law books.

CD-ROMs can be found in our homes and offices and contain software, text, music, or movies. Legal publishers make material found in law books available on CD-ROM and sell the disks to their customers. With CD-ROMs, a large law firm with a centralized library can make portions of its library available to other areas of the firm, making access to the library more convenient. One problem with CD-ROMs is that their data are often not current. Law firms have been reluctant to replace law books with CD-ROMs and have had problems with CD-ROM technology.

E-mail and telefacsimile (fax) machines send documents from one location to another electronically over telephone lines. As law firm libraries are stepping into their role of information centers, they must have access to a variety of information that may be needed by researchers. Large firms with large libraries often lend materials to other firms and provide library materials to their branch offices via e-mail and fax machines.

The Internet is the information superhighway that is absorbing other legal media types, such as print, CD-ROM, and on-line database services. Access to federal and state statutes and court decisions is available on the Internet for free. However, as of this writing, the Internet is not a better research tool than other, conventional types of technology used in law libraries. However, the Internet is an important medium of gathering and disseminating information in new and powerful ways.

The emergence of electronic legal research has created the need for new methods of citing the material. The American Association of Law Libraries (AALL) recognized the need for a new citation format for these materials and recommended that an electronic legal cite include the case name, year of the decision, specific court, a consecutively assigned case number, and paragraph number for the exact location of the quote. Many other groups have also made recommendations for citing electronic documents, including the American Psychological Association and the Modern Language Association of America (MLA). As of 1999, no universally accepted citation system for electronic documents exists.

Court form, form files, and knowledge banks are found in law libraries. Every law office must have an adequate supply of court forms, which are form documents used in a specific court. Court forms must be located quickly. There are three methods of storing court forms: manually, on masters that are photocopied, and computer programs. Court forms are normally organized alphabetically by subject matter. Problems with storage and access to court forms are solved with computer-generated forms. Forms other than court forms are also used by a law office.

The knowledge of employees is a firm's most valuable asset and must be gathered into a knowledge bank. A knowledge bank contains briefs, research memoranda, opinion letters, pleadings, discovery requests, contracts, leases, and articles that may be useful in a future case. When legal assistants and attorneys prepare a complex document or do comprehensive research on a subject, a copy of the document or research is deposited in the firm's knowledge bank.

Before a knowledge bank is useful, its contents must be accessible. There are two types of work retrieval systems used: manual and automated. A manual system is used by small firms and consists of documents kept in three-ring binders, with one binder containing documents for one subject. Automated work retrieval systems are used by medium and large firms that have large knowledge banks.

There are four types of automated work retrieval systems: full text, index, abstracts, and a combination of these. An automated system allows a user to search a knowledge bank database according to a number of parameters, including author, date, client, type, and subject. An automated system on a firm's network or intranet makes a knowledge bank available from each person's computer terminal. Documents in knowledge banks become obsolete with changes in the law and must be updated periodically.

The role of a law librarian is changing with the information explosion. With the advent of technology, a librarian's role is changing into that of an information manager. Among the duties of a law librarian are research, collection development, library maintenance, indexing, establishing library policy, organization, training, management, personnel management, planning, and Web maintenance. In addition, some librarians have additional duties outside the library, such as managing legal assistant or secretarial staff. A law librarian devotes full time to a firm's library and is found in large firms with large libraries.

CHAPTER ILLUSTRATION

The law firm of Black, White, & Greene has a skeletal library consisting of state statutes, state reporters, court rules, and some form books. The firm also has a set of tax codes and books relating to tax law for Grant. The library is decentralized throughout the office. Shelves of library books line the office's walls. Employees retrieve the books they need and use them in their individual offices. If a person needs more room for research, they use the conference room.

The conference room is used more for research than for conferences. The employees refer to it as the "war room" because stacks of books and papers are scattered all over the conference room table. If the conference room is needed for a conference, at least two hours' notice is required so that it can be cleaned up.

Tricia, as office manager, was responsible for maintaining the library. As pocket parts and advance sheets would come in, they would pile up in Tricia's office until she had time to update the library. However, she never had the time, and the updating got way behind. The attorneys started to complain about the condition of the library, so Tricia delegated library maintenance to Kay, the file clerk.

"That's an easy job," said Kay, cheerfully. "Sure, I'll do it. It shouldn't take much time."

Kay accepted her new responsibility with a smile. As pocket parts and advance sheets would come in, Kay would insert them in the books. Tricia was impressed that Kay did not allow the library updates to get behind.

One day, as Robert retrieved the court rules, he noticed that it would not close completely. He then noticed a pocket part in the court rules. He showed the book to Tricia. "What's going on here?" he asked. "There's pocket parts in the court rules and advance sheets in the statutes."

"Oh no!" said Tricia. "I'll talk to Kay about it to find out what's going on."

Tricia approached Kay and asked her how she was updating the library. "Fine," said Kay. "Is there a problem?"

"Yes." Tricia said. "The problem is that pocket parts are put in the court rules, and form books and advance sheets are inserted in the statutes!" exclaimed Tricia.

"What's a pocket part?" asked Kay. "I've never heard of an advance sheet."

"What? You said this would be an easy assignment when I gave it to you," said Tricia. "I assumed you knew how a law library was updated."

"It was easy," said Kay. "I watched you do it, and it looked easy. I didn't know they had to be put in specific books. I'm sorry, Tricia," said Kay.

"Don't worry about it, Kay," said Tricia. "We'll fix it. By the way, you don't have to worry about updating the library anymore."

Every book in the entire library had to be reviewed and updated. No one in the firm had time to do it, so Tricia called Law Library Services, a company that comes to law firms to maintain their libraries. The library consultants came in and updated the entire law library. They also agreed to come to the firm once a month to take care of the library updates and to make sure that the library was in good order.

Tricia received a request from George for a set of restatements that he thought would help him with a case he was working on. Tricia checked her library budget and approved the order. The firm was quickly running out of library space to store the new volumes of statutes and reporters that were delivered each month. When the restatements arrived, there was not enough shelf space to store them. The only space available for the restatements was in George's office. Tricia contacted a cabinetmaker to build new shelves in George's office for the restatements, as this would be the only space left in the office for books. The firm had no room left for new volumes or updates.

At the monthly management meeting, Tricia discussed the library space problem and told the attorneys that soon there would be no space left to store new volumes of reporters as they came in. Patrizia recommended that the firm consider using CD-ROMs for their reporters, replacing the books with the CDs.

"Just think of the shelf space we would save," said Patrizia. "One whole section of books, 250 of them, can be put on one CD. When we need to do research, all we need to do is insert the CD into our computer. The computer searches the CD so that we can find the case we need. It is really fast and convenient. As changes are made, we get a new CD replacing the outdated one. It's really nifty."

"Yes," said George. "Some firms have a lot of volumes on CDs. Some have hundreds of CDs instead of thousands of books. It's the wave of the future. They store all these CDs in a jukebox, which is accessible from the firm's network. Everyone has access to the library from their computers. There's no books to put away, no lost books, no books to look for, and, uh, the conference room is always clean!"

"How much does it cost?" asked Tricia.

"I'm not real sure," said George. "I think the cost of CDs is comparable to the cost of books. I read somewhere that legal publishers have package deals where you can get discounts if you're an established customer."

"I heard that the Internet was the wave of the future," said Dennis. "You can find all the statutes on the Internet. And, it's free."

"Yeah," said George, "but you can't find all the cases. As of now, case law on the Internet goes back only to 1970 or so. I think all the federal statutes are on the Internet, but I'm not sure about all the state statutes."

Patrizia responded, "My problem with the Internet is that it's hard to know how reliable it is. It's hard to know if a Web site can be trusted to be accurate and current. Government and university Web sites are reliable, but I don't know about the rest. If you want to do research on the Internet, what about an on-line legal database such as Westlaw? It costs a fee, but they guarantee that their information is current and accurate."

Robert chimed in, "Hey, let me tell you about Internet research. I had to find a law regarding interstate trucking licensing requirements, so I did a search on the Web. I put the words "interstate trucking license" into a search engine and got 43,768 results. It took me hours to weed them out to find the information I needed. There's no way I can charge the client for all the time I spent. The Internet may be free, but it's very expensive in terms of time."

Tricia said, "I can see that we have a lot of options to expand our library without expanding our space requirements. I'll do a cost analysis to find out what is best and submit my report to you at the next meeting."

At the next meeting, Tricia reported her findings. The attorneys agreed that the firm will establish an account with Westlaw, which will give them access to all the law they will need. The legal database will be put on the firm's intranet and be accessible by everyone in the firm from their computers.

"My research indicates that most firms charge their clients for the cost of on-line legal research," said Tricia. "Therefore, the service should pay for itself."

"Sounds good," said George. "Now, I can hold my conferences in the conference room!"

CHAPTER REVIEW

1. What are the four categories of laws?

2. What are the three classes of law?

3. What is a skeletal library, and what type of attorneys utilize a skeletal library?

4. What is the difference between a complete library and a large library?

5. Describe the three types of library organization.

6. Describe the three types of library checkout systems.

7. Describe the five types of library technology.

8. Describe how court forms are organized.

9. How is a manual knowledge bank organized?

10. What are the four types of automated work retrieval systems?

11. What are the duties of a law librarian?

EXAMPLES FOR DISCUSSION

1. The Mismanaged Library

The law firm of Smith & Jones is a medium-size firm located in Cincinnati. It has an average-size centralized library that contains a large worktable in the center of the library. The attorneys and legal assistants do research at the table as well as in their individual offices. The firm has no law librarian and has delegated the function of library maintenance to a le-

gal assistant, Cindy Anderson, with the help of the receptionist, Marion Malloy.

The library is a constant mess. Books are left on the table in piles and are missing from the shelves and cannot be found. Boxes of new pocket parts, updates, and supplements have been stacked to the ceiling for months. The attorneys and legal assistants constantly complain to Cindy that they cannot find the information they need to complete their projects. Cindy is assigned to a very large case that is going to trial soon. There is a lot of work to do on the case and very little time to complete her projects. She is under constant pressure.

Cindy has stayed late and come in on Saturdays to maintain the library. However, she spends most of her time looking for books that are scattered all over the firm. Once the books are put away, the day is gone. Marion tries to help Cindy, but as soon as she goes into the library, the phone rings. She cannot get away from her desk. New updates keep coming in. Cindy is at her wits' end.

1. What are the problems with this library?
2. If you were the manager, what would you do to remedy the problem?
3. Assume there is no money for a librarian's salary. What systems and controls would you implement?
4. If you were Cindy, how would you handle the problem?
5. How could technology help this situation?

2. *The Problem Attorney*

Dennis Vaughan is the librarian for a large firm in Chicago. He has implemented a library card checkout system for the library. Each attorney, legal assistant, and law clerk has a box in which library cards are placed if a book leaves the library.

Dennis has had great success with this system. Most of the firm's employees are diligent about using the system when they check out books. One attorney, however, refuses to use the system. She removes books from the library without placing the library cards in her box. She often takes books home and to court, and Dennis spends hours trying to locate them. Dennis has talked to her many times about complying with the system's requirements, but to no avail.

1. If you were Dennis, how would you remedy this problem?
2. Would you change the checkout system? If so, how? With no additional funds in the library budget? With unlimited funds in the library budget?
3. How could technology help this problem?

3. *The Virtual Library*

This chapter discusses the various types of technology used in law libraries. Do you foresee a bookless library? If so, why? If not, why not? Describe what technology would be the dominant technology in a virtual (bookless) library. Is it the Internet? If so, what are the advantages and disadvantages to an Internet virtual library? A CD-ROM virtual library? How would a virtual library affect the practice of law?

ASSIGNMENTS

1. Go to a library near you and ask to use its microfilm to find an article on a subject that interests you. Note how to place the microfilm in the reader. Print a copy of the article and bring to your instructor. Write a procedural manual informing other students how to use microfilm.

2. Tour law libraries in your area. Tour a large centralized library, a scattered library, and a satellite library. Write a descriptive report of your tour and include the following:
   a. How the library materials are organized and distributed
   b. The checkout procedures
   c. The advantages and disadvantages of each style of organization
   d. Whether each library has a librarian (if so, describe the duties of the librarian; if not, report who is responsible for maintaining the library and what that person's duties are)
   e. Whether the libraries use technology (if so, report what type)

3. You are the librarian for a large firm with a large library. On a piece of graph paper, illustrate how you would organize the library. Include placement of the following:
   a. Statutes
   b. Reporters
   c. Treatises
   d. Encyclopedias
   e. Dictionary
   f. Knowledge bank
   g. Form files

4. You are the librarian for a large firm. The managing partner wants to purchase an additional set of your state's statutes and asked you to prepare a cost analysis of acquiring an additional set of statutes. Research the cost of the statutes, including update service. Consider CD-ROM and on-line legal databases in your analysis. Make a recommendation at the end of your report. Also include a yearly budget for the cost of the statutes.

5. Go to the Internet sites listed on page 497 and research the current status of electronic citation recommendations of the various groups. Prepare a report to the class and include your opinion as to which system is the best.

SELF-TEST

How well did you grasp the material in the chapter? Test yourself by answering the following questions and check your answers against the answers found in Appendix A.

1. How has a law library been a symbol of the practice of law?
2. What does a law library symbolize?
3. What are the two types of knowledge?
4. What is the highest law in the land?
5. What is the highest law in a state?
6. How are federal laws created?
7. By what laws is each individual governed?
8. Why should a legal assistant be comfortable in a law library?
9. What is the first step in understanding a law library?
10. What is the second step in understanding a law library?
11. Who maintains a library in a small firm?
12. On what two types of law is our legal system based?
13. On what is civil law based?
14. From what was civil law derived?
15. How early were laws written?
16. What are the two main sources of written law?
17. What is common law?
18. Where did common law originate?
19. Reports of court decisions were first compiled into what?
20. What is stare decisis?
21. How was stare decisis established?
22. Where did most laws of the United States originate?
23. What does codify mean?
24. What is the classification of law?
25. When and where was the classification process introduced?
26. What was the name of the first legal index?
27. Why are laws categorized?
28. How are laws categorized?
29. How many laws are made each year?
30. How is case law classified?
31. What are the four functions of law?
32. What are the two types of legal actions filed?
33. Who is the plaintiff in a criminal action?
34. Why are criminal cases prosecuted by the government?
35. What are the two types of remedies available in a civil case?
36. What is monetary relief?
37. What is equitable relief?
38. What are the two types of laws that apply to individuals?

39. What are public laws?
40. What are private laws?
41. What are the two natures of law?
42. What are substantive laws?
43. What are damages?
44. What are procedural laws?
45. What are the sources of law?
46. What are the three classes of law?
47. Of what does primary authority consist?
48. Who enacts primary authority?
49. Who enacts procedural law?
50. Who creates laws governing the rules and procedures of the court system?
51. What are local rules?
52. What types of law is primary authority?
53. How are statutes organized?
54. What do large libraries contain?
55. What are annotated statutes?
56. What are unannotated statutes?
57. Where are annotated statutes placed in a library?
58. Where are unannotated statutes placed?
59. How are new laws published?
60. What is a pocket part?
61. What numbering system does a pocket part use?
62. How often is a new edition of the statutes published?
63. Where are pocket parts placed in a book?
64. Why should pocket parts not be allowed to accumulate?
65. What are books that contain judicial opinions called?
66. How are the volumes of a report numbered?
67. What is a series?
68. When does a publisher produce a new series of reporters?
69. How are reporters placed in a library?
70. Why do many libraries not contain the first series in a reporter set?
71. What is a slip opinion?
72. What is an advance sheet?
73. When are advance sheets sent to law libraries?
74. Where are advance sheets placed in a library?
75. What is done with advance sheets when a new volume has been printed?
76. When were court rules first developed?
77. What are court rules?
78. What are the three purposes of court rules?
79. What are local rules?
80. Where are court rules placed in a library?
81. Who updates court rules?
82. Who establishes an administrative agency?

83. Who publishes opinions from administrative agencies?

84. How are state agency administrative regulations and decisions published?

85. What type of library contains administrative rulings?

86. What is secondary authority?

87. Why was secondary authority developed?

88. How is secondary authority used?

89. What types of documents does secondary authority include?

90. What is a treatise, and what is its purpose?

91. What are periodicals, and what are their purpose?

92. Why are indexes published?

93. What is the name of the most established index service?

94. What is a legal dictionary?

95. What are encyclopedias, and how are they organized?

96. How are encyclopedias categorized?

97. How are the volumes of secondary authority placed in library?

98. Where is a dictionary placed in a library?

99. When are treatises updated?

100. What is the purpose of search tools?

101. When are search tools cited?

102. What is a digest?

103. How is a digest arranged?

104. What is a citator?

105. What happens when a statute is repealed?

106. What are form books?

107. What determines a library's organization?

108. How are law libraries described?

109. What is a skeletal library?

110. What does a skeletal library contain?

111. What are complete law libraries?

112. Where are complete law libraries found?

113. What is the largest complete law library in the United States?

114. What are the three types of library organization?

115. What is a centralized library?

116. What size firm has a centralized library?

117. What is a library cooperative?

118. What is a decentralized library?

119. Where do attorneys and legal assistants use the books in a decentralized library?

120. What types of firms have decentralized libraries?

121. What are the three advantages to a decentralized library?

122. What are the disadvantages to a decentralized library?

123. What is a satellite library?

124. What type of firm has a satellite library?

125. Where are satellite libraries located?

126. What are the most common satellite libraries?

127. Why must a library be maintained so that it is always current?

128. What is an update service?

129. When should law books be updated?

130. Where is most of a law library's budget spent?

131. What are the three most common checkout systems used in law libraries?

132. What are some problems with an out card system?

133. What is a bar code system?

134. What is a library card system?

135. How are law libraries getting smaller?

136. What are the five types of technology used in law libraries?

137. What is an on-line legal database?

138. What is computer-assisted legal research (CALR)?

139. What does "full text" mean?

140. What is a modem?

141. What are the two primary CALR systems?

142. What is an abstract system?

143. What is a nonlegal database?

144. How can a legal database be accessed from the Internet?

145. What is microform?

146. What is microfilm?

147. What is microfiche?

148. How many books does a 100-foot rill of microfilm contain?

149. How many microfiche cards are needed to photograph one book?

150. After documents are put on microfilm, how is it viewed?

151. Why is microform useful for preserving volumes of books?

152. What is the lifetime of microfilm?

153. What does "CD-ROM" stand for?

154. How many books can a CD-ROM store?

155. What is a megabyte?

156. How is material on a CD-ROM accessed?

157. What is a jukebox?

158. How many CD-ROMs does a jukebox hold?

159. Why are CD-ROMs not current?

160. What is a user interface?

161. What is the lifetime of a CD?

162. How have e-mail and the fax machine reduced the number of lost library materials?

163. According to the 1999 Technology Survey conducted by the NFPA, what percentage of responding paralegals conducted research on the Internet?

164. What factors contributed to law being put on the Internet?

165. What type of information is not found on the Internet?
166. What is a problem with conducting research over the Internet?
167. Why does it take longer to do research on the Internet?
168. What book is used as a guide to legal citations?
169. What electronic citation system did the AALL recommend?
170. What electronic citation system did the ABA recommend?
171. What electronic citation system is universally accepted?
172. For what are court forms used?
173. What are the three methods of storing court forms?
174. Where are manual court forms stored, and how are they filed?
175. Where are photocopier-created court forms stored?
176. What are computer-generated court forms?
177. Who is responsible for distributing new court forms?
178. What does a knowledge bank contain?
179. How does utilizing a knowledge bank increase efficiency?
180. What are the two types of work product retrieval systems?
181. What type of firm uses a manual work product retrieval system?
182. How are documents filed in a manual system?
183. What is required to locate a document in a manual system?
184. How is an index prepared?
185. How is the document indexed if it has more than one subject matter?
186. What is a research index memorandum form, and what is its purpose?
187. What type of firm uses an automated work product retrieval system?
188. Why must a large knowledge bank be automated?
189. What are the four types of automated work product retrieval system?
190. What is required for a knowledge bank to be available on each employee's computer system?
191. Where are knowledge banks found if a firm does not have a network?
192. What has been responsible for the changing role of the law librarian?
193. What are the duties of a law librarian?
194. What additional duties may a law librarian have outside of the library?
195. In what type of law firm may a law librarian be found?
196. What type of degree do most librarians in a large firm have?

KEY WORDS

Abstract system
Advance sheet
Affirm
Annotated
Computer-assisted legal research
CD-ROM
CD-ROM drive
Citator
Codify
Complete library
Damages
Digest

Equitable relief
Full text
Library cooperative
Local rules
Megabyte
Modem
Monetary relief
Overrule
Pocket part
Procedural law
Repeal

Reporter
Restatement
Series
Skeletal library
Slip opinion
Stare decisis
Substantive law
Telefacsimile
Unannotated
Update service
User interface

Glossary of Terms

Abstract system: A collection of abstracted, or summarized, documents.

Accounts payable: Accounts that a business owes for goods or services rendered.

Actual cost: True cost without consideration of mark-up for profit.

Add-on: A software application that can be purchased to enhance the features of another software application; also called a plug-in.

Administrative microsystem: A system relating to the management of a firm.

Admonition: A reprimand given to a lawyer.

Advance: To pay money before it is due; to loan money.

Advance sheet: A softcover book of decisions that is circulated soon after a decision is rendered.

Affirm: To confirm an existing judicial opinion.

Aging: Calculating the number of days an account has been unpaid.

Amicus curiae: Friend-of-the-court brief that states the position of the author relating to a case pending before the court.

Annotated: Referring to a publication that contains the law and other pertinent information about the law.

Annual billable hours requirement: The number of hours a timekeeper is required to bill in a year.

Application: Software that has a specific function, such as word processing, spreadsheet, or database.

Arbitration: The resolution of a dispute without court involvement.

Attrition: A reduction in workforce due to death, termination, retirement, or resignation.

Autocratic: Government by one person with unlimited power.

Automatic data collection: The data entry method used in bar code technology.

Autonomous: Self-governing; independent; subject to its own methods of management.

Backup: Substitute; in computer systems, a copy of a system on a different disk.

Bait-and-switch: A tactic used in advertising to attract customers to a sale item and switch that item with one that is not on sale.

Best evidence rule: The requirement that courts must admit the best evidence that is available to a party and procurable under the existing situation.

Billable hour: Sixty minutes of time that are billed to a client.

Blind insert: An entry in a form document alerting the preparer to insert material; seen on the computer screen but not printed.

Block billing: Charging a client for services rendered in one large block of time rather than itemizing the tasks performed in that period.

Bookmarking: A part of browser software that marks a Web site so that its URL is accessible without searching for it.

Boolean search: A method of defining search criteria.

Boutique: A law firm that offers services in one area of law only.

Brief bank: A collection of documents that are used as a template to prepare new documents.

Browser: A software program that allows viewing and interaction with various kinds of resources available on the Internet.

Buddy system: Putting two employees together for training purposes.

Capper: A person who is paid to obtain cases for an attorney.

Case sensitive: Requiring that all letters be in a specific case. If a letter is in the wrong case, the information cannot be read.

Cash payments journal: Record of all checks written or cash disbursed.

Cash receipts journal: Record of all deposits and cash received.

CD-ROM: Compact disk read-only memory. A computer disk that stores a large amount of data.

CD-ROM drive: A device that is connected to the computer that reads CD-ROM disks.

Ceiling: The maximum number of hours that may be spent on nonbillable projects.

CEMEC principle: An acronym to describe employee expectations. Stands for communication, education, motivation, evaluation and compensation.

Central file control: A system that documents the location of each file.

Certificate of service: A document appended to the end of a legal document that contains the date and place of mailing.

Charging lien: A lien placed on a client's proceeds or judgment for payment of an attorney's fees.

Check kiting: Using other clients' funds until a check clears the bank.

Chinese wall: Prohibits a person from working on or discussing a case if that person has a conflict of interest.

Citator: A set of books that provide the judicial history and interpretation of reported decisions.

CLA: Acronym meaning Certified Legal Assistant which is granted after passing an exam given by the National Association of Legal Assistants.

Classification: The process of separating items into categories.

Client funds account: A bank account established exclusively for clients' funds; an attorney may not use the funds for any other purpose; also called a client trust account.

Client security fund: A fund established to reimburse clients who have been damaged because of their attorney's fraudulent abuse of the trust account.

Closed file list: A list of closed files by name, number, and closed file number.

Codify: To arrange laws by subject.

Commingle: Mixing one person's funds with another person's funds.

Compensation expenses: Employee expenses, including wages and benefits.

Complete library: A library containing a comprehensive collection of material.

Compulsory organization: An organization to which all persons of the same class must belong.

Computer-assisted legal research: Legal research on a legal database accessed by computer.

Cone of silence: A construct prohibiting a person from working on or discussing a case.

Confirm: To corroborate or verify (ratify) the ruling of a lower court.

Constructive criticism: Negative performance evaluation that is given for the purpose of giving instruction and direction.

Consumer price index: Index that determines the annual increase in the cost of living.

Contingency: A case in which the client pays an attorney a percentage of the amount recovered in a lawsuit.

Contingency fee: A fee consisting of a percentage of the possible recovery from a lawsuit.

Contract attorney: Attorneys who work for law firms on an assignment basis, or as an independent contractor.

Contract basis: Working as an independent contractor on a per case or assignment basis. The person is not an employee of the firm.

Controlled access: The access and retrieval of a firm's files are controlled by a specific system.

Controller: Also called a comptroller, an employee charged with certain duties relating to the financial affairs of the business.

Cost recovery system: A utility program that allows data to be transferred to a billing program by copier or telephone systems.

Costs: Expenses of one side of a lawsuit that a judge orders the other side to reimburse; includes filing fees, service fees, and recording fees.

Courtesy copy: A document that is sent to a person for informational purposes only.

CPA: Acronym for Certified Public Accountant.

Creditable nonbillable hours: The time that is applied to an annual billable hours requirement.

Cross-index: To mark a document so that it can be easily found in a system.

Cryptography: The method of scrambling information so that it is unreadable except by the person who holds the key to unscramble the information.

Culture: Law firm working environment consisting of intangible factors such as the social environment, employee relationships, and attitudes.

Cumulative: Increasing by successive addition; running total of each month's services and costs.

Custodial: Relating to a person who has custody of another person or thing and is expected to act in its best interests.

Cybertort: Actions for damages resulting from libelous material posted on the Internet; also included is posting material that is protected by copyright or trademarks, such as magazines and photos.

Damages: Compensation for a wrong or an injury.

Data validation: A feature in automated docket control software that will not allow an incorrect entry.

Database: A collection of information for computer retrieval.

Date stamp: To stamp a document with the date it was received.

Decrypt: A way of decoding information so that it may be read.

Default: Failure to respond within the required time.

Deponent: A person whose deposition is taken.

Digest: A collection embodying the chief matter of numerous books, articles, court decisions, and so on, usually arranged alphabetically.

Digital ID: A personal ID number that is encrypted and can be read only by the extranet.

Direct conflict: When an attorney or firm has a relationship with a person who may be involved in the conflict or when the attorney or firm has a financial interest in an entity involved in the conflict.

Direct profitability factors: Factors that affect a firm's profitability in a short period of time, usually one year.

Disbarment: The taking away of a lawyer's license to practice law.

Discovery: The acquisition of notice or knowledge of given acts or facts; that which was previously unknown.

Disengagement letter: Letter informing the client that the case is closed and the representation has ceased.

Dividends: Distribution of a corporation's profits to shareholders.

Docket: An abstract or brief entry or the book or record containing such entries.

Docket coordinator: A person in charge of a firm's docketing process.

Domain name: A unique name that identifies an Internet site.

Download: The method by which users access and retrieve a document, software, or other files from a central computer to their computers.

Downsize: To reduce staff and expenses because of reduced income.

Drop-down list: A list of activities that are listed in an area of the screen that is visible if the list is chosen.

Electronic mail (e-mail): An electronic message sent from one person to another through their computers.

E-mail filters: Software that manages e-mail and that can be programmed to delete e-mails that contain profanity or offensive material.

Emoticons: Symbols used to express feelings in written e-mail communication.

Encrypt: A way of coding the information so that if it is intercepted by a third party, it cannot be read.

Engagement letter: A letter summarizing the scope of representation and the fee agreement between a lawyer and a client.

Equitable relief: Compensation other than money for an injury.

Equity: Referring to the ownership of the firm entitled to a portion of the profits.

Equity partner: A partner who is entitled to a portion of the firm's profits and is responsible for a portion of the firm's losses.

Ergonomics: Area concerned with health factors in the workplace.

Executive committee: Committee comprised of heads of the various committees in a law firm.

Exempt: Professional status that exempts an employee from overtime compensation.

Expert witness: Person who testifies at trial, based on the professional expertise of the witness.

Extranet: A Web-based interface to a private network; used to communicate directly with clients.

Extraordinary fee: A fee that is awarded in addition to statutory fees and that compensates an attorney for extra work required by the circumstances of the case.

Fee adjustment memorandum: A form used by attorney to increase or decrease a client's bill as appropriate.

Fee allocation: When a percentage of the bill is given to the originating or supervising attorney as compensation.

Fiduciary: Of, relating to, or involving great confidence and trust; a person who transacts business for another person, necessitating great confidence and trust by the second party and a high degree of good faith by the first.

File number index: An index containing sequential file numbers and case names indicating the next available file number.

File Transfer Protocol (FTP): A protocol that allows files to be transferred between computers.

Firewall: A protective electronic barrier constructed around a network so that unauthorized persons cannot get through.

Fiscal year: Annual accounting year.

Flame: An angry or a derogatory e-mail message.

Flat fee: A client is charged one fee for the entire case.

Floppy disks: Computer diskettes as distinguished from internal hard drives.

FLSA: Fair Labor Standards Act.

Forecasting: Planning for the future by anticipating future events.

Foreclosure: To shut out; a termination of all rights of the mortgagor in the property covered by the mortgage.

Form files: A collection of copies of form documents and frequently used documents; these documents act as a guide when developing similar documents.

Formal evaluation: Procedure where employees' work performance is evaluated and rated in writing. Occurs annually or biannually.

Freelance paralegal: A freelance paralegal contracts his/her services out to law offices and work under the supervision of an attorney.

Freeware: Free software.

Full text: Consisting of a verbatim text that allows every word in a document to be retrieved by a researcher.

General counsel: Attorney in charge of the corporate legal department. Often an officer of the corporation.

General ledger: An accounting term used to describe the book that summarizes a business's financial accounts.

Contains a separate account for every asset, liability, and expense.

General practitioner: Attorney who does not specialize in a particular area of law. Accepts cases in all areas of law.

Goodwill letter: Letter written to create rapport and good relations.

Gopher: A protocol that organizes Internet information for search and retrieval.

Gross income: Income received before payment of expenses.

Groupware: Software created for and used by an intranet or extranet.

Hard copy: A copy of computer records on a sheet of paper.

Hard costs: Costs incurred for filing fees, service fees, deposition expenses, and so on.

Hiring specifications: The requirements for a position.

Home page: The starting point of a Web presentation that contains a table of contents for the information that is available at the Web site, offering direct links to the different parts of the site.

Human resource audit: To determine strengths and weaknesses of current employees.

Hyperlinks: A connection to another page or site that allows a person to navigate the Web.

Hypertext Markup Language (HTML): A software language used by documents posted on the World Wide Web.

Hypertext Transfer Protocol (HTTP): The protocol used by the World Wide Web.

Icon: A picture that symbolizes a software application or function of an application.

If clause: A clause inserted in a form document alerting the preparer to insert the appropriate paragraph.

Imaging: The process of scanning a paper document into a computer system.

Incarcerated: Imprisoned; confined to a jail or penitentiary.

Independent paralegal: A person who does law-related work for the general public without the supervision of an attorney.

Indigent: Poor or needy.

Indirect profitability factors: Factors that affect a firm's profitability over a longer period, more than one year.

Informal evaluation: Procedure where an employee's work is evaluated verbally. Occurs in an informal manner.

In-house counsel: An attorney who is an employee of a corporation and works in the corporation's legal department.

Integrated software: A program that combines many different software applications into one program to make it easier to use.

Internet Service Provider (ISP): A private company that provides access to the Internet for a fee.

Intranet: A private collection of information that is viewed by Internet Web browser software and is accessible only to authorized members of a private network; a private Internet site.

Joint venture: A grouping of two or more persons for a common goal.

Jukebox: A device that contains many CD-ROMs and allows retrieval of a document on request.

Lawyer hopping: Going from lawyer to lawyer for advice and representation.

Legal administrator: Experienced manager who is hired to manage a law firm. Has the authority of a management partner.

Legal clinic: Low-cost firms with standard fees for standard services.

Legal and nonlegal databases: A legal database contains statutes, case law, administrative rulings, and legal memoranda. A nonlegal database contains nonlegal information, such as medical information, business statistics, and so on.

Leverage: The ability to make money from the work of others.

Leverage ratio: A formula used to identify the number of income producing employees per owner.

Liaison: A person responsible for communication between groups. Spokesperson.

Library cooperative: A group organized to pool library resources for the benefit of the group.

Limited liability company: A company formed to shield its owners and their assets from liability arising from the misconduct of other owners or employees.

Listserv: A group of people who exchange information about a particular topic on the Internet.

Local area network (LAN): A number of computers that are connected together. If information is inserted in one computer, each computer connected to the network receives the information.

Local rules: Rules created by an individual court that applies in that court only.

Lodestar: A method of calculating an attorney's fee using the attorney's hourly rate multiplied by the number of hours worked on a case.

Lurking: Not responding to messages posted on a listserv.

Manual calendar: A calendar that is maintained by hand rather than by computer.

Mark-up: To add a percentage on the cost of an item for profit.

Master calendar: Calendar that contains hearing and deposition dates for each attorney in the firm.

Master client list: A list of active clients; does not include closed files.

MBA: Acronym for masters of business administration degree.

Megabyte: A computer term used to measure data; One megabyte contains about one million characters.

Megafirm: Firm that employs more than 300 attorneys and has branch offices throughout the world.

Merger: Union of two or more law firms to form one law firm.

Microfiche: Sheets of film on which documents are photographed.

Microfilm: Film on which documents are photographed.

Microform: The process of storing information photographically.

Misappropriation: Using funds in the trust account for personal purposes.

Mitigated: To make less severe; alleviation, reduction, abatement, or diminution of a penalty or punishment imposed by law.

Modem: A device that allows remote computers to transmit and receive data using telephone lines; short for modulator/demodulator.

Modified cash basis: Based on cash but including some accrual basis concepts.

Monetary relief: Compensation by money for an injury.

Multipliers: An amount that is added to attorney's lodestar fee to compensate for time limitations and risks.

Netiquette: An informal code of conduct that governs e-mail communication.

Netvertising: Advertising services on the Internet.

Network: Two or more computers connected to each other so they can share resources.

New case memorandum: A form used to provide information about a case so that a file may be opened.

Noncreditable nonbillable hours: The time that is not applied to an annual billable hours requirement.

Nonequity partner: Partner that is not entitled to a portion of the profits and is not responsible for a portion of the losses of the firm.

Nonexempt: Nonprofessional status that requires payment of overtime.

Nonlegal database: An organized collection of nonlegal information, such as medical information, business statistics, and so on.

Nonlegal subsidiary: A nonlegal company that is owned by a law firm.

Numeric index: An index in numeric order that lists files and the date opened. The purpose is to inform the file clerk of the next number in sequence when opening files.

Of-counsel: An attorney affiliated with a firm on a part-time basis.

Office manager: A person hired to assist a Managing Partner or Legal Administrator with management functions of a firm.

On-line: Connected to the Internet or the World Wide Web.

Open questions: Questions that require a narrative answer and cannot be answered yes or no.

Operating expenses: Expenses other than compensation expenses that include occupancy costs, office operating costs, costs of professional activities, and general business expenses.

Ouch formula: Acronym for proper interview questions. Includes objective, uniform, consistence, and have job relatedness.

Outside counsel: Law firm retained to do legal work for a corporate legal department.

Outsourcing: A firm's use of outside services for support functions.

Overrule: To reject or supersede an existing judicial opinion; to invalidate.

P.C.: Acronym for professional corporation.

Pad: To expand in a fraudulent manner.

Pathname: The URL address showing the path of where a certain document may be found on a Web site.

Per diem: Latin term meaning "by the day."

Per unit cost: The amount of money it costs to produce a product or provide a service.

Permanent associates: Employed attorneys who are not eligible for partner or ownership of the firm.

Personal calendar: An individual's calendar that contains the same information as a master calendar but also includes appointment dates, follow-up, deadlines, and personal information.

Pocket part: An addition to a book that updates its contents.

Portal-to-portal: Of or relating to the time spent traveling from one place to another.

Position description: Document that describes the duties and responsibilities of a position.

Positional conflict: An attorney's or firm's representation of the competition of a client.

Positioning: Determining a firm's strengths and weaknesses in relation to those of other firms in the community.

Postconviction writs: A written judicial order to perform a specified act or giving authority to have it done after a criminal conviction.

Potential conflict: Arises when an attorney has an indirect relationship with a person who may be involved in the conflict.

Precedent: A court decision on a question of law that gives authority or direction on how to decide a similar question of law in a later case with similar facts.

Preclient: A person who consults an attorney but does not formally retain the services of the attorney.

Preclient file: A file containing notes of interview or consultation to be retrieved if the client retains the firm.

Preliminary bill: A bill prepared for an attorney's review and consideration for adjustment.

Preventative law: Legal information designed to avoid legal problems before they occur.

Primary case name: The name used to identify a case, consisting of the first-named plaintiff and the first-named defendant.

Primary recipient: A person to whom a document is directed or addressed.

Pro bono: Latin for "for the good"; used to describe work or services performed free of charge for indigent people.

Pro se: For one's own behalf; appearing for oneself in court.

Probate: A court procedure by which a will is proved to be valid or invalid; refers to the legal process wherein the estate of a decedent is administered.

Probation: A form of discipline that allows a person convicted of an offense to forgo more drastic punishment under supervised conditions.

Procedural law: A law that defines procedures of a lawsuit.

Proof of service by mail: A document that informs the recipient of the date the attached document was mailed.

Protocol: The set of rules that two computers use to communicate with each other.

Prune: To discard unnecessary documents from file.

Purge: To clear or discard.

Quota: An assigned goal.

Rainmaker: An attorney responsible for client development for a firm.

Reader-printer: A machine that accommodates microfilm and microfiche.

Realization: The process of turning time into cash.

Realization rate: The hourly rate of a timekeeper that the firm actually realizes when all accounts have been collected compared to the total amount billed.

Reasonable attorney's fee: The amount of an attorney's fee determined by a governing entity to be reasonable.

Redline: Marking a document to indicate changes made by other parties.

Rehabilitation: Restoration to a useful life through education and therapy.

Reinstatement: The restoration of a right that had ceased.

Remedial: Affording a remedy; giving means of obtaining redress.

Repeal: To abrogate or annul an existing law by the enactment of a statute that declares the former law revoked.

Reporter: A published volume of court decisions.

Reprimand: A formal rebuke; to strongly criticize.

Restatement: A series of volumes authored by legal scholars that describe the law, its changes, and future direction of the law.

Retaining lien: A lien placed on property that belongs to a client and is in attorney's possession.

Retroactive event recalculation: A feature in automated docketed software programs that automatically recalculates dates in the event of a change in a corresponding date.

Rich media: Image-based technology that is visual rather than text oriented.

Scanned: Entering text or graphics into a computer by electronically changing the characters into a computer-readable format.

School: A group of persons under common influence or sharing the same belief.

Scrivener: A clerk or scribe; a notary.

Search engine: An independent company that has indexed Internet sites and categorized them so that they can be found easily.

Secondary recipient: A person to whom a document is sent for informational purposes only.

Segregation of cash: Keeping clients' funds separate from law firm funds.

Series: A set of reporters in numeric order.

Server: A large computer that contains a large amount of information and directs customers' inquiries to the Internet.

Service of process: Personally delivering summons, complaints, or other legal document to a defendant or respondent.

Shareware: Software that is distributed without initial cost. If the user likes the software, a nominal payment is expected.

Skeletal library: A small library containing only essential material.

Slip opinion: A printed copy of a judicial opinion that is distributed soon after the decision is rendered.

Snail mail: The process of sending mail through the U.S. Postal Service.

Soft costs: Costs incurred for photocopy expense, long-distance telephone calls, fax, and so on.

Sole practitioner: Attorney who practices law by himself. Does not employ other attorneys.

Sole proprietorship: Business that has one individual owner. May employ other attorneys.

Source codes: The coding used by HTML to program a Web site's material.

Spam: To send unsolicited commercial e-mail messages to large numbers of people on the Internet on an indiscriminate basis.

Staff attorney: An employee of a law firm who has no advancement opportunities.

Stare decisis: The legal principle that a court will follow the decision of another court in a similar case.

Static calendar programs: A calendaring program that requires entries to be made manually.

Statute of limitations: The time period after an offense within which a lawsuit must be filed.

Substantive law: A law that creates, defines, or regulates rights.

Substantive microsystem: A system of providing legal services to a client.

Supra: Latin term meaning "above."

Suspension: The temporary cessation of the right to practice law as punishment for wrongdoing.

Symbology: Language used in bar code technology.

Target market: A group of people a firm wants as clients.

Team approach: Management theory of management and employees working together for the benefit of the organization.

Team churning: Making frequent changes in the legal team.

Telefacsimile: A system of transmitting documents over telephone wires.

Telephone tag: A situation in which someone calls a person who is unavailable and leaves a message and then is unavailable when the person returns the call.

Telnet: A protocol that allows a computer to connect with a remote computer.

Template: A form document used as a guide to prepare new documents.

Temporary restraining order: An emergency judicial remedy of brief duration that may be issued only in exceptional circumstances and only until the trial court can hear arguments or evidence on the issue.

Tickler system: A system of controlling deadlines.

Tort: A legal wrong done to a person; a civil wrong that is not based on a contract.

Trigger date: The date of an event that starts the clock running on a deadline.

Type identifier: A suffix attached to a domain name that identifies the type of organization.

Unannotated: Referring to a publication that contains the text of a law only.

Uniform Resource Locator (URL): An address of a Web site that directs a person to the information.

Unlawful detainer: A statutory procedure whereby a landlord can legally evict a tenant in default on the rent.

Update service: A service that keeps books current.

User interface: The method of operation developed by a legal publisher for its CD-ROM products.

Voice mail: Electronic recording device that allows a person to deliver a message to another person if they are unable to answer the telephone.

Web site: A collection of linked pages grouped in a certain order.

Web-based technology: Internet-like software applications.

Write-down: A decrease in the amount owed because of a discount.

Write-off: A credit for the total amount owed.

Write-up: An increase in the amount owed because of a premium.

Zeal: Enthusiastic and diligent devotion.

Answers to Self-Test Questions

CHAPTER 1

The Legal Marketplace

1. The four things that determine the structure and organization of a law office are size, specialty, management style, and form.

2. The size of a law office is measured by the number of attorneys employed by that office and includes branch offices.

3. The geographic location of the office determines the size differential of a law office.

4. The majority of lawyers prefer to practice in small firms.

5. The four types of large law firms are local, regional, national, and international.

6. The merger boom of the 1980s created the megafirm.

7. The complexity of the law has forced attorneys to specialize.

8. Specialty areas determine the firm's clientele, its need for staff, equipment, and resources.

9. A cybertort is an action for damages resulting from libelous material posted on the Internet. It also includes posting material that is protected by copyright or trademarks, such as magazines and photos.

10. A law office's culture is its working environment. It consists of intangible elements, such as the social environment, employee relationships, and attitudes.

11. The five management styles are autocratic, democratic, managing partner, committees, and combination.

12. An autocratic form of governance is when one attorney is responsible for all management and decision-making responsibilities.

13. The two types of the democratic form of governance are those in which all attorneys in the firm have a vote on management policy and those in which only owners of the law firm have a vote in management policy.

14. A Legal Administrator is an experienced manager who is hired to manage a law firm and has the authority of a managing partner.

15. An office manager is a person hired to assist a managing partner or legal administrator with the management functions of a firm.

16. The managing partner is encouraged to practice law to keep legal skills sharp.

17. An executive committee is composed of heads of various committees.

18. A combination management style is a combination of the following management styles: autocratic, democratic, managing partner, and committee.

19. The two forms of management are centralized and decentralized.

20. A sole proprietor is one attorney who owns the law firm.

21. A general practitioner is an attorney who does not specialize in a particular area of law.

22. The five most common specialties for sole proprietors are family law, real estate, torts and personal injury, criminal defense, and probate and estate planning.

23. The advantages of sole practice are the following:
    1. Receives all of the profits
    2. Has more freedom and independence
    3. Makes all the decisions for the firm
    4. Familiar with all facets of the firm's operation

24. The disadvantages of sole practice are the following:
    1. Responsible for all expenses
    2. Has no assistance with caseload and court appearances from other attorneys
    3. Usually lower income
    4. No guaranteed paycheck
    5. Difficult to take time off for vacations
    6. Long work hours
    7. Must handle all areas of the business—management, bringing in clients, document preparation, and court appearances
    8. Difficult to specialize
    9. Usually unable to afford latest equipment, technology, or large library
    10. Clients abandoned if attorney should die or become incapacitated

25. Contract attorneys work only for other attorneys.

26. The three classes of attorneys that work in a partnership are partners, associates, and nontraditional.

27. A full partner has an equal voice in management policies and has an equal share of the profits of the firm.

28. A junior partner has little input in management policies and is entitled to a smaller portion of the firm's profits.

29. A "nonequity" or "special" partner has not contributed to the firm partnership, which would entitle the partner to a full share of the profits.

30. An LLC is a limited liability company formed to shield its owners and their assets from liability arising from the misconduct of other owners or employees.

31. Only attorneys may be shareholders of a professional legal corporation.

32. The board of directors of a professional corporation are elected by its shareholders and is the policy-making body of the corporation.

33. A boutique firm is a small firm in which the attorneys specialize in one area of law.

34. The two types of office-sharing arrangements are the suite concept and the firm concept.

35. Cost-control motivates an attorney to seek an office-sharing arrangement.

36. Legal clinics are lower-cost law firms with standard fees for standard services. They emphasize low overhead and high volume.

37. The two factors responsible for legal clinics' success are television advertisement and client convenience.

38. High overhead, low compensation, nonstandard fee structure, and mismanagement caused legal clinics' failure.

39. Some legal clinics may take litigation cases with complex issues, but the majority of cases are standard divorces, bankruptcies, probate, and wills.

40. An outside counsel is an attorney retained by a corporation.

41. Preventative law avoids legal problems before they occur.

42. A corporate legal department functions as a part of the whole corporation around the projects of the corporation.

43. The head attorney in a corporate legal department is called general counsel.

44. Corporate legal departments have both centralized and decentralized forms of organization.

45. In-house counsel are attorneys employed by the corporation.

46. Some of the areas in private industry that legal assistants have utilized their paralegal training are the following:
    1. Insurance underwriter
    2. Recruiting coordinator
    3. Rehabilitation counselor
    4. Consultant
    5. Sales representative
    6. Employee benefits manager
    7. Law firm administrator
    8. Law firm marketing specialist
    9. Corporate personnel director
    10. Commercial arbitrator
    11. Corporate bond department manager
    12. Association manager
    13. Writer
    14. Career counselor
    15. Sales marketer
    16. Convention marketer
    17. Teacher
    18. Litigation consultant
    19. Environmental specialist
    20. Paralegal program director
    21. Editor
    22. Legal software trainer
    23. Politician
    24. Negotiator
    25. Investigator
    26. Real estate broker
    27. Civil rights analyst
    28. Stockbroker
    29. Computer-related careers
    30. Law librarian

47. A freelance paralegal service provides services to firms on a contract basis. The legal assistants are not firm employees.

48. An independent paralegal is a person who does law-related work for the general public without the supervision of an attorney.

49. Freelance paralegals may work in the attorney's office, rent their own offices, or work out of their homes.

50. A freelance legal assistant should have at least five years of experience because the majority of attorneys utilizing freelance legal assistants are new sole practitioners. They are not experienced enough to supervise a new legal assistant adequately.

51. The four types of government agencies that employ legal assistants are federal agencies, state agencies, county agencies, and city agencies.

52. The three largest employers of legal assistants in the federal government are the Department of Health and Human Services, the Department of Justice, and the Department of Treasury.

53. The General Schedule is the government's largest white-collar pay system that lists legal assistant positions.

54. The legal clerk/technician is a stepping-stone to a paralegal specialist position.

55. The Legal Services Corporation of the federal government establishes legal service offices in communities to serve indigent people of the community.

56. Among the opportunities at the county level are county counsel (who represents the county when the county is sued), district attorney offices, public defender offices, public administrator, and court clerk.

57. A paralegal specialist is classified under GS-950.

58. The events that have affected the practice of law are the following:
    1. The *Bates v. State Bar of Arizona* decision, which introduced advertising into the legal marketplace
    2. Increasing emphasis on management and profitability of firms
    3. Declining public perception of attorneys and the legal profession
    4. Increasing number of attorneys in the United States

59. Nonlegal subsidiaries are related, nonlegal businesses owned by attorneys.

60. Prepaid group legal services are legal insurance plans.

CHAPTER 2

The Legal Team

1. The advent of the legal assistant and legal administrator has changed the traditional law firm.

2. The legal assistant and legal administrator professions were created to increase lawyers' efficiency and incomes.

3. Legal assistants performing routine tasks and legal administrators performing management duties has increased a lawyer's efficiency.

4. The factors contributing to the growth of the legal assistant profession are the following:
    1. Promotion by bar associations
    2. Growth of paralegal education
    3. Organization of legal assistants and managers
    4. Restructuring of other professions

5. The size and specialty of the firm determines the firm's need for personnel.

6. The five categories of attorneys are the following:
    1. Rainmakers
    2. Owners
    3. Associates and senior associates
    4. Junior associates
    5. Of-counsel

7. Rainmakers bring in the clients that provide the firm with work.

8. Associates do the work. Senior associates supervise junior associates.

9. Leveraging is making a profit on the work of others.

10. A leverage ratio is the number of attorneys and legal assistants per owner.

11. A permanent associate is an employed attorney who is not eligible for an ownership interest in a firm.

12. A staff attorney is an employee of a law firm who has no advancement opportunities.

13. "Of-counsel" is an attorney affiliated with a firm on a part-time basis.

14. A legal administrator is responsible for the management of the law firm.

15. The administrator is responsible for making major business decisions for the firm. An office manager is under the direction of the legal administrator or managing partner and does not have the authority of the administrator.

16. The three major differences between an administrator and office manager are the following:
    1. The administrator attends all partnership or committee meetings, although the

administrator has no right to vote on issues.

2. An administrator has authority to hire and discharge staff personnel and administer salaries within approved guidelines.

3. An administrator has authority to make major purchases of furniture and equipment and make financial decisions for the firm.

17. A legal administrator in a large firm enjoys the same status and compensation as an attorney.

18. The legal administrator may be referred to as the chief operating officer or executive director.

19. In a small firm, the legal administrator has the same responsibilities as an administrator in a large firm, but on a smaller scale. This person may have other duties in addition to management duties, such as paralegal or accounting work.

20. The seven main areas of an administrator's responsibilities are the following:

   1. Financial management
   2. Personnel management
   3. Systems management
   4. Facilities management
   5. General management
   6. Practice management
   7. Marketing

21. The size of the firm and the amount of authority given the administrator determine the administrator's responsibilities.

22. Other types of law office managers are the following:

   1. Financial manager
   2. Personnel manager
   3. Administrative manager
   4. Facilities manager
   5. Marketing manager
   6. Legal assistant manager

23. A legal assistant manager's responsibilities are the following:

   1. Direct legal assistant personnel matters and act as a liaison between legal assistants and firm management
   2. Supervise legal assistants
   3. Coordinate paralegal workload and assign responsibilities
   4. Train legal assistants
   5. Verify that paralegal duties are performed in accordance with the attorney's instructions and act as a liaison between the legal assistants and attorneys
   6. Evaluate legal assistants' performance (see Chapter 3)

   7. Oversee firm's paralegal program
   8. Establish policies and guidelines relating to the effective utilization of legal assistants
   9. Recruit and interview new legal assistants
   10. Conduct orientation and training for new legal assistants
   11. Maintain legal assistant personnel records

24. A tiered paralegal program provides upward mobility for the legal assistant by establishing categories of paralegal positions.

25. Paralegals advance by demonstrating abilities.

26. The majority of legal assistants specialize in litigation.

27. Members of the Legal Assistant Management Association indicated that a bachelors degree should be the minimum educational requirement for a legal assistant.

28. A law clerk is a law student.

29. Some firms have elaborate programs to attract the best law students from the best law schools. They want to establish a relationship with the student so that the student will consider being employed by that firm on graduation.

30. The law clerk's duties are legal research, writing memorandum of law, and case briefs.

31. The differences between a law clerk and a legal assistant are the following:

   1. Law clerks are temporary employees of the firm.
   2. While law clerks are educated in the law, they receive very little practical procedural education. Although a law clerk may draft a motion, chances are the clerk does not know the format and the requirements and how to get the document filed with the court.
   3. A law clerk has little practical knowledge of forms required for an action.
   4. A clerk's time may or may not be billed to the client.
   5. Law clerks will not make a career of clerking.

32. Legal secretaries are responsible for clerical tasks.

33. Receptionists are responsible for answering the telephone and greeting clients.

34. Law librarians manage information and the firm's library.

35. Investigators investigate cases and interview witnesses.

36. Messengers run errands for the firm.

37. Recruiters recruit new attorneys and law clerks.

38. Process servers are responsible for service of process.

39. Case coordinators have the responsibility for the successful management of a case.

40. Outsourcing is the use of outside service companies for support staff functions.

41. An attorney service picks up documents from the firm and files them with the court. It also does service of process and other services.

42. Paralegal services work for attorneys on a contract basis.

43. Advantages of using a temporary agency are the following:

  1. Temps are available quickly.

  2. Temps provide additional help without adding employees.

  3. Temps can be billed to the client at lower rates than the employed legal assistant billing rate.

  4. Temps are not entitled to firm benefits, and employee taxes are paid by the agency.

44. Disadvantages of using a temporary agency are the following:

  1. Use of many temps in the same capacity results in an incontinuity of work flow.

  2. Temps may lack commitment to the firm's goals.

  3. Temps may lack the firm's choice in the skills of the temporary worker.

  4. Confidentiality or conflict of interest problems may arise.

CHAPTER 3

Personnel Relations

1. A firm's personnel are its most important resource.

2. Finding the right place to work is important for personal character building, self-esteem, and overall happiness in life.

3. A manager's performance can be measured by two characteristics: effectiveness and efficiency.

4. The three main objectives of a law firm are the following:

  1. Provide quality legal services to the client

  2. Provide growth and profit for the firm

  3. Provide growth and satisfaction of the employees

5. The three main objectives of a government office are the following:

  1. Provide quality legal services to the government or the people

  2. Operate within the budget set by the government

  3. Provide growth and satisfaction of the employees

6. The three main objectives of a corporate legal department are the following:

  1. Provide quality legal services to the corporation

  2. Keep outside legal costs low and operate within the budget set by the corporation

  3. Provide growth and satisfaction of the employees

7. External conditions that affect management consist of economic conditions, government regulations, and laws.

8. Internal conditions that affect management include the nature and structure of the firm, the nature of the work, and the nature of the employees.

9. The five functions of a personnel manager, or law office manager responsible for personnel relations, are the following:

  1. Planning

  2. Controlling

  3. Organizing

  4. Leading

  5. Staffing

10. Forecasting includes strategic planning and long-range planning for the firm.

11. The four areas of human resource planning are the following:

  1. Establishing human resource objectives

  2. Assessing current human resource conditions

  3. Designing and evaluating human resource activities

  4. Monitoring and evaluating the results of activities

12. The goal of human resource planning is to develop personnel policies and programs that will achieve the firm's objectives.

13. Controlling can be defined as the process of ensuring that actions conform to the plans.

14. The three main elements of control are the following:

  1. Establishing standards of performance

  2. Measuring current performance and comparing it against established standards

  3. Taking action to correct performance that does not meet established standards.

15. If standards are set too high, employee frustration develops.

16. If standards are set too low, employees will not be challenged in their work.

17. The consequences of win-lose management are the following:
    1. The atmosphere in the office becomes competitive and hostile.
    2. Time and energy are diverted from the main issues.
    3. Creativity, sensitivity, and empathy are eliminated from the office environment.
    4. Authority conflicts become more frequent and bitter.
    5. Important organizational decisions are increasingly made by an isolated, elitist group.
    6. New ideas are discouraged.
    7. Deadlocks are created and decisions are delayed.
    8. Nonaggressive people are discouraged from participation.
18. The organization function requires the manager to coordinate the resources of the firm to maximize productivity and effectiveness.
19. Leadership involves determining what is to be accomplished and how to accomplish it.
20. Staffing includes such functions as recruitment, screening, interviewing, testing, hiring, firing, job analysis, job description, and keeping personnel records.
21. The four steps in the hiring process are the following:
    1. Planning
    2. Recruitment
    3. Selection
    4. Training
22. Four advantages of promoting from within the firm are the following:
    1. Costs: The selection cost of hiring a new employee is eliminated.
    2. Productivity: The employee already knows the structure and procedures of the firm, so loss in productivity is reduced.
    3. Loyalty: Promotions encourage employee loyalty.
    4. Morale: The promoted employee receives recognition, which increases employee morale.
23. Prospective employees are recruited through employment agencies, newspaper advertising, legal assistant associations, and word of mouth.
24. Questions on the application that pertain to an applicant's age, sex, race, height, or weight violate federal regulations.
25. The ouch formula is an acronym for proper interview questions. Questions must be the following:

1. Objective
2. Uniform
3. Consistent
4. Have job relatedness

26. Casual conversation at the beginning is one method to give an applicant the opportunity to relax.
27. Some danger signs a manager should look for when interviewing an applicant are the following:
    1. Job hopping
    2. Distance from home
    3. Health
    4. Improper termination notice to previous employer
    5. Reasons for leaving
    6. Poor relationship with previous employer
28. The CEMEC principle is an acronym that describes employee expectations, as follows:
    1. Communication
    2. Education
    3. Motivation
    4. Evaluation
    5. Compensation
29. Fear is the inhibiting factor of open communication: fear of rejection, fear of looking stupid, and fear of losing the respect of co-workers.
30. The buddy system is used when the firm pairs a new employee with another employee in the same job capacity for training purposes.
31. A mentor is an experienced legal assistant or attorney from whom the new legal assistant can learn.
32. Poor working conditions increase turnover and decrease efficiency.
33. Good working conditions decrease turnover and increase efficiency.
34. Working conditions consist of the following:
    1. Policy: reasonable office policies fully set forth in an office manual with grievance procedures and appeal process established and explained
    2. Health and safety: good lighting and a clean, comfortable environment with regulated heating and air conditioning
    3. Tools: updated tools and equipment
35. The two types of evaluation are the following:
    1. Formal evaluation
    2. Informal evaluation
36. Formal evaluation is in writing and is followed by a performance interview with the employee and evaluators.

37. Informal evaluation occurs daily when employees' mistakes are corrected or they are told that they did a good job on a project.

38. Some of the areas considered in a formal performance evaluation are the following:
    1. Courtesy to clients
    2. Punctuality
    3. Dependability
    4. Communication skills
    5. Leadership capabilities
    6. Initiative
    7. Work habits
    8. Willingness to work overtime
    9. Skills rating
    10. Job performance

39. If a legal assistant is unhappy with the formal performance evaluation, the legal assistant should contact the firm's administrator to determine what steps can be taken to remedy the situation.

40. To establish a basic compensation structure, firms consider the following:
    1. The marketplace: what other firms in the area pay their employees
    2. Job analysis: a study of the job activities, duties, and responsibilities of each job
    3. Job description: a detailed description of the job and the skills required to perform the job
    4. Job evaluation: establishes the value of the job and puts a monetary value on the job

41. Raises are based on the consumer price index and merit, tenure, incentives, or base salary.

42. Bonuses are based on merit, tenure, incentive, or base salary.

43. When calculating raises, the consumer price index is often considered.

44. Merit raises and bonuses acknowledge above-average quality and quantity of work.

45. Raises and bonuses based on tenure occur when an employee is rewarded for longevity with the firm.

46. A small firm usually offers fewer benefits than does a large firm.

47. FLSA stands for the Federal Labor Standards Act.

48. The Federal Labor Standards Act (FLSA) designates the parameters within which an employee may be designated exempt or nonexempt.

49. Employees who are exempt are paid an annual or monthly salary and are not entitled to overtime pay.

50. Employees who are nonexempt are paid by the hour and are entitled to overtime pay for all hours worked in excess of forty per week.

51. The basic theory behind the team approach is as follows: By aligning the organization's needs with the needs of the employees, the organization will benefit from employees' personal motivation, energy, and drive as well as benefiting employees by being a vehicle by which they can achieve their personal goals.

52. Studies have shown that the team approach plays an important role in the following:
    1. The personal satisfaction of employees
    2. The success of the enterprise
    3. Good service to the client

53. The five Cs of the team approach are the following:
    1. Commitment
    2. Competency
    3. Constructive feedback
    4. Creativity
    5. Cooperation

54. Each employee should be committed to the following:
    1. Providing quality legal services to the client
    2. Contributing to the profitability of the firm
    3. Deriving personal satisfaction and growth from work

55. Making a commitment requires trust in the organization and trust in the people.

56. Education, experience, on-the-job training, and continuing education are the keys to competency.

57. Continuing legal education is essential to keep abreast of changes in the law.

58. The following attributes increase creativity:
    1. An open mind
    2. Curiosity
    3. Ability to concentrate
    4. Persistence
    5. Cooperation

59. The business of law is more stressful than other industries because of the constant deadlines and needs of clients.

60. The basis of most personality conflicts is lack of communication.

61. If a legal assistant observes unethical behavior, the legal assistant should bring the situation to the attention of the perpetrator or the office manager.

CHAPTER 4

The Attorney-Client Relationship

1. The four things that have affected the traditional attorney-client relationship are the following:
   1. Economics
   2. The demand for varied specialties
   3. Marketing
   4. Business management changes

2. A state bar's Code of Professional Responsibility provides a joint-venture approach to the attorney-client relationship and provides a model in which the responsibilities in any representation are allocated between the attorney and the client.

3. The American Bar Association (ABA) adopted rules of ethics known as the Model Code of Professional Responsibility (Model Code). The most recent version is known as the Model Rules of Professional Responsibility.

4. As a client's representative, a lawyer performs three functions (the three As):
   1. Adviser
   2. Advocate
   3. Agent

5. As an adviser to the client, the lawyer will:
   1. Exercise independent judgment for the client
   2. Be candid no matter how unpleasant the advice may be
   3. Discourage illegal or fraudulent conduct
   4. Inform the client of adverse consequences
   5. Apprise the client of the proposed course of action

6. As a client's advocate, the lawyer will:
   1. Represent a client before a court or tribunal
   2. Make reasonable efforts to expedite litigation consistent with the interest of the client
   3. Not bring a claim that has no basis in fact to harass another

7. As a client's agent, the lawyer will:
   1. Seek results advantageous to the client while being honest and fair with others
   2. Be a spokesperson for the client
   3. Negotiate on the client's behalf
   4. Abide by the client's decisions after informing the client of the issues of the case and ramifications of the client's decision

8. The attorney is ultimately responsible for the attorney-client relationship.

9. The attorney is responsible for the legal assistant's actions.

10. Legal assistants are not bound by the Rules of Professional Responsibility of state bar associations.

11. Legal assistants are considered lawyers' agents.

12. Every legal assistant is ethically obligated to comply with the state bar's Code of Professional Responsibility for lawyers.

13. The four factors clients want most from attorneys are the following:
    1. Commitment
    2. Integrity
    3. Commentary
    4. Fairness in fees

    The most important is commitment.

14. Satisfied clients are the best source of new clients for a firm.

15. A recent study indicated that 50 percent of new clients come from recommendations of existing and former clients and that 30 percent come from recommendations of people who are not clients but who would be clients if the occasion should arise (friends, associates, relatives).

16. Twenty percent of new clients come from marketing activities.

17. A firm's marketing activities are stated in a marketing plan.

18. Positioning a law firm is when the marketing manager analyzes the information from client surveys to determine the firm's strengths, weaknesses, opportunities, and roadblocks.

19. A target market is a group the firm wants to attract as clients.

20. Advertising was banned by the ABA to avoid "extravagant, artful, self-laudatory brashness" that could mislead laypersons and cause public distrust of the legal system. It was also considered demeaning and was believed that advertising had a negative effect on society.

21. The U.S. Supreme Court ruled that the ban on lawyer advertising was a violation of First Amendment guarantees of lawyers' right to advertise

22. The term *dignified manner* was defined in case law.

23. Yellow Page ads are the most common method of lawyer advertising.

24. The key considerations in evaluating the content of lawyer television advertising is that it not be false, misleading, or deceptive.

25. The ABA promotes the Dignity in Lawyer Advertising Award to illustrate what it feels is a dignified television ad.

26. Fewer lawyers are participating in television advertising because it is not cost-effective and is not a wise expenditure of an advertising budget.

27. Netvertising is advertising products or services on the Internet.

28. Model Rule 7.1 applies to Netvertising.

29. Some problems associated with advertising on the Internet include applying each state's Code of Professional Responsibility to multistate advertising and monitoring misleading information.

30. False and misleading information and attorney comparisons are prohibited in attorneys' Internet advertising.

31. Large firms are most likely to sponsor seminars for their clients.

32. Seminars keep corporate clients informed and create a personal rapport with clients.

33. A firm newsletter can help a firm attain a variety of goals, including the following:
    1. Reminding clients of their obligation to file reports with government agencies
    2. Informing clients about new developments in the law
    3. Informing clients about services available from the firm

34. A combination of four different trends have contributed to the success of the law firm newsletter:
    1. Desktop publishing and laser printers
    2. The increased usage of personal computers in law firms
    3. The awareness of increasing demands for technical support
    4. The spread of multiple offices that are connected to a computer network

35. Public relations is developing and maintaining a favorable public image between the law firm and the community.

36. Advertising is purchased; public relations is not. Also, a firm has no control over public relations and has total control over advertising. Advertising allows a firm to repeat an ad as often as it would like and can be directed to specific times and places.

37. Public relations has more credibility than advertising since its source is presumably objective and nonbiased.

38. The general rule is that a lawyer may not solicit legal business from a potential client to whom he or she is not related or with whom he or she has had no prior professional relationship when the solicitation is for the lawyer's monetary gain.

39. The justification for the prohibition is that lawyers are trained in the art of persuasion and that people in need of legal services may be emotionally vulnerable and subject to overreaching.

40. The U.S. Supreme Court Ruled in *Shapero v. Kentucky Bar Association* that direct-mail solicitation is constitutionally protected free speech.

41. Spam is the indiscriminate posting of e-mail messages promoting a product or service. A Phoenix lawyer was suspended for spamming.

42. A capper is paid to get business for an attorney.

43. Exempt from solicitation accusations are the following:
    1. Public defenders and district attorneys because they are employed by a county or state government and receive a salary from taxpayer dollars
    2. Sponsored attorney referral services
    3. Attorneys employed by prepaid legal insurance plans
    4. Attorneys who communicate directly with a family member, current or former client, or pro bono client regarding legal services
    5. Lawyers who provide information to a potential client at their request

44. Types of potential cappers include insurance adjusters, medical personnel, and police officers.

45. An attorney may inform a potential client of services if no financial benefits will be gained, except if the case is a high-profile case.

46. A problem occurs if the employee is compensated for the referral.

47. It is considered improper for an attorney to try to persuade clients to leave the firm with the attorney because clients belong to a firm, not an individual attorney. However, it is the client's decision to choose the attorney or the firm.

48. Among the elements of the attorney-client relationship are trust, loyalty, honesty, openness, and understanding.

49. Case law determines when the attorney-client relationship begins.

50. The Iowa Supreme Court used three factors to test when an attorney-client relationship exists:
    1. The client sought legal advice.
    2. The advice sought was within areas of lawyer's competence.

3. The lawyer gave, or agreed to give, the advice sought

51. Paying a fee is not essential to create an attorney-client relationship.

52. The five Cs of client relations are the following:
    1. Competence
    2. Commitment
    3. Communication
    4. Conflict of interest
    5. Confidentiality

53. Four things are required to represent the client competently:
    1. Legal knowledge
    2. Legal skill
    3. Thoroughness
    4. Preparation

54. Required legal skills include technical skills such as the ability to draft documents, review documents, conduct research, and perform administrative tasks, such as record keeping.

55. The standard of thoroughness as required by the ABA Model Rules is that degree of thoroughness ordinarily employed by lawyers undertaking similar matters.

56. Adequate preparation consists of necessary legal research and investigation of the facts of the case.

57. If an attorney is inexperienced in an area of law, the attorney need not decline the case if the attorney makes an effort to become knowledgeable in that area without jeopardizing the client's case.

58. A lawyer who knows that he or she does not have the necessary skills to undertake a complex matter is bound by the Code of Professional Responsibility to either decline the case or associate another attorney on the case who is competent in the subject matter.

59. If a lawyer chooses to associate another lawyer on a case, the lawyer must obtain the client's consent.

60. No. The fees charged the client cannot be increased because of the involvement of the additional lawyer.

61. The lawyer is responsible for the legal assistant's work.

62. Commitment to a client's case forbids a lawyer to neglect the case.

63. Some examples of a lack of commitment to a client's case are the following:
    1. Failure to begin an action
    2. Failure to appear at hearing
    3. Failure to file pleadings

    4. Filing carelessly drafted pleadings
    5. Failure to respond to interrogatories
    6. Failure to respond to correspondence from opposing counsel
    7. Failure to correct a known defect in a case
    8. Failure to notify clients of lawyers' new office address or telephone number

64. The term *zeal* suggests the frame of mind appropriate in advocacy but not appropriate in the lawyer's role as advisor.

65. The attorney's failure to communicate with clients is the most common complaint clients have about attorneys.

66. A lawyer can keep clients informed by the following:
    1. Advising them of the status of their affairs
    2. Responding to their requests for information
    3. Responding to letters sent by clients
    4. Notifying clients of changes in a lawyer's address and telephone number
    5. Apprising clients of any reason that the lawyer cannot provide them with diligent representation
    6. Advising clients of the proper course of action and the risks involved and possible alternative action
    7. Informing clients of their rights, especially in criminal cases
    8. Advising clients on both the legal and the practical aspects of a matter
    9. Providing clients with copies of all documents received or prepared in their cases

67. Providing the client with information relates to two areas of the client's case: informing the client of the status of the case and advising the client of the law to allow the client to make informed decisions concerning the case.

68. A lawyer may not represent one client whose interests are adverse to another client, even if the two representations are unrelated, unless the client consents and the lawyer believes that the representation will not adversely affect a client.

69. It is generally agreed that a greater obligation is owed to a former client than to a potential client.

70. When a client retains an attorney in a law firm, the client retains every attorney in the firm.

71. Two attorneys in the same firm cannot represent two sides of a dispute because to do so would be a conflict of interest.

72. A direct conflict of interest is when an attorney or firm has a relationship with a person who

may be involved in the conflict or when the attorney or firm has a financial interest in an entity involved in the conflict.

73. A potential conflict arises when an attorney has an indirect relationship with a person who may be involved in the conflict.

74. A positional conflict arises when an attorney or firm represents a client's competition.

75. One of the major factors that differentiates a law firm from other industries is the requirement that all matters within that office be kept confidential.

76. The primary justification for the strict rules on confidentiality is the desirability of complete candor between client and lawyer. Confidentiality not only facilitates the full development of facts essential to proper representation but also encourages people to seek legal assistance at an early stage.

77. The exceptions to the confidentiality rule are the following:

   1. A client may consent to a lawyer's divulging confidential information but only after full disclosure and consultation.
   2. A lawyer may reveal a client's intentions to commit a crime and the information necessary to prevent a crime.
   3. If the client commits perjury, the attorney has an obligation to reveal the perjury. Perjury is a fraud on the court, and the Model Code requires total candor with the court. The Model Code further forbids lawyers to "knowingly use perjured testimony or false evidence" or to "knowingly make a false statement of law or fact." It is the lawyer's obligation to encourage the client to rectify the fraud and reveal the fraud to the court.
   4. If a law or a court order requires the lawyer to disclose otherwise confidential information, the lawyer may do so.
   5. A lawyer may reveal a client's confidences to collect fees and defend him- or herself against claims of criminal or unethical conduct arising out of the lawyer's representation of the client.

78. Attorney-client privilege permits a client to refuse to testify and to keep an attorney from testifying in a legal proceeding about communications made between the two in strict confidence.

79. In order for a communication between an attorney and client to be privileged, three factors must be present:

   1. Communication must be made in confidence.
   2. Communication must be to obtain legal advice.
   3. Communication must be with an attorney.

80. The differences between confidentiality and attorney-client privilege are the following:

   1. Attorney-client privilege protects only information covered by attorney-client communication. It does not protect the facts generating the confidences or the knowledge of the client.
   2. Information that is open to the public is not covered by attorney-client privilege. However, the lawyer's obligation to keep information confidential includes information that is public.
   3. Attorney-client privilege includes information that the lawyer obtains from the client only. Confidentiality includes all information "relating to the representation of a client" regardless of its source.
   4. Attorney-client privilege prevents disclosure in the litigation process. Confidentiality prevents disclosure anywhere at any time, even after the death of the client.
   5. Attorney-client privilege does not include conversations between government attorneys and officials in response to investigations that might involve criminal law issues.

81. The attorney work-product doctrine requires that information the attorney learns in representation of a client be kept confidential and may not be revealed to third parties.

82. Some examples of legal assistants' work product that are subject to the work-product doctrine include the following:

   1. Interoffice memoranda discussing case status or case strategy
   2. Telephone memos of conversations with clients and witnesses and those related to the investigation
   3. Notes of meetings with clients
   4. Document-screening and site inspection notes
   5. Investigation memos and interview notes
   6. Document production notes
   7. Case memoranda and task assignment documents

83. A client may terminate the attorney-client relationship at any time without justifying the termination.

84. If a lawyer wants to end the relationship with a client and the client will not release the lawyer from the obligation, in most cases the lawyer must have the court's permission.

85. Under the ABA Model Rules, a lawyer may terminate the attorney-client relationship under the following circumstances:
    1. The client insists on a claim or defense that cannot be supported by a good-faith argument on existing law.
    2. The client acts unlawfully or insists that the lawyer do so.
    3. The client makes it unreasonably difficult for the lawyer to be effective.
    4. Before a case goes to court, the client insists that the lawyer act contrary to the lawyer's judgment and advice.
    5. The client deliberately disregards an agreement with the lawyer as to fees or expenses.
    6. The lawyer's continued employment is likely to result in a violation of an ethics rule.
    7. The lawyer is unable to work with cocounsel, to the detriment of his client's interest.
    8. The lawyer has physical or mental problems that make it difficult to provide the client with an effective representation.
    9. The client consents to the withdrawal.
    10. Any other reason found by the court to be good cause for withdrawal.

86. A lawyer must still protect the client's interest even after the lawyer has either withdrawn or been terminated from the case. The lawyer must do the following:
    1. Give reasonable notice to the client of his intention to withdraw
    2. Allow the client time to find another lawyer and cooperate with that lawyer
    3. Return to the client papers, property, and unearned advanced fees to which the client is entitled

87. The state bar or other agency may impose discipline on the lawyer in any one of five ways:
    1. Admonition
    2. Reprimand
    3. Probation
    4. Suspension
    5. Disbarment

88. An admonition is the least severe form of discipline. The state bar or other attorney disciplinary agency will declare the attorney's conduct improper but will keep the information private.

89. A reprimand is a form of public discipline that publicly declares the attorney's conduct improper. The state bar or other attorney disciplinary agency will publish the name of the attorney, facts surrounding the discipline, and the form of reprimand in newspapers, magazines, journals, and other publications.

90. When an attorney is on probation, the state bar or disciplinary agency will impose certain conditions that must be met in order for the lawyer to continue to practice law. Probation may be ordered alone or with an admonition or a reprimand. Probation also may be imposed as a condition on reinstatement of a suspended or disbarred attorney.

91. A more severe form of discipline, suspension means that an attorney may not practice law for a specific period of time, usually from six months to three years.

92. Disbarment, the most drastic of attorney's discipline, terminates the lawyer's status as a lawyer and cancels the attorney's license to practice law.

93. Some state bar associations do not have the ultimate authority to disbar an attorney. Since disbarment has a devastating effect on the attorney's livelihood that directly affects the attorney's ability to make a living, most states require that all disbarment proceedings be appealed or reviewed by the state's high court.

94. Disbarment is not always permanent. An attorney may apply for reinstatement after a sufficient amount of time has elapsed (usually about five years).

95. Other forms of discipline for an attorney are the following:
    1. Restitution (if the lawyer steals a client's funds)
    2. Payment of costs
    3. Limitation on practice
    4. Requirement that the lawyer take the Professional Responsibility exam

96. If the attorney fails to act competently or represent a client diligently, the client may sue the attorney for malpractice.

97. If an attorney is negligent, the attorney may be sued for malpractice.

98. Personal injury plaintiff firms are sued for malpractice most often.

99. Client satisfaction is the basis for measuring a law firm's performance?

CHAPTER 5

Legal Assistant Ethics and Client Relations

1. Family, friends, religious upbringing, education, environment, and past experiences contribute to our ethical values.

2. The *Living Webster Encyclopedic Dictionary* defines ethics as "the principles of morality, or the field of study of morals or right conduct."

3. Ethics cannot be defined as honest versus dishonest, right versus wrong, or good versus bad because there are many gray areas in between.

4. Our personal characteristics influence the degree to which we can recognize ethical issues.

5. People with good intentions sometimes violate ethical standards because they are unaware of ethical boundaries or do not give their actions serious thought.

6. The foundation of ethical standards is established through education and knowledge of ethics and professional responsibility.

7. National and state bar associations; national, state, and local paralegal associations; and the courts have developed ethical guidelines for paralegals to follow.

8. Legal assistants are not lawyers and are therefore not bound by the attorney's state bar code of ethics, by which attorneys must abide.

9. Legal assistants are lawyers' agents.

10. A legal assistant cannot be prosecuted by a state bar or governing agency for unethical behavior.

11. The client and employing firm or attorney suffer from a paralegal's unethical conduct.

12. Legal assistants comply with ethical codes to protect their employers from liability.

13. The paralegal profession was born in the 1960s out of concern for the legal profession as it was structured.

14. A study conducted by the ABA in the early 1960s revealed that lawyers' businesses were not as profitable as other professionals, such as doctors, dentists, and architects.

15. Other professions were professionally managed and used assistants.

16. The ABA considered the use of legal assistants and determined that it would do three things:

    1. Increase lawyers' efficiency
    2. Decrease costs to the client
    3. Increase the attorney's profitability

17. The ABA established a committee on legal assistants in 1968, now called the ABA Standing Committee on Legal Assistants.

18. The first formal paralegal educational programs were established in the early 1970s.

19. The ABA began its approval process of paralegal programs in 1975.

20. The two national paralegal associations are the National Federation of Paralegal Associations (NFPA) and the National Association of Legal Assistants (NALA).

21. The NFPA may impose any of the following sanctions for violation of its code of ethics:

    1. Letter of reprimand
    2. Counseling
    3. Attendance at an ethics course approved by committee
    4. Probation
    5. Suspension of authority to practice
    6. Revocation of authority to practice
    7. Imposition of a fine
    8. Assessment of costs
    9. Referral to the appropriate authority if criminal activity is found

22. It has been a problem to monitor adherence to the organization's ethics code because unless a violation is reported to the association, it is unaware of the violation.

23. The five Cs of client relations are 1 competence, 2 commitment, 3 communication, 4 conflict of interest, and 5 confidentiality.

24. The four aspects of a lawyer's competency that apply to legal assistants are legal knowledge, skill, thoroughness, and preparation.

25. Legal knowledge is acquired in school and through continuing legal education.

26. Skill is created by applying that knowledge to clients' cases.

27. Knowledge and skill are increased by experience and continuing legal education.

28. Thoroughness is created by adequate preparation.

29. Failing to prepare a document correctly or being sloppy in work habits affect thoroughness.

30. Technology has been responsible for a lack in thoroughness because a task can be accomplished faster, and it is easy to rely on technology to be thorough for us. We tend to be lazy in the details.

31. The eight areas that indicate a lack of commitment to a client's case are the following:

1. Failure to begin an action
2. Failure to appear at a hearing
3. Failure to file pleadings
4. Filing carelessly drafted pleadings
5. Failure to respond to interrogatories
6. Failure to respond to correspondence from opposing counsel
7. Failure to correct a known defect in a case
8. Failure to notify clients of lawyers' new office address or telephone number

32. Legal assistants can greatly assist an attorney in communicating with clients by answering a client's request for information about a case, easing a client's concerns, and responding to a client's correspondence or request for a status report.

33. A goodwill letter is a letter written to create rapport and good relations.

34. Only an attorney may give legal advice to a client.

35. A general guideline for legal advice is this: If a legal assistant applies knowledge of the law to the facts of a case and renders an opinion, it is legal advice.

36. The following activities constitute legal advice:
    1. Recommending a course of conduct or action to a client
    2. Evaluating a case and predicting the possible outcome
    3. Evaluating a case and suggesting a course of action
    4. Explaining the client's rights or obligations to a client
    5. Independently interpreting statutes, decisions, or legal documents to a client

37. The prohibition against giving legal advice is difficult for experienced paralegals because they know the law and the answers to questions.

38. If a paralegal is asked a question that requires legal advice, she or he must ask the attorney for the answer even though she or he may know the answer.

39. No. A legal assistant may draft the letter for the attorney's approval and signature, but the legal assistant may not sign the letter.

40. A "jailhouse lawyer" may give legal advice, and a legal assistant may give legal advice to a client she or he is representing at an administrative hearing, if the administrative agency allows nonattorney representation.

41. The case of *Johnson v. Avery*, 393 U.S. 484 (1969), created the "jailhouse lawyer."

42. When communicating with clients, legal assistants must always identify themselves as a legal assistant so that the client understands that the legal assistant is not an attorney. This will ensure that no one is confused as to the paralegal's status.

43. A legal assistant may not accept a case because accepting a case creates an attorney-client relationship, for which the attorney is responsible.

44. Nonlawyer conflict of interest is when a legal assistant learns of confidential information about a case during employment with one firm and then goes to work for the opposing firm.

45. A Chinese wall prohibits a person from working on or discussing a case.

46. A Chinese wall prohibits a legal assistant from working on any case with the legal assistant's former employer and imposes the following restrictions:
    1. The firm must educate all employees about the importance of the Chinese wall.
    2. The isolated person may not discuss the case with others or be near others who are working on the case. All firm employees must be aware of the wall that is constructed around the employee.
    3. The isolated person may not have access to files and documents of the case. The subject case files must be "flagged" in a manner that is identifiable from a distance and is obvious to all who see the file that it is subject to a Chinese wall.
    4. The client must be notified of the potential conflict and of the firm's efforts to isolate the person from those working on the case.

47. A freelance paralegal must keep a list of cases she or he has worked on because, if a freelance legal assistant worked on a case for one firm, she or he may not work on the same case for another firm.

48. A legal assistant keeps a client's matter confidential by the following:
    1. Not discussing the case outside the office
    2. Making sure that the surroundings are private when discussing a case with a co-worker
    3. Concealing a client's file from others outside the office
    4. Making sure that a client's e-mail is not subject to the view of others
    5. Not accepting a telephone call from a client while in conference with another client
    6. Not exposing client documents on a computer screen

49. An e-mail must be sent to a client on a secure server to protect confidentiality.

50. The exceptions to the confidentiality rule are the following:
    1. A client may consent to a lawyer's divulging confidential information, but only after full disclosure and consultation.
    2. A lawyer may reveal a client's intentions to commit a crime and the information necessary to prevent a crime.
    3. If the client commits perjury, the attorney has an obligation to reveal the perjury. Perjury is a fraud on the court, and the Model Code requires total candor with the court. The Model Code further forbids lawyers to "knowingly use perjured testimony or false evidence" or to "knowingly make a false statement of law or fact." It is the lawyer's obligation to encourage the client to rectify the fraud and reveal the fraud to the court.
    4. If a law or a court order requires the lawyer to disclose otherwise confidential information, the lawyer may do so.
    5. A lawyer may reveal a client's confidences to collect fees and defend him- or herself against claims of criminal or unethical conduct arising out of the lawyer's representation of the client.

51. The activities that constitute the unauthorized practice of law are subject to case law interpretation of each state.

52. The three activities that have been determined to be the unauthorized practice of law are the following:
    1. Representing clients in court or government agency proceedings
    2. Preparing legal documents without supervision of an attorney
    3. Giving legal advice

53. Paralegals may represent clients before many federal or state administrative agencies if the agency allows nonattorney representation.

54. No. While paralegals may attend depositions with their supervising attorney, they may not ask the deponent questions.

55. In many states, unauthorized practice of law occurs when legal documents are prepared without the attorney's direct supervision.

56. Legal documents includes preprinted legal forms.

57. Courts have ruled that completing a court form for a client requires knowledge obtained by a law school education and constitutes giving legal advice. There have been other court rulings that said that even informing a person what form to use is an unauthorized practice of law.

58. Many courts have a program to help pro se parties complete their paperwork, consisting of legal forms for dissolutions, restraining orders, and small-claims cases.

59. Courts employ nonattorneys to help people complete their paperwork because wrong and incomplete forms are filed, causing delays in the court system.

60. No, a legal assistant may not sign a pleading.

61. An attorney must sign a pleading because the attorney's signature is verification that the attorney read and knows the contents of the document.

62. In the *Dacey* case, the court ruled that publication of forms and instructions on how to complete the forms did not constitute legal advice if the instructions were directed toward the public and not individual clients.

63. The Texas Supreme Court investigated Nolo Press to determine whether its books and software are the unauthorized practice of law and whether Nolo books and software should be banned in Texas.

64. Legal "kits" contain the requisite forms for a particular area, such as wills, trusts, and dissolutions of marriage, along with instructions on how to complete the forms.

65. The courts ruled that the legal "kits" did not constitute the unauthorized practice of law because they are directed to the public rather than to an individual client.

66. Legal "kits" for dissolution of marriage, bankruptcy, and will preparation are available in most stationery stores.

67. A problem arises when the information in a legal "kit" is applied directly to an individual client's matter.

68. Independent paralegals provide legal services directly to the public in areas such as divorce, bankruptcy, immigration, and landlord-tenant matters at reduced rates.

69. Freelance paralegals work for attorneys on an independent contractor basis under their direct supervision.

70. Independent paralegals provide legal services to the public, and freelance paralegals provide legal services to attorneys.

71. The Wave Project is a chain of do-it-yourself divorce centers.

72. Wave centers provided typing and information services to the public.

73. Rosemary Furman was convicted of the unauthorized practice of law for giving her clients legal advice on the correct information

to insert on legal forms and prohibited her from helping customers complete the forms. The court eventually imposed a jail sentence on her for failing to abide by its order.

74. Rosemary Furman's jail sentence was commuted after she agreed to close her business.

75. In the 1980s, the State Bar of California formed the Public Protection Committee to study whether independent paralegal services could meet the need of legal services to low- and middle-income people.

76. The Public Protection Committee held hearings of laypersons and members of the legal community to determine whether there was a need for independent paralegal services.

77. The Public Protection Committee found that independent paralegals could help meet the need of legal services to the indigent.

78. The Public Protection Committee issued a report that recommended that the California Supreme Court adopt a rule authorizing independent paralegals to engage in the practice of law in bankruptcy, family law, and landlord-tenant law in uncomplicated, routine cases.

79. The report caused an uproar in the State Bar of California, and its president at the time vowed that it would "never see the light of day."

80. In late 1998, California enacted SB 1418, which allows paralegals to do "scrivener-type" services for the public if they register with their county.

81. Independent paralegals may make legal information available to customers but may not offer legal advice.

82. Independent paralegals are identified as "legal document assistants" and "Unlawful Detainer Assistants" under SB 1418.

83. In 2003, SB 1418 expires and will be reconsidered at that time.

84. The North Carolina Bar Association's Real Estate Section hired a consumer protection advocate to investigate independent and freelance paralegals who work in the real estate area without proper supervision by an attorney.

85. HALT stands for Help Abolish Legal Tyranny.

86. HALT promotes the public's use of independent paralegals.

87. Traditional paralegals work under the direct supervision of an attorney.

88. Traditional paralegals object to the title "legal document assistants" because it is too close to the title "legal assistant." CAPA stated that independent paralegal activities are scrivener-type work, and it sees the role of paralegals as much more substantive.

89. Other terms for independent paralegals are "legal technician," "legal document assistant," "public paralegal," and "limited law advisers."

90. The case that identifies activities that are not considered to constitute the unauthorized practice of law is *People v. Landlords Professional Services,* 215 Cal. App. 3d 1599; 264 Cal. Rptr. 548 (1989).

91. The lack of regulation of the paralegal profession, especially independent paralegal services, has created problems for the paralegal profession as a whole.

92. "Fly-by-night" paralegal programs are programs or independent paralegal services that are unqualified and that damage their customers and the paralegal profession.

93. "Fly-by-night" paralegal programs are dangerous because the public has no way of knowing whether the independent paralegal service is operated by knowledgeable, experienced paralegals or one with no paralegal training.

94. The lack of regulation allows unqualified paralegals to proliferate.

95. To ensure professionalism, paralegals must be committed to the following:

1. Public service
2. Education
3. High standards of ethical conduct
4. Excellence
5. Strong work ethic
6. Integrity and honor
7. Development of the whole person
8. Exercising good judgment, common sense, and communication skills

CHAPTER 6

Legal Fees

1. At the time of the Roman republic, legal services were free of charge—rendered for the honor and personal satisfaction the advocate received by providing the service.

2. The different types of fees are the following:

1. Retainer fees
2. Hourly fees
3. Flat (fixed) fees
4. Task-based fees
5. Contingency fees
6. Statutory fees
7. Referral fees
8. Premiums
9. Combination

3. The four types of retainer fees are the following:
   1. True retainer
   2. Nonrefundable chargeable retainer
   3. Nonrefundable nonchargeable retainer
   4. Refundable retainer

4. A true retainer fee is paid to the law firm to ensure the firm's availability to the client.

5. A true retainer fee was used to secure a firm's loyalty to a client.

6. A nonrefundable chargeable retainer fee is paid in advance of representation and is not refundable to the client in most circumstances. It is applied to the client's bill.

7. A nonrefundable nonchargeable retainer fee is paid to the firm at the beginning of the case and is not applied to the client's bill. It is not refundable if the firm is discharged.

8. Many firms use nonrefundable retainers to ensure client loyalty to the firm and to test a client's commitment to the case.

9. A refundable retainer fee is applied to the total fee and is refundable if the client terminates the attorney-client relationship.

10. Hourly fees are when clients are charged by the hour for each hour or portion of an hour spent on the case.

11. Hourly rates vary according to specialty, geographic area, and the lawyer's years of experience.

12. A blended hourly rate is the average hourly rate of the people working on the case.

13. The six factors used to determine hourly rates are the following:
    1. Planned or budgeted expenses, excluding partner or shareholder compensation and benefits
    2. Anticipated billable time by a partner, an associate, or a legal assistant
    3. Desired profit percentage
    4. Reasonable allocation of expenses by a partner, an associate, or a legal assistant
    5. Firm collection rate—billings divided by cash receipts
    6. Billing rate—work-in-progress billable time versus past billed hours

14. An hourly fee is the most common fee found in law offices.

15. A flat (fixed) fee is a set fee for a service rendered.

16. A per diem flat fee is a fee charged by the attorney for a day's work.

17. Minimum/maximum flat fees are based on the outcome of the matter. If the outcome of the matter is extremely satisfying for the client, the maximum fee is charged. If the outcome is not as the client had hoped, the minimum fee is charged.

18. A law firm knows by experience about how long it takes to complete a certain type of case. The attorney's and legal assistant's time are estimated, and a flat fee is established by applying the attorney's and legal assistant's hourly rates for completion of the case.

19. Each phase of a case contains a list of tasks, and each task contains activities. Each task is given a specific fee or hourly rate that is appropriate to the level of complexity of the task.

20. A contingency fee is a fee based on a percentage of the client's recovery in a case.

21. The two methods of calculating the attorney's fee are the gross fee method and the net fee method.

22. The difference between the gross fee method and net fee method of calculation is that the attorney's fee is deducted before the costs in the gross fee method. In the net fee method, the attorney's fee is calculated after deducting costs.

23. A client receives more money when a contingency fee is calculated by the net fee method.

24. In a modified contingency fee case, the lawyer is paid a percentage of the difference between the amount at issue and the amount of the final judgment.

25. The four considerations in taking a case on a contingency basis are the following (RISC):
    1. Risk
    2. Inflation
    3. Significant expense
    4. Cash flow

26. Several states have put limits on contingency fees because they felt that doing so would discourage lawsuits.

27. Statutory fees are fees set by state statute.

28. According to Model Rule 1.5(e), the three occasions when a lawyer may divide a fee with another lawyer are the following:
    1. If the division is in proportion to the services rendered by the lawyer or by written agreement with the client
    2. If the client agrees to the division
    3. If the total fee is reasonable

29. According to Model Rule 5.4, the three occasions when a lawyer may divide a fee with a nonlawyer are the following:
    1. It is payment to a lawyer's widow or widower after the lawyer's death

2. A lawyer purchases a law practice of a deceased or disabled lawyer

3. The firm has a profit-sharing or retirement plan for employees

30. Lawyers are prohibited from fee splitting with nonlawyers because it may allow the lawyer's independent judgment to be controlled by a nonlawyer who is interested in his own profit rather than the legal needs of the client. It also discourages nonlawyers from engaging in the unauthorized practice of law and referring clients to the lawyer for a percentage of the fee, known as capping.

31. According to Model Rule 7.2(c), the three occasions when an attorney may pay a referral fee are the following:

    1. For advertising purposes
    2. For a lawyer referral service
    3. For payment of a law practice

32. The four arguments against referral fees are the following:

    1. The fee may increase the client's bill.
    2. Referral fees have a damaging effect on a lawyer's image.
    3. Most clients are offended by referral fees.
    4. Referral fees are beneath the dignity of the profession.

33. The two arguments for referral fees are the following:

    1. Clients benefit by being referred to the most competent attorney.
    2. Clients are protected from increased fees by other rules of professional conduct.

34. Premiums can be best described as tips. If the attorney obtains an especially favorable result for the client, the client will give the firm a premium fee in addition to the usual attorney's fee, whether it is a contingency fee, flat fee, or hourly rate.

35. Combination fees are a combination of all the types of fees.

36. Hard costs (also called direct costs) are directly attributable to the client's case, such as filing fees, service fees, deposition expenses, and so on.

37. Costs are recoverable by the prevailing party in some cases, and expenses are not recoverable.

38. Modern-day reasoning for not allowing attorneys to pay for the expenses of litigation is to discourage lawyers from putting their own recovery before that of the client and therefore creating a conflict of interest.

39. Soft costs (also known as indirect costs) cannot be directly attributable to a client's case until applied to the client's case.

40. Examples of soft costs include the following:

    1. Photocopies
    2. Attorney's time in preparing forms or other multiple-use documents
    3. Use of conference rooms
    4. Use of substantive systems (see Chapter 9)
    5. Local and long-distance telephone charges
    6. Meals and transportation on occasions of overtime
    7. Telex and fax
    8. Supplies
    9. Storage of documents
    10. Use of computer and computer database
    11. Destruction of documents
    12. Housekeeping services for meetings and depositions
    13. Interest on accounts receivable
    14. Outside services
    15. Document production
    16. Postage

41. The ABA established rules and guidelines concerning legal fees (1) to preserve the effectiveness, integrity, and independence of the profession and (2) to give society reasonable access to the legal system.

42. The eight considerations of determining a reasonable fee are the following:

    1. Time and labor required
    2. Other employment opportunities
    3. Customary fees in community
    4. Amount involved and results obtained
    5. Time limitations
    6. Professional relationship with client
    7. Experience, reputation, and ability of lawyer
    8. Type of fee; fixed or contingent

43. Calculation of a lodestar equation is accomplished by determining the number of hours reasonably spent in a case and applying the attorney's hourly rate thereto to arrive at a reasonable fee.

44. If the court determines that lodestar does not adequately compensate for all factors of the case, the court may apply a multiplier to the lodestar figure, thereby increasing the fee. Multipliers are additional fees.

45. The two types of liens that a lawyer may place on a case are a charging lien and a retaining lien.

46. A charging lien is placed on a client's judgment that the lawyer obtained for the client.

47. A retaining lien allows a lawyer to retain papers, money, or other property received from a client until the lawyer is paid the fee.

48. In addition to a charging and a retaining lien, an attorney may secure payment of fees by

having the client sign a promissory note secured by a deed on the client's property. Lawyers also may hold the pink slip to a client's car to secure payment of fees.

49. The lawyer has full responsibility for a client's fee.

50. Legal assistants must comply with attorneys' guidelines concerning fees because they are agents of the attorney.

51. Case law has ruled that a person must have a law school education to quote fees.

52. Attorneys or law firm management have the responsibility to set fees.

53. The case of *Missouri v. Jenkins,* 109 S. Ct. 2463 (1989), ruled that legal assistant fees are recoverable.

54. A misunderstanding about fees is frequently a source of disputes between a client and a lawyer and erodes the attorney-client relationship.

55. All fee agreements should be in writing.

56. According to Model Rule 1.5(c), all contingency fee agreements must be in writing.

57. Written fee agreements are desirable for the following reasons:
    1. They prevent misunderstandings.
    2. They enhance the attorney-client relationship.
    3. They provide protection for the lawyer in case of a fee dispute.

Chapter 7

Timekeeping

1. The knowledge and expertise of lawyers and legal assistants are the products that law firms sell to their clients. Time is the vehicle by which the product is produced.

2. Inaccurate time records result in inaccurate client billing and management reports. Inaccurate billing causes law firms to lose clients and client goodwill. Inaccurate management records cause management to make decisions on the basis of incorrect information.

3. If time is not documented, its value is lost, and the firm loses its product.

4. Lawyers and legal assistants are the primary timekeepers in a law office.

5. The annual billable hour requirement is the minimum number of billable hours that must be produced by each timekeeper per year.

6. Billable hours are hours directly applied to clients' matters.

7. Nonbillable hours are not applied to clients' matters.

8. The two types of nonbillable hours are creditable and noncreditable.

9. Creditable nonbillable hours are credited toward the annual billable hours requirements and include the following:
    1. Time spent serving on firm committees
    2. Pro bono work
    3. Participating in management functions (i.e., completing reports, firm meetings, and so on)
    4. Administrative functions
    5. Training

10. Noncreditable nonbillable hours are not credited toward the annual billable hours requirement and include the following:
    1. Educational activities, consisting of attending seminars, attending paralegal association conferences, and reading trade journals
    2. Time spent on personal matters
    3. Paralegal association work

11. Crediting time spent in educational activities and paying for educational activities are ways a firm encourages continuing education for its timekeepers.

12. Most firms give attorneys a higher creditable nonbillable hours allowance than legal assistants because attorneys are expected to participate in more marketing activities for the firm.

13. Some activities included in an attorney's nonbillable hour allowance are the following:
    1. Working on pro bono cases
    2. Speaking at seminars
    3. Cultivating clients
    4. Participating in community organizations

14. Nonbillable hour information will tell law firm management about the efforts being expended by the timekeeper on the firm's behalf. These records are considered when an employee is evaluated and considered for a raise or bonus.

15. The most common method of calculating time is tenths of an hour.

16. The most commonly used minimum charge is 0.2 of an hour.

17. The billable hour is different from an actual hour in that the actual hour contains sixty minutes, while a billable hour may contain as little as five minutes or as much as eight hours.

18. Management utilizes time records for the following seven purposes:

1. Billing clients
2. Compensating hourly employees
3. Calculating employee productivity
4. Planning
5. Monitoring work in progress
6. Projecting profitability
7. Forecasting income

19. Time records assist management in its marketing activities by determining what types of cases the firm is attracting.

20. Type of case reports derived from time records provide management with information on the time it takes to complete a certain type of case. A set fee can then be established.

21. Work-in-progress reports derived from time records give attorneys and legal assistants a realistic idea of their caseload and allow management to allocate work accordingly.

22. Time records allow management to project a timekeeper's profitability by checking to see whether a timekeeper is meeting her or his quota.

23. A firm calculates the profitability of the contingency case by multiplying the amount of time spent on the case by the attorney's and legal assistant's hourly rate and comparing that figure with the amount of money received on the case.

24. Management forecasts its income on the basis of projected income derived by timekeepers meeting their annual billable hour quotas.

25. The seven elements of time sheets are the following:

    1. Name of timekeeper
    2. Date
    3. File name
    4. Client number
    5. File number
    6. Amount of time expended in tenths of an hour
    7. Description of work performed

26. Firms may require the following additional information on time sheets:

    1. Department code
    2. Name of supervising attorney
    3. Type of case code number

27. Firms developed codes for each function to expedite the timekeeping process.

28. Contingency law firms keep time records to monitor the profitability of the case and monitor work in progress. Time records are also important if the attorney must file a lien or prove that time was spent on a case. Time records also assist attorneys in determining a case's settlement value.

29. Corporate legal departments require time records to prepare management reports, keep track of departmental use of the legal services, and prepare departmental budgets.

30. Government legal offices use time records for budget proposals and management reports.

31. The four basic features of timekeeping software are the following:

    1. Record time, expense, and payment entries
    2. Produce client billing statements
    3. Age and track accounts receivable
    4. Produce management and productivity reports

32. A timekeeper may not do the following six things:

    1. Bill clients for work not performed
    2. Pad time sheets
    3. Bill a client for time spent on personal matters
    4. Double-bill
    5. Bill multiple clients for one activity
    6. Apply an attorney's hourly rate to a paralegal's services

33. Double billing is working on two matters at the same time and billing each client separately for the time.

34. Padding timesheets is fraudulently adding time to a client's matter that was not spent.

35. Personal telephone calls are considered nonbillable noncreditable time.

36. Preparing the time sheet is the first thing a legal assistant does in the morning.

37. Completing the time sheet is the last thing a legal assistant does in the evening.

38. A legal assistant should not wait until the end of the day to complete time sheets because many short activities will be forgotten and lost.

39. Timekeepers should not estimate their time because surveys have shown that timekeepers underestimate their time when time is estimated.

40. It is the attorney's responsibility to reduce the cost of a project.

41. A timekeeper should record all nonbillable time to show the firm's management that time was spent on the firm's activities and not wasted. It is also a good method of determining whether time was spent productively. By monitoring all nonbillable time, a timekeeper can determine whether she or he exceeded the time allowed for nonbillable matters and adjust her or his activities accordingly.

42. Listing projects on a to-do list will help the legal assistant prioritize time and structure the day.

43. A time sheet should be completed when an activity is completed. If a paralegal is working on one project that exceeds one day, a time sheet should be completed at the end of each day.

CHAPTER 8

Billing and Financial Management

1. The four essential elements of the billing process are communication, understanding, regular and frequent billing, and descriptive bills.

2. The most important aspect of the billing process is communication.

3. It is the lawyer's responsibility to communicate the fee agreement to the client.

4. The legal assistant may discuss the situation with the client in an empathic manner but may not give advice or suggest a solution to the problem.

5. The responsible attorney or administrator has the authority to adjust a client's bill.

6. When communicating with clients, a legal assistant may not discuss the duration of a case and may not estimate the cost of a matter, give an opinion as to the possible outcome of a matter, or discuss the lawyer's strategy.

7. When a legal assistant has a communication with a client, she or he must document all client communication.

8. A client's complete understanding of the case will reward a firm in prompt payment of the firm's invoices.

9. An engagement letter is a letter that summarizes the scope of representation and the fee agreement between a lawyer and a client.

10. Billing should be regular and frequent because delaying the billing process is very costly for a firm.

11. Small firms and sole proprietors have difficulties meeting a monthly billing schedule, especially if the legal team is working hard to meet approaching deadlines.

12. A client should be billed as soon as possible after the matter is completed.

13. As time goes by, a client's perception of legal services decreases.

14. Monthly billing is the most common method of billing.

15. Clients prefer to receive smaller monthly bills than larger infrequent bills.

16. The elements of an average bill are the following:
    1. Name of case
    2. Billing period
    3. Date of work
    4. Description of work performed
    5. Time increment of the work
    6. Who performed the work
    7. Hourly rate of person performing work
    8. Cost of work
    9. Itemization of costs
    10. Total costs
    11. Total of fees and costs
    12. Payment terms

17. A preliminary bill is prepared for the attorney's review and consideration for adjustment.

18. A fee adjustment memorandum is a form used by an attorney to increase or decrease a client's bill.

19. Traditionally, attorneys do not determine their clients' ability to pay legal fees, and this has caused firms to experience collection problems.

20. The two methods used by firms to extend credit to clients are bank loans and credit cards.

21. The ABA issued the following guidelines regarding the use of credit cards:
    1. No directory of any kind shall be printed or published with the names of individual attorney members who subscribe to the credit card plan.
    2. No promotional materials of any kind will be supplied by the credit card company to a participating attorney except possibly a small insignia to be tactfully displayed in the attorney's office indicating his participation in the use of the credit card.
    3. A lawyer shall not encourage participation in the plan, but his position must be that he accepts the plan as a convenience for clients who desire it, and the lawyer may not because of his participation increase his fee for legal services rendered to the client.
    4. Charges made by lawyers to clients pursuant to a credit card plan shall be only for services actually rendered or cash actually paid on behalf of a client.
    5. In participating in a credit card program the attorney shall scrupulously observe his obligation to preserve the confidences and secrets of his client.

22. Fee allocation is a percentage of a bill that is given to the originating or supervising attorney as compensation.

23. A cost recovery system is a utility program that allows data to be transferred to a billing program by a copier or telephone system.

24. The style of the bill depends on the type of client, the type of case, and the policy of the firm.

25. The rule of thumb is to be as descriptive as necessary to get the bill paid.

26. The two styles of hourly bills are detailed and brief.

27. A gross contingency fee accounting is when an attorney deducts his or her fee percentage before deducting costs.

28. A net contingency fee accounting is when an attorney deducts his or her fee percentage after deducting costs.

29. Collection activities begin when an account is thirty days past due.

30. A lawyer will become involved in collection activities when the account is ninety days past due.

31. If an attorney withdraws from a case because of nonpayment of fees, the attorney must take steps to protect the client's interest. The attorney must give the client reasonable notice and time to employ a new attorney.

32. The nine things a lawyer must consider before withdrawing from a case are the following:
    1. The client's financial condition at the beginning of the representation and whether the lawyer had knowledge of the client's ability to pay
    2. The client's sophistication as a consumer of legal services
    3. Whether the fees and expenses were explained fully to the client
    4. Whether the lawyer offered several different fee arrangements and the client selected a payment option with knowledge of the consequences of the selection
    5. Whether the client has received periodic notice about costs as they were incurred and whether the actual charges remained in the range predicted
    6. How long the fee has been outstanding
    7. Efforts the client has made to submit partial payment
    8. Efforts of the lawyer to negotiate a more lenient fee payment schedule
    9. Whether there is a dispute about the fee

33. If a firm sues the client, the firm has the burden of proving the extent of the services rendered and the reasonableness of the fee.

34. Suing a client should be the last resort.

35. It is standard practice for a firm to give a client at least two weeks' notice of collection agency involvement.

36. Billing methods and disputes have contributed to the public's negative perception of lawyers.

37. The four most common areas of unethical billing practices are the following:
    1. Applying a client's funds
    2. Charging more than the client agreed to pay
    3. Charging for services not rendered to the client
    4. Increasing a flat fee

38. Legal fee agreements are held to a higher standard than other contracts because of the fiduciary relationship between attorney and client.

39. A fiduciary is a person who transacts business for another person, necessitating great confidence and trust by one party and a high degree of good faith by the other party.

40. Any ambiguity in a fee agreement will be construed against the lawyer.

41. A legal auditor is a person or company that audits legal bills.

42. A legal auditor is paid to find discrepancies in a law firm's bill.

43. The two major problems clients complain about are ambiguous bills and high legal costs.

44. The following ten problems are major contributors to ambiguous bills:
    1. Incomprehensible format
    2. Surprise total
    3. Perceived poor work
    4. Team churning
    5. Too much conference time
    6. Nickel-and-dime billing
    7. Errors in arithmetic
    8. Other glaring errors
    9. Bill received months after work is completed
    10. Bill directed to wrong person

45. Of the complaints received by bar associations, most of them are complaints of legal fees.

46. Team churning is making frequent changes in the legal team.

47. Padding is fraudulently increasing a bill when the fee is not warranted.

48. Block billing is charging a client for services rendered in one large block of time rather than itemizing the tasks performed in that period of time.

49. Client-directed billing policies are when clients, usually large corporations and insurance companies, have developed their own billing policies for their attorneys to follow.

50. Some attorneys object to client-directed billing because they say that the policies illegally restrict their practice of law. They say they are contrary to the code of professional responsibility and create a conflict of interest between the independence of outside counsel and their clients.

51. Once a firm has been advised of a dispute regarding a bill, a firm may not take steps to collect the amount. The firm may not send collection letters, telephone the client, or sue the client until the dispute has been resolved.

52. To keep fee disputes out of the court system, most state bar associations have developed arbitration programs to resolve fee disputes.

53. Arbitration is a process of dispute resolution in which a neutral third party (arbitrator) renders a decision after a hearing at which both parties have an opportunity to be heard.

54. Discovery is the acquisition or knowledge of facts or that which was previously unknown.

55. The organization of a firm's finance function depends on the size of the firm.

56. Direct profitability factors are factors that affect a firm's profitability in a short period of time, usually one year.

57. To be profitable, a task should be delegated to the least expensive employee capable of performing the task.

58. Leveraging is the ability to make money from the work of others.

59. A leverage ratio is a formula used to identify the number of leveraged income earners per partner. Some firms may have a one-to-four ratio (one profit contributor per four attorneys) or a four-to-one ratio (four profit contributors per attorney).

60. The two types of expenses are compensation expenses and operating expenses.

61. Compensation expenses include employees' compensation and are categorized into three categories: associates' and legal assistants' compensation, administrative staff salaries, and employee benefits.

62. The four categories of operating expenses are occupancy costs, office operating costs, costs of professional activities, and general business expenses.

63. Occupancy costs include office rental, storage facilities, and utilities.

64. Office operating costs include the day-to-day expenses involved in running the office, such as office equipment, computers, janitorial services, stationery, copying costs, and miscellaneous supplies.

65. Professional activity costs include professional dues, continuing education, and client entertainment.

66. General business expenses include telephone costs, library costs, insurance, taxes, and interest expenses.

67. Indirect profitability factors are factors that indirectly affects a firm's profitability over a long period, more than one year.

68. A law firm's culture is the firm's environment, including intangible factors such as employee behavior patterns, social policies, and employees' values.

69. Reward systems include compensation plans, bonus plans, and other professional and personal reward systems for motivating people to contribute to the firm's profitability.

70. The environment affects profitability because it affects a firm's employees. Employees must have a thriving environment within which to contribute their best effort. Without such an environment, employees are not productive, therefore affecting a firm's profitability.

71. In a small firm, the finance function is performed by the attorney or office manager with the assistance of an outside bookkeeper or CPA.

72. Small firms use outside services because it is more cost-effective than hiring a full-time employee to perform these functions.

73. CPA is an acronym for certified public accountant.

74. In a medium firm, the finance function is managed by a controller or office administrator.

75. In some medium firms, the finance function is divided into two groups: a general ledger group and a billing and collections group.

76. The general ledger group consists of a general ledger accountant, payroll clerk, cashier, and accounts payable clerk.

77. The billing and collections group consists of billing clerk, timekeeping clerk, and collection clerk.

78. In a large firm, the finance function is managed by the controller or office administrator.

79. Among the supervisors found in a large firm are the following:
    1. Billing and collections supervisor
    2. Payroll supervisor
    3. Accounts payable supervisor
    4. Cashier supervisor
    5. Financial reporting accountant
    6. General ledger accountant
    7. Partners' accounts accountant
    8. Special projects accountant

80. In a megafirm with many branch offices, a director of finance or chief financial officer is in charge of the finance function of the firm.

81. A corporate legal department's financial functions are handled by the corporation's finance department.

82. Realization is the process of turning time into cash.

83. The five steps of the realization process are getting, doing, recording, billing, and collecting for the work.

84. A realization rate is the rate that the firm actually receives for work done.

85. Management uses the realization rate to prepare the firm's budget.

86. A number of factors affect the realization rate: nonbillable time, write-ups, write-downs, and write-offs.

87. A firm will write up a client's bill when the client receives a substantial benefit from the firm's work on the case and agrees to give the firm a premium.

88. A firm will write down a client's bill when some of the timekeeper's time is not billed to the client or is discounted.

89. A write-off is when a firm credits an account for the total amount owed.

90. An 80 percent realization rate is common in a law firm.

91. To arrive at a timekeeper's realization rate, multiply the number of annual billable hours by the hourly rate and take the realization percentage of that figure.

92. Legal clinics average the highest ratio of legal assistants to attorney.

93. Large firms average the lowest ratio of legal assistants to attorney.

94. A client report can be cumulative or individual. A cumulative report lists all the firm's clients and their billing histories. An individual report lists one client's billing history.

95. A transaction activity report gives daily transaction entries per timekeeper.

96. A file maintenance report describes client file information and makes changes to file information, including client address and the responsible attorney and legal assistant.

97. A work-in-progress report describes details of unbilled hours and costs per timekeeper, including client totals.

98. A billing report consist of the following:
    1. Unbilled time and disbursements per client or case
    2. Draft bills
    3. Summary of bills with client totals and timekeeper totals
    4. Summary of client billing history, including amounts billed, amounts collected, and amounts uncollected
    5. Total amount of bills generated per month compared to budgeted amounts indicating variances

99. Aging accounts receivable is calculating how long an account has been unpaid. The aging process alerts management to which accounts require collection activities.

100. An accounts receivable report describes the amount of outstanding bills with an aging report.

101. A cash receipts report describes income received per day, per week, per month, per quarter, or per year.

102. A practice management report includes the following:
    1. Client investment summary
    2. Billing realization report
    3. Staff utilization report
    4. Fee analysis report
    5. Type-of-case summary

103. A compensation report gives a summary of the firm's payroll, employee benefits, and tax liability.

104. An accounts payable report is a summary of all accounts payable, including year-to-date balances and aging report.

105. A budget performance report is a comparison of the firm's actual income and expenditures with budgeted income and expenditures.

106. A cash flow projection report is used to anticipate monthly cash availability and is used to plan periodic partner distributions and a firm's investments.

107. A cumulative summary report informs management whether the firm's projected income expectations are being met.

108. A total hours report provides management with a total number of hours billed to date and per hour average.

109. A year-to-date report lists totals for each client and assists management in its client relations program.

110. An adjustments report provides management with the total amount of adjustments made in the bills as reflected on the fee adjustment memorandum.

111. A timekeeper summary report is a summary of billable hours for each timekeeper that includes monthly charges and year-to-date totals. This report informs management if each timekeeper is producing the required billable hours.

112. A work log summary report informs management of each timekeeper's workload.

113. A work category summary report shows the charges and income by type of case and informs management of the volume of cases in a certain category.

114. A budget is the key to a law firm's profitability.

115. When developing a budget, a firm's management projects income, projects personnel costs, and projects operating expenses.

116. To project a firm's gross income for the year, management must estimate the amount of work required for existing clients and anticipate work from new clients.

117. Factors used to determine income from new clients include the economic environment, the firm's marketing activities and strategic planning, past experience in producing new clients, and competitive pressures.

118. Factors considered when projecting a firm's income are income generated from each timekeeper, annual billable hours, hourly rate, and realization rate for each timekeeper.

119. Budgeting for personnel costs requires management to anticipate associates' compensation, administrative staff salaries, employee benefit costs, and employee taxes.

120. Management calculates an expense percentage by dividing expenses by income.

121. A firm's anticipated profit is calculated by deducting the expense percentage of each timekeeper's gross fees.

122. The average expense percentage is 60 percent.

Chapter 9

Managing the Clients' Funds Trust Account

1. The clients' funds trust account is a bank account established exclusively for client funds.

2. A fiduciary is a person who holds the character of a trustee.

3. Each state's bar association has rules governing the client funds trust account.

4. Segregation of cash is keeping client funds completely separate from office and personal bank accounts.

5. A firm usually has one account for the funds of all its clients.

6. If a firm anticipates that a case will have many large transactions, the firm may open a separate trust account for that case only.

7. Probate is the administration of a deceased person's estate.

8. The type of funds held in the trust account are funds for estate proceeds, escrow funds, settlements, and judgment payments.

9. Law firms that handle real estate transactions will accept a down payment for the property and keep those funds in the trust account pending transfer of the property.

10. The payments are paid from the law firm's trust account so that there is a record that the payment was made.

11. People prefer adversarial financial transactions to be completed with the assistance of an intermediary to eliminate misappropriation allegations.

12. An attorney may not withdraw the funds until the fees are earned and a monthly accounting is sent to the client.

13. Nonrefundable nonchargeable, or true retainer, fees that secure an attorney's availability may be deposited directly into the attorney's operating account.

14. True retainer fees are not required to be deposited directly into the trust account because they are considered "earned on receipt" and are not considered prepayment for the attorney's services.

15. Legal assistants are often given the responsibility of maintaining a trust account, especially in small firms.

16. Some legal malpractice insurance companies require that manual records of the trust account be kept in addition to electronic records.

17. Manual records are necessary in case of computer failure, energy shortages, and other disasters.

18. The nine steps of proper trust fund accounting are the following:

    1. Preparing the client ledger sheet
    2. Maintaining journals

3. Communicating with clients
4. Documenting transactions
5. Disbursing funds
6. Reconciling the account
7. Preparing monthly statements
8. Closing an account
9. Keeping records

19. The client ledger sheet documents the amount of fees and costs billed, amount paid, and trust account funds received and disbursed.

20. If the client gives the firm money to deposit in the trust account, that transaction is listed separately on the client ledger card.

21. A hard copy is a copy of computer records on a sheet of paper.

22. All money received for the trust account is entered in the cash receipts journal.

23. All checks written from the trust account are entered in the cash payments journal.

24. The following seven items must be entered into the journals:

    1. Date of transaction
    2. Name of payer
    3. Name of client
    4. Name of case
    5. Amount of transaction
    6. Check number
    7. Purpose and description of transaction (e.g., deposition of Harry Snow)

25. The client ledger sheets, cash receipts journal, and cash payments journal must balance with the clients' funds account.

26. When trust account bank statements are received each month, the statement must be reconciled immediately.

27. A client must be notified that funds were received immediately on receipt of the funds.

28. If a check is made payable to both the client and lawyer, the client must endorse the check first so it can be deposited into the trust account for disbursement.

29. If the client cannot come into the office to endorse the check, it should be sent to the client by certified mail and mailed back to the lawyer by certified mail.

30. Before a check is deposited into the trust account, copies of the deposit slip and the front and back of the check are made.

31. The copies of the check are filed in the client's file, and a copy is filed in a trust account receipts file.

32. A trust account receipts file is a file of copies of checks deposited in the trust account.

33. When entering a deposit on a client ledger sheet, include the payer, check number, and exact date of deposit.

34. A check must clear the bank before any funds are disbursed.

35. Funds must be disbursed promptly after receipt to avoid allegations of commingling.

36. The responsible attorney or office manager signs a trust account check.

37. All disbursements should have some written documentation describing what the payment is for.

38. Disbursements for payment of attorneys' fees and costs may be made after a statement is prepared for the client.

39. The trust account must be reconciled to the bank statement immediately after receipt of the statement.

40. The account must balance to the penny.

41. A statement must be sent to each client informing him or her of the status of his or her trust account each month.

42. A client's trust account is ready to be closed when a case has ended and all checks have cleared the bank.

43. Most firms wait until all checks have cleared the bank before closing.

44. All the funds in the account must be disbursed before closing, and each transaction must be documented on the client ledger sheet.

45. Records of a trust account must be kept for auditing purposes or in the event of a malpractice claim.

46. Trust account records should be kept for at least five years.

47. Interest on trust accounts is sent to state bar associations.

48. The funds are used to fund legal programs for the indigent.

49. IOLTA stands for Interest on Lawyers' Trust Accounts.

50. The IOLTA program was begun in England, Canada, and Australia in the 1960s.

51. Florida was the first state in the United States to adopt an IOLTA program.

52. The three types of IOLTA participation are the following:

    1. Mandatory: All lawyers in the state must participate in IOLTA.
    2. Voluntary: All lawyers may choose whether to participate in IOLTA.
    3. Opt-out: All lawyers must participate unless they affirmatively choose not to participate.

53. The money received for interest is transferred to the state bar or state bar foundation.

54. The IOLTA funds sponsor law-related public interest programs for the indigent, elderly, or disabled, including legal aid, victim assistance programs, and client security funds.

55. A client security fund is a fund established to reimburse clients who have been damaged because of their attorney's fraudulent abuse of the trust account.

56. Many attorneys were not supportive of the IOLTA program because of the additional administrative tasks the program requires.

57. The legality of IOLTA programs was challenged in the 1998 case of *Phillips v. Washington Legal Foundation* (96-1578).

58. The U.S. Supreme Court ruled that interest earned on client funds held in IOLTA accounts is the private property of the client.

59. The Conference of State Supreme Court Chief Justices issued a unanimous resolution urging "continued operation of IOLTA programs in every jurisdiction."

60. IOLTA programs continue to function as usual since the Supreme Court's ruling, and they are confident that the constitutionality of their programs will be upheld.

61. Attorneys who abuse their trust accounts may be disciplined by the state bar association.

62. The state bar association audits attorneys' trust accounts.

63. In some states, the state bar may audit a firm's trust account at any time without provocation or reason, and other states audit only those accounts whose abuse is suspected.

64. Some state bar associations require banks to automatically notify it of any trust account overdrafts or bounced checks, whether they were honored or not.

65. An overdraft is an indication of mishandling a trust account.

66. Common abuses of the client funds account include the following:
    1. Misappropriation
    2. Using client funds to cover office expenses
    3. Withdrawing funds from the trust account of one client to meet another client's trust account obligations
    4. Check kiting
    5. Commingling funds
    6. Failure to promptly notify clients of receipt of funds
    7. Failure to promptly disburse funds
    8. Failure to provide clients with an accounting of trust account funds

67. Misappropriation is writing personal checks from a trust account.

68. If an attorney writes a personal check from the trust account, the attorney is essentially stealing clients' money.

69. No office expense may be paid from the trust account.

70. Check kiting is when money is withdrawn from a recently deposited check before the check has cleared the bank, thereby using other clients' funds to cover the check.

71. Commingling is mixing law firm funds with client funds.

72. The only time an attorney may deposit a firm's funds into the clients' trust account is to cover monthly bank charges, such as service charges and check charges.

73. The attorney is ultimately responsible for the condition of the trust account.

74. A legal assistant not familiar with trust funds accounting principles may be exposing the firm to serious liability if allowed to maintain the firm's client funds account.

75. If a client terminates the attorney-client relationship, all funds in the client funds account that have not been earned must be immediately returned to the client.

76. In most states, a lawyer must have a client's permission to apply funds in the trust account to an outstanding legal bill.

77. If an attorney who works for a law firm that is a partnership abuses the trust account, each partner may also be subject to disciplinary proceedings.

78. Managing the client funds account accurately has the following benefits:
    1. Reduced legal malpractice insurance costs
    2. Reduced ethics problems
    3. Reduced client complaints
    4. Reduced stress and anxiety

CHAPTER 10

Technology in the Law Office

1. The primary challenge is keeping current with the latest technology.

2. To be trained adequately, employees must be trained often.

3. Access to the Internet has resulted in information overload, which must be managed properly in order for members of the legal team to be able to locate it.

4. Software applications are developed specifically for the operating system used by the firm's computers.

5. There are currently three major operating systems: Windows, Macintosh, and Unix.

6. Microsoft's Windows operating system is the most popular and widely used operating system used in law offices today.

7. The Windows operation system has its origin in an operating system that was used in the 1970s and 1980s called MS-DOS (Microsoft Disk Operating System).

8. Most software in use today is designed for the Windows operating system.

9. Macintosh operating system was the first to use a graphical user interface.

10. The Unix operating system was created for computer programmers developing software and is generally used by very large computers and servers.

11. A custom software application is created exclusively for the law firm.

12. Off-the-shelf applications are created by software companies that market and distribute the software to the public.

13. Custom computer applications are created by computer programmers according to the parameters set by the customer.

14. Off-the-shelf applications are created by software companies.

15. Integrated software applications combine many software applications into one program.

16. An advantage of an integrated system is that the commands in the software are uniform, making the program easy to use.

17. A disadvantage to an integrated system is that the individual features are generally less powerful than an individual application.

18. Office suites combine several separate software applications, such as word processing, spreadsheet, database, and presentation programs, into one package.

19. Some advantages to an office suite are that the applications have similar interfaces that interact with one another, making them easily integrated. Training time is reduced, and the features of the software are easier to use. It is also less expensive than purchasing each application individually.

20. Most law firms use off-the-shelf computer applications and office suites.

21. Word processing software has been a standard application used in law firms since the 1960s.

22. The two most popular word processing systems used in law offices today are Corel's WordPerfect and Microsoft's MS Word.

23. Until the late 1990s, WordPerfect was the standard word processor for law firms with 97 percent of small firms and 84 percent of large firms using it.

24. Many law firms have switched to Microsoft Word because of the following:

    1. Firms use the Windows operating system, and because Microsoft makes both products, they feel that Word integrates better with Windows.
    2. Most clients use Word, and the firm can easily exchange documents with clients via disk or e-mail.
    3. Third-party software for WordPerfect, such as document management programs, are not as abundant as those for MS Word.

25. Add-ons (or plug-ins) are software created to enhance the features of other software and are used in conjunction with other software.

26. Add-on software adds features to other applications.

27. A spreadsheet application is used to crunch numbers.

28. A database application is a powerful application used by law firms and other businesses to manage information.

29. Law firms use a database for its client list, to log marketing efforts, and to manage its brief bank.

30. Time and billing software prepares timekeeping reports and numerous other management reports.

31. Time and billing software is used by all the timekeepers in a firm.

32. The timekeeping system is connected to the firm's billing system so that client invoices are automatically generated.

33. Case management software is used to control calendars, monitor deadlines, and track essential law firm tasks.

34. The benefits of a case management application are guarding against missed deadlines, reducing employee time to enter due dates, and updating rules when rules are changed.

35. Other features of a case management application are document assembly and conflict-of-interest checking.

36. Litigation support software manage a complex litigation case.

37. Complex litigation cases often involve thousands and sometimes millions of documents. These documents must be reviewed and organized in a manner that allows the legal team fast access to them. By inputting each document into a litigation support database, the information can be screened, sorted, and located quickly.

38. There are four types of litigation support software: abstract, full-text retrieval, document imaging, and a combination of these.

39. A document abstract system prepares an abstract, or summary, of a document's contents.

40. A full-text retrieval contains the entire document instead of a summary.

41. Scanning is entering text or graphics into a computer by electronically changing the characters into a computer-readable format.

42. Substantive law software is developed for use in a specific area of law.

43. Court-forms-generating software prepares court forms. The software is stored on the firm's server and is accessible by each workstation. The software program guides the user in preparing the forms, and they are printed on the firm's laser printer.

44. A browser is a software program that allows viewing and interaction with various kinds of resources available on the Internet.

45. A browser is used to access the Internet.

46. As of this writing, there are two major browser software: Netscape's Netscape Navigator and Microsoft's Internet Explorer.

47. Small firms are more likely to restrict Internet use to certain employees.

48. The Internet is a worldwide cooperative network of networks.

49. The Internet was designed by the RAND Corporation.

50. The Internet was designed for the U.S. Department of Defense in the 1960s.

51. The Internet's purpose was to be a means of communication that would withstand nuclear war or other disaster.

52. The name of the first Internet was ARPANET.

53. ARPANET stands for the Advanced Research Projects Agency of the Department of Defense, which funded it.

54. In 1983, ARPANET split into two networks: ARPANET and MILNET.

55. The Department of Defense controlled MILNET, and the National Science Foundation controlled ARPANET.

56. The name of the new Internet became NSFNET.

57. Access to NSFNET was provided free to any U.S. research and educational institution for noncommercial purposes.

58. NSFNET was used primarily by scientists, academics, and nonprofit organizations.

59. Commercial use of NSFNET was allowed in 1991.

60. NREN stands for the National Research and Education Network.

61. NREN was a $2 billion project approved by Congress to upgrade the NSFNET backbone.

62. No one owns the Internet.

63. The two things needed to access the Internet are browser software and an Internet Service Provider (ISP).

64. An Internet Service Provider (ISP) is a private company that provides access to the Internet for a fee.

65. A modem is a term that is short for modulator/demodulator. It is a device that allows remote computers to transmit and receive data using telephone lines.

66. An ISP's computers are known as servers.

67. The ISP's server is connected either to larger regional networks or directly to the backbone sites that direct traffic on the Internet.

68. An ISP gets its access from telephone companies and charge a fee for their service.

69. A protocol is a set of rules that ensures that different network software products can work together.

70. Protocols dictate how the various systems on the Internet operate.

71. Protocol standards are set by the Internet Engineering Task Force (IETF).

72. The IETF is a large international community of network designers, operators, vendors, and researchers concerned with the smooth operation of the Internet.

73. A FTP, or File Transfer Protocol, is a protocol that allows files to be transferred between computers.

74. Telnet protocol is a protocol that allows a computer to connect with a remote computer as if it were local.

75. A gopher protocol organizes Internet information into an index that can be searched and retrieved.

76. Gopher was developed by two University of Minnesota students who named it after the school's mascot.

77. The five factors that attributed to the Internet's sudden growth and prominence are the following:
    1. Widespread use of personal computers and graphical user interfaces, such as the Windows operating system
    2. Elimination of commercial use prohibitions
    3. The creation of software applications specifically for use on the Internet
    4. The existence of a large body of electronically stored data
    5. Technological advances in computer hardware, such as modems and monitors

78. A domain name is a unique name that identifies an organization on the Internet.

79. Domain names were created in 1986 by the National Science Foundation (NSF), AT&T, and Network Solutions, Inc. (NSI).

80. The domain name project was called the InterNIC project.

81. There have been many concerns over issuance of domain names, including the following:
    1. A rise in conflicts between trademark owners and domain name registrants
    2. An increase in the commercial value of domain names, requiring a more formal management system
    3. Internationalization of the Internet
    4. Too much U.S. government involvement in Internet activities

82. The name of the government's policy toward domain name registration is the White Paper.

83. The government proposes to turn the domain name system over to a private U.S. corporation, the Internet Corporation for Assigned Names and Numbers (ICANN), comprised of an international group of Internet users.

84. A type identifier is a suffix at the end of a domain name that describes the type of organization.

85. The six categories of type identifiers are commercial, educational institution, nonprofit organization, military organization, network provider, and government institution.

86. Countries are identified on the Internet by an additional extension after their domain name identifying the country.

87. To obtain a domain name, one must register with NSI or another registration service and pay the required fee.

88. The World Wide Web (WWW, or Web) is one of the protocols that operate via the Internet.

89. The Web was developed by Tim Berners-Lee in 1990 at the European Laboratory for Particle Physics (CERN) in Switzerland.

90. The Web is managed by the World Wide Web Consortium (W3C), also known as the World Wide Web Initiative (www.w3c.org).

91. The W3C is run by the Massachusetts Institute of Technology (MIT) and the French National Institute for Research in Computer Science (INRIA).

92. The W3C is funded by a number of large corporate members, including AT&T; Adobe Systems, Inc.; Microsoft Corporation; and Sun Microsystems, Inc.

93. The W3C's purpose is to promote the Web by developing specification and reference software that will be freely available to everyone.

94. The protocol used by the Web is called Hypertext Transfer Protocol (HTTP).

95. The specific software language used by all documents on the Web is Hypertext Markup Language (HTML).

96. In order for a computer to read the HTML language, it needs browser software.

97. Shareware is software that is distributed without initial cost. If the user likes the software, a nominal payment is expected.

98. The difference between shareware and freeware is that a payment is expected with shareware but not with freeware.

99. A hyperlink is a connection to another page or site that allows a person to navigate the web.

100. Hyperlinks enable readers to navigate through the Web.

101. A collection of hyperlinks, grouped together in an orderly manner, is called a Web site.

102. The first page of a Web site is known as the home page.

103. The legal profession uses the Web to publicize cases and manage the media in high-profile cases by posting exhibits and other information on the Web.

104. The three basic ways to locate specific information on the Internet are the following:
    1. Uniform Resource Locator (URL)
    2. Keyword search
    3. Topical index

105. A Uniform Resource Locator (URL) is an address of a Web site that directs a person to the information.

106. The four main elements of a URL are the following:
    1. Protocol
    2. Address of server where the data are located
    3. Domain name
    4. Type identifier

107. Almost all companies and corporations use a ".com" identifier.

108. ".com" means that it is a commercial site.

109. To locate a Web site outside the United States, substitute the type identifier with the country code, as follows: http://www.louvre.fr.

110. A pathname is the URL address showing the path of where a certain document may be found on a Web site.

111. Subsequent pages in a URL are separated by a forward slash, as follows: Protocol://server.domainname/pathname/name of document (http://www.microsoft.com/products/msword).

112. Certain rules apply to all URLs. There are no spaces in a URL. Each word of a domain name is run together (except some words in a domain name may be connected by a dash). A forward slash (/) is always used instead of backward slash (\). Domain names are not uppercase but are entered in all lowercase letters.

113. Each browser has a search feature that allows a keyword search. Enter the keyword of the desired site or information, and the browser will retrieve the Web sites that contain information about the words inserted.

114. A Boolean search is a method of defining search criteria.

115. A Boolean search creates sets of words so that a search engine can narrow the search.

116. A search engine is an independent company that has indexed Internet sites and categorized them so that they can be found easily.

117. A search engine categorizes Internet sites into groupings of related fields, such as government, law, judiciary, and so on.

118. Bookmarking is a part of browser software that marks a Web site so that its URL is accessible without searching for it.

119. Commercial Web sites of reputable companies warrant the accuracy of their Web sites, as do most created by law librarians and archivists.

120. The seven things you can do to verify the accuracy of a Web site are the following:
    1. Check to see whether the author of the Web site is identified.
    2. Determine the purpose of the Web site. Is it for the reader's benefit or the author's benefit?
    3. Do not judge a Web site by its home page. Home pages can be professional looking but may promote quack remedies or illegal activities.
    4. Look for the date of the last update. If one is not available, the site may be outdated.
    5. Look at the site's links. If some have disappeared, it is a clue that the site is outdated.
    6. Verify the information elsewhere. Some experts recommend verifying information by two other sources.
    7. Consult Web site review guides.

121. The federal government is the largest contributor of material on the Web.

122. Many of the law-related Web sites were developed by the government, law schools, law libraries, bar associations, and other legal organizations.

123. The federal government operates the Government Information Locator Services (GILS) to help find precise information from the vast number of materials on the Web.

124. An intranet is a law firm's internal information distribution system that is based on Web technology.

125. Web-based technology is Internet-like software applications.

126. An intranet differs from the Web because it is private and is accessible only by designated individuals, normally firm employees.

127. Groupware is software created for and used by an intranet and an extranet.

128. Intranets are custom made and designed according to a firm's specifications by professional intranet designers or in-house computer specialists.

129. An intranet is used to distribute information electronically to its members.

130. The term "on-line" means connected to the Internet or the Web.

131. A brief bank is a collection of documents that are used as a template to prepare new documents.

132. A template is a form document used as a guide to prepare new documents.

133. Large law firms realize the most benefits of an intranet.

134. The benefits of an intranet are the following:
    1. Enhanced efficiency
    2. Maximized use of a firm's resources

3. Reduced overhead
4. Increased employee productivity and satisfaction
5. Centralized operations from one source so that information can be found quickly and easily
6. Information distributed electronically, reducing the use of paper
7. Allow a firm's work product to be reused easily, reducing duplication of effort

135. An extranet is a Web-based interface to a private network.

136. An extranet offers the same benefits as an intranet: efficiency, improved quality of work, and enhancement of communication among people working together.

137. The difference between an intranet and an extranet is that an extranet is directed to different people and has different uses.

138. A firm-centered extranet is where a law firm creates an extranet connection to its clients, especially large corporate clients.

139. A client-centered extranet is where a client provides its law firm(s) with an extranet.

140. The difference between a firm-centered and a client-centered extranet is that a firm-centered extranet gives a firm control over its content and access, and a client-centered Extranet gives a client control of its content and access.

141. A brokered extranet is where a third party provides access to an extranet for a fee.

142. The two types of security risks with an extranet are restricting access so that unauthorized persons cannot access the system and protecting information in transit to and from other members in the extranet.

143. A firewall is a protective electronic barrier constructed around a network so that unauthorized persons cannot get through.

144. The easiest security method to implement is to place the extranet in an undisclosed address on the Web.

145. The most common security method is to require each user to use a special ID and password to gain entry to the extranet.

146. A digital ID is a personal ID number that is encrypted and can be read only by the extranet.

147. Users with digital IDs can obtain certificates from an outside vendor that will certify that the user is who he or she purports to be.

148. A Secure Sockets Layer (SSL) is a protocol used to verify a server's identity to a client and a client's identity to a server.

149. Secure HTTP (SHTTP) is a protocol that is used with the HTTP protocol and is more extensive than SSL.

150. Cryptography is the process of securing private information that is passed through public networks.

151. Cryptography mathematically scrambles information in a way that makes it unreadable to anyone except the person holding the mathematical key that can unscramble it.

152. The two types of cryptography that are in use today are same key and public key.

153. Same-key cryptography is when a message is encrypted and decrypted using the same key, which is passed along from one party to another.

154. Public-key cryptography uses a pair of different keys (one public, one private). A message encrypted with one key can be decrypted only with the other key and vice versa.

155. Electronic mail (e-mail) is an electronic message sent from one person to another through their computers.

156. Snail mail is the process of sending mail through the U.S. Postal Service.

157. E-mail passes to its destination through servers.

158. An ISP provides each customer with an e-mail address that allows the customer to use the ISP's server.

159. The three main parts of an e-mail address are username, domain name, and type identifier.

160. A username contains no spaces and no uppercase letters.

161. The username and domain name are separated by an axon symbol (@), which symbolizes the word "at."

162. E-mail addresses are always in lowercase letters.

163. "Case sensitive" means that all letters must be in a specific case. If a letter is the wrong case, the information cannot be read.

164. E-mail addresses and Web addresses are different. A Web address has a URL, and an e-mail message is sent to a section of the URL.

165. A listserv is a group of people who exchange information about a particular topic on the Internet.

166. Newsgroups are public discussions on topics of general interest in which anyone with newsreader software can participate. A listserv contains a mailing list of e-mail addresses of people interested in the same subject.

167. Lurking is not responding to messages posted on a listserv.

168. Listservs are either public or private and consist of two types: announcement type and discussion type.

169. An announcement-type listserv allows you to receive messages, but you cannot respond to the message.

170. A discussion-type listserv allows every member to participate in the discussion.

171. A moderated listserv allows all messages to be sent to a list moderator who reviews them and makes a determination of whether it is appropriate to be distributed to the group.

172. An unmoderated listserv does not review each message, which is automatically sent to the group regardless of content.

173. Netiquette is an informal code of conduct that governs e-mail communication.

174. Netiquette rules are enforced by the people using them.

175. You should not assume that your e-mail is private because a firm's system administrator has access to e-mails to maintain the system and e-mails are easily forwarded to others.

176. You should never give your user ID or password to another person because another person can wreck havoc with your e-mail account.

177. You should keep messages short and to the point because most busy people resent long e-mails that contain information not relevant to the subject matter.

178. Quotations should be edited to include only the relevant material to keep messages short.

179. An e-mail should be limited to one subject to keep e-mails short.

180. A signature footer should include your name, position, affiliation, and e-mail address. It should not exceed four lines. A telephone number can be included.

181. You should not use words in all caps because it is considered shouting.

182. You should use asterisks (*) to emphasize a point because some Web browsers cannot bold a word for emphasis.

183. You should use underscores (_) before and after a book title because some Web browsers cannot italicize words and phrases.

184. Never send chain letters because they clutter the system.

185. Spell out dates because of the international nature of the Internet. Do not list dates by the numbers (12/21/YY). Always spell out the month to avoid confusion: Dec 24, 2005, or 24 Dec 05.

186. A flame is an angry or a derogatory e-mail message.

187. You should not forward personal e-mail because it is considered extremely rude to forward a personal e-mail to members of a listserv without the original author's permission.

188. An emoticon is a symbol used to express feelings in e-mail.

189. Be careful with humor because without verbal communication and body language that can communicate your intent, e-mails can be misinterpreted.

190. Use acronyms to keep e-mail messages short.

191. You should know your firm's e-mail policy because e-mail sent to persons within the firm are subject to the firm's e-mail policy.

192. You must clearly identify yourself when communicating with clients or others regarding a case because it is important that your status indicates that you are not an attorney.

193. You should check your e-mail daily because important information requires an immediate response and e-mails can pile up, making review and response a time-consuming activity.

194. Spam is junk e-mail that is unsolicited. Spamming is the practice of promoting a product or service by e-mail to a group of people.

195. You should use punctuation sparingly because many periods can separate thoughts (. . . . .), but the use of many exclamation marks looks like anger (!!!!!). Many question marks also signify strong emotion (??????????).

196. E-mails that contain important information should not be deleted but should be stored permanently on the firm's server or printed and put in the file.

197. An E-mail filter is software that manages e-mail and that can be programmed to delete e-mails that contain profanity or offensive material.

198. E-mail sent to clients that contain legal advice must be kept confidential to protect attorney-client privilege.

199. One method that ensures a confidential e-mail message is encryption.

200. Most states say that Web sites are advertising.

201. The four advertising prohibitions that apply to Web sites are the following:

1. It cannot contain a misrepresentation.
2. It cannot contain an omission of fact making a statement misleading.
3. It cannot create an unjustified expectation about the results the lawyer can achieve.
4. It cannot compare the lawyer's services with those of other lawyers.

202. Attorneys have been accused of soliciting in their Web sites if their Web sites are considered misleading.

203. Source codes are the coding used by HTML to program the Web site's material.

CHAPTER 11

Law Office Systems

1. The purpose of a system is to streamline a task so that members of the legal team do not do unnecessary work, waste firm resources, or make a mistake.

2. The goals of a system are to maximize productivity, minimize waste, conserve resources, reduce errors, and produce high-quality work.

3. Systems are used to do the following seven things:

   1. Guarantee that the firm's products maintain their excellence
   2. Guarantee that the firm's commodity (time) is used to its maximum potential
   3. Give each member of the legal team the benefit of the experience of another
   4. Substitute for recollection
   5. Improve language and legal skills
   6. Promote delegation
   7. Preserve methods

4. The four types of systems are macrosystems, microsystems, minisystems, and subsystems.

5. A macrosystem is a large system within which microsystems are contained.

6. A law firm is comprised of a macrosystem, two microsystems (substantive and administrative), many minisystems, and many subsystems.

7. A firm's macrosystem consists of affiliated industries within which a firm must operate.

8. The three main elements that affect a firm's macrosystem are technology, the economy (U.S. and local), and government laws and regulations.

9. A law firm has two microsystems.

10. The two microsystems in a law firm are administrative and substantive.

11. The administrative microsystem consists of the firm's goals and objectives, resources, culture, and management style.

12. A firm's substantive microsystem is responsible for delivering legal services to the client.

13. The number of substantive microsystems in a firm varies according to the areas of law in which the firm practices.

14. The three methods of acquiring substantive microsystems are to develop the system, to evolve the system, and to buy the system.

15. A minisystem is a system within the microsystem.

16. The type and number of minisystems depend on the individual system users and the efforts of the firm to develop systems.

17. Minisystems are constantly changing because parts of the minisystem are improved, expanded, or changed as the law changes and as its users become more experienced.

18. Each step in a minisystem is considered a subsystem.

19. The number of subsystems in a minisystem depends on the procedural aspects of the case.

20. Systems development is thinking through and documenting in detail the way to get the job done.

21. The lawyer has ultimate responsibility for the management and supervision of a system.

22. The four stages of systems development are analyze, synthesize, organize, and finalize.

23. The four steps of system analysis are review, separate, evaluate, and communicate.

24. Coding each step allows the legal assistant to identify the status of each step quickly.

25. It is important to discuss each step of the system with co-workers because they will be expected to participate in the system.

26. The three steps of the synthesis process are eliminate, delegate, and consolidate.

27. When delegating functions, it is important to understand the limits within which support staff can function.

28. A systems developer consolidates by combining the new elements.

29. The two steps of the organization process are chronological sequencing and developing a master task list.

30. The master task list is the skeleton from which the system will be developed.

31. The purpose of a master task list is to do the following:
    1. Give a description of each task
    2. Describe specifically when each task is due
    3. Indicate the documents required to complete the task
    4. List the person responsible for completing the task and preparing the documents
    5. Give the order in which each task is to be completed
    6. List all actions to be taken (e.g., telephone client)
    7. Include telephone calls or court appearances
    8. Direct the person to the appropriate checklist

32. The four steps of the finalization process are forms and checklists, written instructions, system checks and follow-up, and revision.

33. A form letter is a letter that contains standardized language and can be customized for a particular case.

34. A blind insert is an entry in a form document alerting the preparer to insert material. It is seen on the computer screen but is not printed.

35. A checklist includes each step of the system and lists the responsible team member.

36. Checklists are maintained in the computer so that they may be changed easily.

37. Form documents are numbered so that they are easily identified.

38. Written instructions are important because they explain how to use a system.

39. Information for written instructions is obtained from the final master task list.

40. The four sections to the written instructions are information, requirements, instructions, and examples of forms and checklists.

41. The information section of written instructions contains information about the goal and purpose of the system and the specific area of law for which the system was developed.

42. All the system's requirements are listed in the requirements section and includes the following:
    1. Computer hardware requirements
    2. List of software used (including version)
    3. Titles of team members using the system
    4. Outside services, such as attorney service and courier
    5. Other supplies and requirements necessary

43. The instructions section should inform the reader when to use the system and how to use the system and provide an explanation of each step of the system.

44. The master task list is the beginning of the instructions section.

45. Written instructions are the basis of the system's evaluation.

46. The forms and checklist section contains a hard copy of all forms and checklists in the order they are used.

47. As the system is tested, necessary changes are noted.

48. The revision process consists of the entire systems development process but on a smaller scale.

49. The best method of storing a system is in a three-ring binder.

50. A system is divided into sections by using a binder with tabbed dividers to separate sections of the system.

51. There should be an original and one copy of a system.

52. Essential skills for systems development are sharp analytical skills, good work habits, good planning and scheduling skills, and good time management skills.

53. The four common problems of systems development are more steps, fewer steps, updates, and using the system as a source.

54. During the course of working in a particular area of law, checklists, form documents, and form files are developed. These are the beginning of a system.

55. A commercial substantive minisystem is one that is purchased from an outside company.

56. When purchasing a system, a person must be sure that the system is current and expandable. It is also important that the forms in the system comply with the court's requirements.

Chapter 12

Docket Control Systems

1. According to recent statistics, 50 percent of all legal malpractice claims are a result of a missed court date or a critical deadline.

2. Secretaries and/or legal assistants in small firms may have total responsibility for the docket system.

3. In large firms, maintaining a firm's docket is the responsibility of docket coordinators or docket clerks.

4. A legal assistant must have knowledge of docket control systems because she or he is responsible for the day-to-day maintenance of a case.

5. A docket control system contains trial dates, court and hearing dates, deposition dates, meeting dates, filing deadlines, reminder dates, follow-up dates, appointments, and reminder dates.

6. A missed deadline can result in a legal malpractice suit, disciplinary proceedings, and/or damage to a firm's reputation.

7. The six functions of a good docket control system are the following:
   1. Meet time requirements
   2. Expedite completion of tasks
   3. Promote good client relations
   4. Ensure that professional liability insurance requirements are satisfied
   5. Reduce stress
   6. Avoid financial loss by reducing malpractice claims

8. The characteristics of a good docket control system are the following:
   1. Provides immediate and automatic calendaring
   2. Provides a double-check of entries
   3. Allows sufficient lead time in advance for completion of tasks
   4. Provides for follow-up to ensure actual performance of work
   5. Is easily maintained and operated

9. The two types of calendars used in a law office are master and personal.

10. The master calendar contains trial dates, hearing dates, and deposition dates for each attorney in the firm.

11. The purpose of the master calendar is to be able to locate the attorney in case of an emergency and for future scheduling.

12. Large firms normally distribute master calendars daily.

13. A small firm that has few changes in the master calendar distributes it less often, normally weekly.

14. Firms with an intranet do not distribute hard copies of master calendars because employees have immediate access to the most recent changes to the calendars on their desktops.

15. Essential information on a master calendar includes the following:
   1. The first initial and last name of the attorney or the initials of the attorney
   2. Type of matter (trial, hearing, deposition)
   3. Time
   4. Name of case
   5. Location

16. A personal calendar contains two types of information: primary and secondary.

17. Primary information includes court trials and hearings, depositions, and statutes of limitations.

18. A statute of limitations is the time period within which an action must be commenced.

19. Secondary information includes the following:
   1. Dates and times of appointments with clients
   2. Dates and times of conferences
   3. Other dates, such as bar association luncheons or continuing education obligations
   4. Personal reminders, such as birthdays and vacations dates

20. It is recommended that a manual system be used in addition to a computerized system as a backup in the event that the computer system should be unavailable for some reason and to double-check against missed deadlines.

21. A manual calendar consisting of primary and secondary information may be a large appointment book, a small appointment book, a desk calendar, or an electronic calendar device. It may also be a hard copy of the information stored in the computer.

22. A legal secretary is usually given the responsibility of keeping the calendars current.

23. Personal calendars should be updated daily, and the updated information should be shared with other members of the legal team.

24. Events are docketed as soon as they occur.

25. Documents from opposing parties that require a response or other action are entered into the docket system as they are received.

26. A stamp or an initial on a document means that the event was docketed.

27. The absence of a stamp or an initial on a document means that the event was not docketed.

28. A calendar meeting is often a short, informal meeting.

29. A docket coordinator is a person in charge of a firm's docketing process.

30. A docket request sheet is a form that contains docketing information that is directed to a docketing coordinator for insertion into a firm's docket system.

31. A docket request sheet contains the following information:
    1. Name or initials of person requesting the docket entry
    2. Responsible attorney
    3. Name of case and file number, if applicable
    4. Type of matter (trial, deposition)
    5. Date and time
    6. Place (if court, indicate courtroom)
    7. Reminder dates
    8. Date the event was docketed
    9. Signature or initials of docket clerk indicating completion

32. Each docket request sheet should have an original and three copies, with each page a different color (e.g., white, blue, pink, and yellow).

33. As a secretary or legal assistant completes the top white sheet, three copies of the information are automatically made. The requesting party keeps the bottom pink sheet as a record that the request was made. The remaining original and two copies are transferred to the docket coordinator. A docket clerk enters the information and signs and dates the docket sheet. The docket coordinator keeps the yellow sheet and returns the white original and blue copy to the requesting party, indicating that the docket entry was made. The secretary or legal assistant keeps the white original as a record that the event was docketed and as a reminder to enter the information into the manual calendars. The blue copy is given to the attorney so that he or she can enter the information into a manual calendar.

34. A docket request sheet is used to inform other members of the legal team that an event was docketed so that they can insert the information into their calendars.

35. It is important to keep all calendars, whether they are computerized or manual, out of the view of clients to protect the confidentiality of the information.

36. A tickler system is a method of controlling deadlines.

37. If no tickler system is implemented, a legal team would have no method to control deadlines.

38. An integrated tickler system is combined with the firm's calendar.

39. A legal assistant enters the daily schedule on the left side of a personal calendar.

40. A legal assistant enters tickler dates on the right side of a personal calendar.

41. The three dates considered when determining due dates are the trigger date, the due date, and the mail date

42. A trigger date begins the clock running on an event.

43. A due date is the date a document is due, which is also known as the drop-dead date.

44. If a due date falls on a holiday or weekend day, the due date is the next business day.

45. A mail date is the date a document must be mailed to reach its destination by the due date.

46. The exact number of days that should be set aside for mailing is determined by statute.

47. When counting days to determine the due date of a document, the first day is excluded.

48. When counting days to determine the due date of a document, the last day is included.

49. The first day after the trigger date, including holidays and weekend days, is the first day counted (the due date is the last day counted).

50. Yes, weekends and holidays are counted.

51. Weekends and holidays are not counted when a response is due in eight days or less of the trigger date.

52. A state's requirements for counting weekend and holiday dates are found in statutes.

53. You compensate for mail time when determining due dates by adding the correct number of days for mailing.

54. The tickler system reminds a legal team that a deadline is approaching.

55. The four reminder dates are reminder, urging, warning, and due date.

56. The time intervals between reminder dates are flexible.

57. The time intervals between reminder dates are determined by the firm's management.

58. Time intervals between reminder dates must be adjustable and flexible to accommodate holidays, weekend days, and other events.

59. Monitoring statutes of limitations is extremely important because if a statute of limitations is missed, a client is prohibited from proceeding.

60. A one-year statute of limitation has four reminder dates.

61. A four-year statute of limitations has five reminder dates.

62. A standard thirty-day deadline has three reminder dates.

63. For a document that must be filed within fifteen days, two reminders are sufficient.

64. A default is a failure to respond within the required time.

65. When entering the due dates of opposing parties, one reminder is sufficient.

66. Various methods are used to differentiate the due dates of opposing parties. If a computerized system is used, clients' information can be entered in italics, bold, or color. If a manual system is used, the information may be entered in red for a client and black for an opposing party, or an asterisk (*) may be inserted by information concerning a client and a "C" for a client and "O" for an opposing party.

67. If a document is mailed to a client and is subject to other deadlines, an entry must be made in a legal assistant's tickler system when the document is expected back.

68. If a client, opposing counsel, or other person agrees to provide a legal assistant with verbal information on a certain date, an entry is made to a tickler system to remind the legal assistant that the information is coming.

69. If an attorney is unexpectedly ill and must be out of the office for a period of time, the tickler system is consulted by other attorneys in the office who will temporarily take over the absent attorney's workload.

70. The basic rule of a tickler system is that no item is removed from the system until it is completed.

71. If information is verbally communicated, chances are that the information will get lost in a myriad of other matters on the minds of the attorney and legal assistant.

72. Docketing due dates and reminder dates correctly is only half the battle; getting the job done is the other half.

73. The two types of computerized docketing systems are static calendar programs and automated docketing programs.

74. A static calendar program is a calendar program that requires entries to be made manually.

75. Both primary and secondary information are entered into a static calendar program.

76. All dates, including tickler dates, are inserted manually into a static calendar program.

77. Static calendar programs are similar to manual, hand-written systems.

78. Static calendar programs are prone to error.

79. Static calendar programs are found in small firms.

80. Two areas of automated docketing software set them apart from static calendaring programs: they prevent users from entering data incorrectly, and they apply preprogrammed court rules to schedule events.

81. Automated docketing programs contain databases that are preprogrammed with docketing rules so that the correct rule and its time frame are automatically applied to a client's matter.

82. A malpractice alert report lists all cases that have no activity scheduled for them.

83. The key features of an automated docketing program are the following:
    1. Preprogrammed court rules
    2. Automatic date scheduling
    3. Automatic reminders
    4. Data validation
    5. Holiday scheduling
    6. Retroactive event recalculation
    7. Group scheduling
    8. Scheduling reports

84. Automatic date scheduling allows a user to enter a key event date, such as a trigger date, and the due date and reminder dates are automatically calculated and scheduled.

85. The data validation feature will automatically validate client matters so that an incorrect entry cannot be made. This feature prevents the possibility that two schedules are prepared for one client.

86. The holiday scheduling feature must be flexible to allow the user to insert other holidays that may be jurisdiction specific.

87. The retroactive event recalculation feature allows entries to be recalculated if a rule changes.

88. The group scheduling feature is important so that all members of the team receive important information relating to the group in their calendars.

89. The information in an automated docketing system is displayed in a calendar that resembles a personal calendar.

90. The advantages to an automated docketing program are that it will increase accuracy, increasing productivity and thus the firm's profits.

91. Some firms use a manual tickler system as their primary system, and others use it in addition to a computerized system as a backup in the event the computer system should be unavailable for some reason and as an extra precaution against missed deadlines.

92. The manual tickler system that has been used by law firms since 1915 is the Basic System.

93. A docket request sheet is used with a manual tickler system. These sheets come in multipart

sets, with each page a different color. If docket request sheets are purchased from a legal supply store, it must have at least four pages in different colors. The original white page is for the due date, the pink slip for the warning date, the blue slip for the urging date, and the yellow slip for the reminder date (or other color coding scheme as the firm may choose). When a docket request sheet is completed, each page is inserted behind its corresponding date. Each morning, the tickler slips are pulled, and the appropriate action is taken. When the current month ends, there should be no tickler sheets left behind a daily divider in that month. The daily divider cards in the current month are then transferred to the first month without daily divider cards. Tickler slips behind that month are then put behind the appropriate daily divider. Yearly index cards are used for long-range dates for events such as judgment renewal dates, stockholder meetings, tax return dates, statute of limitations, and review dates for wills and contracts.

94. Red sticker dots can be put on those cards that represent weekend or holiday dates.

95. A file review system is a system in which a file cannot be ignored.

96. Each file should be reviewed monthly.

97. An attorney should not postpone a file review because doing so defeats its purpose and results in loose habits.

98. When a file is reviewed, the review date is inserted on a file review sheet, which is inserted into the file or taped to the cover of the file folder.

99. File review promotes good client relations because it gives the firm an opportunity to communicate with a client.

CHAPTER 13

File and Records Management

1. For the law firm, the four benefits of a well-organized records management system are the following:
   1. Increased access to information
   2. Easier identification and processing of documents that require special handling
   3. Increased organization of the office as a result of established procedures in document retention
   4. Reduced costs in clerical expenses, photocopy expenses, filing equipment expenses, and storage costs

2. For the employees, the four benefits of a well-organized records management system are the following:
   1. Improved work product: Necessary files and documentation are easily obtained to support each person's work.
   2. Improved organization: Unnecessary material is eliminated.
   3. Increased productivity: The legal assistant can spend time on billable projects rather than on trying to find files, documents, and pertinent information.
   4. Improved use of office space: A better arrangement of necessary equipment and space produces a comfortable working environment.

3. The eight considerations of a records management system are the following:
   1. Ability to find what you want when you want it
   2. Employee time involved in operating the system
   3. The amount and cost of floor space required for the system
   4. Capital investment of durable equipment
   5. Cost of supplies to maintain the system
   6. Appearance of files and equipment
   7. Confidentiality of files
   8. Safety of files

4. A legal assistant cannot bill a client for time spent searching for a file.

5. Disorganization is a cause of employee dissatisfaction.

6. Employee time spent operating a records management system constitutes 80 percent of the cost of most systems.

7. If the records management system is so complicated that it takes many people to keep it functioning, or too much employee time to maintain it, it is not cost effective and is a poor system.

8. The possibility of losing records because of misfiling is greater in a complicated system because employees consider misfiling easier than trying to figure out the system.

9. Filing cabinets and a storage system ordinarily constitute 10 percent of the total cost of a filing system.

10. Supplies for maintaining a records management system constitute another 10 percent of the total cost of a filing system.

11. If a specialized file folder is required for a system, it may not be readily available and can cause a backlog in a system.

12. A filing system must preserve the confidentiality of clients' files.

13. A firm's records must be protected from theft, fire, and other natural elements.

14. The eight elements of an effective filing system are the following:
    1. Retrievability
    2. Functionality
    3. Suitability
    4. Flexibility
    5. Consistency
    6. Economy
    7. Disposability
    8. Security

15. When each function has been identified, categories can be developed within each function.

16. It is important to keep a filing system simple because the more complex a system, the less suitable it is for employees.

17. In large offices, active files increase more than 25 percent a year, doubling in size every four years.

18. To avoid confusion, a system must be consistent in its structure.

19. The economy of a filing system includes the use of time and space.

20. Records are eliminated from an active system when they become inactive.

21. Retention of inactive records that do not need to be retained uses valuable space and increases the time it takes to use and maintain a system.

22. The three types of filing systems are centralized, decentralized, and automated.

23. A centralized filing system has all files in one location.

24. A centralized filing system is managed by a file coordinator or clerk.

25. Large firms and many medium-size firms use centralized filing systems.

26. Controlled access is access and retrieval of a firm's files that is controlled by a specific system.

27. A decentralized filing system has files in different locations, usually divided by department or category.

28. The files are stored in or near the responsible attorney's work area, and each attorney is responsible for maintaining his or her own files.

29. A small firm will have a decentralized system.

30. An automated filing system uses the computer to classify files and folders in the same way a manual system does.

31. The three parts of an automated filing system are document entry, scanning, and retrieval.

32. Imaging is the process of scanning a paper document into a computer system.

33. A user may search the database to find a file. The system will display the files that match the criteria and will display the documents in the file. A user can review, print, or fax documents directly from the system.

34. Classification is the process of separating items into categories.

35. A good classification system increases accessibility and reduces complexity.

36. The four major categories for most law firm files are function, subject, topic, and subtopic.

37. Before a document can be found, the function of its file must be known.

38. After the function is identified, records are divided into subjects.

39. After the subject is identified, it is further divided into topics.

40. Topics may be further divided into subtopics.

41. A coding system is a method used to store files in a specified sequence.

42. The three methods of coding files are alphabetical, numeric, and alphanumeric.

43. An alphabetical coding system is the most common coding system used by sole proprietors and small firms.

44. An alphabetical coding system is the easiest coding system to maintain.

45. An alphabetical coding system files a client's files alphabetically by the surname of the client.

46. The first unit of an individual client's file is his or her surname.

47. The first unit of a business client's file name is the first word of the business name.

48. File nothing before something.

49. The word "the" is always considered the last unit.

50. Ignore all punctuation when alphabetizing.

51. Arabic and roman numerals are filed sequentially before alphabetical letters.

52. The call letters of a television station are considered one unit.

53. Cross-referencing a file is documenting other names that might be used.

54. If a client is the sole plaintiff in a case, his name would be the first name in a case name.

55. If a client is the defendant, his name would be the second name in the case name.

56. "Adversus," as opposed to instead of "versus," indicates that the client is a defendant.

57. A primary case name is the name used to identify a case. It consists of the first-named plaintiff and the first-named defendant.

58. In an insurance defense firm or corporate legal department with only one client, the client's name is not indicated on the label since that name is the same for each file.

59. Subject alphabetical coding for clients' files is more difficult than straight alphabetical coding because a user must know the subject before a file is accessible.

60. Firms that code files by subject must cross-index the case in an alphabetical listing by a client's name to locate the files.

61. The six types of numeric systems are the following:

    1. Straight numbering
    2. Coded numbering
    3. Calendar numbering
    4. Standard numbering
    5. Account numbering
    6. Combination numbering

62. Straight numbering is consecutive numbering: 1, 2, 3, 4.

63. Straight numbering is the least complicated numeric numbering system.

64. Straight numbering usually begins at 100.

65. Coded numbering combines numbers with letters of the alphabet.

66. Coded numbering allows files in one category to be filed together.

67. Calendar numbering inserts the month and year the file was opened as part of the file number.

68. Calendar numbering will keep all files opened in one year together.

69. A calendar numbering system will inform the firm how many files are opened in the year and in the month.

70. Standard numbering separates categories of numbers by a space, comma, period, or dash.

71. A standard numbering system provides the user with information by just reading the file number. It tells the user the responsible attorney, type of case, file number, and volume number.

72. A subfile is known as a volume.

73. Account numbering gives each client a permanent number, and all subsequent cases are filed with that account number.

74. All the files for one client are filed together.

75. Combination numeric numbering is a combination of the five numeric numbering systems.

76. Alphanumeric coding system is a numeric system that codes files alphabetically.

77. Files in an alphanumeric coding system are filed in alphabetical and numeric order.

78. Advantages of an alphanumeric coding system is that it can increase retrieval and filing speed up to six times, misfilings are reduced, and a cross-index is in alphabetical and numeric order.

79. A cross-index is a cross-reference of clients' files. All numeric coding systems must have an alphabetical cross-index of clients with corresponding file numbers. In a firm with many cases, it is impossible to remember the file number of each case.

80. A numeric index informs the person assigning file numbers of the next number in sequence to be assigned.

81. Color coding is used to further categorize files.

82. Color coding can convey information such as type of case, type of document, responsible attorney, branch office, area of law, or the year a file was opened.

83. A colored dot or sticker may be added to the label to add additional information.

84. When numbers are given a color, misfilings are easily spotted because a file with the contrasting color "pops out" from the rest of the files.

85. According to statistics, about 3 percent of documents are misfiled.

86. Noncompliance with retrieval procedures results in lost files.

87. In small firms, a secretary or legal assistant may be responsible for file system maintenance in addition to other duties.

88. In large firms, file clerks or file coordinators are employed whose sole responsibility is to maintain the system.

89. An efficient system has a central person who is responsible for maintaining a system's procedures.

90. Requests for files from a centralized system are initiated by a file requisition form.

91. A written request has one important advantage over an oral request: It provides a record that the request was made.

92. Files may be in a location other than a file room for various reasons, including the following:

    1. An attorney is reviewing it.

    2. A legal assistant is working on it.

    3. A secretary is working on it.

    4. A law clerk has it in the library doing research.

    5. It is in the copy center having documents copied.

93. An out card is the size of a file folder, made of heavy vinyl, and has lines on the front on which to put names and dates. When a file is removed from the filing area, the responsible party inserts his or her name or initials and date on the out card. The out card is then placed in the location of the removed file.

94. Advantages to the out card system include the following:

    1. It shows that the file is being used and has not been misplaced.

    2. It enables a user to know the location of files at all times.

    3. It acts as a marker to indicate the proper place for a file.

95. Problems occur with an out card system when employees do not put their names on the out card or do not use an out card.

96. Out folders are the same as out cards, except that they allow documents to be inserted into them.

97. Law offices use bar coding as a method of managing records.

98. Automatic data collection is a data entry method used in bar code technology.

99. Symbologies are languages used in bar code technology.

100. Firms using bar codes have reported that the system provides them with more efficient document handling, an automated rather than manual master index, a more accurate index of files stored off-site, and decreased retrieval time.

101. Whenever a file is removed from a central filing area, its bar code label is scanned by a portable data entry terminal that communicates its information back to the firm's computer via radio frequency.

102. As a file moves around the office, its location can be determined by using a portable bar code scanner.

103. Medium and large firms especially benefit from using bar code technology for their files.

104. The six benefits of using bar code technology are the following:

    1. Accuracy

    2. Ease of use

    3. Uniform data collection

    4. Timely feedback

    5. Improved productivity

    6. Increased profitability

105. A preclient is a person who consults an attorney but does not formally retain the services of the attorney.

106. A file is opened immediately after a client retains the firm.

107. A conflict check entails checking each new client for a possible conflict of interest.

108. A conflict check database is maintained with clients' names and the names of all parties to a matter in which the firm was involved.

109. A conflict check is the most important aspect of file opening procedures.

110. Each time a party makes an appearance in a case, a firm's client database must be checked to determine the new party's relationship to the firm, if any.

111. If the person conducting the conflict search suspects that there may be a potential conflict with the representation, the attorney or manager must be notified immediately.

112. A file number index is an index containing sequential file numbers and case names. It is used to indicate the next available file number.

113. A new case memorandum is used as a checklist to complete file opening procedures.

114. When a file is opened the date on which the statute of limitations expires must be put into the firm's tickler system to monitor it.

115. When opening a file, a clerk obtains billing information from a new case memorandum.

116. The name of the person who referred the client to the firm is entered into the system so that the firm can send an acknowledgment or thank you to the referring party.

117. Type-of-case information is used by a law firm's management for statistics and marketing information.

118. In large firms, where potential conflicts are often not readily recognized, the firm will circulate a list of new clients and opposing parties to determine whether a potential conflict exists.

119. It is important that file opening procedures and information be accurate because the information is used in timekeeping, billing, and docketing programs and because any errors at the file opening stage will affect other programs.

120. The legal assistant is responsible for maintaining clients' files in good order.

121. Now, documents consist of electronic documents, e-mails, photographs, video clips, digital images, diskettes, and CD-ROMs.

122. Rich media is image-based technology that is visual rather than text oriented.

123. The transition from text-based to image-based documents is one of the biggest changes facing records management today.

124. The first step in file maintenance is categorizing its documents.

125. Correspondence is filed together in chronological order, with the most recent on top.

126. In a small case, all notes are filed together in chronological order, with the most recent on top, and pleadings are filed together in chronological order, with the most recent on top.

127. In a small case, correspondence is inserted on the left side of the folder in chronological order, with the most recent on top.

128. In a small case, pleadings are inserted on the right side in chronological order, with the most recent on top.

129. In a large case, documents are further categorized by section.

130. Case cover sheets are used to monitor the status of the case and are a synopsis of the events of the case. By looking at the case cover sheet, the attorney or legal assistant can see the current status of a case.

131. The case cover sheet is put on top of the folder or documents in the file so that it can be viewed immediately on opening the file.

132. Some firms keep case cover sheets, or a copy of them, in a binder or computer so that the status of each case can be updated and available without pulling the file from the file room.

133. Indexes are used to direct the person to the document's exact location in the file.

134. Each document is given a number that is put on a tab so that it can be found quickly. The tab is then inserted on a divider sheet and protrudes so that it can be seen easily.

135. A document is inserted between each divider. A divider sheet with the document's number on the tab is inserted in front of the document so that the document can be located by lifting up the tab.

136. The number, title of document, date, and party are inserted on an index sheet, which is placed on top of the applicable section.

137. Indexes should be developed for every category of the file, except correspondence and miscellaneous notes.

138. Photographs should be taped onto a large piece of paper or put into an envelope.

139. Documents are generated in a law office in one of two ways: developed or received.

140. A document's purpose must be determined before its life cycle can be identified.

141. The three values of a document are operational, technical, and legal.

142. Operational value is determining whether a document or information is needed on a day-to-day basis.

143. A document that is referred to at least once a month has high operational value. A document that is referred to less than once a month has low operational value.

144. Technical value is whether a document or information contains technical or procedural information.

145. A document has legal value if its information is covered by statute or regulation.

146. To determine the value of a document, the following questions should be asked:

    1. Why would anyone refer to this document again?
    2. To what degree is this document needed for day-to-day business?
    3. When will the information in this document lose its validity? Two weeks? One month?
    4. Will this document be referred to often?
    5. Will this document be helpful information in the type of law in which I am working?
    6. Is this document covered by a statute or regulation?
    7. Has the statute of limitations expired on this document?

147. Keeping unnecessary documents is a waste of space and therefore costly for a firm. They also clutter files and make files less manageable.

148. Purging a file means to discard or clear it of outdated information.

149. Time management experts advise that document management decisions be made as soon as a document is received.

150. Among the documents found in a typical law office are the following:

1. Correspondence (client correspondence, a law firm's business correspondence, promotional mail and advertisements, and miscellaneous correspondence)
2. Clients' case documents, such as pleadings
3. Interoffice memos and reports
4. Photocopies
5. Meeting notes (notes from client conferences, a law firm's business meetings, and miscellaneous meetings, such as educational seminars)
6. Rough drafts
7. Articles and newspaper clippings

151. Filing experts have estimated that correspondence constitutes most of the documents received.

152. If a document was faxed, the fax cover sheet must also be saved to show the date and origin of the fax.

153. Date stamping is marking documents with the date it was received, even fax cover sheets.

154. Date stamping correspondence when it arrives makes it easier to respond to a document in a timely manner and will eliminate paper glut.

155. Envelopes need not be saved unless the correspondence was mailed certified or special delivery or unless the postmark or return address is important to a client's case.

156. The person to whom correspondence is sent is responsible for deciding whether to keep the material.

157. No document pertaining to a client's case may be discarded.

158. If a document's importance or validity to a case is unclear, the responsible attorney should be consulted.

159. All documents pertaining to employment reviews or benefits are retained.

160. If a photocopy contains notes or highlighting that makes it different from the original, it should be retained.

161. A courtesy copy is a copy of a document sent to the recipient as a courtesy or for information purposes only.

162. A secondary recipient receives a copy of a document as a courtesy only and has no responsibility to retain the document.

163. A primary recipient is the person to whom correspondence is addressed.

164. A secondary recipient has no responsibility to retain the document.

165. Notes taken in a meeting with a client or on a client's behalf are always retained.

166. If the note taker was in charge of the meeting, was required to report on the meeting, or was to do something as a result of the meeting, the notes are retained.

167. No rough draft of a contract is destroyed until the agreement has been fully negotiated and signed.

168. Rough drafts of correspondence or pleadings are destroyed when the final document is completed.

169. The article's source, volume number, and date of its source must be indicated on the article.

170. The files and subfiles into which electronic documents are stored must be similar in structure to the filing system for paper documents.

171. "Read only" access allows documents to be accessible to others in the firm but protects them from alteration.

172. Documents should never be removed from a file because they are likely to get lost.

173. The advantages of electronic documents are that they are stored in less space, are accessible at your fingertips, and are easily edited.

174. The disadvantages of electronic documents are that they are difficult to manage, are easily lost without a good filing system in place, and are difficult to search and review without opening the file.

175. The functions of an automated document management system are the following:

1. It keeps track of clients, cases, authors, keywords, and other relevant information.
2. A user can search the database for a document.
3. It can locate any document.
4. It calculates how much time attorneys, legal assistants, and secretaries spend editing documents and automatically enters that information into the billing system.
5. It moves seldom-used documents to remote storage.
6. It provides extra copies of documents in case the system fails.
7. It archives documents after a prearranged retention period is determined.

8. It keeps track of versions of documents.
9. It calculates the number of keystrokes typed and the number of pages printed for each document. The information is automatically transferred into a time and billing system.
10. It makes a backup copy of the document.

176. Most automated document management packages are integrated with a firm's word processing system and can be integrated with other firm software applications, such as docketing and calendar programs, e-mail, and spreadsheet programs.

177. Once prepared, a document is saved on the firm's network or intranet.

178. A law office must have naming and saving rules for its electronic documents.

179. Everyone in a firm should adhere to the rules; otherwise, a system will fail.

180. The characteristics of a good system for electronic documents are that it is easy to use, is easy to remember, and is universally accepted by all employees.

181. A popular electronic filing system that is used in some law firms contains three components: the first four or five letters of the client's name or surname, the date of the document, and a code that indicates the type of document (e.g., CMP = complaint, ANS = answer, INT = interrogatories, LTR = letter).

182. One can look at the name of the document and get an idea of the document's contents.

183. When a case is completed, the following procedures must be followed before closing the file:

1. The file must be reviewed to make sure that all final documents have been completed.
2. The final bill must be paid by the client.
3. A disengagement letter must be sent to the client.
4. The file must be pruned for closing.
5. The status of file must be changed from active to inactive.
6. Original documents must be returned to the client.
7. Electronic records must be deleted from the firm's computer system.

184. A disengagement letter promotes client relations and substantiates that the client's perception of the status of the case is the same as the attorney's.

185. Pruning a file is discarding unnecessary documents from the file.

186. A file closing memorandum acts as a checklist for file closing procedures.

187. A file must be reviewed to make sure that all final documents have been completed.

188. The final bill must be paid before a file is closed.

189. It is often a legal assistant's responsibility to draft a disengagement letter for an attorney's signature.

190. It is often a legal assistant's or secretary's responsibility to prune files.

191. Some experts recommend that the person pruning the file do so with the responsible attorney so that nothing is overlooked.

192. Other experts say that an attorney reviewing files for closing is a waste of the attorney's time and therefore too costly for a firm.

193. Changing the status changes a file from an active to inactive.

194. The conflict-of-interest database should be double-checked to determine whether all parties are in it.

195. A file's retention period must be determined when a file is closed.

196. Legal assistants are often responsible for determining the retention period, but other file closing tasks are usually delegated to a secretary.

197. Original wills are stored in a safe deposit box or other secure area.

198. Electronic documents that are stored in a client's file on the firm's computer system are deleted from the system. Before doing so, they should be reviewed to determine whether they should be put into the firm's form files and knowledge bank. The electronic documents may be put on a diskette and the diskette inserted in the closed file.

199. Inactive records should not be stored in the main filing area because they waste valuable floor and filing space.

200. A firm must employ an indexing system to locate and retrieve inactive files and records.

201. Inactive records are usually stored in filing cabinets or storage boxes outside the main storage area.

202. Each container, whether a cabinet or box, must be properly marked and labeled.

203. Storage areas include a basement, back storage room, or off-site storage facility.

204. Micrographics consists of microfilm and microform.

205. Large firms and firms that store a lot of records benefit from micrographics.

206. Smaller firms often cannot justify the expense of micrographics.

207. Imaging is when documents are scanned into a computer system and an image of the document is saved on CD-ROMs.

208. An image system consists of a control unit with a monitor, scanner and printer, CD-ROM storage unit, and software.

209. A CD-ROM will hold 250,000 documents on one disk.

210. A jukebox is a device that contains many CD-ROMs and allows retrieval of a document on request.

211. The imaging software will generate an index of all documents and identify the CD-ROM on which a document is found.

212. The best evidence rule permits the introduction of a microfilmed duplicate as evidence if the original document has been lost or destroyed, if certain conditions are met.

213. Congress has enacted two statutes that pertain to microfilmed records: the Uniform Photographic Copies of Business and Public Records as Evidence Act of 1949 (UPA) and Uniform Rules of Evidence of 1974.

214. The closed file number and location are inserted on a closed file index for retrieval purposes.

215. Firms that use an alphabetical coding system find that storing closed files alphabetically requires frequent reorganization.

216. Calendar numbering is the preferred method for coding closed files.

217. A closed file index is a list of closed files.

218. The information on a closed file index should be in alphabetical order according to the client's surname and should include the location of all files.

219. The following information should be inserted on a closed file index:

1. File name
2. Active file number, if applicable
3. Closed file number
4. Date file opened
5. Date file closed
6. Location in storage (box or cabinet number; if microfilm, the number of the roll of film, frame on the film, and location of the film)
7. Short description of the disposition of the matter
8. Date the file may be destroyed

220. The information for a closed file index is obtained from a closed file index form.

221. A closed file index form is completed by the person responsible for closing files.

222. The form is inserted in the file or taped to the front of the file folder. A copy of the form can be used as a closed file index log.

223. Records retention is the time period during which records must be maintained by an organization because they may be needed for legal, operational, historical, or other purposes.

224. Record retention time periods are established by state and federal law.

225. Inactive records may be needed for legal, operational, historical, or other purposes.

226. Records may be destroyed after the retention period expires.

227. Research has shown that 95 percent of all references to closed files occur within the first two years of closing.

228. The responsibility for setting a retention period rests with management after researching legal requirements.

229. A retention schedule is a schedule of retention periods categorized according to type of document.

230. A legal assistant should not rely on an automated retention schedule because a case may contain circumstances that a computer cannot analyze.

231. For business records, the following factors are considered:

1. Statute or regulation
2. Future need for records
3. Statute of limitations

232. The future need for business records is determined by a firm's management.

233. The six considerations for retaining client records are the following:

1. Statute or regulation
2. Future need for records
3. Statute of limitations
4. If minors are involved, applicable age of majority
5. Time requirements for appeal
6. Malpractice and business concerns

234. The future need for records can be anticipated by the responsible attorney.

235. The statute of limitations on a minor's action does not begin until the child has reached the age of majority.

236. To ensure confidentiality, records should never be disposed of in the trash can.

237. To prepare records for shredding, all clamps, paper clips, staples, and plastic covers must be removed.

238. Witnessed records destruction is when a disposal company will haul the records off-site and destroy them in the presence of a supervisor.

239. For smaller shredding projects, a firm shreds the documents.

240. It is inappropriate to leave a shredder unattended because the confidentiality of the documents will not be protected.

241. Only white paper is recyclable.

242. Some state bar associations require that attorneys notify their clients by letter before destroying their files.

243. A notification letter regarding file destruction contains the following information:
    1. The date the file is scheduled for destruction.
    2. The client's right to obtain or inspect the file.
    3. Notice to the client that, if s/he chose to preserve the file, s/he would be responsible for the cost thereof.

244. Some firms insert their file closing and destruction policies in their retainer agreements.

245. Law firm personnel should not remove a file from the office because they may be lost or damaged while in transit from the office to home.

246. It is imperative that conflict checks be performed often.

247. If a client terminates the attorney-client relationship, the file must be returned to the client promptly so that the client can continue legal representation elsewhere.

248. Once a records retention schedule is established, it must be reviewed and approved by an attorney.

249. A file must not be destroyed until its retention period has expired because to do so would expose the firm to sanctions and/or fines.

250. Knowledge of file and records management procedures is important to the smooth operation of a law office.

CHAPTER 14

Law Library Organization and Management

1. Libraries are used as the background for law firm photographs and are displayed in the background of television commercials as attorneys advertise their services.

2. A library communicates a message of an attorney's expertise and knowledge of the law.

3. The two types of knowledge are knowledge we have about a subject and knowledge of where to find information about a subject.

4. The highest law in the land is the U.S. Constitution.

5. The highest law in a state is the state constitution.

6. Federal laws are enacted by Congress.

7. Each individual in the country is bound by the U.S. Constitution, state constitution, federal law, federal agency law, state law, state agency law, county ordinances, and city ordinances.

8. A legal assistant must be comfortable in a library setting because success as a legal assistant depends on it.

9. Acquiring knowledge of libraries is the first step in understanding a law library.

10. Gaining knowledge of the contents of a law library is the second step in understanding a law library.

11. In small and medium firms, legal assistants and experienced legal secretaries act as librarians.

12. Our legal system is based on a combination of civil law and common law.

13. Civil law is based on a series of written laws.

14. Civil law was derived from Roman law.

15. In advanced countries, laws were written as early as 2100 B.C.

16. The two main sources of written law are constitutions and statutes.

17. Common law is law derived from court decisions.

18. Common law originated in England, where there were no written laws.

19. Accounts of court decisions were compiled into a series called the Yearbooks.

20. Stare decisis is the legal principle that a court will follow the decision of another court in a similar case.

21. Courts would consult the Yearbooks when making a ruling, establishing the doctrine of stare decisis.

22. Most laws of the United States originated from English common law and were codified, or arranged, into written laws.

23. "Codify" means to arrange laws by subject.

24. The classification process entails placing law into categories.

25. Classification of the law was introduced in England in 1490.

26. The Abridgment of the Yearbooks was the first legal index published.

27. Placing laws into categories helps us find them quickly.

28. Laws are categorized according to function.

29. There are four million case laws and 45,000 to 50,000 court decisions made each year.

30. Case law is classified according to its subject matter.

31. The four functions of law are the following:
    1. Type of legal action
    2. Individuals involved
    3. Nature of the law
    4. Source of the law

32. The two types of legal actions are civil and criminal.

33. In a criminal action, the government (state or federal) is the plaintiff in the action.

34. Crimes are considered an injury to society, so they are prosecuted by the government.

35. The two types of remedies available in a civil case are monetary relief and equitable relief.

36. Monetary relief is when a party is paid money as compensation for an injury.

37. Equitable relief is when relief other than money acts as compensation for an injury (e.g., the return of a person's property that was wrongfully taken).

38. The two types of laws that apply to individuals are public laws and private laws.

39. Public laws apply to everyone.

40. Private laws apply only to individuals who fall under the jurisdiction of the law by circumstance.

41. The two natures of law are substantive and procedural.

42. Substantive laws are laws that govern society. They create, define, and regulate rights.

43. Damages are compensation for a wrong or an injury.

44. Procedural laws give direction on how to recover damages.

45. The sources of law are constitutional law, which encompasses the U.S. Constitution and the constitution of each state; federal statutory law, which encompasses laws passed by the U.S. Congress; state statutory law, which encompasses laws passed by state legislatures and local governments; and case law, which encompasses court decisions resulting from legal controversies.

46. The three classes of law are primary authority, secondary authority, and search tools.

47. Primary authority consists of constitutions, statutes, judicial opinions, court rules, and administrative regulations and decisions.

48. Primary authority consists of laws made by the three branches of government: executive, legislative, and judicial. Primary authority is given the most weight and consideration in a case.

49. The legislature also enacts procedural law.

50. The judicial branch creates laws governing the rules and procedures of the court system.

51. Local rules are rules that are created by an individual court and that apply to that court only.

52. Procedural laws and court rules are primary authority.

53. Statutes are organized according to subject matter.

54. Large libraries contain administrative rulings.

55. Annotated statutes contain historical information concerning amendments and additions to the statute, citations to judicial opinions interpreting the statute, and references to secondary sources that are relevant to the statute.

56. Unannotated statutes contain the statute, delete repealed statutes, and insert all amendments and additions to the statute.

57. Annotated statutes are placed where they are most accessible.

58. Unannotated statutes are often placed in the attorney's or legal assistant's office so that they are accessible whenever needed.

59. New laws are published in pocket parts.

60. A pocket part is an addition to a book that updates its contents.

61. A pocket part uses the same numbering system as the bound volume.

62. A new edition of the U.S. Code is published with supplements being incorporated into the new volumes every five or six years.

63. Pocket parts are inserted into a pocket inside the back cover of the applicable volume.

64. Pocket parts should not be allowed to accumulate because employees will not have the most recent law at their disposal.

65. Reporters contain the text of judicial opinions as they are made.

66. Reporters are numbered consecutively.

67. A series is a set of reporters numbered in numeric order.

68. When the volumes reach a high number, a publisher will name a new series and begin numbering its volumes from 1.

69. Reporters should be placed in numeric order according to series, starting with the first series.

70. Some libraries, especially small libraries, do not contain a first series because of its outdated nature and a library's limited space.

71. A slip opinion is a printed copy of a judicial opinion that is distributed soon after the decision is rendered.

72. An advance sheet is a softcover book of decisions that is circulated soon after a decision is rendered.

73. Advance sheets are sent to law libraries weekly.

74. Advance sheets are placed at the end of a reporter set.

75. Once a new volume is received, the advance sheets may be discarded and the new volume placed at the end of the set.

76. Court rules were first developed by the Judiciary Act of 1789, passed at the first session of Congress.

77. Court rules are court procedures that must be followed in cases before that court.

78. Court rules have three purposes:
    1. Aid the court in expediting the business that comes before it
    2. Establish uniform procedures for the conduct of a court's business
    3. Provide parties to a lawsuit with procedural information and instructions on bringing the matter before a court

79. Local rules are rules governing local courts.

80. Court rules are placed in a library where they can be retrieved quickly.

81. Court rules are updated by a publisher or the particular court.

82. Administrative agencies are established by Congress and are government entities, other than a court or legislative body, that affect the rights of people through their rules and decisions.

83. Some agencies publish their own opinions, and a few private publishers publish administrative and judicial opinions on particular subjects.

84. State agency administrative regulations and decisions are published chronologically, although some states codify their regulations. Some state administrative rulings are privately published in looseleaf reports or by services. State administrative agency rulings are not as uniformly published as federal administrative rulings.

85. Large libraries contain administrative rulings.

86. Secondary authority is anything other than primary authority that aids a court in reaching a decision. Secondary authority is used to persuade. It is not considered in lieu of primary authority but is used in addition to primary authority.

87. Secondary authority was developed to provide aids in identifying and explaining the law.

88. Secondary authority is used to persuade.

89. Secondary authority includes treatises, periodicals, dictionaries, and encyclopedias.

90. A treatise is a legal commentary on a particular subject of law. The purpose of a treatise is to simplify and explain the law.

91. Periodicals are booklets containing articles about the law.

92. Indexes are published to provide access to all the articles published in a legal periodical.

93. The most established index service is the *Index to Legal Periodicals,* which dates back to 1908.

94. A legal dictionary is considered secondary authority and can be quoted if the meaning of a word is in dispute.

95. Encyclopedias are volumes that contain statements on principles of law and are organized alphabetically by subject matter.

96. Encyclopedias are categorized into broad topics that are subdivided into narrower topics and that act as an index and guide to the law.

97. Secondary authority is placed according to the numeric order of the volumes.

98. Dictionaries are usually placed in a central area of a library.

99. Many treatises are updated by pocket parts, restatements are rewritten, and the new material is contained in an updated series. Other treatises are updated as the law changes.

100. Search tools assist the researcher in finding primary authority.

101. Search tools are never cited as a source of law; they are tools only.

102. A digest is a collection embodying the chief matter of numerous books, articles, and court decisions.

103. A digest is usually arranged alphabetically.

104. A citator is a set of books that provide the judicial history and interpretation of reported decisions.

105. If a statute is repealed, it is abrogated, or annulled.

106. Form books assist the attorney and legal assistant in drafting legal documents and assist in the procedures of a case.

107. The manner in which a firm's library resources are managed determines a library's organization.

108. Law libraries are described according to size.

109. Small libraries that contain only those books essential for the lawyers' needs are skeletal law libraries.

110. Skeletal libraries contain state statutes, case reporters for a specific jurisdiction in which the lawyers practice, form books, and a legal dictionary. A skeletal library may also contain a treatise in a particular area of law.

111. Libraries that contain a comprehensive collection of the laws of the country are complete law libraries. A complete law library has over 300,000 hard-cover volumes, microform, and computer databases.

112. Complete law libraries are found in large law schools, some large agencies, courthouses, and major city libraries.

113. The largest complete law library in the United States is the Library of Congress in Washington, D.C., with two million volumes.

114. The three types of library organization are centralized, decentralized, and satellite.

115. A centralized library is found in one location that has been set aside by a firm.

116. Most large firms have a centralized library.

117. A library cooperative is a group organized to pool library resources for the benefit of the group.

118. A decentralized library is distributed throughout a firm.

119. Attorneys and legal assistants use the books in their individual offices.

120. Sole practitioners and small firms have decentralized libraries.

121. A decentralized library has three advantages:
    1. The books are close to the attorneys and legal assistants using the them.
    2. The books are decorative and give the office a nice appearance.
    3. The books act as a noise buffer, keeping an office quieter.

122. The disadvantages to a decentralized library are that books not readily accessible when needed, are often misplaced, and are kept in offices and not returned to the shelf.

123. A satellite library is a small library maintained outside the main library area.

124. Satellite libraries are found in large firms with a large centralized library.

125. Some firms will remove specialty books from a central library and put a satellite library close to the employees using these books.

126. Tax and labor libraries are the most common satellite libraries.

127. It is important that supplement material be inserted into the proper books as soon as possible so that the attorneys and legal assistants have current law at their disposal.

128. Legal publishing companies provide an update service called Advance Legislative Service.

129. Law books must be updated constantly.

130. Ninety percent of a law library's budget is spent to update law resources.

131. The three most common checkout systems used in law firm libraries are out card, bar code, and library card systems.

132. Problems arise with an out card system when employees do not take the time to write their names on the card or the cards fall off the shelf out of place.

133. Some firms have bar codes placed on their books to track the books electronically.

134. Each book has a library card placed in a pocket on the inside cover of the book. A library card contains the book's name, author, and other pertinent information about the book. As the book leaves the library, the

library card is placed into a card box or card holder behind the person's name taking the book. When the book is returned, the person replaces the card in the book.

135. Law libraries are getting smaller because they are implementing technology by combining it with law books. Fewer books and more technology are being purchased.

136. The five types of technology used in law libraries are the following:
    1. On-line legal and nonlegal databases
    2. Microform
    3. CD-ROM
    4. E-mail and telefacsimile (fax) transmission
    5. The Internet

137. An on-line legal database is a database of laws compiled by a publisher that charges customers to use it.

138. Computer-assisted legal research (CALR) is doing legal research on a legal database.

139. "Full text" means that the entire text of the document is displayed.

140. A modem is a device that is connected to a computer and that allows a telephonic connection with a database or other computer.

141. The two primary CALR systems are Westlaw, from IT Thompson's West Group, and Lexis, from Reed Elsevier, both of which provide access to full-text legal documents through a computer.

142. An abstract system does not provide the full text of a decision but instead provides an abstract, or summary, of a law.

143. A nonlegal database operates the same as a legal database but contains nonlegal information.

144. To access a database from the Internet, one needs an account and a password and must pay the requisite fees. Accessing a database from the Internet requires no specialized software (except a browser) and can be accessed from an individual computer.

145. Microform is the process of storing information photographically. It is the term used to describe any form of printing on film or paper containing miniature images of a document.

146. Microfilm is 35-millimeter film that stores a large number of pages that run continuously in sequence and that need no alteration.

147. Microfiche is a sheet of microfilm in the form of a card that is used to store a small number of pages that require updating.

148. One 100-foot roll of microfilm contains five large books.

149. Six microfiche cards are needed to photograph one book.

150. After documents have been photographed, the film is inserted into a reader/printer that enlarges the document on a screen for viewing.

151. Volumes of books are put on microfilm and stored in a small desk drawer. Many books can be stored in the same desk drawer.

152. Microfilm will last about 200 years.

153. "CD-ROM" stands for "compact disk read-only memory."

154. A CD-ROM can store about 300,000 manuscript pages, or 250 large law books.

155. A megabyte is a computer term used to measure data; one megabyte contains about one million characters.

156. A CD-ROM drive is needed to access material on a CD-ROM.

157. A jukebox is a CD-ROM storage device.

158. A jukebox can hold as few as six and as many as 500 CD-ROMs.

159. As laws change, a disk must be updated by its publisher. Since laws change daily, providing current material has been a challenge for legal CD-ROM publishers. Because of the time and processes needed to produce and ship them, they are out of date when they are received.

160. A user interface is a method of operation developed by a legal publisher for its CD-ROM products.

161. The lifetime of a CD-ROM is currently ten to thirty years—not long enough to replace microform's longevity.

162. Bar association libraries that provide library services to their members deliver materials by e-mail or fax machine. Previously, legal assistants and other law firm personnel had to go to a library to copy materials.

163. According to the 1999 Technology Survey conducted by the NFPA, more than 75 percent of the respondents conduct legal and factual research on the Internet.

164. Access to law on the Internet is partially due to the assertive position of government agencies in placing their information on the Internet and to entrepreneurs who seek to bring viewers to their legal Web sites.

165. A great deal of information that lawyers and librarians need is not available on the Internet, such as secondary authority material.

166. A problem with conducting legal research over the Internet is its poor classification system, making law difficult to locate.

167. It takes longer to do research on the Internet because of its poor classification system.

168. The *Harvard Blue Book: A Uniform System of Citation* is used as a guide to legal citation.

169. The AALL recognized the need for a new citation format for electronic materials and recommended that a legal cite include the case name, year of the decision, specific court, a consecutively assigned case number, and paragraph number for the exact location of the quote.

170. In 1996, the ABA adopted the AALL's recommendation but suggested that the traditional site be included.

171. As of 1999, no universally accepted citation system for electronic documents exists.

172. Every law office must have an adequate supply of court forms, which are form documents used in a specific court.

173. The three methods of storing court forms are manually, on masters that are photocopied, and computer programs.

174. Court forms that are stored manually are filed in filing cabinets and are normally organized alphabetically by subject matter.

175. Photocopier-created forms are stored in three-ring binders to save space. The binders are indexed and divided into subjects. Only one copy of each form, the master form, is inserted into a binder. That form is photocopied when it is needed.

176. Computer-generated forms are software programs that provide court forms and that assist a user in completing them. They are printed after completion.

177. Some courts undertake responsibility for distributing new court forms. Most courts, however, do not want to be burdened with this responsibility and so delegate it to a printing company, court form software company, or court forms service. The legal industry supports many court form service companies that will print and distribute forms to their subscribers. They will automatically send new and updated forms when these forms become effective. Automated court forms software is updated by the publisher.

178. A knowledge bank contains samples of research and documents prepared by a firm and are used in the same manner as form books.

179. Eighty percent of work done in most law firms is not new. The work of attorneys and legal assistants is often similar to a previous case. If a firm can realize increased efficiencies on 80 percent of its work, it will increase productivity, resulting in increased profits. Keeping copies of briefs and research memoranda regarding an issue or subject saves employees' time in researching that issue again should a similar case arise.

180. The two types of work product retrieval systems are manual and automated.

181. A manual system is used by small firms.

182. With a manual system, documents in a knowledge bank are filed alphabetically by subject to allow searchers to locate a document quickly, like court forms.

183. A comprehensive index is required to locate a document in a manual system.

184. An index is prepared alphabetically by subject matter and contains the law or rule to which the document applies.

185. If a document has more than one subject matter, it is cross-referenced to other topics.

186. When a document is inserted into a knowledge bank, it is incorporated into the system by a research index memorandum form.

187. Automated work product retrieval systems are used by medium and large firms that have large knowledge banks.

188. A large knowledge bank must be automated to manage the high number of documents in it.

189. The four types of automated work product retrieval system are full text, index, abstracts, and a combination of these.

190. A network or an intranet is required for a knowledge bank to be available on each person's computer terminal.

191. Without a network, a knowledge bank is found on a dedicated computer in the library.

192. The role of a law librarian is changing with the information explosion.

193. Among the duties of a law librarian are the following:
  1. Research
  2. Collection development
  3. Library maintenance

4. Indexing
5. Establishing library policy
6. Organization
7. Training
8. Management
9. Personnel management
10. Planning
11. Web maintenance

194. Some librarians have additional duties outside the library, such as managing legal assistant or secretarial staff and managing a central filing area.

195. A law librarian devotes full time to a firm's library and is found in large firms with large libraries.

196. Most librarians in large firms have a master of library science degree, and+ some have a law degree.

Associations for Legal Assistants, Legal Secretaries, and Managers

American Association for Paralegal Education (AAfPE)
2965 Flowers Rd. S.
Atlanta, GA 30341
(770) 452-9877
www.aafpe.org

American Association of Law Librarians (AALL)
53 W. Jackson Blvd., #940
Chicago, IL 60604
(312) 939-4764
www.aallnet.org

American Bar Association, Standing Committee on Legal Assistants
750 N. Lake Shore Dr.
Chicago, IL 60611
(312) 988-5618
www.abanet.org

Association of Legal Administrators (ALA)
175 E. Hawthorn Pkwy, #325
Vernon Hills, IL 60061-1428
(708) 816-1212
www.alanet.org

Association of Trial Lawyers of America (ATLA)
1050 31st St. N.W.
Washington, DC 20007-4499
(202) 965-3500

Legal Assistant Management Association (LAMA)
638 Prospect Ave.
Hartford, CT 06105

(860) 586-7507
www.lamanet.org

Legal Marketing Association
401 N. Michigan Ave.
Chicago, IL 60611
(312) 245-1592
www.legalmarketing.org

National Association for Independent Paralegals
635 5th St. W.
Sonoma, CA 95476

National Association of Legal Assistants (NALA)
1516 S. Boston, #200
Tuba, OK 74119
918-587-6828
www.nala.org.

National Association of Legal Secretaries (International) (NALS)
2448 E. 81st St., #3400
Tuba, OK 74137-4238
(918) 493-3540

National Black American Paralegal Association (NBAPA)
P.O. Box 28024
Washington, DC 20038-8024
(202) 452-7485

National Federation of Paralegal Associations (NFPA)
P.O. Box 33108
32 W. Bridle Spur Terr.
Kansas City, MO 64114
(816) 941-4000
www.paralegals.org

State and Territorial

Alabama

Alabama Association of Legal Assistants
P.O. Box 55921
Birmingham, AL 35255

Huntsville Association of Paralegals
P.O. Box 244
Huntsville, AL 35804-0244

Mobile Association of Legal Assistants
P.O. Box 1988
Mobile, AL 36333

Alaska

Alaska Association of Legal Assistants
P.O. Box 101956
Anchorage, AK 99510-1956
Alaska@paralegals.org

Fairbanks Association of Legal Assistants
P.O. Box 73503
Fairbanks, AK 99707

Juneau Legal Assistants Association
P.O. Box 22336
Juneau, AK 99802

Arizona

Arizona Association of Professional Paralegals
P.O. Box 25111
Phoenix, AZ 85002

Arizona Paralegal Association
P.O. Box 392
Phoenix, AZ 85001
602-258-0121

Legal Assistants of Metropolitan
Phoenix
P.O. Box 13005
Phoenix, AZ 85002

Southeast Valley Association of
Legal Assistants
1707 N. Temple
Mesa, AZ 85203

Tucson Association of Legal
Assistants
P.O. Box 257
Tucson, AZ 85702-0257

Arkansas

Arkansas Association of Legal
Assistants
P.O. Box 2162
Little Rock, AR 72203-2162

California

California Alliance of Paralegal
Associations
P. O. Box 2234
San Francisco, CA 94126
415-576-3000

California Association of
Freelance Paralegals
P. O. Box 3267
Berkeley, CA 94703-0267

California Association of
Independent Paralegals
39120 Argonaut Way, #114
Fremont, CA 94538
CAIndependent@paralegals.org

Central Coast Legal Assistant
Association
P.O. Box 93
San Luis Obispo, CA 93406

Central Valley Paralegal
Association
P. O. Box 4086
Modesto, CA 95352

East Bay Association of
Paralegals
P.O. Box 29082
Oakland, CA 94604

Inland Counties Paralegal
Association
P.O. Box 292
Riverside, CA 92502-0292

Kern County Paralegal
Association
P.O. Box 2673
Bakersfield, CA 93303

Legal Assistants Association of
Santa Barbara
P.O. Box 2695
Santa Barbara, CA 93120
(805) 965-7319

Los Angeles Paralegal
Association
P.O. Box 241928
Los Angeles, CA 90024
(213) 251-3755

Marin Association of Legal
Assistants
P.O. Box 13051
San Rafael, CA 94913-3051
(415) 456-6020

Orange County Paralegal
Association
P.O. Box 8512
Newport Beach, CA 92658-8512
(714) 744-7747

Paralegal Association of Santa
Clara County
P.O. Box 26736
San Jose, CA 95159

Redwood Empire Association of
Legal Assistants
1275 4th St., Box 226
Santa Rosa, CA 95404

Sacramento Association of Legal
Assistants
P.O. Box 453
Sacramento, CA 95812-0453
(916) 763-7851
Sacramento@Paralegals.org

San Diego Association of Legal
Assistants
P.O. Box 87449
San Diego, CA 92138-7449
(619) 491-1994
SanDiego@paralegals.org

San Francisco Association of
Legal Assistants
P.O. Box 2110
San Francisco, CA 94126-2110
(415) 777-2390
San Francisco@paralegals.org

San Joaquin Association of Legal
Assistants
P.O. Box 1306
Fresno, CA 93715

Sequoia Paralegal Association
P.O. Box 3884
Visalia, CA 93278-3844

Ventura County Association of
Legal Assistants
P.O. Box 24229
Ventura, CA 93002

Colorado

Association of Legal Assistants of
Colorado
4150 Novia Dr.
Colorado Springs, CO 80911

Rocky Mountain Legal Assistants
Association
P.O. Box 304
Denver, CO 80201
(303) 369-1606

Connecticut

Central Connecticut Association
of Legal Assistants
P.O. Box 230594
Hartford, CT 06123-0594

Connecticut Association of
Paralegals, Fairfield County
P.O. Box 134
Bridgeport, CT 06604

Connecticut Association of
Paralegals, New Haven
P.O. Box 862
New Haven, CT 06504-0862

Legal Assistants of Southeastern
Connecticut
P.O. Box 409
New London, CT 06320

Delaware

Delaware Paralegal Association
P.O. Box 1362
Wilmington, DE 19899

District of Columbia

National Capital Area Paralegal
Association
1155 Connecticut Ave. N.W.
Washington, DC 20036-4306
(202) 659-0243

Florida

Broward County Paralegal
Association
P.O. Box 1900
Ft. Lauderdale, FL 33302

Dade Association of Legal
Assistants
14027 S.W. 84th St
Miami, FL 33183

Florida Legal Assistants
P.O. Box 503
Bradenton, FL 34206

Jacksonville Legal Assistants
P.O. Box 52264
Jacksonville, FL 32201

Orlando Legal Assistants
P.O. Box 231
Orlando, FL 32802

Pensacola Legal Assistants
226 S. Palafox St.
Pensacola, Fl 32581

Volusia Association of Legal
Assistants
P.O. Box 15075
Daytona Beach, FL 32115-5075

Georgia

Georgia Association of Legal
Assistants
P.O. Box 1802
Atlanta, GA 30301

Southeastern Association of Legal
Assistants of Georgia
2215 Bacon Park Dr.
Savannah, GA 31406

South Georgia Association of
Legal Assistants
L. Andrew Smith, P.C.
P.O. Box 1026
Valdosta, GA 31603-1026

Hawaii

Hawaii Association of Legal
Assistants
P.O. Box 674
Honolulu, HI 96809

Idaho

Idaho Association of Legal
Assistants
P.O. Box 1254
Boise, ID 83701

Illinois

Central Illinois Paralegal
Association
GTE North Inc.
1312 E. Empire St.
Bloomington, IL 61701

Independent Contractors
Association of Illinois
6400 Woodward Ave.
Downers Grove, IL 60516

Peoria Paralegal Association
1308 Autumn La.
Peoria, IL 60604

Indiana

Indiana Legal Assistants
14669 Old State Rd.
Evansville, IN 47711

Indiana Paralegal Association
P.O. Box 44518, Federal Station
Indianapolis, IN 46204

Michiana Paralegal Association
P.O. Box 11458
South Bend, IN 46634

Iowa

Iowa Association of Legal
Assistants
P.O. Box 335
Des Moines, IA 50302-0337

Paralegals of Iowa, Ltd.
P.O. Box 1943
Cedar Rapids, IA 52406

Kansas

Kansas Association of Legal
Assistants
700 Fourth Financial Center
Wichita, KS, 67202

Kansas City Association of Legal
Assistants
P.O. Box 1657
Topeka, KS 66601

Kentucky

Kentucky Paralegal Association
P.O. Box 2675
Louisville, KY 40201-2657

Lexington Paralegal Association
P.O. Box 574
Lexington, KY 40586

Louisville Association of
Paralegals
P.O. Box 962
Louisville, KY 40201

Louisiana

Baton Rouge Paralegal Association
P.O. Box 306
Baton Rouge, LA 70821

Lafayette Paralegal Association
P.O. Box 2775
Lafayette, LA 70502

Louisiana State Paralegal
Association
P.O. Box 56
Baton Rouge, LA 70821-0056

New Orleans Paralegal Association
P.O. Box 30604
New Orleans, LA 70190

Northwest Louisiana Paralegal
Association
P.O. Box 1913
Shreveport, LA 71166-1913

Southwest Louisiana Association
of Paralegals
P.O. Box 1143
Lake Charles, LA 70602-1143

Maine

Maine Association of Paralegals
P.O. Box 7554
Portland, ME 04112

Maryland

Baltimore Association of Legal
Assistants
P.O. Box 13244
Baltimore, MD 21203
(301) 576-BALA

Massachusetts

Berkshire Association for
Paralegals and Legal Secretaries
54 Wendell Ave.
Pittsfield, MA 01201

Central Massachusetts Paralegal
Association
P.O. Box 444
Worcester, MA 01614

Massachusetts Paralegal
Association
P.O. Box 423
Boston, MA 02102
(617) 642-8338

Western Massachusetts Paralegal
Association
P.O. Box 30005
Springfield, MA 01102-0005

Michigan

Legal Assistants Association of
Michigan
315 S. Woodward
Royal Oak, MI 48067

Legal Assistant Section
State Bar of Michigan
306 Townsend St.
Lansing, MI 48933-2083
(517) 372-9030

Minnesota

Minnesota Association of Legal
Assistants
P.O. Box 15165
Minneapolis, MN 55415

Minnesota Paralegal Association
724 S.W. First Ave.
Rochester, MN 55902

Mississippi

Gulf Coast Paralegal Association
942 Beach Dr.
Gulfport, MS 39507

Mississippi Association of Legal
Assistants
P. O. Box 996
600 Heritage Bldg.
Jackson, MS 39205

Paralegal Association of
Mississippi
P.O. Box 22887
Jackson, MS 39205

Missouri

Gateway Paralegal Association
P.O. Box 50233
St. Louis, MO 63105

Kansas City Association of Legal
Assistants
P.O. Box 13223
Kansas City, MO 64199
(913) 381-4458

Southwest Missouri Paralegal
Association
2148 S. Oak Grove
Springfield, MO 66504-2708

St. Louis Association of Legal
Assistants
P.O. Box 9690
St. Louis, MO 63122

Montana

Big Sky Paralegal Association
P.O. Box 2753
Great Falls, MT 59403

Montana Paralegal Association
P.O. Box 693
Billings, MT 59101

Nebraska

Nebraska Association of Legal
Assistants
P.O. Box 24943
Omaha, NE 68124

Nevada

Clark County Organization of
Legal Assistants
3800 S. Nellis, # 235
Las Vegas, NV 89121

Sierra Nevada Association of
Paralegals
P.O. Box 40638
Reno, NV 89504

New Hampshire

Paralegal Association of New
Hampshire
P.O. Box 808
Manchester, NH 03305

New Jersey

Central Jersey Paralegal
Association
P.O. Box 1115
Freehold, NJ 07728

Legal Assistants Association of
New Jersey
P.O. Box 142
Caldwell, NJ 07006

South Jersey Paralegal
Association
P.O. Box 355
Haddonfield, NJ 08033

New Mexico

Legal Assistants of New Mexico
P.O. Box 1113
Albuquerque, NM 87103-1113
(505) 260-7104

New York

Adirondack Paralegal Association
1 Washington St., Box 2168
Glen Falls, NY 12801

Legal Professionals of Dutchess
County
51 Maloney Rd.
Wappingers Falls, NY 12590

Long Island Paralegal Association
P.O. Box 31
Deer Park, NY 11729

Manhattan Paralegal Association
200 Park Ave., #303 East
New York, NY 10116
(212) 986-2304

Paralegal Association of Rochester
P.O. Box 40567
Rochester, NY 14604

Southern Tier Association of
Paralegals
P.O. Box 2555
Binghamton, NY 13902

Western New York Paralegal
Association
P.O. Box 207
Buffalo, NY 14202
(716) 862-6132

West/Roc Paralegal Association
Box 101
95 Mamaroneck Ave.
White Plains, NY 10601

North Carolina

Cumberland County Paralegal
Association
P.O. Box 1358
Fayetteville, NC 28302

Metrolina Paralegal Association
P.O. Box 36260
Charlotte, NC 28236

North Carolina Paralegal Association
P.O. Box 1121
Goldsboro, NC 27533-1121

Raleigh Wake Paralegal Association
P.O. Box 1427
Raleigh, NC 27602

Triad Paralegal Association
Drawer U
Greensboro, NC 27402

North Dakota

Red River Valley Legal Assistants
P.O. Box 1954
Fargo, ND 58106

Western Dakota Association of
Legal Assistants
P.O. Box 7304
Bismarck, ND 58502

Ohio

Cincinnati Paralegal Association
P.O. Box 1515
Cincinnati, Ohio 45201
(513) 244-1266

Cleveland Association of Paralegals
P.O. Box 14247
Cleveland, OH 44114

Legal Assistants of Central Ohio
P.O. Box 15182
Columbus, OH 43215-0812
(614) 224-9700

Northeastern Ohio Paralegal
Association
P.O. Box 9236
Akron, OH 44305

Toledo Association of Legal
Assistants
P.O. Box 1322
Toledo, OH 43603

Oklahoma

Oklahoma Paralegal Association
P.O. Box 18476
Oklahoma City, OK 73154

Tulsa Association of Legal
Assistants
P.O. Box 1484
Tulsa, OK 74101

Oregon

Oregon Legal Assistants Association
P.O. Box 8523
Portland, OR 97207

Pacific Northwest Legal Assistants
P.O. Box 1835
Eugene, OR 97440

Pennsylvania

Berks County Paralegal Association
544 Court St.
Reading, PA 19601
(215) 375-4591

Central Pennsylvania Paralegal
Association
P.O. Box 11814
Harrisburg, PA 17108

Keystone Legal Assistant
Association
3021 Guineveer, Apt. B4
Harrisburg, PA 17110

Lancaster Area Paralegal
Association
41 E. Orange St.
Lancaster, PA 17602

Paralegal Association of
Northwestern Pennsylvania
P.O. Box 1504
Erie, PA 16507

Philadelphia Association of
Paralegals
1411 Walnut St., #200
Philadelphia, PA 19102
(215) 564-0525

Pittsburgh Paralegal Association
P.O. Box 2845
Pittsburgh, PA 15230

Wilkes-Barre Area Group
6 E. Green St.
West Hazleton, PA 18201

Rhode Island

Rhode Island Paralegal Association
P.O. Box 1003
Providence, RI 02901

South Carolina

Charleston Association of Legal
Assistants
P.O. Box 1511
Charleston, SC 29402

Columbia Association of Legal
Assistants
P.O. Box 11634
Columbia, SC 29211-1634

Greenville Association of Legal
Assistants
P.O. Box 10491 F.S
Greenville, SC 29603

Paralegal Association of the Pee Dee
P.O. Box 5592
Florence, SC 29502-5592

South Dakota

South Dakota Legal Assistants
Association
P.O. Box 1443
Sioux Falls, SD 57101-1443

Tennessee

Memphis Paralegal Association
P.O. Box 3646
Memphis, TN 38173-0646

Middle Tennessee Paralegal
Association
P.O. Box 198006
Nashville, TN 37219

Southeast Tennessee Paralegal
Association
P. O. Box 1252
Chattanooga, TN 37401

Tennessee Paralegal Association
P.O. Box 11172
Chattanooga, TN 37401

Texas

Alamo Area Professional Legal
Assistants
P.O. Box 524
San Antonio, TX 78292

Capital Area Paralegal
Association
111 Congress, #1700
Austin, TX 78701

Dallas Association of Legal
Assistants
P.O. Box 117885
Carrollton, TX 75011-7885

El Paso Association of Legal
Assistants
P.O. Box 121
El Paso, TX 79941-0121

Fort Worth Paralegal Association
P.O. Box 17021
Fort Worth, TX 76102

Houston Legal Assistants
Association
P.O. Box 52266
Houston, TX 77052

Legal Assistant Division
State Bar of Texas
P.O. Box 12487
Austin, TX 78711
(512) 463-1383

Legal Assistants Association
Permian Basin
P.O. Box 10683
Midland, TX 79702

Legal Assistants Professional
Association (Brazos Valley)
P.O. Box 925
Madisonville, TX 79702

Northeast Texas Association of
Legal Assistants
P.O. Box 2284
Longview, TX 75606

Nueces County Association of
Legal Assistants
P.O. Box 480
Corpus Christi, TX 78403

Southeast Texas Association of
Legal Assistants
8335 Homer
Beaumont, TX 77708

Texarkana Association of Legal
Assistants
P.O. Box 6671
Texarkana, TX 75505

Texas Panhandle Association of
Legal Assistants
P.O. Box 189
Amarillo, TX 79105

Tyler Area Association of Legal
Assistants
P.O. Box 1178
Tyler, TX 75711-1178

West Texas Association of Legal
Assistants
P.O. Box 1499
Lubbock, TX 79408

Utah

Legal Assistants Association of
Utah
P.O. Box 112001
Salt Lake City, UT 84147-2001
(801) 531-0331

Vermont

Vermont Paralegal Association
P.O. Drawer 351
Middlebury, VT 05753

Virginia

American Academy of Legal
Assistants
1022 Paul Ave. N.E.
Norton, VA 24273

Peninsula Legal Assistants
P.O. Box 12888
Newport News, VA 23612

Richmond Association of Legal
Assistants
1 James Center
Richmond, VA 23219

Roanoke Valley Paralegal
Association
P.O. Box 1505
Roanoke, VA 24001
(703) 224-8000

Tidewater Association of Legal
Assistants
1800 Sovran Center
Norfolk, VA 23510

Virgin Islands

Virgin Islands Paralegals
P.O. Box 6276
St. Thomas, VI 00804

Washington

Washington Legal Assistant
Association
2033 6th Ave., #804
Seattle, WA 98121
(206) 441-6020

West Virginia

Legal Assistants of West Virginia
P.O. Box 2506
Charleston, WV 25329-2506

Wisconsin

Paralegal Association of
Wisconsin
P.O. Box 92882
Milwaukee, WI 53202
(414) 272-7168

Wyoming

Legal Assistants of Wyoming
123 W. First St.
Casper, WY 82601

Federal Employment Laws

This list identifies the key purpose of each federal regulation pertaining to employment.

◆ Fifth Amendment to the Constitution (1791) states, "No person shall . . . be deprived of life, liberty or property, without due process of law, . . . "

◆ . . . Civil Rights Act of 1866 states, "All persons within . . . the United States shall have the same right . . . to make and enforce contracts . . . as is enjoyed by white persons." This act provides federal court jurisdiction regarding Thirteenth Amendment matters. It applies primarily to racial discrimination.

◆ Fourteenth Amendment to the Constitution (1868) states, "No State shall make or enforce any law which shall abridge the privileges or immunities of citizens of the United States, nor shall any State deprive any person of life, liberty or property, without due process of law; nor deny to any person within its jurisdiction the equal protection of the laws," and "the Congress shall have the power to enforce, by appropriate legislation, the provisions of this article."

◆ Civil Rights Act of 1871 states, "Every person who, under color of any statute [law], . . . causes . . . the deprivation of any rights . . . shall be liable to the person injured . . . " This Act provides federal court jurisdiction regarding Fourteenth Amendment matters. It applies to discrimination based on race, sex and national origin.

◆ Age Discrimination Act of 1967, amended 1978, prohibits employment discrimination based on age 40–70 years, unless such policies exist as part of an established seniority or benefit plan or age is a bona fide occupational qualification (BFOQ).

◆ Equal Employment Opportunity Act of 1972 expanded the coverage of Title VII and empowered the Equal Employment Opportunity Commission (EEOC) with authority to prosecute unfair employment practices/policies.

◆ Rehabilitation Act of 1973 protects handicapped persons from discrimination in federally assisted programs. It is enforced by the Department of Labor's Office of Federal Contract Compliance Programs (FOC).

◆ Vietnam Veterans Readjustment Act of 1974 prohibits discrimination of Vietnam veterans by federal agencies and government contractors. It is also enforced by the FOC.

◆ Pregnancy Discrimination Amendment of 1978 to Title VII prohibits sex discrimination in employment based on pregnancy, child birth or related medical conditions.

◆ Executive Order 1141, 1964, declares a public policy making it a violation of federal policy to discriminate against employees or applicants because of age.

◆ Executive Order 11246, 1965, established the Affirmative Action Plans as a means of implementing the Civil Rights Act of 1964.

◆ Executive Order 12067, 1978, transfers, by way of Reorganization Plan Number 1, all the functions of the Equal Employment Opportunity Commission. It further charges the EEOC with the responsibility of providing leadership and coordination of federal statutes, executive orders, regulations and policies related to equal employment opportunity.

◆ Executive Order 12106, 1978, transfers, by way of Reorganization Plan Number 1, all the functions relating to enforcement of equal employment programs from the Civil Service Commission to the EEOC.

◆ Executive Order 112107, 1978, changes office designations such as Civil Service Commission to the Office of Personnel Management and creates new offices such as the Merit Systems Protection Board under Reorganization Plan Number 2.

◆ Uniform Guidelines on Employee Selection Procedures, 1978, sets forth uniform procedures to be followed by the EEOC, the Civil Service Commission, the Department of Justice and the Department of Labor in the employee selection process, as they relate to discrimination on grounds of race, color, religion, sex or national origin.

◆ Executive Order 12144, 1979, transfers certain equal pay and age discrimination in employment enforcement functions from the Department of Labor to the EEOC.

◆ Affirmative Action Guidelines, 1979, provide interpretative guidance to the EEOC to follow in enforcing Title VII of the Civil Rights Act of 1964.

◆ Older Workers Benefit Protection Act, 1990, amends the Age Discrimination and Employment Act with respect to employee benefit plans.

In addition to these federal regulations, you should identify and comply with any existing local, state, or county regulations pertaining to EEOC.

Source: Reprinted with permission of Richard K. Hrebik.

111 Ways a Nonlawyer Can Help a Firm's Marketing and Client Relations
by Jay G. Foonberg

Effective, tasteful, professional marketing is essential to profitability and the existence of a law firm. This is a list of marketing activities that lawyers would like done but don't have the time to do. I've accumulated this list by teaching law firms how to market at their marketing retreats and offices. Most lawyers would rather practice law than devote nonbillable time to marketing or client relations activities. An obvious way to reconcile the client relations and marketing needs of a firm with the desire of the lawyers to practice law is to use a nonlawyer marketing person to do the "Busy Work" which effective, tasteful, professional, good marketing requires.

The most important and compelling reason to use a nonlawyer to do the firm marketing and client relations work is that the work will never get done if left to the practicing lawyers. There are other distinct advantages to using a nonlawyer marketing or client relations person to help a firm's marketing efforts. A lawyer can bill enough in three or four hours to pay the nonlawyer's salary for a week. The lawyer will be happier and more effective doing what he or she went to school to learn to do and was hired to do. The nonlawyer will be happier and more effective doing what he or she was hired to do and will be happy doing it.

This list can be used as a menu. The lawyers, through the Marketing Partner or the Marketing Committee or through the General Administration of the firm can select the priority of the tasks. The nonlawyer marketing person can then begin doing the work. The lawyers should do that marketing activity which the lawyer can do best (calling the client, meeting and entertaining the client, keeping the client informed of the progress on the case, bringing marketing data to the nonlawyer, etc. to name just a few). The nonlawyer can do the rest of the work.

There is no order of priority in this list. The priority of what should be done first depends on the types of clients and cases the firm wants.

This list is not a complete menu for marketing or client relations because it omits most of what the lawyers have to do as their contribution to the firm's activities. Additionally, the list only tells a marketing person what to do, it does not tell the person how to do it (my book, *How to Get and Keep Good Clients,* is of great help in telling you how to do it).

As the title of the list indicates, a nonlawyer can help the firm, but only a lawyer should be in charge of making policy decisions. Unless a person has been trained as a lawyer and has practiced law recently, he or she is not likely to be as current as practicing lawyers on the true problems and opportunities which the practicing lawyers face on a daily basis. The nonlawyer may be more up-to-date on the mechanics of getting the job done, once the lawyer has decided on the job to be done. It takes law practice experience and legal training to anticipate the ethical problems and professional problems which will arise due to erroneous short-term marketing decisions. Erroneous decisions may bring in a particular client or case which may be harmful to the firm's long-range professional standing and goals. If the firm is destroyed, the nonlawyer simply looks for a new job; the lawyer may have to look for a new career.

I would have preferred to title this article, 101 Things a Nonlawyer Can Do . . . since 101 is a catchy number and a better marketing device, but in marketing this article, as in marketing legal services, one should only promise what one can deliver.

Please feel free to reproduce the list, but please give me copyright credit when you do so.

1. Calendar, purchase and send appropriate greeting and birthday cards and put the data into the tickler system.

2. Do all the leg work in arranging all of the details of a seminar.

3. Maintain all firm and individual client and referral lists. Maintain the data in the data bank.

4. Periodically meet with the attorneys in the firm to interview them to get the data about them

and the clients needed for the firm's data banks (similar to debriefing sessions in the military).

5. Rewrite and distribute legal research memos into articles for publication in newspapers, trade journals, etc. (or work with outside public relations firm to do this).

6. Help set realistic goals for the firm's marketing effort, for example, to penetrate a particular company or industry, or to increase business by cross selling, or to get a certain number of new clients, or to increase total business by a certain percentage or to penetrate or expand a particular area of law or practice group.

7. Prepare press releases and send them where and when appropriate. Enlist the help of a public relations firm if necessary.

8. Monitor news items concerning existing and target clients in order to be able to disseminate the information in the firm and to send congratulatory cards and notes where appropriate. Get a public relations or professional clipping service to help if needed.

9. Periodically update firm brochures and handouts to reflect the kind of clients the firm has and/or is seeking.

10. Develop departmental brochures and individual attorney fact sheets to be used by departments and individual attorneys as supplements to the firm brochure where appropriate.

11. Arrange for outside lecturers and for consultants where appropriate to come to the firm to help in sales training, printing, public relations, etc., unless the marketing person is trained and skilled in these areas.

12. Track and monitor referrals in and referrals out to see if the firm and the clients are benefiting from the referrals.

13. Track new business sources from client intake forms.

14. Track new business sources by interviewing firm lawyers and nonlawyers.

15. Prepare biannual marketing training featuring outside instructors and in-house lecturers.

16. Survey present and former clients (if trained in how to do it) in order to develop new business and to learn client perceived strengths and weaknesses.

17. Assist in preparing bids or proposals requested by potential clients.

18. Do cold calls via telemarketing if the firm is willing to do this type of marketing.

19. Arrange for and supervise use of single and season tickets for entertainment of firm clients. Be sure that all tickets intended for client promotion get used for client promotion. Include athletic, cultural, charitable and political events, etc. Work with ticket brokers to get needed tickets as required for various events where the firm wants to be seen in public with a client or to send to a client.

20. Work with attorneys to be sure their current individual biographies and Martindale-Hubbell list and other directory listings reflect what the firm currently wants to emphasize. Do this on a periodic basis.

21. Work with a printer or public relations consultant to design firm or department logos or logotype signatures.

22. Work with the public relations firm to decide in which white pages and in which yellow pages the firm wants to be listed and under which specialties or areas of practice the firm or individual lawyers and the firm name are to be listed. Also decide the nature and extent of yellow page listings and whether to emphasize by red ink or yellow highlighting the white page listings.

23. Hound attorneys for materials for client newsletters and client alerts and be sure that present, past and potential clients and targeted clients and referrers of clients get the newsletters and alerts.

24. Help set and administer the firm budget for advertising and listings in charity programs, etc.

25. Get appropriate media coverage for the activities of individual attorneys and the firm in appropriate public service or community activities. Get assistance from a public relations firm if necessary.

26. Develop media contacts through an outside public relations firm to get members of the firm into the media as "experts." Get quoted by the media on new developments and decisions in the areas of law in which the firm wants to be recognized as experts.

27. Ascertain which attorneys and nonattorneys are obstacles in the firm's marketing efforts and educate them as to the importance of the firm's marketing efforts. Let them know that their careers and the careers of all the firm lawyers and staff are at stake.

28. Take appropriate steps to be sure that all client data and marketing data and firm data are safeguarded from unauthorized disclosure or dissemination. Mark computer data and lists to secure commercial protection. This should be done as directed by a knowledgeable lawyer.

29. Assist each lawyer in the firm in developing and executing a personal marketing plan to coordinate each attorney's interest and abilities with the needs of the firm as decided by the firm.

30. Assist each department or practice group in preparing and executing its annual medium-term (3 year) and long-term (5 year) marketing plan in accordance with the anticipated needs and plans of the firm and its clients.

31. Monitor the performance of each individual attorney and practice groups vis à vis their performance of their marketing plans. Report performance or nonperformance to the responsible marketing attorney partner.

32. Locate and prepare a directory of ghostwriters to assist attorneys in getting special articles ghost written where necessary for publication as firm articles. Get a public relations firm's help if necessary.

33. Act as the central clearinghouse for inquiries from prospective clients. Direct inquirers to the lawyer or practice group or department or rainmaker attorney most likely to make a favorable impression on the inquirer.

34. Act as a central clearinghouse for in-house cross-marketing opportunities for the firm.

35. Work with accounting department to conform invoices or billing procedures to meet the specific needs of specific clients.

36. Follow up on marketing leads when applied by lawyers and others.

37. Work with internal or external information specialists (librarians) to access electronic and hard copy data bases and directories to get the most complete publicly available information about prospective and current target clients.

38. Work with specialists to design, perform, analyze and follow up on information obtained from client surveys.

39. Work with word processing or information services department to set up and maintain desk top publishing formats and mailing lists for client alerts, newsletters, internal communications and other communications.

40. Circulate the names of the attorneys, the nonattorneys and the referrers of clients who are instrumental in bringing in new clients or increased business from existing clients (everyone likes to see their name in print).

41. Share marketing information obtained with conflicts department to head off the firm devoting large resources to seek clients the firm can't represent and to provide the conflicts database with more up-to-date information.

42. Plan and coordinate to get maximum media coverage for firm special events that have public relations or media value.

43. Maintain a communications or publications data base to direct the distribution of firm publications and communications. Send appropriate information to special clients and targets. Augment the firm's database with new information. Work with a public relations firm if necessary.

44. Secure permission from present and former clients to use their names in client lists and references.

45. Write the firm's history while there are still people around who know it.

46. Coordinate or hire inside or outside copywriters to rewrite firm research memoranda into various levels of understanding for publication in various publications.

47. Handle client complaints if you are trained how to do it. Alternatively, work with a person who is trained to handle complaints or perceived problems with clients.

48. Work with practice groups or departments or individual lawyers to help maintain on a consistent basis good attorney/client relations by spotting and correcting problems or deficiencies at an early stage.

49. Conduct internal audits of the firm's marketing practices and client relations to spot problems early on.

50. Get involved immediately in all follow-ups on potential new business to provide assistance to the lawyers having contact with the prospect. Do not allow lawyers to "drop the ball."

51. Contact clients by survey or directly to ask if they are happy with the firm's billing format, or if they have special requirements.

52. Work with attorneys to promote and maintain new outward-bound referral firms and institutions for cases and clients that the firm does not want to handle or cannot handle due to conflict.

53. Work with firm attorneys to develop other lawyers, firms and institutions as inward-bound sources of clients, either by offering referrals back or by offering referral fees where appropriate and if in accordance with firm policies or by offering perks and benefits.

54. Survey attorneys and marketing publications to determine the existence of various marketing networks and affiliations to determine if the network can supply the types of work the firm wants.

55. Provide accurate information to the Committee that allocates client origination credits or percentages . . . between attorneys for new business.

56. Work with hiring committee or recruiting committee to identify lawyers who have special qualifications or backgrounds that will fit into the firm's long or medium range marketing plan.

57. Monitor and train telephone receptionists and . . . those having telephone contact with callers to be sure that clients and prospective clients are not alienated by the phone handling.

58. Train lawyers how to make formal presentations to prospective clients.

59. Coordinate with outside experts in training lawyers how to tastefully and professionally market the firm, their department and themselves.

60. Prepare audiovisual aids for dog and pony presentations to prospective clients.

61. Coordinate desktop publishing, client data base, press releases and attorneys to be able to get out a client communication within hours of an important case, new law or important event to attempt to be the first firm to inform the client. (Consider sending a one-paragraph fax the same day informing the client that there has been a major development and then the client will shortly get more information.)

62. Assist attorneys in handling media requests, or deal with media for the attorney after getting information from the attorney.

63. Convince attorneys that the negligible time they spend in helping with marketing will offset the limited amount of billable time they might lose and that most good marketing does not require any lost billable time.

64. Monitor clients to ensure that the firm does not overcommunicate, by seminars or client visits from different practice groups, to the point where the client is annoyed or feels that the firm is pressing too hard.

65. Be sure that individual and practice group marketing plans are not overkilling in one area, while ignoring or giving insufficient attention in another area.

66. Work with a public relations firm to hire celebrities, actors, politicians, etc., to attend client seminars and social events.

67. Work with a public relations firm to keep clients' names and cases in or out of the media to protect their legal interests, or their cases in progress.

68. Determine which local events the firm might wish to sponsor (if any) to get community recognition (10Ks, walkathons, local teams, local cultural events, local educational television, local educational events, etc.).

69. Prepare periodic reports showing where marketing programs and efforts are working and where they are not succeeding.

70. Maintain and supervise the marketing master calendar to be sure that all events and promotions underway are proceeding as scheduled.

71. Contact clients directly or through lawyers to determine which new or repeat subjects clients want or need as seminar topics.

72. Determine directly from clients or through attorneys whether clients want seminars at their location or at the firm location or other location and when the best day and time would be for maximum attendance of appropriate personnel.

73. Keep records of attendees for post-seminar follow-ups and for invitations to future seminars. Use attendance lists to work with various continuing education accreditation entities to get appropriate credits for attendees at firm seminars. (Referring attorneys, CPAs, financial planners, police officers, physicians, social workers, lawyers, etc.)

74. Determine which occupational groups not currently being served require continuing education credits and whether there is any marketing value in doing seminars with or for these groups.

75. Get and tabulate evaluations on a continuing, long-term basis from seminar attendees to ascertain which subjects and speakers and locations are most effective in getting new clients and in getting more business from existing clients.

76. Follow up on all marketing leads from all sources and report back to the sources so that people in the firm can see that their marketing intelligence is being acted on and is not being ignored.

77. Coordinate with billing and data processing departments to get reports on clients and or referrers or other sources where there has been no face-to-face contact for specific time periods. If necessary call or have a lawyer call these noncontacted people just to ask if there is anything the person would like from the firm. The best person to make the call would be one of the firm's lawyers, but it is better for the

marketing administrator to call them than for no one to call.

78. Interview associates, partners and support staff on a regular basis to seek new information from them or to get their input on new projects that could be instituted or implemented or new marketing possibilities.

79. Work with the accounting department to develop a list of all organizational membership dues and fees paid over the last five years to determine which groups have been a worthwhile source of clients and new business and which groups have not. Use the information developed to work with attorneys to determine which types of organizational activities to emphasize and which to eliminate or strengthen. Some groups will probably be worthy of firm support even if there is nothing in it for the firm, but this should be a matter of conscious informed decision and not by accident. In other words, separate marketing expense and purely charitable donations.

80. Work with the firm's attorneys to determine which nonlawyer support staff should have firm cards or names on stationery and which should not. (For example, after six months or after one year or for secretaries or messengers, etc.)

81. Work with attorneys and personnel department and individuals involved to determine what titles to give people on their cards to best encourage their making appropriate usage of the card. For example: Librarian or Information Specialist or Electronic Data Base Specialist, File Clerk or Archivist, Secretary or Legal Secretary or Legal Assistant or Assistant to Attorney Jones, Legal Assistant or Paralegal, Key Puncher or Electronic Data Processing Specialist, Word Processor or Document Production Specialist, Personnel Clerk or Human Resources Specialist. What you call people and what they call themselves can affect their pride in their job and their firm and whether they will try to help the firm's marketing efforts.

82. Work with firm's personnel department to be sure that firm lawyers and nonlawyers have adequate supplies of the cards they are supposed to have.

83. Initiate the firm's first conscious marketing activities.

84. Be involved in the client complaint process if you have been trained how to handle complaints. Either take charge and be the input point for client complaints or work closely with a person who is trained on how to handle complaints and monitor client complaints to correct developing problems. Train attorneys and receptionist how to channel angry people. Gather information on perceived or actual problems and follow up on eliminating the problems where appropriate.

85. Do a dog and pony show for potential clients coming into the office. Have a 20 minute set routine developed to show off the technology and facilities of the firm so that a nonlawyer can, where appropriate, take the client or potential client around. Prioritize on a time needed basis which firm assets to emphasize first (art work, computers, conference rooms, form files, etc.).

86. Order appropriate items with firm logo or name to put out for conferences where nonfirm members will be present. Common items are yellow pads, pens, pencils, matches (unless the firm has a strong no smoking position), candy jars, etc.

87. When a potential client comes to the office, be sure that there are trade publications for that person from that particular client's industry in the reception room, the conference rooms that will be used and in the offices of the attorneys who will be meeting with the clients. If there are articles about that particular client in the periodical, the article should be drawn to the attention of all people participating in the meetings. Trade association publications are among the best type of periodicals. It may be necessary to consult with the attorneys hosting the meeting or conference in advance to be sure that the appropriate publications are available for each meeting. It may be necessary to change the publications two or three times per day so that each visitor gets the appropriate publications displayed and available.

88. Before an open house or a reception, or seminar, spread around copies of the industry publications of the people who will be there so they will feel that you have an interest or an expertise in their industry. Place article in periodicals to coincide with your open house or dog and pony presentations to potential clients to show them your current interest or expertise in the area(s) of interest to them.

89. Alert the receptionist as to who is expected that day. One way is to check the reservations for the conference rooms for conferences and depositions and check with the attorney who reserved them for the expected people. When the person(s) arrive, have the receptionist say,

"Welcome, Mr. Smith. We've been expecting you. I'll notify Ms. Jones that you're here. I've been asked to give you this issue of the Widget Makers Association Journal in case you wanted to look at it while you're waiting." This will impress the client or potential client that you are well organized as well as having an interest in that area of law or industry. If there are other people in the reception area within hearing range do not mention aloud the name of the welcomed person, as their presence may be a matter of confidentiality in the particular matter. There's no harm in doing this (following the same welcoming procedure) for the client of the other lawyer. It may give the other lawyer's client a good impression of your firm, so that you'll be considered when the other lawyer's client needs to use or recommend a different law firm (for a conflicts situation in the appropriate circumstances, for example). Even if there is no new business in it for the firm, the other lawyer's client may gain a respect for the organization of the firm which could inure to the benefit of your client in the matter.

90. Have the receptionist notify you of all conferences or visitors expected (as a back-up to attorneys notifying you) so you'll be prepared for the visit.

91. Assume or accept responsibility for periodically walking through the reception room, conference rooms and other public areas to be sure that they are neat, clean and convey the image the firm wants conveyed. It may be appropriate for you to correct problems through the general administration of the firm rather than interpose yourself between other personnel and their own chain of command.

92. Survey clients who have been referred out in order to remind them that you still consider them to be your clients and in order to be sure that the clients are happy with the firms you are using.

93. Survey clients who have been referred to you in order to show the results of the survey to the people who refer work to you.

94. Arrange in advance for Continuing Professional Education credits for those who can receive them for attending firm seminars. It may be necessary to submit program materials or keep attendance records or submit attendance records for the program.

95. Identify other law firms or accounting firms or institutions for cosponsoring seminars in order to extend client lists and to reduce costs of seminars.

96. Learn the Continuing Professional Education requirements for each group which you want to attract to your seminars.

97. Maintain an adequate supply of appropriate form letters or cards to send on special occasions such as birthdays, religious holidays, births, deaths, illness, etc.

98. Learn and accumulate the death and funeral customs of various religions so that the firm or the individual lawyer will do the appropriate thing when the death of a client or client's family member occurs. Determine whether flowers, candy, cards, donations, etc., are appropriate.

99. Be sure that every job applicant, including those who will not get hired, receives a certain amount of information and materials about the firm and its specialty areas. Those not hired often go to work at other firms and can refer that firm's business to your firm or simply do their own referring to the firm. Applicants who don't get hired can be considered similar to clients whose matters are not accepted. They are still potentially a source of future business.

100. Work with the personnel department to keep track of firm "alumni" who have left the firm under friendly circumstances. Keep them on mailing lists for possible referrals when their current companies might need your firm.

101. Locate and work with list brokers to provide specialized lists for mailings or for other purposes.

102. Work with the data processing department to calendar ahead for known time-triggered client legal needs. Typical examples of work generated from closed files include lease renewals, will reviews, judgment renewals, trusts terminating, etc.

103. Publicize attorney's activities in service, professional and charitable causes. Many clients and potential clients will be in accord with the goals of the organizations supported by the attorney and some will express it by becoming closer to the attorney or the firm. This type of press coverage is usually obtainable in the local press where the information can be accumulated and used as filler. It is incumbent on the attorneys to keep the marketing people advised on what they're doing.

104. "Debrief" attorneys after they attend a bar meeting to get names and addresses of other lawyers they met in order to put the other lawyers' names into the database to receive selected mailings.

105. Work with the budget committee to get a budget for each individual attorney to do marketing (expense reimbursement) and for departments and rainmakers (memberships, season subscriptions, major contributions, etc.).

106. Determine if there are any local radio programs or cable TV programs which have an audience that the firm wants to reach and determine what kind of program(s) the firm might want to sponsor.

107. Determine if the firm can fund small annual prizes to graduates or local high schools, universities or law schools to get recognition and long-range name familiarity with academic committees.

108. Put together CLE retreats for lawyers from law firms which refer your clients.

109. Ride circuit to branch offices or get reports from branch offices to determine what marketing opportunities are available for development and to determine what help they want or need.

110. Periodically analyze existing directories in which the firm could list itself to determine which, if any, the firm should choose.

111. Obtain copies of the Codes of Professional Responsibility or Ethics governing your attorneys and ask an attorney to explain it to you so you can recognize problems. Obtain a copy for every attorney in the firm.

Source: Reprinted with permission from *Law Office Economics and Management* (33, no. 1, published by Clark Boardman Callaghan, 155 Pfingsten Road, Deerfield, Illinois 60015, [800] 323-1336) and Jay G. Foonberg, Esq., author of *How to Start and Build a Law Practice* (Chicago: American Bar Association) and *How to Get and Keep Good Clients* (Boston: Lawyers Weekly Publications).

Time Management for Paralegals by Deanna Jean Brown

Time and time again, there's no time to spare.

The paralegal's challenge in effectively managing time is to do many tasks in one day, and give them your immediate attention under intense time pressures while dealing with people and situations out of your control.

Or, is the challenge to prioritize tasks and deadlines, to manage all the crises that occur simultaneously and still churn out those billable hours?

How can you manage time when your time is not your own, when other people haven't done their homework, the computer is down, the courthouse didn't deliver, the client forgot to, well, what was that again? How do you know which of the squeaky wheels really needs the grease and which wheel is stuck and not making a sound but will be the first to fall apart?

What a challenge! All over the country paralegals rise to the occasion, master the situation and thrive. How do they manage? How is it done?

One key is to recognize that the one law in every jurisdiction is Murphy's Law. Learning to work your way around it and minimize its effects gives you venue in Murphy's court of appeals. Careful planning and clarity of purpose combined with a sense of humor might even get Murphy to settle out of court.

Time traps can be avoided by learning to recognize them. One of the biggest time traps is dealing with people—attorneys, clients, staff—who don't know what they are doing and understand even less about your role in the process. Quite often, it's simply a missed line of communication.

For example, you are the one who fills out the forms. When your attorney fills one out it's the wrong form, or an obsolete form that was in the desk and hasn't been tossed when the revised ones were issued. A clear constant line of communication helps minimize misunderstandings.

People in crises, meetings, interruptions, phone calls and deadlines that crop up at the last minute are other time traps.

Meetings

It goes without saying that meetings are very time consuming. The next best thing to eliminating meetings altogether is to take charge and run them yourself. Armed with an agenda, you can plow through items quickly and efficiently. The attorneys may scratch their heads or stare at the ceiling, but you are finished in half the time.

In any case, make sure there is an agenda, even if you have to provide it yourself. This structures the meeting and provides leverage when you prompt people to stay focused.

Meetings held to develop trial strategy are, by their very nature, time consuming. There's no way out, nor should there be. Simply avoid side issues and stick to the matter at hand.

The routine weekly meeting is counterproductive. These kinds of items can be covered in a memo. There's no reason to sit around and discuss what was discussed before. That's a waste of billable time.

The goal of every meeting should be to make life easier. When you must attend repetitive meetings, use the time to make lists, outline a report or organize schedules. People will think you're taking notes.

How do you notify the person running the meeting and running on at the mouth that the meeting is over? Stand up. Say, "Great, you've given me what I need to know. You've covered everything on the agenda. Now I know exactly what to do. Thanks."

During this little speech, others will have started getting their things together too. They may even push their chairs back from the table.

You do run the risk of being told to sit down because the speaker isn't finished. If this is the case, simply cover yourself by saying, "Sorry, but things were explained so well that I was ready to get back to work at once."

Managing Deadlines

Managing deadlines is so much easier when you have your own tickler file. Use it as your personal docket control system. It will help you make first things FIRST. A tickler file will also clarify priorities and organize time, tasks, people and support systems.

Know how to cut corners when facing a deadline crunch. Make sure you specify in advance which corners may need to be cut and agree upon them with your attorney or the key people on the project.

Be specific about which things you do, which things you don't do right now and which you don't do at all. Insist on being taken seriously.

Make your time count. Develop techniques for getting to the right person or finding another contact who can help you. When the crunch comes, you've given yourself an edge.

Using false deadlines is another way of giving yourself a cushion. This is particularly effective with clients.

Discipline yourself to keep in touch with everything that is happening. Constantly update every piece of information in your calendar, tickler file, or database.

Discipline puts you in a position to make all the pieces fit together, even when bombarded by forces out of your control. Knowing every detail keeps deadlines within your jurisdiction.

Interruptions

Interruptions do more than take up your time. They break the rhythm of your work, intrude on your train of thought and limit productivity. Managing interruptions is simply a matter of shifting gears. Being clear about your priorities helps arm you against interruption fallout.

When people drop by, be polite, answer their questions, acknowledge what they have to say and return to your work.

If it is the lead attorney with co-counsel, then it really isn't an interruption, no matter what you were working on when they stop by.

Saying, "No," "Not now," or "Later," allows you to minimize the time that interruptions take and reduce the opportunities you give others to use up your precious time.

Most paralegals are interrupted by phone calls. The easiest way to avoid this type of interruption is to simply not answer the phone. After all, it's not God calling. Of course, it might be a partner, which is almost the same thing.

When policies dictate that you answer your own phone, learn to handle each call quickly. When you are bombarded with callers who demand immediate attention, tell them you will get back with them after you have pulled their file and can address the issue more fully. Set a time for the return call so you can fit it into your schedule.

Phone tag is not a problem when people leave complete messages when they call. If it's a request for information, pull the information, have someone else give it to them, or call and leave a message with their office. Setting a time for calling people back keeps you in control.

Taking all your calls is a very service-related approach which may be critical to good staff and client relations. Which approach is best for you? The one consistent with office policy and the one that gives you the results you need to do a good job.

Developing Lists

Lists, lists, lists. Lists are at the heart of an effective time management strategy. Your list keeps you focused and frees your mind for other things. It also gives you a measure for accomplishment. Cross off items on a "to do" list with brightly colored markers for a cheery morale booster.

If you don't have time to make your list, you won't have time to get things done.

Gather your thoughts 15 minutes before the end of the day and make your "to do" list for tomorrow. This gives you a jump on the next day's work even before you leave the office. You could also make your "to do" list the first thing in the morning when you are fresh and clear.

You may even be fortunate enough to have your secretary present you with a list of priorities when you walk into the office. Then you can dive in.

Besides realizing your priorities, know the amount of time involved in completing work. This helps you decide which strategies work and which ones won't.

Good record keeping helps you stay on target, provides information at your fingertips and builds a strong foundation for your next project. It keeps your list current and relevant.

Learning to say "No" enables you to stick to your list and stay focused. You won't take on more work than you can handle and you won't be faced with your mission unaccomplished.

Never cut quality for quantity. It weakens your effectiveness and encourages careless work. If you can't do it right, don't start it in the first place. Knowing when you can deliver and when you can't will give you a reputation for reliability and credibility. It will keep you from going into overload. Remember, asking for a continuance is an attorney's prerogative, not yours.

Stamina

Stamina, both mental and physical, is vital in dealing with the stress of time pressures.

Stamina gives you the ability to make quick decisions when needed and the wit to know when an immediate decision isn't necessary. It gives you the endurance to sit at your desk for endless periods of time and the strength to be constantly on the move at other times.

If you are wading through boxes and boxes of documents, you need the fortitude to stay awake while avoiding the hypnotic effect of watching print march across page after page. In this instance, take short breaks to help you stay awake and alert.

Eating right, staying fit and getting enough sleep all play a role in providing the extra effort needed to pull papers together for the 4 a.m. messenger pick-up.

Most of all, believing your work is important gives you strength to draw from when you need a clear head and surge of energy to be more than your best.

A given in the world of law and justice is that there are times things won't go smoothly. Using effective time management principles will help you do more than simply get things done. Your life will be easier and you will feel a sense of pride in your accomplishments.

Source: "Time Management for Paralegals," by Deanna Jean Brown, published summer 1991 in *Outlook*. Reprinted with permission of the Illinois Paralegal Association.

How to Develop a Client Survey by Suzanne B. O'Neill and Doug Magee

Law firms are increasingly striving to fine-tune the services they offer in order to meet rapid changes in client needs and expectations. In addition, they are devoting attention to improving the quality of service produced and delivered. Firms that do know what their clients believe in terms of the firm's needed improvements and areas of excellence have gained this insight by asking the clients. Armed with this knowledge, firms can better direct client service efforts.

This article discusses the importance of obtaining client information and how best to go about the surveying process.

Eliciting Feedback

To improve its quality of service, the firm must possess valid information. Data must be gathered, not only from within the firm, but also from clients. Clients shape their perceptions of service quality based on their interactions with lawyers and staff. Many lawyers erroneously assume they already know what their clients think, without really asking. However, if a client is dissatisfied or disappointed, he or she will readily express that feeling to an average of eight other people without prompting, during conversations on unrelated topics. In contrast, clients who are pleased only offer their opinion about their lawyers and firms to approximately three others—generally in response to a direct inquiry. The sources of dissatisfaction or satisfactions often stem from factors other than those which lawyers and firms would suppose.

To find out how clients view the quality of service received, a firm has various options, depending on the specific objective. Opinions can be obtained from a certain group of clients, such as the firm's largest-paying clients or from clients within a particular industry, or from a sample of companies and individuals drawn from its entire client base. In deciding whether to undertake any type of client survey, some firm members may express reservations. "If we survey our clients, will they think we are in deep trouble?" The reality is a resounding "No." In fact, clients tend to wonder why they have not been asked before whether they are pleased and how the firm can serve them better.

Five-Step Survey Process

There is a five-step process for developing a survey of attitudes about the quality of service from the firm's client base, as distinguished from a specific group of clients. These steps are discussed in the following subsections and a time-table appears in Exhibit F.1.

Defining Objectives

First, before embarking on any effort to determine client attitudes and level of satisfaction, it is essential to define the objectives to be accomplished through the survey. To formulate objectives, questions to be addressed include:

What do we need to know?

Why do we need the information?

How will the information be used?

Who will use the information?

Who is the primary audience for the results?

When do we need the information?

Step 1—Weeks 1–2, Determine Goals and Objectives

Step 2—Weeks 1–2, Establish Method for Conducting Survey

Step 3—Weeks 3–4, Create the Necessary Research Tools

Step 4—Weeks 5–6, Collect and Analyze Information

Step 5—Weeks 7–8, Apply and Report the Results, Implications and Recommendations

---

EXHIBIT F.1   Time-table for Developing and Completing Client Survey

For example, a firm might decide to survey a sample of clients who have used the firm within the past year, as well as a sample of individuals and companies who have become former clients within the last three years. In setting objectives, a word of caution is in order. Some firms have used a client service survey tool in a thinly veiled attempt simply to find out whether there are immediate opportunities to obtain additional business from responding clients. Questions calculated to elicit such information readily reveal to clients that, contrary to the expressed purpose of the survey, the firm is not really interested in the respondents' opinions of the firm's service or in suggestions for improvement.

Survey Method and Data Analysis

After the goals and objectives for the study have been formulated, the second step is to establish the method that will be used to undertake and complete it. During this step, the firm evaluates the advantages and trade-offs among the various approaches. In making evaluations and selections the following matters should be considered.

How much time do we have?

What type of data do we want—qualitative, quantitative or both?

Who will collect the information?

If quantitative data are desired, the following must be considered:

1. sample size needed to accomplish the objectives;
2. how the information will be collected (such as by telephone interview, mail or in person);
3. how the sample respondents will be selected; and
4. the degree of accuracy needed (acceptable margin of error)

For example, there are trade-offs to evaluate when deciding whether to collect data by telephone interviews or by a mailed questionnaire. A telephone survey allows a high degree of administrative control, that is, question order and participation rate can be controlled, as well as the desired number of interviews to be completed. A telephone survey also allows the interviewer to elicit complete responses by asking sub-questions. A mailed questionnaire is less expensive, but can result in a lower percentage of responses. In addition, biased information can result from a mailed questionnaire if, for example, certain types of clients respond in greater number than others.

Creating the Research Instrument

After working through step two, the firm will have gained an understanding of how the survey process will proceed. The next step is to create the necessary research instrument using the following tasks:

1. Select the sample size of clients to be interviewed.
2. Draft questions and develop the format for the questionnaire (telephone interview, mailed questionnaire or in-person interview).
3. Conduct a pilot test of the questionnaire to determine whether the questions are clear, readily understandable and of the desired length. For example, if the time it takes to administer the telephone questionnaire exceeds the desired length of interview time, the instrument can be modified.
4. Brief the interviewers who will collect the information on how to use the questionnaire. (This assumes trained professional interviewers are being used.) As stated earlier, interviewers will need to ask clarifying questions from time to time to obtain complete data.
5. Establish specific quality control procedures to ensure that the interview process will be carried out accurately and completed on time. For example, if a mailed questionnaire is used, a follow-up notification/reminder system must be formulated to maximize the percentage of timely responses.

The sources of client dissatisfaction or satisfaction often stem from factors other than those which lawyers and firms would suppose.

Collecting and Analyzing Data

The fourth step consists of collecting the data from the respondents and then analyzing the findings. If quantitative data will be collected, market research expertise is particularly important to identify significance within the data scientifically. To process quantitative data, the following tasks are required: (1) verification of the data to ensure its accuracy; (2) coding and categorization of all verbatim responses (that is, responses to open ended questions); (3) organization and computerization of the data, which must be reviewed for inconsistencies; and (4) analysis of the data using either a review of frequencies and percentages or appropriate statistical techniques.

Data should not simply be analyzed question by question. Cross tabulation analyses (comparisons between questions) also can yield a wealth of additional findings. For example, if the cross-tabulation analysis indicates that certain client segments have responded to a group of questions similarly, these findings may suggest specific implications about this client subgroup.

When surveying the client base, it is generally important to use an outside specialist to collect the data and perform the analysis to ensure objectivity and a uniformly applied analysis. In addition, an outside source can ensure confidentiality of responses and therefore, help obtain candid opinions and suggestions for improvement. If a mailed questionnaire was used, the respondents would send the completed questionnaire directly to that outside source. If a telephone questionnaire interview was used, the interviews would be performed by the outside source. That third party would not disclose to the firm the identity of the clients from whom specific responses had been obtained.

Interpretation and Application

The fifth and final step toward developing a client survey is interpreting the data and applying it to the objectives that were formulated in step one. A good report is generally a mix of scientific and journalistic skills, carefully structured and precisely written. A report usually follows this progression:

1. Introduction that reviews the research goals and methodology used;

2. Analysis of the data that is organized to lead the reader from one set of ideas to the next, typically from the general to the specific;

3. Implications of the data from the frame of reference of those who will be reading and using it; and

4. Recommendations that describe how to proceed in acting on the data, whether a definitive action, program or additional research.

Conclusion

It is strongly recommended that the client study be coupled with a similar internal survey designed to determine how the lawyers and staff view the quality of service performed, according to the same criteria in the client survey. The analysis from comparing internal and external responses will identify and help focus the similarities and discrepancies between perceptions held within the firm and those held by the clients.

A client survey allows a law firm to obtain objective evaluations of its strengths and weaknesses in delivering service to clients. With the findings in hand, a law firm can identify and prioritize specific improvements to make and, with follow-up surveys, can measure the effectiveness of changes over time.

Source: Reprinted with permission from the *Colorado Lawyer* (1993), which is the official publication of the Colorado Bar Association. All rights reserved.

Definitions and Code of Ethics of National Paralegal Associations

National Association of Legal Assistants

Preamble

A legal assistant must adhere strictly to the accepted standards of legal ethics and to the general principles of proper conduct. The performance of the duties of the legal assistant shall be governed by specific canons as defined herein so that justice will be served and goals of the profession attained (See NALA Model Standards and guidelines for Utilization of Legal Assistants, Section II).

The canons of ethics set forth hereafter are adopted by the National Association of Legal Assistants, Inc., as a general guide intended to aid legal assistants and attorneys. The enumeration of these rules does not mean there are not others of equal importance although not specifically mentioned. Court rules, agency rules and statutes must be taken into consideration when interpreting the canons.

Definition

The National Association of Legal Assistants adopted the following definition in 1984:

Legal assistants, also known as paralegals, are a distinguishable group of persons who assist attorneys in the delivery of legal services. Through formal education, training, and experience, legal assistants have knowledge and expertise regarding the legal system and substantive and procedural law which qualify them to do work of a legal nature under the supervision of an attorney.

Code of Ethics

Canon I

A legal assistant must not perform any of the duties that attorneys only may perform nor take any actions that attorneys may not take.

Canon II

A legal assistant may perform any task which is properly delegated and supervised by an attorney, as long as the attorney is ultimately responsible to the client, maintains a direct relationship with the client, and assumes professional responsibility for the work product.

Canon III

A legal assistant must not:

a) engage in, encourage, or contribute to any act which could constitute the unauthorized practice of law;

b) establish attorney-client relationships, set fees, give legal opinions or advice or represent a client before a court or agency unless so authorized by that court or agency; and

c) engage in conduct or take any action which would assist or involve the attorney in a violation of professional ethics or give the appearance of professional impropriety.

Canon IV

A legal assistant must use discretion and professional judgment commensurate with knowledge and experience but must not render independent legal judgment in place of an attorney. The services of an attorney are essential in the public interest whenever such legal judgment is required.

Canon V

A legal assistant must disclose his or her status as a legal assistant at the outset of any professional relationship with a client, attorney, a court or administrative agency or personnel thereof, or a member of the general public. A legal assistant must act prudently in determining the extent to which a client may be assisted without the presence of an attorney.

Canon VI

A legal assistant must strive to maintain integrity and a high degree of competency through education and training with respect to professional responsibility, local rules and practice, and through continuing education in substantive areas of law to better assist the legal profession in fulfilling its duty to provide legal service.

Canon VII

A legal assistant must protect the confidences of a client and must not violate any rule or statute now in effect or hereafter enacted controlling the doctrine of privileged communications between a client and an attorney.

Canon VIII

A legal assistant must do all other things incidental, necessary, or expedient for the attainment of the ethics and responsibilities as defined by statute or rule of court.

Canon IX

A legal assistant's conduct is guided by bar associations' code of professional responsibility and rules of professional conduct.

Standards and Guidelines

The Guidelines represent a statement of how the legal assistant may function. The Guidelines are not intended to be a comprehensive or exhaustive list of the proper duties of a legal assistant. Rather, they are designed as guides to what may or may not be proper conduct for the legal assistant. In formulating the Guidelines, the reasoning and rules of law in many reported decisions of disciplinary cases and unauthorized practice of law cases have been analyzed and considered. In addition, the provisions of the American Bar Association's Model Rules of Professional Conduct, as well as the ethical promulgation of various state courts and bar associations, have been considered in the development of the Guidelines.

These Guidelines form a sound basis for the legal assistant and the supervising attorney to follow. This Model will serve as a comprehensive resource document and as a definitive, well-reasoned guide to those considering voluntary standards and guidelines for legal assistants.

1. Preamble

Proper utilization of the services of legal assistants contributes to the delivery of cost-effective, high-quality legal services. Legal assistants and the legal profession should be assured that measures exist for identifying legal assistants and their role in assisting attorneys in the delivery of legal services. Therefore, the National Association of Legal Assistants, Inc., hereby adopts these Standards and Guidelines as an educational document for the benefit of legal assistants and the legal profession.

Comment

The three most frequently raised questions concerning legal assistants are (1) How do you define a legal assistant; (2) Who is qualified to be identified as a legal assistant; and (3) What duties may a legal assistant perform? The definition adopted in 1984 by the National Association of Legal Assistants answers the first question. The Model sets forth minimum education, training and experience through standards which will assure that an individual utilizing the title "legal assistant" has the qualifications to be held out to the legal community and the public in that capacity. The Guidelines identify those acts which the reported cases hold to be proscribed and give examples of services which the legal assistant may perform under the supervision of a licensed attorney.

These Guidelines constitute a statement relating to services performed by legal assistants, as defined herein, as approved by court decisions and other sources of authority. The purpose of the Guidelines is not to place limitations or restrictions on the legal assistant profession. Rather, the Guidelines are intended to outline for the legal profession an acceptable course of conduct. Voluntary recognition and utilization of the Standards and Guidelines will benefit the entire legal profession and the public it serves.

2. Definition

The National Association of Legal Assistants adopted the following definition in 1984:

Legal assistants, also known as paralegals, are a distinguishable group of persons who assist attorneys in the delivery of legal services. Through formal education, training, and experience, legal assistants have knowledge and expertise regarding the legal system and substantive and procedural law which qualify them to do work of a legal nature under the supervision of an attorney.

Comment

This definition emphasizes the knowledge and expertise of legal assistants in substantive and procedural law obtained through education and work experience. It further defines the legal assistant or paralegal as a professional working under the supervision of an attorney as distinguished from a non-lawyer who delivers services directly to the public without any intervention or review of work product by an attorney. Statutes, court rules, case law and bar associations are additional sources for legal assistant or paralegal definitions. In applying the Standards and Guidelines, it is important to remember that they were developed to apply to the legal assistant as defined herein.

Lawyers should refrain from labeling those who do not meet the criteria set forth in this definition, such as secretaries and other administrative staff, as legal assistants.

For billing purposes, the services of a legal secretary are considered part of overhead costs and are not recoverable in fee awards. However, the courts have held that fees for paralegal services are recoverable as long as they are not clerical functions, such as organizing files, copying documents, checking docket, updating files, checking court dates and delivering papers. As established in *Missouri v. Jenkins,* 491 U.S. 274, 109 S.Ct. 2463, 2471, n.10 (1989), tasks performed by legal assistants must be substantive in nature which, absent the legal assistant, the attorney would perform.

There are also case law and Supreme Court Rules addressing the issue of a disbarred attorney serving in the capacity of a legal assistant.

3. Standards

A legal assistant should meet certain minimum qualifications. The following standards may be used to determine an individual's qualifications as a legal assistant:

1. Successful completion of the Certified Legal Assistant ("CLA") certifying examination of the National Association of Legal Assistants, Inc.;

2. Graduation from an ABA approved program of study for legal assistants;

3. Graduation from a course of study for legal assistants which is institutionally accredited but not ABA approved, and which requires not less than the equivalent of 60 semester hours of classroom study;

4. Graduation from a course of study for legal assistants, other than those set forth in (2) and (3) above, plus not less than six months of in-house training as a legal assistant;

5. A baccalaureate degree in any field, plus not less than six months in-house training as a legal assistant;

6. A minimum of three years of law-related experience under the supervision of an attorney, including at least six months of in-house training as a legal assistant; or

7. Two years of in-house training as a legal assistant.

For purposes of these Standards, "in-house training as a legal assistant" means attorney education of the employee concerning legal assistant duties and these Guidelines. In addition to review and analysis of assignments, the legal assistant should receive a reasonable amount of instruction directly related to the duties and obligations of the legal assistant.

Comment

The Standards set forth suggest minimum qualifications for a legal assistant. These minimum qualifications, as adopted, recognize legal related work backgrounds and formal education backgrounds, both of which provide the legal assistant with a broad base in exposure to and knowledge of the legal profession. This background is necessary to assure the public and the legal profession that the employee identified as a legal assistant is qualified.

The Certified Legal Assistant ("CLA") examination established by NALA in 1976 is a voluntary nationwide certification program for legal assistants. The CLA designation is a statement to the legal profession and the public that the legal assistant has met the high levels of knowledge and professionalism required by NALA's certification program. Continuing education requirements, which all certified legal assistants must meet, assure that high standards are maintained. The CLA designation has been recognized as a means of establishing the qualifications of a legal assistant in supreme court rules, state court and bar association standards and utilization guidelines.

Certification through NALA is available to all legal assistants meeting the educational and experience requirements. Certified Legal Assistants may also pursue advanced specialty certification ("CLAS") in the areas of bankruptcy, civil litigation, probate and estate planning, corporate and business law, criminal law and procedure, real estate, intellectual property, and may also pursue state certification based on state laws and procedures in California, Florida, Louisiana and Texas.

4. Guidelines

These Guidelines relating to standards of performance and professional responsibility are intended to aid legal assistants and attorneys. The ultimate responsibility rests with an attorney who employs legal assistants to educate them with respect to the duties they are assigned and to supervise the manner in which such duties are accomplished.

Comment

In general, a legal assistant is allowed to perform any task which is properly delegated and supervised by an attorney, as long as the attorney is ultimately responsible to the client and assumes complete professional responsibility for the work product.

ABA Model Rules of Professional Conduct, Rule 5.3 provides:

With respect to a non-lawyer employed or retained by or associated with a lawyer:

(a) a partner in a law firm shall make reasonable efforts to ensure that the firm has in effect measures giving reasonable assurance that the person's conduct is compatible with the professional obligations of the lawyer;

(b) a lawyer having direct supervisory authority over the non-lawyer shall make reasonable efforts to ensure that the person's conduct is compatible with the professional obligations of the lawyer; and

(c) a lawyer shall be responsible for conduct of such a person that would be a violation of the rules of professional conduct if engaged in by a lawyer if:

(1) the lawyer orders or, with the knowledge of the specific conduct ratifies the conduct involved; or

(2) the lawyer is a partner in the law firm in which the person is employed, or has direct supervisory authority over the person, and knows of the conduct at a time when its consequences can be avoided or mitigated but fails to take remedial action.

There are many interesting and complex issues involving the use of legal assistants. In any discussion of the proper role of a legal assistant, attention must be directed to what constitutes the practice of law. Proper delegation to legal assistants is further complicated and confused by the lack of an adequate definition of the practice of law.

Kentucky became the first state to adopt a Paralegal Code by Supreme Court Rule. This Code sets forth certain exclusions to the unauthorized practice of law:

For purposes of this rule, the unauthorized practice of law shall not include any service rendered involving legal knowledge or advice, whether representation, counsel or advocacy, in or out of court, rendered in respect to the acts, duties, obligations, liabilities or business relations of the one requiring services where:

A. The client understands that the paralegal is not a lawyer;

B. The lawyer supervises the paralegal in the performance of his or her duties; and

C. The lawyer remains fully responsible for such representation including all actions taken or not taken in connection therewith by the paralegal to the same extent as if such representation had been furnished entirely by the lawyer and all such actions had been taken or not taken directly by the attorney. Paralegal Code, Ky. S.Ct. R3.700, Sub-Rule 2.

South Dakota Supreme Court Rule 97-25 Utilization Rule a(4) states:

The attorney remains responsible for the services performed by the legal assistant to the same extent as though such services had been furnished entirely by the attorney and such actions were those of the attorney.

Guideline 1

Legal assistants should:

1. Disclose their status as legal assistants at the outset of any professional relationship with a client, other attorneys, a court or administrative agency or personnel thereof, or members of the general public;

2. Preserve the confidences and secrets of all clients; and

3. Understand the attorney's Rules of Professional Responsibility and these Guidelines in order to avoid any action which would involve the attorney in a violation of the Rules, or give the appearance of professional impropriety.

Comment

Routine early disclosure of the legal assistant's status when dealing with persons outside the attorney's office is necessary to assure that there will be no misunderstanding as to the responsibilities and role of the legal assistant. Disclosure may be made in any way that avoids confusion. If the person dealing with the legal assistant already knows of his/her status, further disclosure is unnecessary. If at any time in written or oral communication the legal assistant becomes aware that the other person may believe the legal assistant is an attorney, immediate disclosure should be made as to the legal assistant's status.

The attorney should exercise care that the legal assistant preserves and refrains from using any confidence or secrets of a client, and should instruct the legal assistant not to disclose or use any such confidences or secrets.

The legal assistant must take any and all steps necessary to prevent conflicts of interest and fully disclose such conflicts to the supervising attorney. Failure to do so may jeopardize both the attorney's representation of the client and the case itself.

Guidelines for the Utilization of Legal Assistant Services adopted December 3, 1994 by the Washington State Bar Association Board of Governors states:

"Guideline 7: A lawyer shall take reasonable measures to prevent conflicts of interest resulting from a legal assistant's other employment or interest insofar as such other employment or interests would present a conflict of interest if it were that of the lawyer."

In Re Complex Asbestos Litigation, 232 Cal. App. 3d 572 (Cal. 1991), addresses the issue wherein a law firm was disqualified due to possession of attorney-client confidences by a legal assistant employee resulting from previous employment by opposing counsel.

The ultimate responsibility for compliance with approved standards of professional conduct rests with the supervising attorney. The burden rests upon the attorney who employs a legal assistant to educate the latter with respect to the duties that may be assigned and then to supervise the manner in which the legal assistant carries out such duties. However, this does not relieve the legal assistant from an independent obligation to refrain from illegal conduct. Additionally, and notwithstanding that the Rules are not binding upon non-lawyers, the very nature of a legal assistant's employment imposes an obligation not to engage in conduct which would involve the supervising attorney in a violation of the Rules.

The attorney must make sufficient background investigation of the prior activities and character and integrity of his or her legal assistants. Further, the attorney must take all measures necessary to avoid and fully disclose conflicts of interest due to other employment or interests. Failure to do so may jeopardize both the attorney's representation of the client and the case itself.

Legal assistant associations strive to maintain the high level of integrity and competence expected of the legal profession and, further, strive to uphold the high standards of ethics.

NALA's Code of Ethics and Professional Responsibility states "A legal assistant's conduct is guided by bar associations' codes of professional responsibility and rules of professional conduct."

Guideline 2

Legal assistants should not:

1. Establish attorney-client relationships; set legal fees; give legal opinions or advice; or represent a client before a court, unless authorized to do so by said court; nor
2. Engage in, encourage, or contribute to any act which could constitute the unauthorized practice law.

Comment

Case law, court rules, codes of ethics and professional responsibilities, as well as bar ethics opinions now hold which acts can and cannot be performed by a legal assistant. Generally, the determination of what acts constitute the unauthorized practice of law is made by State Supreme Courts.

Numerous cases exist relating to the unauthorized practice of law. Courts have gone so far as to prohibit the legal assistant from preparation of divorce kits and assisting in preparation of bankruptcy forms and, more specifically, from providing basic information about procedures and requirements, deciding where information should be placed on forms, and responding to questions from debtors regarding the interpretation or definition of terms.

Cases have identified certain areas in which an attorney has a duty to act, but it is interesting to note that none of these cases state that it is improper for an attorney to have the initial work performed by the legal assistant. This again points out the importance of adequate supervision by the employing attorney.

An attorney can be found to have aided in the unauthorized practice of law when delegating acts which cannot be performed by a legal assistant.

Guideline 3

Legal assistants may perform services for an attorney in the representation of a client, provided:

1. The services performed by the legal assistant do not require the exercise of independent professional legal judgment;
2. The attorney maintains a direct relationship with the client and maintains control of all client matters;
3. The attorney supervises the legal assistant;
4. The attorney remains professionally responsible for all work on behalf of the client, including any actions taken or not taken by the legal assistant in connection therewith; and
5. The services performed supplement, merge with and become the attorney's work product.

Comment

Legal assistants, whether employees or independent contractors, perform services for the attorney in the representation of a client. Attorneys should delegate work to legal assistants commensurate with their knowledge and experience and provide appropriate instruction and supervision concerning the delegated work, as well as ethical acts of their employment. Ultimate responsibility for the work product of a legal assistant rests with the attorney. However, a legal assistant must use discretion and professional judgment and must not render independent legal judgment in place of an attorney.

The work product of a legal assistant is subject to civil rules governing discovery of materials prepared in anticipation of litigation, whether the legal assistant is viewed as an extension of the attorney or as another representative of the party itself. Fed. R. Civ. P. 26 (b)(2).

Guideline 4

In the supervision of a legal assistant, consideration should be given to:

1. Designating work assignments that correspond to the legal assistant's abilities, knowledge, training and experience;

2. Educating and training the legal assistant with respect to professional responsibility, local rules and practices, and firm policies;

3. Monitoring the work and professional conduct of the legal assistant to ensure that the work is substantively correct and timely performed;

4. Providing continuing education for the legal assistant in substantive matters through courses, institutes, workshops, seminars and in-house training; and

5. Encouraging and supporting membership and active participation in professional organizations.

Comment

Attorneys are responsible for the actions of their employees in both malpractice and disciplinary proceedings. In the vast majority of cases, the courts have not censured attorneys for a particular act delegated to the legal assistant, but rather, have been critical of and imposed sanctions against attorneys for failure to adequately supervise the legal assistant. The attorney's responsibility for supervision of his or her legal assistant must be more than a willingness to accept responsibility and liability for the legal assistant's work. Supervision of a legal assistant must be offered in both the procedural and substantive legal areas. The attorney must delegate work based upon the education, knowledge and abilities of the legal assistant and must monitor the work product and conduct of the legal assistant to insure that the work performed is substantively correct and competently performed in a professional manner.

Michigan State Board of Commissioners has adopted Guidelines for the Utilization of Legal Assistants (April 23, 1993). These guidelines, in part, en-

courage employers to support legal assistant participation in continuing education programs to ensure that the legal assistant remains competent in the fields of practice in which the legal assistant is assigned.

The working relationship between the lawyer and the legal assistant should extend to cooperative efforts on public service activities wherever possible. Participation in pro bono activities is encouraged in ABA Guideline 10.

Guideline 5

Except as otherwise provided by statute, court rule or decision, administrative rule or regulation, or the attorney's rules of professional responsibility, and within the preceding parameters and proscriptions, a legal assistant may perform any function delegated by an attorney, including, but not limited to the following:

1. Conduct client interviews and maintain general contact with the client after the establishment of the attorney-client relationship, so long as the client is aware of the status and function of the legal assistant, and the client contact is under the supervision of the attorney.

2. Locate and interview witnesses, so long as the witnesses are aware of the status and function of the legal assistant.

3. Conduct investigations and statistical and documentary research for review by the attorney.

4. Conduct legal research for review by the attorney.

5. Draft legal documents for review by the attorney.

6. Draft correspondence and pleadings for review by and signature of the attorney.

7. Summarize depositions, interrogatories and testimony for review by the attorney.

8. Attend executions of wills, real estate closings, depositions, court or administrative hearings and trials with the attorney.

9. Author and sign letters providing the legal assistant's status is clearly indicated and the correspondence does not contain independent legal opinions or legal advice.

Comment

The United States Supreme Court has recognized the variety of tasks being performed by legal assistants and has noted that use of legal assistants encourages cost-effective delivery of legal services, *Missouri v. Jenkins,* 491 U.S. 274, 109 S.Ct. 2463, 2471, n.10 (1989). In Jenkins, the court further held that legal assistant time should be included in compensation for attorney fee awards at the rate in the relevant community to bill legal assistant time.

Courts have held that legal assistant fees are not a part of the overall overhead of a law firm. Legal assistant services are billed separately by attorneys, and decrease litigation expenses. Tasks performed by legal assistants must contain substantive legal work under the direction or supervision of an attorney, such that if the legal assistant were not present, the work would be performed by the attorney.

In Taylor v. Chubb, 874 P. 2d 806 (Okla. 1994), the Court ruled that attorney fees awarded should include fees for services performed by legal assistants and, further, defined tasks which may be performed by the legal assistant under the supervision of an attorney including, among others: interview clients; draft pleadings and other documents; carry on legal research, both conventional and computer aided; research public records; prepare discovery requests and responses; schedule depositions and prepare notices and subpoenas; summarize depositions and other discovery responses; coordinate and manage document production; locate and interview witnesses; organize pleadings, trial exhibits and other documents; prepare witness and exhibit lists; prepare trial notebooks; prepare for the attendance of witnesses at trial; and assist lawyers at trials.

Except for the specific proscription contained in Guideline 1, the reported cases do not limit the duties which may be performed by a legal assistant under the supervision of the attorney.

An attorney may not split legal fees with a legal assistant, nor pay a legal assistant for the referral of legal business. An attorney may compensate a legal assistant based on the quantity and quality of the legal assistant's work and value of that work to a law practice.

Conclusion

These Standards and Guidelines were developed from generally accepted practices. Each supervising attorney must be aware of the specific rules, decisions and statutes applicable to legal assistants within his/her jurisdiction.

Reprinted with permission of the National Association of Legal Assistants. Updated 1997.

* * * * * *

National Federation of Paralegal Associations

Definition

A paralegal/legal assistant is a person qualified through education, training or work experience to perform substantive legal work that requires knowledge of legal concepts and is customarily, but not exclusively, performed by a lawyer. This person may be retained or employed by a lawyer, law office, governmental agency or other entity or may be authorized by administrative, statutory or court authority to perform this work.

Adopted 1987

Model Code of Ethics and Professional Responsibility and Guidelines for Enforcement

Preamble

The National Federation of Paralegal Associations, Inc. ("NFPA") is a professional organization comprised of paralegal associations and individual paralegals throughout the United States and Canada. Members of NFPA have varying backgrounds, experiences, education and job responsibilities that reflect the diversity of the paralegal profession. NFPA promotes the growth, development and recognition of the paralegal profession as an integral partner in the delivery of legal services.

In May 1993 NFPA adopted its Model Code of Ethics and Professional Responsibility ("Model Code") to delineate the principles for ethics and conduct to which every paralegal should aspire.

Many paralegal associations throughout the United States have endorsed the concept and content of NFPA's Model Code through the adoption of their own ethical codes. In doing so, paralegals have confirmed the profession's commitment to increase the quality and efficiency of legal services, as well as recognized its responsibilities to the public, the legal community, and colleagues.

Paralegals have recognized, and will continue to recognize, that the profession must continue to evolve to enhance their roles in the delivery of legal services. With increased levels of responsibility comes the need to define and enforce mandatory rules of professional conduct. Enforcement of codes of paralegal conduct is a logical and necessary step to enhance and ensure the confidence of the legal community and the public in the integrity and professional responsibility of paralegals.

In April 1997 NFPA adopted the Model Disciplinary Rules ("Model Rules") to make possible the enforcement of the Canons and Ethical Considerations contained in the NFPA Model Code. A concurrent determination was made that the Model Code of Ethics and Professional Responsibility, formerly aspirational in nature, should be recognized as setting forth the enforceable obligations of all paralegals.

The Model Code and Model Rules offer a framework for professional discipline, either voluntarily or through formal regulatory programs.

§1. NFPA MODEL DISCIPLINARY RULES AND ETHICAL CONSIDERATIONS

1.1 A PARALEGAL SHALL ACHIEVE AND MAINTAIN A HIGH LEVEL OF COMPETENCE.

Ethical Considerations

EC-1.1(a) A paralegal shall achieve competency through education, training, and work experience.

EC-1.1(b) A paralegal shall participate in continuing education in order to keep informed of current legal, technical and general developments.

EC-1.1(c) A paralegal shall perform all assignments promptly and efficiently.

1.2 A PARALEGAL SHALL MAINTAIN A HIGH LEVEL OF PERSONAL AND PROFESSIONAL INTEGRITY.

Ethical Considerations

EC-1.2(a) A paralegal shall not engage in any ex parte communications involving the courts or any other adjudicatory body in an attempt to exert undue influence or to obtain advantage or the benefit of only one party.

EC-1.2(b) A paralegal shall not communicate, or cause another to communicate, with a party the paralegal knows to be represented by a lawyer in a pending matter without the prior consent of the lawyer representing such other party.

EC-1.2(c) A paralegal shall ensure that all timekeeping and billing records prepared by the paralegal are thorough, accurate, honest, and complete.

EC-1.2(d) A paralegal shall not knowingly engage in fraudulent billing practices. Such practices may include, but are not limited to: inflation of hours billed to a client or employer; misrepresentation of the nature of tasks performed; and/or submission of fraudulent expense and disbursement documentation.

EC-1.2(e) A paralegal shall be scrupulous, thorough and honest in the identification and maintenance of all funds, securities, and other assets of a client and shall provide accurate accounting as appropriate.

EC-1.2(f) A paralegal shall advise the proper authority of non-confidential knowledge of any dishonest or fraudulent acts by any person pertaining to the handling of the funds, securities, or other assets of a client.

The authority to whom the report is made shall depend on the nature and circumstances of the possible misconduct (e.g., ethics committees of law firms, corporations and/or paralegal associations, local or state bar associations, local prosecutors, administrative agencies, etc.). Failure to report such knowledge is in itself misconduct and shall be treated as such under these rules.

1.3 A PARALEGAL SHALL MAINTAIN A HIGH STANDARD OF PROFESSIONAL CONDUCT.

Ethical Considerations

EC-1.3(a) A paralegal shall refrain from engaging in any conduct that offends the dignity and decorum of proceedings before a court or other adjudicatory body and shall be respectful of all rules and procedures.

EC-1.3(b) A paralegal shall avoid impropriety and the appearance of impropriety and shall not engage in any conduct that would adversely affect his/her fitness to practice. Such conduct may include, but is not limited to: violence, dishonesty, interference with the administration of justice, and/or abuse of a professional position or public office.

EC-1.3(c) Should a paralegal's fitness to practice be compromised by physical or mental illness, causing that paralegal to commit an act that is in direct violation of the Model Code/Model Rules and/or the rules and/or laws governing the jurisdiction in which the paralegal practices, that paralegal may be protected from sanction upon review of the nature and circumstances of that illness.

EC-1.3(d) A paralegal shall advise the proper authority of non-confidential knowledge of any action of another legal professional that clearly demonstrates fraud, deceit, dishonesty, or misrepresentation. The authority to whom the report is made shall depend on the nature and circumstances of the possible misconduct (e.g., ethics committees of law firms, corporations and/or paralegal associations, local or state bar associations, local prosecutors, administrative agencies, etc.). Failure to report such knowledge is in itself misconduct and shall be treated as such under these rules.

EC-1.3(e) A paralegal shall not knowingly assist any individual with the commission of an act that is in direct violation of the Model Code/Model Rules and/or the rules and/or laws governing the jurisdiction in which the paralegal practices.

EC-1.3(f)   If a paralegal possesses knowledge of future criminal activity, that knowledge must be reported to the appropriate authority immediately.

1.4 A PARALEGAL SHALL SERVE THE PUBLIC INTEREST BY CONTRIBUTING TO THE DELIVERY OF QUALITY LEGAL SERVICES AND THE IMPROVEMENT OF THE LEGAL SYSTEM.

Ethical Considerations

EC-1.4(a)   A paralegal shall be sensitive to the legal needs of the public and shall promote the development and implementation of programs that address those needs.

EC-1.4(b)   A paralegal shall support bona fide efforts to meet the need for legal services by those unable to pay reasonable or customary fees for example, participation in pro bono projects and volunteer work.

EC-1.4(c)   A paralegal shall support efforts to improve the legal system and access thereto and shall assist in making changes.

1.5 A PARALEGAL SHALL PRESERVE ALL CONFIDENTIAL INFORMATION PROVIDED BY THE CLIENT OR ACQUIRED FROM OTHER SOURCES BEFORE, DURING, AND AFTER THE COURSE OF THE PROFESSIONAL RELATIONSHIP.

Ethical Considerations

EC-1.5(a)   A paralegal shall be aware of and abide by all legal authority governing confidential information in the jurisdiction in which the paralegal practices.

EC-1.5(b)   A paralegal shall not use confidential information to the disadvantage of the client.

EC-1.5(c)   A paralegal shall not use confidential information to the advantage of the paralegal or of a third person.

EC-1.5(d)   A paralegal may reveal confidential information only after full disclosure and with the client's written consent; or, when required by law or court order; or, when necessary to prevent the client from committing an act that could result in death or serious bodily harm.

EC-1.5(e)   A paralegal shall keep those individuals responsible for the legal representation of a client fully informed of any confidential information the paralegal may have pertaining to that client.

EC-1.5(f)   A paralegal shall not engage in any indiscreet communications concerning clients.

1.6 A PARALEGAL SHALL AVOID CONFLICTS OF INTEREST AND SHALL DISCLOSE ANY POSSIBLE CONFLICT TO THE EMPLOYER OR CLIENT, AS WELL AS TO THE PROSPECTIVE EMPLOYERS OR CLIENTS.

Ethical Considerations

EC-1.6(a)   A paralegal shall act within the bounds of the law, solely for the benefit of the client, and shall be free of compromising influences and loyalties. Neither the paralegal's personal or business interest, nor those of other clients or third persons, should compromise the paralegal's professional judgment and loyalty to the client.

EC-1.6(b)   A paralegal shall avoid conflicts of interest that may arise from previous assignments, whether for a present or past employer or client.

EC-1.6(c)   A paralegal shall avoid conflicts of interest that may arise from family relationships and from personal and business interests.

EC-1.6(d)   In order to be able to determine whether an actual or potential conflict of interest exists a paralegal shall create and maintain an effective recordkeeping system that identifies clients, matters, and parties with which the paralegal has worked.

EC-1.6(e)   A paralegal shall reveal sufficient non-confidential information about a client or former client to reasonably ascertain if an actual or potential conflict of interest exists.

EC-1.6(f)   A paralegal shall not participate in or conduct work on any matter where a conflict of interest has been identified.

EC-1.6(g)   In matters where a conflict of interest has been identified and the client consents to continued representation, a paralegal shall comply fully with the implementation and maintenance of an Ethical Wall.

1.7 A PARALEGAL'S TITLE SHALL BE FULLY DISCLOSED.

Ethical Considerations

EC-1.7(a)   A paralegal's title shall clearly indicate the individual's status and shall be disclosed in all business and professional communications to avoid misunderstandings and misconceptions about the paralegal's role and responsibilities.

EC-1.7(b)   A paralegal's title shall be included if the paralegal's name appears on business cards, letterhead, brochures, directories, and advertisements.

EC-1.7(c)   A paralegal shall not use letterhead, business cards or other promotional materials to create a fraudulent impression of his/her status or ability to practice in the jurisdiction in which the paralegal practices.

EC-1.7(d)   A paralegal shall not practice under color of any record, diploma, or certificate that has been illegally or fraudulently obtained or issued or which is misrepresentative in any way.

EC-1.7(e)   A paralegal shall not participate in the creation, issuance, or dissemination of fraudulent records, diplomas, or certificates.

1.8 A PARALEGAL SHALL NOT ENGAGE IN THE UNAUTHORIZED PRACTICE OF LAW.

Ethical Considerations

EC-1.8(a)   A paralegal shall comply with the applicable legal authority governing the unauthorized practice of law in the jurisdiction in which the paralegal practices.

§2. NFPA GUIDELINES FOR THE ENFORCEMENT OF THE MODEL CODE OF ETHICS AND PROFESSIONAL RESPONSIBILITY.

2.1 BASIS FOR DISCIPLINE.

2.1(a)   Disciplinary investigations and proceedings brought under authority of the Rules shall be conducted in accord with obligations imposed on the paralegal professional by the Model Code of Ethics and Professional Responsibility.

2.2 STRUCTURE OF DISCIPLINARY COMMITTEE.

2.2(a)   The Disciplinary Committee ("Committee") shall be made up of nine (9) members including the Chair.

2.2(b)   Each member of the Committee, including any temporary replacement members, shall have demonstrated working knowledge of ethics/professional responsibility-related issues and activities.

2.2(c)   The Committee shall represent a cross-section of practice areas and work experience. The following recommendations are made regarding the members of the Committee.

1) At least one paralegal with one to three years of law-related work experience.

2) At least one paralegal with five to seven years of law-related work experience.

3) At least one paralegal with over ten years of law-related work experience.

4) One paralegal educator with five to seven years of work experience; preferably in the area of ethics/professional responsibility.

5) One paralegal manager.

6) One lawyer with five to seven years of law-related work experience.

7) One lay member.

2.2(d)   The Chair of the Committee shall be appointed within thirty (30) days of its members' induction. The Chair shall have no fewer than ten (10) years of law-related work experience.

2.2(e)   The terms of all members of the Committee shall be staggered. Of those members initially appointed, a simple majority plus one shall be appointed to a term of one year, and the remaining members shall be appointed to a term of two years. Thereafter, all members of the Committee shall be appointed to terms of two years.

2.2(f)   If for any reason the terms of a majority of the Committee will expire at the same time, members may be appointed to terms of one year to maintain continuity of the Committee.

2.2(g)   The Committee shall organize from its members a three-tiered structure to investigate, prosecute and/or adjudicate charges of misconduct. The members shall be rotated among the tiers.

2.3 OPERATION OF COMMITTEE

2.3(a)   The Committee shall meet on an as-needed basis to discuss, investigate, and/or adjudicate alleged violations of the Model Code/Model Rules.

2.3(b)   A majority of the members of the Committee present at a meeting shall constitute a quorum.

2.3(c)   A Recording Secretary shall be designated to maintain complete and accurate minutes of all Committee meetings. All such minutes shall be kept confidential until a decision has been made that the matter will be set for hearing as set forth in Section 6.1.

2.3(d)   If any member of the Committee has a conflict of interest with the Charging Party, the Responding Party, or the allegations of misconduct, that member shall not take part in any hearing or deliberations concerning those allegations. If the absence of that member creates a lack of a quorum for the Committee, then a temporary replacement for the member shall be appointed.

2.3(e)   Either the Charging Party or the Responding Party may request that, for good cause shown, any member of the Committee not participate in a hearing or deliberation. All such requests shall be honored. If the absence of a Committee member under those circumstances creates a lack of a quorum for the Committee, then a temporary replacement for that member shall be appointed.

2.3(f)   All discussions and correspondence of the Committee shall be kept confidential until a decision has been made that the matter will be set for hearing as set forth in Section 6.1.

2.3(g)   All correspondence from the Committee to the Responding Party regarding any charge of misconduct and any decisions made regarding the charge shall be mailed certified mail, return receipt requested, to the Responding Party's last known address and shall be clearly marked with a "Confidential" designation.

2.4 PROCEDURE FOR THE REPORTING OF ALLEGED VIOLATIONS OF THE MODEL CODE/DISCIPLINARY RULES

2.4(a)   An individual or entity in possession of non-confidential knowledge or information concerning possible instances of misconduct shall make a confidential written report to the Committee within thirty (30) days of obtaining same. This report shall include all details of the alleged misconduct.

2.4(b)   The Committee so notified shall inform the Responding Party of the allegation(s) of misconduct no later than ten (10) business days after receiving the confidential written report from the Charging Party.

2.4(c)   Notification to the Responding Party shall include the identity of the Charging Party, unless, for good cause shown, the Charging Party requests anonymity.

2.4(d)   The Responding Party shall reply to the allegations within ten (10) business days of notification.

2.5 PROCEDURE FOR THE INVESTIGATION OF A CHARGE OF MISCONDUCT

2.5(a)   Upon receipt of a Charge of Misconduct ("Charge"), or on its own initiative, the Committee shall initiate an investigation.

2.5(b)   If, upon initial or preliminary review, the Committee makes a determination that the charges are either without basis in fact or, if proven, would not constitute professional misconduct, the Committee shall dismiss the allegations of misconduct. If such determination of dismissal cannot be made, a formal investigation shall be initiated.

2.5(c)   Upon the decision to conduct a formal investigation, the Committee shall:

1) mail to the Charging and Responding Parties within three (3) business days of that decision notice of the commencement of a formal investigation. That notification shall be in writing and shall contain a complete explanation of all Charge(s), as well as the reasons for a formal investigation and shall cite the applicable codes and rules;

2) allow the Responding Party thirty (30) days to prepare and submit a confidential response to the Committee, which response shall address each charge specifically and shall be in writing; and 3) upon receipt of the response to the notification, have thirty (30) days to investigate the Charge(s). If an extension of time is deemed necessary, that extension shall not exceed ninety (90) days.

2.5(d)   Upon conclusion of the investigation, the Committee may:

1) dismiss the Charge upon the finding that it has no basis in fact;

2) dismiss the Charge upon the finding that, if proven, the Charge would not constitute Misconduct;

3) refer the matter for hearing by the Tribunal; or

4) in the case of criminal activity, refer the Charge(s) and all investigation results to the appropriate authority.

2.6 PROCEDURE FOR A MISCONDUCT HEARING BEFORE A TRIBUNAL

2.6(a)   Upon the decision by the Committee that a matter should be heard, all parties shall be notified and a hearing date shall be set. The hearing shall take place no more than thirty (30) days from the conclusion of the formal investigation.

2.6(b) The Responding Party shall have the right to counsel. The parties and the Tribunal shall have the right to call any witnesses and introduce any documentation that they believe will lead to the fair and reasonable resolution of the matter.

2.6(c) Upon completion of the hearing, the Tribunal shall deliberate and present a written decision to the parties in accordance with procedures as set forth by the Tribunal.

2.6(d) Notice of the decision of the Tribunal shall be appropriately published.

2.7 SANCTIONS

2.7(a) Upon a finding of the Tribunal that misconduct has occurred, any of the following sanctions, or others as may be deemed appropriate, may be imposed upon the Responding Party, either singularly or in combination:

1) letter of reprimand to the Responding Party; counseling;
2) attendance at an ethics course approved by the Tribunal;
3) probation;
4) suspension of license/authority to practice; revocation of license/authority to practice;
5) imposition of a fine; assessment of costs; or
6) in the instance of criminal activity, referral to the appropriate authority.

2.7(b) Upon the expiration of any period of probation, suspension, or revocation, the Responding Party may make application for reinstatement. With the application for reinstatement, the Responding Party must show proof of having complied with all aspects of the sanctions imposed by the Tribunal.

2.8 APPELLATE PROCEDURES

2.8(a) The parties shall have the right to appeal the decision of the Tribunal in accordance with the procedure as set forth by the Tribunal.

Definitions

"Appellate Body" means a body established to adjudicate an appeal to any decision made by a Tribunal or other decision-making body with respect to formally-heard Charges of Misconduct.

"Charge of Misconduct" means a written submission by any individual or entity to an ethics committee, paralegal association, bar association, law enforcement agency, judicial body, government agency, or other appropriate body or entity, that sets forth non-confidential information regarding any instance of alleged misconduct by an individual paralegal or paralegal entity.

"Charging Party" means any individual or entity who submits a Charge of Misconduct against an individual paralegal or paralegal entity.

"Competency" means the demonstration of: diligence, education, skill, and mental, emotional, and physical fitness reasonably necessary for the performance of paralegal services.

"Confidential Information" means information relating to a client, whatever its source, that is not public knowledge nor available to the public. ("Non-Confidential Information" would generally include the name of the client and the identity of the matter for which the paralegal provided services.)

"Disciplinary Hearing" means the confidential proceeding conducted by a committee or other designated body or entity concerning any instance of alleged misconduct by an individual paralegal or paralegal entity.

"Disciplinary Committee" means any committee that has been established by an entity such as a paralegal association, bar association, judicial body, or government agency to: (a) identify, define and investigate general ethical considerations and concerns with respect to paralegal practice; (b) administer and enforce the Model Code and Model Rules and; (c) disciplinary individual paralegal or paralegal entity found to be in violation of same.

"Disclose" means communication of information reasonably sufficient to permit identification of the significance of the matter in question.

"Ethical Wall" means the screening method implemented in order to protect a client from a conflict of interest. An Ethical Wall generally includes, but is not limited to, the following elements: (1) prohibit the paralegal from having any connection with the matter; (2) ban discussions with or the transfer of documents to or from the paralegal; (3) restrict access to files; and (4) educate all members of the firm, corporation, or entity as to the separation of the paralegal (both organizationally and physically) from the pending matter. For more information regarding the Ethical Wall, see the NFPA publication entitled "The Ethical Wall—Its Application to Paralegals."

"Ex parte" means actions or communications conducted at the instance and for the benefit of one party only, and without notice to, or contestation by, any person adversely interested.

"Investigation" means the investigation of any charge(s) of misconduct filed against an individual paralegal or paralegal entity by a Committee.

"Letter of Reprimand" means a written notice of formal censure or other proof administered to an individual paralegal or paralegal entity for unethical or improper conduct.

"Misconduct" means the knowing or unknowing commission of an act that is indirect violation of those Canons and Ethical Considerations of any and all applicable codes and/or rules of conduct.

"Paralegal" is synonymous with "Legal Assistant" and is defined as a person qualified through education, training, or work experience to perform substantive legal work that requires knowledge of legal concepts and is customarily, but not exclusively performed by a lawyer. This person may be retained or employed by a lawyer, law office, governmental agency, or other entity or may be authorized by administrative, statutory, or court authority to perform this work.

"Proper Authority" means the local paralegal association, the local or state bar association, Committee(s) of the local paralegal or bar association(s), local prosecutor, administrative agency, or other tribunal empowered to investigate or act upon an instance of alleged misconduct.

"Responding Party" means an individual paralegal or paralegal entity against whom a Charge of Misconduct has been submitted.

"Revocation" means the recision of the license, certificate or other authority to practice of an individual paralegal or paralegal entity found in violation of those Canons and Ethical Considerations of any and all applicable codes and/or rules of conduct.

"Suspension" means the suspension of the license, certificate or other authority to practice of an individual paralegal or paralegal entity found in violation of those Canons and Ethical Considerations of any and all applicable codes and/or rules of conduct.

"Tribunal" means the body designated to adjudicate allegations of misconduct.

Docket Calculation Chart

Find the due date with this handy docket calculation chart. The trigger date is in the left-hand column. Once you have determined the trigger date, go across the grid to find the due date according to the applicable number of days. The dates do not reflect weekends or holidays. Once you have located the correct date, check the calendar to determine whether it is a weekend or a holiday date. If it is, the due date is the first business day after the weekend or holiday date. (Note: Does not apply to leap years.)

Date	+10	+15	+20	+25	+30	+35	+45	+60	+140	−10	−14	−20
Jan 01	01/11	01/16	01/21	01/26	01/31	02/05	02/15	03/02	05/21	12/22	12/18	12/12
Jan 02	01/12	01/17	01/22	01/27	02/01	02/06	02/16	03/03	05/22	12/23	12/19	12/13
Jan 03	01/13	01/18	01/23	01/28	02/02	02/07	02/17	03/04	05/23	12/24	12/20	12/14
Jan 04	01/14	01/19	01/24	01/29	02/03	02/08	02/18	03/05	05/24	12/25	12/21	12/15
Jan 05	01/15	01/20	01/25	01/30	02/04	02/09	02/19	03/06	05/25	12/26	12/22	12/16
Jan 06	01/16	01/21	01/26	01/31	02/05	02/10	02/20	03/07	05/26	12/27	12/23	12/17
Jan 07	01/17	01/22	01/27	02/01	02/06	02/11	02/21	03/08	05/27	12/28	12/24	12/18
Jan 08	01/18	01/23	01/28	02/02	02/07	02/12	02/22	03/09	05/28	12/29	12/25	12/19
Jan 09	01/19	01/24	01/29	02/03	02/08	02/13	02/23	03/10	05/29	12/30	12/26	12/20
Jan 10	01/20	01/25	01/30	02/04	02/09	02/14	02/24	03/11	05/30	12/31	12/27	12/21
Jan 11	01/21	01/26	01/31	02/05	02/10	02/15	02/25	03/12	05/31	01/01	12/28	12/22
Jan 12	01/22	01/27	02/01	02/06	02/11	02/16	02/26	03/13	06/01	01/02	12/29	12/23
Jan 13	01/23	01/28	02/02	02/07	02/12	02/17	02/27	03/14	06/02	01/03	12/30	12/24
Jan 14	01/24	01/29	02/03	02/08	02/13	02/18	02/28	03/15	06/03	01/04	12/31	12/25
Jan 15	01/25	01/30	02/04	02/09	02/14	02/19	03/01	03/16	06/04	01/05	01/01	12/26
Jan 16	01/26	01/31	02/05	02/10	02/15	02/20	03/02	03/17	06/05	01/06	01/02	12/27
Jan 17	01/27	02/01	02/06	02/11	02/16	02/21	03/03	03/18	06/06	01/07	01/03	12/28
Jan 18	01/28	02/02	02/07	02/12	02/17	02/22	01/04	03/19	06/07	01/08	01/04	12/29
Jan 19	01/29	02/03	02/08	02/13	02/18	02/23	03/05	03/20	06/08	01/09	01/05	12/30
Jan 20	01/30	02/04	02/09	02/14	02/19	02/24	03/06	03/21	06/09	01/10	01/06	12/31
Jan 21	01/31	02/05	02/10	02/15	02/20	02/25	03/07	03/22	06/10	01/11	01/07	01/01
Jan 22	02/01	02/06	02/11	02/16	02/21	02/26	03/08	03/23	06/11	01/12	01/08	01/02
Jan 23	02/02	02/07	02/12	02/17	02/22	02/27	03/09	03/24	06/12	01/13	01/09	01/03
Jan 24	02/03	02/08	02/13	02/18	02/23	02/28	03/10	03/25	06/13	01/14	01/10	01/04
Jan 25	02/04	02/09	02/14	02/19	02/24	03/01	03/11	03/26	06/14	01/15	01/11	01/05
Jan 26	02/05	02/10	02/15	02/20	02/25	03/02	03/12	03/27	06/15	01/16	01/12	01/06
Jan 27	02/06	02/11	02/16	02/21	02/26	03/03	03/13	03/28	06/16	01/17	01/13	01/07
Jan 28	02/07	02/12	02/17	02/22	02/27	03/04	03/14	03/29	06/17	01/18	01/14	01/08
Jan 29	02/08	02/13	02/18	02/23	02/28	03/05	03/15	03/30	06/18	01/19	01/15	01/09

Date	+10	+15	+20	+25	+30	+35	+45	+60	+140	−10	−14	−20
Jan 30	02/09	02/14	02/19	02/24	03/01	03/06	03/16	03/31	06/19	01/20	01/16	01/10
Jan 31	02/10	02/15	02/20	02/25	03/02	03/07	03/17	04/01	06/20	01/21	01/17	01/11
Feb 01	02/11	02/16	02/21	02/26	03/03	03/08	03/18	04/02	06/21	01/22	01/18	01/12
Feb 02	02/12	02/17	02/22	02/27	03/04	03/09	03/19	04/03	06/22	01/23	01/19	01/13
Feb 03	02/13	02/18	02/23	02/28	03/05	03/10	03/20	04/04	06/23	01/24	01/20	01/14
Feb 04	02/14	02/19	02/24	03/01	03/06	03/11	03/21	04/05	06/24	01/25	01/21	01/15
Feb 05	02/15	02/20	02/25	03/02	03/07	03/12	03/22	04/06	06/25	01/26	01/22	01/16
Feb 06	02/16	02/21	02/26	03/03	03/08	03/13	03/23	04/07	06/26	01/27	01/23	01/17
Feb 07	02/17	02/22	02/27	03/04	03/09	03/14	03/24	04/08	06/27	01/28	01/24	01/18
Feb 08	02/18	02/23	02/28	03/05	03/10	03/15	03/25	04/09	06/28	01/29	01/25	01/19
Feb 09	02/19	02/24	03/01	03/06	03/11	03/16	03/26	04/10	06/29	01/30	01/26	01/20
Feb 10	02/20	02/25	03/02	03/07	03/12	03/17	03/27	04/11	06/30	01/31	01/27	01/21
Feb 11	02/21	02/26	03/03	03/08	03/13	03/18	03/28	04/12	07/01	02/01	01/28	01/22
Feb 12	02/22	02/27	03/04	03/09	03/14	03/19	03/29	04/13	07/02	02/02	01/29	01/23
Feb 13	02/23	02/28	03/05	03/10	03/15	03/20	03/30	04/14	07/03	02/03	01/30	01/24
Feb 14	02/24	03/01	03/06	03/11	03/16	03/21	03/31	04/15	07/04	02/04	01/31	01/25
Feb 15	02/25	03/02	03/07	03/12	03/17	03/22	04/01	04/16	07/05	02/05	02/01	01/26
Feb 16	02/26	03/03	03/08	03/13	03/18	03/23	04/02	04/17	07/06	02/06	02/02	01/27
Feb 17	02/27	03/04	03/09	03/14	03/19	03/24	04/03	04/18	07/07	02/07	02/03	01/28
Feb 18	02/28	03/05	03/10	03/15	03/20	03/25	04/04	04/19	07/08	02/08	02/04	01/29
Feb 19	03/01	03/06	03/11	03/16	03/21	03/26	04/05	04/20	07/09	02/09	02/05	01/30
Feb 20	03/02	03/07	03/12	03/17	03/22	03/27	04/06	04/21	07/10	02/10	02/06	01/31
Feb 21	03/03	03/08	03/13	03/18	03/23	03/28	04/07	04/22	07/11	02/11	02/07	02/01
Feb 22	03/04	03/09	03/14	03/19	03/24	03/29	04/08	04/23	07/12	02/12	02/08	02/02
Feb 23	03/05	03/10	03/15	03/20	03/25	03/30	04/09	04/24	07/13	02/13	02/09	02/03
Feb 24	03/06	03/11	03/16	03/21	03/26	03/31	04/10	04/25	07/14	02/14	02/10	02/04
Feb 25	03/07	03/12	03/17	03/22	03/27	04/01	04/11	04/26	07/15	02/15	02/11	02/05
Feb 26	03/08	03/13	03/18	03/23	03/28	04/02	04/12	04/27	07/16	02/16	02/12	02/06
Feb 27	03/09	03/14	03/19	03/24	03/29	04/03	04/13	04/28	07/17	02/17	02/13	02/07
Feb 28	03/10	03/15	03/20	03/25	03/30	04/04	04/14	04/29	07/18	02/18	02/14	02/08
Mar 01	03/11	03/16	03/21	03/26	03/31	04/05	04/15	04/30	07/19	02/19	02/15	02/09
Mar 02	03/12	03/17	03/22	03/27	04/01	04/06	04/16	05/01	07/20	02/20	02/16	02/10
Mar 03	03/13	03/18	03/23	03/28	04/02	04/07	04/17	05/02	07/21	02/21	02/17	02/11
Mar 04	03/14	03/19	03/24	03/29	04/03	04/08	04/18	05/03	07/22	02/22	02/18	02/12
Mar 05	03/15	03/20	03/25	03/30	04/04	04/09	04/19	05/04	07/23	02/23	02/19	02/13
Mar 06	03/16	03/21	03/26	03/31	04/05	04/10	04/20	05/05	07/24	02/24	02/20	02/14
Mar 07	03/17	03/22	03/27	04/01	04/06	04/11	04/21	05/06	07/25	02/25	02/21	02/15
Mar 08	03/18	03/23	03/28	04/02	04/07	04/12	04/22	05/07	07/26	02/26	02/22	02/16
Mar 09	03/19	03/24	03/29	04/03	04/08	04/13	04/23	05/08	07/27	02/27	02/23	02/17
Mar 10	03/20	03/25	03/30	04/04	04/09	04/14	04/24	05/09	07/28	02/28	02/24	02/18
Mar 11	03/21	03/26	03/31	04/05	04/10	04/15	04/25	05/10	07/29	03/01	02/25	02/19
Mar 12	03/22	03/27	04/01	04/06	04/11	04/16	04/26	05/11	07/30	03/02	02/26	02/20
Mar 13	03/23	03/28	04/02	04/07	04/12	04/17	04/27	05/12	07/31	03/03	02/27	02/21
Mar 14	03/24	03/29	04/03	04/08	04/13	04/18	04/28	05/13	08/01	03/04	02/28	02/22
Mar 15	03/25	03/30	04/04	04/09	04/14	04/19	04/29	05/14	08/02	03/05	03/01	02/23
Mar 16	03/26	03/31	04/05	04/10	04/15	04/20	04/30	05/15	08/03	03/06	03/02	02/24
Mar 17	03/27	04/01	04/06	04/11	04/16	04/21	05/01	05/16	08/04	03/07	03/03	02/25
Mar 18	03/28	04/02	04/07	04/12	04/17	04/22	05/02	05/17	08/05	03/08	03/04	02/26
Mar 19	03/29	04/03	04/08	04/13	04/18	04/23	05/03	05/18	08/06	03/09	03/05	02/27
Mar 20	03/30	04/04	04/09	04/14	04/19	04/24	05/04	05/19	08/07	03/10	03/06	02/28

Date	+10	+15	+20	+25	+30	+35	+45	+60	+140	−10	−14	−20
Mar 21	03/31	04/05	04/10	04/15	04/20	04/25	05/05	05/20	08/08	03/11	03/07	03/01
Mar 22	04/01	04/06	04/11	04/16	04/21	04/26	05/06	05/21	08/09	03/12	03/08	03/02
Mar 23	04/02	04/07	04/12	04/17	04/22	04/27	05/07	05/22	08/10	03/13	03/09	03/03
Mar 24	04/03	04/08	04/13	04/18	04/23	04/28	05/08	05/23	08/11	03/14	03/10	03/04
Mar 25	04/04	04/09	04/14	04/19	04/24	04/29	05/09	05/24	08/12	03/15	03/11	03/05
Mar 26	04/05	04/10	04/15	04/20	04/25	04/30	05/10	05/25	08/13	03/16	03/12	03/06
Mar 27	04/06	04/11	04/16	04/21	04/26	05/01	05/11	05/26	08/14	03/17	03/13	03/07
Mar 28	04/07	04/12	04/17	04/22	04/27	05/02	05/12	05/27	08/15	03/18	03/14	03/08
Mar 29	04/08	04/13	04/18	04/23	04/28	05/03	05/13	05/28	08/16	03/19	03/15	03/09
Mar 30	04/09	04/14	04/19	04/24	04/29	05/04	05/14	05/29	08/17	03/20	03/16	03/10
Mar 31	04/10	04/15	04/20	04/25	04/30	05/05	05/15	05/30	08/18	03/21	03/17	03/11
Apr 01	04/11	04/16	04/21	04/26	05/01	05/06	05/16	05/31	08/19	03/22	03/18	03/12
Apr 02	04/12	04/17	04/22	04/27	05/02	05/07	05/17	06/01	08/20	03/23	03/19	03/13
Apr 03	04/13	04/18	04/23	04/28	05/03	05/08	05/18	06/02	08/21	03/24	03/20	03/14
Apr 04	04/14	04/19	04/24	04/29	05/04	05/09	05/19	06/03	08/22	03/25	03/21	03/15
Apr 05	04/15	04/20	04/25	04/30	05/05	05/10	05/20	06/04	08/23	03/26	03/22	03/16
Apr 06	04/16	04/21	04/26	05/01	05/06	05/11	05/21	06/05	08/24	03/27	03/23	03/17
Apr 07	04/17	04/22	04/27	05/02	05/07	05/12	05/22	06/06	08/25	03/28	03/24	03/18
Apr 08	04/18	04/23	04/28	05/03	05/08	05/13	05/23	06/07	08/26	03/29	03/25	03/19
Apr 09	04/19	04/24	04/29	05/04	05/09	05/14	05/24	06/08	08/27	03/30	03/26	03/20
Apr 10	04/20	04/25	04/30	05/05	05/10	05/15	05/25	06/09	08/28	03/31	03/27	03/21
Apr 11	04/21	04/26	05/01	05/06	05/11	05/16	05/26	06/10	08/29	04/01	03/28	03/22
Apr 12	04/22	04/27	05/02	05/07	05/12	05/17	05/27	06/11	08/30	04/02	03/29	03/23
Apr 13	04/23	04/28	05/03	05/08	05/13	05/18	05/28	06/12	08/31	04/03	03/30	03/24
Apr 14	04/24	04/29	05/04	05/09	05/14	05/19	05/29	06/13	09/01	04/04	03/31	03/25
Apr 15	04/25	04/30	05/05	05/10	05/15	05/20	05/30	06/14	09/02	04/05	04/01	03/26
Apr 16	04/26	05/01	05/06	05/11	05/16	05/21	05/31	06/15	09/03	04/06	04/02	03/27
Apr 17	04/27	05/02	05/07	05/12	05/17	05/22	06/01	06/16	09/04	04/07	04/03	03/28
Apr 18	04/28	05/03	05/08	05/13	05/18	05/23	06/02	06/17	09/05	04/08	04/04	03/29
Apr 19	04/29	05/04	05/09	05/14	05/19	05/24	06/03	06/18	09/06	04/09	04/05	03/30
Apr 20	04/30	05/05	05/10	05/15	05/20	05/25	06/04	06/19	09/07	04/10	04/06	03/31
Apr 21	05/01	05/06	05/11	05/16	05/21	05/26	06/05	06/20	09/08	04/11	04/07	04/01
Apr 22	05/02	05/07	05/12	05/17	05/22	05/27	06/06	06/21	09/09	04/12	04/08	04/02
Apr 23	05/03	05/08	05/13	05/18	05/23	05/28	06/07	06/22	09/10	04/13	04/09	04/03
Apr 24	05/04	05/09	05/14	05/19	05/24	05/29	06/08	06/23	09/11	04/14	04/10	04/04
Apr 25	05/05	05/10	05/15	05/20	05/25	05/30	06/09	06/24	09/12	04/15	04/11	04/05
Apr 26	05/06	05/11	05/16	05/21	05/26	05/31	06/10	06/25	09/13	04/16	04/12	04/06
Apr 27	05/07	05/12	05/17	05/22	05/27	06/01	06/11	06/26	09/14	04/17	04/13	04/07
Apr 28	05/08	05/13	05/18	05/23	05/28	06/02	06/12	06/27	09/15	04/18	04/14	04/08
Apr 29	05/09	05/14	05/19	05/24	05/29	06/03	06/13	06/28	09/16	04/19	04/15	04/09
Apr 30	05/10	05/15	05/20	05/25	05/30	06/04	06/14	06/29	09/17	04/20	04/16	04/10
May 01	05/11	05/16	05/21	05/26	05/31	06/05	06/15	06/30	09/18	04/21	04/17	04/11
May 02	05/12	05/17	05/22	05/27	06/01	06/06	06/16	07/01	09/19	04/22	04/18	04/12
May 03	05/13	05/18	05/23	05/28	06/02	06/07	06/17	07/02	09/20	04/23	04/19	04/13
May 04	05/14	05/19	05/24	05/29	06/03	06/08	06/18	07/03	09/21	04/24	04/20	04/14
May 05	05/15	05/20	05/25	05/30	06/04	06/09	06/19	07/04	09/22	04/25	04/21	04/15
May 06	05/16	05/21	05/26	05/31	06/05	06/10	06/20	07/05	09/23	04/26	04/22	04/16
May 07	05/17	05/22	05/27	06/01	06/06	06/11	06/21	07/06	09/24	04/27	04/23	04/17
May 08	05/18	05/23	05/28	06/02	06/07	06/12	06/22	07/07	09/25	04/28	04/24	04/18
May 09	05/19	05/24	05/29	06/03	06/08	06/13	06/23	07/08	09/26	04/29	04/25	04/19

Date	+10	+15	+20	+25	+30	+35	+45	+60	+140	−10	−14	−20
May 10	05/20	05/25	05/30	06/04	06/09	06/14	06/24	07/09	09/27	04/30	04/26	04/20
May 11	05/21	05/26	05/31	06/05	06/10	06/15	06/25	07/10	09/28	05/01	04/27	04/21
May 12	05/22	05/27	06/01	06/06	06/11	06/16	06/26	07/11	09/29	05/02	04/28	04/22
May 13	05/23	05/28	06/02	06/07	06/12	06/17	06/27	07/12	09/30	05/03	04/29	04/23
May 14	05/24	05/29	06/03	06/08	06/13	06/18	06/28	07/13	10/01	05/04	04/30	04/24
May 15	05/25	05/30	06/04	06/09	06/14	06/19	06/29	07/14	10/02	05/05	05/01	04/25
May 16	05/26	05/31	06/05	06/10	06/15	06/20	06/30	07/15	10/03	05/06	05/02	04/26
May 17	05/27	06/01	06/06	06/11	06/16	06/21	07/01	07/16	10/04	05/07	05/03	04/27
May 18	05/28	06/02	06/07	06/12	06/17	06/22	07/02	07/17	10/05	05/08	05/04	04/28
May 19	05/29	06/03	06/08	06/13	06/18	06/23	07/03	07/18	10/06	05/09	05/05	04/29
May 20	05/30	06/04	06/09	06/14	06/19	06/24	07/04	07/19	10/07	05/10	05/06	04/30
May 21	05/31	06/05	06/10	06/15	06/20	06/25	07/05	07/20	10/08	05/11	05/07	05/01
May 22	06/01	06/06	06/11	06/16	06/21	06/26	07/06	07/21	10/09	05/12	05/08	05/02
May 23	06/02	06/07	06/12	06/17	06/22	06/27	07/07	07/22	10/10	05/13	05/09	05/03
May 24	06/03	06/08	06/13	06/18	06/23	06/28	07/08	07/23	10/11	05/14	05/10	05/04
May 25	06/04	06/09	06/14	06/19	06/24	06/29	07/09	07/24	10/12	05/15	05/11	05/05
May 26	06/05	06/10	06/15	06/20	06/25	06/30	07/10	07/25	10/13	05/16	05/12	05/06
May 27	06/06	06/11	06/16	06/21	06/26	07/01	07/11	07/26	10/14	05/17	05/13	05/07
May 28	06/07	06/12	06/17	06/22	06/27	07/02	07/12	07/27	10/15	05/18	05/14	05/08
May 29	06/08	06/13	06/18	06/23	06/28	07/03	07/13	07/28	10/16	05/19	05/15	05/09
May 30	06/09	06/14	06/19	06/24	06/29	07/04	07/14	07/29	10/17	05/20	05/16	05/10
May 31	06/10	06/15	06/20	06/25	06/30	07/05	07/15	07/30	10/18	05/21	05/17	05/11
June 01	06/11	06/16	06/21	06/26	07/01	07/06	07/16	07/31	10/19	05/22	05/18	05/12
June 02	06/12	06/17	06/22	06/27	07/02	07/07	07/17	08/01	10/20	05/23	05/19	05/13
June 03	06/13	06/18	06/23	06/28	07/03	07/08	07/18	08/02	10/21	05/24	05/20	05/14
June 04	06/14	06/19	06/24	06/29	07/04	07/09	07/19	08/03	10/22	05/25	05/21	05/15
June 05	06/15	06/20	06/25	06/30	07/05	07/10	07/20	08/04	10/23	05/26	05/22	05/16
June 06	06/16	06/21	06/26	07/01	07/06	07/11	07/21	08/05	10/24	05/27	05/23	05/17
June 07	06/17	06/22	06/27	07/02	07/07	07/12	07/22	08/06	10/25	05/28	05/24	05/18
June 08	06/18	06/23	06/28	07/03	07/08	07/13	07/23	08/07	10/26	05/29	05/25	05/19
June 09	06/19	06/24	06/29	07/04	07/09	07/14	07/24	08/08	10/27	05/30	05/26	05/20
June 10	06/20	06/25	06/30	07/05	07/10	07/15	07/25	08/09	10/28	05/31	05/27	05/21
June 11	06/21	06/26	07/01	07/06	07/11	07/16	07/26	08/10	10/29	06/01	05/28	05/22
June 12	06/22	06/27	07/02	07/07	07/12	07/17	07/27	08/11	10/30	06/02	05/29	05/23
June 13	06/23	06/28	07/03	07/08	07/13	07/18	07/28	08/12	10/31	06/03	05/30	05/24
June 14	06/24	06/29	07/04	07/09	07/14	07/19	07/29	08/13	11/01	06/04	05/31	05/25
June 15	06/25	06/30	07/05	07/10	07/15	07/20	07/30	08/14	11/02	06/05	06/01	05/26
June 16	06/26	07/01	07/06	07/11	07/16	07/21	07/31	08/15	11/03	06/06	06/02	05/27
June 17	06/27	07/02	07/07	07/12	07/17	07/22	08/01	08/16	11/04	06/07	06/03	05/28
June 18	06/28	07/03	07/08	07/13	07/18	07/23	08/02	08/17	11/05	06/08	06/04	05/29
June 19	06/29	07/04	07/09	07/14	07/19	07/24	08/03	08/18	11/06	06/09	06/05	05/30
June 20	06/30	07/05	07/10	07/15	07/20	07/25	08/04	08/19	11/07	06/10	06/06	05/31
June 21	07/01	07/06	07/11	07/16	07/21	07/26	08/05	08/20	11/08	06/11	06/07	06/01
June 22	07/02	07/07	07/12	07/17	07/22	07/27	08/06	08/21	11/09	06/12	06/08	06/02
June 23	07/03	07/08	07/13	07/18	07/23	07/28	08/07	08/22	11/10	06/13	06/09	06/03
June 24	07/04	07/09	07/14	07/19	07/24	07/29	08/08	08/23	11/11	06/14	06/10	06/04
June 25	07/05	07/10	07/15	07/20	07/25	07/30	08/09	08/24	11/12	06/15	06/11	06/05
June 26	07/06	07/11	07/16	07/21	07/26	07/31	08/10	08/25	11/13	06/16	06/12	06/06
June 27	07/07	07/12	07/17	07/22	07/27	08/01	08/11	08/26	11/14	06/17	06/13	06/07
June 28	07/08	07/13	07/18	07/23	07/28	08/02	08/12	08/27	11/15	06/18	06/14	06/08

Date	+10	+15	+20	+25	+30	+35	+45	+60	+140	−10	−14	−20
June 29	07/09	07/14	07/19	07/24	07/29	08/03	08/13	08/28	11/16	06/19	06/15	06/09
June 30	07/10	07/15	07/20	07/25	07/30	08/04	08/14	08/29	11/17	06/20	06/16	06/10
July 01	07/11	07/16	07/21	07/26	07/31	08/05	08/15	08/30	11/18	06/21	06/17	06/11
July 02	07/12	07/17	07/22	07/27	08/01	08/06	08/16	08/31	11/19	06/22	06/18	06/12
July 03	07/13	07/18	07/23	07/28	08/02	08/07	08/17	09/01	11/20	06/23	06/19	06/13
July 04	07/14	07/19	07/24	07/29	08/03	08/08	08/18	09/02	11/21	06/24	06/20	06/14
July 05	07/15	07/20	07/25	07/30	08/04	08/09	08/19	09/03	11/22	06/25	06/21	06/15
July 06	07/16	07/21	07/26	07/31	08/05	08/10	08/20	09/04	11/23	06/26	06/22	06/16
July 07	07/17	07/22	07/27	08/01	08/06	08/11	08/21	09/05	11/24	06/27	06/23	06/17
July 08	07/18	07/23	07/28	08/02	08/07	08/12	08/22	09/06	11/25	06/28	06/24	06/18
July 09	07/19	07/24	07/29	08/03	08/08	08/13	08/23	09/07	11/26	06/29	06/25	06/19
July 10	07/20	07/25	07/30	08/04	08/09	08/14	08/24	09/08	11/27	06/30	06/26	06/20
July 11	07/21	07/26	07/31	08/05	08/10	08/15	08/25	09/09	11/28	07/01	06/27	06/21
July 12	07/22	07/27	08/01	08/06	08/11	08/16	08/26	09/10	11/29	07/02	06/28	06/22
July 13	07/23	07/28	08/02	08/07	08/12	08/17	08/27	09/11	11/30	07/03	06/29	06/23
July 14	07/24	07/29	08/03	08/08	08/13	08/18	08/28	09/12	12/01	07/04	06/30	06/24
July 15	07/25	07/30	08/04	08/09	08/14	08/19	08/29	09/13	12/02	07/05	07/01	06/25
July 16	07/26	07/31	08/05	08/10	08/15	08/20	08/30	09/14	12/03	07/06	07/02	06/26
July 17	07/27	08/01	08/06	08/11	08/16	08/21	08/31	09/15	12/04	07/07	07/03	06/27
July 18	07/28	08/02	08/07	08/12	08/17	08/22	09/01	09/16	12/05	07/08	07/04	06/28
July 19	07/29	08/03	08/08	08/13	08/18	08/23	09/02	09/17	12/06	07/09	07/05	06/29
July 20	07/30	08/04	08/09	08/14	08/19	08/24	09/03	09/18	12/07	07/10	07/06	06/30
July 21	07/31	08/05	08/10	08/15	08/20	08/25	09/04	09/19	12/08	07/11	07/07	07/01
July 22	08/01	08/06	08/11	08/16	08/21	08/26	09/05	09/20	12/09	07/12	07/08	07/02
July 23	08/02	08/07	08/12	08/17	08/22	08/27	09/06	09/21	12/10	07/13	07/09	07/03
July 24	08/03	08/08	08/13	08/18	08/23	08/28	09/07	09/22	12/11	07/14	07/10	07/04
July 25	08/04	08/09	08/14	08/19	08/24	08/29	09/08	09/23	12/12	07/15	07/11	07/05
July 26	08/05	08/10	08/15	08/20	08/25	08/30	09/09	09/24	12/13	07/16	07/12	07/06
July 27	08/06	08/11	08/16	08/21	08/26	08/31	09/10	09/25	12/14	07/17	07/13	07/07
July 28	08/07	08/12	08/17	08/22	08/27	09/01	09/11	09/26	12/15	07/18	07/14	07/08
July 29	08/08	08/13	08/18	08/23	08/28	09/02	09/12	09/27	12/16	07/19	07/15	07/09
July 30	08/09	08/14	08/19	08/24	08/29	09/03	09/13	09/28	12/17	07/20	07/16	07/10
July 31	08/10	08/15	08/20	08/25	08/30	09/04	09/14	09/29	12/18	07/21	07/17	07/11
Aug 01	08/11	08/16	08/21	08/26	08/31	09/05	09/15	09/30	12/19	07/22	07/18	07/12
Aug 02	08/12	08/17	08/22	08/27	09/01	09/06	09/16	10/01	12/20	07/23	07/19	07/13
Aug 03	08/13	08/18	08/23	08/28	09/02	09/07	09/17	10/02	12/21	07/24	07/20	07/14
Aug 04	08/14	08/19	08/24	08/29	09/03	09/08	09/18	10/03	12/22	07/25	07/21	07/15
Aug 05	08/15	08/20	08/25	08/30	09/04	09/09	09/19	10/04	12/23	07/26	07/22	07/16
Aug 06	08/16	08/21	08/26	08/31	09/05	09/10	09/20	10/05	12/24	07/27	07/23	07/17
Aug 07	08/17	08/22	08/27	09/01	09/06	09/11	09/21	10/06	12/25	07/28	07/24	07/18
Aug 08	08/18	08/23	08/28	09/02	09/07	09/12	09/22	10/07	12/26	07/29	07/25	07/19
Aug 09	08/19	08/24	08/29	09/03	09/08	09/13	09/23	10/08	12/27	07/30	07/26	07/20
Aug 10	08/20	08/25	08/30	09/04	09/09	09/14	09/24	10/09	12/28	07/31	07/27	07/21
Aug 11	08/21	08/26	08/31	09/05	09/10	09/15	09/25	10/10	12/29	08/01	07/28	07/22
Aug 12	08/22	08/27	09/01	09/06	09/11	09/16	09/26	10/11	12/30	08/02	07/29	07/23
Aug 13	08/23	08/28	09/02	09/07	09/12	09/17	09/27	10/12	12/31	08/03	07/30	07/24
Aug 14	08/24	08/29	09/03	09/08	09/13	09/18	09/28	10/13	01/01	08/04	07/31	07/25
Aug 15	08/25	08/30	09/04	09/09	09/14	09/19	09/29	10/14	01/02	08/05	08/01	07/26
Aug 16	08/26	08/31	09/05	09/10	09/15	09/20	09/30	10/15	01/03	08/06	08/02	07/27
Aug 17	08/27	09/01	09/06	09/11	09/16	09/21	10/01	10/16	01/04	08/07	08/03	07/28

Date	+10	+15	+20	+25	+30	+35	+45	+60	+140	−10	−14	−20
Aug 18	08/28	09/02	09/07	09/12	09/17	09/22	10/02	10/17	01/05	08/08	08/04	07/29
Aug 19	08/29	09/03	09/08	09/13	09/18	09/23	10/03	10/18	01/06	08/09	08/05	07/30
Aug 20	08/30	09/04	09/09	09/14	09/19	09/24	10/04	10/19	01/07	08/10	08/06	07/31
Aug 21	08/31	09/05	09/10	09/15	09/20	09/25	10/05	10/20	01/08	08/11	08/07	08/01
Aug 22	09/01	09/06	09/11	09/16	09/21	09/26	10/06	10/21	01/09	08/12	08/08	08/02
Aug 23	09/02	09/07	09/12	09/17	09/22	09/27	10/07	10/22	01/10	08/13	08/09	08/03
Aug 24	09/03	09/08	09/13	09/18	09/23	09/28	10/08	10/23	01/11	08/14	08/10	08/04
Aug 25	09/04	09/09	09/14	09/19	09/24	09/29	10/09	10/24	01/12	08/15	08/11	08/05
Aug 26	09/05	09/10	09/15	09/20	09/25	09/30	10/10	10/25	01/13	08/16	08/12	08/06
Aug 27	09/06	09/11	09/16	09/21	09/26	10/01	10/11	10/26	01/14	08/17	08/13	08/07
Aug 28	09/07	09/12	09/17	09/22	09/27	10/02	10/12	10/27	01/15	08/18	08/14	08/08
Aug 29	09/08	09/13	09/18	09/23	09/28	10/03	10/13	10/28	01/16	08/19	08/15	08/09
Aug 30	09/09	09/14	09/19	09/24	09/29	10/04	10/14	10/29	01/17	08/20	08/16	08/10
Aug 31	09/10	09/15	09/20	09/25	09/30	10/05	10/15	10/30	01/18	08/21	08/17	08/11
Sep 01	09/11	09/16	09/21	09/26	10/01	10/06	10/16	10/31	01/19	08/22	08/18	08/12
Sep 02	09/12	09/17	09/22	09/27	10/02	10/07	10/17	11/01	01/20	08/23	08/19	08/13
Sep 03	09/13	09/18	09/23	09/28	10/03	10/08	10/18	11/02	01/21	08/24	08/20	08/14
Sep 04	09/14	09/19	09/24	09/29	10/04	10/09	10/19	11/03	01/22	08/25	08/21	08/15
Sep 05	09/15	09/20	09/25	09/30	10/05	10/10	10/20	11/04	01/23	08/26	08/22	08/16
Sep 06	09/16	09/21	09/26	10/01	10/06	10/11	10/21	11/05	01/24	08/27	08/23	08/17
Sep 07	09/17	09/22	09/27	10/02	10/07	10/12	10/22	11/06	01/25	08/28	08/24	08/18
Sep 08	09/18	09/23	09/28	10/03	10/08	10/13	10/23	11/07	01/26	08/29	08/25	08/19
Sep 09	09/19	09/24	09/29	10/04	10/09	10/14	10/24	11/08	01/27	08/30	08/26	08/20
Sep 10	09/20	09/25	09/30	10/05	10/10	10/15	10/25	11/09	01/28	08/31	08/27	08/21
Sep 11	09/21	09/26	10/01	10/06	10/11	10/16	10/26	11/10	01/29	09/01	08/28	08/22
Sep 12	09/22	09/27	10/02	10/07	10/12	10/17	10/27	11/11	01/30	09/02	08/29	08/23
Sep 13	09/23	09/28	10/03	10/08	10/13	10/18	10/28	11/12	01/31	09/03	08/30	08/24
Sep 14	09/24	09/29	10/04	10/09	10/14	10/19	10/29	11/13	02/01	09/04	08/31	08/25
Sep 15	09/25	09/30	10/05	10/10	10/15	10/20	10/30	11/14	02/02	09/05	09/01	08/26
Sep 16	09/26	10/01	10/06	10/11	10/16	10/21	10/31	11/15	02/03	09/06	09/02	08/27
Sep 17	09/27	10/02	10/07	10/12	10/17	10/22	11/01	11/16	02/04	09/07	09/03	08/28
Sep 18	09/28	10/03	10/08	10/13	10/18	10/23	11/02	11/17	02/05	09/08	09/04	08/29
Sep 19	09/29	10/04	10/09	10/14	10/19	10/24	11/03	11/18	02/06	09/09	09/05	08/30
Sep 20	09/30	10/05	10/10	10/15	10/20	10/25	11/04	11/19	02/07	09/10	09/06	08/31
Sep 21	10/01	10/06	10/11	10/16	10/21	10/26	11/05	11/20	02/08	09/11	09/07	09/01
Sep 22	10/02	10/07	10/12	10/17	10/22	10/27	11/06	11/21	02/09	09/12	09/08	09/02
Sep 23	10/03	10/08	10/13	10/18	10/23	10/28	11/07	11/22	02/10	09/13	09/09	09/03
Sep 24	10/04	10/09	10/14	10/19	10/24	10/29	11/08	11/23	02/11	09/14	09/10	09/04
Sep 25	10/05	10/10	10/15	10/20	10/25	10/30	11/09	11/24	02/12	09/15	09/11	09/05
Sep 26	10/06	10/11	10/16	10/21	10/26	10/31	11/10	11/25	02/13	09/16	09/12	09/06
Sep 27	10/07	10/12	10/17	10/22	10/27	11/01	11/11	11/26	02/14	09/17	09/13	09/07
Sep 28	10/08	10/13	10/18	10/23	10/28	11/02	11/12	11/27	02/15	09/18	09/14	09/08
Sep 29	10/09	10/14	10/19	10/24	10/29	11/03	11/13	11/28	02/16	09/19	09/15	09/09
Sep 30	10/10	10/15	10/20	10/25	10/30	11/04	11/14	11/29	02/17	09/20	09/16	09/10
Oct 01	10/11	10/16	10/21	10/26	10/31	11/05	11/15	11/30	02/18	09/21	09/17	09/11
Oct 02	10/12	10/17	10/22	10/27	11/01	11/06	11/16	12/01	02/19	09/22	09/18	09/12
Oct 03	10/13	10/18	10/23	10/28	11/02	11/07	11/17	12/02	02/20	09/23	09/19	09/13
Oct 04	10/14	10/19	10/24	10/29	11/03	11/08	11/18	12/03	02/21	09/24	09/20	09/14
Oct 05	10/15	10/20	10/25	10/30	11/04	11/09	11/19	12/04	02/22	09/25	09/21	09/15
Oct 06	10/16	10/21	10/26	10/31	11/05	11/10	11/20	12/05	02/23	09/26	09/22	09/16

Date	+10	+15	+20	+25	+30	+35	+45	+60	+140	−10	−14	−20
Oct 07	10/17	10/22	10/27	11/01	11/06	11/11	11/21	12/06	02/24	09/27	09/23	09/17
Oct 08	10/18	10/23	10/28	11/02	11/07	11/12	11/22	12/07	02/25	09/28	09/24	09/18
Oct 09	10/19	10/24	10/29	11/03	11/08	11/13	11/23	12/08	02/26	09/29	09/25	09/19
Oct 10	10/20	10/25	10/30	11/04	11/09	11/14	11/24	12/09	02/27	09/30	09/26	09/20
Oct 11	10/21	10/26	10/31	11/05	11/10	11/15	11/25	12/10	02/28	10/01	09/27	09/21
Oct 12	10/22	10/27	11/01	11/06	11/11	11/16	11/26	12/11	03/01	10/02	09/28	09/22
Oct 13	10/23	10/28	11/02	11/07	11/12	11/17	11/27	12/12	03/02	10/03	09/29	09/23
Oct 14	10/24	10/29	11/03	11/08	11/13	11/18	11/28	12/13	03/03	10/04	09/30	09/24
Oct 15	10/25	10/30	11/04	11/09	11/14	11/19	11/29	12/14	03/04	10/05	10/01	09/25
Oct 16	10/26	10/31	11/05	11/10	11/15	11/20	11/30	12/15	03/05	10/06	10/02	09/26
Oct 17	10/27	11/01	11/06	11/11	11/16	11/21	12/01	12/16	03/06	10/07	10/03	09/27
Oct 18	10/28	11/02	11/07	11/12	11/17	11/22	12/02	12/17	03/07	10/08	10/04	09/28
Oct 19	10/29	11/03	11/08	11/13	11/18	11/23	12/03	12/18	03/08	10/09	10/05	09/29
Oct 20	10/30	11/04	11/09	11/14	11/19	11/24	12/04	12/19	03/09	10/10	10/06	09/30
Oct 21	10/31	11/05	11/10	11/15	11/20	11/25	12/05	12/20	03/10	10/11	10/07	10/01
Oct 22	11/01	11/06	11/11	11/16	11/21	11/26	12/06	12/21	03/11	10/12	10/08	10/02
Oct 23	11/02	11/07	11/12	11/17	11/22	11/27	12/07	12/22	03/12	10/13	10/09	10/03
Oct 24	11/03	11/08	11/13	11/18	11/23	11/28	12/08	12/23	03/13	10/14	10/10	10/04
Oct 25	11/04	11/09	11/14	11/19	11/24	11/29	12/09	12/24	03/14	10/15	10/11	10/05
Oct 26	11/05	11/10	11/15	11/20	11/25	11/30	12/10	12/25	03/15	10/16	10/12	10/06
Oct 27	11/06	11/11	11/16	11/21	11/26	12/01	12/11	12/26	03/16	10/17	10/13	10/07
Oct 28	11/07	11/12	11/17	11/22	11/27	12/02	12/12	12/27	03/17	10/18	10/14	10/08
Oct 29	11/08	11/13	11/18	11/23	11/28	12/03	12/13	12/28	03/18	10/19	10/15	10/09
Oct 30	11/09	11/14	11/19	11/24	11/29	12/04	12/14	12/29	03/19	10/20	10/16	10/10
Oct 31	11/10	11/15	11/20	11/25	11/30	12/05	12/15	12/30	03/20	10/21	10/17	10/11
Nov 01	11/11	11/16	11/21	11/26	12/01	12/06	12/16	12/31	03/21	10/22	10/18	10/12
Nov 02	11/12	11/17	11/22	11/27	12/02	12/07	12/17	01/01	03/22	10/23	10/19	10/13
Nov 03	11/13	11/18	11/23	11/28	12/03	12/08	12/18	01/02	03/23	10/24	10/20	10/14
Nov 04	11/14	11/19	11/24	11/29	12/04	12/09	12/19	01/03	03/24	10/25	10/21	10/15
Nov 05	11/15	11/20	11/25	11/30	12/05	12/10	12/20	01/04	03/25	10/26	10/22	10/16
Nov 06	11/16	11/21	11/26	12/01	12/06	12/11	12/21	01/05	03/26	10/27	10/23	10/17
Nov 07	11/17	11/22	11/27	12/02	12/07	12/12	12/22	01/06	03/27	10/28	10/24	10/18
Nov 08	11/18	11/23	11/28	12/03	12/08	12/13	12/23	01/07	03/28	10/29	10/25	10/19
Nov 09	11/19	11/24	11/29	12/04	12/09	12/14	12/24	01/08	03/29	10/30	10/26	10/20
Nov 10	11/20	11/25	11/30	12/05	12/10	12/15	12/25	01/09	03/30	10/31	10/27	10/21
Nov 11	11/21	11/26	12/01	12/06	12/11	12/16	12/26	01/10	03/31	11/01	10/28	10/22
Nov 12	11/22	11/27	12/02	12/07	12/12	12/17	12/27	01/11	04/01	11/02	10/29	10/23
Nov 13	11/23	11/28	12/03	12/08	12/13	12/18	12/28	01/12	04/02	11/03	10/30	10/24
Nov 14	11/24	11/29	12/04	12/09	12/14	12/19	12/29	01/13	04/03	11/04	10/31	10/25
Nov 15	11/25	11/30	12/05	12/10	12/15	12/20	12/30	01/14	04/04	11/05	11/01	10/26
Nov 16	11/26	12/01	12/06	12/11	12/16	12/21	12/31	01/15	04/05	11/06	11/02	10/27
Nov 17	11/27	12/02	12/07	12/12	12/17	12/22	01/01	01/16	04/06	11/07	11/03	10/28
Nov 18	11/28	12/03	12/08	12/13	12/18	12/23	01/02	01/17	04/07	11/08	11/04	10/29
Nov 19	11/29	12/04	12/09	12/14	12/19	12/24	01/03	01/18	04/08	11/09	11/05	10/30
Nov 20	11/30	12/05	12/10	12/15	12/20	12/25	01/04	01/19	04/09	11/10	11/06	10/31
Nov 21	12/01	12/06	12/11	12/16	12/21	12/26	01/05	01/20	04/10	11/11	11/07	11/01
Nov 22	12/02	12/07	12/12	12/17	12/22	12/27	01/06	01/21	04/11	11/12	11/08	11/02
Nov 23	12/03	12/08	12/13	12/18	12/23	12/28	01/07	01/22	04/12	11/13	11/09	11/03
Nov 24	12/04	12/09	12/14	12/19	12/24	12/29	01/08	01/23	04/13	11/14	11/10	11/04
Nov 25	12/05	12/10	12/15	12/20	12/25	12/30	01/09	01/24	04/14	11/15	11/11	11/05

Date	+10	+15	+20	+25	+30	+35	+45	+60	+140	−10	−14	−20
Nov 26	12/06	12/11	12/16	12/21	12/26	12/31	01/10	01/25	04/15	11/16	11/12	11/06
Nov 27	12/07	12/12	12/17	12/22	12/27	01/01	01/11	01/26	04/16	11/17	11/13	11/07
Nov 28	12/08	12/13	12/18	12/23	12/28	01/02	01/12	01/27	04/17	11/18	11/14	11/08
Nov 29	12/09	12/14	12/19	12/24	12/29	01/03	01/13	01/28	04/18	11/19	11/15	11/09
Nov 30	12/10	12/15	12/20	12/25	12/30	01/04	01/14	01/29	04/19	11/20	11/16	11/10
Dec 01	12/11	12/16	12/21	12/26	12/31	01/05	01/15	01/30	04/20	11/21	11/17	11/11
Dec 02	12/12	12/17	12/22	12/27	01/01	01/06	01/16	01/31	04/21	11/22	11/18	11/12
Dec 03	12/13	12/18	12/23	12/28	01/02	01/07	01/17	02/01	04/22	11/23	11/19	11/13
Dec 04	12/14	12/19	12/24	12/29	01/03	01/08	01/18	02/02	04/23	11/24	11/20	11/14
Dec 05	12/15	12/20	12/25	12/30	01/04	01/09	01/19	02/03	04/24	11/25	11/21	11/15
Dec 06	12/16	12/21	12/26	12/31	01/05	01/10	01/20	02/04	04/25	11/26	11/22	11/16
Dec 07	12/17	12/22	12/27	01/01	01/06	01/11	01/21	02/05	04/26	11/27	11/23	11/17
Dec 08	12/18	12/23	12/28	01/02	01/07	01/12	01/22	02/06	04/27	11/28	11/24	11/18
Dec 09	12/19	12/24	12/29	01/03	01/08	01/13	01/23	02/07	04/28	11/29	11/25	11/19
Dec 10	12/20	12/25	12/30	01/04	01/09	01/14	01/24	02/08	04/29	11/30	11/26	11/20
Dec 11	12/21	12/26	12/31	01/05	01/10	01/15	01/25	02/09	04/30	12/01	11/27	11/21
Dec 12	12/22	12/27	01/01	01/06	01/11	01/16	01/26	02/10	05/01	12/02	11/28	11/22
Dec 13	12/23	12/28	01/02	01/07	01/12	01/17	01/27	02/11	05/02	12/03	11/29	11/23
Dec 14	12/24	12/29	01/03	01/08	01/13	01/18	01/28	02/12	05/03	12/04	11/30	11/24
Dec 15	12/25	12/30	01/04	01/09	01/14	01/19	01/29	02/13	05/04	12/05	12/01	11/25
Dec 16	12/26	12/31	01/05	01/10	01/15	01/20	01/30	02/14	05/05	12/06	12/02	11/26
Dec 17	12/27	01/01	01/06	01/11	01/16	01/21	01/31	02/15	05/06	12/07	12/03	11/27
Dec 18	12/28	01/02	01/07	01/12	01/17	01/22	02/01	02/16	05/07	12/08	12/04	11/28
Dec 19	12/29	01/03	01/08	01/13	01/18	01/23	02/02	02/17	05/08	12/09	12/05	11/29
Dec 20	12/30	01/04	01/09	01/14	01/19	01/24	02/03	02/18	05/09	12/10	12/06	11/30
Dec 21	12/31	01/05	01/10	01/15	01/20	01/25	02/04	02/19	05/10	12/11	12/07	12/01
Dec 22	01/01	01/06	01/11	01/16	01/21	01/26	02/05	02/20	05/11	12/12	12/08	12/02
Dec 23	01/02	01/07	01/12	01/17	01/22	01/27	02/06	02/21	05/12	12/13	12/09	12/03
Dec 24	01/03	01/08	01/13	01/18	01/23	01/28	02/07	02/22	05/13	12/14	12/10	12/04
Dec 25	01/04	01/09	01/14	01/19	01/24	01/29	02/08	02/23	05/14	12/15	12/11	12/05
Dec 26	01/05	01/10	01/15	01/20	01/25	01/30	02/09	02/24	05/15	12/16	12/12	12/06
Dec 27	01/06	01/11	01/16	01/21	01/26	01/31	02/10	02/25	05/16	12/17	12/13	12/07
Dec 22	01/07	01/12	01/17	01/22	01/27	02/01	02/11	02/26	05/17	12/18	12/14	12/08
Dec 29	01/08	01/13	01/18	01/23	01/28	02/02	02/12	02/27	05/18	12/19	12/15	12/09
Dec 30	01/09	01/14	01/19	01/24	01/29	02/03	02/13	02/28	05/19	12/20	12/16	12/10
Dec 31	01/10	01/15	01/20	01/25	01/30	02/04	02/14	03/01	05/20	12/21	12/17	12/11

Bankruptcy Petition Preparers 11 U.S.C. § 110

§ 110. Penalty for persons who negligently or fraudulently prepare bankruptcy petitions.

(a) In this section—

  (1) "bankruptcy petition preparer" means a person, other than an attorney or an employee of an attorney, who prepares for compensation a document for filing; and

  (2) "document for filing" means a petition or any other document prepared for filing by a debtor in a United States bankruptcy court or a United States district court in connection with a case under this title.

(b) (1) A bankruptcy petition preparer who prepares a document for filing shall sign the document and print on the document the preparer's name and address.

  (2) A bankruptcy petition preparer who fails to comply with paragraph (1) may be fined not more than $500 for each such failure unless the failure is due to reasonable cause.

(c) (1) A bankruptcy petition preparer who prepares a document for filing shall place on the document, after the preparer's signature, an identifying number that identifies individuals who prepared the document.

  (2) For purposes of this section, the identifying number of a bankruptcy petition preparer shall be the Social Security account number of each individual who prepared the document or assisted in its preparation.

  (3) A bankruptcy petition preparer who fails to comply with paragraph (1) may be fined not more than $500 for each such failure if the failure is due to reasonable cause.

(d) (1) A bankruptcy petition preparer shall, not later than the time which a document for filing is presented for the debtor's signature, furnish to the debtor a copy of the document.

  (2) A bankruptcy petition preparer who fails to comply with paragraph (1) may be fined not more than $500 for each such failure unless the failure is due to reasonable cause.

(e) (1) A bankruptcy petition preparer shall not execute any document on behalf of a debtor.

  (2) A bankruptcy petition preparer may be fined not more than $500 for each document executed in violation of paragraph (1).

(f) (1) A bankruptcy petition preparer shall not use the word "legal" or any similar term in any advertisements, or advertise under any category that includes the word "legal" or any similar term.

  (2) A bankruptcy petition preparer shall be fined not more than $500 for each violation of paragraph (1).

(g) (1) A bankruptcy petition preparer shall not collect or receive any payment from the debtor or on behalf of the debtor for the court fees in connection with filing the petition.

  (2) A bankruptcy petition preparer shall be fined not more than $500 for each violation of paragraph (1).

(h) (1) Within 10 days after the date of the filing of a petition, a bankruptcy petition preparer shall file a declaration under penalty of perjury disclosing any fee received from or on behalf of the debtor within 12 months immediately prior to the filing of the case, and any unpaid fee charged to the debtor.

  (2) The court shall disallow and order the immediate turnover to the bankruptcy trustee of any fee revalue of services rendered for the documents prepared. An individual debtor may exempt any funds so recovered under section 522(b).

  (3) The debtor, the trustee, a creditor, or the United States trustee may file a motion for an order under paragraph (2).

  (4) A bankruptcy petition preparer shall be fined not more than $500 for each failure to comply with a court order to turn over funds within 30 days of service of such order.

(i) (1) If bankruptcy case or related proceeding is dismissed because of the failure to file bankruptcy papers, including papers specified in section 521(1) of this title, the negligence of intentional disregard of this title or the Federal Rules of Bankruptcy Procedure by a bankruptcy petition preparer, or if a bankruptcy petition preparer violates this section or commits any fraudulent, unfair, or deceptive act, the bankruptcy court shall certify that fact to the district court, and the district court, on motion of the debtor, the trustee, or the creditor and after a hearing, shall order the bankruptcy petition preparer to pay the debtor—

(A) the debtor's actual damages;

(B) the greater of—

(i) $2,000; or

(ii) twice the amount paid by the debtor to the bankruptcy petition preparer for the preparer's services; and

(C) reasonable attorneys' fees and costs in moving for damages under this subsection.

(2) If the trustee or creditor moves for damages on behalf of the debtor under this subsection, the bankruptcy petition preparer shall be ordered to pay the movant the additional amount of $1,000 plus reasonable attorneys' fees and costs incurred.

(j) (1) A debtor for whom a bankruptcy petition preparer has prepared a document for filing, the trustee, a creditor, or the United States trustee in the district in which the bankruptcy petition preparer resides, has conducted business, or the United States trustee in any other district in which the debtor resides may bring a civil action to enjoin a bankruptcy petition preparer from engaging in any conduct in violation of this section or from further acting as a bankruptcy petition preparer.

(2) (A) In an acting under paragraph (1), if the court finds that—

(i) a bankruptcy petition preparer has—

(I) engaged in conduct in violation of this section or of any provision of this title a violation of which subjects a person to criminal penalty;

(II) misrepresented the preparer's experience or education as a bankruptcy petition preparer; or

(III) engaged in any other fraudulent, unfair, or deceptive conduct; and

(ii) injunctive relief is appropriate to prevent the recurrence of such conduct,

the court may enjoin the bankruptcy petition preparer from engaging in such conduct.

(B) If the court finds that a bankruptcy petition preparer has continually engaged in conduct described in subclause (I), (II), or (III) of subclause (I) and that injunction prohibiting such conduct would not be sufficient to prevent such person's interference with the proper administration of this title, or has not paid a penalty imposed under this section, the court may enjoin the person from acting as a bankruptcy petition preparer.

(3) The court shall award to a debtor, trustee, or creditor that brings a successful action under this subsection reasonable attorney's fees and costs of the action, to be paid by the bankruptcy petition preparer.

(k) Nothing in this section shall be constructed to permit activities that are otherwise prohibited by law, including rules and laws that prohibit the unauthorized practice of law.

Bibliography

Chapter 1

Anderson, Eugene, Randy Paar, and Joshua Gold. "Safety Net May Not Hold." *National Law Journal,* October 9, 1995.

Beardsley, Dee. "Leveling the Playing Field." @ *LAW,* spring 1997.

Blodgett, Nancy. "How Best to Organize a Law Firm." *Legal Management,* March/April 1995.

Brewster, Christopher. "Kids May Be Polled if Parents Are Told." *Legal Management,* December 1997.

Coburn, Jeff. "Practice Group Planning—the New Frontier." *Legal Management,* March/April 1995.

Cox, Gail Diane. "Now, It's Jacoby vs. Meyers." *National Law Journal,* July 15, 1995.

Denny, Robert. "Developing Managers." *Legal Management,* July/August 1998.

Donovan, Karen. "Should SEC Cases Await DOJ Action?" *National Law Journal,* March 24, 1997.

Editor. "An 'Eat What You Kill' Ethos Can Harm Law Firms." *National Law Journal,* June 16, 1997.

Editor. "First Interactive Legal Brief Filed." *Legal Management,* March/April 1997.

Editor. "Organizing Your Practice for Success and Avoiding Malpractice Claims." *Law Practice Management Solutions,* autumn 1995.

Editor. "Paralegals Online." *Legal Assistant Today,* January/February 1998.

Editor. "Practice Area Growth." *Of Counsel,* April 21, 1997.

Editor. "Preliminary of Counsel 700 Survey Data Shows Shrewd Niche Marketing by Firms Nationwide." *Of Counsel* 16, no. 8 (April 1997).

Editor. "A Sample of Recent General Trends." *Law Practice Management Solutions,* autumn 1995.

Fisk, Margaret Cronin. "What Lawyers Earn." *National Law Journal,* July 15, 1996.

———. "What's Hot in the Job Market?" *National Law Journal,* August 23, 1999.

Foreman, Johnathon. "Seeking the Best, Both In-House and Outhouse." *National Law Journal,* December 2, 1996.

———. "Working out Relations with Outside Counsel." *National Law Journal,* March 24, 1997.

France, Mike. "Legal Clinics: Lights Go out for Store Fronts." *National Law Journal,* December 12, 1994.

———. "Administrative Law Tops Earnings List." *National Law Journal,* June 27, 1995.

———. "IP's Hot, Tax Is Not, in Mid-'90s Practice." *National Law Journal,* February 26, 1996.

Galbenski, David J. "'Tis the Season to Be in IP Law." *National Law Journal,* August 23, 1999.

Griffith, Cary. "Knowledge to the Nth Power." *Legal Management,* September/October 1996.

Hayes, Arthur S. "ABA Group: Change in the Air." *National Law Journal,* June 27, 1995.

Hazard, Geoffrey C. "The Firm's Muddy Mission." *National Law Journal,* July 15, 1995.

Hildebrant, Bradford W. "Learning from Firms That Failed." *National Law Journal,* April 25, 1994.

Ibelle, Bill. "Temp Lawyers: Should You Hire One?" *Lawyers Weekly USA,* March 10, 1997.

Klein, Chris. "Associate Job 1: Land Clients." *National Law Journal,* March 31, 1997.

Leibowitz, Wendy R. "Go Solo, Go High-Tech." *National Law Journal,* March 8, 1999.

Petropulos, Diane. "Choosing a Legal Specialty." *Legal Assistant Today,* May/June 1993.

———. "Paralegal Jobs beyond the Law Office." *Legal Assistant Today,* May/June 1997.

Resnick, Rosalind. "Cybertort: The New Era." *National Law Journal,* July 18, 1994.

Rovella, David E. "Non-Traditionals Surge in New Legal Market." *National Law Journal,* October 9, 1995.

Smith, William Carl. "A Sociologist's Look at Small-Firm Lawyers." *Lawyers Weekly USA,* March 10, 1997.

Smock, John. "Feeling Short Handed." *Legal Management,* January/February 1998.

Stock, Richard G. "Reaching over the Border." *Legal Management,* May/June 1996.

———. "Tools to Navigate a Firm Plan." *Legal Management,* November/December 1996.

Stoddard, Debbie. "Little Firm on the Prairie." @*LAW,* spring 1997.

Van Duch, Darryl L. "Some Firms Hesitate to Adopt L.L.P." *National Law Journal,* May 5, 1997.

Whiteside, Frances B. "Career Alternatives for Paralegals." *Legal Assistant Today,* January/February 1993.

———. "Dinner at Dux." *The Legal Professional Career News,* spring 1994.

———. "Paralegal Roles and Responsibilities." *National Paralegal Reporter,* fall 1998.

Chapter 2

Anderson, Robert. "All That Glitters." *Legal Management,* January/February 1996.

Arron, Deborah. "Temping Is Big, Even for Hot-Shots." *National Law Journal,* April 12, 1999.

Barge, Jeff. "Paralegals Make 'Partner.' " *Legal Assistant Today,* May/June 1996.

Behan, Kevin J. "Small Firms Require More." *Legal Assistant Today,* May/June 1997.

Blazek, Glenn E. "Court Reporters Now Offer a Diversity of Services." *National Law Journal,* Monday, September 22, 1997.

Blodgett, Nancy. "Back-Up Child Care Centers for Law Firms on the Rise." *Legal Management,* November/December 1993.

Carrier, Pamela Hastings. "Family and Medical Leave Act of 1993." *Orange County Paralegal Association Compendium,* July 1994.

Cazares, Leanne, and Nicole Kording. "For Love or Money." *Legal Assistant Today,* January/February 1997.

Coburn, Jeff. "The Changing Role of the Large Firm Administrator." *Legal Management,* November/December 1993.

Cohn, Steven. "California Association Proposes Specialty Exams, Certification." *Legal Assistant Today,* March/April 1994.

———. "NALA Survey Shows Paralegals Changing Jobs Sooner." *Legal Assistant Today,* March/April 1994.

———. "Land of the Giants." *Legal Assistant Today,* March/April 1995.

Conrad, Sherri L., and Ronald E. Mallen. "Legal Profession." *National Law Journal,* July 17, 1995.

Conti, Al. "The Administrator as Coach: Developing a Winning Team." *Legal Management,* May/June 1997.

Coyle, Marcia. "Panic over Definition of 'Partner.' " *National Law Journal,* May 26, 1997.

Damp, Dennis. "General Schedule—White Collar/Professional/Administative." *Internet Career Connection,* October 31, 1998.

Davis, Ann. "Rainmakers Score High on Test." *National Law Journal,* September 30, 1996.

Donovan, Karen. "Firms Shed '&'s and Commas." *National Law Journal,* August 1996.

Editor. "ALA Announces Certification for Legal Managers." *Legal Management,* May/June 1997.

Editor. "End the Secretary Shortage by Turning Top Secretaries into Practice Mangers." *Law Office Administrator,* December 1997.

Editor. "Firm Environment and Utilization." http://www.nala.org/Sec.2web.htm, August 13, 1998.

Editor. "Floaters Are an Alternative to Temporary Staffing." *Law Office Administrator,* September 1997.

Editor. "Getting Along." *National Law Journal,* June 17, 1996.

Editor. "*Handbook on Paralegal Utilization.*" California Alliance of Paralegal Associations, July 1997.

Editor. "In the Courts." *The Legal Professional Career News,* fall 1994.

Editor. "Lawsuits Filed against Paralegal Businesses." *National Federation of Paralegal Assistants Reporter,* January 1998.

Editor. "Model Guidelines for the Utilization of Legal Assistant Services." American Bar Association Standing Committee on Legal Assistants, August 19, 1997.

Editor. "New ABA Definition of 'Legal Assistant.' " American Bar Association Standing Committee on Legal Assistants, August 19, 1997.

Editor. "New York's Finest Law Firms." *Legal Assistant Today,* May/June 1996.

Editor. "Paralegal Compensation and Benefits Report." National Federation of Paralegal Associations, November 1997.

Editor. "The Role of the Senior Administrator—Does Law Firm Size Make a Difference?" *Law Practice Management,* December 1995.

Editor. "'Round the Industry." *Legal Management,* January/February 1998.

Editor. "Schaming Congratulates History's First Certified Legal Managers: 11 Pass First CLM Exam." *Legal Management,* January/February 1998.

Editor. "Special Report." *American Library Association News,* November/December 1996.

Editor. "Survey Finds Interpersonal Skills Most Important for Administrator Success." *Legal Assistant Today,* November/December 1997.

Editor. "The Surveys Say!" *Legal Management,* May/June 1997.

Editor. "The Traditional Law Partnership Track: Does It Still Exist? Quo Vadis?" *Law Practice Management,* December 1995.

Editor. "Where Is the Profession Today?" *National Paralegal Reporter,* December 1997.

Emmons, Natasha. "ABA Refines Definition of Paralegal." *Legal Assistant Today,* January/February 1998.

———. "ABA Paralegal Utilization Survey Reveals Trends." *Legal Assistant Today,* November/December 1998.

Evans, James. "Legal Sites: Paralegal Resources." *California Lawyer,* January 1998.

Evans, Larry. "Ten Commandments for Legal Secretaries." *The Docket,* July/August 1998.

Finkelstein, James. "MJL Founder Looks Back at Profession's Changes." *National Law Journal,* September 21, 1998.

Foonberg, Jay G. "Telephone Receptionists: Marketing's Front Line." *National Law Journal,* April 25, 1994.

Garber, Chris, Marisella Jorgenson, and Rita Madnick. "1997 OCPA Salary Survey." Orange County Paralegal Association, September 15, 1997.

Gladwell, Gina M. "The Issues Affecting Paralegals Then and Now." *Legal Assistant Today,* September/October 1997.

Healy, Deborah J. "Are You a Paralegal? Or Are You a Banker?" *National Paralegal Reporter,* fall 1998.

Hershkowitz, William. "Career Comparison between Paralegals/Secretaries." *Legal Assistant Today,* May/June 1998.

Horowitz, Jay B., and William Kummel. "Improve Profit through Contract Legal Services." *Accounting for Law Firms* 10, no. B (August 1997).

Hunt, Stacey. "The Paralegal as Office Manager? You Bet!" *Orange County Paralegal Association Compendium,* July 1994.

Infanti, Patricia E. "Now Is the Time for All Legal Secretaries to Go Back to School." @ *LAW,* fall 1998.

Kanofsky, Florence. "Legal Administrators Today: Success Strategies for a Changing Profession." *Legal Management,* September/October 1995.

Kaufman, Monty. "Outsourcing—Once a Curiosity, Now a Necessity." *Legal Management,* January/February 1995.

Klein, Chris. "Big-Firm Partners: Profession Sinking." *National Law Journal,* May 26, 1997.

Kummel, William, and Jay B. Horowitz. "Short Time Gone." *Legal Management,* September/October 1996.

Leiter, Richard. "Your Role as Librarian." *Legal Assistant Today,* January/February 1997.

Leonard, Cari A., and Charles E. Stinnett. "Legal Administrators in the New Millenium." *Legal Management,* November/December 1998.

Lurie, Sylvia. "Legal Administrators Rate Their Quality of Life." *Legal Management,* November/December 1993.

———. "The Quality of Life among Legal Administrators." *Legal Management,* September/October 1994.

Mallen, Ronald E. "Of Counsel, Affiliates May Trigger Firm Liability." *National Law Journal,* November 10, 1997.

McClean, Frances M. "What Will the Legal Secretary Need to Know to Be Successful in the Year 2000?" @ *LAW,* fall 1996.

Melhe, Kathy. "Visiting the Year 2005." *National Paralegal Reporter,* December 1997.

Messmer, Max. "Alleviate the Full-Time Press." *Legal Management,* September/October 1996.

Middleton, Martha. "Firms Find New Ways to Save." *National Law Journal,* January 24, 1995.

Miller, Nancy. "Administration 2000." *Legal Management,* September/October 1996.

National Federation of Paralegal Associations. "NFPA's Internet Connection," *The Reporter,* December 1997.

Orlik, Deborah K. "A Career Alternative for Beginning Paralegals." *Legal Assistant Today,* January/February 1998.

Petropulos, Diane. "A Step in the Right Direction." *Legal Assistant Today,* January/February 1998.

Rowland, Caroline. "Freelance Paralegals: Fees Upheld in California." *Paralegal Headliner,* December 1993.

Shepherd, Ritchenya. "Law Firm Management." *National Law Journal,* October 5, 1998.

Slind-Flor, Victoria. "A Piece of the Action." *National Law Journal,* June 17, 1996.

Solomon, Robin. "No Satisfaction?" *National Paralegal Reporter,* December 1997.

Sparrow, Vince, and Ron Stratton. "Strategic Outsourcing." *Legal Management,* July/August 1995.

Sperber, Robert. "58% Paralegal Job Increase by Year 2005." *Legal Assistant Today,* May/June 1997.

———. "In-House Intellectual Property Paralegals Net Big Bucks." *Legal Assistant Today,* May/June 1997.

Stell, Camille Stucky. "North Carolina Bar Association Forms Legal Assistants Division." *Legal Assistant Today,* January/February 1998.

Stock, Richard. "A Sense of Place." *Legal Assistant Today,* March/April 1996.

Wainess, Marcia Watson. "If You Build It, Will It Serve?" *Legal Management,* July/August 1998.

Walker, Bruce. "Legal Secretary Opportunities in Prosecutor's Office." *The Docket,* spring 1996.

Weidlich, Thom. "After Slump, Paralegal Work on Rebound." *National Law Journal,* April 25, 1994.

Weston, I. Perrin. "Additional Progress Made at October Conclave Meeting." *Legal Assistant Today,* January/February 1998.

———. "Paralegal Certificate v. Bachelor Degree." *Legal Assistant Today,* January/February 1998.

———. "Paralegal Student." *Legal Assistant Today,* January/February 1998.

Widoff, Shelly G. "Working the Night Shift." *Legal Assistant Today,* January/February 1998.

Wood, Steven M. "Experienced Legal Secretary Salaries Reaching Higher and Higher." *The Docket,* spring 1996.

Chapter 3

Abrahams, Sharon Meit. "Teach Your Employees Well." *Legal Management,* January/February 1998.

Atherton, Marjorie R. "What Is a Legal Administrator?" *Legal Management,* November 1986.

Baber, Brad. "The Road to In-House Training." *Legal Assistant Today,* January/February 1998.

Bauer, E.G. "Are You a Good Team Player?" *Working Together,* October 1996.

Blackwell, Mary Ann. "Five Steps to Ask for a Raise." *Law Office Administrator,* July 1998.

Blodgett, Nancy. "Self-Directed Work Teams: A New Way to Operate Your Business." *Legal Management,* September/October 1995.

Boone, Norlene. "Effective Staff Benefits Are Still Possible—Even on a Tight Budget." *Law Office Administrator,* August 1997.

Brashear, Sally. "You Are Not Alone." *Legal Management,* May/June 1997.

Brimm, Jack L. "Managerial Training: Don't Leave It to Chance." American Library Association, March/April 1996.

Brown, James G. "Law Office Current Labor Issues." *The Docket,* September/October 1994.

Burnett, Terrill Hill. "Mediation: An Effective Tool in Law Firm Management." *Legal Management,* March/April 1995.

Carey, Theresa W., Mike Heck, and Mike Hogan. "Human Resources." *PC World,* Reader No. 660, October 1997.

Caudron, Shari. "Understanding Law." *Legal Assistant Today,* July/August 1995.

———. "Overtime Pay: Overrated or Making Ends Meet?" *Legal Assistant Today,* January/February 1996.

Delaney, Joan. "Rave Reviews." *Your Company,* spring 1994.

Editor. "A Look at Hours Worked under the Fair Labor Standards Act." U.S. Department of Labor, February 1980.

Editor. "Cost per Hire Example." *Legal Management,* September/October 1996.

Editor. "Developing a Performance Plan." Q.\\Training\MPM\Ratt\copm.docrevised, May 22, 1997.

Editor. "Employees' Rights, after Hours." *Manager's Legal Bulletin,* June 1996.

Editor. "Factors in Setting Law Firm Goals and Objectives." *Law Practice Management,* December 1995.

Editor. "Handy Reference Guide to the Fair Labor Standards Act." U.S. Department of Labor, October 1978.

Editor. "The HR Power Guide," Champlain, NY.: William Steinberg Consultants, Inc. fall 1994.

Editor. "Legal Assistant Salary and Compensation Levels." http://www.nala.org/Sec.4web.htm, August 13, 1998.

Editor. "Nearly 1/3 of Attorneys Would Teach as Alternate Career Choice." *Legal Management,* November/December 1997.

Editor. "The Pryor Report." *The Pryor Report Management Newsletter* 11, no. 1a, July 1996.

Editor. "Purchasing and Supply Management." National Association of Purchasing Management, August 1996.

Editor. "Survey Shows U.S. Corporations Now Widely Use Alternative Dispute Resolution over Litigation." *Legal Management,* July/August 1997.

Editor. "Where Is the Profession Today?" *National Paralegal Reporter,* July 1997.

Editor. "You Can't Please Everyone." *Executive Female,* January/February 1997.

Ellis, Diane M. "Reviews a la Carte." *Legal Assistant Today,* September/October 1996.

Emmons, Natasha. "Military Outreach Task Force Formed." *Legal Assistant Today,* March/April 1998.

Estrin, Chere B. "Stop Bonusing Paralegals for Billable Hours Start Rewarding for Achieving Instead." California Alliance of Paralegal Associations, winter 1997.

Gurowitz, Edward M. "Flexible Leadership Styles Let You Keep Current with Firm Needs." *Legal Management,* May/June 1997.

Haserot, Phyllis Weiss. "Relationship Management: The Primary Focus of Quality Improvement." *Legal Management,* September/October 1994.

Hayes, Arthur S. "Tough Guys Argue in Court." *National Law Journal,* September 25, 1995.

Hedrick, Alexandra Kreuger. "Ten Commandments of Personal Management." *Legal Assistant Today,* July/August 1994.

Hunt, Stacey. "Paralegals Deemed Production Workers." *Legal Assistant Today,* July/August 1996.

———. "The Paralegal 'X' Files." *Legal Assistant Today,* July/August 1997.

Hutchinson, Jennifer E. "Peer Review: A Good Way to Help Improve Law Firm Procedures." *Legal Management,* September/October 1995.

Jeffries, John A. "Wage and Hour Law Applications for Paralegals." *Legal Administrator,* March/April 1988.

Kording, Nicole, and Leanne Cazares. "A Dream Job." *Legal Assistant Today,* November/December 1996.

Kornreich, Wendy L. "Quick Reference for Selected Employment Laws." @ *LAW,* January 1998.

Kramer, Thomas J., Lori O. Lewis, and Ellen Harshman. "What's Missing from This Picture?" *Legal Management,* July/August 1999.

Luebke, Robert. "Designing the Effective Team in a Law Firm Environment." *Legal Management,* September/October 1995.

McKenna, Patrick J. "Best Law Firm Management Practices." *Legal Management,* September/October 1994.

Messmer, Max. "The Many Faces of Motivation." *Legal Management,* September/October 1997.

———. "The Good Ones Are Gone: Lack of Growth Opportunities Cause Top Employees to Resign." *Legal Management,* March/April 1999.

Miles, Breanda W. "Benefits and Perks in the Legal Field." @ *LAW,* spring 1997.

Nelson, Bob, and Peter Economy. "Managing Today Requires New Skills." *The PriceCo Connection,* March 1993.

Newman, Ruth G. "Appraising Performance: What Every Good Coach Knows." *Self Employed Professional,* May/June 1996.

Patterson, Cynthia L. "Pricing Legal Assistant Services." *Topics in Legal Assistant Utilization,* November 1988.

Petropulos, Diane. "Make Your First Count." *Legal Assistant Today,* November 1998.

Smith, Charlsye. "Brief Survey Shows What Attorneys Expect from the Paralegal Staff." *Law Office Administrator,* September 1997.

Sokolosky, Valerie. "On the Job Satisfaction." *Spirit,* November 1998.

Stewart, Patrick J. "Salaried Personnel: Are They Really Exempt from Minimum Wage and Overtime Requirements?" *Legal Management,* January/February 1990.

Stoddard, Debbie. "Get the Job Credit and the Raise with a Self-Evaluation." *Law Office Administrator,* August 1997.

Tate, John R. "Profitability Formulas and Paralegal/Associate Comparisons." *The Docket,* spring 1997.

Ward, Frances D. "All for One." *Legal Management,* September/October 1997.

Wertheim, Lynda F., and Robert J. Berkow. "A Hot Topic in Management Committee Meetings." *Legal Assistant Today,* November/December 1987.

Williams, Monci. "The Manager as Servant." *Executive Female,* March/April 1997.

Chapter 4

Allen, Ronald J. "Dead Men Need Not Talk." *National Law Journal,* July 6, 1998.

Berman, Bruce. " 'Niche' Firms Can Target Other Firms." *National Law Journal,* March 10, 1997.

Blumberg, John P. "Is It Really Legal Practice?" *California Lawyer,* February 1999.

Coburn Jeff, and Eva Ginsburg. "Create Client Satisfaction Surveys That Give You More than Useless Information." *Legal Management,* September 1998.

Cooper, Alan. "Soliciting by Mail Approved." *National Law Journal,* January 19, 1998.

Coyle, Marcia. "Fla. Bar Asks High Court to Take a Hard Look at Ads." *National Law Journal,* January 23, 1995.

———. "High Court Eyes Client Trust Fund." *National Law Journal,* January 19, 1998.

———. "D.C. Circuit Trims Client Privilege." *National Law Journal,* September 15, 1997.

———. "Ad Decision Could Spur a Rollback." *National Law Journal,* July 3, 1995.

Davis, Ann. "Calif. Offenders Can be Disbarred Permanently." *National Law Journal,* September 1996.

———. "Profit Connection: Ohio-Naples, Fla." *National Law Journal,* November 4, 1996.

DeBenedicts, Don J. "State Bar Questions Simpson Commercials." *Orange County Reporter,* March 24, 1999.

Editor. "The ABA Commission on Advertising." American Bar Association, June 4, 1995.

Editor. "Attorney Advertising on the Internet." http://personal.law.miami.edu/-rappapor/imternet.html, November 5, 1998.

Editor. "From the Other Side: What Should a Client Expect for a Lawyer?" *Orange County Paralegal Association Compendium,* December 1996.

Editor. "From the Chair." *Lawyer Advertising News* 5, no. 1 (August 1995).

Editor. "Let ALA Give You a Hand!" American Library Association, October 5, 1995.

Editor. "Oklahoma Undue Hardship Analysis Reveals System's Inconsistencies." *Consumer Bankruptcy News,* August 1, 1996.

Editor. " 'Round the Industry." *Legal Management,* March/April 1998.

Editor. "Special Supplement." *Lawyer Advertising News,* June 21, 1995.

Editor. "Walking a Tight Rope: Preserving the Attorney-Client Privilege." *The New York Professional Responsibility Report,* April 1998.

Editor. "What Happens When the Attorney-Client Relationship Ends?" State Bar of California, 1996.

Editor. "Yellow Pages Lawyer Advertising: An Analysis of Effective Elements." American Bar Association, May 1992.

Filip, Christine S., and Anne E. Johnston. "Misleading Message May Spark a Suit." *National Law Journal,* November 10, 1997.

Fischer, James. "When Does a Client Become a Client?" *National Law Journal,* March 10, 1997.

Gallagher, Mike. "Minimizing Internet Security Risks." *Law Technology Product News,* April 1998.

Gerstman, Sharon Stern. "Advertising a Practice Specialty." *The New York Professional Responsibility Report,* April 1998.

Graham, John R. "Redefine Your Views on Marketing." *Legal Management,* January/February 1998.

Harguindeguy, Bernard. "Wavering Attorney-Client Privelege On-Line." *Law Technology News,* January 1999.

Harned, Billie Jo. "Why Manage Risk?" American Library Association, July/August 1998.

Hazard, Geoffrey C. "It Pays to Be Alert about Unforeseen Conflicts." *National Law Journal,* February 1, 1996.

———. "The Would-Be Client II." *National Law Journal,* February 1, 1996.

———. "More Talk of Walls to Protect Confidentiality." *National Law Journal,* August 22, 1997.

Helle, Steven. "Attorney Advertising after Peel." *Illinois Bar Journal* 78, no. 11 (November 1990).

Hoffmann Elinor R., and S. Calvin Walden. "Transactions." *National Law Journal,* December 1, 1997.

Hornsby, William E. "Ethics Rules for Ads May Cover Web Sites." *National Law Journal,* January 29, 1996.

Jaffe, Jay M. "Bold Ads Help Firms Position Themselves." *National Law Journal,* March 18, 1996.

Jones, Arnold W. "Withdrawal from Representation of a Client." *The Docket,* September/October 1994.

Leibowitz, Wendy R. "Client Conflict Software: No Panacea." *National Law Journal,* July 21, 1997.

———. "Legal Ethics in an Electronic Age: Where No One Has Gone Before?" *National Law Journal,* March 24, 1997.

———. "Even Authorized Off-Site Parties Imperil Security." *National Law Journal,* January 12, 1998.

———. "Lawyers Find Niches in the 'Net.' " *National Law Journal,* November 23, 1998.

Luce, Charles F. "Confidentiality, Cell Phones and E-Mail." *Legal Ethics and the Practice of Law Online,* November 4, 1998.

———. "Ethics in Attorney Advertising and Solicitation." http://www.mgovg.com/ethics/11advert.htm, November 4, 1998.

Meyers, Harriet S. "When Their Fingers Do the Walking; Effectively Reach Potential Clients Through Yellow Pages." *American Library Association News,* November 5, 1998.

Micheletti, Mary. "Internet Has Transformed Prepaid Legal Services." *Orange County Reporter,* March 24, 1999.

Orlik, Deborah K. "What Exactly Is Confidentiality?" *Legal Assistant Today,* May/June 1992.

Perkins. "Client Trust Accounts: Disasters Waiting to Happen?" *Lawyers Weekly USA,* March 10, 1997.

Piatt, Pearl J. "You Say You Want a Revolution?" *Los Angeles Daily Journal,* September 1997.

———. "Lawyer Advertising." *Orange County Reporter,* October 4, 1997.

———. "Getting the Word Out." *Los Angeles Daily Journal,* October 27, 1997.

Pike, Robert. "Making IOLTA Voluntary May Not Affect Every State." *Orange County Reporter,* August 22, 1997.

Schmidt, Sally. "Individual Lawyer Marketing Plans." *Memorandum,* October 23, 1998.

Shaw, B. "Court Split over IOLTA Fund Case." *Orange County Reporter,* January 15, 1998.

Shepherd, Ritchenya. "Marketers Seen Running Firms." *National Law Journal,* March 22, 1999.

———. "Why MoFo Teams with KPMG." *National Law Journal,* August 23, 1999.

Simpson, Richard A. "Legal View." *Cyberspace Lawyer* 6, no. 3 (December 1998).

Solovy, Jerold S., and Robert L. Byman. "When Is Work Protectable as Work Product?" *National Law Journal,* September 21, 1998.

Spivak, Cary. "Fight over Ban on Direct Mail." *National Law Journal,* March 18, 1996.

Stiefel, David. "Cooperation Helps Publicists Polish a Firm's Image." *National Law Journal,* October 9, 1995.

Verstegen. "Client Trust Accounting Discipline Issues." *National Law Journal,* February 6, 1996.

Weidlich, Thom. "Ten Ways to Cut Malpractice Risk." *National Law Journal,* June 3, 1994.

Zitrin, Richard A., and Carol M. Langford. "Ethics in Ashes." *California Lawyer,* November 1998.

Zwicker, Milton W. "What Clients Really Want for Their Lawyers." *Law Practice Management,* September 1994.

Chapter 5

Anderson, Judy. "Components for Ethics for Legal Support Staff." *The Docket,* fall 1995.

Baskette, Elsbeth, Kaye Aoki, Elizabeth Jackman, and Kathleen Nevins. *Manual for the Lawyers Assistant.* St. Paul: West Publishing, 1988.

Bielec, Laurel. "A Giant Leap toward Regulation." *Legal Assistant Today,* November/December 1998.

Bogen, Deborah. "Social Security Paralegal under Investigation." *Legal Assistant Today,* November/December 1998.

Cannon, Teresa. *Ethics and Professional Responsibility for Legal Assistants.* Boston: Little, Brown, 1992.

Chapman, Elwood N. *From Campus to Career Success.* New York: Pergamon, 1978.

Clas, Camille Stucky. "UPL Attacked in North Carolina." *Legal Assistant Today,* January/February 1998.

Committee on Paralegal Education and Regulation. "Law." Los Angeles Mission College Paralegal Studies Program, August 12, 1998.

———. "New Jersey Report." Los Angeles Mission College Paralegal Studies Program, August 12, 1998.

Cooper, David, and Michael Gibson. *An Introduction to Paralegal Studies.* Cincinnati: South-Western Publishing, 1994.

Council, John. "No Sale for Unlicensed Cyber-Lawyer." http://www.ljx.com/tech/nocyber.htm, April 20, 1999.

Editor. "Case Law." *National Paralegal Reporter,* fall 1998.

Editor. "It's Time to Tell Staff about the Little Errors That Cause Malpractice." *Law Office Management,* July 1998.

Editor. "Lawsuit Filed against Paralegal Businesses." *National Federation of Paralegal Associations Reporter,* January 1998.

Editor. "Making News." *National Federation of Paralegal Associations Reporter,* fall 1998.

Editor. "New 'Legal Document Assistants' Opposed by Paralegals." *Notary Bulletin*, December 1998.

Editor. "Parabriefs." *Legal Assistant Today*, September/October 1998.

Editor. "Report of the Licensing of Legal Assistants Committee of the Legal Assistant Division of the Utah State Bar." Legal Assistants Committee of Utah, May 6, 1998.

Emmons, Natasha. "Case against California Independents Dropped." *Legal Assistant Today*, November/December 1998.

———. "Nolo Press Wins Latest Round." *Legal Assistant Today*, November/December 1998.

Gust, Steve. "Public Opinion Poll Underway." *Legal Assistant Today*, November/December 1998.

Hazard, Geoffrey C. "Erecting a Wall to Prevent Conflicts of Interest." *National Law Journal*, July 21, 1997.

Heller, Nancy B. "Paralegal Ethics." *National Paralegal Reporter*, fall 1998.

Howery, Susan. "Hawaii Attacks Document Prep Services." *Legal Assistant Today*, May/June 1999.

Hughes, Rod. "NoLo Wins Battle in Texas." *Legal Assistant Today*, July/August 1999.

Levy, Debra. "Parent Advocate Accused of UPL." *Legal Assistant Today*, March/April 1999.

Lowell, Abbe David. "Lawyer-Client Privilege Is Absolute." *National Law Journal*, May 26, 1997.

Micheletti, Mary. "Maine Regulation Moves Ahead." *Legal Assistant Today*, July/August 1999.

Nakaahiki, Victorialei. "Hawaii Paralegals Head toward Certification through Federal Court." *National Paralegal Reporter*, fall 1998.

Orlik, Deborah K. *Ethics for the Legal Assistant.* Glenview, Ill.: Scott, Foresman, 1986.

———. "What Exactly Is Confidentiality?" *Legal Assistant Today*, May/June 1992.

Rosen, Barbara. "When Are You Giving Legal Advice?" *Legal Assistant Today*, July/August 1995.

Samborn, Hope Viner. "Defining Paralegal Ethics." *Legal Assistant Today*, January/February 1995.

Simon, Stephanie. "Opting for Cut-Rate Legal Eagles." *Los Angeles Times*, June 21, 1997.

Sperber, Robert. "NFPA Issues Two Cyberspace Ethics Opinions." *Legal Assistant Today*, May/June 1997.

———. NFPA Adopts Model Disciplinary Rules at Annual Meeting." *Legal Assistant Today*, July/August 1997.

———. "Oregon Legislature Moves toward Licensing Independent Paralegals." *Legal Assistant Today*, July/August 1997.

Statsky, William P. *Introduction to Paralegalism, Perspectives, Problems, and Skills.* 4th ed. St. Paul: West Publishing, 1996.

Wallach, Joni Mcdonald. "Where Do We Stand?" *Legal Assistant Today*, March/April 1999.

Westin, I. Perrin. "NFPA Revises Its Model Ethic Codes and Definition of Paralegalism." *Legal Assistant Today*, November/December 1997.

———. "Paralegal Defeats Ex-Firm's Efforts to Prevent Move to Competitor." *Legal Assistant Today*, January/February 1998.

———. "Bill Regulating Independent Paralegals Passes First Hurdle." *Legal Assistant Today*, May/June 1998.

Chapter 6

Alexander, Karen. "Was It a 'Premium' or an Inflated Bill?" *National Law Journal*, April 6, 1998.

Allen, Rae L. "NFPA Database Covers Wide Range of Cases." *National Paralegal Reporter*, December 1997.

Altonji, Joseph B. "Calculating the Costs of Providing Legal Services." *Accounting for Law Firms Newsletter*, August 1997.

———. "Knowing the Costs of Legal Services." *National Law Journal*, December 2, 1996.

Blum, Andrew. "When Getting Your Fee Gets Tough." *National Law Journal*, April 1, 1996.

Cohn, Steven. "Tow Appeals Courts Rule Paralegal Fees Recoverable at Market Rate." *Legal Assistant Today*, July/August 1994.

Cox, Gail Diane. "Cost-Cutting Targets One of Its Own." *National Law Journal*, February 17, 1997.

———. "Plaintiffs Reap Payoff from Auditor's Aid." *National Law Journal*, June 30, 1997.

———. "Excessive Fees Are Attacked across the Board." *National Law Journal*, November 4, 1996.

Davis, Ann. "No Bill to Client for Training." *National Law Journal*, August 10, 1996.

———. "Temps Use Sparks Ire in Client Ranks." *National Law Journal*, December 23, 1996.

Donovan, Karen. "Is $1,109 an Hour Too Much?" *National Law Journal*, July 21, 1997.

Dooley, Laurel Ann. "Alston Bird, Others Win Total $1.89M." *National Law Journal*, December 22, 1997.

Dresslar, Tom. "Contingency Fee Appeals Eyed." *Orange County Reporter*, May 11, 1998.

Dubin, Lawrence A. "Ethics." *National Law Journal*, December 8, 1993.

———. "Court Blasts Non-Refundable Fee." *National Law Journal*, October 1994.

Dwight, Jennifer. "How Alternative Billing Will Affect Your Firm and Your Job." *Legal Assistant Today*, May/June 1995.

Editor. "Alternative Fee Arrangements—Panacea or Placebo?" *Legal Management*, May/June 1994.

Editor. "Compensation for Associates Generally Grows with Firm Size." *National Law Journal*, November 4, 1996.

Editor. "Fee Changes in Effect." *California Lawyer*, March 1993.

Editor. "O.J. Simpson Defense." *USA Today,* August 5, 1994.

Editor. "Pro Bono." *National Law Journal,* March 10, 1997.

Editor. "Recovery of Paralegal Fees Table of Authorities." In *Handbook on Paralegal Utilization.* San Francisco, CA.: California Alliance of Paralegal Associations, 1986.

Editor. "Watch out for the Billing Practices That Kill the Clients." *Law Office Administrator,* August 1997.

Editor. "What Can a Legal Fee Agreement Do for Me?" State Bar of California, 1997.

Editor. "Windy City Paralegal Rates." *Legal Assistant Today,* November/December 1998.

Eigles, Jack T. "Take It to the Bank." *Legal Administrator,* November/December 1997.

Emmons, Natasha. "Firm Denied Recovery of Fees for Paralegals Who Crossed the Line." *Legal Assistant Today,* January/February 1998.

———. "NFPA Releases Survey Results." *Legal Assistant Today,* January/February 1998.

———. "Fees Reduced for Work That 'Could Have' Been Done by Paralegals." *Legal Assistant Today,* March/April 1998.

Estrin, Chere B. "Looking into the Compensation Crystal Ball." *Legal Assistant Today,* May/June 1997.

Fisk, Margaret Cronin. "Corporate Firms Try Contingency." *National Law Journal,* June 20, 1996.

Jessen, Nancy A. "The Task at Hand: Making Task-Based Billing a Working Reality in Your Firm." *Legal Management,* March/April 1996.

Kummel, William. "Things Change." *Legal Management,* May/June 1996.

Leibowitz, Wendy R. "Lawyers and Technology." *National Law Journal,* June 22, 1998.

MacLachlan, Claudia. "DOE in Dark on Defense Fees." *National Law Journal,* July 17, 1994.

———. "Court Sides with Lawyer on Expenses." *National Law Journal,* April 15, 1995.

Marshall Joseph L., and Elizabeth D. Hersey. "Take a Closer Look at Value Billing before the Compensation Does." *Legal Management,* November/December 1994.

Prohaska, Ronald R. "Are You Setting Your Fees Too Low?" *Lawyers Weekly USA,* March 10, 1997.

Samborn, Randall. "Contingent Fee Arrangements Get ABA Nod." *National Law Journal,* January 30, 1995.

Statsky, Bill. "Summary-Billing for Lexis and Westlaw." *National Law Journal,* November 6, 1998.

Van Duch, Darryl. "Fee Challenged in Conn. Case." *National Law Journal,* November 6, 1995.

Van Voris, Bob. "That $10 Billion Fee." *National Law Journal,* November 30, 1998.

Weston, I. Perrin. "NY Governor Disallows Fee Recovery for Paralegal Services." *Legal Assistant Today,* January/February 1998.

Chapter 7

Editor. "Billing Rates." http://www.nala.org/Sec.3web.htm, August 21, 1999.

Editor. "Do Not Squander Time." *Legal Management,* July/August 1999.

Editor. "1996 Average Annual Associate Billable Hours at 10 Firms." *National Law Journal,* August 22, 1997.

Editor. "1996 Median Billable Hours of Lawyers Nationwide." *National Law Journal,* August 22, 1997.

Editor. "Time and Billing Solutions for Legal Professionals." In *Client Success and Satisfaction.* Manual for Status Pro, Bellview, WA.: CSS, Inc., 1998.

Goldstein, David A. "Task-Based Timekeeping: Technology's Role in Solving the Puzzle." *Legal Management,* March/April 1996.

Hunt, Stacey. "Making Time Count." *Legal Assistant Today,* May/June 1999.

Lovett, Wayne J. "It's Time Software Fit a Lawyer's Bill." *National Law Journal,* November 20, 1995.

Neser, Arlin P. "Is Your Law Firm Losing the War with Time?" *Law Office Computing,* February/March 1997.

Russo, Michael A. *Timeslips Deluxe for Windows CD-ROM.* Dallas, TX.: Timeslips Corporation, 1996.

Thompson, Mark. "Pay Me Right, and I'll Bill You Honestly." @ *LAW,* March 1, 1999.

Chapter 8

Blodgett, Nancy. "Articulating the Values of Your Law Firm." *Legal Management,* January/February 1996.

Bollar, Robert W., and Robert D. Sheehan. "Alternative Billing Options to Keep Clients Satisfied." *Legal Management,* July/August 1994.

Cioccio, Diana Di. "No More Smoke and Mirrors." *Legal Management,* November/December 1996.

Coburn, Jeff, and Michael Preston. "Management: Survey Reveals How Firms Use Profit Centers as Strategic Tools." *Legal Management,* July/August 1997.

Correl, Bruce. "Tracking Non-Chargeables Can Keep Firm Afloat." *National Law Journal,* April 25, 1994.

Cotterman, James D. "Developing Rational Capital Structures for Law Firms." *Accounting for Law Firms* 10, no. 7 (July 1997).

Drucker, Bruce D. "Some Firms Still Vexed by Audits of Legal Bills." *National Law Journal,* July 25, 1994.

Editor. "Billable Hours." *Wall Street Journal,* May 27, 1994.

Editor. "Don't Let Billable Time in the Library Get Written Off." *Law Office Administrator,* July 1997.

Editor. "Editor's In-Box." Legal Management, July/August 1997.

Editor. "55 of the Top 200 Corporate Legal Departments Use Compinfo Lawpack." *Legal Management,* November/December 1997.

Editor. *Getting Started with INTEGRA*™. Dawson Creek, Canada: Power Soft Innovations Corp., 1997.

Editor. "Have Go-Go '80s Returned?" *National Law Journal,* September 1997.

Editor. "Internet Law Researcher*." Legal Management,* March/April 1997.

Editor. "Juris Eases Compliance with Special Billing Requirements." *Legal Management,* November/December 1997.

Editor. "New Products." *Legal Management,* March/April 1995.

Editor. "Tailored Training Programs Help Some Firms Play the RFP Game." *National Law Journal,* March 3, 1997.

Editor. "Time & Billing Software." *National Law Journal,* December 21, 1998.

Editor. "U.S Law Firms: Gross Receipts Improve, Profit Lags." *Legal Management,* November/December 1998.

Editor. "Watch Out For the Billing Practices That Kill the Clients." *Law Office Administrator,* 6, no. 8 (August 1997).

Editor. "What Lawyers Earn." *National Law Journal,* June 2, 1997.

Editor. "What Partners Bill Each Year." *National Law Journal,* August 22, 1997.

Estrin, Chere B. "The Old Billable Hours Game." *Legal Assistant Today,* March/April 1997.

Ford, Chris. "Is There a Cure for the Billable-Hour Blues?" *Cyber Esq.,* spring 1999.

France, Mike. "Clock's Running on Billable Hours." *National Law Journal,* December 19, 1994.

Hayes, Arthur. "Uniform Task-Based Billing." *National Law Journal,* June 22, 1998.

Kulpa, Bob. "10 Things—and Then One More—to Do with a Balance Sheet." *Legal Management,* January/February 1998.

Lewis, Geraldine A. "A New Era in Billing Practices." *California Lawyer,* September 1998.

Neath, James J. "Task-Based Billing—the Way of the Future." *Legal Management,* March/April 1995.

Nilsson, David S. "There Must Be 60 Ways to Lead Your Finances." *Legal Management,* July/August 1997.

Orlik, Deborah K. "Those Elusive Billable Hours." *Legal Assistant Today,* May/June 1995.

———. "A Question of Billing." *Compendium,* December 1995.

Preston, Michael. "Managing Partners Voice Their Views on Profit Center Measurement." *Legal Management,* September/October 1997.

Pritchard, Grant, and John R. Tate. Law Office Economics & Management Manual. *Orientation to Law Firm Accounting.* Deerfield, IL.: Callaghan & Co., 1991.

Schley, Sandra G. "Don't Stop Thinking about Tomorrow." *Legal Management,* November/December 1996.

Singleton, Ruth. "How Billing Rates React to the Larger Economy." *National Law Journal,* December 8, 1997.

Slind, Victoria. " 'Grown-Up' Lawyers Do Non-Billables." *National Law Journal,* November 13, 1995.

Smith, Colin. "Grow Your Own Way." *Legal Management,* November/December 1996.

Snyder, Theda. "Complaints about Legal Billing Practices." *Law Practice Management,* April 1999.

Sturgill, Stephen J. "New System Offers Easier and More Exact Billing." *National Law Journal,* October 17, 1994.

Turnbow, Richard B. "Be Proactive—Explain Your Law Firm's Billing Practices to Clients." *Legal Management,* July/August 1995.

———. "Revising Your Billing Practices Can Fund Your Tech Upgrades." *Law Technology News,* March 1999.

Van Duch, Darryl. "Troubled Firms Must Act Fast." *National Law Journal,* September 22, 1997

———. "Test Case for Insurers' Billing Rules." *National Law Journal,* January 25, 1999.

Wilke, John T. "Know What to Look for When Analyzing Income Trends." *Legal Management,* July/August 1997.

Yost, Sandra L. "Alternative Billing Strategies—New Wave or Passing Fad." *Legal Management,* March/April 1994.

Chapter 9

Coyle, Marcia. "Critics: Now We'll See Where IOLTA Funds Go." *National Law Journal,* June 29, 1998.

Editor. Accounting for Law Firms 10, no. 6 (June 1997).

Editor. "Brief Accounting." http://www.briefaccounting.com/pages/trust.htm, August 21, 1999.

Editor. *The Case for Integra™.* Dawson Creek, Canada: Power Soft Innovations Corp., 1998.

Editor. "Trust Accounting." http://www.stilegal.com/trustacc.html, August 21, 1999.

Oster, Patrick. "IOLTA Redux." *National Law Journal,* June 29, 1998.

Thomas, Richard. "IOLTA Funds Are Clients." *National Law Journal,* September 30, 1996.

Chapter 10

Alberts, Alan. "The Integrated Desktop: Budgeting and Strategic Planning for Your Next Upgrade." *Legal Management,* March/April 1997.

Alizadeh, Steve. "Predictions from an Expert." *Legal Management,* November/December 1998.

Ambrogi, Robert J. "Finding Ethics via the World Wide Web." *Law Technology Product News,* December 1998.

Ballon, Ian C. *Selected Issues in the Emerging Law of the Internet.* Legal Works 98. Little Falls, N.J.: Glasser Legal Works, 1998.

Bendell, Adam S. *State-of-the-Art Document Management.* Legal Works 97. Little Falls, N.J.: Glasser Legal Works, 1997.

Berg, Martin. "Lawyers in Federal Court Say They're Tickled by Elmo." *Cyber Esq.,* spring 1999.

Biddle, Brad. "Public Key Infrastructure and 'Digital Signature' Legislation: Ten Public Policy Questions." *Cyberspace Lawyer* 2, no. 2 (1997).

Burrows, Jennifer. "Searching for Answers." *WebSite Journal* 2, no. 26 (June 30, 1999).

Butler, Charles. "Knowledge Is Power." *Legal Management,* March/April 1999.

Caddell, Douglas D. "Bridge the Gap." *Legal Management,* March/April 1999.

Calhoun, Richard A. "Automation Requirements for the Year 2000." *Legal Management,* May/June 1995.

Canfield, Curt A. "Dismiss Groupware at Your Own Peril." *Law Technology Product News,* March 1998.

Cohen, Steve. *Maintaining a Secure Legal Extranet.* Legal Works 98. Little Falls, N.J.: Glasser Legal Works, 1998.

Curreri, Michael. *Networking Counsel Efforts: Extranets for Litigation and Matter Management.* Legal Works 98. Little Falls, N.J.: Glasser Legal Works, 1998.

Davis, Susan E. "Duty to Surf." *California Lawyer,* November 1998.

Dean, Martin L. "The Portable Lawyer." *California Lawyer,* November 1998.

Diboise, James. "E-Mail Security, Section 998 Offers, and Clean Air Act Liability." *California Lawyer,* August 1998.

Editor. "Accessibility and Distribution of Information on the Web." http://www.wwwmetrics.com/, August 20, 1999.

Editor. "Advanced Web Searching Techniques." http://www.learnthenet.com/english/html/77advance.htm, April 11, 1999.

Editor. "All about News Groups." http://www.learnthenet.com. April 5, 1999.

Editor. "Anatomy of an E-Mail Message." http://www.learnthenet.com/english/html/21e_anat.htm, April 5, 1999.

Editor. "Best of the Web." @ *LAW,* fall–winter 1998.

Editor. "Case Management Software." *Legal Assistant Today,* March/April 1997.

Editor. "Dataviz Debuts Web Buddy 1.1." *Legal Management,* June 1997.

Editor. "Direct Contact with Prospective Clients." ABA Professional Conduct on the Internet White Paper, July 1998.

Editor. "Electronic Communications." http://www.learnthenet.com. April 5, 1999.

Editor. "Florida Firm Uses E-Mail to Solve Phone Problems." *Law Office Administrator,* July 1998.

Editor. "Frequently Asked Questions." http://www.learnthenet.com/english/toolbar/faq.htm, March 29, 1999.

Editor. "How E-Mail Works." http//www.learnthenet.com/english/html/20how.htm, March 28,1999.

Editor. "How to Find People's E-Mail Addresses." http://www.cis.ohiostate.edu/hypertext/faq/usenet/finding-addresses/faq.html, April 5, 1999.

Editor. "How Law Firms Use the Internet." *California Lawyer,* July 1997.

Editor. "The Internet and the Practice of Law." *Web Counsel.* LLC. March 20, 1998.

Editor. "Internet Survey Results." *Cyber Esq./California Lawyer,* spring 1998.

Editor. "Interview: The ILPN Talks with Will Hornsby about Internet Ethics." *National Law Journal,* November 18, 1996.

Editor. "IOMA Site." *Law Technology Product News,* mid-April 1998.

Editor. "The Law Firm Intranet." *Internet Law Researcher,* March 1998.

Editor. "Lawyers Reluctant to Use Internet for Confidential Correspondence." *Legal Management,* May/June 1998.

Editor. "Legal Software Directory." *Legal Assistant Today,* September/October 1997.

Editor. "Legal Software Directory." *Legal Assistant Today,* November/December 1998.

Editor. "Legal Technology Purchasing Guide." *Daily Journal.* June 21, 1998.

Editor. "Mailing Lists." http://www.learnthenet.com/english/html/24mlists.htm, April 5, 1999.

Editor. "1997 Survey Show Internet Is Hot." American Bar Association, July 1997.

Editor. "One Firm's New Policy." *Legal Management,* March/April 1998.

Editor. "Penetrating the U.S. Market." *Legal Integrations, USA,* May 1999.

Editor. "Products and Services for the Legal Community." *Legal Assistant Today,* May/June 1997.

Editor. "Recent Technology Survey Provides New Information." *National Federation of Paralegal Associations Reporter,* January 1998.

Editor. "Smileys." http://www.learnthenet.com/english/html/25smile.htm, April 5, 1999.

Editor. "Starting Salaries for Legal Support Professionals Will Rise in 1999, Survey Says." *Legal Management,* March/April 1999.

Editor. "State Developments." *Cyberspace Lawyer* 2, no. 2 (1997).

Editor. "Subscribing." http://www.learnthenet.com/english/html/28subscr.htm, April 5, 1999.

Editor. "Tips and Timesavers." *Legal Assistant Today,* July/August 1998.

Editor. "21st Century Lawyer—Case and Trial Management in the Same Program." *Law Office Technology Solutions,* March 1997.

Editor. "Understanding E-Mail Addresses." http://www.learnthenet.com/english/html/22email.htm, April 5, 1999.

Editor. "Web Stop." *Legal Assistant Today,* November/December 1998.

Estrin, Chere B., and Kevin J. Behan. "Enter the Net." *Legal Assistant Today,* July/August 1999.

Evans, Cheryl D. "Legal Sites: Findlaw." *California Lawyer,* May 1998.

———. "Legal Sites: Know Your Bill." *California Lawyer,* July 1998.

Forrest, Elizabeth. "What's the Word." *Legal Management,* March/April 1999.

Fox, John C. "Electronic Lawyers Assist Employers." *National Law Journal,* November 20, 1995.

Freeling, Kenneth A., and Ronald E. Wiggings. "States Develop Rules for Using Digital Signatures." *National Law Journal,* October 20, 1997.

George, Molly. *Electronic Discovery Litigation's Newest Challenge to Corporate Records.* Legal Works 97. Little Falls, N.J.: Glasser Legal Works, 1997.

Glickenhaus, Lee H. "Untangling the Web: Secure Extranets as a Legal Management and Collaboration Tool." *Legal Assistant Today,* November/December 1998.

———. "Knowledge." *Law Practice Management,* March 1999.

———. *Extranets Merge Virtues of Internet and Intranets.* Legal Works 99. Little Falls, N.J.: Glasser Legal Works, 1999.

Goldsborough, Reid. "Internet Information May Warrant a Double Check." *Inside the Internet,* winter 1997.

Gonzalez, Sandra. "If You Build It Right, They Will Come." *Law Technology Product News,* mid-September 1998.

Gottesman, Ben Z. "The Web Workplace." *PC Magazine,* June 22, 1999.

Griffith, Cary. "Lawyers Can't Afford Not to Automate Case Management." *U.S. Business Litigation,* March 1997.

———. "Put the Web to Work." *Legal Management,* November/December 1997.

Hobbs, Allen. "The Internet Offers Expanded Alternatives for Law Firm Marketing." *National Law Journal,* April 3, 1995.

Hornsby, William E. "The Regulation of Technology-Based Lawyer Advertising and Internet Use Policies." *Legal Management,* July 1998.

Johnson, Amy. "Courtroom of the Future Gets Raves from Lawyers." *Lawyers Weekly USA,* March 10, 1997.

Kashi, Joseph L. *How to Conduct On-Premises Discovery of Computer Records.* Legal Works 98. Little Falls, N.J.: Glasser Legal Works, 1998.

———. *Upgrading Older Computers: What's New, Smart and Cost-Effective?* Legal Works 98. Little Falls, N.J.: Glasser Legal Works, 1998.

Klau, Richard P. *Litigation Management through the Use of Secure Internet-Based Networks.* Legal Works 99. Little Falls, N.J.: Glasser Legal Works, 1999.

Kohlmann, Susan. *Internet: Domain Name System To Be Restructured.* Legal Works 98. Little Falls, N.J.: Glasser Legal Works, 1998.

Kohn, Lawrence M., and Lisa Ellis. "Market the Megabyte$." *Legal Management,* March/April 1999.

Kozlowski, Ken. "Around the Legal Web Sites." *Internet Law Researcher* 3, no. 11 (February 1999).

Krakaur, Peter. *Intranets and Extranets: Using Internet Technology to Enhance the Practice of Law.* Legal Works 97. Little Falls, N.J.: Glasser Legal Works, 1997.

Lake, Matt. "Journey to the Ends of the Search Tools and Prevail." *PC World,* June 1999.

Leibowitz, Wendy R. "E-Mail Policy on Trial." *National Law Journal,* November 9, 1998.

———. "Lawyers and Technology." *Law Technology Center,* March 3, 1999.

———. "Is Every Web Store a Law Breaker?" *National Law Journal,* August 23, 1999.

———. "Future Law Tech. Visions." *National Law Journal,* September 13, 1999.

Levin, Carol. "Little Devices Will Think." *PC Magazine,* June 22, 1999.

Loundy, David. "E-Law: Rising Awareness Shown in Three New Encryption Bills." *Cyberspace Lawyer* 2, no. 2 (1997).

Lovett, Wayne J. "Document Software Called to Assembly." *National Law Journal,* June 26, 1995.

Macleod, Don. *Legal Research and the Internet.* Legal Works 97. Little Falls, N.J.: Glasser Legal Works, 1997.

Mattiano, Paul. "Get the Skinny on Thin-Client-Server Computing." *Legal Management,* July/August 1999.

McKenzie, Diana. "Business in Cyberspace Calls for Cautious Dealings." *National Law Journal,* June 26, 1995.

McQueen, Howard, and Jean E. DeMatteo. "A CIO's Perspective on Intranet Development." *Internet Professional,* no. 4 (November/December 1998).

Middlehurst, Carl. *Intranets for Legal Departments.* Legal Works 97. Little Falls, N.J.: Glasser Legal Works, 1997.

Miller, Michael J. "Also on the Horizon." *PC Magazine,* June 22, 1999.

———. "Computers Will Be More Human." *PC Magazine,* June 22, 1999.

Nadler, David M. "New Encryption Export Rules: Two Views." *Cyberspace Lawyer* 3, no. 10 (1999).

Nagel, Rebecca Thompson. "Bonnie Hill's Web Picks." *Legal Assistant Today,* March/April 1998.

———. "ABA Tech Survey Released." *Legal Assistant Today,* November/December 1998.

Overly, Michael R. "E-eek!" *Legal Management,* November/December 1998.

Ozolin, Peter J. "Leveraging the Internet to Better Serve Clients." *Law Technology Product News,* April 1998.

Pacifici, Sabrina. *Law Firms Intranets: Harnessing the Power of Knowledge Resources.* Legal Works 98. Little Falls, N.J.: Glasser Legal Works, 1998.

Piatt, Pearl J. "Greedy Lawyers on Line." *Cyber Esq.*, spring 1999.

Putnam, Melanie. "The Internet Guide to Reference Resources." *Internet Law Researcher* 3, no. 11 (February 1999).

Rinaldi, Arlene. "Lister VS/Mailing Lists/Discussion Groups." *The Net: Users Guidelines and Netiquette*, April 5, 1999.

Robson, Gary D. "Cybercasts Pose Alternatives to Videoconferencing." *National Law Journal*, July 1997.

Rogers, James. "Space Odyssey: Law Offices for the 21st Century." *National Law Journal*, January 30, 1995.

Ross, Susan B. "Balance Your Practice, the Internet and Ethics." *Legal Management*, November/December 1997.

Rothbart, George. *Designing, Building and Maintaining a Web Site*. Legal Works 99. Little Falls, NJ.: Glasser Legal Works, 1999.

Rovner, Jeffery S. "Law Firm Extranets: The New Kid on the Block." *Legal Works '98*. Little Falls, N.J.: Glasser Legal Works.

———. "Three Benefits of a Law Firm Intranet" *Law Technology News*, September 1998.

Rupley, Sebastian. "The Web Will Be Smart." *PC Magazine*, June 22, 1999.

Saxon, Steve. "Voice Recognition Software Makes You George Jetson." *Legal Management*, March/April 1999.

Sevy, Monica. *Live Demonstration III Word 97 and Word Perfect 7.0*. Legal Works 97. Little Falls, N.J.: Glasser Legal Works, 1997.

Snider, Anna. "Web Photos Pulled." *National Law Journal*, March 8, 1999.

Socha, George. *Processing the Electronic Ore: Reconstructing and Analyzing the Other Side's Electronic Evidence*. Legal Works 97. Little Falls, N.J.: Glasser Legal Works, 1997.

Sommers, Robert L. *Client Development on the Internet*. Legal Works 98. Little Falls, N.J.: Glasser Legal Works, 1998.

———. *Surf Rider*. Legal Works 98. Little Falls, N.J.: Glasser Legal Works, 1998.

Statsky, Bill. "Websites and UPL's." *New York Opinion*, October 24, 1998.

———. "If Operating Systems Ran the Airlines." *The Internet*, BillStatsky@Delmar.com, August 20, 1999.

Steele, Eric H., and Thomas Scharbach. "Efficiently Set up an Intranet/Extranet?" *Law Technology News*, January, 1999.

Steinberg, Marty. "Why Extranets Are Gaining Litigators' Trust." *Law Technology Product News*, mid-September 1998.

Stoddard, Sonia Von Mott. "E-Mail Etiquette." *Legal Assistant Today*, March/April 1998.

Teshima, Daryl. "Eight Predictions for 1998." *Legal Assistant Today*, March/April 1998.

Wallach, McDonald J. "Bookmarking Basics." *Legal Assistant Today*, July/August 1998.

Wright, Benjamin. "Electronic Commerce Litigation: Frequently Asked Questions." *Cyberspace Lawyer* 2, no. 2 (1997).

Yelin, Andrea B. "Staying Professionally Connected." *Legal Assistant Today*, January/February 1998.

Chapter 11

Dodge, John A. "Outside Your Windows." *Wall Street Journal*, April 19, 1999.

Grimes, Linda A. "Teamwork Is Essential in Systems Management." *National Law Journal*, January 30, 1995.

Hunt, Stacey. "NALA Announces 1998 Member Exchange Presentations." *Legal Assistant Today*, March/April 1998.

Editor. "Paralegals Online." *Legal Assistant Today*, May/June 1998.

Editor. "What Corporate Clients Think of Outside Counsel Billings." *National Law Journal*, January 30, 1995.

Messmer, Max. "The Human Side of New Technology in Law Firms." @ *LAW*, fall–winter 1998.

Meyers, Harriet S. "Everybody's Gone Surfing." *Legal Management*, September/October 1997.

Nagel, Rebecca Thompson, "Plugged in and on Top." *Legal Assistant Today*, March/April 1998.

Chapter 12

Davis, Susan E. "Docket Science." *CompuLaw*, October 1998.

Dean, Martin L. "Software Guaranteed to Save Money." *California Lawyer*, November 1989.

Dodge, John A. "Outside Your Windows." *Wall Street Journal*, April 19, 1999.

Editor. "Insurance Discounts." *CompuLaw*, September 1998.

Editor. "Paralegals Online." *Legal Assistant Today*, May/June 1998.

Editor. "Pays for Itself." *CompuLaw*, September 1998.

Editor. "Polk Research." *CompuLaw*, October 1998.

Editor. "What Corporate Clients Think of Outside Counsel Billings." *National Law Journal*, January 30, 1995.

Grier, John. "It's on the Calendar!" *Legal Management*, November/December 1996.

Grimes, Linda A. "Teamwork Is Essential in Systems Management." *National Law Journal*, January 30, 1995.

Hunt, Stacey. "NALA Announces 1998 Member Exchange Presentations." *Legal Assistant Today*, March/April 1998.

———. "Ten Tips for Implementing a Case Management System." *Legal Assistant Today*, November/December 1997.

Kaplan, Ronald E. "Reaping the Benefits of a Computerized Calendar System." *CompuLaw*, October 1998.

Messmer, Max. "The Human Side of New Technology in Law Firms." *LAW,* fall–winter 1998.

Meyers, Harriet S. "Everybody's Gone Surfing." *Legal Management,* September/October 1997.

Murai, Ray. "Bringing Hi-Tech Docket Calendaring to the Nation's Premier Hi-Tech Law Firm." @ *LAW,* July 1996.

Nagel, Rebecca Thompson. "Plugged in and on Top." *Legal Assistant Today,* March/April 1998.

Schilling, Joan. "Law Office Management: Calendaring Is Critical." *California Lawyer,* January 1998.

Yellen, Howard. "Risk Reduction." *CompuLaw,* October 1998.

Chapter 13

Baldwin, Merri A., and Pamela Phillips. "Client Files: Handle with Care." *California Lawyer,* May 1998.

Barr, Jean G. "Computers Are the Future for Keeping Track of Files. But First You Have to Get Ready." *Legal Assistant Today,* November/December 1993.

Bendell, Adam S. "State-of-the-Art Document Management." *American Law Technology,* spring 1997.

Davis, Susan. "Getting down to Cases." *California Lawyer,* June 1996.

Dwight, Jennifer. "The Nuts and Bolts of Civil Case Organization." *Legal Assistant Today,* March/April 1995.

Editor. "About Bar Coding." http://www.learnthenet.com, May 15, 1999.

Editor. "Ask ETHICSearch." http://www.learnthenet.com, February 26, 1999.

Editor. "DFS-General Information." Applied Engineering Management Corporation. May 8, 1999.

Editor. "Effective Record Management." *The Docket,* July/August 1993.

Editor. "Is That New Client Bringing the Firm a Malpractice Risk?" *Legal Office Administrator,* 7, no. 7 (July 1998).

Editor. "Large Firms." *Law Technology Product News,* August 1998.

Editor. "1999 Legal Products and Services Directory." *Legal Assistant Today,* May/June 1999.

Editor. "Slow down the Paper Chase by Making Full Use of the Record System." *Law Office Administrator,* August 1997.

Editor. "Twelve Steps in Automating Your Files." *The Docket,* July/August 1993.

Editor. "Watch Out for the Risks in the Client Engagement Letter." *Legal Office Administrator,* 7, no. 4 (April 1998).

Emmons, Natasha. "The Specialty Star." *Legal Assistant Today,* May/June 1999.

Fienman, Harvey B. "Trends in Automated Litigation Document Management." *Internet,* http://.lib.polyu.edu.hk/electdb/DATAPRO/57529-1.htm. May 7, 1999.

Ford, Chris. "Bank on It." *Cyber Esq.,* spring 1999.

Gable, Julie. "Records Management in Electronic Document Management." *Internet,* http://.lib.polyu.edu.hk/electdb/DATAPRO/57529-1.htm. September 9, 1998.

Glanell, Barry. "A Solo Creates Defacto Document Management." *Law Technology News,* May 1999.

Gold, Gloria. "Set the Records Straight." *Legal Management,* March/April 1999.

Greenwald, David, and Guy Wiggins. "Document Management Shootout." *Law Office Computing,* June/July 1997.

Jones, Nancy B. "Risk Management." *The Docket,* March/April 1994.

Kanofsky, Florence. "The Automated Office—Technical Skills for Legal Secretaries." *The Docket,* September/October 1994.

Katz, Stanley. "For the Record." *Legal Management,* January/February 1996.

Kazemi, Dana L. "Tips and Timesavers." *Legal Assistant Today,* July/August 1994.

Morgan, Barbara D. "Transfer: Breaking Boundaries with Web-Based Networks." *Law Practice Management,* March 1999.

Myers, Gini. "Law Office Technology: Systems Filing." @ *LAW,* July 1996.

Polisar, Lisa. "Converting a Large Firm to Automated Imaging." *Law Technology Product News,* August 1998.

Pollan, Lynne E. "Every Law Office Needs a Good Filing System." *National Law Journal,* October 17, 1994.

Reed, Richard C. "The Lawyer: Brain Power vs. Computer Power." *Law Practice Management,* March 1999.

Shill, Rhonda. "Beyond Search and Retrieval." *Law Technology Product News,* March 1998.

Simon, Roy. "Do I Have to Keep These Old Files?" *The New York Professional Responsibility Report,* April 1998.

Skupsky, Donald S. "Records Retention Programs for Law Firms." *Legal Management,* January/February 1995.

Solomon, Barry. *Choosing a Relationship Management System.* Legal Works 98. Little Falls, N.J.: Glasser Legal Works, 1998.

Zaben, Alan S. "Managing Electronic Documents, Including E-mail." http://www.learnthenet.com, May 5, 1999.

Chapter 14

Aarons, Anthony. "From Free to Fee." *Cyber Esq.,* July 1998.

Baker, Brian L. "Librarians Might Get Entangled in the Web." *National Law Journal,* October 2, 1995.

Beyer, Robin. "Controlling Costs in the Law Library." *Legal Management,* January/February 1994.

Bohill, Ruth. "Electronic Citation Guide for Legal Materials." *Internet,* http://law.anu.edu.au/nglrw/lr3.htm. May 28, 1999.

Davis, Susan E. "Books versus Bytes." *California Lawyer,* July 1998.

Davis, Ann. "Swapping Books for 'Jukebox.'" *National Law Journal,* November 6, 1995.

Editor. "Inmagic® Tech Flash." http://www.learnthenet.com, May 25, 1999.

Editor. "MLA Style." http://www.learnthenet.com, May 28, 1999.

Editor. "Recent Technology Surveys." http://www.learnthenet.com, April 15, 1999.

Editor. "Query Help." http://www.learnthenet.com, May 28, 1999.

Emrick, Nicholas. "Storehouse of Legal Expertise." *The Docket,* July/August 1993.

Estes, Mark. "Try These Eight Tactics to Cut the Cost of Library Subscriptions." *Law Office Administrator,* July 1997.

Freriks, David. "Library of Progress." *Legal Management,* March/April 1997.

Giangrande, Mark. "Research Tools for Today." *National Law Journal,* July 17, 1995.

Glickenhaus, Lee H. *Knowledge.* Legal Works 99. Little Falls, N.J.: Glasser Legal Works, 1998.

Leibowitz, Wendy R. "Big-Firm Librarians to Publishers: Get Your CD-ROM Acts Together." *National Law Journal,* October 20, 1997.

Leiter, Richard A. "The Five Laws of Library Science." *Legal Assistant Today,* November/December 1996.

Mingo, Michael. "Developing Your Own Online Research Strategy." *Law Technology News,* April 1999.

Orlik, Deborah K. "Technology and the Law." *Legal Assistant Today,* May/June 1996.

Platt, Nina. "Managing a (High-Tech) Library Effectively." *Law Technology Product News,* October 1997.

Relles, George, and Richard C. Solomon. "Law Office Management, Charging for Online Research and CD-ROM." *California Lawyer,* April 1998.

Scarbrough, Bill. "The Library 'Space' Race." *Legal Management,* March/April 1999.

Schorr, Morriss E. "Will CD-ROMs Replace Books in Law Libraries?" *Law Technology Product News,* April 1999.

Shimpock-Vieweg, Kathy. "Work Product Retrieval: Design and Implementation." *Legal Assistant Today,* March/April 1994.

———. "Library Cost Control: Trimming the Fat." *Legal Assistant Today,* July/August 1994.

Stathis Andrew L. "Technology Offers Incentive to Downsize Law Libraries." *National Law Journal,* October 2, 1995.

Sternfeld, Donald O. "Facilitating Document Retrieval." *National Law Journal,* March 21, 1994.

Teshima, Daryl. "Finding Needles in Digital Haystacks." *Legal Assistant Today,* January/February 1998.

———. "The Challenge: Westlaw.com and Lexis-Nexis Xchange." *Legal Assistant Today,* July/August 1998.

Index